University Casebook Series

June, 1990

ACCOUNTING AND THE LAW, Fourth Edition (1978), with Problems Pamphlet (Successor to Dohr, Phillips, Thompson & Warren)

George C. Thompson, Professor, Columbia University Graduate School of Business.
Robert Whitman, Professor of Law, University of Connecticut.
Ellis L. Phillips, Jr., Member of the New York Bar.
William C. Warren, Professor of Law Emeritus, Columbia University.

ACCOUNTING FOR LAWYERS, MATERIALS ON (1980)

David R. Herwitz, Professor of Law, Harvard University.

ADMINISTRATIVE LAW, Eighth Edition (1987), with 1989 Case Supplement and 1983 Problems Supplement (Supplement edited in association with Paul R. Verkuil, Dean and Professor of Law, Tulane University)

Walter Gellhorn, University Professor Emeritus, Columbia University.
Clark Byse, Professor of Law, Harvard University.
Peter L. Strauss, Professor of Law, Columbia University.
Todd D. Rakoff, Professor of Law, Harvard University.
Roy A. Schotland, Professor of Law, Georgetown University.

ADMIRALTY, Third Edition (1987), with Statute and Rule Supplement

Jo Desha Lucas, Professor of Law, University of Chicago.

ADVOCACY, see also Lawyering Process

AGENCY, see also Enterprise Organization

AGENCY—PARTNERSHIPS, Fourth Edition (1987)

Abridgement from Conard, Knauss & Siegel's Enterprise Organization, Fourth Edition.

AGENCY AND PARTNERSHIPS (1987)

Melvin A. Eisenberg, Professor of Law, University of California, Berkeley.

ANTITRUST: FREE ENTERPRISE AND ECONOMIC ORGANIZATION, Sixth Edition (1983), with 1983 Problems in Antitrust Supplement and 1989 Case Supplement

Louis B. Schwartz, Professor of Law, University of Pennsylvania.
John J. Flynn, Professor of Law, University of Utah.
Harry First, Professor of Law, New York University.

BANKRUPTCY, Second Edition (1989)

Robert L. Jordan, Professor of Law, University of California, Los Angeles.
William D. Warren, Professor of Law, University of California, Los Angeles.

BANKRUPTCY AND DEBTOR–CREDITOR LAW, Second Edition (1988)

Theodore Eisenberg, Professor of Law, Cornell University.

UNIVERSITY CASEBOOK SERIES—Continued

BUSINESS CRIME (1990)

Harry First, Professor of Law, New York University.

BUSINESS ORGANIZATION, see also Enterprise Organization

BUSINESS PLANNING, Temporary Second Edition (1984)

David R. Herwitz, Professor of Law, Harvard University.

BUSINESS TORTS (1972)

Milton Handler, Professor of Law Emeritus, Columbia University.

CHILDREN IN THE LEGAL SYSTEM (1983) with 1988 Supplement

Walter Wadlington, Professor of Law, University of Virginia.
Charles H. Whitebread, Professor of Law, University of Southern California.
Samuel Davis, Professor of Law, University of Georgia.

CIVIL PROCEDURE, see Procedure

CIVIL RIGHTS ACTIONS (1988), with 1989 Supplement

Peter W. Low, Professor of Law, University of Virginia.
John C. Jeffries, Jr., Professor of Law, University of Virginia.

CLINIC, see also Lawyering Process

COMMERCIAL AND DEBTOR–CREDITOR LAW: SELECTED STATUTES, 1990 EDITION

COMMERCIAL LAW, Second Edition (1987)

Robert L. Jordan, Professor of Law, University of California, Los Angeles.
William D. Warren, Professor of Law, University of California, Los Angeles.

COMMERCIAL LAW, Fourth Edition (1985)

E. Allan Farnsworth, Professor of Law, Columbia University.
John Honnold, Professor of Law, University of Pennsylvania.

COMMERCIAL PAPER, Third Edition (1984)

E. Allan Farnsworth, Professor of Law, Columbia University.

COMMERCIAL PAPER, Second Edition (1987) (Reprinted from COMMERCIAL LAW, Second Edition (1987))

Robert L. Jordan, Professor of Law, University of California, Los Angeles.
William D. Warren, Professor of Law, University of California, Los Angeles.

COMMERCIAL PAPER AND BANK DEPOSITS AND COLLECTIONS (1967), with Statutory Supplement

William D. Hawkland, Professor of Law, University of Illinois.

COMMERCIAL TRANSACTIONS—Principles and Policies (1982)

Alan Schwartz, Professor of Law, University of Southern California.
Robert E. Scott, Professor of Law, University of Virginia.

COMPARATIVE LAW, Fifth Edition (1988)

Rudolf B. Schlesinger, Professor of Law, Hastings College of the Law.
Hans W. Baade, Professor of Law, University of Texas.
Mirjan P. Damaska, Professor of Law, Yale Law School.
Peter E. Herzog, Professor of Law, Syracuse University.

UNIVERSITY CASEBOOK SERIES—Continued

COMPETITIVE PROCESS, LEGAL REGULATION OF THE, Fourth Edition (1990), with 1989 Selected Statutes Supplement

Edmund W. Kitch, Professor of Law, University of Virginia.
Harvey S. Perlman, Dean of the Law School, University of Nebraska.

CONFLICT OF LAWS, Ninth Edition (1990)

Willis L. M. Reese, Professor of Law, Columbia University.
Maurice Rosenberg, Professor of Law, Columbia University.
Peter Hay, Professor of Law, University of Illinois.

CONSTITUTIONAL LAW, Eighth Edition (1989), with 1989 Case Supplement

Edward L. Barrett, Jr., Professor of Law, University of California, Davis.
William Cohen, Professor of Law, Stanford University.
Jonathan D. Varat, Professor of Law, University of California, Los Angeles.

CONSTITUTIONAL LAW, CIVIL LIBERTY AND INDIVIDUAL RIGHTS, Second Edition (1982), with 1989 Supplement

William Cohen, Professor of Law, Stanford University.
John Kaplan, Professor of Law, Stanford University.

CONSTITUTIONAL LAW, Eleventh Edition (1985), with 1989 Supplement (Supplement edited in association with Frederick F. Schauer, Professor of Law, University of Michigan)

Gerald Gunther, Professor of Law, Stanford University.

CONSTITUTIONAL LAW, INDIVIDUAL RIGHTS IN, Fourth Edition (1986), (Reprinted from CONSTITUTIONAL LAW, Eleventh Edition), with 1989 Supplement (Supplement edited in association with Frederick F. Schauer, Professor of Law, University of Michigan)

Gerald Gunther, Professor of Law, Stanford University.

CONSUMER TRANSACTIONS (1983), with Selected Statutes and Regulations Supplement and 1987 Case Supplement

Michael M. Greenfield, Professor of Law, Washington University.

CONTRACT LAW AND ITS APPLICATION, Fourth Edition (1988)

Arthur Rosett, Professor of Law, University of California, Los Angeles.

CONTRACT LAW, STUDIES IN, Third Edition (1984)

Edward J. Murphy, Professor of Law, University of Notre Dame.
Richard E. Speidel, Professor of Law, Northwestern University.

CONTRACTS, Fifth Edition (1987)

John P. Dawson, late Professor of Law, Harvard University.
William Burnett Harvey, Professor of Law and Political Science, Boston University.
Stanley D. Henderson, Professor of Law, University of Virginia.

CONTRACTS, Fourth Edition (1988)

E. Allan Farnsworth, Professor of Law, Columbia University.
William F. Young, Professor of Law, Columbia University.

CONTRACTS, Selections on (statutory materials) (1988)

CONTRACTS, Second Edition (1978), with Statutory and Administrative Law Supplement (1978)

Ian R. Macneil, Professor of Law, Cornell University.

COPYRIGHT, PATENTS AND TRADEMARKS, see also Competitive Process; see also Selected Statutes and International Agreements

COPYRIGHT, PATENT, TRADEMARK AND RELATED STATE DOCTRINES, Third Edition (1990), with 1989 Selected Statutes Supplement and 1981 Problem Supplement

Paul Goldstein, Professor of Law, Stanford University.

COPYRIGHT, Unfair Competition, and Other Topics Bearing on the Protection of Literary, Musical, and Artistic Works, Fifth Edition (1990), with 1990 Statutory Supplement

Ralph S. Brown, Jr., Professor of Law, Yale University.
Robert C. Denicola, Professor of Law, University of Nebraska.

CORPORATE ACQUISITIONS, The Law and Finance of (1986), with 1989 Supplement

Ronald J. Gilson, Professor of Law, Stanford University.

CORPORATE FINANCE, Third Edition (1987)

Victor Brudney, Professor of Law, Harvard University.
Marvin A. Chirelstein, Professor of Law, Columbia University.

CORPORATION LAW, BASIC, Third Edition (1989), with Documentary Supplement

Detlev F. Vagts, Professor of Law, Harvard University.

CORPORATIONS, see also Enterprise Organization

CORPORATIONS, Sixth Edition—Concise (1988), with Statutory Supplement (1990)

William L. Cary, late Professor of Law, Columbia University.
Melvin Aron Eisenberg, Professor of Law, University of California, Berkeley.

CORPORATIONS, Sixth Edition—Unabridged (1988), with Statutory Supplement (1990)

William L. Cary, late Professor of Law, Columbia University.
Melvin Aron Eisenberg, Professor of Law, University of California, Berkeley.

CORPORATIONS AND BUSINESS ASSOCIATIONS—STATUTES, RULES, AND FORMS (1990)

CORPORATIONS COURSE GAME PLAN (1975)

David R. Herwitz, Professor of Law, Harvard University.

CORRECTIONS, SEE SENTENCING

CREDITORS' RIGHTS, see also Debtor-Creditor Law

CRIMINAL JUSTICE ADMINISTRATION, Third Edition (1986), with 1989 Case Supplement

Frank W. Miller, Professor of Law, Washington University.
Robert O. Dawson, Professor of Law, University of Texas.
George E. Dix, Professor of Law, University of Texas.
Raymond I. Parnas, Professor of Law, University of California, Davis.

CRIMINAL LAW, Fourth Edition (1987)

Fred E. Inbau, Professor of Law Emeritus, Northwestern University.
Andre A. Moenssens, Professor of Law, University of Richmond.
James R. Thompson, Professor of Law Emeritus, Northwestern University.

CRIMINAL LAW AND APPROACHES TO THE STUDY OF LAW (1986)

John M. Brumbaugh, Professor of Law, University of Maryland.

CRIMINAL LAW, Second Edition (1986)

Peter W. Low, Professor of Law, University of Virginia.
John C. Jeffries, Jr., Professor of Law, University of Virginia.
Richard C. Bonnie, Professor of Law, University of Virginia.

CRIMINAL LAW, Fourth Edition (1986)

Lloyd L. Weinreb, Professor of Law, Harvard University.

CRIMINAL LAW AND PROCEDURE, Seventh Edition (1989)

Ronald N. Boyce, Professor of Law, University of Utah.
Rollin M. Perkins, Professor of Law Emeritus, University of California, Hastings College of the Law.

CRIMINAL PROCEDURE, Third Edition (1987), with 1989 Supplement

James B. Haddad, Professor of Law, Northwestern University.
James B. Zagel, Chief, Criminal Justice Division, Office of Attorney General of Illinois.
Gary L. Starkman, Assistant U. S. Attorney, Northern District of Illinois.
William J. Bauer, Chief Judge of the U.S. Court of Appeals, Seventh Circuit.

CRIMINAL PROCESS, Fourth Edition (1987), with 1989 Supplement

Lloyd L. Weinreb, Professor of Law, Harvard University.

DAMAGES, Second Edition (1952)

Charles T. McCormick, late Professor of Law, University of Texas.
William F. Fritz, late Professor of Law, University of Texas.

DECEDENTS' ESTATES AND TRUSTS, Seventh Edition (1988)

John Ritchie, late Professor of Law, University of Virginia.
Neill H. Alford, Jr., Professor of Law, University of Virginia.
Richard W. Effland, late Professor of Law, Arizona State University.

DISPUTE RESOLUTION, Processes of (1989)

John S. Murray, President and Executive Director of The Conflict Clinic, Inc., George Mason University.
Alan Scott Rau, Professor of Law, University of Texas.
Edward F. Sherman, Professor of Law, University of Texas.

DOMESTIC RELATIONS, see also Family Law

DOMESTIC RELATIONS, Second Edition (1990)

Walter Wadlington, Professor of Law, University of Virginia.

EMPLOYMENT DISCRIMINATION, Second Edition (1987), with 1989 Supplement

Joel W. Friedman, Professor of Law, Tulane University.
George M. Strickler, Professor of Law, Tulane University.

EMPLOYMENT LAW (1987), with 1987 Statutory Supplement and 1989 Case Supplement

Mark A. Rothstein, Professor of Law, University of Houston.
Andria S. Knapp, Adjunct Professor of Law, University of California, Hastings College of Law.
Lance Liebman, Professor of Law, Harvard University.

ENERGY LAW (1983) with 1986 Case Supplement

Donald N. Zillman, Professor of Law, University of Utah.
Laurence Lattman, Dean of Mines and Engineering, University of Utah.

ENTERPRISE ORGANIZATION, Fourth Edition (1987), with 1987 Corporation and Partnership Statutes, Rules and Forms Supplement

Alfred F. Conard, Professor of Law, University of Michigan.
Robert L. Knauss, Dean of the Law School, University of Houston.
Stanley Siegel, Professor of Law, University of California, Los Angeles.

ENVIRONMENTAL POLICY LAW 1985 Edition, with 1985 Problems Supplement (Supplement in association with Ronald H. Rosenberg, Professor of Law, College of William and Mary)

Thomas J. Schoenbaum, Professor of Law, University of Georgia.

EQUITY, see also Remedies

EQUITY, RESTITUTION AND DAMAGES, Second Edition (1974)

Robert Childres, late Professor of Law, Northwestern University.
William F. Johnson, Jr., Professor of Law, New York University.

ESTATE PLANNING, Second Edition (1982), with 1985 Case, Text and Documentary Supplement

David Westfall, Professor of Law, Harvard University.

ETHICS, see Legal Profession, Professional Responsibility, and Social Responsibilities

ETHICS OF LAWYERING, THE LAW AND (1990)

Geoffrey C. Hazard, Jr., Professor of Law, Yale University.
Susan P. Koniak, Professor of Law, University of Pittsburgh.

ETHICS AND PROFESSIONAL RESPONSIBILITY (1981) (Reprinted from THE LAWYERING PROCESS)

Gary Bellow, Professor of Law, Harvard University.
Bea Moulton, Legal Services Corporation.

EVIDENCE, Sixth Edition (1988 Reprint)

John Kaplan, Professor of Law, Stanford University.
Jon R. Waltz, Professor of Law, Northwestern University.

EVIDENCE, Eighth Edition (1988), with Rules, Statute and Case Supplement (1989)

Jack B. Weinstein, Chief Judge, United States District Court.
John H. Mansfield, Professor of Law, Harvard University.
Norman Abrams, Professor of Law, University of California, Los Angeles.
Margaret Berger, Professor of Law, Brooklyn Law School.

FAMILY LAW, see also Domestic Relations

FAMILY LAW Second Edition (1985), with 1988 Supplement

Judith C. Areen, Professor of Law, Georgetown University.

FAMILY LAW AND CHILDREN IN THE LEGAL SYSTEM, STATUTORY MATERIALS (1981)

Walter Wadlington, Professor of Law, University of Virginia.

UNIVERSITY CASEBOOK SERIES—Continued

FEDERAL COURTS, Eighth Edition (1988), with 1989 Supplement

Charles T. McCormick, late Professor of Law, University of Texas.
James H. Chadbourn, late Professor of Law, Harvard University.
Charles Alan Wright, Professor of Law, University of Texas, Austin.

FEDERAL COURTS AND THE FEDERAL SYSTEM, Hart and Wechsler's Third Edition (1988), with 1989 Case Supplement, and the Judicial Code and Rules of Procedure in the Federal Courts (1989)

Paul M. Bator, Professor of Law, University of Chicago.
Daniel J. Meltzer, Professor of Law, Harvard University.
Paul J. Mishkin, Professor of Law, University of California, Berkeley.
David L. Shapiro, Professor of Law, Harvard University.

FEDERAL COURTS AND THE LAW OF FEDERAL–STATE RELATIONS, Second Edition (1989), with 1989 Supplement

Peter W. Low, Professor of Law, University of Virginia.
John C. Jeffries, Jr., Professor of Law, University of Virginia.

FEDERAL PUBLIC LAND AND RESOURCES LAW, Second Edition (1987), with 1990 Case Supplement and 1990 Statutory Supplement

George C. Coggins, Professor of Law, University of Kansas.
Charles F. Wilkinson, Professor of Law, University of Oregon.

FEDERAL RULES OF CIVIL PROCEDURE and Selected Other Procedural Provisions, 1990 Edition

FEDERAL TAXATION, see Taxation

FOOD AND DRUG LAW (1980), with Statutory Supplement

Richard A. Merrill, Dean of the School of Law, University of Virginia.
Peter Barton Hutt, Esq.

FUTURE INTERESTS (1958)

Philip Mechem, late Professor of Law Emeritus, University of Pennsylvania.

FUTURE INTERESTS (1970)

Howard R. Williams, Professor of Law, Stanford University.

FUTURE INTERESTS AND ESTATE PLANNING (1961), with 1962 Supplement

W. Barton Leach, late Professor of Law, Harvard University.
James K. Logan, formerly Dean of the Law School, University of Kansas.

GOVERNMENT CONTRACTS, FEDERAL, Successor Edition (1985), with 1989 Supplement

John W. Whelan, Professor of Law, Hastings College of the Law.

GOVERNMENT REGULATION: FREE ENTERPRISE AND ECONOMIC ORGANIZATION, Sixth Edition (1985)

Louis B. Schwartz, Professor of Law, Hastings College of the Law.
John J. Flynn, Professor of Law, University of Utah.
Harry First, Professor of Law, New York University.

HEALTH CARE LAW AND POLICY (1988)

Clark C. Havighurst, Professor of Law, Duke University.

UNIVERSITY CASEBOOK SERIES—Continued

HINCKLEY, JOHN W., JR., TRIAL OF: A Case Study of the Insanity Defense (1986)

Peter W. Low, Professor of Law, University of Virginia.
John C. Jeffries, Jr., Professor of Law, University of Virginia.
Richard C. Bonnie, Professor of Law, University of Virginia.

INJUNCTIONS, Second Edition (1984)

Owen M. Fiss, Professor of Law, Yale University.
Doug Rendleman, Professor of Law, College of William and Mary.

INSTITUTIONAL INVESTORS, (1978)

David L. Ratner, Professor of Law, Cornell University.

INSURANCE, Second Edition (1985)

William F. Young, Professor of Law, Columbia University.
Eric M. Holmes, Professor of Law, University of Georgia.

INSURANCE LAW AND REGULATION (1990)

Kenneth S. Abraham, University of Virginia.

INTERNATIONAL LAW, see also Transnational Legal Problems, Transnational Business Problems, and United Nations Law

INTERNATIONAL LAW IN CONTEMPORARY PERSPECTIVE (1981), with Essay Supplement

Myres S. McDougal, Professor of Law, Yale University.
W. Michael Reisman, Professor of Law, Yale University.

INTERNATIONAL LEGAL SYSTEM, Third Edition (1988), with Documentary Supplement

Joseph Modeste Sweeney, Professor of Law, University of California, Hastings.
Covey T. Oliver, Professor of Law, University of Pennsylvania.
Noyes E. Leech, Professor of Law Emeritus, University of Pennsylvania.

INTRODUCTION TO LAW, see also Legal Method, On Law in Courts, and Dynamics of American Law

INTRODUCTION TO THE STUDY OF LAW (1970)

E. Wayne Thode, late Professor of Law, University of Utah.
Leon Lebowitz, Professor of Law, University of Texas.
Lester J. Mazor, Professor of Law, University of Utah.

JUDICIAL CODE and Rules of Procedure in the Federal Courts, Students' Edition, 1989 Revision

Daniel J. Meltzer, Professor of Law, Harvard University.
David L. Shapiro, Professor of Law, Harvard University.

JURISPRUDENCE (Temporary Edition Hardbound) (1949)

Lon L. Fuller, late Professor of Law, Harvard University.

JUVENILE, see also Children

JUVENILE JUSTICE PROCESS, Third Edition (1985)

Frank W. Miller, Professor of Law, Washington University.
Robert O. Dawson, Professor of Law, University of Texas.
George E. Dix, Professor of Law, University of Texas.
Raymond I. Parnas, Professor of Law, University of California, Davis.

LABOR LAW, Tenth Edition (1986), with 1989 Case Supplement and 1986 Statutory Supplement

Archibald Cox, Professor of Law, Harvard University.
Derek C. Bok, President, Harvard University.
Robert A. Gorman, Professor of Law, University of Pennsylvania.

LABOR LAW, Second Edition (1982), with Statutory Supplement

Clyde W. Summers, Professor of Law, University of Pennsylvania.
Harry H. Wellington, Dean of the Law School, Yale University.
Alan Hyde, Professor of Law, Rutgers University.

LAND FINANCING, Third Edition (1985)

The late Norman Penney, Professor of Law, Cornell University.
Richard F. Broude, Member of the California Bar.
Roger Cunningham, Professor of Law, University of Michigan.

LAW AND MEDICINE (1980)

Walter Wadlington, Professor of Law and Professor of Legal Medicine, University of Virginia.
Jon R. Waltz, Professor of Law, Northwestern University.
Roger B. Dworkin, Professor of Law, Indiana University, and Professor of Biomedical History, University of Washington.

LAW, LANGUAGE AND ETHICS (1972)

William R. Bishin, Professor of Law, University of Southern California.
Christopher D. Stone, Professor of Law, University of Southern California.

LAW, SCIENCE AND MEDICINE (1984), with 1989 Supplement

Judith C. Areen, Professor of Law, Georgetown University.
Patricia A. King, Professor of Law, Georgetown University.
Steven P. Goldberg, Professor of Law, Georgetown University.
Alexander M. Capron, Professor of Law, University of Southern California.

LAWYERING PROCESS (1978), with Civil Problem Supplement and Criminal Problem Supplement

Gary Bellow, Professor of Law, Harvard University.
Bea Moulton, Professor of Law, Arizona State University.

LEGAL METHOD (1980)

Harry W. Jones, Professor of Law Emeritus, Columbia University.
John M. Kernochan, Professor of Law, Columbia University.
Arthur W. Murphy, Professor of Law, Columbia University.

LEGAL METHODS (1969)

Robert N. Covington, Professor of Law, Vanderbilt University.
E. Blythe Stason, late Professor of Law, Vanderbilt University.
John W. Wade, Professor of Law, Vanderbilt University.
Elliott E. Cheatham, late Professor of Law, Vanderbilt University.
Theodore A. Smedley, Professor of Law, Vanderbilt University.

LEGAL PROFESSION, THE, Responsibility and Regulation, Second Edition (1988)

Geoffrey C. Hazard, Jr., Professor of Law, Yale University.
Deborah L. Rhode, Professor of Law, Stanford University.

LEGISLATION, Fourth Edition (1982) (by Fordham)

Horace E. Read, late Vice President, Dalhousie University.
John W. MacDonald, Professor of Law Emeritus, Cornell Law School.
Jefferson B. Fordham, Professor of Law, University of Utah.
William J. Pierce, Professor of Law, University of Michigan.

LEGISLATIVE AND ADMINISTRATIVE PROCESSES, Second Edition (1981)

Hans A. Linde, Judge, Supreme Court of Oregon.
George Bunn, Professor of Law, University of Wisconsin.
Fredericka Paff, Professor of Law, University of Wisconsin.
W. Lawrence Church, Professor of Law, University of Wisconsin.

LOCAL GOVERNMENT LAW, Second Revised Edition (1986)

Jefferson B. Fordham, Professor of Law, University of Utah.

MASS MEDIA LAW, Fourth Edition (1990)

Marc A. Franklin, Professor of Law, Stanford University.
David A. Anderson, Professor of Law, University of Texas.

MUNICIPAL CORPORATIONS, see Local Government Law

NEGOTIABLE INSTRUMENTS, see Commercial Paper

NEGOTIATION (1981) (Reprinted from THE LAWYERING PROCESS)

Gary Bellow, Professor of Law, Harvard Law School.
Bea Moulton, Legal Services Corporation.

NEW YORK PRACTICE, Fourth Edition (1978)

Herbert Peterfreund, Professor of Law, New York University.
Joseph M. McLaughlin, Dean of the Law School, Fordham University.

OIL AND GAS, Fifth Edition (1987)

Howard R. Williams, Professor of Law, Stanford University.
Richard C. Maxwell, Professor of Law, University of California, Los Angeles.
Charles J. Meyers, late Dean of the Law School, Stanford University.
Stephen F. Williams, Judge of the United States Court of Appeals.

ON LAW IN COURTS (1965)

Paul J. Mishkin, Professor of Law, University of California, Berkeley.
Clarence Morris, Professor of Law Emeritus, University of Pennsylvania.

PENSION AND EMPLOYEE BENEFIT LAW (1990)

John H. Langbein, Professor of Law, University of Chicago.
Bruce A. Wolk, Professor of Law, University of California, Davis.

PLEADING AND PROCEDURE, see Procedure, Civil

POLICE FUNCTION, Fourth Edition (1986), with 1989 Case Supplement

Reprint of Chapters 1–10 of Miller, Dawson, Dix and Parnas's CRIMINAL
JUSTICE ADMINISTRATION, Third Edition.

PREPARING AND PRESENTING THE CASE (1981) (Reprinted from THE LAW-YERING PROCESS)

Gary Bellow, Professor of Law, Harvard Law School.
Bea Moulton, Legal Services Corporation.

UNIVERSITY CASEBOOK SERIES—Continued

PROCEDURE (1988), with Procedure Supplement (1989)

Robert M. Cover, late Professor of Law, Yale Law School.
Owen M. Fiss, Professor of Law, Yale Law School.
Judith Resnik, Professor of Law, University of Southern California Law Center.

PROCEDURE—CIVIL PROCEDURE, Second Edition (1974), with 1979 Supplement

The late James H. Chadbourn, Professor of Law, Harvard University.
A. Leo Levin, Professor of Law, University of Pennsylvania.
Philip Shuchman, Professor of Law, Cornell University.

PROCEDURE—CIVIL PROCEDURE, Sixth Edition (1990)

Richard H. Field, late Professor of Law, Harvard University.
Benjamin Kaplan, Professor of Law Emeritus, Harvard University.
Kevin M. Clermont, Professor of Law, Cornell University.

PROCEDURE—CIVIL PROCEDURE, Fifth Edition (1990)

Maurice Rosenberg, Professor of Law, Columbia University.
Hans Smit, Professor of Law, Columbia University.
Rochelle C. Dreyfuss, Professor of Law, New York University.

PROCEDURE—PLEADING AND PROCEDURE: State and Federal, Sixth Edition (1989)

David W. Louisell, late Professor of Law, University of California, Berkeley.
Geoffrey C. Hazard, Jr., Professor of Law, Yale University.
Colin C. Tait, Professor of Law, University of Connecticut.

PROCEDURE—FEDERAL RULES OF CIVIL PROCEDURE, 1990 Edition

PRODUCTS LIABILITY AND SAFETY, Second Edition, (1989), with 1989 Statutory Supplement

W. Page Keeton, Professor of Law, University of Texas.
David G. Owen, Professor of Law, University of South Carolina.
John E. Montgomery, Professor of Law, University of South Carolina.
Michael D. Green, Professor of Law, University of Iowa

PROFESSIONAL RESPONSIBILITY, Fourth Edition (1987), with 1990 Selected National Standards Supplement

Thomas D. Morgan, Dean of the Law School, Emory University.
Ronald D. Rotunda, Professor of Law, University of Illinois.

PROPERTY, Sixth Edition (1990)

John E. Cribbet, Professor of Law, University of Illinois.
Corwin W. Johnson, Professor of Law, University of Texas.
Roger W. Findley, Professor of Law, University of Illinois.
Ernest E. Smith, Professor of Law, University of Texas.

PROPERTY—PERSONAL (1953)

S. Kenneth Skolfield, late Professor of Law Emeritus, Boston University.

PROPERTY—PERSONAL, Third Edition (1954)

Everett Fraser, late Dean of the Law School Emeritus, University of Minnesota.
Third Edition by Charles W. Taintor, late Professor of Law, University of Pittsburgh.

PROPERTY—INTRODUCTION, TO REAL PROPERTY, Third Edition (1954)

Everett Fraser, late Dean of the Law School Emeritus, University of Minnesota.

UNIVERSITY CASEBOOK SERIES—Continued

PROPERTY—FUNDAMENTALS OF MODERN REAL PROPERTY, Second Edition (1982), with 1985 Supplement

Edward H. Rabin, Professor of Law, University of California, Davis.

PROPERTY, REAL (1984), with 1988 Supplement

Paul Goldstein, Professor of Law, Stanford University.

PROSECUTION AND ADJUDICATION, Third Edition (1986), with 1989 Case Supplement

Reprint of Chapters 11–26 of Miller, Dawson, Dix and Parnas's CRIMINAL JUSTICE ADMINISTRATION, Third Edition.

PSYCHIATRY AND LAW, see Mental Health, see also Hinckley, Trial of

PUBLIC UTILITY LAW, see Free Enterprise, also Regulated Industries

REAL ESTATE PLANNING, Third Edition (1989), with 1989 Problem and Statutory Supplement

Norton L. Steuben, Professor of Law, University of Colorado.

REAL ESTATE TRANSACTIONS, Revised Second Edition (1988), with Statute, Form and Problem Supplement (1988)

Paul Goldstein, Professor of Law, Stanford University.

RECEIVERSHIP AND CORPORATE REORGANIZATION, see Creditors' Rights

REGULATED INDUSTRIES, Second Edition, (1976)

William K. Jones, Professor of Law, Columbia University.

REMEDIES, Second Edition (1987)

Edward D. Re, Chief Judge, U. S. Court of International Trade.

REMEDIES, (1989)

Elaine W. Shoben, Professor of Law, University of Illinois.
Wm. Murray Tabb, Professor of Law, Baylor University.

SALES, Second Edition (1986)

Marion W. Benfield, Jr., Professor of Law, University of Illinois.
William D. Hawkland, Chancellor, Louisiana State Law Center.

SALES AND SALES FINANCING, Fifth Edition (1984)

John Honnold, Professor of Law, University of Pennsylvania.

SALES LAW AND THE CONTRACTING PROCESS (1982)

Reprint of Chapters 1–10 of Schwartz and Scott's Commercial Transactions.

SECURED TRANSACTIONS IN PERSONAL PROPERTY, Second Edition (1987) (Reprinted from COMMERCIAL LAW, Second Edition (1987))

Robert L. Jordan, Professor of Law, University of California, Los Angeles.
William D. Warren, Professor of Law, University of California, Los Angeles.

SECURITIES REGULATION, Sixth Edition (1987), with 1989 Selected Statutes, Rules and Forms Supplement and 1989 Cases and Releases Supplement

Richard W. Jennings, Professor of Law, University of California, Berkeley.
Harold Marsh, Jr., Member of California Bar.

UNIVERSITY CASEBOOK SERIES—Continued

SECURITIES REGULATION, Second Edition (1988), with Statute, Rule and Form Supplement (1988)

Larry D. Soderquist, Professor of Law, Vanderbilt University.

SECURITY INTERESTS IN PERSONAL PROPERTY, Second Edition (1987)

Douglas G. Baird, Professor of Law, University of Chicago.
Thomas H. Jackson, Professor of Law, Harvard University.

SECURITY INTERESTS IN PERSONAL PROPERTY (1985) (Reprinted from Sales and Sales Financing, Fifth Edition)

John Honnold, Professor of Law, University of Pennsylvania.

SOCIAL RESPONSIBILITIES OF LAWYERS, Case Studies (1988)

Philip B. Heymann, Professor of Law, Harvard University.
Lance Liebman, Professor of Law, Harvard University.

SOCIAL SCIENCE IN LAW, Second Edition (1990)

John Monahan, Professor of Law, University of Virginia.
Laurens Walker, Professor of Law, University of Virginia.

TAXATION, FEDERAL INCOME (1989)

Stephen B. Cohen, Professor of Law, Georgetown University

TAXATION, FEDERAL INCOME, Second Edition (1988), with 1989 Supplement

Michael J. Graetz, Professor of Law, Yale University.

TAXATION, FEDERAL INCOME, Sixth Edition (1987)

James J. Freeland, Professor of Law, University of Florida.
Stephen A. Lind, Professor of Law, University of Florida and University of California, Hastings.
Richard B. Stephens, late Professor of Law Emeritus, University of Florida.

TAXATION, FEDERAL INCOME, Successor Edition (1986), with 1989 Legislative Supplement

Stanley S. Surrey, late Professor of Law, Harvard University.
Paul R. McDaniel, Professor of Law, Boston College.
Hugh J. Ault, Professor of Law, Boston College.
Stanley A. Koppelman, Professor of Law, Boston University.

TAXATION, FEDERAL INCOME, VOLUME II, Taxation of Partnerships and Corporations, Second Edition (1980), with 1989 Legislative Supplement

Stanley S. Surrey, late Professor of Law, Harvard University.
William C. Warren, Professor of Law Emeritus, Columbia University.
Paul R. McDaniel, Professor of Law, Boston College.
Hugh J. Ault, Professor of Law, Boston College.

TAXATION, FEDERAL INCOME, OIL AND GAS, NATURAL RESOURCES TRANSACTIONS (1990)

Peter C. Maxfield, Professor of Law, University of Wyoming.
James L. Houghton, CPA, Partner, Ernst and Young.
James R. Gaar, CPA, Partner, Ernst and Young.

TAXATION, FEDERAL WEALTH TRANSFER, Successor Edition (1987)

Stanley S. Surrey, late Professor of Law, Harvard University.
Paul R. McDaniel, Professor of Law, Boston College.
Harry L. Gutman, Professor of Law, University of Pennsylvania.

UNIVERSITY CASEBOOK SERIES—Continued

TAXATION, FUNDAMENTALS OF CORPORATE, Second Edition (1987), with 1989 Supplement

Stephen A. Lind, Professor of Law, University of Florida and University of California, Hastings.
Stephen Schwarz, Professor of Law, University of California, Hastings.
Daniel J. Lathrope, Professor of Law, University of California, Hastings.
Joshua Rosenberg, Professor of Law, University of San Francisco.

TAXATION, FUNDAMENTALS OF PARTNERSHIP, Second Edition (1988)

Stephen A. Lind, Professor of Law, University of Florida and University of California, Hastings.
Stephen Schwarz, Professor of Law, University of California, Hastings.
Daniel J. Lathrope, Professor of Law, University of California, Hastings.
Joshua Rosenberg, Professor of Law, University of San Francisco.

TAXATION, PROBLEMS IN THE FEDERAL INCOME TAXATION OF PARTNERSHIPS AND CORPORATIONS, Second Edition (1986)

Norton L. Steuben, Professor of Law, University of Colorado.
William J. Turnier, Professor of Law, University of North Carolina.

TAXATION, PROBLEMS IN THE FUNDAMENTALS OF FEDERAL INCOME, Second Edition (1985)

Norton L. Steuben, Professor of Law, University of Colorado.
William J. Turnier, Professor of Law, University of North Carolina.

TORT LAW AND ALTERNATIVES, Fourth Edition (1987)

Marc A. Franklin, Professor of Law, Stanford University.
Robert L. Rabin, Professor of Law, Stanford University.

TORTS, Eighth Edition (1988)

William L. Prosser, late Professor of Law, University of California, Hastings.
John W. Wade, Professor of Law, Vanderbilt University.
Victor E. Schwartz, Adjunct Professor of Law, Georgetown University.

TORTS, Third Edition (1976)

Harry Shulman, late Dean of the Law School, Yale University.
Fleming James, Jr., Professor of Law Emeritus, Yale University.
Oscar S. Gray, Professor of Law, University of Maryland.

TRADE REGULATION, Second Edition (1983), with 1987 Supplement

Milton Handler, Professor of Law Emeritus, Columbia University.
Harlan M. Blake, Professor of Law, Columbia University.
Robert Pitofsky, Professor of Law, Georgetown University.
Harvey J. Goldschmid, Professor of Law, Columbia University.

TRADE REGULATION, see Antitrust

TRANSNATIONAL BUSINESS PROBLEMS (1986)

Detlev F. Vagts, Professor of Law, Harvard University.

TRANSNATIONAL LEGAL PROBLEMS, Third Edition (1986) with Documentary Supplement

Henry J. Steiner, Professor of Law, Harvard University.
Detlev F. Vagts, Professor of Law, Harvard University.

TRIAL, see also Evidence, Making the Record, Lawyering Process and Preparing and Presenting the Case

UNIVERSITY CASEBOOK SERIES—Continued

TRUSTS, Fifth Edition (1978)

George G. Bogert, late Professor of Law Emeritus, University of Chicago.
Dallin H. Oaks, President, Brigham Young University.

TRUSTS AND SUCCESSION (Palmer's), Fourth Edition (1983)

Richard V. Wellman, Professor of Law, University of Georgia.
Lawrence W. Waggoner, Professor of Law, University of Michigan.
Olin L. Browder, Jr., Professor of Law, University of Michigan.

UNFAIR COMPETITION, see Competitive Process and Business Torts

WATER RESOURCE MANAGEMENT, Third Edition (1988)

The late Charles J. Meyers, formerly Dean, Stanford University Law School.
A. Dan Tarlock, Professor of Law, II Chicago-Kent College of Law.
James N. Corbridge, Jr., Chancellor, University of Colorado at Boulder, and
    Professor of Law, University of Colorado School of Law.
David H. Getches, Professor of Law, University of Colorado School of Law.

WILLS AND ADMINISTRATION, Fifth Edition (1961)

Philip Mechem, late Professor of Law, University of Pennsylvania.
Thomas E. Atkinson, late Professor of Law, New York University.

WRITING AND ANALYSIS IN THE LAW (1989)

Helene S. Shapo, Professor of Law, Northwestern University
Marilyn R. Walter, Professor of Law, Brooklyn Law School
Elizabeth Fajans, Writing Specialist, Brooklyn Law School

University Casebook Series

CRIMINAL LAW:

CASES AND MATERIALS

SECOND EDITION

By

PETER W. LOW

Hardy Cross Dillard Professor of Law,
University of Virginia

JOHN CALVIN JEFFRIES, JR.

Professor of Law, University of Virginia

and

RICHARD J. BONNIE

Professor of Law, University of Virginia

Mineola, New York
THE FOUNDATION PRESS, INC.
1986

COPYRIGHT © 1982 THE FOUNDATION PRESS, INC.
COPYRIGHT © 1986 By THE FOUNDATION PRESS, INC.
All rights reserved
Printed in the United States of America

Library of Congress Cataloging in Publication Data
Low, Peter W., 1937–
  Criminal law.

  (University casebook series)
  Includes index.
  1. Criminal law—United States—Cases. I. Jeffries,
John Calvin, 1948–   . II. Bonnie, Richard J.
III. Title. IV. Series.
KF9218.L68 1986   345.73   86–9823
ISBN 0–88277–325–9   347.305

L., J. & B. Cs.Crim.Law 2nd Ed. UCB
5th Reprint—1990

PREFACE TO THE SECOND EDITION

This book has been substantially revised, chiefly with an eye to improving teachability. Nonetheless, comments made in the preface to the first edition remain applicable:

"The first thing one notices about this book is the prevalence of notes. Main cases occupy only about half of the pages. The rest are devoted to narrative exposition and excerpts. The prevalence of notes is consistent with our objective to bring the student as quickly as possible to a point of readiness to confront interesting issues. To that end, we have used notes not only to ask questions and to suggest lines of analysis, but also to recount historical background, to summarize settled doctrine, and to provide additional information relevant to discussion of the issue at hand. For the most part, therefore, main cases have been selected and edited not simply to convey information, but to provide expansive opportunities for discussion and analysis of issues of genuine scope and importance in the criminal law.

"A second objective has been to strike an appropriate balance between structure and flexibility. With respect to the former, we have tried to structure these materials so that the arrangement of topics is, in itself, instructive. This concern is especially evident in the materials on the criminal act and the criminal mind (Chapters I and II, respectively). ... At the same time, we have tried to preserve the greatest possible flexibility for the individual instructor to pick and choose among the additional subjects to be covered. This concern predominates in the later chapters, many of which have been arranged in discrete units designed to make the materials freely adaptable to a variety of course-plans and interests. ...

"Our third objective has been to ensure that the materials do full justice both to the tradition of the common law and to the contribution of modern statutes. To date, more than half the states have adopted revised criminal codes, and others have proposals pending. All of these modern codes derive in one or another degree from the American Law Institute's Model Penal Code. We therefore have included frequent and detailed reference to the Model Penal Code and to other modern statutes. Additionally, we have reprinted the bulk of the Model Code and selected other statutes [in appendices]. We also recognize, however, that no contemporary study of this field can afford to neglect the heritage of the common law. For one thing, the common law continues to provide the essential structure of crime definition in a substantial number of American jurisdictions. Moreover, the legacy of the common law continues to make itself felt, even in those jurisdictions that have adopted revised codes.

We have resisted, therefore, the temptation to treat the common law as a matter of merely historical interest and instead have tried to deal with that tradition on its own terms."

As in the first edition, we have conformed all citations to our usage. That usage is standard save for the omission of citations to subsequent history—e.g., rehearing denied or reversed on other grounds. Many citations have been deleted without specific indication, but the omission of anything more than a citation is indicated by brackets or ellipses. Original footnote numbers have been retained in all quoted materials; our footnotes are lettered rather than numbered. Acknowledgment of permission to reprint excerpts from the literature appears at appropriate places in the text.

PWL
JCJjr
RJB

Charlottesville, Virginia
March, 1986

SUMMARY OF CONTENTS

	Page
PREFACE TO THE SECOND EDITION	xix
TABLE OF CASES	xlix

INTRODUCTION: THE PURPOSES OF PUNISHMENT — 1

CHAPTER I: THE CRIMINAL ACT — 29

Section 1: The Requirement of Previously Defined Conduct — 29
  Subsection A: The Principle of Legality — 29
  Subsection B: The Vagueness Doctrine — 45
Section 2: Conduct in the Definition of the Offense — 85
  Subsection A: Acts — 85
  Subsection B: Omissions — 107
Section 3: Minimum Conduct Requirements for the Imposition of Penal Sanctions — 122
  Subsection A: Minimum Conduct Requirements and Anticipatory Offenses — 126
  Subsection B: Minimum Conduct Requirements in Completed Offenses — 140
  Subsection C: Minimum Conduct Requirements and Voluntariness — 152

CHAPTER II: THE CRIMINAL MIND — 193

Section 1: Culpability in the Definition of the Offense — 193
  Subsection A: Culpability at Common Law — 193
  Subsection B: Culpability in Modern Statutes — 233
Section 2: Ignorance or Mistake — 246
  Subsection A: Ignorance or Mistake of Fact — 246
  Subsection B: Ignorance or Mistake as to Criminality — 257
  Subsection C: Other Mistakes of Law — 268
Section 3: The Significance of Intoxication — 274
Section 4: Strict Liability — 291
  Subsection A: Regulatory Offenses — 291
  Subsection B: Constitutional Limits on Strict Liability — 308
  Subsection C: Strict Liability in Serious Crimes — 313
  Subsection D: A Concluding Problem of Mens-Rea Policy — 323
  Subsection E: The Abandonment of Mens Rea for All Crimes — 334
Section 5: The Relation of Culpability and Conduct — 339
  Subsection A: The Mens Rea of Attempt — 342
  Subsection B: Impossibility and Attempt — 353
  Subsection C: Equivocal Conduct in Completed Offenses — 366
  Subsection D: Abandonment in Attempt and Other Offenses — 371

CHAPTER III: LIABILITY FOR THE CONDUCT OF ANOTHER ... 379

Section 1: Complicity ... 379

Subsection A: The Conduct Required for Complicity ... 383

Subsection B: The Culpability Required for Complicity ... 392

Subsection C: Guilt of the Principal ... 404

Subsection D: Limits of Accomplice Liability ... 412

Section 2: Vicarious Liability ... 414

Section 3: Corporate Criminality ... 420

Section 4: Conspiracy ... 434

Subsection A: The Objectives That Make Conspiracy Criminal ... 437

Subsection B: Conspiracy as an Inchoate Offense ... 445

Subsection C: The Relation of Conspiracy to Complicity ... 463

Subsection D: Scope and Duration of Conspiracy ... 480

Subsection E: Limits on Liability for Conspiracy ... 500

CHAPTER IV: JUSTIFICATION AND EXCUSE ... 511

Section 1: Justification ... 512

Subsection A: The General Principle of Justification ... 512

Subsection B: The Effect of Mistake ... 530

Subsection C: Defense Against Aggression ... 537

Subsection D: Public Authority ... 581

Section 2: Situational Excuse ... 604

CHAPTER V: CRIMINAL RESPONSIBILITY ... 631

Section 1: Immaturity ... 632

Section 2: Mental Abnormality ... 654

Subsection A: The Insanity Defense and Major Mental Disorder ... 664

Subsection B: The Insanity Defense and the Control Inquiry ... 686

Subsection C: The Insanity Defense and Intoxication ... 720

Subsection D: Disposition of Mentally Disordered Offenders ... 733

Subsection E: Mental Abnormality and Mens Rea ... 752

Subsection F: Abolition of the Insanity Defense ... 770

CHAPTER VI: HOMICIDE: A PROBLEM OF CULPABILITY AND GRADING ... 779

Section 1: Capital Homicide ... 786

Subsection A: The Supreme Court and Capital Punishment ... 792

Subsection B: Administration of Modern Capital Sentencing Statutes ... 816

Page

**CHAPTER VI: HOMICIDE: A PROBLEM OF CULPABILI-
TY AND GRADING**—Continued
Section 2: Grading of Non-Capital Homicides 882
    Subsection A: Intentional Homicide 882
    Subsection B: Unintentional Homicide 905
Section 3: Causation 923
Section 4: Felony Murder 932

**CHAPTER VII: PROOF, PROPORTIONALITY, AND
CRIMINALIZATION** 967
Section 1: Proof Beyond a Reasonable Doubt 967
    Subsection A: Mitigations and Defenses 968
    Subsection B: Presumptions 993
Section 2: Proportionality 1004
    Subsection A: Proportionality and Capital Punishment 1004
    Subsection B: Proportionality and Imprisonment 1028
Section 3: Criminalization 1053

APPENDICES

A. The Model Penal Code A–1
Introductory Note on the Model Penal Code A–1
Model Penal Code A–4
Table of Model Penal Code References A–97
B. Selected Penal Statutes B–1
Virginia Homicide Statutes B–1
Pre-*Furman* Georgia Homicide Statutes B–5
New York Homicide Statutes B–6
Oregon Homicide and Assault Offenses and Provisions on
    Attempt B–9
Capital Punishment Statutes Before the Supreme Court in
    1976 Decisions B–12
Additional Contemporary Capital Sentencing Statutes B–19

Index .... [1]

*

TABLE OF CONTENTS

Page

PREFACE TO THE SECOND EDITION _____ xix

TABLE OF CASES _____ xlix

INTRODUCTION: THE PURPOSES OF PUNISHMENT

RETRIBUTION _____ 2
    1. The Criminal Law as a Moral Statement _____ 3
    2. Retribution as a Limiting Concept: Blameworthiness 4
    3. Retribution as a Limiting Concept: Proportionality ___ 7

GENERAL DETERRENCE _____ 7
    1. The Concept _____ 8
    2. Criticisms of Deterrence Theory _____ 10
    3. The Limits of Deterrence _____ 12
    4. Deterrence and Blameworthiness _____ 13
    5. The Socializing Effect of the Criminal Law _____ 15
    6. Measuring Deterrence _____ 16
    7. The Relation of Severity and Certainty _____ 17

INDIVIDUAL PREVENTION _____ 21
    1. Special Deterrence _____ 21
    2. Incapacitation _____ 22
    3. Rehabilitation _____ 24
    4. The Limits of Individual Prevention _____ 27

CHAPTER I: THE CRIMINAL ACT

SECTION 1: THE REQUIREMENT OF PREVIOUSLY DEFINED
  CONDUCT _____ 29
Subsection A: The Principle of Legality _____ 29
Rex v. Manley _____ 29
Notes on *Manley* and the Common Law _____ 31
    1. Introduction to the Common Law _____ 31
    2. Later English Cases _____ 32
    3. Questions and Comments on Judicial Crime Creation _____ 33
Notes on the Principle of Legality _____ 33
    1. Introduction _____ 33
    2. European Origins _____ 34
    3. The American Experience: Encounter With the Common Law _____ 36
    4. Recent Experience _____ 38
    5. Growing Acceptance and Evolving Meaning _____ 39
Note on the Continuing Significance of the Common Law 43

Page

SECTION 1: THE REQUIREMENT OF PREVIOUSLY DEFINED CONDUCT—Continued

Subsection B: The Vagueness Doctrine 45

Parker, Warden, et al. v. Levy 45

Notes on *Parker v. Levy* 61

    1.   Prior Constructions of Arts. 133 and 134 61

    2.   The Specifications 61

    3.   Significance of the Military Context 62

Notes on the Vagueness Doctrine 64

    1.   Rationales of the Vagueness Doctrine 64

    2.   Limits of the Vagueness Rationales 64

    3.   Illustrative Cases: *Coates and Papachristou* 66

    4.   Tolerable Vagueness and the Demands of Necessity 68

    5.   Tolerable Vagueness and Questions of Degree 69

    6.   Intolerable Vagueness and the Impact of Indefinite Laws on Protected Freedoms 71

    7.   Concluding Questions and Comments 72

Notes on the Relationship of Vagueness and Overbreadth 72

    1.   *Parker v. Levy* Revisited 72

    2.   The Relation Between Vagueness and Overbreadth: As Applied vs. Facial Review 73

    3.   Concluding Questions and Comments 75

Notes on Obscenity: A Case Study of the Vagueness Doctrine 76

    1.   The Obscenity Problem 76

    2.   *Roth* and *Memoirs* 76

    3.   Redefining Obscenity: The 1973 Decisions 78

    4.   The Brennan Dissent 81

    5.   Questions and Comments on Vagueness and Obscenity 84

SECTION 2: CONDUCT IN THE DEFINITION OF THE OFFENSE 85

Subsection A: Acts 85

Keeler v. Superior Court of Amador County 85

People v. Sobiek 94

Notes on *Keeler* and *Sobiek* 97

    1.   Questions on *Keeler* and *Sobiek* 97

    2.   Relation to *Manley* 98

    3.   *Bouie:* Background of a Constitutional Precedent 98

    4.   The Meaning of *Bouie* 100

Notes on the Doctrine of Strict Construction 101

    1.   Origin of the Doctrine 101

    2.   The Legislative Response 102

    3.   Modern Application: *McBoyle v. United States* ... 103

    4.   Modern Application: *United States v. Bass* 104

Page

SECTION 2: CONDUCT IN THE DEFINITION OF THE OFFENSE—Continued

Subsection B: Omissions _____ 107

    Jones v. United States _____ 107

    Notes on Omissions _____ 109

        1. A Duty to Act _____ 109

        2. Illustrative Cases _____ 110

            (i) *People v. Beardsley* _____ 110

            (ii) *Regina v. Instan* _____ 111

        3. A General Duty to Rescue? _____ 111

        4. Omissions Outside the Law of Homicide _____ 113

    Barber v. Superior Court of Los Angeles County _____ 114

    Notes on the Omission of Life-Sustaining Treatment _____ 117

        1. Questions and Comments on *Barber* _____ 117

        2. Report of the President's Commission _____ 118

        3. Differentiating Acts From Omissions _____ 120

        4. Legislative Solutions _____ 120

    Note on Possession _____ 121

SECTION 3: MINIMUM CONDUCT REQUIREMENTS FOR THE IMPOSITION OF PENAL SANCTIONS _____ 122

    Notes on the Significance of Conduct in the Penal Law ___ 122

        1. The Importance of the Act Requirement _____ 122

        2. Jeffries & Stephan _____ 123

        3. Packer _____ 123

        4. Questions and Comments on the Act Requirement 125

Subsection A: Minimum Conduct Requirements and Anticipatory Offenses _____ 126

    Introductory Note on Attempt _____ 126

    People v. Bowen and Rouse _____ 127

    Notes on Preparation vs. Attempt _____ 132

        1. The Last-Proximate-Act Doctrine _____ 132

        2. Other Common-Law Tests _____ 132

            (i) The Physical-Proximity Test _____ 132

            (ii) The Indispensable-Element Test _____ 133

            (iii) The Dangerous-Proximity Test _____ 134

            (iv) The Res-Ipsa-Loquitur Test _____ 134

        3. The Model Code Approach _____ 136

        4. Questions _____ 137

    Notes on Minimum Conduct Requirements and Solicitation 137

        1. *People v. Adami* _____ 137

        2. Solicitation as an Independent Offense _____ 139

        3. Footnote on Conspiracy _____ 139

SECTION 3: MINIMUM CONDUCT REQUIREMENTS FOR THE IMPOSITION OF PENAL SANCTIONS—Continued

Subsection B: Minimum Conduct Requirements in Completed Offenses 140
    Introductory Note on Completed Offenses 140
    People v. Valot 141
    Notes on Minimum Conduct Requirements in Completed Offenses 144
        1. Possession 144
        2. Constructive Possession 145
        3. Being in a Place 146
        4. Traditional Vagrancy and Loitering Laws 146
        5. *People v. Berck* and Modern Loitering Statutes .. 148
        6. *Kolender v. Lawson* and "Stop-and-Identify" Statutes 151

Subsection C: Minimum Conduct Requirements and Voluntariness 152
    Introductory Notes on the Voluntary Act 152
        1. The Requirement of a Voluntary Act 152
            (i) Physically Coerced Movement 153
            (ii) Reflex Movements 153
            (iii) Muscular Contraction or Paralysis Produced by Disease 153
            (iv) Unconsciousness 153
        2. Forms of Impaired Consciousness 153
            (i) Concussion 154
            (ii) Somnambulism 154
            (iii) Hypnosis and Hypoglycemia 154
        3. Codification 155
        4. Comments and Observations 156
            (i) Content and Function 156
            (ii) Involuntary Act in a Voluntary Course of Conduct 156
            (iii) Relation to Other Doctrines 157
    Robinson v. California 158
    Powell v. Texas 168
    Notes on *Robinson* and *Powell* 182
    Notes on Non-Criminal Methods of Coercive Intervention 183
        1. Quarantine and Civil Commitment 183
        2. Principles Governing Control Interventions 184
            (i) Purpose 184
            (ii) Legality 184
            (iii) Limits 186
        3. The Difference Between Treatment and Punishment 186
            (i) Civil Commitment of Narcotics Addicts 186
            (ii) Mentally Disordered Sex Offenders 187
            (iii) Children in Need of Supervision 188
            (iv) Treatment for Venereal Disease 188
         4. Alcoholism and Drug Dependence: Recent Trends 189

CHAPTER II: THE CRIMINAL MIND

Page

SECTION 1: CULPABILITY IN THE DEFINITION OF THE OF-
FENSE _____ 193
Subsection A: Culpability at Common Law _____ 193
    Introductory Note on the Emergence of Mens Rea at Com-
    mon Law _____ 193
    Regina v. Faulkner _____ 196
    Notes on Mens-Rea Terminology and Meaning _____ 198
        1. The Language of *Mens Rea* _____ 198
        2. *Mens Rea* as General Malevolence _____ 199
        3. *Mens Rea* as a Particular State of Mind _____ 201
        4. *Regina v. Cunningham* _____ 201
        5. *Faulkner* and *Cunningham* Compared _____ 203
    Director of Public Prosecutions v. Smith _____ 204
    Note on the Presumption of Natural and Probable Conse-
    quences _____ 209
    Notes on General Intent at Common Law _____ 211
        1. Holmes' Theory _____ 211
        2. Negligence as the Basis for Criminal Liability ___ 214
        3. The Concept of General Intent _____ 219
        4. Footnote on Strict Liability _____ 220
        5. Mens Rea and Legal Fictions _____ 220
        6. Statutory Response to *Smith* in England _____ 221
    Morissette v. United States _____ 221
    Notes on Specific Intent at Common Law _____ 228
        1. Questions on *Morissette* _____ 228
        2. Background on Theft Offenses _____ 228
        3. Holmes Revisited _____ 229
        4. The Concept of Specific Intent _____ 231

Subsection B: Culpability in Modern Statutes _____ 233
    Introductory Note on the Model Penal Code _____ 233
        1. The Actus Reus _____ 233
        2. The Mens Rea _____ 235
    Model Penal Code Culpability Provisions _____ 235
    Notes on the Model Penal Code Culpability Structure _____ 237
        1. Minimum Requirements of Culpability _____ 237
            (i) Strict Liability _____ 237
            (ii) Types of Culpability _____ 237
            (iii) Material Element _____ 238
            (iv) Each Material Element _____ 238
        2. Purpose _____ 238
        3. Knowledge _____ 238
        4. Recklessness _____ 239
            (i) Advertence to the Risk _____ 239
            (ii) Application of External Standard _____ 239
            (iii) Substantial and Unjustifiable Risk _____ 239
            (iv) The Actor's Situation _____ 240

SECTION 1: CULPABILITY IN THE DEFINITION OF THE OF-
FENSE—Continued

     5.   Negligence _____ 240

     6.   Offense Silent on Culpability _____ 241

     7.   Ambiguous Provision of Culpability _____ 242

        (i) False Imprisonment _____ 242

        (ii) Reckless Burning _____ 243

        (iii) Escape _____ 243

        (iv) Hindering Prosecution _____ 243

     8.   Hierarchy of Model Penal Code Culpability Terms 244

     9.   Illustrative Problems _____ 245

    10.   Application of Model Code to Previously Consid-
ered Cases _____ 245

SECTION 2: IGNORANCE OR MISTAKE _____ 246

Subsection A: Ignorance or Mistake of Fact _____ 246

   United States v. Short _____ 246

   Notes on Mistake of Fact at Common Law _____ 248

     1.   Summary of Common-Law Methodology _____ 248

     2.   Specific Intent _____ 248

     3.   General Intent as Negligence _____ 250

     4.   *State v. Walker* _____ 250

     5.   General Intent as Recklessness _____ 252

     6.   General-Intent Elements of Specific-Intent Crimes 253

     7.   Grading Elements _____ 253

   Model Penal Code _____ 254

   Notes on Mistake of Fact and the Model Penal Code _____ 255

     1.   Methodology of the Model Code _____ 255

     2.   Innovations of the Model Code _____ 255

     3.   Application of the Model Code _____ 256

     4.   The Model Code and Grading Elements _____ 256

Subsection B: Ignorance or Mistake as to Criminality _____ 257

   State v. Downs _____ 257

   Notes on Ignorance or Mistake as to Criminality _____ 258

     1.   Application of the Maxim _____ 258

        (i) *Rex v. Esop* _____ 258

        (ii) *Hopkins v. State* _____ 259

     2.   Problems With the Maxim _____ 259

     3.   Justifications for the Maxim _____ 260

     4.   The Model Penal Code _____ 263

     5.   Proposals for Reform _____ 263

        (i) Perkins _____ 263

        (ii) Revised New Jersey Code _____ 264

   State v. Striggles _____ 264

SECTION 2: IGNORANCE OR MISTAKE—Continued

Notes on Official Misstatement of Criminal Law 265

    1. The *O'Neil* Case 265

    2. Questions on *Striggles* and *O'Neil* 266

    3. Statutory Provisions on Official Misstatement of Criminal Law 267

Subsection C: Other Mistakes of Law 268

    State v. Woods 268

Notes on Other Mistakes of Law 270

    1. Introduction 270

    2. The Common Law 270

    3. Background on Bigamy 271

    4. Questions and Comments on *Woods* 271

    5. The Model Penal Code 272

    6. Categorization of Mistakes Under the Common Law 273

    7. Categorization of Mistakes Under the Model Penal Code 274

SECTION 3: THE SIGNIFICANCE OF INTOXICATION 274

    Director of Public Prosecutions v. Majewski 274

Notes on Intoxication and Mens Rea 283

    1. Introduction 283

    2. General-Intent Crimes 283

    3. Specific-Intent Crimes 285

        (i) Restrictive Positions 285

        (ii) Lack of Capacity vs. Factual Relevance 286

        (iii) Burden of Persuasion 288

    4. Creation of a Separate "Dangerous Intoxication" Offense 288

Note on Mental Abnormality and Mens Rea 290

SECTION 4: STRICT LIABILITY 291

Subsection A: Regulatory Offenses 291

Introductory Note on the Origins and Nature of Regulatory Offenses 291

Introductory Notes to *United States v. Park* 292

    1. *United States v. Dotterweich* 293

    2. *United States v. Wiesenfeld Warehouse Co.* 295

United States v. Park 295

Notes on Strict Liability in Regulatory Offenses 304

    1. Questions on *Park* 304

    2. The Strict-Liability Debate 304

    3. Alternatives to Strict Liability 307

Subsection B: Constitutional Limits on Strict Liability 308

Lambert v. California 308

Note on *Lambert* 312

SECTION 4: STRICT LIABILITY—Continued

Subsection C: Strict Liability in Serious Crimes_____ 313

    *United States v. Freed*_____ 313

    Notes on Strict Liability in Serious Crimes_____ 317

        1.   Questions on *Freed* _____ 317

        2.   *Regina v. Prince* _____ 317

        3.   *United States v. Yermian* _____ 320

Subsection D: A Concluding Problem of Mens-Rea Policy_____ 323

    Liparota v. United States _____ 323

    Notes on *Liparota*_____ 333

        1.   Questions on *Liparota* _____ 333

        2.   *United States v. International Minerals & Chemicals Corp.* _____ 333

Subsection E: The Abandonment of Mens Rea for All Crimes___ 334

    Notes on the Abandonment of Mens Rea for All Crimes__ 334

        1.   Lady Wootton's Proposal to Abandon Mens Rea 334

        2.   Responses to Lady Wootton _____ 337

SECTION 5: THE RELATION OF CULPABILITY AND CONDUCT_____ 339

    Introductory Notes on the History and Grading of Attempt 339

        1.   Origins of the Crime of Attempt _____ 339

        2.   Attempts in the United States _____ 340

        3.   The Model Penal Code _____ 341

Subsection A: The Mens Rea of Attempt_____ 342

    Thacker v. Commonwealth _____ 342

    Notes on the Mens Rea of Attempt _____ 344

        1.   *People v. Acevedo*_____ 344

        2.   Rationale for Specific-Intent Requirement _____ 345

        3.   Circumstance Elements _____ 346

            (i) Statutory Rape_____ 346

            (ii) Burglary _____ 347

         4.   Completed Conduct But No Result_____ 348

        5.   *Gentry v. State*_____ 350

    Notes on the Model Penal Code Attempt Provisions_____ 351

        1.   The Text of the Model Code _____ 351

        2.   Explanation of the Model Code Text_____ 351

        3.   Questions on the Model Code _____ 352

Page

SECTION 5: THE RELATION OF CULPABILITY AND CON-
DUCT—Continued

Subsection B: Impossibility and Attempt _____ 353
    People v. Jaffe _____ 353
    Notes on Impossibility and Attempt _____ 356
      1. The Impossibility Problem _____ 356
      2. Some Approaches to the Impossibility Problem __ 358
        (i) Previously Consummated Attempt _____ 358
        (ii) Primary and Secondary Intent _____ 359
        (iii) The Defendant's Reasonable Expectations ___ 360
        (iv) The Model Penal Code _____ 361
        (v) The Importance of the Actus Reus _____ 363
        (vi) The Principle of Legality _____ 365
      3. True Legal Impossibility _____ 366

Subsection C: Equivocal Conduct in Completed Offenses _____ 366
    Bronston v. United States _____ 366
    Notes on Equivocal Conduct in Completed Offenses _____ 370
      1. Questions on *Bronston* _____ 370
      2. *United States v. Remington* _____ 371

Subsection D: Abandonment in Attempt and Other Offenses _____ 371
    People v. Staples _____ 371
    Notes on Abandonment in Attempt and Other Offenses ___ 374
      1. The Traditional Position on Abandonment _____ 374
      2. Comments and Questions on the Traditional Posi-
          tion _____ 375
      3. The Model Penal Code _____ 376
      4. Scope of the Defense _____ 376

**CHAPTER III: LIABILITY FOR THE CONDUCT OF
ANOTHER**

SECTION 1: COMPLICITY _____ 379
    Introductory Notes on Parties to Crime _____ 379
      1. The Common Law _____ 379
      2. Abrogation of the Common Law _____ 380
      3. Accessories After the Fact _____ 381

Subsection A: The Conduct Required for Complicity _____ 383
    Rex v. Russell _____ 383
    Notes on the Conduct Required for Complicity _____ 386
      1. Questions and Comments on *Russell* _____ 386
        (i) Accomplice Liability _____ 386
        (ii) Independent Liability _____ 386
      2. *State v. Walden* _____ 387
      3. *McGhee v. Virginia* _____ 388
      4. *State v. Tally* _____ 389
      5. Describing the Proscribed Conduct: Modern Stat-
          utes and the Common Law _____ 390
      6. A Problem and an Analogy _____ 391

SECTION 1: COMPLICITY—Continued
Subsection B: The Culpability Required for Complicity_____ 392
    United States v. Peoni _____ 392
    Backun v. United States _____ 393
    Notes on the Culpability Required for Complicity_____ 395
        1. Culpability Required for Conduct: Knowledge vs.
             Stake in the Venture_____ 395
        2. Compromise Solutions and the Offense of Facilita-
             tion _____ 397
        3. Culpability Required for Results _____ 398
        4. Culpability Required for Circumstances_____ 399
    *People v. Durham*_____ 400
    Note on the Rule of Natural and Probable Consequences 403

Subsection C: Guilt of the Principal_____ 404
    Regina v. Cogan and Leak _____ 404
    Notes on Liability of a Secondary Party Where There Is No
    Principal_____ 406
        1. Questions on *Cogan and Leak* _____ 406
        2. *Dusenberry v. Commonwealth*: A Contrary View 406
        3. The Abandonment of Derivative Liability? _____ 407
        4. The Theory of the Excusable Wrong_____ 408
        5. Perjury: A Hypothetical _____ 409
        6. *Regina v. Richards* and Degrees of Liability _____ 409
        7. The Model Code and Modern Statutes _____ 411
        8. Study Problems_____ 411

Subsection D: Limits of Accomplice Liability _____ 412
    *Regina v. Tyrrell*_____ 412
    Notes on the Limits of Accomplice Liability_____ 413
        1. Implied Exemption_____ 413
        2. Withdrawal_____ 413

SECTION 2: VICARIOUS LIABILITY_____ 414
    *Commonwealth v. Koczwara*_____ 414
    Notes on Vicarious Liability _____ 417
        1. Background_____ 417
        2. The Relevance of the Sanction _____ 418
        3. *Iowa City v. Nolan* _____ 419

SECTION 3: CORPORATE CRIMINALITY _____ 420
    Commonwealth v. Beneficial Finance Co. _____ 420
    Notes on Corporate Criminal Responsibility_____ 425
        1. Liability for the Acts of an Agent_____ 425
        2. Corporate Criminality and the Problem of Sanc-
             tions_____ 426
        3. RICO_____ 429
        4. Partnerships and Other Unincorporated Associa-
             tions_____ 430
        5. Bibliography _____ 431

TABLE OF CONTENTS

Page

SECTION 3: CORPORATE CRIMINALITY—Continued
Note on Individual Responsibility for Corporate Acts......... 432

SECTION 4: CONSPIRACY... 434
   Introductory Notes on the Law of Conspiracy 434
     1. Background... 434
     2. The Co-Conspirator's Exception to the Hearsay
        Rule 434
     3. Joint Trial... 435
     4. Venue 436
     5. Pervasive Issues.................................... 436

Subsection A: The Objectives That Make Conspiracy Criminal .. 437
   Commonwealth v. Donoghue.................................. 437
   Notes on the Objectives That Make Conspiracy Criminal.. 440
     1. Rationale for the Common-Law Rule 440
     2. The Principle of Legality 440
     3. Conspiracy to Defraud the United States 442
     4. Modern State Statutes 444
     5. The *Powell* Doctrine............................... 444

Subsection B: Conspiracy as an Inchoate Offense 445
   People v. Burleson 445
   Notes on Conspiracy as an Inchoate Offense 448
     1. Introduction.. 448
     2. Actus Reus: The Necessity of Agreement 449
     3. Actus Reus: The Sufficiency of Agreement 450
     4. Actus Reus: Bilateral or Unilateral Agreement 453
     5. Mens Rea 457
        (i) Conduct 458
        (ii) Results 458
        (iii) Circumstances 458
     6. Impossibility 460
     7. Renunciation and Withdrawal 461
   Note on Conspiracy and Cumulative Punishment 461

Subsection C: The Relation of Conspiracy to Complicity....... 463
   People v. Lauria.. 463
   Notes on the Conspiracy-Complicity Relationship 469
     1. The Conspiracy-Complicity Relationship............. 469
     2. *United States v. Feola*........................... 470
     3. Additional Note on Mens Rea 472
   Pinkerton v. United States 473
   Notes on the *Pinkerton* Rule 476
     1. The Scope of Liability for Conspiracy 476
     2. Evaluating the *Pinkerton* Rule 477
     3. *State v. Stein*................................... 478

SECTION 4: CONSPIRACY—Continued

Subsection D: Scope and Duration of Conspiracy _____ 480
   Braverman v. United States _____ 480
   Notes on the Scope of Conspiracy—The Object Dimension 482
     1. *Lievers v. State* _____ 482
     2. Questions and Comments on *Braverman* and
        Lievers _____ 483
     3. The Model Code Approach _____ 483
   United States v. Bruno _____ 484
   Notes on the Scope of Conspiracy—The Party Dimension 485
     1. Wheels and Chains _____ 485
     2. The Model Code Approach _____ 486
     3. *Kotteakos v. United States* _____ 487
     4. *Blumenthal v. United States* _____ 489
     5. *United States v. Borelli* _____ 490
   Grunewald v. United States _____ 493
   Notes on the Duration of Conspiracy _____ 499
     1. Duration Generally _____ 499
     2. Conspiracies to Conceal _____ 499

Subsection E: Limits on Liability for Conspiracy _____ 500
   Gebardi v. United States _____ 500
   Iannelli v. United States _____ 502
   Note on *Gebardi* and *Iannelli* _____ 509

CHAPTER IV: JUSTIFICATION AND EXCUSE

   Introductory Note on Justification and Excuse _____ 511

SECTION 1: JUSTIFICATION _____ 512

Subsection A: The General Principle of Justification _____ 512
   State v. Warshow _____ 512
   Notes on the Defense of Necessity _____ 518
     1. Common-Law Necessity and the *Warshow* Case __ 518
     2. Modern Statutory Formulations _____ 519
     3. Illustrative Cases _____ 520
        (i) Deprogramming _____ 520
        (ii) Economic Necessity _____ 521
        (iii) Medical Necessity _____ 521
     4. Necessity as a Justification for Homicide: *Dudley*
        and Stephens _____ 523
     5. Necessity Created by Fault of the Actor _____ 526
     6. The Desirability of a General Defense of Necessity 526

Subsection B: The Effect of Mistake _____ 530
   Notes on the Effect of Mistake in Claims of Justification 530
     1. Introduction _____ 530
     2. Reasonable Mistake _____ 530
     3. Unreasonable Mistake _____ 531
     4. Unreasonable Mistake and Imperfect Justification 532
     5. The Model Penal Code _____ 532

TABLE OF CONTENTS

Page

SECTION 1: JUSTIFICATION—Continued

6. Alternative Statutory Formulations................ 533
7. Accidental Justification 534
8. Mistake of Law in Claims of Justification.......... 535
9. Strict Liability in Claims of Justification 536

Subsection C: Defense Against Aggression 537
Crawford v. State.................................... 537
Notes on Defense of Self and Property 540
1. Introduction.................................... 540
2. Common-Law Doctrines Justifying Deadly Force 540
    (i) Self-Defense 540
    (ii) Defense of Habitation.................... 540
    (iii) Prevention of Dangerous Felonies 541
    (iv) Questions on Crawford 541
3. Approaches to Defensive Use of Deadly Force.... 542
    (i) The Law of Nature 542
    (ii) Social Utility 543
    (iii) Accommodating Autonomy and Proportionality.................................... 544
    (iv) Questions and Comments................ 545
4. Modern Statutory Provisions 545
5. Excessive Use of Defensive Force 545
6. Prevention of Escape........................... 546
Notes on the Requirement of Retreat 547
1. The Retreat Rule.............................. 547
2. The Wisdom of Rules.......................... 549
3. The "Castle" Exception 550
State v. Wanrow 551
Notes on the Requirement of "Reasonable" Belief 555
1. Introduction.................................... 555
2. The Traditional Objective Standard 556
3. Subjective Standards of Reasonableness......... 558
4. The Case for a Subjective Approach 559
5. The Model Penal Code......................... 559
State v. Kelly.. 559
Notes on Domestic Violence and the Law of Self-Defense 568
1. Questions and Comments on Kelly and the Battered Woman Syndrome 568
2. Self-Defense by a Battered Chief: Jahnke v. State 570
People v. Young 573
Note on Defense of Others 580

Subsection D: Public Authority 581
Introductory Note on Public Authority................ 581
Tennessee v. Garner................................. 581
Notes on the Use of Deadly Force.................... 589
1. Questions and Comments on Garner 589
2. The Authority of Private Citizens.............. 589

Page

SECTION 1: JUSTIFICATION—Continued

Problem Based on *United States v. Ehrlichman* 591

Notes on Mistakes by Public Officials Regarding Their Own
Authority 595

    1. *Ehrlichman* and Ignorantia Juris 595

    2. Special Rules for Official Mistakes of Law 595

    3. The Debate on Official Mistake 595

Problem Based on *United States v. Barker* 597

Notes on Citizen Reliance on Apparent Official Authority 602

    1. Introduction 602

    2. Compliance With Official Orders or Requests 602

SECTION 2: SITUATIONAL EXCUSE 604

Introductory Notes on the Defense of Duress 604

    1. Duress and Involuntariness 604

    2. Elements of the Defense 606

    3. Duress as a Defense to Murder 607

    4. Voluntary Exposure to Duress 608

United States v. Bailey 609

Notes on Duress and Situational Compulsion 619

    1. Relation of Duress and Necessity 619

    2. Questions and Comments on *Bailey* 621

       (i) Justification 621

       (ii) Excuse 622

    3. A General Principle of Situational Compulsion? 622

    4. Situational Excuse and Mens Rea 624

    5. Brainwashing or Coercive Persuasion 624

Notes on the Defense of Entrapment 625

    1. The Entrapment Defense 625

       (i) *People v. Barraza* 626

       (ii) Approaches to the Defense 627

       (iii) Questions on the Defense 628

    2. *Cox v. Louisiana* 629

CHAPTER V: CRIMINAL RESPONSIBILITY

Introductory Note on Criminal Responsibility 631

SECTION 1: IMMATURITY 632

Introductory Notes on the Infancy Defense and the Juvenile
Court 632

    1. The Common-Law Presumptions 632

    2. Antecedents of the Juvenile Court 633

    3. The Juvenile-Court Movement 634

    4. Contemporary Reform of Juvenile Justice 636

In re Davis 640

Notes on Mens Rea and Responsibility in Delinquency Proceedings 642

    1. Mens Rea and Delinquency 642

    2. The Relevance of Statutory Purpose 643

Page

SECTION 1: IMMATURITY—Continued
    3.   *In re Gladys R.* 644
    4.   Minimum Age for Delinquency Jurisdiction 645
In re Dahl 646
Notes on Transfer of Juveniles to Criminal Court 649
    1.   Introduction 649
    2.   The Responsibility of Older Adolescents 650
    3.   The Contemporary Debate 652
    4.   Questions on *In re Dahl* 653

SECTION 2: MENTAL ABNORMALITY 654
Introductory Notes on the Insanity Defense 654
    1.   Introduction 654
    2.   Early History 656
    3.   *M'Naghten's* Case 658
    4.   Other Common-Law Formulations 659
         (i) The Product Test 660
         (ii) The Control Test 660
    5.   The Model Penal Code 661
    6.   The *Hinckley* Case 663
    7.   Current Law 663

Subsection A: The Insanity Defense and Major Mental Disorder ... 664
The Case of Joy Baker 664
Notes on the Insanity Defense and Major Mental Disorder 673
    1.   Introduction 673
    2.   Joy Baker's Credibility 673
    3.   The Existence of Mental Disease 673
    4.   Mental Disorder and Criminal Responsibility 675
    5.   Applying the *M'Naghten* Test to Joy Baker 677
         (i) Knowledge of the Act 677
         (ii) Knowledge of Wrongfulness 677
         (iii) The Value of Expert Testimony 678
    6.   The Meaning of "Knowing" 680
    7.   The Significance of Cognitive Impairment 682
    8.   Applying Control Tests to Psychotic Defendants 685

Subsection B: The Insanity Defense and the Control Inquiry 686
The Case of Francis Pollard 686
Notes on Volitional Criteria of Responsibility 695
    1.   Relation of Control Inquiry to Other Doctrines .. 695
    2.   The Control Tests: Criticism and Defense 696
    3.   Responsibility and Unconscious Motivation 700
    4.   Illustrative Claims of Insanity 704
         (i) *Barnes* 705
         (ii) *Chester* 706
         (iii) *Ellingwood* 708
         (iv) *Murdock* 709

TABLE OF CONTENTS

Page

SECTION 2: MENTAL ABNORMALITY—Continued

Notes on the Boundaries of Criminal Responsibility 709
1. The Significance of Mental Disease.................... 709
    (i) Restrictive Definition......................... 710
    (ii) Intermediate Position 711
    (iii) Abandonment of the Requirement............. 712
    (iv) Questions on the Mental-Disease Requirement 712
2. Compulsive Gambling: *United States v. Torniero* 713
3. Drug Dependence: *United States v. Moore* 716

Subsection C: The Insanity Defense and Intoxication 720
People v. Kelly.. 720
Notes on the Insanity Defense and Intoxication 725
1. Introduction.. 725
2. Non-Culpable Intoxication........................... 725
3. Alcohol-Related Insanity 726
4. Insanity Related to the Use of Other Drugs 728
    (i) Psychoactive Effects of Intoxication............. 728
    (ii) Precipitation of a "Functional" Psychosis ... 729
    (iii) Toxic Psychosis 730
5. Pathological Intoxication: The Problem of Unanticipated Effects 731

Subsection D: Disposition of Mentally Disordered Offenders........ 733
Introductory Notes on the Disposition of Mentally Disordered Offenders.. 733
1. Background... 733
2. Commitment of Persons Incompetent to Stand Trial 733
3. Special Sentencing Provisions 734
4. Commitment of Persons Acquitted by Reason of Insanity.. 734
In re Torsney... 735
Notes on the Disposition of Persons Acquitted by Reason of Insanity 743
1. The Statutory Response to *Torsney*................ 743
2. *State v. Gebarski*................................ 744
3. Questions on *Torsney* and *Gebarski*............. 745
4. *Jones v. United States*.......................... 746
    (i) Automatic Commitment of Insanity Acquittees 746
    (ii) Commitment and Proportionality 747
5. Relation Between Automatism and Insanity Defense 749
Note on the Verdict of Guilty But Mentally Ill 750

Page

SECTION 2: MENTAL ABNORMALITY—Continued

Subsection E: Mental Abnormality and Mens Rea 752

    Introductory Note on the Meaning of Diminished Responsibility 752

        (i)   Rule of Logical Relevance 752

        (ii) Partial Responsibility 753

    Regina v. Stephenson 754

    Notes on Mental Abnormality and Mens Rea 756

        1.   The Rule of Relevance 756

        2.   The Case for Exclusion 758

        3.   *People v. Wetmore* 762

    United States v. Bright 764

    Notes on the Boundaries of Psychiatric Testimony on Mens Rea 767

        1.   Introduction 767

        2.   Lack of Capacity vs. Actual State of Mind 767

        3.   The Significance of Mental Disease 767

        4.   Proper Subjects for Expert Testimony 768

    Note on Bifurcation of Insanity and Mens Rea 769

Subsection F: Abolition of the Insanity Defense 770

    Notes on Abolition of the Insanity Defense 770

        1.   Approaches to Abolition 770

            (i)   The Sentencing Approach 770

            (ii) The Mens-Rea Approach 771

        2.   Effect on Case Outcome 772

        3.   Dispositional Considerations 773

            (i)   Sentencing the Mentally Disordered Offender 773

            (ii) Disposition of Persons Lacking Mens Rea Due to Mental Disease 774

        4.   Blameworthiness Considerations 775

CHAPTER VI: HOMICIDE: A PROBLEM OF CULPABILITY AND GRADING

Introductory Notes on the History of Criminal Homicide 779

    1.   The Early Law 779

    2.   The Distinction Between Murder and Manslaughter .. 780

    3.   The Premeditation-Deliberation Formula 781

        (i)   The Pennsylvania Construction 781

        (ii) *People v. Anderson* 784

        (iii) Modern Utility of the Formula 785

SECTION 1: CAPITAL HOMICIDE 786

    Introductory Note on the Use of the Death Penalty 786

    Introductory Note on the Efficacy and Morality of the Death Penalty 787

TABLE OF CONTENTS

Page

SECTION 1: CAPITAL HOMICIDE—Continued

Subsection A: The Supreme Court and Capital Punishment 792
Introductory Notes on the Supreme Court and Capital Punishment 792
    1. Background.. 792
    2. *McGautha v. California*... 792
    3. *Furman v. Georgia*... 793
        (i) Brennan and Marshall 793
        (ii) Douglas, Stewart, and White 794
        (iii) The Dissenters 794
    4. The Aftermath of *Furman*....................................... 795
    5. The 1976 Decisions 795
    6. *Lockett* and *Eddings* 799
    7. *Zant v. Stephens* 800
Godfrey v. Georgia... 801
Notes on *Godfrey* 813
    1. The Constitutional Defect in Godfrey's Death Sentence 813
    2. The Proper Role of the Supreme Court 813
    3. Subsequent History 813
    4. The Structure of Modern Capital Sentencing Statutes: An Overview.. 814
        (i) Criteria of Inclusion 814
        (ii) Criteria of Exclusion 814
        (iii) Criteria of Mitigation and Selection 815
        (iv) Comparative Review 815

Subsection B: Administration of Modern Capital Sentencing Statutes... 816
State v. Moose.. 816
Notes on Substantive Predicates for Imposition of the Death Penalty... 824
    1. Questions and Comments on *Moose*..................... 824
    2. Statutory Criteria of Inclusion............................... 824
        (i) Identity of the Victim................................... 825
        (ii) Accompanying Criminal Offenses................ 825
        (iii) Hazardous Conduct 825
        (iv) Pecuniary Motive.. 825
        (v) Hindrance of Law Enforcement.................. 826
        (vi) Unusual Cruelty or Depravity..................... 826
        (vii) In Custody 826
        (viii) Prior Criminal Conduct............................... 826
        (ix) Prediction of Future Criminal Conduct..... 826
    3. Relevance of the Premeditation-Deliberation Formula 827
State of Alabama v. Judith Ann Neelley............................ 827
Neelley v. State 834

xlii

SECTION 1: CAPITAL HOMICIDE—Continued

Notes on Criteria of Mitigation and Selection in Capital Cases _____ 837

    1. Questions on *Neelley* _____ 837

    2. Statutory Mitigating Circumstances _____ 838

    3. Youth _____ 838

        (i) *State v. Valencia* _____ 839

        (ii) *Trimble v. State* _____ 839

    4. Degree of Participation _____ 840

    5. Duress or Domination By Another _____ 840

    6. Diminished Responsibility _____ 841

        (i) Extreme Mental or Emotional Disturbance 842

        (ii) Impaired Capacity for Appreciation or Control _____ 843

    7. The Double-Edged Sword _____ 843

    8. Limits on Mitigating Evidence _____ 847

    9. Limits on Discretion to Be Lenient _____ 847

    10. Intracase Disparity as a Basis for Leniency _____ 848

Introductory Note on Comparative Review of Death Sentences _____ 850

        (i) Case-by-Case Proportionality Review _____ 850

        (ii) Comparative Review _____ 851

State v. Yates _____ 851

State v. Young _____ 855

Notes on Comparative Review of Death Sentences _____ 859

    1. Questions on *Yates* and *Young* _____ 859

    2. Methodology of Comparative Review Defining the Universe of Relevant Cases _____ 859

        (i) Should Comparison Be Limited to Cases in Which Death Sentences Were Imposed? 860

        (ii) Should Comparison Be Limited to Cases in Which the Prosecution Sought a Death Sentence? _____ 861

    3. Methodology of Comparative Review: Selecting and Comparing "Similar" Cases _____ 864

    4. *Godfrey* Reconsidered _____ 866

    5. *Pulley v. Harris* _____ 867

    6. Efficacy of Comparative Review _____ 867

Notes on Race and the Death Penalty _____ 868

    1. Introduction _____ 868

    2. The Gross and Mauro Study _____ 869

    3. The Baldus, Pulaski, and Woodworth Study _____ 876

    4. *McCleskey v. Zant* _____ 879

SECTION 2: GRADING OF NON–CAPITAL HOMICIDES 882
Subsection A: Intentional Homicide 882
    Freddo v. State 882
    Notes on the Mitigation of Murder to Manslaughter at
    Common Law 884
      1. The Provocation Formula 884
      2. Rationale for the Provocation Formula 886
        (i) Defendant in Fact Provoked 886
        (ii) Legally Adequate Provocation 887
        (iii) The Objective Standard 887
      3. Cooling Time 890
      4. Characteristics of the Objective Standard 892
      5. The Relevance of Mistake 893
      6. The Relevance of Mental Abnormality 895
        (i) Provocation 895
        (ii) "Imperfect" Justification 895
    People v. Casassa 896
    Notes on "Extreme Emotional Disturbance" as a Mitigation
    of Murder to Manslaughter 902
      1. Questions and Comments on *Casassa* 902
      2. Diminished Responsibility in England 903
      3. Diminished Responsibility Under the "Extreme
        Emotional Disturbance" Formulation 904
      4. Burden of Persuasion 904

Subsection B: Unintentional Homicide 905
    Essex v. Commonwealth 905
    Notes on the Grading of Unintentional Homicide at Common Law 911
      1. The Degree of Culpability Sufficient for Murder 911
        (i) *Commonwealth v. Malone* 911
        (ii) Comments and Questions on *Essex* and *Malone* 912
      2. The Degree of Culpability Sufficient for Involuntary Manslaughter 912
        (i) *Commonwealth v. Sostilio* 913
        (ii) *Commonwealth v. Agnew* 913
    People v. Register 914
    Notes on the Grading of Unintentional Homicide Under
    Modern Statutes 921
      1. The Degree of Culpability Sufficient for Murder 921
      2. *Northington v. State* 921
      3. The Degree of Culpability Sufficient for Manslaughter and Negligent Homicide 922

SECTION 3: CAUSATION 923
    People v. Kibbe 923
    Notes on Causation 926
      1. The Relevance of Causation............................ 926
      2. The Common-Law Approach to Causation 928

TABLE OF CONTENTS

Page

SECTION 3: CAUSATION—Continued
3. The Model Code Approach _____ 929
4. Problems With the Model Code _____ 930
(i) Concurrent Causes _____ 930
(ii) Transferred Intent _____ 931
(iii) Volitional Human Intervention_____ 931

SECTION 4: FELONY MURDER _____ 932
Introductory Notes on Felony Murder_____ 932
1. The Rule and Its Traditional Limitations_____ 932
2. Rationale of the Rule_____ 933
3. Judicial Rejection of the Rule: *People v. Aaron* 935
4. The Model Penal Code and Modern Statutes_____ 937
State v. Goodseal _____ 938
State v. Underwood _____ 946
Notes on Felony Murder _____ 949
1. Questions and Comments on *Goodseal* and *Underwood* _____ 949
(i) Merger _____ 949
(ii) Determination of Inherent Dangerousness 951
(iii) Lesser-Included-Offense Instruction_____ 951
(iv) Defenses and Mitigations_____ 952
2. Distribution of Controlled Substances _____ 952
(i) *Heacock v. Commonwealth* _____ 953
(ii) *Sheriff, Clark County v. Morris* _____ 953
(iii) *State v. Randolph*_____ 954
3. Attempted Felony Murder _____ 954
People v. Antick _____ 954
Further Notes on Felony Murder_____ 959
1. Homicide Committed by a Non-Participant_____ 959
2. *People v. Washington* _____ 960
3. Relation to Principles of Causation_____ 962
(i) Application of the Felony-Murder Rule_____ 962
(ii) Independent Prosecution for Murder_____ 962
4. Relation to Principles of Accessorial Liability ____ 962
(i) Application of the Felony-Murder Rule_____ 962
(ii) Independent Prosecution for Murder_____ 963
5. Duration of the Felony _____ 963
6. Modern Statutes _____ 964
Note on Misdemeanor Manslaughter _____ 965

CHAPTER VII: PROOF, PROPORTIONALITY, AND CRIMINALIZATION

Page

SECTION 1: PROOF BEYOND A REASONABLE DOUBT 967
   Introductory Note on *In re Winship* 967

Subsection A: Mitigations and Defenses................................. 968
   Mullaney v. Wilbur 968
   Patterson v. New York... 975
   Notes on Burden of Proof for Mitigations and Defenses.... 986
    1. The Distinction Between *Mullaney* and *Patterson* 986
    2. The Procedural Interpretation of *Winship*............ 986
    3. Criticisms of the Procedural Approach................. 989
    4. An Alternative Reformulation of *Mullaney:* The *Patterson* Dissent 991
    5. Burden of Proof and Substantive Justice 991

Subsection B: Presumptions... 993
   Sandstrom v. Montana 993
   Notes on Burden of Proof and Presumptions.................1000
    1. Introduction.....................................1000
    2. Conclusive Presumptions 1000
    3. Rebuttable Presumptions 1001
    4. Shift in the Burden of Production 1001
    5. Permissive Inferences 1002
    6. Defenses, Presumptions, and Legislative Candor 1002

SECTION 2: PROPORTIONALITY 1004
Subsection A: Proportionality and Capital Punishment.............1004
   Coker v. Georgia...1004
   Notes on Proportionality and Capital Punishment 1019
    1. Questions and Comments on *Coker* 1019
    2. *Eddings v. Oklahoma*..............................1019
    3. *Enmund v. Florida* 1020
      (i) Debate About Indicators of Societal Judgment.....................................1021
      (ii) Debate About "Ultimate" Judgment 1024
      (iii) Questions on *Coker* and *Enmund* 1028

Subsection B: Proportionality and Imprisonment.....................1028
   Solem v. Helm 1028
   Notes on Proportionality and Imprisonment 1048
    1. Pre-*Rummel* Decisions 1048
    2. *Rummel v. Estelle*................................1049
    3. *Hutto v. Davis* 1050
    4. Questions and Comments on *Solem v. Helm*.......1051
    5. Footnote on Proportionality and Sentencing 1051

Page

SECTION 3: CRIMINALIZATION _____1053
   Introductory Note on Criminalization _____1053
   John Stuart Mill, On Liberty _____1053
   Notes on the Enforcement of Morals _____1059
      1.   Stephen's Response _____1059
      2.   The Wolfenden Report _____1059
      3.   Lord Devlin's Response _____1060
      4.   Hart's Rejoinder _____1065
      5.   Questions on the Hart-Devlin Debate _____1067
      6.   Offenses Against Decency _____1067
      7.   Paternalism in Health and Safety _____1071
   Notes on the Effects of Criminalization _____1073
      1.   Introduction _____1073
      2.   Assessing Benefits _____1074
      3.   Assessing Costs _____1075
         (i)   Deterrence of Socially Valuable Behavior 1075
         (ii)   Enforcement Expenditures_____1076
         (iii)   Effects on the Individual _____1076
         (iv)   Effects on Privacy _____1076
         (v)   Crimogenic Effects _____1077
         (vi)   Costs of Under-Enforcement _____1077
         (vii)   The Crime Tariff_____1079
      4.   Weighing Costs and Benefits _____1080
   Notes on Drug Offenses: A Case Study in Criminalization 1081
      1.   Background_____1081
      2.   Prohibition or Regulation _____1082
      3.   Consumption-Related Offenses _____1083

APPENDICES

A: **THE MODEL PENAL CODE** _____ A–1
   Introductory Note on the Model Penal Code _____ A–1
   Model Penal Code_____ A–4
   Table of Model Penal Code References _____ A–97

B: **SELECTED PENAL STATUTES** _____ B–1
   Virginia Homicide Statutes _____ B–1
   Pre-*Furman* Georgia Homicide Statutes _____ B–5
   New York Homicide Statutes_____ B–6
   Oregon Homicide and Assault Offenses and Provisions on
     Attempt _____ B–9
   Capital Punishment Statutes Before the Supreme Court
     in 1976 Decisions_____ B–12
   Additional Contemporary Capital Sentencing Statutes __ B–19

Index_____ [1]

*

TABLE OF CASES

The principal cases are in italic type.   Cases cited or discussed are in roman type.   References are to Pages.

A. & P. Trucking Co., United States v., 430
Aaron, People v., 935, 936, 952
Abbott v. The Queen, 607
Abbott, State v., 547, 549, 550
Acevedo, People v., 344, 345, 348, 349, 350, 352, 921, 927
Ackerly, State v., 269, 271
Adami, People v., 137, 139
Adams v. State, 640
Agnew, Commonwealth v., 913, 922
Alabama, State of v. Judith Ann Neelley, 827
Alexander, United States v., 709
American Tobacco Co., United States v., 69, 70
Amlotte v. Florida, 954
Anderson, People v., 784
Antick, People v., 954, 960, 962, 963, 964
Arambasich, United States v., 329
Arnold's Case, 657
Attorney General, State ex rel. v. Tally, 389
Audette, State v., 269

Backun v. United States, 393, 395, 469
Bailey, Rex v., 259
Bailey, United States v., 601, *609,* 619, 621, 622, 623, 624
Bainbridge, Regina v., 467
Baker v. Marcus, 908
Balint, United States v., 310, 311, 312, 314, 328, 332
Barber v. Superior Court of Los Angeles County, 114, 117, 120, 121
Barraza, People v., 626, 627, 628
Bass, United States v., 104, 105, 106
Batchelor, United States v., 625
Battin, People v., 219
Beardsley, People v., 108, 110, 111
Beasley v. State, 726, 729
Beck v. Alabama, 951
Bedder v. Director of Public Prosecutions, 892, 903
Bell v. State, 710, 1025
Bell v. United States, 508
Beneficial Finance Co., Commonwealth v., 420, 425, 426
Berck, People v., 148, 150, 151
Berge, State v., 922
Bernstein, State v., 265
Bess, State v., 557, 559, 560, 565, 566
Bethea v. United States, 758, 759, 761, 767, 769, 770
Bey, State v., 940
Biondi v. State, 848

Bishop, United States v., 200
Blackwell v. State, 909
Blumenthal v. United States, 489, 490
Boddie v. Connecticut, 1048
Booth v. State, 356, 366
Borelli, United States v., 490
Bouie v. City of Columbia, 59, 89, 90, 96, 98, 99, 100, 101
Bowen and Rouse, People v., 127, 137
Bowling, State v., 442
Boyett, State v., 260
Bradford, State v., 941
Brailsford, Rex v., 30
Bratty v. Attorney-General for Northern Ireland, 749
Braverman v. United States, 480, 482, 483, 484
Brawner, United States v., 660, 712, 718, 719, 720, 758, 771
Bray, People v., 273, 274
Bright, United States v., 764, 767, 768, 769
Briscoe v. United States, 705
Brody, People v., 95
Bronston v. United States, 366, 370, 371, 375
Brown v. United States, 548, 549, 550
Brown, State v., 820, 821
Bruno, United States v., 484, 486, 487, 489, 491
Buckman, State v., 38
Buckoke's Case, 527
Burleson, People v., 445, 448, 449, 461
Byrne, Regina v., 903

C.I.T. Corp. v. United States, 423
Cali, Commonwealth v., 113, 114
Callanan v. United States, 440, 462, 471, 504
Calley, United States v., 603
Camara v. Municipal Court, 593
Cameron, State v., 678
Camodeca, People v., 356
Canola, State v., 960, 961, 962, 963
Capitolo, Commonwealth v., 519
Carroll, Commonwealth v., 782
Carter v. McClaughry, 507
Casassa, People v., 896, 902, 904
Chaplinsky v. New Hampshire, 65
Charlson, Regina v., 749
Chavez, People v., 90, 93, 94
Chermansky, Commonwealth v., 590
Chester, Commonwealth v., 706
Chittum v. Commonwealth, 285, 907
City of (see name of city)
Clark, State v., 941, 945, 948, 949, 950, 952

Cleveland v. Municipality of Anchorage, 519
Coates v. City of Cincinnati, 53, 66, 72
Coates v. Regina, 154
Cofield v. State, 847
Cogan and Leak, Regina v., 404, 406, 407, 408, 409, 411
Coker v. Georgia, 7, 545, 585, 796, *1004,* 1019, 1021, 1022, 1024, 1026, 1027, 1028, 1032, 1033, 1034
Coleman, People v., 129
Collins, Regina v., 358
Commonwealth v. ——— (see opposing party)
Coney, Regina v., 385
Connally v. General Construction Co., 64, 89, 90
Coolidge, United States v., 37
Copeland, State v., 853, 861
Costello v. Wainwright, 27
Cox v. Louisiana, 629, 630
Craig, People v., 147
Crawford v. State, 537, 540, 541, 545, 546
Crimmins, United States v., 459, 470
Crouse, Ex parte, 633, 634
Cunningham, Regina v., 201, 203, 220, 935

Dahl, In re, 646, 649, 650, 653
Darry v. People, 922
Davis, In re, 640, 642, 643, 644, 649
Davis v. Davis, 1049, 1050, 1051
Davis v. United States, 971
Davis v. Zahradnick, 1044
Davis, State v., 347
Dawson, State v., 44
De La O, In re, 186
Decina, People v., 156, 157
Delamater v. South Dakota, 265
Direct Sales Co. v. United States, 464, 465, 467
Director of Public Prosecutions v. Beard, 277, 282
Director of Public Prosecutions v. Majewski, 274, 283, 284, 285, 288, 351, 723
Director of Public Prosecutions v. Smith, 204, 209, 210, 211, 213, 214, 215, 217, 218, 219, 220, 221, 911, 921, 1000
Director of Public Prosecutions for Northern Ireland v. Lynch, 607
Dixon, State v., 44
Doherty, Regina v., 287
Donnelly, Regina v., 356
Donoghue, Commonwealth v., 38, 39, *437,* 440, 441
Dorsey, State v., 519
Dotterweich, United States v., 178, 293, 295, 297, 298, 299, 302, 304, 307, 310, 312, 314, 328, 419
Downey v. Perini, 1048
Downs, State v., 257, 258, 259, 266
Drew, People v., 723
Drope v. Missouri, 733
Dudley, Regina v., 523, 526, 623
Dunn, State v., 200
Durham v. United States, 660, 676

Durhan, People v., 400, 403, 477
Dusenberry v. Commonwealth, 406, 407, 411
Dynes v. Hoover, 48, 57

Eagleton, Regina v., 132
Ealey v. State, 141
Earl of Devon's Case, 1031
Eddings v. Oklahoma, 800, 839, 1019
Egan v. United States, 423
Ehrlichman, United States v., 595, 597
Ellingwood, State v., 708
Elliott, State v., 900
Ellis, State v., 264, 553
Enmund v. Florida, 584, 799, 800, 814, 840, 854, 952, 1020, 1028, 1032, 1034, 1035
Escobar, People v., 744
Esop, Rex v., 258, 259
Essex v. Commonwealth, 905, 912, 913, 922
Estelle v. Gamble, 617
Evers v. State, 285, 286
Evilsizer v. State, 730
Ex parte (see name of party)

Fain v. Commonwealth, 154
Falcone, United States v., 464, 465, 466
Faulkner v. State, 532, 935
Faulkner, Regina v., 196, 199, 200, 201, 203, 207, 220, 254
Feagley, People v., 187
Felton, State v., 567
Feola, United States v., 459, 470, 472
Ferlin, People v., 957, 958
Fisher, Commonwealth v., 636
Flack, People v., 226
Fletcher, United States v., 48, 49
Freddo v. State, 882, 885, 886, 902
Freed, United States v., 313, 317, 320, 328, 333
Freeman, People v., 157
Fulcher v. State, 750
Furman v. Georgia, 786, 791, 793, 795, 796, 797, 798, 800, 804, 807, 808, 809, 811, 812, 815, 816, 848, 867, 869, 876, 880, 881, 1006, 1007, 1018, 1033

Gaetano v. United States, 519
Gaskins, State v., 868
Gault, In re, 640
Gebardi v. United States, 500, 509
Gebarski, State v., 744, 745
Gentry v. State, 350, 954
Gervin v. State, 43, 44
Giarratano v. Commonwealth, 907
Gilbert, People v., 957
Gilbert, State v., 854, 855, 859
Gilmore v. Utah, 790
Glecker, People v., 841
Godfrey v. Georgia, 801, 813, 814, 824, 826, 843, 847, 865, 866, 1026
Goodard, United States ex rel. v. Vaughn, 288
Gooding v. Wilson, 73
Goodman v. Commonwealth, 910, 911

1

Goodseal, State v., *938*, 947, 948, 949, 951, 952
Gore v. Leeke, 44
Gould, United States v., 716
Gounagais, State v., 887, 890, 892, 902
Grant, People v., 750
Grayned v. City of Rockford, 55
Green .v. State, 248, 254
Gregg v. Georgia, 795, 800, 801, 802, 803, 804, 805, 806, 807, 808, 809, 812, 813, 847, 848, 860, 879, 1004, 1005, 1006, 1007, 1025
Gretzler, State v., 846
Grimley, In re, 47, 50
Grunewald v. United States, 493, 499

H., In re Elizabeth, 146
H.M. Advocate v. Fraser, 154
Haas v. Henkel, 442
Haldeman, United States v., 200, 443
Hall, State v., 729, 730, 732
Hamilton v. Commonwealth, 907
Hamm v. City of Rock Hill, 100
Hammerschmidt v. United States, 442
Hanaphy, State v., 265
Harris, People v., 350
Harris, State v., 541
Harrison v. Commonwealth, 907
Hart v. Coiner, 1049, 1050
Hayes, State v., 411
Heacock v. Commonwealth, 953
Hearst, United States v., 624
Heart of Atlanta Motel v. United States, 100
Helm, State v., 1036, 1048, 1050
Henderson v. Kibbe, 926
Higgins, Rex v., 30, 339
Hill, State v., 44
Hodges v. Humkin, 1031
Hogan, State v., 648, 649
Hopkins v. State, 259, 266
Houston v. State, 847
Hudson and Goodwin, United States v., 37
Hunt, State v., 858, 859
Hutton v. Davis, 1032, 1040, 1044, 1050
Hyde v. United States, 134, 474

Iannelli v. United States, 502, 507
Ibn-Tamas v. United States, 568
In re (see name of party)
Inmates, D.C. Jail v. Jackson, 27
Instan, Regina v., 111
International Minerals & Chemical Corp., United States v., 328, 332, 333, 334
Iowa City v. Nolan, 419

Jackson v. Indiana, 733
Jackson, State v., 858, 859
Jacobellis v. Ohio, 82
Jaffe, People v., 352, *353,* 356, 358, 359, 360, 362, 364, 365, 366
Jahnke v. State, 570, 573
Jenkins v. Georgia, 80, 940
Jernatowski, People v., 917

Johnson v. State, 582
Jones v. Randall, 31
Jones v. State, 550, 676
Jones v. United States, 107, 109, 110, 111, 113, 746, 747
Jurek v. Texas, 795

Kane v. United States, 731
Kane, People v., 925
Kansas v. Warbritton, 210
Katz, People v., 575
Katzenbach v. McClung, 100
Keeler v. Superior Court of Amador County, 85, 97, 98, 100, 101, 103, 106
Kelly, People v., 720, 728, 729, 730
Kelly, State v., 559, 568, 569, 570, 573
Kemp, Regina v., 749
Kemp, State v., 440
Kent v. United States, 638
Kibbe v. Henderson, 926, 927, 928, 930, 932
Kibbe, People v., 923, 926
Kinder, United States v., 603
King v. Barker, 134, 135, 603, 604, 630
King v. Creighton, 661
Kirby, United States v., 614
Knuller v. Director of Public Prosecutions, 33
Koczwara, Commonwealth v., 414, 418
Kolender v. Lawson, 151, 152
Kotteakos v. United States, 487, 489, 490, 491
Krizka, People v., 519
Kroncke, United States v., 519
Krosky, United States v., 200
Krovarz, People v., 347, 348
Krulewitch v. United States, 435, 436, 491, 495, 496, 497, 499

Lafferty, State v., 716
Lambert v. California, 308, 312, 313, 314, 317, 419, 993
Lanzetta v. New Jersey, 53, 55, 64, 89, 90
Lauria, People v., 463, 469
Le Gras v. Bailiff of Bishop of Winchester, 1031
Lee, State v., 890
Leggett v. State, 731
Leland v. Oregon, 664, 974, 977, 978
Levin v. Gallman, 200
Levy v. Parker, 46
Lewellyn, United States v., 716
Lievers v. State, 482, 483, 484
Liparota v. United States, 323, 333, 334
Lipman, Regina v., 279
Lockett v. Ohio, 799, 800, 838, 847, 865, 1020, 1025
Long v. State, 272
Lorentzen, People v., 1049
Louisiana v. Elzie, 219
Lovercamp, People v., 621
Luciano, People v., 477
Lutwak v. United States, 495, 496, 499
Lynch, In re, 1049
Lyons, United States v., 664

McBoyle v. United States, 103, 104, 105, 106
McCleskey v. Kamp, 879, 882
McCleskey v. Zant, 879, 882
McCollum v. McConaugy, 265
McCombs, State v., 541
McCray v. State, 44
McDonald v. United States, 711, 718
McDougle v. Maxwell, 1048
McFarland v. American Sugar Rfg. Co., 980
McGautha v. California, 792, 793, 795, 809
McGhee v. Virginia, 388
McIlvoy, State v., 841
McKinnon v. State, 836
McLaughlin, People v., 466
McQuirk v. State, 246
Machekequonabe, Regina v., 556
Maher v. People, 885, 886, 892
Maik, State v., 729
Malone, Commonwealth v., 911, 912, 921
Manley, Rex v., 29, 31, 32, 33, 34, 98, 320, 441
Marshall, People v., 398
Martarella v. Kelley, 188
Martin v. State, 176
Mathew v. Nelson, 185
Matter of (see name of party)
Mayfield, State v., 521
Memoirs v. Massachusetts, 76, 77, 78, 82
Merrit v. Commonwealth, 344
Michael, In re, 642, 643, 644
Miller v. California, 78, 80, 81, 82, 84
Miller v. State, 844, 849
Minneapolis v. Altimus, 725
Minor, Regina v., 154
M'Naghten's Case, Daniel, 658, 659, 660, 661, 662, 663, 674, 676, 677, 678, 680, 681, 682, 683, 686, 697, 698, 699, 710, 723, 724, 726, 903, 904
Mochan, Commonwealth v., 38, 39
Moe, State v., 521
Moffitt, State v., 940, 942, 946, 947, 948, 949, 951
Monahan, State v., 651, 652
Monkhouse, Regina v., 287
Monzie v. Bagazo, 556
Moore, United States, v., 190, 716
Moose, State v., 816, 824, 825, 826
Moreira, Commonwealth v., 536
Morgan, Regina v., 405
Morissette v. United States, 176, 178, 193, 221, 228, 229, 245, 291, 314, 316, 317, 324, 325, 328, 333, 334, 998, 999, 1000
Mullane v. Central Hanover Bank & Trust Co., 310
Mullaney v. Wilbur, 228, *968*, 976, 980, 981, 982, 983, 984, 985, 986, 988, 989, 991, 993, 994, 999, 1000, 1001, 1002
Murdock, United States v., 709
Musser v. Utah, 441
Musser, State v., 442

N.A.A.C.P. v. Button, 72
Nash v. United States, 69, 70, 84, 97

Nearing, United States v., 424
Neelley v. State, 834, 837, 838, 839, 843, 848
Nelson v. State, 186, 558
New Mexico v. Viscarra, 219
New York Central & Hartford R.R. v. United States, 423, 425
Northington v. State, 921

O'Connor v. Donaldson, 184, 188
Oliver, State v., 823, 824
O'Malley, Commonwealth v., 229
O'Neil v. Vermont, 266, 1032, 1045
O'Neil, State v., 265
Ott, State v., 903

Palmer v. Regina, 546
Papachristou v. City of Jacksonville, 55, 66, 67, 147, 149, 151
Paris Adult Theatre I v. Slaton, 81
Park, United States v., 292, *295*, 304, 307, 308, 419, 433, 434
Parker v. State, 728
Parker, Warden v. Levy, 45, 61, 62, 63, 64, 72, 75, 101
Parsons v. State, 661, 710
Patrick, People v., 520
Patrick, United States v., 520
Patterson v. New York, 288, 898, 899, *975*, 986, 989, 900, 904, 991, 993, 994, 997, 999, 1002
Peak, People v., 220
Peaslee, Commonwealth v., 131, 134
Pennsylvania v. Gillespie, 37
Peoni, United States v., 392, 395, 469, 485
People v. _____ (see opposing party)
People By and Through Russel v. District Court, 922
Petrillo, United States v., 68, 77, 152
Pierce v. Turner, 728
Pike, State v., 660
Pinch, State v., 860
Pinkerton v. United States, 404, *473*, 476, 477, 478, 486, 491, 499
Pippin, People v., 131, 137
Ploof v. Putnam, 513
Pollard v. United States, 686
Pond v. People, 538
Poplis, People v., 917
Porter, Rex v., 30
Powell v. Texas, 168, 182, 183, 186, 190, 283, 717, 720
Powell, People v., 444
Prince, Regina v., 317, 319, 320
Prince, United States v., 381
Problem Based on United States v. Barker, 597
Problems Based on United States v. Ehrlichman, 591
Proffitt v. Florida, 71, 795
Pugh v. Commonwealth, 906
Pulley v. Harris, 815, 867

Quick, Regina v., 750
Quinlan, Matter of, 116

R., In re, Gladys, 644, 649
Raley v. Ohio, 629
Randall, United States v., 522, 523
Randolph, State v., 954
Read, United States v., 461
Reddick v. State, 43
Redline, Commonwealth v., 960
Redrup v. New York, 78, 82
Reed, State v., 941
Reese, State v., 43
Reese, United States v., 56, 64
Regina v. _____ (see opposing party)
Register, People v., 914, 921
Regle v. Maryland, 453
Remington, United States v., 371, 375
Rewis v. United States, 326
Rex v. _____ (see opposing party)
Reynolds v. McNichols, 189
Richards, Regina v., 409, 410, 411
Richardson, United States v., 522
Rivera v. Delaware, 664
Rizzo, People v., 133, 137
Roberts v. Collins, 1049
Roberts v. Louisiana, 795, 796, 1006, 1007, 1017
Robinson v. California, 158, 170, 174, 175, 177, 178, 179, 181, 182, 183, 186, 187, 190, 283, 717, 993, 1004, 1026, 1032, 1033, 1034
Robinson, Commonwealth v., 606
Roe v. Wade, 519
Rogers, Commonwealth v., 660
Rojas, People v., 356
Romine v. State, 847
Rood, State v., 141
Rose v. Mitchell, 881
Roth v. United States, 76, 77, 78, 80, 81, 82, 83
Rummel v. Estelle, 1030, 1032, 1033, 1034, 1037, 1038, 1039, 1040, 1041, 1042, 1043, 1044, 1047, 1048, 1049, 1050, 1051
Rundle, United States v., 96
Russell, Rex v., 383, 386, 387, 388, 390, 391, 392
Russell, United States v., 628

St. Christopher, State v., 453, 456
St. Louis, City of v. Klocker, 519
Sall, United States v., 474
Sandstrom v. Montana, 211, 288, *993,* 1000, 1001, 1002
Satchell, People v., 943, 944, 945, 946
Schmidt, People v., 678
Scofield, Rex v., 339
Seven Minors, In re, 653
Shaw v. Director of Public Prosecutions, 32, 33, 34, 441
Shelton, People v., 900, 901
Sheriff, Clark County v. Morris, 953
Sherman v. United States, 627
Shevlin-Carpenter Co. v. Minnesota, 309, 310, 312
Shiflet v. State, 907
Short, United States v., 246, 248
Sidley, Rex v., 31

Sigma Reproductive Health Center v. State, 519
Sikora, State v., 566, 701
Sledge v. State, 541
Smith v. Goguen, 51, 53
Smith v. Whitney, 48, 49
Smith, Regina v., 356, 357
Smith, State v., 350
Sobiek, People v., 94, 97, 98, 103, 106
Solem v. Helm, 558, 587, 993, *1028,* 1051
Sorrells v. United States, 627, 628
Sostilio, Commonwealth v., 913, 922
Sparf v. United States, 303
Spaziano v. Florida, 838, 848
Speiser v. Randall, 977
Standard Oil Co. v. United States, 69, 70
Staples, People v., 371, 374
Stasiun, Commonwealth v., 422
State v. _____ (see opposing party)
State ex rel. v. _____ (see opposing party)
State of (see name of state)
Steele v. State, 770
Stein, State v., 478
Stephenson, Regina v., 523, 623 *754,* 756, 757, 767
Story v. United States, 398
Strasburg, State v., 771
Striggles, State v., 263, 264, 265, 266
Sullivan, Regina v., 750
Sutton v. State, 483
Swaim v. United States, 49
Sweet v. Parsley, 308
Sykes v. Director of Public Prosecutions, 467

Tally, State v., 389, 390, 391
Taylor, Commonwealth v., 38
Taylor, People v., 958, 963
Tender v. State, 482
Tennessee v. Garner, 581, 589, 591
Terminiello v. Chicago, 160
Thacker v. Commonwealth, 342, 345, 348, 349, 350, 351, 352, 927
Thomas, Regina v., 466
Thomas, State v., 558, 568
Thomas, United States v., 460, 461
Thompson v. Washington, 950
Thornton v. Mitchell, 408, 411
Tichnell v. State, 861
Tolson, Regina v., 271, 272, 273
Tomlins, People v., 550
Torniero, United States v., 713, 714
Torsney, In re, 735, 743, 747, 749
Toscano, State v., 606
Tot v. United States, 980
Tribett, State v., 553
Trimble v. State, 838, 839
Trop v. Dulles, 792, 1007
Tyrrell, Regina v., 412, 413, 502, 509

Underwood, State v., 946, 949, 951, 952
United States v. _____ (see opposing party)

liii

United States ex rel. v. ——— (see opposing party)
United States Gypsum Co., United States v., 325, 998, 999, 1000

Valencia, State v., 839
Valot, People v., 141, 145, 146
Vaughn, United States ex rel. Goddard v., 288
Villa, People v., 402

Wahrlich v. Arizona, 760
Wakefield, Regina v., 154
Walden, State v., 387, 392
Walker, State v., 250, 252, 254
Walters v. Lunt, 405, 406
Wanrow, State v., 551, 556, 558, 559, 580, 950
Warshow, State v., 512, 518, 519, 520, 523, 623
Washington v. Bingham, 785
Washington, People v., 956, 957, 959, 960
Watson, People v., 908
Weems v. United States, 1032, 1034, 1042, 1045, 1050
Wells, People v., 896
Welsh, Regina v., 886
Wetmore, People v., 762, 764, 770
Whisenant, State v., 857, 859
White, Rex v., 357

Whiteford v. Commonwealth, 910, 911
Wiesenfeld Warehouse Co., United States v., 295, 300
Wilberger, United States v., 101
Williams, State v., 860, 864
Willis, State v., 44
Wilson v. State, 200
Winship, In re, 926, 967, 968, 971, 972, 973, 974, 977, 980, 981, 982, 983, 984, 985, 986, 987, 988, 989, 992, 994, 997, 998
Winters v. New York, 53
Withers v. Director of Public Prosecutions, 32
Witherspoon v. Illinois, 787
Woodruff v. Superior Court, 958
Woods, State v., 268, 270, 271, 272, 273, 274
Woodson v. North Carolina, 795, 1006, 1007, 1045

Yanz, State v., 893, 894, 903
Yates, State v., 851, 859, 860
Yermian, United States v., 320, 322, 327, 328, 329, 330
York, Commonwealth v., 970, 971
Young, People v., 573, 579, 580
Young, State v., 855, 859, 860, 865, 866
Youngs, People v., 131, 137

Zant v. Stephens, 800, 814, 848

CRIMINAL LAW:

CASES AND MATERIALS

*

Introduction

THE PURPOSES OF PUNISHMENT

This book is about the substantive criminal law. Its focus is on crime definition and the elements of criminal liability. Broadly speaking, there are three main components of criminal liability: the criminal act (the actus reus), the criminal state of mind (the mens rea), and the absence of a defense of justification or excuse. Each of these topics is considered in the chapters that follow.

It is essential to the study of substantive criminal law to focus on the purpose of the enterprise—that is, to ask why the criminal process is used to punish people who engage in designated behavior. This inquiry requires consideration of the rationales or purposes of punishment. Debate over the purposes of punishment has engaged a wide range of disciplines for many years. The intention here is not to attempt an authoritative resolution of this debate but to introduce the terms of inquiry and the principal points of dispute.[a]

The literature of the criminal law typically identifies four main goals of punishment: retribution, deterrence, incapacitation, and rehabilitation. Each of these concepts represents a complex series of moral assertions, beliefs about human nature, and aspirations for the criminal justice system. It is important to understand that the criminal process is not the only way in which society can seek to accomplish one or more of these goals. For example, an award of punitive damages in a civil case may be imposed in retribution or to deter future misconduct. Incapacitation may be accomplished through the civil commitment of those who are dangerous to themselves or others. Rehabilitation may be attempted by therapeutic intervention wholly outside the scope of the criminal law. The purpose here, therefore, is to focus upon the unique manner in which the criminal process pursues the commonly stated goals of punishment and upon the limitations on criminal punishment implied by these goals and by constraints that may be derived from other sources.

There are at bottom only two contending philosophical views regarding the ultimate purpose of punishment. One is utilitarian—that punishment is threatened and imposed in order to achieve beneficial social consequences. In more direct terms, the ultimate purpose of punishment is to prevent or minimize criminal behavior. The other is

[a] An accessible introduction to the purposes of punishment and their relation to the substantive criminal law can be found in Part I of Professor Herbert Packer's book, The Limits of the Criminal Sanction 3–145 (1968). Professor Packer's effort is an admirable summary of many of the issues to be encountered in this casebook and is highly recommended as supplementary reading. Also excellent is Kent Greenawalt's article on Punishment for the Encyclopedia of Crime and Justice (S. Kadish, ed.), published separately as Greenawalt, Punishment, 74 J.Crim.L. & Crim. 343 (1983).

retributive—that punishment is deserved because the offender has engaged in a wrongful act. By this view, the ultimate purpose of punishment is to impose just deserts upon the criminal. Neither of these two contending positions dominates the existing criminal justice system to the exclusion of the other. Rather, the present system can be seen as a series of uneasy compromises between these two ideas.

RETRIBUTION

The premise of retribution is that individuals are responsible moral agents capable of making choices between right and wrong. Punishment is appropriate for wrong choices. This premise is a normative assertion; it is not empirically verifiable, nor does it depend on pragmatic justification. It is right to punish the offender against societal norms because it is wrong to violate these norms. The same point is sometimes put in terms of expiation. It is essential for the offender to right a wrong or, to use the common vernacular, to "pay" for a crime. The offender "owes a debt to society" for essentially retributive reasons; having violated societal norms, the offender must now atone for that sin by suffering punishment for the transgression.[b]

One of the best known spokesmen for the retributive point of view was Sir James Fitzjames Stephen, a 19th-century English judge and historian of the criminal law. In 2 A History of the Criminal Law of England 81–82 (1883), he said:

"[N]o one in this country regards murder, rape, arson, robbery, theft, or the like, with any feeling but detestation. I do not think it admits of any doubt that law and morals powerfully support and greatly intensify each other in this matter. Everything which is regarded as enhancing the moral guilt of a particular offence is recognized as a reason for increasing the severity of the punishment awarded to it. On the other hand, the sentence of the law is to the moral sentiment of the public in relation to any offence what a seal is to hot wax. It converts into a permanent final judgment what might otherwise be a transient sentiment. The mere general suspicion or knowledge that a man has done something dishonest may never be brought to a point, and the disapprobation excited by it may in time pass away, but the fact that he has been convicted and punished as a thief stamps a mark upon him for life. In short, the infliction of punishment by law gives definite expression and a solemn ratification and justification to the hatred which is excited by the commission of the offense. . . .   The criminal law thus proceeds upon the principle that it is morally right to hate

[b] Cf. H.L.A. Hart, Punishment and Responsibility 158–59 (1968):

"This . . . conception of punishment . . . makes primary the meting out to a responsible wrongdoer of his just deserts. Dostoevsky passionately believed that society was morally justified in punishing people simply because they had done wrong; he also believed that psychologically the criminal needed his punishment to heal the laceration of the bonds that joined him to his society. So, in the end, Raskolnikov the murderer thirsts for his punishment."

criminals, and it confirms and justifies that sentiment by inflicting upon criminals punishments which express it. . . .

"These views are regarded by many people as being wicked, because it is supposed that we never ought to hate, or wish to be revenged upon, any one. The doctrine that hatred and vengeance are wicked in themselves appears to me to contradict plain facts, and to be unsupported by any argument deserving of attention. Love and hatred, gratitude for benefits, and the desire of vengeance for injuries, imply each other as much as convex and concave. . . . The unqualified manner in which [these views] have been denounced is in itself a proof that they are deeply rooted in human nature. No doubt they are peculiarly liable to abuse, and in some states of society are commonly in excess of what is desirable, and so require restraint rather than excitement, but unqualified denunciations of them are as ill-judged as unqualified denunciations of sexual passion. The forms in which deliberate anger and righteous disapprobation are expressed, and the execution of criminal justice is the most emphatic of such forms, stand to the one set of passions in the same relation in which marriage stands to the other. . . ."

Today, the retributive argument is not often put so bluntly. Yet the concept of retribution contains a number of important implications. Among them are the following:

1. **The Criminal Law as a Moral Statement.** Professor Henry Hart explored what was meant by the concept of crime in an essay prepared for first-year students on the threshold of studying criminal law. In The Aims of the Criminal Law, 23 Law & Contemp. Probs. 401, 404 (1958), he concluded that "[w]hat distinguishes a criminal from a civil sanction and all that distinguishes it, it is ventured, is the judgment of community condemnation which accompanies and justifies its imposition."[c] While this observation may be overstated, it makes an important point. The conviction of crime is itself an important moral statement. Whatever features of the criminal process distinguish it from other kinds of legal sanctions, one cannot gainsay the uniqueness of the moral overtones underlying the impact (as well as the vocabulary) of a criminal conviction. Stephen made the point in the observation, quoted above, that the fact that a person "has been convicted and punished as a thief stamps a mark upon him for life." The label "criminal" is highly stigmatic. The criminal law speaks in terms of the "guilt" or "innocence" of the offender. And the very

---

[c] Cf. Royal Comm'n on Capital Punishment, Minutes of Evidence, 9th Day, Dec. 1, 1949, Memorandum submitted by the Rt. Hon. Lord Denning, p. 207:

"Punishment is the way in which society expresses its denunciation of wrong doing: and, in order to maintain respect for law, it is essential that the punishment inflicted for grave crimes should adequately reflect the revulsion felt by the great majority of citizens for them. It is a mistake to consider the objects of punishment as being deterrent or reformative or preventive and nothing else. . . . The truth is that some crimes are so outrageous that society insists on adequate punishment, because the wrong-doer deserves it, irrespective of whether it is a deterrent or not.

". . . In my view the ultimate justification of any punishment is, not that it is a deterrent, but that it is the emphatic denunciation by the community of a crime. . . ."

concept of "punishment," which implies "blame" and "responsibility," carries strong moral connotations uniquely associated with the criminal law. The same stigmatic labels are not attached to one who breaks a contract or who engages in other conduct that warrants only "civil" sanctions.

It would be possible to argue that the law achieves an important deterrent effect from this aspect of the criminal process and that the moral condemnation of criminals is therefore justified for deterrent reasons. Any such deterrence, however, is dependent upon the underlying credibility of the moral statement made by a criminal conviction. The stigma of conviction can work as a deterrent only if it accords with common moral conceptions that commission of a criminal act "deserves" such moral disapprobation. The label "rapist" or "murderer" or "thief" conveys strong moral signals. That the label may aid deterrent objectives does not detract from the fact that its stigmatic effect is derived from strong feelings of moral disapproval. Nor does it detract from the fact that the criminal process is influenced—perhaps inescapably so [d]—by retributive features. The stigma of condemnation is one of the distinctive characteristics, if not *the* distinctive characteristic, differentiating the criminal law from other kinds of legal sanctions.

2. **Retribution as a Limiting Concept: Blameworthiness.** As noted above, some philosophers have asserted that retribution is the ultimate purpose of punishment. According to this view, punishment of blameworthy wrongdoers, in proportion to the evil of their deeds, is an ethical imperative; in a word, retribution *requires* punishment. However, even if one rejects this view in favor of the idea that the legitimacy of punishment depends upon its social consequences, it is still possible to accept the ethical postulates of retribution as principles of limitation. Specifically, the concepts of blameworthiness and proportionality may be seen as limiting the occasions for, and severity of, punishment that is otherwise justifiable on purely utilitarian grounds.

The premise of retribution—that individuals are responsible moral agents capable of free choice—is considered by many to be the central ethical predicate for the imposition of criminal sanctions. It follows from this premise that people should not be punished unless they are blameworthy. Moreover, blame can be assessed only through certain inquiries about the nature of the defendant's behavior at the time the offending conduct occurred. Thus the law must ask such questions as: Was the conduct a product of the defendant's voluntary choice? What

---

[d] The development of the concept of juvenile delinquency, elaborated in more detail at pages 632–54, infra, is instructive on this point. The original idea was that rehabilitative concepts should govern the disposition and treatment of juvenile offenders and that all stigmatic and condemnatory features of the law should be removed. To this end, a separate system for dealing with juveniles was established. It included those who had committed traditionally criminal behavior and those who had not engaged in criminal conduct but were otherwise in need of state intervention. The result, over time, was that the term "juvenile delinquent" became a stigmatic label in spite of the benevolent objectives of the founders of the juvenile-offender movement and came to be applied to an even broader range of persons than those who in some sense "deserved" to be stigmatized because of the commission of criminal acts.

was the defendant's state of mind at the time of the offense? Was the defendant too young to have made a responsible choice? Or too severely afflicted with mental illness? Was the defendant's conduct justified by special circumstances, as in the case of self-defense? As subsequent materials reveal, many of the doctrines of the criminal law are in large part answers to questions such as these. On the retributive premise, punishment is appropriate only if the answers show that the defendant properly can be blamed for having made a wrong choice.

This relatively simplistic view of the relationship between blame and punishment is regarded as unsatisfactory by many people, partly because of modern reluctance to embrace the full-blown concept of retribution as a justification for punishment. Many of these same people, however, fully embrace the concept that the criminal law should be premised on responsibility, free choice, and an inquiry into the blameworthiness of the defendant's conduct.

H.L.A. Hart is one of the more articulate spokesmen for this point of view. In his collection of essays published in book form as Punishment and Responsibility 180–83 (1968),* he makes essentially two arguments. The first is that "[t]here are values quite distinct from those of retributive punishment" that are maintained by adhering to the premise that man is a responsible moral agent, namely the "nearly universal ideas of fairness or justice and of the value of individual liberty." The premise, he concludes, "could rest on the simple idea that unless a man has the capacity and a fair opportunity or chance to adjust his behavior to the law its penalties ought not to be applied to him. Even if we punish men not as wicked but as nuisances, this is something we still should respect." This emphasis on individual freedom and autonomy maximizes the breathing space of the individual.

> "[It allows us] to predict and plan the future course of our lives within the coercive framework of the law. For the system which makes liability to the law's sanctions dependent upon a voluntary act not only maximizes the power of the individual to determine by his choice his future fate; it also maximizes his power to identify in advance the space which will be left open to him free from the law's interference. Whereas a system from which responsibility was eliminated so that he was liable for what he did by mistake or accident would leave each individual not only less able to exclude the future interference by the law with his life, but also less able to foresee the times of the law's interference."

Hart's second point is that this normative view as to how the law ought to function is also descriptive of the way people actually treat each other. "[P]ersons interpret each other's movements as manifestations of intention and choices, and these subjective factors are often more important to their social relations than the movements by which they are manifested or their effects." When one person strikes another, Hart argues, "[i]f the blow was light but deliberate, it has a significance for the person struck quite different from an accidental much heavier blow." [e] He concludes that:

> "This is how human nature in human society actually is and as yet we have no power to alter it. The bearing of this fundamental fact on law is this. If as our legal moralists maintain it is important for the law to reflect common judgments of morality, it is surely even more important that it should in general reflect in its judgments on human conduct distinctions which not only underly morality, but pervade the whole of our social life. This it would fail to do if it treated men as merely alterable, predictable, curable or manipulable things."

Hart's arguments—that the law should proceed from the premise that people are responsible moral agents because individual freedom is thereby maximized and because the law should reflect the way people in fact treat each other—also suggest an answer to those who would reject the concept of free will and embrace principles of determinism. The debate concerning free will and determinism has engaged various disciplines for many centuries. This debate, argues Hart,[f] is beside the point as far as the criminal law is concerned. The underlying premise of the criminal law is that it is morally right to *treat* people as responsible moral agents, whatever the fact of the matter, because any other view would be inconsistent with the values of individual autonomy and freedom that the law should reflect and with the perceptions of each other on which people at least think they are governing their daily lives. Determinism is rejected by the criminal law, in other words, because it *should be* rejected in light of the proper normative premises on which the criminal law should function.

It should also be noted, however, that many people who embrace these views would not argue that the criminal law should concern itself exclusively with the blameworthiness of the offender. To say that determining the blameworthiness of the offender is an *important* function of the criminal law is not necessarily to say that it is the *only* function. Other principles of punishment may condition the law's acceptance of the concept of blameworthiness and may require compromise in order to accommodate other goals. Indeed, the question of when and where to compromise the concept of blameworthiness with other goals of punishment presents a central and difficult theme cutting across many of the policy issues in the criminal law. As H.L.A. Hart has said in a different context, "[w]hat is needed is the realization that different principles . . . are relevant at different points in any morally acceptable account of punishment." [g]

[e] Cf. O. Holmes, The Common Law 3 (1881):

"Vengeance imports a feeling of blame, and an opinion, however distorted by passion, that a wrong has been done. It can hardly go very far beyond the case of a harm intentionally inflicted: even a dog distinguishes between being stumbled over and being kicked."

[f] In addition to H.L.A. Hart, Punishment and Responsibility 28–53 (1968), see H. Packer, The Limits of the Criminal Sanction 74–75 (1968).

[g] H.L.A. Hart, Punishment and Responsibility 3 (1968).

3. **Retribution as a Limiting Concept: Proportionality.** The concept of retribution implies another important limitation on the uses of the criminal law, namely the principle of proportionality. Blame is a question of degree. To say that it was bad for someone to do something suggests the further question: "How bad?" A simple illustration makes the point. No one would argue that a petty thief should be punished as severely as one who kills for money. But why not? The answer that life imprisonment or the death penalty for the petty thief would be viewed as monstrously disproportionate to the offense is derived from an essentially retributive evaluation of the behavior. The degree of wrong-doing involved in such a case, most people would conclude, does not justify such extreme punishment. In the language of retribution, the offender did not "deserve" to be punished so severely.

The idea of proportionality is reflected in the criminal law in at least two ways. The first is through the grading of offenses, i.e., establishing by legislation some measure of the relative severity of offenses. For centuries, the law has reflected this concern by recognizing the category of "felony" for more serious offenses and "misdemeanor" for less serious crimes. The legislature "grades" offenses by establishing the maximum penalty that can be imposed upon conviction, and the relative seriousness of a given offense can be determined by comparing that sanction with those authorized for other offenses. Today, it is common to distinguish among six to 10 categories of crime, ranked according to relative seriousness, as a device for grading offenses.[h]

The second way that proportionality is reflected in the law is by assessing whether the sentence actually imposed is "just" or "fair" in relation to the blameworthiness of the offender and the gravity of the offense. The question here, in other words, is whether a particular sentence is or is not disproportionate for a particular crime, taking into account all of the facts and circumstances surrounding the offense. This is one factor, among others, that a judge takes into account at the time of sentencing. This idea is also reflected in the holding of the Supreme Court in Coker v. Georgia, 433 U.S. 584, 592 (1977),[i] that "a sentence of death is grossly disproportionate and excessive punishment for the crime of rape and is therefore forbidden . . . ."

GENERAL DETERRENCE

The concept of deterrence is typically divided into *special* deterrence and *general* deterrence. *Special* deterrence, sometimes called deterrence by intimidation, refers to steps taken to dissuade the particular offender from repeating his crime. The hope is that the conviction and sentence will bring the consequences of further criminal behavior dramatically to the offender's attention and thereby induce him to refrain from such conduct in the future. *General* deterrence, often called general prevention or deterrence by example, refers to the

[h] See Sections 6.01, 6.06, and 6.08 of the Model Penal Code, reproduced in Appendix A, pages 49, 51–52, infra.

[i] Reprinted infra, at 1004–19.

impact of sentence and conviction on others. The idea is that other people will be deterred from criminal behavior once they see what happens to those who commit crimes. Both of these concepts, in their classical form, are based on an essentially hedonistic calculus of pain and pleasure. If the costs of crime are set high enough to assure that the gains to be derived from it are not profitable, the rational man will not commit crimes. General deterrence brings home to the public generally the costs of crime; special deterrence brings the costs home to the individual offender. It will facilitate consideration of these concepts if special deterrence is laid to one side for the moment and general deterrence is considered independently.

1. **The Concept.** The outlines of the classical concept of deterrence are revealed in the following excerpts from J. Bentham, The Rationale of Punishment 19–41 (1830):

"Pain and pleasure are the great springs of human action. When a man perceives or supposes pain to be the consequence of an act, he is acted upon in such a manner as tends, with a certain force, to withdraw him, as it were, from the commission of that act. If the apparent magnitude, or rather value *of that pain be greater than the apparent magnitude or value of the pleasure or good he expects to be the consequence of the act, he will be absolutely prevented from performing it. The mischief which would have ensued from the act, if performed, will also by that means be prevented. . . . j

"General prevention is effected by the denunciation of punishment, and by its application, which, according to the common expression, *serves for an example.* The punishment suffered by the offender presents to every one an example of what he himself will have to suffer if he is guilty of the same offence.

"General prevention ought to be the chief end of punishment, as it is its real justification. If we could consider an offence which has been committed as an isolated fact, the like of which would never recur, punishment would be useless. It would only be adding one evil to another. But when we consider that an unpunished crime leaves the path of crime open, not only to the same delinquent, but also to all those who may have the same motives and opportunities for entering upon it, we perceive that the punishment inflicted on the individual becomes a source of security to all. That punishment, which, considered in itself, appeared base and repugnant to all generous sentiments, is elevated to the first rank of benefits, when it is regarded not as an act of wrath or of vengeance against a guilty or unfortunate

" * I say *value*, in order to include the circumstances of *intensity, proximity, certainty*, and *duration*; which magnitude, properly speaking, does not. . . ."

j As Bentham says later, "[t]he profit of the crime is the force which urges a man to delinquency—the pain of the punishment is the force employed to restrain him from it. If the first of these forces be the greater, the crime will be committed ["that is to say, committed by those who are only restrained by the laws, and not by any other tutelary motives, such as benevolence, religion, or honour"; if the second, the crime will not be committed." [Footnote by eds.]

individual who has given way to mischievous inclinations, but as an indispensable sacrifice to the common safety. . . .

"All punishment being in itself evil, upon the principle of utility, if it ought at all to be admitted, it ought only to be admitted in as far as it promises to exclude some greater evil.

"It is plain, therefore, that in the following cases punishment ought not to be inflicted:—(i) Where it is *groundless* [e.g., where "the mischief is *outweighed* by the production of a benefit of greater value"]; (ii) Where it must be *inefficacious*; because it cannot act so as to prevent the mischief [e.g., where "the penal provision, though it were conveyed to the individual's notice, *could produce no effect* with respect to preventing his engaging in the act prohibited; as in the cases of extreme *infancy, insanity,* and *intoxication*"]; (iii) Where it is *unprofitable* or too *expensive* [i.e., if "the evil of the punishment exceed the evil of the offence, the punishment will be unprofitable, the legislator will have produced more suffering than he has prevented. He will have purchased exemption from one evil at the expense of a greater"]; (iv) Where it is *needless*; because the mischief may be prevented or cease of itself without it [i.e., a "punishment is needless, where the purpose of putting an end to the practice may be attained as effectually at a cheaper rate" by using devices other than the criminal law]. . . .

"The observation of rules of proportion between crimes and punishments has been objected to as useless, because they seem to suppose, that a spirit of calculation has place among the passions of men, who, it is said, never calculate. But dogmatic as this proposition is, it is altogether false. In matters of importance, every one calculates. Each individual calculates with more or less correctness, according to the degrees of his information, and the power of the motives which actuate him, but all calculate. It would be hard to say that a madman does not calculate. Happily, the passion of cupidity, which on account of its power, its constancy, and its extent, is most formidable to society; is the passion which is most given to calculation. This, therefore, will be more successfully combated, the more carefully the law turns the balance of profit against it." [k]

---

[k] Bentham also defends a rule of proportionality in grading:

"*When two offences come in competition, the punishment for the greater offence must be sufficient to induce a man to prefer the less.*

"Two offences may be said to be in competition, when it is in the power of an individual to commit both. When thieves break into a house, they may execute their purpose in different manners; by simply stealing, by theft accompanied with bodily injury, or murder, or incendiarism. If the punishment is the same for simple theft, as for theft and murder, you give the thieves a motive for committing murder, because this crime adds to the facility of committing the former, and the chance of impunity when it is committed.

"The great inconvenience resulting from the infliction of great punishments for small offenses, is, that the power of increasing them in proportion to the magnitude of the offense is thereby lost."

[Footnote by eds.]

Bentham's argument makes plain that general deterrence is essentially utilitarian in focus. It is not backward-looking in the sense of repaying the offender for a crime or requiring the offender to repay society, but forward-looking in the sense of preventing or reducing the incidence of such behavior in the future. The central utilitarian premise is one of social control. Society has the right (and the obligation) to protect itself from certain forms of behavior and is entitled to take preventive steps in order to protect itself and individuals who live within it from harm.

Bentham's principal contention that the prevention of socially harmful behavior ought to be regarded as the primary aim of the criminal law is widely accepted today. Moreover, an important segment of the current research being conducted on deterrence is based on an economic model that predicts behavior based on a rational calculus of costs and benefits. A modern statement of this point of view is reflected in the following excerpt from R. Posner, Economic Analysis of Law 164–65 (2d ed. 1977):

> "The notion of the criminal as a rational calculator will strike many readers as highly unrealistic, especially when applied to criminals having little education or to crimes not committed for pecuniary gain. But . . . the test of a theory is not the realism of its assumptions but its predictive power. A growing empirical literature on crime has shown that criminals respond to changes in opportunity costs, in the probability of apprehension, in the severity of punishment, and in other relevant variables, as if they were indeed the rational calculators of the economic model—and this regardless of whether the crime is committed for pecuniary gain or out of passion, or by well or by poorly educated people."

Posner's assertion about the results of recent empirical research can be questioned, but general deterrence is widely believed to have the effects he describes. More importantly, as noted, the objective of achieving these effects is frequently regarded as the proper motivating aim of the criminal law.[1]

There are a number of aspects of general deterrence that should be isolated for separate consideration. They are developed below:

2. **Criticisms of Deterrence Theory.** One of the more effective and widely known proponents of a modern concept of general deterrence is Johannes Andenaes, a Norwegian criminologist who is a professor of law at the University of Oslo.[m] In his article, the General Preventive Effects of Punishment, 114 U.Pa.L.Rev. 949, 955–57 (1966),[*]

---

[1] H.L.A. Hart in Punishment and Responsibility 6 (1968) put the point this way: "[The] question is: Why are certain kinds of action forbiden by law and so made crimes or offences? The answer is: To announce to society that these actions are not to be done and to secure that fewer of them are done. These are the common immediate aims of making any conduct a criminal offence. . . ."

[m] A series of articles written by Professor Andenaes appears in book form under the title Punishment and Deterrence (1974).

[*] Reprinted by permission of the University of Pennsylvania Law Review and Fred B. Rothman & Company from the University of Pennsylvania Law Review, Vol. 114, pp. 955–57.

he observed that "certain untenable contentions are frequently introduced in various forms into discussions of general prevention" and responded to five such contentions as follows:

"1. *'Our knowledge of criminals shows us that the criminal law has no deterrent effects.'*

"The fallacy of this argument is obvious. If a man commits a crime, we can only conclude that general prevention has not worked *in his case.* If I interview 1000 prisoners, I collect information about 1000 men in whose cases general prevention has failed. But I cannot infer from this data that general prevention is ineffective in the cases of all those who have *not* committed crimes. General prevention is more concerned with the psychology of those obedient to the law than with the psychology of criminals.

"2. *'The belief in general prevention rests on an untenable rationalistic theory of behavior.'*

"It is true that the extreme theories of general prevention worked out by people like Bentham and Feuerbach were based on a shallow psychological model in which the actions of men were regarded as the outcome of a rational choice whereby gains and losses were weighed against each other. Similar simplified theories are sometimes expressed by police officials and by authors of letters to newspaper editors asking for heavier penalties. But if we discard such theories, it does not follow that we have to discard the idea of general prevention. Just as fear enters the picture when people take a calculated risk in committing an offense, fear may also be an element in behavior which is not rationally motivated. . . . [M]odern theories of general prevention take into account both deterrence and moral influence, and they concede that the effects involved may be 'unconscious and emotional, drawing upon deep rooted fears and aspirations.'
. . .

"3. *'Legal history shows that general prevention has always been overestimated.'*

"It is true that in the course of history there have been contentions about general prevention which seem fantastic today. There was a time when distinguished members of the House of Lords rose to warn their countrymen that the security of property would be seriously endangered if the administration of justice were weakened by abolition of capital punishment for shoplifting of items having a value of five shillings. Even today, one might find people with exaggerated conceptions of what can be accomplished by means of strong threats of punishment. But the fact that the general-preventive effects of punishment might have been exaggerated does not disprove the existence of such effects.

"4. *'Because people generally refrain from crimes on moral grounds, threats of penalty have little influence.'*

"The premise contains a large measure of truth, but it does not justify the conclusion. Three comments are necessary. (i) Even if people on the whole do not require the criminal law to keep them from committing more serious offenses, this is not true for offenses which are subject to little or no moral reprobation. (ii) Even though moral inhibitions today are adequate enough to prevent the bulk of the population from committing serious crimes, it is a debatable question whether this would continue for long if the hazards of punishment were removed or drastically minimized. It is conceivable that only a small number of people would fall victim to temptation when the penalties were first abolished or greatly reduced, but that with the passage of time, crime would attract the weaker souls who had become demoralized by seeing offenses committed with impunity. The effects might gradually spread through the population in a chain reaction. (iii) Even though it be conceded that law-abiding conduct in certain areas predominantly depends upon non-legal conditions, this does not mean that the effects of the legal machinery are not extremely valuable from a community point of view. Let us imagine a fictitious city which has 1,000,000 adult male inhabitants who commit 100 rapes annually. Suppose, then, that abolishing the crime of rape led to an increase in the number of rape cases to 1,000. From a social-psychological point of view one might conclude that the legal measures were quite insignificant: 999,000 males do not commit rape even when the threat of penalty is absent. If observed from the view point of the legal machinery, however, the conclusion is entirely different. A catastrophic increase of serious cases of violence has occurred. In other words, the increase in rape has demonstrated the tremendous social importance of general prevention.

"5. *'To believe in general prevention is to accept brutal penalties.'*

"This reasoning is apparent in Zilboorg's statement that 'if it is true that the punishment of the criminal must have a deterrent effect, then the abolition of the drawing and quartering of criminals was both a logical and penological mistake. Why make punishment milder and thus diminish the deterrent effect of punishment?'

"Here we find a mixture of empirical and ethical issues. It was never a principle of criminal justice that crime should be prevented at all costs. Ethical and social considerations will always determine which measures are considered 'proper.' As Ball has expressed it: '[A] penalty may be quite effective as a deterrent, yet undesirable.' Even if it were possible to prove that cutting off thieves' hands would effectively prevent theft, proposals for such practice would scarcely win many adherents today. . . ."

3. **The Limits of Deterrence**. Andenaes' last point, that "[i]t was never a principle of criminal justice that crime should be prevented at

all costs," deserves special emphasis. It has been argued that, standing alone:

> "[D]eterrent theory offers no clear standards by which either the kind or amount of punishment can be determined. How is the legislature to measure in advance the quantum of punishment necessary to prevent a given form of conduct in the various social circumstances in which it may appear? How is the danger to social interests of such behavior to be reflected proportionately in the penalties applied? This inherent uncertainty may result either in an excess or a deficiency of punishment. In times of stress and insecurity the effort to deter may result in draconian measures with consequent injury to individual and social interests." [n]

It seems clear that certain sanctions—torture, cutting off thieves' hands, branding—are morally repulsive in modern society and that any desire to employ such sanctions will be tempered by a sense of appropriate moral limits, no matter what deterrence theory may suggest about their effectiveness in reducing crime. Similarly, even though rigid adherence to deterrence theory might seem to suggest adoption of the most effective traditional sanctions that are likely to achieve the social control objective—however long or oppressive those sanctions turn out to be—most persons would agree that general deterrence needs to be tempered by the concept of proportionality. These points do not, however, exhaust the problem. How does the deterrent theorist choose between a five-year sentence and a 10-year sentence for a particular crime? Between a three-year sentence and a 20-year sentence? By what calipers does the concept of general deterrence give answers in the precise detail that a legislature needs in choosing authorized sentences or a judge in imposing an actual sentence? [o]

   4. **Deterrence and Blameworthiness.** The implications of deterrence for the concept of blameworthiness must also be taken into account. Recall that Bentham argued that punishment ought not to be inflicted in cases where it would be inefficacious and used as examples persons who would not be blameworthy for having engaged in otherwise criminal behavior. H.L.A. Hart has argued in Punishment and Responsibility 18–20 (1968) [*] that deterrence theory alone cannot justify Bentham's conclusion:

> "Utilitarians have made strenuous, detailed efforts to show that restriction of the use of punishment to those who have voluntarily broken the law is explicable on purely utilitarian lines. Bentham's efforts are the most complete and their failure is an instructive warning to contemporaries. . . .

[n] F. Allen, The Borderland of Criminal Justice 86 (1964). Professor Allen was summarizing the views of Raffaele Garofalo, a 19th-century Italian criminologist, not stating his own views.

[o] Indeed, implementation of deterrence theory may be even more deeply problematic. For an insightful investigation of some of the complexities involved, see Seidman, Soldiers, Martyrs, and Criminals: Utilitarian Theory and the Problem of Crime Control, 94 Yale L.J. 315 (1984).

[*] Copyright © Oxford University Press 1968. The excerpts below are reprinted by permission of the author and Oxford University Press.

"Bentham's argument is in fact a spectacular non sequitur. He sets out to prove that to *punish* the mad, the infant child or those who break the law unintentionally or under duress or even under 'necessity' must be inefficacious; but all that he proves (at the most) is the quite different proposition that the *threat* of punishment will be ineffective so far as the class of persons who suffer from these conditions is concerned. Plainly it is possible that though (as Bentham says) the *threat* of punishment could not have operated on them, the actual *infliction* of punishment on those persons, may secure a higher measure of conformity to law on the part of normal persons than is secured by the admission of excusing conditions. If this is so and if utilitarian principles only were at stake, we should, without any sense that we were sacrificing any principle of value or were choosing the lesser of two evils, drop from the law the restriction on punishment entailed by the admission of excuses: Unless, of course, we believed that the terror or insecurity or misery produced by the operation of laws so draconic was worse than the lower measure of obedience to law secured by the law which admits excuses.

"This objection to Bentham's rationale of excuses is not merely a fanciful one. Any increase in the number of conditions required to establish criminal liability increases the opportunity for deceiving courts or juries by the pretence that some condition is not satisfied. When the condition is a psychological factor the chances of such pretence succeeding are considerable. Quite apart from the provision made for mental disease, the cases where an accused person pleads that he killed in his sleep or accidentally or in some temporary abnormal state of unconsciousness show that deception is certainly feasible. From the utilitarian point of view this may lead to two sorts of 'losses.' The belief that such deception is feasible may embolden persons who would not otherwise risk punishment to take their chance of deceiving a jury in this way. Secondly, a criminal who actually succeeds in this deception will be left at large, though belonging to the class which the law is concerned to incapacitate."

Acceptance of Hart's argument does not require, of course, that the concept of blameworthiness must be abandoned by one who regards social control as the primary objective of the criminal law, although that is one conclusion to which it could lead. The alternative is to recognize that constraints derived from sources other than deterrence theory must be used if one is to retain the blameworthiness concept.[p]

p Cf. A. Ewing, The Morality of Punishment 44–45 (1929):

"While the retributive theory seems to break down in practice, certain general principles for which it stands are of very great importance and value. It condemns the punishment of the innocent, i.e., of those who have not deliberately committed offences against definite laws in force prior to their commission; it demands that a lighter offence should not be punished more severely than a much graver one; it insists that considerations of expediency, or apparent expediency, should not be easily allowed to outweigh the general rule that the guilty are to be punished. These principles, however they may be justified, must be recognized as of great ethical importance. The retributive theory, though it is often stigmatised as 'brutal,' should defend the criminal against an excessive severity as unjust, and is far easier to

5. **The Socializing Effect of the Criminal Law.** Many people have observed that the deterrent effect of the criminal law reaches considerably beyond the fear of punishment it may induce in one who is contemplating a criminal offense. This has sometimes been described as the socializing effect of the criminal law, i.e., the capacity of the law to reinforce attitudes and values and to become a part of the conditioning that leads individuals not to commit crime as a matter of habit or life-style, quite apart from day-to-day calculation of its effects. Indeed, one reasonably could take the position that the real importance of general deterrence lies not in its effect on the calculus of one who may be contemplating a criminal offense but elsewhere.[q] Andenaes makes the point in General Prevention—Illusion or Reality, 43 J.Crim.L., C. & P.S. 176, 179–80 (1952),[*] as follows:

"By general prevention we mean the ability of criminal law and its enforcement to make citizens law-abiding. If general prevention were 100 per cent effective there would be no crime at all. General prevention may depend on the mere frightening or deterrent effect of punishment—the risk of discovery and punishment outweighing the temptation to commit crime. . . . Later theory puts much stress on the ability of penal law to arouse or strengthen inhibitions of another sort. In Swedish discussion the *moralizing*—in other words the *educational*—function has been greatly stressed. The idea is that punishment as a concrete expression of society's disapproval of an act helps to form and to strengthen the public's moral code and thereby creates conscious and unconscious inhibitions against committing crime. Unconscious inhibitions against committing forbidden acts can also be aroused without appealing to the individual's concepts of morality. Purely as a matter of habit, with fear, respect for authority, or social imitation as connecting links, it is possible to induce favorable attitudes toward this or that action and unfavorable attitudes toward another action. We find the clearest example of this in the military, where extended inculcation of discipline and stern reaction against breach thereof can induce a purely automatic, habitual response—not only where obeying specific orders is concerned, but also with regard to general orders and regulations. We have another example in the relationship between an occupying power and an occupied population. The regulations set down by the occupier are not regarded by the people as morally binding; but by a combination of terror and habit formation a great measure of obedience can be elicited—at any

reconcile with our horror at the deliberate infliction of punishment on the innocent for reasons of expediency than any merely utilitarian theory."

[q] Cf. Section 7.01(1)(c) of the Model Penal Code: "The court shall deal with a person who has been convicted of a crime without imposing a sentence of imprisonment unless, having regard to the nature and circumstances of the crime and the history, character and condition of the defendant, it is of the opinion that his imprisonment is necessary for protection of the public because . . . a lesser sentence will depreciate the seriousness of the defendant's crime."

[*] Reprinted by special permission of the Journal of Criminal Law and Criminology, © 1952 by Northwestern University School of Law.

rate in response to commands which do not conflict too greatly with national feelings.

"We can say that punishment has three sorts of general-preventive effects: it may have a *deterrent* effect, it may strengthen *moral inhibitions* (a *moralizing* effect), and it may stimulate *habitual law-abiding conduct*. I have reason to emphasize this, since many of those who are most skeptical of general prevention think only of the deterrent effect. Even if it can be shown that conscious fear of punishment is not present in certain cases, this is by no means the same as showing that the secondary effects of punishment are without importance. To the lawmaker, the achievement of inhibition and habit is of greater value than mere deterrence. For these apply in cases where a person need not fear detection and punishment, and they can apply without the person ever having knowledge of the legal prohibition."

6. **Measuring Deterrence.** It was noted above that retribution is essentially a normative theory and that as such it cannot be empirically verified or tested. The utilitarian concept of deterrence, on the other hand, justifies punishment in preventive terms and as such makes an assertion that in principle is subject to empirical verification. We should be able to find out, in other words, whether criminal punishment in fact deters people from committing crimes and, more precisely, which sanctions and in what amounts provide the most effective deterrents. Yet to date, we have been unable to do so in a manner that can claim general recognition and acceptance in the scientific community.

In a paper entitled "General Deterrence: A Review of the Empirical Evidence" prepared for the National Academy of Sciences,[r] Daniel Nagin offered the following conclusions on the state of scientific research on deterrence:

"A decade ago there were virtually no empirical analyses of the deterrence hypothesis for non-capital sanctions. Many people held strong positions for and against deterrence, but these opinions had virtually no scientific basis. The explicit empirical analyses of deterrence were almost exclusively limited to capital punishment, and these analyses suggested that capital punishment had no marginal deterrent effect beyond extended imprisonment.

"The past decade has witnessed a burgeoning of analyses directed at testing the deterrence hypothesis for non-capital sanctions. In this critique over 20 published analyses are cited, and even this list is less than exhaustive. Yet, despite the intensity of the research effort, the empirical evidence is still not sufficient for providing a rigorous confirmation of the existence of a deterrent effect. Perhaps more important, the evidence is

[r] Published in A. Blumstein, J. Cohen, & D. Nagin, eds., Deterrence and Incapacitation: Estimating the Effects of Criminal Sanctions on Crime Rates 95, 135–36 (1978).

woefully inadequate for providing a good estimate of the magnitude of whatever effect may exist.

"The development of public policy directed explicitly at crime control is dependent upon sound estimates of the magnitude of deterrent effects. Thus, policy suggestions, based upon the existing evidence, can only be made with a clear recognition of the inadequacy of the evidence. Accordingly, such suggestions must be very limited and posed with great caution.

"This is in stark contrast to some of the presentations in public discussion that have unequivocally concluded that sanctions deter and that have made sweeping suggestions that sanctioning practices be changed to take advantage of the presumed deterrent effect. Certainly, most people will agree that increasing sanctions will deter crime somewhat, but the critical question is, By how much? There is still considerable uncertainty over whether that effect is trivial (even if statistically detectable) or profound. Any unequivocal policy conclusion is simply not supported by valid evidence.

"Although more punitive sanctioning practices might legitimately be argued as a responsible ethical response to a truly significant crime problem, arguing such a policy on the basis of the empirical evidence is not yet justified because it offers a misleading impression of scientific validity. Policy makers in the criminal justice system are done a disservice if they are left with the impression that the empirical evidence, which they themselves are frequently unable to evaluate, strongly supports the deterrence hypothesis. Furthermore, such distortions ultimately undermine the credibility of scientific evidence as inputs to public-policy choices. A more critical assessment of the evidence is needed if we are to see progress in the development of knowledge about deterrent effectiveness and its application to effective public policy."

7. **The Relation of Severity and Certainty.** Finally, it must be kept in mind that the magnitude and terms of the criminal sanction are not the only factors that must be considered in determining the deterrent effect of punishment. As Bentham recognized, the proximity and certainty of punishment—the probability of conviction and imposition of a criminal sanction—must also be taken into account. Andenaes offered the following observations on the relationship between these factors in The General-Preventive Effects of Punishment, 114 U.Pa.L.Rev. 949, 960–70 (1966): *

"The efficiency of the system could be changed . . . by intensifying or reducing the effort of the police or by altering the rules of criminal procedure so as to increase or lower the probabilities that criminals will escape punishment. Even the simplest kind of common sense indicates that the degree of risk

* Reprinted by permission of the University of Pennsylvania Law Review and Fred B. Rothman & Company from the University of Pennsylvania Law Review, Vol. 114, pp. 960–70.

of detection and conviction is of paramount importance to the preventive effects of the penal law. Very few people would violate law if there were a policeman on every doorstep. It has even been suggested that the insanity of an offender be determined by asking whether he would have performed the prohibited act 'with a policeman at his elbow.'

"Exceptions would occur, however. Some crimes are committed in such a state of excitement that the criminal acts without regard to the consequences. In other cases the actor accepts the penalty as a reasonable price for carrying out the action—we may think of the attitude a busy salesman has toward parking regulations. Further a political assassin may deliberately sacrifice his life to his cause. But there is good reason to believe that certainty of rapid apprehension and punishment would prevent *most* violations.

"On the other hand, there is evidence that the lack of enforcement of penal laws designed to regulate behavior in morally neutral fields may rapidly lead to mass infringements. Parking regulations, currency regulations, and price regulations are examples of such laws. The individual's moral reluctance to break the law is not strong enough to secure obedience when the law comes into conflict with his personal interests.

". . . At least since the time of Beccaria, it has been commonly accepted that the certainty of detection and punishment is of greater consequence in deterring people from committing crimes than is the severity of the penalty.[s] This notion has undoubtedly contributed significantly to the abolition of brutal penalties, and there is certainly a large measure of truth in it. Part of the explanation is that one who ponders the possibility of detection and punishment before committing a crime must necessarily consider the total social consequences, of which the penalty is but a part. A trusted cashier committing embezzlement, a

[s] Econometric analysis has produced numerous empirical studies on the general-deterrent effect of punishment. If a criminal calculates the costs of an activity as the severity of the penalty times the probability of apprehension, a change in either variable should, theoretically, have the same impact on the calculation. Studies have suggested, however, that an increase in the severity of the penalty will not have as great an effect on the volume of crime as an increase in the probability of apprehension. In Antunes & Hunt, The Impact of Certainty and Severity of Punishment on Levels of Crime in American States, 64 J.Crim.L. & Crim. 486, 492–93 (1973), it is concluded that "certainty, considered by itself, has a moderate deterrent effect for all crimes, while severity acting alone is not associated with lower rates of crime. . . . [I]ncreasing severity in a condition of low certainty will have little effect on crime rates." But see Nagel, Trade-offs in Crime Reduction Among Certainty, Severity, and Crime Benefits, 35 Rut.L.Rev. 100 (1982) (concluding that certainty is more important than severity only in certain contexts).

Further studies on the relation of certainty of punishment to criminal behavior include M. Silver, Punishment, Deterrence, and Police Effectiveness: A Survey and Critical Interpretation of the Recent Econometric Literature (1974), and Erickson, Gibbs, & Jensen, The Deterrence Doctrine and the Perceived Certainty of Legal Punishments, 42 Am.Soc.Rev. 305 (1977). Two important collections of essays on the economics of deterrence are G. Becker & W. Landes, eds., Essays in the Economics of Crime and Punishment (1974), and A. Blumstein, J. Cohen, & D. Nagin, eds., Deterrence and Incapacitation: Estimating the Effects of Criminal Sanctions on Crime Rates (1978). [Footnote by eds.]

minister who evades payment of his taxes, a teacher making sexual advances towards minors, and a civil servant who accepts bribes have a fear of detection which is more closely linked with the dread of public scandal and subsequent social ruin than with apprehensions of legal punishment. Whether the punishment is severe or mild thus appears to be rather unimportant. However, in cases of habitual criminals or juvenile delinquents from the slums the situation may be quite different.

"Even if we accept Beccaria's position, it does not follow that the severity of penalties is without importance. It is difficult to increase the likelihood of detection and punishment because the risk of detection usually depends on many conditions beyond the reach of the authorities, and because improvement of police effectiveness requires money and human resources. Accordingly, when the legislators and courts attempt to check any apparent rise in the crime rate they generally increase the severity of penalties. On the other hand, for those who wish to make the criminal law more humane the problem is one of determining how far it is possible to proceed in the direction of leniency without weakening the law's total preventive effects. It is impossible to avoid the question of how important a change in the severity of the punishment may be under standard conditions of detection, apprehension, and conviction. For the judge this is the only form in which the problem presents itself.

"A potential criminal who reflects upon the possibilities of punishment may pay attention to the severity of the penalty to which he exposes himself, as well as to the risks of detection. He may be willing to run the risk of a year's imprisonment but he might not gamble 10. The situation is similar to those in which nature herself attaches penalties to certain actions. Sexual promiscuity has always brought with it the risk of undesired children and of venereal diseases, and consideration of these risks has certainly in the course of time persuaded many people to exercise self-restraint. The progress of civilization has led to a diminishing of the former risk and rendered the latter less formidable. Few people will deny that these changes have had a considerable bearing on the development of sexual mores in the Western world. . . .

"It seems reasonable to conclude that as a general rule, though not without exceptions, the general-preventive effect of the criminal law increases with the growing severity of penalties. Contemporary dictatorships display with almost frightening clarity the conformity that can be produced by a ruthlessly severe justice.

"However, it is necessary to make two important reservations. In the first place . . . what is decisive is not the actual practice but how this practice is conceived by the public. Although little research has been done to find out how much the general public knows about the penal system, presumably most people have only vague and unspecified notions. Therefore, only quite substantial changes will be noticed. Only rarely does a single sentence bring about significant preventive effects.

"In the second place, the prerequisite of general prevention is that the law be enforced. Experience seems to show that excessively severe penalties may actually reduce the risk of conviction, thereby leading to results contrary to their purpose. When the penalties are not reasonably attuned to the gravity of the violation, the public is less inclined to inform the police, the prosecuting authorities are less disposed to prosecute and juries are less apt to convict. . . ."

Consider also the following position, advanced arguendo in R. Posner, Economic Analysis of Law 170 (2d ed. 1977): *

"If we must continue to rely heavily on the sanction of imprisonment, there is an argument for combining heavy prison terms for the convicted criminal with low probabilities of apprehension and conviction. An example will suggest why this might be an economically attractive trade-off. Consider the choice between combining a .1 probability of apprehension and conviction with a ten-year prison term, and a .2 probability of apprehension and conviction with a five-year term. Under the second approach, twice as many individuals are imprisoned, but for only half as long a time, so the total costs of imprisonment are likely to be the same or similar under the two approaches. But the costs of police, court officials, etc., are clearly less under the first approach, since under it the probability of apprehension and conviction is only half of what it is under the second.

"It is sometimes objected that a system under which probabilities of punishment are low is unfair, because it creates ex post inequality among offenders: many go scot-free; others serve longer prison sentences than they would if more offenders were caught. But to object to this result is like saying that all lotteries are unfair because, ex post, they create wealth differences among the players. In an equally significant sense, both the criminal-justice system that creates low probabilities of apprehension and conviction and the lottery are fair so long as the ex ante costs and benefits are equalized among the participants.

"Another factor to be considered in the design of an optimal system of criminal sanctions is preference for and against risk. If risk aversion is prevalent among criminals, that reinforces the argument for combining low probabilities of apprehension and conviction with high levels of severity, for this method of creating punishment costs imposes greater risk on the criminal than would a less severe and more certain punishment. Conversely, the risk-preferring criminal would prefer a low probability of a severe punishment to a high probability of a mild punishment,

* R. Posner, Economic Analysis of Law,
Little Brown and Company: Boston, 1977,
p. 170. Reprinted by permission.

even if the expected punishment costs of the two forms of sanction were the same." [t]

INDIVIDUAL PREVENTION

It is convenient to consider the remaining elements of the traditional list of the purposes of punishment under the single rubric of individual prevention. Each, in the last analysis, is based on the utilitarian conception that once a person has been identified as an offender by the commission of a criminal offense, the system should devote its resources to preventing that offender from committing another offense. The focus here shifts from the effect of punishment on the general population to the effect of punishment on the identified offender. The ultimate objective—prevention of future criminality—remains the same.

1. **Special Deterrence.** The concept of special deterrence is difficult to separate from rehabilitation, since normally a criminal sanction—be it probation, imprisonment, a fine, or some combination of the three—will have at least both objectives. The justification for a sentence to probation, for example, might well be both that the offender will be intimidated by the exposure to the criminal process, the fact of conviction, and the threat of future sanctions for violations of the conditions of release, and that the offender will be rehabilitated by official supervision during the period of probation. Similarly, a prison sentence may be expected to have intimidating effects, but it frequently is coupled with rehabilitative objectives sought to be accomplished during the period of imprisonment. In the latter case, moreover, incapacitative objectives may also be served.

It is for this reason that the literature on special deterrence is slim.[u] Virtually all modern studies of prison effectiveness concern rehabilitative programs rather than the isolated effect of special deterrence or incapacitation.[v] To the extent, moreover, that special deterrence is isolated, it is often asserted that recidivism rates, i.e., the rates at which offenders repeat their offenses, are so high that this fact alone demonstrates that the idea of special deterrence does not work.[w] To this point, however, it can be responded that there may indeed be types

[t] In addition to the materials on deterrence cited elsewhere in these notes, other useful treatments include R. Hauge, ed., Drinking and Driving in Scandinavia (1980); J. Gibbs, Crime, Punishment, and Deterrence (1975); F. Zimring & G. Hawkins, Deterrence: The Legal Threat in Crime Control (1973); C. Tittle, Sanctions and Social Deviance: the Question of Deterrence (1980); Andenaes, General Prevention Revisited: Research and Policy Implications, 66 J.Crim.L. & Crim. 338 (1975); Chambliss, Types of Deviance and the Effectiveness of Legal Sanctions, 1967 Wisc.L.Rev. 703; Clarke, "Situational" Crime Prevention: Theory and Practice, 20 Brit.J. Criminology 136 (1980); Grasmick & Bryjak, The Deterrent Effect of Perceived Severity of Punishment, 59 Social Forces 471 (1980). [Footnote by eds.]

[u] For theoretical analyses of special deterrence, see F. Zimring & G. Hawkins, Deterrence: The Legal Threat in Crime Control 224–48 (1973); H. Packer, The Limits of the Criminal Sanction 45–48 (1968).

[v] See, e.g., J. Martin & D. Webster, The Social Consequences of Conviction (1971); R. Hood & R. Sparks, Key Issues in Criminology 171–92 (1970).

[w] For an analysis of recidivism rates and what they seem to show, see D. Glaser, The Effectiveness of a Prison and Parole System (1964).

of offenders who do not respond to efforts to intimidate them from the commission of future offenses and that by and large these offenders make up the bulk of the prison population and the recidivism statistics. This does not establish, however, that there are neither other types of offenders nor other individual offenders who learn simply from the fact of conviction or from realistic exposure to the possibility of severe sanctions that they do not want to become involved in the criminal process again. Indeed, the so-called "split sentence" has become more widely used in recent years on just this theory.[x]

Finally it should be noted that to the extent that special deterrence can be isolated as a separate theory of punishment it would seem subject to the same criticisms and limitations that have been discussed above in connection with general deterrence. In particular, the empirical foundation for assertions about specific deterrence has not been established to a level that has received general recognition and acceptance in the scientific community. Also, the need for independently developed limitations on the extent to which special deterrence is used as a justifying aim of punishment seems just as great.

2. **Incapacitation.** Incapacitation as a goal of punishment is in many ways the cleanest form of individual prevention. Its objective is to deny, or at least greatly reduce, the opportunity to commit future offenses. By increasing the rigor of the incapacitative regime, moreover, absolute prevention—if that is the sole objective and if limitations derived from other sources are ignored—can very nearly be achieved.

The goal of incapacitation as a utilitarian method of achieving individual prevention thus avoids some of the more vexing empirical problems posed by general and special deterrence. We know that incapacitation prevents crime. On the other hand, another empirical problem of imposing dimensions immediately emerges. As a utilitarian objective, the incapacitative theory teaches that incapacitation should be used only in cases where it is needed, i.e., only in cases where it is necessary to restrain the offender from committing a future offense. In cases where the offender would not commit another offense anyway, incapacitation is unnecessary and should not be used. This theoretical implication in turn involves the problem of prediction: Do we know enough about human behavior to be able to predict what an offender will do in the future?

A task force of the American Psychological Association addressed this problem in 1978. Its report, published in 33 Am. Psychologist 1099, 1110 (1978), concludes that:

"It does appear from reading the research that the validity of psychological predictions of violent behavior, at least in the sentencing and release situations we are considering, is extremely poor, so poor that one could oppose their use on the strictly

[x] A "split sentence" is a sentence that uses a short jail term (for the purpose of giving the offender a taste of what it is like to be confined) followed by a period of probation. Its use is described and defended in ABA Standards for Criminal Justice ch. 18, pp. 100–07 (2d ed. 1980).

empirical grounds that psychologists are not professionally competent to make such judgments."

Similarly, the following conclusion is expressed in Diamond, The Psychiatric Prediction of Dangerousness, 123 U.Pa.L.Rev. 439, 452 (1974):

"Neither psychiatrists nor other behavioral scientists are able to predict the occurrence of violent behavior with sufficient reliability to justify the restriction of freedom of persons on the basis of the label of potential dangerousness. Accordingly, it is recommended that courts no longer ask such experts to give their opinion of the potential dangerousness of any person, and that psychiatrists and other behavioral scientists acknowledge their inability to make such predictions when called upon to do so by courts and other legal agencies." [y]

To this can be added a range of imposing moral difficulties. What statistical margin of error is permissible, if, indeed, such statistics can even be developed? If there is only a 30-per-cent chance that a violent offender with certain characteristics will commit another violent offense, is imprisonment nonetheless ethically appropriate? For how long? Until the chances are reduced to 10 per cent? Until there is *no* chance? And suppose the predicted future offense does not involve violence. For how long should a petty thief be incapacitated if there is a 90-per-cent chance of future petty thefts? If it could be shown (as many people believe has been shown) that certain kinds of murderers are virtually certain not to kill again, does this mean that incapacitation is for them an illegitimate goal of punishment? [z]

The difficulty of these problems should be drawn out in at least two respects. The first was captured by Professor Packer in The Limits of the Criminal Sanction 50–51 (1968):

"The case for incapacitation is strongest in precisely those areas where the offender is least capable of controlling himself, where his conduct bears the least resemblance to the kind of purposeful, voluntary conduct to which we are likely to attach moral con-

---

[y] A more moderate position is taken in J. Monahan, The Clinical Prediction of Violent Behavior (1981). Professor Monahan states his ambivalence in the opening paragraph of his preface:

"At several points in its gestation [this book] had a working subtitle. When I was beginning the monograph, it was 'Why You Can't Do It.' About halfway through writing it, I changed the subtitle to 'How to Do It and Why You Shouldn't.' By the time I was finished, I was toying with 'How to Do It and When to Do It.' The development of my thinking on the prediction of violence is reflected quite well in these changes: from an empirical distaste for the task, to an ethical aversion to engaging in it, to a reluctant concession that there may be circumstances in which prediction is both empirically possible and ethically appropriate."

[z] An even broader moral challenge to the use of prediction as a basis for punishment is reflected in the following comment from A. von Hirsch, Doing Justice: The Choice of Punishments 26 (1976):

"[P]redictive restraint poses special ethical problems. The fact that the person's liberty is at stake reduces the moral acceptability of mistakes of overprediction. Moreover, one may question whether it is ever just to *punish* someone more severely for what he is expected to do, even if the prediction was accurate."

See also von Hirsch, The Ethics of Selective Incapacitation: Observations on the Contemporary Debate, 30 Crime & Delinq. 175 (1984). But see J. Wilson, Thinking About Crime (1983) (urging greater emphasis on selective incapacitation).

demnation. Baldly put, the incapacitative theory is at its strongest for those who, in retributive terms, are the least deserving of punishment."

A person who can be identified as a kleptomaniac, for example, presents a strong case for incapacitation, yet a weak case for retribution since it seems immoral to "blame" one who acts under an abnormally strong impulse to steal. Packer also made the second point, again in the context of the kleptomaniac:

"The logic of the incapacitative position drives us to say that until the offender stops being a danger we will continue to restrain him. What this means, pushed to its logical conclusion, is that offenses that are universally regarded as relatively trivial may be punished by imprisonment for life. It means that, at least, unless we have some basis for asserting that lengthy imprisonment is a greater evil than the prospect of repeated criminality."

It should also be noted that the utilitarian rationale of incapacitation as a measure of individual prevention is not necessarily the justification for all sentences of imprisonment. Imprisonment can be used for retributive purposes or for general deterrent purposes as well, and arguably is so used for certain homicides where the emotional situation that provoked the actor to kill is so unlikely to recur that it can be predicted that he or she will not kill again. It should not be assumed, in other words, that all sentences of imprisonment are justified by the goal of incapacitation as it is normally understood as a rationale for punishment.

3. **Rehabilitation.** Rehabilitation as a goal of punishment is often not thought of as a utilitarian form of individual prevention, but rather as an humanitarian effort to improve the lot of convicted criminals and to make them more productive members of society. Packer suggested why the humanitarian focus may be inappropriate as a goal of punishment in The Limits of the Criminal Sanction 53–54 (1968): "However benevolent the purpose of reform, however better off we expect its object to be, there is no blinking the fact that what we do to the offender in the name of reform is being done to him by compulsion and for *our* sake, not for his." In this view, the purpose of criminal punishment cannot be a generalized desire to help people and to make them better. Such an approach would raise fundamental problems of individual liberty and autonomy and would lead the state to intervention in people's lives to a far greater extent than could be justified in contemporary American society. The intervention of the criminal law is coercive and is based on previously committed conduct, and if rehabilitation is to have a place as a goal of the criminal process, it would seem to follow that the purpose, as in the case of special deterrence and incapacitation, should be to prevent repetition of the criminal behavior, i.e., to accomplish the objective of individual prevention.

Even so confined, however, the proper role of rehabilitation as a measure of individual prevention is not clear. Partly this is for reasons that have been explored above in other contexts. It should come as no surprise that, just as we do not know the actual effects of deterrence and are limited in our ability to predict human behavior, we also do not know very much about how to change people's behavior.[a] Even if we did know how to cure some people of their propensity towards crime, moreover, there is the question of how long the cure should be permitted to take and what to do with those who cannot be cured. The goal of rehabilitation does not itself suggest its own time limitations. To return to the example of kleptomania, many would find it morally offensive to imprison a petty thief for life if there were no cure or for 30 years if it took that long to effect the necessary reformation. In this sense, rehabilitation shares with other individual-prevention rationales the need for compromise with other values in order to keep the length of coercive intervention within reasonable bounds. Finally, there are serious ethical questions involved in any effort at coercive cure. As Packer has said, even if we finally do learn how to rehabilitate people— even if "the day of the good-behavior pill comes"—is "it quixotic to assert that man has a right to be bad?" Do we have the moral right to attempt fundamental, coerced personality change?[b]

The response of many modern criminologists to these points is that rehabilitation is not itself a proper goal of punishment, but rather a collateral objective to be sought by moderate means within a system of sanctions created with other objectives in mind. If a decision to imprison is made for retributive, general-deterrent, or incapacitative reasons, it is proper to seek to reform the offender within the limits of imprisonment set by these goals, at least by methods that give him the opportunity for self-improvement (education, job training) rather than methods that coerce unwanted reform (psychosurgery). It is not appropriate, on the other hand, to impose a sentence of imprisonment or any other criminal punishment in order to accomplish rehabilitative objectives.[c] This view is reflected in the following excerpt from N. Morris & G. Hawkins, Letter to the President on Crime Control 67–68 (1977): *

"The fact is that rehabilitation programs for convicted criminals in prison do not overcome the socially alienative effects

---

[a] Two major studies on the failure of therapeutic programs in prisons are G. Kassebaum, D. Ward, & D. Wilner, Prison Treatment and Parole Survival: An Empirical Assessment (1971) and D. Lipton, R. Martinson, & J. Wilks, The Effectiveness of Correctional Treatment: A Survey of Evaluation Studies (1975). One author of the second study, Robert Martinson, has written a highly influential summary of his conclusions called "What Works? Questions and Answers About Prison Reform" in 35 Pub.Int. 22 (Spring 1974). Martinson has since moderated his views somewhat and now believes that some rehabilitative programs, particularly parole supervision, work better than others. See Martinson, New Findings; New Views: A Note of Caution Regarding Sentencing Reform, 7 Hofstra L.Rev. 243 (1979).

[b] Voluntary forms of rehabilitation in prisons stir little controversy, but moral objections become acute when prisoners are forced to undergo personality transformations through various kinds of behavior control, such as psychotropic drugs, aversion therapy (popularized in A Clockwork Orange), electric shock therapy, and particularly psychosurgery. See Gobert, Psychosurgery, Conditioning, and the Prisoner's Right to Refuse "Rehabilitation", 61 Va.L.Rev. 155 (1975); Shapiro, Legislating Control of Behavior Control, 47 So.Cal.L.Rev. 237 (1974); Note, 45 So.Cal.L.Rev. 616 (1972).

[c] But cf. Section 7.01(1)(b) of the Model Penal Code: "The court shall deal with a

---

* See note * on page 26.

and other disadvantages of conviction and imprisonment. The cage is not a sensible place in which to cure the criminal, even when the medical analogy makes sense, which it rarely does. But this does *not* mean that such treatment programs as we now have in prisons should be abandoned; quite the contrary, they urgently need expansion. No one of any sensitivity can visit any of our mega-prisons without recognizing that they contain, as in all countries, populations that are disproportionately illiterate, unemployed, vocationally untrained, undereducated, psychologically disturbed, and socially isolated. It is both in the prisoners' and in the community's best interest to help them to remedy these deficiencies.

"Nevertheless, it should be recognized that rehabilitative programs to that end are not *the* purpose, or even *one* purpose of imprisonment. 'Rehabilitation,' whatever it means and whatever the programs that give it meaning, must cease to be the claimed purpose of imprisonment. We should avoid hypocrisy: we send men to prison as punishment for what they have done; sometimes also to deter those who are like-minded, and sometimes because we do not know what else to do with them. We cage them for what they have done; it is an injustice to cage them also for what they *are* in order to change them, to attempt to cure them coercively. There is a sharp distinction between the purposes of imprisonment and the opportunities for the training and assistance of prisoners that may properly be pursued within those purposes.

"The rejection of the model of coercive curing of criminals flows not from lack of power to change human behavior if human rights and the concept of a just-desert limiting punishment are ignored. Coercive curing must be rejected as a punishment because of certain centrally important issues concerning the relationship between individual freedom and state authority. We must stay out of the business of forcibly remaking man. The central point is this: Punishment, not cure, is the business of the criminal law. The purposes of the criminal law are easy to state, though difficult to achieve: the criminal law should, with justice and mercy, parsimoniously punish those whose punishment is both deserved by their conduct and necessary for the common good. When the agents of the criminal law seek to extend their reach beyond these purposes, they imperil fundamental values on which this country was built."

person who has been convicted of a crime without imposing a sentence of imprisonment unless, having regard to the nature and circumstances of the crime and the history, character and condition of the defendant, it is of the opinion that his imprisonment is necessary for protection of the public because . . . the defendant is in need of correctional treatment that can be provided most effectively by his commitment to an institution. . . ."

* Reprinted from Letter to the President on Crime Control by N. Morris & G. Hawkins with permission of the University of Chicago Press. © 1977 The University of Chicago Press.

It is fair to say, moreover, that there has been a decided shift towards this point of view in much of the recent literature on sentencing.[d]

4. **The Limits of Individual Prevention.** As has been stated, special deterrence, incapacitation, and rehabilitation as goals of individual prevention are focused on the particular offender and what can be done to induce self-restraint. An important aspect of such measures that must be taken into account in an assessment of their effectiveness is the criminogenic effect of punishment itself. The idea that punishments may actually cause more crime than they prevent is reflected in the claims, found in much of the recent criminological literature, that prisons breed crime by exposing otherwise unlikely recidivists to criminal role models and underworld contacts and that the stigmatizing effects of a criminal conviction can increase the likelihood of recidivism by "labelling" a person as a criminal and thereby changing the individual's self-image.[e] Thus, assessment of both incapacitative and non-incapacitative punishments ultimately requires sophisticated predictive inquiries: What would the offender have done in the absence of intervention? What will be the impact of various types of intervention on his future behavior? Will the conviction or the sentence make the offender worse rather than better, more of a threat to society than he already is?

Related to these concerns is the effect of conditions of confinement on convicted criminals. In Costello v. Wainwright, 397 F.Supp. 20, 38 (M.D.Fla.1975), the court observed that:

> "severe overcrowding in the prison system tends to perpetuate antisocial behavior and foster recidivism. . . . A free democratic society cannot cage inmates like animals in a zoo or stack them like chattels in a warehouse and expect them to emerge as decent, law abiding, contributing members of the community. In the end, society becomes the loser."

In a similar but more detailed vein, the court in Inmates, D.C. Jail v. Jackson, 416 F.Supp. 119 (D.D.C.1976), made the following observations:

> "The court is . . . persuaded that the conditions and practices in the D.C. Jail are not rational means of advancing a valid state interest, and that the reality of conditions at the jail subvert the legitimate purposes of incarceration.

> "It is apparent, therefore, that the conditions in which inmates are housed at the D.C. Jail constitute cruel and unusual punishment in the sense currently contemplated in American society. These conditions simply are not to be tolerated in a civilized society, much less in our national capital. These are

---

[d] The recent literature is exhaustively reviewed in ABA Standards for Criminal Justice ch. 18, pp. 5–14, 25–332 (2d ed. 1980). Deserving of special mention is Francis A. Allen's thoughtful essay, The Decline of the Rehabilitative Ideal: Penal Policy and Social Purpose (1981).

[e] E.g., Leger, Labelling and its Consequences in a Closed Social System, 21 Brit.J. Criminology 109 (1981); Farrington, Osborn & West, The Persistence of Labelling Effects, 18 Brit.J. Criminology 277 (1978); Farrington, The Effects of Public Labelling, 17 Brit.J. Criminology 112 (1977).

conditions which turn men into animals, which degrade and dehumanize. In some senses the punishment they inflict is more painful and enduring than the stocks or the rack, long since discarded as barbaric or primitive. Imprisonment in conditions such as these absolutely guarantees that the inmates will never be able to return to civilized society, will never feel any stake in playing by its rules. For imprisonment under such conditions, where a man may be stuffed into a tiny cell with another, surrounded by the nocturnal moans or screams of mentally disturbed but untreated fellow inmates, plagued by rats and roaches, sweltering by summer and shivering by winter, unable to maintain significant contact with his family in the outside world, sometimes going for long periods without real exercise or recreation, can only have one message for him: society does not acknowledge your existence as a fellow human being. And when that message is delivered in the D.C. Jail, whatever small chance may have existed that a person might act as though he were a member of a civilized society is obliterated, along with his decency and humanity."

It is of course true that not all prisons fit this description. On the other hand, too many do. To the extent that imprisonment can be described in such terms, it seems plain that the goal of individual prevention is undermined by the very measures taken to punish offenders. It thus may not be too cynical to observe that one of the major purposes of criminal sanctions ought to be merely to avoid making the offender worse.

*   *   *   *   *

As was noted at the outset, this book is concerned with the substantive criminal law and the elements of criminal liability. It is clear that the concepts of retribution and general deterrence have major implications for these issues, as do other values reflected in contemporary society—such as individual liberty and equality—that are not properly thought of as goals of punishment but that plainly constrain any concept of just punishment. These ideas, therefore, are never far from the surface in the following materials. Indeed, most of the issues that are addressed can be seen as accommodations between the preventive goals of punishment and ethical considerations relating to blameworthiness, liberty, and equality.

By contrast, considerations of individual prevention—special deterrence, incapacitation, and rehabilitation—are relevant mainly to decisions about sentencing. It can be argued, moreover, that these goals of punishment should not play a prominent role in determinations of the substantive content of the criminal law or the minimum conditions of criminal liability. As the preceding discussion emphasizes, individual prevention necessarily suggests a predictive inquiry focused on the particular offender. Individual freedom and autonomy are seriously threatened when the criterion for intervention by the criminal law is a prediction of what a person may do rather than a demonstration of what that individual has done.

Chapter I

THE CRIMINAL ACT

SECTION 1: THE REQUIREMENT OF PREVIOUSLY DEFINED CONDUCT

SUBSECTION A: THE PRINCIPLE OF LEGALITY

REX v. MANLEY
Court of Criminal Appeal, 1932.
[1933] 1 K.B. 529.

Appeal against conviction, a certificate of fitness for appeal having been granted by the Recorder of London.

On November 18, 1932, the appellant, Elizabeth Manley, was charged at the Central Criminal Court on an indictment containing two counts, the first count being that she "on September 10, 1932, did, by means of certain false statements, to wit that on that day a man whose description she then gave had hit her with his fist and taken from her handbag, six 10s. notes, nine 1l. notes, 15s. in silver, and a receipt, cause officers of the metropolitan police maintained at public expense for the public benefit to devote their time and services to the investigation of false allegations, thereby temporarily depriving the public of the services of these public officers, and rendering liege subjects of the king liable to suspicion, accusation and arrest, and in so doing did unlawfully effect a public mischief"; and the second count being that on September 15, 1932, she made a statement that on September 10, 1932, a man whose description she gave came up behind her and that she then felt a blow in the back and that her bag containing 12l. 12s. 6d. had been taken from under her arm.

The appellant pleaded not guilty.

On behalf of the prosecution evidence was called to support the allegations in the indictment.

On behalf of the appellant these allegations were not denied and no evidence was called, but the submission was made that the indictment disclosed no offence known to the law, and that there was no cause to go to the jury.

In giving judgment on that submission the Recorder said: "It is my clear view that this act is one which may tend to a public mischief. It would be intolerable that our police force, already hard pressed to preserve law and order in a time of increasing lawlessness, should have

29

their services deflected in order to follow up charges which are entirely bogus to the knowledge of those making them. In my view, taking the times—you must consider the times in which we live—such an act may distinctly tend to the public mischief. . . . I hold as a matter of law that this indictment discloses a common-law misdemeanour."

The jury found on the evidence that the appellant had done the acts which she was alleged to have done and that she was guilty of the offence with which she was charged.

The Recorder postponed sentence, and granted a certificate that the case was fit for an appeal to the Court of Criminal Appeal on the question whether he was right in holding that the indictment disclosed a common-law misdemeanour; and he bound the appellant over to come up for judgment when the Court of Criminal Appeal had decided the question of law. . . .

LORD HEWART, C.J. The appellant in this case was indicted at the Central Criminal Court before the learned Recorder of London for having effected a public mischief. [His Lordship read the counts of the indictment, and continued:] The appellant was convicted, and was bound over to come up for judgment when called upon to do so after this court had decided the question of law now raised. It was then submitted on her behalf, as it is submitted now, that she had committed no offence; but before that proposition can be assented to it is necessary, as counsel for the prosecution has indicated, to consider two questions.

The first is whether it is true at the present day to say that there is a misdemeanour of committing an act tending to the public mischief. In our opinion that question ought to be answered in the affirmative. We think that the law remains as it was stated to be by Lawrence, J., in Rex v. Higgins, 1801 2 East 5, 21: "All offences of a public nature, that is, all such acts or attempts as tend to the prejudice of the community, are indictable." That case was referred to with approval in the case of Rex v. Brailsford, [1905] 2 K.B. 730, and in the still more recent case of Rex v. Porter, [1910] 1 K.B. 369, 372, where Lord Alverstone, C.J., in delivering the judgment of the court, said: "We are of opinion that it is for the court to direct the jury as to whether such an act may tend to the public mischief, and that it is not in such a case an issue of fact upon which evidence can be given."

The second question is whether the appellant did acts which constitute a public mischief. As counsel has said, the facts stated in the indictment are not in dispute, and it is admitted that what is there alleged to have been done by the appellant was done by her. In the opinion of the Court the indictment aptly describes two ingredients of public mischief or prejudice to the community, one of these being that officers of the metropolitan police were led to devote their time and services to the investigation of an idle charge, and the other being that members of the public, or at any rate those of them who answered a certain description, were put in peril of suspicion and arrest.

For these reasons the court is of opinion that the conviction should stand and that the appeal should be dismissed.

Appeal dismissed.

_____

NOTES ON *MANLEY* AND THE COMMON LAW

1. **Introduction to the Common Law.** *Manley* is an excellent illustration of the methodology of the "common law." That phrase has a variety of meanings, but it is used chiefly to refer to judge-made law. In fact, most of the ancient English offenses were judicial in origin. By the accession of Elizabeth I (1558), the English courts had created and defined felonies of murder, suicide,[a] manslaughter, arson, burglary, robbery, mayhem, larceny, sodomy, and rape. Additionally, various lesser wrongs were punished as misdemeanors. Offenses in both categories were created by judges who acted without aid of statute to protect societal interests as they saw them. The legacy of the common law, therefore, was a judicial assumption of broad authority to adapt broad principles to new situations as the occasion arose.

Over time, the exercise of this authority gradually became more constrained. For one thing, with the evolution of the idea of precedent, the common-law tradition bred its own limitation. As an ever more elaborate body of precedent built up, opportunities for judicial innovation were reduced. Moreover, increasing activity by parliament lessened the need for activism by the courts. The earliest legislative efforts were usually addressed to gaps in the common law. As parliament met more often and grew in power and prestige, more and more statutes were enacted to supplement or correct the law as declared by judges. Gradually, the locus of crime creation shifted from the courts to the legislature. As early as 1600, judicial creation of new felonies was already a thing of the past. New misdemeanors, on the other hand, continued to be recognized, albeit infrequently, throughout the 17th and 18th centuries. The judges who decided these cases often spoke of the residual authority of courts, absent statutory intervention, to punish as criminal any conduct contra bonos mores et decorum—in more modern phrasing, any conduct tending to outrage decency or to corrupt public morals. The most famous early assertion of this power was Rex v. Sidley, 82 E.R. 1036 (1663), where Sir Charles Sidley was found guilty of a common-law misdemeanor for standing naked on a balcony at Covent Garden. Others were held liable for such things as blasphemy, publication of an obscene book, undressing on a public beach, and digging up corpses for anatomical inspection. Decisions of this sort were made sporadically at least through 1774, when the underlying claim of continuing common-law authority was endorsed by the great Lord Mansfield. "Whatever is contra bonos mores et decorum," said Mansfield, "the principles of our law prohibit, and the king's court, as the general censor and guardian of the public manners, is bound to restrain and punish." Jones v. Randall, [1774] 98 E.R. 706, 707.

_____

[a] Actually, it is unclear whether suicide was an independent offense or a species of murder. See ALI, Model Penal Code and Commentaries § 210.5, pp. 90–91 (1980), and the sources cited therein.

By the late 19th century, the power of the courts to punish all conduct tending to corrupt morals or to create public mischief had fallen into disuse and apparent disrepute. The intervening years saw an accelerating reliance on statute and a deepening quiescence in the courts. In 1883 the claim of continuing common-law authority to create new crimes was denounced by no less an authority than Sir James Fitzjames Stephen, a successor to Mansfield on the Queen's Bench and pre-eminent Victorian historian of the criminal law: "Though the existence of this power as inherent in the judges has been asserted by several high authorities for a great length of time, it is hardly probable that any attempt would be made to exercise it at the present day; and any such attempt would be received with great opposition, and would place the bench in an invidious position." 3 J. Stephen, A History of the Criminal Law of England 359–60 (1883). Later judges sometimes echoed the assertions of their ambitious predecessors but did not try to exercise such authority. The result was that *Manley*, decided half a century after Stephen's pronouncement, came as a surprise and provoked something of a furor in English legal circles.[b]

2. **Later English Cases.** *Manley* might be dismissed as anachronistic were it not for subsequent English cases applying the same principle. In Shaw v. Director of Public Prosecutions, [1961] 2 All E.R. 446, the defendant was convicted of the common-law misdemeanor of conspiracy to corrupt public morals. The facts as stated by Viscount Simonds were as follows:

"When the Street Offences Act, 1959, came into operation, it was no longer possible for prostitutes to ply their trade by soliciting in the streets, and it became necessary for them to find some other means of advertising the services that they were prepared to render. It occurred to [Shaw] that he could with advantage to himself assist them to this end. The device that he adopted was to publish on divers days . . . a magazine or booklet which was called 'Ladies Directory'. It contained the names, addresses and telephone numbers of prostitutes with photographs of nude female figures, and in some cases details which conveyed to initiates willingness to indulge not only in ordinary sexual intercourse but also in various perverse practices."

Shaw appealed his conviction on the ground that the law of England no longer recognized a generic offense of conspiracy to corrupt public morals. Alternatively, he argued that if such a crime did exist, it should be limited to factual circumstances previously declared to fall within its scope. The House of Lords rejected both contentions and upheld the conviction. This decision was not based on narrow grounds.

---

[b] For criticism of *Manley* and a discussion of its aftermath in England and other Commonwealth jurisdictions, see G. Williams, Criminal Law: The General Part 596–600 (2d ed. 1961), and the authorities cited in id. at 596 n. 2. See also Withers v. Director of Public Prosecutions, [1975] A.C. 842, in which *Manley* is expressly repudiated.

On the contrary, Viscount Simonds' rendition of judicial authority to declare the law is as broad as those issued two centuries before:

". . . In the sphere of criminal law, I entertain no doubt that there remains in the courts of law a residual power to enforce the supreme and fundamental purpose of the law, to conserve not only the safety and order but also the moral welfare of the state, and that it is their duty to guard it against attacks which may be the more insidious because they are novel and unprepared for. . . . When Lord Mansfield, speaking long after the Star Chamber had been abolished, said that the Court of King's Bench was the custos morum of the people and had the superintendency of offences contra bonos mores, he was asserting, as I now assert, that there is in that court a residual power, where no statute has yet intervened to supersede the common law, to superintend those offences which are prejudicial to the public welfare." [c]

A similar decision was reached in Knuller v. Director of Public Prosecutions, [1972] 2 All E.R. 898. In *Knuller* the publishers of a "progressive" magazine were convicted of conspiracy to corrupt public morals for running classified ads by male homosexuals. Relying on the authority of *Shaw,* the House of Lords sustained this charge despite an act of parliament decriminalizing private homosexual acts between consenting adults.[d]

3. **Questions and Comments on Judicial Crime Creation.** What, exactly, is wrong with the decision in *Manley*? Is there reason to doubt that the defendant should have been punished on the facts presented? Would you object to that result if the defendant had been convicted of violating a statute such as Section 241.5 of the Model Penal Code? If not, what reasons exist for criticizing the result in the case?

NOTES ON THE PRINCIPLE OF LEGALITY

1. **Introduction.** The "principle of legality" is not in any ordinary sense a rule of law. It is more nearly a statement of an ideal. The following discussion should be taken, therefore, as a look at a fundamental normative proposition about the criminal law. That is not to say that the principle has no practical application. On the contrary, it is a very widely accepted ideal, and familiarity with it is essential to understanding the law as it stands.

Put simply, the principle of legality forbids the retroactive definition of crime. Often reduced to the maxim, nulla poena (or nullum crimen)

[c] For criticism of *Shaw,* see W. Friedmann, Law in a Changing Society 54–62 (1972); H.L.A. Hart, Law, Liberty and Morality 7–12 (1963); Davies, The House of Lords and the Criminal Law, 6 J. Soc. Pub. Tchrs. Law 104 (1961); Comment, 75 Harv.L.Rev. 1652 (1962). For a favorable reaction by Professor Arthur Goodhart, see 77 L.Q.Rev. 560 (1961).

[d] Like *Shaw* and *Manley, Knuller* quickly became subject to critical academic comment. See, e.g., Finch, Stare Decisis and Changing Standards in English Law, 51 Can.L.Rev. 523 (1973); Comment, Conspiracies Contra Bonos Mores, 19 McGill L.J. 136 (1973). For a more favorable view, see Comment, 19 McGill L.J. 130 (1973).

sine lege, this construct condemns judicial crime creation of the sort involved in *Manley* and *Shaw*. The essential idea is that no one should be punished for a crime that has not been so defined in advance by the appropriate institutional authority. Generally speaking, the appropriate institution for crime definition is the legislature, although this question is more complicated than at first appears. For most purposes, therefore, the principle of legality may be taken to signify *the desirability in principle of advance legislative specification of criminal conduct.*

Note that the insistence on advance crime definition has no necessary relation to the content of the offenses so defined. The principle of legality does not speak to the question of what should be declared criminal. Rather, it states a normative expectation regarding how that decision should be made. In other words, the principle concerns the process of crime definition rather than the content of specific offenses.

The same point may be put in terms of the relation of law to morals. That the criminal law derives from moral values cannot be doubted; some notion of right and wrong necessarily underlies the decision of what to punish. The principle of legality, however, does not identify which values the penal law should seek to enforce; it merely specifies the appropriate way to make that decision. In other words, the principle of legality asserts that certain constraints on the process of crime definition are essential to the ethical integrity of the criminal law as a system of rules, and it seeks to maintain those constraints without regard to the content of the rules chosen.

Today, few would dispute the desirability in principle of advance legislative specification of criminal conduct. This goal is widely recognized as the cornerstone of the penal law. Yet the very fact of widespread acceptance has worked to inhibit full exploration of the legality concept. For one thing, the principle of legality, like many truly fundamental propositions, is seldom put squarely in issue. Only infrequently is there occasion for reasoned defense or elaboration of what legality really means. Moreover, the generality with which the legality principle is usually stated (here as elsewhere) tends to obscure the variety of concerns comprehended by this label and to ignore its dynamic character. While the idea of nulla poena sine lege is undoubtedly of long standing, its significance has evolved over time as emphasis has shifted from one to another rationale for the legality ideal. Indeed, contemporary explanations of the legality principle reveal a surprisingly modern conception of the essential characteristics of an ethical system of criminal law. This discussion begins, therefore, with a look at the history of the principle of legality and its changing role in American penal law.[a]

2. **European Origins.** Although there may have been ancient antecedents,[b] the categorical insistence on advance legislative crime definition seems to have arisen in late 18th-century Europe. The idea

[a] For an examination of the philosophical underpinnings of legality, see Zupančič, On Legal Formalism: The Principle of Legality in Criminal Law, 27 Loyola L.Rev. 369 (1981).

[b] See J. Hall, General Principles of the Criminal Law 27–35 (2d ed. 1960).

sprang from the intellectual movement known as the Enlightenment, and its origins are deeply embedded in the premises and purposes of Enlightenment thought.

Though adequate summary of Enlightenment ideology far exceeds the scope of this note, two aspects of that tradition may be identified as specially relevant to the concept of nulla poena sine lege. First, at the level of individual behavior, Enlightenment thinkers viewed man as rational and hedonistic. Since individual conduct presumably was based on a utilitarian calculation of pain and pleasure, criminal acts could be deterred by a credible threat of a penalty sufficient to outweigh the expected gain from wrongdoing. In order for this scheme to work, crimes and punishments had to be specified in advance. Second, at the level of societal organization, Enlightenment thought emphasized contractual notions of the legitimacy of government. The state owed its authority to the aggregate surrenders of individual freedom necessary to the formation of the social compact. Thus, everyone gave up some freedom in order to secure the benefits of an ordered society, and the punishment of individual citizens was legitimate to the extent that it was based on laws established for the protection of society as a whole. Implicit in such a conception is a commitment to representative government, at least as an ideal of political organization. Accordingly, Enlightenment thinkers identified the legislature as the only legitimate institution for assessing the needs of society and for implementing those judgments through penal laws. Thus, Enlightenment ideology insisted not only that crime definition be prospective in nature but also that it be specifically legislative in origin.

Enlightenment thinkers who proved specially influential in the development of criminal law were Montesquieu and Cesare Beccaria. In a republic, according to Montesquieu, "the people should have the sole power to enact laws." [c] The legislature, as the branch of government most directly responsive to the popular will, was therefore the only legitimate source of crime definition. Judges were to enforce statutes; they were not to exercise any independent authority over the penal law:

> "[T]here is no liberty if the judiciary power be not separated from the legislative and executive. Were it joined with the legislative, the life and liberty of the subject would be exposed to arbitrary control; for the judge would be then the legislator. Were it joined to the executive power, the judge might behave with violence and oppression.
>
> "There would be an end of everything, were the same man or the same body . . . to exercise those three powers, that of enacting laws, that of executing the public resolutions, and of trying the causes of individuals." [d]

Beccaria followed Montesquieu in insisting on legislative action as indispensable to political legitimacy but placed greater emphasis on the notion that precise and prospective definition of offenses was essential

[c] Montesquieu, The Spirit of the Laws 13 (T. Nugent, trans., 1897).   [d] Id. at 152.

to crime control. Indeed, he argued that crime was actually caused, in part, by the obscurity and irrationality of the penal law. By creating clear, precise, and reasonable laws, with penalties proportionate to the gravity of the offense and sufficiently harsh to offset any gain to the offender, the legislature could attack the problem of crime. Judicial innovation, on the other hand, would lead to arbitrariness and inconsistency. Results would depend on "the good or bad logic of the judge; and this will depend on his good or bad digestion; on the violence of his passion; on the rank and condition of the accused, or on his connections with the judge . . . ." [e] The upshot of such disarray would be impairment of the law's capacity to exert a restraining influence on the passions of men. Thus, for reasons of efficiency as well as political theory, Beccaria endorsed nulla poena sine lege as a cardinal principle of the penal law.

3. **The American Experience: Encounter with the Common Law.** In many ways the newly independent American nation was fertile soil for the doctrine of nulla poena sine lege. For one thing, there was the pervasive influence of Enlightenment thought generally.[f] There was also specific familiarity with the principal works on penal law. Montesquieu and Beccaria were widely read, and their ideas were a prominent feature of the American intellectual landscape at the time of the Revolution. Their insistence on a sharp differentiation of legislative, executive, and judicial functions found practical expression in the American scheme of separation of powers. That concept called for a division of responsibilities among three branches of government. The power to make laws generally was assumed to rest with the legislature. Perhaps most importantly, the insistence on legislative action as essential to the political legitimacy of crime definition was a natural corollary of the American ideal of popular sovereignty through republican government.

In light of these factors, one might have expected nulla poena sine lege quickly to take its place as the first principle of American criminal law. In fact, the story is much more complicated. "English law—as authority, as legitimizing precedent, as embodied principle, and as the framework of historical understanding—stood side by side with Enlightenment rationalism" in influencing the American revolutionaries.[g] In the United States, unlike Europe, the theoretical insistence on legislative crime definition ran up against the ancient, familiar, and entrenched tradition of the English common law.

The conflict between the common-law heritage and Enlightenment ideals of political organization was nowhere more apparent than in the debate whether to allow criminal prosecution for non-statutory offenses. At the federal level, the ultimate answer was "no," though not without a struggle. Mr. Justice Story, an eminent scholar and authority on American law, had argued that "all offences against the sover-

[e] C. Beccaria, On Crimes and Punishments 23–24 (E. Ingraham, trans., 1819).

[f] On the influence of the Enlightenment on the American revolution, see generally B. Bailyn, The Ideological Origins of the American Revolution (1967), and Gay, America The Paradoxical, 62 Va.L.Rev. 843 (1976).

[g] B. Bailyn, The Ideological Origins of the American Revolution 31 (1967).

eignty, the public rights, the public justice, the public peace, the public trade and the public police of the United States, are crimes and offences against the United States," whether or not specifically proscribed by statute.[h]   The view prevailed, however, that there was no federal common law of crimes.   This was announced by the Supreme Court in United States v. Hudson and Goodwin, 11 U.S. (7 Cranch) 32 (1812), and subsequently confirmed in United States v. Coolidge, 14 U.S. (1 Wheat.) 415 (1816).   The result in *Hudson and Goodwin* was based in part on the general objection to judicial crime creation as an illegitimate usurpation of legislative authority.   In part, however, the rejection of common-law crimes was derived from the federal structure of the Constitution and the consequent limitation of the powers of the national government vis-a-vis the states.   As the Supreme Court put it, "[t]he powers of the general government are made up of concessions from the several states; whatever is not expressly given to the former the latter expressly reserve."   11 U.S. (7 Cranch) at 33.   Thus, in the context of federal law, judicial enforcement of non-statutory crimes would have implicated *both* the separation of powers among the branches of the national government *and* the limitations imposed on the national government by its place in a federal structure.   Together these ideas proved strong enough to oust the tradition of the common law and to vindicate an insistence on statutory definition of all federal offenses.

At the state level, the story was entirely different.   Despite the efforts of early law reformers,[i] all of the original states, and most of the later ones, adopted English common law insofar as it was deemed applicable to local conditions.   This "reception" of the common law, as it came to be called, was accomplished either by express statutory or constitutional provision or by judicial decision.   It usually included English law of a general nature as of a certain date.   Many states used 1607, when the first colony was founded, while others used 1775 or 1776, when the break with the mother country occurred.   Whatever the date used, the reception of English common law included not only the roster of offenses previously defined by the English courts, but also the familiar and intimately related assumption that the courts had residual authority to adapt old principles to new situations should the need arise.[j]

That this assumption was widely entertained is evident from the cases and from the observations of commentators.   An early example is Pennsylvania v. Gillespie, 1 Add. 267 (1795), where the defendant was indicted for "unlawfully, forcibly and contemptuously tearing down" an

[h] United States v. Coolidge, 25 Fed.Cas. 619, 620 (1813).   Story issued this ruling in his capacity as Circuit Justice.   His decision was overruled by the Supreme Court in United States v. Coolidge, 14 U.S. (1 Wheat.) 415 (1816).

[i] See generally Beckman, Three Penal Codes Compared, 10 Am.J.Leg.Hist. 148 (1966), and Bloomfield, William Sampson and the Codifiers: The Roots of American Legal Reform, 1820–1830, 11 Am.J.Leg. Hist. 234 (1967).

[j] Hall, The Common Law: An Account of Its Reception in the United States, 4 Vand.L.Rev. 791 (1951).   The reception of the English law usually included not only decisional law, but also parliamentary enactments in aid thereof.   This practice led to the odd result that rules of law originally created by an act of parliament were received in this country as part of the common law, even though that phrase usually signifies judge-made law rather than statute.

advertisement for a tax sale. The court reasoned that since taking down an advertisement for a private sale would give rise to a private tort claim, "when the sale is under a public law, for public use, an indictment should lie for the injury done to the public." Similarly, in State v. Buckman, 8 N.H. 203 (1836), the defendant was indicted for putting a dead animal into another person's well. The court upheld the conviction on the ground that the act was analogous to selling unwholesome food and to poisoning food or drink intended for human consumption, both of which were indictable at common law. The overarching rationale for such innovations was explained by the Supreme Court of Pennsylvania in Commonwealth v. Taylor, 5 Binn. 277, 281 (Pa.1812):

> "It is impossible to find precedents for all offenses. The malicious ingenuity of mankind is constantly producing new inventions in the art of disturbing their neighbors. To this invention must be opposed general principles, calculated to meet and punish them."

This approach to judicial innovation was endorsed by respected commentators. As late as 1892, Professor Bishop rebuked those who sought to limit the common-law methodology to non-criminal contexts with the following comment:

> "No well-founded reason can be given why, if we are to have a common law, it should not be applied to acts injurious to the entire community, as well as to those violative only of individual rights. If a difference must be made, rather let the civil part be abrogated, but preserve the criminal."

J. Bishop, Commentaries on the Criminal Law 18 (8th ed. 1892).

4. **Recent Experience.** In the United States, contemporary instances of judicial crime creation are increasingly hard to find. In fact, there appear to be only two unambiguous examples in this century. The more recent is Commonwealth v. Mochan, 177 Pa.Super. 454, 110 A.2d 788 (1955). The defendant was indicted for making obscene telephone calls, despite the absence of either statute or precedent specifically proscribing such conduct. The Superior Court of Pennsylvania nevertheless affirmed a misdemeanor conviction, noting that "[a]ny act is indictable at common law which from its nature scandalously affects the morals or health of the community." An analogous example of judicial crime creation in the context of group conduct is Commonwealth v. Donoghue, 250 Ky. 343, 63 S.W.2d 3 (1933).[k] There the defendant's alleged participation in a loansharking operation was the basis of an indictment for common-law conspiracy. Specifically, the indictment charged that the defendant had engaged "in the business of lending money in small amounts to poor and necessitous wage earners at excessive, exorbitant and usurious rates of interest . . . ." The defendant demurred on the ground that no statute or prior decision made usury a crime, but the court held that participation in "a nefarious plan for the habitual exaction of gross usury" would be

[k] This case is excerpted and discussed in the materials on conspiracy at pages 437–44, infra.

punishable despite the absence of any prior definition of such an offense.

Today, decisions such as *Mochan* and *Donoghue* are widely viewed as relics. Most judges no longer feel free to respond to new situations as the occasion demands but increasingly regard themselves as bound to enforce only those offenses previously declared to exist. In part, this development is due to the growing consensus, among both courts and commentators, that judicial crime creation is in principle unacceptable. In part, however, the decline in such activity is due simply to the fact that legislatures sit more frequently and for longer sessions than was formerly true. Penal statutes accumulate over time, and there seems to be little difficulty in focusing legislative sentiment on the need to prohibit conduct perceived as anti-social. It is a rare legislative session that does not add to the list of offenses, often by proscribing in more particularistic terms misconduct already covered by existing statutes. The result is such a comprehensiveness, not to say redundancy, of penal legislation that judicial crime creation is rendered unnecessary as well as objectionable.

5. **Growing Acceptance and Evolving Meaning.** Even as the legality concept has won increasing acceptance as a cardinal principle of the penal law, its meaning has undergone considerable evolution. Today, few would regard punishment for any non-statutory offense as necessarily violative of any great principle. What is condemned by contemporary understanding of the legality ideal is not enforcement of a crime that is non-statutory in origin, but enforcement of a crime not previously declared to exist. Where prior judicial decisions have given adequate notice of the content of the law, criminal punishment is not generally thought to offend the legality concept, despite the absence of any statutory base. In other words, what is currently seen as essential is not so much the *fact* of legislative crime definition as the *characteristics* of that process. Those characteristics include prospectivity and generality; a crime is defined in advance of the actor's conduct and without particular reference to an identified defendant. Judicial crime creation is disapproved chiefly because it lacks these characteristics; it is done retrospectively and specifically. Continued application of *prior* judicial decisions, however, may meet the essential requirements of acceptable crime definition even without legislative participation.

Moreover, evolution in the meaning of the legality ideal has been accompanied by a changing emphasis in the rationales advanced to support it. Today, few would take seriously Beccaria's idea that advance legislative crime definition plays a crucial role in the practical business of controlling criminal conduct. Identification of legality with a strictly utilitarian concern for effective deterrence would strike most modern observers as a bit off point. For one thing, the mechanisms of deterrence are less direct than is suggested in Beccaria's model of the rational hedonist who regularly consults the criminal code. Moreover, it seems far-fetched to believe that the social problem of crime results in significant degree from the failure of citizens to know what is forbidden. Of much greater importance are the actor's assessment of the probability that punishment will actually be imposed and the magnitude of the penalty that would be inflicted. It seems likely that most criminals know that their conduct is illegal but believe that they will not be caught. For these reasons, the principle of legality today is seldom advanced as an aid to deterrence. Instead, it is defended chiefly as a normative proposition—arguably essential to the ethical integrity of the criminal law but not to its efficiency.

By contrast, the political-legitimacy rationale for insisting on advance legislative crime definition no doubt survives, though perhaps with somewhat less force than formerly. Separation of powers remains a fundamental principle of American government, and lawmaking continues to be regarded as primarily the responsibility of the legislative branch. To this extent, Montesquieu's ideas survive and flourish. It is also true, however, that the last few decades have seen an enormous upsurge in the restriction of legislative choice through constitutional adjudication. The result is a significant shift of power from legislatures to courts. While that development has not escaped criticism, it may nevertheless reflect some glacial retreat from the 18th-century insistence on the primacy of legislative authority.

In any event, it is clear that the political-legitimacy rationale for preferring legislative to judicial crime creation does not tell the whole story behind the contemporary commitment to legality. Modern explanations of that ideal also emphasize fairness to the individual defendant as a central goal of the legality construct. In particular, modern theorists view the principle of legality as an important prophylaxis against the arbitrary and abusive exercise of discretion in the enforcement of the penal law.

The connection between this evil and an insistence on advance legislative crime definition may not be immediately apparent. On the contrary, it is a matter of some subtlety. Consider the argument of Herbert Packer, as advanced in The Limits of the Criminal Sanction 88–91 (1968): *

> "It is plain, then, that the objectives of criminal law . . . require a set of institutions for detecting the commission of offenses, apprehending offenders, and determining whether they should be held for the adjudicative process. In short, it is essential to have police and prosecutors. But is is also essential to have checks on the exercise of discretion in the initiating phase of criminal prosecution . . . . And it is here that we can see the real importance of the principle of legality in the criminal law today; for this principle operates primarily to control the discretion of the police and of prosecutors rather than that of judges.

> "In the judicial process the principle of legality is not essential to guarding against abuses of discretion because other checks accomplish the same thing. Courts operate in the open through

* Reprinted from The Limits of the Criminal Sanction by Herbert L. Packer, with the permission of the publishers, Stanford University Press. © 1968 by Herbert L. Packer.

what has been described as a process of reasoned elaboration. They have to justify their decisions. It is not enough to say: this man goes to jail because he did something bad. There is an obligation to relate the particular bad thing that this man did to other bad things that have been treated as criminal in the past. The system of analogical reasoning that we call the common-law method is a very substantial impediment to arbitrary decision-making. The fact that courts operate in the open according to a system of reasoning that is subjected to the scrutiny of an interested audience, both professional and lay, militates against any but the most marginal invasions of the values represented by the principle of legality.

"By contrast, the police and the official prosecutors operate in a setting of secrecy and informality. Their processes are subjected to public scrutiny in only the most sporadic and cursory ways. Although some courts (particularly low-level courts in large cities faced with the necessity for dispensing assembly-line justice) at times behave with the informality and lack of articulation that [characterize] the police and prosecutors, no one has ever discovered a police or prosecutorial organization that behaves like a court. When judges deviate from the model of openness, even-handedness, and rationality, it is recognized and deplored as a deviation from their ideal role. But no one expects the police or the prosecutors to behave the way a court is supposed to behave; that is simply not their role, and they are not subjected to even the minimal psychological constraints that flow from self-perceived deviation from an acknowledged role.

"The principle of legality, then, is important for the allocation of competences not between the legislative and judicial branches, but among those who initiate the criminal process through the largely informal methods of investigation, arrest, interrogation, and charge that characterize the operation of criminal justice. [The existence of these largely informal decisions] poses problems in the exercise of power to which the principle of legality is an important response.

"Does this mean, then, that the conventional focus of the principle of legality, which is on defining the respective roles of legislatures and courts, is distorted? Does it really make no difference whether the operative law is 'made' by legislatures, declaring certain kinds of conduct criminal before they occur, or by courts, looking backward at the conduct whose criminality they are called upon to adjudicate? Not at all. The conventional focus is perfectly correct although not, as we have seen, for conventional reasons. It is correct because in a system that lodges the all-important initiating power in the hands of officials who operate, as they must, through informal and secret processes, there must be some devices to insure that the initiating decisions are, to the greatest extent possible, fair, evenhanded, and rational. Most of these devices . . . are in the nature of post-audits on the decisions taken by the police and prosecutors. But the most important single device is the requirement . . . that the police and prosecutors confine their attention to the catalogue of what has already been defined as criminal. . . .

"If criminal law can be made a posteriori by judges, rather than a priori, by legislatures, then the enforcement officials are under strong temptation to guess what the judges will do in a particular case. This temptation cannot be eliminated . . ., but it can be minimized through the habits of thought acquired by enforcement officials who work under the principle of legality. To take a modern [1968] instance, consider the problem of dangerous drugs such as LSD. If judges had as broad a lawmaking power as legislatures do, any policeman who thought that taking LSD was a bad thing that should be treated as criminal and any prosecutor who agreed with him could combine to put the criminal process in motion against people who took LSD. And if they could find one judge (among hundreds in a jurisdiction) who agreed with them, they could obtain a criminal conviction. And if a majority of the members of the appellate court in the jurisdiction agreed with them, they would carry the day.

"In fact, nothing of the sort has occurred, despite the sentiment, probably greater among law enforcement officials than among the public at large, for the suppression of LSD. Aside from a little informal harassment of the kind that no legal system can effectively preclude, members of the deviant subculture composed of LSD takers remained free to follow their bent until legislative bodies began declaring, according to their mode of operation that, henceforth or from a certain day forward, anyone who takes LSD will be committing a crime. This kind of certainty and regularity is particularly to be prized . . . ."

Note the centrality to Packer's argument of his assumption that it is desirable to protect the "deviant subculture" of LSD users from discretionary repression by the agencies of law enforcement. The particular example may be dated, but modern American society continues to spawn "subcultures" that contravene, and sometimes openly flout, community standards of morals or behavior. Such factors as race, ethnic identity, religious practice, sexual preference, and an endless variety of lifestyle choices may set one or another group of citizens against the mainstream of the culture in which they live. That the institutions of law should be arrayed to protect such diversity may seem obvious in a liberal democracy, but it is far from commonplace, either historically or among contemporary cultures. Would you expect, for example, that a Puritan theocracy, or a primitive tribe, or a Communist dictatorship would have a comparable commitment to protect "deviant subcultures" within their societies? Would you expect any tightly integrated community to construct a legal system around values of pluralism and diversity? That is not to say, of course, that other cultures and other ideologies are inferior, but only that the commitment to the principle of legality as a fundamental ideal of the penal law is especially compatible with the modern tradition of liberal democracy and its underlying assumptions about the appropriate relation of the state to individual citizens.

NOTE ON THE CONTINUING SIGNIFICANCE OF THE COMMON LAW

As the foregoing notes indicate, judicial crime creation is largely a thing of the past. It is important to remember, however, that the rejection of the methodology of the common law does not necessarily mean that the results of that tradition have also been abandoned. On the contrary, the common law of crimes has continuing significance, even as the exercise of common-law authority to create new crimes recedes into history.

Well into this century, a majority of American states enforced previously declared common-law offenses without aid of statute. As of 1947, fully 31 American jurisdictions recognized the continued viability of the common law insofar as it had not been superseded by legislation.[a] Over the next three decades, the number of states taking this position declined sharply. The greatest single factor in this change was the widespread adoption of revised criminal codes, virtually all of which follow Section 1.05 of the Model Penal Code in eliminating non-statutory crimes. Nevertheless, as late as 1980, at least 15 states continued to allow prosecution for non-statutory offenses.[b] In these jurisdictions, the full list of crimes for which a citizen may be punished cannot even today be found in the statute books, but requires as well a look at the precedents, both local and English, that declare one or another kind of conduct an offense at common law.

Modern prosecutions for non-statutory offenses are infrequent, but instances do arise. In 1959 a Maryland court upheld a conviction for forgery despite doubtful coverage by the relevant statute. The court found that, however the statute might be construed, the analogous common-law crime remained applicable.[c] In 1961 the Supreme Court

----

[a] Note, Common Law Crimes in the United States, 47 Colum.L.Rev. 1332 (1947).

[b] Fla.Stat.Ann. § 775.01; Md.Const. art. 5; Mass.Gen. Laws Ann.Const. pt. 2, ch. 6, art. 6; Mich.Comp. Laws Ann.Const. art. 3, § 7; Miss. Code § 99–1–3; N.M.Stat.Ann. § 30–1–3; N.C.Gen.Stat. § 4–1; R.I.Gen. Laws § 11–1–1 (Supp.1979); S.C. Code § 14–1–50; 1 Vt.Stat.Ann. § 271; Va. Code § 1–10; Rev. Code Wash.Ann. § 9A.04.060; W.Va. Code § 2–1–1; Wyo.Stat. § 8–1–107. In Tennessee there is no express statute but case law indicates that prosecution for common-law crimes continues. E.g., Gervin v. State, 212 Tenn. 653, 371 S.W.2d 449 (1963). Finally, Code of Ala. § 13A–1–4 appears on its face to abolish common-law crimes: "No act or omission is a crime unless made so by this title or by other applicable statute or lawful ordinance." The commentary to this provision, however, puts the issue in doubt:

> "The original draft of this section included an explicit provision to abolish common-law crimes . . . but the Advisory Committee considered such provision impolitic and also, unnecessary under a comprehensive Criminal Code, so it was deleted. . . . Thus § 1–3–1 [a general statute enacted in 1907 and adopting the 'common law of England'], which continues in force the common law 'except as from time to time it may be altered or repealed by the legislature,' remains intact, although its future field of operation may be reduced."

[c] Reddick v. State, 219 Md. 95, 148 A.2d 384 (1959). Cf. State v. Reese, 283 Md. 86,

of North Carolina sustained an indictment for attempt to commit suicide. No statute proscribed such conduct, but the court relied on English precedents punishing suicide as a common-law felony.[d] Some years later, the North Carolina courts also upheld a conviction for the non-statutory offense of "going armed with unusual and dangerous weapons to the terror of the people."[e] In 1963 the Supreme Court of Tennessee ruled, without aid of legislation, that the common-law crime of solicitation was an indictable offense in that state,[f] and in 1970 the Supreme Court of South Carolina affirmed a conviction for the common-law crime of assault and battery.[g] None of these decisions was based on statute, yet none was widely perceived to violate the principle of legality. In each case, the result reached, whatever its merits as a matter of policy, was adequately based on prior precedent describing the activity in question as an offense at common law. These cases illustrate the continuing readiness of some jurisdictions to enforce existing common-law crimes, despite a nearly uniform unwillingness to create new ones.

Of far greater consequence than the occasional prosecution for a non-statutory offense, however, is the pervasive role of the common law as an aid to statutory construction. Indeed, a few jurisdictions expressly adopt the common law as the background for interpreting penal legislation. Thus, for example, Kansas provides that "where a crime is denounced by any statute of this state, but not defined, the definition of such crime at common law shall be applied."[h] More often, the point is left to implication, as in the common legislative practice of assigning penalties for "manslaughter" without defining that crime.[i] In such instances, courts must resort to the common law in order to ascertain the meaning of the legislative enactment. Even when a statute purports to define a crime, it often does no more than memorialize the common-law definition. In such cases, interstitial ambiguity in the statutory formulation frequently is resolved by reference to the common-law understanding. All of these uses of the common law as an aid to the construction of statutes are illustrated in subsequent cases and need not be dwelt on here. For present purposes, it is enough to note that the common law of crimes, although rarely enforced as such, remains important to the student of the modern penal law.

---

388 A.2d 122 (1978) (holding the evidence insufficient to support a conviction for common-law forgery).

[d] State v. Willis, 255 N.C. 473, 121 S.E.2d 854 (1961).

[e] State v. Dawson, 272 N.C. 535, 159 S.E.2d 1 (1968). See also State v. Dixon, 8 N.C.App. 37, 173 S.E.2d 540 (1970).

[f] Gervin v. State, 212 Tenn. 653, 371 S.W.2d 449 (1963).

[g] State v. Hill, 254 S.C. 321, 175 S.E.2d 227 (1970). Cf. McCray v. State, 271 S.C. 185, 246 S.E.2d 230 (1978) (affirming a conviction for common-law assault and bat-tery); Gore v. Leeke, 261 S.C. 308, 199 S.E.2d 755 (1973) (upholding application of common-law felony murder despite absence of statutory authority).

[h] Kan.Stat.Ann. § 21–3102. Cf. Nev.Rev.Stat. § 193.050 (stating that the "provisions of the common law relating to the definition of public offenses apply to any public offense which is so prohibited but is not defined, or which is so prohibited but is incompletely defined").

[i] See, e.g., the Virginia statutes reprinted in Appendix B, pages 1–3, infra.

SUBSECTION B: THE VAGUENESS DOCTRINE

PARKER, WARDEN, et al. v. LEVY

Supreme Court of the United States, 1974.
417 U.S. 733.

MR. JUSTICE REHNQUIST delivered the opinion of the Court.

Appellee Howard Levy, a physician, was a captain in the Army stationed at Fort Jackson, South Carolina. He had entered the Army under the so-called "Berry Plan," under which he agreed to serve for two years in the Armed Forces if permitted first to complete his medical training. From the time he entered on active duty in July 1965 until his trial by court-martial, he was assigned as Chief of the Dermatological Service of the United States Army Hospital at Fort Jackson. On June 2, 1967, appellee was convicted by a general court-martial of violations of Arts. 90, 133, and 134 of the Uniform Code of Military Justice, and sentenced to dismissal from the service, forfeiture of all pay and allowances, and confinement for three years at hard labor.

The facts upon which his conviction rests are virtually undisputed. The evidence admitted at his court-martial trial showed that one of the functions of the hospital to which appellee was assigned was that of training Special Forces aide men. As Chief of the Dermatological Service, appellee was to conduct a clinic for those aide men. In the late summer of 1966, it came to the attention of the hospital commander that the dermatology training of the students was unsatisfactory. After investigating the program and determining that appellee had totally neglected his duties, the commander called appellee to his office and personally handed him a written order to conduct the training. Appellee read the order, said that he understood it, but declared that he would not obey it because of his medical ethics. Appellee persisted in his refusal to obey the order, and later reviews of the program established that the training was still not being carried out.

During the same period of time, appellee made several public statements to enlisted personnel at the post, of which the following is representative:

"The United States is wrong in being involved in the Viet Nam War. I would refuse to go to Viet Nam if ordered to do so. I don't see why any colored soldier would go to Viet Nam: they should refuse to go to Viet Nam and if sent should refuse to fight because they are discriminated against and denied their freedom in the United States, and they are sacrificed and discriminated against in Viet Nam by being given all the hazardous duty and they are suffering the majority of casualties. If I were a colored soldier I would refuse to fight. Special Forces personnel are liars and thieves and killers of peasants and murderers of women and children."

Appellee's military superiors originally contemplated non-judicial proceedings against him under Art. 15 of the Uniform Code of Military Justice, . . . but later determined that court-martial proceedings were appropriate. The specification under Art. 90 alleged that appellee willfully disobeyed the hospital commandant's order to establish the training program, in violation of that article, which punishes anyone subject to the Uniform Code of Military Justice who "willfully disobeys a lawful command of his superior commissioned officer." [2] Statements to enlisted personnel were listed as specifications under the charges of violating Arts. 133 and 134 of the Code. Article 133 provides for the punishment of "conduct unbecoming an officer and a gentleman," [3] while Art. 134 proscribes, inter alia, "all disorders and neglects to the prejudice of good order and discipline in the armed forces." [4]

The specification under Art. 134 alleged that appellee "did, at Fort Jackson, South Carolina, . . . with design to promote disloyalty and disaffection among the troops, publicly utter [certain] statements to divers enlisted personnel at divers times . . . ." The specification under Art. 133 alleged that appellee did "while in the performance of his duties at the United States Army Hospital . . . wrongfully and dishonorably" make statements variously described as intemperate, defamatory, provoking, disloyal, contemptuous, and disrespectful to Special Forces personnel and to enlisted personnel who were patients or under his supervision.

Appellee was convicted by the court-martial, and his conviction was sustained on his appeals within the military. After he had exhausted this avenue of relief, he sought federal habeas corpus in the United States District Court for the Middle District of Pennsylvania, challenging his court-martial conviction on a number of grounds. The District Court, on the basis of the voluminous record of the military proceedings and the argument of counsel, denied relief. . . .

The Court of Appeals reversed, holding in a lengthy opinion that Arts. 133 and 134 are void for vagueness. Levy v. Parker, 478 F.2d 772 (3d Cir. 1973). . . . [a]

[2] Article 90 of the Uniform Code of Military Justice, 10 U.S.C. § 890, provides:

"Any person subject to this chapter who . . .

(2) willfully disobeys a lawful command of his superior commissioned officer;

shall be punished, if the offense is committed in time of war, by death or such other punishment as a court-martial may direct, and if the offense is committed at any other time, by such punishment, other than death, as a court-martial may direct."

[3] Article 133 of the Uniform Code of Military Justice, 10 U.S.C. § 933, provides:

"Any commissioned officer, cadet, or midshipman who is convicted of conduct unbecoming an officer and a gentleman

shall be punished as a court-martial may direct."

[4] Article 134 of the Uniform Code of Military Justice, 10 U.S.C. § 934, provides:

"Though not specifically mentioned in this chapter, all disorders and neglects to the prejudice of good order and discipline in the armed forces, all conduct of a nature to bring discredit upon the armed forces, and crimes and offenses not capital, of which persons subject to this chapter may be guilty, shall be taken cognizance of by a general, special, or summary court-martial, according to the nature and degree of the offense, and shall be punished at the discretion of that court."

[a] Note that Capt. Levy was convicted under Art. 90, as well as under Arts. 133 and 134. A single sentence was imposed for all

Appellants appealed to this Court pursuant to 28 U.S.C. § 1252.
. . .

I

This Court has long recognized that the military is, by necessity, a specialized society separate from civilian society. We have also recognized that the military has, again by necessity, developed laws and traditions of its own during its long history. The differences between the military and civilian communities result from the fact that "it is the primary business of armies and navies to fight or be ready to fight wars should the occasion arise." In In re Grimley, 137 U.S. 147, 153 (1890), the Court observed: "An army is not a deliberative body. It is the executive arm. Its law is that of obedience. No question can be left open as to the right to command in the officer, or the duty of obedience in the soldier." More recently we noted that "[t]he military constitutes a specialized community governed by a separate discipline from that of the civilian," and that "the rights of men in the armed forces must perforce be conditioned to meet certain overriding demands of discipline and duty . . . ."

Just as military society has been a society apart from civilian society, so "[m]ilitary law . . . is a jurisprudence which exists separate and apart from the law which governs in our federal judicial establishment." And to maintain the discipline essential to perform its mission effectively, the military has developed what "may not unfitly be called the customary military law" or "general usage of the military service."

An examination of the British antecedents of our military law shows that the military law of Britain had long contained the forebears of Arts. 133 and 134 in remarkably similar language. The Articles of the Earl of Essex (1642) provided that "[a]ll other faults, disorders and offenses, not mentioned in these Articles, shall be punished according to the general customs and laws of war." One of the British Articles of War of 1765 made punishable "all Disorders or Neglects . . . to the Prejudice of good Order and Military Discipline . . . ." that were not mentioned in the other articles. Another of those articles provided:

> "Whatsoever Commissioned Officer shall be convicted before a General Court-martial, of behaving in a scandalous infamous Manner, such as is unbecoming the Character of an Officer and a Gentleman, shall be discharged from Our Service."

three offenses. As the Court of Appeals correctly noted, "[t]he general rule governing a single sentence imposed upon convictions on several charges is that the sentence will be upheld on appeal if any one of the convictions is valid, and the sentence imposed is within the statutorily authorized maximum for the valid charge, despite the fact that convictions on the other charges may not be valid." 478 F.2d at 778. The Court of Appeals found no independent defect in the Art. 90 conviction but reversed on the ground that, on the particular facts of this case, trial of the Art. 90 charge along with the assertedly unconstitutional charges under Arts. 133 and 134 might have prejudiced trial of the Art. 90 offense. Thus, the Art. 90 conviction was set aside for reasons that depended on the supposed invalidity of the convictions under Arts. 133 and 134, and the constitutionality of those statutes was put squarely in issue before the Supreme Court. [Footnote by eds.]

In 1775 the Continental Congress adopted this last article, along with 68 others for the governance of its army. The following year it was resolved by the Congress that "the committee on spies be directed to revise the rules and articles of war; this being a committee of five, consisting of John Adams, Thomas Jefferson, John Rutledge, James Wilson and R. R. Livingston . . . ." The article was included in the new set of articles prepared by the Committee, which Congress adopted on September 20, 1776. After being once more re-enacted without change in text in 1786, it was revised and expanded in 1806, omitting the terms "scandalous" and "infamous," so as to read:

"Any commissioned officer convicted before a general court-martial of conduct unbecoming an officer and a gentleman, shall be dismissed [from] the service."

From 1806, it remained basically unchanged through numerous congressional re-enactments until it was enacted as Art. 133 of the Uniform Code of Military Justice in 1951. . . .

Decisions of this Court during the last century have recognized that the longstanding customs and usages of the services impart accepted meaning to the seemingly imprecise standards of Arts. 133 and 134. In Dynes v. Hoover, 61 U.S. (20 How.) 65 (1857), this Court upheld the Navy's general article, which provided that "[a]ll crimes committed by persons belonging to the navy, which are not specified in the foregoing articles, shall be punished according to the laws and customs in such cases at sea." The Court reasoned:

"[W]hen offences and crimes are not given in terms or by definition, the want of it may be supplied by a comprehensive enactment, such as the 32d article of the rules for the government of the navy, which means that courts martial have jurisdiction of such crimes as are not specified, but which have been recognised to be crimes and offences by the usages in the navy of all nations, and that they shall be punished according to the laws and customs of the sea. Notwithstanding the apparent indeterminateness of such a provision, it is not liable to abuse; for what those crimes are, and how they are to be punished, is well known by practical men in the navy and army, and by those who have studied the law of courts martial, and the offences of which the different courts martial have cognizance."

In Smith v. Whitney, 116 U.S. 167 (1886), this Court refused to issue a writ of prohibition against Smith's court-martial trial on charges of "[s]candalous conduct tending to the destruction of good morals" and "[c]ulpable inefficiency in the performance of duty." The Court again recognized the role of "the usages and customs of war" and "old practice in the army" in the interpretation of military law by military tribunals.

In United States v. Fletcher, 148 U.S. 84 (1893), the Court considered a court-martial conviction under what is now Art. 133, rejecting Captain Fletcher's claim that the court-martial could not properly have held that his refusal to pay a just debt was "conduct unbecoming an officer and a gentleman." The Court of Claims decision which the

Court affirmed in *Fletcher* stressed the military's "higher code termed honor, which holds its society to stricter accountability" and with which those trained only in civilian law are unfamiliar. In Swaim v. United States, 165 U.S. 553 (1897), the Court affirmed another Court of Claims decision, this time refusing to disturb a court-martial conviction for conduct "to the prejudice of good order and military discipline" in violation of the articles of war. The Court recognized the role of "unwritten law or usage" in giving meaning to the language of what is now Art. 134. In rejecting Swaim's argument that the evidence failed to establish an offense under the article, the Court said:

> "[T]his is the very matter that falls within the province of courts-martial, and in respect to which their conclusions cannot be controlled or reviewed by the civil courts. As was said in *Smith* v. *Whitney*, supra, 'of questions not depending upon the construction of the statutes, but upon unwritten military law or usage, within the jurisdiction of courts-martial, military or naval officers, from their training and experience in the service, are more competent judges than the courts of common law.' "

The Court of Claims had observed that cases involving "conduct to the prejudice of good order and military discipline," as opposed to conduct unbecoming an officer, "are still further beyond the bounds of ordinary judicial judgment, for they are not measurable by our innate sense of right and wrong, of honor and dishonor, but must be gauged by an actual knowledge and experience of military life, its usages and duties."

II

The differences noted by this settled line of authority, first between the military community and the civilian community, and second between military law and civilian law, continue in the present day under the Uniform Code of Military Justice. That Code cannot be equated to a civilian criminal code. It, and the various versions of the Articles of War which have preceded it, regulate aspects of the conduct of members of the military which in the civilian sphere are left unregulated. While a civilian criminal code carves out a relatively small segment of potential conduct and declares it criminal, the Uniform Code of Military Justice essays more varied regulation of a much larger segment of the activities of the more tightly knit military community. In civilian life there is no legal sanction—civil or criminal—for failure to behave as an officer and a gentleman; in the military world, Art. 133 imposes such a sanction on a commissioned officer. The Code likewise imposes other sanctions for conduct that in civilian life is not subject to criminal penalties: disrespect toward superior commissioned officers; cruelty toward, or oppression or maltreatment of subordinates; negligent damaging, destruction, or wrongful disposition of military property of the United States; improper hazarding of a vessel; drunkenness on duty; and malingering.

But the other side of the coin is that the penalties provided in the Code vary from death and substantial penal confinement at one extreme to forms of administrative discipline which are below the threshold of what would normally be considered a criminal sanction at the other. Though all of the offenses described in the Code are punishable "as a court-martial may direct," and the accused may demand a trial by court-martial, Art. 15 of the Code also provides for the imposition of non-judicial "disciplinary punishments" for minor offenses without the intervention of a court-martial. The punishments imposable under that article are of a limited nature. With respect to officers, punishment may encompass suspension of duty, arrest in quarters for not more than 30 days, restriction for not more than 60 days, and forfeiture of pay for a limited period of time. In the case of enlisted men, such punishment may additionally include, among other things, reduction to the next inferior pay grade, extra fatigue duty, and correctional custody for not more than seven consecutive days. Thus, while legal proceedings actually brought before a court-martial are prosecuted in the name of the government, and the accused has the right to demand that he be proceeded against in this manner before any sanctions may be imposed upon him, a range of minor sanctions for lesser infractions are often imposed administratively. Forfeiture of pay, reduction in rank, and even dismissal from the service bring to mind the law of labor-management relations as much as the civilian criminal law.

In short, the Uniform Code of Military Justice regulates a far broader range of the conduct of military personnel than a typical state criminal code regulates of the conduct of civilians; but at the same time the enforcement of that Code in the area of minor offenses is often by sanctions which are more akin to administrative or civil sanctions than to civilian criminal ones.

The availability of these lesser sanctions is not surprising in view of the different relationship of the government to members of the military. It is not only that of law-giver to citizen, but also that of employer to employee. Indeed, unlike the civilian situation, the government is often employer, landlord, provisioner, and law-giver rolled into one. That relationship also reflects the different purposes of the two communities. As we observed in In re Grimley, 137 U.S. 147, at 153, the military "is the executive arm" whose "law is that of obedience." While members of the military community enjoy many of the same rights and bear many of the same burdens as do members of the civilian community, within the military community there is simply not the same autonomy as there is in the larger civilian community. The military establishment is subject to the control of the civilian commander in chief and the civilian departmental heads under him, and its function is to carry out the policies made by those civilian superiors.

Perhaps because of the broader sweep of the Uniform Code, the military makes an effort to advise its personnel of the contents of the Uniform Code, rather than depending on the ancient doctrine that everyone is presumed to know the law. Article 137 of the Uniform Code requires that the provisions of the Code be "carefully explained to each enlisted member at the time of his entrance on active duty, or within six days thereafter" and that they be "explained again after he has completed six months of active duty . . . ." Thus the numerically largest component of the services, the enlisted personnel, who might be expected to be a good deal less familiar with the Uniform Code than commissioned officers, are required by its terms to receive instructions in its provisions. Article 137 further provides that a complete text of the Code and of the regulations prescribed by the president "shall be made available to any person on active duty, upon his request, for his personal examination."

With these very significant differences between military law and civilian law and between the military community and the civilian community in mind, we turn to appellee's challenges to the constitutionality of Arts. 133 and 134.

III

Appellee urges that both Art. 133 and Art. 134 (the general article) are "void for vagueness" under the due process clause of the fifth amendment [b]. . . . We have recently said of the vagueness doctrine:

> "The doctrine incorporates notions of fair notice or warning. Moreover, it requires legislatures to set reasonably clear guidelines for law enforcement officials and triers of fact in order to prevent 'arbitrary and discriminatory enforcement.' Where a statute's literal scope, unaided by a narrowing state-court interpretation, is capable of reaching expression sheltered by the first amendment,[c] the doctrine demands a greater degree of specificity than in other contexts." Smith v. Goguen, 415 U.S. 566, 572–573 (1974).

Each of these articles has been construed by the United States Court of Military Appeals or by other military authorities in such a manner as to at least partially narrow its otherwise broad scope.

The United States Court of Military Appeals has stated that Art. 134 must be judged "not in vacuo, but in the context in which the years have placed it." Article 134 does not make "every irregular, mischievous, or improper act a court-martial offense," but its reach is limited to conduct that is " 'directly and palpably—as distinguished from indirectly and remotely—prejudicial to good order and discipline.' " It applies only to calls for active opposition to the military policy of the United States and does not reach all "[d]isagreement with, or objection to, a policy of the government."

The Manual for Courts-Martial restates these limitations on the scope of Art. 134. It goes on to say that "[c]ertain disloyal statements by military personnel" may be punishable under Art. 134. "Examples are utterances designed to promote disloyalty or disaffection among troops, as praising the enemy, attacking the war aims of the United States, or denouncing our form of government." Extensive additional

[b] The fifth amendment to the Constitution of the United States provides, in pertinent part, that no person shall "be deprived of life, liberty, or property without due process of law." [Footnote by eds.]

[c] The first amendment to the Constitution of the United States provides, in pertinent part, that "Congress shall make no law . . . abridging the freedom of speech." [Footnote by eds.]

interpretative materials are contained in the portions of the Manual devoted to Art. 134, which describe more than 60 illustrative offenses.

The Court of Military Appeals has likewise limited the scope of Art. 133. Quoting from W. Winthrop, Military Law and Precedents 711–12 (2d ed. 1920), that court has stated:

"To constitute therefore the conduct here denounced, the act which forms the basis of the charge must have a double significance and effect. Though it need not amount to a crime, it must offend so seriously against law, justice, morality or decorum as to expose to disgrace, socially or as a man, the offender, and at the same time must be of such a nature or committed under such circumstances as to bring dishonor or disrepute upon the military profession which he represents."

The effect of these constructions of Arts. 133 and 134 by the Court of Military Appeals and by other military authorities has been twofold: It has narrowed the very broad reach of the literal language of the articles, and at the same time has supplied considerable specificity by way of examples of the conduct which they cover. It would be idle to pretend that there are not areas within the general confines of the articles' language which have been left vague despite these narrowing constructions. But even though sizable areas of uncertainty as to the coverage of the articles may remain after their official interpretation by authoritative military sources, further content may be supplied even in these areas by less formalized custom and usage. And there also cannot be the slightest doubt under the military precedents that there is a substantial range of conduct to which both articles clearly apply without vagueness or imprecision. It is within that range that appellee's conduct squarely falls, as the Court of Appeals recognized:

"Neither are we unmindful that the Manual for Courts-Martial offers as an example of an offense under Article 134, 'praising the enemy, attacking the war aims of the United States, or denouncing our form of government.' With the possible exception of the statement that 'Special Forces personnel are liars and thieves and killers of peasants and murderers of women and children,' it would appear that each statement for which [Levy] was court-martialed could fall within the example given in the Manual."

The Court of Appeals went on to hold, however, that even though Levy's own conduct was clearly prohibited, the void-for-vagueness doctrine conferred standing upon him to challenge the imprecision of the language of the articles as they might be applied to hypothetical situations outside the considerable area within which their applicability was similarly clear.

We disagree with the Court of Appeals both in its approach to this question and in its resolution of it. This Court has on more than one occasion invalidated statutes under the due process clause of the fifth or 14th [d] amendment because they contained no standard whatever by

[d] The 14th amendment to the Constitution of the United States provides, in pertinent part, that no state "shall . . . deprive any person of life, liberty, or

which criminality could be ascertained, and the doctrine of these cases has subsequently acquired the shorthand description of "void for vagueness." Lanzetta v. New Jersey, 306 U.S. 451 (1939); Winters v. New York, 333 U.S. 507 (1948). In these cases, the criminal provision is vague "not in the sense that it requires a person to conform his conduct to an imprecise but comprehensible normative standard, but rather in the sense that no standard of conduct is specified at all." Coates v. City of Cincinnati, 402 U.S. 611, 614 (1971).

But the Court of Appeals found in this case, and we agree, that Arts. 133 and 134 are subject to no such sweeping condemnation. Levy had fair notice from the language of each article that the particular conduct which he engaged in was punishable. This is a case, then, of the type adverted to in *Smith* v. *Goguen*, supra, in which the statutes "by their terms or as authoritatively construed apply without question to certain activities, but whose application to other behavior is uncertain." . . .

We have noted in *Smith* v. *Goguen*, supra, that more precision in drafting may be required because of the vagueness doctrine in the case of regulation of expression. For the reasons which differentiate military society from civilian society, we think Congress is permitted to legislate both with greater breadth and with greater flexibility when prescribing the rules by which the former shall be governed than it is when prescribing rules for the latter. But each of these differentiations relates to how strict a test of vagueness shall be applied in judging a particular criminal statute. None of them suggests that one who has received fair warning of the criminality of his own conduct from the statute in question is nonetheless entitled to attack it because the language would not give similar fair warning with respect to other conduct which might be within its broad and literal ambit. One to whose conduct a statute clearly applies may not successfully challenge it for vagueness. . . .[e]

Reversed.

MR. JUSTICE MARSHALL took no part in the consideration or decision of this case.

MR. JUSTICE BLACKMUN, with whom THE CHIEF JUSTICE joins, concurring.

I wholly concur in the Court's opinion. I write only to state what for me is a crucial difference between the majority and dissenting views in this case. My Brother Stewart complains that men of common intelligence must necessarily speculate as to what "conduct unbecoming an officer and a gentleman" or conduct to the "prejudice of good order and discipline in the armed forces" or conduct "of a nature to bring discredit upon the armed forces" really means. He implies that the average soldier or sailor would not reasonably expect, under the general articles, to suffer military reprimand or punishment for engaging in

property without due process of law." [Footnote by eds.]

[e] The Court also held explicitly that Levy's "conduct, that of a commissioned officer publicly urging enlisted personnel to refuse to obey orders which might send them into combat, was unprotected under the most expansive notions of the first amendment." [Footnote by eds.]

sexual acts with a chicken, or window peeping in a trailer park, or cheating while calling bingo numbers. He argues that "times have surely changed" and that the articles are "so vague and uncertain as to be incomprehensible to the servicemen who are to be governed by them."

These assertions are, of course, no less judicial fantasy than that which the dissent charges the majority of indulging. In actuality, what is at issue here are concepts of "right" and "wrong" and whether the civil [criminal?] law can accommodate, in special circumstances, a system of law which expects more of the individual in the context of a broader variety of relationships than one finds in civilian life.

In my judgment, times have not changed in the area of moral precepts. Fundamental concepts of right and wrong are the same now as they were under the Articles of the Earl of Essex (1642), or the British Articles of War of 1765, or the American Articles of War of 1775, or during the long line of precedents of this and other courts upholding the general articles. And, however unfortunate it may be, it is still necessary to maintain a disciplined and obedient fighting force.

A noted commentator, Professor Bishop of Yale, has recently stated that "[a]lmost all of the acts actually charged under [Articles 133 and 134], notably drug offenses, are of a sort which ordinary soldiers know, or should know, to be punishable." J. Bishop, Justice Under Fire 87–88 (1974). I agree. The subtle airs that govern the command relationship are not always capable of specification. The general articles are essential not only to punish patently criminal conduct, but also to foster an orderly and dutiful fighting force. One need only read the history of the permissive—and short-lived—regime of the Soviet Army in the early days of the Russian Revolution to know that command indulgence of an undisciplined rank and file can decimate a fighting force. Moreover, the fearful spectre of arbitrary enforcement of the articles, the engine of the dissent, is disabled, in my view, by the elaborate system of military justice that Congress has provided to servicemen, and by the self-evident, and self-selective, factor that commanders who are arbitrary with their charges will not produce the efficient and effective military organization this country needs and demands for its defense. . . .

Relativistic notions of right and wrong, or situation ethics, as some call it, have achieved in recent times a disturbingly high level of prominence in this country, both in the guise of law reform, and as a justification of conduct that persons would normally eschew as immoral and even illegal. The truth is that the moral horizons of the American people are not footloose . . . . The law should, in appropriate circumstances, be flexible enough to recognize the moral dimension of man and his instincts concerning that which is honorable, decent, and right.

[The dissenting opinion of Mr. Justice Douglas is omitted.]

MR. JUSTICE STEWART, with whom MR. JUSTICE DOUGLAS and MR. JUSTICE BRENNAN join, dissenting.

Article 133 of the Uniform Code of Military Justice makes it a criminal offense to engage in "conduct unbecoming an officer and a gentleman." Article 134 makes criminal "all disorders and neglects to the prejudice of good order and discipline in the armed forces," and "all conduct of a nature to bring discredit upon the armed forces." The Court today, reversing a unanimous judgment of the Court of Appeals, upholds the constitutionality of these statutes. I find it hard to imagine criminal statutes more patently unconstitutional than these vague and uncertain general articles, and I would, accordingly, affirm the judgment before us.

I

As many decisions of this Court make clear, vague statutes suffer from at least two fatal constitutional defects. First, by failing to provide fair notice of precisely what acts are forbidden, a vague statute "violates the first essential of due process of law." As the Court put the matter in Lanzetta v. New Jersey, 306 U.S. 451, 453 (1939): "No one may be required at peril of life, liberty, or property to speculate as to the meaning of penal statutes. All are entitled to be informed as to what the state commands or forbids." "Words which are vague and fluid . . . may be as much of a trap for the innocent as the ancient laws of Caligula."

Secondly, vague statutes offend due process by failing to provide explicit standards for those who enforce them, thus allowing discriminatory and arbitrary enforcement. Papachristou v. City of Jacksonville, 405 U.S. 156, 165–71 (1972). "A vague law impermissibly delegates basic policy matters to policemen, judges, and juries for resolution on an ad hoc and subjective basis. . . ." Grayned v. City of Rockford, 408 U.S. 104, 108–09 (1972). The absence of specificity in a criminal statute invites abuse on the part of prosecuting officials, who are left free to harass any individuals or groups who may be the object of official displeasure.

It is plain that Arts. 133 and 134 are vague on their face; indeed, the opinion of the Court does not seriously contend to the contrary. Men of common intelligence—including judges of both military and civilian courts—must necessarily speculate as to what such terms as "conduct unbecoming an officer and a gentleman" and "conduct of a nature to bring discredit upon the armed forces" really mean. In the past, this Court has held unconstitutional statutes penalizing "misconduct," conduct that was "annoying," "reprehensible," or "prejudicial to the best interests" of a city, and it is significant that military courts have resorted to several of these very terms in describing the sort of acts proscribed by Arts. 133 and 134.

Facially vague statutes may, of course, be saved from unconstitutionality by narrowing judicial construction. But I cannot conclude, as does the Court, that the facial vagueness of the general articles has been cured by the relevant opinions of either the Court of Military Appeals or any other military tribunal. In attempting to give meaning to the amorphous words of the statutes, the Court of Military Appeals has repeatedly turned to Winthrop's Military Law and Precedents, an 1886 treatise. That work describes "conduct unbecoming an officer and a gentleman" in the following manner:

> "To constitute therefore the conduct here denounced, the act which forms the basis of the charge must have a double significance and effect. Though it need not amount to a crime, it must offend so seriously against law, justice, morality, or decorum as to expose to disgrace, socially or as a man, the offender, and at the same time must be of such a nature or committed under such circumstances as to bring dishonor or disrepute upon the military profession which he represents."

As to the predecessor statute of Art. 134, Col. Winthrop read it as applicable to conduct whose prejudice to good order and discipline was *"reasonably direct and palpable,"* as opposed to that conduct which is simply *"indirectly or remotely"* prejudicial—whatever that may mean. These passages, and the decisions of the Court of Military Appeals that adopt them verbatim, scarcely add any substantive content to the language of the general articles. At best, the limiting constructions referred to by the Court represent a valiant but unavailing effort to read some specificity into hopelessly vague laws. Winthrop's definitions may be slightly different in wording from Arts. 133 and 134, but they are not different in kind, for they suffer from the same vagueness as the statutes to which they refer.

If there be any doubt as to the absence of truly limiting constructions of the general articles, it is swiftly dispelled by even the most cursory review of convictions under them in the military courts. Article 133 has been recently employed to punish such widely disparate conduct as dishonorable failure to repay debts, selling whiskey at an unconscionable price to an enlisted man, cheating at cards, and having an extramarital affair. Article 134 has been given an even wider sweep, having been applied to sexual acts with a chicken, window peeping in a trailer park, and cheating while calling bingo numbers. Convictions such as these leave little doubt that "[a]n infinite variety of other conduct, limited only by the scope of a commander's creativity or spleen, can be made the subject of court-martial under these articles."

In short, the general articles are in practice as well as theory "catch-alls," designed to allow prosecutions for practically any conduct that may offend the sensibilities of a military commander. Not every prosecution of course, results in a conviction, and the military courts have sometimes overturned convictions when the conduct involved was so marginally related to military discipline as to offend even the loosest interpretations of the general articles. But these circumstances can hardly be thought to validate the otherwise vague statutes. As the Court said in United States v. Reese, 92 U.S. 214, 221 (1876): "It would certainly be dangerous if the legislature could set a net large enough to catch all possible offenders, and leave it to the courts to step inside and say who could be rightfully detained, and who should be set at large."

At best, the general articles are just such a net, and suffer from all the vices that our previous decisions condemn.

II

Perhaps in recognition of the essential vagueness of the general articles, the Court today adopts several rather periphrastic approaches to the problem before us. Whatever the apparent vagueness of these statutes to us civilians, we are told, they are models of clarity to "'practical men in the navy and army.'" Moreover, the Court says, the appellee should have been well aware that his conduct fell within the proscriptions of the general articles, since the Manual for Courts-Martial gives specific content to these facially uncertain statutes. I believe that neither of these propositions can withstand analysis.

A

It is true, of course, that a line of prior decisions of this Court . . . have upheld against constitutional attack the ancestors of today's general articles. With all respect for the principle of stare decisis, however, I believe that these decisions should be given no authoritative force in view of what is manifestly a vastly "altered historic environment."

It might well have been true in 1858 or even 1902 that those in the Armed Services knew, through a combination of military custom and instinct, what sorts of acts fell within the purview of the general articles. But times have surely changed. Throughout much of this country's early history, the standing army and navy numbered in the hundreds. The cadre was small, professional, and voluntary. The military was a unique society, isolated from the mainstream of civilian life, and it is at least plausible to suppose that the volunteer in that era understood what conduct was prohibited by the general articles.

It is obvious that the Army into which Dr. Levy entered was far different. It was part of a military establishment whose members numbered in the millions, a large percentage of whom were conscripts or draft-induced volunteers, with no prior military experience and little expectation of remaining beyond their initial period of obligation. Levy was precisely such an individual, a draft-induced volunteer whose military indoctrination was minimal, at best. To presume that he and others like him who served during the Vietnam era were so imbued with the ancient traditions of the military as to comprehend the arcane meaning of the general articles is to engage in an act of judicial fantasy. In my view, we do a grave disservice to citizen soldiers in subjecting them to the uncertain regime of Arts. 133 and 134 simply because these provisons did not offend the sensibilities of the federal judiciary in a wholly different period of our history. In today's vastly "altered historic environment," the *Dynes* case and its progeny have become constitutional anachronisms, and I would retire them from active service.

B

The Court suggests that the Manual for Courts-Martial provides some notice of what is proscribed by the general articles, through its Appendix containing "Forms for Charges and Specifications." These specimen charges, which consist of "fill-in-the-blank" accusations covering various fact situations, do offer some indication of what conduct the drafters of the Manual perceived to fall within the prohibitions of Arts. 133 and 134. There are several reasons, however, why the form specifications cannot provide the sort of definitive interpretation of the general articles necessary to save these statutes from unconstitutionality.

For one thing, the specifications covering Arts. 133 and 134 are not exclusive; the military courts have repeatedly held conduct not listed in the Manual's Appendix as nonetheless violative of the general articles. Nor can it be said that the specifications contain any common thread or unifying theme that gives generic definition to the articles' vague words; the specimen charges in the Manual list such widely disparate conduct as kicking a public horse in the belly, subornation of perjury, and wrongful cohabitation as violative of Art. 134. Moreover, the list of offenses included in the Appendix is ever-expanding; the 1951 Manual contained 59 Art. 134 offenses, while the list has increased to 63 in 1969. In view of the non-exclusive and transient character of the specification list, a serviceman wishing to conform his conduct to the requirements of the law would simply find definitive guidance from the Manual impossible.

More significantly, the fact that certain conduct is listed in the Manual is no guarantee that it is in violation of the general articles. The Court of Military Appeals has repeatedly emphasized that the sample specifications are only procedural guides and timesavers for military prosecutors beset by poor research facilities, and are not intended to *create* offenses under the general articles. Consequently, the Court has on several occasions disapproved Art. 134 convictions, despite the fact that the precise conduct at issue was listed in the form specifications as falling under that article.

Despite all this, the Court indicates that Levy should have been aware that *his* conduct was violative of Art. 134, since one of the specimen charges relates to the making of statements "disloyal to the United States." That specification, and the brief reference to such conduct in the text of the Manual, is itself so vague and overbroad as to have been declared unconstitutional by one federal court. But even if a consensus as to the meaning of the word "disloyal" were readily attainable, I am less than confident that Dr. Levy's attacks upon our Vietnam policies could be accurately characterized by such an adjective. However foreign to the military atmosphere of Fort Jackson, the words spoken by him represented a viewpoint shared by many American citizens. Whatever the accuracy of these views, I would be loath to impute "disloyalty" to those who honestly held them. In short, I think it is clear that the form specification concerning disloyal statements cannot be said to have given Levy notice of the illegality of his conduct. The specimen charge is no better than the article that spawned it. It merely substitutes one set of subjective and amorphous phraseology for another.[40]

III

What has been said above indicates my view that the general articles are unconstitutionally vague under the standards normally and repeatedly applied by this Court. The remaining question is whether, as the Court concludes, the peculiar situation of the military requires application of a standard of judicial review more relaxed than that embodied in our prior decisions.

It is of course common ground that the military is a "specialized community governed by a separate discipline from that of the civilian." A number of [servicemen's] individual rights must necessarily be subordinated to the overriding military mission, and I have no doubt that the military may constitutionally prohibit conduct that is quite permissible in civilian life, such as questioning the command of a superior. But this only begins the inquiry. The question before us is not whether the military may adopt substantive rules different from those that govern civilian society, but whether the serviceman has the same right as his civilian counterpart to be informed as to precisely what conduct those rules proscribe before he can be criminally punished for violating them. More specifically, the issue is whether the vagueness of the general articles is required to serve a genuine military objective.

The Solicitor General suggests that a certain amount of vagueness in the general articles is necessary in order to maintain high standards of conduct in the military, since it is impossible to predict in advance every offense that might serve to affect morale or discredit the service. It seems to me that this argument was concisely and eloquently rebutted by Judge Aldisert in the Court of Appeals:

"[W]hat high standard of conduct is served by convicting an individual of conduct he did not reasonably perceive to be criminal? Is not the essence of high standards in the military, first, knowing one's duty, and secondly, executing it? And, in this regard, would not an even higher standard be served by delinea-

---

[40] . . . The words of arts. 133 and 134 are vague beyond repair; I am no more able to discern objective standards of conduct from phrases such as "conduct unbecoming an officer and a gentleman" and "conduct of a nature to bring discredit upon the armed forces" than I am from such words as "bad" or "reprehensible." Given this essential uncertainty, I cannot conclude that the statutory language clearly warned [Levy] that his speech was illegal. It may have been, of course, that Dr. Levy had a subjective feeling that his conduct violated (some) military law. But that is not enough, for as we pointed out in Bouie v. City of Columbia, 378 U.S. 347, 355–56 n. 5 (1964): "The determination whether a criminal statute provides fair warning of its prohibitions must be made on the basis of the statute itself and the other pertinent law, rather than on the basis of an ad hoc appraisal of the subjective expectations of particular defendants."

tion of the various offenses under Article 134, followed by obedience to these standards?"

It may be that military necessity justifies the promulgation of substantive rules of law that are wholly foreign to civilian life, but I fail to perceive how any legitimate military goal is served by enshrouding these rules in language so vague and uncertain as to be incomprehensible to the servicemen who are to be governed by them.[41] Indeed, I should suppose that vague laws, with their serious capacity for arbitrary and discriminatory enforcement, can in the end only hamper the military's objectives of high morale and esprit de corps.

In short, I think no case has been made for finding that there is any legitimate military necessity for perpetuation of the vague and amorphous general articles. In this regard, I am not alone. No less an authority than Kenneth J. Hodson, former Judge Advocate General of the Army and Chief Judge of the Army Court of Military Review, has recommended the abolition of Art. 134 because "[w]e don't really need it, and we can't defend our use of it in this modern world." Hodson, The Manual for Courts-Martial—1984, 57 Mil.L.Rev. 1, 12 (1972).[42] No different conclusion can be reached as to Art. 133. Both are anachronisms, whose legitimate military usefulness, if any, has long since disappeared.

It is perhaps appropriate to add a final word. I do not for one moment denigrate the importance of our inherited tradition that the commissioned officers of our military forces are expected to be men of honor, nor do I doubt the necessity that servicemen generally must be orderly and dutiful. An efficient and effective military organization depends in large part upon the character and quality of its personnel, particularly its leadership. The internal loyalty and mutual reliance indispensable to the ultimate effectiveness of any military organization can exist only among people who can be counted on to do their duty. It is, therefore, not only legitimate but essential that in matters of promotion, retention, duty assignment, and internal discipline, evaluations must repeatedly be made of a serviceman's basic character as reflected in his deportment, whether he be an enlisted man or a commissioned officer. But we deal here with criminal statutes. And I cannot believe that such meaningless statutes as these can be used to send men to prison under a Constitution that guarantees due process of law.

---

[41] Cf. J. Heller, Catch-22 395 (Dell ed. 1973):

"We accuse you also of the commission of crimes and infractions we don't even know about yet. Guilty or innocent?

"I don't know, sir. How can I say if you don't tell me what they are."

"How can we tell if we don't know?"

[42] General Hodson suggests that in place of Art. 134, the Department of Defense and various military commanders could promulgate specific sets of orders, outlawing particular conduct. Those disobeying these orders could be prosecuted under Art. 92 of the UCMJ, 10 U.S.C. § 892, which outlaws the failure to obey any lawful order. See also Note, Taps for the Real Catch-22, 81 Yale L.J. 1518, 1537–41 (1972), containing a similar suggestion.

NOTES ON *PARKER* v. *LEVY*

1. **Prior Constructions of Arts. 133 and 134.** Note that even the *Parker* majority did not suggest that the bare texts of Arts. 133 and 134 would pass muster under conventional standards of vagueness review. Indeed, the Court seemed implicitly to concede that punishment of civilians under criteria as uncertain as "conduct unbecoming an officer and a gentleman" and conduct "to the prejudice of good order and discipline" would be unconstitutional. For the majority, however, several factors called for a different result.

One such factor was the construction given these statutes in prior judicial decisions. Art. 133 had been read to apply only to conduct having the "double significance and effect" of exposing the offender to personal disgrace and of bringing the military into disrepute. Art. 134 had been construed to reach only acts "directly and palpably—as distinguished from indirectly and remotely—prejudicial to good order and discipline." The dissenters did not dispute the relevance of prior judicial construction, but they did dispute the extent to which these interpretations had narrowed the statutory uncertainty. According to Mr. Justice Stewart, the prior constructions quoted above were merely an "unavailing effort to read some specificity into hopelessly vague laws." Do you agree?

2. **The Specifications.** Another factor emphasized by the *Parker* majority was the effect of fill-in-the-blank specifications, or charges, in reducing certain aspects of Arts. 133 and 134 to relative specificity. These form specifications are listed in the Manual for Courts-Martial. The Manual is a comprehensive guide to enforcement of military law. It is issued and periodically updated by executive order of the President. Though lacking the force of statute, the Manual is in most respects an authoritative statement of military law.

Under Art. 134 the Manual currently lists 62 form specifications. Most of them are relatively precise, but they do not reveal much in the way of a common theme. Thus, for example, the charges listed under Art. 134 include abusing an animal, adultery, bigamy, bribery, disorderly drunkenness, fleeing the scene of an accident, negligent homicide, impersonating an officer, indecent acts with a child, tampering with the mail, perjury, breaking medical quarantine, soliciting another to commit an offense, receiving stolen property, straggling, and wearing an unauthorized decoration. The Art. 133 list is more limited. It includes only charges against copying an examination paper, being drunk or disorderly in uniform, and dishonorably failing to repay a debt.

Obviously, none of the Art. 133 form specifications addresses the conduct of Capt. Levy. Apparently, the Art. 133 prosecution went forward under the policy, as described in the Manual for Courts-Martial, that conduct punishable under any other article of the Uniform Code is also an offense under Art. 133 if such conduct is judged unbecoming an officer and a gentleman. See Manual for Courts-Martial ¶ 212. Thus, in essence, the Art. 133 offense was made to piggyback on the conduct violative of Art. 134. Significantly, that conduct was more or less precisely proscribed by a form specification published under Art. 134 in the Manual for Courts-Martial. That specification, which has since been modified slightly, then read as follows:

"In that _____ did, on or about _____, 19__, with design to promote disloyalty and disaffection among the troops, utter to _____ the following statement, to wit: '_____,' or words to that effect, which statement was disloyal to the United States."

Capt. Levy was in fact prosecuted under an elaborated version of this specification, with the statements quoted in the Court's opinion forming the basis for the charge.

Given the prior existence of this specification, how persuasive is the claim of lack of notice in the enforcement of Art. 134? Is it plausible to believe, as the dissenting opinion suggests, that Capt. Levy was unfairly surprised by the charges brought against him?

On one view, therefore, the debate about Art. 134 boils down to this: Should an area of residual indeterminacy render invalid a statute whose enforcement in the instant case is reasonably clear? In other words, if Capt. Levy was given adequate notice by the specification quoted above, should it matter that the statute may be applied in future cases in ways that cannot be anticipated? The *Parker* majority and dissent obviously part company on this point. Which is the stronger position? Does not the choice turn in part on one's conception of the essential rationale of the vagueness doctrine?

3. **Significance of the Military Context.** The analysis of the *Parker* majority is not limited to the various sources of the meaning of Arts. 133 and 134. The Court's conclusion also rests on considerations arising from the military context.

One such factor mentioned by the Court is the existence within the armed forces of the system of non-judicial and less severe punishment for minor offenses under Art. 15 of the Uniform Code of Military Justice. Art. 15 is not substantive; by its own force it defines no crime. It merely defines a mechanism for enforcing other provisions of the Code, including Arts. 133 and 134. The summary procedure set forth in Art. 15 is carried out by the commander without resort to lawyers or a trial or any of the elaborate adversarial proceedings typical of the criminal law. The commander makes an initial decision whether to proceed under Art. 15 or by court-martial, but the defendant always has the option of refusing punishment under Art. 15 and requesting trial by court-martial. The accused who elects court-martial thereby becomes entitled to procedural protections generally comparable to civilian justice, but he also becomes subject to the kinds of penalties imposed by civilian laws, as distinct from the lesser sanctions available under Art. 15. As a practical matter, therefore, the accused who expects to lose at trial and who wishes to minimize the consequences usually accepts an offer of summary punishment under Art. 15.

The *Parker* opinion describes this system of summary punishment but does not explain why it matters. What is the relevance of Art. 15

to this case? Should the validity of Arts. 133 and 134 be affected by the existence of a system of non-judicial proceedings which, in any event, was not invoked here? If so, how? If not, what point does the Court hope to make by its discussion of Art. 15 or, more generally, by Part II of its opinion?

A second contention arises from the need to maintain a disciplined and effective fighting force. The *Parker* majority apparently believed that the exigencies of the military situation justified penal legislation of greater breadth and flexibility than would have been permitted in civilian laws. Essentially, this is the argument of necessity. Vague laws must be tolerated where they are necessary, and the need of the military is especially great. Do you agree? Would a more rigorous requirement of advance crime definition undermine the ability of a commander to accomplish his mission? Could that consequence be avoided by greater reliance on Art. 90?

Finally, there is the related but distinct point that the traditional characteristics of military society work to ameliorate the dangers of indefinite laws. The contention is not that the military situation makes vague laws essential but rather that it renders them relatively less harmful. The underlying assumption is that there is a relation between the characteristics of any given society and the significance in that society of the concerns of the vagueness doctrine. Arguably, notice of proscribed conduct and restraint of arbitrary enforcement are especially important in a diverse, pluralistic, fragmented society but less so in a tightly knit, conformist, and authoritarian environment. Is the modern military a highly integrated society of the sort described above? Or is it more nearly a reflection of contemporary American civilian society?

In this connection, note the close analogy between the progressive particularization of Arts. 133 and 134 and the common-law method of crime creation. Just as the Manual for Courts-Martial and the accumulation of precedent gradually specify particular applications of the general articles, the common-law courts of medieval England gradually spelled out various criminal offenses. And just as Arts. 133 and 134 retain an elastic potential to punish wrongs not previously specified, the common-law method asserted a residual power in the courts to define new crimes or particularize old ones as the occasion demanded. Moreover, the decision upholding Arts. 133 and 134 is based in part on an assessment that the military environment is similar to the highly structured society that gave rise to the common law. And the dissenters reject the military analogue to the common-law method at least partly because of a differing perception of life in the military. For both majority and dissent, the acceptability of indeterminacy in the penal law seems to turn in part on the characteristics of the society in which the law is enforced.

NOTES ON THE VAGUENESS DOCTRINE

1. **Rationales of the Vagueness Doctrine.** As Justice Stewart noted in his *Parker* dissent, a vague statute has at least two flaws. First, it fails to give adequate notice of what conduct is proscribed. The danger is that criminal punishment may be imposed without fair warning. This fair warning rationale is a recurrent theme in vagueness decisions. As the Court said in Lanzetta v. New Jersey, 306 U.S. 451, 453 (1939), "[n]o one may be required at peril of life, liberty or property to speculate as to the meaning of penal statutes," and in Connally v. General Construction Co., 269 U.S. 385, 391 (1926), "a statute which either forbids or requires the doing of an act in terms so vague that men of common intelligence must necessarily guess at its meaning and differ as to its application, violates the first essential of due process of law."

A second problem with an indefinite law is that it invites arbitrary and discriminatory enforcement. In essence, the power to define a vague statute is left to those who enforce it. The fear is that the strictures of the penal law will be determined on ad hoc and potentially illegitimate bases. As the Supreme Court noted over a century ago, "[i]t would certainly be dangerous if the legislature could set a net large enough to catch all possible offenders, and leave it to the courts to step inside and say who could be rightfully detained, and who should be set at large." United States v. Reese, 92 U.S. 214, 221 (1876). And, of course, a vague law also leaves police and prosecutors dangerously unconstrained in the performance of their duties. The result is a drift toward arbitrariness in the administration of justice and a consequent undermining of the rule of law.

2. **Limits of the Vagueness Rationales.** Virtually every modern vagueness decision focuses on fair warning and non-discriminatory enforcement as rationales for invalidating vague laws, but neither justification can be accepted without qualification. The fair-warning rationale, in particular, is hard to take at face value. Invalidating some laws because they do not give adequate notice of their content presupposes that other laws effectively provide such notice. Yet there is something inescapably fictive in the notion that potential criminals learn what is forbidden from the words of a statute. That assumption may hold true for those who seek advice of counsel, but the ordinary citizen is not likely to have such an opportunity. Indeed, most prospective offenders are not even likely to have either access to the statute books or the skill to unravel the legislative language should they find it. How realistic is it, given such circumstances, to speak of a lack of fair warning as the fatal defect of an indefinite law?

The rationale of fair warning is weakened further by the rule that the precision required of a penal statute need not appear on its face. Instead, the courts recognize that facial uncertainty may be resolved by judicial construction. Thus, review of a state statute for unconstitutional vagueness often turns not on the text of the law as it stands on the books but on its meaning as construed by the state courts. A good example is Chaplinsky v. New Hampshire, 315 U.S. 568 (1942). In that case, the Supreme Court upheld a law making it criminal for any person to "address any offensive, derisive or annoying word to any other person who is lawfully in any street or other public place . . . ." In the Court's view, "offensive, derisive or annoying" was made sufficiently specific by a state court ruling that the phrase should be applied only to words having "a direct tendency to cause acts of violence" by the persons to whom they are addressed. Absent this interpretation, the ordinance would probably have been found unconstitutional. Similarly, federal courts dealing with federal legislation often supply their own narrowing constructions in order to save acts of Congress from invalidation for vagueness. In such situations, the reach of the penal law is ascertainable only through a process of research and interpretation. Yet the courts hold that determinacy of meaning, no matter how difficult it may be to discover, is nevertheless sufficient answer to a vagueness challenge. Does not this position undercut the traditional reliance on fair warning as the rationale for vagueness review?

The concern for non-discriminatory enforcement of the penal law is also not without difficulty. It is true that the vagueness doctrine results in the invalidation of laws which, because they are standardless, are especially susceptible to arbitrary enforcement. In this respect the doctrine makes an important contribution to evenhandedness in the administration of justice. Yet it is revealing to note how imperfect is the law's commitment to that goal. A vague statute may *invite* arbitrary enforcement, but virtually any law *allows* it. The difference may not be so great as the rhetoric of vagueness decisions suggests. After all, even an ideally precise statute is subject to discretionary, and hence potentially discriminatory, administration. The police decide which laws to enforce and whom to arrest. Prosecutors decide whether to bring charges and for which offenses. Prosecutors also may elect to accept or reject offers of guilty pleas and to make or withhold recommendations of sentence. In all of these respects, the exercise of discretion is virtually uncontrolled. Only in the truly exceptional case where the defendant can prove that the prosecutorial decision was made on some plainly illegitimate basis—notably race or religion—is there possibility of redress for arbitrary or selective enforcement. Perhaps most dramatic of all is the enormous discretion involved in sentencing. Legislatively authorized penalties for any given offense typically cover a wide range. The judge's selection of a particular sentence within that range may be the most consequential decision of the entire enforcement process. Yet sentences traditionally are imposed on an individualized and highly discretionary basis, and the law of most jurisdictions imposes few restraints on sentencing variations among offenders. Where there is jury sentencing, the process is entirely ad hoc; it lacks even the advantages of institutional continuity. Judicial sentencing may be less various than jury determinations, but the predilections of the sentencing judge remain critically important. There is usually no requirement that a particular sentence be justified by a statement of reasons, and in many states sentences are not subject to appellate review. Even where review is authorized, it is only in the rare case of a demonstrable abuse of discretion that an initial decision will be overturned on appeal.[a]

What, if anything, does the prevalence of discretionary authority throughout the criminal justice system reveal about the strength of the non-discriminatory enforcement rationale of the vagueness doctrine? Does the pervasive potential for ad hoc and arbitrary enforcement of any penal statute undermine the policy of invalidating some laws for failure to provide determinate standards? Or is the vagueness doctrine nevertheless justified as an important, though arguably insufficient, corollary of the rule of law? [b]

3. **Illustrative Cases: *Coates* and *Papachristou*.** Prior vagueness decisions illustrate the relevance of both of the traditional rationales for the vagueness doctrine. The potential of an indefinite law to deny fair warning to prospective offenders is depicted by Coates v. City of Cincinnati, 402 U.S. 611 (1971). A municipal ordinance made it a crime for "three or more persons to assemble . . . on any of the sidewalks . . . and there conduct themselves in a manner annoying to persons passing by . . . ." This law was upheld by a state court whose principal contribution to its construction was a dictionary definition of the verb "annoy." [c] The Supreme Court reversed, noting espe-

---

[a] General sources on discretion in the administration of criminal justice include K. Davis, Discretionary Justice (1969), and Vorenberg, Narrowing the Discretion of Criminal Justice Officials, 1976 Duke L.J. 651. There is also a rich literature focusing specifically on police discretion and on various possibilities for securing greater regularity in the exercise of police authority. See, e.g., K. Davis, Police Discretion (1975); J. Skolnick, Justice Without Trial: Law Enforcement in Democratic Society (2d ed. 1975); Allen, The Police and Substantive Rule-Making: Reconciling Principle and Expediency, 125 U.Pa.L.Rev. 62 (1976); Goldstein, Police Discretion Not to Invoke the Criminal Process: Low-Visibility Decisions in the Administration of Justice, 69 Yale L.J. 543 (1960).

For discussion of the exercise of discretion by prosecutors in charging, and in negotiating and accepting guilty pleas, see Vorenberg, Decent Restraint of Prosecutorial Power, 94 Harv.L.Rev. 1521 (1981); LaFave, The Prosecutor's Discretion in the United States, 18 J.Comp.L. 532 (1970); Alschuler, The Prosecutor's Role in Plea Bargaining, 36 U.Chi.L.Rev. 50 (1968). For an informative recent study of federal prosecutorial discretion, see Frase, The Decision to File Federal Criminal Charges: A Quantitative Study, 47 U.Chi.L.Review 246 (1980).

For a review of the highly discretionary nature of traditional sentencing schemes,

see M. Frankel, Criminal Sentences—Law Without Order (1973). For discussion of recent reforms, see American Bar Association, Standards for Criminal Justice: Sentencing Alternatives and Procedures (2d ed. 1980); Alschuler, Sentencing Reform and Prosecutorial Power: A Critique of Recent Proposals for "Fixed" and "Presumptive" Sentencing, 126 U.Pa.L.Rev. 550 (1978).

[b] For a critical account of the vagueness doctrine as a "conscious interpretive construct" used to mask or avoid political choices in the application of the criminal law, see Kelman, Interpretive Construction in the Substantive Criminal Law, 33 Stan.L.Rev. 591, 652–62 (1981). For a more sanguine view of the contribution of the vagueness doctrine to the rule of law, see Jeffries, Legality, Vagueness, and the Construction of Penal Statutes, 71 Va.L.Rev. 189, 201–19 (1985).

[c] "The ordinance prohibits, inter alia, 'conduct . . . annoying to persons passing by.' The word 'annoying' is a widely used and well understood word; it is not necessary to guess its meaning. 'Annoying' is the present participle of the transitive verb 'annoy' which means to trouble, to vex, to impede, to incommode, to provoke, to harass or to irritate."

21 Ohio St.2d 66, 69, 255 N.E.2d 247, 249 (1970).

cially the failure of the state court to narrow the statute's reach and the consequent difficulty of knowing what was prohibited:

> "If three or more people meet together on a sidewalk or street corner, they must conduct themselves so as not to annoy any police officer or other person who should happen to pass by. In our opinion this ordinance is unconstitutionally vague . . . .

> "Conduct that annoys some people does not annoy others. Thus, the ordinance is vague, not in the sense that it requires a person to conform his conduct to an imprecise but comprehensible normative standard, but rather in the sense that no standard of conduct is specified at all. As a result, 'men of common intelligence must necessarily guess at its meaning.' "

Similarly, the case of Papachristou v. City of Jacksonville, 405 U.S. 156 (1972), is richly suggestive of the potential for arbitrary and discriminatory enforcement of vague laws. The ordinance there considered is so extravagant and yet so typical of the municipal legislation of a certain era that it merits reprinting in full:

> "Rogues and vagabonds, or dissolute persons who go about begging, common gamblers, persons who use juggling or unlawful games or plays, common drunkards, common night walkers, thieves, pilferers or pickpockets, traders in stolen property, lewd, wanton and lascivious persons, keepers of gambling places, common railers and brawlers, persons wandering or strolling around from place to place without any lawful purpose or object, habitual loafers, disorderly persons, persons neglecting all lawful business and habitually spending their time by frequenting houses of ill fame, gaming houses, or places where alcoholic beverages are sold or served, persons able to work but habitually living upon the earnings of their wives or minor children shall be deemed vagrants and, upon conviction in the Municipal Court shall be punished as provided . . . ."

This ordinance was applied against two white women and two black men who were arrested while driving on the main thoroughfare of Jacksonville. The arresting officers denied that the racial composition of the group had any impact on their decision to arrest, but the Court was plainly worried:

> "Those generally implicated by the imprecise terms of the ordinance—poor people, non-conformists, dissenters, idlers—may be required to comport themselves according to the lifestyle deemed appropriate by the Jacksonville police and the courts. Where, as here, there are no standards governing the exercise of the discretion granted by the ordinance, the scheme permits and encourages an arbitrary and discriminatory enforcement of the law. It furnishes a convenient tool for 'harsh and discriminatory enforcement by local prosecuting officials, against particular groups deemed to merit their displeasure.' . . . It results in a regime in which the poor and the unpopular are permitted to 'stand on a public sidewalk . . . only at the whim of any police officer.' . . . Under this ordinance, '[I]f some carefree

type of fellow is satisfied to work just so much, and no more, as will pay for one square meal, some wine, and a flophouse daily, but a court thinks this kind of living subhuman, the fellow can be forced to raise his sights or go to jail as a vagrant.' Amsterdam, Federal Constitutional Restrictions on the Punishment of Crimes of Status, Crimes of General Obnoxiousness, Crimes of Displeasing Police Officers, and the Like, 3 Crim.L.Bull. 205, 226 (1967).

". . . Of course, vagrancy statutes are useful to the police. Of course, they are nets making easy the roundup of so-called undesirables. But the rule of law implies equality and justice in its application. Vagrancy laws of the Jacksonville type teach that the scales of justice are so tipped that even-handed administration of the law is not possible. The rule of law, evenly applied to minorities as well as majorities, to the poor as well as the rich, is the great mucilage that holds society together."

Are these illustrations sufficient to suggest some continuing vitality in the articulated rationales for vagueness review?

4. **Tolerable Vagueness and the Demands of Necessity.** The point, of course, is not that the traditional justifications for the vagueness doctrine are invalid, but only that our commitment to them is not unqualified. Fair warning and non-discriminatory enforcement are highly valued in the penal law, but they are ideals, not rules of decision. Endorsement of them does not lead ineluctably to the invalidation of particular laws, for there is no yardstick of specificity against which a challenged statute can be measured. The inquiry is evaluative rather than mechanistic. It calls for a judgment concerning not merely the degree of vagueness, but also the acceptability of vagueness in particular situations. Context affects results. Thus, vagueness decisions cannot be understood as linear extrapolations from the rationales of fair warning and non-discriminatory enforcement. A number of other factors may intrude on those concerns and skew the judicial attitude toward accepting or rejecting statutory indeterminacy.

One such factor is the feasibility of being more precise. Imprecision is an inevitable feature of generality. Laws drawn to regulate future conduct necessarily speak in abstract terms, and the reduction of general language to specific results is often uncertain. Indeed, nothing is more common than a statutory standard that is intelligible in concept though unclear in its application to particular facts. Yet the courts are reluctant to invalidate for vagueness laws that cannot reasonably be made more precise. To do so would be to withdraw the subject matter of the law from the legislative grasp and thus to leave government without means to accomplish its purpose. This is drastic medicine, and the courts are unwilling to administer it in any doubtful case. Thus, the demands of necessity often move the courts to accept in some contexts a degree of indeterminacy that might not be permitted elsewhere.

An unusually explicit example of such reasoning comes from United States v. Petrillo, 332 U.S. 1 (1947). A provision of the Federal

Communications Act made it criminal to use any means to coerce or compel a broadcast licensee to employ "any person or persons in excess of the number of employees needed by such licensee . . .". The defendant challenged the law for vagueness, and the trial court agreed that the reference to "number of employees needed" was too indefinite to give fair warning of the meaning of the law. The Supreme Court reversed, noting that:

"Clearer and more precise language might have been framed by Congress to express what it meant by 'number of employees needed.' But none occurs to us, nor has any better language been suggested, effectively to carry out what appears to have been the congressional purpose. The argument really seems to be that it is impossible for a jury or court ever to determine how many employees a business needs, and that, therefore, no statutory language could meet the problem Congress had in mind. If this argument should be accepted, the result would be that no legislature could make it an offense for a person to compel another to hire employees, no matter how unnecessary they were, and however desirable a legislature might consider suppression of the practice to be.

"The Constitution presents no such insuperable obstacle to legislation. We think that the language Congress used provides an adequate warning as to what conduct falls under its ban, and marks boundaries sufficiently distinct for judges and juries fairly to administer the law in accordance with the will of Congress. That there may be marginal cases in which it is difficult to determine the side of the line on which a particular fact situation falls is no sufficient reason to hold the language too ambiguous to define a criminal offense. . . . The Constitution has erected procedural safeguards to protect against conviction for crime except for violation of laws which have clearly defined conduct thereafter to be punished; but the Constitution does not require impossible standards."

5. **Tolerable Vagueness and Questions of Degree.** The concern that legislatures not be required to meet "impossible standards" of precision comes directly into play for questions of degree. The most famous judicial pronouncement on this subject appears in Nash v. United States, 229 U.S. 373 (1913). *Nash* involved a vagueness challenge to criminal prosecution under the Sherman Antitrust Act. Section 1 of that statute declared illegal "[e]very contract, combination in the form of trust or otherwise, or conspiracy in restraint of trade or commerce . . .". Of course, it is the essence of contract to restrict future choice. If read literally, therefore, the Sherman Act could be taken to forbid any commercial agreement. The Supreme Court avoided this absurdity by declaring, in the context of civil antitrust litigation, that the Sherman Act should be interpreted according to a "rule of reason." See Standard Oil Co. v. United States, 221 U.S. 1 (1911), and United States v. American Tobacco Co., 221 U.S. 106 (1911). By this construction, the Court transformed the condemnation of "every"

restraint of trade to one that reached only an *undue* restraint of trade. It was the criminal application of this test of liability that was challenged in *Nash*. Writing for the Court, Mr. Justice Holmes responded as follows:

"The objection to the criminal operation of the statute is thought to be warranted by *Standard Oil Co.* v. *United States* and *United States* v. *American Tobacco Co.* Those cases may be taken to have established that only such contracts and combinations are within the act as, by reason of intent or the inherent nature of the contemplated acts, prejudice the public interests by unduly restricting competition or unduly obstructing the course of trade. And thereupon it is said that the crime thus defined by the statute contains in its definition an element of degree as to which estimates may differ, with the result that a man might find himself in prison because his honest judgment did not anticipate that of a jury of less competent men. . . .

"But . . . the law is full of instances where a man's fate depends on his estimating rightly, that is, as the jury subsequently estimates it, some matter of degree. If his judgment is wrong, not only may he incur a fine or a short imprisonment, as here; he may incur the penalty of death. . . . 'The criterion in such cases is to examine whether common social duty would, under the circumstances, have suggested a more circumspect conduct.' "

The Sherman Act is still on the books and occasionally is enforced by criminal prosecution. Do you think the statute sufficiently precise to meet the concerns of the vagueness doctrine? Can fair warning be derived from a law against contracts "unduly" restrictive of competition? In evaluating the adequacy of notice, should it matter that an antitrust statute is likely to be applied against persons who have the means and opportunity to seek advice of counsel?

Lastly and perhaps most importantly, how much should it matter that insistence on a more precise statutory standard for antitrust violations might have hamstrung the development of that body of law? Is the difficulty of doing better a sufficient justification for a vague law? Or should the government have been forced to rely on civil remedies unless and until more determinate penal laws could be drafted?

Whatever one's views on the merits of these questions, it is clear that Mr. Justice Holmes' remarks on the prevalence of distinctions of degree remain descriptively accurate. Today, as in 1913, the law is full of instances where the fact or grade of criminal liability turns on an estimate of degree. Assault, for example, may be a felony or a misdemeanor depending on whether the attack caused "serious" bodily harm.[d] The distinction between murder and manslaughter may hinge on whether the defendant suffered from "extreme" emotional distur-

---

[d] See, e.g., N.H.Rev.Stat.Ann. §§ 631:1 and 631:2. The concept of "serious bodily harm" is defined under New Hampshire law to include "harm to the body which causes severe, permanent, or protracted loss of or impairment to the health or the function of any bodily organ." N.H.Rev.Stat.Ann. § 625:11(VI). This definition may clarify the meaning of the phrase, but it does not obviate the necessity to make distinctions of degree.

bance.[e] Indeed, even imposition of the death penalty may depend on whether the accused had a "significant" history of prior criminal activity [f] or whether the circumstances of his crime revealed were "especially" heinous.[g]

In all of these cases and a great many others besides, the law requires that a line be drawn somewhere along a spectrum of infinite gradation. The exact location of that line cannot be known until, as Mr. Justice Holmes noted, "the jury subsequently estimates it." And jury evaluations of this sort are inevitably somewhat ad hoc. Thus, the indefiniteness attendant on questions of degree seems to implicate both of the underlying concerns of the vagueness doctrine. The fact that such uncertainty nonetheless is widely tolerated reflects the importance in the law of distinctions of degree and the perceived impossibility of making such distinctions without marginal vagueness.

6. **Intolerable Vagueness and the Impact of Indefinite Laws on Protected Freedoms.** As the preceding discussion indicates, the difficulty of being more precise is an important factor favoring judicial acceptance of statutory indeterminacy. An equally significant factor cutting the other way is the impact of indefinite laws on constitutionally protected rights. Judicial scrutiny under the vagueness doctrine is most rigorous when the subject matter of the law in question implicates the first-amendment freedoms of speech and press. In no other context is the search for specificity likely to be so demanding; in no other area is the impossibility of more exact legislation so unlikely to be accepted as a justification for vagueness.

The rationale for heightened vagueness scrutiny of laws touching first-amendment freedoms is not hard to discern. Vagueness in this context is especially costly. It is costly not merely in terms of the usual concerns of the vagueness doctrine—lack of fair notice and the prospect of arbitrary enforcement—but also in terms of the unwanted deterrence of constitutionally protected activities. Courts fear that a law of uncertain reach will produce an indiscriminate inhibition of primary conduct. The danger is that a prohibition of indefinite scope will cast a shadow over actions that may not be prohibited. In the traditional terminology of the first amendment, the evil of an imprecise law is that it may have a "chilling effect" on the exercise of protected rights. Thus, the due-process requirement of specificity in the penal law is

[e] See, e. g., 11 Del.Code Ann. § 632(3) (1975); N.Y. Penal Law §§ 125.20(2) and 125.25(1)(a). These statutes are based on the Model Penal Code formulation, which imposes liability for manslaughter where "a homicide which would otherwise be murder is committed under the influence of *extreme* mental or emotional disturbance for which there is reasonable explanation or excuse." MPC § 210.3(1)(b) (emphasis added). Cf. 17–A Me.Rev.Stat.Ann. § 203(1) (B) ("extreme anger or extreme fear"); N.H.Rev.Stat.Ann. § 630:2(I)(a) ("extreme mental or emotional disturbance caused by extreme provocation").

[f] The Arkansas, Florida, and Utah death penalty statutes list among the mitigating circumstances to be considered in determining sentence the fact that the "defendant has no significant history of prior criminal activity." Ark.Stats. § 41–1304(6); Fla.Stat.Ann. § 921.141(6)(a); Utah Code Ann. § 76–3–207(1) (a).

[g] See, e.g., Fla.Stat. § 921.141(5) (identifying as an aggravating circumstance for determination of sentence that the "capital felony was especially heinous, atrocious or cruel"), upheld in Proffitt v. Florida, 428 U.S. 242 (1976).

enforced with special rigor where it also serves to avoid incidental impairment of first-amendment freedoms.

This point was well put by the Supreme Court in N.A.A.C.P. v. Button, 371 U.S. 415 (1963). After noting that the "standards of permissible statutory vagueness are strict in the area of free expression," the Court gave the following justification for this special version of vagueness review:

"The objectionable quality of vagueness and overbreadth does not depend upon absence of fair notice to a criminally accused or upon unchanneled delegation of legislative powers, but upon the danger of tolerating, in the area of first-amendment freedoms, the existence of a penal statute susceptible of sweeping and improper application. These freedoms are delicate and vulnerable, as well as supremely precious in our society. The threat of sanctions may deter their exercise almost as potently as the actual application of sanctions. Because first-amendment freedoms need breathing space to survive, government may regulate in the area only with narrow specificity. . . ." [h]

7. **Concluding Questions and Comments.** One way of putting the disagreement between Justices Rehnquist and Stewart is by asking whether, in Rehnquist's words, Capt. Levy should have "standing" to challenge—that is, be allowed to raise the issue of—the vagueness of arts. 133 and 134 as they might be applied in other cases. The Court of Appeals agreed that Levy's conduct was clearly prohibited by art. 134 but feared its application in other contexts. Justice Rehnquist's response was that some statutes (he cited *Coates v. Cincinatti*) were so vague that they could not constitutionally be invoked against anyone, while other statutes could be applied to conduct clearly prohibited, even though they might be vague in their application to other situations. In the view of the majority, arts. 133 and 134 were in the latter category, and Capt. Levy was not allowed to raise the question of their vagueness in other cases.

With which part or parts of this analysis did Justice Stewart disagree? Did he find arts. 133 and/or 134 vague as applied to the conduct of Capt. Levy? Or was he willing to allow Capt. Levy to raise the issue of their application in other contexts? More generally, what conception of the vagueness doctrine underlies these alternatives?

NOTES ON THE RELATIONSHIP OF VAGUENESS AND OVERBREADTH

1. ***Parker v. Levy* Revisited.** In addition to the issues already considered, part III of the *Parker* opinion dealt with an "overbreadth" attack on arts. 133 and 134. On that issue, Justice Rehnquist said:

[h] Of special relevance to this discussion is Amsterdam, The Void-for-Vagueness Doctrine in the Supreme Court, 109 U.Pa.L.Rev. 67 (1960). Though perhaps a bit dated, Amsterdam's article remains the classic analysis of the vagueness doctrine.

"We likewise reject [Levy's] contention that arts. 133 and 134 are facially invalid because of their 'overbreadth.' In Gooding v. Wilson, 405 U.S. 518, 520–21 (1972), the Court said:

> 'It matters not that the words appellee used might have been constitutionally prohibited under a narrowly and precisely drawn statute. At least when statutes regulate or proscribe speech . . . , the transcendent value to all society of constitutionally protected expression is deemed to justify allowing "attacks on overly broad statutes with no requirement that the person making the attack demonstrate that his own conduct could not be regulated by a statute drawn with the requisite narrow specificity." '
> . . .

"This Court has . . . repeatedly expressed its reluctance to strike down a statute on its face where there were a substantial number of situations to which it might be validly applied. Thus, even if there are marginal applications in which a statute would infringe on first amendment values, facial invalidation is inappropriate if the 'remainder of the statute . . . covers a whole range of easily identifiable and constitutionally proscribable . . . conduct.' . . .

"There is a wide range of the conduct of military personnel to which arts. 133 and 134 may be applied without infringement of the first amendment. While there may lurk at the fringes of the articles, even in the light of their narrowing construction by the United States Court of Military Appeals, some possibility that conduct which would be ultimately held to be protected by the first amendment could be included within their prohibition, we deem this insufficient to invalidate either of them at the behest of [Levy]. His conduct, that of a commissioned officer publicly urging enlisted personnel to refuse to obey orders which might send them into combat, was unprotected under the most expansive notions of the first amendment. Articles 133 and 134 may constitutionally prohibit that conduct, and a sufficiently large number of similar or related types of conduct so as to preclude their invalidation for overbreadth."

2. **The Relation Between Vagueness and Overbreadth: As Applied vs. Facial Review**. The doctrines of vagueness and overbreadth are conceptually distinct, even though they are often factually coincident. The vagueness doctrine states a requirement that meaning be determinable. It is a feature of due process and applies specially, if not exclusively, to the penal law. Any kind of criminal statute, however, may be implicated, for the vices of unfair warning and arbitrary enforcement are not limited by subject matter. Overbreadth, by contrast, is a concern of the first amendment. The term describes the relation of statutory coverage to the constitutionally protected freedoms of speech and press. Specifically, a law is overbroad if it purports to prohibit not only acts that the legislation may forbid, but also acts that the first amendment makes immune to such regulation.

Such a statute is overbroad, as it were, with respect to the permissible scope of legislative power. And since first-amendment freedoms may be impaired by civil statutes as well as by those carrying penal sanctions, the overbreadth doctrine applies in more or less identical terms to both civil and criminal law.

There is, however, more to overbreadth than a name for excessive coverage. The heart of the matter is a posture of judicial review. The doctrine asserts that the constitutionality of an overbroad law should be judged on its face. The result is that the statute is upheld or invalidated in toto and not as it applies in a particular case. This approach is called "facial" review. It permits a person against whom a law is constitutionally enforced to challenge the validity of its potential application in other situations. In essence, the defendant is allowed to raise someone else's rights by attacking the statute as it might be applied to someone else. And if the consideration of these other situations leads to the conclusion that the enactment is overbroad and thus unconstitutional, the litigant in the instant case reaps the windfall benefit of the law's invalidation *with respect to that litigant.*

Facial review is not the usual method of determining constitutionality. A less controversial alternative is to review the constitutionality of a law as it is applied in a particular case. The choice between "as-applied" and "facial" review presents an issue of great subtlety that is principally a subject for debate in constitutional law. Only the essentials of the argument can be noted here. An as-applied decision contributes to a piecemeal reformation of an overbroad law to make it conform to constitutional limitations. At the same time, the legislative will is given effect within its legitimate reach. Thus, as-applied review serves to minimize conflict between courts and legislatures and to give maximum permissible scope to the decisions of the politically responsive branches of government. Additionally, as-applied review may be thought to enhance the quality of judicial decision-making if, as is traditionally supposed, courts function best when confined to the context of a particular case as it is developed through the adversary process.

Facial review, by contrast, extrapolates judicial decision-making far beyond the circumstances of the pending litigation. It calls for the adjudication of constitutional claims only tangentially connected to the case at hand and is therefore a departure from the usual style and context of judicial reasoning. Perhaps most importantly, facial review precipitates confrontation between courts and legislatures. Under its aegis, courts are authorized to invalidate statutes on the basis of hypothetical situations that may never actually arise and thus to deny the legislative judgment even in circumstances where it is entitled to prevail.

It should be clear that judging the constitutionality of a statute on its face rather than as applied contradicts the usual canons of restraint in the exercise of judicial review. The justification for this approach lies in a special solicitude for first-amendment freedoms. As one commentator made the point, the rationale for facial scrutiny "rests on a recognition that the actual application of overbroad laws against privileged activity is not their only vice." Note, The First Amendment Overbreadth Doctrine, 83 Harv.L.Rev. 844, 853 (1970). Even if an overbroad law is never actually invoked against privileged behavior, the apparent sweep of its continued presence on the statute books might cast a shadow of illegality over the exercise of constitutional rights. Facial review therefore "emphasizes the need to eliminate an overbroad law's deterrent impact—or 'chilling effect'—on protected primary conduct." It is a judicial stratagem designed to avoid the in terrorem inhibition of free expression by an overbroad law.

Obviously, the rationale for facial review of overbroad statutes is exactly the same as that advanced to justify intensified vagueness scrutiny of laws touching first-amendment freedoms. Thus, the relation between vagueness and overbreadth is not limited to factual overlap. Where they do overlap, the policies of dealing with the offending statute under one or the other rubric also tend to converge. As the note cited above stated:

> "Both doctrines are responsive to the fact that precision and predictability of governmental intervention are vital to persons planning the exercise of fundamental rights. Both vague and overbroad statutes covering first-amendment activities tend to deter privileged conduct. These facts should not be thought to exclude any independent concern for statutory failure to give fair warning of coverage quite apart from the possibility of first-amendment overbreadth. But [when first-amendment freedoms are involved], the two constitutional vices appear in practice to merge. . . ."

It should not be surprising, therefore, that the courts often blur the distinctions between the concepts and "[use] the idioms of due-process vagueness and first-amendment overbreadth interchangeably." In most cases, this blending of doctrines is inconsequential, but it may promote analytical clarity to think of them separately. It is at least useful to keep in mind that the length and breadth of the vagueness doctrine is not aptly described by those cases in which it serves chiefly as a vehicle for overbreadth concerns.[a]

3. **Concluding Questions and Comments.** Why did the *Parker* majority reject the overbreadth claim of Capt. Levy? Was this argument stronger or weaker than his vagueness claim? Compare the approach of Justice Stewart. Was Stewart using the vagueness doctrine to achieve the kind of facial review normally associated with overbreadth? Or did his opinion rest on a different ground?

---

[a] The best general source on the overbreadth doctrine is the Harvard Law Review note cited in text. For the relation of vagueness and overbreadth, see especially 83 Harv.L.Rev. at 871–75 and L.Tribe, American Constitutional Law §§ 12–28, –29 (1978).

NOTES ON OBSCENITY: A CASE STUDY OF THE VAGUENESS DOCTRINE

1. **The Obscenity Problem.** The first amendment to the Constitution of the United States provides that "Congress shall make no law . . . abridging the freedom of speech . . .". The 14th amendment applies the same limitation to the laws of the states. One might assume that the effect of these provisions is to invalidate any legislative restraint on expression. The law has long been settled, however, that certain instances of "speech" fall outside the protections of the first amendment and thus are subject to legislative regulation. Obscenity is one such instance. At least in the view of the Supreme Court, obscenity is not constitutionally protected speech and may validly be suppressed by appropriate legislation.

Of course, the exclusion of obscenity from the protections of the first amendment is not beyond debate. On the contrary, it is the subject of continuing controversy and disagreement. If that debate is laid to one side, however, there remain imposing difficulties in the use of the criminal law to regulate obscenity. Given that obscenity is excluded from the realm of constitutionally protected speech, it is obviously necessary to define what "obscenity" is. And if the criminal law is to be used to suppress obscenity, the distinct constitutional concern for specificity must be satisfied. The history of the Supreme Court's consideration of the obscenity question centers on the continuing search for precision in the controlling definition. Because precision is hard to attain in this context, the Court's obscenity decisions present an interesting case study in analysis and application of the vagueness doctrine.

2. *Roth* **and** *Memoirs.* The Supreme Court's effort to define obscenity began in Roth v. United States, 354 U.S. 476 (1957). The California statute at issue in *Roth* provided misdemeanor sanctions for "every person who, wilfully and lewdly, . . . writes, composes, stereotypes, prints, publishes, sells, distributes, keeps for sale, or exhibits any obscene or indecent writing, paper, or book; or designs, copies, draws, engraves, paints, or otherwise prepares any obscene or indecent picture or print; or molds, cuts, casts, or otherwise makes any obscene or indecent figure." A companion case involved a federal statute that declared non-mailable, and hence punishable by criminal penalties, "[e]very obscene, lewd, lascivious, or filthy book, pamphlet, picture, paper, letter, writing, print, or other publication of an indecent character . . .." These laws were attacked both on the ground that obscenity should be brought within the "freedom of speech" protected by the first amendment and on the claim that, in any event, the reliance on such words as "obscene" and "indecent" rendered the laws unconstitutionally vague.

The *Roth* Court upheld both statutes. First, the Court held that "obscenity is not within the area of constitutionally protected speech . . .." Then, the Court undertook to formulate a constitutional definition of "obscenity." The test ultimately adopted was this: "whether to the average person, applying contemporary community standards, the dominant theme of the material taken as a whole appeals to the prurient interest." This concept was elaborated by a dictionary definition of "prurient" as meaning "[i]tching; longing; uneasy with desire or longing; of persons having itching, morbid or lascivious longings; of desire, curiosity, or propensity, lewd."

Finally, the *Roth* Court faced and rejected the claim of impermissible vagueness:

> "It is argued that the statutes do not provide reasonably ascertainable standards of guilt and therefore violate the constitutional requirements of due process. The federal obscenity statute makes punishable the mailing of material that is 'obscene, lewd, lascivious, or filthy . . . .'. The California statute makes punishable, inter alia, the keeping for sale or advertising material that is 'obscene or indecent.' The thrust of the argument is that these words are not sufficiently precise because they do not mean the same thing to all people, all the time, everywhere.

> "Many decisions have recognized that these terms of obscenity statutes are not precise. This Court, however, has consistently held that lack of precision is not itself offensive to the requirements of due process. '. . . [T]he Constitution does not require impossible standards'; all that is required is that the language 'conveys sufficiently definite warning as to the proscribed conduct when measured by common understanding and practices. . . .' United States v. Petrillo, 332 U.S. 1, 7–8 (1947). These words, applied according to the proper standard for judging obscenity, already discussed, give adequate warning of the conduct proscribed and mark '. . . boundaries sufficiently distinct for judges and juries fairly to administer the law . . . .' That there may be marginal cases in which it is difficult to determine the side of the line on which a particular fact situation falls is no sufficient reason to hold the language too ambiguous to define a criminal offense.'

> "In summary, then, we hold that these statutes, applied according to the proper standard for judging obscenity, do not offend constitutional safeguards against convictions based upon protected material, or fail to give men in acting adequate notice of what is prohibited."

The years following *Roth* saw increasing disarray in the Supreme Court's approach to obscenity. The test itself was restated and expanded by a plurality of the Court in Memoirs v. Massachusetts, 383 U.S. 413 (1966). This reformulation became known as the *Roth-Memoirs* test and governed obscenity litigation for the next several years. It required the coalescence of three elements:

> "[I]t must be established that (i) the dominant theme of the material taken as a whole appeals to a prurient interest in sex; (ii) the material is patently offensive because it affronts contemporary community standards relating to the description or repre-

sentation of sexual matters; and (iii) the material is utterly without redeeming social value."

This test had the support of a decisive bloc of justices, but since no one approach could command majority support, the Court in Redrup v. New York, 386 U.S. 767 (1967), began the practice of summarily reversing obscenity convictions whenever five justices, using their individual criteria for decision, could agree as to that result. Between 1967 and 1973, some 31 cases were decided by the *Redrup* procedure. As the Court itself noted, no justification other than "the necessity of circumstances" was ever offered for this approach. Miller v. California, 413 U.S. 15, 22 n.3 (1973).

3. **Redefining Obscenity: The 1973 Decisions.** In 1973 the Supreme Court undertook a full scale re-examination of the obscenity area, and a series of decisions announced in June of that year attempted to restructure the inquiry along more manageable lines. The lead case was Miller v. California, 413 U.S. 15 (1973). *Miller* involved the California obscenity statute excerpted below. Note the extent to which the California legislature had based its statute on the *Roth-Memoirs* test for the constitutionality of obscenity:

"Section 311. Definitions.

"As used in this chapter:

"(a) 'Obscene' means that to the average person, applying contemporary standards, the predominant appeal of the matter, taken as a whole, is to prurient interest, i. e., a shameful or morbid interest in nudity, sex, or excretion, which goes substantially beyond customary limits of candor in description or representation of such matters and is matter which is utterly without redeeming social importance.

"(b) 'Matter' means any book, magazine, newspaper, or other printed or written material, or any picture, drawing, photograph, motion picture, or other pictorial representation or any statue or other figure, or any recording, transcription or mechanical, chemical or electrical reproduction or any other articles, equipment, machines or materials. . . .

"Section 311.2. Sending or bringing into state for sale or distribution; printing, exhibiting, distributing or possessing within state.

"(a) Every person who knowingly: sends or causes to be sent, or brings or causes to be brought, into this state for sale or distribution, or in this state prepares, publishes, prints, exhibits, distributes, or offers to distribute, or has in his possession with intent to distribute or to exhibit or offer to distribute, any obscene matter is guilty of a misdemeanor. . . . "

The defendant in *Miller* had been convicted for conducting a mass-mailing campaign to advertise "adult" books bearing such titles as "Intercourse," "Sex Orgies Illustrated," and "An Illustrated History of Pornography." Illustrated brochures advertising these products were mailed, unsolicited, to the homes of California residents. The brochures themselves were found to constitute "obscene matter" within the meaning of the statute.

The Supreme Court affirmed in an opinion by Chief Justice Burger:

"This much has been categorically settled by the Court, that obscene material is unprotected by the first amendment. . . . We acknowledge, however, the inherent dangers of undertaking to regulate any form of expression. State statutes designed to regulate obscene materials must be carefully limited. As a result, we now confine the permissible scope of such regulation to works which depict or describe sexual conduct. That conduct must be specifically defined by the applicable state law, as written or authoritatively construed. A state offense must also be limited to works which, taken as a whole, appeal to the prurient interest in sex, which portray sexual conduct in a patently offensive way, and which, taken as a whole, do not have serious literary, artistic, political, or scientific value.

"The basic guidelines for the trier of fact must be: (i) whether 'the average person, applying contemporary community standards' would find that the work, taken as a whole, appeals to the prurient interest; (ii) whether the work depicts or describes, in a patently offensive way, sexual conduct specifically defined by the applicable state law; and (iii) whether the work, taken as a whole, lacks serious literary, artistic, political, or scientific value. . . .

"We emphasize that it is not our function to propose regulatory schemes for the states. That must await their concrete legislative efforts. It is possible, however, to give a few plain examples of what a state statute could define for regulation under part (ii) of the standard announced in this opinion, supra:

"(a) Patently offensive representations or descriptions of ultimate sexual acts, normal or perverted, actual or simulated.

"(b) Patently offensive representations or descriptions of masturbation, excretory functions, and lewd exhibition of the genitals.

"Sex and nudity may not be exploited without limit by films or pictures exhibited or sold in places of public accommodation any more than live sex and nudity can be exhibited or sold without limit in such public places. At a minimum, prurient, patently offensive depiction or description of sexual conduct must have serious literary, artistic, political, or scientific value to merit first-amendment protection. For example, medical books for the education of physicians and related personnel necessarily use graphic illustrations and descriptions of human anatomy. In resolving the inevitably sensitive questions of fact and law, we must continue to rely on the jury system, accompanied by the safeguards that judges, rules of evidence, presumption of innocence, and other protective features provide, as we do with rape, murder, and a host of other offenses against society and its individual members. [9] . . ."

Additional portions of the *Miller* opinion dealt with the "contemporary community standards" aspect of the definition of obscenity. The majority rejected the contention that there had to be a fixed, national standard for determining what is obscene. In the course of this discussion, the Court threw additional light on the kinds of judgments it expected jurors to make in deciding obscenity cases:

"Under a national Constitution, fundamental first-amendment limitations on the powers of the states do not vary from community to community, but this does not mean that there are, or should or can be, fixed, uniform national standards of precisely what appeals to the 'prurient interest' or is 'patently offensive.' These are essentially questions of fact, and our nation is simply too big and too diverse for this Court to reasonably expect that such standards could be articulated for all 50 states in a single formulation, even assuming the prerequisite consensus exists. When triers of fact are asked to decide whether 'the average person, applying contemporary community standards' would consider certain materials 'prurient,' it would be unrealistic to require that the answer be based on some abstract formulation. The adversary system, with lay jurors as the usual ultimate factfinders in criminal prosecutions, has historically permitted triers of fact to draw on the standards of their community, guided always by limiting instructions on the law. . . . [a]

"It is neither realistic nor constitutionally sound to read the first amendment as requiring that the people of Maine or Mississippi accept public depiction of conduct found tolerable in Las Vegas, or New York City. People in different states vary in their tastes and attitudes, and this diversity is not to be strangled by the absolutism of imposed uniformity. . . . [T]he primary concern with requiring a jury to apply the standard of 'the average person, applying contemporary community standards' is to be certain that, so far as material is not aimed at a deviant group, it will be judged by its impact on an average person, rather than a particularly susceptible or sensitive person—or

"[9] The mere fact juries may reach different conclusions as to the same materials does not mean that constitutional rights are abridged. As this Court observed in *Roth*, 'it is common experience that different juries may reach different results under any criminal statute. That is one of the consequences we accept under our jury system.'"

[a] To what extent does this approach remit the determination of obscenity to the unreviewable discretion of a jury? Does the jury provide an effective safeguard against arbitrary and discriminatory application of a vague concept? Is the *Miller* decision based on the assumption that it does?

In this connection note that the Supreme Court has established that at least some jury determinations of obscenity will not be upheld. In Jenkins v. Georgia, 418 U.S. 153 (1974), the Court reversed an obscenity conviction based on the determination of a Georgia jury that the film "Carnal Knowledge" (starring Candice Bergen and Jack Nicholson) was obscene. Speaking for a unanimous Court, Mr. Justice Rehnquist stated that the justices' own viewing of the film had convinced them that it was not obscene within the *Miller* standards. [Footnote by eds.]

indeed a totally insensitive one. We hold that the requirement that the jury evaluate the materials with reference to 'contemporary standards of the state of California' serves this protective purpose and is constitutionally adequate."

A companion case was decided on the same day. In Paris Adult Theatre I v. Slaton, 413 U.S. 49 (1973), a local district attorney filed a civil complaint seeking injunctive relief against the showing of two movies said to violate the Georgia criminal obscenity statute. The Georgia statute was similar to the California provision considered in *Miller*. The contention advanced to distinguish the two cases was that the movie theaters should be treated differently because they were open only to consenting adults (recall that *Miller* involved unsolicited mailings). The Supreme Court found this difference constitutionally insignificant and remanded the case for proceedings not inconsistent with *Miller*.

4. **The Brennan Dissent.** In *Paris Adult Theatre*, Mr. Justice Brennan filed a 41-page dissenting opinion on behalf of himself and Justices Stewart and Marshall. This dissent focuses on the facts of *Paris Adult Theatre* but responds generally to the issues dealt with in *Miller*. It begins as follows:

"This case requires the Court to confront once again the vexing problem of reconciling state efforts to suppress sexually oriented expression with the protections of the first amendment . . . . No other aspect of the first amendment has, in recent years, demanded so substantial a commitment of our time, generated such disharmony of views, and remained so resistant to the formulation of stable and manageable standards. I am convinced that the approach initiated 16 years ago in *Roth*, and culminating in the Court's decision today, cannot bring stability to this area of the law without jeopardizing fundamental first-amendment values, and I have concluded that the time has come to make a significant departure from that approach." [b]

The new approach suggested by Justice Brennan was to hold unconstitutional all laws punishing obscenity as such. He left open the question whether narrower statutes dealing with such particular problems as the distribution of obscenity to juveniles or exhibition to unconsenting adults could be sustained. He thus indicated that he might vote to affirm a conviction on the facts involved in *Miller*, but only under a more narrowly drawn law.

It is important to note that Justice Brennan did not base his suggested new approach on the contention that obscenity is constitutionally protected speech. He indicated in a footnote that he found that view plausible, at least as to consenting adults, but he expressly disclaimed reliance on this rationale.[c] Instead, he grounded his attack squarely on the concerns of vagueness:

"In *Roth*, the Court held that obscenity, although expression, falls outside the area of speech or press constitutionally protected

[b] Mr. Justice Brennan wrote the opinion of the Court in *Roth*. [Footnote by eds.]

[c] "Whether or not a class of 'obscene' and thus entirely unprotected speech does

under the first and 14th amendments against state or federal infringement. . . . [T]hat approach has been endorsed by all but two members of this Court who have addressed the question since *Roth.* Yet our efforts to implement that approach demonstrate that agreement on the existence of something called 'obscenity' is still a long and painful step from agreement on a workable definition of that term.

"Recognizing that 'the freedoms of expression . . . are vulnerable to gravely damaging yet barely visible encroachments,' we have demanded that 'sensitive tools' be used to carry out the 'separation of legitimate from illegitimate speech.' The essence of our problem in the obscenity area is that we have been unable to provide 'sensitive tools' to separate obscenity from other sexually oriented but constitutionally protected speech, so that efforts to suppress the former do not spill over into the suppression of the latter."

Justice Brennan then recounted the history of *Roth* and *Memoirs.* He described the *Miller* Court's redefinition of obscenity as "a slightly altered formulation of the basic *Roth* test" and launched an attack on the entire approach:

"Our experience with the *Roth* approach has certainly taught us that the outright suppression of obscenity cannot be reconciled with the fundamental principles of the first and 14th amendments. For we have failed to formulate a standard that sharply distinguishes protected from unprotected speech, and out of necessity, we have resorted to the *Redrup* approach, which resolves cases as between the parties, but offers only the most obscure guidance to legislation, adjudication by other courts, and primary conduct. . . .

"Of course, the vagueness problem would be largely of our own creation if it stemmed primarily from our failure to reach a consensus on any one standard. But after 16 years of experimentation and debate I am reluctantly forced to the conclusion that none of the available formulas, including the one announced today, can reduce the vagueness to a tolerable level . . . . Any effort to draw a constitutionally acceptable boundary on state power must resort to such indefinite concepts as 'prurient interest,' 'patent offensiveness,' 'serious literary value,' and the like. The meaning of these concepts necessarily varies with the experience, outlook, and even idiosyncrasies of the person defining them. Although we have assumed that obscenity does exist and that we 'know it when [we] see it,' Jacobellis v. Ohio, 378 U.S. 184, 197 (1964) (Stewart, J., concurring), we are manifestly unable to describe it in advance except by reference to concepts so elusive that they fail to distinguish clearly between protected and unprotected speech. . . .

exist, I am forced to conclude that the class is incapable of definition with sufficient clarity to withstand attack on vagueness grounds. Accordingly, it is on principles of the void-for-vagueness doctrine that this opinion exclusively relies."

"The vagueness of the standards in the obscenity area produces a number of separate problems, and any improvement must rest on an understanding that the problems are to some extent distinct. First, a vague statute fails to provide adequate notice to persons who are engaged in the type of conduct that the statute could be thought to proscribe. . . . In this context, even the most painstaking efforts to determine in advance whether certain sexually oriented expression is obscene must inevitably prove unavailing. For the insufficiency of the notice compels persons to guess not only whether their conduct is covered by a criminal statute, but also whether their conduct falls within the constitutionally permissible reach of the statute. The resulting level of uncertainty is utterly intolerable, not alone because it makes '[b]ookselling . . . a hazardous profession,' but as well because it invites arbitrary and erratic enforcement of the law.

"In addition to problems that arise when any criminal statute fails to afford fair notice of what it forbids, a vague statute in the areas of speech and press creates a second level of difficulty. We have indicated that 'stricter standards of permissible statutory vagueness may be applied to a statute having a potentially inhibiting effect on speech; a man may the less be required to act at his peril here, because the free dissemination of ideas may be the loser.' . . .

"The problems of fair notice and chilling protected speech are very grave standing alone. But it does not detract from their importance to recognize that a vague statute in this area creates a third, although admittedly more subtle, set of problems. These problems concern the institutional stress that inevitably results where the line separating protected from unprotected speech is excessively vague. In *Roth* we conceded that 'there may be marginal cases in which it is difficult to determine the side of the line on which a particular fact situation falls. . . .' Our subsequent experience demonstrates that almost every case is 'marginal.' And since the 'margin' marks the point of separation between protected and unprotected speech, we are left with a system in which almost every obscenity case presents a constitutional question of exceptional difficulty."

On the basis of these difficulties, Justice Brennan concluded that the approach initiated in *Roth* should be abandoned. He then discussed alternative approaches to the regulation of obscenity and surveyed the various state interests involved. He concluded as follows:

"I would hold, therefore, that at least in the absence of distribution to juveniles or obtrusive exposure to unconsenting adults, the first and 14th amendments prohibit the state and federal governments from attempting wholly to suppress sexually oriented materials on the basis of their allegedly 'obscene' contents. Nothing in this approach precludes those governments from taking action to serve what may be strong and legitimate interests through regulation of the manner or distribution of sexually oriented material.

". . . I do not pretend to have found a complete and infallible answer to what Mr. Justice Harlan called 'the intractable obscenity problem.' Difficult questions must still be faced, notably in the areas of distribution to juveniles and offensive exposure to unconsenting adults. Whatever the extent of state power to regulate in those areas, it should be clear that the view I espouse today would introduce a large measure of clarity to this troubled area, would reduce the institutional pressure on this Court and the rest of the state and federal judiciary, and would guarantee fuller freedom of expression while leaving room for the protection of legitimate governmental interests. . . ."

5. **Questions and Comments on Vagueness and Obscenity**. Is Justice Brennan justified in claiming that his approach would bring "a large measure of clarity" to the regulation of obscenity? Does the answer depend on the position he would take with respect to legislation prohibiting the distribution of obscenity to juveniles or its exhibition to unconsenting adults? If, under Brennan's approach, the state and federal governments would remain free to address those problems, would it not still be necessary to adopt a constitutional definition of obscenity? How else could the law distinguish expression that may be barred as to juveniles from expression that may not be constrained? And if obscenity can be defined satisfactorily for the purpose of controlling dissemination to children, why does that same definition not also suffice for legislation of a broader scope?

On the other hand, adoption of Brennan's position would preclude application of arguably vague obscenity statutes to situations involving consenting adults. To this extent, his solution would reduce the impact of an indefinite standard of penal liability. As a matter of social policy, moreover, this is the context in which obscenity legislation is most controversial. This solution, however, would have its costs. If, Brennan's position would achieve "a large measure of clarity" in the context of consenting adults, it would do so at the cost of substantially negating legislative authority to suppress obscene matter. And Brennan admits, at least for purposes of this opinion, that legislative action to achieve that end is constitutionally permissible. Thus, the upshot of Brennan's approach would be to deny legislative authority to control obscenity because of a lack of acceptable means to accomplish its purpose. Is this result justified? Should the vagueness doctrine be invoked where there is no reasonable prospect of greater precision? Is the majority position in *Miller* defensible on this basis? Does it matter why the legislature wants to punish obscenity? Whether speech that borders on the obscene is regarded as constitutionally important? Recall the discussion in *Nash* v. *United States*, quoted at pages 69–70, supra. Would Justice Brennan's analysis suggest that the decision was wrong? Or are *Nash* and the obscenity cases distinguishable?

Finally, it should be noted that the vagueness of the constitutional definition of obscenity is not in any meaningful sense attributable to legislative error. Justice Brennan is arguing for invalidation of a standard conceived and formulated by judges. Of course, that fact has little, if any, impact on the concerns of fair warning and non-discriminatory enforcement. At a minimum, therefore, the obscenity dispute confirms that the vagueness doctrine has less to do with separation of powers and the allocation of authority among institutions of government than it does with the unfairness that may result from an indefinite standard of liability.

SECTION 2: CONDUCT IN THE DEFINITION OF THE OFFENSE

SUBSECTION A: ACTS

KEELER v. SUPERIOR COURT OF AMADOR COUNTY

Supreme Court of California, 1970.
2 Cal.3d 619, 87 Cal.Rptr. 481, 470 P.2d 617.

Mosk, J. In this proceeding for [a] writ of prohibition we are called upon to decide whether an unborn but viable fetus is a "human being" within the meaning of the California statute defining murder, Cal.Penal Code § 187. We conclude that the legislature did not intend such a meaning, and that for us to construe the statute to the contrary and apply it to this petitioner would exceed our judicial power and deny petitioner due process of law.

The evidence received at the preliminary examination may be summarized as follows: Petitioner and Teresa Keeler obtained an interlocutory decree of divorce on September 27, 1968. They had been married for 16 years. Unknown to petitioner, Mrs. Keeler was then pregnant by one Ernest Vogt, whom she had met earlier that summer. She subsequently began living with Vogt in Stockton, but concealed the fact from petitioner. Petitioner was given custody of their two daughters, aged 12 and 13 years, and under the decree Mrs. Keeler had the right to take the girls on alternate weekends.

On February 23, 1969, Mrs. Keeler was driving on a narrow mountain road in Amador County after delivering the girls to their home. She met petitioner driving in the opposite direction; he blocked the road with his car, and she pulled over to the side. He walked to her vehicle and began speaking to her. He seemed calm, and she rolled down her window to hear him. He said, "I hear you're pregnant. If you are you had better stay away from the girls and from here." She did not reply, and he opened the car door; as she later testified, "He assisted me out of the car. . . . [I]t wasn't roughly at this time." Petitioner then looked at her abdomen and became "extremely upset."

He said, "You sure are. I'm going to stomp it out of you." He pushed her against the car, shoved his knee into her abdomen, and struck her in the face with several blows. She fainted, and when she regained consciousness petitioner had departed.

Mrs. Keeler drove back to Stockton, and the police and medical assistance were summoned. She had suffered substantial facial injuries, as well as extensive bruising of the abdominal wall. A caesarian section was performed and the fetus was examined in utero. Its head was found to be severely fractured, and it was delivered stillborn. The pathologist gave as his opinion that the cause of death was skull fracture with consequent cerebral hemorrhaging, that death would have been immediate, and that the injury could have been the result of force applied to the mother's abdomen. There was no air in the fetus' lungs, and the umbilical cord was intact.

Upon delivery the fetus weighed five pounds and was 18 inches in length. Both Mrs. Keeler and her obstetrician testified that fetal movements had been observed prior to February 23, 1969. The evidence was in conflict as to the estimated age of the fetus; the expert testimony on the point, however, concluded "with reasonable medical certainty" that the fetus had developed to the stage of viability, i.e., that in the event of premature birth on the date in question it would have had a 75 per cent to 96 per cent chance of survival.

An information was filed charging petitioner, in count I, with committing the crime of murder in that he did "unlawfully kill a human being, to wit Baby Girl Vogt, with malice aforethought." . . . His motion to set aside the information for lack of probable cause was denied, and he now seeks a writ of prohibition. . . .

Penal Code Section 187 provides: "Murder is the unlawful killing of a human being, with malice aforethought." The dispositive question is whether the fetus which petitioner is accused of killing was, on February 23, 1969, a "human being" within the meaning of the statute. If it was not, petitioner cannot be charged with its "murder" and prohibition will lie.

Section 187 was enacted as part of the Penal Code of 1872. Inasmuch as the provision has not been amended since that date, we must determine the intent of the legislature at the time of its enactment. But Section 187 was, in turn, taken verbatim from the first California statute defining murder, part of the Crimes and Punishments Act of 1850. Penal Code Section 5 (also enacted in 1872) declares: "The provisions of this code, so far as they are substantially the same as existing statutes, must be construed as continuations thereof, and not as new enactments." We begin, accordingly, by inquiring into the intent of the legislature in 1850 when it first defined a murder as the unlawful and malicious killing of a "human being."

It will be presumed, of course, that in enacting a statute the legislature was familiar with the relevant rules of the common law, and, when it couches its enactment in common-law language, that its intent was to continue those rules in statutory form. This is particularly appropriate in considering the work of the first session of our legislature: its precedents were necessarily drawn from the common law, as modified in certain respects by the Constitution and by legislation of our sister states.

We therefore undertake a brief review of the origins and development of the common law of abortional homicide. [An extensive review of English cases and authorities revealed that an infant could not be the subject of criminal homicide at common law unless it had been born alive.]

By the year 1850 this rule of the common law had long been accepted in the United States. As early as 1797 it was held that proof the child was born alive is necessary to support an indictment for murder . . . .

While it was thus "well settled" in American case law that the killing of an unborn child was not homicide, a number of state legislatures in the first half of the 19th century undertook to modify the common law in this respect. [The court then discussed the enactment in New York and in a few other states, but not in California, of statutes specially directed against feticide.]

We conclude that in declaring murder to be the unlawful and malicious killing of a "human being" the legislature of 1850 intended that term to have the settled common-law meaning of a person who had been born alive, and did not intend the act of feticide—as distinguished from abortion—to be an offense under the laws of California.

Nothing occurred between the years 1850 and 1872 to suggest that in adopting the new penal code on the latter date the legislature entertained any different intent. The case law of our sister states, for example, remained consonant with the common law. . . .

Any lingering doubt on this subject must be laid to rest by a consideration of the legislative history of the Penal Code of 1872. The act establishing the California Code Commission required the commissioners to revise all statutes then in force, correct errors and omissions, and "recommend all such enactments as shall, in the judgment of the commission, be necessary to supply the defects of and give completeness to the existing legislation of the state. . . ." In discharging this duty the statutory schemes of our sister states were carefully examined, and we must assume the commissioners had knowledge of the feticide laws noted hereinabove. Yet the commissioners proposed no such law for California, and none has been adopted to this day. . . .

It is the policy of this state to construe a penal statute as favorably to the defendant as its language and the circumstances of its application may reasonably permit; just as in the case of a question of fact, the defendant is entitled to the benefit of every reasonable doubt as to the true interpretation of words or the construction of language used in a statute. We hold that in adopting the definition of murder in Penal Code Section 187 the legislature intended to exclude from its reach the act of killing an unborn fetus.

The People urge, however, that the sciences of obstetrics and pediatrics have greatly progressed since 1872, to the point where with proper medical care a normally developed fetus prematurely born at 28 weeks or more has an excellent chance of survival, i.e., is "viable"; that the common-law requirement of live birth to prove the fetus had become a "human being" who may be the victim of murder is no longer in accord with scientific fact, since an unborn but viable fetus is now fully capable of independent life; and that one who unlawfully and maliciously terminated such a life should therefore be liable to prosecution for murder under Section 187. We may grant the premises of this argument; indeed, we neither deny nor denigrate the vast progress of medicine in the century since the enactment of the Penal Code. But we cannot join in the conclusion sought to be deduced: we cannot hold this petitioner to answer for murder by reason of his alleged act of killing an unborn—even though viable—fetus. To such a charge there are two insuperable obstacles, one "jurisdictional" and the other constitutional.

Penal Code Section 6 declares in relevant part that "[n]o act or omission" accomplished after the code has taken effect "is criminal or punishable, except as prescribed or authorized by this code, or by some of the statutes which it specifies as continuing in force and as not affected by its provisions, or by some ordinance, municipal, county, or township regulation. . . ." This section embodies a fundamental principle of our tripartite form of government, i.e., that subject to the constitutional prohibition against cruel and unusual punishment, the power to define crimes and fix penalties is vested exclusively in the legislative branch. Stated differently, there are no common-law crimes in California. . . .

Settled rules of construction implement this principle. Although the Penal Code commands us to construe its provisions "according to the fair import of their terms, with a view to effect its objects and to promote justice," Cal.Penal Code § 4, it is clear the courts cannot go so far as to create an offense by enlarging a statute, by inserting or deleting words, or by giving the terms used false or unusual meanings. Penal statutes will not be made to reach beyond their plain intent; they include only those offenses coming clearly within the import of their language. . . .

Applying these rules to the case at bar, we would undoubtedly act in excess of the judicial power if we were to adopt the People's proposed construction of Section 187. As we have shown, the legislature has defined the crime of murder in California to apply only to the unlawful and malicious killing of one who has been born alive. We recognize that the killing of an unborn but viable fetus may be deemed by some to be an offense of similar nature and gravity; but as Chief Justice Marshall warned long ago, "[i]t would be dangerous, indeed, to carry the principle, that a case which is within the reason or mischief of a statute, is within its provisions, so far as to punish a crime not enumerated in the statute, because it is of equal atrocity, or of kindred character, with those which are enumerated." Whether to thus extend liability for murder in California is a determination solely within the province of the legislature. For a court to simply declare, by judicial fiat, that the time has now come to prosecute under Section 187 one who kills an unborn but viable fetus would indeed be to rewrite the statute under the guise of construing it. Nor does a need to fill an asserted "gap" in the law between abortion and homicide—as will appear, no such gap in fact exists—justify judicial legislation of this nature: to make it a "judicial function 'to explore such new fields of crime as they may appear from time to time' is wholly foreign to the American concept of criminal justice" and "raises very serious questions concerning the principle of separation of powers."

The second obstacle to the proposed judicial enlargement of Section 187 is the guarantee of due process of law. Assuming arguendo that we have the power to adopt the new construction of this statute as the law of California, such a ruling, by constitutional command, could operate only prospectively, and thus could not in any event reach the conduct of petitioner on February 23, 1969.

The first essential of due process is fair warning of the act which is made punishable as a crime. "That the terms of a penal statute creating a new offense must be sufficiently explicit to inform those who are subject to it what conduct on their part will render them liable to its penalties, is a well-recognized requirement, consonant alike with ordinary notions of fair play and the settled rules of law." Connally v. Gen. Const. Co., 269 U.S. 385, 391 (1926). "No one may be required at peril of life, liberty or property to speculate as to the meaning of penal statutes. All are entitled to be informed as to what the state commands or forbids." Lanzetta v. New Jersey, 306 U.S. 451, 453 (1939).
. . .

This requirement of fair warning is reflected in the constitutional prohibition against the enactment of ex post facto laws, U.S.Const. art. I, §§ 9, 10; Cal.Const. art. I, § 16. When a new penal statute is applied retrospectively to make punishable an act which was not criminal at the time it was performed, the defendant has been given no advance notice consistent with due process. And precisely the same effect occurs when such an act is made punishable under a pre-existing statute but by means of an unforeseeable *judicial* enlargement thereof. Bouie v. City of Columbia, 378 U.S. 347 (1964).

In *Bouie* two Negroes took seats in the restaurant section of a South Carolina drugstore; no notices were posted restricting the area to whites only. When the defendants refused to leave upon demand, they were arrested and convicted of violating a criminal trespass statute which prohibited entry on the property of another "after notice" forbidding such conduct. Prior South Carolina decisions had emphasized the necessity of proving such notice to support a conviction under the statute. The South Carolina Supreme Court nevertheless affirmed the convictions, construing the statute to prohibit not only the act of entering after notice not to do so but also the wholly different act of remaining on the property after receiving notice to leave.

The United States Supreme Court reversed the convictions, holding that the South Carolina court's ruling was "unforeseeable" and when an "unforeseeable state-court construction of a criminal statute is applied retroactively to subject a person to criminal liability for past conduct, the effect is to deprive him of due process of law in the sense of fair warning that his contemplated conduct constitutes a crime." Analogizing to the prohibition against retrospective penal legislation, the high court reasoned "Indeed, an unforeseeable judicial enlargement of a criminal statute, applied retroactively, operates precisely like an ex post facto law, such as Art. I, § 10, of the Constitution forbids. An ex post facto law has been defined by this Court as one 'that makes an action done before the passing of the law, and which was *innocent* when done, criminal; and punishes such action,' or 'that *aggravates* a *crime*, or makes it *greater* than it was, when committed.' If a state legislature is barred by the ex post facto clause from passing such a law, it must follow that a state supreme court is barred by the due process clause from achieving precisely the same result by judicial construction. The fundamental principle that 'the required criminal law must have existed when the conduct in issue occurred,' must apply to bar retroactive criminal prohibitions emanating from courts as well as from legislatures. If a judicial construction of a criminal statute is 'unexpected and indefensible by reference to the law which had been expressed prior to the conduct in issue,' it must not be given retroactive effect."

. . .

It is true that Section 187, on its face, is not as "narrow and precise" as the South Carolina statute involved in *Bouie*; on the other hand, neither is it as vague as the statutes struck down in *Connally* and *Lanzetta*. Rather, Section 187 bears a plain, common-sense meaning, well settled in the common law and fortified by its legislative history in California. In *Bouie*, moreover, the Court stressed that a breach of the peace statute was also in force in South Carolina at the time of the events, and that the defendants were in fact arrested on that ground and prosecuted (but not convicted) for that offense. Here, too, there was another statute on the books which petitioner could well have believed he was violating: Penal Code Section 274 defines the crime of abortion, in relevant part, as the act of "[e]very person who . . . uses or employs any instrument *or any other means whatever*, with intent thereby to procure the miscarriage" of any woman, and does not come within the exceptions provided by law. The gist of the crime is the performance, with the requisite intent, of any of the acts enumerated in the statute. It is therefore no defense to a charge of violating Section 274 that the act was committed unusually late in the woman's pregnancy or by a method not commonly employed for that purpose.

. . .

Turning to the case law, we find no reported decisions of the California courts which should have given petitioner notice that the killing of an unborn but viable fetus was prohibited by Section 187.

. . .

Properly understood, the often cited case of People v. Chavez, 77 Cal.App.2d 621, 176 P.2d 92 (1947), does not derogate from this rule. There the defendant was charged with the murder of her newborn child, and convicted of manslaughter. She testified that the baby dropped from her womb into the toilet bowl; that she picked it up two or three minutes later, and cut but did not tie the umbilical cord; that the baby was limp and made no cry; and that after 15 minutes she wrapped it in a newspaper and concealed it, where it was found dead the next day. The autopsy surgeon testified that the baby was a full-term, nine-month child, weighing six and one-half pounds and appearing normal in every respect; that the body had very little blood in it, indicating the child had bled to death through the untied umbilical cord; that such a process would have taken about an hour; and that in his opinion "the child was born alive, based on conditions he found and the fact that the lungs contained air and the blood was extravasated or pushed back into the tissues, indicating heart action."

On appeal, the defendant emphasized that a doctor called by the defense had suggested other tests which the autopsy surgeon could have performed to determine the matter of live birth; on this basis, it was contended that the question of whether the infant was born alive "rests entirely on pure speculation." The Court of Appeals found only an insignificant conflict in that regard, and focused its attention instead on testimony of the autopsy surgeon admitting the possibility that the evidence of heart and lung action could have resulted from the child's breathing "after presentation of the head but before the birth was completed."

The court cited [various] mid-19th century English infanticide cases . . . and noted that the decisions had not reached uniformity on whether breathing, heart action, severance of the umbilical cord, or some combination of these or other factors established the status of "human being" for the purposes of the law of homicide. The court then adverted to the state of modern medical knowledge, discussed the phenomenon of viability, and held that "a viable child *in the process of being born* is a human being within the meaning of the homicide statutes, whether or not the process has been fully completed. It should at least be considered a human being where it is a living baby and where in the natural course of events *a birth which is already started* would naturally be successfully completed." (Italics added.) Since the testimony of the autopsy surgeon left no doubt in that case that a live birth had at least begun, the court found "the evidence is sufficient here to support the implied finding of the jury that this child *was born alive and became a human being within the meaning of the homicide statutes.*" (Italics added.)

Chavez thus stands for the proposition—to which we adhere—that a viable fetus "in the process of being born" is a human being within the meaning of the homicide statutes. But it stands for no more; in particular it does not hold that a fetus, however viable, which is *not* "in the process of being born" is nevertheless a "human being" in the law of homicide. On the contrary, the opinion is replete with references to the common-law requirement that the child be "born alive," however that term is defined, and must accordingly be deemed to reaffirm that requirement as part of the law of California. . . .

We conclude that the judicial enlargement of Section 187 now urged upon us by the People would not have been foreseeable to this petitioner, and hence that its adoption at this time would deny him due process of law.

Let a peremptory writ of prohibition issue restraining respondent court from taking any further proceedings on Count I of the information, charging petitioner with the crime of murder.

BURKE, ACTING C.J. [dissenting].   The majority hold that "Baby Girl" Vogt, who, according to medical testimony, had reached the 35th week of development, had a 96 percent chance of survival, and was "definitely" alive and viable at the time of her death, nevertheless was not a "human being" under California's homicide statutes.   In my view, in so holding, the majority ignore significant common-law precedents, frustrate the express intent of the legislature, and defy reason, logic and common sense.   . . .

The majority opinion suggests that we are confined to common-law concepts, and to the common-law definition of murder or manslaughter. However, the legislature, in Penal Code Sections 187 and 192, has defined those offenses: homicide is the unlawful killing of a "human being."   These words need not be frozen in place as of any particular time, but must be fairly and reasonably interpreted by this court to promote justice and to carry out the purposes of the legislature in adopting a homicide statute.   Thus, Penal Code Section 4, which was enacted in 1872 along with Sections 187 and 192, provides: "The rule of the common law, that penal statutes are to be strictly construed, has no application to this code.   All its provisions are to be construed according to the fair import of their terms, with a view to effect its objects and to promote justice."   . . .

Penal Code Section 4, which abolishes the common-law principle of the strict construction of penal statutes,   . . .   permits this court fairly to construe the terms of those statutes to serve the ends of justice.   Consequently, nothing should prevent this court from holding that Baby Girl Vogt was a human ("belonging or relating to man; characteristic of man")[4] being ("existence, as opp. to nonexistence; specif. life")[5] under California's homicide statutes.

We commonly conceive of human existence as a spectrum stretching from birth to death.   However, if this court properly might expand the definition of "human being" at one end of that spectrum, we may do so at the other end.   Consider the following examples: All would agree that "shooting or otherwise damaging a corpse is not homicide . . . ."   In other words, a corpse is not considered to be a "human being" and thus cannot be the subject of a "killing" as those terms are used in the homicide statutes.   However, it is readily apparent that our concepts of what constitutes a "corpse" have been and are being continually modified by advances in the field of medicine, including new techniques for life revival, restoration and resuscitation such as artificial respiration, open heart massage, transfusions, transplants and

[4] Webster's New International Dictionary (2d ed. 1959), page 1211, column 3.

[5] Id.   at 247.

a variety of life-restoring stimulants, drugs and new surgical methods. Would this court ignore these developments and exonerate the killer of an apparently "drowned" child merely because that child would have been pronounced dead in 1648 or 1850? Obviously not. Whether a homicide occurred in that case would be determined by medical testimony regarding capability of the child to have survived prior to the defendant's act. And that is precisely the test which this court should adopt in the instant case.

The common-law reluctance to characterize the killing of a quickened fetus as a homicide was based solely upon a presumption that the fetus would have been born dead. This presumption seems to have persisted in this country at least as late as 1876. Based upon the state of the medical art in the 17th, 18th and 19th centuries, that presumption may have been well-founded. However, as we approach the 21st century, it has been apparent that "This presumption is not only contrary to common experience and the ordinary course of nature, but it is contrary to the usual rule with respect to presumptions followed in this state." *People* v. *Chavez*, supra.

There are no accurate statistics disclosing fetal death rates in "common-law England," although the foregoing presumption of death indicates a significantly high death experience. On the other hand, in California the fetal death rate [6] in 1968 is estimated to be 12 deaths in 1,000, a ratio which would have given Baby Girl Vogt a 98.8 per cent chance of survival. If, as I have contended, the term "human being" in our homicide statutes is a fluid concept to be defined in accordance with present conditions, then there can be no question that the term should include the fully viable fetus.

The majority suggests that to do so would improperly create some new offense. However, the offense of murder is no new offense. Contrary to the majority opinion, the legislature has not "defined the crime of murder in California to apply only to the unlawful and malicious killing of one who has been born alive." Instead, the legislature simply used the term "human being" and directed the courts to construe that term according to its "fair import" with a view to effect the objects of the homicide statutes and promote justice. Cal.Penal Code § 4. What justice will be promoted, what objects effectuated, by construing "human being" as excluding Baby Girl Vogt and her unfortunate successors? Was defendant's brutal act of stomping her to death any less an act of homicide than the murder of a newly born baby? No one doubts that the term "human being" would include the elderly or dying persons whose potential for life has nearly lapsed; their proximity to death is deemed immaterial. There is no sound reason for denying the viable fetus, with its unbounded potential for life, the same status.

The majority also suggest that such an interpretation of our homicide statutes would deny defendant "fair warning" that his act was punishable as a crime. Aside from the absurdity of the underlying

[6] I.e., fetal deaths of 20 weeks or more gestation.

premise that defendant consulted Coke, Blackstone or Hale before kicking Baby Girl Vogt to death, it is clear that defendant had adequate notice that his act could constitute homicide. Due process only precludes prosecution under a new statute insufficiently explicit regarding the specific conduct proscribed, or under a pre-existing statute "by means of an unforeseeable *judicial* enlargement thereof."

Our homicide statutes have been in effect in this state since 1850. The fact that the California courts have not been called upon to determine the precise question before us does not render "unforeseeable" a decision which determines that a viable fetus is a "human being" under those statutes. Can defendant really claim surprise that a 5-pound, 18-inch, 34-week-old, living, viable child is considered to be a human being?

The fact is that the foregoing construction of our homicide statutes easily could have been anticipated from strong dicta in *People* v. *Chavez*, supra, wherein the court reviewed common-law precedents but disapproved their requirement that the child be born alive and completely separated from its mother. . . . In dicta, the court discussed the question when an unborn infant becomes a human being under the homicide statutes, as follows: ". . . While it may not be possible to draw an exact line applicable to all cases, the rules of law should recognize and make some attempt to follow the natural and scientific facts to which they relate. . . . [I]t would be a mere fiction to hold that a child is not a human being because the process of birth has not been fully completed, when it has reached that state of viability when the destruction of the life of its mother would not end its existence and when, if separated from the mother naturally or by artificial means, it will live and grow in the normal manner."

Thus the *Chavez* case explodes the majority's premise that a viability test for defining the "human being" under our homicide statutes was unforeseeable. . . . I would conclude that defendant had sufficient notice that the words "human being" could include a viable fetus.

. . . .

PEOPLE v. SOBIEK

California Court of Appeals, 1973.
30 Cal.App.3d 458, 106 Cal.Rptr. 519.

BRAY, J. . . . By an indictment filed in the San Mateo County Superior Court respondent was indicted for four counts of violation of Penal Code Section 487 (grand theft) [a] . . . . He moved to quash the

---

[a] Cal.Penal Code § 487 does not actually define grand theft. It merely differentiates grand theft from the lesser offense of petty theft. The generic crime of theft is defined in Cal.Penal Code § 484(a), which reads in pertinent part as follows:

"Every person who shall feloniously steal, take, carry, lead, or drive away the personal property of another, or who shall fraudulently appropriate property which has been entrusted to him, or who shall knowingly and designedly, by any false or fraudulent representation or pretense, defraud any other person of money, labor or real or personal property . . . is guilty of theft."

[Footnote by eds.

indictment.   After a hearing, the court granted his motion . . . .
The People appeal.

The charges arise out of a situation in San Mateo County where a group of 15 friends organized the Empire Investment Club whose purpose was to invest money in second mortgages.   Respondent, an insurance and real estate field representative, was elected president. Each member originally invested $100 and paid into the club's fund $25 per month thereafter.

It is unnecessary to detail the various acts of respondent in gradually assuming practically unlimited control of the making of loans and in finally appropriating to his own use considerable sums of the group's money.   The evidence on the hearing of the motion under Penal Code Section 995 to set aside the indictment clearly and amply shows reasonable cause for holding respondent to answer on all the charges unless, as contended by respondent and found by the court, Section 487 cannot apply to a member of a group such as this on the theory that a partner may not steal nor embezzle the property of his partnership.

In People v. Brody, 29 Cal.App.2d 6, 83 P.2d 952 (1938), the defendant and his friends contributed money for the purpose of operating bingo games.   A partnership was formed for profit-making purposes and an agreement executed.   The defendant used some of the funds for his own purposes and was charged with grand theft.   The court held: "The evidence is, as defendant claims, insufficient *in law* to sustain the judgment.   Viewed as a charge of embezzlement the uncontradicted evidence showed that the defendant and his associates were partners. However, it is settled law that a general partner cannot be convicted of embezzling partnership property which comes into his possession or under his control during the course of the partnership business by reason of his being a partner."   (Italics added.)

The basic thought behind the decisions sustaining the rule that a partner may not steal partnership property seems to be that as each partner is the ultimate owner of an undivided interest in all the partnership property and as no one can be guilty of stealing or embezzling what belongs to him, a general partner cannot be convicted of embezzling partnership property, i.e., the property must be "of another."   This rule, when thus broadly stated, goes further than the simple statutory requirement that the property be "of another."   When thus stated, the rule requires that the property be wholly that of another because a part interest by the defendant prevents a conviction. . . .

[The court then proceeded to review a number of California precedents restating the rule that a partner cannot be guilty of a theft of partnership funds.   The court found that, despite the frequency with which it was repeated, the rule was based on "misinterpretation and dicta."]

The broad rule that a partner cannot embezzle from a partnership has been rejected by the American Law Institute.   In Model Penal Code Section 223.0(7), "property of another" is defined to include property in which any person other than the actor has an interest which the actor is not privileged to infringe, regardless of the fact that the actor also has an interest in the property. This is the equivalent of the former, tentative definition under Section 206.1(4) (Tent.Draft No. 1, 1953), in which it is stated that the purpose of that definition is to nullify the concept that each of the joint owners has complete title to the jointly owned property so that a joint owner cannot misappropriate what already belongs to him. The draft states that, whatever might be merits of such notions in the civil law, it is clear they have no relevance to the criminal law's effort to deter deprivations of other people's economic interests. Modern statutes, including those of Minnesota, Wisconsin, and Illinois, either expressly or impliedly reach the same result. . . .

It is both illogical and unreasonable to hold that a partner cannot steal from his partners merely because he has an undivided interest in the partnership property. Fundamentally, stealing that portion of the partners' shares which does not belong to the thief is no different from stealing the property of another person. There is nothing in Penal Code Section 484 which requires an interpretation different from that in Model Penal Code Section 223.0(7). . . .

[The court then turned to the contention that applying this new construction to the defendant would violate the federal Constitution. It reasoned as follows:]

The prohibition in the federal Constitution against ex post facto legislation was placed in Article I, Section 10, which governs legislative powers, and is not in the article relating to the judiciary, Article III. It has been held that that provision, according to the natural import of its term, is a restraint upon legislative power and concerns the making of law, not [its] construction, by the courts. However, due process does apply to the construction of statutes by the courts, and principles similar to those involved in ex post facto doctrine have evolved. Thus, in Bouie v. City of Columbia, 378 U.S. 347 (1964), which applied the lack-of-due-process rule to a prosecution of persons involved in a sit-in where no statute or ordinance prohibited such conduct, the reviewing court held that enlarging a certain statute to cover the conduct in question was an unforeseeable judicial enlargement of a criminal statute applied retroactively. That was an entirely different situation from the one at bench where not only is the interpretation of the grand theft [statute] reasonable, but the respondent must have known that his act was immoral and that he was taking the property of another.

In United States v. Rundle, 255 F.Supp. 936 (E.D.Pa.1966), [the court distinguished *Bouie* with the following remarks:]

"It is not always true that where the definition of a crime is extended by judicial construction, a conviction which results therefrom is a denial of due process" and, quoting Mr. Justice Holmes, ". . . the law is full of instances where a man's fate depends on his estimating rightly, that is, as the jury subsequently estimates it, some matter of degree. If his judgment is wrong, not only may he incur a fine or a short imprisonment, as here; he may incur the penalty of death. . . . '*The criterion in such cases is to examine whether common social duty would, under the*

*circumstances, have suggested a more circumspect conduct.' Nash
v. United States.* (Emphasis added)."

Similarly, in the case at bar, "common social duty" would have
forewarned respondent that "circumspect conduct" prohibited robbing
his partners and also would have told him that he was stealing
"property of another."

Keeler v. Superior Court, 2 Cal.3d 619, 87 Cal.Rptr. 481, 470 P.2d
617 (1970), at first blush seems to support respondent's contention that
the construction of Section 487 placed upon it by this court deprives
respondent of due process. However, a study of *Keeler* shows that it is
not in point. *Keeler* held that the brutal killing of a fetus did not
violate Section 187 of the Penal Code, which defines murder as "the
unlawful killing of a human being," because, as the court expends a
number of pages to prove, a fetus is not a "human being" and "the
legislature intended to exclude from its reach the act of killing an
unborn fetus." The court then states that were the court to determine
that an infant in utero was a human being within the meaning of the
murder statute, such determination would have met jurisdictional and
constitutional barriers. That this is dictum cannot be gainsaid, for
once the court determined the fetus was not a human being there was
nothing more that needed to be determined. Dictum is not binding on
this court.

Moreover, the circumstances applying to Section 187 are entirely
different from those applying to Section 487. The court in *Keeler* said
that, prior to the killing, the defendant had no notice from any cause
that destroying a viable fetus might be murder. As to the grand-theft
statute, Section 487, there is no indication that the legislature did not
intend to include in "property of another" the property of partners
other than the one stealing such property, or of the partnership itself.
. . .

As we have shown, respondent's defense relies upon an interpretation of the law which is improper because it is based upon mere dictum.
If respondent, at the time he stole his partner's property, relied on a
mistaken dictum of court, traditional notions of fair play and substantial justice are not offended by applying to his act the clear meaning of
Sections 484 and 487.

The order appealed from is reversed.

NOTES ON *KEELER* AND *SOBIEK*

1. **Questions on *Keeler* and *Sobiek*.** Can you reconcile *Keeler*
and *Sobiek*? It is arguable that *Sobiek* involved a departure from prior
understanding more substantial than that involved in *Keeler*. Would
that necessarily mean that *Sobiek* was wrongly decided? Or do you
think *Keeler* was the case in error?

Can *Keeler* be explained on grounds other than those stated in the
opinion? In this connection, consider the amendment to the murder

statute adopted by the California legislature shortly after the *Keeler* decision:

"Section 187. Murder defined; death of fetus.

"(a) Murder is the unlawful killing of a human being, or a fetus, with malice aforethought.

"(b) This section shall not apply to any person who commits an act which results in the death of a fetus if any of the following apply:

(1) The act complied with the Therapeutic Abortion Act.
. . .

(2) The act was committed by a holder of a physician's and surgeon's certificate . . . in a case where, to a medical certainty, the result of childbirth would be death of the mother of the fetus or where her death from childbirth, although not medically certain, would be substantially certain or more likely than not.

(3) The act was solicited, aided, abetted, or consented to by the mother of the fetus.

"(c) Subdivision (b) shall not be construed to prohibit the prosecution of any person under any other provision of law."

Was the effect of this statute simply to overturn *Keeler*? Does the amendment to Section 187 achieve a solution different from that which would have resulted if *Keeler* had come out the other way? Is the difference consequential?

2. **Relation to *Manley***. The fact that *Keeler* and *Sobiek* involved questions of statutory interpretation seems to differentiate these cases from the *Manley* decision. Yet in another sense, all three courts were called upon to engage in the retrospective definition of criminal conduct. Does the statutory context make a difference? Is the process of judicial decision-making illustrated in *Sobiek* and suggested by the *Keeler* dissent really any different from that adopted in *Manley*? [a]

3. ***Bouie*: Background of a Constitutional Precedent**. The Supreme Court's opinion in *Bouie* is featured prominently in both *Keeler* and *Sobiek*. That case arose during one of the "sit-in" demonstrations of the early 1960's, the object of which was to secure equal access to places of public accommodation for blacks. Throughout the South blacks were refused service in many restaurants, lunch counters, hotels, motels, and similar establishments otherwise open to the public.

The fight for equal access was waged on two fronts. First, the courts were asked to recognize a constitutional right based on the equal-protection clause of the 14th amendment. There was, however, a formidable obstacle to this line of attack. The equal-protection clause applies only to actions by a "state"—i.e., to actions in some way

[a] For an opinionated review of *Keeler* and *Sobiek* and an argument that these cases are importantly different from *Manley*, see Jeffries, Legality, Vagueness, and the Construction of Penal Statutes, 71 Va.L.Rev. 189, 223–34 (1985). For a very thoughtful analysis of these issues from a British perspective, see A.T.H. Smith, Judicial Law Making in Criminal Law, 100 Law Q.R. 46 (1984).

commanded or authorized by government. Racial discrimination in privately owned places of public accommodation falls outside the traditional conception of "state action." Whether that concept can be stretched to encompass such discrimination presents a difficult and unresolved question of constitutional law. The second arena of battle was the Congress of the United States. As early (or as late) as 1946, President Truman initiated an unsuccessful effort to deal legislatively with some aspects of racial discrimination. In 1957 and again in 1960, civil-rights proposals were threatened by filibuster and were enacted only in compromise versions. As passed, neither statute prohibited racial discrimination in privately owned places of public accommodation.

While the legislative effort remained stalled, resort to the courts accelerated. In the years 1960–63, the Supreme Court faced some 33 cases involving essentially the same factual pattern. A group of blacks would seek service at a "white" lunch counter or other place of public accommodation. When denied service, the demonstrators would refuse to leave. The management would then call the police, who would arrest the demonstrators for such offenses as criminal trespass, breach of the peace, and disorderly conduct. In the resulting prosecutions, the defendants would renew the claim to a constitutional right to equal treatment. In each of these 33 cases, the Supreme Court reversed the criminal convictions but did not endorse the equal-protection argument advanced by the protestors. Instead, the Court came up with a series of ingenious, if not disingenuous, reasons for holding the convictions invalid. At the very least, the Court bent over backwards to require scrupulous fairness in sit-in prosecutions and subjected convictions on such charges to far more rigorous scrutiny than would ordinarily be applied in criminal cases.

Many observers thought that the Court's 1963 term would provide the answer to the equal-protection question that had been so deliberately postponed. On June 10, 1963, the Court granted certiorari in four sit-in cases, including *Bouie*, and consolidated them for argument with a fifth case scheduled for re-argument. All five cases were argued on October 14 and 15, 1963. On November 18, 1963, the Solicitor General, who had appeared as an amicus supporting reversal of the convictions on various narrow grounds, was invited, by a five-to-four vote, "to file a brief . . . expressing the views of the United States . . . [on] the broader constitutional issues which have been mooted." This extremely unusual invitation was accepted by the Solicitor General, who filed a brief on January 7, 1964, in which he offered additional narrow grounds for reversal, followed by some 140 pages of argument supporting recognition of the constitutional claim asserted by the convicted defendants.

Meanwhile, events were also progressing on the legislative front. On February 28, 1963, President Kennedy transmitted recommendations to the House pertaining to civil-rights legislation he intended to propose, and the resulting bill, including a public-accommodations provision, finally reached the floor of the Senate on March 9, 1964.

The traditional filibuster then began, and on May 12 became the longest in Senate history. Finally, on June 18, 1964, the filibuster ended after 82 days, 6,300 pages in the Congressional Record, and 10 million words. Enactment followed on July 3, 1964. The law provided, in substance, that "[a]ll persons shall be entitled to the full and equal enjoyment of the goods, services, facilities, privileges, advantages, and accommodations of any place of public accommodation [defined to include inns, motels, hotels, restaurants, lunch counters, gas stations, theaters, sports arenas, etc., with a few exceptions not here relevant] without discrimination or segregation on the ground of race, color, religion, or national origin." 42 U.S.C. § 2000a. The effect of this legislation was to provide a statutory right to non-discriminatory access to public accommodations and thus substantially to obviate any practical necessity for a constitutional pronouncement to that effect.

The Supreme Court may have had its eye on events across the street in Congress. Four days after the filibuster was broken, on June 22, 1964, the five sit-in cases which had been pending since October were decided. All convictions were reversed, in each case on grounds that did not address the merits of the equal-protection claim [b] and in several cases, including *Bouie*, on grounds that had not even been argued. During the Court's next term, the public-accommodations provision of the 1964 Civil Rights Act was upheld as constitutional [c] and also was found to be retroactive in effect,[d] so that it voided all pending sit-in prosecutions based on events that occurred prior to the passage of the statute. The Supreme Court still has not had the occasion to address the constitutional question that it so carefully avoided.

4. **The Meaning of *Bouie*.** The *Keeler* majority correctly recounts the reasoning of the Court in *Bouie*. There can be no doubt, moreover, that the principles enunciated in *Bouie* are sound. In view, however, of the Supreme Court's invalidation of the sit-in convictions on any available ground other than the equal-protection claim, it is fair speculation that the Court's application of those principles to the *Bouie* facts was somewhat more rigid than would have been the case if a more ordinary trespass was involved. That the Supreme Court itself understands the context of *Bouie* as qualifying its message is illustrated by the fact that *Bouie* has not become a substantial constraint on the interpretation of ambiguities in subsequently construed federal criminal statutes.

[b] In fact, six of the justices addressed the equal-protection question, three on each side. Chief Justice Warren and Justices Douglas and Goldberg voted to uphold the constitutional claim, and Justices Black, Harlan, and White voted to reject it. Justices Brennan, Stewart, and Clark took no view on these questions, but confined their votes to reverse to other "narrower" grounds. For a discussion of the views expressed in these five cases, see Paulsen, The Sit-in Cases of 1964, But Answer Came There None, 1964 Sup.Ct.Rev. 137.

[c] See Heart of Atlanta Motel v. United States, 379 U.S. 241 (1964); Katzenbach v. McClung, 379 U.S. 294 (1964). For a consideration of the constitutional debate involved in these decisions, see G. Gunther, Cases and Materials on Constitutional Law 195–211 (10th ed. 1980).

[d] Hamm v. City of Rock Hill, 379 U.S. 306 (1964).

Finally, one exchange between Justice Brennan's opinion for the Court in *Bouie* and Justice Black's dissent should be noted. Justice Black argued, in part, that fair notice was not denied to the defendants because the whole point of their exercise was to get arrested and thereby to raise a legal challenge to the segregation practices of the lunch counter involved. Justice Brennan's answer appeared in a footnote:

> "We think it irrelevant that petitioners at one point testified that they had intended to be arrested. The determination whether a criminal statute provides fair warning of its prohibitions must be made on the basis of the statute itself and the other pertinent law, rather than on the basis of an ad hoc appraisal of the subjective expectations of particular defendants. But apart from that, the record is silent as to what petitioners intended to be arrested for, and in fact what they *were* arrested for was not trespass but breach of the peace—on which charge they were not convicted. Hence there is no basis for an inference that petitioners intended to be arrested *for violating this statute*, either by remaining on the premises after being asked to leave or by any other conduct." (Emphasis in original.)

Is Justice Brennan's answer persuasive? Recall the debate on fair warning between Justices Rehnquist and Stewart in *Parker* v. *Levy*. Do Rehnquist and Black, on the one hand, and Stewart and Brennan, on the other, share common conceptions of the function of fair notice as a constitutional doctrine?

NOTES ON THE DOCTRINE OF STRICT CONSTRUCTION

1. **Origin of the Doctrine**. Recall the statement of the *Keeler* court that "[i]t is the policy of this state to construe a penal statute as favorably to the defendant as its language and the circumstances of its application may reasonably permit . . . ." This is the doctrine of strict construction. It requires that ambiguity in the interpretation of criminal statutes be resolved in favor of the accused. The history of this doctrine is described in Hall, Strict or Liberal Construction of Penal Statutes, 48 Harv.L.Rev. 748, 749–51 (1935): *

> " 'The rule that penal laws are to be construed strictly, is perhaps not much less old than construction itself.' [4] Thus did Chief Justice Marshall pay his respects more than 100 years ago to the antiquity of this rule. It did not spring into existence as soon as there were any statutes to construe. It arose to meet a very definite situation, and for a very definite purpose.
>
> "Some history of benefit of clergy is necessary for a proper understanding of the growth of the rule. Benefit of clergy

"[4] United States v. Wilberger, 5 Wheat. 76, 95 (U.S.1820)."

(freedom from the usual death penalty for common-law felonies) did not become really important until the growing literacy among laymen in the latter part of the 14th century made a considerable number of them eligible to claim it under the literacy test adopted some years earlier. A century later the number of successful claimants became so large that the first of many statutes ousting benefit of clergy in specified crimes was passed, applying to a lay person murdering his lord or master.

"In the reign of Henry VIII, who is said to have executed 72,000 of his subjects, numerous statutes were passed to exclude from benefit of clergy persons convicted as principals or accessories before the fact in a number of specified felonies. These statutes were repealed by Edward VI in 1547 except as to principals in five named felonies, to which accessories were added in 1557. A few other felonies were made non-clergyable by Elizabeth and James I.

"It was against this background of unmitigated severity in serious crimes that the doctrine of strict construction emerged. Prior to the 17th century there were only a few cases where it was employed, and there were others where it was rejected. It did not become a general rule of conscious application until the growing humanitarianism of 17th century England came into serious conflict with the older laws of the preceding century. During this period there seems to have been no further non-clergyable offenses created. But from 1691 to 1765 benefit of clergy was ousted in various forms of fraud, embezzlement, and aggravated larceny, and a conflict ensued between the legislature on the one hand and courts, juries, and even prosecutors on the other. The former was committed by inertia, or pressure from property owners, to a policy of deterrence through severity, while the latter tempered this severity with strict construction carried to its most absurd limits, verdicts contrary to the evidence, and waiver of the non-clergyable charge in return for a plea of guilty to a lesser offense. It was from cases and text writers in England of this period that the doctrine of strict construction was brought to this country.

"The 19th century, both here and in England, marked the end of the death penalty as the chief mode of punishment for serious crimes. And with its passing, the factor which had brought the doctrine of strict construction into existence as literally in favorem vitae disappeared—yet the doctrine itself lived, the sole relic of what had once been a veritable conspiracy for administrative nullification."

2. **The Legislative Response**. Faced with this persistent frustration of statutory purpose, 19th-century legislatures tried to overrule the doctrine of strict construction. The original suggestion came from the Field Code proposed for New York:

"The rule of the common law that penal statutes are to be strictly construed has no application to this code. All its provisions are to be construed according to the fair import of their terms, with a view to effect its objects and to promote justice."

D. Field, W. Noyes & A. Bradford, Draft of a Penal Code for the State of New York § 10 (1864). As the *Keeler* case points out, this proposal was adopted verbatim as Section 4 of the California Code of 1872. Additionally, some 18 other states, most of them west of the Mississippi, passed similar statutes in the years before World War I. In a few cases, the enactment of such laws seems immediately to have altered the terms of judicial construction, but in other jurisdictions the courts continued to invoke the doctrine of strict construction despite express legislative direction to the contrary. See Hall, Strict or Liberal Construction of Penal Statutes, 48 Harv.L.Rev. 748, 752–56 (1935).

Modern penal codes typically include some statement on statutory construction. Often, they simply carry forward a variant of the Field Code proposal quoted above. See, e.g., N.Y.Penal Code § 5.00. Other states have followed the more elaborate formulation in Section 1.02 of the Model Penal Code:

"(1) The general purposes of the provisions governing the definition of offenses are:

(a) to forbid and prevent conduct that unjustifiably and inexcusably inflicts or threatens substantial harm to individual or public interests;

(b) to subject to public control persons whose conduct indicates that they are disposed to commit crimes;

(c) to safeguard conduct that is without fault from condemnation as criminal;

(d) to give fair warning of the nature of the conduct declared to constitute an offense;

(e) to differentiate on reasonable grounds between serious and minor offenses. . . .

"(3) The provisions of the Code shall be construed according to the fair import of their terms but when the language is susceptible of differing constructions it shall be interpreted to further the general purposes stated in this Section and the special purposes of the particular provision involved. . . ."

For examples of modern enactments based on this model, see 18 Consol.Penn.Stat. §§ 104, 105; N.J.Stat.Ann. § 2C:1–2.

3. **Modern Application:** *McBoyle* v. *United States*. As *Keeler* and *Sobiek* suggest, the doctrine of strict construction continues to be invoked, albeit selectively, as an aid in the interpretation of penal statutes. Today, however, the policy most often advanced to support this approach is not aversion to the severity of penal sanctions but rather the concern for fair notice of what is proscribed. In the words of Professor Packer, the modern principle of strict construction "may perhaps be viewed as something of a junior version of the vagueness doctrine." H. Packer, The Limits of the Criminal Sanction 95 (1968).

One of the earliest and most famous illustrations of this approach comes from McBoyle v. United States, 283 U.S. 25 (1931). McBoyle was convicted of interstate transportation of a stolen "motor vehicle." That term was defined to include "an automobile, automobile truck, automobile wagon, motorcycle, or any other self-propelled vehicle not designed for running on rails." Speaking through Mr. Justice Holmes, the Supreme Court found that McBoyle's act of transporting a stolen airplane did not qualify:

"The question is the meaning of the word 'vehicle' in the phrase, 'any other self-propelled vehicle not designed for running on rails.' No doubt etymologically it is possible to use the word to signify a conveyance working on land, water or air, and sometimes legislation extends the use in that direction . . . . But in everyday speech 'vehicle' calls up the picture of a thing moving on land. . . . Airplanes were well known in 1919 when this statute was passed; but it is admitted that they were not mentioned in the reports or in the debates in Congress. It is impossible to read words that so carefully enumerate the different forms of motor vehicles and have no reference to any kind of aircraft, as including airplanes under a term that usage more and more precisely confines to a different class. . . .

"Although it is not likely that a criminal will carefully consider the text of the law before he murders or steals, it is reasonable that a fair warning should be given to the world in language that the common world will understand, of what the law intends to do if a certain line is passed. To make the warning fair, so far as possible the line should be clear. When a rule of conduct is laid down in words that evoke in the common mind only the picture of vehicles moving on land, the statute should not be extended to aircraft simply because it may seem to us that a similar policy applies, or upon the speculation that, if the legislature had thought of it, very likely broader words would have been used."

Mr. Justice Holmes' speculation as to what the legislature would have done had it thought of the situation was confirmed when Congress amended the law to cover interstate transportation of a stolen motor vehicle "or aircraft." 59 Stat. 536 (1945). "Aircraft" was defined to include "any contrivance now known or hereafter invented, used, or designed for navigation of or for flight in the air."

What should the Supreme Court do if this statute, now codified as 18 U.S.C. § 2312, were invoked against the interstate transportation of a stolen boat?

4. **Modern Application:** *United States* v. *Bass*. United States v. Bass, 404 U.S. 336 (1971), illustrates an additional dimension of the application of strict construction to federal statutes. First, however, a preliminary comment on the jurisdictional structure of federal offenses is required.

The Constitution of the United States speaks in terms of certain enumerated powers of the national government. A good example is the power accorded Congress under Article I "to regulate commerce with foreign nations, and among the several states." No federal enactment is constitutionally valid unless it pertains to one or another of these enumerated powers. In practice, however, the various sources of federal power have been construed very expansively. As a result, virtually any exercise of federal legislative authority will be upheld, even if the connection with one of the designated federal powers is remote or tangential. Nonetheless, at least theoretically, the federal government's power to punish criminal misconduct is not plenary but must be related to a legitimate federal interest within the enumerated powers.

This theoretical limitation of the national government to the enumerated powers has an important consequence for federal crime definition. Most federal offenses include components specifically addressed to the underlying federal power being exercised. These are called "jurisdictional" elements. Typically, the basis of federal jurisdiction is stated together with the description of proscribed conduct as part of the definition of the offense. Thus, for example, federal law does not directly punish incitement to riot. Instead, it forbids travel in interstate or foreign commerce, or use of any facility of interstate or foreign commerce with intent to incite a riot. 18 U.S.C. § 2101. The "interstate transportation" component of the offense involved in *McBoyle* is another example. Among the commonly employed jurisdictional bases (in addition to those dealing with interstate commerce) are use of the mails, the status of the offender as a federal employee, or involvement of property owned, licensed, or insured by the federal government. Under current law, these jurisdictional components are part of the definition of federal crimes and must be proved to the jury beyond a reasonable doubt just as any other element of the offense charged.

United States v. *Bass* involved one of the many federal criminal statutes based on the power over interstate commerce. Specifically, 18 U.S.C. § 1202(a) punishes anyone previously convicted of a felony "who receives, possesses, or transports in commerce or affecting commerce" any firearm. The issue before the Supreme Court was whether the phrase "in commerce or affecting commerce" applied only to transporting or whether it also limited the scope of the receiving and possessing offenses. Given the precedents in this field, it is virtually certain that either construction would be upheld as a constitutionally valid exercise of federal power.

The Court held that the phrase "in commerce or affecting commerce" should be read to apply to all three aspects of the offense. The Court was not persuaded to reach this result by the face of the statute or by its legislative history. Instead, it adopted the "narrower reading" in recognition of "two wise principles this Court has long followed." The first principle was that "ambiguity concerning the ambit of criminal statutes should be resolved in favor of lenity":

> "In various ways over the years, we have stated that 'when choice has to be made between two readings of what Congress has made a crime, it is appropriate, before we choose the harsher alternative, to require that Congress should have spoken in

language that is clear and definite.' This principle is founded on two policies that have long been part of our tradition. First, 'a fair warning should be given to the world in language that the common world will understand, of what the law intends to do if a certain line is passed. To make the warning fair, so far as possible the line should be clear.' McBoyle v. United States, 283 U.S. 25, 27 (1931) (Holmes, J.). Second, because of the seriousness of criminal penalties, and because criminal punishment usually represents the moral condemnation of the community, legislatures and not courts should define criminal activity. This policy embodies 'the instinctive distaste against men languishing in prison unless the lawmaker has clearly said they should.' Thus, where there is ambiguity in a criminal statute, doubts are resolved in favor of the defendant. Here, we conclude that Congress has not 'plainly and unmistakably' made it a federal crime for a convicted felon simply to possess a gun absent some demonstrated nexus with interstate commerce."

The second principle was that "unless Congress conveys its purpose clearly, it will not be deemed to have significantly changed the federal-state balance":

"Congress has traditionally been reluctant to define as a federal crime conduct readily denounced as criminal by the states. . . . In traditionally sensitive areas, such as legislation affecting the federal balance, the requirement of clear statement assures that the legislature has in fact faced, and intended to bring into issue, the critical matters involved in the judicial decision. . . . In the instant case, the broad construction urged by the government renders traditionally local criminal conduct a matter for federal enforcement and would also involve a substantial extension of federal police resources. Absent proof of some interstate-commerce nexus in each case, Section 1202(a) dramatically intrudes upon traditional state criminal jurisdiction. [T]he legislative history provides scanty basis for concluding that Congress faced these serious questions and meant to affect the federal-state balance in the way now claimed by the government. Absent a clearer statement of intention from Congress than is present here, we do not interpret Section 1202(a) to reach the 'mere possession' of firearms."

Is the Court's second (or "federalism") principle applicable only to "jurisdictional" elements of federal offenses? Could it have been applied with equal force in *McBoyle*? Do you see why it would not be applicable in such cases as *Keeler* and *Sobiek*? On the other hand, does the Court's first (or "strict construction") principle apply with less force to *Bass* and *McBoyle* than to *Keeler* and *Sobiek*? Note that in *Bass* and *McBoyle* the question was not so much whether the underlying conduct was criminal as it was whether state or federal authorities would prosecute. Should the courts be especially concerned about fair notice that certain misconduct violates a federal statute as well as state law?

Are there other reasons to support "strict construction," even in the context of federal jurisdictional provisions?

———

SUBSECTION B: OMISSIONS

———

JONES v. UNITED STATES

United States Court of Appeals for the District of Columbia Circuit, 1962.
308 F.2d 307.

WRIGHT, CIRCUIT JUDGE.   Appellant, together with one Shirley Green, was tried on [an] indictment charging them jointly with . . . involuntary manslaughter through failure to perform their legal duty of care for Anthony Lee Green, which failure resulted in his death. . . . [A]ppellant was convicted of involuntary manslaughter. Shirley Green was found not guilty. . . .

A summary of the evidence, which is in conflict upon almost every significant issue, is necessary. . . .   In late 1957, Shirley Green became pregnant, out of wedlock, with a child, Robert Lee, subsequently born August 17, 1958. Apparently to avoid the embarrassment of the presence of the child in the Green home, it was arranged that appellant, a family friend, would take the child to her home after birth. Appellant did so, and the child remained there continuously until removed by the police on August 5, 1960. Initially, appellant made some motions toward the adoption of Robert Lee, but they came to nought, and shortly thereafter it was agreed that Shirley Green was to pay appellant $72 a month for his care. According to appellant, these payments were made for only five months. According to Shirley Green, they were made up to July, 1960.

Early in 1959 Shirley Green again became pregnant, this time with the child Anthony Lee, whose death is the basis of appellant's conviction. This child was born October 21, 1959. Soon after birth, Anthony Lee developed a mild jaundice condition, attributed to a blood incompatibility with his mother. The jaundice resulted in his retention in the hospital for three days beyond the usual time, or until October 26, 1959, when, on authorization signed by Shirley Green, Anthony Lee was released by the hospital to appellant's custody. Shirley Green, after a two or three day stay in the hospital, also lived with appellant for three weeks, after which she returned to her parents' home, leaving the children with appellant. She testified she did not see them again, except for one visit in March, until August 5, 1960. Consequently, though there does not seem to have been any specific monetary agreement with Shirley Green covering Anthony Lee's support, appellant had complete custody of both children until they were rescued by the police.

With regard to medical care, the evidence is undisputed. In March, 1960, appellant called a Dr. Turner to her home to treat Anthony Lee for a bronchial condition. Appellant also telephoned the doctor at various times to consult with him concerning Anthony Lee's diet and health. In early July, 1960, appellant took Anthony Lee to Dr. Turner's office where he was treated for "simple diarrhea." At this time the doctor noted the "wizened" appearance of the child and told appellant to tell the mother of the child that he should be taken to a hospital. This was not done.

On August 2, 1960, two collectors for the local gas company had occasion to go to the basement of appellant's home, and there saw the two children. Robert Lee and Anthony Lee at this time were age two years and 10 months respectively. Robert Lee was in a "crib" consisting of a framework of wood, covered with a fine wire screening, including the top which was hinged. The "crib" was lined with newspaper, which was stained, apparently with feces, and crawling with roaches. Anthony Lee was lying in a bassinet and was described as having the appearance of a "small baby monkey." One collector testified to seeing roaches on Anthony Lee.

On August 5, 1960, the collectors returned to appellant's home in the company of several police officers and personnel of the Women's Bureau. At this time, Anthony Lee was upstairs in the dining room in the bassinet, but Robert Lee was still downstairs in his "crib." The officers removed the children to the D.C. General Hospital where Anthony Lee was diagnosed as suffering from severe malnutrition and lesions over large portions of his body, apparently caused by severe diaper rash. Following admission, he was fed repeatedly, apparently with no difficulty, and was described as being very hungry. His death, 34 hours after admission, was attributed without dispute to malnutrition. At birth Anthony Lee weighed six pounds, 15 ounces—at death at age 10 months, he weighed seven pounds, 13 ounces. Normal weight at this age would have been approximately 14 pounds. . . .

Appellant . . . takes exception to the failure of the trial court to charge that the jury must find beyond a reasonable doubt, as an element of the crime, that appellant was under a legal duty to supply food and necessities to Anthony Lee. . . .

The problem of establishing the duty to take action which would preserve the life of another has not often arisen in the case law of this country. The most commonly cited statement of the rule is found in People v. Beardsley, 150 Mich. 206, 113 N.W. 1128 (1907):

> "The law recognizes that under some circumstances the omission of a duty owed by one individual to another, where such omission results in the death of the one to whom the duty is owing, will make the other chargeable with manslaughter. . . . This rule of law is always based upon the proposition that the duty neglected must be a legal duty, and not a mere moral obligation. It must be a duty imposed by law or by contract, and the omission to perform the duty must be the immediate and direct cause of death. . . ."

There are at least four situations in which the failure to act may constitute breach of a legal duty. One can be held criminally liable:

first, where a statute imposes a duty to care for another; second, where one stands in a certain status relationship to another; third, where one has assumed a contractual duty to care for another; and fourth, where one has voluntarily assumed the care of another and so secluded the helpless person as to prevent others from rendering aid.

It is the contention of the government that either the third or fourth ground is applicable here. However, it is obvious that in any of the four situations, there are critical issues of fact which must be passed on by the jury—specifically in this case, whether appellant had entered into a contract with the mother for the care of Anthony Lee or, alternatively, whether she assumed the care of the child and secluded him from the care of his mother, his natural protector. On both of these issues, the evidence is in direct conflict, appellant insisting that the mother was actually living with appellant and Anthony Lee, and hence should have been taking care of the child herself, while Shirley Green testified she was living with her parents and was paying appellant to care for both children.

In spite of this conflict, the instructions given in the case failed even to suggest the necessity for finding a legal duty of care. The only reference to duty in the instructions was the reading of the indictment which charged, inter alia, that the defendants "failed to perform their legal duty." A finding of legal duty is the critical element of the crime charged and failure to instruct the jury concerning it was plain error.

. . .

Reversed and remanded.

NOTES ON OMISSIONS

1. **A Duty to Act**. As *Jones* makes clear, criminal liability may be based on an omission only where there is a legal duty to act. Mere moral obligation will not do. Of course, many criminal statutes expressly punish failure to act. For example, there are laws against failure to register for the draft, failure to file a tax return, failure to stop at a red light, etc. In such cases, the statute defining the criminal offense itself creates the duty to act. The same may be said of the host of penal statutes proscribing some combination of act and omission—e.g., driving without a license. Enforcement of such offenses yields no special difficulty.

Problems arise, however, where the offense in question does not expressly proscribe an omission but covers any conduct producing a given result. The classic example is homicide. Typically, criminal homicide statutes punish one who "causes the death of another human being." A more elaborate formulation might say "does or omits to do anything that causes death of another." In this case, the reach of the penal statute is limited by the rule, applied in *Jones*, that failure to act suffices only when it breaches a legal duty. And the legal duty is not found on the face of the statute defining the offense but in the other

sources of law, both statutory and decisional, that specify legal obligations among citizens.

The chief categories of legal duty are stated in the *Jones* opinion.
They include duties based on statute (e.g., the common provision that a
driver involved in an automobile accident must stop and render assistance); duties based on relationship (e.g., parent and minor child);
duties based on contract (e.g., the employment responsibilities of a
lifeguard); and duties based on voluntary assumption of responsibility
that effectively precludes aid from others (e.g., the person who takes a
foundling home and thus secretes it from the agencies of public assistance). Legal duties may also be based on control over the conduct of
another, as in the obligation of an employer to oversee employees, and
sometimes on the existence of a peril for which the actor was in some
way responsible. Finally, a landowner or businessman may have a
legal duty to provide for the safety of persons invited onto the property.
An extensive summary of recognized legal duties may be found in
Kirchheimer, Criminal Omission, 55 Harv.L.Rev. 615, 619–36 (1942),
and a more modern survey appears in Robinson, Criminal Liability for
Omissions: A Brief Summary and Critique of the Law in the United
States, 29 N.Y.L.S.L.Rev. 101 (1984).

2. **Illustrative Cases**. In connection with the preceding statement
of doctrine, consider the following two cases:

(i) *People v. Beardsley*. The decision quoted in *Jones* is People
v. Beardsley, 150 Mich. 206, 113 N.W. 1128 (1907). Defendant arranged
with one Blanche Burns to spend the weekend in his rooms. They
drank more or less steadily for two days. Additionally, and without his
consent, she obtained and took some morphine. When defendant began
to expect the return of his wife, he arranged for Blanche to be moved to
the room of a friend, whom he asked to look after her and to let her out
the back way when she awoke. Some hours later she died.

Defendant was convicted of manslaughter for his failure to render
reasonable care, but the Supreme Court of Michigan reversed:

"It is urged by the prosecutor that the [defendant] 'stood
towards this woman for the time being in the place of her
natural guardian and protector, and as such owed her a clear
legal duty which he completely failed to perform.' The cases
cited and digested establish that no such legal duty is created
based upon a mere moral obligation. The fact that this woman
was in his house created no such legal duty as exists in law and
is due from a husband towards his wife, as seems to be intimated
by the prosecutor's brief. Such an inference would be very
repugnant to our moral sense. . . . Had this been a case
where two men under like circumstances had voluntarily gone on
a debauch together, and one had attempted suicide, no one would
claim that this doctrine of legal duty could be invoked to hold the
other criminally responsible for omitting to make an effort to
rescue his companion. How can the fact that in this case one of
the parties was a woman change the principle of law applicable
to it?"

Beardsley has been condemned as a "savage proclamation that the wages of sin is death." Hughes, Criminal Omissions, 67 Yale L.J. 590, 624 (1958). Do you agree? Is it, as Professor Hughes continued, reflective of a morality which is "smug, ignorant, and vindictive," or is there some other justification for the result? Should the outcome hinge on the character and duration of the defendant's relationship with the deceased? Would the result have been different if, for example, the defendant and the deceased had been living together for some time? If so, why?

(ii) *Regina* v. *Instan*. Another famous case is Regina v. Instan, [1893] Cox C.C. 602. Defendant lived with, and was supported by, her aunt. Some 10 days before her death, the aunt contracted gangrene. Defendant continued to live in the aunt's house and to take in food supplied by tradespeople, but she neither procured medical attention nor notified anyone else of the aunt's condition. The aunt died of gangrene and neglect, and defendant was found guilty of manslaughter. The court upheld the conviction:

> "It is not correct to say that every moral obligation is a legal duty, but every legal duty is founded upon a moral obligation. In this case, as in most cases, the legal duty can be nothing else than taking upon oneself the performance of the moral obligation. There is no question whatever that it was this woman's clear duty to impart to the deceased so much of that food which was taken into the house and paid for by the deceased as was necessary to sustain her life. . . ."

Is *Instan* correct? Into which of the four categories described in *Jones* does *Instan* fit? Is it critical that the defendant was supported by the deceased? Would a different result have been reached if the defendant had her own income? Would liability have attached merely because the defendant was the only person who knew of the aunt's condition? If so, would the same rule apply to a neighbor who happened to discover the situation but did nothing to rectify it?

3. **A General Duty to Rescue**? An underlying issue in all these cases is whether there should be a general duty to rescue. Rather than focusing on particular legal duties based on contract or status, why should not the law simply recognize a generalized duty to give reasonable assistance to a person in peril? Consider, for example, the principal case. Why, on those facts, should it be necessary to prove that the defendant had contracted with the child's mother for maintenance or that she had acted to seclude the child from his mother's protection? Why should it not suffice that the defendant, at no special cost or danger to herself, could have saved a child's life and that she chose not to do so?

A defense of the traditional view against a general duty to rescue was attempted by Lord Macaulay. In his notes on a proposed Indian penal code, Macaulay undertook to assess the extent to which omissions productive of evil consequences should be punished on the same footing as affirmative misconduct leading to those results. After rejecting the categorical alternatives of "always" and "never," Macaulay explained the drafters' choice of a "middle course":

"What we propose is this: that where acts are made punishable on the ground that they have caused, or have been intended to cause, or have been known to be likely to cause, a certain evil effect, omissions which have caused, which have been intended to cause, or which have been known to be likely to cause the same effect, shall be punishable in the same manner, provided that such omissions were, on other grounds, illegal. An omission is illegal if it be an offense, if it be a breach of some direction of law, or if it be such a wrong as would be a good ground for a civil action.

"We cannot defend this rule better than by giving a few illustrations of the way in which it will operate. *A* omits to give *Z* food, and by that omission voluntarily causes *Z*'s death. Is this murder? Under our rule it is murder if *A* was *Z*'s jailer, directed by the law to furnish *Z* with food. It is murder if *Z* was the infant child of *A*, and had, therefore, a legal right to sustenance, which right a civil court would enforce against *A*. It is murder if *Z* was a bedridden invalid, and *A* a nurse hired to feed *Z*. . . . It is not murder if *Z* is a beggar, who has no other claim on *A* than that of humanity. . . .

"We are sensible that in some of the cases which we have put, our rule may appear too lenient; but we do not think that it can be made more severe without disturbing the whole order of society. It is true that the man who, having abundance of wealth, suffers a fellow-creature to die of hunger at his feet is a bad man—a worse man, probably, than many of those for whom we have provided very severe punishment. But we are unable to see where, if we make such a man legally punishable, we can draw the line. If the rich man who refuses to save a beggar's life at the cost of a little copper is a murderer, is the poor man just one degree above beggary also to be a murderer if he omits to invite the beggar to partake his hard-earned rice? Again, if the rich man is a murderer for refusing to save the beggar's life at the cost of a little copper, is he also to be a murderer if he refuses to save the beggar's life at the cost of a thousand rupees? . . . The distinction between a legal and an illegal omission is perfectly plain and intelligible; but the distinction between a large and a small sum of money is very far from being so, not to say that a sum which is small to one man is large to another. . . .

"It is, indeed, most highly desirable that men should not merely abstain from doing harm to their neighbors, but should render active services to their neighbors. In general, however, the penal law must content itself with keeping men from doing positive harm, and must leave to public opinion, and to the teachers of morality and religion, the office of furnishing men with motives for doing positive good. . . ."

T. Macaulay, Notes on the Indian Penal Code, in 4 Miscellaneous Works 251–56 (1880).

Is Macaulay's argument persuasive? Are the line-drawing problems so intractable as to preclude recognition of a general duty to rescue? Might this difficulty be alleviated by drawing the line very far to one side—as, for example, in a rule imposing a duty to rescue only where there is no appreciable risk or expense to the actor? Would not such a rule cover the *Jones* case? For an interesting analysis of this question, see Woozley, A Duty to Rescue, 69 Va.L.Rev. 1273 (1983).

4. **Omissions Outside the Law of Homicide**. It is no accident that the great majority of omission cases concern criminal homicide. Unlike most penal legislation, homicide statutes typically do not describe the prohibited conduct. Instead, they cover any act or omission that causes death of another. The need therefore arises to consider which omissions should suffice. Of course, an analogous problem can occur in any "result" crime—that is, any crime defined by reference to the consequences of the actor's conduct rather than to the nature of the conduct itself. However, result crimes are very much the exception rather than the rule. Indeed, at one time criminal homicide was probably the only offense structured in this way. Thus, it is plain that the emergence of a general doctrine on omissions played an important, albeit indirect, role in defining the actus reus of criminal homicide.

The question arises, however, whether the law of omissions has significant application outside that context. Consider the case of Commonwealth v. Cali, 247 Mass. 20, 141 N.E. 510 (1923). Defendant was indicted under a statute punishing one who, "with intent to injure the insurer, burns a building or any goods, wares, merchandise or other chattels belonging to himself or another and which are at the time insured against loss or damage by fire." Defendant was charged with arson of a building belonging to his wife. He testified that he set the fire accidentally and then merely failed to give an alarm, but the jury was instructed that even if he did cause the fire accidentally, liability could be found if defendant subsequently realized that he could put the fire out and failed to do so in order to defraud the insurer. The Supreme Judicial Court of Massachusetts affirmed the conviction, in essence basing liability for arson on an omission.

Is *Cali* correct? If you had to decide the case, what kind of analysis would you think appropriate to the issue? Is it a question of the "law of omissions"? Is it more broadly a question of social policy governing attempts to defraud insurers? Or is it simply a question of statutory construction—whether the verb "burns" should be construed to include intentional failure to put out a fire accidentally begun? Is such a construction defensible? Would the result be easier to defend under a subsequent amendment changing the statute to reach one who "sets fire to, or attempts to set fire to, or . . . *causes to be burned*" a building, etc.?

Finally, note that the facts of the *Cali* case are covered by the Model Penal Code under a separate provision on failure to control or report a dangerous fire. Section 220.1(3) provides that one "who knows that a fire is endangering life or a substantial amount of property of another and fails to take reasonable measures to put out or control the fire, when he can do so without substantial risk to himself, or to give a prompt fire alarm, commits a misdemeanor if . . . the fire was started, albeit lawfully, by him or with his assent, or on property in his custody or control." This provision explicitly creates a duty to act, though only in carefully circumscribed situations, and punishes failure to do so as a minor offense. Obviously, an enactment of this sort would be unnecessary in a jurisdiction adhering to the *Cali* interpretation of the arson offense. Do the differences between this provision and the *Cali* construction of the statute there considered suggest reasons to prefer one or the other way of handling this problem? Which solution is better?

BARBER v. SUPERIOR COURT OF LOS ANGELES COUNTY

California Court of Appeal for the Second District, 1983.
147 Cal.App.3d 1006, 195 Cal.Rptr. 484.

COMPTON, ASSOCIATE JUSTICE.

In these consolidated proceedings we consider petitions for writs of prohibition filed by two medical doctors who are charged . . . with the crimes of murder and conspiracy to commit murder—both felonies.

At the close of a lengthy preliminary hearing the magistrate ordered the complaint dismissed. On motion of the People, . . . the superior court ordered the magistrate to reinstate the complaint. These proceedings followed. . . .

Deceased Clarence Herbert underwent surgery for closure of an ileostomy. Petitioner Robert Nejdl, M.D., was Mr. Herbert's surgeon and petitioner Neil Barber, M.D. was his attending internist. Shortly after the successful completion of the surgery, and while in the recovery room, Mr. Herbert suffered a cardio-respiratory arrest. He was revived by a team of physicians and nurses and immediately placed on life support equipment.

Within the following three days, it was determined that Mr. Herbert was in a deeply comatose state from which he was not likely to recover. Tests and examinations performed by several physicians, including petitioners herein, each specializing in relevant fields of medicine indicated that Mr. Herbert had suffered severe brain damage, leaving him in a vegetative state, which was likely to be permanent.

At that time petitioners informed Mr. Herbert's family of their opinion as to his condition and chances for recovery. While there is some dispute as to the precise terminology used by the doctors, it is clear that they communicated to the family that the prognosis for recovery was extremely poor. At that point, the family convened and drafted a written request to the hospital personnel stating that they wanted "all machines taken off that are sustaining life" (sic). As a result, petitioners, either directly or as a result of orders given by them, caused the respirator and other life-sustaining equipment to be removed. Mr. Herbert continued to breathe without the equipment but showed no signs of improvement. The family remained at his bedside and requested of the nursing staff that Mr. Herbert not be disturbed. They even objected to certain routine procedures followed by hospital personnel in caring for comatose patients.

After two more days had elapsed, petitioners, after consulting with the family, ordered removal of the intravenous tubes which provided hydration and nourishment. From that point until his death, Mr. Herbert received nursing care which preserved his dignity and provided a clean and hygienic environment.

The precise issue for determination by this court is whether the evidence presented before the magistrate was sufficient to support his determination that petitioners should not be held to answer to the charges of murder. . . .

Murder is the *unlawful* killing of a human being, . . . with malice aforethought." Penal Code, § 187 (italics added) . . .

The term "malice" is an amorphous and ill-defined state of mind which the law considers sufficiently culpable to make an unlawful killing murder rather than some lesser form of criminal homicide such as manslaughter. While the law is settled that motive is irrelevant to a determination of whether a killing amounts to murder; the lack of precision in defining malice often makes it difficult to disentangle motive from a determination of what constitutes malice.

For the purposes of this decision, however, we accept the superior court judge's analysis that if petitioners unlawfully and intentionally killed Mr. Herbert, the malice could be presumed regardless of their motive.

The use of the term "unlawful" in defining a criminal homicide is generally to distinguish a criminal homicide from those homicides which society has determined to be "justifiable" or "excusable." Euthanasia, of course, is neither justifiable nor excusable in California. . . .

Historically, death has been defined in terms of cessation of heart and respiratory function. Matter of Quinlan, 70 N.J. 10, 355 A.2d 647 (1976). Health and Safety Code section 7180(a)(2) now provides for an alternative definition in terms of irreversible cessation of all brain function. . . .

Of course it is conceded by all that at the time petitioners terminated further treatment, Mr. Herbert was not "dead" by either statutory or historical standards since there was still some minimal brain activity. If Mr. Herbert had in fact been "brain dead," this prosecution could not have been instituted because one cannot be charged with killing another person who is already dead. . . .

We thus turn to an analysis of the superior court's determination that petitioners' conduct was "unlawful" as a matter of law. . . .

As a predicate to our analysis of whether the petitioners' conduct amounted to an "unlawful killing," we conclude that the cessation of "heroic" life support measures is not an affirmative act but rather a withdrawal or omission of further treatment.

Even though these life support devices are, to a degree, "self-propelled," each pulsation of the respirator or each drop of fluid introduced into the patient's body by intravenous feeding devices is comparable to a manually administered injection or item of medication. Hence "disconnecting" of the mechanical devices is comparable to withholding the manually administered injection or medication.

Further we view the use of an intravenous administration of nourishment and fluid, under the circumstances, as being the same as the use of the respirator or other form of life support equipment. . . .

In the final analysis, since we view petitioners' conduct as that of omission rather than affirmative action, the resolution of this case turns on whether petitioners had a duty to continue to provide life sustaining treatment.

There is no criminal liability for failure to act unless there is a legal duty to act. Thus the critical issue becomes one of determining the duties owed by a physician to a patient who has been reliably diagnosed as in a comatose state from which any meaningful recovery of cognitive brain function is exceedingly unlikely. . . .

A physician has no duty to continue treatment, once it has proved to be ineffective. Although there may be a duty to provide life-sustaining machinery in the *immediate* aftermath of a cardio-respiratory arrest, there is no duty to continue its use once it has become futile in the opinion of qualified medical personnel. . . .

Of course, the difficult [determination] that must be made under these principles is the point at which further treatment will be of no reasonable benefit to the patient, who should have the power to make that decision and who should have the authority to direct termination of treatment.

No precise guidelines as to when or how these decisions should be made can be provided by this court since this determination is essentially a medical one to be made at a time and on the basis of facts which will be unique to each case. If specific procedural rules are to be adopted in this area in order to protect the public interest, they must necessarily come from that body most suited for the collection of data and the reaching of a consensus—the Legislature. However, we would be derelict in our duties if we did not provide some general guidelines for future conduct in the absence of such legislation. . . .

Of course the patient's interests and desires are the key ingredients of the decision making process. When dealing with patients for whom the possibility of full recovery is virtually non-existent, and who are incapable of expressing their desires, there is . . . something of a consensus on the standard to be applied.

"[T]he focal point of decision should be the prognosis as to the reasonable possibility of return to cognitive and sapient life, as distinguished from the forced continuance of that biological vegetative existence . . . . " *Matter of Quinlan*, supra, 355 A.2d at p. 669. . . .

The evidence presented at the preliminary hearing supports the conclusion that petitioners reasonably concluded that Mr. Herbert had

virtually no chance of recovering his cognitive or motor functions.
. . . .

Given the general standards for determining when there is a duty to provide medical treatment of debatable value, the question still remains as to who should make these vital decisions. Clearly, the medical diagnoses and prognoses must be determined by the treating and consulting physicians under the generally accepted standards of medical practice in the community and, whenever possible, the patient himself should then be the ultimate decision-maker.

When the patient, however, is incapable of deciding for himself, because of his medical condition or for other reasons, there is no clear authority on the issue of who . . . is to make the final decision [and under what procedure].

Under the circumstances of this case, the wife was the proper person to act as a surrogate for the patient with the authority to decide issues regarding further treatment . . . and would have so qualified had judicial approval been sought. There is no evidence that there was any disagreement among the wife and children. Nor was there any evidence that they were motivated in their decision by anything other than love and concern for the dignity of their husband and father.

Furthermore, in the absence of legislative guidance, we find no legal requirement that prior judicial approval is necessary before any decision to withdraw treatment can be made. . . .

In summary we conclude that the petitioners' omission to continue treatment under the circumstances, though intentional and with knowledge that the patient would die, was not an unlawful failure to perform a legal duty. . . . Let a peremptory writ of prohibition issue to restrain the Superior Court of Los Angeles County from taking any further action in this matter . . . .

ROTH, P.J., and BEACH, J., concur.

NOTES ON THE OMISSION OF LIFE–SUSTAINING TREATMENT

1. **Questions and Comments on *Barber*.** *Barber* is a very rare reported prosecution of medical personnel for conduct that probably occurs with some frequency. The court's resolution of the issue accords with prevailing medical practice, both in upholding the acceptability of terminating life-sustaining treatment and in grounding that result in a distinction between act and omission.[a]

[a] See, e.g., § 2.11 of the Opinions of the Judicial Council of the American Medical Association (1982), where it is stated: "For humane reasons, with informed consent a physician may do what is medically necessary to alleviate severe pain, or cease or omit treatment to let a terminally ill patient die, but he should not intentionally cause death." For a comprehensive but economical treatment of the "right to stop treatment" of incompetent patients, see J. Robertson, The Rights of the Critically Ill 49–70 (1983).

Does the distinction make sense? Does it accord with traditional legal doctrine that regards homicide by omission as criminal whenever there is a duty to act? Does a physician have a duty to continue life-sustaining treatment of a patient with an irreversible disease process? On what considerations would the existence of such a duty depend? Is the question properly susceptible to ad hoc determination by physicians? By the family? By a court? Moreover, if the physician and/or the patient's family are competent to decide when the duty to treat has ended, why are they not equally competent to decide whether there should be an affirmative action to end the patient's suffering? Do the considerations at stake properly depend on the distinction between act and omission?

2. **Report of the President's Commission.** In connection with the above questions, consider the views of the President's Commission for the Study of Ethical Problems in Medicine and Biomedical and Behavioral Research. The significance of the act/omission distinction was extensively discussed in a report entitled "Deciding to Forego Life-Sustaining Treatment." The Commission began with the observation that a distinction between act and omission is widely followed by medical personnel dealing with the irreversibly ill:

"Physicians commonly acquiesce in the wishes of competent patients not to receive specified treatments, even when failure to provide those treatments will increase the chance—or make certain—that the patient will die soon. When some patients are dying of a disease process that cannot be arrested, physicians may, for example, write orders not to provide resuscitation if the heart should stop, forego antibiotic treatment of pneumonia and other infections, cease use of respirators, or withhold aggressive therapy from overwhelmingly burned patients. Courts have sanctioned such decisions by guardians for incompetent patients, as well as by competent patients who might have lived for an indefinite period if treated. Although declining to start or continue life-sustaining treatment is often acceptable, health care providers properly refuse to honor a patient's request to be directly killed. Not only would killing, as by violence or strychnine, be outside the bounds of accepted medical practice, but as murder it would be subject to a range of criminal sanctions, regardless of the provider's motives."

The Commission then undertook to identify the possible grounds for differentiating between acts and omissions:

"Usually, one or more of several factors make fatal actions worse than fatal omissions:

(i) The motives of an agent who acts to cause death are usually worse (for example, self-interest or malice) than those of someone who omits to act and lets another die.

(ii) A person who is barred from acting to cause another's death is usually thereby placed at no personal risk of harm; whereas, especially outside the medical context, if a person were forced to intercede to save another's life (instead of standing by and omitting to act), he or she would often be put at substantial risk.

(iii) The nature and duration of future life denied to a person whose life is ended by another's act is usually much greater than that denied to a dying person whose death comes slightly more quickly due to an omission of treatment.

(iv) A person, especially a patient, may still have some possibility of surviving if one omits to act, while survival is more often foreclosed by actions that lead to death.

Each of these factors—or several in combination—can make a significant moral difference in the evaluation of any particular instance of acting and omitting to act. Together they help explain why most actions leading to death are correctly considered morally worse than most omissions leading to death."

The Commission recognized, however, that not all of these factors can plausibly be invoked in the medical context. Specifically, (i) health care professionals could be "equally merciful" in acting or omitting; (ii) medical personnel usually act at no personal risk to themselves and indeed have a "special role-related duty" to act on behalf of their patients; and (iii) they often face special situations concerning the "nature and duration of future life." "Only the final factor," therefore, "can apply as much in medical settings as elsewhere":

"Indeed, this factor has particular relevance here since the element of uncertainty—whether a patient really will die if treatment is ceased—is sometimes unavoidable in the medical setting. A valid distinction may therefore arise between an act causing certain death (for example, a poisoning) and an omission that hastens or risks death (such as not amputating a gangrenous limb). But sometimes death is as certain following withdrawal of a treatment as following a particular action that is reliably expected to lead to death.

"Consequently, merely determining whether what was done involved a fatal act or omission does not establish whether it was morally acceptable. Some actions that lead to death can be acceptable: very dangerous but potentially beneficial surgery or the use of hazardous doses of morphine for severe pain are examples. Some omissions that lead to death are very serious wrongs: deliberately failing to treat an ordinary patient's bacterial pneumonia or ignoring a bleeding patient's pleas for help would be totally unacceptable conduct for that patient's physician."

In view of this reasoning, one might have thought that the Commission would recommend abandoning the act/omission distinction. But that was not the case:

"Although there are some cases in which the acting-omitting distinction is difficult to make and although its moral importance originates in other considerations, the commonly accepted prohibition of active killing helps to produce the correct decision in the great majority of cases. Furthermore, weakening the legal prohibition to allow a deliberate taking of life in extreme circumstances would risk allowing wholly unjustified taking of life in less extreme circumstances. . . . Thus, the Commission concludes that the current interpretation of the legal prohibition of active killing should be sustained."

Is this conclusion sound? Is it defensible on the ground stated? On any other ground?

3. **Differentiating Acts From Omissions.** Even if one accepts that there is a difference in principle between acting and omitting to act in this context, there remains the difficulty of differentiating acts from omissions. The tendency in medical practice is to demark that difference with terms that are both descriptive and conclusory. Thus, unacceptable conduct leading to death of a patient is often identified as "killing," a word that connotes both the affirmative act and its unacceptability. Acceptable conduct, by contrast, is usually described as "allowing to die."

In some cases the distinction seems clear. If a terminally ill patient experiences spontaneous cardio-respiratory arrest, the physician who foregoes heroic attempts at resuscitation has, whatever the moral or legal import of this conclusion, omitted to act. Less clear is the termination of a treatment already underway. Is turning off the respirator an act or an omission? Many physicians, who are ready to *withhold* treatment in appropriate cases, are nevertheless reluctant to *withdraw* treatment once begun. The former conduct seems an acceptable omission, while the latter comes dangerously close to an act.[b]

The *Barber* court obviated this difficulty by construing turning off the respirator and withdrawing intravenous feeding as omissions rather than acts. Is this characterization persuasive? Is there a meaningful distinction to be made between not turning on a respirator and later turning it off? Between turning off the respirator and withdrawing sustenance? Between any of these "omissions" and the apparent "act" of injecting a lethal dose of morphine?

4. **Legislative Solutions.** Increasingly, situations such as that presented in *Barber* are handled under special legislation. Most common is the statutory provision for a "living will," an advance declaration of the patient's wishes regarding the withdrawal of life-sustaining treatment. Such laws are various entitled "Death with Dignity" or "Natural Death" acts, and they vary in detail. The common theme,

[b] Ironically, the distinction between withholding and withdrawing treatment may sometimes be medically perverse. The President's Commission received testimony that the fear that a therapy once begun could not be discontinued has "unduly raised the threshold" for vigorous intervention on behalf of defective newborns. The Commission's view was that, contrary to the usual formulation, the decision to withhold treatment should actually require a *greater* justification than the decision to withdraw treatment. "Whether a particular treatment will have positive effects is often highly uncertain before the therapy has been tried. If a trial of therapy makes clear that it is not helpful to the patient, this is actual evidence (rather than mere surmise) to support stopping because the therapeutic benefit that earlier was a possibility has been found to be clearly unobtainable." The President's Commission for the Study of Ethical Problems in Medicine and Biomedical and Behavioral Research, Deciding to Forego Life-Sustaining Treatment 75–76 (1983).

however, is to enable a patient to direct that medical treatment be stopped under specified circumstances even though the patient is at that point incompetent to address the issue. Under the terms of these statutes, physicians who follow such directives are protected from civil or criminal liability for doing so. Thus, for example, if Mr. Herbert had executed a "living will" in accordance with California's Natural Death Act, the prosecution in *Barber* would never have occurred.

Interestingly, there is support for the view that a "living will" may be legally valid even where it is not specially authorized by statute. The argument seems to be that the physician's obligation is only to treat the patient to the extent of his or her consent. If the patient directs that medical care be stopped in certain circumstances, the physician is then free, or perhaps required, to withhold treatment should those circumstances arise. Of course, this argument is necessarily based on the distinction between act and omission, as there is no suggestion that a patient may validly consent to being actively killed by his or her physician. And there is also tension between this conclusion and the traditional doctrine that consent of the victim is not a defense to murder. See, e.g., § 2.11(2) of the Model Penal Code, which, because of the definition of "conduct" in § 1.13(5), applies both to acts and to omissions.

Less widespread are legislative provisions for designation of a proxy to speak on the patient's behalf in the event that he or she becomes incompetent. This may be accomplished as part of the "living will" legislation or as an amendment to a "durable power-of-attorney" statute. The idea is that the proxy will make the critical decision regarding continuation of life-sustaining care in light of the patient's wishes and the medical situation. Without explicit legislative authorization, however, the legal status of such arrangements may well be doubted.[c]

NOTE ON POSSESSION

As the preceding materials indicate, criminal liability may be based either on an affirmative act proscribed by law or on failure to perform an act required by law. There is also a third possibility—liability for possession. Possession may be thought of as a status that begins with the act of acquisition and that is continued by a failure to divest. Alternatively, possession may be viewed simply as an indirect way of proving the act of acquisition. In any event, possession is very widely employed as a basis of criminal liability. The Model Penal Code merely confirms existing law when it identifies possession, along with acts and omissions, as possible grounds for criminal liability. Section 2.01(4) provides that, "[p]ossession is an act . . . if the possessor knowingly procured or received the thing possessed or was aware of his control thereof for a sufficient period to have been able to terminate his

[c] This subject is treated in J. Robertson, The Rights of the Critically Ill 97–115 (1983). Additionally, a detailed examination of one of the most recently enacted and most comprehensive statutes in this field appears in Note, Proxy Decisionmaking for the Terminally Ill: The Virginia Approach, 70 Va.L.Rev. 1269 (1984).

possession." At least as so defined, there seems to be no objection in principle to punishing crimes of possession. In other words, there seems to be no reason to regard possession as an inherently inappropriate basis for imposing penal sanctions. That is not to say, however, that there are not serious questions arising from the definition and construction of contemporary possession offenses. These questions are considered at some length in the next section of these materials, specifically in the subsection on Minimum Conduct Requirements in Completed Offenses, at pages 140–52, infra. For the moment, it is only important to note that possession often figures largely in the actus reus of criminal offenses.

SECTION 3: MINIMUM CONDUCT REQUIREMENTS FOR THE IMPOSITION OF PENAL SANCTIONS

NOTES ON THE SIGNIFICANCE OF CONDUCT IN THE PENAL LAW

1. **The Importance of the Act Requirement**. Settled doctrine requires that criminal liability be based on conduct. More than that, it requires that the conduct be in some sense voluntary. A subsequent subsection of these materials will examine the question of voluntariness. For the present, however, it is useful to put voluntariness to one side and to focus instead on the significance of conduct as a prerequisite to penal sanctions.

The law is clear that conduct is an essential component of crime definition. The traditional understanding on this point is well and succinctly put in G. Williams, Criminal Law: The General Part 1 (2d ed. 1961):

> "That crime requires an act is invariably true if the proposition be read as meaning that a private thought is not sufficient to found responsibility. . . . 'So long as an act rests in bare intention,' said Mansfield, 'it is not punishable by our laws;' and this is so even though the intention be abundantly proved by the confession of the accused."

As the quotation suggests, it has long been established that criminal liability may not be premised on a mere intention or bare desire to do wrong. Increasingly, the requirement of conduct is also taken to bar the infliction of punishment for a mere personal characteristic or status. Instead, criminal liability is reserved for behavior. At least within the confines of the Anglo-American tradition, the starting point for any definition of crime is a statement of proscribed conduct.

It is important to remember, of course, that adherence to the requirement of conduct does not limit the penal law to the redress of positive wrongdoing. On the contrary, it is clear that the law may proscribe as criminal either an act or a failure to act. It may even punish possession—a condition begun by an act of acquisition and continued by a failure to divest. But conduct in some form—an act, omission, or possession by the accused—remains everywhere accepted as an essential prerequisite of criminal conviction and punishment.

This requirement of conduct is so fundamental to our understanding of the criminal law that it is only rarely put in issue. Obvious though it may seem, however, the requirement of conduct is a matter of great significance to the conceptual structure of the penal law. The excerpts that follow support this conclusion.

2. **Jeffries & Stephan**. A short summary of the traditional view of the act requirement appears in Jeffries & Stephan, Defenses, Presumptions, and Burden of Proof in the Criminal Law, 88 Yale L.J.1325, 1371 n. 130 (1979): *

"The significance of the act requirement should not be understated. First, it serves a critical evidentiary function in corroborating other proof going to the existence of evil intent. The inevitable risk of error in assessing mental attitude is intolerably great when state of mind is not anchored in evidence of objectively demonstrable conduct. Thus, proof of conduct is necessary to establish culpability.

"Second, the act requirement serves an equally important function in differentiating daydreams from fixed intentions. Mental attitude is not only difficult to demonstrate; it is also evanescent, fluid, and various. When there is no real prospect that evil thought will be translated into evil deed, there is no legitimate occasion for punishment. The act requirement therefore precludes criminal penalty for fantasy, wish, or conjecture. It insists that anti-social thought be manifest in behavior tending toward the harm ultimately feared. Thus, proof of conduct is necessary to establish dangerousness as well as culpability.

"Finally, the act requirement preserves the liberty of the individual citizen by constraining penal liability within a tolerable sphere. It states a limit on the coercive power of the state and marks a boundary of individual accountability to the collective will. As Herbert Packer put the point, the act requirement provides a locus poenitentiae to enable the law-abiding citizen to avoid criminal liability. . . ."

3. **Packer.** The final reference in the preceding excerpt is to H. Packer, The Limits of the Criminal Sanction 73–75 (1968).** Packer's

* Reprinted by permission of The Yale Law Journal Company and Fred B. Rothman & Company from The Yale Law Journal, Vol. 88, p. 1371.

with the permission of the publishers, Stanford University Press. © 1968 by Herbert L. Packer.

** Reprinted from The Limits of the Criminal Sanction by Herbert L. Packer,

development of the point is sufficiently subtle to warrant extensive quotation:

"It may hardly seem a startling notion that criminal law, or law in general for that matter, is concerned with conduct—people's actions (including their verbal and other expressive actions) and their failures to act. Yet there is nothing in the nature of things that compels this focus. The criminal law could be concerned with people's thoughts and emotions, with their personality patterns and character structures. It is true that if this rather than conduct was the focus, it would still be expedient in most cases to ascertain these essentially internal characteristics through inquiry into conduct. But if these internal characteristics were the focus, conduct would simply be evidence of what we are interested in rather than the thing itself; and we would not hesitate to use other evidence to the extent that it became available. If, for example, we could determine through projective tests like the Rohrschach or through other and more sophisticated forms of psychological testing that a given individual was likely to inflict serious physical injury on someone, someday, somewhere, and if we viewed conduct [as merely evidentiary rather than as a prerequisite of liability], we would presumably not hesitate to inflict punishment on that person for his propensities, or, as the old cliche has it, for thinking evil thoughts. . . .

"Why do we not do so? The obvious historical answer is that, aside from a few antiquarian anomalies such as the offense of imagining the King's death, we have not been sufficiently stirred by the danger presented or sufficiently confident of our ability to discern propensities in the absence of conduct to use the instruments of the criminal law in this fashion. For some it may be enough to rejoice that historically this was so and to rest on that historical accident for the present and the future, but I think that a further answer is required. This answer turns, in my view, on the idea of culpability. . . .

"Among the notions associated with the concept of 'culpability' are those of free will and human autonomy. I do not mean this in any deep philosophical sense but in a contingent and practical social sense. It is important, especially in a society that likes to describe itself as 'free' and 'open,' that a government should be empowered to coerce people only for what they do and not for what they are.

"If this is important for law generally, it is a fortiori important for that most coercive of legal instruments, the criminal law. Now, this self-denying ordinance can be and often is attacked as being inconsistent with the facts of human nature. People may in fact have little if any greater capacity to control their conduct . . . than their emotions or their thoughts. It is therefore either unrealistic or hypocritical, so the argument runs, to deal with conduct as willed or to treat it differently from personality and character.

"This attack is, however, misconceived. Neither philosophic concepts nor psychological realities are actually at issue in the criminal law. The idea of free will in relation to conduct is not, in the legal system, a statement of fact, but rather a value preference having very little to do with the metaphysics of determinism and free will. . . . Very simply, the law treats man's conduct as autonomous and willed, not because it is, but because it is desirable to proceed as if it were. It is desirable because the capacity of the individual human being to live his life in reasonable freedom from socially imposed external constraints (the only kind with which the law is concerned) would be fatally impaired unless the law provided a locus poenitentiae, a point of no return beyond which external constraints may be imposed but before which the individual is free—not free of whatever compulsions determinists tell us he labors under but free of the very specific social compulsions of the law. . . ."

4. **Questions and Comments on the Act Requirement**. Professor Packer mentions, as a hypothetical, the possibility of using sophisticated psychological testing to determine in advance that a given individual is likely to engage in violent conduct. Recent research suggests that the prospect may not be entirely fanciful. Take, for example, the findings reported in Abel, Barlow, Blanchard & Guild, The Components of Rapists Sexual Arousal, 34 Arch.Gen.Psychiatry 895 (1977). There the researchers used the degree of penile erection to measure sexual arousal in males. Both rapists and non-rapists were read vivid descriptions of two types of sexual encounters: consensual intercourse actively enjoyed by both parties and coercive intercourse against the will of the female. The responses of the two groups differed significantly. Rapists experienced sexual arousal in both situations. Non-rapists experienced comparable arousal in the descriptions of consensual intercourse but markedly lower responses to the descriptions of coercive encounter. As the researchers reported their conclusion, "[u]sing explicit descriptions of rape and non-rape behavior as stimuli, rapists can be separated from non-rapists on the basis of their erection responses."

Suppose, hypothetically, that this technique were sufficiently refined to allow accurate predictions of rape behavior. Suppose, to be specific, that persons extremely likely to engage in violent rape could be identified in advance of such conduct. If such a procedure were feasible, would you favor using it as a basis for criminal prosecution? For involuntary commitment? Or would you remain convinced of the wisdom of awaiting the actual conduct before coercive state intervention? In other words, if the evidentiary functions of the act requirement could be satisfied by reliable scientific testing, would you still take the position, as does Professor Packer, that it would remain essential to limit the criminal law to the punishment of conduct? Or would you think that the societal costs of allowing such conduct to occur might then become too high?

———

SUBSECTION A: MINIMUM CONDUCT REQUIREMENTS AND ANTICIPATORY OFFENSES

INTRODUCTORY NOTE ON ATTEMPT

Although minimum conduct requirements are a matter of pervasive importance in the penal law, the issue has received surprisingly little doctrinal development. Indeed, the only doctrinal formulations addressed to this problem come from the law of anticipatory offenses, specifically from the law of attempt.

Attempt is an anticipatory offense in the sense that it reaches conduct preliminary to completion of the crime contemplated. Attempt is defined chiefly by reference to the requirements of the underlying offense. Thus, there can be no attempt standing alone. There must be an attempt to commit murder, rape, larceny, or some other substantive offense. In each instance, the actor takes some step toward completion of the underlying crime. The question therefore arises: How much conduct is enough? How far must the actor proceed towards completion of the underlying offense for attempt liability to attach? Doctrinally, this question is put as the distinction between criminal attempt and mere preparation. The former is punishable, while the latter is not. The line between preparation and attempt marks the point at which the actor's conduct becomes sufficient to support the imposition of penal sanctions.

In order to isolate the question of how much conduct is enough, it is necessary to assume that all other requirements of the law of attempt have been met. In particular, one must take as given that the actor has been shown to have the state of mind required for the crime of attempt. For present purposes, one should assume (and this turns out to be very nearly correct) that the state of mind required for attempt is purpose.[a] The actor must have a conscious objective or desire to complete a course of conduct proscribed as criminal. In each of the situations discussed below, the trier of fact is prepared to conclude, beyond a reasonable doubt, that the actor had such a purpose. The question, therefore, is whether his actions toward fulfilling that purpose were sufficient to support criminal liability. Various approaches to answering that question are revealed by the following case.

----

[a] This issue is explored more fully at pages 342–52, infra.

PEOPLE v. BOWEN AND ROUSE

Court of Appeals of Michigan, 1968.
10 Mich.App. 1, 158 N.W.2d 794.

LEVIN, JUDGE. Defendants, Sherrel Bowen and William Rouse, appeal their convictions of attempted larceny in a building.

On January 19, 1965, at approximately eight o'clock p. m., the defendants and two female companions were admitted to the home of one Matilda Gatzmeyer, an 80-year-old woman. The defendants' car was observed parked in front of Miss Gatzmeyer's residence and a neighbor, believing the defendants to have designs upon her property, called the police. Two police officers arrived and entered the home along with the neighbor. The defendants were found in the rear of the house near or on the basement steps. The two female companions were seated on either side of Miss Gatzmeyer, apparently engaged with her in conversation. The bedroom of the house was in a state of disarray.

The police ordered defendants to come to the front of the house and sit in the living room. Defendant Rouse seated himself within a foot of the TV, and some time thereafter one of the police officers spotted under the TV set two rings belonging to Miss Gatzmeyer. The neighbor testified she found a necklace on the staircase near where defendant Bowen had been standing when he was first sighted by the police. When the neighbor's discovery was called to the attention of one of the police officers, he and Miss Gatzmeyer went to the staircase and found the necklace in that location.

After interrogation, the defendants were arrested and charged with larceny of "rings and necklace" in a building in violation of Mich.Comp.Laws Ann. § 28.592.[b]

Bowen had been to the Gatzmeyer home on a number of prior occasions, ostensibly as a handyman, the same reason he gave Miss Gatzmeyer for appearing on the night in question. Miss Gatzmeyer testified that on this occasion the defendants sought to hire themselves out to clean and to do some masonry work on the chimney. She complained about the high prices charged by Bowen and his failure to do work as agreed, and that Bowen's helper (the role allegedly filled by Rouse at the time of the incident) generally helped himself to things that belonged to her.

The neighbor testified that she had met Bowen on three occasions prior to the one in question and that on one occasion Bowen had induced Miss Gatzmeyer to go with him to the bank, but it was not clear whether the visit to the bank was to withdraw money to pay Bowen that which was due him or unlawfully to separate Miss Gatzmeyer from her money.

The neighbor testified that she visited with Miss Gatzmeyer daily and assisted her in various chores and generally in getting around.

---

[b] The statute provides, in pertinent part, as follows:

"Any person who shall commit the crime of larceny by stealing in any dwelling house . . . or any building used by the public shall be guilty of a felony."

[Footnote by eds.]

She stated that when she and the police officers arrived on the night in question the dresser drawers in the bedroom were all pulled out and everything thrown all over the bed. This was not the way Miss Gatzmeyer generally kept the house according to the neighbor: "she has a very neat house, everything is in its place." The neighbor further testified that "after Miss Gatzmeyer cleaned up (presumably after the police left) she found more jewelry back of the pillows" on the couch Bowen sat on during his interrogation by the police.

Miss Gatzmeyer testified that the defendants removed the jewelry from her bedroom without her consent.

At the beginning of his charge to the jury, the trial judge stated that because he doubted whether the case properly could be submitted to the jury on the original charge of larceny in a building he had decided to submit it to the jury solely on the included offense of attempt to commit larceny in a building.

I

There was sufficient evidence to support the defendants' conviction of attempt to commit larceny. The jury could properly infer from the testimony that the defendants did in fact ransack Miss Gatzmeyer's bedroom and furniture without her permission, remove the two rings which were found under the TV set and the necklace found on the staircase. Such a finding would justify conviction of attempted larceny, the elements of which are a felonious intent to commit larceny and an overt act going beyond mere preparation towards the commission of the crime. It is the jury's function to weigh the evidence and to determine therefrom whether such intent is manifest and in doing so the jury may draw reasonable inferences from the facts.

II

We do find error in the judge's failure properly to charge the jury on the necessity of finding an overt act [towards commission of larceny in a building]. It has been said that the overt act "is the essence of the offense" or the "gravamen of the offense." Not only did the trial judge fail to charge the jury at all concerning the necessity of finding an overt act, but he also incorrectly charged that the jury could convict if it found that the defendants came to or entered Miss Gatzmeyer's house with the intention of committing larceny.

During the charge, the trial judge stated:

"The theory of the People is that the evidence in this case, that is, the age of the complainant, Mrs. Gatzmeyer, the lateness of the visit to the house, the presence of two women to talk to the complainant, and the condition of the bedroom which it is claimed indicated ransacking and the attempt of the defendants to hide when the police were called, bear upon and indicate that the two defendants *came there with the intention* of committing larceny in the dwelling. The offense of larceny isn't clear but the attempt to commit larceny it is charged by the People . . . is clear.

"Now, the defense is rather brief and that is that the testimony given here does not tend to prove beyond a reasonable doubt that the defendants *entered the place with the intent* or for the purpose of attempting to commit larceny. In other words, the defense is that the testimony that is shown here is not sufficient to convict the defendants beyond a reasonable doubt of *coming* into that building or *going into the building* on the night in question *with the intent* to commit larceny." (Emphasis supplied.)

There was ample evidence from which the jury could have found felonious intent. There are the circumstances related by the judge in his charge, as well as the other evidence previously set forth in this opinion. We must assume that, in convicting the defendants, the jury followed the judge's instructions and found the requisite felonious intent.

. . . [T]he trial judge's failure to charge the jury on the necessity of finding commission of an overt act, as a separate ingredient or element, might not be error if he were correct in charging the jury that if it found defendants "came" to or "entered" Miss Gatzmeyer's house with intent to commit larceny it could bring in a verdict of guilty. If defendants' coming to, or entering, Miss Gatzmeyer's house with felonious intent was an "overt act", the jury verdict of guilty could be viewed as a finding of the requisite overt act.

Thus, the narrow question before us is whether the defendants when they came to or entered Miss Gatzmeyer's house with the intent to commit larceny committed an overt act that would support their conviction of attempted larceny. In our opinion, their mere coming to or entry of Miss Gatzmeyer's house was not an overt act, under the circumstances that Mr. Bowen and other helpers had rightfully been in the house on prior occasions and were admitted to the house by Miss Gatzmeyer on the night in question. . . .

In People v. Coleman, 350 Mich. 268, 86 N.W.2d 281 (1957), the Supreme Court stated that a defendant may not be convicted of an attempt unless he has "gone beyond acts of an ambiguous nature" or those that are "equivocal," [7] and that a "thoughtful test for the resolution of the equivocal act has been phrased by Turner in his article,

---

[7] . . . Other courts have said much the same thing in describing the overt act as one that can have "no other purpose" or "apparent result" than the commission of the principal crime—the "natural and probable" effect test is of the same genre; and then there are the judicial and text statements which speak of the overt act as an act that "commences" or has a "direct tendency" or "sufficient proximity" or "sufficient nearness" to the commission of the principal offense that (some add, hav-

ing in mind the seriousness and enormity of the principal offense), in the opinion of the court, the actor's purpose is clear. Whether the differences in language used by the courts bring about different results or merely permit the courts that speak in terms of proximity or nearness or the like to explain their results with greater ease is beyond the scope of this opinion. On the question before us, we found substantial uniformity in results, if not in their explanation.

'Attempts to Commit Crimes' in 5 Camb.L.J. 230, 237–38 (1933), in these words:

> 'If the acts of the accused, taken by themselves, are unambig-
> uous, and cannot, in reason, be regarded as pointing to any other
> end than the commission of the specific crime in question, then
> they constitute a sufficient actus reus. In other words, his acts
> must be *unequivocally referable* to the commission of the specific
> crime. They must, as the late Sir John Salmond said, "speak for
> themselves." If the example may be permitted, it is as though a
> cinematograph film, which has so far depicted merely the ac-
> cused person's acts without stating what was his intention, had
> been suddenly stopped, and the audience were asked to say to
> what end those acts were directed. If there is only one reasona-
> ble answer to this question then the accused has done what
> amounts to an "attempt" to attain that end. If there is more
> than one reasonably possible answer, then the accused has not
> yet done enough.' "   .   .   .

It has been suggested that the basic function of the overt act is corroboration of the felonious intent. However, that analysis can become somewhat circular if we permit intent to be gleaned from the overt act itself.

The testimony in this case was that defendant Bowen had, on a number of prior occasions, been in Miss Gatzmeyer's house with help-ers. With that in mind and even if it be assumed (on the basis of the jury finding) that the defendants entered her house with a felonious intent, their mere presence there did not indicate, let alone "corrobo-rate," that intention. The defendants did not break into Miss Gatzmeyer's house—they were voluntarily admitted by her. At the time of defendants' admission to Miss Gatzmeyer's house their *acts* were entirely "ambiguous" and "equivocal." It is the acts thereafter allegedly committed (but as to which we have no finding from the jury) [10] that were neither ambiguous nor equivocal.

Our analysis of the authorities convinces us that the function of the overt act is not to "corroborate," but rather to demonstrate that the defendant has converted resolution into action. Man being what he is, evil thoughts and intentions are easily formed. Fortunately, for socie-ty, most felonious thoughts are not fulfilled. The law does not punish evil intent or even every act done with the intent to commit a crime. The requirement that the jury find an overt act proceeds on the assumption that the devil may lose the contest, albeit late in the hour.

---

[10] The only jury finding before us is a finding that the defendants came to Miss Gatzmeyer's house with a felonious intent. While we proceed on the assumption that in convicting the defendants the jury con-cluded that the defendants came to or en-tered Miss Gatzmeyer's house with a felo-nious intent, we cannot similarly assume that the jury found that the defendant ransacked Miss Gatzmeyer's room or re-moved her personal belongings from her bedroom or were responsible for the fact that they were found under the TV set or on the staircase, where the only issue sub-mitted to the jury was whether the "defen-dants *came there* with intention of commit-ting larceny." The jury could have found such *intention* on the basis of evidence other than the ransacking and the atypical locations of her personal belongings.

The overt act is not any act. In this connection, "overt" is used in the sense of "manifest" or symbolic. The act must manifest, or be symbolic of, the crime. Considering that Bowen and helpers had been in Miss Gatzmeyer's house on previous occasions (and, whatever her differences with Bowen may have been, she nevertheless admitted him on the night in question), the fact that the defendants came to and entered Miss Gatzmeyer's house would not manifest or symbolize the crime . . . which they were convicted of attempting to commit. . . .

Attempt patterns vary widely. No rule can be laid down applicable to all cases. Most cases will in the end turn on their own facts.

> "It is a question of degree . . . .. [T]he degree of proximity held sufficient may vary with the circumstances, including among other things the apprehension which the particular crime is calculated to excite." Commonwealth v. Peaslee, 177 Mass. 267, 272, 59 N.E. 55, 56 (1901) [per Holmes, J.].

In the last cited case the defendant arranged combustibles in a building, then left the building. Later he set out for the building with the intention of lighting it, but changed his mind and turned back. Held not to be an attempt.

In People v. Pippin, 316 Mich. 191, 25 N.W.2d 164 (1946), defendant, who had on a prior occasion been convicted of gross indecency, was found guilty of parole violation on evidence that he had invited a 13-year-old boy to enter his automobile. The Supreme Court said the question was whether the defendant could be convicted of attempt to commit the crime of gross indecency. The court assumed arguendo that intent had been established (just as we assume in this case that the jury found the defendants here before us harbored a felonious intent) but ruled that an overt act had not been established—"the act [committed by Pippin], at most can be considered no more than preparation for the attempt."

In People v. Youngs, 122 Mich. 292, 81 N.W. 114 (1899), the defendant armed himself with a revolver, purchased cartridges, obtained an armed accomplice, carried slippers to perpetrate a silent entry of the intended victim's house, purchased chloroform to be used in the commission of the crime, and had already set out for the selected scene of the crime when he was arrested. Our Supreme Court reversed the conviction, holding that the defendant had not gone beyond preparation. . . .

Where entry or attempted entry upon the victim's premises has been held in itself sufficient to constitute an overt act, such entry or attempted entry has been without permission, or the defendant came armed or with burglary tools or other means of committing the crime. . . .

Reversed and remanded for a new trial.

NOTES ON PREPARATION VS. ATTEMPT

1. **The Last-Proximate-Act Doctrine.** The earliest case to undertake a general distinction between preparation and attempt was Regina v. Eagleton, 6 Cox C.C. 559 (Crim.App.1855). The defendant in that case contracted with the public authorities to deliver to the poor of the parish loaves of bread weighing three and one-half pounds each. In fact, he delivered loaves weighing less. He then attempted to obtain full credit in his accounts with the public authorities, but the shortfall was discovered before payment was made. In an opinion affirming defendant's conviction for attempt to commit fraud, Baron Parke made the following comments:

"The mere intention to commit a misdemeanor is not criminal, some act is required; and we do not think that all acts towards committing a misdemeanor are indictable. Acts remotely leading towards the commission of the offence are not to be considered as attempts to commit it; but acts immediately connected with it are; and if in this case after the credit with the relieving officer for the fraudulent overcharge, any further step on the part of the defendant had been necessary to obtain payment, as the making out a further account, or producing the vouchers to the board, we should have thought that the obtaining credit in account with the relieving officer would not have been sufficiently proximate to the obtaining of the money.

"But on the statement in this case no other act on the part of the defendant would have been required. It was the last act depending on himself towards the payment of the money, and therefore it ought to be considered as an attempt."

These remarks gave rise to the doctrine of the "last proximate act." Under this approach, an attempt is made out when the actor does all that he intends to do to accomplish the crime. Thus, for example, a would-be murderer commits the last proximate act when he or she shoots at the intended victim. If, however, the actor is apprehended while lying in wait, the final act remains undone. Obviously, this is a very demanding standard for the actus reus of attempt, and, despite Baron Parke's apparently mandatory phrasing, the courts have not insisted on it. At least in this country, commission of the last proximate act has long been regarded as sufficient but not necessary to constitute an attempt. A number of tests have been advanced to specify what *is* necessary.

2. **Other Common-Law Tests.** The drafters of the Model Penal Code attempt provision referred to the formulation of a general standard for distinguishing preparation from attempt as "the most difficult problem in defining attempt liability." Model Penal Code § 5.01, Commentary at 39 (Tent. Draft No. 10, 1958). This judgment is confirmed by the judicial experience in trying to resolve that issue. The following tests have been suggested:

(i) **The Physical-Proximity Test.** Many courts have emphasized the physical proximity of the actor's conduct to the completed offense. The focus here is not on what has already been done but on what yet remains to be done to complete the crime. Under this view, the actor's separation from the criminal objective—whether in terms of time, distance, or necessary steps not yet taken—becomes the critical factor.

Application of the physical-proximity test is illustrated by the well known case of People v. Rizzo, 246 N.Y. 334, 158 N.E. 888 (1927). Defendant and three others made plans to rob one Charles Rao, a payroll clerk for a construction company. The men armed themselves and set off in a car to find their intended victim. They went to the bank from which he was supposed to draw the money and to the company's various construction sites, but they located neither the clerk nor the money. They succeeded, however, in attracting the attention of the police, with the result that the defendants were convicted of attempt to commit robbery. The courts construed New York law to require that the actor come "*very near* to the accomplishment of the crime" in order to be liable for attempt. Applying this standard, the Court of Appeals reversed the conviction with the following remarks:

> "To constitute the crime of robbery, the money must have been taken from Rao by means of force or violence, or through fear. The crime of attempt to commit robbery was committed, if these defendants did an act tending to the commission of this robbery. Did the acts above described come dangerously near to the taking of Rao's property? Did the acts come so near the commission of robbery that there was reasonable likelihood of its accomplishment but for the interference [of the police]? Rao was not found; the defendants were still looking for him; no attempt to rob him could be made, at least until he came in sight . . . . . Men would not be guilty of an attempt at burglary if they had planned to break into a building and were arrested while they were hunting about the streets for the building not knowing where it was. Neither would a man be guilty of an attempt to commit murder if he armed himself and started out to find the person whom he had planned to kill but could not find him. So here these defendants were not guilty of an attempt to commit robbery . . . when they had not found or reached the presence of the person they intended to rob."

(ii) **The Indispensable-Element Test.** A variation on the proximity approach is the indispensable-element test. Under this view, no attempt can be committed if the actor has yet to acquire control over an indispensable element of the criminal endeavor. The standard illustration is the criminal scheme requiring action by a third party. Thus, one who plans to defraud an insurer by having another file a false claim could not be guilty of attempt until the other actually filed the claim or at least agreed to do so. The same reasoning applies when control over some object is indispensable to commission of the offense. Thus, a would-be whiskey smuggler would not become liable for attempt until he or she actually took possession of the whiskey. In such cases, liability would be precluded on the ground that the requisite proximity could not be shown if the actor has yet to assert effective control over an indispensable element of the planned offense.

(iii) **The Dangerous-Proximity Test.** An expanded version of the proximity test was advanced by Justice Holmes. Under this approach the issue of the actor's nearness to completion of the offense is subsumed in a broader inquiry that also encompasses the gravity of the harm threatened, the degree of apprehension aroused, and the probability that the conduct would result in the intended offense. Evaluating all these factors, the courts should ask whether there was a "dangerous proximity to success" in the actor's conduct. Hyde v. United States, 225 U.S. 347, 388 (1912) (Holmes, J., dissenting). See also Commonwealth v. Peaslee, 177 Mass. 267, 59 N.E. 55 (1901) (discussed in the principal case).

This approach—in common with other variations on the proximity doctrine—can be defended on the view that the essential purpose of the law of attempt is to punish dangerous conduct. The ultimate harms to be avoided are those identified by substantive crimes. Where the substantive offense is complete, the danger has been realized, and punishment is warranted. Where the offense is not complete, however, the danger has not been realized, and the case for punishment is weaker. Only where the anticipatory conduct comes dangerously close to accomplishing the harm ultimately feared is there sufficient justification for punishment of the actor, even though he may have done his best to commit a criminal offense.

Do you agree with this reasoning? Are there other objectives that ought to be served by the law of attempt? If so, how would they suggest that the focus of the various proximity tests should be changed?

(iv) **The Res-Ipsa-Loquitur Test.** An entirely different approach to the problem of distinguishing preparation from attempt is suggested by the res-ipsa-loquitur test. This position was first expounded by Justice Salmond of New Zealand. As he stated the doctrine in King v. Barker, [1924] N.Z.L.R. 865, 874:

> "An act done with intent to commit a crime is not a criminal attempt unless it is of such a nature as to be in itself sufficient evidence of the criminal intent with which it is done. A criminal attempt is an act which shows criminal intent on the face of it. The case must be one in which res ipsa loquitur."

See also J. Salmond, Jurisprudence 350–52 (3d ed. 1910).

Unlike the various proximity doctrines, the res-ipsa-loquitur test looks to what the actor has already done rather than to what yet remains to be done. The object of this inquiry is not to assess the dangerousness of the anticipatory conduct itself, but to focus on the dangerousness of the actor who engaged in it. The premise is that the individual who has demonstrated a resolute commitment to a criminal endeavor poses a threat to the social order and therefore may properly be subject to criminal punishment. The argument is that the objectives of the criminal law are well served by focusing on the actor's demonstrated propensity toward criminal misbehavior rather than solely on the dangerousness of the completed conduct.

The difficulty with this view is that it calls for a prediction of arguably doubtful validity. Where an individual is judged dangerous on some basis other than the demonstrated dangerousness of his completed conduct (as the proximity tests would require), the possibility of error seems great. How can society be confident in such a case that the coercive sanctions of the criminal law are used only where warranted? The problem is the potential for over-prediction of dangerousness, and the question is whether a focus on the dangerous propensities of individuals can separate those who are truly intent on criminal misconduct from those who may not complete the offense.

The res-ipsa-loquitur test responds to these concerns in two ways. First, the requirement that the actor's criminal purpose be evident on the face of his conduct precludes criminal liability based solely on confessions or other representations of purpose. In other words, the requirement of unequivocal conduct demands manifest evidence of the actor's blameworthiness. It protects against conviction based on inadequate or unreliable proof of criminal purpose. Second, the res-ipsa-loquitur test may also be justified on the closely related ground of ensuring adequate evidence of the actor's commitment to the criminal purpose. Requiring conduct that speaks for itself would work to differentiate daydream from fixed intention and thus to limit liability for attempt to persons firmly resolved to violate societal interests.

Criticism of the res-ipsa test may be directed to its feasibility. The question is whether any conduct truly speaks for itself. Consider, for example, the hypotheticals offered in Salmond's *Barker* opinion, [1924] N.Z.L.R. at 875–76:

> "To buy a box of matches with intent to use them in burning a haystack is not an attempt to commit arson, for it is in itself and in appearance an innocent act, there being many other reasons than arson for buying matches. The act does not speak for itself of any guilty design. The criminal intent is not manifested by any overt act sufficient for that purpose. But he who takes matches to a haystack and there lights one of them, and blows it out on finding that he is observed, has done an act which speaks for itself, and he is guilty of a criminal attempt accordingly."

Does the latter conduct really speak for itself? Does it show criminal intent on the face of it, or are there other possible explanations for lighting a match near a haystack? The underlying concern is that the res-ipsa-loquitur test would disable the law of attempt in cases where liability should obtain. Glanville Williams used a variation of Salmond's hypothetical to support his view that liability should attach in at least some instances where unequivocality cannot be shown:

> "*D* goes up to a haystack, fills his pipe, and lights a match. The act of lighting the match, even to a suspicious-minded person, is ambiguous. It may indicate only that *D* is going to light his pipe; but perhaps, on the other hand, the pipe is only a

'blind' and *D* is really bent on setting fire to the stack. We do not know. Therefore, on the equivocality test, the act is not proximate. But suppose that as a matter of actual fact *D*, after his arrest, confesses to the guilty intent, and suppose that that confession is believed. We are now certain of the intent and the only question is as to proximity. It becomes clear that the act satisfies all the requirements for a criminal attempt."

G. Williams, Criminal Law: The General Part 630 (2d ed. 1961). Do you agree with Williams' reliance on subjective indicia of intent, or do you think Salmond is right in insisting on conduct which is "in itself sufficient evidence of the intent with which it is done"?

3. **The Model Code Approach.** The Model Penal Code standard for distinguishing preparation from attempt is stated in Section 5.01(1)(c). That provision allows conviction for attempt where the actor engages in "an act or omission constituting a substantial step in a course of conduct planned to culminate in his commission of the crime." The content of this standard is spelled out in Section 5.01(2):

"Conduct shall not be held to constitute a substantial step under Subsection (1)(c) of this Section unless it is strongly corroborative of the actor's criminal purpose. Without negating the sufficiency of other conduct, the following, if strongly corroborative of the actor's criminal purpose, shall not be held insufficient as a matter of law:

(a) lying in wait, searching for or following the contemplated victim of the crime;

(b) enticing or seeking to entice the contemplated victim of the crime to go to the place contemplated for its commission;

(c) reconnoitering the place contemplated for the commission of the crime;

(d) unlawful entry of a structure, vehicle or enclosure in which it is contemplated that the crime will be committed;

(e) possession of materials to be employed in the commission of the crime, which are specially designed for such unlawful use or which can serve no lawful purpose of the actor under the circumstances;

(f) possession, collection or fabrication of materials to be employed in the commission of the crime, at or near the place contemplated for its commission, where such possession, collection or fabrication serves no lawful purpose of the actor under the circumstances;

(g) soliciting an innocent agent to engage in conduct constituting an element of the crime."

Thus, under the Model Code there is a general requirement of a substantial step strongly corroborative of the actor's criminal purpose and a further specification of particular conduct that should not be deemed, as a matter of law, inadequate to support liability for attempt.

At least as compared to the proximity tests, the Model Code approach significantly broadens liability for attempt. The fact that the actor has not yet done the last act contemplated, or come dangerously close to completing the crime, or acquired control over some indispensable element of the design would not bar conviction for attempt—provided that the completed conduct constitutes a substantial step strongly corroborative of criminal purpose. In this respect—the focus on what has been done rather than on what remains to be done—the Model Code is based on the view that the proximity approach unduly compromises the social-control function of the penal law. The rationales for the Model Code conduct requirement are the same as those advanced to support the res-ipsa-loquitur test. Both standards are based on the view that the distinction between preparation and attempt serves chiefly to avoid speculative and undisciplined inquiry into state of mind. Both standards seek to ensure that the actor's criminal purpose and the firmness of his commitment to it are substantiated by objectively demonstrable conduct. Unlike the res-ipsa test, however, the Model Code does not require that the actor's conduct be *in itself* sufficient evidence of criminal purpose. Instead, it demands only that the actor's conduct *strongly corroborate* the existence of a criminal purpose that may be shown by other means. In essence, therefore, the Model Code provision is an effort to recast the conceptual focus of the res-ipsa-loquitur test into a more manageable standard for imposing liability. The ultimate objectives are to protect individuals against free-wheeling inquiries into criminal purpose and at the same time to broaden the scope of attempt so as to facilitate early police intervention and the effective neutralization of dangerous persons.

4. **Questions.** How would you apply the Model Code approach to *Bowen and Rouse*? To *Rizzo*? To the *Pippin* and *Youngs* cases discussed in *Bowen and Rouse*? Would the Model Code formulation necessarily change the results in those cases? Would it change the nature of the inquiry? Is the shift in focus desirable?

NOTES ON MINIMUM CONDUCT REQUIREMENTS AND SOLICITATION

1. *People* v. *Adami.* In connection with the preceding materials, consider the case of People v. Adami, 36 Cal.App.3d 452, 111 Cal.Rptr. 544 (1973). The court stated the facts as follows:

"Defendant was under investigation for sales of narcotics. Agent Thomas Dell'Ergo, who was conducting the undercover investigation, made several purchases of cocaine from defendant. During the course of their dealings, defendant mentioned to Dell'Ergo that he was having marital problems with his wife, and he was interested in getting rid of her. He expressed concern that his wife would inform the local authorities of his drug dealings. This conversation took place on November 1, 1972, over the telephone. Later that day Dell'Ergo met with defendant to negotiate the purchase of cocaine, and once again defendant mentioned that he wanted to get rid of his wife. He suggested arranging a fatal automobile accident.

"On the following day Dell'Ergo telephoned defendant regarding the purchase of cocaine, and defendant said he really wanted to have something done about his wife because she had stolen $5,000 in cash from him. Defendant said that he was interested in having Dell'Ergo be the one to do something about it.

"On the evening of November 6, 1972, Dell'Ergo contacted defendant and advised him that he had been in touch with an individual who would be willing to kill defendant's wife for a price. Dell'Ergo advised defendant that a $500 deposit was required, and it would be necessary for the defendant to furnish a photograph of his wife. Defendant agreed, and Dell'Ergo advised him that he would set up a meeting for the following day.

"Dell'Ergo met with defendant at a restaurant parking lot on November 7, 1972, in the afternoon, and drove him to the Laurel Motor Inn, where Inspector King of the San Francisco Police Department was waiting in the room. Dell'Ergo introduced King to defendant as the would-be assassin. Defendant gave King $500 and furnished him with a photograph of his wife. Defendant then wrote her description out in detail and told King of her possible whereabouts.

"King testified that defendant told him that he wanted to get rid of his wife, that there was some talk about an insurance policy with a double indemnity clause that defendant had on his wife, and that they discussed the most profitable way of killing her. King then asked defendant to write out his wife's name, her physical description, where she was living (defendant and his wife were separated), the description of any cars she might be driving, and anything else that might come to defendant's mind. Defendant wrote this information on Laurel Motor Inn stationery. King told defendant the price would be $2,000 and that he wanted $500 as a down-payment with the balance to be paid upon completion of the agreement. King then asked defendant if he was going to change his mind. Defendant replied that he was not going to change his mind and when King asked him if he was sure he wanted his wife dead, defendant replied 'yes'. Defendant then left."

Of course, Inspector King did not carry out the plan but instead had the defendant arrested. Defendant was indicted for attempt to commit murder, but the court refused to allow that charge to go forward. The defect, said the court, was that since neither the defendant nor the undercover agent had taken direct steps coming dangerously close to the commission of the contemplated crime, there was at most mere preparation, not a criminal attempt. Apparently, defendant's liability for attempt required some active participation by the person whom he solicited to commit the crime. Do you agree with this result? Should the course of conduct described above be insufficient to support liability for attempt?

2. **Solicitation as an Independent Offense.** In many American jurisdictions, prosecution on the facts of *Adami* would have to go forward under a charge of attempt. The difficulty of securing conviction for attempt in this situation, however, has led to the fairly widespread enactment of independent provisions on criminal solicitation. The prototype is Section 5.02 of the Model Penal Code:

"A person is guilty of solicitation to commit a crime if with the purpose of promoting or facilitating its commission he commands, encourages or requests another to engage in specific conduct which would constitute such crime or an attempt to commit such crime. . . ."

The enactment of such provisions is based on the view that purposeful solicitation of criminal conduct by another warrants preventive intervention by the police and is sufficiently indicative of criminality to support penal sanctions. More importantly, perhaps, recognizing solicitation as an independent offense renders immaterial the fact that the person solicited may not actually intend to commit the crime. This position reflects a judgment that the guilt or innocence of the person solicited should have no bearing on the liability of the initiating party. For a more detailed exposition of this view, along with a useful review of the common-law history of solicitation, see Wechsler, Jones & Korn, The Treatment of Inchoate Crimes in the Model Penal Code of the American Law Institute: Attempt, Solicitation, and Conspiracy, Part I, 61 Colum.L.Rev. 571, 621–28 (1961).

Do you accept the rationale for an independent offense of criminal solicitation? If so, do you think the Model Code effort is successful? Why does the provision not have a requirement analogous to the "substantial step" provision in the definition of attempt? Is *every* solicitation sufficiently informative to serve as the basis of penal liability? Or should some gloss be put on the words of the statute? For a discussion of some of these issues and an argument that solicitation should be limited to cases where the underlying offense is serious, see Note, Reforming the Law of Inchoate Crimes, 59 Va.L.Rev. 1235, 1260–68 (1973).

3. **Footnote on Conspiracy.** A third inchoate offense is criminal conspiracy. Traditionally, conspiracy is defined as an agreement between two or more persons to do an unlawful act or to do a lawful act by an unlawful means. The offense is inchoate or anticipatory in nature because liability is based on the preliminary step of agreement rather than on completed misconduct. The question therefore arises whether the act of agreement is a sufficient basis in conduct to support the imposition of penal sanctions. This and other aspects of the law of conspiracy are examined in detail at pages 435–510, infra.

SUBSECTION B: MINIMUM CONDUCT REQUIREMENTS IN COMPLETED OFFENSES

INTRODUCTORY NOTE ON COMPLETED OFFENSES

The issue of minimum conduct requirements for the imposition of penal sanctions has received scant theoretical attention outside the law of anticipatory offenses. Indeed, the distinction between criminal attempt and mere preparation may be the only established doctrine squarely addressed to determining how much conduct is enough. Yet the problem is pervasive throughout the criminal law.

Of course, some crimes require that the actor's conduct be complete—complete in the sense that it must actually bring about the harm ultimately feared. Homicide is the premier example. The actor actually must cause death of another for the offense to be made out. Many crimes, however, do not require actual harm as a condition of liability. Thus, for example, a false statement may be punished as perjury, even though the trial outcome is not affected. Similarly, bribery of a public servant is a crime, even though no official action is influenced. And various kinds of risk creation may be criminal, even where no injury results. In all of these cases, the law proscribes conduct preliminary to the harm ultimately feared. The issue therefore arises: How early in a course of conduct leading to actual harm should liability attach? This, of course, is exactly the same question posed by the distinction between attempt and preparation, but here it is considered in the context of defining substantive crimes. Furthermore, since the definition of offenses is necessarily fairly general, the same issue comes up in the application of those definitions to particular fact situations. In both contexts it may be necessary to consider whether the preliminary conduct in question is sufficiently indicative of blameworthiness and dangerousness to support the imposition of penal sanctions.

The point is most obvious in offenses, such as burglary, that punish some form of inchoate wrongdoing as a completed crime. The traditional common-law definition of burglary required breaking and entering the dwelling of another in the nighttime with intent to commit a felony therein. Since burglary is a more serious crime than breaking and entering without such intent, the grade of liability turns on having a purpose to engage in conduct that need not actually take place. In that respect, the offense reaches inchoate or anticipatory behavior, even though it is formally a completed crime. Moreover, some modern statutes exaggerate the inchoate aspect of the offense by diluting the actus reus to require only unauthorized entry rather than breaking and entering. Obviously, enforcement of such provisions may raise difficult questions about the sufficiency of the actor's conduct to support a finding of intent to commit a felony. Conceptually, this is the same issue as the sufficiency of the actor's conduct to support a finding of criminal purpose in the law of attempt. And in light of the conflicting resolutions of this issue in the law of attempt, it should not be surprising that the courts have also made differing interpretations of the minimum conduct requirements of modern burglary statutes. Compare, for example, State v. Rood, 11 Ariz.App. 102, 462 P.2d 399 (1969), where unauthorized but non-forcible entry of another's home was found inadequate to support a finding of intent to steal, with Ealey v. State, 139 Ga.App. 604, 229 S.E.2d 86 (1976), where the opposite conclusion was reached on similar facts.

Analogous issues of minimum conduct requirements in traditional crimes are presented later. It is important to note, however, that the problem is equally acute in the context of relatively minor offenses, often of recent origin, that are designed to facilitate law enforcement by identifying various preliminary steps as completed crimes. The case and notes following are illustrative.

PEOPLE v. VALOT

Court of Appeals of Michigan, 1971.
33 Mich.App. 49, 189 N.W.2d 873.

CHURCHILL, JUDGE. Defendant, Harold Valot, was charged with having had possession and control of marijuana contrary to the provisions of Mich.Comp.Laws Ann. § 335.153.[a] He was convicted by non-jury trial. The judgment of sentence refers to possession of marijuana. The trial judge's recited findings at the conclusion of the trial make it clear that the conviction was based on findings of control. Possession and control are separate offenses under the statute.

Defendant asserts on appeal . . . that there was no evidence of his possession or control of the drug to support the conviction. . . .

Three Redford Township policemen went to a motel in their township in response to a call from a motel employee. Upon answering they learned from the motel manager that he was concerned about the continued use of one of the motel rooms by a number of "hippie-type people." The room had been rented about three days before. The rent was paid until noon of that day. The police were called and arrived in the early afternoon. The officers examined the registration card and learned that the motel room was registered in the name of Harold Valot. . . .

The policemen went to the room with the motel manager. The manager knocked on the door. There was no response. The manager opened the door with a key. The manager and the policemen walked in and observed five persons in the room, all apparently asleep or in beds. One of the officers recognized the defendant by description and the officers observed marijuana about the room. Defendant was arrested. The marijuana was seized. . . .

[a] The statute then provided in pertinent part that "any person . . . who shall possess or have under his or her control any narcotic drug shall be deemed guilty of a felony. . . ." A related provision included marijuana in the statutory definition of a "narcotic" drug. Mich.Comp. Laws Ann. § 335.151. [Footnote by eds.]

Defendant personally registered for the room on September 27, 1968, three days before the arrest, and paid one day's room rent. A girl paid rent on the day before the arrest. Defendant testified that he rented the room for two other persons, and that he had been sleeping there since about 7 a. m. or 8 a. m. on the day of the arrest. He said that he knew that Paul Silver carried and used marijuana and that he, Valot, previously chased Silver out, but that Silver was there when he was aroused by the police. He said that he was unaware of the presence of marijuana in the room until that time.

The room, upon police entry, was in complete disarray. There was a strong odor of marijuana in the room. There were four hand-rolled marijuana cigarettes and a brass water pipe of a type used for smoking marijuana on tables, including one on a table next to the bed occupied by defendant and another. Later examination disclosed traces of marijuana in the pipe. Two marijuana cigarette butts were in the room, one of them being on the floor beside defendant's bed. Defendant's record player was in the room. . . .

The legislature used the words "possession" and "control" in the narcotics statute in their commonly understood sense, and not in a restricted, technical sense. The trial judge conceded the possibility that someone, unbeknownst to defendant, brought the marijuana into the room, but nevertheless did not have a reasonable or fair doubt as to defendant's control thereof. It was a fact question. There was strong circumstantial evidence to support the court's findings. Defendant's control of the marijuana in the room was a fact reasonably inferred from the evidence. . . .

His conviction is affirmed.

LEVIN, JUDGE (dissenting). I dissent because it is not a crime to be in control of a room where marijuana is found and because the People failed to prove that the defendant, Harold Eugene Valot, Jr., was in possession or control of marijuana.

Time and again the courts of this and other states have ruled that where the People's case is based on circumstantial evidence the prosecution has the burden of proving "that there is no innocent theory possible which will, without violation of reason, accord with the facts." In this case the People failed to negate every reasonable theory consistent with Valot's innocence of the crime charged.

When the police entered the motel room they observed five persons all apparently asleep. There were four marijuana cigarettes on a desk. There was also a water pipe, with marijuana residue in the pipe near where Valot and his girl friend were sleeping. Next to the water pipe was a marijuana cigarette butt. On another bed a man was sleeping and near him on the floor was another marijuana cigarette butt. Sprawled on the floor somewhere was another man and another woman. Valot had paid the rent for one day. His girl friend paid the rent for the second day; he offered to reimburse her but she refused. The rent for the third day had not been paid.

The trial judge found that Valot was in control of the room and was aware at least of the fact that others in the room had marijuana. Those inferences and findings are reasonably supported by the evidence. From the fact that Valot had paid the rent for the first day, had offered to pay for the second day, and, by his own testimony, had kicked someone out of the room, it is reasonable to conclude that he was in control of the room. In light of the manager's testimony that shortly before his arrest Valot was awake, it is reasonable to conclude that he was aware that marijuana was being used or, at least, that it had been used in the room.

One or more of the persons in the room possessed or controlled the marijuana that was in it. There was, however, no evidence as to who brought the marijuana into the room or who used it. The People did not prove by direct or circumstantial evidence that Valot, rather than another person or persons in the room, was himself in actual possession of the marijuana found in the room. There was no evidence, direct or circumstantial, that Valot ever used marijuana or did so on this occasion. The trier of fact's disbelief of Valot's testimony does not support a conclusion that the opposite of his testimony is true in the absence of independent evidence affirmatively supporting that conclusion.

If Valot did not bring the marijuana into the room or smoke it—and, again, there was no evidence that he had—then someone else did. It is not reasonable to infer from Valot's *control of the room* and his knowledge that others in the room possessed or were using marijuana, and I quote from the majority opinion, that Valot, rather than one or another of the other persons in the room, was in "control of the marijuana in the room." . . .

Plainly, the prosecution failed in this case to negate the reasonable inference that persons in the room other than Valot were in control of the marijuana in the room. Plainly, to infer from the fact that a person is in control of a room that he is in control of marijuana in the possession of other persons in the room is not a reasonable inference. It is not a reasonable inference beyond a reasonable doubt. It is not even more probable than not . . . that Valot was in control of marijuana possessed by others in the room. . . .

The legislature may, if it wishes, amend the statute to make presence in a room where marijuana is in use a crime. In the meantime, enforcement of the law prohibiting possession and control of marijuana is not, in my opinion, of sufficient overriding public importance to justify departure from fundamental principles long established.

The legislature made possession and control of marijuana a crime. It is not a crime for one in possession or control of a motel room to invite or allow hippy [sic] types in the room or to fail to evict guests smoking marijuana. The legislature has not yet made a citizen responsible for the indulgence of others in his presence.

NOTES ON MINIMUM CONDUCT REQUIREMENTS IN COMPLETED OFFENSES

1. **Possession.** Possession is a common basis of criminal liability. Generally, the term denotes exclusive dominion and control over the thing possessed. Punishment for possession is particularly important in the areas of controlled substances and unauthorized weapons, but it is not limited to those contexts. A survey of the California Penal Code reveals more than 20 additional categories of possession offenses, ranging from a typical provision against possession of burglar's tools to an unusual series of offenses regulating possession for sale of wearing apparel manufactured in non-California prisons. New York is typical of jurisdictions with modern revised codes in maintaining a less extensive, but still imposing, list of possession offenses. The items there covered include burglar's tools, dangerous drugs, eavesdropping or wiretapping devices, forged instruments, forgery devices, gambling devices, hypodermic instruments, obscene materials, stolen property, usurious loan records, and weapons.

Possession offenses may be divided into two broad types. Offenses of the first type cover various items of contraband—i.e., things that may not legitimately be possessed by anyone or only by certain well-defined categories of persons. Examples include designated types of firearms that are not permitted for lawful use, and narcotics and other controlled substances in the hands of persons who do not have either a prescription for medical use or a permit for scientific research. The second type of possession offense concerns items with both lawful and unlawful uses where it is not possible to classify the article as contraband or to limit its authorized possession to well-defined groups. In these situations, the offense is therefore typically defined as possession of the article with intent to employ it in an unlawful way. Examples include possession of burglar's tools with intent to use them in illegal activity and possession of narcotics paraphernalia with intent to engage in unlawful use of a controlled substance.

In offenses of either type, possession is typically punished as an indirect means of reaching something else. Only rarely is possession an evil in itself. More often, it is proscribed as a proxy for use, distribution, or sale of the item possessed. The principal justification for focusing on possession rather than solely on the underlying activity of use or sale is the resulting simplification of the practical and evidentiary burdens of law enforcement. Often possession can be proved more easily than use, and the finding generally rests on more reliable evidence.

Moreover, crimes of possession allow the police to intervene in a course of criminal conduct at an earlier stage than might otherwise be possible. Thus, for example, the police do not need to wait until actual use of narcotics is at hand; instead they can arrest for the completed and continuing offense of possession whenever it occurs. Similarly, offenses such as possession of burglar's tools allow the police to arrest and prosecute suspected burglars in the preparation stage, before conduct that would constitute a criminal attempt to commit burglary. For these reasons, possession offenses are extremely useful to law enforcement and correspondingly popular with legislatures. The danger, of course, is that in some cases punishment of possession may impose criminal liability with arguably insufficient basis in any demonstrated wrongdoing by the accused.

2. **Constructive Possession.** In the usual run of cases, punishing possession as a legislative short-cut to proscribing use probably presents no serious problem. At least in the context of contraband, such as narcotics, where there is no occasion for legitimate possession, exclusive dominion and control over the thing possessed arguably furnishes an adequate basis for imposing penal sanctions. Specifically, the actor has engaged in the conduct of acquisition followed by a failure to divest. The demonstrated basis for criminal punishment is fairly strong.

Difficulty arises, however, when the concept of possession is stretched to include borderline situations. Often the result is called *constructive* possession, presumably to indicate that liability is to be imposed even though actual possession or exclusive control cannot be found. As *Valot* illustrates, the problem is especially acute in the context of group arrests. Several persons may be found in a single room or apartment with an illegal drug. It is clear that someone, and perhaps everyone, possessed the forbidden item, but the link to any given individual is unclear. In some cases, the courts have emphasized presence plus a proprietary interest in the premises where the drug was found as the basis of liability for possession. Thus, the owner or lessee of a dwelling might be convicted of possessing a controlled substance found in the presence of a number of guests. Presumably, that explains why Valot, rather than one of his several companions, was charged with possession of the marijuana found in his motel room. Does a proprietary or possessory interest in the premises justify distinguishing one person from among several present as the possessor of illegal drugs found therein? Does the answer depend on where within the premises the contraband was found? What if it is found in the owner's bedroom or in some other location to which guests ordinarily would not have access?

A related problem is presented by married persons and others who live together. If contraband is found in the marital bedroom, are both parties guilty of possessing it? Is neither? Does it depend on whose bureau contained the substance, or on whether it was found in a place used indiscriminately by both?

Finally, note that the statute in *Valot* punished in the alternative possession *or* control of a narcotic drug. Does this formulation change the analysis? Even if you think that Valot was not proved to have possessed the marijuana, could you not say that he nevertheless controlled marijuana which others brought into his motel room? If the room was registered in his name and paid for by him, he presumably had the right to control access to it. Should that be sufficient conduct to support criminal conviction?

For a trenchant attack on the doctrine of constructive possession and a suggested analytic framework for resolving close questions, see Whitebread & Stevens, Constructive Possession in Narcotics Cases: To Have and Have Not, 58 Va.L.Rev. 751 (1972).

3. **Being in a Place.** The dissent in *Valot* accuses the majority of converting Michigan's possession-or-control statute into a law against being in a place where marijuana is used. In the dissent's view, it was up to the legislature rather than the court to accomplish that result. Interestingly, several state legislatures have done just that. An illustration is Section 11365 of the California Health and Safety Code, which declares it unlawful "to visit or to be in any room or place where any controlled substances . . . are being unlawfully smoked or used with knowledge that such activity is occurring." Is this approach sound?

In this connection, consider the case of In re Elisabeth H., 20 Cal.App.3d 323, 97 Cal.Rptr. 565 (1971). The defendant was apprehended along with four other minors in a parked car at 4:00 a. m. A passing police officer signalled the car to dim its lights and then pulled alongside to repeat the request. The driver saw the police car and abruptly drove off. When the officer stopped the car, he saw smoke and smelled marijuana. Marijuana was found in a boy's jacket and in a packet thrown from the car during the search. There was no direct evidence that the defendant had smoked or possessed marijuana. She neither owned nor operated the car, and the officers subsequently could not identify where she was seated at the time the car was stopped.

The defendant, a juvenile, was declared a ward of the court for violating the predecessor to California's being-in-a-place statute. The appellate court reversed that order on the ground that it failed to comply with a narrowing construction by the highest state court. Based on that precedent, the appellate court concluded that, despite the statute's literal reach, something more than voluntary presence and knowledge of illegal activity would be required for conviction. The court confessed some confusion as to exactly what else would be needed but referred to control over the premises, aiding others in the use of narcotics, and failing to take sufficient steps to stop narcotics use as possibly relevant factors.

Do you agree that the statute should not be given its literal sweep? If so, what additional conduct should be required? What, in this context, would furnish a minimally acceptable basis for imposing criminal liability? For a useful account of the history of the California provision and a criticism of the approach it reflects, see Note, No Place for "Being in a Place": The Vanishing of Health and Safety Code Section 11,556, 23 Stan.L.Rev. 1009 (1971).

4. **Traditional Vagrancy and Loitering Laws.** Traditional vagrancy and loitering laws provide another context of acute concern with the minimum conduct requirements for criminal liability. Historically, vagrancy and loitering were catch-all offenses aimed at social control of undesirables. Such laws typically included multiple descriptions of proscribed conduct. A good example is the vagrancy ordinance found

unconstitutionally vague in Papachristou v. City of Jacksonville, 405 U.S. 156 (1972) (set forth in full at page 67, supra). Among those punished as vagrants were "common drunkards" and "common gamblers," "dissolute persons who go about begging," "lewd, wanton and lascivious persons," and "persons able to work but habitually living upon the earnings of their wives or minor children." The crime of loitering was an outgrowth of common-law vagrancy and was distinguished from its parent chiefly in excluding from coverage mere idleness or indolence. Nonetheless, traditional loitering statutes were like vagrancy laws in imposing criminal liability with little or no requirement of actual misconduct by the accused. Instead, these offenses generally focused on a status derived from *past* criminality (e.g., "common night walkers, thieves, pilferers or pickpockets") or on behavior suggestive of *future* criminality (e.g., "persons wandering or strolling around from place to place without any lawful purpose or object"). In neither aspect was the imposition of penal sanctions firmly grounded in proof of specific anti-social conduct.

The vices of such laws are apparent. They provide little notice of what is forbidden, and they allow police unbridled discretion to decide whom to arrest. Sometimes vagrancy and loitering statutes have been invoked against persons suspected of specific criminal acts that could not be proved. See, e.g., People v. Craig, 152 Cal. 42, 91 P. 997 (1907). Sometimes such laws have been enforced to suppress lawful conduct deemed socially objectionable. Thus, for example, it was probably no accident that the group of "vagrants" involved in *Papachristou* were two white women and two black men riding together down the city's main thoroughfare. Finally, perhaps the predominant use of traditional vagrancy and loitering provisions has been simply to clear streets and parks of derelicts, alcoholics, and other aesthetically undesirable elements. See Foote, Vagrancy-Type Law and Its Administration, 104 U.Pa.L.Rev. 603 (1956). For these reasons, old-style vagrancy and loitering statutes have come under strong constitutional attack. Many such provisions have been invalidated under the vagueness doctrine, and most of those that remain on the books are enforced so rarely that they persist in name only.

One response to the widespread invalidation of vagrancy laws has been an effort to redraft these provisions in order to address legitimate law-enforcement objectives more precisely. Section 250.6 of the Model Penal Code is representative of this new generation of laws:

> "A person commits a violation if he loiters or prowls in a place, at a time, or in a manner not usual for law-abiding individuals under circumstances that warrant alarm for the safety of persons or property in the vicinity. Among the circumstances which may be considered in determining whether such alarm is warranted is the fact that the actor takes flight upon appearance of a peace officer, refuses to identify himself, or manifestly endeavors to conceal himself or any object. Unless flight by the actor or other circumstance makes it impracticable, a peace officer shall prior to any arrest for an offense under this

section afford the actor an opportunity to dispel any alarm which would otherwise be warranted, by requesting him to identify himself and explain his presence and conduct. No person shall be convicted of an offense under this section if the peace officer did not comply with the preceding sentence, or if it appears at trial that the explanation given by the actor was true and, if believed by the peace officer at the time, would have dispelled the alarm."

This statute differs from older vagrancy laws in several ways. It eschews any attempt to base criminal liability on a status derived from prior misconduct and focuses instead directly on the problem of incipient criminality. Thus, the catch-all approach of prior law is abandoned in favor of a more targeted effort to control behavior that "warrant[s] alarm for the safety of persons or property in the vicinity." Additionally, an effort has been made to allay the concerns of the vagueness doctrine by elaborating the standard of liability and by specifying the circumstances that may be considered in making the required determination. It seems plain, however, that the vices of prior law have not been completely eradicated in the Model Code provision and, indeed, cannot be entirely eliminated in any statute that attempts to reach such preliminary conduct. The continuing dispute over the wisdom and constitutionality of modern vagrancy and loitering statutes is illustrated in the next note.

5. *People* v. *Berck* and Modern Loitering Statutes. People v. Berck, 32 N.Y.2d 567, 300 N.E.2d 411 (1973), involved a constitutional challenge to New York Penal Code § 240.35(6). That statute provided in pertinent part as follows:

"A person is guilty of loitering when he . . .

"6. Loiters, remains or wanders in or about a place without apparent reason and under circumstances which justify suspicion that he may be engaged or about to engage in crime, and, upon inquiry by a peace officer, refuses to identify himself or fails to give a reasonably credible account of his conduct and purposes."

By a vote of four to three, the New York Court of Appeals held this provision unconstitutional. Excerpts from Judge Burke's majority opinion explain that conclusion:

"The statute in the case before us is not informative on its face and utterly fails to give adequate notice of the behavior it forbids. The statute contains two substantive elements: (i) loitering 'in or about a place without apparent reason', (ii) under circumstances which 'justify suspicion' that a person 'may be engaged or about to engage in crime'. Certainly, . . . the first element standing alone could not possibly be held to give sufficient notice of the conduct proscribed. The second element—that the loitering be done under circumstances which justify suspicion that a person is engaged in or about to engage in crime—is similarly obscure. Assuredly, there [is] no commonly understood set of suspicious circumstances of which all citizens are aware and to which applicability of the statute is restricted.

In other words, this additional language does not condemn any identifiable act or omission or restrict the operation of the statute to a particular place or a clearly defined set of circumstances but, rather, it merely indicates that a person may be held for loitering if suspicion of criminality happens to be created in the mind of the arresting officer. . . .

"Not only is Subdivision 6 of Section 240.35 of the Penal Law unconstitutionally vague for the reason that it fails to give adequate notice of the conduct to be avoided and punished but also because it places virtually unfettered discretion in the hands of the police and thereby encourages arbitrary and discriminatory enforcement. . . .

"Still another aspect of vagueness fatally afflicts Subdivision 6. By authorizing an arrest for loitering 'under circumstances which justify suspicion that [a person] may be engaged or about to engage in crime,' Subdivision 6 of Section 240.35 plainly undercuts the constitutional requirement that arrests are lawful only upon a showing of 'probable cause.' As the Supreme Court pointed out in the *Papachristou* case:

'We allow our police to make arrests only on "probable cause" . . . .. Arresting a person on suspicion, like arresting a person for investigation, is foreign to our system, even when the arrest is for past criminality.'

'A direction by a legislature to the police to arrest all "suspicious" persons would not pass constitutional muster. A vagrancy prosecution may be merely the cloak for a conviction which could not be obtained on the real but undisclosed grounds for the arrest.'

"Manifestly, this constitutional infirmity of general vagrancy ordinances—that they may be used by the police to obtain custody of a person whom they suspect of more serious offenses but whom they cannot lawfully arrest for such crimes because there is no probable cause to support such an arrest—is equally inherent in the general loitering provision in the present case. . . .

"In this case, the defendant may very well have been conscious of the importance of protecting the identity of a young lady who was 'the other party' on a 'sparking expedition.' Manifestly, prohibiting such harmless conduct serves no reasonable state interest . . . ..

"Accordingly, the judgment of conviction should be reversed and the complaint dismissed as Section 240.35(6) of the New York Penal Law is unconstitutional."

In dissent, Judge Breitel responded as follows:

"In this case, the police had been advised that certain residential premises would be temporarily unoccupied. On patrol, they observed defendant standing behind a tree, at 1:00 a.m., seeming to be examining the unoccupied premises. When questioned by the police, he refused to explain his presence, but more important, or even to identify himself. No other person was present and there was, of course, no indication of a tryst.

"The statute, it is suggested, is not so vague as to preclude the denotation of conduct giving justifiable belief that a crime is being or is about to be committed. It requires the following elements in conjunction:

"(i) Loitering without apparent reason.

"(ii) Additional circumstances giving rise to suspicion of present or intended criminal activity.

"(iii) Refusal to respond to inquiry by a peace officer by identifying one's self and explaining the questioned conduct.

"The arrest and conviction are not for any one of these grounds but were and must have been for all three. Moreover, to satisfy the important second requirement referring to 'circumstances' there must be objective facts justifying suspicion. The measure would be the factual circumstances and not the police officer's idiosyncratic capacity for suspicion. The quality of the factual circumstances and the strength of the inference that the defendant 'may be engaged or about to engage in crime' would be for the courts to assess.

"These elements are amply supplied in this case: the sparsely populated residential area involved; the temporarily unoccupied residence; the defendant standing behind a tree in front of the residence; the unusual hour of 1:00 a.m.; and the absence of any other persons until the patrol car came along. Those circumstances bespeak 'casing' the house for a possible burglary; but, as with any inchoate offense, there was no action sufficient to establish even a criminal attempt. These circumstances did not make unreasonably intrusive the police inquiry, and when that inquiry was denied, even as to defendant's identity, simple reason suggests removing the defendant from the scene. As the prosecutor argued on the appeal, what else were the police to do at that hour, unless they were to drive away and let happen what might happen. . . .

"Accordingly, I dissent and vote to affirm the conviction."

The debate in these opinions focuses chiefly on the vagueness doctrine. An underlying issue, however, is whether it should ever be permissible, under any formulation, to punish a person for merely "suspicious" behavior. Efforts to do so necessarily reach very far back in an "inchoate" course of conduct and punish actions far more preliminary than would be covered by the law of attempt. Are the essential concerns of the act requirement adequately respected by statutes such as the one in *Berck*? Does the conduct required by this law corroborate the actor's evil intent? Does it confirm the actor's dangerousness? Does it provide a sufficiently definite locus poenitentiae to enable the law-abiding citizen to avoid penal sanctions? If not, what alternative measures should be taken? Will the police be left powerless to intervene in situations such as *Berck*? Should they be?

6. ***Kolender* v. *Lawson* and "Stop-and-Identify" Statutes.** In light of the continuing uncertainty as to the constitutionality and/or wisdom of conventional loitering statutes, it is not surprising that legislatures have sought other ways of enabling police to deal with incipient crime. One alternative is a so-called "stop and identify" statute. California's version of such a law was held unconstitutional by the United States Supreme Court in Kolender v. Lawson, 461 U.S. 352 (1983).

The law in question was Cal.Penal Code § 647(e). It declared guilty of a misdemeanor every person "[w]ho loiters or wanders upon the streets or from place to place without apparent reason or business and who *refuses to identify himself and to account for his presence when requested by any peace officer to do so,* if the surrounding circumstances are such as to indicate to a reasonable man that the public safety demands such identification." [Emphasis added.] A state court had construed the statute to require "credible and reliable" identification to a police officer who acted on reasonable suspicion of criminal activity. "Credible and reliable" was specified to mean "carrying reasonable assurance that the identification is authentic and providing means for later getting in touch with the person who has identified himself."

The Supreme Court, speaking through Justice O'Connor, found the statute unconstitutionally vague:

"Section 647(e), as presently drafted and construed by the state courts, contains no standard for determining what a suspect has to do in order to satisfy the requirement to provide a 'credible and reliable' identification. As such, the statute vests virtually complete discretion in the hands of the police to determine whether the suspect has satisfied the statute and must be permitted to go on his way in the absence of probable cause to arrest. An individual, whom police may think is suspicious but do not have probable cause to believe has committed a crime, is entitled to continue to walk the public streets 'only at the whim of any police officer' who happens to stop that individual under § 647(e) . . . .

"Section 647(e) is not simply a 'stop-and-identify' statute. Rather, the statute requires that the individual provide a 'credible and reliable' identification that carries a 'reasonable assurance' of authenticity, and that provides 'means for later getting in touch with the person who has identified himself' . . . .

"It is clear that the full discretion accorded to the police to determine whether the suspect has provided a 'credible and reliable' identification necessarily 'entrust[s] lawmaking "to the moment-to-moment judgment of the policeman on his beat."' Section 647(e) 'furnishes a convenient tool for "harsh and discriminatory enforcement by local prosecuting officials, against particular groups deemed to merit their displeasure"' [citing *Papachristou,* Casebook pp. 67–68], and 'confers on police a virtually unrestrained power to arrest and charge persons with a violation.'

"[The state stresses] the need for strengthened law enforcement tools to combat the epidemic of crime that plagues our nation. The concern of our citizens with curbing criminal activity is certainly a matter requiring the attention of all branches of government. As weighty as this concern is, however, it cannot justify legislation that would otherwise fail to meet constitutional standards for definiteness and clarity. Section 647(e), as presently construed, requires that 'suspicious' persons satisfy some undefined identification requirement, or face criminal punishment. Although due process does not require 'impossible standards' of clarity [citing *Petrillo*, Casebook pp. 68–69], this is not a case where further precision in the statutory language is either impossible or impractical."

Justice White, with whom Justice Rehnquist joined, dissented.

Although Justice O'Connor asserted that further precision in the statutory language was neither impossible nor impractical, she did not spell out what the statute should have said. What would you suggest? Can you think of language to resolve this problem, or is the difficulty more fundamental than sloppy draftsmanship? *

———

SUBSECTION C: MINIMUM CONDUCT REQUIREMENTS AND VOLUNTARINESS

———

INTRODUCTORY NOTES ON THE VOLUNTARY ACT

1. **The Requirement of a Voluntary Act.** As has been noted, settled doctrine requires not only that criminal liability be based on conduct, but also that the conduct be in some sense voluntary. This is called the requirement of a voluntary "act," but it applies as well to omissions and to possession. The classical definition of a voluntary act is one that results from an exercise of the will.[a] This formulation raises philosophical questions of some difficulty, and theoretical debate over the meaning of the concept continues.[b] The law, however, has

---

* The facts of the case are suggestive. Edward Lawson is a black man of unconventional appearance who walked, often late at night and often in wealthy and predominantly white residential areas. He had been stopped on at least 15 occasions before the statute was declared unconstitutional. For analysis of race as a factor in a police intervention, see Johnson, Race and the Decision to Detain a Suspect, 93 Yale L.J. 214 (1983). For a more focused analysis of the issues presented by *Kolender*, see Williams, Constitutional Reflections on California's Request for Identification Law, 8 Black L.J. 177 (1983).

[a] See J. Austin, Lectures in Jurisprudence 284–91 (4th ed. 1873); J. Salmond, Jurisprudence 367–69 (10th ed. 1947); O. Holmes, The Common Law 53–55 (1881).

[b] Perhaps the most elegant attack on the classical formulation is H.L.A. Hart, Acts of Will and Responsibility, in Punishment and Responsibility at 90 (1968). Hart's views were in turn criticized in Murphy, Involuntary Acts and Criminal Responsibility, 81 Ethics 332 (1971), where the author proposes a reformulation of the traditional focus on an exercise of the will.

largely been content to "define" by example, and thus it is that most accounts of the voluntary-act requirement feature illustrations of acts that are not voluntary. Among the generally accepted instances of involuntary conduct are the following:

(i) **Physically Coerced Movement.** If A, without B's assent or cooperation, shoves B into C and thus knocks C into the path of a passing car, B's act is plainly involuntary. Indeed, it may be more idiomatic in this case to say that B has engaged in no "act" at all, for the "act" is attributed to A, not B. Under either formulation, B is not liable.

(ii) **Reflex Movements.** The usual example is the reaction of a person suddenly attacked by a swarm of bees. According to most authorities, a person so afflicted while driving a car could not be held liable for the resulting loss of control over the vehicle.

(iii) **Muscular Contraction or Paralysis Produced by Disease.** Some disorders of the central nervous system, including epilepsy and chorea, cause muscular contractions beyond the control of the individual. Others, such as a stroke, may suddenly restrict movement or induce partial paralysis. Obviously, a person who has no control over his limbs cannot be said to act voluntarily with respect to their movements.

(iv) **Unconsciousness.** A relatively complete obliteration of consciousness, ranging from coma to normal sleep, ordinarily involves a cessation of most motor functions. In some cases, however, unconscious acts may occur. A sleeping mother may roll over her child and smother it. A person may suffer unconsciousness due to stroke, epilepsy, narcolepsy, or some other neurophysiological disturbance. Obviously, physical movements or omissions during these intervals are not, in any meaningful sense, voluntary.

The common theme in these situations is that the actor's bodily movement or omission is not directed by any conscious mental process. As H.L.A. Hart once put the point, what is "missing in such a case is the minimum link between mind and body, indispensable for any form of criminal responsibility." [c]

2. **Forms of Impaired Consciousness.** The above examples describe situations where the individual lacks any mental control over his physical acts. Such acts are plainly involuntary. In other recognized instances of involuntariness, however, some link between mind and body remains, but that link is sufficiently attenuated to preclude criminal responsibility. These situations characteristically involve disturbances of consciousness in persons who nonetheless retain the capacity to engage in goal-directed conduct based on prior learned responses. Because conscious awareness of one's acts is absent during such episodes, such behavior may be said to be "automatic" and the individual so afflicted an "automaton." Hence the law sometimes has dealt with such conditions under the rubric of "automatism" even though use of

[c] H.L.A. Hart, Acts of Will and Responsibility, in Punishment and Responsibility at 92 (1968).

this term is medically appropriate only in cases of epilepsy. The two most important examples are concussion and somnambulism.

(i) **Concussion.** Temporary brain damage due to physical trauma sometimes produces a "black-out" or "confusional state," during which a person may engage in previously learned behavior without full awareness thereof. An example is the football player who continues to go through the motions of the game even though he is not consciously aware of his actions and may not remember them afterwards. More pertinent, perhaps, to the present discussion is the fact that concussion can compromise the functioning of those brain centers that mediate and inhibit behavioral manifestation of emotion. A person who injures another while in such a state may do what he (unconsciously) wanted to do but would not have done had he had conscious control over his behavior. Some courts have found such conduct to be involuntary.[d]

(ii) **Somnambulism.** There is a well recognized continuum of sleep disorders, ranging from ordinary nightmares to sleepwalking to a more severe form of disturbance known as "night terrors." [e] During mild sleepwalking episodes, the "sleeping" person may move about, although generally in a poorly coordinated, automatic manner. "Night terrors" are characterized by extreme fear and panic, intense vocalization, and frenzied motor activity. Aberrant behavior, including violence, can occur. Moreover, any interference with a person experiencing a somnambulistic episode may precipitate a violent reaction. The courts have generally regarded acts committed during such episodes as involuntary. In one famous English case, an 1859 grand jury refused to indict a woman who, after dreaming that her house was on fire, arose in a panic, screamed "Save my children!," and threw her baby out the window.[f]

(iii) **Hypnosis and Hypoglycemia.** There are other situations involving impaired consciousness for which the sufficiency of the "link between mind and body" appears to be an open question. One such instance involves acts performed under hypnosis or pursuant to post-hypnotic suggestion. The uncertainty here is not so much conceptual as scientific. It is simply not clear whether and to what extent hypnosis can abrogate the control that a person normally has over his own conduct.[g]

Another unsettled question concerns the behavioral effects of hypoglycemia, or abnormally low blood sugar. Because blood sugar is the exclusive source of energy for brain metabolism, hypoglycemia can lead to impaired functioning of the central nervous system. This condition

---

[d] For cases dealing with concussion, see Regina v. Wakefield, 75 W.N. 66 (New South Wales 1957); Coates v. Regina, 96 C.L.R. 353 (1957); Regina v. Minor, 112 Can. Crim. Cases 29 (1959).

[e] See generally Kales et al., Somnambulism, 37 Arch. Gen. Psychiat. 1406 (1980); Kales et al., Night Terrors, 37 Arch. Gen. Psychiat. 1413 (1980).

[f] This case is described in N. Walker, Crime and Insanity in England 168–69

(1968). Other well-known somnambulism cases include Fain v. Commonwealth, 78 Ky. 183 (1879), and H.M. Advocate v. Fraser, 4 Couper 70 (Scotland 1878). For an especially intriguing case, see Morris, Somnambulistic Homicide: Ghosts, Spiders and North Koreans, 5 Res. Judicatae 29 (1959).

[g] For discussions of this issue, see the various papers on anti-social behavior and hypnosis published in 20 Int'l J. of Clin. and Experimental Hypnosis (No. 2, 1972).

usually arises when a diabetic takes too much insulin or fails to get sufficient food or sleep. It can also occur, however, in a non-diabetic but biologically susceptible individual whose blood sugar is reduced by starvation or muscular over-exertion. In many such cases, the condition is precipitated by the ingestion of alcohol. Additionally, the condition can occur as a result of liver disease or endocrine disturbance. Hypoglycemic symptoms include tremors, poor coordination, confusion, and irritation. Although the condition may be associated with aggressive behavior, current understanding does not permit confident generalization about the effect of hypoglycemia on control over one's conduct.[h] The question, simply put, is whether this condition differs significantly from any of a number of other metabolic conditions that may lower a person's threshold for aggressive behavior without rendering such conduct involuntary.

3. **Codification.** As has been noted, the voluntariness requirement was an established feature of common-law doctrine. It did not originate in legislation but developed through the case-by-case exercise of judicial authority. Accordingly, courts have tended to regard the voluntary-act requirement as existing independent of statute and have enforced the requirement in the absence of supporting legislation.

Older American statutes did sometimes require a "voluntary act" without further explication, e.g., Smith-Hurd Ill.Ann.Stat. § 4–1, or exempt from liability persons who acted "without being conscious thereof," e.g., Cal. Penal Code § 26. More elaborate formulation was undertaken by the drafters of the Model Penal Code, who attempted in Section 2.01 to spell out the scope of the voluntary-act requirement:

"(1) A person is not guilty of an offense unless his liability is based on conduct which includes a voluntary act or the omission to perform an act of which he is physically capable.

"(2) The following are not voluntary acts within the meaning of this Section:

(a) a reflex or convulsion;

(b) a bodily movement during unconsciousness or sleep;

(c) conduct during hypnosis or resulting from hypnotic suggestion;

(d) a bodily movement that otherwise is not a product of the effort or determination of the actor, either conscious or habitual."

See also N.J.Stat.Ann. § 2C:2–1. Note that this formulation continues the tradition of definition by example and that the list of involuntary acts does not purport to be exhaustive. On the contrary, the Model Code provision plainly contemplates that judges will continue the case-by-case development of the voluntary-act requirement under the rubric of identifying acts that are "not [products] of the effort or determination of the actor, either conscious or habitual."

[h] See generally Shah and Roth, Biological and Psychophysiological Factors in Criminality, in D. Glaser, ed., Handbook of Criminology 101, 125–26 (1974).

   4. **Comments and Observations.** It is probably not possible to devise any test that precisely differentiates voluntary from involuntary acts. Perhaps as good as any is the Model Penal Code formulation of "a bodily movement that . . . is not a product of the effort or determination of the actor, either conscious or habitual." Ultimately, however, the requirement of a voluntary act poses a question of judgment rather than definition. In the final analysis, interpretation of the voluntary-act requirement rests on a normative view of the appropriate reach of penal sanctions and of the appropriate relationship of voluntariness to other exculpatory doctrines of the criminal law. The dimensions of that assessment cannot be reduced to any simple formula, but the following observations may help to place the inquiry in context.

   (i) **Content and Function.** At the outset, it is important to understand the consequence of invoking the voluntary-act requirement. Under settled principles, commission of a voluntary act is a necessary, though not sufficient, condition of criminal liability. Holding an act involuntary precludes liability for that act. It is not a question of which among several possible offenses should apply but an absolute bar to penal liability based on the involuntary conduct. The result is a complete exoneration of the actor and a correspondingly total sacrifice of the social-control objectives implicated by his conduct.

   Not surprisingly, the complete exculpation that results from a finding of involuntariness has tended to narrow the interpretation of that concept. Many acts that in a meaningful sense are coerced by circumstances are found nevertheless to satisfy the voluntary-act requirement. An example might be the person who steals bread because he has no other way to feed his child. It may seem a bit strained to describe such a theft as voluntary, but it is everywhere agreed that the voluntary-act requirement would be met in such a case. The point is that the legal construct of voluntariness is not merely descriptive. The meaning of the concept is informed by its function, and the function of the voluntary-act requirement is to identify cases where an individual's responsibility for his own conduct is so sharply interrupted as to preclude altogether the just imposition of penal sanctions.

   (ii) **Involuntary Act in a Voluntary Course of Conduct.** A second observation concerns the case of an involuntary act embedded in an otherwise voluntary course of conduct. Here the Model Penal Code formulation is instructive. It does not flatly preclude liability based on involuntary conduct; instead, it requires that liability be based on "conduct which includes" a voluntary act. The point of this phrasing is to leave open the possibility of penal sanctions for a course of conduct that includes some involuntary aspects.

   The issue is raised by the famous case of People v. Decina, 2 N.Y.2d 133, 138 N.E.2d 799 (1956). The defendant suffered an epileptic seizure while driving and ran over and killed several children. He was convicted under a statute punishing negligent homicide in a motor vehicle.[i] It was agreed, of course, that the seizure itself was involuntary and could not support penal liability. The state, however, proceeded on the theory that the defendant was liable for the negligent and voluntary act of driving a car with knowledge that he was subject to epileptic seizures. The indictment was sustained on the ground that the admittedly involuntary character of the seizure did not vitiate the defendant's responsibility for his voluntary acts prior to losing consciousness:

> "To hold otherwise would be to say that a man may freely indulge himself in liquor in the same hope that it will not affect his driving, and if it later develops that ensuing intoxication causes dangerous and reckless driving resulting in death, his unconsciousness or involuntariness at that time would relieve him from prosecution under the statute. His awareness of a condition which he knows may produce such consequences as these, and his disregard of the consequences, [render] him liable for culpable negligence. . . . To have a sudden sleeping spell, an unexpected heart or other disabling attack, without any prior knowledge or warning thereof, is an altogether different situation. . . ."

This is not to say, of course, that it is necessarily negligent to drive with knowledge of a potentially disabling medical condition, but only that the act of doing so may serve in an appropriate case as the basis for criminal liability.[j]

(iii) **Relation to Other Doctrines.** Finally, it must be emphasized that the voluntary-act requirement is not the only exculpatory doctrine of the criminal law that is animated by concerns about voluntariness. As is explained in Chapter IV, a person whose capacity for free choice is constrained by external circumstances beyond his control may be excused from criminal liability. The prototypical case is duress, where a person commits a criminal act because someone is holding a gun to his head. Also, in many jurisdictions a person whose capacity to conform his behavior to societal norms is compromised by mental illness may be relieved from criminal liability on grounds of insanity. The analytical boundaries separating these doctrines from the voluntary-act requirement are not always well marked. It is important, however, to keep in mind that specifying the "minimum link between mind and body" of the act requirement does not exhaust the law's receptivity to claims turning on lack of free choice. Finding an act to be "voluntary" for purposes of the act requirement does not

[i] N.Y. Penal Law § 1053–a provided punishment for anyone "who operates or drives any vehicle of any kind in a reckless or culpably negligent manner, whereby a human being is killed . . . ."

[j] While this position seems consistent with the voluntary-act requirement, the point is not entirely free from doubt. In particular, debate may arise over whether the specific voluntary act committed by the defendant was the act proscribed by the offense. Essentially, this is an issue of statutory construction. It turns not on whether a particular act may be punished as criminal, but on whether the legislature has in fact chosen to make it so. For discussions evidencing some concern with this problem, see the dissent in People v. Decina, 2 N.Y.2d 133 at 140, 138 N.E.2d 799 at 804, and the earlier decision in People v. Freeman, 61 Cal.App.2d 110, 142 P.2d 435 (1943).

lead inexorably to liability; it merely forecloses one of several potential grounds of exculpation.

ROBINSON v. CALIFORNIA
Supreme Court of the United States, 1962.
370 U.S. 660.

MR. JUSTICE STEWART delivered the opinion of the Court.

A California statute makes it a criminal offense for a person to "be addicted to the use of narcotics." [1] This appeal draws into question the constitutionality of that provision of the state law, as construed by the California courts in the present case.

The appellant was convicted after a jury trial in the Municipal Court of Los Angeles. The evidence against him was given by two Los Angeles police officers. Officer Brown testified that he had had occasion to examine the appellant's arms one evening on a street in Los Angeles some four months before the trial. The officer testified that at that time he had observed "scar tissue and discoloration on the inside" of the appellant's right arm, and "what appeared to be numerous needle marks and a scab which was approximately three inches below the crook of the elbow" on the appellant's left arm. The officer also testified that the appellant under questioning had admitted to the occasional use of narcotics.

Officer Lindquist testified that he had examined the appellant the following morning in the Central Jail in Los Angeles. The officer stated that at that time he had observed discolorations and scabs on the appellant's arms, and he identified photographs which had been taken of the appellant's arms shortly after his arrest the night before. Based upon more than 10 years of experience as a member of the Narcotic Division of the Los Angeles Police Department, the witness gave his opinion that "these marks and the discoloration were the result of the injection of hypodermic needles into the tissue into the vein that [were] not sterile." He stated that the scabs were several days old at the time of his examination, and that the appellant was neither under the influence of narcotics nor suffering withdrawal symptoms at the time he saw him. This witness also testified that the appellant had admitted using narcotics in the past.

---

[1] The statute is Section 11721 of the California Health and Safety Code. It provides:

"No person shall use, or be under the influence of, or be addicted to the use of narcotics, excepting when administered by or under the direction of a person licensed by the state to prescribe and administer narcotics. It shall be the burden of the defense to show that it comes within the exception. Any person convicted of violating any provision of this section is guilty of a misdemeanor and shall be sentenced to serve a term of not less than 90 days nor more than one year in the county jail. The court may place a person convicted hereunder on probation for a period not to exceed five years and shall in all cases in which probation is granted require a condition thereof that such person be confined in the county jail for at least 90 days. In no event does the court have the power to absolve a person who violates this section from the obligation of spending at least 90 days in confinement in the county jail."

The appellant testified in his own behalf, denying the alleged conversations with the police officers and denying that he had ever used narcotics or been addicted to their use. He explained the marks on his arms as resulting from an allergic condition contracted during his military service. His testimony was corroborated by two witnesses.

The trial judge instructed the jury that the statute made it a misdemeanor for a person "either to use narcotics, or to be addicted to the use of narcotics. . . . That portion of the statute referring to the 'use' of narcotics is based upon the 'act' of using. That portion of the statute referring to 'addicted to the use' of narcotics is based upon a condition or status. They are not identical. . . . To be addicted to the use of narcotics is said to be a status or condition and not an act. It is a continuing offense and differs from most other offenses in the fact that [it] is chronic rather than acute; that it continues after it is complete and subjects the offender to arrest at any time before he reforms. The existence of such a chronic condition may be ascertained from a single examination, if the characteristic reactions of that condition be found present."

The judge further instructed the jury that the appellant could be convicted under a general verdict if the jury agreed *either* that he was of the "status" *or* had committed the "act" denounced by the statute. "All that the People must show is either that the defendant did use a narcotic in Los Angeles County, or that while in the City of Los Angeles he was addicted to the use of narcotics . . . ."

Under these instructions the jury returned a verdict finding the appellant "guilty of the offense charged." An appeal was taken to the Appellate Department of the Los Angeles County Superior Court, "the highest court of a state in which a decision could be had" in this case. 28 U.S.C. § 1257. Although expressing some doubt as to the constitutionality of "the crime of being a narcotic addict," the reviewing court in an unreported opinion affirmed the judgment of conviction, citing two of its own previous unreported decisions which had upheld the constitutionality of the statute. We noted probable jurisdiction of this appeal, because it squarely presents the issue whether the statute as construed by the California courts in this case is repugnant to the 14th amendment of the Constitution.

The broad power of a state to regulate the narcotic-drugs traffic within its borders is not here in issue. More than 40 years ago this Court explicitly recognized the validity of that power: "There can be no question of the authority of the state in the exercise of its police power to regulate the administration, sale, prescription and use of dangerous and habit-forming drugs. . . . The right to exercise this power is so manifest in the interest of the public health and welfare, that it is unnecessary to enter upon a discussion of it beyond saying that it is too firmly established to be successfully called in question."

Such regulation, it can be assumed, could take a variety of valid forms. A state might impose criminal sanctions, for example, against the unauthorized manufacture, prescription, sale, purchase, or possession of narcotics within its borders. In the interest of discouraging the violation of such laws, or in the interest of the general health or welfare of its inhabitants, a state might establish a program of compulsory treatment for those addicted to narcotics.[7] Such a program of treatment might require periods of involuntary confinement. And penal sanctions might be imposed for failure to comply with established compulsory treatment procedures. Or a state might choose to attack the evils of narcotics traffic on broader fronts also—through public-health education, for example, or by efforts to ameliorate the economic and social conditions under which those evils might be thought to flourish. In short, the range of valid choice which a state might make in this area is undoubtedly a wide one, and the wisdom of any particular choice within the allowable spectrum is not for us to decide. Upon that premise we turn to the California law in issue here.

It would be possible to construe the statute under which the appellant was convicted as one which is operative only upon proof of the actual use of narcotics within the state's jurisdiction. But the California courts have not so construed this law. Although there was evidence in the present case that the appellant had used narcotics in Los Angeles, the jury were instructed that they could convict him even if they disbelieved that evidence. The appellant could be convicted, they were told, if they found simply that the appellant's "status" or "chronic condition" was that of being "addicted to the use of narcotics." And it is impossible to know from the jury's verdict that the defendant was not convicted upon precisely such a finding.

The instruction of the trial court, implicitly approved on appeal, amounted to "a ruling on a question of state law that is as binding on us as though the precise words had been written" into the statute. Terminiello v. Chicago, 337 U.S. 1, 4 (1949). "We can only take the statute as the state courts read it." Indeed, in their brief in this Court counsel for the state have emphasized that it is "the proof of addiction by circumstantial evidence . . . by the tell-tale track of needle marks and scabs over the veins of his arms, that remains the gist of the section."

This statute, therefore, is not one which punishes a person for the use of narcotics, for their purchase, sale or possession, or for anti-social or disorderly behavior resulting from their administration. It is not a law which even purports to provide or require medical treatment. Rather, we deal with a statute which makes the "status" of narcotic addiction a criminal offense, for which the offender may be prosecuted "at any time before he reforms." California has said that a person can be continuously guilty of this offense, whether or not he has ever used or possessed any narcotics within the state, and whether or not he has been guilty of any anti-social behavior there.

It is unlikely that any state at this moment in history would attempt to make it a criminal offense for a person to be mentally ill, or a leper, or to be afflicted with a venereal disease. A state might

---

[7] California appears to have established just such a program in Sections 5350–5361 of its Welfare and Institutions Code. The record contains no explanation of why the civil procedures authorized by this legislation were not utilized in the present case.

determine that the general health and welfare require that the victims of these and other human afflictions be dealt with by compulsory treatment, involving quarantine, confinement, or sequestration. But, in the light of contemporary human knowledge, a law which made a criminal offense of such a disease would doubtless be universally thought to be an infliction of cruel and unusual punishment in violation of the eighth and 14th amendments.

We cannot but consider the statute before us as of the same category. In this Court counsel for the state recognized that narcotic addiction is an illness. Indeed, it is apparently an illness which may be contracted innocently or involuntarily.[9] We hold that a state law which imprisons a person thus afflicted as a criminal, even though he has never touched any narcotic drug within the state or been guilty of any irregular behavior there, inflicts a cruel and unusual punishment in violation of the 14th amendment. To be sure, imprisonment for 90 days is not, in the abstract, a punishment which is either cruel or unusual. But the question cannot be considered in the abstract. Even one day in prison would be a cruel and unusual punishment for the "crime" of having a common cold.

We are not unmindful that the vicious evils of the narcotics traffic have occasioned the grave concern of government. There are, as we have said, countless fronts on which those evils may be legitimately attacked. We deal in this case only within an individual provision of a particularized local law as it has so far been interpreted by the California courts.

Reversed.

MR. JUSTICE FRANKFURTER took no part in the consideration or decision of this case.

MR. JUSTICE DOUGLAS, concurring.

While I join the Court's opinion, I wish to make more explicit the reasons why I think it is "cruel and unusual" punishment in the sense of the eighth amendment to treat as a criminal a person who is a drug addict.

. . . The addict is a sick person. He may, of course, be confined for treatment or for the protection of society. Cruel and unusual punishment results not from confinement, but from convicting the addict of a crime. The purpose of Section 11721 is not to cure, but to penalize. Were the purpose to cure, there would be no need for a mandatory jail term of not less than 90 days. Contrary to my Brother Clark, I think the means must stand constitutional scrutiny, as well as the end to be achieved. A prosecution for addiction, with its resulting stigma and irreparable damage to the good name of the accused, cannot be justified as a means of protecting society, where a civil commitment would do as well. Indeed, in Section 5350 of the Welfare and Institutions Code, California has expressly provided for civil proceedings for

---

[9] Not only may addiction innocently result from the use of medically prescribed narcotics, but a person may even be a narcotics addict from the moment of his birth. [Citing various medical authorities.]

the commitment of habitual addicts. Section 11721 is, in reality, a direct attempt to punish those the state cannot commit civilly.[5] This prosecution has no relationship to the curing of an illness. Indeed, it cannot, for the prosecution is aimed at penalizing an illness, rather than at providing medical care for it. We would forget the teachings of the eighth amendment if we allowed sickness to be made a crime and permitted sick people to be punished for being sick. This age of enlightenment cannot tolerate such barbarous action.

MR. JUSTICE HARLAN, concurring.

I am not prepared to hold that on the present state of medical knowledge it is completely irrational and hence unconstitutional for a state to conclude that narcotics addiction is something other than an illness nor that it amounts to cruel and unusual punishment for the state to subject narcotics addicts to its criminal law. Insofar as addiction may be identified with the use or possession of narcotics within the state (or, I would suppose, without the state), in violation of local statutes prohibiting such acts, it may surely be reached by the state's criminal law. But in this case the trial court's instructions permitted the jury to find the appellant guilty on no more proof than that he was present in California while he was addicted to narcotics.* Since addiction alone cannot reasonably be thought to amount to more than a compelling propensity to use narcotics, the effect of this instruction was to authorize criminal punishment for a bare desire to commit a criminal act.

If the California statute reaches this type of conduct, and for present purposes we must accept the trial court's construction as binding, it is an arbitrary imposition which exceeds the power that a state may exercise in enacting its criminal law. Accordingly, I agree that the application of the California statute was unconstitutional in this case and join the judgment of reversal.

MR. JUSTICE CLARK, dissenting.

The Court finds Section 11721 of California's Health and Safety Code, making it an offense to "be addicted to the use of narcotics," violative of due process as "a cruel and unusual punishment." I cannot agree.

[5] The difference between Section 5350 and Section 11721 is that the former aims at treatment of the addiction, whereas Section 11721 does not. The latter cannot be construed to provide treatment, unless jail sentences, without more, are suddenly to become medicinal. A comparison of the lengths of confinement under the two sections is irrelevant, for it is the purpose of the confinement that must be measured against the constitutional prohibition of cruel and unusual punishments. . . .

* The jury was instructed that "it is not incumbent upon the People to prove the unlawfulness of defendant's use of narcotics. All that the People must show is *either* that the defendant did use a narcotic in Los Angeles County, *or* that while in the City of Los Angeles he was addicted to the use of narcotics." (Emphasis added.) Although the jury was told that it should acquit if the appellant proved that his "being addicted to the use of narcotics was administered [sic] by or under the direction of a person licensed by the state of California to prescribe and administer narcotics," this part of the instruction did not cover other possible lawful uses which could have produced the appellant's addiction.

The statute must first be placed in perspective. California has a comprehensive and enlightened program for the control of narcotism based on the overriding policy of prevention and cure. It is the product of an extensive investigation made in the mid-Fifties by a committee of distinguished scientists, doctors, law enforcement officers and laymen appointed by the then attorney general, now governor, of California. The committee filed a detailed study entitled "Report on Narcotics Addiction" which was given considerable attention. No recommendation was made therein for the repeal of Section 11721, and the state legislature in its discretion continued the policy of that section.

Apart from prohibiting specific acts such as the purchase, possession and sale of narcotics, California has taken certain legislative steps in regard to the status of being a narcotic addict—a condition commonly recognized as a threat to the state and to the individual. The Code deals with this problem in realistic stages. At its incipiency narcotic addiction is handled under Section 11721 of the Health and Safety Code which is at issue here. It provides that a person found to be addicted to the use of narcotics shall serve a term in the county jail of not less than 90 days nor more than one year, with the minimum 90-day confinement applying in all cases without exception. Provision is made for parole with periodic tests to detect re-addiction.

The trial court defined "addicted to narcotics" as used in Section 11721 in the following charge to the jury:

"The word 'addicted' means, strongly disposed to some taste or practice or habituated, especially to drugs. In order to inquire as to whether a person is addicted to the use of narcotics is in effect an inquiry as to his habit in that regard. Does he use them habitually. To use them often or daily is, according to the ordinary acceptance of those words, to use them habitually."

There was no suggestion that the term "narcotic addict" as here used included a person who acted without volition or who had lost the power of self-control. Although the section is penal in appearance—perhaps a carry-over from a less sophisticated approach—its present provisions are quite similar to those for civil commitment and treatment of addicts who have lost the power of self-control, and its present purpose is reflected in a statement which closely follows Section 11721: "The rehabilitation of narcotic addicts and the prevention of continued addiction to narcotics is a matter of statewide concern." Cal. Health and Safety Code § 11728.

Where narcotic addiction has progressed beyond the incipient, volitional stage, California provides for commitment of three months to two years in a state hospital. Cal. Welfare and Institutions Code § 5355. For the purposes of this provision, a narcotic addict is defined as

"any person who habitually takes or otherwise uses *to the extent of having lost the power of self-control* any opium, morphine, cocaine, or other narcotic drug as defined in Article I of Chapter 1 of Division 10 of the Health and Safety Code." Cal. Welfare and Institutions Code § 5350. (Emphasis supplied.)

This proceeding is clearly civil in nature with a purpose of rehabilitation and cure. Significantly, if it is found that a person committed under Section 5355 will not receive substantial benefit from further hospital treatment and is not dangerous to society, he may be discharged—but only after a minimum confinement of three months.

Thus, the "criminal" provision applies to the incipient narcotic addict who retains self-control, requiring confinement of three months to one year and parole with frequent tests to detect renewed use of drugs. Its overriding purpose is to cure the less seriously addicted person by preventing further use. On the other hand, the "civil" commitment provision deals with addicts who have lost the power of self-control, requiring hospitalization up to two years. Each deals with a different type of addict but with a common purpose. This is most apparent when the sections overlap: if after civil commitment of an addict it is found that hospital treatment will not be helpful, the addict is confined for a minimum period of three months in the same manner as is the volitional addict under the "criminal" provision.

In the instant case the proceedings against the petitioner were brought under the volitional-addict section. There was testimony that he had been using drugs only four months with three to four relatively mild doses a week. At arrest and trial he appeared normal. His testimony was clear and concise, being simply that he had never used drugs. The scabs and pocks on his arms and body were caused, he said, by "overseas shots" administered during army service preparatory to foreign assignment. He was very articulate in his testimony but the jury did not believe him, apparently because he had told the clinical expert while being examined after arrest that he had been using drugs, as I have stated above. The officer who arrested him also testified to like statements and to scabs—some 10 or 15 days old—showing narcotic injections. There was no evidence in the record of withdrawal symptoms. Obviously he could not have been committed under Section 5355 as one who had completely "lost the power of self-control." The jury was instructed that narcotic "addiction" as used in Section 11721 meant strongly disposed to a taste or practice or habit of its use, indicated by the use of narcotics often or daily. A general verdict was returned against petitioner, and he was ordered confined for 90 days to be followed by a two-year parole during which he was required to take periodic Nalline tests.

The majority strikes down the conviction primarily on the grounds that petitioner was denied due process by the imposition of criminal penalties for nothing more than being in a status. This viewpoint is premised upon the theme that Section 11721 is a "criminal" provision authorizing a punishment, for the majority admits that "a state might establish a program of compulsory treatment for those addicted to narcotics" which "might require periods of involuntary confinement." I submit that California has done exactly that. The majority's error is in instructing the California legislature that hospitalization is the *only treatment* for narcotics addiction—that anything less is a punishment denying due process. California has found otherwise after a study which I suggest was more extensive than that conducted by the Court. Even in California's program for hospital commitment of non-volitional narcotic addicts—which the majority approves—it is recognized that some addicts will not respond to or do not need hospital treatment. As to these persons its provisions are identical to those of Section 11721— confinement for a period of not less than 90 days. Section 11721 provides this confinement as treatment for the volitional addicts to whom its provisions apply, in addition to parole with frequent tests to detect and prevent further use of drugs. The fact that Section 11721 might be labeled "criminal" seems irrelevant,* not only to the majority's own "treatment" test but to the "concept of ordered liberty" to which the states must attain under the 14th amendment. The test is the overall purpose and effect of a state's act, and I submit that California's program relative to narcotic addicts—including both the "criminal" and "civil" provisions—is inherently one of treatment and lies well within the power of a state.

However, the case in support of the judgment below need not rest solely on this reading of California law. For even if the overall statutory scheme is ignored and a purpose and effect of punishment is attached to Section 11721, that provision still does not violate the 14th amendment. The majority acknowledges, as it must, that a state can punish persons who purchase, possess or use narcotics. Although none of these acts are [sic] harmful to society *in themselves*, the state constitutionally may attempt to deter and prevent them through punishment because of the grave threat of future harmful conduct which they pose. Narcotics addiction—including the incipient, volitional addiction to which this provision speaks—is no different. California courts have taken judicial notice that "the inordinate use of a narcotic drug tends to create an irresistible craving and forms a habit for its continued use until one becomes an addict, and he respects no convention or obligation and will lie, steal, or use any other base means to gratify his passion for the drug, being lost to all considerations of duty or social position." . . . Can this Court deny the legislative and judicial judgment of California that incipient, volitional narcotic addiction poses a threat of serious crime similar to the threat inherent in the purchase or possession of narcotics? And if such a threat is inherent in addiction, can this Court say that California is powerless to deter it by punishment?

It is no answer to suggest that we are dealing with an involuntary status and thus penal sanctions will be ineffective and unfair. The section at issue applies only to persons who use narcotics often or even daily but not to the point of losing self-control. When dealing with involuntary addicts California moves only through Section 5355 of its Welfare and Institutions Code which clearly is not penal. Even if it could be argued that Section 11721 may not be limited to volitional addicts, the petitioner in the instant case undeniably retained the power of self-control and thus to him the statute would be constitution-

---

* Any reliance upon the "stigma" of a misdemeanor conviction in this context is misplaced, as it would hardly be different from the stigma of a civil commitment for narcotics addiction.

al. Moreover, "status" offenses have long been known and recognized in the criminal law. A ready example is drunkenness, which plainly is as involuntary after addiction to alcohol as is the taking of drugs.

Nor is the conjecture relevant that petitioner may have acquired his habit under lawful circumstances. There was no suggestion by him to this effect at trial, and surely the state need not rebut all possible lawful sources of addiction as part of its prima facie case.

The argument that the statute constitutes a cruel and unusual punishment is governed by the discussion above. Properly construed, the statute provides a treatment rather than a punishment. But even if interpreted as penal, the sanction of incarceration for three to 12 months is not unreasonable . . . when compared to the provisions for three to 24 months' confinement under Section 5355 which the majority approves.

I would affirm the judgment.

MR. JUSTICE WHITE, dissenting.

If appellant's conviction rested upon sheer status, condition or illness or if he was convicted for being an addict who had lost his power of self-control, I would have other thoughts about this case. But this record presents neither situation. And I believe the Court has departed from its wise rule of not deciding constitutional questions except where necessary and from its equally sound practice of construing state statutes, where possible, in a manner saving their constitutionality.

I am not at all ready to place the use of narcotics beyond the reach of the states' criminal laws. I do not consider appellant's conviction to be a punishment for having an illness or for simply being in some status or condition, but rather a conviction for the regular, repeated or habitual use of narcotics immediately prior to his arrest and in violation of the California law. As defined by the trial court,[2] addiction *is* the regular use of narcotics and can be proved only by evidence of such use. To find addiction in this case the jury had to believe that appellant had frequently used narcotics in the recent past.[3] California is entitled to have its statute and the record so read, particularly where the state's only purpose in allowing prosecutions for addiction was to supersede its own venue requirements applicable to prosecutions for the

[2] The court instructed the jury that, "The word 'addicted' means, strongly disposed to some taste or practice or habituated, especially to drugs. In order to inquire as to whether a person is addicted to the use of narcotics is in effect an inquiry as to his habit in that regard. . . . To use them often or daily is, according to the ordinary acceptance of those words, to use them habitually."

[3] This is not a case where defendant is convicted "even though he has never touched any narcotic drug within the state or been guilty of any irregular behavior there." The evidence was that appellant lived and worked in Los Angeles. He ad-mitted before trial that he had used narcotics for three or four months, three or four times a week, usually at his place with his friends. He stated to the police that he had last used narcotics at 54th and Central in the City of Los Angeles on January 27, eight days before his arrest. According to the state's expert, no needle mark or scab found on appellant's arm was newer than three days old and the most recent mark might have been as old as 10 days, which was consistent with appellant's own pretrial admissions. The state's evidence was that appellant had used narcotics at least seven times in the 15 days immediately preceding his arrest.

use of narcotics and in effect to allow convictions for use where there is no precise evidence of the county where the use took place.[4]

Nor do I find any indications in this record that California would apply Section 11721 to the case of the helpless addict. I agree with my Brother Clark that there was no evidence at all that appellant had lost the power to control his acts. There was no evidence of any use within three days prior to appellant's arrest. The most recent marks might have been three days old or they might have been 10 days old. The appellant admitted before trial that he had last used narcotics eight days before his arrest. At the trial he denied having taken narcotics at all. The uncontroverted evidence was that appellant was not under the influence of narcotics at the time of his arrest nor did he have withdrawal symptoms. He was an incipient addict, a redeemable user, and the state chose to send him to jail for 90 days rather than to attempt to confine him by civil proceedings under another statute which requires a finding that the addict has lost the power of self-control. In my opinion, on this record, it was within the power of the state of California to confine him by criminal proceedings for the use of narcotics or for regular use amounting to habitual use.

The Court clearly does not rest its decision upon the narrow ground that the jury was not expressly instructed not to convict if it believed appellant's use of narcotics was beyond his control. The Court recognizes no degrees of addiction. The 14th amendment is today held to bar any prosecution for addiction regardless of the degree or frequency of use, and the Court's opinion bristles with indications of further consequences. If it is "cruel and unusual punishment" to convict appellant for addiction, it is difficult to understand why it would be any less offensive to the 14th amendment to convict him for use on the same evidence of use which proved he was an addict. It is significant that in purporting to reaffirm the power of the states to deal with the narcotics traffic, the Court does not include among the obvious powers of the state the power to punish for the use of narcotics. I cannot think that the omission was inadvertent.

The Court has not merely tidied up California's law by removing some irritating vestige of an outmoded approach to the control of narcotics. At the very least, it has effectively removed California's

---

[4] The typical case under the narcotics statute, as the state made clear in its brief and argument, is the one where the defendant makes no admissions, as he did in this case, and the only evidence of use or addiction is presented by an expert who, on the basis of needle marks and scabs or other physical evidence revealed by the body of the defendant, testifies that the defendant has regularly taken narcotics in the recent past. . . . Under the local venue requirements, a conviction for simple use of narcotics may be had only in the county where the use took place and in the usual case evidence of the precise location of the use is lacking. Where the charge is addiction, venue under § 11721 of the Health and Safety Code may be laid in any county where the defendant is found. Under California law a defendant has no constitutional right to be tried in any particular county, but under statutory law, with certain exceptions, "an accused person is answerable only in the jurisdiction where the crime, or some part or effect thereof, was committed or occurred." A charge of narcotics addiction is one of the exceptions and there are others. Venue is to be determined from the evidence and is for the jury, but it need not be proved beyond a reasonable doubt. . . . In reviewing convictions in narcotics cases, appellate courts view the evidence of venue "in the light most favorable to the judgment."

power to deal effectively with the recurring case under the statute where there is ample evidence of use but no evidence of the precise location of use. Beyond this it has cast serious doubt upon the power of any state to forbid the use of narcotics under threat of criminal punishment. I cannot believe that the Court would forbid the application of the criminal laws to the use of narcotics under any circumstances. But the states, as well as the federal government, are now on notice. They will have to await a final answer in another case.

Finally, I deem this application of "cruel and unusual punishment" so novel that I suspect the Court was hard put to find a way to ascribe to the framers of the Constitution the result reached today rather than to its own notions of ordered liberty. If this case involved economic regulation, the present Court's allergy to substantive due process would surely save the statute and prevent the Court from imposing its own philosophical predilections upon state legislatures or Congress. I fail to see why the Court deems it more appropriate to write into the Constitution its own abstract notions of how best to handle the narcotics problem, for it obviously cannot match either the states or Congress in expert understanding.

I respectfully dissent.

POWELL v. TEXAS

Supreme Court of the United States, 1968.
392 U.S. 514.

MR. JUSTICE MARSHALL announced the judgment of the Court and delivered an opinion in which THE CHIEF JUSTICE, MR. JUSTICE BLACK, and MR. JUSTICE HARLAN join.

In late December 1966, appellant was arrested and charged with being found in a state of intoxication in a public place, in violation of Texas Penal Code, art. 477 (1952), which reads as follows:

"Whoever shall get drunk or be found in a state of intoxication in any public place, or at any private house except his own, shall be fined not exceeding one hundred dollars."

Appellant was tried in the Corporation Court of Austin, Texas, found guilty, and fined $20. He appealed to the County Court at Law No. 1 of Travis County, Texas, where a trial de novo was held. His counsel urged that appellant was "afflicted with the disease of chronic alcoholism," that "his appearance in public [while drunk was] not of his own volition," and therefore that to punish him criminally for that conduct would be cruel and unusual, in violation of the eighth and 14th amendments to the United States Constitution.

The trial judge in the county court, sitting without a jury, made certain findings of fact, but ruled as a matter of law that chronic alcoholism was not a defense to the charge. He found appellant guilty, and fined him $50. There being no further right to appeal within the Texas judicial system, appellant appealed to this Court; we noted probable jurisdiction.

I

The principal testimony was that of Dr. David Wade, a Fellow of the American Medical Association, duly certificated in psychiatry. His testimony consumed a total of 17 pages in the trial transcript. Five of those pages were taken up with a recitation of Dr. Wade's qualifications. In the next 12 pages Dr. Wade was examined by appellant's counsel, cross-examined by the state, and reexamined by the defense, and those 12 pages contain virtually all the material developed at trial which is relevant to the constitutional issue we face here. Dr. Wade sketched the outlines of the "disease" concept of alcoholism; noted that there is no generally accepted definition of "alcoholism"; alluded to the ongoing debate within the medical profession over whether alcohol is actually physically "addicting" or merely psychologically "habituating"; and concluded that in either case a "chronic alcoholic" is an "involuntary drinker," who is "powerless not to drink," and who "loses his self-control over his drinking." He testified that he had examined appellant, and that appellant is a "chronic alcoholic," who "by the time he has reached [the state of intoxication] is not able to control his behavior, and [who] has reached this point because he has an uncontrollable compulsion to drink." Dr. Wade also responded in the negative to the question whether appellant has "the willpower to resist the constant excessive consumption of alcohol." He added that in his opinion jailing appellant without medical attention would operate neither to rehabilitate him nor to lessen his desire for alcohol.

On cross-examination, Dr. Wade admitted that when appellant was sober he knew the difference between right and wrong, and he responded affirmatively to the question whether appellant's act of taking the first drink in any given instance when he was sober was a "voluntary exercise of his will." Qualifying his answer, Dr. Wade stated that "these individuals have a compulsion, and this compulsion, while not completely overpowering, is a very strong influence, and this compulsion coupled with the firm belief in their mind that they are going to be able to handle it from now on causes their judgment to be somewhat clouded."

Appellant testified concerning the history of his drinking problem. He reviewed his many arrests for drunkenness; testified that he was unable to stop drinking; stated that when he was intoxicated he had no control over his actions and could not remember them later, but that he did not become violent; and admitted that he did not remember his arrest on the occasion for which he was being tried. On cross-examination, appellant admitted that he had one drink on the morning of the trial and had been able to discontinue drinking. . . .

Evidence in the case then closed. The state made no effort to obtain expert psychiatric testimony of its own, or even to explore with appellant's witness the question of appellant's power to control the frequency, timing, and location of his drinking bouts, or the substantial disagreement within the medical profession concerning the nature of the disease, the efficacy of treatment and the prerequisites for effective treatment. It did nothing to examine or illuminate what Dr. Wade might have meant by his reference to a "compulsion" which was "not completely overpowering," but which was "an exceedingly strong influence," or to inquire into the question of the proper role of such a "compulsion" in constitutional adjudication. Instead, the state contented itself with a brief argument that appellant had no defense to the charge because he "is legally sane and knows the difference between right and wrong."

Following this abbreviated exposition of the problem before it, the trial court indicated its intention to disallow appellant's claimed defense of "chronic alcoholism." Thereupon defense counsel submitted, and the trial court entered, the following "findings of fact":

"(i) That chronic alcoholism is a disease which destroys the afflicted person's will power to resist the constant, excessive consumption of alcohol.

"(ii) That a chronic alcoholic does not appear in public by his own volition but under a compulsion symptomatic of the disease of chronic alcoholism.

"(iii) That Leroy Powell, defendant herein, is a chronic alcoholic who is afflicted with the disease of chronic alcoholism."

Whatever else may be said of them, those are not "findings of fact" in any recognizable, traditional sense in which that term has been used in a court of law; they are the premises of a syllogism transparently designed to bring this case within the scope of this Court's opinion in Robinson v. California, 370 U.S. 660 (1962). Nonetheless, the dissent would have us adopt these "findings" without critical examination; it would use them as the basis for a constitutional holding that "a person may not be punished if the condition essential to constitute the defined crime is part of the pattern of his disease and is occasioned by a compulsion symptomatic of the disease."

The difficulty with that position, as we shall show, is that it goes much too far on the basis of too little knowledge. In the first place, the record in this case is utterly inadequate to permit the sort of informed and responsible adjudication which alone can support the announcement of an important and wide-ranging new constitutional principle. We know very little about the circumstances surrounding the drinking bout which resulted in this conviction, or about Leroy Powell's drinking problem, or indeed about alcoholism itself. The trial hardly reflects the sharp legal and evidentiary clash between fully prepared adversary litigants which is traditionally expected in major constitutional cases. The state put on only one witness, the arresting officer. The defense put on three—a policeman who testified to appellant's long history of arrest for public drunkenness, the psychiatrist, and appellant himself.

Furthermore, the inescapable fact is that there is no agreement among members of the medical profession about what it means to say that "alcoholism" is a "disease." One of the principal works in this field states that the major difficulty in articulating a "disease concept of alcoholism" is that "alcoholism has too many definitions and disease has practically none." This same author concludes that "*a disease is what the medical profession recognizes as such.*" In other words, there is widespread agreement today that "alcoholism" is a "disease," for the simple reason that the medical profession has concluded that it should attempt to treat those who have drinking problems. There the agreement stops. Debate rages within the medical profession as to whether "alcoholism" is a separate "disease" in any meaningful biochemical, physiological or psychological sense, or whether it represents one peculiar manifestation in some individuals of underlying psychiatric disorders. . . .

The trial court's "finding" that Powell "is afflicted with the disease of chronic alcoholism," which "destroys the afflicted person's will power to resist the constant, excessive consumption of alcohol" covers a multitude of sins. Dr. Wade's testimony that appellant suffered from a compulsion which was "not completely overpowering" is at least more carefully stated, if no less mystifying. Jellinek [whom the Court characterized as "one of the outstanding authorities on the subject"] insists that conceptual clarity can only be achieved by distinguishing carefully between "loss of control" once an individual has commenced to drink and "inability to abstain" from drinking in the first place. Presumably a person would have to display both characteristics in order to make out a constitutional defense, should one be recognized. Yet the "findings" of the trial court utterly fail to make this crucial distinction, and there is serious question whether the record can be read to support a finding of either loss of control or inability to abstain.

Dr. Wade did testify that once appellant began drinking he appeared to have no control over the amount of alcohol he finally ingested. Appellant's own testimony concerning his drinking on the day of the trial would certainly appear, however, to cast doubt upon the conclusion that he was without control over his consumption of alcohol when he had sufficiently important reasons to exercise such control. However that may be, there are more serious factual and conceptual difficulties with reading this record to show that appellant was unable to abstain from drinking. Dr. Wade testified that when appellant was sober, the act of taking the first drink was a "voluntary exercise of his will," but that this exercise of will was undertaken under the "exceedingly strong influence" of a "compulsion" which was "not completely overpowering." Such concepts, when juxtaposed in his fashion, have little meaning. . . .

It is one thing to say that if a man is deprived of alcohol his hands will begin to shake, he will suffer agonizing pains and ultimately he will have hallucinations; it is quite another to say that a man has a "compulsion" to take a drink, but that he also retains a certain amount of "free will" with which to resist. It is simply impossible, in the present state of our knowledge, to ascribe a useful meaning to the latter statement. This definitional confusion reflects, of course, not merely the undeveloped state of the psychiatric art but also the conceptual difficulties inevitably attendant upon the importation of scientific and medical models into a legal system generally predicated upon a different set of assumptions.

II

Despite the comparatively primitive state of our knowledge of the subject, it cannot be denied that the destructive use of alcoholic beverages is one of our principal social and public-health problems. The lowest current informed estimate places the number of "alcoholics" in America (definitional problems aside) at 4,000,000, and most authorities are inclined to put the figure considerably higher. The problem is compounded by the fact that a very large percentage of the alcoholics in this country are "invisible"—they possess the means to keep their drinking problems secret, and the traditionally uncharitable attitude of our society towards alcoholics causes many of them to refrain from seeking treatment from any source. Nor can it be gainsaid that the legislative response to this enormous problem has in general been inadequate.

There is as yet no known generally effective method for treating the vast number of alcoholics in our society. Some individual alcoholics have responded to particular forms of therapy with remissions of their symptomatic dependence upon the drug. But just as there is no agreement among doctors and social workers with respect to the causes of alcoholism, there is no consensus as to why particular treatments have been effective in particular cases and there is no generally agreed upon approach to the problem of treatment on a large scale. Most psychiatrists are apparently of the opinion that alcoholism is far more difficult to treat than other forms of behavioral disorders, and some believe it is impossible to cure by means of psychotherapy; indeed, the medical profession as a whole, and psychiatrists in particular, have been severely criticized for the prevailing reluctance to undertake the treatment of drinking problems. Thus it is entirely possible that, even were the manpower and facilities available for a full-scale attack upon chronic alcoholism, we would find ourselves unable to help the vast bulk of our "visible"—let alone our "invisible"—alcoholic population.

However, facilities for the attempted treatment of indigent alcoholics are woefully lacking throughout the country. It would be tragic to return large numbers of helpless, sometimes dangerous and frequently unsanitary inebriates to the streets of our cities without even the opportunity to sober up adequately which a brief jail term provides. Presumably no state or city will tolerate such a state of affairs. Yet the medical profession cannot, and does not, tell us with any assurance that, even if the buildings, equipment and trained personnel were made available, it could provide anything more than slightly higher-class jails for our indigent habitual inebriates. Thus we run the grave risk that nothing will be accomplished beyond the hanging of a new sign—reading "hospital"—over one wing of the jailhouse.

One virtue of the criminal process is, at least, that the duration of penal incarceration typically has some outside statutory limit; this is universally true in the case of petty offenses, such as public drunkenness, where jail terms are quite short on the whole. "Therapeutic civil commitment" lacks this feature; one is typically committed until one is "cured." Thus, to do otherwise than affirm might subject indigent alcoholics to the risk that they may be locked up for an indefinite period of time under the same conditions as before, with no more hope than before of receiving effective treatment and no prospect of periodic "freedom."

Faced with this unpleasant reality, we are unable to assert that the use of the criminal process as a means of dealing with the public aspects of problem drinking can never be defended as rational. The picture of the penniless drunk propelled aimlessly and endlessly through the law's "revolving door" of arrest, incarceration, release and re-arrest is not a pretty one. But before we condemn the present practice across-the-board, perhaps we ought to be able to point to some clear promise of a better world for these unfortunate people. Unfortunately, no such promise has yet been forthcoming. If, in addition to the absence of a coherent approach to the problem of treatment, we consider the almost complete absence of facilities and manpower for the implementation of a rehabilitation program, it is difficult to say in the present context that the criminal process is utterly lacking in social value. This Court has never held that anything in the Constitution requires that penal sanctions be designed solely to achieve therapeutic or rehabilitative effects, and it can hardly be said with assurance that incarceration serves such purposes any better for the general run of criminals than it does for public drunks.

Ignorance likewise impedes our assessment of the deterrent effect of criminal sanctions for public drunkenness. The fact that a high percentage of American alcoholics conceal their drinking problems, not merely by avoiding public displays of intoxication but also by shunning all forms of treatment, is indicative that some powerful deterrent operates to inhibit the public revelation of the existence of alcoholism. Quite probably this deterrent effect can be largely attributed to the harsh moral attitude which our society has traditionally taken toward intoxication and the shame which we have associated with alcoholism. Criminal conviction represents the degrading public revelation of what Anglo-American society has long condemned as a moral defect, and the existence of criminal sanctions may serve to reinforce this cultural taboo just as we presume it serves to reinforce other, stronger feelings against murder, rape, theft, and other forms of anti-social conduct.

Obviously, chronic alcoholics have not been deterred from drinking to excess by the existence of criminal sanctions against public drunkenness. But all those who violate penal laws of any kind are by definition undeterred. The long-standing and still raging debate over the validity of the deterrence justification for penal sanctions has not reached any sufficiently clear conclusions to permit it to be said that such sanctions are ineffective in any particular context or for any particular group of people who are able to appreciate the consequences of their acts. Certainly no effort was made at the trial of this case, beyond a monosyllabic answer to a perfunctory one-line question, to determine the effectiveness of penal sanctions in deterring Leroy Powell in particular or chronic alcoholics in general from drinking at all or from getting drunk in particular places or at particular times.

III

Appellant claims that his conviction on the facts of this case would violate the cruel and unusual punishment clause of the eighth amendment as applied to the states through the 14th amendment.   The primary purpose of that clause has always been considered, and properly so, to be directed at the method or kind of punishment imposed for the violation of criminal statutes; the nature of the conduct made criminal is ordinarily relevant only to the fitness of the punishment imposed.

Appellant, however, seeks to come within the application of the cruel and unusual punishment clause announced in *Robinson* v. *California*, supra, which involved a state law making it a crime to "be addicted to the use of narcotics."   This Court held there that "a state law which imprisons a person thus afflicted [with narcotic addiction] as a criminal, even though he has never touched any narcotic drug within the state or been guilty of any irregular behavior there, inflicts a cruel and unusual punishment . . . ."

On its face the present case does not fall within that holding, since appellant was convicted, not for being a chronic alcoholic, but for being in public while drunk on a particular occasion.   The state of Texas thus has not sought to punish a mere status, as California did in *Robinson*; nor has it attempted to regulate appellant's behavior in the privacy of his own home.   Rather, it has imposed upon appellant a criminal sanction for public behavior which may create substantial health and safety hazards, both for appellant and for members of the general public, and which offends the moral and esthetic sensibilities of a large segment of the community.   This seems a far cry from convicting one for being an addict, being a chronic alcoholic, being "mentally ill, or a leper   . . . ."

Robinson so viewed brings this Court but a very small way into the substantive criminal law.   And unless *Robinson* is so viewed it is difficult to see any limiting principle that would serve to prevent this Court from becoming, under the aegis of the cruel and unusual punishment clause, the ultimate arbiter of the standards of criminal responsibility, in diverse areas of the criminal law, throughout the country.

It is suggested in dissent that *Robinson* stands for the "simple" but "subtle" principle that "[c]riminal penalties may not be inflicted upon a person for being in a condition he is powerless to change."   . . .   In that view, appellant's "condition" of public intoxication was "occasioned by a compulsion symptomatic of the disease" of chronic alcoholism, and thus, apparently, his behavior lacked the critical element of mens rea.   Whatever may be the merits of such a doctrine of criminal responsibility, it surely cannot be said to follow from *Robinson*.   The entire thrust of *Robinson*'s interpretation of the cruel and unusual punishment clause is that criminal penalties may be inflicted only if the accused has committed some act, has engaged in some behavior, which society has an interest in preventing, or perhaps in historical common law terms, has committed some actus reus. It thus does not deal with the question of whether certain conduct cannot constitutionally be punished because it is, in some sense, "involuntary" or "occasioned by a compulsion."

Likewise, as the dissent acknowledges, there is a substantial definitional distinction between a "status," as in *Robinson*, and a "condition," which is said to be involved in this case. Whatever may be the merits of an attempt to distinguish between behavior and a condition, it is perfectly clear that the crucial element in this case, so far as the dissent is concerned, is whether or not appellant can legally be held responsible for his appearance in public in a state of intoxication. The only relevance of *Robinson* to this issue is that because the Court interpreted the statute there involved as making a "status" criminal, it was able to suggest that the statute would cover even a situation in which addiction had been acquired involuntarily. That this factor was not determinative in the case is shown by the fact that there was no indication of how Robinson himself had become an addict.

Ultimately, then, the most troubling aspect of this case, were *Robinson* to be extended to meet it, would be the scope and content of what could only be a constitutional doctrine of criminal responsibility. In dissent it is urged that the decision could be limited to conduct which is "a characteristic and involuntary part of the pattern of the disease as it afflicts" the particular individual, and that "[i]t is not foreseeable" that it would be applied "in the case of offenses such as driving a car while intoxicated, assault, theft, or robbery." That is limitation by fiat. In the first place, nothing in the logic of the dissent would limit its application to chronic alcoholics. If Leroy Powell cannot be convicted of public intoxication, it is difficult to see how a state can convict an individual for murder, if that individual, while exhibiting normal behavior in all other respects, suffers from a "compulsion" to kill, which is an "exceedingly strong influence," but "not completely overpowering." Even if we limit our consideration to chronic alcoholics, it would seem impossible to confine the principle within the arbitrary bounds which the dissent seems to envision.

It is not difficult to imagine a case involving psychiatric testimony to the effect that an individual suffers from some aggressive neurosis which he is able to control when sober; that very little alcohol suffices to remove the inhibitions which normally contain these aggressions, with the result that the individual engages in assaultive behavior without becoming actually intoxicated; and that the individual suffers from a very strong desire to drink which is an "exceedingly strong influence" but "not completely overpowering." Without being untrue to the rationale of this case, should the principles advanced in dissent be accepted here, the Court could not avoid holding such an individual constitutionally unaccountable for his assaultive behavior.

Traditional common-law concepts of personal accountability and essential considerations of federalism lead us to disagree with appellant. We are unable to conclude, on the state of this record or on the current state of medical knowledge, that chronic alcoholics in general, and Leroy Powell in particular, suffer from such an irresistible compulsion to drink and to get drunk in public that they are utterly unable to control their performance of either or both of these acts and thus cannot be deterred at all from public intoxication. . . .

We cannot cast aside the centuries-long evolution of the collection of interlocking and overlapping concepts which the common law has utilized to assess the moral accountability of an individual for his anti-social deeds. The doctrines of actus reus, mens rea, insanity, mistake, justification, and duress have historically provided the tools for a constantly shifting adjustment of the tension between the evolving aims of the criminal law and changing religious, moral, philosphical, and medical views of the nature of man. . . .

It is simply not yet the time to write into the Constitution formulas cast in terms whose meaning, let alone relevance is not yet clear either to doctors or to lawyers.

Affirmed.

MR. JUSTICE BLACK, whom MR. JUSTICE HARLAN joins, concurring. . . .

I agree with Mr. Justice Marshall that the findings of fact in this case are inadequate to justify the sweeping constitutional rule urged upon us. I could not, however, consider any findings that could be made with respect to "voluntariness" or "compulsion" controlling on the question whether a specific instance of human behavior should be immune from punishment as a constitutional matter. When we say that appellant's appearance in public is caused not by "his own" volition but rather by some other force, we are clearly thinking of a force that is nevertheless "his" except in some special sense.[1] The accused undoubtedly commits the proscribed act and the only question is whether the act can be attributed to a part of "his" personality that should not be regarded as criminally responsible. Almost all of the traditional purposes of the criminal law can be significantly served by punishing the person who in fact committed the proscribed act, without regard to whether his action was "compelled" by some elusive "irresponsible" aspect of his personality. [P]unishment of such a defendant can clearly be justified in terms of deterrence, isolation, and treatment. On the other hand, medical decisions concerning the use of a term such as "disease" or "volition," based as they are on the clinical problems of diagnosis and treatment, bear no necessary correspondence to the legal decision whether the overall objectives of the criminal law can be furthered by imposing punishment. For these reasons, much as I think that criminal sanctions should in many situations be applied only to those whose conduct is morally blameworthy, see Morissette v. United

---

[1] If an intoxicated person is actually carried into the street by someone else, "he" does not do the act at all, and of course he is entitled to acquittal. E.g., Martin v. State, 31 Ala.App. 334, 17 So.2d 427 (1944).

States, 342 U.S. 246 (1952), I cannot think the states should be held constitutionally required to make the inquiry as to what part of a defendant's personality is responsible for his actions and to excuse anyone whose action was, in some complex, psychological sense, the result of a "compulsion."

The rule of constitutional law urged by appellant is not required by *Robinson* v. *California*, supra. In that case we held that a person could not be punished for the mere status of being a narcotics addict. We explicitly limited our holding to the situation where no conduct of any kind is involved, stating:

> "We hold that a state law which imprisons a person thus afflict-ed as a criminal, *even though he has never touched any narcotic drug within the state or been guilty of any irregular behavior there*, inflicts a cruel and unusual punishment in violation of the 14th amendment." (Emphasis added.)

The argument is made that appellant comes within the terms of our holding in *Robinson* because being drunk in public is a mere status or "condition." Despite this many-faceted use of the concept of "condi-tion," this argument would require converting *Robinson* into a case protecting actual behavior, a step we explicitly refused to take in that decision.

A different question, I admit, is whether our attempt in *Robinson* to limit our holding to pure status crimes, involving no conduct whatever, was a sound one. I believe it was. Although some of our objections to the statute in *Robinson* are equally applicable to statutes that punish conduct "symptomatic" of a disease, any attempt to explain *Robinson* as based solely on the lack of voluntariness encounters a number of logical difficulties. Other problems raised by status crimes are in no way involved when the state attempts to punish for conduct, and these other problems were, in my view, the controlling aspects of our deci-sion.

Punishment for a status is particularly obnoxious, and in many instances can reasonably be called cruel and unusual, because it in-volves punishment for a mere propensity, a desire to commit an offense; the mental element is not simply one part of the crime but may constitute all of it. This is a situation universally sought to be avoided in our criminal law; the fundamental requirement that some action be proved is solidly established even for offenses most heavily based on propensity, such as attempt, conspiracy, and recidivist crimes. In fact, one eminent authority has found only one isolated instance, in all of Anglo-American jurisprudence, in which criminal responsibility was imposed in the absence of any act at all.[5]

The reasons for this refusal to permit conviction without proof of an act are difficult to spell out, but they are nonetheless perceived and universally expressed in our criminal law. Evidence of propensity can be considered relatively unreliable and more difficult for a defendant to rebut; the requirement of a specific act thus provides some protection

[5] G. Williams, Criminal Law: The Gener-al Part 11 n. 4 (2d ed. 1961).

against false charges. . . . Perhaps more fundamental is the difficulty of distinguishing, in the absence of any conduct, between desires of the daydream variety and fixed intentions that may pose a real threat to society; extending the criminal law to cover both types of desire would be unthinkable, since "[t]here can hardly be anyone who has never thought evil. When a desire is inhibited it may find expression in fantasy; but it would be absurd to condemn this natural psychological mechanism as illegal."

In contrast, crimes that require the state to prove that the defendant actually committed some proscribed act involve none of these special problems. In addition, the question whether an act is "involuntary" is, as I have already indicated, an inherently elusive question, and one which the state may, for good reasons, wish to regard as irrelevant. In light of all these considerations, our limitation of our *Robinson* holding to pure status crimes seems to me entirely proper.

The rule of constitutional law urged upon us by appellant would have a revolutionary impact on the criminal law, and any possible limits proposed for the rule would be wholly illusory. If the original boundaries of *Robinson* are to be discarded, any new limits too would soon fall by the wayside and the Court would be forced to hold the states powerless to punish any conduct that could be shown to result from a "compulsion," in the complex, psychological meaning of that term. The result, to choose just one illustration, would be to require recognition of "irresistible impulse" as a complete defense to any crime; this is probably contrary to present law in most American jurisdictions.

The real reach of any such decision, however, would be broader still, for the basic premise underlying the argument is that it is cruel and unusual to punish a person who is not morally blameworthy. I state the proposition in this sympathetic way because I feel there is much to be said for avoiding the use of criminal sanctions in many such situations. See *Morissette* v. *United States*, supra. But the question here is one of constitutional law. The legislatures have always been allowed wide freedom to determine the extent to which moral culpability should be a prerequisite to conviction of a crime. E.g., United States v. Dotterweich, 320 U.S. 277 (1943). The criminal law is a social tool that is employed in seeking a wide variety of goals, and I cannot say the eighth amendment's limits on the use of criminal sanctions extend as far as this viewpoint would inevitably carry them.

But even if we were to limit any holding in this field to "compulsions" that are "symptomatic" of a "disease," in the words of the findings of the trial court, the sweep of that holding would still be startling. Such a ruling would make it clear beyond any doubt that a narcotics addict could not be punished for "being" in possession of drugs or, for that matter, for "being" guilty of using them. A wide variety of sex offenders would be immune from punishment if they could show that their conduct was not voluntary but part of the pattern of a disease. More generally speaking, a form of the insanity defense would be made a constitutional requirement throughout the nation, should the Court now hold it cruel and unusual to punish a person whenever his conduct was part of the pattern of his disease and occasioned by a compulsion symptomatic of the disease. . . .

The impact of . . . the proposed new constitutional rule would be devastating, for constitutional questions would be raised by every state effort to regulate the admissibility of evidence relating to "disease" and "compulsion," and by every state attempt to explain these concepts in instructions to the jury. The test urged would make it necessary to determine, not only what constitutes a "disease," but also what is the "pattern" of the disease, what "conditions" are "part" of the pattern, what parts of this pattern result from a "compulsion," and finally which of these compulsions are "symptomatic" of the disease. . . . The range of problems created would seem totally beyond our capacity to settle at all, much less to settle wisely, and even the attempt to define these terms and thus to impose constitutional and doctrinal rigidity seems absurd in an area where our understanding is even today so incomplete. . . .

I join in affirmance of this conviction.

MR. JUSTICE WHITE, concurring in the result.

If it cannot be a crime to have an irresistible compulsion to use narcotics, *Robinson* v. *California*, supra, I do not see how it can constitutionally be a crime to yield to such a compulsion. Punishing an addict for using drugs convicts for addiction under a different name. Distinguishing between the two crimes is like forbidding criminal conviction for being sick with flu or epilepsy but permitting punishment for running a fever or having a convulsion. Unless *Robinson* is to be abandoned, the use of narcotics by an addict must be beyond the reach of the criminal law. Similarly, the chronic alcoholic with an irresistible urge to consume alcohol should not be punishable for drinking or for being drunk.

Powell's conviction was for the different crime of being drunk in a public place. Thus even if Powell was compelled to drink, and so could not constitutionally be convicted for drinking, his conviction in this case can be invalidated only if there is a constitutional basis for saying that he may not be punished for being in public while drunk. . . .

The trial court said that Powell was a chronic alcoholic with a compulsion not only to drink to excess but also to frequent public places when intoxicated. Nothing in the record before the trial court supports the latter conclusion, which is contrary to common sense and to common knowledge. The sober chronic alcoholic has no compulsion to be on the public streets; many chronic alcoholics drink at home and are never seen drunk in public. Before and after taking the first drink, and until he becomes so drunk that he loses the power to know where he is or to direct his movements, the chronic alcoholic with a home or financial resources is as capable as the non-chronic drinker of doing his drinking in private, of removing himself from public places and, since he knows or ought to know that he will become intoxicated, of making plans to avoid his being found drunk in public. For these reasons, I cannot say that the chronic alcoholic who proves his disease and a compulsion to drink is shielded from conviction when he has knowingly failed to take feasible precautions against committing a criminal act, here the act of going to or remaining in a public place. On such facts the alcoholic is like a person with smallpox, who could be convicted for being on the street but not for being ill, or, like the epileptic, who could be punished for driving a car but not for his disease.

The fact remains that some chronic alcoholics must drink and hence must drink *somewhere*. Although many chronics have homes, many others do not. For all practical purposes the public streets may be home for these unfortunates, not because their disease compels them to be there, but because, drunk or sober, they have no place else to go and no place else to be when they are drinking. This is more a function of economic station than of disease, although the disease may lead to destitution and perpetuate that condition. For some of these alcoholics I would think a showing could be made that resisting drunkenness is impossible and that avoiding public places when intoxicated is also impossible. As applied to them this statute is in effect a law which bans a single act for which they may not be convicted under the eighth amendment—the act of getting drunk.

It is also possible that the chronic alcoholic who begins drinking in private at some point becomes so drunk that he loses the power to control his movements and for that reason appears in public. The eighth amendment might also forbid conviction in such circumstances, but only on a record satisfactorily showing that it was not feasible for him to have made arrangements to prevent his being in public when drunk and that his extreme drunkenness sufficiently deprived him of his faculties on the occasion in issue.

These prerequisites to the possible invocation of the eighth amendment are not satisfied on the record before us. . . .   For the purpose of this case, it is necessary to say only that Powell showed nothing more than that he was to some degree compelled to drink and that he was drunk at the time of his arrest. He made no showing that he was unable to stay off the streets on the night in question. . . .

MR. JUSTICE FORTAS, with whom MR. JUSTICE DOUGLAS, MR. JUSTICE BRENNAN, and MR. JUSTICE STEWART join, dissenting. . . .

The sole question presented is whether a criminal penalty may be imposed upon a person suffering the disease of "chronic alcoholism" for a condition—being "in a state of intoxication" in public—which is a characteristic part of the pattern of his disease and which, the trial court found, was not the consequence of appellant's volition but of "a compulsion symptomatic of the disease of chronic alcoholism." We must consider whether the eighth amendment, made applicable to the states through the 14th amendment, prohibits the imposition of this penalty in these rather special circumstances as "cruel and unusual punishment." This case does not raise any question as to the right of the police to stop and detain those who are intoxicated in public, whether as a result of the disease or otherwise; or as to the state's power to commit chronic alcholics for treatment. Nor does it concern the responsibility of an alcoholic for criminal *acts*. We deal here with the mere *condition* of being intoxicated in public.[2]

As I shall discuss, consideration of the eighth amendment issue in this case requires an understanding of "the disease of chronic alcoholism" with which, as the trial court found, appellant is afflicted, which has destroyed his "will power to resist the constant, excessive consumption of alcohol," and which leads him to "appear in public [not] by his own volition but under a compulsion symptomatic of the disease of chronic alcoholism." . . .

Although there is some problem in defining the concept, its core meaning, as agreed by authorities, is that alcoholism is caused and maintained by something other than the moral fault of the alcoholic, something that, to a greater or lesser extent depending upon the physiological or psychological makeup and history of the individual, cannot be controlled by him. . . .

Authorities have recognized that a number of factors may contribute to alcoholism. Some studies have pointed to physiological influences, such as vitamin deficiency, hormone imbalance, abnormal metabolism, and hereditary proclivity. Other researchers have found more convincing a psychological approach, emphasizing early environment and underlying conflicts and tensions. Numerous studies have indicated the influence of sociocultural factors. It has been shown, for example, that the incidence of alcoholism among certain ethnic groups is far higher than among others.

The manifestations of alcoholism are reasonably well identified. . . . It is well established that alcohol may be habituative and "can be physically addicting." It has been said that "the main point for the non-professional is that alcoholism is not within the control of the person involved. He is not willfully drinking." . . .

Robinson stands upon a principle which, despite its subtlety, must be simply stated and respectfully applied because it is the foundation of individual liberty and the cornerstone of the relations between a civilized state and its citizens: Criminal penalties may not be inflicted upon a person for being in a condition he is powerless to change. In all probability, *Robinson* at some time before his conviction elected to take narcotics. But the crime as defined did not punish this conduct. The statute imposed a penalty for the offense of "addiction"—a condition which Robinson could not control. Once Robinson had become an addict, he was utterly powerless to avoid criminal guilt. He was powerless to choose not to violate the law.

[2] It is not foreseeable that findings such as those which are decisive here—namely that appellant's being intoxicated in public was a part of the pattern of his disease and due to a compulsion symptomatic of that disease—could or would be made in the case of offenses such as driving a car while intoxicated, assault, theft, or robbery. Such offenses require independent acts or conduct and do not typically flow from and are not part of the syndrome of the disease of chronic alcoholism. If an alcoholic should be convicted for criminal conduct which is not a characteristic and involuntary part of the pattern of the disease as it afflicts him, nothing herein would prevent his punishment.

In the present case, appellant is charged with a crime composed of two elements—being intoxicated and being found in a public place while in that condition. The crime, so defined, differs from that in *Robinson*. The statute covers more than a mere status. But the essential constitutional defect here is the same as in *Robinson*, for in both cases the particular defendant was accused of being in a condition which he had no capacity to change or avoid. The trial judge sitting as a trier of fact found, upon the medical and other relevant testimony, that Powell is a "chronic alcoholic." He defined appellant's "chronic alcoholism" as "a disease which destroys the afflicted person's will power to resist the constant, excessive consumption of alcohol." He also found that "a chronic alcoholic does not appear in public by his own volition but under a compulsion symptomatic of the disease of chronic alcoholism." I read these findings to mean that appellant was powerless to avoid drinking; that having taken his first drink, he had "an uncontrollable compulsion to drink" to the point of intoxication; and that, once intoxicated, he could not prevent himself from appearing in public places. . . .

The findings in this case, read against the background of the medical and sociological data to which I have referred, compel the conclusion that the infliction upon appellant of a criminal penalty for being intoxicated in a public place would be "cruel and inhuman punishment" within the prohibition of the eighth amendment. This conclusion follows because appellant is a "chronic alcoholic" who, according to the trier of fact, cannot resist the "constant excessive consumption of alcohol" and does not appear in public by his own volition but under a "compulsion" which is part of his condition.

I would reverse the judgment below.

NOTE ON *ROBINSON* AND *POWELL*

Robinson and *Powell* involve two distinct levels of inquiry. The first is constitutional: What requirements does the Constitution of the United States impose on state criminal law? More specifically, what is the appropriate role of the Supreme Court in articulating constitutional limitations on the policy choices made by legislatures and by state courts? The second level of inquiry concerns the content of the policy choices reflected in the criminal law: Are the approaches reflected in *Robinson* and *Powell* appropriate ways to deal with the problems of drug dependency and alcoholism? With other kinds of arguably involuntary conduct?

The *Powell* dissenters would have read *Robinson* to stand for the "subtle but simple" principle that "[c]riminal penalties may not be inflicted upon a person for a condition he is powerless to change." Would this principle also extend to such acts as are inevitably incident to such a condition? Would it extend, for example, to possession or use of heroin by an addict? To the purchase of heroin for the addict's own use? To theft or robbery committed in order to get money to pay for the heroin? Where, in terms of voluntariness, can the line be drawn?

Are you satisfied with the answer to these questions suggested by the *Powell* dissenters?

On the other hand, is it not clear that some version of the principle advanced by the *Powell* dissenters is essential to the ethical integrity of the criminal law? Can a person fairly be blamed for being in "a condition he is powerless to change"? Does the answer depend on how he got into that condition in the first place? If the actor really had no choice in the matter, how can society justly condemn and punish him for the failure to do otherwise?

Robinson and *Powell* illustrate a divergence between the social-control objectives of the penal law and the ethical foundations of just punishment. One possible escape from this conflict is to seek non-criminal means of social control. Arguably at least, civil intervention may enable society to safeguard its legitimate interests without imposing morally unjustified punishment. The following series of notes examines this possibility.

NOTES ON NON–CRIMINAL METHODS OF COERCIVE INTERVENTION

1. **Quarantine and Civil Commitment.** A determination that a person should not be criminally punished for the status of addiction or for acts symptomatic of that condition does not mean that the state must leave the person alone. Recall Mr. Justice Stewart's observation in *Robinson* that a "state might determine that the . . . general health and welfare might require that the victims [of disease] be dealt with by compulsory treatment involving quarantine, confinement or sequestration." Similarly, the *Powell* dissenters emphasized that "this case does not raise any question as to . . . the state's power to commit chronic alcoholics for treatment."

As these observations suggest, criminal punishment is not the only method of coercive state intervention. Governmental authority to confine persons afflicted by such contagious diseases as smallpox, tuberculosis, or venereal disease is well established. So too is the state's power to confine persons found to be mentally ill and dangerous to themselves or others.

Statutes of this type, which are said to be "civil" rather than "criminal" in nature, represent a model of coercive intervention that differs both in its premises and in its method from the model of criminal punishment. This non-criminal type of coercive intervention is often called the "treatment" or "control" model. Whereas the predicate for criminal punishment is a finding that the actor engaged in an act, omission, or possession in violation of the penal law, the predicate for control interventions is a determination that the person has a condition or status declared by the legislature to warrant preventive intervention. Criminal prosecution is reconstructive or backward-looking; civil adjudication is predictive or forward-looking. It looks to the person's present condition and to a prediction of the dangers posed by that condition. It is true, of course, that predictive considerations frequently are considered in sentencing the criminal offender, and equally true that a person's past conduct often has evidentiary significance in a civil proceeding requiring a prediction of future behavior. However, these similarities should not obscure the fundamental theoretical and operational differences between the two models of coercive intervention.

2. **Principles Governing Control Interventions.** Statutes prescribing control interventions were largely ignored by academic commentators—and by the courts—until the 1960's. The literature, now voluminous,[a] raises fundamental questions concerning the purposes and methods of the "therapeutic state."

(i) **Purpose.** Coercive treatment of persons afflicted with tuberculosis or venereal disease and civil commitment of the mentally ill usually reflect mixed motivations. One purpose may be benevolent— curing the person's illness or improving the condition. Another purpose may be the prevention of harm to others. Questions arise concerning the kind of harm that may legitimately trigger preventive restraint. For example, may the state compel a person addicted to cigarette smoking to undergo treatment? Is the state permitted to hospitalize mentally ill persons merely in order to prevent behavior which is troubling to their families or offensive to others? It should also be noted that the legitimacy of a control intervention may depend upon whether treatment is available to alleviate or cure the harmful condition. For example, one of the most divisive questions in the area of civil commitment is whether a person found to be mentally ill and dangerous may be restrained indefinitely when his condition is determined to be "untreatable." [b]

(ii) **Legality.** To what extent should the policies explored in this chapter be taken into account in the formulation and proof of the criteria governing control interventions? Critics argue that the civil-commitment laws are fatally flawed by the vagueness and elasticity of the terms "mental illness" and "dangerousness," a problem aggravated by the unreliability of psychiatric diagnoses and behavioral predic-

---

[a] See, e.g., N. Kittrie, The Right to be Different: Deviance and Enforced Therapy (1971); Wexler, Therapeutic Justice, 57 Minn.L.Rev. 289 (1972); Livermore, Malmquist & Meehl, On the Justifications for Civil Commitment, 117 U.Pa.L.Rev. 75 (1968); Note, Developments in the Law— Civil Commitment of the Mentally Ill, 87 Harv.L.Rev. 1190 (1974).

[b] The outer boundaries of civil commitment authority were sketched by the Supreme Court in O'Connor v. Donaldson, 422 U.S. 563, 575–76 (1975):

"May the state confine the mentally ill merely to ensure them a living standard superior to that they enjoy in the private community? That the state has a proper interest in providing care and assistance to the unfortunate goes without saying. But the mere presence of mental illness

does not disqualify a person from preferring his home to the comforts of an institution. Moreover while the state may arguably confine a person to save him from harm, incarceration is rarely if ever a necessary condition for raising the living standards of those capable of surviving safely in freedom, on their own or with the help of family or friends.

"May the state fence in the harmless mentally ill solely to save its citizens from exposure to those whose ways are different? One might as well ask if the state, to avoid public unease could incarcerate all who are physically unattractive or socially eccentric. Mere public intolerance or animosity cannot constitutionally justify the deprivation of a person's physical liberty."

tions.[c] To what extent are the policies underlying the vagueness doctrine applicable to control interventions? In recent years concerns about vagueness have led to greater specificity in commitment criteria, especially in the definition of the type of behavior which the intervention is designed to avoid. Consider, for example, the relevant provision of Illinois law that permits involuntary commitment of any person

"who is mentally ill and who because of his illness is reasonably expected to inflict serious physical harm upon himself or another in the near future; or . . . who is mentally ill and who because of his illness is unable to provide for his basic physical needs so as to guard himself from serious harm." [d]

Is this provision sufficiently precise to withstand a vagueness challenge? Does your answer depend on any empirical assumptions about the accuracy of behavioral predictions?

Several courts have held that the state is constitutionally required to prove the occurrence of a recent "overt act" as an essential predicate for a finding of future dangerousness in a civil commitment proceeding. What is the basis for such a requirement? Are the policies underlying the "act" requirement in the criminal law applicable to control interventions?

In Mathew v. Nelson, 461 F.Supp. 707 (N.D.Ill.1978), the court upheld the predecessor of the Illinois provision quoted above despite its failure to require proof of past dangerous behavior. The court emphasized that the challenge was based on the claim that clinical predictions of future dangerousness are most likely to be accurate in cases where the person has recently behaved in a dangerous manner. However, the court found:

". . . that there are instances in which a psychiatrist can determine from a psychiatric clinical examination that a mentally ill person is reasonably likely to injure himself or another even though the person's history does not include a recent overt act. . . . These cases may be relatively few, but they are not so insignificant that they can be discarded. . . . If we are to [conclude that an overt act is constitutionally required], we would be holding that Illinois is powerless to protect the mentally ill person and society in these cases. We are unwilling to reach such a conclusion even though in most cases a somewhat more reliable prediction can be made if there is a history of a recent overt act." [e]

[c] See, e.g., Morse, Crazy Behavior, Morals and Science: An Analysis of Mental Health Law, 51 So.Cal.L.Rev. 527 (1978).

[d] Smith-Hurd Ill.Ann.Stat. ch. 91-½ § 1–119.

[e] There is no significant body of empirical research on the accuracy of clinical predictions of "imminent" violence. More specifically, there are no studies of the predictive value of the actor having committed "a recent overt act or threat." Research in another context, however, suggests caution in relying on such predictions. Long-term follow-up studies of persons released from institutions for the mentally ill indicate that predictions that violence *will* occur at *any* time after release are accurate in no more than one out of every three cases. In this context, past violent behavior is regarded as an essential prerequisite for prediction of future violence. See generally J. Monahan,

Even if the *Nelson* court's empirical conclusion is correct, can you think of other reasons why a control intervention should be precluded in the absence of proof of dangerous conduct?

(iii) **Limits.** One of the pervasive difficulties with control interventions is the absence of any internally derived limitations on the duration of the intervention or on the "therapeutic" measures that may be undertaken.[f] Recall, for example, Mr. Justice Marshall's observation in *Powell* that "one virtue of the criminal process is, at least, that the duration of penal incarceration typically has some outside limit." In contrast, as he pointed out, a person who is civilly committed may lose his liberty indefinitely. The "outside limit" on criminal punishment derives from the idea that the severity of the sanction must not be disproportionate to the seriousness of the offense. When the justifying purpose of the intervention is treatment or restraint, as distinct from punishment, the duration of the intervention is logically limited only by the duration of the danger. Similarly, the measures that may be undertaken to cure a person's dangerous condition or to modify his dangerous behavior are logically limited only by available technology. Contemporary attention to such concerns has led legislatures to set outside limits on the duration of civil commitments and to restrict or regulate the use of "intrusive" modalities of treatment.[g]

A few modern commentators have expressed grave reservations about the legitimacy of all control interventions, especially involuntary hospitalization of the mentally ill. They have argued that these laws should be repealed and that mentally ill persons should be subject to coercive intervention only on the same terms as everyone else—that is, they should be punished for their offending conduct and otherwise left alone.[h] Although these views are unlikely to prevail, they represent a useful counterpoint to those expressed in the *Powell* dissent.

3. **The Difference Between Treatment and Punishment.** *Robinson* is generally thought to stand for the proposition that conduct is a constitutionally required predicate for the imposition of criminal liability. In addition, *Robinson* has also been taken to establish constitutional boundaries on control interventions: Courts and commentators commonly say that a nominally "civil" commitment scheme may be found unconstitutional if the deprivations imposed as a consequence of the intervention are indistinguishable from those that would be entailed by "criminal punishment." Such a result would run afoul of *Robinson*, it is said, because the result would be the imposition of criminal punishment "for" status alone. Such claims have been litigated in a variety of contexts.

(i) **Civil Commitment of Narcotic Addicts.** The issue arose in California immediately after the *Robinson* decision in In re De La O, 59

The Clinical Prediction of Violent Behavior (1981).

[f] See generally Wexler, Therapeutic Justice, 57 Minn.L.Rev. 289 (1972).

[g] See, e.g., Cal. Welfare and Institutions Code §§ 5150–5212 (durational limits on civil commitment), 5325–5326 (limits on psychosurgery and electroconvulsive treatment).

[h] See, e.g., Morse, A Preference for Liberty: The Case Against Involuntary Commitment of the Mentally Disordered, 70 Cal.L.Rev. 54 (1982).

Cal.2d 128, 28 Cal.Rptr. 489, 378 P.2d 793 (1963). De La O was convicted of violating the same penal statute involved in *Robinson*. However, acting on his own motion, the arraigning judge suspended the criminal proceedings—entering no judgment and imposing no sentence—and certified De La O to the appropriate court for civil commitment under California Penal Code Section 6450. (The provisions of this section are similar to those summarized by Mr. Justice Clark at pages 163–65, supra.) After a medical examination and an adversarial commitment hearing, the court adjudged De La O to be "a narcotic drug addict" and committing him to the custody of the Department of Corrections for a period of up to five years.

De La O thereafter petitioned for a writ of habeas corpus on the ground, among others, that Section 6450 imposed "criminal penalties for an illness" in violation of the eighth and 14th amendments. In support of this contention, he argued that the conditions of his confinement were substantially the same as they would have been if he had been sentenced to prison. Although acknowledging the presence of some "indicia of criminality"—especially the fact that the program was "under the direction and control of the Director of Corrections"—the Supreme Court of California concluded that the statutory scheme was "civil" rather than penal in purpose and effect, and hence "petitioner's commitment and confinement thereunder did not constitute cruel and unusual punishment within the meaning of *Robinson* . . . ."

(ii) **Mentally Disordered Sex Offenders.** Many states provide for indeterminate civil commitment of persons convicted of specified sex offenses who are found, in a subsequent proceeding, to be "sexual psychopaths" or "mentally disordered sex offenders." Courts typically have held that these statutes are non-penal in character, the legislative purpose being to treat the person's condition rather than to punish him for the particular offense which triggered the commitment. That is, the predicate for the intervention is the actor's status rather than his offending conduct. However, persons subject to such commitments have argued that there is no significant difference between their situation and confinement in the penitentiary.

Such a challenge was successful in People v. Feagley, 14 Cal.3d 338, 121 Cal.Rptr. 509, 535 P.2d 373 (1975). Feagley was charged with molesting two eight-year-old girls by stroking their hair. He pleaded guilty to one count of simple battery, a misdemeanor punishable by a maximum confinement of one year in jail. Subsequently, in a separate proceeding, he was found to be a "mentally disordered sex offender." However, because the court also found that he would not "benefit by treatment in a state hospital" he was committed to the Department of Corrections. After reviewing the conditions of confinement in the "institutional units" set aside by the Corrections Department for "mentally disordered sex offenders," the Supreme Court of California concluded that such offenders "are incarcerated in penal units among the general population and are customarily detained without treatment." Accordingly, the court held that the statutory scheme imposed criminal punishment for the status of being a mentally disordered sex offender in violation of the eighth and 14th amendments.

(iii) **Children in Need of Supervision.** As is described more fully in the materials on juvenile offenders, see pages 632–54, infra, persons under a designated age (usually 18) who commit criminal offenses are not subject to criminal prosecution but are subject instead to "delinquency" adjudication in a juvenile court. Although the juvenile court began as a benevolent and paternalistic innovation, the modern tendency is to reshape the administration of juvenile justice to conform to a different premise—that the youth is being punished for offending conduct. In particular, the criminal-law doctrines described in this book are now regarded as generally applicable to the definition and proof of juvenile delinquency.

However, juvenile courts have jurisdiction not only over delinquents, but also over youths found to be "persons in need of supervision." This so-called "PINS" determination does not depend upon proof of the occurrence of specific conduct previously declared to be an offense. Instead, such non-delinquent conduct as truancy, running away from home, or habitual disobedience is regarded as evidence of the status or condition upon which preventive intervention is predicated. Is the state permitted to place "persons in need of supervision" in the same institutions as persons being "punished" for their delinquent acts? In Martarella v. Kelley, 349 F.Supp. 575 (S.D.N.Y.1972), persons alleged or adjudicated to be PINS under Section 732 of the Family Court Act of New York[i] challenged the constitutionality of their detention in three "maximum security" facilities for juvenile delinquents. After reviewing the conditions at these facilities, the court concluded that the conditions at one of them were so punitive that juveniles committed as PINS could not constitutionally be held there.[j]

(iv) **Treatment for Venereal Disease.** A Denver ordinance authorizes the police to issue "walk in" orders to any person "reasonably suspected" of having venereal disease. A person receiving such an order is required to report to the Department of Health for examination

[i] A "person in need of supervision" is defined in Section 712(b) of the Act as "a male less than 16 years of age and a female less than 18 years of age who does not attend school in accordance with . . . the education law or who is incorrigible, ungovernable or habitually disobedient and beyond the lawful control of parent or other lawful authority. . . ."

[j] The *Martarella* court also found that youths committed to any of these facilities for a long term were entitled to "adequate treatment" and that because such treatment had not been provided, their detention was unconstitutional. This facet of the court's decision is characteristic of the so-called "right-to-treatment" cases in which persons subject to control intervention have claimed that the state is constitutionally obligated not only to refrain from imposing criminal punishment but also to provide adequate treatment. In a variety of commitment settings, courts have held that to the extent that the justifying purpose of the intervention is "treatment," the state is constitutionally required to establish conditions which afford the committed individual a reasonable opportunity to improve his condition. In other words, the state is constitutionally bound to take steps to effectuate the benevolent purposes that justify the intervention. As noted above, however, the justifying purpose of some control interventions may be protective custody or restraint. If such a purpose is a legitimate one, the state may be required only to afford the confined individual a safe and humane environment. The issue is discussed by Chief Justice Burger in O'Connor v. Donaldson, 422 U.S. 563 (1975).

and for treatment if the diagnosis is confirmed. Another local ordinance authorizes the police to detain—in jail—any person who is arrested for prostitution or solicitation of prostitution and who is reasonably suspected of having venereal disease. Under this "hold-and-treat" ordinance, persons thus detained are ineligible for release on bond until completion of the examining process, which takes 48 hours. Occasionally, persons detained under the ordinance are released immediately if they will agree to take penicillin without an examination. Criminal charges against persons detained and treated under this ordinance are routinely dismissed. Are persons who are detained in jail for examination and treatment under this ordinance being punished for having venereal disease? In Reynolds v. McNichols, 488 F.2d 1378 (10th Cir. 1973), Roxanne Reynolds, a self-acknowledged prostitute living and working in Denver, challenged the constitutionality of the "hold-and-treat" ordinance as it had been applied to her. The court upheld the ordinance as a legitimate public health regulation, finding no significance in the fact that the "suspected person" is detained in jail.

4. Alcoholism and Drug Dependence: Recent Trends.[k] During the 18th and 19th centuries, state statutes and local ordinances commonly punished public drunkenness. Additionally, "habitual drunkards" were typically included in the list of social undesirables subject to restraint under vagrancy statutes. No special provisions existed for treatment of such persons, for the alcohol habit was regarded as a sympton of moral weakness. This attitude also shaped the initial legislative response to drug addiction during the last part of the 19th century.

Between 1890 and 1920 most states enacted commitment statutes for "inebriates" or "addicts" who had lost the "power of self-control" over their drinking or drug use. These statutes were responsive to the claims by the medical profession that alcoholism and drug addiction were diseases curable by compulsory treatment in sanitoria established for this purpose. By the time of the Depression, however, the therapeutic optimism underlying the inebriate-commitment statutes had waned, and responsibility for dealing with the chronic alcohol and drug users was left primarily to the criminal law.

The therapeutic approach to alcoholism and drug dependency revived during the late 1950's. In 1961 and 1962, legislatures in California and New York established institutions for treatment of opiate-dependent persons and authorized civil commitment of such persons in lieu of criminal prosecution. Congress enacted a similar scheme in 1966. Although long-term institutional treatment of drug-dependent persons is now regarded as therapeutically unnecessary, these schemes

[k] This note summarizes a more extensive discussion of this subject which can be found in Bonnie, "Reaching Out: Origins of the Interventionist Strategy" in R. Bonnie and M. Sonnenreich, Legal Aspects of Drug Dependence 25–63 (1975). See also D. Musto, The American Disease: Origins of Narcotics Control (1973); Report of the National Commission on Marihuana and Drug Abuse, Drug Use in America: Problem in Perspective 242–77, 304–46 (1973).

originally were seen as enlightened alternatives to the traditional punitive approach.

Many legal commentators interpreted the *Robinson* decision as an indication of the Court's willingness to constitutionalize a non-criminal approach to alcoholism and drug addiction. However, the practical effect of the *Powell* decision was to leave to the Congress and the state legislatures the responsibility for making public policy in this field. In Addiction and Criminal Responsibility, 84 Yale L.J. 413, 444 (1975), Professor Fingarette argued in defense of *Powell* that "coordinating the attack on the complex problem of drug abuse is preeminently a legislative responsibility": "For the courts to assume that addictive drug use or addiction-related conduct is involuntary, and to build such an unworthy assumption into constitutional and common-law doctrine, would be a grave error."

The legislatures have been active in the years since *Powell* was decided, and prevailing policies have tilted strongly toward a therapeutic approach to the problems of alcoholism and drug dependence. In 1969, the American Medical Association and the American Bar Association released a joint statement urging state governments to adopt comprehensive legislation establishing and funding treatment programs for alcoholics and other intoxicated persons, and precluding use of criminal sanctions. In 1971, the National Conference of Commissioners on Uniform State Laws promulgated the Uniform Alcoholism and Intoxication Treatment Act to aid the states to implement such a policy.[l] In 1974, Congress made special grants available to states which had adopted "the basic provisions" of the Uniform Act. In particular, eligibility for the grants was predicated upon a determination that "the state and each of its political subdivisions are committed to the concept of care for alcoholism and alcohol abuse through community health and social service agencies and . . . have repealed those portions of their criminal statutes and ordinances under which drunkenness is the gravamen of a petty criminal offense. . . ."[m] Although the conditional funding requirement was later repealed, two-thirds of the states have adopted the essential provisions of the Uniform Act.

Possession of drugs and other acts incidental to drug consumption are still criminal offenses; no state has provided, either by statute or judicial decision, that a defendant's dependency precludes criminal prosecution for any of these offenses. In fact, several courts have rejected such claims.[n] However, the legal situation of the drug-dependent person has changed considerably during the years since the *Powell*

[l] Section 1 of the Uniform Act provides:

"It is the policy of this state that alcoholics and intoxicated persons may not be subjected to criminal prosecution because of their consumption of alcoholic beverages but rather should be afforded a continuum of treatment in order that they may lead normal lives as productive members of society."

It should be noted, however, that § 12(b) of the Uniform Act authorizes involuntary protective custody for up to 48 hours of persons incapacitated by intoxication.

[m] Comprehensive Alcohol Abuse and Alcoholism Prevention Treatment and Rehabilitation Act of 1970, as amended § 310(b)(1).

[n] See, e.g., United States v. Moore, 486 F.2d 1139 (D.C.Cir. 1973), discussed in the materials on volitional impairment and criminal responsibility at pages 716–20, infra.

decision. Substantial advances have been made in understanding and treating drug dependence, and each state now has a network of community-based treatment facilities for drug users. Many persons arrested for consumption-related criminal offenses are routinely referred to these programs in lieu of, or in conjunction with, the normal operation of the criminal process. These pretrial "diversion" programs reflect a systematic effort to employ the "criminal justice system as a process for identifying drug-dependent persons and for securing their entry into a treatment system." ° If the defendant agrees to participate in a treatment program and cooperates thereafter, the charges against him may be dismissed, or, if a conviction has been entered, the record may be expunged. Hence, these diversion programs represent a hybrid species of coercive intervention.

Modification of the legal regimes governing alcoholism and drug dependence reflect a societal redefinition of the nature of these behaviors. Sociologists have called this the "medicalization of deviance." ᴾ Are these reforms sound? Does the legitimacy or usefulness of coercive intervention for alcoholics depend on whether they end up in jail or in a detoxification facility? Is it appropriate to use the threat of criminal prosecution to persuade someone to undergo treatment? Does it matter whether the treatment works? Or is it enough that treatment is a more humane alternative to criminal prosecution and punishment?

° Drug Use in America: Problem in Perspective, Final Report of the National Commission on Marihuana and Drug Abuse 269 (1973).

ᴾ See Conrad and Schreider, Deviance and Medicalization: From Badness to Sickness (1980). For one of the few reported studies on the impact of the Uniform Act, see Fagan and Mauss, Padding the Revolving Door: An Initial Assessment of the Uniform Alcoholism and Intoxication Treatment Act in Practice, 26 Social Prob. 232 (1978).

*

Chapter II

THE CRIMINAL MIND

SECTION 1: CULPABILITY IN THE DEFINITION OF THE OFFENSE

SUBSECTION A: CULPABILITY AT COMMON LAW

INTRODUCTORY NOTE ON THE EMERGENCE OF MENS REA AT COMMON LAW

The requirement of a "guilty mind" or "mens rea" is generally regarded as an essential predicate for the imposition of criminal liability. It is captured in the ancient maxim "actus reus non facit reum nisi mens sit rea," which means "the act is not guilty unless the mind is guilty." The materials in this chapter address the variety of doctrines that effectuate and qualify this fundamental policy.

The modern significance of mens rea was emphasized by Justice Jackson in Morissette v. United States, 342 U.S. 246 (1952):

"The contention that an injury can amount to a crime only when inflicted by intention is no provincial or transient notion. It is as universal and persistent in mature systems of law as belief in freedom of the human will and a consequent ability and duty of the normal individual to choose between good and evil. A relation between some mental element and punishment for a harmful act is almost as instinctive as the child's familiar exculpatory 'But I didn't mean to,' . . . . Unqualified acceptance of this doctrine by English common law in the 18th century was indicated by Blackstone's sweeping statement that to constitute any crime there must first be a 'vicious will.' Common-law commentators of the 19th century early pronounced the same principle . . . .

"Crime, as a compound concept, generally constituted only from concurrence of an evil-meaning mind with an evil-doing hand, was congenial to an intense individualism and took deep and early root in American soil. As the states codified the common law of crimes, even if their enactments were silent on the subject, their courts assumed that the omission did not signify disapproval of the principle but merely recognized that intent was so inherent in the idea of the offense that it required no statutory affirmation. Courts, with little hesitation or division, found an implication of the requirement as to offenses that were taken over from the common law. The unanimity with which they have adhered to the central thought that wrongdoing must be conscious to be criminal is emphasized by the variety, disparity and confusion of their definitions of the requisite but elusive mental element. However, courts of various jurisdictions, and for the purposes of different offenses, have devised working formulae, if not scientific ones, for the instruction of juries around such terms as 'felonious intent,' 'criminal intent,' 'malice aforethought,' 'guilty knowledge,' 'fraudulent intent,' 'wilfulness,' 'scienter,' to denote guilty knowledge, or 'mens rea,' to signify an evil purpose or mental culpability. By use or combination of these various tokens, they have sought to protect those who were not blameworthy in mind from conviction of infamous common-law crimes. . . .

The origins of the common-law mens-rea requirement are obscure. With respect to some offenses, early criminal law apparently focused on harms caused and not on the motive or intent of the actor. It is clear, however, that for most offenses a general requirement of mens rea has existed for many centuries. The early development of this concept is admirably treated in Sayre, Mens Rea, 45 Harv.L.Rev. 974 (1932),* from which the following excerpts are taken. As to the primitive criminal law, Sayre concluded:

"The truth is that the surviving records relating to the administration of justice in early days are so scanty that no one knows exactly what was the law in action. So far as the law in the ancient books is concerned, there are numerous isolated passages pointing to criminality in certain cases without criminal intent. But one has to remember that there was no distinction in those days between crime and tort. From such records as remain some of our ablest legal students have concluded that primitive English law started from a basis bordering on absolute liability.[6] The law, which was seeking to supplant the blood feud by inducing the victim or his kin to accept money payments in place of taking violent revenge, seemed to concentrate its gaze rather upon the outraged victims or would-be avengers who must be brought under control than upon the actual blameworthiness of the accused."

Professor Sayre then pointed out that by the end of the 12th century, two significant influences were making themselves strongly felt. The first was the Roman law and the second was the canon law,

---

* Copyright © 1932 Harvard Law Review Association. Reprinted with permission.

[6] "'. . . The doer of a deed was responsible whether he acted innocently or inadvertently, because he was the doer; the owner of an instrument which caused harm was responsible because he was the owner, though the instrument had been wielded by a thief; the owner of an animal, the master of a slave, was responsible because he was associated with it as owner, as master; . . . one who merely attempted an evil was not liable because there was no evil result to attribute to him . . . .' Wigmore, Responsibility for Tortious Acts, 7 Harv.L.Rev. 315, 317–18 (1894)."

both of which contained strong elements of insistence upon moral guilt. He continued:

"Mens rea, in the period following Bracton [who wrote in the middle of the 13th century], thus smacked strongly of general moral blameworthiness. The transition from the more primitive concept of liability was all the easier because . . . most of the 13th century felonies from their very nature already involved an intentional element. Robbery and rape necessitate a design; they cannot possibly be committed through mischance. Burglary had not yet developed the requirement of an accompanying felonious intent, but a breaking into a house was of itself an act necessitating a design. Although the appeal of larceny might be brought against one in possession of stolen goods not himself a thief, the penal element of the action was based upon an original theft, a taking by design. Arson was not felonious unless intentional. Homicide included negligent and accidental, as well as intentional, killings; but already by the 13th century, the killer by misadventure, though strictly a felon and liable to forfeiture of goods, was being relieved from the ordinary felon's punishment of death.

"That the 13th century felonies did thus involve an intentional element is perhaps only another illustration of the fact that crime in general always depended and always will depend upon deep-lying ethico-psychological concepts. The early felonies were roughly the external manifestations of the heinous sins of the day. The point is not that morality first began to make its appearance in the law, but that an increasing and now conscious emphasis upon morality necessitated a new insistence upon psychical elements in determining criminality. Perhaps it is more correct to say that the newer concept of criminal liability involved, not so much a transition of thought, as a shift of emphasis and change in the angle of approach, which resulted in the recognition of new legal doctrines and attitudes."

Professor Sayre then turned to subsequent refinements in the meaning of mens rea. The next stage consisted of the conversion of a requirement of general moral blameworthiness into a series of sharper and more specific inquiries varying with the particular crime involved. For the crime of larceny, for example, he noted three stages of evolution: (i) the initial formulation permitting action against one in possession of stolen goods without regard to wrongful intent and whether or not that person was the thief; (ii) the later idea that the proper inquiry was whether the actor was morally blameworthy in the sense that the conduct was wicked or evil; (iii) and finally, the modern concept that the mens rea for larceny should focus on the defendant's state of mind at the time of the taking, as reflected in what became the traditional common-law definition of larceny: "the taking and carrying away of the personal property of another with the intent permanently to deprive the other of his or her interest in the property." Professor Sayre then stated his general conclusions:

"A study of the historical development of the mental requisites of crime leads to certain inescapable conclusions. In the first place, it seems clear that mens rea, the mental factor necessary to prove criminality, has no fixed continuing meaning. The conception of mens rea has varied with the changing underlying conceptions and objectives of criminal justice. At the beginning when the object of criminal administration was to restrict and supplant the blood feud, the mental factor was of importance insofar as it determined the provocative nature of the offense; a malicious burning of another's dwelling house being far more provocative than an accidental one, judges must distinguish between malicious and accidental burnings. Under the dominating influence of the canon law and the penitential books the underlying objective of criminal justice gradually came to be the punishment of evil-doing; as a result the mental factors necessary for criminality were based upon a mind bent on evil-doing in the sense of moral wrong. Our modern objective tends more and more in the direction, not of awarding adequate punishment for moral wrong-doing, but of protecting social and public interests. To the extent that this objective prevails, the mental element requisite for criminality . . . is coming to mean, not so much a mind bent on evil-doing as an intent to do that which unduly endangers social or public interests. As the underlying objective of criminal administration has almost unconsciously shifted, and is shifting, the basis of the requisite mens rea has imperceptibly shifted, lending a change to the flavor, if not to the actual content, of the criminal state of mind which must be proved to convict."

REGINA v. FAULKNER

Ireland, Court of Crown Cases Reserved, 1877.
13 Cox C.C. 550.

[The defendant was a seaman on a ship carrying a cargo of rum, sugar, and cotton. He was not permitted in the cargo area where the rum was stored, but ignoring the prohibition in order to satisfy his thirst, he entered the storage hold, poked a hole in a rum cask, and helped himself. In order to plug the hole after he was finished, he lit a match to see. The rum caught fire, which injured him and destroyed the ship. He was indicted for arson, on the charge that he "feloniously, unlawfully, and maliciously did set fire to the said ship, with intent thereby to prejudice" the owners of the ship. It was conceded that he had no actual intention to set fire to the vessel, and no instruction was requested as to his recklessness or his knowledge of the probable consequences of his act.

[The prosecutor's theory was that since the defendant was stealing rum when he started the fire, his felonious intent with respect to the arson was established by his intent with respect to the theft. The trial judge accepted this theory in the instructions, and the jury convicted.

On appeal, the prosecutor argued that " 'the terms malice and malicious are used in a general sense, as denoting a wicked, perverse, and incorrigible disposition.' Here the felonious act of the prisoner showing a wicked, perverse, and incorrigible disposition supplies the malice required . . . ." One member of the court, Justice Keogh, accepted the theory, noting that he was of the opinion "that the conviction should stand, as I consider all questions of intention and malice are closed by the finding of the jury, that the prisoner committed the act with which he was charged whilst engaged in the commission of a substantive felony. On this broad ground, irrespective of all refinements as to 'recklessness' and 'wilfulness,' I think the conviction is sustained."

[The majority of the appellate court, however, voted to quash the conviction. Excerpts from some of their opinions follow.]

FITZGERALD, J. . . . I am . . . of opinion that in order to establish the charge . . . , the intention of the accused forms an element in the crime to the extent that it should appear that the defendant intended to do the very act with which he is charged, or that it was the necessary consequence of some other felonious or criminal act in which he was engaged, or that having a probable result which the defendant foresaw, or ought to have foreseen, he, nevertheless, persevered in such other felonious or criminal act. The prisoner did not intend to set fire to the ship—the fire was not the necessary result of the felony he was attempting; and if it was a probable result, which he ought to have foreseen, of the felonious transaction on which he was engaged, and from which a malicious design to commit the injurious act with which he is charged might have been fairly imputed to him, that view of the case was not submitted to the jury. On the contrary, it was excluded from their consideration on the requisition of the counsel for the prosecution. Counsel for the prosecution in effect insisted that the defendant, being engaged in the commission of, or in an attempt to commit a felony, was criminally responsible for every result that was occasioned thereby, even though it was not a probable consequence of his act or such as he could have reasonably foreseen or intended. No authority has been cited for a proposition so extensive, and I am of opinion that it is not warranted by law. . . .

FITZGERALD, B. . . . The utmost which I can conceive the jury to have found over and above the facts stated is, that at the time when the prisoner set fire to this ship he was actuated by a felonious intent, which no doubt is malice; but I must take this not to have been the particular malicious intent of burning the vessel, but the particular felonious intent, which is an element of larceny. Its whole force, therefore, in the present case (if any) is as evidence of malice in general . . . . In my opinion, this general malice might have been sufficiently connected with the overt act in this case, from which the injury resulted, if the jury had found that the injury was a reasonable consequence—that is to say, a consequence which any man of reason might have anticipated as probable of an act or acts . . . . Now, however clearly I may be satisfied that the jury ought, as a matter of fact, if the question had been left to it, to have found that injury was the reasonable consequence of an act or acts done with a felonious intent, I cannot draw the conclusion as a matter of law. . . . I am quite satisfied that in cases like the present, if the overt act from which injury resulted be actuated by any malice, and the injury is the reasonable consequence of such overt act so actuated, malice would be sufficiently established. . . . I am clearly of opinion that there was evidence on which the jury might have found the malice necessary to sustain the indictment . . . , yet I think the question of malice was not left to the jury at all—the conviction cannot be sustained.

PALLES, C.B. I concur in the opinion of the majority of the Court . . . . I agree with my brother Keogh that from the facts proved the inference might have been legitimately drawn that the setting fire to the ship was malicious . . . . I am of opinion that that inference was one of fact for the jury, and not a conclusion of law at which we can arrive upon the case before us. There is one fact from which, if found, that inference would, in my opinion, have arisen as matter of law, as that the setting fire to the ship was the probable result of the prisoner's act in having a lighted match in the place in question; and if that had been found I should have concurred in the conclusion at which Mr. Justice Keogh has arrived. In my judgment the law imputes to a person who wilfully commits a criminal act an intention to do everything which is the probable consequence of the act constituting the corpus delicti which actually ensues. In my opinion this inference arises irrespective of the particular consequence which ensued being or not being foreseen by the criminal, and whether his conduct is reckless or the reverse. . . .

NOTES ON MENS–REA TERMINOLOGY AND MEANING

1. **The Language of Mens Rea.** The first lesson to be learned about common-law mens-rea terminology is that the words used often do not mean what one would expect. There is remarkably little correlation between their common usage or dictionary meaning and their legal usage to describe an offender's state of mind. Before mens-rea terms can be understood in their special legal sense, therefore, one must face the problem of translation. Just as one begins the study of a foreign language by learning the English equivalent of the words to be used, and gradually learns to use the foreign vocabulary without the intermediate step of constant translation, it is useful to treat common-law mens-rea terms, and indeed much of the language of the law, as words that must be translated into ordinary language before one can learn what they mean and how to use them.

The difficulty of the terminology is compounded by the colorful variety of mens-rea terms in common usage. They include "corruptly," "scienter," "wilfully," "maliciously," "fraudulently," "wantonly," "feloniously," "wilful neglect," "recklessly," "negligently," "wanton and wilful," "specific intent," "general intent," and many more. Learning to use these terms would not be too problematic if their meaning and the differences among them were settled. This is not the case, however, even though courts and scholars have been centuries in the effort. To return to the foreign language analogy, there are no accepted meanings into which these terms invariably can be translated. Different courts translate them differently, and usages are frequently inconsistent and confusing. What is required of the student, therefore, is not memorization and assimilation of accepted definitions, but sensitive assessment and analysis, informed by the realization that context is essential to understanding.

There is at least one further difficulty. It is typical in American legislation based on common-law terminology and tradition for a collection of common-law mens-rea terms to be strung together, without focus or attention in the enactment process on what they mean, how they relate to each other, or how they might be construed. An example of the origins of the practice is the phrase "feloniously, unlawfully, and maliciously" contained in the indictment in the *Faulkner* case. A study of modern federal criminal legislation is also instructive:

". . . The 'mental element' of federal crimes is specified in the definitions of the crimes, which definitions are frequently modified, if not indeed distorted, in judicial decisions. If one looks to the statutes alone, the specifications of mental states form a staggering array: [Here some 78 different combinations of words are extracted from various federal statutes. Examples are 'willfully and corruptly,' 'willfully and maliciously,' 'willfully or maliciously,' 'willfully and unlawfully,' 'willfully and knowingly,' 'willfully, deliberate, malicious, and premeditated,' 'unlawfully and willfully,' 'knowingly and willfully,' 'knowingly or willfully,' 'fraudulently or wrongfully,' 'from a premeditated design unlawfully and maliciously to,' 'knowingly, willfully, and corruptly,' 'willfully neglects,' and 'improperly.']

"Unsurprisingly, the courts have been unable to find substantive correlates for all these varied descriptions of mental states, and, in fact, the opinions display far fewer mental states than the statutory language. Not only does the statutory language not reflect accurately or consistently what are the mental elements of the various crimes; there is no discernible pattern or consistent rationale which explains why one crime is defined or understood to require one mental state and another crime another mental state or indeed no mental state at all."

1 National Commission on Reform of Federal Criminal Laws, Working Papers 119–20 (1970). The same study concludes with respect to the word "willfully" that "the courts, including the Supreme Court, have endowed the requirement of willfulness with the capacity to take on whatever meaning seems appropriate in the statutory context." The same comment could be made about many other common-law mens-rea terms.

2. **Mens Rea as General Malevolence.** Sayre described the emerging notion of mens rea in the 13th century as a concept of "general moral blameworthiness." By that he appears to have meant

an unfocused judgment about the general character and disposition of the actor. There is a remarkable similarity between this position and the argument advanced by the prosecutor in *Faulkner*. Recall the argument: " '[T]he terms malice and malicious are used in a general sense, as denoting a wicked, perverse, and incorrigible disposition.' Here the felonious act of the prisoner [stealing rum] showing a wicked, perverse, and incorrigible disposition supplies the malice required . . . ." The word "malice" is not being used here in a particularly artificial sense. In common usage it means "badness," "wickedness," "active ill-will," or the like. Yet the appellate court, reflecting the changes in the law over time that Sayre recounted, rejected this common-sense definition of the term and substituted a different measure of the defendant's blameworthiness.

To what extent has modern law followed the pattern outlined by Sayre and rejected the "general moral blameworthiness" inquiry as the appropriate standard of liability? The answer is: To a large extent, but not completely. Consider the following statements by modern American courts:

"The court, in fact, has recognized that the word, 'willfully' in those statutes generally connotes a voluntary, intentional violation of a known legal duty. It has formulated the requirement of willfulness as 'bad faith or evil intent,' . . . or 'evil motive and want of justification' . . . ." United States v. Bishop, 412 U.S. 346, 360 (1973).

"The main distinction between specific and general intent is the element of bad or evil purpose which is required for the former." United States v. Haldeman, 559 F.2d 31, 114 n. 226 (D.C.Cir.1976).

"An act is done 'willfully' if done . . . with bad purpose . . . . Willfulness includes an evil motive." United States v. Krosky, 418 F.2d 65, 67 (6th Cir.1969).

"[A] felony requires the existence of felonious intent; stated conversely, without a felonious intent there is no felony. . . . [A]n act feloniously done proceeds from an evil heart or purpose . . . ." Wilson v. State, 303 A.2d 638, 640–41 (Del.1973).

"[T]he word 'maliciously,' when used in a legislative enactment pertaining to the crime of arson, denotes that malice which characterizes all acts done with an evil disposition, a wrong and unlawful motive or purpose . . . ." State v. Dunn, 199 N.W.2d 104, 107 (Iowa 1972).

" '[W]illful' is generally construed to mean an act done with evil motive, bad purpose or corrupt design." Levin v. Gallman, 49 A.D.2d 434, 435, 375 N.Y.S.2d 185, 187 (1975).

Statements such as these could be multiplied indefinitely, though in each case they seem more to reflect a refusal to think seriously about the meaning of mens rea than a considered judgment indicating that Sayre was wrong. One might speculate that the reason such language persists is that judges have failed to adjust their vocabulary as the law progressed from the second stage described by Sayre to the third. Most modern legislation, supported by modern academic commentary, rejects such loose talk. Nonetheless, it is still found in casual statements by courts and, more importantly, in jury instructions. As is indicated in materials to follow, one of the major objectives of modern reform efforts in American criminal law has been to eradicate such remnants of a former era and to achieve more understanding and agreement about the language and content of culpability.

3. **Mens Rea as a Particular State of Mind.** The indictment in *Faulkner* described the mens rea required by the offense as "feloniously, unlawfully, and maliciously . . . with intent thereby to prejudice" the owners of the ship. Do the various opinions reflect serious disagreement about the meaning of these words? Do they focus on the defendant's attitude towards the act of lighting the match or his attitude towards destruction of the ship by fire? Or could some other mental state (or lack of it) have led to his conviction had the jury been properly instructed? If Faulkner had been a seaman whose job it was periodically to inspect the hold in which the rum was kept, could he have been convicted if, while performing that duty, he lit a match in order to see and carelessly caused the same destruction?

Whatever the answer to these questions, it is clear that the judges are using the string of mens-rea words in the indictment in a way that is foreign to their ordinary-language meaning. How do the various opinions in *Faulkner* fit within the progression of attitudes towards mens rea described by Sayre?

4. ***Regina v. Cunningham.*** The following case concerns mens-rea terminology similar to that interpreted in *Faulkner,* applied by the trial judge in a manner similar to the way the trial judge and prosecutor reasoned in *Faulkner.* As in *Faulkner,* the appellate court, this time the English Court of Criminal Appeals, rejected the trial court instruction and suggested the outlines of an appropriate instruction. As you read the following excerpts, ask yourself whether there are important differences between the criteria employed by the two courts.

In Regina v. Cunningham, 41 Crim.App. 155 (1957), the defendant was convicted and sentenced to five years' imprisonment for violating the following statute:

"Whosoever shall unlawfully and maliciously administer to or cause to be administered to or taken by any other person any poison or other destructive or noxious thing, so as thereby to endanger the life of such person, or so as thereby to inflict upon such person any grievous bodily harm, shall be guilty of felony."

The facts, as recited by the appellate court, were that:

"[T]he appellant was engaged to be married and his prospective mother-in-law was the tenant of a house, No. 7a, Bakes Street, Bradford, which was unoccupied but which was to be occupied by the appellant after his marriage. Mrs. Wade and her husband, an elderly couple, lived in the house next door. At one time the two houses had been one, but when the building was converted into two houses a wall had been erected to divide the cellars of the two houses, and that wall was composed of rubble loosely cemented. On the evening of January 17 last the appellant went to the cellar of No. 7a, Bakes Street, wrenched the gas meter from the gas pipes and stole it, together with its contents, and in a second indictment he was charged with the larceny of the gas meter and its contents. To that indictment he pleaded guilty and was sentenced to six months' imprisonment. In respect of that matter he does not appeal. The facts were not really in dispute, and in a statement to a police officer the appellant said: 'All right I will tell you. I was short of money, I had been off work for three days, I got eight shillings from the gas meter. I tore it off the wall and threw it away.' Although there was a stop tap within two feet of the meter, the appellant did not turn off the gas, with the result that a very considerable volume of gas escaped, some of which seeped through the wall of the cellar and partially asphyxiated Mrs. Wade, who was asleep in her bedroom next door, with the result that her life was endangered."

The trial judge instructed the jury as follows:

"You will observe that there is nothing [in the statute] about 'with intention that that person should take [the noxious substance].' He has not got to intend that it should be taken; it is sufficient that by his unlawful and malicious act he causes it to be taken. What you have to decide here, then, is whether, when he loosed that frightful cloud of coal gas into the house which he shared with this old lady, he caused her to take it by his unlawful and malicious action. 'Unlawful' does not need any definition. It is something forbidden by law. What about 'malicious'? 'Malicious' for this purpose means wicked—something which he has no business to do and perfectly well knows it. 'Wicked' is as good a definition as any other which you would get. The facts . . . are these. [T]he prisoner quite deliberately, intending to steal the money that was in the meter, . . . broke the gas mains away from the supply pipes and thus released the main supply of gas at large into that house. When he did that he knew that this old lady and her husband were living next door to him. The gas meter was in a cellar. The wall which divided his cellar from the cellar next door was a kind of honeycomb wall through which gas could very well go, so that when he loosed that cloud of gas into that place he must have known perfectly well that gas would percolate all over the house. If it were part of this offence—which it is not—that he intended to poison the old lady, I should have left it to you to decide, and I should have told you that there was evidence on which you could find that he intended that, since he did an action which he must have known would result in that. As I have already told you, it is not necessary to prove that he intended to do it; it is quite enough that what he did was done unlawfully and maliciously."

The appellate court quashed the conviction. Excerpts from the opinion follow:

" 'In any statutory definition of a crime, malice must be taken not in the old vague sense of wickedness in general but as requiring either (i) an actual intention to do the particular kind of harm that in fact was done; or (ii) recklessness as to whether such harm should occur or not (i.e., the accused has foreseen that the particular kind of harm might be done and yet has gone on to take the risk of it). It is neither limited to nor does it indeed require any ill will towards the person injured.' . . . We think that this is an accurate statement of the law. . . . In our opinion, the word 'maliciously' in a statutory crime postulates foresight of consequence. . . .

"With the utmost respect to the learned judge, we think it is incorrect to say that the word 'malicious' in a statutory offence merely means wicked. We think the learned judge was in effect telling the jury that if they were satisfied that the appellant acted wickedly—and he had clearly acted wickedly in stealing the gas meter and its contents—they ought to find that he had acted maliciously in causing the gas to be taken by Mrs. Wade so as thereby to endanger her life.

"In our view, it should have been left to the jury to decide whether, even if the appellant did not intend the injury to Mrs. Wade, he foresaw that the removal of the gas meter might cause injury to someone but nevertheless removed it. We are unable to say that a reasonable jury, properly directed as to the meaning of the word 'maliciously' in the [statute], would without doubt have convicted.

"In these circumstances this court has no alternative but to allow the appeal and quash the conviction."

5. ***Faulkner and Cunningham* Compared.** By now you should have concluded that the content of "maliciously" as construed by the *Cunningham* and *Faulkner* courts was quite different, though in both cases its meaning diverges considerably from that used in ordinary discourse. Does the *Cunningham* court focus on the defendant's attitude toward the act of allowing the gas to escape or his attitude toward the safety of another person? Or could some other mental state (or lack of it) have led to his conviction had the jury been properly instructed? If Cunningham had been a meter repairman who allowed the gas to escape and endanger Mrs. Wade when he dismantled the meter and returned to his shop to get a spare part, could he have been convicted under the approach taken by the *Cunningham* court? How does the *Cunningham* opinion fit within the progression of mens-rea attitudes described by Sayre?

DIRECTOR OF PUBLIC PROSECUTIONS v. SMITH
House of Lords, 1960.
[1960] 3 All.E.R. 161, [1961] A.C. 290.

VISCOUNT KILMUIR, L.C.: My Lords, the respondent, Jim Smith, was convicted on April 7, 1960, of the wilful murder on March 2, 1960, of Leslie Edward Vincent Meehan, a police officer acting in the execution of his duty. Such a crime constitutes capital murder under Section 5 of the Homicide Act, 1957, and, accordingly, the respondent was sentenced to death. [The conviction was set aside by the Court of Criminal Appeal and the case was then brought by the prosecution to the House of Lords.] There was never any suggestion that the respondent meant to kill the police officer, but it was contended by the prosecution that he intended to do the officer grievous bodily harm as a result of which the officer died. . . .

The facts can be summarised as follows: At about 7:30 p.m. on March 2, 1960, the respondent, accompanied by a man named Artus, was driving a Ford Prefect motor car through Woolwich. In the boot and the back of the car were sacks containing scaffolding clips that they had just stolen. The car was stopped in Beresford Square by the police officer on point duty in the normal course of traffic control and, while so stopped, P[olice] C[onstable] Meehan, who was acquainted with the respondent, came to the driver's window and spoke to him. No doubt as a result of what P.C. Meehan saw in the back of the car, he told the respondent when the traffic was released to draw in to his near-side. The respondent began to do so, and P.C. Meehan walked beside the car. Suddenly, however, the respondent accelerated along Plumstead Road and P.C. Meehan began to run with the car shouting to the officer on point duty to get on to the police station. Despite the fact that the respondent's car had no running board, P.C. Meehan succeeded in hanging on and never let go until some 130 yards up Plumstead Road when he was thrown off the car and under a bubble car coming in the opposite direction, suffering a crushed skull and other injuries from which he died. . . .

After P.C. Meehan had been thrown off, the respondent drove his car a little further up Plumstead Road and into a side turning where he and Artus threw the sacks of clips out of the car. Artus then went off but the respondent returned to the scene. According to P.C. Weatherill, the respondent first asked: "Is he dead?" and then, on being told that it was believed so, he said: "I knew the man, I wouldn't do it for the world. I only wanted to shake him off." The respondent, however, denied that he had spoken the last few words. The respondent was taken to the police station. On being arrested and cautioned, he said: "I didn't mean to kill him but I didn't want him to find the gear." The respondent then made and signed a statement in which, inter alia, he said:

> "P.C. Meehan jumped on the side of the car and I got frightened. I don't know what I got frightened about. I don't think I thought of the stolen gear I had on board. I don't know

what I did next in respect of driving the car. All I know is when he fell off he must have been hurt. I knew he fell off, and I then took a turning off the Plumstead Road. I drove up this turning some way and turned right down a back street.

"I stopped the car in the back street, as George wanted to get out of it. I got out too and chucked the gear out of the car on to the pavement. I got rid of it, because I was scared the police would find it in my motor."

The respondent gave evidence at the trial. He said that, when P.C. Meehan jumped on the side of the car, his foot went down on the accelerator and he was scared. "I was scared very much. I was very much frightened." He agreed that he did not take his foot off the accelerator.

"I never thought of it, sir. I was frightened. I was up in the traffic. I never thought of it. It happened too quick."

Asked why he did not take his foot off the accelerator, he said: "I would have done, but when he jumped on the side he took my mind off what I was doing." "When he jumped on I was frightened. I was up the road before it happened. It all happened in a matter of seconds." He further said that, when going up Plumstead Road, he didn't realise that the officer was still hanging on to the car. Asked about his car swerving, he said: "My motor was swaying because of the load in the back."

. . . It is said that the jury were misdirected as to the intent which has to be proved in order to constitute the necessary ingredient of malice. The passages complained of are these:

"The intention with which a man did something can usually be determined by a jury only by inference from the surrounding circumstances including the presumption of law that a man intends the natural and probable consequences of his acts.
. . .

"If you feel yourselves bound to conclude from the evidence that the accused's purpose was to dislodge the officer, then you ask yourselves this question: Could any reasonable person fail to appreciate that the likely result would be at least serious harm to the officer? If you answer that question by saying that the reasonable person would certainly appreciate that, then you may infer that that was the accused's intention, and that would lead to a verdict of guilty on the charge of capital murder. . . .

"Now the only part of that evidence of P.C. Weatherill which the accused challenges is the part that incriminates him, namely, 'I only wanted to shake him off.' He says he did not say that. Well, you may think it is a curious thing to imagine, and further it may well be the truth—he did only want to shake him off; but if the reasonable man would realise that the effect of doing that might well be to cause serious harm to this officer, then, as I say, you would be entitled to impute such an intent to the accused, and, therefore, to sum up the matter as between murder and manslaughter, if you are satisfied that when he drove his car erratically up the street, close to the traffic on the other side, he must as a reasonable man have contemplated that grievous bodily harm was likely to result to that officer still clinging on, and that such harm did happen and the officer died in consequence, then the accused is guilty of capital murder, and you should not shrink from such a verdict because of its possible consequences.

"On the other hand, if you are not satisfied that he intended to inflict grievous bodily harm upon the officer—in other words, if you think he could not as a reasonable man have contemplated that grievous bodily harm would result to the officer in consequence of his actions—well, then, the verdict would be guilty of manslaughter."

The main complaint is that the learned judge was there applying what is referred to as an objective test, namely, the test of what a reasonable man would contemplate as the probable result of his acts, and therefore, would intend, whereas the question for the jury, it is said, was what the respondent himself intended. This, indeed, was the view of the Court of Criminal Appeal who said:

"[T]he present case [is] one in which the degree of likelihood of serious injury to the police officer depended on which of the not always consistent versions of the facts given by witnesses for the prosecution was accepted. It was one in which it could not be said that there was a certainty that such injury would result; and it was one in which there always remained the question whether the appellant really did during the relevant 10 seconds realise what was the degree of likelihood of serious injury. If the jury took the view that the appellant [the present respondent] deliberately tried to drive the body of the police officer against oncoming cars, the obvious inference was open to them that the appellant intended serious injury to result; if, however, they concluded he merely swerved or zigzagged to shake off the officer, or if they concluded that for any reason he may not have realised the degree of danger to which he was exposing the officer, a different situation would arise with regard to the inferences to be drawn. . . . "

. . . [T]he Court of Criminal Appeal . . . were saying that it was for the jury to decide, whether, having regard to the panic in which he said he was, the respondent in fact at the time contemplated that grievous bodily harm would result from his actions or, indeed, whether he contemplated anything at all. Unless the jury were satisfied that he in fact had such contemplation, the necessary intent to constitute malice would not, in their view, have been proved. This purely subjective approach involves this, that, if an accused said that he did not in fact think of the consequences and the jury considered that that might well be true, he would be entitled to be acquitted of murder.

My Lords, the proposition has only to be stated thus to make one realise what a departure it is from that on which the courts have always acted. The jury must of course in such a case as the present make up their minds on the evidence whether the accused was unlawfully and voluntarily doing something to someone. The unlawful and voluntary act must clearly be aimed at someone in order to eliminate cases of negligence or of careless or dangerous driving. Once, however, the jury are satisfied as to that, it matters not what the accused in fact contemplated as the probable result, or whether he ever contemplated at all, provided he was in law responsible and accountable for his actions . . . . On the assumption that he is accountable for his actions, the sole question is whether the unlawful and voluntary act was of such a kind that grievous bodily harm was the natural and probable result. The only test available for this is what the ordinary responsible man would, in all the circumstances of the case, have contemplated as the natural and probable result. That, indeed, has always been the law and I would only make a few citations.

The true principle is well set out in that persuasive authority The Common Law by Holmes, J. After referring to Stephens' Digest of the Criminal Law and the statement that foresight of the consequences of the act is enough, he says:

> "But again, what is foresight of consequence? It is a picture of a future state of things called up by knowledge of the present state of things, the future being viewed as standing to the present in the relation of effect to cause. Again, we must seek a reduction to lower terms. If the known present state of things is such that the act done will very certainly cause death, and the probability is a matter of common knowledge, one who does the act, knowing the present state of things, is guilty of murder, and the law will not inquire whether he did actually foresee the consequence or not. The test of foresight is not what this very criminal foresaw, but what a man of reasonable prudence would have foreseen."

And again:

> "But furthermore, on the same principle, the danger which in fact exists under the known circumstances ought to be of a class which a man of reasonable prudence could foresee. Ignorance of a fact and inability to foresee a consequence have the same effect on blameworthiness. If a consequence cannot be foreseen, it cannot be avoided. But there is this practical difference, that whereas, in most cases, the question of knowledge is a question of the actual condition of the defendant's consciousness, the question of what he might have foreseen is determined by the standard of the prudent man, that is, by general experience."

In Regina v. Faulkner, 13 Cox C.C. 550 (1877), the Court of Crown Cases Reserved for Ireland [on grounds immaterial to this case quashed a conviction] for arson of a sailor who with intent to steal tapped a cask of rum. He was holding a lighted match and the rum caught fire and the vessel was destroyed. Palles, C.B., said:

> "In my judgment the law imputes to a person who willfully commits a criminal act an intention to do everything which is

the probable consequence of the act constituting the corpus delicti which actually ensues. In my opinion this inference arises irrespective of the particular consequences which ensued being or not being foreseen by the criminal, and whether his conduct is reckless or the reverse . . . ."

[At this point, Viscount Kilmuir discussed a number of other authorities.]

My Lords, the law being as I have endeavoured to define it, there seems to be no ground on which the approach by the trial judge in the present case can be criticised. [H]e asked the jury to consider what were the exact circumstances at the time as known to the respondent and what were the unlawful and voluntary acts which he did towards the police officer. The learned judge then prefaced the passages of which complaint is made by saying, in effect, that if, in doing what he did, he must as a reasonable man have contemplated that serious harm was likely to occur then he was guilty of murder. My only doubt concerns the use of the expression "a reasonable man," since this to lawyers connotes the man on the Clapham omnibus by reference to whom a standard of care in civil cases is acertained. In judging of intent, however, it really denotes an ordinary man capable of reasoning who is responsible and accountable for his actions, and this would be the sense in which it would be understood by a jury.

Another criticism of the summing-up and one which found favour in the Court of Criminal Appeal concerned the manner in which the trial judge dealt with the presumption of law that a man intends the natural and probable consequences of his acts. . . . It is said that the reference to this being a presumption of law without explaining that it was rebuttable amounted to a misdirection. Whether the presumption is one of law or of fact or, as has been said, of common sense, matters not for this purpose. The real question is whether the jury should have been told that it was rebuttable. In truth, however, as I see it, this is merely another way of applying the test of the reasonable man. Provided that the presumption is applied, once the accused's knowledge of the circumstances and the nature of his acts have been ascertained, the only thing that could rebut the presumption would be proof of incapacity to form an intent . . . . In the present case, therefore, there was no need to explain to the jury that the presumption was rebuttable.

. . . While, however, I can see no possible criticism of the trial judge in regard to the use he made of the presumption in the present case, I cannot help feeling that it is a matter which might well be omitted in summing up to a jury. The phrase "presumption of law" and the reference, if it has to be made, to the presumption being "rebuttable" are only apt to confuse a jury. In my opinion, the test of the reasonable man, properly understood, is a simpler criterion. It should present no difficulty to a jury and contains all the necessary ingredients of malice aforethought. . . .

In the result, the appeal should, in my opinion, be allowed and the conviction of capital murder restored.

NOTE ON THE PRESUMPTION OF NATURAL AND PROBABLE CONSEQUENCES

The reference in *Smith* to "the presumption of law that a man intends the natural and probable consequences of his acts" illustrates one of the wonderful ambiguities of the common law. Until very recently, this phrase was widely used in American jury instructions, generally without clarification. Numerous meanings have been attributed to the phrase, only two of which are important for present purposes.

First, the presumption can be used consistently with the views of the Court of Criminal Appeal. Normally, when we care about what another person intended, we are prepared to assume, absent a plausible explanation to the contrary, that people know what they are doing and desire, or at least foresee, the results that usually flow from particular conduct. An observer watching the events that transpired in *Smith* might well conclude that Smith deliberately threw Officer Meehan off the car and was unconcerned by any serious injuries that might result, though he realized their probability. Given Smith's testimony, on the other hand, it is at least plausible that he panicked, did not really understand what he was doing, and neither wanted to hurt his friend nor thought he was going to. If Smith's actual foresight of the likely consequences is the appropriate measure of his liability for murder, a jury might conclude that he was not guilty.

On this view of the applicable mens rea, the presumption can be seen to serve a common-sense evidentiary function. It brings to the jury's attention the fact that it is legitimate to draw inferences of foresight of consequences from conduct, but it does not require that the inference be drawn. It describes, in other words, a "permissive inference" that need not be made if the evidence suggests that it should not be. While the need for such an instruction to the jury can be debated,[a] it can be defended on practical grounds. If the law requires an inquiry into the actual state of mind of the defendant at the time of the offense, it is asking a question that will be very hard for the prosecutor to answer with direct proof. Only the defendant can answer the relevant question with certainty, and the defendant is not likely to be a reliable prosecution witness. Moreover, in this country, the constitutional privilege against self-incrimination forecloses the prosecution from using the defendant as a source of evidence without consent and permits the defendant not to take the stand at all. In this context, the presumption can be seen as a reminder to the jury that it is legitimate to infer the crucial element and that the prosecutor cannot be expected to prove it directly. The jury still can be admonished, however, that a specific finding of actual foresight should be made on the basis of all the evidence.[b]

---

[a] One might think that in the absence of such an instruction, the jury would be inclined to draw such common-sense inferences anyway.

[b] Cf. 3 W. Holdsworth, A History of English Law 374–75 (3rd ed. 1923):

"The general rule of the common law is that crime cannot be imputed to a man

Passages in the trial court's instruction in *Smith* support this view of the presumption. The first paragraph is certainly consistent with it. The second paragraph, after asking whether any reasonable person could fail to appreciate that serious harm to the officer was the likely result, tells the jury that it "may infer that that was the accused's intention." In the next paragraph, moreover, the jury is told that it "would be entitled to impute such an intent to the accused." Standing alone, this language could be construed as telling the jury that it may, but need not, conclude that Smith understood the risks of his conduct.

The remainder of the instruction, however, speaks in different language. The third paragraph concludes by asking the jury whether "he must as a reasonable man have contemplated" the likelihood of harm. The final paragraph says that he will be guilty of a lesser offense only if "he *could not* as a reasonable man have contemplated" the harm. The instruction as a whole is therefore ambiguous as to whether the jury (i) was entitled to draw the inference, but not required to do so,[c] or (ii) was required by the law to draw the inference. This ambiguity, indeed, was the basis of the defendant's appeal and of his victory in the intermediate appellate court.

The House of Lords held, in effect, that it made no difference how the jury resolved this ambiguity because the appropriate standard of liability was objective in any event. Though the Lords indicated that reference to the presumption should be omitted, their holding illustrates a second way in which the presumption has been used. By this view, to say that the law presumes that one intends the natural and probable results of one's conduct means that actual foresight of consequences is irrelevant. Fault is measured not by whether the defendant actually foresaw the consequences, but by whether a reasonable person would have. As Viscount Kilmuir said, the presumption "is merely another way of applying the test of the reasonable man." As so used, the presumption is a fictional construct. It uses the language of a subjective inquiry but actually invokes an objective standard. The presumption in this sense can thus be said to be "mandatory" or "conclusive." It applies no matter what the evidence shows as to the defendant's actual perceptions or intention.

without mens rea. It is, of course, quite another question how the existence of that mens rea is to be established. The thought of man is not triable by direct evidence; but if the law grounds liability upon intent it must endeavor to try it by circumstantial evidence. Much of that circumstantial evidence will be directed to show that a man of ordinary ability, situated as the accused was situated, and having his means of knowledge, could not have acted as he acted without having that mens rea which it is sought to impute to him. In other words, we must adopt an external standard in adjudicating upon the weight of the evidence adduced to prove or disprove mens rea. That, of course, does not mean that the law bases criminal liability upon non-compliance with an external standard. So to argue is to confuse the evidence for a proposition with the proposition proved by that evidence."

[c] In which case, as Viscount Kilmuir indicated in the last full paragraph of his opinion, the presumption might be said to be "rebuttable." For an example of this language in a recent American decision, see Kansas v. Warbritton, 211 Kan. 506, 509, 506 P.2d 1152, 1155 (1973):

"The presumption is rebuttable and may be overcome by evidence to the contrary. . . . It is not a conclusive presumption in the sense that it is a rule of substantive law which applies regardless of facts and which cannot be contradicted by evidence to the contrary."

There are, as noted above, other meanings that have been assigned to the presumption.[d] It is sufficient for present purposes to observe that the presumption of natural and probable consequences can be used in service of either a subjective or an objective line of inquiry, and that Viscount Kilmuir plainly used it in the latter sense. It is not at all clear in the general run of cases, however, what the presumption is supposed to mean or how the jury will interpret it. When included in a jury instruction in this country, it normally has been part of a boiler-plate recitation without elaboration or explanation. Rarely has the presumption been discussed helpfully in American appellate opinions, though this can be expected to change in light of the recent Supreme Court decisions considered at pages 967–1004, infra. A useful discussion of the presumption and the *Smith* decision can be found in G. Williams, Criminal Law: The General Part 89–99, 894–96 (2d ed. 1961).

NOTES ON GENERAL INTENT AT COMMON LAW

1. **Holmes' Theory.** Oliver Wendell Holmes defended an approach similar to *Smith* (and was quoted approvingly in *Smith*) in The Common Law, first published in 1881. He argued that the mens-rea inquiry for any offense turns on a resolution of the tension between a retributive theory of criminal justice and a deterrent theory. Retribution calls into question the extent to which the offender is actually and personally to blame. Deterrence or prevention, on the other hand, looks to public protection. It is not unusual, he argued, for society to sacrifice individual welfare for the protection of the whole:

> "No society has ever admitted that it could not sacrifice individual welfare for its own existence. If conscripts are necessary for its army, it seizes them, and marches them, with bayonets in their rear, to death. It runs highways and railroads through old family places in spite of the owner's protest, paying in this instance the market value, to be sure, because no civilized government sacrifices the citizen more than it can help, but still sacrificing his will and his welfare to that of the rest."

He then argued:

> "[T]here can be no case in which the law-maker makes certain conduct criminal without his thereby showing a wish and purpose to prevent that conduct. Prevention would accordingly

[d] In technical terms, they involve various shades of formally shifting to the defendant the burden of production of evidence, the burden of persuasion, or both. Frequently, they qualify the use of the presumption in the first sense described above. These uses of presumptions in general and this presumption in particular will be considered elsewhere in these materials. In Sandstrom v. Montana, 442 U.S. 510 (1979), the Supreme Court held the presumption of natural and probable consequences unconstitutional in a particular application to a Montana murder prosecution. The announced reasons for this conclusion are not related to the underlying purpose for which *Smith* is considered here, namely to explore traditional common-law standards of culpability and to introduce the language and content of mens rea. The constitutional underpinnings of the *Sandstrom* decision, the *Sandstrom* case itself, and the burden-of-proof consequences of presumptions in a broader setting are considered at pages 967–1004, infra.

seem to be the chief and only universal purpose of punishment. The law threatens certain pains if you do certain things, intending thereby to give you a new motive for not doing them. If you persist in doing them, it has to inflict the pains in order that its threats may continue to be believed.

"If this is a true account of the law as it stands, the law does undoubtedly treat the individual as a means to an end, and uses him as a tool to increase the general welfare at his own expense. It has been suggested above, that this course is perfectly proper; but even if it is wrong, our criminal law follows it, and the theory of our criminal law must be shaped accordingly. . . .

"If the foregoing arguments are sound, it is already manifest that liability to punishment cannot be finally and absolutely determined by considering the actual personal unworthiness of the criminal alone. That consideration will govern only so far as the public welfare permits or demands.[a] And if we take into account the general result which the criminal law is intended to bring about, we shall see that the actual state of mind accompanying a criminal act plays a different part from what is commonly supposed.

"For the most part, the purpose of the criminal law is only to induce external conformity to rule. All law is directed to conditions of things manifest to the senses. And whether it brings those conditions to pass immediately by the use of force, as when it protects a house from a mob by soldiers, or appropriates private property to public use, or hangs a man in pursuance of a judicial sentence, or whether it brings them about mediately through men's fears, its object is equally an external result. In directing itself against robbery or murder, for instance, its purpose is to put a stop to the actual physical taking and keeping of other men's goods, or the actual poisoning, shooting, stabbing, and otherwise putting to death of other men. If those things are not done, the law forbidding them is equally satisfied, whatever the motive.

"Considering this purely external purpose of the law together with the fact that it is ready to sacrifice the individual so far as necessary in order to accomplish that purpose, we can see more readily than before that the actual degree of personal guilt involved in any particular transgression cannot be the only element, if it is an element at all, in the liability incurred. . . .

"It is not intended to deny that criminal liability . . . is founded on blameworthiness. Such a denial would shock the moral sense of any civilized community; or, to put it another

---

a Holmes had earlier observed that "[i]f punishment stood on the moral grounds which are proposed for it, the first thing to be considered would be those limitations in the capacity for choosing rightly which arise from abnormal instincts, want of education, lack of intelligence, and all the other defects which are most marked in the criminal classes." Yet, he continued, the criminal law has never been structured to take these elements into account. [Footnote by eds.]

way, a law which punished conduct which would not be blame-worthy in the average member of the community would be too severe for that community to bear. It is only intended to point out that, when we are dealing with that part of the law which aims more directly than any other at establishing standards of conduct, we should expect there more than elsewhere to find that the tests of liability are external, and independent of the degree of evil in the particular person's motives or intentions. The conclusion follows directly from the nature of the standards to which conformity is required. These are not only external, as was shown above, but they are of general application. They do not merely require that every man should get as near as he can to the best conduct possible for him. They require him at his own peril to come up to a certain height. They take no account of incapacities, unless the weakness is so marked as to fall into well-known exceptions, such as infancy or madness. They as-sume that every man is as able as every other to behave as they command. If they fall on any one class harder than on another, it is on the weakest. For it is precisely to those who are most likely to err by temperament, ignorance, or folly, that the threats of the law are the most dangerous.

"The reconciliation of the doctrine that liability is founded on blameworthiness with the existence of liability where the party is not to blame . . . is found in the conception of the average man, the man of ordinary intelligence and reasonable prudence. Liability is said to arise out of such conduct as would be blame-worthy in him. But he is an ideal being, represented by the jury when they are appealed to, and his conduct is an external or objective standard when applied to any given individual. That individual may be morally without stain, because he has less than ordinary intelligence or prudence. But he is required to have those qualities at his peril. If he has them, he will not, as a general rule, incur liability without blameworthiness."

Holmes illustrated his theory by considering a number of offenses. One of them was murder, and his remarks on that subject directly support the result reached in *Smith*. In the law of murder, said Holmes, "malice" obviously does not mean ill will, for "[i]t is just as much murder to shoot a sentry for the purpose of releasing a friend, as to shoot him because you hate him." Rather, the term "malice" is used to signify the mens rea required by the law. The test for mens rea, according to Holmes, should be not whether the actor actually desired or foresaw the death of another, but whether "a man of reasonable prudence" would have anticipated that consequence and would there-fore have refrained from acting. The key, said Holmes, is that the actor be aware of the existence of those circumstances that render conduct dangerous and that would put the reasonably prudent person on notice to desist:

"It is enough that such circumstances were actually known as would have led a man of common understanding to infer from them the rest of the group making up the present state of things. For instance, if a workman on a housetop at mid-day knows that the space below him is a street in a great city, he knows facts from which a man of common understanding would infer that there were people passing below. He is therefore bound to draw that inference, or, in other words, is chargeable with knowledge of that fact also, whether he draws the inference or not. If then, he throws down a heavy beam into the street, he does an act which a person of ordinary prudence would foresee is likely to cause death, or grievous bodily harm, and he is dealt with as if he foresaw it, whether he does so in fact or not. If a death is caused by the act, he is guilty of murder. But if the workman has reasonable cause to believe that the space below is a private yard from which every one is excluded, and which is used as a rubbish-heap, his act is not blameworthy, and the homicide is a mere misadventure. . . .

"But furthermore, on the same principle, the danger which in fact exists under the known circumstances ought to be of a class which a man of reasonable prudence could foresee. Ignorance of a fact and inability to foresee a consequence have the same effect on blameworthiness. If a consequence cannot be foreseen, it cannot be avoided. But there is this practical difference, that whereas, in most cases, the question of knowledge is a question of the actual condition of the defendant's consciousness, the question of what he might have foreseen is determined by the standard of the prudent man, that is, by general experience. For it is to be remembered that the object of the law is to prevent human life being endangered or taken; and that, although it so far considers blameworthiness in punishing as not to hold a man responsible for consequences which no one, or only some exceptional specialist, could have foreseen, still the reason for this limitation is simply to make a rule which is not too hard for the average member of the community. As the purpose is to compel men to abstain from dangerous conduct, and not merely to restrain them from evil inclinations, the law requires them at their peril to know the teachings of common experience, just as it requires them to know the law. Subject to these explanations, it may be said that the test of murder is the degree of danger to life attending the act under the known circumstances of the case."

Do you follow Holmes' logic? Does it support his conclusion with respect to the appropriate mens rea for murder? Does acceptance of Holmes' general thesis compel agreement with the result reached in *Smith?* Or can his thesis be accepted as sometimes appropriate for implementation in the criminal law, but not in the context of *Smith?* You should consider the material in the following note as you think about these questions.

2. **Negligence as the Basis for Criminal Liability.** The concept of "negligence" has frequently formed the basis upon which both civil and criminal liability have been imposed under the Anglo-American

legal system. Holmes is an eloquent spokesmen for the position that negligence is a proper basis for the imposition of criminal liability. Although the result in *Smith* is testimony to the force of the idea underlying his position, there is much criticism of this view.[b]

The argument against negligence as an appropriate basis for criminal liability proceeds from the central premise that blame is an essential ethical predicate for use of the criminal sanction. The assumption is that one cannot properly be blamed for inadvertent behavior or for unforeseen results. H.L.A. Hart, in Punishment and Responsibility at 136 (1968),[*] argued the contrary position:

> " 'I didn't *mean* to do it: I just didn't think.' 'But you should have thought.' Such an exchange, perhaps over the fragments of a broken vase destroyed by some careless action, is not uncommon; and most people would think that, in ordinary circumstances, such a rejection of 'I didn't think' as an excuse is quite justified. No doubt many of us have our moments of scepticism about both the justice and the efficacy of the whole business of blaming and punishment; but, if we are going in for the business at all, it does not appear unduly harsh, or a sign of archaic or unenlightened conceptions of responsibility, to include gross, unthinking carelessness among the things for which we blame and punish. . . . There seems a world of difference between punishing people for the harm they unintentionally but carelessly cause, and punishing them for the harm which no exercise of reasonable care on their part could have avoided."

Most opponents of negligence as a basis for criminal liability concede this much, and respond with a point anticipated in Hart's next paragraph:

> "So 'I just didn't think' is not in ordinary life, in ordinary circumstances, an excuse; nonetheless it has its place in the rough assessments which we make, outside the law, of the gravity of different offences which cause the same harm. To break your Ming china, deliberately or intentionally, is worse than to knock it over while waltzing wildly round the room and not thinking of what might get knocked over. Hence, showing that the damage was not intentional, but the upshot of thoughtlessness or carelessness, has its relevance as a mitigating factor affecting the quantum of blame or punishment."

The question then becomes whether the "quantum of blame or punishment" for thoughtlessness or carelessness is sufficient to justify use of the criminal sanction. This is the fighting issue.

---

[b] See, e.g., Wasserstrom, H.L.A. Hart and the Doctrine of Mens Rea and Criminal Responsibility, 35 U.Chi.L.Rev. 92 (1967); Hall, Negligent Behavior Should be Excluded from Penal Liability, 63 Colum.L. Rev. 632 (1963). But see Brady, Punishment for Negligence: A Reply to Professor Hall, 22 Buff.L.Rev. 107 (1972).

The argument in favor of negligence as an appropriate basis for criminal liability can proceed from two sorts of premises. The first, illustrated by Holmes, is essentially utilitarian, based on the need for effective social control tempered by limitations based on blameworthiness. The second is that liability for negligence is consistent with liability based on blame. The argument is that the central characteristic that justifies blame in any case is present when liability is based on negligence. H.L.A. Hart also takes this position. His thesis is worth elaboration.

There is widespread agreement that criminal liability is appropriate at some level in cases where the actor intended the harm caused or where there was foresight of consequences and the actor nonetheless took the risk that they would occur. Hart asks why blame is appropriate under such circumstances and whether negligence is importantly different. His answer is revealed in the following passage:

"[Those who oppose negligence as a basis for criminal liability think] that unless a man 'has in his mind the idea of harm to someone' it is not only bad law, but morally objectionable, . . . to punish him. But here we should ask why, in or out of law courts, we should attach this crucial importance to foresight of consequences, to the 'having of an idea in the mind of harm to someone.' On what theory of responsibility is it that the presence of this particular item of mental furniture is taken to be something which makes it perfectly satisfactory to hold that the agent is responsible for what he did? And why should we necessarily conclude that in its absence an agent cannot be decently held responsible? I suspect, in [the view of those who object to liability for negligence, it is] a form of the ancient belief that possession of knowledge of consequences is a sufficient and necessary condition of the capacity for self control, so that if the agent knows the consequences of his action we are bound to say 'he could have helped it'; and, by parity of reasoning, if he does not know the consequences of his action, even though he failed to examine or think about the situation before acting, we are bound to say that he could not have helped it.

"Neither of these views [is] acceptable. The first is not only incompatible with what large numbers of scientists and lawyers and plain men now believe about the capacity of human beings for self control. But it is also true that there is nothing to compel us to say 'He could not have helped it' in *all* cases where a man omits to think about or examine the situation in which he acts and harm results which he has not foreseen. [Consider] the case of a signalman whose duty it is to signal a train . . . . He may say after the disaster, 'Yes, I went off to play a game of cards. I just didn't stop to think about the 10:15 when I was asked to play'. Why, in such a case, should we say 'He could not help it—because his mind was a blank as to the consequences'? The kind of evidence we have to go upon in distinguishing those omissions to . . . think about the situation, and to assess its risks before acting, which we treat as culpable, from those omissions (e.g., on the part of infants or mentally deficient persons) for which we do not hold the agent responsible, is not different from the evidence we have to use whenever we say of anybody who has failed to do something 'He could not have done it' or 'He could have done it.' The evidence in such cases relates to the general capacities of the agent; it is drawn, not only from the facts of the instant case, but from many sources, such as his previous behaviour, the known effect upon him of instruction or punishment, etc. Only a theory that mental operations like . . . thinking about . . . a situation are somehow 'either there or not there', and so utterly outside our control, can lead to the theory that we are *never* responsible if, like the signalman who forgets to pull the signal, we fail to think or remember. And this theory of the uncontrollable character of mental operations would, of course, be fatal to responsibility for even the most cold-blooded, deliberate action performed by an agent with the maximum 'foresight'. For just as the signalman . . . might say 'My mind was a blank' or 'I just forgot' or 'I just didn't think, I could not help not thinking' so the cold-blooded murderer might say 'I just decided to kill; I couldn't help deciding'. In the latter case we do not normally allow this plea because we know from the general history of the agent, and others like him, that he could have acted differently. This general evidence is what is relevant to the question of responsibility, not the mere presence or absence of foresight. We should have doubts . . . even in the case of deliberate murder, if it were shown that in spite of every warning and every danger and without a comprehensible motive the agent had deliberately and repeatedly planned and committed murder. After all, a hundred times a day persons are blamed outside the law courts for not being more careful, for being inattentive and not stopping to think; in particular cases, their history or mental or physical examination may show that they could not have done what they omitted to do. In such cases they are not responsible; but *if* anyone is *ever* responsible for *anything*, there is no general reason why men should not be responsible for such omissions to think, or to consider the situation and its dangers before acting."

Hart argues that there are analytical similarities between liability for negligence and liability where there is foresight of consequences. But does his position establish that the *degree* of blame for inadvertent harm is the moral equivalent of the *degree* of blame for advertent harm? Recall his concession that a showing of careless as opposed to intentional harm is relevant to "the quantum of blame or punishment." Is the amount of blame due one who is negligent sufficient to justify invoking criminal sanctions? How would you resolve this debate? Is *Smith* wrong because criminal liability should never turn on the standard it establishes? Or is it right for the reasons given by Holmes or Hart?

Three additional points should be considered as you think about these questions. First, whatever the merits of the theoretical debate, liability for negligence in English and American criminal law has a long history, pervades many areas of the law, and persists in recently reformed statutes. It is often asserted that there is general agreement that the occasions for invoking liability based on negligence should be limited, though some of the materials to follow may cast doubt on how "general" the agreement really is. Nonetheless, criminal liability for negligence in some form exists in every American jurisdiction and in all probability will continue to do so.

Second, the correlation between negligence and "the quantum of blame or punishment" that justifies criminal sanctions is frequently reflected in efforts to define criminal negligence as an especially egregious sort of callousness that is different in kind or degree from "ordinary" or civil negligence. Consider, for example, the comments of Jerome Hall, in General Principles of Criminal Law 124 (2d ed. 1960), on early English efforts to come to grips with this problem:

> "For many years [the judges] relied on adjectives qualifying 'negligence' to carry their meaning; and they continued to do this long after the adjectives were regarded as mere 'vituperative epithets.' Nor has so-called 'criminal negligence' been clarified by judicial efforts to distinguish it from civil negligence. The opinions run in terms of 'wanton and wilful negligence,' 'gross negligence,' and more illuminating yet, 'that degree of negligence that is more than the negligence required to impose tort liability.' The apex of this infelicity is 'wilful, wanton negligence,' which suggests a triple contradiction—'negligence' implying inadvertence; 'wilful,' intention; and 'wanton,' recklessness."

How "criminal negligence" should be defined is examined in context as the question arises in subsequent materials.

Third, "the quantum of blame or punishment" that is deserved for negligence does not necessarily present an all-or-nothing choice. Sanctions authorized for given offenses, as well as the labels attached, are ranked in some sequence reflecting proportional gravity. Murder is punished more severely than assault; rape more severely than indecent exposure. All jurisdictions, moreover, classify negligent homicide as a far less serious offense than capital murder.[c] The real problem with *Smith* may be not that criminal liability for negligence is never appropriate but that liability for *capital murder* based on negligence is too severe a classification.[d] Is "the quantum of blame or punishment" deserved by Smith the same as that for a robber who calmly kills the

---

[c] For example, the Model Penal Code reflects current practice by classifying murder as a first-degree felony (carrying the highest sanctions authorized by law) and negligent homicide as a third-degree felony (carrying a five-year maximum sentence). See MPC §§ 210.2, 210.4, 6.06.

[d] Professor Rhoda Berkowitz of the University of Toledo College of Law informed the editors that, in response to the curiosity of her students, she checked with the Home Office in England to find out whether Smith was actually executed. He was not, she learned; his sentence was commuted to life imprisonment. Did that solve the problem?

victim? Is Holmes wrong because he too fails to take account of the proper grading of criminal homicide?

3. **The Concept of General Intent.** The phrase "general intent" will be encountered frequently in subsequent materials. What it means, however, is problematical. Most courts use the term without explanation as though everyone understood it. When an explanation is offered, one suspects the court does not really mean what it says or at least is not willing to generalize its explanation across offenses. Consider, for example, the following assertions:

"'General intent' occurs when the act is knowingly or wilfully done." People v. Battin, 77 Cal.App.3d 635, 658 n. 19, 143 Cal. Rptr. 731, 746 n. 19 (1978).

"The trial court instructed the jury that one of the material allegations which must be proved [in a prosecution for receiving stolen property] was . . . that in the concealing of such property he had a wrongful intent with respect thereto. 'Wrongful intent' means wicked or felonious intent. . . . We believe it falls within the category of general criminal intent . . . . Criminal intent is a mental state, a conscious wrongdoing." New Mexico v. Viscarra, 84 N.M. 217, 218, 501 P.2d 261, 262 (1972).

Additional uses of the term will be encountered in subsequent materials, where the student should be alert to the need to extrapolate the intended meaning from the context. For present purposes, however, two possible meanings should be noted. The first refers to a negligence-type inquiry involving blameworthy inadvertence. Illustrative is a Louisiana statute, which states that general intent exists: "when the circumstances indicate that the offender, in the ordinary course of human experience, must have adverted to the prescribed criminal consequences as reasonably certain to result from his act or failure to act." La.Rev.Stat. § 14:10(2).[e] Use of the term in this sense is to ask whether a reasonable person in the defendant's situation would have appreciated the risks posed by the defendant's conduct and, if so, whether the defendant should have refrained from acting. One could thus say that *Smith* defined murder as a general-intent offense and that Holmes thought general intent in this sense would suffice for murder.

Secondly, "general intent" can be used to refer to a concept of recklessness involving actual awareness of risk and a blameworthy judgment to take the risk when one should not have. Recklessness in this sense involves an inquiry into the defendant's actual understanding of the risks involved in conduct, but also shares with negligence the idea that deciding whether the defendant should or should not have taken the risk is to be measured by an external standard.[f] Although he

[e] In Louisiana v. Elzie, 343 So.2d 712, 714 (La.1977), the court paraphrased the statute by observing that "general intent exists when from the circumstances the prohibited result may reasonably be expected to follow from the offender's voluntary act, irrespective of any subjective desire on his part to have accomplished such result."

[f] It should be noted that the term "recklessness" is not invariably defined by the courts in this manner, as might be expected. This usage is convenient, however, both because it is becoming the generally

is critical of those who use the term "general intent," Glanville Williams defines the mens rea that is generally sufficient for criminal liability in this manner. In Criminal Law: The General Part 31, 34, 53 (2d ed. 1961), he states that "the mental element necessary for [a] particular crime . . . may be either *intention* to do the immediate act or bring about the consequences or (in some crimes) *recklessness* as to such act or consequence." "Intention" he defines as "knowledge of . . . surrounding circumstances" or "the desire that . . . specified consequences shall follow . . . ." "Recklessness" he defines as occurring "when the actor does not desire the consequence, but foresees the possibility and consciously takes the risk." Those who object to negligence as a basis for criminal liability typically embrace a similar formulation as the minimum culpability that will suffice for crime.[g] One might also ascribe this view to the court in *Cunningham*, page 201, supra.

4. **Footnote on Strict Liability.** "Strict" or "absolute" liability refers to offenses where no mens rea is required with respect to one or more elements. A common example is statutory rape, which is usually defined to include sexual intercourse with a person below a specified age, with or without force and irrespective of consent by the victim. Typically, no mens rea is required as to the age of the victim.

As can be imagined, there is considerable controversy about the use of strict liability in the criminal law. Those who object to liability for negligence, for example, could hardly be expected to approve of liability without fault. It is sufficient at this point, nonetheless, simply to note the possibility of strict liability. The legitimacy of its use and the contexts in which it might be used are developed later.

5. **Mens Rea and Legal Fictions.** One encounters many instances in the common law when the judges seem to be playing games of make-believe. You should be alert to this possibility. Examine the quotation in *Smith* from the *Faulkner* case. What do you think it means to say that the law "imputes" an "intention" to someone? Does it mean the law pretends the intent exists even if in fact it does not? That the law seeks to talk in language of intent even though it has no concern with actual intent? Are there any advantages to be gained by such talk? You will see many examples of a similar use of language in common-law opinions,[h] both in this course and in others. In each instance, they should signal the need to translate into more direct terms the court's actual meaning and perhaps to question why such an indirect means was chosen to accomplish its objective.

recognized meaning of the term and because it serves as a convenient basis for comparison to the concept of negligence.

[g] For an elaborate development of this thesis, see J. Hall, General Principles of Criminal Law 105–70 (2d ed. 1960).

[h] Cf. People v. Peak, 66 Cal.App.2d 894, 902, 153 P.2d 464, 467 (1944):

"There are some crimes in which a wrongful intent is . . . based solely upon the commission of the act itself. If intent is not made an affirmative element in an offense . . . , the law imputes a criminal intent. The law assumes an intent as an element of a crime. . . . It is only in offenses where the voluntary commission of an unlawful act is based upon the essential element of specific intent that intent should be alleged and proved."

6. Statutory Response to *Smith* in England. The decision in *Smith* provoked a critical response in England and elsewhere. The following statute was enacted to overrule it:

> "A court or jury in determining whether a person has committed an offense,—
>
> > (a) shall not be bound in law to infer that he intended or foresaw a result of his actions by reason only of its being a natural and probable consequence of those actions; but
> >
> > (b) shall decide whether he did intend or foresee that result by reference to all the evidence, drawing such inferences from the evidence as appear proper in the circumstances."

Criminal Justice Act of 1967, c. 80, pt. I, § 8. This statute was defended by its drafters on the ground that the common law traditionally required a subjective focus on the mens rea for murder, Holmes notwithstanding, and that the inferences to be drawn from the natural and probable consequences of one's conduct should be permissive but not mandatory. Whether it has in fact accomplished the objective of overruling *Smith* is a matter of some controversy.[i]

MORISSETTE v. UNITED STATES

Supreme Court of United States, 1952.
342 U.S. 246.

MR. JUSTICE JACKSON delivered the opinion of the Court.

This would have remained a profoundly insignificant case to all except its immediate parties had it not been so tried and submitted to the jury as to raise questions both fundamental and far-reaching in federal criminal law, for which reason we granted certiorari.

On a large tract of uninhabited and untilled land in a wooded and sparsely populated area of Michigan, the government established a practice bombing range over which the Air Force dropped simulated bombs at ground targets. These bombs consisted of a metal cylinder about 40 inches long and eight inches across, filled with sand and enough black powder to cause a smoke puff by which the strike could be located. At various places about the range signs read "Danger—Keep Out—Bombing Range." Nevertheless, the range was known as good deer country and was extensively hunted.

Spent bomb casings were cleared from the targets and thrown into piles "so that they will be out of the way." They were not stacked or piled in any order but were dumped in heaps, some of which had been

[i] The statute can be interpreted as establishing only an evidentiary proposition, i.e., *how* intent or foresight must be proved in cases where the substantive law requires it to be proved. What the statute does not say, on the other hand, is *when* intent or foresight must in fact be proved as a matter of substantive law. *Smith* can be read as speaking to this latter point—to a redefinition of the substantive law of murder to the effect that intent or foresight need not be proved in the first place—and thus may escape unscathed by the enactment of the quoted statute. See J. Smith & B. Hogan, Criminal Law 285–91 (4th ed. 1978).

accumulating for four years or upwards, were exposed to the weather and rusting away.

Morissette, in December of 1948, went hunting in this area but did not get a deer. He thought to meet expenses of the trip by salvaging some of these casings. He loaded three tons of them on his truck and took them to a nearby farm, where they were flattened by driving a tractor over them. After expending this labor and trucking them to market in Flint, he realized $84.

Morissette, by occupation, is a fruit stand operator in summer and a trucker and scrap iron collector in winter. An honorably discharged veteran of World War II, he enjoys a good name among his neighbors and has had no blemish on his record more disreputable than a conviction for reckless driving.

The loading, crushing and transporting of these casings were all in broad daylight, in full view of passers-by, without the slightest effort at concealment. When an investigation was started, Morissette voluntarily, promptly and candidly told the whole story to the authorities, saying that he had no intention of stealing but thought the property was abandoned, unwanted and considered of no value to the government. He was indicted, however, on the charge that he "did unlawfully, wilfully and knowingly steal and convert" property of the United States of the value of $84, in violation of 18 U.S.C. § 641 [2] . . . .. Morissette was convicted and sentenced to imprisonment for two months or to pay a fine of $200. The Court of Appeals affirmed, one judge dissenting.

On his trial, Morissette, as he had at all times told investigating officers, testified that from appearances he believed the casings were cast-off and abandoned, that he did not intend to steal the property, and took it with no wrongful or criminal intent. The trial court, however, was unimpressed, and ruled:

> "[H]e took it because he thought it was abandoned and he knew he was on government property. . . . That is no defense . . . .. I don't think anybody can have the defense [that] they thought the property was abandoned on another man's piece of property."

The court stated:

> "I will not permit you to show this man thought it was abandoned. . . . I hold in this case that there is no question of abandoned property."

The court refused to submit or to allow counsel to argue to the jury whether Morissette acted with innocent intention. It charged:

> "And I instruct you that if you believe the testimony of the government in this case, he intended to take it. . . . He had no right to take this property. [A]nd it is no defense to claim

---

[2] Section 641, so far as pertinent, reads:

"Whoever embezzles, steals, purloins, or knowingly converts to his use or the use of another . . . any . . . thing of value of the United States [s]hall be fined not more than $10,000 or impris-
oned not more than ten years, or both; but if the value of such property does not exceed the sum of $100, he shall be fined not more than $1,000 or imprisoned not more than one year, or both."

that it was abandoned, because it was on private property . . ..
And I instruct you to this effect: That if this young man took
this property (and he says he did), without any permission (he
says he did), that was on the property of the United States
Government (he says it was), that it was of the value of one cent
or more (and evidently it was), that he is guilty of the offense
charged here. If you believe the government, he is guilty.
. . . The question on intent is whether or not he intended to
take the property. He says he did. Therefore, if you believe
either side, he is guilty."

Petitioner's counsel contended, "But the taking must have been with a
felonious intent." The court ruled, however: "That is presumed by his
own act."

The Court of Appeals suggested that "greater restraint in expression
should have been exercised," but affirmed the conviction because, "[a]s
we have interpreted the statute, appellant was guilty of its violation
beyond a shadow of doubt, as evidenced even by his own admissions."
Its construction of the statute is that it creates several separate and
distinct offenses, one being knowing conversion of government property. The court ruled that this particular offense requires no element of
criminal intent. This conclusion was thought to be required by the
failure of Congress to express such a requisite.

I.

. . . Stealing, larceny, and its variants and equivalents, were
among the earliest offenses known to the law that existed before
legislation; they are invasions of rights of property which stir a sense
of insecurity in the whole community and arouse public demand for
retribution, the penalty is high and, when a sufficient amount is
involved, the infamy is that of a felony, which, says Maitland, is ". . .
as bad a word as you can give to man or thing." State courts of last
resort, on whom fall the heaviest burden of interpreting criminal law in
this country, have consistently retained the requirement of intent in
larceny-type offenses. If any state has deviated, the exception has
neither been called to our attention nor disclosed by our research.

Congress, therefore, omitted any express prescription of criminal
intent from the enactment before us in the light of an unbroken course
of judicial decision in all constituent states of the Union holding intent
inherent in this class of offense, even when not expressed in a statute.
Congressional silence as to mental elements in an act merely adopting
into federal statutory law a concept of crime already so well defined in
common law and statutory interpretation by the states [does not warrant the inference that intent is not required as an element of the
offense]. Nor do exhaustive studies of state-court cases disclose any
well-considered decisions applying the doctrine of crime without intent
to such enacted common-law offenses . . . .

The government asks us by a feat of construction radically to change
the weights and balances in the scales of justice. The purpose and
obvious effect of doing away with the requirement of a guilty intent is

to ease the prosecution's path to conviction, to strip the defendant of such benefit as he derived at common law from innocence of evil purpose, and to circumscribe the freedom heretofore allowed juries. Such a manifest impairment of the immunities of the individual should not be extended to common-law crimes on judicial initiative.

The spirit of the doctrine which denies to the federal judiciary power to create crimes forthrightly admonishes that we should not enlarge the reach of enacted crimes by constituting them from anything less than the incriminating components contemplated by the words used in the statute. And where Congress borrows terms of art in which are accumulated the legal tradition and meaning of centuries of practice, it presumably knows and adopts the cluster of ideas that were attached to each borrowed word in the body of learning from which it was taken and the meaning its use will convey to the judicial mind unless otherwise instructed. In such case, absence of contrary direction may be taken as satisfaction with widely accepted definitions, not as a departure from them.

We hold that mere omission from § 641 of any mention of intent will not be construed as eliminating that element from the crimes denounced.

II.

It is suggested, however, that the history and purposes of § 641 imply something more affirmative as to elimination of intent from at least one of the offenses charged under it in this case. The argument does not contest that criminal intent is retained in the offenses of embezzlement, stealing and purloining, as incorporated into this section. But it is urged that Congress joined with those, as a new, separate and distinct offense, knowingly to convert government property, under circumstances which imply that it is an offense in which the mental element of intent is not necessary.

Congress has been alert to what often is a decisive function of some mental element in crime. It has seen fit to prescribe that an evil state of mind, described variously in one or more such terms as "intentional," "wilful," "knowing," "fraudulent" or "malicious," will make criminal an otherwise indifferent act, or increase the degree of the offense or its punishment. Also, it has at times required a specific intent or purpose which will require some specialized knowledge or design for some evil beyond the common-law intent to do injury. . . . In view of the care that has been bestowed upon the subject, it is significant that we have not found, nor has our attention been directed to, any instance in which Congress has expressly eliminated the mental element from a crime taken over from the common law.

The section with which we are here concerned was enacted in 1948, as a consolidation of four former sections of Title 18. . . . We find no other purpose in the 1948 re-enactment than to collect from scattered sources crimes so kindred as to belong in one category. Not one of these had been interpreted to be a crime without intention and no purpose to differentiate between them in the matter of intent is disclosed. No inference that some were and some were not crimes of intention can be drawn from any difference in classification or punishment. [E]ach is, at its least, a misdemeanor, and if the amount involved is $100 or more each is a felony. If one crime without intent has been smuggled into a section whose dominant offenses do require intent, it was put in ill-fitting and compromising company. The government apparently did not believe that conversion stood so alone when it drew this one-count indictment to charge that Morissette "did unlawfully, wilfully and knowingly steal and convert to his own use."

Congress, by the language of this section, has been at pains to incriminate only "knowing" conversions. But, at common law, there are unwitting acts which constitute conversions. In the civil tort, except for recovery of exemplary damages, the defendant's knowledge, intent, motive, mistake, and good faith are generally irrelevant.[31] If one takes property which turns out to belong to another, his innocent intent will not shield him from making restitution or indemnity, for his well-meaning may not be allowed to deprive another of his own.

Had the statute applied to conversions without qualification, it would have made crimes of all unwitting, inadvertent and unintended conversions. Knowledge, of course, is not identical with intent and may not have been the most apt words of limitation. But knowing conversion requires more than knowledge that defendant was taking the property into his possession. He must have had knowledge of the facts, though not necessarily the law, that made the taking a conversion. In the case before us, whether the mental element that Congress required be spoken of as knowledge or as intent, would not seem to alter its bearing on guilt. For it is not apparent how Morissette could have knowingly or intentionally converted property that he did not know could be converted, as would be the case if it was in fact abandoned or if he truly believed it to be abandoned and unwanted property.

It is said, and at first blush the claim has plausibility, that, if we construe the statute to require a mental element as part of criminal conversion, it becomes a meaningless duplication of the offense of stealing, and that conversion can be given meaning only by interpreting it to disregard intention. But here again a broader view of the evolution of these crimes throws a different light on the legislation.

It is not surprising if there is considerable overlapping in the embezzlement, stealing, purloining and knowing conversion grouped in this statute. What has concerned codifiers of the larceny-type offense is that gaps or crevices have separated particular crimes of this general class and guilty men have escaped through the breaches. The books

[31] The rationale underlying [this rule] is that when one clearly assumes the rights of ownership over property of another no proof of intent to convert is necessary. It has even been held that one may be held liable in conversion even though he reasonably supposed that he had a legal right to the property in question. . . . [Such cases] leave no doubt that Morissette could be held liable for a civil conversion for his taking of the property here involved, and the instructions to the jury might have been appropriate in such a civil action. This assumes of course that actual abandonment was not proven, a matter which petitioner should be allowed to prove if he can.

contain a surfeit of cases drawing fine distinctions between slightly different circumstances under which one may obtain wrongful advantages from another's property. The codifiers wanted to reach all such instances. Probably every stealing is a conversion, but certainly not every knowing conversion is a stealing. . . . Conversion . . . may be consummated without any intent to keep and without any wrongful taking, where the initial possession by the converter was entirely lawful. Conversion may include misuse or abuse of property. It may reach use in an unauthorized manner or to an unauthorized extent of property placed in one's custody for limited use. Money rightfully taken into one's custody may be converted without any intent to keep or embezzle it merely by commingling it with the custodian's own, if he was under a duty to keep it separate and intact. It is not difficult to think of intentional and knowing abuses and unauthorized uses of government property that might be knowing conversions but which could not be reached as embezzlement, stealing or purloining. Knowing conversion adds significantly to the range of protection of government property without interpreting it to punish unwitting conversions.

The purpose which we here attribute to Congress parallels that of codifiers of common law in England and in the states and demonstrates that the serious problem in drafting such a statute is to avoid gaps and loopholes between offenses. It is significant that the English and state codifiers have tried to cover the same type of conduct that we are suggesting as the purpose of Congress here, without, however, departing from the common-law tradition that these are crimes of intendment.

We find no grounds for inferring any affirmative instruction from Congress to eliminate intent from any offense with which this defendant was charged.

III.

As we read the record, this case was tried on the theory that even if criminal intent were essential its presence (i) should be decided by the court (ii) as a presumption of law, apparently conclusive, (iii) predicated upon the isolated act of taking rather than upon all of the circumstances. In each of these respects we believe the trial court was in error.

Where intent of the accused is an ingredient of the crime charged, its existence is a question of fact which must be submitted to the jury. State court authorities cited to the effect that intent is relevant in larcenous crimes are equally emphatic and uniform that it is a jury issue. The settled practice and its reason are well stated by Judge Andrews in People v. Flack, 125 N.Y. 324, 334, 26 N.E. 267, 270 (1891):

"It is alike the general rule of law, and the dictate of natural justice, that to constitute guilt there must be not only a wrongful act, but a criminal intention. Under our system, (unless in exceptional cases), both must be found by the jury to justify a conviction for crime. However clear the proof may be, or however incontrovertible may seem to the judge to be the inference of a criminal intention, the question of intent can never be ruled as a question of law, but must always be submitted to the jury. Jurors may be perverse; the ends of justice may be defeated by unrighteous verdicts, but so long as the functions of the judge and jury are distinct, the one responding to the law, the other to the facts, neither can invade the province of the other without destroying the significance of trial by court and jury. . . ."

It follows that the trial court may not withdraw or prejudge the issue by instruction that the law raises a presumption of intent from an act. It often is tempting to cast in terms of a "presumption" a conclusion which a court thinks probable from given facts. . . .

We think presumptive intent has no place in this case. A conclusive presumption which testimony could not overthrow would effectively eliminate intent as an ingredient of the offense. A presumption which would permit but not require the jury to assume intent from an isolated fact would prejudge a conclusion which the jury should reach of its own volition. A presumption which would permit the jury to make an assumption which all the evidence considered together does not logically establish would give to a proven fact an artificial and fictional effect. . . . Such incriminating presumptions are not to be improvised by the judiciary. . . .

Moreover, the conclusion supplied by presumption in this instance was one of intent to steal the casings, and it was based on the mere fact that defendant took them. The court thought the only question was, "Did he intend to take the property?" That the removal of them was a conscious and intentional act was admitted. But that isolated fact is not an adequate basis on which the jury should find the criminal intent to steal or knowingly convert, that is, *wrongfully* to deprive another of possession of property. Whether that intent existed, the jury must determine, not only from the act of taking, but from that together with defendant's testimony and all of the surrounding circumstances.

Of course, the jury, considering Morissette's awareness that these casings were on government property, his failure to seek any permission for their removal and his self-interest as a witness, might have disbelieved his profession of innocent intent and concluded that his assertion of a belief that the casings were abandoned was an afterthought. Had the jury convicted on proper instructions it would be the end of the matter. But juries are not bound by what seems inescapable logic to judges. They might have concluded that the heaps of spent casings left in the hinterland to rust away presented an appearance of unwanted and abandoned junk, and that lack of any conscious deprivation of property or intentional injury was indicated by Morissette's good character, the openness of the taking, crushing and transporting of the casings, and the candor with which it was all admitted. They might have refused to brand Morissette as a thief. Had they done so, that too would have been the end of the matter.

Reversed.

MR. JUSTICE DOUGLAS concurs in the result.

MR. JUSTICE MINTON took no part in the consideration or decision of this case.

NOTES ON SPECIFIC INTENT AT COMMON LAW

1. **Questions on *Morissette*.** Justice Jackson repeatedly asserted that the government's theory of the case, adopted by the trial judge, dispensed with the requirement of a "guilty intent." Is this a fair characterization of the government's position? The trial judge instructed the jury that Morissette should be convicted if he was found to have taken the casings without the government's permission from land which he knew to be federal property. Did this instruction dispense with a requirement of mens rea? What would have been the proper instruction in the Supreme Court's view?

Did the Supreme Court properly construe the statutory language? Can the statute reasonably be construed to support the government's position? If so, what factors should the Court have taken into account in deciding how to construe it? Consider the material in the following notes as you think about these questions.

2. **Background on Theft Offenses.** The common-law crime of larceny required a trespassory taking of the personal property of another with intent to appropriate. The taking was said to be "trespassory" when the initial acquisition of the property violated rights of possession created by applicable laws of personal property. For this reason, larceny was often said to be an offense against possession.

It is plain, however, that theft can occur in contexts where the actor does not "trespass" on the possessory rights of others to obtain the property. Bank tellers, servants, and agents, for example, have the right to possess property that belongs to others; for many purposes they are lawful custodians of other people's property. They are not, however, entitled to treat such property as their own, as when the teller bets bank money at the track. When they deprive owners of their property, such persons should be as guilty of theft as the person who acquires the property by trespass.

The Anglo-American legal system reached this conclusion slowly. The earliest forms of larceny were concerned with misappropriations by violence or stealth. Over the years, and often through legal fictions, the concept of trespassory taking was expanded to encompass a variety of means by which one can misappropriate property of another. For example, "larceny by trick" covered a class of cases where a "constructive" trespass was said to have occurred if the property was obtained under specified fraudulent circumstances. In particular, if one had the intent to steal property at the time its temporary use was lawfully obtained from the owner, this form of larceny would have been committed. Thus, for example, one who intended to steal a car at the time it was rented would be guilty of larceny by trick. On the other hand, if one rented a car and decided to steal it after the rental agreement was consummated, the law's ability to perceive a fictional trespass would have been exceeded, and no larceny would have occurred. Indeed, for a substantial period of common-law history, no crime at all would have been committed if property was obtained under such circumstances.

Perhaps the most important effort to close this gap was begun in England in 1799 by the enactment of the statutory offense of embezzlement. Originally, embezzlement was designed to deal with situations where a master's property was received from a third person by a servant and the servant proceeded to steal it. Subsequently the offense was expanded by additional statutes, both in this country and in England, to cover most variations of the situation where a lawful custodian misappropriates custodial property. In separate developments, offenses also emerged to deal with obtaining property by false pretenses, extortion, and the like.[a]

The technical distinctions that emerged between these various theft offenses were extremely complicated. Moreover, the procedures of the early common law were such that it mattered a great deal that the prosecutor charged the right offense at the outset of the case. If, for example, the prosecutor charged larceny by trick, the defendant could defend successfully on the ground that what really happened was embezzlement. It was possible in this country for the defendant then to be charged with embezzlement, but the defense in the second trial might then be that the crime really was larceny by trick.[b]

Statutes such as the one involved in *Morissette* were enacted to avoid such technicalities and to make sure, as the Court says, that gaps between the various theft offenses were filled. More comprehensive consolidation of theft offenses was suggested by the Model Penal Code, and most modern statutes have followed its approach. The provisions of article 223 of the Model Code consolidate the law of theft into a single, comprehensive offense.[c] The principal thrust of these provisions is to eliminate technical distinctions between separately defined crimes that turn on how the property was acquired. As can be seen from the detail of article 223, however, this approach does not eliminate the need to draft limitations, many of which could be found in the common law, designed to confine the crime of theft within appropriate limitations.

3. **Holmes Revisited.** Even the strongest adherents of the view that criminal liability should be based on an external standard concede

---

[a] For a more detailed review of the history of larceny, embezzlement, and related offenses, see J. Hall, Theft, Law and Society (2d ed. 1952); W. LaFave & A. Scott, Criminal Law 618–712 (1972); R. Perkins & R. Boyce, Criminal Law 292–452 (3d ed. 1982).

[b] The example may sound fanciful but, as reported in J. Michael & H. Wechsler, Criminal Law and Its Administration 545 (1940), the "books are replete with dismissals and reversals on the ground that the indictment or the conviction was for the wrong crime." They cite Commonwealth v. O'Malley, 97 Mass. 584 (1867), as an illustration. In that case the defendant was acquitted of larceny and later convict-

ed of embezzlement. The conviction was then set aside on the ground that the evidence proved larceny.

[c] For a general discussion of the purpose of consolidation and some of the problems of implementation, see ALI, Model Penal Code and Commentaries § 223.1, pp. 127–38 (1980). At least 30 states have adopted consolidated theft provisions since the promulgation of the Model Penal Code in 1962. The Model Code was not the first effort at consolidation, though it has been by far the most influential. An earlier treatment of the consolidation issue can be found in J. Michael & H. Wechsler, Criminal Law and Its Administration 545–52 (1940).

that there are occasions where a subjective inquiry is desirable. Holmes illustrated this proposition in a discussion of the crimes of attempt and larceny:

"There is [a] class of cases in which intent plays an important part . . . . The most obvious examples of this class are criminal attempts. . . .

"Some acts may be attempts . . . which could not have effected the crime unless followed by other acts on the part of the wrong-doer. For instance, lighting a match with intent to set fire to a haystack has been held to amount to a criminal attempt to burn it, although the defendant blew out the match on seeing that he was watched. . . .

"In such cases the law goes on a new principle, different from that governing most substantive crimes. The reason for punishing any act must generally be to prevent some harm which is foreseen as likely to follow that act under the circumstances in which it is done. In most substantive crimes the ground on which that likelihood stands is the common working of natural causes as shown by experience. But when an act is punished the natural effect of which is not harmful under the circumstances, that ground alone will not suffice. The probability does not exist unless there are grounds for expecting that the act done will be followed by other acts in connection with which its effect will be harmful, although not so otherwise. But as in fact no such acts have followed, it cannot, in general, be assumed, from the mere doing of what has been done, that they would have followed if the actor had not been interrupted. They would not have followed it unless the actor had chosen, and the only way generally available to show that he would have chosen to do them is by showing that he intended to do them when he did what he did. The accompanying intent in that case renders the otherwise innocent act harmful, because it raises a probability that it will be followed by such other acts and events as will all together result in harm. The importance of the intent is not to show that the act was wicked, but to show that it was likely to be followed by hurtful consequences. . . .

"There remain to be considered certain substantive crimes, which differ in very important ways from murder and the like, and for the explanation of which the foregoing analysis of intent in criminal attempts . . . will be found of service.

"The type of these is larceny. Under this name acts are punished which of themselves would not be sufficient to accomplish the evil which the law seeks to prevent, and which are treated as equally criminal, whether the evil has been accomplished or not. Murder, manslaughter, and arson, on the other hand, are not committed unless the evil is accomplished, and they all consist of acts the tendency of which under the surrounding circumstances is to hurt or destroy person or property by the mere working of natural laws.

"In larceny the consequences immediately flowing from the act are generally exhausted with little or no harm to the owner. Goods are removed from his possession by trespass, and that is all, when the crime is complete. But they must be permanently kept from him before the harm is done which the law seeks to prevent. A momentary loss of possession is not what has been guarded against with such severe penalties. What the law means to prevent is the loss of it wholly and forever, as is shown by the fact that it is not larceny to take for a temporary use without intending to deprive the owner of his property. If then the law punishes the mere act of taking, it punishes an act which will not of itself produce the evil effect sought to be prevented, and punishes it before that effect has in any way come to pass.

"The reason is plain enough. The law cannot wait until the property has been used up or destroyed in other hands than the owner's, or until the owner has died, in order to make sure that the harm which it seeks to prevent has been done. And for the same reason it cannot confine itself to acts likely to do that harm. For the harm of permanent loss of property will not follow from the act of taking, but only from the series of acts which constitute removing and keeping the property after it has been taken. After these preliminaries, the bearing of intent upon the crime is easily seen.

"According to Mr. Bishop, larceny is 'the taking and removing, by trespass, of personal property which the trespasser knows to belong either generally or specially to another, with the intent to deprive such owner of his ownership therein . . . .'

"There must be an intent to deprive such owner of his ownership therein, it is said. But why? Is it because the law is more anxious not to put a man in prison for stealing unless he is actually wicked, than it is not to hang him for killing another? That can hardly be. The true answer is, that the intent is an index to the external event which probably would have happened, and that, if the law is to punish at all, it must, in this case, go on probabilities, not on accomplished facts. The analogy to the manner of dealing with attempts is plain. Theft may be called an attempt to permanently deprive a man of his property, which is punished with the same severity whether successful or not. If theft can rightly be considered in this way, intent must play the same part as in other attempts. An act which does not fully accomplish the prohibited result may be made wrongful by evidence that but for some interference it would have been followed by other acts co-ordinated with it to produce that result. This can only be shown by showing intent. In theft the intent to deprive the owner of his property establishes that the thief would have retained, or would not have taken steps to restore, the stolen goods. . . ."

4. **The Concept of Specific Intent.** The term "specific intent" is encountered with some frequency in the common law. In contrast to

most of the mens rea terms mentioned previously, however, the meaning of "specific intent" has become fairly well settled. It refers to an inquiry into the defendant's actual state of mind. Moreover, courts typically do not permit presumptions to displace a determination by the jury that the defendant actually performed the mental operations described in the "specific intent" component of an offense. There are no fictions here.

There are essentially three types of situations to which the term is applied. The first is in cases where the criminal offense is defined in terms of specified conduct committed with a purpose that other conduct will follow. Assault with intent to rape is an example. As Holmes indicates, attempt and larceny are also examples. These are all commonly referred to as "specific intent" offenses. "Specific intent" in this sense, therefore, refers to some plan to engage in designated conduct in the future. Exactly what "specific" intent is required in a given case is determined by the definition of the particular offense involved.

The second is closely related. It occurs when the crime requires that the defendant engage in behavior with the hope or expectation that some consequence will result without the need for any further conduct by the defendant. For example, criminal coercion can be defined as threatening to take official action with the purpose of unlawfully restricting the freedom of action of another person. This offense could be committed by a public official who threatens to do something, with the hope or expectation that the threat will cause another person to engage in conduct which that person is not legally obligated to undertake. Another illustration is the offense of hindering prosecution, which can be defined as volunteering false information to a law enforcement officer with the purpose of hindering the apprehension or prosecution of another. In this case the intended effect of the conduct of volunteering false information to a law enforcement officer is that the apprehension or prosecution of another person will be hindered without the need for the defendant to engage in any further conduct.

The third context in which common-law courts sometimes use the term "specific intent" is to refer to a requirement that the actor actually be aware of the existence of certain circumstances pertinent to the criminality of the conduct. An example would be an offense punishing the making of false entries in a record, knowing them to be false. Another example would be the crime of receiving stolen property, knowing it to have been stolen. In both crimes the defendant must know that specified actus reus elements have occurred, i.e., must know that the record entry is false or must know that the property had been stolen.

The differences between these uses of the term, then, are that the first refers to the defendant's plan to engage in future conduct, the second refers to results the defendant hopes will follow from conduct, and the third refers to the defendant's awareness that conduct is of a certain character. The similarity shared by all three is that each asks a subjective question, that is, each focuses on what the defendant was actually thinking or planning at the time of the offense. Some variant of purpose or knowledge, in the ordinary sense of these words, is therefore meant when the label "specific intent" is applied to a common-law offense.

SUBSECTION B: CULPABILITY IN MODERN STATUTES

INTRODUCTORY NOTE ON THE MODEL PENAL CODE

The Model Penal Code introduced a new approach to the mens-rea inquiry. The approach is new both in analytical structure and in proposed changes on questions of policy. It builds, however, on the common-law tradition and works a skillful blending of the old and the new. As many as half of the states have adopted culpability provisions that are derived from the analytical structure of the Model Code and that in many cases follow the substance of its provisions. The remainder of the states still base the culpability inquiry on the common law, but even in these states the Model Code has had an important impact on the decisional law.

The Model Code abandons much of the terminology of common-law culpability. It proposes instead a tightly integrated structure built on definitions that are more faithful to the ordinary sense of language. It is difficult, at first imposingly so, and requires careful and repeated study. The following notes are designed to draw out the analytical structure of the Model Code and to illustrate the application of its provisions.[a]

1. **The Actus Reus.** The starting point is the Model Code conception of the criminal act. The act components of an offense are broken down into three categories: "conduct," "circumstances," and "results." The "conduct" elements are those that describe the acts or omissions required to commit the charged offense. Examples are "taking and carrying away" in common-law larceny, "breaking and entering" in common-law burglary, and the like. Every offense must contain some "conduct" as so defined, although sometimes the exact nature of the conduct is not described. For example, murder usually is defined to encompass any act (or omission in the face of a legal duty to act) that causes the death of another person (with the appropriate mens rea). For murder, some "conduct" by the defendant must occur, and the total universe of potential conduct that may lead to another's death is included in the offense by the failure to be more specific. For common-law larceny or burglary, on the other hand, only conduct properly described as a "taking," a "breaking," etc., suffices. In cases where the conduct element of the offense is specifically designated, nice questions

[a] For an extensive consideration of the analytical structure of the Model Code, see Robinson and Grall, Element Analysis in Defining Criminal Liability: The Model Penal Code and Beyond, 35 Stanford L.Rev. 681 (1983).

can arise as to whether it is satisfied. For example, does reaching through an open window (and breaking the plane fixed by the window) constitute a "breaking" for purposes of burglary?

"Circumstance" elements consist of external facts that must exist in order for the crime to be committed. Common-law larceny, for example, requires the taking and carrying away "of the personal property of another." The circumstance elements are that the object taken must be "personal property" (do growing crops count?) that belongs to "another" (is partnership property included?). Other examples of circumstance elements are "the dwelling of another in the nighttime" that must be the subject of common-law burglary, the status of a person as an FBI agent in the federal crime of killing an FBI agent, the age of the victim where made relevant by the definition of the crime, and so on.

"Result" elements are the consequences of the defendant's conduct that are incorporated in the offense. The obvious example is murder, which requires the death of a person as a result. Other results that may be required include "serious bodily injury" in an assault-and-battery statute, "fear of bodily injury" induced in an assault victim, and the like. Most offenses are defined only in terms of conduct and circumstances, with no result specified. For example, only conduct and circumstance elements are contained in the common-law definition of larceny as "the taking and carrying away of the personal property of another with the intent permanently to deprive the other of his interest in the property." Note also that in cases where results are specified, an additional element of a causal relation between the defendant's conduct and the prohibited result is necessarily included.

These three categories are necessarily somewhat arbitrary. It would be relatively easy to develop a different terminology or to categorize some elements differently within the same terminology. Indeed, difficulties can be encountered in applying this construct to offenses defined by the Model Penal Code itself. For example, in rape as defined in § 213.1(1)(a), the actor is guilty if "he compels [the victim] to submit by force." Is it intuitively clear how each of these elements should be classified? Does the quoted phrase describe conduct or a result? Fortunately, in most situations nothing turns on an improper categorization of a given element. The principal purpose of adopting this structure is satisfied by the exercise of focusing on each element separately rather than treating the actus reus of the offense as an undifferentiated whole. Separating the actus-reus elements in this manner is an essential analytical step in approaching any criminal offense under the Model Code or under any statute based upon it.

There are cases, particularly those involving the crime of attempt, where proper categorization of some elements is crucial. These are considered in due course below. For now, it is sufficient that the student experiment with the classification scheme, and be aware of the ambiguities and difficulties that a given classification entails. To this end, a useful exercise would be to select a variety of substantive offenses defined by the Model Code and, before reading on, to classify each element (other than those which obviously deal with state of mind) within the specified categories. This should be done enough times so that it becomes an automatic first step in *every* analysis of a problem to be dealt with under the Model Code or a similar statute.

2. **The Mens Rea.** The next step in the Model Penal Code analysis is consideration of the required mens rea. The Model Code is based on the proposition that four culpability concepts are both necessary and sufficient to define criminal offenses. They are "purpose," "knowledge," "recklessness," and "negligence." Each of these terms is carefully defined. The analytical key to the Model Code is that the mental elements of a given crime must be determined by ascertaining which of these four terms applies to *each* of the actus-reus components of the offense. Thus, once the crime is broken down into its conduct, circumstance, and result components, one of the four culpability concepts will be applied to each component in order to determine the level of mens rea required for that offense.

To illustrate, common-law larceny was defined above as "the taking and carrying away of the personal property of another with the intent permanently to deprive the other of his interest in the property." One would first classify "taking" and "carrying away" as conduct elements, and ask whether that conduct has occurred. One would then ask which of the four culpability terms applies to each element. The same analysis would then be followed for the circumstance elements "personal property" and "of another." One could then describe the mens rea for larceny as consisting of the applicable culpability term applied to each actus-reus element of the offense *in addition to* the specified intent permanently to deprive the other of his or her interest in the property. This additional intent element is required, of course, because the definition of the offense says so; it would not be a part of the mens rea of an offense that did not contain comparable language.

At this point, the student should study carefully the provisions of § 2.02. In that connection, it would be useful to re-examine the offenses selected for the purpose of classifying the actus-reus elements and see if this time the appropriate mens-rea elements can be added. This too should be done enough times so that it becomes an automatic step in the analysis of *every* problem confronted under the Model Code or a statute derived from it. The notes beginning on page 237, infra, are designed to assist you in this task.

––––––

MODEL PENAL CODE CULPABILITY PROVISIONS

Section 2.02. General Requirements of Culpability

(1) <u>Minimum Requirements of Culpability</u>. Except as provided in Section 2.05, a person is not guilty of an offense unless he acted purposely, knowingly, recklessly or negligently, as the law may require, with respect to each material element of the offense.

(2) Kinds of Culpability Defined.

(a) Purposely.

A person acts purposely with respect to a material element of an offense when:

(i) if the element involves the nature of his conduct or a result thereof, it is his conscious object to engage in conduct of that nature or to cause such a result; and

(ii) if the element involves the attendant circumstances, he is aware of the existence of such circumstances or he believes or hopes that they exist.

(b) Knowingly.

A person acts knowingly with respect to a material element of an offense when:

(i) if the element involves the nature of his conduct or the attendant circumstances, he is aware that his conduct is of that nature or that such circumstances exist; and

(ii) if the element involves a result of his conduct, he is aware that it is practically certain that his conduct will cause such a result.

(c) Recklessly.

A person acts recklessly with respect to a material element of an offense when he consciously disregards a substantial and unjustifiable risk that the material element exists or will result from his conduct. The risk must be of such a nature and degree that, considering the nature and purpose of the actor's conduct and the circumstances known to him, its disregard involves a gross deviation from the standard of conduct that a law-abiding person would observe in the actor's situation.

(d) Negligently.

A person acts negligently with respect to a material element of an offense when he should be aware of a substantial and unjustifiable risk that the material element exists or will result from his conduct. The risk must be of such a nature and degree that the actor's failure to perceive it, considering the nature and purpose of his conduct and the circumstances known to him, involves a gross deviation from the standard of care that a reasonable person would observe in the actor's situation.

(3) Culpability Required Unless Otherwise Provided. When the culpability sufficient to establish a material element of an offense is not prescribed by law, such element is established if a person acts purposely, knowingly or recklessly with respect thereto.

(4) Prescribed Culpability Requirement Applies to All Material Elements. When the law defining an offense prescribes the kind of culpability that is sufficient for the commission of an offense, without distinguishing among the material elements thereof, such provision shall apply to all the material elements of the offense, unless a contrary purpose plainly appears.

(5) <u>Substitutes for Negligence, Recklessness and Knowledge.</u> When the law provides that negligence suffices to establish an element of an offense, such element also is established if a person acts purposely, knowingly or recklessly. When recklessness suffices to establish an element, such element also is established if a person acts purposely or knowingly. When acting knowingly suffices to establish an element, such element also is established if a person acts purposely. . . .

NOTES ON THE MODEL PENAL CODE
CULPABILITY STRUCTURE

The following notes are designed to help you draw out the meaning of the provisions of § 2.02. The first eight notes are keyed to the particular subdivisions of § 2.02 and are an explanation of what they mean. The remaining notes contain a series of exercises designed to test the application of the provisions in specific contexts.

1. **Minimum Requirements of Culpability.** There are four points to be noted about this provision:

(i) **Strict Liability.** Section 2.05, to which reference is made in the opening phrase of Subsection (1) of § 2.02, concerns a category of strict-liability offenses which the Model Code calls "violations." Under § 1.04, violations are not "crimes" and carry only fines, forfeitures, or other civil penalties. The tradition from which this recommendation grows is dealt with at pages 291–92, infra. For now it is sufficient to note that there is a category of offenses to which the basic culpability structure of the Model Code does not apply. Because of their non-criminal status and the limited sanctions that can be imposed, offenses in this category are generally governed by considerations different from those that control the serious offenses dealt with throughout most of these materials.

(ii) **Types of Culpability.** Subsection (1) also introduces the four mainstays of the culpability structure—purpose, knowledge, recklessness, and negligence. Each of these terms is defined in Subsection (2), and other common-law mens-rea terms are discarded. The applicable mens rea for the elements of a given offense is determined by what "the law may require." What "the law may require" is discovered, first, by examining the definition of the offense together with § 2.02(4) and, second, if no answer is forthcoming from that examination, by applying the interpretive provision specified in § 2.02(3).

The provision of only four basic levels of culpability—five if you count strict liability—represents one of the important insights underlying the Model Code. The Model Code position is that these concepts are both necessary and sufficient—necessary because the distinctions among them are required as a basis for crime definition and for discriminating among crimes as to relative seriousness, and sufficient because additional generalized discriminations would be superfluous. This proposition can be tested by asking yourself whether any concepts were encountered in the previously studied common-law materials that cannot be translated into one or more of these four ideas.

(iii) **Material Element.** The term "material element" is defined in § 1.13(9) and (10). The important point for present purposes is that the definition explicitly includes "(i) such conduct or (ii) such attendant circumstances or (iii) such a result of conduct as . . . is included . . . in the definition of the offense." Section 1.13 thus establishes the basic division of the actus reus of an offense into its conduct, circumstance, and result components. As has been noted, application of § 2.02 to an offense requires the allocation of each of the actus-reus elements of an offense to one of these three categories.

(iv) **Each Material Element.** In many ways, the word "each" is the most important word in Section 2.02(1). It requires that you ask about the level of culpability—purpose, knowledge, recklessness, or negligence—that the law makes applicable to "each" conduct, circumstance, and result element of the actus reus of an offense. Thus every actus-reus element of an offense has its own culpability requirement.

As an analytical matter, this provision represents one of the most important contributions of the Model Code. Thinking about mens rea separately for each element of the offense permits far more precision than was contemplated by the common-law tradition. This is true both for legislatures that seek to specify what the law should provide and for courts and juries that must implement legislative decisions in particular cases. Note that this analytical insight does not require the legislature to select any particular mens-rea requirement for a given element or offense. The legislature is completely free to set the mens rea at any one of the four levels it chooses. The structure simply requires the mens-rea question to be asked as to each element; it does not itself give the answer to that question. The answer is provided in the definition of the individual offense and in further provisions of § 2.02 discussed below.

2. **Purpose.** "Purpose" is defined in the ordinary-language sense of conscious objective or desire. Many enactments based on the Model Code have used the word "intent" to mean the same thing. Why, however, has the Model Code defined the term differently for conduct and result elements of the actus reus on the one hand and circumstance elements on the other? The answer is that, as a matter of common sense, circumstances cannot be intended. They concern matters external to the actor (property belongs to another, nighttime, age of the victim, status of the victim as a public officer) that either exist or do not exist. The actor can be aware of their existence or believe or hope that they exist, but it is a bit strained to think that a defendant has a purpose that it now be nighttime.

3. **Knowledge.** "Knowledge" is defined as awareness. Why in this case are conduct and circumstances distinguished from results? The answer is that one cannot "know" that results will flow from conduct. Common experience will indicate the degree of likelihood, but cause and effect are always matters of probability. "Knowledge" under the Model Code scheme is satisfied if the actor is "practically certain"

that the result will follow. Whether the result is desired is irrelevant to such knowledge, though of course it would be relevant to whether there was a purpose to cause the result. It should be noted that for most offenses either purpose or knowledge suffices and it is rarely important to distinguish between them.

4. **Recklessness.** Application of the Model Code concept of recklessness requires careful dissection of the definition in § 2.02(2)(c).[b] Unlike "purpose" and "knowledge," it applies in the same terms to conduct, circumstances, and results. One can be reckless as to the existence of a circumstance or to the likelihood that a result will follow from conduct in many different ways. Whether one can be reckless as to the nature of conduct is more problematical, and has led some drafters of modern statutes to apply the definition only to circumstances and results and to require at least knowledge for all conduct. Can you understand why one might want to make such a distinction?[c]

Application of the definition of recklessness involves four different steps:

(i) **Advertence to the Risk.** One must determine the extent to which the actor was aware of the risk that the material element exists or will result. The actor must then have made a conscious decision to disregard the risk and nonetheless engage in the conduct. The common-law parallel is to those situations where actual foresight of risk was required.

(ii) **Application of External Standard.** One must then ask whether the defendant was blameworthy for having taken the risk. This determination will be made by the jury or, in bench trials, by the judge. It requires evaluation of the "quantum of blame" involved in taking the risk, made by asking whether disregard of the risk "involve[d] a gross deviation from the standard of conduct that a law-abiding person would observe in the actor's situation." While this language is obviously not self-executing, it is designed to inform the blameworthiness inquiry by indicating that only serious deviations from the norm should give rise to criminal liability.

(iii) **Substantial and Unjustifiable Risk.** Obviously relevant to the blameworthiness judgment are the likelihood or predictability that the risk will be realized and the justifications one might have for taking it. Physicians are frequently called upon to take very substantial risks, but such risks can be entirely justifiable given the alternatives. Application of the external standard to the defendant's behavior thus must take into account whether the risk was substantial and justifiable in the context presented. In addition, the language of § 2.02(3)(c) requires that "the nature and purpose of the actor's conduct

[b] The meaning of recklessness under the Model Code is extensively discussed in Treiman, Recklessness and the Model Penal Code, 9 Am.J.Crim.Law 281 (1981). Professor Treiman also considers in detail how the Model Code's concept of recklessness has been implemented in jurisdictions with recent criminal code revisions and proposals.

[c] One of its costs is that it puts a premium on being able to distinguish conduct elements from circumstances and results. Thus the inevitably somewhat arbitrary process of categorization could become crucial in determining the appropriate level of culpability.

and the circumstances known to him" be considered. This, together with the requirement that the defendant actually be aware of the risk, means that the defendant must also have been aware of the factors that make the risk substantial and unjustifiable, though of course the defendant need not have believed that the risk should not have been taken. In effect, therefore, what the decision-maker must ask is whether, given all that was known about the risks, the defendant deviated in a gross manner from law-abiding behavior by engaging in the conduct and taking the risk.

(iv) **The Actor's Situation.** The word "situation" contains an important and deliberate ambiguity. Suppose, for example, that the defendant is blind or suffers from some other physical disability that impairs perception or judgment. Should such a person be held to the same standard of law-abiding behavior as everyone else? Or suppose the defendant is drunk. Should such a person be held to the standard of the drunk law-abiding person, or the sober law-abiding person? The function of the word "situation" is to permit the courts to personalize the standard in situations where it seems appropriate, and not to do so in situations where it seems inappropriate. A decision was made by the drafters of the Model Code not to resolve such questions in advance but to leave the matter to judicial evolution. Mitigation or exoneration based on individual characteristics of the offender can substantially undermine the functions of the criminal law if taken to extremes. This does not mean, however, that the criminal law should never take individual disabilities into account. One of the serious tensions of the law is where lines of this sort should be drawn. The problem surfaces in numerous places and raises policy questions of the most fundamental kind. The decision reflected in the Model Code is to leave it in this case to judicial resolution.

One final observation should be added about the recklessness inquiry and its relation to the definition of "knowledge." When dealing with result elements, it might be argued, there is a fine line between being "practically certain" that a result will ensue and disregarding a "substantial and unjustifiable risk" that the result will ensue. Does this draw too fine a line to be intelligible? The answer is that maybe it does, but it makes little practical difference. Most cases turning on the occurrence of results involve one or another form of criminal homicide. There are special rules to deal with this problem in the law of homicide, even under the Model Penal Code. This issue will be dealt with at pages 905–23, infra, and need not be of concern now. Few offenses other than homicide turn on results actually caused, and even fewer turn on the difference between results caused knowingly and results caused recklessly. The problem does arise, however, as in the provisions of § 211.1(2)(b) of the Model Code, which defines aggravated assault as occurring, inter alia, when one "knowingly causes bodily injury to another with a deadly weapon." Can you make sense of the difference between knowledge and recklessness in this context? If not, what should be done about it?

5. **Negligence.** The major difference between recklessness and negligence is that negligence is based on inattention to risk. The first

step in application of the concept is for the decision-maker to identify the risks that actually existed, given the defendant's conduct. This requires an independent judgment, i.e., independent of the defendant's own perceptions, of the substantiality of the risk and the justifications for taking it. Once this has been determined, the question is whether the defendant was blameworthy for not having perceived the risk— whether the defendant should have perceived it and behaved different- ly. This judgment is made by asking whether the actor's failure to perceive the risk "involve[d] a gross deviation from the standard of care that a reasonable person would observe in the actor's situation." Again, the decision-maker is to determine what the defendant actually knew about the situation and what the defendant's purposes were. The question, then, is given what the defendant knew and meant to do, did the failure to perceive the risks involve a "gross deviation" from the perceptions we might expect to govern the conduct of a reasonable person in that situation? As with recklessness, the word "situation" is designedly ambiguous, permitting personalization of the external stan- dard in cases where it is deemed appropriate.

The Model Code thus reflects the judgment that criminal liability may legitimately be predicated upon negligence. Yet a review of the specific offenses in the Model Code demonstrates that the drafters rarely chose to base liability on negligence. The most important negligence offense is negligent homicide (§ 210.4) and there are few others (e.g., § 211.1(1)(b)). But the minimum culpability established by the Model Code for most criminal offenses is recklessness. Indeed, as subsequent materials explain, it seems clear that the Model Code relies less on negligence as the basis for criminal liability than did the common law. While the Model Code has not accepted the arguments of the critics of negligence liability, it has stimulated a significant modifi- cation of the law in this respect.

6. **Offense Silent on Culpability.** Section 2.02(3) establishes a drafting convention followed by the Model Code, and also an important substantive conclusion. These two points should be separately consid- ered.

Section 2.02(3) states that recklessness is the minimum culpability required for every element of every offense, absent specific provision to the contrary in a particular definition. As a drafting matter, such a provision is a great convenience. It eliminates the necessity to state a culpability requirement for each separate actus-reus element of an offense and thus makes the defining process less cumbersome. It permits implementation of an important analytical insight of the Model Code—that culpability should be established in advance for each ele- ment of an offense—without unnecessary verbiage in the definitions themselves.

Section 2.02(3) also expresses an important substantive judgment. It provides that a minimum culpability of recklessness is required for each element of a criminal offense, absent particular provision to the contrary in the definition. As noted above, this goes a long way towards reducing the incidence of negligence liability in the criminal law. It indicates that liability based on negligence should be viewed as exceptional and that, if adopted, the decision to do so should be based on a particularized judgment and not on a generalized assumption that negligence is usually, or even frequently, appropriate.

It should be noted that § 2.02(3) is defended by its drafters as a statement of the usual common-law position on minimum culpability in the absence of specific statement. Whether this assertion is descriptively accurate can be doubted and is called into question in some of the materials that follow. In any event, § 2.02(3) expresses an important normative proposition, the correctness of which can be debated independently of the analytical structure established by the Model Code culpability provisions.

7. **Ambiguous Provision of Culpability.** A second drafting convention is established by § 2.02(4). It is intended merely to resolve grammatical ambiguities, but its application is not always as straightforward as might at first appear. Four illustrations are given below: the first two are cases where the application of § 2.02(4) presents little difficulty; the third is a straightforward application of § 2.02(3); the last raises a common point of confusion between § 2.02(3) and § 2.02(4), where the answer intended by the drafters of the Model Code is clear but how that answer is derived from the text of § 2.02(4) is not.

(i) **False Imprisonment.** Section 212.3 punishes one who "knowingly restrains another unlawfully so as to interfere substantially with his liberty." Must the defendant know that a substantial interference with liberty has resulted? The answer provided by § 2.02(4) is "yes."

The key to understanding § 2.02(4) is first to break the offense into its actus reus components. Here, there are four: "restrains," "another [person]," "unlawfully," and "so as to interfere substantially with his liberty." The next step is to ask why the word "knowingly" is included in the definition of the offense. The answer is that it *at least* establishes that the defendant must know that one of the actus reus elements (the restraint) has occurred.

As a grammatical matter, the definition in § 212.3 is ambiguous. One cannot tell from reading the definition alone whether the word "knowingly" was intended to modify only the word "restrains" or whether it was intended to modify the remaining words in the sentence. Section 2.02(4) was included for the purpose of resolving such a grammatical ambiguity, *and only for that purpose.* It applies when a mens rea term is included in the definition of an offense to establish whether the defendant must have a purpose that an actus reus element occur, must know that it occurred, or must be reckless or negligent as to its occurrence. It says that "unless a contrary purpose plainly appears" from the definition of the offense, a mens rea term that provides the culpability for one actus reus element also provides the culpability for all of the other actus reus elements. Since it is not clear from reading the definition in § 212.3 whether "knowingly" applies only to "restrains" or whether it also is meant to apply to the other actus reus elements of the offense, the mens rea of "knowingly" should be applied to all of them.

(ii) **Reckless Burning.** Section 220.1(2)(a) punishes one who "purposely starts a fire . . . and thereby recklessly places another person in danger of death or bodily injury." Does § 2.02(4) mean that the defendant must "purposely" create the danger of death or bodily injury to another? Plainly not. Here the definition is clear that "recklessly" modifies the element "places another person in danger of death or bodily injury," and there is no ambiguity for § 2.02(4) to resolve.

(iii) **Escape.** Section 242.6(1) covers one who "fails to return to official detention following temporary leave granted for a . . . limited period." What is the mens rea for the "limited period" component of the offense? Must the defendant know that the length of time for which leave was granted has expired? The answer is that "recklessness" is the mens rea as to this element. No mens rea term is included in the definition of the offense, and § 2.02(3) provides that recklessness is required as to all actus reus elements in such a case.

(iv) **Hindering Prosecution.** Section 242.3(5) provides that a person commits an offense "if, with purpose to hinder the apprehension, prosecution, conviction or punishment of another for crime, he . . . volunteers false information to a law enforcement officer." What is the mens rea for the element "false?"

Section 2.02(4) might be read to say that if a culpability term is used anywhere in the definition of the offense, it applies to every element of the offense "unless a contrary purpose plainly appears." Under this reading, purpose would apply to all elements of § 242.3(5) since the defendant must have a "purpose to hinder" and since there is no indication that this purpose need not accompany the commission of each element of the offense. Since "purpose" means "knowledge" as to circumstance elements under § 2.02(2)(a)(ii), "knowledge" would be required for the circumstance element "false" under this reading of § 2.02(4).

Although this is certainly a plausible reading of § 2.02(4), it is not the reading the drafters intended. The intended reading can be derived from the following reasoning. As in the false imprisonment example above, the first step is to isolate the actus reus elements of the offense. Here they are "volunteers," "false," "information," and "to a law enforcement officer." The next step is to ask whether there are any mens rea words in the offense designed to state whether the frame of mind described as purpose, knowledge, recklessness, or negligence applies to one of these actus reus elements. There are no such mens rea words in this offense. Here the purpose of including the mens rea phrase in the definition of the offense is not to designate the mens rea required for any given actus reus element, but to describe a collateral objective or motive that must accompany the defendant's conduct. The defendant must, in effect, hope that the conduct will have the described impact on law enforcement. That impact need not in fact occur; the defendant is still guilty even if the officer disbelieves the defendant and does nothing in response to the false information.[d] The motive or purpose must exist independently of any mens rea that may or may not be required for each of the actus reus elements of the offense.

The intent of the drafters of § 2.02(4) is that collateral motives or purposes of this sort should be ignored in applying the drafting conventions of § 2.02. Such motives or purposes are additional mens rea elements of the crimes in which they are required; they are not intended to supply the mens rea for any of the actus reus elements of the offense.[e] Instead, one must ask whether the offense contains any mens rea words that are plainly intended to describe the mental state the defendant must have as to whether an actus reus element of the offense has occurred. Section 242.3(5) has no such mens rea words, and hence the mens rea for "false" would be "reckless," derived from the provisions of § 2.02(3).

Contrast the situation that would occur if the definition of the offense were "if, with purpose to hinder the apprehension, prosecution, conviction or punishment of another for crime, he knowingly volunteers false information to a law enforcement officer." In that case, the function of the word "knowingly" would be at least to describe the mens rea for the element "volunteers"; it has nothing to do with any collateral motives or objectives that the defendant must have, but is at least intended to require that the defendant "know" that certain conduct has occurred. If this were the definition of the offense, the mens rea for "false" would be "knowledge," derived from the provisions of § 2.02(4) as in the false imprisonment example given above.[f]

8. **Hierarchy of Model Penal Code Culpability Terms.** Section 2.02(5) ranks the four Model Code culpability terms. It provides that if negligence is the mens rea required for a given element the prosecution can establish its case by proving purpose, knowledge, recklessness, or negligence. Plainly, if negligence is sufficient, the defendant is *more* culpable, not less, if purpose, knowledge, or recklessness can be proved.

[d] Recall the discussion of common law "specific intent" crimes by Holmes, pages 229–31, supra. A crime is often defined to include a collateral motive or objective, independently of the mens rea required for its actus reus elements, where the objective is to prevent a particular kind of harm from occurring and to intervene before the harm has actually occurred. Such motives or objectives are also frequently used for grading purposes. In the case of hindering prosecution, for example, there is a sense in which the law is intervening before the ultimate harm of actual interference with apprehension, prosecution, conviction, or punishment has occurred, and there is also a grading differential between volunteering false information that would be punished by § 242.3 and similar behavior, committed for other purposes, that would be punished by § 241.5.

[e] This is the common-law position in this situation. In common-law terms, as illustrated at page 253, infra, general-intent mistake rules were applied to the actus reus elements of specific-intent crimes where the function of the specific intent was to state a collateral motive or objective with which the crime was committed and where the mistake was not relevant to the existence of the collateral motive or objective.

[f] Compare the definition of falsely incriminating another in § 241.5 of the Model Code. That crime is committed if one "knowingly gives false information to any law enforcement officer with purpose to implicate another." Applying § 2.02(4), the mens rea for the element "false" would be "knowledge." If the word "knowingly" were omitted from the definition and it was otherwise worded the same, the mens rea for "false" would be recklessness. Section 2.02(4) would not apply, and the answer would be derived from § 2.02(3).

Similarly, if recklessness is required by the definition of a particular offense, proof of knowledge or purpose should also suffice. Section 2.02(5) thus stands for the common-sense proposition that if the prosecutor proves the defendant more blameworthy than is required by the offense charged, the defendant should be convicted.

9. **Illustrative Problems.** As should be apparent by now, the Model Penal Code culpability structure is neither self-executing nor easy to apply. It requires careful thought and analysis. Moreover, many questions yet to be considered will turn on correct application of its provisions. At this stage, therefore, the student should work through § 2.02 and the preceding notes carefully, and should test understanding by examining particular crimes defined by the Model Code and by isolating the actus-reus and mens-rea elements of each offense. Can you answer the following questions?

(i) What is the mens rea for "thing which may be useful for escape" in § 242.7(1)?

(ii) What is the mens rea for "likely to provoke violent or disorderly response" in § 250.4(2)?

(iii) What is the mens rea for "unless . . . the actor is licensed or privileged to enter" in burglary, contained in § 221.1(1)?

(iv) What is the mens rea for the elements "dwelling at night" in § 221.2(1) of the Model Code? For "building or occupied structure"? For "not licensed or privileged to do so"? Must the defendant in fact not be licensed or privileged to enter?

(v) What is the mens rea for "less than 10 years old" in § 213.1(1)(d)? For "less than [16] years old" in § 213.3(1)(a)? Be careful with these two questions. You need to take account of §§ 213.6(1) and 1.13(16) in your answers.

10. **Application of Model Code to Previously Considered Cases.** Another useful exercise to test your understanding of the Model Code is to analyze how actual cases previously considered would have been decided under the Model Code. For example:

(i) On the facts of *Morissette,* page 221, supra, would the defendant be entitled to defend on the basis that he thought the casings were abandoned if he were prosecuted under § 223.2(1) of the Model Code?

(ii) For what offenses could Faulkner (page 196, supra) be prosecuted under the Model Code? What mens rea would have to be established for each possibility?

SECTION 2: IGNORANCE OR MISTAKE

SUBSECTION A: IGNORANCE OR MISTAKE OF FACT

UNITED STATES v. SHORT

United States Court of Military Appeals, 1954.
4 C.M.A. 437, 16 C.M.R. 11.

QUINN, CHIEF JUDGE. [The defendant was convicted of assault with intent to commit rape. The trial was a general court martial held in Japan. The defendant testified that he thought the alleged victim, Tomobe, was a prostitute and that he thought she was consenting to his advances. Tomobe testified that she was forcibly assaulted. The defendant sought an instruction to the effect that "in order to constitute an offense, the accused must think [the] victim is not consenting because he must intend not only to have carnal knowledge of the woman but to do so by force." This instruction was not given. On appeal, the majority held that it was correctly withheld.]

[T]he accused argues that this instruction sought, in essence, to present a defense of mistake of fact. . . . We assume for the purposes of this case that sufficient evidence appears in the record from which it may reasonably be inferred the accused believed that Tomobe consented to his "proposition." However, the question still to be answered is whether the instruction requested is legally correct. The accused stresses the similarity of the requested instruction to that in McQuirk v. State, 84 Ala. 435, 4 So. 775 (1888). In that case the accused was charged with rape. The evidence showed that the prosecutrix was weak-minded. The defendant maintained that he believed she had consented to the act. He requested the following instruction which was denied by the trial judge:

"If the jury believe, from the evidence, that the conduct of the prosecutrix was such towards the defendant, at the time of the alleged rape, as to create in the mind of the defendant the honest and reasonable belief that she had consented, or was willing for defendant to have connection with her, they must acquit the defendant."

On appeal the conviction was reversed because of the failure of the trial judge to give the requested instruction.

It is immediately apparent that the requested instruction in this case is markedly different from that in *McQuirk*. It fails to qualify the accused's belief by requiring that it be reasonable and honest. This omission is substantial. The requested instruction also assumes too much. When consent is in issue, whether or not it was given is a question of fact for the court.[a] It, not the accused, must determine whether the woman's conduct was such as to lead the accused to believe she had consented to his acts. The accused's personal evaluation of the circumstances is but one factor to be considered by the court; it is not conclusive. . . .

The decision . . . is affirmed.

BROSMAN, JUDGE [dissenting]. . . . Rape . . . has ordinarily been treated as requiring only a general criminal intent. . . . However, assault with intent to commit rape would seem to occupy a quite different position—since the very designation of the offense indicates the requirement of a specific intent. . . . An *unreasonable* mistake of fact could perhaps not serve to deny criminal liability for a consummated rape. But could it negative the prerequisites for a finding of guilt of assault with intent to commit rape . . . ?

Assault with intent to commit rape demands proof of an assault on the prosecutrix accompanied by an intent to have unlawful sexual intercourse by force and without her consent—a purpose to overcome any resistance by force. If the woman consents to the application of force to her body, there would presumably be no assault in the first instance. Of course, if she had consented to sexual intercourse—that is, if her "will" favored such a result—she would also ordinarily have consented to that fondling which frequently precedes the act of coition. Thus, acts like those before us here would not partake of their usual character of a battery.

Ignorance or mistake of fact—if reasonable—normally provides a defense to an accused. . . . I would suppose that the type of consent with which we are now dealing is "factual" in nature, and that a mistake as to the woman's attitude would constitute one of fact. Thus, if the accused believed reasonably that the Japanese girl here was consenting to his proposals, he would be exonerated, I should think, even from the crime of assault. On the other hand, an unreasonable mistake on his part would not affect his liability for assault. . . .

But if an assault is to be found here—on the theory there was neither consent nor a reasonable mistake with regard thereto—does not the accused's mistake reenter the picture? One possibility is that the trier of fact may conclude that the girl did not consent, and that no reasonable man would have thought she did, but that the accused . . . genuinely believed that she was acquiescent. His purpose simply was to enjoy sexual relations with her under the circumstances presented to him. Those circumstances he unreasonably construed to amount to an invitation on her part. However, he did not intend coitus under any other circumstances. This might be because (i) he did not desire intercourse without full consent; or (ii) because he was just not the sort of person who worries about hypothetical problems. When an accused fondles a woman against a background of the frame of mind just mentioned, I would suppose him to be wanting in that variety of

[a] The reference to the "court" means the panel that in court-martial proceedings under the military system performs the function of a jury in a civilian case. [Footnote by eds.]

criminal purpose required for assault with intent to rape. One may well lack an intention to overcome resistance when nothing is present which seems to suggest the possibility of its presence.

It may be regarded as anomalous to conclude that an accused may be exonerated from guilt of assault with intent to commit rape because of an unreasonable mistake, whereas he could have been convicted lawfully of rape had penetration been effected under the same misapprehension. It is to be observed, however, that the anomaly is no greater than that involved in holding that an assault with intent to murder requires a specific intent to kill, whereas the crime of murder may be made out with a lesser intent. The fact of the matter is that a specific intent is, by definition, required for the present finding. The evidence, in my view, raised the possibility that a mistake of fact on the accused's part precluded that intent. . . .

It follows from what has been said that, as to mere assault, the accused is not entitled to an instruction on mistake of fact, unless the possibility of a *reasonable* mistake was raised by the evidence. On the other hand, as to assault with intent to rape, he is so entitled *regardless* of reasonableness. . . .

I would reverse the decision . . . .

———

NOTES ON MISTAKE OF FACT AT COMMON LAW

1. **Summary of Common-Law Methodology.** The traditional approach of the common law to mistakes of fact begins by differentiating between specific intent and general intent offenses. If the offense falls into the specific-intent category, then any honest mistake of fact that negates the specific intent is a defense. If the offense falls into the general-intent category, then the mistake must have been both honest and reasonable in order to constitute a defense.[a] Moreover, if the crime required a specific intent but the mistake was relevant to an element of the offense other than the specific intent, the courts followed the general-intent rule. Was the traditional approach followed in the majority opinion in *Short?* In the dissent? Are you concerned with the "anomaly" referred to in the next-to-last paragraph of the dissent?

2. **Specific Intent.** The common-law rule as to specific intent may be analyzed as simply a rule of logical relevance. Consider, for example, the facts of Green v. State, 153 Tex.Cr.R. 442, 221 S.W.2d 612 (1949). The defendant drove into a woodland and killed several hogs. He then loaded them into his car and took them home for dressing. The police arrived, correctly identified the hogs as belonging to someone else, and returned them to their owner. The defendant was prosecuted for stealing the hogs and testified that he had some hogs

---

[a] "If no specific intent or other special mental element is required for guilt of the offense charged, a mistake of fact will not be recognized as an excuse unless it was based upon reasonable grounds." Perkins, Ignorance and Mistake in Criminal Law, 88 U.Pa.L.Rev. 35, 56 (1939).

running on the range at the time and thought the hogs he killed were his own.

Larceny is traditionally defined as the taking and carrying away of the personal property of another with the intent permanently to deprive the other of his interest. While the defendant in *Green* unquestionably committed the actus reus of this offense, his testimony raises the question whether he had the required "intent permanently to deprive the other of his interest." The position that he is entitled to acquittal if his testimony is believed can be stated in either of two ways. First, the prosecutor must prove the existence of the "specific-intent" requirement in the definition of larceny. If the jury believes the defendant, the prosecution plainly has failed to prove its case. The defendant's testimony, in other words, is logically relevant to the existence of a required element of the offense. If his testimony is believed and if it effectively disproves an essential ingredient of the crime charged, he should be acquitted. Second, one can make the same point in the form of a "defense" of mistake: an honest mistake of fact, i.e., a mistake actually made by the defendant, is a defense to a specific-intent crime. For reasons that are obscured by history, judges trained in the common law preferred this second description.

One possible explanation for this preference can be derived from the normal progression of a trial that raises these issues. On the *Green* facts, the prosecutor would prove that the defendant killed the hogs, took them home, and was beginning to do things to them supporting the inference that he intended to treat them as his own. The prosecutor would then prove that the hogs belonged to someone else, and ask the jury to infer that the defendant knew this and intended to appropriate them from the owner. The prosecutor would try to substantiate this inference with such other evidence as might be available—e.g., statements by the defendant to the police or others, the method of acquiring the hogs (perhaps a surreptitious taking at night as opposed to an open taking in the daytime), the fact that the defendant had never owned hogs before, etc. At this point, the prosecutor would rest the case, and if the defendant introduced no evidence it would be up to the jury to decide whether the defendant in fact entertained the required intent. On the other hand, if the defendant testified that he owned hogs in the area, that he thought these were his hogs, that his hogs were of the same type and general appearance, that hogs in that area generally carried no clear marks of identification, etc., the complexion of the case would change completely. It could then be said that the defendant had raised a "mistake-of-fact defense" by his evidence, and the jury would be told that an honest mistake of fact is a defense in order to make sure that they understood the significance of the defendant's evidence.

Whatever the explanation for the common-law position, in any event, evidence of mistake of fact will normally be introduced in the first instance by the defendant, i.e., the defendant will ordinarily bear the initial burden of producing evidence. Indeed, an instruction on mistake will not be given unless the defendant has borne this burden or unless the possibility of a mistake is suggested by the prosecutor's evidence. But it should be noted that calling mistake of fact a defense generally has no consequence as to the prosecutor's ultimate burden of persuasion. The prosecutor has the burden of proving the specific intent beyond a reasonable doubt, and the defendant is thus entitled to prevail if the evidence merely raises a reasonable doubt in the mind of the jury as to the existence of the required intent.

3. **General Intent as Negligence.** The common-law rule as to general intent is more complex. Principally, this is because the meaning of "general intent" is obscure. At one level, the rule as to general intent could be analyzed in the same terms presented above as to specific intent—i.e., by saying that an honest and reasonable mistake of fact is a defense to a general-intent crime because "general intent" means negligence and a reasonable mistake is by definition not negligent.

Such a straightforward analysis does not dispose of the problem, however, even on the view that "general intent" states a negligence-type inquiry. One reason for this is that "negligence" as a mens-rea requirement is usually defined with considerably more elaboration than is typical in a "reasonable mistake-of-fact" instruction. Cases of negligent homicide, for example, typically identify the "quantum of blame or punishment" required for criminal negligence by rather elaborate instructions defining the term as some form of gross inadvertence. Care must therefore be taken in equating "negligence," as that term is frequently understood, to the "general intent" that is reflected in a reasonable mistake-of-fact instruction. Simply saying that "general intent" can be inferred from the natural and probable consequences of the defendant's conduct and that only a reasonable mistake of fact can negate the inference sets a much less demanding standard than is frequently meant by the term "negligence" in a criminal case.

4. **State v. Walker.** Consider also in connection with the previous note the rather subtle position reflected in State v. Walker, 35 N.C.App. 182, 241 S.E.2d 89 (1978). The defendant was charged with child abduction. Prior law was clear that the statute was violated only in cases of abduction where neither parent consented. The defendant and his son abducted a seven-year-old boy and a five-year-old girl as they were leaving a school bus in front of their school. They left with the two children in their care, and about five minutes later the girl was found walking back to the school. The boy was still missing at the time of trial. The boy was the grandson of the defendant, and the appellate court dismissed the case as to his abduction, on the ground that the father of the boy participated in the affair and thereby obviously gave his consent. The girl, however, was unrelated to the two men. The defendant's contention as to her is revealed in the following excerpt from the court's opinion:

> "[D]efendant contends that the trial judge erred in failing to instruct the jury on the defense of mistake of fact. In support of this argument defendant cites evidence tending to show that defendant and his son were operating under the mistaken belief

that the female child whom they allegedly abducted was Joy Walker, the granddaughter of defendant.

"It is an elementary principle that general criminal intent is an essential component of every malum-in-se criminal offense. Where *specific intent* is not an element of the offenses charged, '[a] person is presumed to intend the natural consequences of his act . . . .' Thus, an inference of general criminal intent is raised by evidence tending to show that the defendant committed the acts comprising the elements of the offense charged. The presumption of intent establishes a prima-facie case for the state, and if no opposing inferences are raised by the evidence, the trial judge is not required to instruct on general criminal intent. On the other hand, if an inference that the defendant committed the act without criminal intent is raised by the evidence then the presumption dissolves and the law with respect to intent 'becomes a part of the law of the case which should be explained and applied by the court to the evidence in the cause.'

"An examination of the evidence presented by the defendant reveals that the general principles recited above are applicable to the present case. The defendant testified that when he took the little girl, Vickie Irby, he believed that she was his granddaughter, Joy Walker; that he discerned the true identity of the child after he and his son had driven one-half mile from the school; that upon realizing that the child was not his granddaughter, he returned to the school and let the child out of the automobile. According to this evidence, if the facts had been as the defendant supposed, he would have committed no crime in taking Joy Walker since he was acting under the authority and with the consent of her father. The evidence viewed in this light obviously permits the inference that defendant in taking Vickie Irby was laboring under a mistake as to the identity of the little girl which could negate any criminal intent. In appropriate cases, culpable negligence has been considered the equivalent of criminal intent. Accordingly, in order to negate criminal intent, the mistake under which the defendant was acting must have been made in good faith and with due care.

"In accordance with the principles set forth, we hold that the trial judge erred in not declaring and explaining the law on a substantial feature of the case arising from the evidence that the defendant believed that he and his son were taking the latter's daughter, Joy Walker, when they were in fact taking Vickie Irby. . . . ."

If the defendant had offered no evidence of mistake, how would the jury have been instructed on the need for the prosecution to prove "general intent"? What function is performed on this assumption by the presumption of natural and probable consequences? Would it be correct to say on this assumption that "general intent" states a standard of negligence? Or would it be more correct to say that intent was fictionally and automatically "imputed" to the defendant? Does the mens-rea standard then change when the defendant offers evidence of mistake? Do you see why one would describe mistake of fact as a "defense" under the *Walker* decision rather than the statement of a rule of logical relevance? Is the *Walker* approach sound?

5. **General Intent as Recklessness.** Some do not agree that general intent refers to a mens rea of negligence. Instead, they argue that the minimum appropriate level of culpability is recklessness and that recklessness should be taken to require actual perception of the risk by the defendant. If this is an accurate description of what the common law meant by the term "general intent," how can the common-law rule as to mistake of fact be explained? If, in other words, the prosecutor must prove that the defendant actually was aware of the risk that the element of the offense existed or would result and nonetheless chose to run the risk, why is it that the defendant can defend on grounds of mistake only if the failure to perceive the risk was reasonable? There is an inconsistency, is there not, between establishing a mens rea of recklessness and permitting only a reasonable mistake as a defense?

The easy answer is that inclusion of the word "reasonable" in the statement of the common-law rule as to mistakes of fact in general-intent offenses is wrong. This has been the conclusion of many who have argued that recklessness is (or ought to be) the minimum meaning of mens rea in cases where no specific intent is required.[b] Nonetheless, the requirement that the mistake be reasonable is persistently stated in the cases and elsewhere in the literature.[c] Would it be possible to defend or explain the position that recklessness is the required mens rea but that only a reasonable mistake of fact will warrant an acquittal?

One possible explanation lies in the history of the common law and the common-law mode of thought as to such matters. As Sayre pointed out, pages 194–96, supra, there was a time when mens rea was regarded as a general state of wickedness of mind. During this period, defenses to criminal conduct were either non-existent or at the most primitive stages of development. Eventually, the law came to regard mens rea as more specifically related to the harms associated with particular offenses, and more sophisticated defenses related to culpability were established. This development did not occur of a piece, however, and it seems probable that the definition of "general intent" and the rule as to a mistake-of-fact defense were seen as two entirely different problems, or at least developed along essentially independent paths. The insight that mens rea and mistake should be treated as two sides of the same coin came later, and at a time when the law had assumed a settled course that the judges were not disposed to change. This line of speculation would suggest, in any event, that the integral relationship between these two ideas simply did not occur to the early common-law

[b] See, e.g., G. Williams, Criminal Law: The General Part 30–31, 53–59, 201–05 (2d ed. 1961); J. Hall, General Principles of Criminal Law 163–70, 366–72 (2d ed. 1960); cf. Keedy, Ignorance and Mistake in the Criminal Law, 22 Harv.L.Rev. 75, 84–85 (1908).

[c] See Howard, The Reasonableness of Mistake in the Criminal Law, 4 U.Queensland L.J. 45 (1961).

mind, and that by the time it did, the law had already crystallized in an acceptable and practical form.

A rationalization can also be advanced. Consider the following argument. The prosecutor must prove mens rea beyond a reasonable doubt, including the inference—typically based on objective facts and circumstantial evidence—that the defendant was reckless. Requiring a finding as to the defendant's subjective state of mind serves the philosophical objectives underlying the emphasis on fault in the criminal law and operates as a check on the extent to which circumstantial evidence can result in conviction. On the other hand, the defendant who seeks to rebut this subjective inference typically will do so through his or her own testimony. Since self-interest may induce stretching the truth, some restraint is necessary in order to give the jury a standard by which to judge the defendant's credibility. We may not be completely confident, in other words, that the jury will be able to sort out those defendants who testify truthfully from those who do not. This restraint is supplied by requiring that the defendant's testimony be corroborated by objective circumstances supporting the reasonableness of the conclusions the jury is being asked to draw. The law as to mistake of fact in general-intent crimes thus may be viewed as a special rule necessitated by the desire to control the reliability of evidence offered to support a claimed exculpation. Arguably, therefore, the common-law rule might be defended as a practical compromise that may not make sense to the theoretical purist, but that works pretty well in the everyday world of the criminal courtroom.

Is this a persuasive line of reasoning? It is essential that *some* rationale be advanced for the rules of mistake that are applied to modern cases. Is historical momentum sufficient? What should the rules be?

6. **General-Intent Elements of Specific-Intent Crimes.** Consider the following hypothetical. The common-law definition of burglary is "breaking and entering the dwelling house of another in the nighttime with the intent to commit a felony therein." The defendant lived in a subdivision where all houses looked alike, it was dark, the house was locked and the defendant had no keys, and the defendant made a mistake and broke into someone else's house in the belief that it was the defendant's house. Once there, the defendant realized the mistake and took some valuable jewelry. The defendant is plainly guilty of theft, which, you should assume, is a less serious offense than burglary. Should the defendant be acquitted of burglary if the defense evidence is believed? How would you expect the jury to be charged on the relevance of this defense? Can you see another mens-rea defense that might be raised?

7. **Grading Elements.** The common-law formulation of the mistake of fact rule applicable to general-intent crimes is usually qualified in the following manner:

> "If an actor honestly and reasonably, although mistakenly, believed the facts to be other than they were, and if his conduct would not have been criminal had the facts been as he believed

them to be, then his mistake is a defense if he is charged with a crime which requires 'mens rea' . . . ."

J. Michael & H. Wechsler, Criminal Law and Its Administration 756 (1940). Compare the Texas statute at issue in the *Green* case, page 248, supra:

> "If a person laboring under a mistake as to a particular fact shall do an act which would otherwise be criminal he is guilty of no offense, but the mistake of fact which will excuse must be such that the person so acting under a mistake would have been excusable had his conjecture as to the fact been correct, and it must also be such mistake as does not arise from a want of proper care on the part of the person so acting." [d]

Consider the following hypothetical in connection with these rules. The defendant commits a theft of jewelry actually valued at $5000. The defendant thought the item stolen was merely costume jewelry, and can prove that it was fenced for $100. Assume that the defendant's belief was reasonable under the circumstances. If the dividing line between grand larceny and petty larceny is $500, would evidence of the defendant's mistake be admissible as a basis for reducing the conviction to petty larceny? Or would the evidence be excluded and the defendant convicted of grand larceny no matter how reasonable the mistake? Is it correct to say that the effect of the rules as stated above is that strict liability is imposed for elements of a crime that are relevant only to grading?

Does the common-law rule reach the right answer in this context? Compare the *Faulkner* case, page 196, supra. There, the fact that the defendant had a "criminal" state of mind (intending to steal rum) was not sufficient to support conviction for another offense (arson) without independent proof of culpability as to the other offense. Is convicting the jewelry thief of grand larceny consistent with *Faulkner?* Is the common-law rule a remnant of the second stage in the evolution of mens rea described by Sayre on pages 194–96, supra, or is it a statement of appropriate contemporary culpability principles?

MODEL PENAL CODE

Section 2.04. Ignorance or Mistake

(1) Ignorance or mistake as to a matter of fact or law is a defense if:

    (a) the ignorance or mistake negatives the purpose, knowledge, belief, recklessness or negligence required to establish a material element of the offense; or

[d] See also R. Perkins & R. Boyce, Criminal Law 1045 (3d ed. 1982); Keedy, Ignorance and Mistake in the Criminal Law, 22 Harv.L.Rev. 75, 81–82 (1908). The excerpt from the *Walker* case, page 251, supra, also contains a similar statement of the rule.

(b) the law provides that the state of mind established by such ignorance or mistake constitutes a defense.

NOTES ON MISTAKE OF FACT AND THE MODEL PENAL CODE

1. **Methodology of the Model Code.** Section 2.04(1)(a) of the Model Code states a tautology. Ignorance or mistake of fact is a defense if, and only if, it shows that the defendant did not have the mens rea required for an element of an offense. Evidence of ignorance or mistake of fact is thus governed by a rule of logical relevance. If it is relevant to an assertion that the mens rea did not exist, the evidence is admissible to show that it did not. If it is irrelevant, the evidence is inadmissible. The Model Code position on mistakes of fact thus requires as a first step that one ascertain the appropriate mens rea for each of the elements of the offense involved. This is done by application of the culpability structure outlined in the preceding section. Once this is accomplished, the process of assessing the availability of a mistake-of-fact defense is mechanical and logical. The defendant who has the requisite mens rea is guilty. The defendant who does not must be acquitted.

Consider also the meaning of § 2.04(1)(b). Can you find examples in the Model Code of cases where "the law provides . . . a defense" based on assertions of ignorance or mistake of fact? Does § 230.1(1) contain some illustrations? Section 223.1(3)? Section 212.4? The answer is "yes" in all three instances.

2. **Innovations of the Model Code.** The combination of §§ 2.04(1)(a) and 2.02(3) of the Model Code would effect a substantial change in the law of mistake of fact as usually stated by the common law for "general-intent" crimes. Section 2.02(3) provides that recklessness is the minimum level of culpability for a criminal offense unless the definition of the offense specifies otherwise, and the occasions in the Model Code where a lesser culpability suffices are infrequent. Recklessness requires awareness of risk. Thus a defendant who was unaware of a risk that should have been perceived—who in other words made an honest but unreasonable mistake that led to a failure to perceive the risks associated with conduct—would be entitled to an acquittal under the Model Code approach. In most instances, the common law would describe such an offense as requiring a "general intent" and would foreclose a defense based on an unreasonable mistake. Is there a substantial difference between one who is reckless in the Model Code sense of that term and one whose mistake is not "honest and reasonable" as those words are used in the typical common-law formulation? Would it matter to the defendant which of the two formulations is chosen? To the prosecutor?

In addition to this important substantive innovation, it should also be borne in mind that § 2.04(1)(a) makes a significant analytical point that is independent of the conclusions reflected in § 2.02(3). To say that the relevance of mistakes of fact is simply a function of the mens rea required for a particular offense is not necessarily to say what level of mens rea should be required. Section 2.02(3), in other words, makes a substantive policy judgment about the level of mens rea generally to be required in the absence of legislative specification. The legislature remains free either to reject this conclusion or to dilute its effect by specifying different culpability levels in the definition of particular offenses. Section 2.02(3) can thus be regarded as wrong in general or in particular instances without affecting the basic analytical proposition underlying § 2.04(1)(a), namely that mistakes of fact are relevant only to the extent that they negate culpability and that the real issue to be faced in a mistake-of-fact case is what culpability is required for the element of the offense in question. Is this an improvement over the common-law approach? Why or why not?

3. **Application of the Model Code.** Consider how the common-law mistake cases previously studied would be decided under the Model Code. If Short (page 246, supra) had completed the act of intercourse, how would the jury be instructed if he were charged with rape under § 213.1? How would the jury be instructed if Green (page 248, supra) were charged with theft under § 223.2(1)? How would the jury be instructed if Walker (page 250, supra) were charged with interference with custody under § 212.4?

Now reconsider the burglary hypothetical in note 6, page 253, supra. If the defendant were charged with burglary under § 221.1 of the Model Code, how would the jury be instructed as to the relevance of the mistake?

4. **The Model Code and Grading Elements.** Now consider the larceny hypothetical in note 7, page 253, supra. How would the jury be instructed on the relevance of the defendant's mistake to the proper grade of theft if the defendant were charged under §§ 223.1(2) and 223.2(1) of the Model Code? Are grading factors "material elements" of the offense to which the culpability structure of § 2.02 applies? Is § 2.04(2) relevant to your answer? Does the Model Code treatment of this issue reach a different result than the common law? A better result?

Most modern statutes based on the Model Penal Code are ambiguous on the effect of mistakes of fact that relate only to grading elements. The federal code proposed by the Brown Commission (but not enacted by the Congress) was explicit on the point:

> "Except as otherwise expressly provided, culpability is not required with respect to any fact which is solely a basis . . . for grading."

Final Report of the National Commission on Reform of Federal Criminal Laws § 302(3)(c) (1971). The revised statute in Maine (title 17–A) seems to be to the same effect. Culpability is required in § 34(1) for each "element" of a crime. "Element" is defined in § 32 as "the forbidden conduct; the attendant circumstances specified in the definition of the crime; . . . and any required result." Section 34(4) then states that:

"Unless otherwise expressly provided, a culpable mental state need not be proved with respect to . . . [a]ny fact which is solely a basis for sentencing classification." [a]

SUBSECTION B: IGNORANCE OR MISTAKE AS TO CRIMINALITY

STATE v. DOWNS

Supreme Court of North Carolina, 1895.
116 N.C. 1064, 21 S.E. 689.

Indictment for the unlawful sale of spirituous liquors within two miles of Bethel Methodist Church in Macon County, tried before Shuford, J., and a jury, at Fall Term, 1894, of Macon Superior Court. The defendants were found guilty—under a special verdict—and appealed from the judgment thereon. The special verdict was as follows:

"The jury for their verdict say, that the defendants within two years before the finding of this bill of indictment sold spirituous liquor at the place of manufacture in Macon County, to-wit, one gallon to one David Lewis, within two miles of Bethel Church, in Macon County. Acts of 1881, chapter 234.[b]

"That before making said sale the defendants inquired of two reputable attorneys, who practice law in said county, if the said Bethel Church was incorporated [in the statute], and were informed by said attorneys that said church was not incorporated, and that it would be no violation of the law for them, the said defendants, to sell spirituous liquors at said place of manufacture in quantities not less than a gallon. . . .

"That the defendants did not intend to violate the law when they made said sale.

"If, from the foregoing facts, the court is of the opinion that the defendants are guilty, then the jury find them guilty; and if, from said facts, the court should be of the opinion that the defendants are not guilty, then the jury find them not guilty."

[a] To take one illustrative Maine offense, the definition of burglary is stated in Subsection (1) of § 401. Subsection (2) then states that burglary "is classified" into three levels of offenses based on various grading factors. The accompanying commentary refers to Subsection (2) as the "sentencing provisions" of the statute. It thus would appear that no culpability is required as to the grading factors contained in Subsection (2).

[b] This statute, extending over nine pages in the Laws of North Carolina 440 (1881), is a morass of detail. It contains lists by name of towns, counties, churches, schools, etc., as to which the sale of liquor is prohibited within one mile, two miles, and so on up to five. It puts the legality of sales to local option in some places, prohibits manufacture in others, and contains a series of exceptions to liability, the detail of which is illustrated by the proviso "that any law heretofore enacted prohibiting the sale of spirituous liquors near any church or school-house in Edgecombe county, is hereby repealed, except Draughan's school-house." The two-miles list extends for two and a half pages, and refers to the church here in question as "Bethel Church in Macon County." [Footnote by eds.]

CLARK, JUDGE. The indictment charges the sale of spirtuous liquor within two miles of Bethel Methodist Church in Macon County. The statute and the verdict both describe the church simply as Bethel Church in Macon County. There is nothing to indicate that the church is not one and the same. The added word "Methodist" in the indictment is simply harmless surplusage or immaterial variance. There is nothing tending to show that there was any ambiguity or more than one Bethel Church in the county or that the defendants were in any wise prejudiced in their defense or misled as to the church which was meant. It was not necessary that the indictment should specify the kind of spiruous liquor sold. That was a matter of evidence.

. . . Neither was it any defense that before making sale of the liquor the defendants on inquiry of counsel were told that the church was not incorporated and that it would be no violation of the law for the defendants to sell within two miles thereof at the place of manufacture in quantities not less than a gallon. "Ignorance of the law excuses no one," and the vicarious ignorance of counsel has no greater value. The law does not encourage ignorance in either. If ignorance of counsel would excuse violations of the criminal law, the more ignorant counsel could manage to be the more valuable and sought for, in many cases, would be his advice.

[Affirmed.]

NOTES ON IGNORANCE OR MISTAKE AS TO CRIMINALITY

1. **Application of the Maxim.** The *Downs* case illustrates the maxim, ignorantia juris neminem excusat.[a] As will be seen, the maxim is susceptible to misapplication and increasingly subject to exceptions. It is nevertheless descriptive of the dominant policy of the penal law with respect to awareness of illegality. Generally speaking, criminal liability does not depend on the actor's awareness of the illegality of conduct. Thus, ignorance or mistake regarding the criminality of one's act is no defense to criminal prosecution. In more familiar phrasing, "ignorance of the law is no excuse."

The idea that mistake or ignorance as to criminality should not have defensive significance is deeply embedded in the law. Some idea of the law's commitment to this policy may be illustrated by the following cases:

(i) **Rex v. Esop.** Esop was indicted for an "unnatural offence" committed aboard an East India ship lying in an English harbor. The accused was a native of Baghdad, and it was urged on his behalf that his act was no crime in that place. His counsel contended that "a person who comes into this country and does an act, believing that it is a perfectly innocent one, cannot be convicted according to the law of

[a] Sometimes given as ignorantia legis neminem excusat or as ignorantia juris non excusat.

England." The judges, however, were unanimously of the opinion that this was no defense.[b] Rex v. Esop, 173 Eng.Rep. 203 (Cent.Crim.Ct. 1836).

In the same vein, see Rex v. Bailey, 168 Eng.Rep. 651 (C.C. 1800). In that case, the defendant was tried for an assault committed on board ship. The statute under which the indictment was returned had been enacted while the defendant was at sea. There was no way he could have known of the enactment. The judges agreed that these facts made out a basis for requesting executive clemency but did not excuse the offense.

(ii) *Hopkins v. State.* The Reverend William F. Hopkins specialized in weddings. In an apparent attempt to discourage this enterprise, the legislature made it unlawful to erect or maintain any sign intended to aid in the solicitation or performance of marriages. Hopkins then sought the advice of the local state's attorney as to the legality of certain signs he proposed to erect. After receiving assurances that they would not violate the law, Hopkins put up one sign with the words, "Rev. W. F. Hopkins" and another with the legend, "W. F. Hopkins, Notary Public, Information."

Three years later, Hopkins was indicted for violating the anti-sign law. His offer of proof regarding the assurances by the state's attorney was excluded from evidence, and conviction resulted. In Hopkins v. State, 193 Md. 489, 499, 69 A.2d 456, 460 (1950), the state supreme court affirmed:

> "If the right of a person to erect a sign of a certain type and size depends upon the construction and application of a penal statute, and the right is somewhat doubtful, he erects the sign at his peril. In other words, a person who commits an act which the law declares to be criminal cannot be excused from punishment upon the theory that he misconstrued or misapplied the law."

The fact that the misconstruction was confirmed by the state's attorney was thought inconsequential.

2. **Problems With the Maxim.** Is it obvious that the claims of Downs, Seaman Esop, and Rev. Hopkins should have been rejected? Or is there something wrong with criminal conviction in such cases?

Some have argued that criminal punishment without regard to awareness of illegality is objectionable because it is ineffective. See Cass, Ignorance of the Law: A Maxim Reexamined, 17 Wm. & Mary L.Rev. 671, 684–85 (1976). The argument seems to be that the threat of penal sanctions can have no deterrent effect if the actor reasonably believes conduct to be lawful. The infliction of punishment in such cases is therefore seen as gratuitous and hence unjustified. Do you agree with this analysis? Why is it assumed that a reasonable belief in the legality of one's conduct vitiates the deterrent function of the law? Would not the imposition of penal sanctions in cases such as *Downs*, *Esop*, and *Hopkins* diminish the likelihood of such cases arising in the

---

[b] As it happened, the defense produced evidence from which "it appeared that the witnesses for the prosecution acted under the influence of spite and ill will," and thereby secured a verdict of acquittal.

future? Consider in this connection the following observations by Hall and Seligman, in Mistake of Law and Mens Rea, 8 U.Chi.L.Rev. 641, 648 (1941):

"This problem of educating the community by law is a practical one. A conviction for doing that which violates a new law, although not regarded as wrong in the community, is a matter of considerable interest and does a great deal to educate the community; an acquittal for violation of such a law, on the ground of a mistake of law, would scarcely cause a ripple in the current of community thought. As de Saint-Exupery has his airline manager say, to justify cutting pilots' punctuality bonuses whenever their planes started late, even where it was due to the weather and was not their fault: 'If you only punish men enough, the weather will improve.' It is a hard doctrine, but an effective one."

A different contention is that punishment on these facts is objectionable because it is unfair. Do you agree with this argument? In what sense is it unfair to punish without regard to awareness of illegality? Is the element of unfairness the same in each of the cases referred to above?

In connection with these questions, consider the following possible justifications for adherence to the traditional policy regarding ignorance of the law.

3. **Justifications for the Maxim.** Ignorantia juris neminem excusat is often associated with the statement that "everyone is presumed to know the law." At one time this "presumption" may have been a fair approximation of reality. Certainly, awareness of illegality would be especially likely in a legal system where the penal law was used almost exclusively to redress depredations against the person or property of another. It was with respect to such offenses, sometimes called mala in se, that one court commented that "every one has an innate sense of right and wrong, which enables him to know when he violates the law, and it is of no consequence, if he be not able to give the name, by which the offence is known in the law books, or to point out the nice distinctions between the different grades of offence." State v. Boyett, 32 N.C. 336, 343–44 (1849).

However plausible this view may have seemed at one time, the situation today is hardly comparable. Modern laws define a great many crimes that are not mala in se but only mala prohibita. For such offenses, no "innate sense of right and wrong" suffices, and the presumption that everyone knows the law seems an obvious fiction. Not surprisingly, it is precisely in the context of modern regulatory offenses that plausible claims of ignorance of the law most commonly arise. In such cases, the policy of ignorantia legis must be explained as something other than an attempt to describe reality. Consider the following efforts to provide a rationale for the ignorantia-legis concept:

(i) 1 J. Austin, Lectures on Jurisprudence 498–99 (3d ed. 1869):

"The only *sufficient* reason for the rule in question, seems to be this: that if ignorance of law were admitted as a ground of exemption, the courts would be involved in questions which it were scarcely possible to solve, and which would render the administration of justice next to impracticable. If ignorance of law were admitted as a ground of exemption, ignorance of law would always be alleged by the party, and the court, in every case, would be bound to decide the point.

"But, in order that the court might decide the point, it [is] incumbent upon the court to examine the following questions of fact: First, was the party ignorant of the law at the time of the alleged wrong? Second, assuming that he was ignorant of the law at the time of the wrong alleged, was his ignorance of the law *inevitable* ignorance, or had he been previously placed in such a position that he might have known the law, if he had duly tried?

"It is manifest that the latter question is not less material than the former. If he might have known the law in case he had duly tried . . . the conduct in question [is] imputable, in the last result, to his *negligence.*

"Now either of these questions [is] next to insoluble. Whether the party was *really* ignorant of the law, and was *so* ignorant of the law that he had no *surmise* of its provisions, could scarcely be determined by any evidence accessible to others. And for the purpose of determining the *cause* of his ignorance (its *reality* being ascertained), it [would be] incumbent upon the tribunal to unravel his previous history, and to search his whole life for the elements of a just solution."

(ii) O. Holmes, The Common Law 47–48 (1881):

"Ignorance of the law is no excuse for breaking it. This substantive principle is sometimes put in the form of a rule of evidence, that every one is presumed to know the law. It has accordingly been defended by Austin and others, on the ground of difficulty of proof. If justice requires the fact to be ascertained, the difficulty of doing so is no ground for refusing to try. But every one must feel that ignorance of the law could never be admitted as an excuse, even if the fact could be proved by sight and hearing in every case. Furthermore, now that parties can testify, it may be doubted whether a man's knowledge of the law is any harder to investigate than many questions which are gone into. The difficulty, such as it is, would be met by throwing the burden of proving ignorance on the law-breaker.

"The principle cannot be explained by saying that we are not only commanded to abstain from certain acts, but also to find out that we are commanded. For if there were such a second command, it is very clear that the guilt of failing to obey it would bear no proportion to that of disobeying the principal command if known, yet the failure to know would receive the same punishment as the failure to obey the principal law.

"The true explanation of the rule is the same as that which accounts for the law's indifference to a man's particular temperament, faculties, and so forth. Public policy sacrifices the individual to the general good. It is desirable that the burden of all should be equal, but it is still more desirable to put an end to robbery and murder. It is no doubt true that there are many cases in which the criminal could not have known that he was breaking the law, but to admit the excuse at all would be to encourage ignorance where the law-maker has determined to make men know and obey, and justice to the individual is rightly outweighed by the larger interests on the other side of the scale."

(iii) J. Hall, General Principles of Criminal Law 380–83 (2d ed. 1960): *

"Holmes' thesis, that to allow the defense would 'encourage ignorance where the lawmaker has determined to make men know and obey,' is surely questionable. [P]enal policy is not to make men know the law, as such, but to help them inhibit harmful conduct. The influence of penal law results not from men's learning criminal law as amateur lawyers, but from the significance of the public condemnation of, and imposition of punishment for, certain highly immoral acts. . . .

"A defensible theory of ignorantia juris must, it is suggested, find its origin in the central fact . . . that the meaning of the rules of substantive penal law is unavoidably vague, the degree of vagueness increasing as one proceeds from the core of the rules to their periphery. It is therefore possible to disagree indefinitely regarding the meaning of these words. But in adjudication, such indefinite disputation is barred because that is opposed to the character and requirements of a legal order, as is implied in the principle of legality. Accordingly, a basic axiom of legal semantics is that legal rules do or do not include certain behavior; and the linguistic problem must be definitely solved one way or the other, on that premise. These characteristics of legal adjudication imply a degree of necessary reliance upon authority. The debate must end and the court must decide one way or the other within a reasonable time. The various needs are met by prescribing a rational procedure and acceptance of the decisions of the 'competent' officials as authoritative. Such official declaration of the meaning of a law is what the law is, however circuitously that is determined.

"Now comes a defendant who truthfully pleads that he did not know that his conduct was criminal, implying that he thought it was legal. This may be because he did not know that any relevant legal prohibition existed (ignorance) or, if he did know any potentially relevant rule, that he decided it did not include his intended situation or conduct (mistake). In either case, such defenses always imply that the defendant thought he

* Reprinted with the permission of the author and Bobbs-Merrill Co., Inc.

was acting legally. If that plea were valid, the consequence would be: Whenever a defendant in a criminal case thought the law was thus and so, he is to be treated as though the law were thus and so, i.e., *the law actually is thus and so.* But such a doctrine would contradict the essential requisites of a legal system, the implications of the principle of legality.

"To permit an individual to plead successfully that he had a different opinion or interpretation of the law would contradict the . . . postulates of a legal order. For there is a basic incompatibility between asserting that the law is what certain officials declare it to be after a prescribed analysis, and asserting also, that those officials *must* declare it to be, i.e. that the law is, what defendants or their lawyers believed it to be. A legal order implies the rejection of such contradiction. It opposes objectivity to subjectivity, judicial process to individual opinion, official to lay, and authoritative to non-authoritative declarations of what the law is. This is the rationale of ignorantia juris neminem excusat."

4. **The Model Penal Code.** Section 2.02(9) of the Model Code provides that:

"Neither knowledge or recklessness or negligence as to whether conduct constitutes an offense or as to the existence, meaning or application of the law determining the elements of an offense is an element of such offense, unless the definition of the offense or the Code so provides."

The effect of this provision is to continue the ignorantia legis principle as part of the Model Code culpability structure.

Note that the Model Code provision suspends application of the ignorance-of-the-law concept in cases where "the Code so provides." An example is § 2.04(3), which is discussed following *Striggles*, the next main case.

5. **Proposals for Reform.** There have been occasional suggestions that the time has come for amelioration of the ignorantia juris concept. Consider the following two illustrations.

(i) **Perkins.** In Ignorance and Mistake in Criminal Law, 88 U.Pa.L.Rev. 35, 45 (1939), Professor Perkins argued that a defense should be given in the following situation:

"If the meaning of a statute is not clear, and has not been judicially determined, one who has acted in 'good faith' should not be held guilty of crime if his conduct would have been proper had the statute meant what he 'reasonably believed' it to mean, even if the court should decide later that the proper construction is otherwise."

If a court can be persuaded in the face of "fair warning" arguments that a statute should be construed to include the defendant's conduct, should the defendant also be able to argue that a reasonable construction of the statute to the contrary should be a defense? Is Perkins' suggestion consistent with the arguments that favor the ignorantia juris principle? Would it undermine that principle if his proposal were adopted?

(ii) **Revised New Jersey Code.** The revised New Jersey penal code provides that a belief that one's conduct does not constitute a crime is a defense if the mistake is reasonable and if the actor "diligently pursues all means available to ascertain the meaning and application of the offense to his conduct and honestly and in good faith concludes his conduct is not an offense in circumstances in which a law-abiding and prudent person would also so conclude." N.J.Stat.Ann. § 2C:2–4(c)(3). This provision is derived from an early and now superseded proposal for revision of the law of California. See Cal. Joint Leg. Comm. for Revision of the Pen.Code, Pen.Code Revision Project § 500(2)(b)(ii) (Tent. Draft No. 2, 1968). Would you support its adoption? Would any of the cases discussed above be decided differently if this provision were law? What would be the costs or potential dangers of following the New Jersey approach? Are they justified?

STATE v. STRIGGLES

Supreme Court of Iowa, 1926.
202 Iowa 1318, 210 N.W. 137.

ALBERT, J. We gather from the record and arguments of counsel the following history of the case at bar:

It appears that in the early part of 1923 there was installed in several places of business in the city of Des Moines a gum or mint vending machine. The machine and its workings are fully set out in the opinion in the case of State v. Ellis, 200 Iowa 1228, 206 N.W. 105 (1925), filed at the November, 1925, sitting of this court. In that opinion it was judicially determined that such machine was a gambling device within the inhibition of the statute.

On August 1, 1923, in several proceedings then pending in the municipal court of the city of Des Moines, a decision was rendered holding that such machine was not a gambling device. The distributors of the machine in question thereupon secured a certified copy of said decree, and equipped themselves with a letter from the county attorney, and also one from the mayor of the city, stating that such machine was not a gambling device. Thus equipped they presented themselves to appellant, Striggles, who conducted a restaurant in the city of Des Moines, and induced him to allow them to install a machine in his place of business.

Subsequent thereto, in the early part of 1925, the Polk County grand jury returned an indictment against appellant in which it charged that he did "willfully and unlawfully keep a house, shop, and place . . . resorted to for the purpose of gambling, and he . . . did then and there willfully and unlawfully permit and suffer divers persons, . . . in said house, shop, and place . . . to play a certain machine . . . being then and there a gambling device." On entering a plea of not guilty, the appellant was put on trial. He offered in evidence the aforesaid certified copy of the judgment decree of the court, and the letters from the county attorney and the mayor, which were properly objected to and the objection sustained. The appellant while testifying was permitted by the court to say that the exhibits had been presented to him before he permitted the machine to be installed. He was then asked by his counsel whether he relied on the contents of the papers when he gave his permission for installation of the machine. Objection to this line of testimony was sustained. He was also asked whether he would have permitted the machine to be installed had he believed it to be a gambling device. He was not permitted to answer this question.

It is first urged in this case that the certified copy of the judgment from the municipal court was admissible in evidence on the strength of the case of State v. O'Neil, 147 Iowa 513, 126 N.W. 454 (1910). A careful reading of the case, however, shows that it has no application to the case at bar. A certain statute of this state was held to be violative of the Constitution of the United States, and therefore void, in State v. Hanaphy, 117 Iowa 15, 90 N.W. 601 (1902), and State v. Bernstein, 129 Iowa 520, 105 N.W. 1015 (1906). The United States Supreme Court then decided Delamater v. South Dakota, 205 U.S. 93 (1907), [holding that a similar North Dakota statute was not unconstitutional]. On the strength of this opinion of the United States Supreme Court, we then overruled the *Hanaphy* and *Bernstein* cases, in McCollum v. McConaugy, 141 Iowa 172, 119 N.W. 539 (1909).

The crime with which O'Neil was charged was committed by him between the time of the filing of the opinion by this court and the filing of the opinion by the United States Supreme Court. We held in that case that the appellant could not be guilty because he was entitled to rely on the decision of this court, which held the law in question unconstitutional.

Cases cited from other jurisdictions in appellant's argument are in line with the *O'Neil* case. There is no case cited, nor can we find one on diligent search, holding that the decision of an inferior court can be relied upon to justify the defendant in a criminal case in the commission of the act which is alleged to be a crime. We are disposed to hold with the *O'Neil* case that, when the highest court of a jurisdiction passes on any given proposition, all citizens are entitled to rely upon such decision; but we refuse to hold that the decisions of any court below, inferior to the supreme court, are available as a defense under similar circumstances.

Affirmed.

NOTES ON OFFICIAL MISSTATEMENT OF CRIMINAL LAW

1. **The *O'Neil* Case.** The *Striggles* opinion refers to State v. O'Neil, 147 Iowa 513, 126 N.W. 454 (1910). The defendant in that case was prosecuted under a statute prohibiting the solicitation or acceptance of any order for the purchase, sale, shipment, or delivery of

intoxicating liquor. The Supreme Court of Iowa had previously declared the law invalid as an unconstitutional burden on interstate commerce. A contrary pronouncement by the United States Supreme Court prompted reassessment of that question, and the state court reversed its position. The acts with which O'Neil was charged had occurred after the decision invalidating the statute and before the decision announcing its revival. Defendant was convicted in the trial court on the basis of ignorantia juris, but the state supreme court reversed:

"[W]e think it would strike any reasonable and fair person as manifestly unjust that one should be adjudged criminal in having done an act not morally wrong, but only wrong because prohibited by statute, that is, an act malum prohibitum, and not malum in se, relying upon the decisions of the highest court in the state holding such statute to be wholly invalid because in excess of the power of the legislature to enact it. . . .

"To the ordinary mind it would smack of absurdity to say that defendant ought to have known that the statute was constitutional, and would in case he violated it be enforced against him, although the supreme court of the state had fully considered the validity of the statute as against the claim that it was unconstitutional, and had unanimously held that it was in excess of state legislative power as to its entire subject-matter, and therefore invalid. Under such circumstances, it is plain that there should be some relief to defendant from punishment, for the very purpose of punishment is defeated, if unreasonably and arbitrarily imposed. Respect for law, which is the most cogent force in prompting orderly conduct in a civilized community, is weakened, if men are punished for acts which according to the general consensus of opinion they were justified in believing to be morally right and in accordance with law."

2. **Questions on *Striggles* and *O'Neil*.** Assume, arguendo, that the *O'Neil* case was rightly decided. Why, then, did it not require a contrary result in *Striggles*? Is the reasoning in *O'Neil* inapplicable to *Striggles*? In particular, why is it any less "manifestly unjust" to convict Striggles simply because the official misstatement on which he relied originated with a lower court? With respect to him, is not the municipal court authoritative? Can the "ordinary mind" differentiate the two cases on this basis, or is there some other explanation?

On the other hand, perhaps *O'Neil* is the faulty decision. Given the generally steadfast adherence to ignorantia juris, what justifies an exception on the *O'Neil* facts? Is fairness to the defendant an adequate explanation? Recall the *Downs* case, where the defendants secured the advice of "two reputable attorneys," or *Hopkins,* where the defendant sought assurances from the local district attorney. Did not those defendants do all that they could have done to ascertain the law? Is conviction of them despite their best efforts any less "manifestly unjust" than conviction of O'Neil? Or does the exculpation of O'Neil address some concern other than that covered by the court's explanation? It was clear that Striggles actually relied on the municipal court opinion and that he believed he was not violating the law. Would it matter whether O'Neil actually knew about the decision declaring the statute invalid? If he did not, does this mean that Striggles had a better claim for exculpation?

3. **Statutory Provisions on Official Misstatement of Criminal Law.** As noted above, the Model Penal Code embraces the ignorantia-juris concept in § 2.02(9), with exceptions for cases where the definition of the offense or some other explicit provision of the Code otherwise provides. Section 2.04 provides a limited exception in the following terms:

"(3) A belief that conduct does not legally constitute an offense is a defense to a prosecution for that offense based upon such conduct when:

(a) the statute or other enactment defining the offense is not known to the actor and has not been published or otherwise reasonably made available prior to the conduct alleged; or

(b) he acts in reasonable reliance upon an official statement of the law, afterward determined to be invalid or erroneous, contained in (i) a statute or other enactment; (ii) a judicial decision, opinion or judgment; (iii) an administrative order or grant of permission; or (iv) an official interpretation of the public officer or body charged by law with responsibility for the interpretation, administration or enforcement of the law defining the offense.

"(4) The defendant must prove a defense arising under Subsection (3) of this Section by a preponderance of the evidence."

This provision has been defended on several grounds. First, it is argued that persons who fall within the exception will have engaged in behavior that is consistent with a law-abiding character, that the likelihood of collusion between the defendant and those upon whom he might rely is small, and that it will not be difficult in such a context to determine whether the statute has "reasonably [been] made available" or whether the defendant acted "in reasonable reliance" upon the named official sources. Second, and more broadly, it is observed that the exception is most likely to apply in regulatory contexts, where there are not significant moral overtones to the defendant's conduct. In such cases, only deliberate and repeated violations are appropriately punished by criminal sanctions.

Provisions based on the Model Code proposal have been enacted in at least 17 states, though several restrict the defense even more than does the Model Code. The language of Tex.Penal Code art. 8.03 is illustrative:

"(a) It is no defense to prosecution that the actor was ignorant of the provisions of any law after the law has taken effect.

"(b) It is an affirmative defense to prosecution that the actor reasonably believed the conduct charged did not constitute a crime and that he acted in reasonable reliance upon:

(1) an official statement of the law contained in a written order or grant of permission by an administrative agency charged by law with responsibility for interpreting the law in question; or

(2) a written interpretation of the law contained in an opinion of a court of record or made by a public official charged by law with responsibility for interpreting the law in question.

"(c) Although an actor's mistake of law may constitute a defense to the offense charged, he may nevertheless be convicted of a lesser included offense of which he would be guilty if the law were as he believed."

Have the Texas drafters improved or unduly restricted the Model Code proposal?

SUBSECTION C: OTHER MISTAKES OF LAW

STATE v. WOODS

Supreme Court of Vermont, 1935.
107 Vt. 354, 179 A. 1.

BUTTLES, SUPERIOR JUDGE. [The defendant was convicted of violating a statute euphemistically called the "Blanket Act":

"Section 8602. Parties found in bed together. A man with another man's wife, or a woman with another woman's husband, found in bed together, under circumstances affording presumption of an illicit intention, shall each be imprisoned in the state prison not more than three years or fined not more than one thousand dollars."

Defendant had driven to Reno with her three children and a married man. She was unmarried at the time. The man obtained in Reno what later turned out to be an invalid divorce, and married the defendant. They then returned to Vermont to live. Her argument on appeal and its rejection were explained by the court in the following language:]

The respondent does not challenge . . . the submission to the jury of the questions of fact upon which the determination below of the invalidity of the attempted Nevada divorce for the purposes of this case was based. Neither does she challenge the manner in which questions were submitted nor the determination by the court below that said attempted divorce is, for the purposes of this case, invalid. The verdict of the jury and the rulings of the trial court as to the invalidity of the attempted Nevada divorce are therefore conclusive upon the rights of the respondent in this case. . . .

The respondent contends . . . that an honest belief in the validity of the Reno divorce and of her subsequent marriage . . . would be a defense to this prosecution. There is much diversity of view as to whether a mistaken belief as to a fact, based upon reasonable grounds, may or may not constitute a defense in a criminal action of a nature similar to this one. In State v. Ackerly, 79 Vt. 69, 64 A. 450 (1906), this court held that an honest belief that his wife was dead was not a defense in a prosecution for bigamy, the respondent having attempted to remarry. . . .

But in State v. Audette, 81 Vt. 400, 70 A. 833 (1908), it was held that, under the circumstances of that case, ignorance of the fact that the woman whom the respondent attempted to marry had a husband living was available as a defense in a prosecution for adultery, he having been misled by her false statements as to that fact.

Here the respondent relies upon a mistake of law rather than of fact. Her presence in Reno and her marriage . . . immediately after the supposed divorce was granted by the judge who granted the decree indicate that she must have known all about the facts and circumstances of that proceeding. No claim is made that she did not know the facts. Her mistake, if one she made, was as to the legal effect in Vermont of the Nevada decree. The maxim, "ignorantia legis non excusat," and the corresponding presumption that everyone is conclusively presumed to know the law, are of unquestioned application in Vermont as elsewhere, both in civil and in criminal cases.

This presumption applies as well in prosecutions for adultery . . . .

It remains to consider whether this presumption is applicable in this case in view of the phraseology of [the statute] under which the respondent was prosecuted. Clearly it does apply if the words "under circumstances affording presumption of an illicit intention" mean that the act which the respondent intends to do is forbidden and not that the respondent must have acted with a guilty mind.

Obviously the real purpose of this section of the statute is to punish and prevent the commission of adultery. We perceive no reason why the rule regarding ignorance of the law should be any differently applied to a prosecution under this section than it would be if the prosecution were for adultery under one of the two preceding sections of the statute. Furthermore, the practical necessity for this rule if the criminal law is to be adequately enforced is as great with respect to this offense as any other. Our public policy as evidenced by our divorce statutes and our refusal to recognize the validity of attempted foreign divorces, under certain circumstances, would have little force if people could use such attempted foreign divorce coupled with a plea of ignorance of the law as a defense in prosecutions for sexual offenses.

When it is proved that the parties were found in bed together under circumstances affording presumption of an intention to commit the act as charged in the indictment or information, then the requirement of the statute is met and ignorance of the law cannot be urged as a defense.

Judgment that there is no error in the record.

NOTES ON OTHER MISTAKES OF LAW

1. **Introduction.** The materials studied thus far support two broad generalizations. First, ignorance or mistake as to the existence, scope, or meaning of the criminal law is generally not a defense to crime. Second, a mistake of fact that negates a required mens rea generally is a defense. The issue now to be considered concerns a third kind of mistake and the defensive significance it should be given.

The situation arises when the defendant makes a mistake of non-criminal law relevant to the criminality of conduct. Many crimes— larceny and burglary to name two—involve invasions of the property rights of others. The criminal law is not the general source of property rights. These rights are created by an elaborate body of civil law that determines their scope and the extent to which ordinary civil remedies can be invoked for their protection. The question to be considered is this: If the defendant makes a mistake as to the relevant law of property and wrongly comes to the conclusion that he or she "owns" certain property, is it a defense if the actor then does things with or to the property that would otherwise constitute larceny or burglary? The problem is a pervasive one. Can a mistake as to the validity of a divorce be offered as a defense to a charge of adultery, bigamy, or violation of the infamous "Blanket Act?" Can a mistake as to child-custody rights be a defense to abduction? *Woods* and the following notes deal with the response of the criminal law to these questions.

2. **The Common Law.** The common law, at least as it has emerged in modern times, was very clear on at least one aspect of this problem. If the offense required a specific intent or some other special mental element, a mistake of the non-criminal law that negated the required mens rea was a defense. Thus, for example, a mistake as to ownership of property is a defense to larceny because the requisite intent to deprive another would be lacking. The offense of persistent non-support as defined in § 230.5 of the Model Penal Code is another illustration: "A person commits a misdemeanor if he persistently fails to provide support which he can provide and which he knows he is legally obliged to provide to a spouse, child or other dependent." The legal obligation to provide support arises from the general provisions of family law and, in particular cases, may be governed by a support decree or some other specific court order. Since the offense as defined requires that one "know" of the legal obligation to provide support, any mistake as to the scope of the legal duty would be a defense under the common-law rule summarized above, as it would be under the Model Code itself.

The harder case for the common law was one where no special or specific intent was required. The rule as to general-intent crimes was often said to be that mistakes of this character were not a defense. Rarely were adequate reasons given to support this conclusion. Sometimes this result was said to be required by the policies underlying the particular offense before the court and thus not dictated by a generally applicable rule. More often, it was explained by a reflexive invocation of the principle that "ignorance of the law is no excuse."

3. **Background on Bigamy.** A special mens-rea policy frequently has been applied to the offense of bigamy. The original statute, adopted in England in 1603, imposed a mandatory death penalty on persons who married while already married. It established several specified situations in which remarriage was permitted: if the prior marriage had been annulled, dissolved by divorce, or was void because the parties had not reached the age of consent; if the prior spouse had been absent within the commonwealth for seven years and was not known to be alive; or if the prior spouse "shall be continually remaining beyond the seas by the space of seven years." [a] Derivative American statutes generally took a similar approach.[b] The pattern of early judicial interpretations was that the listed exceptions were exclusive and that no other remarriages would be excused. This led to the conclusion that bigamy was an offense of strict liability if the precise terms of the statutory exceptions were not met.

This view was rejected in the well known case of Regina v. Tolson, 23 Q.B.D. 168 (1889). The defendant's husband had deserted her in December of 1881. Defendant's inquiries about his whereabouts were met with the information that he had sailed for America and had been lost at sea when the ship sunk with no survivors. She remarried in January of 1887, before the expiration of the seven years specified by the bigamy statute, and he then reappeared in December of that year. A divided court held that a defense based on Tolson's good faith and reasonable belief that the husband was dead should have been permitted. The effect of the decision was that bigamy was declared a general-intent offense, and the normal rules as to mistake of fact became applicable.

American courts continue to divide on the question whether bigamy should be a strict-liability offense if the specified exceptions have not been met. The *Ackerly* decision, referred to in *Woods,* is thus illustrative of a line of decisions, rejected in *Tolson,* for which there is considerable precedential support.[c] Would you expect the defense raised in *Woods* to be successful if asserted by Woods' new husband to a charge of bigamy?

4. **Questions and Comments on Woods.** Consider the following variation of the *Woods* facts. Assume that no Reno divorce was involved, but that the defendant claimed that her purported spouse had

[a] 1 James 1, ch. 11, § 2 (1603).

[b] See, e.g., 12 Hening's Stat. 691 (Va. 1788), which also originally authorized the death penalty.

[c] More elaborate treatment of the history of the bigamy offense, as well as modern statutes, can be found in ALI, Model Penal Code and Commentaries, § 230.1, pp. 380–91 (1980).

told her that he had never been married, that she believed him, and that her mistake was reasonable. Would the Vermont court give her a defense if she could establish all of these points? If she could establish only that she honestly believed him but made an unreasonable mistake? Of what relevance is the statutory language "under circumstances affording presumption of an illicit intention" to your response? Does the Blanket Act establish an offense of specific intent, general intent, or strict liability?

One possible resolution of these questions is that the Blanket Act states a general-intent offense to which the traditional common-law doctrine regarding reasonable mistake of fact would be applicable. If this is so, *Woods* would seem to stand for the proposition that reasonable mistakes of fact will be a defense in situations in which functionally equivalent mistakes as to the non-criminal law will not.[d] The announced reason for this conclusion, moreover, is that "everyone is conclusively presumed to know the law." Does this follow? Was Woods more blameworthy than she would have been if her mistake had been one of fact? Less blameworthy? Do the reasons underlying the ignorantia juris concept apply to a case such as *Woods?*[e] Can you defend a distinction between general and specific intent in this context? If *Woods* is right, are the specific-intent cases wrong?

5. **The Model Penal Code.** Re-examine § 2.04(1)(a) of the Model Penal Code. Notice that it reads "[i]gnorance or mistake as to a matter of fact *or law* is a defense if . . . ." What is the function of the words "or law" in this formulation? The Model Code contains no adultery offense, but if it did contain one in identical language to the Blanket Act, what mens rea would be required for the element "with another woman's husband?" Would Woods have a defense if her mistake had

---

[d] The court in Long v. State, 44 Del. 262, 65 A.2d 489 (1949), was explicit on this point. *Long* was a bigamy prosecution based on remarriage following an invalid out-of-state divorce. The defendant had very carefully secured the best legal advice he could as to the validity of the divorce and, from all appearances, had acted reasonably and in good faith. The court noted its agreement with *Tolson* that bigamy should not be regarded as a strict-liability offense. Its discussion then included the following observations:

"The defense of mistake of fact is important only because it negatives a 'criminal mind,' general criminal intent. [W]e accept the view that the statute does not exclude as a defense the absence of general criminal intent; that is, the intent to do what would constitute a crime if the surrounding circumstances were such as a reasonable man in the defendant's position would likely believe them to be (the criminality . . . being measured by an objective standard).

"We turn now to the ground that this is a case to which the ignorance-of-law maxim applies. In many crimes involving a *specific* criminal intent, an honest mistake of law constitutes a defense if it negatives the specific intent [citing larceny and embezzlement cases]. As to crimes not involving a specific intent, an honest mistake of law is usually, though not invariably, held not to excuse conduct otherwise criminal. A mistake of law, where not a defense, may nevertheless negative a general criminal intent as effectively as would an exculpatory mistake of fact. Thus, mistake of law is disallowed as a defense in spite of the fact that it may show an absence of the criminal mind. . . . "

[e] In *Long*, the court followed the portion of its opinion quoted in the preceding footnote with an elaborate discussion of the rationale of the ignorantia juris concept and concluded, uniquely for an American court at that time, in favor of an exception in terms remarkably similar to the language of the New Jersey statute, quoted at page 264, supra. Was it necessary for the court to be so elaborate? Could the case have been resolved on a simpler and more direct ground?

been one of fact? Under what jury instruction? Would she have a defense in the case as it actually arose? Under what jury instruction?

Your understanding of § 2.04(1)(a) can be tested further by considering the following situations. (i) How would the *Tolson* case be decided if she were prosecuted under § 230.1 of the Model Penal Code? (ii) What result on the facts of *Woods* if the man were prosecuted for bigamy under § 230.1 of the Model Code? (iii) Assume that *A* lived with *B* long enough and under such conditions that under the law of the relevant jurisdiction their relationship amounted to a common-law marriage. *A*, unaware that the law has attached this conclusion to her relationship with *B*, marries *C*. *B* complains to the police and *A* is prosecuted for bigamy under § 230.1 of the Model Code. Is *A*'s evidence of ignorance of law admissible, and if so, under what jury instruction?

6. **Categorization of Mistakes under the Common Law.** Can you argue that Woods' mistake was one of fact? What is the difference between a mistake of law and a mistake of fact in this situation?

Consider in this connection People v. Bray, 52 Cal.App.3d 494, 124 Cal.Rptr. 913 (1975). The defendant was convicted on two counts of being a felon in possession of a concealable firearm. There was no doubt that he had possessed two concealable firearms; the question was whether he was a convicted felon. His only prior conviction had occurred in Kansas some years before, where he had pleaded guilty to being an accessory after the fact and had been sentenced to, and successfully served, a period of probation. Even the prosecutor was not sure that the offense involved was a felony under Kansas law. He sought to introduce expert testimony at the trial to the effect that it was. On numerous occasions, the defendant had been required to fill out forms asking if he had a prior felony conviction. On most, he had answered that he did not know and made full disclosure of the situation. California officials had permitted him to vote in the face of such disclosures. Would you characterize Bray's ignorance as of law or of fact? Is it different in kind from the mistake made by Ms. Woods? How would you expect the Vermont Supreme Court to decide the *Bray* case?

The California court that decided *Bray* never mentioned the possibility that Bray was ignorant of law. Instead, it reversed on the ground that the jury had not been properly instructed on the doctrine of mistake of fact:

> "Although the district attorney had great difficulty in determining whether the Kansas offense was a felony or a misdemeanor, he expects the layman Bray to know his status easily. There was no doubt Bray knew he had committed an offense; there was, however, evidence to the effect he did not know the offense was a felony. Without this knowledge Bray would be ignorant of the facts necessary for him to come within the proscription of [the statute]. Under these circumstances the requested instructions on mistake or ignorance of fact and knowledge of the facts which make the act unlawful should have been given."

Assume that California follows the common-law position illustrated by *Woods* and that the instruction on mistake of fact to which Bray was entitled was the typical common-law instruction on reasonable mistakes of fact for general-intent offenses. On these assumptions, does the quoted reasoning adequately explain why Bray should be entitled to a mistake defense? Could comparable reasoning have been applied in *Woods?*

7. **Categorization of Mistakes Under the Model Penal Code.** The Model Penal Code does not contain an offense comparable to the one charged in *Bray.* If it did, how would the *Bray* situation be analyzed? Before you answer too quickly, recall that § 2.02(9) extends the ignorantia juris concept to "the existence, meaning or application of the law determining the elements of an offense." Does this provision, or the general provision about mistakes of "fact or law" in Section 2.04(1)(a), apply to the *Bray* situation? By what criteria is the necessary categorization to be made? Can you think of simpler and more typical examples of the need for the language contained in § 2.02(9)? Do they help you answer the previous questions?

SECTION 3: THE SIGNIFICANCE OF INTOXICATION

DIRECTOR OF PUBLIC PROSECUTIONS v. MAJEWSKI

House of Lords, 1976.
[1976] 2 All E.R. 142.

LORD ELWYN-JONES, L.C. My Lords, Robert Stefan Majewski appeals against his conviction [for] assault occasioning actual bodily harm. [H]e was placed on probation for three years. Later he committed a further offence for which he was given an additional sentence of six months imprisonment for the original offences.

The appellant's case was that when the assaults were committed he was acting under the influence of a combination of drugs (not medically prescribed) and alcohol, to such an extent that he did not know what he was doing and that he remembered nothing of the incidents that had occurred. After medical evidence had been called by the defence as to the effect of the drugs and drink the appellant had taken, the learned judge, in the absence of the jury, ruled that he would direct the jury in due course that on the charges of assault occasioning actual bodily harm, the question whether he had taken drink or drugs was immaterial. The learned judge directed the jury that in relation to an offence not requiring a specific intent, the fact that a man has induced in himself a state in which he is under the influence of drink and drugs, is no defence. . . . He concluded ". . . on my direction in law you can ignore the subject of drink and drugs as being in any way a defence to any one or more of the counts in this indictment." . . .

In view of the conclusion to which I have come that the appeal should be dismissed . . . , it is desirable that I should refer in some detail to the facts, which were largely undisputed. During the evening of 19th February 1973 the appellant and his friend, Leonard Stace, who had also taken drugs and drink, went to the Bull public house in Basildon. The appellant obtained a drink and sat down in the lounge bar at a table by the door. Stace became involved in a disturbance. Glasses were broken. The landlord asked Stace to leave and escorted him to the door. As he did so, Stace called to the appellant: "He's putting me out." The appellant got up and prevented the landlord from getting Stace out and abused him. The landlord told them both to go. They refused. The appellant butted the landlord in the face and bruised it, and punched a customer. The customers in the bar and the landlord forced the two out through the bar doors. They re-entered by forcing the outer door, a glass panel of which was broken by Stace. The appellant punched the landlord and pulled a piece of broken glass from the frame and started swinging it at the landlord and a customer, cutting the landlord slightly on his arm. The appellant then burst through the inner door of the bar with such force that he fell on the floor. The landlord held him there until the police arrived. The appellant was violent and abusive and spat in the landlord's face. When the police came, a fierce struggle took place to get him out. He shouted at the police: "You pigs, I'll kill you all, you f . . . pigs, you bastards." P.C. Barkway said the appellant looked at him and kicked him deliberately. . . .

Cross-examined as to the appellant's condition that evening the publican said he seemed to have gone berserk, his eyes were a bit glazed and protruding. A customer said he was "glarey-eyed," and went "berserk" when the publican asked Stace to leave. He was screaming and shouting. A policeman said he was in a fearful temper.

The appellant gave evidence and said that on Saturday, 17th February 1973, he bought, not on prescription, about 440 Dexadrine tablets ("speeds") and early on Sunday morning consumed about half of them. That gave him plenty of energy until he "started coming down." He did not sleep throughout Sunday. On Monday evening at about 6:00 p.m. he acquired a bottle full of sodium nembutal tablets which he said were tranquillisers—"downers," "barbs"—and took about eight of them at about 6:30 p.m. He and his friends went to the Bull. He said he could remember nothing of what took place there save for a flash of recollection of Stace kicking a window. All he recollected of the police cell was asking the police to remove his handcuffs and then being injected.

In cross-examination he admitted he had been taking amphetamines and barbiturates, not on prescription, for two years, in large quantities. On occasions he drank barley wine or Scotch. He had sometimes "gone paranoid." This was the first time he had "completely blanked out."

Dr. Bird, called for the defence, said that the appellant had been treated for drug addiction since November 1971. There was no history in his case of psychiatric disorder or diagnosable mental illness, but the appellant had a personality disorder. Dr. Bird said that barbiturates and alcohol are known to potentiate each other and to produce rapid intoxication and affect a person's awareness of what was going on. In the last analysis one could be rendered unconscious and a condition known as pathological intoxication can occur, but it is uncommon and there are usually well-marked episodes. It would be possible, but unlikely, to achieve a state of automatism as a result of intoxication with barbiturates and alcohol or amphetamines and alcohol. Aggressive behavior is greater. After a concentration of alcohol and barbiturates it was not uncommon for "an amnesic patch" to ensue.

In cross-examination, Dr. Bird said he had never in practice come across a case of "pathological intoxication" and it is an unusual condition. It is quite possible that a person under the influence of barbiturates, amphetamines or alcohol or all three in combination may be able to form certain intentions and execute them, punching and kicking people, and yet afterwards be unable to remember anything about it. During such "disinhibited behaviour" he may do things which he would not do if he was not under the influence of the various sorts of drink and drugs about which evidence has been given.

In a statement Dr. Mitchell expressed the opinion that at the police station on the morning of 20th February, the appellant was completely out of control mentally and physically, which might have been due to "withdrawal symptoms."

The Court of Appeal dismissed the appeal against conviction but granted leave to appeal to your Lordships' House . . . . The appeal raises issues of considerable public importance. In giving the judgment of the Court of Appeal Lawton, L.J. rightly observed:

> "The facts are commonplace—indeed so commonplace that their very nature reveals how serious from a social and public standpoint the consequences would be if men could behave as the appellant did and then claim that they were not guilty of any offence."

Self-induced alcoholic intoxication has been a factor in crimes of violence, like assault, throughout the history of crime in this country. But voluntary drug taking with the potential and actual dangers to others it may cause has added a new dimension to the old problem with which the courts have had to deal in their endeavour to maintain order and to keep public and private violence under control. To achieve this is the prime purpose of the criminal law. I have said "the courts," for most of the relevant law has been made by the judges. A good deal of the argument in the hearing of this appeal turned on that judicial history, for the crux of the case for the Crown was that, illogical as the outcome may be said to be, the judges have evolved for the purpose of protecting the community a substantive rule of law that, in crimes of basic intent as distinct from crimes of specific intent, self-induced intoxication provides no defence and is irrelevant to offences of basic intent, such as assault.

The case of counsel for the appellant was that there was no such substantive rule of law and that if there was, it did violence to logic and ethics and to fundamental principles of the criminal law which had been evolved to determine when and where criminal responsibility should arise. His main propositions were as follows: (i) No man is guilty of a crime (save in relation to offences of strict liability) unless he has a guilty mind. (ii) A man who, though not insane, commits what would in ordinary circumstances be a crime when he is in such a mental state (whether it is called "automatism" or "pathological intoxication" or anything else) that he does not know what he is doing, lacks a guilty mind and is not criminally culpable for his actions. (iii) This is so whether the charge involves a specific (or "ulterior") intent or one involving only a general (or "basic") intent. (iv) The same principle applies whether the automatism was the result of causes beyond the control of the accused or was self-induced by the voluntary taking of drugs or drink. (v) Assaults being crimes involving a guilty mind, a man who in a state of automatism unlawfully assaults another must be regarded as free from blame and be entitled to acquittal. (vi) It is logically and ethically indefensible to convict such a man of assault. . . . (vii) There was accordingly a fatal misdirection. . . .

[Lord Elwyn-Jones began his consideration of these arguments with a general discussion of the meaning of mens rea and the definition of assault. He concluded that assault was a crime of "basic intent" and that recklessness was the minimum culpability ordinarily required. He then continued by asking:]

How does the factor of self-induced intoxication fit into [this] analysis? If a man consciously and deliberately takes alcohol and drugs not on medical prescription, but in order to escape from reality, to go "on a trip," to become hallucinated, whatever the description may be, and thereby disables himself from taking the care he might otherwise take and as a result by his subsequent actions causes injury to another—does our criminal law enable him to say that because he did not know what he was doing he lacked both intention and recklessness and accordingly is entitled to an acquittal?

Originally the common law would not and did not recognise self-induced intoxication as an excuse. . . . The authority which for the last half century has been relied on in this context has been the speech of Lord Birkenhead, L.C. in Director of Public Prosecutions v. Beard, [1920] A.C. 479, 494, [1920] All E.R. 21, 25:

"Under the law of England as it prevailed until early in the 19th century voluntary drunkenness was never an excuse for criminal misconduct; and indeed the classic authorities broadly assert that voluntary drunkenness must be considered rather an aggravation than a defence. This view was in terms based upon the principle that a man who by his own voluntary act debauches and destroys his will power shall be no better situated in regard to criminal acts than a sober man."

Lord Birkenhead, L.C. made an historical survey of the way the common law from the 16th century on dealt with the effect of self-induced intoxication on criminal responsibility. [He] concluded that . . . the decisions . . .

"establish where a specific intent is an essential element in the offence, evidence of a state of drunkenness rendering the accused incapable of forming such an intent should be taken into consideration in order to determine whether he had in fact formed the intent necessary to constitute the particular crime. If he was so drunk that he was incapable of forming the intent required he could not be convicted of a crime which was committed only if the intent was proved. . . . "

From this it seemed clear—and this is the interpretation which the judges have placed on the decision during the ensuing half-century— that it is only in the limited class of cases requiring proof of specific intent that drunkenness can exculpate. Otherwise in no case can it exempt completely from criminal liability. . . .

I do not for my part regard that general principle as either unethical or contrary to the principles of natural justice. If a man of his own volition takes a substance which causes him to cast off the restraints of reason and conscience, no wrong is done to him by holding him answerable criminally for any injury he may do while in that condition. His course of conduct in reducing himself by drugs and drink to that condition in my view supplies the evidence of mens rea, of guilty mind certainly sufficient for crimes of basic intent. It is a reckless course of conduct and recklessness is enough to constitute the necessary mens rea in assault cases . . . . The drunkenness is itself an intrinsic, an integral part of the crime, the other part being the evidence of the unlawful use of force against the victim. Together they add up to criminal recklessness. . . . This approach is in line with the American Model Code [Section 2.08(2)]:

"When recklessness establishes an element of the offence, if the actor, due to self-induced intoxication, is unaware of a risk of which he would have been aware had he been sober, such unawareness is immaterial."

Acceptance generally of intoxication as a defence (as distinct from the exceptional cases where some additional mental element above that of ordinary mens rea has to be proved) would in my view undermine the criminal law and I do not think that it is enough to say, as did counsel for the appellant, that we can rely on the good sense of the jury . . . to ensure that the guilty are convicted. It may well be that parliament will at some future time consider, as I think it should, the recommendation in the Butler Committee Report on Mentally Abnormal Offenders that a new offence of "dangerous intoxication" should be created. But in the meantime it would be irresponsible to abandon the common-law rule, as "mercifully relaxed," which the courts have followed for a century and a half. . . .

LORD SIMON OF GLAISDALE. My Lords, I have had the advantage of reading the speech prepared by my noble and learned friend, Lord Elwyn-Jones, L.C. I agree with it, and I would therefore dismiss the appeal. What follows is by way of marginal comment.

(i) One of the prime purposes of the criminal law, with its penal sanctions, is the protection from certain proscribed conduct of persons who are pursuing their lawful lives. Unprovoked violence has, from time immemorial, been a significant part of such proscribed conduct. To accede to the argument on behalf of the appellant would leave the citizen legally unprotected from unprovoked violence, where such violence was the consequence of drink or drugs having obliterated the capacity of the perpetrator to know what he was doing or what were its consequences.

(ii) Though the problem of violent conduct by intoxicated persons is not new to society, it has been rendered more acute and menacing by the more widespread use of hallucinatory drugs. For example, in Regina v. Lipman, [1969] All E.R. 410, [1970] 1 Q.B. 152, the accused committed his act of mortal violence under the hallucination (induced by drugs) that he was wrestling with serpents.[a] He was convicted of manslaughter. But, on the logic of the appellant's argument, he was innocent of any crime.

(iii) The Butler Committee on Mentally Abnormal Offenders recognised that even the traditional view of the effect of intoxication in relation to conduct prohibited by law left a gap in the protection which the criminal law should afford to innocent citizens; this required, in their view, to be closed by legislation. Their recommendation . . . was:

> ". . . We propose that it should be an offence for a person while voluntarily intoxicated [to] do an act (or make an omission) that would amount to a dangerous offence if it were done or made with the requisite state of mind for such offence."

The maximum sentence recommended for such offence was imprisonment for one year for a first offence or for three years on a second or subsequent offence.

But, on the traditional view, much anti-social conduct is still criminal notwithstanding the intoxication— . . . assault with intent may be reduced to common assault, and stealing a motor car to taking and driving it away without the owner's consent.

On the appellant's arguments, on the other hand, the "Butler gap" is enormously widened. . . .

[T]here is nothing unreasonable or illogical in the law holding that a mind rendered self-inducedly insensible . . . , through drink or drugs, to the nature of a prohibited act or to its probable consequences is as wrongful a mind as one which consciously contemplates the prohibited act and foresees its probable consequences (or is reckless whether they ensue). The latter is all that is required by way of mens rea in a crime of basic intent. But a crime of specific intent requires something more than contemplation of the prohibited act and foresight of its probable consequences. The mens rea in a crime of specific intent requires proof of a purposive element. This purposive element either exists or not; it cannot be supplied by saying that the impairment of mental powers by self-induced intoxication is its equivalent, for it is

---

[a] Lippman killed his companion by stuffing bedclothes down her throat under the delusion, induced by hallucinatory drugs, that he was fighting for his life against snakes. [Footnote by eds.]

not. So . . . the 19th century development of the law as to the effect of self-induced intoxication on criminal responsibility is juristically entirely acceptable . . . .

LORD SALMON. . . . A number of distinguished academic writers support [the defendant's] contention on the ground of logic. As I understand it, the argument runs like this. Intention, whether special or basic (or whatever fancy name you choose to give it), is still intention. If voluntary intoxication by drink or drugs can, as it admittedly can, negative the special or specific intention necessary for the commission of crimes such as murder and theft, how can you justify in strict logic the view that it cannot negative a basic intention, e.g., the intention to commit offences such as assault and unlawful wounding? The answer is that in strict logic this view cannot be justified. But this is the view that has been adopted by the common law of England, which is founded on common sense and experience rather than strict logic. There is no case in the 19th century when the courts were relaxing the harshness of the law in relation to the effect of drunkenness on criminal liability in which the courts ever went so far as to suggest that drunkenness, short of drunkenness producing insanity, could ever exculpate a man from any offence other than one which required some special or specific intent to be proved.

. . . I accept that there is a degree of illogicality in the rule that intoxication may excuse or expunge one type of intention and not another. This illogicality is, however, acceptable to me because the benevolent part of the rule removes undue harshness without imperilling safety and the stricter part of the rule works without imperilling justice. It would be just as ridiculous to remove the benevolent part of the rule (which no one suggests) as it would be to adopt the alternative of removing the stricter part of [the] rule for the sake of preserving absolute logic. . . .

LORD EDMUND-DAVIES. . . . Illogical though the present law may be, it represents a compromise between the imposition of liability on inebriates in complete disregard of their condition (on the alleged ground that it was brought on voluntarily), and the total exculpation required by the defendant's actual state of mind at the time he committed the harm in issue. It is at this point pertinent to pause to consider why legal systems exist. The universal object of a system of law is obvious—the establishment and maintenance of order.

> "The *first* aim of legal rules is to ensure that members of the community are safeguarded in their persons and property so that their energies are not exhausted by the business of self-protection."

The relevant quotations on the purpose of law are endless and they serve to explain (if, indeed, any explanation be necessary) the sense of outrage which would naturally be felt not only by the victims of such attacks as are alleged against the appellant—and still more against Lipman—were he to go scot free. And a law which permitted this would surely deserve and earn the contempt of most people. But not, it seems, of the joint authors of Smith and Hogan, who in the third edition of their valuable book write:

> "While a policy of not allowing a man to escape the consequence of his voluntary drunkenness is understandable, it is submitted that the principle that a man should not be held liable for an act over which he has no control is more important and should prevail."

They add that this is not to say that such a man should in all cases escape criminal liability but that, if he is to be held liable, it should be for the voluntary act of taking the drink or drug. Such a suggestion is far from new. Thus, it appears from Hale's Pleas of the Crown that some lawyers of his day thought that the formal cause of punishment ought to be the drink and not the crime committed under its influence. Edwards expressed concern in 1965 over the possible existence of this gateway to exemption from criminal responsibility and stressed the need for urgent attention to the provision of new statutory powers under which the courts may place such offenders on probation or commit them, as the case may require, to a hospital capable of treating them for the underlying cause of their propensity to automatism. Glanville Williams anticipated in 1961 the Butler Report on Mentally Abnormal Offenders by recommending the creation of an offence of being drunk and dangerous and the committee itself proposed that a new offence of "dangerous intoxication" be punishable on indictment for one year for a first offence or for three years on a second or subsequent offence.

Such recommendations for law reform may receive parliamentary consideration hereafter but this House is presently concerned with the law as it is. The merciful relaxation of the old rule that drunkenness was no defence appears to have worked reasonably well for 150 years. As to the complaint that it is unethical to punish a man for a crime when his physical behaviour was not controlled by a conscious mind, I have long regarded as a convincing theory in support of penal liability for harms committed by voluntary inebriates, the view of Austin, who argued that a person who voluntarily became intoxicated is to be regarded as acting recklessly, for he made himself dangerous in disregard of public safety.

But, to my way of thinking, the nearest approach to a satisfactory refutation of charges of lack of both logic and ethics in punishing the most drunken man for actions which, were he sober, would call for his criminal conviction is that of Stroud, who wrote:

> "It has been suggested by various writers, in explanation of the doctrine respecting voluntary drunkenness as an excuse for crime, that the effect is 'to make drunkenness itself an offence, which is punishable with a degree of punishment varying as the consequences of the act done.' This is not exactly correct, although it is not far from the true explanation of the rule. The true explanation is, that drunkenness is not incompatible with mens rea, in the sense of ordinary culpable intentionality, because mere recklessness is sufficient to satisfy the definition of

mens rea, and drunkenness is itself an act of recklessness. The law therefore establishes a conclusive presumption against the admission of proof of intoxication for the purpose of disproving mens rea in ordinary crimes. Where this presumption applies, it does not make 'drunkenness itself' a crime, but the drunkenness is itself an integral part of the crime, as forming, together with the other unlawful conduct charged against the defendant, a complex act of criminal recklessness.

"This explanation affords at once a justification of the rule of law, and a reason for its inapplicability when drunkenness is pleaded by way of showing absence of full intent, or of some exceptional form of mens rea essential to a particular crime, according to its definition."

Reverting to the same topic immediately after the decision in *Beard,* Stroud added:

"It would be contrary to all principle and authority to suppose that drunkenness can be a defence for crime in general on the ground that a 'person cannot be convicted of a crime unless the mens was rea.' By allowing himself to get drunk, and thereby putting himself in such a condition as to be no longer amenable to the law's commands, a man shows such regardlessness as amounts to mens rea for the purpose of all ordinary crimes. . . . His drunkenness can constitute a defence only in those exceptional cases where some additional mental element, of a more heinous and mischievous description than ordinary mens rea, is required by the definition of the crime charged against him, and is shown to have been lacking in consequence of his drunken condition."

Professor Glanville Williams would probably condemn such an approach as savouring of "judge-made fiction." While generally sharing his dislike of such fictions, in my judgment little can properly be made out of the criticisms that a law which demands the conviction of such persons who behave as the appellant did is both illogical and unethical. It may be that Parliament should look at it, and devise a new way of dealing with drunken or drugged offenders. But, until it does, the continued application of the existing law is far better calculated to preserve order than the recommendation that he and all who act similarly should leave the dock as free men. . . .

Lord Russell of Killowen. My Lords, your Lordships have dealt . . . so fully with the considerations to which this appeal has given rise that I will be brief. I entirely agree that the [appeal should be dismissed]. That the facts of the case give rise to the question [raised], I doubt. The appellant's participation in the events of the evening begin when he is told by the other man that the latter is to be ejected: whereupon the appellant stationed himself before the door to prevent that, which shows comprehension and intention on his part. When the police arrived the appellant called them adjectival pigs, a word which has of recent years been revived as a reference to law enforcement officers, having been current in the early 19th century . . . . This

. . . negatives lack of understanding. Nevertheless, the question requires to be answered, and I agree with the answer proposed. . . .

Appeal dismissed.

NOTES ON INTOXICATION AND MENS REA

1. **Introduction.** In *Majewski* the House of Lords considers the significance of a claim that the defendant's conscious mental functioning at the time of the offense was impaired as a result of intoxication. In rare cases, a defendant might claim, as Majewski did, that he or she was so intoxicated as to lack any conscious awareness of, or control over, behavior; this claim may be thought to be legally significant because it shows that the defendant's conduct was not produced by a "voluntary act." [a] In the more typical case, a defendant who was consciously aware of some aspects of conduct may claim to have lacked the mens rea required for conviction because of unawareness or misperception of legally pertinent circumstances or risks, or may claim to have lacked the type of conscious objective (e.g., purpose to kill) prescribed by the offense. All of these claims may be logically relevant to the elements of the offense. However, as the *Majewski* opinions indicate, there has been a remarkable consensus that evidence of voluntary intoxication should be restricted considerably short of its logical import.[b] How far short has been the question on which the authorities disagree.[c]

2. **General-Intent Crimes.** There is a consensus in American law that the result in *Majewski* is correct, i.e., that intoxication evidence is inadmissible to negate mens rea for general or "basic" intent offenses. In cases where "general intent" is equated to negligence, this result is not surprising. It is clear enough, is it not, that the standard for negligence should not be the "reasonable intoxicated" person? But even the Model Penal Code, which ordinarily requires actual perception of risk, modifies its stance when recklessness is sought to be rebutted by

[a] The voluntary act doctrine is considered at pages 152–58, supra. The claim that the defendant was "unconscious" and that the ensuing conduct was equivalent to an "automatism" should be distinguished from another type of "involuntariness" claim—the contention that a defendant addicted to drugs or alcohol lacks the capacity to refrain from the prohibited conduct. The significance of this claim is considered in connection with the *Robinson* and *Powell* cases, pages 158–83, supra.

[b] As *Majewski* indicates, the law does not distinguish between drugs and alcohol in this context. It should also be noted that the doctrine applied in *Majewski* pertains only to voluntary ingestion of intoxicating substances; involuntary or otherwise non-culpable intoxication is governed by other doctrines, considered at pages 725–26, 731–32, infra. Finally, the restrictive doctrine illustrated by *Majewski* and the notes to follow is qualified by the possibility that a person who ingests alcohol or drugs may become legally insane. The relation between intoxication and the insanity defense is considered at pages 720–32, infra.

[c] Both the constitutionality and the wisdom of restricting the relevance of intoxication evidence are thoughtfully examined in Mandiberg, Protecting Society and Defendants Too: The Constitutional Dilemma of Mental Abnormality and Intoxication Defenses, 53 Fordham L.Rev. 221 (1984). Professor Mandiberg argues that restrictions on attempts to negate mens rea by evidence of intoxication or mental abnormality are unconstitutional and that the social control objectives of such restrictions can be served by the alternative of civil commitment.

evidence of intoxication. Are you persuaded by *Majewski* that this result is correct? The Model Code position has been defended on four grounds: (i) the weight of authority, which is virtually unanimous; (ii) the fairness of postulating a moral equivalence between the act of getting drunk as a risk-taking venture and the risks subsequently created by drunken conduct; (iii) the difficulty of measuring actual foresight when the actor is drunk; and (iv) the rarity of cases in which drunkenness leads to unawareness as opposed to imprudence.[d] Are these reasons persuasive as applied to alcohol? As applied to the types of substances ingested by Majewski? As applied to all drugs? What of Glanville Williams' point that "[i]f a man is punished for doing something when drunk that he would not have done when sober, is he not in plain truth punished for getting drunk?" [e]

Paul Robinson has analyzed the traditional rule regarding voluntary intoxication in Imputed Criminal Liability, 93 Yale L.J. 609, 639–42, 660–63 (1984). He suggests that it is useful to analogize voluntary intoxication to situations where a person causes an innocent agent to commit a crime. One who is culpable as to the ultimate crime may be guilty of that crime for causing an innocent and unsuspecting person to commit the offense; there is here a genuine moral equivalence between the culpability required when the actor commits the crime by his or her own conduct and the culpability required when he or she causes another to do so. Those who argue that one's culpability in getting drunk is morally equivalent to the culpability required for a general-intent offense, however, are ignoring at least two potential disparities: first, that one may be convicted for an offense requiring recklessness even though one may have been merely negligent in that he or she, in the words of § 2.08(5)(b) of the Model Penal Code, "knows or ought to know" that the substance ingested was intoxicating; and second, that one who is reckless or purposeful as to the act of getting drunk is not necessarily reckless or purposeful as to causing a death or engaging in any other elements of a crime. One who causes *another* person to get drunk and to commit an offense, on the other hand, can be liable for the offense committed only if he or she manifested the culpability required for the offense at the time of causing the other person to get drunk and commit the offense. Professor Robinson suggests a similar rule here: that "one must inquire into the actor's state of mind as to the elements of the offense at the time he voluntarily becomes intoxicated" in order to treat the two situations alike.

Professor Robinson also notes that the revised Hawaii penal code has rejected the Model Code solution and forbids any imputation of culpability in cases of voluntary intoxication. This solution too, he

---

[d] Compare Paulsen, Intoxication as a Defense to Crime, 1961 U.Ill.L.F. 1:

"Drinking alcohol impairs judgment, releases inhibitions, and thus permits the drinker to engage in behavior quite different from the normal pattern. 'Alcohol is an anesthetic or depressant, and its action is approximately the same on all human central nervous systems: it is usually described as reducing the speed and accuracy of perception, slowing down reaction time, and diminishing tensions, anxieties and inhibitions.' Drinking 'stimulates' the drinker, but does so by 'loosening the brakes,' not by 'stepping on the gas.' "

[e] G. Williams, Criminal Law: The General Part 564 (2d ed. 1961).

adds, may be wrong because it is based on the "mistaken belief" that imputation of culpability is always improper. Imputation of culpability is improper, he argues, only if it "does not have a proper basis. Whether a basis is proper depends, first, upon the theories for imposing criminal liability on which the jurisdiction is willing to rely, and, second, upon the adherence of the doctrinal formulation to the underlying theory of imputation." Do you find Professor Robinson's position persuasive? If so, can you suggest a theory of criminal liability that would justify in the terms he suggests the rule for which *Majewski* and the Model Penal Code stand? If you cannot, how should the rule be modified?

3. **Specific-Intent Crimes.** There is disagreement in American law on the proposition advanced in *Majewski* that evidence of intoxication is admissible to negate a specific intent. The cases fall into three groups, each of which is summarized below. In addition, the question of burden of persuasion must also be considered.

(i) **Restrictive Positions.** In Chittum v. Commonwealth, 211 Va. 12, 174 S.E.2d 779 (1970), the defendant was convicted of attempted rape. The defendant's argument on appeal, and the terms in which it was rejected, are revealed in the following excerpt from the affirmance of his conviction:

"The issue presented . . . is whether a defendant is entitled to have the jury instructed to the effect that when a specific intent is a necessary element of the crime charged, the drunkenness of defendant, although voluntary, may be considered in determining whether he was capable of forming or entertaining that requisite intent.

"Although a majority of jurisdictions would allow such an instruction, we have held . . . that '[v]oluntary drunkenness, where it has not produced permanent insanity, is *never* an excuse for crime; *except,* where a party is charged with murder, if it appear that the accused was too drunk to be capable of deliberating and premeditating, then he can be convicted only of murder in the second degree.' . . . We think this to be the better rule.

"In [another case involving] a prosecution for robbery, an instruction was offered on the theory that if defendant was too drunk to entertain the specific intent to rob he could not be found guilty. We agreed with the trial court that there was no evidence to support the instruction and said, 'Even if there had been evidence of drunkenness, under the decisions of this court, it would have been no excuse for the crime.'"

The position reflected in this decision is not unique to Virginia, though very few states have adopted a comparable view. Texas appears to exclude the evidence altogether. Section 8.04(a) of its revised Penal Code carries forward prior law in the following blunt language: "Voluntary intoxication does not constitute a defense to the commission of crime." See also Evers v. State, 31 Tex.Cr.R. 318, 20 S.W. 744 (1892), which held that evidence of intoxication was only admissible to establish temporary insanity, which in turn was relevant only to punishment. *Evers* apparently still states the Texas position.[f]

If it is right to reject intoxication evidence offered to negate the awareness required for recklessness, why is it not also right to reject its use in all cases? Is it relevant that there is usually a lesser offense of which the defendant is guilty if specific intent is lacking, i.e., that the "Butler gap" is not large? Consider in this connection the following excerpt from Paulsen, Intoxication as a Defense to Crime, 1961 U.Ill. L.F. 1, 11:

> "The present policy of the law which permits the disproof of knowledge or purpose by evidence of extreme intoxication is sound enough. If a crime (or a degree of crime) requires a showing of one of these elements, it is because the conduct involved presents a special danger, if done with purpose or knowledge or the actor presents a special cause for alarm. A burglar, one who breaks in with a purpose to commit a felony, is more dangerous than the simple housebreaker. The aggravated assaults are punished more severely precisely because of the danger presented by the actor's state of mind. He who passes counterfeit money with knowledge is a greater threat than the actor who transfers it without understanding. If purpose or knowledge are not present, the cause for the lack is not important. The policy served by requiring these elements of culpability will obtain whether or not their absence is established by proof of extreme intoxication or any other evidence."

Are you persuaded? If so, why is recklessness different?

(ii) **Lack of Capacity vs. Factual Relevance.** Modern cases also reflect a division—originating in 19th century English decisions— as to how the rule relating to specific intent should be stated. The dispute is illustrated by two hypothetical instructions drafted for a proposed charge of larceny of a radio by a defendant who was "quite drunk" and based on form instructions for the two states involved. The hypotheticals are contained in Murphy. The Intoxication Defense: An Introduction to Mr. Smith's Article, 76 Dick.L.Rev. 1, 10 (1971–72): *

> "Early in his charge the court would instruct on the elements of larceny, including the intent element and make it clear that the jury cannot convict unless satisfied beyond [a] reasonable doubt as to all elements. If the judge were to use the California form of intoxication charge, he might proceed in this fashion:
>
> > 'In the crime of larceny a necessary element is the existence in the mind of the defendant of the specific intent to deprive the owner permanently of his radio.

[f] Citations to cases and statutes in several other states taking either the Virginia or Texas position on this issue are contained in Robinson, Imputed Criminal Liability, 93 Yale L.J. 609, 661–62 nn. 201, 202 (1984).

* The excerpts below are reprinted with permission of Professor Murphy of the Dickinson School of Law and the Dickinson Law Review.

'If the evidence shows that the defendant was intoxicated at the time of the alleged offense you should consider his state of intoxication in determining if the defendant had that specific intent.' [g]

Were the judge to use the Ohio form he might instruct as follows:

'Intoxication is not an excuse for a crime. However, such evidence is admissible for the purpose of showing that the defendant was so intoxicated he was incapable of forming the intent to deprive the owner permanently of his radio. On this issue, the burden of proof is upon the defendant to establish by a greater weight of the evidence that his mind did not form that intent. If you find by a greater weight of the evidence that the defendant was incapable of forming an intent to deprive the owner permanently of his property then you must find the defendant not guilty.' " [h]

What is there to be said for each of these two formulations? Which one does the Model Penal Code adopt? As you think about these questions, consider Professor Murphy's comments:

"If given no further guidance than the California charge, a juror might believe that an inebriate who acts on impulse never acts with specific intent or that specific intent requires relatively clearheaded thought processes. When the proof shows that a defendant was even moderately drunk, he might feel bound by the accused's testimony that 'I didn't mean to do it' or 'I didn't know what I was doing.' The juror would in effect be insisting on a higher quality of specific intent—a more culpable state of mind—than required by generally accepted legal doctrine.

"The Ohio charge includes a verbal formula which conveys the idea that only extreme intoxication precludes intent. It focuses the inquiry on the defendant's *potential* for forming the required intent and implies that any intent will serve (impulsive or at a low level of awareness?) so long as the defendant is *capable* of the kind of intent required by law. If we accept the premises that the criminal law should treat most people alike,

[g] Cf. Stephen, J., in his charge to the jury in Regina v. Doherty, 16 Cox C.C. 306, 308 (N.P.1887):

"The general rule as to intention is that a man intends the natural consequences of his act. As a rule the use of a knife to stab or of a pistol to shoot shows an intent to do grievous bodily harm, but this is not a necessary inference. In drawing it . . . the question whether the prisoner is drunk or sober [should be considered]. [A]lthough you cannot take drunkenness as an excuse for crime, yet when the crime is such that the intention of the party committing it is one of its constituent elements, you may look at the fact that a man was in drink in considering whether he formed the intention necessary to commit the crime.

. . . [Y]ou have to consider the effect of his drunkenness upon his intention."

[h] Cf. Coleridge, J., in Regina v. Monkhouse, 4 Cox C.C. 55 (1849):

"If the defendant is proved to have been intoxicated, the question becomes a . . . subtle one; . . . namely, was he rendered by intoxication entirely incapable of forming the intent charged. . . . Drunkenness is ordinarily neither a defence nor excuse for crime, and where it is available as a partial answer to a charge, it rests on the prisoner to prove it, and it is not enough that he was excited or rendered more irritable, unless the intoxication was such as . . . to take away from him the power of forming any specific intention."

that specific-intent crimes can be committed by stupid, unstable and quite peculiar people and that intent or conscious purpose does not require a cool head, clear thinking or, indeed, very much in the way of mental activity, the Ohio charge seems more likely to avoid improper verdicts than the California form."

(iii) **Burden of Persuasion.** Perhaps as many as half of the states adopt the Ohio version of the specific-intent rule as stated by Professor Murphy. Typically, these states also follow the practice of placing the burden of persuasion on the defendant. Why do you think the burden is shifted on this issue? Can you articulate reasons why it should or should not be placed on the defendant? [i]

As you think about these questions, notice the anomaly created by Professor Murphy's Ohio instruction and consider his comments thereon:

"The California charge avoids a problem of conflicting burdens of persuasion that is inherent in any instruction which, like the Ohio form, makes incapacity a true affirmative defense. Looking back at our sample Ohio charge, we see that the accused has the burden of persuading the jury that he was so drunk he was unable to form the intent to steal, while the state retains the burden of proving beyond reasonable doubt that the accused had that intent. If the jurors have even a reasonable doubt of the defendant's capacity to form an intent to steal, how can they be convinced beyond reasonable doubt that he did in fact intend to steal? The Ohio charge appears to reconcile the conflicting burdens in the only way it can logically be done—by conceiving the capacity defense as working a partial exception to the prosecutor's normal burden of proving the intent element. The jury is told that on the capacity issue the defendant has the burden of proving 'that his mind did not form the intent.' In many courts, however, which treat incapacity as a true affirmative defense, the jurors are left to resolve the anomaly for themselves."

Is this a serious problem? What is the jury to do?

4. **Creation of a Separate "Dangerous Intoxication" Offense.** The proposals of the Butler Commission are referred to in *Majewski*. Following *Majewski*, the Criminal Law Revision Committee published a report [j] that rejected both the recommendations of the Butler Commission and a revised version of their proposal in favor of a solution based on the Model Penal Code. [k] The suggestion of the Butler Commission

---

[i] There is an argument that placing this burden on the defendant is unconstitutional. The argument cannot be evaluated now, however, because it requires consideration of a series of cases dealt with at pages 967–93, infra. For an example of a case where the argument was made and rejected, see United States ex rel. Goodard v. Vaughn, 614 F.2d 929 (3d Cir.1980) (Delaware instruction, similar to Professor Murphy's Ohio hypothetical, on specific intent required for first-degree murder; defendant had ingested LSD, marihuana, and angel dust shortly before the murder; defendant's arguments based on *Mullaney, Patterson,* and *Sandstrom* rejected).

[j] Offences Against the Person, 14th Report, Cmnd. 7844, pp. 111–16 (March 1980).

[k] Specifically, the Committee recommended that the terms "specific intent" and "basic (or general) intent" be abandoned and that the Model Code formula be adopted in cases where recklessness, defined in terms of actual foresight of risk, is the required culpability.

was rejected because of the insufficiency of the penalty and "the problem of the nomenclature of the offense." As the Report elaborated the latter objection:

> "A conviction of the Butler Committee offence would merely record a conviction of an offence of committing a dangerous act while intoxicated. This is insufficient. The record must indicate the nature of the act committed, for example whether it was an assault or a killing. It would be unfair for a defendant who has committed a relatively minor offence while voluntarily intoxicated to be labelled as having committed the same offence as a defendant who has killed. The penalty suggested is also in our opinion insufficient to deal with serious offences such as killings or rapes while voluntarily intoxicated by drink or drugs."

Professors J.C. Smith and Glanville Williams, members of the Law Revision Commission, accepted this criticism and advanced the following alternative:

> "(1) Intoxication shall be taken into account for the purpose of determining whether the person charged had formed an intention, specific or otherwise, in the absence of which he would not be guilty of the offence.

> "(2) Where a person is charged with an offence and he relies on evidence of voluntary intoxication, whether introduced by himself or by any other party to the case, for the purpose of showing that he was not aware of a risk where awareness of that risk is, or is part of, the mental element required for conviction of the offence, then, if:

> (a) the jury are not satisfied that he was aware of the risk, but

> (b) the jury are satisfied

> (i) that all the elements of the offence other than any mental element have been proved, and

> (ii) that the defendant would, in all the circumstances of the case, have been aware of the risk if he had not been voluntarily intoxicated

> the jury shall find him not guilty of the offence charged but guilty of doing the act while in a state of voluntary intoxication. . . .

> "(5) A person convicted under (2) . . . above shall, where the charge was of murder, be liable to the same punishment as for manslaughter; and in any other case shall be liable to the same punishment as that provided by the law for the offence charged."

The Commission advanced five reasons for rejecting what they called "a separate offense of doing the actus reus while voluntarily intoxicated." They were: (i) that the separate offense would unnecessarily complicate the task of the jury; (ii) that special problems would be created if the jury were convinced that the actus reus was committed but could not agree whether the intoxication showed that the defendant was not in fact reckless or whether the defendant was reckless even though he or she had too much to drink: (iii) that the existence of the separate offense would unnecessarily complicate the pleading process, since the defendant might prefer to plead guilty to the separate offense rather than the offense charged; (iv) that the problem simply is not worth such an elaborate solution; and (v) that the public is likely to be confused by the separate label attached to the offense.[1]

Did the Commission reach the right result?

NOTE ON MENTAL ABNORMALITY AND MENS REA

It is plain that evidence of mental abnormality can be relevant to the mens-rea determinations previously explored. As in the case of intoxication, however, the law has always treated a claim of ignorance or mistake based on mental abnormality as presenting a special problem. The long-standing tradition has been to recognize a separate defense of insanity which, if established, excuses the actor even though the formal elements of actus reus and mens-rea have been proved. Whether evidence of mental abnormality can also be considered on mens-rea issues is a question of considerable difficulty and debate.

It is helpful in understanding why this is so to recognize that the common-law courts saw sanity and insanity as categorical concepts. Insane persons—those who acted in a frenzy induced by madness, in the language of the early days—were said to lack the capacity to entertain a "criminal intent." They were incapable of having "guilty minds." However, a defendant who did not claim to be insane was conclusively presumed to have the capacity to form a criminal intent. There was no middle ground. As a result, evidence of mental abnormality was inadmissible unless it was offered in support of an insanity defense.

This categorical approach to evidence of mental abnormality began to break down during the late 19th and early 20th centuries. One important factor was the emergence of psychiatry as a recognized scientific discipline, a development that was accompanied by efforts to relate advances in psychological understanding to the doctrines of the criminal law. A central theme in the forensic literature of the period was the variety and complexity of mental dysfunction and the difficulty of relating emerging psychiatric concepts to the sane-insane model of the law. Another important influence was the emergence during the same period of integrated approaches to the culpability requirements of the criminal law, including an increased focus on subjective components of mens rea.

----

[1] On this point, the Commission elaborated:

"An example of the type of case in which there is frequently evidence of intoxication is rape. We think the public would find it difficult to understand a verdict to the effect that the defendant was not guilty of rape but guilty of the act. This can only mean that he was guilty of having sexual intercourse without the woman's consent while voluntarily intoxicated, when as far as the victim was concerned she had been raped."

Today there is considerable support for the proposition that evidence of mental abnormality, including expert testimony, should be admissible whenever it is relevant to any issue of culpability in the criminal law. However, some jurisdictions adhere rigorously to the notion that evidence of mental abnormality may be considered only in connection with the insanity defense. Others admit the evidence only on some mens-rea issues, and still others admit it whenever relevant to any mens-rea issue. There is disagreement too—as in the case of intoxication—on how its relevance should be stated in cases where it is admissible. Some jurisdictions, for example, insist that evidence of mental abnormality must show lack of capacity to formulate the required mens rea and that such evidence must be confined to cases where the defendant was afflicted with some recognized disease or illness.

Full explication and evaluation of these issues cannot usefully be undertaken until the separate defense of insanity is considered, an enterprise that is postponed to Chapter V in these materials. Chapter V deals with insanity and then returns to the problems of mens rea and evidence of mental abnormality. Additionally, Chapter VI explores some related problems in the law of homicide.

***

SECTION 4: STRICT LIABILITY

***

SUBSECTION A: REGULATORY OFFENSES

***

INTRODUCTORY NOTE ON THE ORIGINS AND NATURE OF REGULATORY OFFENSES

The most pervasive use of strict liability in the criminal law is in "regulatory" or "public welfare" offenses. A frequently cited summary of the nature of regulatory offenses [a] is contained in Morissette v. United States, 342 U.S. 246 (1952), where Justice Jackson said:

"[There has been] a century-old but accelerating tendency, discernible both here and in England, to call into existence new duties and crimes which disregard any ingredient of intent. The industrial revolution multiplied the number of workmen exposed to injury from increasingly powerful and complex mechanisms, driven by freshly discovered sources of energy, requiring higher precautions by employers. Traffic of velocities, volumes and varieties unheard of came to subject the wayfarer to intolerable casualty risks if owners and drivers were not to observe new cares and uniformities of conduct. Congestion of cities and crowding of quarters called for health and welfare regulations

[a] The history of such offenses is detailed in Sayre, Public Welfare Offenses, 33 Colum.L.Rev. 55 (1933).

undreamed of in simpler times. Wide distributions of goods became an instrument of wide distribution of harm when those who dispersed food, drink, drugs, and even securities, did not comply with reasonable standards of quality, integrity, disclosure and care. Such dangers have engendered increasingly numerous and detailed regulations which heighten the duties of those in control of particular industries, trades, properties or activities that affect public health, safety or welfare.

"While many of these duties are sanctioned by a more strict civil liability, lawmakers, whether wisely or not, have sought to make such regulations more effective by invoking criminal sanctions to be applied by the familiar technique of criminal prosecutions and convictions. This has confronted the courts with a multitude of prosecutions, based on statutes or administrative regulations, for what have been aptly called "public-welfare offenses." These cases do not fit neatly into any of the accepted classifications of common-law offenses, such as those against the state, the person, property, or public morals. Many of these offenses are not in the nature of positive aggressions or invasions, with which the common law so often dealt, but are in the nature of neglect where the law requires care, or inaction where it imposes a duty. Many violations of such regulations result in no direct or immediate injury to person or property but merely create the danger or probability of it which the law seeks to minimize. While such offenses do not threaten the security of the state in the manner of treason, they may be regarded as offenses against its authority, for their occurrence impairs the efficiency of controls deemed essential to the social order as presently constituted. In this respect, whatever the intent of the violator, the injury is the same, and the consequences are injurious or not according to fortuity. Hence, legislation applicable to such offenses, as a matter of policy, does not specify intent as a necessary element. The accused, if he does not will the violation, usually is in a position to prevent it with no more care than society might reasonably expect and no more exertion than it might reasonably exact from one who assumed his responsibilities. Also, penalties commonly are relatively small, and conviction does no grave damage to an offender's reputation. Under such considerations, courts have turned to construing statutes and regulations which make no mention of intent as dispensing with it and holding that the guilty act alone makes out the crime. This has not, however, been without expressions of misgiving."

———

INTRODUCTORY NOTES TO *UNITED STATES v. PARK*

The next main case, *United States v. Park,* is a recent Supreme Court decision in one important area of public-welfare offenses. It involved a criminal prosecution under § 303 of the Federal Food, Drug, & Cosmetic Act, which reads as follows:

"(a) Any person [a] who violates a provision of Section 301 of this title shall be imprisoned for not more than one year or fined not more than $1,000 or both.

"(b) Notwithstanding the provisions of subsection (a) of this section, if any person commits such a violation after a conviction of him under this section has become final, or commits such a violation with the intent to defraud or mislead, such person shall be imprisoned for not more than three years or fined not more than $10,000 or both."

Section 301 in turn provides:

"The following acts and the causing thereof are prohibited:

. . .

"(k) The alteration, mutilation, destruction, obliteration, or removal of the whole or any part of the labeling of, or the doing of any other act with respect to, a food, drug, device, or cosmetic, if such act is done while such article is held for sale (whether or not the first sale) after shipment in interstate commerce and results in such article being adulterated or misbranded."

The term "adulterated" is defined as follows in § 402:

"A food shall be deemed to be adulterated—

"(a) . . . (3) if it consists in whole or in part of any filthy, putrid, or decomposed substance, or if it is otherwise unfit for food; or (4) if it has been prepared, packed, or held under insanitary conditions whereby it may have become contaminated with filth, or whereby it may have been rendered injurious to health . . . ."

Two cases decided prior to *Park* provide the context in which it was decided:

1. ***United States v. Dotterweich.*** United States v. Dotterweich, 320 U.S. 277 (1943), involved the prosecution of the Buffalo Pharmacal Company and Dotterweich, its president and general manager, for shipping adulterated and misbranded drugs in interstate commerce. The drugs had been purchased from their manufacturer, repackaged, and shipped under the Buffalo Pharmacal label. Dotterweich had not been involved personally in the particular incident that was the subject of the prosecution. The jury acquitted the corporation but convicted Dotterweich.[b] He was sentenced to pay a fine and to 60-days' probation. The argument before the Supreme Court was that the word

---

[a] The term "person" is defined to include corporations as well as individuals. [Footnote by eds.]

[b] As to this apparent inconsistency, the Supreme Court observed:

"Equally baseless is the claim of Dotterweich that, having failed to find the corporation guilty, the jury could not find him guilty. Whether the jury's verdict was the result of carelessness or compromise or a belief that the responsible individual should suffer the penalty instead of merely increasing, as it were, the cost of running the business of the corporation, is immaterial. Juries may indulge in precisely such motives or vagaries."

"person" in § 303 applied only to the corporation, an argument that the Court of Appeals had accepted in reversing the conviction. The Supreme Court disagreed and reinstated the conviction. In the course of its opinion, it made the following observations about the scheme of the statute:

"The purposes of this legislation . . . touch phases of the lives and health of people which, in the circumstances of modern industrialism, are largely beyond self-protection. Regard for these purposes should infuse construction of the legislation if it is to be treated as a working instrument of government and not merely as a collection of English words. The prosecution to which Dotterweich was subjected is based on a now familiar type of legislation whereby penalties serve as effective means of regulation. Such legislation dispenses with the conventional requirement for criminal conduct—awareness of some wrongdoing. In the interest of the larger good it puts the burden of acting at hazard upon a person otherwise innocent but standing in responsible relation to a public danger. . . .

"The Circuit Court of Appeals was evidently [concerned by the] fear that an enforcement of § 301(a) as written might operate too harshly by sweeping within its condemnation any person however remotely entangled in the proscribed shipment. But that is not the way to read legislation. Literalism and evisceration are equally to be avoided. To speak with technical accuracy, under § 301 a corporation may commit an offense and all persons who aid and abet its commission are equally guilty. Whether an accused shares responsibility in the business process resulting in unlawful distribution depends on the evidence produced at the trial and its submission—assuming the evidence warrants it—to the jury under appropriate guidance. The offense is committed . . . by all who do have such a responsible share in the furtherance of the transaction which the statute outlaws, namely, to put into the stream of interstate commerce adulterated or misbranded drugs. Hardship there doubtless may be under a statute which thus penalizes the transaction though consciousness of wrongdoing be totally wanting. Balancing relative hardships, Congress has preferred to place it upon those who have at least the opportunity of informing themselves of the existence of conditions imposed for the protection of consumers before sharing in illicit commerce, rather than to throw the hazard on the innocent public who are wholly helpless.

"It would be too treacherous to define or even to indicate by way of illustration the class of employees which stands in such a responsible relation. To attempt a formula embracing the variety of conduct whereby persons may responsibly contribute in furthering a transaction forbidden by an act of Congress, to wit, to send illicit goods across state lines, would be mischievous futility. In such matters the good sense of prosecutors, the wise guidance of trial judges, and the ultimate judgment of juries must be trusted. Our system of criminal justice necessarily depends on 'conscience and circumspection in prosecuting officers,' even when the consequences are far more drastic than they are under the provision of law before us."

2. ***United States v. Wiesenfeld Warehouse Co.*** United States v. Wiesenfeld Warehouse Co., 376 U.S. 86 (1964), involved an interpretation of §§ 301(k) and 402(a)(3) and (4) of the Act. The defendant argued that the mere holding of food in a warehouse under insanitary conditions did not constitute an offense and in particular that the words "the doing of any other act" in § 301(k) required some affirmative conduct that resulted in adulteration. The Supreme Court rejected the argument, explicitly holding that "[i]t is . . . clear from [the] legislative history that Congress intended to proscribe the particular conduct charged in the information filed below—the holding of food under insanitary conditions whereby it may have become contaminated." The Court also added the following observation:

> "It is argued . . . that the government in this case is seeking to impose criminal sanctions upon one 'who is, by the very nature of his business powerless' to protect against this kind of contamination, however high the standard of care exercised. Whatever the truth of this claim, it involves factual proof to be raised defensively at a trial on the merits. We are here concerned only with the construction of the statute as it relates to the sufficiency of the information, and not with the scope and reach of the statute as applied to such facts as may be developed by evidence adduced at a trial."

UNITED STATES v. PARK

Supreme Court of the United States, 1975.
421 U.S. 658.

MR. CHIEF JUSTICE BURGER delivered the opinion of the Court.

We granted certiorari to consider whether the jury instructions in the prosecution of a corporate officer under § 301(k) of the Federal Food, Drug, and Cosmetic Act were appropriate under United States v. Dotterweich, 320 U.S. 277 (1943).

Acme Markets, Inc., is a national retail food chain with approximately 36,000 employees, 874 retail outlets, 12 general warehouses, and four special warehouses. Its headquarters, including the office of the president, respondent Park, who is chief executive officer of the corporation, are located in Philadelphia, Pa. In a five-count information . . . the government charged Acme and respondent with violations of the Federal Food, Drug, and Cosmetic Act. Each count of the information alleged that the defendants had received food that had been shipped in interstate commerce and that, while the food was being held for sale, in Acme's Baltimore warehouse following shipment in interstate commerce, they caused it to be held in a building accessible by rodents and to be exposed to contamination by rodents. These acts were alleged to have resulted in the food's being adulterated within the meaning of [§ 402 of the act] in violation of [§ 301(k)].

Acme pleaded guilty to each count of the information. Respondent pleaded not guilty. The evidence at trial [3] demonstrated that in April 1970 the Food and Drug Administration (FDA) advised respondent by letter of insanitary conditions in Acme's Philadelphia warehouse. In 1971 the FDA found that similar conditions existed in the firm's Baltimore warehouse. An FDA consumer safety officer testified concerning evidence of rodent infestation and other insanitary conditions discovered during a 12-day inspection of the Baltimore warehouse in November and December 1971. He also related that a second inspection of the warehouse had been conducted in March 1972.[5] On that occasion the inspectors found that there had been improvement in the sanitary conditions, but that "there was still evidence of rodent activity in the building and in the warehouses and we found some rodent-contaminated lots of food items."

The government also presented testimony by the Chief of Compliance of the FDA's Baltimore office, who informed respondent by letter of the conditions at the Baltimore warehouse after the first inspection.[6] There was testimony by Acme's Baltimore division vice president, who had responded to the letter on behalf of Acme and respondent and who described the steps taken to remedy the insanitary conditions discovered by both inspections. The government's final witness, Acme's vice president for legal affairs and assistant secretary, identified respondent as the president and chief executive officer of the company and read a bylaw prescribing the duties of the chief executive officer.[7] He testified that respondent functioned by delegating "normal operating duties," including sanitation, but that he retained "certain things, which are the big, broad, principles of the operation of the company," and had "the responsibility of seeing that they all work together."

---

[3] The parties stipulated in effect that the items of food described in the information had been shipped in interstate commerce and were being held for sale in Acme's Baltimore warehouse.

[5] The first four counts of the information alleged violations corresponding to the observations of the inspectors during the November and December 1971 inspection. The fifth count alleged violations corresponding to observations during the March 1972 inspection.

[6] The letter dated, January 27, 1972, included the following:

"We note with much concern that the old and new warehouse areas used for food storage were actively and extensively inhabited by live rodents. Of even more concern was the observation that such reprehensible conditions obviously existed for a prolonged period of time without any detection, or were completely ignored. . . .

"We trust this letter will serve to direct your attention to the seriousness of the problem and formally advise you of the urgent need to initiate whatever measures are necessary to prevent recurrence and ensure compliance with the law."

[7] The bylaw provided in pertinent part:

"The chairman of the board of directors or the president shall be the chief executive officer of the company as the board of directors may from time to time determine. He shall, subject to the board of directors, have general and active supervision of the affairs, business, offices and employees of the company.

. . .

"He shall, from time to time, in his discretion or at the order of the board, report the operations and affairs of the company. He shall also perform such other duties and have such other powers as may be assigned to him from time to time by the board of directors."

At the close of the government's case in chief, respondent moved for a judgment of acquittal on the ground that "the evidence in chief has shown that Mr. Park is not personally concerned in this Food and Drug violation." The trial judge denied the motion, stating that *Dotterweich* was controlling.

Respondent was the only defense witness. He testified that, although all of Acme's employees were in a sense under his general direction, the company had an "organizational structure for responsibilities for certain functions" according to which different phases of its operation were "assigned to individuals who, in turn, have staff and departments under them." He identified those individuals responsible for sanitation, and related that upon receipt of the January 1972 FDA letter, he had conferred with the vice president for legal affairs, who informed him that the Baltimore division vice president "was investigating the situation immediately and would be taking corrective action and would be preparing a summary of the corrective action to reply to the letter." Respondent stated that he did not "believe there was anything [he] could have done more constructively than what [he] found was being done."

On cross-examination, respondent conceded that providing sanitary conditions for food offered for sale to the public was something that he was "responsible for in the entire operation of the company," and he stated that it was one of many phases of the company that he assigned to "dependable subordinates." Respondent was asked about and, over the objections of his counsel, admitted receiving, the April 1970 letter addressed to him from the FDA regarding insanitary conditions at Acme's Philadelphia warehouse. He acknowledged that, with the exception of the division vice president, the same individuals had responsibility for sanitation in both Baltimore and Philadelphia. Finally, in response to questions concerning the Philadelphia and Baltimore incidents, respondent admitted that the Baltimore problem indicated the system for handling sanitation "wasn't working perfectly" and that as Acme's chief executive officer he was responsible for "any result which occurs in our company."

At the close of the evidence, respondent's renewed motion for a judgment of acquittal was denied. The relevant portion of the trial judge's instructions to the jury challenged by respondent is set out in the margin.[9] Respondent's counsel objected to the instructions on the

[9] "In order to find the defendant guilty . . . you must find beyond a reasonable doubt on each count . . . .

"[T]hat John R. Park held a position of authority in the operation of the business of Acme Markets, Incorporated.

". . . The main issue for your determination is . . . whether the defendant held a position of authority and responsibility in the business of Acme Markets. . . .

"The statute makes individuals, as well as corporations, liable for violations. An individual is liable if it is clear, beyond a reasonable doubt, . . . that the individual had a responsible relation to the situation, even though he may not have participated personally.

"The individual is or could be liable under the statute, even if he did not consciously do wrong. However, the fact that the defendant is pres[id]ent and is a

ground that they failed fairly to reflect our decision in *Dotterweich* and to define " 'responsible relationship.' " The trial judge overruled the objection. The jury found respondent guilty on all counts of the information, and he was subsequently sentenced to pay a fine of $50 on each count.

The Court of Appeals reversed the conviction and remanded for a new trial. That court viewed the government as arguing "that the conviction may be predicated solely upon a showing that [respondent] was the president of the offending corporation," and it stated that as "a general proposition, some act of commission or omission is an essential element of every crime." It reasoned that, although our decision in *Dotterweich* had construed the statutory provisions under which respondent was tried to dispense with the traditional element of " 'awareness of some wrongdoing,' " the Court had not construed them as dispensing with the element of "wrongful action." The Court of Appeals concluded that the trial judge's instructions "might well have left the jury with the erroneous impression that Park could be found guilty in the absence of 'wrongful action' on his part and that proof of the element was required by due process. It held, with one dissent, that the instructions did not "correctly state the law of the case" and directed that on retrial the jury be instructed as to "wrongful action," which might be "gross negligence and inattention in discharging . . . corporate duties and obligations or any of a host of other acts of commission or omission which would 'cause' the contamination of food."

. . .

We granted certiorari because of an apparent conflict among the Courts of Appeal with respect to the standard of liability of corporate officers under the Federal Food, Drug, and Cosmetic Act as construed in *Dotterweich* and because of the importance of the question to the government's enforcement program. We reverse.

I

[At this point, the Court summarized the *Dotterweich* decision.]

II

The rule that corporate employees who have "a responsible share in the furtherance of the transaction which the statute outlaws" are subject to the criminal provisions of the act was not formulated in a vacuum. Cases under the Federal Food and Drugs Act of 1906 reflected the view both that knowledge or intent were not required to be proved in prosecutions under its criminal provisions, and that responsible corporate agents could be subjected to the liability thereby imposed. Moreover, the principle had been recognized that a corporate agent, through whose act, default, or omission the corporation committed a

chief executive officer of the Acme Markets does not require a finding of guilt. Though, he need not have personally participated in the situation, he must have had a responsible relationship to the issue. The issue is, in this case, whether the defendant, John R. Park, by virtue of his position in the company, had a position of authority and responsibility in the situation out of which these charges arose."

crime, was himself guilty individually of that crime. The principle had been applied whether or not the crime required "consciousness of wrongdoing," and it had been applied not only to those corporate agents who themselves committed the criminal act, but also to those who by virtue of their managerial positions or other similar relation to the actor could be deemed responsible for its commission.

In the latter class of cases, the liability of managerial officers did not depend on their knowledge of, or personal participation in, the act made criminal by the statute. Rather, where the statute under which they were prosecuted dispensed with "consciousness of wrongdoing," an omission or failure to act was deemed a sufficient basis for a responsible corporate agent's liability. It was enough in such cases that, by virtue of the relationship he bore to the corporation, the agent had the power to prevent the act complained of.

The rationale of the interpretation given the act in *Dotterweich,* as holding criminally accountable the persons whose failure to exercise the authority and supervisory responsibility reposed in them by the business organization resulted in the violation complained of, has been confirmed in our subsequent cases. Thus, the Court has reaffirmed the proposition that "the public interest in the purity of its food is so great as to warrant the imposition of the highest standard of care on distributors." In order to make "distributors of food the strictest censors of their merchandise . . . ," the act punishes "neglect where the law requires care, or inaction where it imposes a duty. . . . " "The accused, if he does not will the violation, usually is in a position to prevent it with no more care than society might reasonably expect and no more exertion than it might reasonably exact from one who assumed his responsibilities." Similarly, in cases decided after *Dotterweich,* the courts of appeals have recognized that those corporate agents vested with the responsibility, and power commensurate with that responsibility, to devise whatever measures are necessary to ensure compliance with the act bear a "responsible relationship" to, or have a "responsible share" in, violations.

Thus *Dotterweich* and the cases which have followed reveal that in providing sanctions which reach and touch the individuals who execute the corporate mission—and this is by no means necessarily confined to a single corporate agent or employee—the act imposes not only a positive duty to seek out and remedy violations when they occur but also, and primarily, a duty to implement measures that will insure that violations will not occur. The requirements of foresight and vigilance imposed on responsible corporate agents are beyond question demanding, and perhaps onerous, but they are no more stringent than the public has a right to expect of those who voluntarily assume positions of authority in business enterprises whose services and products affect the health and well-being of the public that supports them.

The Act does not, as we observed in *Dotterweich,* make criminal liability turn on "awareness of some wrongdoing" or "conscious fraud." The duty imposed by Congress on responsible corporate agents is, we emphasize, one that requires the highest standard of foresight and vigilance, but the act, in its criminal aspect, does not require that which is objectively impossible. The theory upon which responsible corporate agents are held criminally accountable for "causing" violations of the act permits a claim that a defendant was "powerless" to prevent or correct the violation to "be raised defensively at a trial on the merits." United States v. Wiesenfeld Warehouse Co., 376 U.S. 86 (1964). If such a claim is made, the defendant has the burden of coming forward with evidence, but this does not alter the government's ultimate burden of proving beyond a reasonable doubt the defendant's guilt, including his power, in light of the duty imposed by the act, to prevent or correct the prohibited condition. Congress has seen fit to enforce the accountability of responsible corporate agents dealing with products which may affect the health of consumers by penal sanctions cast in rigorous terms, and the obligation of the courts is to give them effect so long as they do not violate the Constitution.

III

We cannot agree with the Court of Appeals that it was incumbent upon the District Court to instruct the jury that the government had the burden of establishing "wrongful action" in the sense in which the Court of Appeals used that phrase. The concept of a "responsible relationship" to, or a "responsible share" in, a violation of the Act indeed imports some measure of blameworthiness; but it is equally clear that the government establishes a prima facie case when it introduces evidence sufficient to warrant a finding by the trier of the facts that the defendant had, by reason of his position in the corporation, responsibility and authority either to prevent in the first instance, or promptly to correct, the violation complained of, and that he failed to do so. The failure thus to fulfill the duty imposed by the interaction of the corporate agent's authority and the statute furnishes a sufficient causal link. The considerations which prompted the imposition of this duty, and the scope of the duty, provide the measure of culpability.

Turning to the jury charge in this case, it is of course arguable that isolated parts can be read as intimating that a finding of guilt could be predicated solely on respondent's corporate position. But this is not the way we review jury instructions, because "a single instruction to a jury may not be judged in artificial isolation, but must be viewed in the context of the overall charge."

Reading the entire charge satisfies us that the jury's attention was adequately focused on the issue of respondent's authority with respect to the conditions that formed the basis of the alleged violations. Viewed as a whole, the charge did not permit the jury to find guilt solely on the basis of respondent's position in the corporation; rather, it fairly advised the jury that to find guilt it must find respondent "had a responsible relation to the situation," and "by virtue of his position . . . had . . . authority and responsibility" to deal with the situation. The situation referred to could only be "food . . . held in unsanitary conditions in a warehouse with the result that it consisted, in part, of filth or . . . may have been contaminated with filth."

Moreover, in reviewing jury instructions, our task is also to view the charge itself as part of the whole trial. "Often isolated statements taken from the charge, seemingly prejudicial on their face, are not so when considered in the context of the entire record of the trial." The record in this case reveals that the jury could not have failed to be aware that the main issue for determination was not respondent's position in the corporate hierarchy, but rather his accountability, because of the responsibility and authority of his position, for the conditions which gave rise to the charges against him.[16]

We conclude that, viewed as a whole and in the context of the trial, the charge was not misleading and contained an adequate statement of the law to guide the jury's determination. Although it would have been better to give an instruction more precisely relating the legal issue to the facts of the case, we cannot say that the failure to provide the amplification requested by respondent was an abuse of discretion. Finally, we note that there was no request for an instruction that the government was required to prove beyond a reasonable doubt that respondent was not without the power or capacity to affect the conditions which founded the charges in the information. In light of the evidence adduced at trial, we find no basis to conclude that the failure of the trial court to give such an instruction sua sponte was plain error or a defect affecting substantial rights. . . .

Reversed.

MR. JUSTICE STEWART, with whom MR. JUSTICE MARSHALL and MR. JUSTICE POWELL join, dissenting.

Although agreeing with much of what is said in the Court's opinion, I dissent from the opinion and judgment, because the jury instructions in this case were not consistent with the law as the Court today expounds it.

As I understand the Court's opinion, it holds that in order to sustain a conviction under § 301(k) of the Federal Food, Drug, and Cosmetic Act the prosecution must at least show that by reason of an individual's corporate position and responsibilities, he had a duty to use care to maintain the physical integrity of the corporation's food products. A jury may then draw the inference that when the food is found to be in such condition as to violate the statute's prohibitions, that condition was "caused" by a breach of the standard of care imposed upon the

---

[16] In his summation to the jury, the prosecutor argued:

"That brings us to . . . whether Mr. John R. Park is responsible for the conditions persisting. . . .

"The point is that, while Mr. Park apparently had a system, and I think he testified the system had been set up long before he got there—he did say that if anyone was going to change the system, it was his responsibility to do so. That very system, the system that he didn't change, did not work in March of 1970 in Philadelphia; it did not work in November of 1971 in Baltimore; it did not work in March of 1972 in Baltimore, and under those circumstances, I submit, that Mr. Park is the man responsible. . . .

"Mr. Park was responsible for seeing that sanitation was taken care of, and he had a system set up that was supposed to do that. This system didn't work. It didn't work three times. At some point in time, Mr. Park has to be held responsible for the fact that his system isn't working . . . ."

responsible official. This is the language of negligence, and I agree with it.

To affirm this conviction, however, the Court must approve the instructions given to the members of the jury who were entrusted with determining whether the respondent was innocent or guilty. Those instructions did not conform to the standards that the Court itself sets out today.

The trial judge instructed the jury to find Park guilty if it found beyond a reasonable doubt that Park "had a responsible relation to the situation . . . . The issue is, in this case, whether the defendant, John R. Park, by virtue of his position in the company, had a position of authority and responsibility in the situation out of which these charges arose." Requiring, as it did, a verdict of guilty upon a finding of "responsibility," this instruction standing alone could have been construed as a direction to convict if the jury found Park "responsible" for the condition in the sense that his position as chief executive officer gave him formal responsibility within the structure of the corporation. But the trial judge went on specifically to caution the jury not to attach such a meaning to his instruction, saying that "the fact that the defendant is pres[id]ent and is a chief executive officer of the Acme Markets does not require a finding of guilt." "Responsibility" as used by the trial judge therefore had whatever meaning the jury in its unguided discretion chose to give it.

The instructions, therefore, expressed nothing more than a tautology. They told the jury: "You must find the defendant guilty if you find that he is to be held accountable for this adulterated food." In other words: "You must find the defendant guilty if you conclude that he is guilty." The trial judge recognized the infirmities in these instructions but he reluctantly concluded that he was required to give such a charge under *Dotterweich*, which, he thought, in declining to define "responsible relation" had declined to specify the minimum standard of liability for criminal guilt.[1]

As the Court today recognizes, the *Dotterweich* case did not deal with what kind of conduct must be proved to support a finding of criminal guilt under the act. *Dotterweich* was concerned rather, with the statutory definition of "person"—with what kind of corporate employees were even "subject to the criminal provisions of the act." The Court held that those employees with "a responsible relation" to the violative transaction or condition were subject to the act's criminal provisions, but all that the Court had to say with respect to the kind of conduct that can constitute criminal guilt was that the act "dispenses with the conventional requirement for criminal conduct—awareness of some wrongdoing."

---

[1] In response to a request for further illumination of what he meant by "responsible relationship" the District Judge said:

"Let me say this, simply as to the definition of the 'responsible relationship.' *Dotterweich* and subsequent cases have indicated this really is a jury question. It says it is not even subject to being defined by the court. As I have indicated to counsel, I am quite candid in stating that I do not agree with the decision; therefore, I am going to stick by it."

In approving the instructions to the jury in this case, . . . the Court approves a conspicuous departure from the long and firmly established division of functions between judge and jury in the administration of criminal justice. As the Court put the matter more than 80 years ago:

"We must hold firmly to the doctrine that in the courts of the United States it is the duty of juries in criminal cases to take the law from the court and apply that law to the facts as they find them to be from the evidence. Upon the court rests the responsibility of declaring the law; upon the jury, the responsibility of applying the law so declared to the facts as they, upon their conscience, believe them to be. Under any other system, the courts, although established in order to declare the law, would for every practical purpose be eliminated from our system of government as instrumentalities devised for the protection equally of society and of individuals in their essential rights. When that occurs our government will cease to be a government of laws, and become a government of men. Liberty regulated by law is the underlying principle of our institutions." Sparf v. United States, 156 U.S. 51, 102–03 (1895).

[*Sparf* and other related decisions] embody a principle fundamental to our jurisprudence: that a jury is to decide the facts and apply to them the law as explained by the trial judge. Were it otherwise, trial by jury would be no more rational and no more responsive to the accumulated wisdom of the law than trial by ordeal. It is the function of jury instructions, in short, to establish in any trial the objective standards that a jury is to apply as it performs its own function of finding the facts.

To be sure, "the day [is] long past when [courts] . . . parsed instructions and engaged in nice semantic distinctions. . . . " But this Court has never before abandoned the view that jury instructions must contain a statement of the applicable law sufficiently precise to enable the jury to be guided by something other than its rough notions of social justice. And while it might be argued that the issue before the jury in this case was a "mixed" question of both law and fact, this has never meant that a jury is to be left wholly at sea, without any guidance as to the standard of conduct the law requires. The instructions given by the trial court in this case, it must be emphasized, were a virtual nullity, a mere authorization to convict if the jury thought it appropriate. Such instructions—regardless of the blameworthiness of the defendant's conduct, regardless of the social value of the Food, Drug, and Cosmetic Act, and regardless of the importance of convicting those who violate it—have no place in our jurisprudence.

We deal here with a criminal conviction, not a civil forfeiture. It is true that the crime was but a misdemeanor and the penalty in this case light. But under the statute even a first conviction can result in imprisonment for a year, and a subsequent offense is a felony carrying a punishment of up to three years in prison. So the standardless conviction approved today can serve in another case tomorrow to support a felony conviction and a substantial prison sentence. However highly the Court may regard the social objectives of the Food, Drug, and Cosmetic Act, that regard cannot serve to justify a criminal conviction so wholly alien to fundamental principles of our law.

The *Dotterweich* case stands for two propositions, and I accept them both. First, "any person" within [§ 303] may include any corporate officer or employee "standing in responsible relation" to a condition or transaction forbidden by the act. Second, a person may be convicted of a criminal offense under the act even in the absence of "the conventional requirement for criminal conduct—awareness of some wrongdoing."

But before a person can be convicted of a criminal violation of this act, a jury must find—and must be clearly instructed that it must find—evidence beyond a reasonable doubt that he engaged in wrongful conduct amounting at least to common-law negligence. There were no such instructions, and clearly, therefore, no such finding in this case.

For these reasons, I cannot join the Court in affirming Park's criminal conviction.

NOTES ON STRICT LIABILITY IN REGULATORY OFFENSES

1. **Questions on *Park*.** Could Park have been convicted if the letters of April, 1970, and January, 1972, had never been sent and the prosecution was based simply on the discoveries made during the various inspections? What, exactly, is the court's holding as to mens rea? Apart from the court's mens-rea holding, does the conduct underlying Park's conviction supply an adequate basis for criminal prosecution?

2. **The Strict-Liability Debate.** The scholarly literature on strict liability is for the most part strongly condemnatory of the use of the criminal law for the purposes illustrated by *Dotterweich* and *Park*. The occasional article defending strict liability [a] is offset by numerous, and often quite vociferous, attacks by some of the most respected scholars of the criminal law.[b]

Consider, for example, the position taken by Professor Henry Hart in The Aims of the Criminal Law, 23 Law & Contemp.Probs. 401, 422–25 (1958).[*] He asserted that cases such as *Dotterweich* "squarely pose the question whether there can be any justification for condemning and punishing a human being as a criminal when he has done nothing which is blameworthy" and answered that "there can be no moral justification for this, and . . . not, indeed, even a rational, amoral justification." In support of this conclusion, he argued that:

[a] E.g., Wasserstrom, Strict Liability in the Criminal Law, 12 Stan.L.Rev. 731 (1960).

[b] In addition to the other materials cited in these notes, see, e.g., J. Hall, General Principles of the Criminal Law 325–59 (2d ed. 1960); G. Williams, Textbook of Criminal Law 905–24 (1978); Packer, Mens Rea and the Supreme Court, 1962 Sup.Ct.Rev. 107.

[*] Copyright © 1958 by the Duke University School of Law. Reprinted with permission.

"1. People who do not know and cannot find out that they are supposed to comply with an applicable command are, by hypothesis, non-deterrable. . . .

"2. If it be said that most people will know of such commands and be able to comply with them, the answer, among others, is that nowhere else in the criminal law is the probable, or even the certain, guilt of nine men regarded as sufficient warrant for the conviction of a 10th. In the tradition of Anglo-American law, guilt of crime is personal. The main body of the criminal law, from the Constitution on down, makes sense on no other assumption.

"3. If it be asserted that strict criminal liability is necessary in order to stimulate people to be diligent in learning the law and finding out when it applies, the answer, among others, is that this is wholly unproved and prima-facie improbable. Studies to test the relative effectiveness of strict criminal liability and well designed civil penalties are lacking and badly needed. Until such studies are forthcoming, however, judgment can only take into account (i) the inherent unlikelihood that people's behavior will be significantly affected by commands that are not brought definitely to their attention; (ii) the long-understood tendency of disproportionate penalties to promote disrespect rather than respect for law, unless they are rigorously and uniformly enforced; (iii) the inherent difficulties of rigorous and uniform enforcement of strict criminal liability and the impressive evidence that it is, in fact, spottily and unevenly enforced; (iv) the greater possibilities of flexible and imaginative adaptation of civil penalties to fit particular regulatory problems, the greater reasonableness of such penalties, and their more ready enforceability; and (v) most important of all, the shocking damage that is done to social morale by open and official admission that crime can be respectable and criminality a matter of ill chance, rather than blameworthy choice.

"4. If it be urged that strict criminal liability is necessary in order to simplify the investigation and prosecution of violations of statutes designed to control mass conduct, the answer, among others, is that (i) maximizing compliance with law, rather than successful prosecution of violators, is the primary aim of any regulatory statute; (ii) the convenience of investigators and prosecutors is not, in any event, the prime consideration in determining what conduct is criminal; (iii) a prosecutor, as a matter of common knowledge, always assumes a heavier burden in trying to secure a criminal conviction than a civil judgment; (iv) in most situations of attempted control of mass conduct, the technique of a first warning, followed by criminal prosecution only of knowing violators, has not only obvious, but proved superiority; and (v) the common-sense advantages of using the criminal sanction only against deliberate violators is confirmed by the policies which prosecutors themselves tend always to follow when they are free to make their own selection of cases to prosecute.[c]

"5. Moral, rather than crassly utilitarian, considerations re-enter the picture when the claim is made, as it sometimes is, that strict liability operates, in fact, only against people who are really blameworthy, because prosecutors only pick out the really guilty ones for criminal prosecution. This argument reasserts the traditional position that a criminal conviction imports moral condemnation. To this, it adds the arrogant assertion that it is proper to visit the moral condemnation of the community upon one of its members on the basis solely of the private judgment of his prosecutors. Such a circumvention of the safeguards with which the law surrounds other determinations of criminality seems not only irrational, but immoral as well.

"6. But moral considerations in a still larger dimension are the ultimately controlling ones. In its conventional and traditional applications, a criminal conviction carries with it an ineradicable connotation of moral condemnation and personal guilt. Society makes an essentially parasitic, and hence illegitimate, use of this instrument when it uses it as a means of deterrence (or compulsion) of conduct which is morally neutral. This would be true even if a statute were to be enacted proclaiming that no criminal conviction hereafter should ever be understood as casting any reflection on anybody. For statutes cannot change the meaning of words and make people stop thinking what they do think when they hear the words spoken. But it is doubly true—it is 10-fold, 100-fold, 1000-fold true—when society continues to insist that some crimes *are* morally blameworthy and then tries to use the same epithet to describe conduct which is not.[d]

"7. To be sure, the traditional law recognizes gradations in the gravity of offenses . . . . [T]he excuse of the Scotch servant girl for her illegitimate baby, that "It was only such a leetle one," is not open to modern legislatures. And since a crime remains a crime, just as a baby is unalterably a baby, it would

[c] Criteria for prosecution of offenders such as Park have not been officially promulgated. There are, however, informal indications of the bases on which selections are made, among them: the seriousness of the violation, evidence of knowledge or intent, the likely effect of prosecution on future conduct by the defendant and others similarly situated, available resources, and the impact of the violation on consumers. It appears that a judgment as to fault is highly relevant to the likelihood of prosecution, and that a warning letter of the sort that Park received usually precedes prosecution. See generally O'Keefe, Criminal Liability: *Park* Update, 32 Food, Drug, Cosmetic L.J. 400–02 (1977); O'Keefe & Shapiro, Personal Criminal Liability under the Federal Food, Drug, and Cosmetic Act: The *Dotterweich* Doctrine, 30 Food, Drug, Cosmetic L.J. 5 (1975). [Footnote by eds.]

[d] Cf. G. Williams, Criminal Law: The General Part 259 (2d ed. 1961):

"[Strict liability] is an abuse of the moral sentiments of the community. To make a practice of branding people as criminals who are without moral fault tends to weaken respect for the law and the social condemnation of those who break it. When it becomes respectable to be convicted, the vitality of the criminal law has been sapped." [Footnote by eds.]

not be a good excuse if it were. Especially is this so since the legislature could avoid the taint of illegitimacy, much more surely than the servant girl, by simply saying that the 'crime' is not a crime, but only a civil violation."

Do you find Hart's arguments persuasive? Bear in mind that he was speaking generally to a wide variety of contexts in which strict liability has been used. How many of his arguments apply to *Park?* Is there any force to the argument that deterrence can be achieved in the *Park* situation? Is strict liability, at least in a context like *Park,* morally justifiable to at least the same extent, and for the same reasons, as liability for negligence? [e] Indeed, given the "powerless" defense, is liability completely "without fault" in *Park?*

3. **Alternatives to Strict Liability.** How should legislatures respond to these criticisms? Consider first the possibility of decriminalization. Following the lead of the Model Penal Code, many states have reclassified such strict-liability regulatory offenses as non-criminal "infractions" or "violations" that are punishable only by monetary penalties and that do not "give rise to any disability or legal disadvantage based on conviction of a criminal offense." [f] Is this a satisfactory solution? Is it subject to the criticism that it perpetuates "the injustice and futility of punishing men for consequences they cannot help"? [g] In what sense are violators "punished" by imposition of such sanctions? How do such sanctions differ from the damages imposed on the defendant in a civil suit for tortious conduct or breach of contract? On the other hand, proponents of the existing law argue that such a reclassification would undermine the preventive purposes of regulatory prohibitions because the threatened penalties exert no meaningful deterrent effect. How do you think corporate officials like Mr. Park would assess the personal "costs" of a criminal conviction and a possible jail term as compared with a $1,000 fine, or even a $10,000 fine, resulting from a "civil" proceeding? [h]

Decriminalization is not the only possible solution. An alternative would be to maintain criminal sanctions for regulatory offenses and to require proof of negligence as an essential predicate for the imposition of liability. Professor Glanville Williams has argued that negligence

[e] Compare the arguments canvassed in the note on negligence as the basis for criminal liability, pages 214–19, supra. Could the same justifications be asserted as the basis for liability on the *Park* facts? On the law as the Supreme Court states it?

[f] MPC § 1.04(5). See also Section 2.05.

[g] G. Williams, Criminal Law: The General Part 261 (2d ed. 1961).

[h] Park was punishable upon conviction under § 301(k) by a maximum sentence of one year; a second offense would have been classified as a felony with a maximum authorized sentence of three years. Sentences of confinement for these lengths would rarely be imposed in a case like

Park, though there are cases in the *Dotterweich-Park* line, all in lower courts, where jail sentences have been imposed. See O'Keefe & Shapiro, Personal Criminal Liability under the Federal Food, Drug, and Cosmetic Act: The *Dotterweich* Doctrine, 30 Food, Drug, Cosmetic L.J. 5, 14, 18 (1975). One case, United States v. H. Wool & Sons, Inc., 215 F.2d 95 (2d Cir. 1954), involved a $1000 fine and six months in jail for repackaging butter held for sale with labels that misrepresented its weight. G. Williams, Criminal Law: The General Part 256 (2d ed. 1961), also refers to an English case where the defendant was fined £1000 and sentenced to 12 months' imprisonment.

"is a halfway house . . . which has not been properly utilized" in such cases. He continues:

> "In nearly all the public-welfare offences coming before the courts there has been at least negligence on the part of the defendant . . . . To put responsibility frankly upon personal negligence would not be a large practical change, but would better accord with the general sense of right, while not weakening the effectiveness of the legislation. It is only rarely that a person is convicted of a public-welfare offence where the real fault was that of a third party over whom the defendant had no control." [i]

Is this a fair compromise? Would the objectives of the Food & Drug Act be undermined if Park could be prosecuted only for negligent supervision? Indeed, how different would a prosecution for negligence be from what the court actually held in *Park?* Is Stewart right in suggesting that the court was really adopting a negligence standard? Or does he re-write the Court's opinion in stating his "understanding" of what it says?

SUBSECTION B: CONSTITUTIONAL LIMITS ON STRICT LIABILITY

LAMBERT v. CALIFORNIA

Supreme Court of the United States, 1957.
355 U.S. 225.

MR. JUSTICE DOUGLAS delivered the opinion of the Court.

Section 52.38(a) of the Los Angeles Municipal Code defines "convicted person" as follows:

> "Any person who, subsequent to January 1, 1921, has been or hereafter is convicted of an offense punishable as a felony in the state of California, or who has been or who is hereafter convicted of any offense in any place other than the state of California, which offense, if committed in the state of California, would have been punishable as a felony."

Section 52.39 provides that it shall be unlawful for "any convicted person" to be or remain in Los Angeles for a period of more than five days without registering; it requires any person having a place of abode outside the city to register if he comes into the city on five occasions or more during a 30-day period; and it prescribes the information to be furnished the chief of police on registering.

---

[i] Id. at 262. Professor Williams cites several English cases where this approach has been taken. He also notes that it has more frequently been used in Australia and Denmark. See also Sweet v. Parsley, [1970] A.C. 132. Note that Section 2.05(2)(b) of the Model Penal Code also contemplates this possibility. [Footnote by eds.]

Section 52.43(b) makes the failure to register a continuing offense, each day's failure constituting a separate offense.

Appellant, arrested on suspicion of another offense, was charged with a violation of this registration law. The evidence showed that she had been at the time of her arrest a resident of Los Angeles for over seven years. Within that period she had been convicted in Los Angeles of the crime of forgery, an offense which California punishes as a felony. Though convicted of a crime punishable as a felony, she had not at the time of her arrest registered under the Municipal Code. At the trial, appellant asserted that Section 52.39 of the code denies her due process of law and other rights under the federal Constitution, unnecessary to enumerate. The trial court denied this objection. The case was tried to a jury which found appellant guilty. The court fined her $250 and placed her on probation for three years.[a] Appellant, renewing her constitutional objection, moved for arrest of judgment and a new trial. This motion was denied. On appeal the constitutionality of the code was again challenged. The Appellate Department of the Superior Court affirmed the judgment, holding there was no merit to the claim that the ordinance was unconstitutional. The case is here on appeal. We noted probable jurisdiction and designated amicus curiae to appear in support of appellant. The case having been argued and reargued, we now hold that the registration provisions of the code as sought to be applied here violate the due-process requirement of the 14th amendment.

The registration provision, carrying criminal penalties, applies if a person has been convicted "of an offense punishable as a felony in the state of California" or, in case he has been convicted in another state, if the offense "would have been punishable as a felony" had it been committed in California. No element of willfulness is by terms included in the ordinance nor read into it by the California court as a condition necessary for a conviction.

We must assume that appellant had no actual knowledge of the requirement that she register under this ordinance, as she offered proof of this defense which was refused. The question is whether a registration act of this character violates due process where it is applied to a person who has no actual knowledge of his duty to register, and where no showing is made of the probability of such knowledge.

We do not go with Blackstone in saying that "a vicious will" is necessary to constitute a crime, for conduct alone without regard to the intent of the doer is often sufficient. There is wide latitude in the lawmakers to declare an offense and to exclude elements of knowledge and diligence from its definition. But we deal here with conduct that is wholly passive—mere failure to register. It is unlike the commission of acts, or the failure to act under circumstances that should alert the doer to the consequences of his deed. Cf. Shevlin-Carpenter Co. v. Minnesota, 218 U.S. 57 (1910); [b] United States v. Balint, 258 U.S. 250

[a] The maximum authorized sentence was a fine of $500 and/or six months in jail. [Footnote by eds.]

[b] *Shevlin-Carpenter* was a civil case imposing double damages for cutting timber on state lands. [Footnote by eds.]

(1922); [c] United States v. Dotterweich, 320 U.S. 277 (1943).[d] The rule that "ignorance of the law will not excuse" is deep in our law, as is the principle that of all the powers of local government, the police power is "one of the least limitable." On the other hand, due process places some limits on its exercise. Engrained in our concept of due process is the requirement of notice. Notice is sometimes essential so that the citizen has the chance to defend charges. Notice is required before property interests are disturbed, before assessments are made, before penalties are assessed. Notice is required in a myriad of situations where a penalty or forfeiture might be suffered for mere failure to act. Recent cases illustrating the point are Mullane v. Central Hanover Bank & Trust Co., 339 U.S. 306 (1950),[e] [and others]. These cases involved only property interests in civil litigation. But the principle is equally appropriate where a person, wholly passive and unaware of any wrongdoing, is brought to the bar of justice for condemnation in a criminal case.

Registration laws are common and their range is wide. Many such laws are akin to licensing statutes in that they pertain to the regulation of business activities. But the present ordinance is entirely different. Violation of its provisions is unaccompanied by any activity whatever, mere presence in the city being the test. Moreover, circumstances which might move one to inquire as to the necessity of registration are completely lacking. At most the ordinance is but a law-enforcement technique designed for the convenience of law-enforcement agencies through which a list of the names and addresses of felons then residing in a given community is compiled. The disclosure is merely a compilation of former convictions already publicly recorded in the jurisdiction where obtained. Nevertheless, this appellant on first becoming aware of her duty to register was given no opportunity to comply with the law and avoid its penalty, even though her default was entirely innocent. She could but suffer the consequences of the ordinance, namely, conviction with the imposition of heavy criminal penalties thereunder. We

[c] *Balint* involved a prosecution for selling a derivative of opium contrary to federal narcotics legislation. The maximum penalty upon conviction was five years in prison. The district court dismissed the indictment because it failed to allege mens rea. The Supreme Court unanimously reversed. The Court noted that normally scienter was required for all crimes, but that "there had been a modification of this view in respect to prosecutions under statutes the purpose of which would be obstructed by such a requirement." The Court then referred to the line of public-welfare offenses and seemed to place the offense at issue in that category. At one point in its opinion, however, the Court said that such offenses "require the punishment of the negligent person though he be ignorant." At another, it referred to the fact that the statute required "every person . . . to ascertain at his peril whether that which he sells comes within the inhibition of the statute" and to penalize him "if he sells the inhibited drug in ignorance of its character." The argument that conviction without mens rea would violate due process was dismissed in one sentence with a citation to *Shevlin-Carpenter*. [Footnote by eds.]

[d] The *Dotterweich* case is summarized at pages 293–95, supra. [Footnote by eds.]

[e] *Mullane* is a case, usually studied in civil procedure courses, involving the adequacy of notice by publication to persons who may be affected by the judicial settlement of accounts by a trustee. The case concerned a common trust fund, participated in by 113 separate trusts, with numerous beneficiaries scattered all over the country. The issue was the kind of notice required in pending litigation to persons who may be affected by the outcome. [Footnote by eds.]

believe that actual knowledge of the duty to register or proof of the probability of such knowledge and subsequent failure to comply are necessary before a conviction under the ordinance can stand. As Holmes wrote in The Common Law, "A law which punished conduct which would not be blameworthy in the average member of the community would be too severe for that community to bear." [f] Its severity lies in the absence of an opportunity either to avoid the consequences of the law or to defend any prosecution brought under it. Where a person did not know of the duty to register and where there was no proof of the probability of such knowledge, he may not be convicted consistently with due process. Were it otherwise, the evil would be as great as it is when the law is written in print too fine to read or in a language foreign to the community.

Reversed.

MR. JUSTICE BURTON dissents because he believes that, as applied to this appellant, the ordinance does not violate her constitutional rights.

MR. JUSTICE FRANKFURTER, whom MR. JUSTICE HARLAN and MR. JUSTICE WHITTAKER join, dissenting.

The present laws of the United States and of the 48 states are thick with provisions that command that some things not be done and others be done, although persons convicted under such provisions may have had no awareness of what the law required or that what they did was wrongdoing. The body of decisions sustaining such legislation, including innumerable registration laws, is almost as voluminous as the legislation itself. The matter is summarized in *Balint:* "Many instances of this are to be found in regulatory measures in the exercise of what is called the police power where the emphasis of the statute is evidently upon achievement of some social betterment rather than the punishment of the crime as in cases of mala in se."

Surely there can hardly be a difference as a matter of fairness, of hardship, or of justice, if one may invoke it, between the case of a person wholly innocent of wrongdoing, in the sense that he was not remotely conscious of violating any law, who is imprisoned for five years for conduct relating to narcotics, and the case of another person who is placed on probation for three years on condition that she pay $250, for failure, as a local resident, convicted under local law of a felony, to register under a law passed as an exercise of the state's "police power." Considerations of hardship often lead courts, naturally enough, to attribute to a statute the requirement of certain mental element—some consciousness of wrongdoing and knowledge of the law's command—as a matter of statutory construction. Then, too, a cruelly disproportionate relation between what the law requires and the sanction for its disobedience may constitute a violation of the eighth amendment as a cruel and unusual punishment, and, in respect to the states, even offend the due process clause of the 14th amendment.

[f] This statement by Holmes appears in a passage quoted at pages 211–14, supra, where it can be read in context. [Footnote by eds.]

But what the Court here does is to draw a constitutional line between a state's requirement of doing and not doing. What is this but a return to Year Book distinctions between feasance and nonfeasance— a distinction that may have significance in the evolution of common-law notions of liability, but is inadmissible as a line between constitutionality and unconstitutionality. One can be confident that Mr. Justice Holmes would have been the last to draw such a line. What he wrote about "blameworthiness" is worth quoting in its context:

> "It is not intended to deny that criminal liability, as well as civil, is founded on blameworthiness. Such a denial would shock the moral sense of any civilized community; or, to put it another way, a law which punished conduct which would not be blameworthy in the average member of the community would be too severe for that community to bear." (This passage must be read in the setting of the broader discussion of which it is an essential part. O. Holmes, The Common Law 49–50 (1881).)

If the generalization that underlies, and alone can justify, this decision were to be given its relevant scope, a whole volume of the United States Reports would be required to document in detail the legislation in this country that would fall or be impaired. I abstain from entering upon a consideration of such legislation, and adjudications upon it, because I feel confident that the present decision will turn out to be an isolated deviation from the strong current of precedents—a derelict on the waters of the law. Accordingly, I content myself with dissenting.

NOTE ON *LAMBERT*

Can a meaningful constitutional limit on the use of strict liability be derived from *Lambert?* In an interesting and provocative article dealing with *Shevlin-Carpenter, Balint, Dotterweich, Lambert,* and related cases, Professor Packer offers the following introductory summation: "Mens rea is an important requirement, but it is not a constitutional requirement, except sometimes." [a] Is it possible to be more specific?

There are at least five factors involved in the *Lambert* prosecution that, separately or together, may serve to explain the result: (i) Ms. Lambert lacked mens rea in the ordinary sense, i.e., she lacked purpose, knowledge, recklessness, or negligence as to her failure to register; (ii) her offense involved an omission rather than affirmative misconduct; (iii) she was unaware of the requirement that she register and the criminality of failure to do so; (iv) the statute carried serious criminal penalties; and (v) though the language of the statute was precise enough, its obscurity and applicability only to a class of persons in whom the police could be expected to have special interest suggests some of the same defects the Court has taken seriously in the vagueness

[a] Packer, Mens Rea and the Supreme Court, [1962] Sup.Ct.Rev. 107. See also Erlinder, Mens Rea, Due Process, and the Supreme Court: Toward a Constitutional Doctrine of Substantive Criminal Law, 9 Am.J.Crim.Law 163 (1981).

context. *Lambert* has often been regarded as having established a constitutionally mandated exception to the ignorantia-juris concept, i.e., as having been based on the third factor listed above. Which of these factors do you regard as crucial to the decision? Are there other factors that deserve consideration?

Consider the following hypotheticals in thinking about these questions:

(i) Defendant is prosecuted for murder. He deliberately allowed his infant son to starve to death, and defends on the ground that he did not know such behavior could be murder.

(ii) Defendant purchased a bottle labeled "aspirin" in a drug store and she believed the label. She is arrested as she leaves the store and is prosecuted for possession of narcotics, which tests prove the bottle contained.

(iii) Defendant, a manufacturer of sulphuric acid, shipped its product by common carrier. Federal regulations require such shipments to be labeled "Corrosive Liquid." Defendant did not so label the shipment, and defends prosecution for violation of the regulation on the ground that it did not know of its existence.

(iv) Defendant is a minister interested in performing marriages who obtained advice from the prosecuting attorney that a particular sign would not violate a law prohibiting the advertising of marriages. The sign is erected and the minister is prosecuted.

Would *Lambert* provide the basis for a constitutional defense in any of these cases? Would Ms. Lambert herself have a defense if her offense were classified as a "violation" under the Model Penal Code approach to regulatory offenses?

SUBSECTION C: STRICT LIABILITY IN SERIOUS CRIMES

UNITED STATES v. FREED
Supreme Court of the United States, 1971.
401 U.S. 601.

Mr. Justice Douglas delivered the opinion of the Court.

The defendants were indicted for possession of unregistered hand grenades in violation of a federal statute that carried a 10-year maximum sentence. The district court dismissed the indictments on the ground, inter alia, that due process was violated by the failure to allege mens rea. The government appealed.

We . . . conclude that the district court erred in dismissing the indictment for absence of an allegation of scienter.

The act requires no specific intent or knowledge that the hand grenades were unregistered. It makes it unlawful for any person "to receive or possess a firearm which is not registered to him." . . .

The presence of a "vicious will" or mens rea was long a requirement of criminal responsibility. But the list of exceptions grew, especially in the expanding regulatory area involving activities affecting public health, safety, and welfare. The statutory offense of embezzlement, borrowed from the common law where scienter was historically required, was in a different category:

"[W]here Congress borrows terms of art in which are accumulated the legal tradition and meaning of centuries of practice, it presumably knows and adopts the cluster of ideas that were attached to each borrowed word in the body of learning from which it was taken and the meaning its use will convey to the judicial mind unless otherwise instructed." [a]

At the other extreme is Lambert v. California, 355 U.S. 225 (1957), in which a municipal code made it a crime to remain in Los Angeles for more than five days without registering if a person had been convicted of a felony. Being in Los Angeles is not per se blameworthy. The mere failure to register, we held, was quite "unlike the commission of acts, or the failure to act under circumstances that should alert the doer to the consequences of his deed." The fact that the ordinance was a convenient law enforcement-technique did not save it:

"Where a person did not know of the duty to register and where there was no proof of the probability of such knowledge, he may not be convicted consistently with due process. Were it otherwise, the evil would be as great as it is when the law is written in print too fine to read or in a language foreign to the community."

In United States v. Dotterweich, 320 U.S. 277 (1943), a case dealing with the imposition of a penalty on a corporate officer whose firm shipped adulterated and misbranded drugs in violation of the Food and Drug Act, we approved the penalty "though consciousness of wrongdoing be totally wanting."

The present case is in the category neither of *Lambert* nor *Morissette*, but is closer to *Dotterweich*. This is a regulatory measure in the interest of the public safety, which may well be premised on the theory that one would hardly be surprised to learn that possession of hand grenades is not an innocent act. They are highly dangerous offensive weapons, no less dangerous than the narcotics involved in United States v. Balint, 258 U.S. 250 (1922), where a defendant was convicted of sale of narcotics against his claim that he did not know the drugs were covered by a federal act. We say with Chief Justice Taft in that case:

"It is very evident from a reading of it that the emphasis of the section is in securing a close supervision of the business of

[a] The quotation is from Morissette v. United States, 342 U.S. 246 (1952), and is set forth in context at page 224, supra. [Footnote by eds.]

dealing in these dangerous drugs by the taxing officers of the government and that it merely uses a criminal penalty to secure recorded evidence of the disposition of such drugs as a means of taxing and restraining the traffic. Its manifest purpose is to require every person dealing in drugs to ascertain at his peril whether that which he sells comes within the inhibition of the statute, and if he sells the inhibited drug in ignorance of its character, to penalize him. Congress weighed the possible injustice of subjecting an innocent seller to a penalty against the evil of exposing innocent purchasers to danger from the drug, and concluded that the latter was the result preferably to be avoided."

Reversed.

Mr. Justice Brennan, concurring in the judgment of reversal.

[A]lthough I reach the same result as the Court on the intent the government must prove to convict, I do so by another route. . . .

The Court's discussion of the intent the government must prove . . . does not dispel the confusion surrounding a difficult, but vitally important, area of the law. This case does not raise questions of "consciousness of wrongdoing" or "blameworthiness." If the ancient maxim that "ignorance of the law is no excuse" has any residual validity, it indicates that the ordinary intent requirement—mens rea— of the criminal law does not require knowledge that an act is illegal, wrong, or blameworthy. Nor is it possible to decide this case by a simple process of classifying the statute involved as a "regulatory" or a "public welfare" measure. To convict appellees of possession of unregistered hand grenades, the government must prove three material elements: (i) that appellees possessed certain items; (ii) that the items possessed were hand grenades; and (iii) that the hand grenades were not registered. The government and the Court agree that the prosecutor must prove knowing possession of the items and also knowledge that the items possessed were hand grenades. Thus, while the Court does hold that no intent at all need be proved in regard to one element of the offense—the unregistered status of the grenades—knowledge must still be proved as to the other two elements. Consequently, the National Firearms Act does not create a crime of strict liability as to all its elements. It is no help in deciding what level of intent must be proved as to the third element to declare that the offense falls within the "regulatory" category.

Following the analysis of the Model Penal Code, I think we must recognize, first, that "[t]he existence of a mens rea is the rule of, rather than the exception to, the principles of Anglo-American criminal jurisprudence;" second, that mens rea is not a unitary concept, but may vary as to each element of a crime; and third, that Anglo-American law has developed several identifiable and analytically distinct levels of intent, e.g., negligence, recklessness, knowledge, and purpose. To determine the mental element required for conviction, each material element of the offense must be examined and the determination made what level of intent Congress intended the government to prove, taking into account constitutional considerations, ... as well as the common-law background, if any, of the crime involved. See Morissette v. United States, 342 U.S. 246 (1952).

Although the legislative history of the amendments to the National Firearms Act is silent on the level of intent to be proved in connection with each element of the offense, we are not without some guideposts. I begin with the proposition stated in *Morissette* that the requirement of mens rea "is no provincial or transient notion. It is as universal and persistent in mature systems of law as belief in freedom of the human will and a consequent ability and duty of the normal individual to choose between good and evil." In regard to the first two elements of the offense, (i) possession of items that (ii) are hand grenades, the general rule in favor of some intent requirement finds confirmation in the case law . . . . [W]e may therefore properly infer that Congress meant that the government must prove knowledge with regard to the first two elements of the offense under the amended statute.

The third element—the unregistered status of the grenades— presents more difficulty. Proof of intent with regard to this element would require the government to show that the appellees knew that the grenades were unregistered or negligently or recklessly failed to ascertain whether the weapons were registered. It is true that such a requirement would involve knowledge of law, but it does *not* involve "consciousness of wrongdoing" in the sense of knowledge that one's actions were prohibited or illegal. Rather, the definition of the crime, as written by Congress, requires proof of circumstances that involve a legal element, namely whether the grenades were registered in accordance with federal law. The knowledge involved is solely knowledge of the circumstances that the law has defined as material to the offense. . . . .

Therefore, as with the first two elements, the question is solely one of congressional intent. And while the question is not an easy one, two factors persuade me that proof of mens rea as to the unregistered status of the grenades is not required. First, . . . the case law under the provisions replaced by the current law dispensed with proof of intent in connection with this element. Second, the firearms covered by the act are major weapons such as machine guns and sawed-off shotguns; deceptive weapons such as flashlight guns and fountain-pen guns; and major destructive devices such as bombs, grenades, mines, rockets, and bazookas. Without exception, the likelihood of governmental regulation of the distribution of such weapons is so great that anyone must be presumed to be aware of it. In the context of a . . . registration scheme, I therefore think it reasonable to conclude that Congress dispensed with the requirement of intent in regard to the unregistered status of the weapon, as necessary to effective administration of the statute.

———

NOTES ON STRICT LIABILITY IN SERIOUS CRIMES

1. **Questions on *Freed*.** Is Justice Douglas correct in analogizing the situation in *Freed* to the line of public-welfare offenses? Is not the penalty alone sufficient to distinguish the two situations? Contrast Justice Brennan's rationale for imposing strict liability on the unregistered status of the grenades. Is his opinion more persuasive?

Notice that none of the Justices took seriously a constitutional argument that Freed could not be convicted. Is *Lambert* applicable? Or is the question simply one of legislative intent on a matter as to which Congress was silent? If so, what principles of construction should apply? Is Justice Jackson's reasoning in *Morissette* (page 221, supra) relevant? Should it be controlling?

2. ***Regina v. Prince.*** Consider the decision in Regina v. Prince, L.R. 2 C.C.R. 154 (1875), in connection with Justice Brennan's *Freed* opinion. The defendant was indicted under a statute that read:

> "Whosoever shall unlawfully take . . . any unmarried girl, being under the age of 16 years, out of the possession and against the will of her father . . . shall be guilty of a misdemeanor . . . ."

The defendant committed the acts proscribed by this statute, but believed that the girl was 18 years old. In fact she was 14, but the jury determined that the defendant's mistaken belief was honest and reasonable. The question was whether such a mistake should be a defense.

The conviction was affirmed. Four opinions were written.[a] Judge Blackburn, joined by nine colleagues, held that the legislature intended that no mens rea be required for the age element. On this view of the offense, it was plain that no mistake as to age would be exculpatory, and these judges therefore voted for conviction. Judge Brett, joined by none of his colleagues, applied the common-law mistake of fact rule summarized on pages 253–54, supra. His view was that the conviction should be reversed because no crime would have been committed had the facts been as the defendant believed them to be. Accordingly, for him an honest and reasonable mistake of fact was a defense. Judge Bramwell, joined by seven colleagues, wrote the opinion that is of present interest. He voted to uphold the conviction because Prince's conduct would have been morally wrong even if the girl had been 18. He explained:

> "The act forbidden is wrong in itself, if without lawful cause; I do not say illegal, but wrong. . . . The legislature has enacted that if anyone does this wrong act, he does it at the risk of her turning out to be under 16. This opinion gives full scope to the doctrine of the mens rea. If the taker believed he had the father's consent, though wrongly, he would have no mens rea; so if he did not know she was in anyone's possession, nor in the care or charge of anyone. In those cases he would not know he was

---

[a] For a thorough consideration of the various opinions in *Prince*, see G. Williams, Criminal Law: The General Part 185–99 (2d ed. 1961).

doing the *act* forbidden by the statute—an act which, if he knew she was in possession and in care or charge of anyone, he would know was a crime or not, according as she was under 16 or not."

Judge Bramwell purported to be stating a general proposition for the interpretation of common-law offenses. His position was that since Prince knew enough about his conduct to make it a morally wrong act, his mistake about the age of the girl should be irrelevant. To put the point another way, mens rea should be required as to those elements central to the wrongfulness of the act. Liability should be strict as to the remaining elements of the offense.[b]

Professor Perkins has taken the position that Judge Bramwell's view in *Prince* is reflected in the current law with respect to some crimes:[*]

"In certain very extreme situations one may be convicted of a true crime although at the time of his deed he was laboring under a mistake of fact based upon reasonable grounds, and of such a nature that the thing done would not have been a crime had the facts been as he reasonably supposed them to be. These are cases in which the deed would have involved a high degree of moral delinquency even under the supposed facts, and the claim for acquittal is based, not upon the ground that defendant thought his deed was proper or lawful but only that he thought it was a type of wrongful conduct for which no criminal penalty had been provided. The common examples fall within the fields of statutory rape, abduction and adultery.

"A man who has illicit sexual intercourse with a girl under the age of consent is guilty of statutory rape although she consented and he mistakenly believed she was older than the limit thus established. This is true no matter how reasonable his mistaken belief may have been, as in cases in which both her appearance and her positive statement indicated she was older than she was in fact, or in which he had exercised considerable pains in the effort to ascertain her age. One who has illicit intercourse with a married person is guilty of adultery even if he has no idea that the other is married. . . .

"It has sometimes been suggested that the reason for this result in such cases is that these are crimes which have no mens-rea requirement. This is quite unsound and should be avoided because it will lead to very unsatisfactory results in certain cases, such as those of *innocent* mistake of fact. The latter problem has arisen most frequently in the adultery cases. If the intercourse

[b] The fourth opinion in *Prince* was written by Judge Denman, who was joined by none of the other judges. Judge Denman voted to affirm the conviction. His view was that Prince was guilty because on the facts as he believed them to be, he would have been civilly liable to the girl's father. Judge Denman's view, in other words, was that strict liability should be applied to those elements of a criminal offense that are not central to whether a civil wrong would have been committed had the facts been as the defendant believed them to be.

* Reprinted by permission of the University of Pennsylvania Law Review and Fred B. Rothman Company from the University of Pennsylvania Law Review, vol. 88, pp. 62–65.

is obviously illicit, the mistaken belief in the unmarried status of the other party is not an *innocent* mistake, however well grounded it may be, since the conduct falls far below the line of social acceptability even under the supposed facts. 'In such a case there is a measure of wrong in the act as the defendant understands it, and his ignorance of the fact that makes it a greater wrong will not relieve him from the legal penalty.' On the other hand, in spite of some indication to the contrary, it is clearly established that if the intercourse follows a marriage ceremony entered into in good faith, with no thought or reason to believe that the other party is already married, it does not constitute the crime of adultery if it does not occur after the mistake has been discovered. . . .

"Mens rea is requisite to guilt of such offenses but there is no *specific* requirement of knowledge. Hence a prima-facie case of guilt is established by proof of the act of intercourse by the defendant with one . . . married to another, without either averment or proof of any such knowledge on his part. After this prima-facie case is established it is possible for the defendant to come forward with proof indicating that although he intentionally indulged in the act of intercourse he did not do so with mens rea, because of a mistake of fact. Whether the proof offered will be sufficient for this purpose depends not only upon whether the mistake was based upon reasonable grounds but also upon the nature of the mistake. And the act under such circumstances as supposed by him may have involved too much of blameworthiness to permit this excuse, even if he could have avoided any criminal penalty had his conjecture been correct."

Is there a case to be made for this position? As to some crimes only? As to all crimes? Is a defendant who has proceeded far enough along a course of conduct so that moral signals should operate to restrain further action properly punishable for not having stopped? Though he ultimately rejects the doctrine, Professor Williams, in Criminal Law: The General Part 188–89 (2d ed. 1961), advances the following argument in support of Judge Bramwell's position in *Prince*:

"The chief attraction of this view is that citizens who break the law frequently do not know the existence or at any rate the precise working of the crime in question, yet may know that they are doing something morally reprehended by the community. To equate mens rea with the knowledge of this moral reprobation has therefore an air of practicality. Thus suppose that there are two men who respectively abduct girls just under 16. The first is told by the girl her true age; the second is told by the girl that she is just over 16. Neither of them knows the law and does not realise the legal importance of the age of 16. If we convict the first man of an offence, as we must, why (it may be asked) should we not convict the second also? It is not as though the second knew the law and thought from what the girl said that he would not be committing an offense. The relevance of the precise age of the girl is a legal technicality not known to the man, and since it does not affect the morality of the matter, mistake as to this age should not be a defence."

Professor Brett, in An Inquiry into Criminal Guilt 149 (1963), goes further and argues that Judge Bramwell is right:

"Which of [the] views [stated in *Prince*] is the better? That of Bramwell, B. is to my mind clearly in accord with principle. It reflects the view that we learn our duties, not by studying the statute book, but by living in a community. A defence of mistake rests ultimately on the defendant's being able to say that he has observed the community ethic, and this Prince could not do. The view of Brett, J. depends ultimately, it seems, on an argument based on deterrence; it involves saying that the defendant was aware of the command of the law, but the command could have no force because on the basis of his beliefs it did not impinge on his conduct. This analysis is reflected in his opinion that Prince could have been found guilty if according to his beliefs he had been committing a lesser kind of wrong forbidden by the criminal law. It is difficult to see why we should stop at this point rather than adopt the view of Denman, J. For the law of tort also uses the deterrent factor to some extent in its commands, albeit a different kind of sanction is used. I would reject both these views on the ground that they reflect too strongly the Austinian view of law as a command, and indeed ultimately rest on the belief that law and ethics are two separate compartments."

On the other hand, whose moral signals are being used to determine the proper stopping point? Compare the *Manley* case, page 29, supra. There, the judges decided that conduct was criminally punishable based on their own moral assessment reached after the conduct was committed. Is Bramwell doing the same thing here, and is he subject to the same criticisms leveled at the *Manley* approach? There is the difference here that Prince actually had engaged in specifically prohibited conduct, and that he knew a good bit, though not precisely all, about the nature of his conduct. Does this difference matter?

Return now to Justice Brennan's opinion in *Freed*. Is he taking essentially the same position as Judge Bramwell in *Prince*? Would you defend that position as stating a principle that should generally determine when a particular element of a serious crime should carry strict liability? Consider, for example, felony murder. The details of the felony-murder rule are developed at pages 932–65, infra. That rule states that anyone who participates in prescribed felonies is guilty of murder if a person is killed during the course of the felony, irrespective of whether the felon(s) manifested the culpability towards death of the victim normally required for a murder conviction. Liability is therefore strict as to the death. Is the felony-murder rule based on the principles involved in *Prince* or *Freed*? Does it seem defensible?

3. ***United States v. Yermian.*** The defendant in United States v. Yermian, 468 U.S. 63 (1984), lied as to his employment history and

criminal record on a security questionnaire [c] which his employer, a defense contractor, required him to fill out because he was to have access to classified information. He was convicted of violating 18 U.S.C. § 1001, which provides:

> "Whoever, in any matter within the jurisdiction of any department or agency of the United States knowingly and willfully . . . makes any false . . . statements . . . shall be fined not more than $10,000 or imprisoned not more than five years, or both."

Yermian admitted at his trial that he had intentionally made false statements on the form so that the information it contained would be consistent with similar false statements he had made on his employment application. His sole defense was that he had no knowledge that his false statements would be transmitted to a federal agency. His attorney requested an instruction to the effect that the jury could not convict unless they found that he knew that the statements were made in a matter within the jurisdiction of a federal agency. The trial judge rejected this request, but instructed the jury that it should convict if it found that the defendant "knew or should have known that the information was to be submitted to a government agency."

The Court of Appeals reversed, but the Supreme Court reinstated the conviction. Justice Powell's opinion for the Court first noted that the language "in any matter within the jurisdiction of any department or agency of the United States" was a "jurisdictional element," that is, an element "whose primary purpose is to identify the factor that makes the false statement an appropriate subject for federal concern." [d] "Jurisdictional language," Justice Powell continued, "need not contain the same culpability requirement as other elements of the offense." He then noted that the statutory language was clear in this case, since the

> "jurisdictional language appears in a phrase separate from the prohibited conduct modified by the terms 'knowingly and willfully.' Any natural reading of § 1001, therefore, establishes that the terms 'knowingly and willfully' modify only the making of 'false . . . statements' and not the predicate circumstance that those statements be made in a matter within the jurisdiction of a federal agency. Once this is clear, there is no basis for requiring proof that the defendant had actual knowledge of federal agency jurisdiction. The statute contains no language suggesting any additional element of intent . . . . On its face, therefore, § 1001 requires that the government prove that false statements were made knowingly and willfully, and it unambiguously dispenses with any requirement that the government also prove

[c] The form was entitled "Department of Defense Personnel Security Questionnaire." The document contained a reference to the "Defense Industrial Security Clearance Office," stated that Yermian's work would require access to "secret" material, and stated explicitly that signing it would grant the "Department of Defense" permission to conduct an investigation. A warning that any false answers would subject him to prosecution under "§ 1001 of the United States Criminal Code" was printed right above the place where Yermian signed the form.

[d] See the discussion on pages 104–05, supra.

that those statements were made with actual knowledge of federal agency jurisdiction."

Justice Powell's reading of the legislative history of the statute confirmed this conclusion. He then turned to the defendant's argument that construed in this manner § 1001 becomes a " 'trap for the unwary' imposing criminal sanctions on 'wholly innocent conduct.' " Justice Powell responded:

"Whether or not respondent fairly may characterize the intentional and deliberate lies prohibited by the statute (and manifest in this case) as 'wholly innocent conduct,' this argument is not sufficient to overcome the express statutory language of § 1001. Respondent does not argue that Congress lacks the power to impose criminal sanctions for deliberately false statements submitted to a federal agency, regardless whether the person who made such statements actually knew that they were being submitted to the federal government. That is precisely what Congress has done here. In the unlikely event that § 1001 could be the basis for imposing an unduly harsh result on those who intentionally make false statements to the federal government, it is for Congress and not this Court to amend the criminal statute.[14] "

Justice Rehnquist dissented, joined by Justices Brennan, Stevens, and O'Connor. He argued that the statute was ambiguous and that the legislative history confirmed that actual knowledge as to the jurisdictional element should be required. He also argued that it should not lightly be inferred that Congress

"intended to criminalize the making of even the most casual false statements so long as they turned out, unbeknownst to their maker, to be material to some federal agency function. The latter interpretation would substantially extend the scope of the statute even to reach, for example, false statements privately made to a neighbor if the neighbor then uses those statements in connection with his work for a federal agency."

He also criticised the Court for not resolving the question whether some lesser culpability was required for the jurisdictional element.

Was *Yermian* correctly decided?

---

[14] "In the context of this case, respondent's argument that § 1001 is a 'trap for the unwary' is particularly misplaced. It is worth noting that the jury was instructed, without objection from the prosecution, that the government must prove that respondent 'knew or should have known' that his false statements were made within the jurisdiction of a federal agency.

"As the government did not object to the reasonable foreseeability instruction, it is unnecessary for us to decide whether that instruction erroneously read a culpability requirement into the jurisdictional phrase. Moreover, the only question presented in this case is whether the government must prove that the false statement was made with *actual* knowledge of federal agency jurisdiction. The jury's finding that federal agency jurisdiction was reasonably foreseeable by the defendant, combined with the requirement that the defendant had actual knowledge of the falsity of those statements, precludes the possibility that criminal penalties were imposed on the basis of innocent conduct."

SUBSECTION D: A CONCLUDING PROBLEM OF MENS–REA POLICY

LIPAROTA v. UNITED STATES

Supreme Court of the United States, 1985.

—— U.S. ——.

JUSTICE BRENNAN delivered the opinion of the Court.

The federal statute governing food stamp fraud provides that "whoever knowingly uses, transfers, acquires, alters, or possess coupons or authorization cards in any manner not authorized by [the statute] or the regulations" is subject to a fine and imprisonment. 7 U.S.C. § 2024(b).[a] The question presented is whether in a prosecution under this provision the government must prove that the defendant knew that he was acting in a manner not authorized by statute or regulations.

I

Petitioner Frank Liparota was the co-owner with his brother of Moon's Sandwich Shop in Chicago, Illinois. He was indicted for acquiring and possessing food stamps in violation of § 2024(b). The Department of Agriculture had not authorized petitioner's restaurant to accept food stamps.[2] At trial, the government proved that petitioner on three occasions purchased food stamps from an undercover Department of Agriculture agent for substantially less than their face value. On the first occasion, the agent informed petitioner that she had $195 worth of food stamps to sell. The agent then accepted petitioner's offer of $150 and consummated the transaction in a back room of the restaurant with petitioner's brother. A similar transaction occurred one week later, in which the agent sold $500 worth of coupons for $350. Approximately one month later, petitioner bought $500 worth of food stamps from the agent for $300.

In submitting the case to the jury, the District Court rejected petitioner's proposed "specific intent" instruction, which would have instructed the jury that the government must prove that "the defendant knowingly did an act which the law forbids, purposely intending to violate the law."[3] Concluding that "[t]his is not a specific intent

---

[a] Violation of this statute is a felony if the value of the coupons or authorization cards is $100 or more. The maximum sentence for a first conviction in such a case is a fine up to $10,000 or imprisonment for not more than five years, or both. If the value of the coupons or cards is less than $100, the offense is a misdemeanor with a maximum penalty of a fine up to $1,000 and imprisonment for not more than one year, or both. [Footnote by eds.]

[2] Food stamps are provided by the government to those who meet certain need-related criteria. They generally may be used only to purchase food in retail food stores. If a restaurant receives proper authorization from the Department of Agriculture, it may receive food stamps as payment for meals under certain special circumstances not relevant here.

[3] The instruction proffered by petitioner was drawn from 1 E. Devitt & C. Blackmar, Federal Jury Practice and Instructions § 14.03 (1977). The instructions read in its entirety:

"The crime charged in this case is a serious crime which requires proof of

crime" but rather a "knowledge case," the District Court instead instructed the jury as follows:

> "When the word 'knowingly' is used in these instructions, it means that the defendant realized what he was doing, and was aware of the nature of his conduct, and did not act through ignorance, mistake, or accident. Knowledge may be proved by defendant's conduct and by all the facts and circumstances surrounding the case."

The District Court also instructed that the government had to prove that "the defendant acquired and possessed food stamp coupons for cash in a manner not authorized by federal statute or regulations" and that "the defendant knowingly and wilfully acquired the food stamps." Petitioner objected that this instruction required the jury to find merely that he knew that he was acquiring or possessing food stamps; he argued that the statute should be construed instead to reach only "people who knew that they were acting unlawfully." The judge did not alter or supplement his instructions, and the jury returned a verdict of guilty.

Petitioner appealed his conviction to the Court of Appeals for the Seventh Circuit, arguing that the District Court erred in refusing to instruct the jury that "specific intent" is required in a prosecution under 7 U.S.C. § 2024(b). The Court of Appeals rejected petitioner's arguments. Because this decision conflicted with recent decisions of three other Courts of Appeals, we granted certiorari. We reverse.

II

The controversy between the parties concerns the mental state, if any, that the government must show in proving that petitioner acted "in any manner not authorized by [the statute] or the regulations." The government argues that petitioner violated the statute if he knew that he acquired or possessed food stamps and if in fact that acquisition or possession was in a manner not authorized by statute or regulations. According to the government, no mens rea, or "evil-meaning mind," Morissette v. United States, 342 U.S. 246, 251 (1952), is necessary for conviction. Petitioner claims that the government's interpretation, by dispensing with mens rea, dispenses with the only morally blameworthy element in the definition of the crime. To avoid this allegedly untoward result, he claims that an individual violates the statute if he knows that he has acquired or possessed food stamps and if he also knows that he has done so in an unauthorized manner.[5] Our task is to determine which meaning Congress intended.

specific intent before the defendant can be convicted. Specific intent, as the term implies, means more than the general intent to commit the act. To establish specific intent the government must prove that the defendant knowingly did an act which the law forbids, purposely intending to violate the law. Such intent may be determined from all the

facts and circumstances surrounding the case."

[5] The required mental state may of course be different for different elements of a crime. In this case, for instance, both parties agree that petitioner must have known that he acquired and possessed food stamps. They disagree over whether any mental element at all is required with re-

The definition of the elements of a criminal offense is entrusted to the legislature, particularly in the case of federal crimes, which are solely creatures of statute.[6] With respect to the element at issue in this case, however, Congress has not explicitly spelled out the mental state required. Although Congress certainly intended by use of the word "knowingly" to require *some* mental state with respect to *some* element of the crime defined in § 2024(b), the interpretations proffered by both parties accord with congressional intent to this extent. Beyond this, the words themselves provide little guidance. Either interpretation would accord with ordinary usage.[7] The legislative history of the statute contains nothing that would clarify the congressional purpose on this point.

Absent indication of contrary purpose in the language or legislative history of the statute, we believe that § 2024(b) requires a showing that the defendant knew his conduct to be unauthorized by statute or regulations.[9] "The contention that an injury can amount to a crime only when inflicted by intention is no provincial or transient notion. It is as universal and persistent in mature systems of law as belief in freedom of the human will and a consequent ability and duty of the normal individual to choose between good and evil." *Morissette v. United States,* supra, at 250.[b] Thus, in United States v. United States

---

spect to the unauthorized nature of that acquisition or possession.

We have also recognized that the mental element in criminal law encompasses more than the two possibilities of "specific" and "general" intent. The Model Penal Code, for instance, recognizes four mental states—purpose, knowledge, recklessness, and negligence. ALI, Model Penal Code § 2.02. In this case, petitioner argues that with respect to the element at issue, knowledge is required. The government contends that no mental state is required with respect to that element.

[6] Of course, Congress must act within any applicable constitutional constraints in defining criminal offenses. In this case, there is no allegation that the statute would be unconstitutional under either interpretation.

[7] One treatise has aptly summed up the ambiguity in an analogous situation:

"Still further difficulty arises from the ambiguity which frequently exists concerning what the words or phrases in question modify. What, for instance, does 'knowingly' modify in a sentence from a . . . criminal statute punishing one who 'knowingly sells a security without a permit' from the securities commissioner? To be guilty must the seller of a security without a permit know only that what he is doing constitutes a sale, or must he also know that the thing he sells is a security, or must he also know that he has no permit to sell the security

he sells? As a matter of grammar the statute is ambiguous; it is not at all clear how far down the sentence the word 'knowingly' is intended to travel— whether it modifies 'sells,' or 'sells a security' or 'sells a security without a permit.' "

W. LaFave & A. Scott, Criminal Law 193 (1972).

[9] The dissent repeatedly claims that our holding today creates a defense of "mistake of law." Our holding today no more creates a "mistake of law" defense than does a statute making knowing receipt of stolen goods unlawful. In both cases, there is a legal element in the definition of the offense. In the case of a receipt of stolen goods statute, the legal element is that the goods were stolen; in this case, the legal element is that the "use, transfer, acquisition," etc., were in a manner not authorized by statute or regulations. It is not a defense to a charge of receipt of stolen goods that one did not know that such receipt was illegal, and it is not a defense to a charge of a § 2024(b) violation that one did not know that possessing food stamps in a manner unauthorized by statute or regulations was illegal. It is, however, a defense to a charge of knowing receipt of stolen goods that one did not know that the goods were stolen, just as it is a defense to a charge of a § 2024(b) violation that one did not know that one's possession was unauthorized.

[b] See page 193, supra. [Footnote by eds.]

Gypsum Co., 438 U.S. 422, 438 (1978), we noted that "[c]ertainly far more than the simple omission of the appropriate phrase from the statutory definition is necessary to justify dispensing with an intent requirement" and that criminal offenses requiring no mens rea have a "generally disfavored status." Similarly, in this case, the failure of Congress explicitly and unambiguously to indicate whether mens rea is required does not signal a departure from this background assumption of our criminal law.

This construction is particularly appropriate where, as here, to interpret the statute otherwise would be to criminalize a broad range of apparently innocent conduct. For instance, § 2024(b) declares it criminal to use, transfer, acquire, alter, or possess food stamps in any manner not authorized by statute or regulations. The statute provides further that "[c]oupons issued to eligible households shall be used by them only to purchase food in retail food stores which have been approved for participation in the food stamp program *at prices prevailing in such stores.*" 7 U.S.C. § 2016(b) (emphasis added). This seems to be the only authorized use. A strict reading of the statute with no knowledge of illegality requirement would thus render criminal a food stamp recipient who, for example, used stamps to purchase food from a store that, unknown to him, charged higher than normal prices to food stamp program participants. Such a reading would also render criminal a nonrecipient of food stamps who "possessed" stamps because he was mistakenly sent them through the mail due to administrative error, "altered" them by tearing them up, and "transferred" them by throwing them away. Of course, Congress could have intended that this broad range of conduct be made illegal, perhaps with the understanding that prosecutors would exercise their discretion to avoid such harsh results. However, given the paucity of material suggesting that Congress did so intend, we are reluctant to adopt such a sweeping interpretation.

In addition, requiring mens rea is in keeping with our long-standing recognition of the principle that "ambiguity concerning the ambit of criminal statutes should be resolved in favor of lenity." Rewis v. United States, 401 U.S. 808, 812 (1971). Application of the rule of lenity ensures that criminal statutes will provide fair warning concerning conduct rendered illegal and strikes the appropriate balance between the legislature, the prosecutor, and the court in defining criminal liability. Although the rule of lenity is not to be applied where to do so would conflict with the implied or expressed intent of Congress, it provides a time-honored interpretive guideline when the congressional purpose is unclear. In the instant case, the rule directly supports petitioner's contention that the government must prove knowledge of illegality to convict him under § 2024(b).

The government argues, however, that a comparison between § 2024(b) and its companion, § 2024(c), demonstrates a congressional purpose not to require proof of the defendant's knowledge of illegality in a § 2024(b) prosecution. Section 2024(c) is directed primarily at stores authorized to accept food stamps from program participants. It provides that "[w]hoever presents, or causes to be presented, coupons for payment or redemption . . . *knowing* the same to have been received, transferred, or used in any manner in violation of [the statute] or the regulations" is subject to fine and imprisonment (emphasis added). The government contrasts this language with that of § 2024(b), in which the word "knowingly" is placed differently: "whoever *knowingly* uses, transfers . . . ." (emphasis added). Since § 2024(c) undeniably requires a knowledge of illegality, the suggested inference is that the difference in wording and structure between the two sections indicates that § 2024(b) does not.

The government urges that this distinction between the mental state required for a § 2024(c) violation and that required for a § 2024(b) violation is a sensible one. Absent a requirement of mens rea, a grocer presenting food stamps for payment might be criminally liable under § 2024(c) even if his customer or employees have illegally procured or transferred the stamps without the grocer's knowledge. Requiring knowledge of illegality in a § 2024(c) prosecution is allegedly necessary to avoid this kind of vicarious, and non-fault-based, criminal liability. Since the offense defined in § 2024(b)—using, transferring, acquiring, altering, or possessing food stamps in an unauthorized manner—does not involve this possibility of vicarious liability, argues the government, Congress had no reason to impose a similar knowledge of illegality requirement in that section.

We do not find this argument persuasive . . . . Grocers are participants in the food stamp program who have had the benefit of an extensive informational campaign concerning the authorized use and handling of food stamps. Yet the government would have to prove knowledge of illegality when prosecuting such grocers, while it would have no such burden when prosecuting third parties who may well have had no opportunity to acquaint themselves with the rules governing food stamps. It is not immediately obvious that Congress would have been so concerned about imposing strict liability on grocers, while it had no similar concerns about imposing strict liability on nonparticipants in the program. Our point once again is not that Congress could not have chosen to enact a statute along these lines, for there are no doubt policy arguments on both sides of the question as to whether such a statute would have been desirable. Rather, we conclude that the policy underlying such a construction is neither so obvious nor so compelling that we must assume, in the absence of any discussion of this issue in the legislative history, that Congress *did* enact such a statute.

The government advances two additional arguments in support of its reading of the statute. First, the government contends that this Court's decision last Term in United States v. Yermian, 468 U.S. __ (1984), supports its interpretation. *Yermian* involved a prosecution for violation of the federal false statement statute, 18 U.S.C. § 1001.[14] All

---

[14] The statute provides:

"Whoever, in any matter within the jurisdiction of any department or agency of the United States knowingly and willfully . . . makes any false . . . statements or representations . . . shall be fined not more than $10,000 or imprisoned not more than five years, or both."

parties agreed that the statute required proof at least that the defendant "knowingly and willfully" made a false statement. Thus, unlike the instant case, all parties in *Yermian* agreed that the government had to prove the defendant's mens rea.[15] The controversy in *Yermian* centered on whether the government also had to prove that the defendant knew that the false statement was made in a matter within the jurisdiction of a federal agency. With respect to this element, although the Court held that the government did not have to prove actual knowledge of federal agency jurisdiction, the Court explicitly reserved the question whether some culpability was necessary with respect even to the jurisdictional element. 468 U.S., at ___, n. 14. In contrast, the government in the instant case argues that *no* mens rea is required with respect to any element of the crime. Finally, *Yermian* found that the statutory language was unambiguous and that the legislative history supported its interpretation. The statute at issue in this case differs in both respects.

Second, the government contends that the § 2024(b) offense is a "public welfare" offense, which the Court defined in United States v. Morissette, 342 U.S., at 252–253, to "depend on no mental element but consist only of forbidden acts or omissions." Yet the offense at issue here differs substantially from those "public welfare offenses" we have previously recognized. In most previous instances, Congress has rendered criminal a type of conduct that a reasonable person should know is subject to stringent public regulation and may seriously threaten the community's health or safety. Thus, in United States v. Freed, 401 U.S. 601 (1971), we examined the federal statute making it illegal to receive or possess an unregistered firearm. In holding that the government did not have to prove that the recipient of unregistered hand grenades knew that they were unregistered, we noted that "one would hardly be surprised to learn that possession of hand grenades is not an innocent act." See also United States v. International Minerals & Chemical Corp., 402 U.S. 558, 564–565 (1971). Similarly, in United States v. Dotterweich, 320 U.S. 277, 284 (1943), the Court held that a corporate officer could violate the Food and Drug Act when his firm shipped adulterated and misbranded drugs, even "though consciousness of wrongdoing be totally wanting." See also United States v. Balint, 258 U.S. 250 (1922). The distinctions between these cases and the instant case are clear. A food stamp can hardly be compared to a hand grenade, nor can the unauthorized acquisition or possession of food stamps be compared to the selling of adulterated drugs.

III

We hold that in a prosecution for violation of § 2024(b), the government must prove that the defendant knew that his acquisition or

---

[15] The fact that both parties in *Yermian* agreed that the government had to prove that the defendant had "knowingly and willfully" made a false statement does not of course indicate that the parties agreed on the mental state applicable to other elements of the offense. What it does mean is that in *Yermian*, unlike this case, all parties agreed that an "evil-meaning mind" was required with respect at least to one element of the crime.

possession of food stamps was in a manner unauthorized by statute or regulations.[16] This holding does not put an unduly heavy burden on the government in prosecuting violators of § 2024(b). To prove that petitioner knew that his acquisition or possession of food stamps was unauthorized, for example, the government need not show that he had knowledge of specific regulations governing food stamp acquisition or possession. Nor must the government introduce any extraordinary evidence that would conclusively demonstrate petitioner's state of mind. Rather, as in any other criminal prosecution requiring mens rea, the government may prove by reference to facts and circumstances surrounding the case that petitioner knew that his conduct was unauthorized or illegal.[17]

Reversed.

JUSTICE POWELL took no part in the consideration or decision of this case.

JUSTICE WHITE, with whom THE CHIEF JUSTICE joins, dissenting.

Forsaking reliance on either the language or the history of § 2024(b), the majority bases its result on the absence of an explicit rejection of the general principle that criminal liability requires not only an actus reus, but a mens rea. In my view, the result below is in fact supported by the statute's language and its history, and it is the majority that has ignored general principles of criminal liability.

I

The Court views the statutory problem here as being how far down the sentence the term "knowingly" travels. See n. 7. Accepting for the moment that if "knowingly" does extend to the "in any manner" language today's holding would be correct—a position with which I take issue below—I doubt that it gets that far. The "in any manner" language is separated from the litany of verbs to which "knowingly" is directly connected by the intervening nouns. We considered an identically phrased statute last Term in *United States v. Yermian.* We found that under the "most natural reading" of the statute, "knowingly and willfully" applied only to the making of false . . . statements and not to the fact of jurisdiction. By the same token, the "most natural reading" of § 2024(b) is that knowingly modifies only the verbs to which it is attached.[1]

---

[16] Although we agree with petitioner concerning his interpretation of the statute, we express no opinion on the "specific intent" instruction he tendered, see n. 2, supra. This instruction has been criticized as too general and potentially misleading, see United States v. Arambasich, 597 F.2d 609, 613 (CA7 1979). A more useful instruction might relate specifically to the mental state required under § 2024(b) and eschew use of difficult legal concepts like "specific intent" and "general intent."

[17] In this case, for instance, the government introduced evidence that petitioner bought food stamps at a substantial discount from face value and that he conducted part of the transaction in a back room of his restaurant to avoid the presence of the other patrons. Moreover, the government asserts that food stamps themselves are stamped "nontransferable." A jury could have inferred from this evidence that petitioner knew that his acquisition and possession of the stamps was unauthorized.

[1] The majority's efforts to distinguish *Yermian* are unavailing. First, it points out that under the statute at issue there, the prosecution had to establish some mens rea because it had to show a knowing falsehood. However, as the majority itself

In any event, I think that the premise of this approach is mistaken. Even accepting that "knowingly" does extend through the sentence, or at least that we should read § 2024(b) as if it does, the statute does not mean what the Court says it does. Rather, it requires only that the defendant be aware of the relevant aspects of his conduct. A requirement that the defendant know that he is acting in a particular manner, coupled with the fact that that manner is forbidden, does not establish a defense of ignorance of the law. It creates only a defense of ignorance or mistake of fact. Knowingly to do something that is unauthorized by law is not the same as doing something knowing that it is unauthorized by law.

This point is demonstrated by the hypothetical statute referred to by the majority, which punishes one who "knowingly sells a security without a permit." See n. 7. Even if "knowingly" does reach "without a permit," I would think that a defendant who knew that he did not have a permit though not that a permit was required, could be convicted.

Section 2024(b) is an identical statute, except that instead of detailing the various legal requirements, it incorporates them by proscribing use of coupons "in any manner not authorized" by law. This shorthand approach to drafting does not transform knowledge of illegality into an element of the crime. As written, § 2024(b) is substantively no different than if it had been broken down into a collection of specific provisions making crimes of particular improper uses. For example, food stamps cannot be used to purchase tobacco. The statute might have said, inter alia, that anyone "who knowingly uses coupons to purchase cigarettes" commits a crime. Under no plausible reading could a defendant then be acquitted because he did not know cigarettes are not "eligible food." But in fact, that is exactly what § 2024(b) does say, it just does not write it out longhand.

The Court's opinion provides another illustration of the general point: someone who used food stamps to purchase groceries at inflated prices without realizing he was overcharged. I agree that such a person may not be convicted, but not for the reason given by the majority. The purchaser did not "knowingly" use the stamps in the proscribed manner, for he was unaware of the circumstances of the transaction that made it illegal.

The majority and I would part company in result as well as rationale if the purchaser knew he was charged higher than normal prices but not that overcharging is prohibited. In such a case, he would have been aware of the nature of his actions, and therefore the purchase

points out elsewhere, see n. 5, different mental states can apply to different elements of an offense. The fact that in *Yermian* mens rea had to be proved as to the first element was irrelevant to the Court's holding that it did not with regard to the second. There is no reason to read this statute differently. Second, the majority states that the language in *Yermian* was "unambiguous." Since it is identical, the language at issue in this case can be no less so. Finally, the majority notes that the Court in *Yermian* did not decide whether the prosecution might have to prove that the defendant "should have known" that his statements were within the agency's jurisdiction. However, that passing statement was irrelevant to the interpretation of the statute's language the Court did undertake.

would have been "knowing." I would hold that such a mental state satisfies the statute. Under the Court's holding, as I understand it, that person could not be convicted because he did not know that his conduct was illegal.[3]

Much has been made of the comparison between § 2024(b) and § 2024(c). The government . . . argues that the express requirement of knowing illegality in subsection (c) supports an inference that the absence of such a provision in subsection (b) was intentional. . . . I view most of this discussion as beside the point. The government's premise seems to me mistaken. Subsection (c) does not impose a requirement of knowing illegality. The provision is much like statutes that forbid the receipt or sale of stolen goods. Just as those statutes generally require knowledge that the goods were stolen, so § 2024(c) requires knowledge of the past impropriety. But receipt of stolen goods statutes do not require that the defendant know that receipt itself is illegal, and similarly § 2024(c) plainly does not require that the defendant know that it is illegal to present coupons that have been improperly used in the past. It is not inconceivable that someone presenting such coupons—again, like someone buying stolen goods—would think that his conduct was above board despite the preceding illegality. But that belief, however sincere, would not be a defense. In short, because § 2024(c) does not require that the defendant know that the conduct for which he is being prosecuted was illegal, it does not create an ignorance of the law defense.[5]

I therefore cannot draw the government's suggested inference. The two provisions are nonetheless fruitfully compared. What matters is not their difference, but their similarity. Neither contains any indication that "knowledge of the law defining the offense [is] an element of the offense." See ALI, Model Penal Code § 2.02, Comment p. 131 (Tent.Draft No. 4, 1955). A requirement of knowing illegality should not be read into either provision. . . .

II

The broad principles of the Court's opinion are easy to live with in a case such as this. But the application of its reasoning might not always

---

[3] The appropriate prosecutorial target in such a situation would of course be the seller rather than the purchaser. I have no doubt that every prosecutor in the country would agree. The discussion of this hypothetical is wholly academic.

For similar reasons, I am unmoved by the spectre of criminal liability for someone who is mistakenly mailed food stamps and throws them out, and do not think the hypothetical offers much of a guide to congressional intent. We should proceed on the assumption that Congress had in mind the run-of-the-mill situation, not its most bizarre mutation. Arguments that presume wildly unreasonable conduct by government officials are by their nature unconvincing, and reliance on them is likely

to do more harm than good. No rule, including that adopted by the Court today, is immune from such contrived defects.

[5] Similarly, it is a valid defense to a charge of theft that the defendant thought the property legally belonged to him, even if that belief is incorrect. But this is not because ignorance of the law is an excuse. Rather, "the legal element involved is simply an aspect of the attendant circumstances, with respect to which knowledge . . . is required for culpability. . . . The law involved is not the law defining the offense; it is some other legal rule that characterizes the attendant circumstances that are material to the offense." ALI, Model Penal Code § 2.02, Comment p. 131 (Tent.Draft No. 4, 1955).

be so benign. For example, § 2024(b) is little different from the basic federal prohibition on the manufacture and distribution of controlled substances. 21 U.S.C. § 841(a) provides:

"Except as authorized by this subchapter, it shall be unlawful for any person knowingly or intentionally—

"(1) to manufacture, distribute, or dispense, or possess with intent to manufacture, distribute or dispense, a controlled substance. . . . "

I am sure that the members of the majority would agree that a defendant charged under this provision could not defend on the ground that he did not realize his manufacture was unauthorized or that the particular substance was controlled. See United States v. Balint, 258 U.S. 250 (1922). On the other hand, it would be a defense if he could prove he thought the substance was something other than what it was. By the same token, I think, someone in petitioner's position should not be heard to say that he did not know his purchase of food stamps was unauthorized, though he may certainly argue that he did not know he was buying food stamps. I would not stretch the term "knowingly" to require awareness of the absence of statutory authority in either of these provisions.

These provisions might be distinguished because of the different placements of the "except as authorized" and the "in any manner not authorized" clauses in the sentences. However, nothing in the majority's opinion indicates that this difference is relevant. Indeed, the logic of the Court's opinion would require knowledge of illegality for conviction under any statute making it a crime to do something "in any manner not authorized by law" or "unlawfully." I suspect that if a case rises in the future where such a result is unacceptable, the Court will manage to distinguish today's decision. But I will be interested to see how it does so.

III

In relying on the "background assumption of our criminal law" that mens rea is required, the Court ignores the equally well-founded assumption that ignorance of the law is no excuse. It is "the conventional position that knowledge of the existence, meaning or application of the law determining the elements of an offense is not an element of that offense. . . . " ALI, Model Penal Code § 2.02, Comment, p. 130 (Tent.Draft No. 4, 1955).

This Court's prior cases indicate that a statutory requirement of a "knowing violation" does not supersede this principle. For example, under the statute at issue in United States v. International Minerals & Chemical Corp., 402 U.S. 558 (1971), the Interstate Commerce Commission was authorized to promulgate regulations regarding the transportation of corrosive liquids, and it was a crime to "knowingly violat[e] any such regulation." Viewing the word "regulations" as "a shorthand designation for specific acts or omissions which violate the act," we adhered to the traditional rule that ignorance of the law is not a defense. The violation had to be "knowing" in that the defendant had to know that he was transporting corrosive liquids and not, for example, merely water. But there was no requirement that he be aware that he was violating a particular regulation. Similarly, in this case the phrase "in any manner not authorized by" the statute or regulations is a shorthand incorporation of a variety of legal requirements. To be convicted, a defendant must have been aware of what he was doing, but not that it was illegal.

[T]he statutory language [in *International Minerals*] lent itself to the approach adopted today if anything more readily than does § 2024(b).[6] I would read § 2024(b) like [that statute], to require awareness of only the relevant aspects of one's conduct rendering it illegal, not the fact of illegality. This reading does not abandon the "background assumption" of mens rea by creating a strict liability offense, and is consistent with the equally important background assumption that ignorance of the law is not a defense.

IV

I wholly agree that "[t]he contention that an injury can amount to a crime only when inflicted by intention is no provincial or transient notion." Morissette v. United States, 342 U.S. 246, 250 (1952). But the holding of the court below is not at all inconsistent with that longstanding and important principle. Petitioner's conduct was intentional; the jury found that petitioner "realized what he was doing, and was aware of the nature of his conduct, and did not act through ignorance, mistake, or accident" (trial court's instructions). Whether he knew which regulation he violated is beside the point.

NOTES ON *LIPAROTA*

1. **Questions on *Liparota*.** The *Liparota* case presents an interesting context in which to review your understanding of the meaning of mens rea and its relation to the principle that ignorance of the criminal law is no excuse. Do you agree with the analysis of the majority or the dissent? Or would some different analysis have been more likely to lead to a correct decision of the case?

2. *United States v. International Minerals & Chemical Corp.* Title 18 U.S.C. § 834(a) gave the Interstate Commerce Commission

---

[6] The Court distinguishes [*International Minerals*] as [a] "public welfare offense" . . . involving inherently dangerous articles of commerce whose users should have assumed were subject to regulation. But see United States v. Freed, 401 U.S., at 612 (Brennan, J., concurring in judgment). Apart from the fact that a reasonable person would also assume food stamps are heavily regulated and not subject to sale and exchange, this distinction is not related to the actual holdings in those cases. The . . . concurrence in *Freed* [did] not discuss this consideration. And the Court's references to the dangerousness of the goods in *International Minerals* were directed to possible due process challenges to convictions without notice of criminality. As today's majority acknowledges, n. 6, there is no constitutional defect with the holding of the court below. The only issue here is one of congressional intent.

power to formulate regulations for the safe transportation of "corrosive liquids." Section 834(f) provided that whoever "knowingly violates any such regulation" was guilty of a criminal offense. Applicable regulations required that the words "Corrosive Liquid" appear on the shipping papers of the acids defendant shipped. They did not appear, the defendant was charged with the criminal offense, and a dismissal of the information was obtained on the ground that defendant did not know of the existence of the applicable regulation. The Supreme Court in United States v. International Minerals & Chemical Corp., 402 U.S. 558, 563 (1971), reversed in an opinion by Justice Douglas holding that:

> "The principle that ignorance of the law is no defense applies whether the law be a statute or a duly promulgated and published regulation. In the context of [this statute] we decline to attribute to Congress the inaccurate view that that act requires proof of knowledge of the law, as well as the facts, and that it intended to endorse that interpretation by retaining the word 'knowingly.' We conclude that the meager legislative history . . . makes unwarranted the conclusion that Congress abandoned the general rule and required knowledge of both the facts and the pertinent law before a criminal conviction could be sustained under this act."

Three justices dissented.

Is *International Minerals* consistent with *Liparota?* On what basis?

SUBSECTION E: THE ABANDONMENT OF MENS REA FOR ALL CRIMES

NOTES ON THE ABANDONMENT OF MENS REA FOR ALL CRIMES

1. **Lady Wootton's Proposal to Abandon Mens Rea.** Notwithstanding the occasional instances of strict liability considered in the preceding materials, the idea that criminal liability should be predicated on proof of a blameworthy state of mind remains one of the fundamental postulates of the penal law. Recall, in this connection, Justice Jackson's observation in *Morissette v. United States,* page 193, supra, that the requirement of mens rea is "universal and persistent in mature systems of law."

However, there have been occasional suggestions that mens rea should be abandoned.[a] In her Hamlyn Lectures, published in Crime

---

[a] E.g., Leivitt, Extent and Function of the Doctrine of Mens Rea, 17 Ill.L.Rev. 578 (1923). For an attempt to draft a statute based on the substantial abandonment of mens rea, see Note, Professor George H. Dession's Final Draft of the Code of Correction for Puerto Rico, 71 Yale L.J. 1050 (1962).

and the Criminal Law (1963),[b] Lady Barbara Wootton advanced the view that the focus of the criminal law on blameworthiness and responsibility is misplaced, that the law should concentrate instead on the occurrence of prohibited conduct, and that mens rea, if relevant at all, should be taken into account only in determining what should be done to prevent recurrence of such conduct. Lady Wootton developed this thesis as follows. She began by asking what is "the object of the whole exercise" and "what it is that [the judge at sentencing] is trying to achieve." She continued: *

"Is he trying to punish the wicked, or to prevent the recurrence of forbidden acts? The former is certainly the traditional answer and is still deeply entrenched both in the legal profession and in the minds of much of the public at large . . . . Those who take this view doubtless comfort themselves with the belief that the two objectives are nearly identical: that the punishment of the wicked is also the best way to prevent the occurrence of prohibited acts. Yet the continual failure of a mainly punitive system to diminish the volume of crime strongly suggests that such comfort is illusory; and it will indeed be a principal theme of these lectures that the choice between the punitive and the preventive concept of the criminal process is a real one; and that, according as that choice is made, radical differences must follow in the courts' approach to their task. I shall, moreover, argue that in recent years a perceptible shift has occurred away from the first and towards the second of these two conceptions of the function of the criminal law; and that this movement is greatly to be welcomed and might with advantage be both more openly acknowledged and also accelerated. . . .

"If . . . the primary function of the courts is conceived as the prevention of forbidden acts, there is little cause to be disturbed by the multiplication of offences of strict liability. If the law says that certain things are not to be done, it is illogical to confine this prohibition to occasions on which they are done from malice aforethought; for at least the material consequences of an action, and the reasons for prohibiting it, are the same whether it is the result of sinister malicious plotting, of negligence or of sheer accident. A man is equally dead and his relatives equally bereaved whether he was stabbed or run over by a drunken motorist or by an incompetent one; and the inconvenience caused by the loss of your bicycle is unaffected by the question whether or no the youth who removed it had the intention of putting it back, if in fact he had not done so at the time of his arrest. It is true, of course, as Professor [H.L.A.] Hart has argued, that the material consequences of an action by no means exhaust its effects. 'If one person hits another, the person

[b] See also B. Wootton, *Crime and Penal Policy* 220–39 (1978).

* Copyright © 1963 by Stevens & Sons. Reprinted with the kind permission of the author, the Baroness Wootton of Abinger CH.

struck does not think of the other as *just* a cause of pain to him. . . . If the blow was light but deliberate, it has a significance for the person struck quite different from an accidental much heavier blow.' To ignore this difference, he argues, is to outrage 'distinctions which not only underlie morality, but pervade the whole of our social life.' That these distinctions are widely appreciated and keenly felt no one would deny. Often perhaps they derive their force from a purely punitive or retributive attitude; but alternatively they may be held to be relevant to an assessment of the social damage that results from a criminal act. Just as a heavy blow does more damage than a light one, so also perhaps does a blow which involves psychological injury do more damage than one in which the hurt is purely physical.

"The conclusion to which this argument leads is, I think, not that the presence or absence of the guilty mind is unimportant, but that mens rea has, so to speak—and this is the crux of the matter—*got into the wrong place.* Traditionally, the require-ment of the guilty mind is written into the actual definition of a crime. No guilty intention, no crime, is the rule. Obviously this makes sense if the law's concern is with wickedness: where there is no guilty intention, there can be no wickedness. But it is equally obvious, on the other hand, that an action does not become innocuous merely because whoever performed it meant no harm. If the object of criminal law is to prevent the occur-rence of socially damaging actions, it would be absurd to turn a blind eye to those which were due to carelessness, negligence or even accident. The question of motivation is *in the first instance* irrelevant.

"But only in the first instance. At a later stage, that is to say, after what is now known as a conviction, the presence or absence of guilty intention is all-important for its effect on the appropriate measures to be taken to prevent a recurrence of the forbidden act. The prevention of accidental deaths presents different problems from those involved in the prevention of wilful murders. The results of the actions of the careless, the mistaken, the wicked and the merely unfortunate may be indis-tinguishable from one another, but each case calls for a different treatment. Tradition, however, is very strong, and the notion that these differences are relevant only after the fact has been established that the accused committed the forbidden act seems still to be deeply abhorrent to the legal mind. . . .

"I am not, of course, arguing that all crimes should immedi-ately be transferred into the strict liability category. To do so would in some cases involve formidable problems of definition— as, for instance, in that of larceny. But I do suggest that . . . strict liability is not the nightmare that it is often made out to be, that it does not promise the decline and fall of the criminal law, and that it is, on the contrary, a sensible and indeed inevitable measure of adaptation to the requirements of the modern world; and above all I suggest that its supposedly nightmarish quality disappears once it is accepted that the primary objective of the criminal courts is preventive rather than punitive. . . . "

2. **Responses to Lady Wootton.** In a review of Lady Wootton's book, published in 74 Yale L.J. 1325 (1965),* H.L.A. Hart observed that "[w]hat she offers in the place of a system of punishment is . . . a system of purely forward-looking social hygiene in which our only concern when we have an offender to deal with is with the future and the rational aim of prevention of further crime." [c] In response to her suggestion that mens rea has "got into the wrong place" and her related argument that mens rea can only make sense as part of a system that justifies punishment as the appropriate response for past wickedness, he said:

"This argument is I think mistaken . . . . It rests . . . on the illusory idea that our only interest in asking whether those whom we punish could at the time of their offence have conformed to the law is to determine whether they were 'wicked' in doing what they did. This altogether ignores an outlook on punishment which is surely common, intelligible and, except perhaps for determinists (among whom Lady Wootton does not number herself) perfectly defensible. According to this outlook we should restrict even punishment designed as 'preventive' to those who at the time of their offence had the capacity and a fair opportunity or chance to obey the law: and we should do this out of considerations of fairness or justice to those whom we punish. This is an intelligible ideal of justice to the individual and remains intelligible even when we punish to protect society from harm in the future and not to 'pay back' the harm that those whom we punish have done. Viewed in this way as a restriction imposed on preventive punishment by considerations of fairness or justice to individuals the doctrine of mens rea presents an aspect neglect of which renders Lady Wootton's argument inconclusive. For such a restriction on punishment has a perfectly 'logical' place even within a preventive theory. To show this we can usefully draw upon the ideas and terminology of economics. Let us consider the idea of maximising a certain variable subject to a restraint. In this case the variable will be the efficiency of the system in reducing harmful crime. Plainly, without any illogicality or inconsistency we might acknowledge this as our purpose in punishing but also wish it to be pursued only subject to certain restraints. Some of these restraints might be held absolute in the sense that no increase in the efficiency of the system would be allowed to compensate for the slightest infringe-

* Reprinted by permission of the author, the Yale Law Journal Company, and Fred B. Rothman & Company from The Yale Law Journal, vol. 74, pp. 1327–31.

[c] Compare the notes on non-criminal methods of coercive intervention, pages 183–91, supra.

ment of the restraint. A veto on the use of torture might, for example, be such an absolute restraint; and it is conceivable (and perhaps desirable) that we should treat as an absolute restraint the principle of mens rea that no one who lacked the capacity or a fair opportunity or chance to conform to law at the time of his offence should be punished. . . .

"More persuasive than the mistaken identification of the doctrine of mens rea with a purely retributive theory of punishment are the practical considerations that Lady Wootton urges against the doctrine at least as it operates in England. It may well be that through the doctrine of mens rea we secure justice for those whom we punish at too great a cost in terms of social security and that this cost would be avoided if we abandoned the restraints imposed by the doctrine and made all offences into crimes of strict liability. . . . Yet important as these practical considerations are, there are equally practical objections to the wholesale elimination of mens rea from the criminal law and to these I think Lady Wootton pays insufficient attention. The first and most important concerns individual freedom. In a system in which proof of mens rea was no longer a necessary condition for conviction the occasions for official interferences in our lives would be vastly increased. If the doctrine of mens rea were abolished, every blow, even if it was apparent that it was accidental or merely careless, and therefore not under the present law a criminal assault, would in principle be a matter for investigation under the new scheme. This is so because the possibilities of a curable condition would have to be investigated and if possible treated. No doubt under the new regime prosecuting authorities would use their common sense; but a very great discretion would have to be entrusted to them to sift from the mass the cases worth investigation for either penal or therapeutic treatment. This expansion of police powers would bring with it great uncertainty for the individual citizen and, though official interference with his life would be more frequent, he will be less able to predict their incidence if any accidental breach of the criminal law may be an occasion for them.

"A second objection is this. Lady Wootton looks forward to the day when 'the formal distinction' between medical and penal treatment and between hospital and prison will have vanished. At present one of the features distinguishing punishment from treatment is that unlike a medical inspection followed by detention in hospital, conviction by a court followed by a sentence of imprisonment is a public act expressing the odium of society for those who break the law, or at least for their conduct in doing so. As long as this odium attaches to conviction and sentence a moral objection to their use on those who could not have helped doing as they did will always remain. On the other hand, if with the operation of the new system, conviction and imprisonment will in time be assimilated to, and no more odious than, a compulsory medical inspection followed by detention in hospital, it seems that the law will lose an important element in its authority and deterrent force. Some would say that this element is more important as a deterrent than the actual punishment administered.

"A third objection needing some careful consideration concerns the claim that a satisfactory criminal code could be framed without the 'illogical' reference to mens rea in the definition of offences. The difficulty is that there are some socially harmful activities which can only be identified by reference to intention or some other mental element. A clear example of this is the idea of an attempt to commit a crime. It is obviously desirable that persons who attempt crimes, even if they fail, should be brought before courts for punishment or treatment; yet what distinguishes an attempt which fails from an innocent activity is, in many cases, just the fact that it is a step taken with the intention of bringing about some harmful consequence."

Objections to a system similar to Lady Wootton's are developed more elaborately in H.L.A. Hart, Punishment and Responsibility (1968), H. Packer, The Limits of the Criminal Sanction 3–145 (1968), and Kadish, The Decline of Innocence, 26 Camb.L.J. 273 (1968). Useful background reading can also be found in F. Allen, The Borderland of Criminal Justice (1964), and J. Andenaes, Punishment and Deterrence (1974). Professor Allen's book is a particularly useful development of the moral and scientific uncertainties inherent in what Hart calls a system of "social hygiene."

SECTION 5: THE RELATION OF CULPABILITY AND CONDUCT

INTRODUCTORY NOTES ON THE HISTORY AND GRADING OF ATTEMPT

1. **Origins of the Crime of Attempt.** The early common law did not punish attempt as a separate category of crime. The seminal decision, written by Lord Mansfield in 1784,[a] involved an attempted arson and was based on the doctrine, as reformulated 17 years later, that "all offenses of a public nature, that is, all such acts or attempts as tend to the prejudice of the community, are indictable" as misdemeanors.[b] By the mid-1830's, it had become settled that an attempt to commit any offense, whether felony or misdemeanor and whether created by statute or by the common law, was itself a misdemeanor.[c]

[a] Rex v. Scofield, Cald. 397 (1784).

[b] Rex v. Higgins, 2 East 5, 102 Eng.Rep. 269 (1801). Compare the discussion of offenses based on this theory at pages 31–33, supra.

[c] The history of the crime of attempt is summarized in J. Hall, General Principles of the Criminal Law 558–74 (2d ed. 1960), and in Sayre, Criminal Attempts, 41 Harv. L.Rev. 821 (1928).

Prior to 1784, there had been scattered convictions for what today would be called an attempt, but no doctrinal formulation of general applicability had emerged. In addition, certain forms of analytically similar conduct had been punished as completed substantive offenses. Indeed, it seems clear that the pressure to create a generic attempt offense emerged so late because many of the more serious forms of attempt had already been recognized as substantive offenses. Larceny, for example, was defined in terms that fell short of requiring a permanent deprivation of property. Assault, defined as an attempt to commit a battery, dealt with efforts to attack a person. Robbery in effect was an aggravated combination of the two—an effort to obtain property by means of assault. Burglary combined an attempt to commit a felony with trespass in a dwelling. These staples of the common law, together with other offenses that emerged as the law matured, constituted piecemeal responses to specific problems of inchoate behavior.

The generic crime of attempt generalized the principle of inchoate liability and thereby criminalized a wide range of behavior that theretofore had escaped criminal sanctions. It punished conduct preliminary to existing offenses, including those that themselves addressed some form of inchoate behavior. Thus, for example, it became a misdemeanor to attempt to commit larceny, a felony itself defined in inchoate terms. The effect was thus to push back toward more preliminary conduct the point at which criminal liability attached. How far back criminality was (and should be) pushed by the crime of attempt raises the distinction between criminal attempt and mere preparation—an issue that has been explored previously at pages 126–37, supra.

2. **Attempts in the United States.** The development of the offense of attempt in England at the turn of the 19th century occurred too late to be received as part of the common law in the United States. The pattern of piecemeal response, inherited from the tradition of the common law, constituted the initial American approach to the problem. Offenses such as larceny, assault, robbery, and burglary had been taken over from the common law. Additional statutory offenses were soon created. In Massachusetts, for example, assault with intent to rob or murder was first made a crime in 1761, assault with intent to kill or maim and assault with intent to rape in 1784, and assault with intent to commit any felony in 1836. Attempted murder first appeared in an 1832 statute, and the first generic attempt statute covering all offenses appeared in 1836.

As noted previously, attempt was a misdemeanor at its inception in England.[d] Early American statutes tended to grade the offense at significantly lower levels than the offense attempted. For example, the 1836 Massachusetts statute authorized a maximum of 10 years for an

---

[d] Classification of an offense as a misdemeanor usually means that the maximum sentence is limited to one year or some comparable figure. This result is provided by statute in most states. At common law, however, the penalty for a misdemeanor was theoretically unlimited. G. Williams, Criminal Law: The General Part 606–07 (2d ed. 1961). Thus, an attempt at common law, though classified as a misdemeanor, could be punished with relative severity.

attempted capital offense, three years for an attempt to commit an offense punishable by more than five years, and one year for an attempt to commit an offense punishable by less than five years, though in this last category the punishment could not exceed one-half the maximum for the completed offense.[e]

Prior to the drafting of the Model Penal Code, the grading of attempt in American statutes followed essentially four patterns: (i) the categorical approach illustrated by the Massachusetts statute summarized above; (ii) statement of the authorized maximum for attempt as a proportion (usually one-half) of the sentence authorized for the completed offense; (iii) a fixed maximum penalty (ranging from one year to five years) for all attempts; and (iv) the provision in three states that the attempt could be punished as severely as the completed offense.[f] Moreover, it was typical to achieve intermediate grading of more serious forms of attempt by punishing various assault-with-intent offenses.[g] In addition, such offenses as larceny, burglary, and robbery were retained either in their traditional form or, more commonly, in broadened language to encompass an even wider range of inchoate behavior.[h] Not surprisingly, so many offenses covering essentially similar behavior rarely resulted in a consistent approach to the grading of related offenses. Instead, curious anomalies resulted. In California, breaking into a car with intent to steal its contents was punishable by a maximum term of 15 years under an expanded burglary statute; stealing the whole car carried a maximum of only 10. In Florida, an attempt to procure perjury from another carried a maximum of five years, but the maximum was only one year if the attempt was successful.[i]

3. **The Model Penal Code.** Section 5.05(1) of the Model Penal Code grades an attempt to commit a first-degree felony as a second-degree felony and treats all other attempts as equivalent in grade to the offense attempted. Modern statutes based on the Model Penal Code generally have increased the grading of attempts over previous levels, though not all have gone as far as equivalent grading of the attempt and the completed offense.[j]

One by-product of the Model Code deserves special attention. The Model Code contains no offenses of the assault-with-intent variety. Such offenses are unnecessary under a scheme in which attempts to

[e] The present Massachusetts statute retains the same categories but substitutes a five-year maximum for the three-year maximum in the middle class of cases. Mass. Gen.Laws Ann. c. 274, § 6.

[f] See Wechsler, Jones & Korn, The Treatment of Inchoate Crimes in the Model Penal Code of the American Law Institute: Attempt, Solicitation, and Conspiracy II, 61 Colum.L.Rev. 957, 1022–24 (1961). See also ALI, Model Penal Code and Commentaries § 5.05 pp. 485–87 (1985).

[g] In addition to modern versions of the statutes cited above, Massachusetts today has at least 10 additional assault-with-intent statutes, including assault on a police officer, assault to collect a loan, assault with a deadly weapon, etc. See Mass.Gen. Laws Ann. c. 265.

[h] For a general discussion of the expansive reach of pre-Model Penal Code burglary statutes, see Note, Statutory Burglary— The Magic of Four Walls and a Roof, 100 U.Pa.L.Rev. 411 (1951). See also pages 139–41, supra.

[i] See Low, Reform of the Sentencing Process, [1971] Camb.L.J. 237, 246.

[j] See, e.g., the Oregon statutes reproduced in Appendix B, pages 9–12, infra.

commit serious offenses can themselves be sanctioned as severely, or almost as severely, as the completed offense. Thus, rape in its most serious form is a first-degree felony under the Model Code (Section 213.1), and an attempt to commit the same rape is a second-degree felony. Assault with intent to commit rape would be needed as an offense of intermediate gravity only if the attempt were punished much less severely.

The Model Code does retain, however, the traditional common-law offenses of robbery and burglary, though in each case it emphasizes particular characteristics that justify more serious grading for the offense than would be warranted for a mere attempt to commit larceny or some other felony.[k] Assault is combined with battery to create a range of lesser offenses against the person. Larceny is retained in its traditional inchoate form but, given the equivalent grading of attempted larceny, the distinction between two different inchoate forms of the same offense—a distinction that was critical under older approaches[l]—is no longer important.[m]

SUBSECTION A: THE MENS REA OF ATTEMPT

THACKER v. COMMONWEALTH

Supreme Court of Appeals of Virginia, 1922.
134 Va. 767, 114 S.E. 504.

WEST, J. This writ of error is to a judgment upon the verdict of a jury finding John Thacker, the accused, guilty of attempting to murder Mrs. J.A. Ratrie, and fixing his punishment at two years in the penitentiary.

The only assignment of error is the refusal of the trial court to set aside the verdict as contrary to the law and the evidence.

The accused, in company with two other young men, Doc Campbell and Paul Kelly, was attending a church festival in Alleghany County, at which all three became intoxicated. They left the church between 10 and 11 o'clock at night, and walked down the country road about one and one-half miles, when they came to a sharp curve. Located in this curve was a tent in which the said Mrs. J.A. Ratrie, her husband, four children, and a servant were camping for the summer. The husband, though absent, was expected home that night, and Mrs. Ratrie, upon

---

[k] See ALI, Model Penal Code and Commentaries §§ 221.1, 222.1, pp. 66–68, 98–99 (1980).

[l] For example, assume that larceny requires a "taking and carrying away" with intent to deprive and is punishable by a five-year maximum sentence. Assume that attempted larceny is punishable by a one-year maximum. Both are inchoate offenses in that their object is to prevent permanent deprivation of property. Yet the large difference in authorized penalties turns on whether the actor engaged in conduct that can be described as a "taking and carrying away." The maximum penalty, moreover, is authorized once these events have occurred, even though the property is immediately recovered, the offense remains inchoate in fact, and the ultimate harm never occurs.

[m] But see page 376 n.h, infra.

retiring, had placed a lighted lamp on a trunk by the head of her bed. After 11 o'clock she was awakened by the shots of a pistol and loud talking in the road near by, and heard a man say, "I am going to shoot that Goddamned light out;" and another voice said, "Don't shoot the light out." The accused and his friends then appeared at the back of the tent, where the flaps of the tent were open, and said they were from Bath County and had lost their way, and asked Mrs. Ratrie if she could take care of them all night. She informed them she was camping for the summer, and had no room for them. One of the three thanked her, and they turned away, but after passing around the tent the accused used some vulgar language and did some cursing and singing. When they got back in the road, the accused said again he was going to shoot the light out, and fired three shots, two of which went through the tent, one passing through the head of the bed in which Mrs. Ratrie was lying, just missing her head and the head of her baby, who was sleeping with her. The accused did not know Mrs. Ratrie, and had never seen her before. He testified he did not know any of the parties in the tent, and had no ill will against either of them; that he simply shot at the light, without any intent to harm Mrs. Ratrie or any one else; that he would not have shot had he been sober, and regretted his action.

The foregoing are the admitted facts in the case.

An attempt to commit a crime is composed of two elements: (i) the intent to commit it; and (ii) a direct, ineffectual act done towards its commission. The act must reach far enough towards the accomplishment of the desired result to amount to the commencement of the consummation.

The law can presume the intention so far as realized in the act, but not an intention beyond what was so realized. The law does not presume, because an assault was made with a weapon likely to produce death, that it was an assault with the intent to murder. And where it takes a particular intent to constitute a crime, that particular intent must be proved either by direct or circumstantial evidence, which would warrant the inference of the intent with which the act was done.

When a statute makes an offense to consist of an act combined with a particular intent, that intent is just as necessary to be proved as the act itself, and must be found as a matter of fact before a conviction can be had; and no intent in law or mere legal presumption, differing from the intent in fact, can be allowed to supply the place of the latter.

In discussing the law of attempts, W. Clark, Criminal Law 111–12 (1894), says:

> "The act must be done with the specific intent to commit a particular crime. This specific intent at the time the act is done is essential. To do an act from general malevolence is not an attempt to commit a crime because there is no specific intent, though the act according to its consequences may amount to a substantive crime. . . . A man actuated by general malevolence may commit murder, though there is not actual intention to kill; to be guilty of an attempt to murder there must be a specific intent to kill."

1 J. Bishop, Criminal Law 731–36 (8th ed. 1892), says:

". . . When we say that a man attempted to do a given wrong, we mean that he intended to do specifically it, and proceeded a certain way in the doing. The intent in the mind covers the thing in full; the act covers it only in part.[a] Thus to commit murder, one need not intend to take life, but to be guilty of an attempt to murder, he must so intend. It is not sufficient that his act, had it proved fatal, would have been murder. We have seen that the unintended taking of life may be murder, yet there can be no attempt to murder without the specific intent to commit it. . . . For example, if one from a housetop recklessly throws down a billet of wood upon the sidewalk where persons are constantly passing, and it falls upon a person passing by and kills him, this would be common-law murder, but if, instead of killing, it inflicts only a slight injury, the party could not be convicted of an assault with attempt to commit murder since, in fact, the murder was not intended."

The application of the foregoing principles to the facts of the instant case shows clearly, as we think, that the judgment complained of is erroneous. While it might possibly be said that the firing of the shot into the head of Mrs. Ratrie's bed was an act done towards the commission of the offense charged, the evidence falls far short of proving that it was fired with the intent to murder her. . . .

[Reversed and remanded for a new trial.]

NOTES ON THE MENS REA OF ATTEMPT

1. **People v. Acevedo.** In People v. Acevedo, 39 A.D.2d 664, 331 N.Y.S.2d 903 (1972), the defendant fired a rifle from a rooftop and seriously wounded several people. He was convicted of attempted murder under the former New York statutes, which defined attempt as "an act, done with intent to commit a crime, and tending but failing to effect its commission" and which defined murder, inter alia, as "[t]he killing of a human being [by] an act imminently dangerous to others, and evincing a depraved mind, regardless of human life, although without a premeditated design to effect the death of any individual." The Appellate Division affirmed by a divided vote, reasoning that the murder statute in effect defined a criminal intent in the nature of "a general and indiscriminate intent to take life" and that this sufficed for an attempt prosecution:

[a] The court paraphrased Bishop in a subsequent case, Merrit v. Commonwealth, 164 Va. 653, 661, 180 S.E. 395, 399 (1935), as follows:

"[T]he indictable attempt exists only when the act, short of the substantive crime, proceeds from the specific intent to do the entire evil thing, thus imparting to so much as is done a special culpability. When we say that a man attempted to do a given wrong, we mean that he intended to do it specifically; and proceeded in a certain way in the doing. The intent in the mind covers the thing in full; the act covers it only in part."

[Footnote by eds.]

"Implicit in the verdict of the jury was a finding that all the elements of murder . . . were present except the actual killing of the three persons endangered and wounded by defendant's acts. The defendant maliciously committed acts 'tending but failing to effect [the] commission' of the particular crime . . . and absurd, indeed, is a holding that he may not be found guilty of an attempt to commit the crime merely because the seriously wounded victims of his acts did not die."

This result was reached even though the prosecutor joined the defendant in arguing that the conviction should be overturned.

The dissent noted that the quoted portion of the murder statute perhaps did include situations where there was a general intent to take life not directed to any particular person, but that it also included situations of extremely reckless behavior. Since a charge of attempted murder requires a specific intent to kill, the dissent concluded, a finding that the defendant satisfied the quoted portion of the murder statute was insufficient. The Court of Appeals unanimously reversed the Appellate Division in ᐧ memorandum order "for the reasons stated in the dissenting opinio   People v. Acevedo, 32 N.Y.2d 807, 345 N.Y.S.2d 555 (1973).

2. **Rationale for Specific-Intent Requirement.** It is clear in both *Thacker* and *Acevedo* that the defendants would have been guilty of murder had someone been killed by their reckless behavior. Both cases thus illustrate the traditional view that the crime of attempt requires a special mens rea beyond that required for the offense attempted. Even though their mens rea would have been adequate had the offense been completed, in other words, they are not guilty of attempt if they lacked the specific intent to kill. Why is this so?

One reason frequently given for the specific-intent requirement was described by Holmes as etymological in origin.[a] It is illustrated by the following passage from Smith, Two Problems in Criminal Attempts, 70 Harv.L.Rev. 422, 434 (1957):

"The conception of attempt seems necessarily to involve the notion of an intended consequence. Thus the word 'attempt' is defined in the Shorter Oxford English Dictionary as 'a putting forth of effort to accomplish what is uncertain or difficult.' When a man attempts to do something he is 'endeavoring' or 'trying' to do it. All these ways of describing an attempt seem to require a desired, or at least an intended, consequence. Recklessness and negligence are incompatible with desire or intention. [T]herefore, in a crime which by definition may be committed recklessly or negligently . . . , it is impossible to conceive of an attempt."

An explanation in these terms is often advanced to show why the crime of attempt requires a specific intent.[b] Do you find this explanation

---

[a] O. Holmes, The Common Law 66 (1881).

[b] Cf. R. Perkins & R. Boyce, Criminal Law 637 (3d ed. 1982): "The word 'attempt' means to try; it implies an effort to bring about a desired result. Hence an attempt to commit any crime requires a specific intent to commit that particular offense."

persuasive? Does it beg the question, or does the fact that it conforms to ordinary usage of the word "attempt" express a policy that the law should take into account? If the latter, can you articulate the policy?

A second line of reasoning in support of the specific-intent requirement is advanced in the passage from Holmes quoted at pages 229–31, supra, which should be re-read at this point. Holmes argued that it is easy to understand why a specific intent should be required in cases where the actor's conduct, viewed against the harms the criminal law is designed to prevent, is incomplete. Holmes illustrated his point with a hypothetical involving an attempt to burn a haystack: "[L]ighting a match with intent to set fire to a haystack has been held to amount to a criminal attempt to burn it, although the defendant blew out the match on seeing that he was watched." Why require a specific intent to set a fire in such a case? Holmes answered that since the act itself (lighting a match near a haystack) is not necessarily harmful under the circumstances, criminal liability should not follow:

> "unless there are grounds for expecting that the act done will be followed by other acts in connection with which its effect will be harmful . . . . But as in fact no such acts have followed, it cannot, in general, be assumed, from the mere doing of what has been done, that they would have followed if the actor had not been interrupted. They would not have followed it unless the actor had chosen, and the only way generally available to show that he would have chosen to do them is by showing that he intended to do them when he did what he did. The accompanying intent in that case renders the otherwise innocent act harmful, because it raises a probability that it will be followed by such other acts and events as will all together result in harm. The importance of the intent is not to show that the act was wicked, but to show that it was likely to be followed by hurtful consequences." [c]

Is Holmes convincing? Can you think of other reasons for the specific-intent requirement? Is it clear that the crime of attempt should require a specific intent to commit each element of every criminal offense? The next two notes explore these questions in more detail.

3. **Circumstance Elements.** Consider the following hypotheticals:

(i) **Statutory Rape.** The crime of statutory rape traditionally is defined as sexual intercourse with a person below a certain age, irrespective of consent. Normally, liability is strict as to the age of the victim. A mistake by the defendant as to age, no matter how reasonable, thus is not a defense. Assume that the

---

[c] Contrast People v. Krovarz, 697 P.2d 378 (Colo.1985), which held that knowledge (rather than purpose) was a sufficient mens rea for a charge of attempted robbery:

"Punishment is justified where the actor intends harm because there exists a high likelihood that his 'unspent' intent will flower into harmful conduct at any mo-ment. The probability of future dangerousness, however, is not confined to actors whose conscious purpose is to perform the proscribed acts or achieve the proscribed results, i.e., those possessing the culpable mental state of specific intent. We believe that this danger is equally present when one acts knowingly."

operative age is 16 and that the defendant has passed beyond mere preparation and is interrupted just prior to actual intercourse. Assume further that the defendant intended intercourse, that the defendant's conduct fully corroborates this intent, and that the victim was in fact 15. Could the actor defend against a charge of attempted statutory rape on the ground that the victim was believed to be 17? The answer would appear to be "yes" if the specific-intent requirement for attempt encompasses *all* of the elements of the completed offense—if, indeed, the defendant must intend "to do the entire evil thing." Is this the right answer as a matter of policy? Is it supported by arguments you can make in favor of the specific-intent requirement for attempt?

(ii) **Burglary.** Assume that burglary is defined in the traditional common-law manner as breaking and entering the dwelling house of another at night with the intent to commit a felony therein. Assume that 7 p.m. is when "night" begins. If the defendant completed the offense and if in fact it occurred at 7:30 p.m., do you think it likely that the defendant's belief that it was only 6:30 would be a valid defense? Based on materials previously studied, how would you expect the jury to be instructed on this issue? If the defendant was caught before the offense was completed, would the belief that it was only 6:30 constitute a defense to an attempted-burglary charge? Should it?

It has been argued that these two hypotheticals illustrate a situation in which no special policy of the law of attempt should displace the mens rea otherwise required for the completed offense—that, in other words, the mens rea as to circumstance elements should be the same for the attempt as it would be for the completed offense. In Smith, Two Problems in Criminal Attempts, 70 Harv.L.Rev. 422, 434–35 (1957),* this position is defended as follows:

"[A]n attempt is so essentially connected with consequences— with that event or series of events which is the principal constituent of the crime—that the only essential intention is an intention to bring about those consequences; and . . . if recklessness, or negligence, or even blameless inadvertence with respect to the remaining constituents of the crime (the . . . circumstances) will suffice for the substantive crime, it will suffice also for the attempt. It must be admitted that there appears to be no authority in support of these propositions,[d] but there appears to

* Copyright © 1957 by The Harvard Law Review Association. Reprinted with permission.

[d] The English Court of Appeal subsequently adopted Professor Smith's view in Regina v. Pigg, [1982] 2 All.E.R. 591, holding that recklessness was sufficient for the "consent" element in a charge of attempted rape. See also Williams, The Problem of Reckless Attempts, [1983] Crim. L.Rev. 365, which defends *Pigg* as the right result even under the subsequently enacted English attempt statute that requires

an "intent to commit an offence" without differentiating among the elements thereof.

There seem to be few American authorities that speak to this point. But see State v. Davis, 108 N.H. 158, 160–61, 229 A.2d 842, 844 (1967), where the court said without elaboration: "The fact that defendant was ignorant of the age of the female or that he did not intend the intercourse to be with a girl of non-age would not prevent his act from constituting [statutory] rape if completed, or an attempt, if it failed." In

be no authority against them and it is submitted that they achieve a common-sense result and are in accordance with principle. . . .

"Since the consequence which is involved in the complete crime must be intended, the emphasis in attempts is naturally on intention. But where *D* intends to produce a consequence which in the actual existing circumstances will constitute the actus reus of a substantive crime, and he does so with the mens rea of that same crime (being reckless or negligent or blamelessly inadvertent, as the case may be, as to a . . . circumstance), is there any reason why he should not be convicted of an attempt if he fails to accomplish his intention? It is submitted that there is not. If *D*'s state of mind is sufficiently blameworthy to ground liability for the complete crime, it is surely sufficiently blameworthy to ground liability for the attempt; and if *D* had done all that he intended to do, his act would have constituted the actus reus of that same crime. He has attempted to produce a consequence which in the existing circumstances is, if accompanied by a particular state of mind, forbidden by law and he has that state of mind which the law prescribes as a condition of guilt."

Is Professor Smith right? Can you identify a special mens-rea policy that ought to obtain in such cases?[e] Does Holmes' argument help?

4. **Completed Conduct But No Result.** *Thacker* and *Acevedo* likewise present situations where it is arguable that no special policy of the law of attempt should elevate the mens rea above what would be required for the completed offense. The law of attempt proceeds on the premise that the deterrent or social-control functions of the criminal law require punishment of those who come dangerously close to the commission of crime or who manifest a dangerous propensity to engage in criminal behavior. Both Thacker and Acevedo completed conduct that created a serious risk of fatality and, for all that appears, were saved from a murder conviction only by fortuitous circumstances. Arguably, both were no less culpable and no less dangerous than they would have been had a death occurred. Moreover, the concern expressed by Holmes—that specific intent is required in attempt offenses in order to show that the defendant was likely to engage in additional conduct that would complete a criminal offense—explains some cases but seems clearly inapplicable to *Thacker* and *Acevedo*. Both completed their planned course of behavior, and no further conduct by them would have been required in order to charge them with murder had a death resulted. If a specific intent is required as to them, therefore,

---

People v. Krovarz, 697 P.2d 378, 383 n. 11 (Colo.1985), the court adverted to the issue but found it not presented by the facts of the case.

[e] In Enker, Mens Rea and Criminal Attempt, 1977 A.B.F.Res.J. 845, 866–78, it is argued that Professor Smith's distinction between results and circumstances "seems to be justified in terms of policy" in cases where the object offense and the attempt require recklessness as to a circumstance element. In cases where negligence or strict liability suffices for the completed offense, however, he argues that there may be a problem of insufficient warning from the conduct of which the actor is aware that a criminal offense is being attempted. If this were so, he concludes, a mens rea of at least recklessness should be required for that element.

some other rationale must be advanced. One possibility is that the requirement of specific intent serves the function of protecting the innocent from unwarranted conviction. However, this interest, which arises frequently in attempt prosecutions, is of serious concern only when the defendant's conduct is ambiguous and there is genuine doubt whether the defendant actually presented the dangers at which the law of attempt is aimed. There is little basis for such concern on the facts of either *Thacker* or *Acevedo*.

How, then, can one explain the consistent conclusion of both the common law and modern statutes that neither Thacker nor Acevedo should be guilty of attempted murder? Are they in fact less dangerous than persons who intend to kill? [f] Is retribution or proportionality the reason? Does your moral assessment of their behavior depend on whether a death actually occurred?

These questions are not easily answered. Part of the answer can be derived from thinking about how the crime of attempt should be graded. Recall that the common law punished attempts less severely than the completed offense and that most early American statutes followed the same tradition. The Model Penal Code, however, grades attempts at the same level as the completed offense, except for the most serious category of crimes. How should attempts be graded? Does it make sense to treat them as equivalent for purposes of punishment to the completed offense? Or is grading at a lower level appropriate? Once you decide how the actor who completes the offense and the actor who specifically intends to complete it should be treated relative to each other, does it follow that the actor who commits reckless homicide and the actor who is plainly reckless with respect to the death of another but who fortuitously does not cause that result should be treated the same way, relative to each other? The answer that the law gives to this question is "no." Can you articulate any reasons for this answer? Are they persuasive?

It is also helpful to broaden the focus of inquiry beyond the law of attempt. Both the common law and modern statutes reflect an often unarticulated policy that causing results or intending to cause results is worse, from the perspective of the purposes of the criminal law, than engaging in conduct that is likely to cause the result but that does not do so. This is illustrated by the absence at common law of an offense comparable to the reckless-endangering provision of the Model Penal Code (Section 211.2) and the absence even from the Model Penal Code of an offense of negligent endangering. It is also illustrated by the fact that even under the Model Penal Code there is a dramatic grading differential between the completed offense and the attempt on the one hand and reckless endangering on the other. One of the questions that must be asked is whether this focus of the law upon results and upon those who intend results reflects a sensible modern penal policy. Can you articulate reasons why this view should or should not be given such prominence? Should there be an offense like Section 211.2 of the

[f] See Enker, Mens Rea and Criminal Attempt, 1977 A.B.F.Res.J. 845, 846–66.

Model Penal Code? Should it be graded less severely (and by how much) than similar conduct that causes death? That is intended to cause death? Should there be an offense of negligent endangering? If so, how should it be graded?

At a more mundane level, it seems clear enough why the courts in implementing modern attempt statutes adhere to the result in these cases. Examine the Oregon statutes in Appendix B, pages 9–12, infra. Aside from attempt, of what offense would Thacker and Acevedo be guilty under these provisions? Can the Oregon attempt statute be construed to convict Thacker or Acevedo of attempted murder? What are the consequences of such a conviction in grading terms? Do you see why the courts would be unlikely to so construe the Oregon attempt statute? Do the Oregon statutes reflect the view that causing or intending results is more serious criminal behavior than creating a risk that they will occur? If so, is it appropriate for the courts to ignore this legislative statement of policy? [g]

5. *Gentry v. State.* In contrast to *Thacker* and *Acevedo,* consider the holding of the court in Gentry v. State, 437 So.2d 1097 (Fla.1983):

"We now hold that there are offenses that may be successfully prosecuted as an attempt without proof of a specific intent to commit the relevant completed offense. The key to recognizing these crimes is to first determine whether the completed offense is a crime requiring specific or general intent. If the state is not required to show specific intent to successfully prosecute the completed crime, it will not be required to show specific intent to successfully prosecute an attempt to commit that crime. We believe there is logic in this approach and that it comports with legislative intent. Second-degree and third-degree murder under our statutes are crimes requiring only general intent.

"In the instant case, the appellant . . . swore at his father, choked him, snapped a pistol several times to his head and when the weapon failed to fire, struck his father in the head with the gun. Had a homicide occurred, there can be no doubt that the appellant could have been successfully prosecuted for second-degree murder without the state adducing proof of a specific intent to kill. The fact that the father survived was not the result of any design on the part of the appellant not to effect death but was simply fortuitous. We can think of no good reason to reward the appellant for such fortuity by imposing upon the state the added burden of showing a specific intent to kill in order to successfully prosecute the attempted offense." [h]

[g] A situation comparable to *Thacker* and *Acevedo* faced the court in State v. Smith, 21 Or.App. 270, 534 P.2d 1180 (1975). The Oregon statutes were graded slightly differently when first enacted and as before the court in *Smith* (the offense defined in Section 163.118 was included in the murder provisions of Section 163.115; Section 163.175 was a class C felony; Section 163.185 was a class B felony). The court held that a charge of attempted reckless murder could not be sustained. For discussion of an interesting series of Illinois decisions coming eventually to the same result, see People v. Harris, 72 Ill.2d 16, 17 Ill.Dec. 838, 377 N.E.2d 28 (1978).

[h] The defendant was drunk when these events occurred, and one issue before the court was the relevance of intoxication to

This is distinctly a minority view. As indicated above, *Thacker* and *Acevedo* illustrate the traditional common-law analysis of this situation. Did the Florida court nonetheless get the right answer?

NOTES ON THE MODEL PENAL CODE ATTEMPT PROVISIONS

1. **The Text of the Model Code.** The Model Code definition of attempt (Section 5.01) reads as follows:

"(1) . . . A person is guilty of an attempt to commit a crime if, acting with the kind of culpability otherwise required for commission of the crime, he:

(a) purposely engages in conduct which would constitute the crime if the attendant circumstances were as he believes them to be; or

(b) when causing a particular result is an element of the crime, does or omits to do anything with the purpose of causing or with the belief that it will cause such result without further conduct on his part; or

(c) purposely does or omits to do anything which, under the circumstances as he believes them to be, is an act or omission constituting a substantial step in a course of conduct planned to culminate in his commission of the crime."

2. **Explanation of the Model Code Text.** Section 5.01(1) is one of the more inartfully drafted provisions of the Model Code. Indeed, its provisions cannot be understood unless you know why various phrases were placed where they appear. The policy resolutions it reflects, however, have been widely influential, and it is therefore important to understand its meaning. The following explanation is derived from the elaborate commentary appearing in Wechsler, Jones & Korn, The Treatment of Inchoate Crimes in the Model Penal Code of the American Law Institute: Attempt, Solicitation, and Conspiracy, 61 Colum.L. Rev. 571, 957 (1961).

Analytically, Subsections (1)(a) and (1)(b) should be read separately from Subsection (1)(c). The former provisions cover cases where the actor engages in all of the planned behavior; the latter provision concerns cases where the actor stops or is interrupted before the planned behavior is completed. When taken together, Subsections (1)(a) and (1)(b) adopt, in effect, the common-law position that attempt requires a specific intent to engage in conduct punished as criminal. There are two modifications of this policy. The more important is that the mens rea for circumstance elements of the attempt is the same as it would be for the completed offense. This is accomplished by the language "acting with the kind of culpability otherwise required for

the charge of second-degree murder. Since the court concluded that no specific intent need be shown, it also concluded that a jury charge relative to voluntary intoxication was properly refused. See the discussion in connection with the *Majewski* case, supra page 283. [Footnote by eds.]

commission of the crime" in the introductory phrase of Subsection (1). Even though this phrase is not keyed explicitly to circumstance elements, it applies to such elements.[a] Subsection (1)(a) requires purpose for conduct elements of the object offense, and Subsection (1)(b) requires purpose (as qualified below) for result elements of the object offense. The effect of the quoted language is therefore to carry forward the mens rea of the object offense only as to circumstance elements.[b] Although Subsections (1)(a) and (1)(b) are separated by an "or," it seems clear that this analysis is intended to apply to an offense that includes both conduct and result elements—purpose would be required as to both the conduct and the result; the mens rea for the circumstances would be governed by the policy of the completed offense.[c]

Subsection (1)(c) is meant to be interpreted similarly to Subsections (1)(a) and (1)(b), although the language hardly says so. Conduct and result elements are governed by a mens rea requirement of purpose, and circumstance elements are governed by the mens rea established for those elements by the completed offense. Thus the words "purposely does" and "planned to culminate in his commission of the crime" must be read as though they applied to conduct and result elements only.

The next question concerns the meaning of the words "if the attendant circumstances were as he believed them to be" in Subsection (1)(a) and the substantially equivalent words in Subsection (1)(c). The short answer is that for all of the issues heretofore addressed, these words should be ignored. They are meant to address the issue that is dealt with in *Jaffe*, which is the next main case. They are *not* designed to establish the Model Code's mens-rea policy for circumstance elements in attempts, even though they could be read to do just that. The function of these words is discussed in the notes following the *Jaffe* decision.

3. **Questions on the Model Code.** Your understanding of the foregoing explanation can be tested by answering the following questions:

(i) How would the *Thacker* and *Acevedo* cases be decided under the Model Code? Could they be guilty of attempted murder? Attempted

---

[a] It would also require that the defendant act with any "specific intent" required by the object offense. Thus, for attempted larceny the defendant would have to have a "purpose to deprive."

[b] Section 5.01 thus is one of the rare instances under the Model Code where proper classification of the elements is crucial. See the discussion of this point in the introductory note on the Model Penal Code culpability structure, page 234, supra.

[c] The second modification of the common-law specific-intent requirement is provided by the language "or with the belief that it will cause such result without fur-

ther conduct on his part" in subsection (1)(b). These words go slightly beyond the common law by including actors who believe that a forbidden result will occur, though they may be indifferent to its occurrence. Consider the following hypothetical. A business rival rigs a competitor's airplane so that it will crash, in order to cause a prospective customer to believe that it is defectively designed. The actor in such a case may believe that the pilot will be killed, but either not care or hope that the pilot is skillful enough to escape in some manner. Such a case, in the view of the Model Code drafters, should be assimilated to one where the actor intends to kill.

manslaughter? Of what offense under the Model Code might they be guilty?

(ii) How would the statutory rape and burglary hypotheticals appearing on pages 346–47, supra, be decided if the Model Code attempt provisions were applied to the definitions of the offenses given in the hypotheticals? How would they be decided under the Model Code definitions in §§ 213.1(1)(d) and 213.3(1)(a) in the rape situation (changing the operative ages accordingly) and § 221.1 in the burglary situation (assuming that sunset occurs at 6:30 p.m. on the night in question)?

SUBSECTION B: IMPOSSIBILITY AND ATTEMPT

PEOPLE v. JAFFE

Court of Appeals of New York, 1906.
185 N.Y. 497, 78 N.E. 169.

WILLARD BARTLETT, J. The indictment charged that the defendant . . . feloniously received 20 yards of cloth . . . knowing that [it] had been . . . stolen . . . . It was found under § 550 of the Penal Code, which provides that a person who buys or receives any stolen property knowing the same to have been stolen is guilty of criminally receiving such property. The defendant was convicted of an attempt to commit the crime charged in the indictment. The proof clearly showed, and the district attorney conceded upon the trial, that the goods which the defendant attempted to purchase . . . had lost their character as stolen goods at the time when they were offered to the defendant and when he sought to buy them. In fact the property had been restored to the owners and was wholly within their control and was offered to the defendant by their authority and through their agency. The question presented by this appeal, therefore, is whether upon an indictment for receiving goods, knowing them to have been stolen, the defendant may be convicted of an attempt to commit the crime where it appears without dispute that the property which he sought to receive was not in fact stolen property.

The conviction was sustained by the Appellate Division chiefly upon the authority of the numerous cases in which it has been held that one may be convicted of an attempt to commit a crime notwithstanding the existence of facts unknown to him which would have rendered the complete perpetration of the crime itself impossible. Notably among these are what may be called the "pickpocket cases," where, in prosecutions for attempts to commit larceny from the person by pickpocketing, it is held not to be necessary to allege or prove that there was anything in the pocket which could be the subject of larceny. . . . Much reliance was also placed [on a case] where a conviction of an attempt to commit the crime of extortion was upheld, although the woman from whom the defendant sought to obtain money by a threat to accuse her of a crime was not induced to pay the money by fear, but was acting at the time as a decoy for the police, and hence could not have been subjected to the influence of fear. In passing upon the question here presented for our determination, it is important to bear in mind precisely what it was that the defendant attempted to do. He simply made an effort to purchase certain specific pieces of cloth. He believed the cloth to be stolen property, but it was not such in fact. The purchase, therefore, if it had been completely effected, could not constitute the crime of receiving stolen property, knowing it to be stolen, since there could be no such thing as knowledge on the part of the defendant of a nonexistent fact, although there might be a belief on his part that the fact existed. [I]t is a mere truism that there can be no receiving of stolen goods which have not been stolen. It is equally difficult to perceive how there can be an attempt to receive stolen goods, knowing them to have been stolen, when they had not been stolen in fact.

The crucial distinction between the case before us and the pickpocket cases, and others involving the same principle, lies not in the possibility or impossibility of the commission of the crime, but in the fact that, in the present case, the act, which it was doubtless the intent of the defendant to commit would not have been a crime if it had been consummated. If he had actually paid for the goods which he desired to buy and received them into his possession, he would have committed no offense under § 550 of the Penal Code, because the very definition in that section of the offense of criminally receiving property makes it an essential element of the crime that the accused shall have known the property to have been stolen or wrongfully appropriated in such a manner as to constitute larceny. This knowledge being a material ingredient of the offense it is manifest that it cannot exist unless the property has in fact been stolen or larcenously appropriated. No man can know that to be so which is not so in truth and in fact. He may believe it to be so but belief is not enough under this statute. In the present case it appeared, not only by the proof, but by the express concession of the prosecuting officer, that the goods which the defendant intended to purchase had lost their character as stolen goods at the time of the proposed transaction. Hence, no matter what was the motive of the defendant, and no matter what he supposed, he could do no act which was intrinsically adapted to the then present successful perpetration of the crime denounced by this section of the Penal Code, because neither he nor any one in the world could know that the property was stolen property inasmuch as it was not, in fact, stolen property. In the pickpocket cases the immediate act which the defendant had in contemplation was an act which, if it could have been carried out, would have been criminal, whereas in the present case the immediate act which the defendant had in contemplation (to wit, the purchase of the goods which were brought to his place for sale) could not have been criminal under the statute even if the purchase had been completed, because the goods had not, in fact, been stolen, but were, at the time when they were offered to him, in the custody and under the control of the true owners.

If all which an accused person intends to do would, if done, constitute no crime, it cannot be a crime to attempt to do with the same purpose a part of the thing intended. . . . The crime of which the defendant was convicted necessarily consists of three elements: First, the act; second, the intent; and, third, the knowledge of an existing condition. There was proof tending to establish two of these elements, the first and the second, but none to establish the existence of the third. This was knowledge of the stolen character of the property sought to be acquired. There could be no such knowledge. The defendant could not know that the property possessed the character of stolen property when it had not in fact been acquired by theft. The language . . . to the effect that "the question whether an attempt to commit a crime had been made is determinable solely by the condition of the actor's mind and his conduct in the attempted consummation of his design," . . . has no application in a case like this, where, if the accused had completed the act which he attempted to do, he would not be guilty of a criminal offense. A particular belief cannot make that a crime which is not so in the absence of such belief. Take, for example, the case of a young man who attempts to vote, and succeeds in casting his vote under the belief that he is but 20 years of age, when he is in fact over 21 and a qualified voter. His intent to commit a crime, and his belief that he was committing a crime, would not make him guilty of any offense under these circumstances, although the moral turpitude of the transaction, on his part, would be just as great as it would if he were in fact under age. So, also, in the case of a prosecution under the statute of this state, which makes it rape in the second degree for a man to perpetrate an act of sexual intercourse with a female not his wife under the age of 18 years. There could be no conviction if it was established upon the trial that the female was in fact over the age of 18 years, although the defendant believed her to be younger and intended to commit the crime. No matter how reprehensible would be his act in morals, it would not be the act forbidden by this particular statute. "If what a man contemplates doing would not be in law a crime, he could not be said, in point of law, to intend to commit the crime. If he thinks his act will be a crime, this is a mere mistake of his understanding where the law holds it not to be such, his real intent being to do a particular thing. If the thing is not a crime, he does not intend to commit one whatever he may erroneously suppose."

The judgment of the Appellate Division and of the Court of General Sessions must be reversed. . . .

CHASE, J. . . . I dissent. Defendant having, with knowledge, repeatedly received goods stolen from a dry-goods firm by one of its employees, suggested to the employee that a certain specified kind of cloth be taken, he was told by the employee that that particular kind of cloth was not kept on his floor, and he then said that he would take a roll of certain Italian cloth. The employee then stole a roll of the Italian cloth and carried it away, but left it in another store where he could subsequently get it for delivery to the defendant. Before it was actually delivered to the defendant the employers discovered that the employee had been stealing from them, and they accused him of the thefts. The employee then confessed his guilt and told them of the piece of cloth that had been stolen for the defendant, but had not actually been delivered to him. The roll of cloth so stolen was then taken by another employee of the firm, and it was arranged at the police headquarters that the employee who had taken the cloth should deliver it to the defendant, which he did, and the defendant paid the employee about one half the value thereof. The defendant was then arrested and this indictment was thereafter found against him. That the defendant intended to commit a crime is undisputed. I think the record shows an attempt to commit the crime of criminally receiving property . . . .

NOTES ON IMPOSSIBILITY AND ATTEMPT

1. **The Impossibility Problem.** Cases such as *Jaffe* have bedeviled the courts throughout the history of the law of attempt. Modern American decisions are divided on the *Jaffe* facts,[a] and courts in both England[b] and New Zealand[c] have supported the *Jaffe* result. The problem is more widely discussed in the literature of attempt than any other aspect of the offense.[d]

Some indication of the variety of contexts in which the so-called "impossibility" problem has arisen is given by the following summary of American decisions in Booth v. State, 398 P.2d 863, 870–71 (Okl.Cr. App.1965) (citations omitted):

"The reason for the 'impossibility' of completing the substantive crime ordinarily falls into one of two categories: (i) where the act if completed would not be criminal, a situation which is usually described as a 'legal impossibility,' and (ii) where the basic or substantive crime is impossible of completion, simply because of some physical or factual condition unknown to the defendant, a situation which is usually described as a 'factual impossibility.'

"The authorities in the various states and the text-writers are in general agreement that where there is a 'legal impossibility' of completing the substantive crime, the accused cannot be successfully charged with an attempt, whereas in those cases in which the 'factual impossibility' situation is involved, the accused may be convicted of an attempt. Detailed discussion of the subject is

---

a E.g., compare Booth v. State, 398 P.2d 863 (Okl.Cr.App.1965) (agreeing with *Jaffe* result but calling for legislative reconsideration), with People v. Camodeca, 52 Cal.2d 142, 338 P.2d 903 (1959) (disagreeing with *Jaffe* result), and People v. Rojas, 55 Cal.2d 252, 10 Cal.Rptr. 465, 358 P.2d 921 (1961) (following *Camodeca*).

b Regina v. Smith, [1975] A.C. 475.

c Regina v. Donnelly, [1970] N.Z.L.R. 980.

d In addition to the materials cited in the remainder of these notes, see, e.g., Elkind, Impossibility in Criminal Attempts: A Theorist's Headache, 54 Va.L.Rev. 20 (1968); Hughes, One Further Footnote on Attempting the Impossible, 42 N.Y.U.L. Rev. 1005 (1967); Smith, Two Problems in Criminal Attempts, 70 Harv.L.Rev. 422 (1957); Smith, Two Problems in Criminal Attempts Re-Examined-II, [1962] Crim.L.R. 212; Williams, Criminal Attempts—A Reply, [1962] Crim.L.R. 300.

unnecessary to make it clear that it is frequently most difficult to compartmentalize a particular set of facts as coming within one of the categories rather than the other. Examples of the so-called 'legal impossibility' situations are:

(i) A person accepting goods which he believes to have been stolen, but which were not in fact stolen goods, is not guilty of an attempt to receive stolen goods.

(ii) It is not an attempt to commit subornation of perjury where the false testimony solicited, if given, would have been immaterial to the case at hand and hence not perjurious.

(iii) An accused who offers a bribe to a person believed to be a juror, but who is not a juror, is not guilty of an attempt to bribe a juror.

(iv) An official who contracts a debt which is unauthorized and a nullity, but which he believes to be valid, is not guilty of an attempt to illegally contract a valid debt.

(v) A hunter who shoots a stuffed deer believing it to be alive is not guilty of an attempt to shoot a deer out of season.

Examples of cases in which attempt convictions have been sustained on the theory that all that prevented the consummation of the completed crime was a 'factual impossibility' are:

(i) The picking of an empty pocket.

(ii) An attempt to steal from an empty receptacle or an empty house.

(iii) Where defendant shoots into the intended victim's bed, believing he is there, when in fact he is elsewhere.

(iv) Where the defendant erroneously believing that the gun is loaded points it at his wife's head and pulls the trigger.

(v) Where the woman upon whom the abortion operation is performed is not in fact pregnant."

To these actual cases can be added a number of other situations that have been discussed in the cases and the literature:

(i) "In the Empty Room, Sherlock Holmes' enemy, Colonel Moran, was induced to fire at a wax image of the detective silhouetted in the window, though Holmes prudently rejected Inspector Lestrade's advice to prefer a charge of attempted murder and so the matter was never tested . . . ." Regina v. Smith, [1975] A.C. 476, 495.

(ii) "[I]n Rex v. White, [1910] 2 K.B. 124 (C.C.A.), a man who put a small quantity of cyanide in a wine glass, too small to kill, was held guilty of attempted murder. . . . But quaere, what would have been the position if the glass . . . had contained pure water, even though the accused believed falsely that it contained cyanide? [Or consider] the situation when a would-be murderer attempts to assassinate a corpse, or a bolster in a bed, believing it to be the living body of his enemy, or when he fires into an empty room believing that it contained an intended victim [or when] the accused fired at a peephole in a roof believing it to be in use by a watching policeman who was in fact a few yards away." Id.

(iii) "Suppose a man takes away an umbrella from a stand with intent to steal it, believing it not to be his own, but it turns out to be his own, could he be convicted of attempting to steal?" Regina v. Collins, 9 Cox C.C. 497, 498 (1864).

(iv) "A defendant . . . endeavors to kill his enemies with a toy pistol or by incantations" or by sticking pins in a voodoo doll. Sayre, Criminal Attempts, 41 Harv.L.Rev. 821, 850 (1928).

(v) "Lady Eldon, when traveling with her husband on the Continent, bought what she supposed to be a quantity of French Lace, which she hid, concealing it from Lord Eldon in one of the pockets of the coach. The package was brought to light by a custom officer at Dover. The lace turned out to be an English manufactured article of little value and, of course, not subject to duty. Lady Eldon had bought it at a price vastly above its value, believing it to be genuine, intending to smuggle it into England." 1 F. Wharton, Criminal Law 304 n. 9 (12th ed. 1932).

(vi) "*D* had sexual intercourse with a girl of 16, believing her to be 15. [Is he] guilty of attempting to have intercourse with a girl under 16 . . . "? G. Williams, Textbook of Criminal Law 394 (1978).

(vii) "*D* receives a bicycle from his seven-year-old child, knowing that it has been taken by the child in circumstances that would amount to larceny for an adult. *D* is not guilty of receiving [stolen property], since the bicycle is not 'stolen' in law" because a seven-year old is incapable of committing a crime. Can he be convicted of attempting to receive stolen property? G. Williams, Criminal Law: The General Part 634 (2d ed. 1961).

2. **Some Approaches to the Impossibility Problem.** How should these various situations be analyzed? Does the distinction between legal and factual impossibility help? What problems of policy are posed? As you think about these questions, consider the following suggested approaches to the impossibility problem:

(i) **Previously Consummated Attempt.** Professors Perkins and Boyce, in Criminal Law 624 (2d ed. 1982),* have argued that in at least some of the situations illustrated above, the actor properly can be viewed as having passed beyond preparation and completed an attempt before any impossibility problem arose. Thus, as to *Jaffe*, they reasoned that:

"[M]uch could be said for [the *Jaffe* result] if nothing was involved except the purchase of property under such circumstances that the buyer firmly, but mistakenly, believed it to be stolen. More was involved, however, in these cases. Property

---

* Copyright © 1982 by The Foundation Press. The two excerpts below are reprinted with permission.

had in fact been stolen, the thief and [the defendant] had made arrangements for [the defendant] to receive it and [the defendant] did receive it. In the meantime the thief had been apprehended and the property recovered. After it had thus lost its stolen character it was returned to the thief to carry out the original plan. The courts overlooked everything except the very last step by which the property was actually handed over. [The defendant] had gone beyond preparation and moved in the direction of receiving stolen property before that last step and should have been convicted . . . ."

Is this a sound approach to at least some of the impossibility cases? How many of the situations posed above would result in convictions under this analysis?

(ii) **Primary and Secondary Intent.** Several scholars have suggested that it is important in impossibility cases to distinguish between two kinds of intent manifested by the actor at the time of the offense. Professors Perkins and Boyce summarize this view as follows: [c]

"Deeply intrenched in the common law is the principle that conviction of crime cannot be based upon intent alone . . . . This raises the question of 'inconsistent intents.' At times one has two different intents which seem only one to him but are so inconsistent that only one is possible of achievement. . . . In such a situation the law regards one intent as primary and the other as secondary and only the primary intent controls . . . .

It has been said that if D takes his own umbrella, thinking it belongs to another and with intent to steal, this does not constitute an attempt to commit larceny. Here . . . we find utterly inconsistent intents unrealized by the actor. He intends to take a particular umbrella (which actually belongs to him). He also has in mind the intent to steal the umbrella of another. His primary intent is to take the umbrella he actually seizes and hence there is nothing wrongful in what is actually done but only in his secondary, inconsistent intent. Hence in such a situation, if there is nothing in his conduct either preceding or following the taking, which manifests a criminal purpose he should not be held guilty of attempted larceny. To convict him merely because he admitted his mistaken notion at a later time would be to convict him on intent alone. But this does not mean that he should not be convicted of attempt to steal if his conduct at the time of the transaction clearly manifested a criminal purpose."

How helpful is the primary-secondary intent distinction? Did the court have it in mind in *Jaffe?* Does it aid analysis, or does it rationalize a result reached for other reasons? Could the argument by Professors Perkins and Boyce be stated in policy terms that did not rely on distinguishing between two kinds of intents?

[c] For more elaborate statements of this position, see Keedy, Criminal Attempts at Common Law, 102 U.Pa.L.Rev. 464 (1954); Perkins, Criminal Attempt and Related Problems, 2 U.C.L.A.L.Rev. 319 (1955).

Suppose *A* aims a gun at *B* and pulls the trigger with intent to kill. If the bullet misses, what is *A*'s primary intent? Is this case different in any important respect from the umbrella situation? From *Jaffe*?

(iii) **The Defendant's Reasonable Expectations.** Professor Sayre, in Criminal Attempts, 41 Harv.L.Rev. 821, 849–51 (1928),* has argued that the key to the impossibility cases lies in the underlying purposes of the criminal law. From such purposes, he extrapolates the following position:

"Under the retributive or expiative theory, the object of criminal justice is conceived to be punishment qua punishment, and the aim is to make the defendant suffer in exact proportion to his guilt. Since the proportionment of an individual's guilt cannot be divorced from moral and psychological considerations, punishment for a criminal attempt under this theory must be determined from an essentially subjective viewpoint, i.e., a defendant will deserve punishment if he actually intended to consummate a crime and committed such acts as *from his viewpoint* would be effective in achieving the crime, quite regardless of whether in the world of fact his acts could or could not cause the criminal consummation desired. If, on the other hand, one follows the more modern utilitarian theory of criminal justice, i.e., that the end of criminal law is to protect public and social interests, and that criminality should depend primarily, therefore, not on moral guilt but on whether or not social or public interests are unduly injured or endangered, then it follows that the question of punishment for a criminal attempt must be determined from an *objective* viewpoint. Under this view the question of the criminality of an attempt will depend primarily not on what may have been passing through the mind of the individual defendant, but on the degree of actual danger to social or public interests arising from his acts.

"At this point many of the followers of the utilitarian theory of criminal justice fall into the error of arguing that if, because of some misconception of fact, the defendant's act in the light of the actual circumstances could not possibly achieve the criminal objective desired, it follows that since there is no actual endangering of social or public interests, the acts of the defendant should not be made punishable. In truth, however, the allowing of such acts to go unpunished might very seriously endanger social interests by encouraging repetition on the part of the defendant or others; the real danger lies in future similar acts when the actor may have learned to guard against his mistakes.

"Whenever a gunman fires to kill and misses, all possible danger from that particular attempt has passed; yet surely even the staunchest adherent of the objective theory would convict such a gunman for a criminal attempt. Even under the objective viewpoint, therefore, when a defendant to achieve some crime commits an act which because of his mistake could not possibly cause the desired criminal consequence, he should be convicted if allowing him to go free would menace social interests through the danger of repetition. This is a question depending upon all the circumstances of the individual case. If from the point of view of a reasonable man in the same circumstances as the defendant the desired criminal consequence could not be expected to result from the defendant's acts, it cannot endanger social interests to allow the defendant to go unpunished, no matter how evil may have been his intentions. A defendant who endeavors to kill his enemies with a toy pistol or by incantations may safely be allowed freely to continue making such attempts. As long as he abstains from acts reasonably adapted to the attainment of the desired criminal consequence, no social or public interests are endangered nor is any sense of social security violated. On the other hand, the gunman who shoots to kill his victim but fails because, unknown to him, a detective had previously slipped a blank cartridge into his gun, is no more able to kill his victim than the man who seeks to kill with a toy pistol or an incantation, but his conduct endangers public and social interests to a far greater degree. Under the objective view of a criminal attempt, therefore, the unsuccessful effort to achieve a criminal consequence should be punished if, and only if, a reasonable man in the same circumstances as the defendant might expect the defendant's acts to cause the consummation of the crime. . . .

"One further word of caution as to the objective view should be added. As has been suggested before, an attempt presupposes an intent to effectuate the crime attempted; no conviction can be had without proof of this specific intent. This must be true whatever be one's theory of an attempt. Even under the objective theory, therefore, the actual subjective intent of the defendant is material and must be proved as the necessary mental element of the crime, just as in every other crime requiring a specific intent. In other words, under the objective theory the defendant to be convicted for a criminal attempt must be proved (i) to have actually *intended* to effectuate what constitutes the crime attempted, and (ii) in pursuance of that intent to have committed some act which a reasonable man in the same circumstances might have supposed would cause the criminal consequence intended."

Is Sayre's approach sound? Does a defendant who acts unreasonably necessarily manifest no danger to social interests? On the other hand, should the voodoo-doctor be convicted?

  (iv) **The Model Penal Code.** The Model Penal Code abandons the common-law distinction between legal and factual impossibility. Its approach to impossibility cases can be extracted from three separate sources. First, § 5.01(1) is drafted on the premise that the defendant's criminality should be judged from the circumstances as he or she viewed them. This is accomplished in Subsection (1)(a) by the language "if the attendant circumstances were as he believes them to be." Thus, in the umbrella case, since the defendant believed the umbrella belonged to someone else, he would be guilty. The same result is specified in comparable language in Subsection (1)(c) for cases where the actor's conduct is incomplete but has passed beyond mere preparation. The same result would also follow under Subsection (1)(b) in a case such as the Sherlock Holmes hypothetical posed at page 357, supra. The actor in that case would have fired at the wax dummy "with the purpose of causing [the death of another] without further conduct on his part."

Second, the provisions of §§ 5.05(2) and 2.12 permit the grade of the offense to be reduced, or in extreme cases the prosecution to be dismissed, when the actor's conduct "is so inherently unlikely to result or culminate in the commission of a crime that neither such conduct nor the actor presents a public danger" or where the actor's conduct "did not actually cause or threaten the harm or evil sought to be prevented by the law defining the offense or did so only to an extent too trivial to warrant the condemnation of conviction." Thus, in a case involving a toy pistol, incantation, or voodoo, the court would have the authority to decide that the actor should be convicted of a lesser offense or no offense at all, based on its evaluation of the dangers presented by the defendant to the interests sought to be protected by the law.

Third, certain substantive offenses, most particularly § 223.6 (receiving stolen property), have been defined so as to eliminate the possibility of acquittal on the basis of an impossibility argument. Section 223.6 provides that an actor is guilty who has received property "believing that it has probably been stolen." On the facts of *Jaffe*, therefore, it is likely that the defendant would be guilty of the completed substantive offense and resort to a charge of attempt would be unnecessary.

These results are defended [f] on the rationale that most defendants in impossibility situations have demonstrated their readiness to violate the criminal law, have manifested the required culpability, and have posed sufficient social danger to justify the invocation of criminal sanctions. Three functions are seen to have been served by the impossibility defense. First, it has functioned as a surrogate for uncertainties on the facts about whether the defendant had the required criminal purpose. Second, it similarly has functioned as a surrogate for the entrapment defense [g] and has thus allowed the courts to express their displeasure at certain law-enforcement techniques involving the use of traps or decoys. Third, the impossibility defense has eliminated from the ambit of the criminal law certain cases where the defendant does not threaten the interests the law is designed to serve. Each of these

[f] See Wechsler, Jones & Korn, The Treatment of Inchoate Crimes in the Model Penal Code of the American Law Institute: Attempt, Solicitation, and Conspiracy, 61 Colum.L.Rev. 571, 578–84 (1961). See also ALI, Model Penal Code and Commentaries § 5.01, pp. 315–17 (1985).

[g] Materials on the entrapment defense are included at pages 625–30, infra.

functions is said to have been sufficiently taken into account in the Model Code provisions. Are you satisfied with the Model Code position? Are there other problems that have not been taken into account? How would the impossibility cases posed above be resolved under the Model Code approach?

(v) **The Importance of the Actus Reus.** Professor Enker, in Impossibility in Criminal Attempts—Legality and the Legal Process, 53 Minn.L.Rev. 665 (1969),* argued that it is important to retain the impossibility defense in certain situations because it reinforces the policies underlying the act requirement. He pointed out that criminal convictions based on equivocal conduct—conduct that does not corroborate the inferences of intent sought to be drawn—create an unacceptable risk of extending the criminal law to innocent behavior. He then argued that:

"[P]rosecution for attempt contains potential for arbitrary ex post facto judgments. But in large measure this danger is mitigated by the following factors: (i) The requirement that the defendant intend to commit the substantive crime: while recklessness or negligence may be adequate for certain substantive crimes, they are not adequate for attempts. This has the effect of limiting the acts which can be held to be attempts to those which appear to be intentionally directed toward the acts defined in the substantive crime, or toward bringing about the illegal result . . . . (ii) The requirement that the act evidence commitment to the criminal venture and corroborate the mens rea: to the extent that this requirement is preserved it prevents the conviction of persons engaged in innocent acts on the basis of a mens rea proved through speculative inferences, unreliable forms of testimony and/or past criminal conduct. (iii) The use of the technique of analogy whereby the decision in each case must be rationalized in comparison with other more or less similar cases which presumably were decided neutrally. (iv) Finally, the alternative to running the risk of occasional erroneous or arbitrary judgment is to prosecute only those attempts which can be carefully defined in advance, a rather intolerable option at least in the case of the more serious crimes.

"Though it does not ordinarily occur to us, our legal system could have adopted a completely different technique for distinguishing culpable attempts from those which are not culpable but are rather, in the conventional terminology, preparations. It would have been possible to eliminate the preparation-attempt dichotomy, thereby eliminating any notion of particular indispensable acts, and simply approach each case in terms of whether the evidence at hand is sufficient to prove the necessary intent, encompassing intent and commitment to the venture, or will. But even the Model Penal Code resolution of the issue does not rely solely on the sufficiency of the evidence to prove intent

---

* The three excerpts below are reprinted with permission of the author and the Minnesota Law Review.

and will. It, too, requires that the act itself be 'a substantial step' toward completion of the crime and that the act corroborate 'the actor's criminal purpose.'

"There are several reasons justifying our reluctance to substitute a sufficiency-of-the-evidence test for the act requirement. Degrees of commitment vary so that we would again lack an objective criterion in cases falling short of consummation. Accomplice testimony and alleged confessions would ordinarily meet the sufficiency hurdles so that this would be an inadequate technique for controlling the jury unless corroboration standards were tightened. Defendants with prior criminal records for similar crimes would be particularly vulnerable under such an approach. And the technique of analogy would be considerably less significant, possibly resulting in less judicial objectivity."

Professor Enker continued by arguing that the actual existence of required actus-reus elements of crime, especially circumstance elements, provides important corroboration of criminal intent that will be lost if the impossibility defense is totally abandoned. He then criticized the Model Code solution as follows:

"The draftsmen of the Model Penal Code have argued that while eliminating legal impossibility as a defense, the Code adequately takes care of these problems by its separate provision requiring that the defendant's act corroborate his mens rea. But the Model Penal Code's requirement that the act corroborate the mens rea applies only to cases in the preparation-attempt continuum. Cases such as *Jaffe* and Lady Eldon are covered by a separate provision which provides that where the defendant does any act which would constitute a crime under the circumstances as he thought them to be, he is guilty of an attempt. The corroboration requirement of Section 5.01(2) does not apply to this section.[40] Perhaps the draftsmen assumed that doing the act defined in the substantive crime will always supply at least as much corroboration of mens rea as is present in the substantive crime itself. If so, what they have failed to see is that the act in its narrow sense of the defendant's physical movements can be perfectly innocent in itself—possession of goods, bringing goods into the country—and that what gives the act character as corroborative of mens rea is often the objective element or the attendant circumstances that the goods possessed are in fact stolen, or that the goods brought into the country are in fact dutiable, or that the goods possessed are in fact narcotics."

The Model Code is defended in the face of these criticisms in ALI, Model Penal Code and Commentaries § 5.01, pp. 319–20 (1985). Three

---

[40] "Impossibility cases are dealt with in Subsections (1)(a) . . . and (1)(b) . . . of Section 5.01. Subsection (1)(c) deals with attempt-preparation cases. The corroboration requirement is contained in the first sentence of Section 5.01(2) which is limited to defining the term 'substantial step' under Subsection (1)(c). Indeed, Subsections (1)(a) and (1)(b) do not require a 'substantial step.' And while some impossibility cases will fit under Section (1)(c), the requirement of substantiality is judged there, too, by reference to 'the circumstances as [the defendant] believes them to be . . . .'"

reasons are advanced in support of the Model Code as drafted: (i) the issue is "more theoretical than practical" because it is unlikely that persons will be prosecuted for innocuous behavior solely on the basis of their admissions; (ii) a requirement of corroboration in the context of completed conduct may lead to the acquittal of persons whose behavior alone is insufficiently corroborative, but whose behavior in light of contemporaneous statements and later admissions provides a sufficient case for guilt; and (iii) contemporaneous statements and later admissions might be thought to be a more reliable indicator of guilt in a case of completed conduct than in a case where the actor has yet to complete proposed behavior.

Is this a persuasive response? Or is Professor Enker right that the Model Code does not adequately protect against the risk of convicting an innocent person?

(vi) **The Principle of Legality.** Professor Enker also argues that the impossibility defense is in certain circumstances an appropriate vehicle for recognition of the principle of legality. He states his position on a case like *Jaffe* as follows:

"We may, therefore, characterize the issue presented by legal impossibility thus: the legislature has defined the substantive crime to require the presence of a particular circumstance; there is no reason why—for cases in which that circumstance is absent but the defendant allegedly thinks it is present—the legislature should delegate to the courts the power or the duty to decide whether that circumstance may be dispensed with; if the legislature were to delegate the issue to the courts—or the courts to assume it—the courts would have no analytic tools for deciding the issue; delegation to the court of the power to define the elements of a crime after the act ʁaises serious issues of legality, particularly when such analytic tools are lacking; and there are in any event good policy reasons favoring retention of the circumstance as an element of the crime.

"It is not the burden of this article to argue that the legislature must preserve the objective element of the crime in all instances. The point is that the defense of legal impossibility is a device which enables the court to return the ball to the legislature to resolve for each crime separately what are its appropriate objective elements and which objective elements may be safely dispensed with. And if, as suggested above, the significance of the objective element may vary from crime to crime, there is reason for the legislature to make discriminating choices to retain the objective element in certain crimes and eliminate it in others rather than deal with the issue in the attempt context which has the unfortunate tendency to generalize its results indiscriminately across the entire spectrum of crimes.

"The problem of legal impossibility, in the final analysis, is not really an attempt problem at all. It is rather a problem of the proper definition of the objective elements of specific crimes, a peculiarly legislative task."

Is this argument convincing? If the Model Code approach were adopted by the legislature, would the legislature then have made the judgment for which Enker calls? Or is his point that it is inappropriate for the legislature to return the ball to the courts in such indiscriminate language?

3. **True Legal Impossibility.** There is one variation of the impossibility situation on which there is virtually unanimous agreement in the cases and the literature. Consider the following variation of the *Jaffe* facts. If the legislature repealed the receiving-stolen-property statute the day before Jaffe's conduct, and if the Model Penal Code approach to impossibility were to be taken, could Jaffe be convicted of attempting to receive stolen property? Would it be relevant that he believed he was committing a crime? How is this situation different from the "legal impossibility" cases summarized in the *Booth* case, page 357, supra? Recall the discussion of the principle of legality at pages 33–43, supra. Do you see why virtually all would agree that Jaffe could not be convicted in this situation? Are there arguments you could make in favor of his conviction? Are they convincing? Do any of the situations described at pages 357–58, supra, pose an analogous problem?

SUBSECTION C: EQUIVOCAL CONDUCT IN COMPLETED OFFENSES

BRONSTON v. UNITED STATES

Supreme Court of the United States, 1973.
409 U.S. 352.

MR. CHIEF JUSTICE BURGER delivered the opinion of the Court.

We granted the writ in this case to consider a narrow but important question in the application of the federal perjury statute, 18 U.S.C. § 1621:[1] whether a witness may be convicted of perjury for an answer, under oath, that is literally true but not responsive to the question asked and arguably misleading by negative implication.

Petitioner is the sole owner of Samuel Bronston Productions, Inc., a company that between 1958 and 1964, produced motion pictures in various European locations. For these enterprises, Bronston Productions opened bank accounts in a number of foreign countries; in 1962, for example, it had 37 accounts in five countries. As president of Bronston Productions, petitioner supervised transactions involving the foreign bank accounts.

---

[1] 18 U.S.C. § 1621 provides:

"Whoever, having taken an oath before a competent tribunal . . . that he will testify . . . truly, . . . willfully and contrary to such oath states or subscribes any material matter which he does not believe to be true, is guilty of perjury, and shall . . . be fined not more than $2,000 or imprisoned not more than five years, or both. . . ."

In June 1964, Bronston Productions petitioned for an arrangement with creditors under . . . the Bankruptcy Act. On June 10, 1966, a referee in bankruptcy held a . . . hearing to determine, for the benefit of creditors, the extent and location of the company's assets. Petitioner's perjury conviction was founded on the answers given by him as a witness at that bankruptcy hearing, and in particular on the following colloquy with a lawyer for a creditor of Bronston Productions:

"Q. Do you have any bank accounts in Swiss banks, Mr. Bronston?

"A. No, sir.

"Q. Have you ever?

"A. The company had an account there for about six months, in Zurich.

"Q. Have you any nominees who have bank accounts in Swiss banks?

"A. No, sir.

"Q. Have you ever?

"A. No, sir."

It is undisputed that for a period of nearly five years, between October 1959 and June 1964, petitioner had a personal bank account at the International Credit Bank in Geneva, Switzerland, into which he made deposits and upon which he drew checks totaling more than $180,000. It is likewise undisputed that petitioner's answers were literally truthful. (i) Petitioner did not at the time of questioning have a Swiss bank account. (ii) Bronston Productions, Inc., did have the account in Zurich described by petitioner. (iii) Neither at the time of questioning nor before did petitioner have nominees who had Swiss accounts. The government's prosecution for perjury went forward on the theory that in order to mislead his questioner, petitioner answered the second question with literal truthfulness but unresponsively addressed his answer to the company's assets and not to his own—thereby implying that he had no personal Swiss bank account at the relevant time.

At petitioner's trial, the District Court instructed the jury that the "basic issue" was whether petitioner "spoke his true belief." Perjury, the court stated, "necessarily involves the state of mind of the accused" and "essentially consists of wilfully testifying to the truth of a fact which the defendant does not believe to be true"; petitioner's testimony could not be found "wilfully" false unless at the time his testimony was given petitioner "fully understood the questions put to him but nevertheless gave false answers knowing the same to be false." The court further instructed the jury that if petitioner did not understand the question put to him and for that reason gave an unresponsive answer, he could not be convicted of perjury. Petitioner could, however, be convicted if he gave an answer "not literally false but when considered in the context in which it was given, nevertheless constitute[d] a false statement." [3] The jury began its deliberations at 11:30 a.m. Several

---

[3] The District Court gave the following example "as an illustration only":

"[I]f it is material to ascertain how many times a person has entered a store

times it requested exhibits or additional instructions from the court, and at one point, at the request of the jury, the District Court repeated its instructions in full.   At 6:10 p.m., the jury returned its verdict, finding petitioner guilty . . . of perjury . . . .

In the Court of Appeals, petitioner contended, as he had in post-trial motions before the District Court, that the key question was imprecise and suggestive of various interpretations.   In addition, petitioner contended that he could not be convicted of perjury on the basis of testimony that was concededly truthful, however unresponsive.   A divided Court of Appeals held that the question was readily susceptible of a responsive reply and that it adequately tested the defendant's belief in the veracity of his answer.   The Court of Appeals further held that "[f]or the purposes of 18 U.S.C. § 1621, an answer containing half of the truth which also constitutes a lie by negative implication, when the answer is intentionally given in place of the responsive answer called for by a proper question, is perjury."   In this Court, petitioner renews his attack on the specificity of the question asked him and the legal sufficiency of his answer to support a conviction for perjury.   The problem of the ambiguity of the question is not free from doubt, but we need not reach that issue.   Even assuming, as we do, that the question asked petitioner specifically focused on petitioner's personal bank accounts, we conclude that the federal perjury statute cannot be construed to sustain a conviction based on petitioner's answer. . . .

There is, at the outset, a serious literal problem in applying § 1621 to petitioner's answer.   The words of the statute confine the offense to the witness who "willfully . . . states . . . any material matter which he does not believe to be true."   Beyond question, petitioner's answer to the crucial question was not responsive if we assume, as we do, that the first question was directed at personal bank accounts. There is, indeed, an implication in the answer to the second question that there was never a personal bank account; in casual conversation this interpretation might reasonably be drawn.   But we are not dealing with casual conversation and the statute does not make it a criminal act for a witness to willfully state any material matter that *implies* any material matter that he does not believe to be true.[4]

on a given day and that person responds to such a question by saying five times when in fact he knows that he entered the store 50 times that day, that person may be guilty of perjury even though it is technically true that he entered the store five times."

The illustration given by the District Court is hardly comparable to petitioner's answer; the answer "five times" is responsive to the hypothetical question and contains nothing to alert the questioner that he may be sidetracked.   Moreover, it is very doubtful that an answer which, in response to a specific quantitative inquiry, baldly understates a numerical fact can be described as even "technically true."   Whether an answer is true must be determined with reference to the question it purports

to answer, not in isolation.   An unresponsive answer is unique in this respect because its unresponsiveness by definition prevents its truthfulness from being tested in the context of the question—unless there is to be speculation as to what the unresponsive answer "implies." . . .

[4] Petitioner's answer is not to be measured by the same standards applicable to criminally fraudulent or extortionate statements.   In that context, the law goes "rather far in punishing intentional creation of false impressions by a selection of literally true representations, because the actor himself generally selects and arranges the representations."   In contrast, "under our system of adversary questioning and cross-examination the scope of disclosure is largely in the hands of counsel

The government urges that the perjury statute be construed broadly to reach petitioner's answer and thereby fulfill its historic purpose of reinforcing our adversary factfinding process. We might go beyond the precise words of the statute if we thought they did not adequately express the intention of Congress, but we perceive no reason why Congress would intend the drastic sanction of a perjury prosecution to cure a testimonial mishap that could readily have been reached with a single additional question by counsel alert—as every examiner ought to be—to the incongruity of petitioner's unresponsive answer. Under the pressures and tensions of interrogation, it is not uncommon for the most earnest witnesses to give answers that are not entirely responsive. Sometimes the witness does not understand the question, or may in an excess of caution or apprehension read too much or too little into it. It should come as no surprise that a participant in a bankruptcy proceeding may have something to conceal and consciously tries to do so, or that a debtor may be embarrassed at his plight and yield information reluctantly. It is the responsibility of the lawyer to probe; testimonial interrogation, and cross-examination in particular, is a probing, prying, pressing form of inquiry. If a witness evades, it is the lawyer's responsibility to recognize the evasion and to bring the witness back to the mark, to flush out the whole truth with the tools of adversary examination.

It is no answer to say that here the jury found that petitioner intended to mislead his examiner. A jury should not be permitted to engage in conjecture whether an unresponsive answer, true and complete on its face, was intended to mislead or divert the examiner; the state of mind of the witness is relevant only to the extent that it bears on whether "he does not believe [his answer] to be true." To hold otherwise would be to inject a new and confusing element into the adversary testimonial system we know. Witnesses would be unsure of the extent of their responsibility for the misunderstandings and inadequacies of examiners, and might well fear having that responsibility tested by a jury under the vague rubric of "intent to mislead" or "perjury by implication."

. . . The cases support petitioner's position that the perjury statute is not to be loosely construed, nor the statute invoked simply because a wily witness succeeds in derailing the questioner—so long as the witness speaks the literal truth. The burden is on the questioner to pin the witness down to the specific object of the questioner's inquiry.

The government does not contend that any misleading or incomplete response must be sent to the jury to determine whether a witness committed perjury because he intended to sidetrack his questioner. As the government recognizes, the effect of so unlimited an interpretation of § 1621 would be broadly unsettling. It is said, rather, that petitioner's testimony falls within a more limited category of intentionally misleading responses with an especially strong tendency to mislead the questioner. In [two prior] federal cases [in which perjury convictions

and presiding officer." MPC § 208.20, Comment at 124 (Tent.Draft No. 6, 1957) [now § 223.3].

were overturned], the government tells us the defendant gave simple negative answers "that were both entirely responsive and entirely truthful. . . . In neither case did the defendant—as did petitioner here—make affirmative statements of one fact that in context constituted denials by negative implication of a related fact." Thus the government isolates two factors which are said to require application of the perjury statute in the circumstances of this case: the unresponsiveness of petitioner's answer and the affirmative cast of that answer, with its accompanying negative implication.

This analysis succeeds in confining the government's position, but it does not persuade us that Congress intended to extend the coverage of § 1621 to answers unresponsive on their face but untrue only by "negative implication." Though perhaps a plausible argument can be made that unresponsive answers are especially likely to mislead, any such argument must, we think, be predicated upon the questioner's being aware of the unresponsiveness of the relevant answer. Yet, if the questioner is aware of the unresponsiveness of the answer, with equal force it can be argued that the very unresponsiveness of the answer should alert counsel to press on for the information he desires. It does not matter that the unresponsive answer is stated in the affirmative, thereby implying the negative of the question actually posed; for again, by hypothesis, the examiner's awareness of unresponsiveness should lead him to press another question or reframe his initial question with greater precision. Precise questioning is imperative as a predicate for the offense of perjury.

It may well be that petitioner's answers were not guileless but were shrewdly calculated to evade. Nevertheless, we [conclude] that any special problems arising from the literally true but unresponsive answer are to be remedied through the "questioner's acuity" and not by a federal perjury prosecution.

Reversed.

NOTES ON EQUIVOCAL CONDUCT IN COMPLETED OFFENSES

1. **Questions on *Bronston*.** What was the basis for the reversal of Bronston's conviction? Would the result be the same if the defendant had been charged with perjury under § 241.1 of the Model Penal Code? With attempted perjury under § 5.01 of the Model Code? Are there similarities between the reasons given by the Chief Justice for reversing Bronston's conviction and the reasons that could be given for not convicting the defendant in certain impossibility-attempt situations? Between the reasons given by the Chief Justice and the reasons underlying the act requirement? [a] Is the impossibility-attempt situation merely symptomatic of a larger and more pervasive problem in the criminal law, one that really has little to do with "impossibility" as a concept or even the crime of attempt?

[a] See pages 122–25, supra.

2. ***United States v. Remington.*** In United States v. Remington, 191 F.2d 246 (2d Cir.1951), a distinguished panel of the Second Circuit (Chief Judge Swan and Judges Augustus and Learned Hand) approved a conviction of perjury on the following facts. Remington was asked before a grand jury whether he had ever been a member of the Communist Party. His response was "no." The fact was that he had not been a member. The court held that a conviction could be sustained, however, on the theory that he *thought* he had been a member and thus *believed* that his answer was untruthful. Since the perjury statute, quoted in *Bronston,* covers one who "wilfully . . . subscribes [to] any material matter which he does not believe to be true," the court concluded that Remington could be convicted for the misrepresentation of his belief contained in his testimony.

Does this conclusion bother you? Is it consistent with the reasoning in *Bronston?* Could Remington be convicted of perjury under § 241.1 of the Model Penal Code? Note that there are occasions where misrepresentation of belief quite properly is the concern of the perjury offense. Thus, an expert who is asked to testify under oath as to his or her "opinion" on a matter or a conscientious objector who is asked under oath to state the religious "belief" that is the foundation for his or her claim may well, if they lie, subvert the process of justice to exactly the same extent as a person who lies about "facts." How could the prosecutor prove that an expert or a conscientious objector lied about an opinion or belief? Are the problems in such cases any different from the problems with Bronston's or Remington's convictions?

If Remington cannot be convicted of perjury under the Model Penal Code, can he be convicted of attempted perjury under § 5.01? Is this an "impossibility" situation, thus permitting his conviction because "if the attendant circumstances were as he believe[d] them to be," he would indeed have lied? It is concluded in ALI, Model Penal Code and Commentaries, § 241.1, pp. 102–08 (1980), that Remington would be guilty neither of perjury nor attempted perjury under the Model Code provisions. Can you see how these conclusions could be defended?

SUBSECTION D: ABANDONMENT IN ATTEMPT AND OTHER OFFENSES

PEOPLE v. STAPLES

California Court of Appeals, 1970.
6 Cal.App.3d 61, 85 Cal.Rptr. 589.

REPPY, J. In October 1967, while his wife was away on a trip, defendant, a mathematician, under an assumed name, rented an office on the second floor of a building in Hollywood which was over the mezzanine of a bank. Directly below the mezzanine was the vault of the bank. Defendant was aware of the layout of the building, specifically of the relation of the office he rented to the bank vault. Defendant paid rent for the period from October 23 to November 23. The landlord had 10 days before commencement of the rental period within which to finish some interior repairs and painting. During the pre-rental period defendant brought into the office certain equipment. This included drilling tools, two acetylene gas tanks, a blow torch, a blanket, and a linoleum rug. The landlord observed these items when he came in from time to time to see how the repair work was progressing. Defendant learned from a custodian that no one was in the building on Saturdays. On Saturday, October 14, defendant drilled two groups of holes into the floor of the office above the mezzanine room. He stopped drilling before the holes went through the floor. He came back to the office several times thinking he might slowly drill down, covering the holes with the linoleum rug. At some point in time he installed a hasp lock on a closet, and planned to, or did, place his tools in it. However, he left the closet keys on the premises. Around the end of November, apparently after November 23, the landlord notified the police and turned the tools and equipment over to them. Defendant did not pay any more rent. It is not clear when he last entered the office, but it could have been after November 23, and even after the landlord had removed the equipment. On February 22, 1968, the police arrested defendant. After receiving advice as to his constitutional rights, defendant voluntarily made an oral statement which he reduced to writing.

Among other things which defendant wrote down were these:

"Saturday, the 14th . . . I drilled some small holes in the floor of the room. Because of tiredness, fear, and the implications of what I was doing, I stopped and went to sleep.

"At this point I think my motives began to change. The [actual] commencement of my plan made me begin to realize that even if I were to succeed a fugitive life of living off of stolen money would not give the enjoyment of the life of a mathematician however humble a job I might have.

"I still had not given up my plan however. I felt I had made a certain investment of time, money, effort and a certain [psychological] commitment to the concept.

"I came back several times thinking I might store the tools in the closet and slowly drill down (covering the hole with a rug of linoleum square). As time went on (after two weeks or so), my wife came back and my life as a bank robber seemed more and more absurd."

Defendant's position in this appeal is that, as a matter of law, there was insufficient evidence upon which to convict him of a criminal attempt . . . .[a] Defendant claims that his actions were all preparatory in nature and never reached a stage of advancement in relation to the substantive crime which he concededly intended to commit (burglary of the bank vault) so that criminal responsibility might attach.

a Defendant was convicted of attempted burglary and was placed on probation. [Footnote by eds.]

In order for the prosecution to prove that defendant committed an attempt to burglarize . . . it was required to establish that he had the specific intent to commit a burglary of the bank and that his acts toward that goal went beyond mere preparation. . . .

The required specific intent was clearly established in the instant case. Defendant admitted in his written confession that he rented the office fully intending to burglarize the bank, that he brought in tools and equipment to accomplish this purpose, and that he began drilling into the floor with the intent of making an entry into the bank.

The question of whether defendant's conduct went beyond "mere preparation" raises some provocative problems. . . .

Defendant relies heavily on the following language: "Preparation alone is not enough [to convict for an attempt], there must be some appreciable fragment of the crime committed, *it must be in such progress that it will be consummated unless interrupted by circumstances independent of the will of the attempter,* and the act must not be equivocal in nature." . . . Defendant argues that while the facts show that he did do a series of acts directed at the commission of a burglary—renting the office, bringing in elaborate equipment and actually starting drilling—the facts do not show that he was interrupted by any outside circumstances. Without such interruption and a voluntary desistance on his part, defendant concludes that under the above stated test, he has not legally committed an attempt. The Attorney General has replied that even if the above test is appropriate, the trial judge, obviously drawing reasonable inferences, found that defendant was interrupted by outside circumstances—the landlord's acts of discovering the burglary equipment, resuming control over the premises, and calling the police.

However, the Attorney General suggests that another test, . . . is more appropriate: "Whenever the design of a person to commit crime is clearly shown, slight acts in furtherance of the design will constitute an attempt." (Note absence of reference to interruption.) The People argue that defendant's felonious intent was clearly set out in his written confession; that the proven overt acts in furtherance of the design, although only needing to be slight, were, in fact, substantial; that this combination warrants the affirmance of the attempt conviction.

[I]t is quite clear that under California law an overt act, which, when added to the requisite intent, is sufficient to bring about a criminal attempt, need not be the last proximate or ultimate step towards commission of the substantive crime. "It is not necessary that the overt act proved should have been the ultimate step toward the consummation of the design. It is sufficient if it was 'the first or some subsequent step in a direct movement towards the commission of the offense after the preparations are made.'"

There was definitely substantial evidence entitling the trial judge to find the defendant's acts had gone beyond the preparation stage. Without specifically deciding where defendant's preparations left off and where his activities became a completed criminal attempt, we can say that his "drilling" activity clearly was an unequivocal and direct step toward the completion of the burglary. It was a fragment of the substantive crime contemplated, i.e., the beginning of the "breaking" element. Further, defendant himself characterized his activity as the *actual commencement of his plan.* The drilling by defendant was obviously one of a series of acts which logic and ordinary experience indicate would result in the proscribed act of burglary. . . .

The instant case provides an out-of-the-ordinary factual situation . . . . Usually the actors [who do not complete all the acts necessary to complete the substantive offense] are intercepted or caught in the act. Here, there was no direct proof of any actual interception. But it was clearly inferable by the trial judge that defendant became aware that the landlord had resumed control over the office and had turned defendant's equipment and tools over to the police. This was the equivalent of interception.

The inference of this non-voluntary character of defendant's abandonment was a proper one for the trial judge to draw. However, it would seem that the character of the abandonment in situations of this type, whether it be voluntary (prompted by pangs of conscience or a change of heart) or non-voluntary (established by inference in the instant case), is not controlling. The relevant factor is the determination of whether the acts of the perpetrator have reached such a stage of advancement that they can be classified as an attempt. Once that attempt is found there can be no exculpatory abandonment.

"One of the purposes of the criminal law is to protect society from those who intend to injure it. When it is established that the defendant intended to commit a specific crime and that in carrying out this intention he committed an act that caused harm or sufficient danger of harm, it is immaterial that for some collateral reason he could not complete the intended crime."

The order is affirmed.

NOTES ON ABANDONMENT IN ATTEMPT AND OTHER OFFENSES

1. **The Traditional Position on Abandonment.** Analytically, the *Staples* case presents two distinct questions. The first is whether the defendant progressed sufficiently beyond "mere preparation" to commit the actus reus of attempted burglary.[a] The second is whether, if he did (and did so with the required specific intent), he is nevertheless entitled to acquittal if he "voluntarily" abandoned his criminal plan. How should this second issue be treated? Should Staples' claim that he changed his mind and relinquished his criminal purpose before any harm was done have any legal significance?

[a] Recall the various tests developed by the law for resolving this problem, discussed at pages 127–37, supra.

In Criminal Attempts, 41 Harv.L.Rev. 821, 847 (1928), Professor Sayre states the usual position of the courts on this question:

"So far as the defendant's criminality is concerned, it would seem to make little or no difference whether the interruption of the defendant's intended acts is due to another's interference or to his own repentance or change of mind. Once the defendant's acts have gone far enough to make him liable for a criminal attempt, no subsequent repentance or change of mind or abstention from further crime can possibly wipe away liability for the crime already committed. Genuine repentance may cause a reduction of sentence, but it cannot free from criminal liability. In the cases where the defendant voluntarily abandons his intended course of conduct, therefore, the problem reduces itself to whether or not the defendant's conduct before the abandonment had gone so far as to constitute an indictable attempt. The burglar who, while trying to force the lock on the front door, decides to abandon the attempt is equally guilty whether his change of mind is due to the voice of his own conscience or the voice of an approaching policeman. Present virtue never wipes away past crimes."

2. **Comments and Questions on the Traditional Position.** Assume that Staples is telling the truth. What purposes are served by punishing a person who abandons his or her criminal intention before committing any completed offense? Does the very fact of voluntary abandonment raise any doubt about the firmness of the actor's original criminal purpose, suggesting that it was only "half-formed or provisional"? [b] Does a voluntary change of mind suggest that the defendant has not, in fact, "gone far enough to show that he has broken through the psychological barrier to crime?" [c] In this sense, is an abandonment defense a desirable complement to a modern reformulation of the actus reus of attempt? To a proper understanding of the intent that should be required for attempt? If there is a problem with Staples' conviction, is it different from the problems endemic to the impossibility situation and to cases such as *Bronston* and *Remington?*

It has been argued that a voluntary renunciation of criminal intentions should be regarded as a praiseworthy act that erases the defendant's original blameworthiness and therefore removes the ethical predicate for criminal liability.[d] Do you agree? Others have claimed that recognition of an abandonment defense would offer an incentive to inchoate offenders to desist from their plan to commit a criminal offense.[e] Is this a plausible hypothesis? [f]

[b] G. Williams, Criminal Law: The General Part 620–21 (2d ed. 1961).

[c] Id. at 379–80.

[d] G. Fletcher, Rethinking the Criminal Law 190 (1978).

[e] "In our view, the most persuasive argument in favour of the provision of a withdrawal defence is that, since the object of the criminal law is to prevent crime, it is equally important to give reasonable encouragement to a conspirator, attempter or inciter to withdraw before a substantive offence is committed as it is to encourage an accomplice to end his participation in that offence. The absence of such a defence may operate to dissuade an individual who might otherwise decide to cease participating in the planning of a crime from taking that decision, since, having

f. See note f on page 376.

3. **The Model Penal Code.** Section 5.01(4) of the Model Penal Code reads as follows:

> "When the actor's conduct would otherwise constitute an attempt under Subsection (1)(b) or (1)(c) of this Section, it is an affirmative defense that he abandoned his effort to commit the crime or otherwise prevented its commission, under circumstances manifesting a complete and voluntary renunciation of his criminal purpose. . . .

> "Within the meaning of this Article, renunciation of criminal purpose is not voluntary if it is motivated, in whole or in part, by circumstances, not present or apparent at the inception of the actor's course of conduct, which increase the probability of detection or apprehension or which make more difficult the accomplishment of the criminal purpose. Renunciation is not complete if it is motivated by a decision to postpone the criminal conduct until a more advantageous time or to transfer the criminal effort to another but similar objective or victim."

Would Staples have a defense under this formulation?

Although the Model Code proposal has been adopted in several states, it has not met with widespread approval in recent American penal-code revisions.[g] Why do you think the proposed defense has been received with so little enthusiasm? Is there a relationship between the grading of attempt and the case for an abandonment defense?

4. **Scope of the Defense.** If provision of an abandonment defense is sound for attempts, are there other offenses to which it should also be applicable? Note that the Model Code includes a comparable defense for solicitation (§ 5.02(3)), conspiracy (§ 5.03(6)), and perjury (§ 241.1(4)). No similar provision is made, however, for larceny or burglary. Are these offenses distinguishable either analytically or as a policy matter? If the actor "exercise[d] unlawful control over . . . property of another with purpose to deprive" (§ 223.2(1)) and at the next instant changed his or her mind, would the situation be any different from a case where the actor tried to exercise unlawful control

---

become a party to the inchoate offence, there is no inducement for him to cease his activities before commission of the substantive offence takes place. It may well be that the type of criminal who is liable to change his mind in this way is a relative newcomer to crime and would, in any event, be given the opportunity to give evidence for the prosecution. But provision of the defence would make it quite clear that the criminal in these circumstances would not be liable to be charged at all."

The Law Commission, Working Paper No. 50, Inchoate Offences 102 (1973).

[f] "How likely is it that a man who is sufficiently far along the path towards committing a criminal offense, that he would be guilty of an attempt if he stopped, and who then decided not to commit it, would change his mind again and decide to carry on, since he realizes he is guilty of the attempt anyway? The argument is farfetched."

M. Wasik, Abandoning Criminal Intent, [1980] Crim.L.Rev. 785, 793.

[g] The English Law Commission also recently rejected a proposal similar to § 5.01(4) of the Model Code. The Law Commission, Report No. 102, Attempt, and Impossibility in Relation to Attempt, Conspiracy and Incitement 68–69 (1980).

and voluntarily desisted after committing an attempt? [h] Should the abandonment defense be applicable, if it is to be recognized at all, to all offenses defined in terms that fall short of ultimate harm? If not, by what criteria should offenses be distinguished?

[h] It was noted above, page 342, that the equivalent grading of larceny and attempted larceny under the Model Code eliminated the importance of the technical determination of precisely when the completed offense occurred. Must this statement now be questioned?

*

Chapter III

LIABILITY FOR THE CONDUCT OF ANOTHER

SECTION 1: COMPLICITY

INTRODUCTORY NOTES ON PARTIES TO CRIME

1. **The Common Law.** At common law, parties to a felony were differentiated as principals in the first and second degree and accessories before and after the fact.[a] The principal in the first degree was normally the primary actor, one who engaged personally in the act or omission proscribed by law. The principal in the second degree aided or abetted the primary actor in the commission of a felony and was present at the perpetration thereof. Presence was essential, but it could be constructive in nature. A typical example was the lookout who was posted some distance from a robbery in order to stand guard. In general, a person was constructively present at a felony whenever he or she was situated to assist the primary actor during commission of the crime. One who aided, counseled, commanded, or encouraged the commission of a felony but who was not present at its perpetration, either actually or constructively, became an accessory before the fact. Finally, liability as an accessory after the fact was imposed on one who assisted a known felon to avoid apprehension, trial, or punishment.

Even at common law, the distinction among principals was a matter of little consequence. Principals in the first and second degree received the same punishment. Since both had to be "present" at the scene of the crime, both were subject to the jurisdiction of the same court. Furthermore, it was not necessary, as a matter of pleading, to specify the degree of a principal's participation; conviction in either capacity could be had upon the same indictment. Finally, liability of one principal did not depend upon the liability of the other. A principal in the second degree could be tried before or after the principal in the first degree and could be convicted even following acquittal of the primary actor.

The distinction between principals and accessories was, by contrast, critically important. Jurisdiction over principals lay where the crime was committed, but an accessory could be tried only where the act of assistance was performed. Moreover, the indictment had to identify

---

[a] In case of treason, all participants were classed as principals. The same was true for misdemeanors, except that there was no fourth degree of participation (no accessory after the fact) to such offenses.

379

correctly the defendant's role as principal or accessory. A person charged as an accessory before the fact could not be convicted if the evidence showed that person to have been constructively present at the scene of the crime. Similarly, one charged as a principal could not be found guilty if the evidence demonstrated liability as an accessory. Most striking of all was the requirement of conviction of the principal as a procedural prerequisite to liability of an accessory. Anything that defeated conviction of the primary actor also barred punishment of an accessory. Thus, if the principal escaped apprehension, or died before trial, or for any reason was found not guilty, the accessory had to go free.

Obviously, this scheme invited evasion of justice. The risk was that liability might be avoided simply by inducing another to perform criminal conduct under circumstances where that person could not be held liable. For example, the infancy, insanity, or innocent mistake of one who actually administered a lethal poison might bar conviction for murder of the person who tricked him or her into doing so. The common-law answer to this problem was the doctrine of innocent agency. Under this view, the guiltless actor was deemed a mere instrumentality of the ultimate wrongdoer. Thus, a person apparently in the posture of an accessory before the fact could be tried and convicted as a principal in the first degree for acting through an innocent agent. Where the immediate actor was less than "innocent," however, his or her conviction remained an essential prerequisite for punishment of any secondary party.[b]

2. **Abrogation of the Common Law.** The common-law concept of accessorial liability was derivative in nature. Since the liability of an accessory necessarily derived from that of the principal offender, establishing the guilt of the latter was an indispensable precondition to punishing the former. Today, virtually every American jurisdiction has modified this scheme by legislation. Older statutes on the subject vary a good deal, but their essential features are to abrogate the various procedural distinctions between principals and accessories before the fact and to allow prosecution of all such parties as principals. Accessories after the fact continue to be treated separately, as is described more fully in a subsequent note.

The California provisions are fairly typical in their redefinition of who may be punished as a principal:

> "All persons concerned in the commission of a crime, whether it be a felony or misdemeanor, and whether they directly commit the act constituting the offense, or aid and abet in its commission, or, not being present, have advised and encouraged its commission, and all persons counseling, advising, or encouraging children under the age of 14 years, lunatics or idiots, to commit any crime, or who, by fraud, contrivance, or force, occasion the

---

[b] For a comprehensive review of the common-law approach to complicity, see Perkins, Parties to Crime, 89 U.Pa.L.Rev. 581 (1941). For an interesting analysis of complicity as only the most obvious instance of a broader conceptual category of "imputed" liability, see Robinson, Imputed Criminal Liability, 93 Yale L.J. 609, 631–39 (1984).

drunkenness of another for the purpose of causing him to commit any crime, or who, by threats, menaces, command, or coercion, compel another to commit any crime, are principals in any crime so committed." Cal. Penal Code § 31.

"The distinction between an accessory before the fact and a principal, and between principals in the first and second degree is abrogated; and all persons concerned in the commission of a crime, who by the operation of other provisions of this code are principals therein, shall hereafter be prosecuted, tried, and punished as principals and no other facts need be alleged in any accusatory pleading against any such person than are required in an accusatory pleading against a principal." Cal. Penal Code § 971.

"An accessory to the commission of a felony may be prosecuted, tried, and punished, though the principal may be neither prosecuted nor tried, and though the principal may have been acquitted." Cal. Penal Code § 972.

Since, for most purposes, it is no longer necessary to distinguish between principals and accessories before the fact, the generic term "accomplice" is often used to designate all such parties.

It must not be supposed, however, that the statutory abrogation of the common law has rendered that tradition entirely irrelevant. On the contrary, in many jurisdictions, the common-law heritage continues to make itself felt in a variety of ways. For one thing, the terminology of the common law is still in use. Even though a statute may have declared that accessories before the fact may be prosecuted as principals, it remains necessary to determine the kinds of involvement that make one liable as a party to crime. Often this question is addressed in the language of the common law. Moreover, even today it is possible to find decisions holding that some vestige of the common-law approach remains in force, despite legislative abrogation of the core of that tradition. Thus, although the common law has been everywhere curtailed, bits and pieces of that legacy may continue to turn up.[c] Finally, and most importantly, the underlying concept of derivative liability continues to influence judicial articulation of the substantive requirements for liability as an accomplice. Thus, although conviction of the principal is no longer a procedural prerequisite to trial of an accessory, it may continue to be necessary to prove, in the prosecution of a secondary party, that the activity of the primary actor amounted to a "crime."[d]

3. **Accessories After the Fact.** Despite the widespread enactment during the 19th century of statutes abrogating the distinctions between accessories before the fact and principals, accessories after the fact continued to be dealt with separately. The chief feature of this

[c] For example, one can find fairly recent expressions of the view that, although conviction of the principal is not a prerequisite to punishment of an accessory, the accessory must be acquitted if his principal is actually tried and acquitted. See, e.g.,

United States v. Prince, 430 F.2d 1324 (4th Cir. 1970).

[d] An important ambiguity in this formulation is explored in Subsection C, infra, pp. 404–11.

separate treatment was a reduction in maximum penalties. The common law made all parties to crime equally liable. Thus, one who helped a murderer escape became subject to the penalties authorized for the original offense, which could be very severe indeed. The chief object of separate statutory treatment was to limit the liability of an accessory after the fact to fixed penalties, usually at the misdemeanor or lower felony level. Again, the California provisions are representative:

> "Every person who, after a felony has been committed, harbors, conceals or aids a principal in such felony, with the intent that said principal may avoid or escape from arrest, trial, conviction or punishment, having knowledge that said principal has committed such felony or has been charged with such felony or convicted thereof, is an accessory to such felony." Cal. Penal Code § 32.

> "Except in cases where a different punishment is prescribed, an accessory is punishable by a fine not exceeding $5,000, or by imprisonment in the state prison, or in a county jail not exceeding one year, or by both such fine and imprisonment." Cal. Penal Code § 33.

Even with this change in the penalty structure, the traditional approach to accessories after the fact remains anachronistic. The notion that one who aids a felon to avoid justice thereby becomes a retroactive participant in the original crime is an heroic fiction. Its only justification is history. As Glanville Williams noted, "[t]he treatment of an accessory after the fact as a party to the felony remains part of the law only because no one troubles to change it." G. Williams, Criminal Law: The General Part 414 (2d ed. 1961). Increasingly, however, the common-law heritage is being abandoned in favor of a more straightforward approach to accessories after the fact.

Section 242.3 of the Model Penal Code is illustrative. It does not deal with parties to crime but defines an independent substantive offense of hindering apprehension of another. The gist of the offense is the purposeful hindering of the apprehension, prosecution, conviction, or punishment of another by any of a number of specified activities—e.g., harboring a fugitive; providing a weapon, transportation, disguise, or other means of effecting escape; or concealing evidence. This offense is based on the rationale that aiding another after consummation of a crime should be punished as a form of obstruction of justice. The focus is on illegitimate interference with law enforcement rather than on the obvious fiction that one who aids a fugitive thereby becomes a party to the original crime. In line with this approach, the Model Code provision is not limited to aiding persons known to be guilty of crime; it also applies to persons merely charged with, or sought for, criminal activity. The core of the offense is obstructive conduct done with the purpose "to hinder the apprehension, prosecution, conviction or punishment of another for crime." Penalties for this offense are similar to those assigned to other forms of obstruction of justice and in no case approach the very serious sanctions provided for major felonies. For a discussion of the statutes in more than half the American jurisdictions that follow this approach, see ALI, Model Penal Code and Commentaries, § 242.3, pp. 223–40 (1980).

SUBSECTION A: THE CONDUCT REQUIRED FOR COMPLICITY

REX v. RUSSELL

Supreme Court of Victoria, 1932.
[1933] Vict. L.R. 59.

CUSSEN, ACTING CHIEF JUSTICE. In this case the accused was charged on the first count of the presentment with having at Sunshine in Victoria on the 11th day of June 1932 murdered Ivy Letitia Russell; on the second count with having at the same time and place murdered Harold George Russell; and on the third count with having at the same time and place murdered Eric Russell. Ivy Letitia Russell was the accused's wife, and the others mentioned their two children, aged three-and-a-half and one-and-a-half years respectively, and the deaths of all were due to drowning. After a trial beginning on Monday the 26th September 1932 and lasting several days, the presiding judge opened his charge to the jury by saying:

"Gentlemen, the prisoner is presented on three counts charging him for that he severally murdered his wife and his two children. . . . These three persons came to their deaths by drowning, and the Crown case is that the prisoner drowned them. If the evidence satisfies you of the truth of that charge, then he was guilty of murder. The opposing theory—and it seems to be the only possible opposing theory—is that they drowned themselves; that is, that the mother destroyed her children and committed suicide. . . ."

His Honour having completed his charge, the jury at 1:10 p.m. on the 30th September, retired to consider its verdict; and at 4:25 returned into court to ask a question. What then took place is as follows:

The Foreman: "Assuming that the woman took the children into the water without the assistance of putting them in the water by the man, but that he stood by, conniving to the act, what is the position from the standpoint of the law?"

His Honour: "One has to be very careful about the facts that you are supposing. As I understand your question, he is looking on?"

The Foreman: "Yes."

His Honour: "Are you supposing a case where he is offering no encouragement or persuasion to her to do it, but simply standing by and watching his wife drown the children? Is that the case?"

The Foreman: "That is the position."

His Honour: "It is a question upon which, before I answer it, I should like to hear some argument from counsel, because the circumstances are very special, having regard to the relationship of these parties; and I will ask you to return to your room, and I will bring you in again and answer it as I understand the law to be."

At 4:28 p.m. the jury again retired, and His Honour discussed with counsel matters arising out of the jury's question . . .. At 4:50 p.m. the jury again returned into court, and His Honour addressed them as follows:

"Mr. Foreman and gentlemen, you have raised a case of some nicety, and I will do my best to put the position clearly before you. On the bare facts as you have stated them to me, and I repeated them to you, the position is that the accused man, being under a duty by reason of his parenthood of caring for the safety of children in his charge and in his power, would come under a duty to take steps to prevent the commission of that crime by his wife, and his failure to discharge that duty—standing by, as you put it, and doing nothing—would make him guilty of the crime of manslaughter. . . ."

[The jury subsequently returned a verdict of guilty of manslaughter on all three counts.]

In my view, which I shall elaborate later, the jury must be taken to have found that though the act immediately resulting in all three deaths was that of the accused's wife, the accused was present "conniving to" the act; and the legal result of such finding was, in the circumstances, that the accused was guilty as a participator or principal or, as it is sometimes called, a principal in the second degree. In these circumstances I think it will be convenient in the first place to cite some authorities relating to the principles of criminal law with regard to the liability of principals in the second degree . . ..

In Lord Mohun's Case, [1692] 12 How.St.Tr. 949, it was said if the person present "doth neither aid nor abet, nor any ways agree to the doing of the thing," i.e., the killing, "it will neither be murder nor manslaughter"; and later it was stated: "for if he never engaged or agreed to the killing of him, nor was there for that purpose, nor at the time did any way act, or join, or assist, in the doing of it; in those cases he is certainly not guilty " . . ..

In 2 W. Hawkins, Pleas of the Crown, ch. 19, § 10 (1716), it is stated: "Also those who by accident are barely present when a felony is committed, and are merely passive, and neither any way encourage it, nor endeavor to hinder it, nor to apprehend the offenders, shall neither be adjudged principals, or accessories . . .."

In M. Dalton, Justice of the Peace 527 (1727), it is stated: "But he that is present at the time of the felony committed (be it in case of murder, robbery, burglary or larceny) is a principal at this day, if he were either a procurer, or mover or aider, comforter or consenter thereto, although at that present he doth nothing." . . . In M. Foster, Crown Law 350 (3d ed. 1809) (originally published in 1762), it is stated: "In order to render a person an accomplice and a principal in a felony, he must be aiding and abetting at the fact, or ready to afford assistance, if necessary: and therefore if *A* happeneth to be present at a murder for instance, and taketh no part in it, nor endeavoureth to prevent it, nor apprehendeth the murderer, nor levyeth hue and cry after him; this strange behaviour of his, though highly criminal, will not of itself render him either principal or accessory. . . ." In Regina v. Coney, [1882] 8 Q.B.D. 534, 539–40, Cave, J. says: "Now it is a general rule in the case of principals in the second degree that there must be participation in the act, and that, although a man is present whilst a felony is being committed, if he takes no part in it, and does not act in concert with those who commit it, he will not be a principal in the second degree merely because he does not endeavour to prevent the felony, or apprehend the felon" . . .. In the same case, Hawkins, J. says:

"In my opinion, to constitute an aider and abettor some active steps must be taken by word, or action, with the intent to instigate the principal, or principals. . . . It is no criminal offense to stand by, a mere passive spectator of a crime, even of a murder. Non-interference to prevent a crime is not itself a crime. But the fact that a person was voluntarily and purposely present witnessing the commission of a crime, and offered no opposition to it, though he might reasonably be expected to prevent and had the power so to do, or at least to express his dissent, might under some circumstances afford cogent evidence upon which a jury would be justified in finding that he wilfully encouraged and so aided and abetted." . . .

Taking these authorities as a whole, I am of the opinion (i) that if a person present at the commission of a crime in the opinion of the jury on sufficient evidence shows his assent to such commission, he is guilty as a principal, and (ii) that assent may in some cases be properly found by the jury to be shown by the absence of dissent, or in the absence of what may be called an effective dissent. Various words, such as "aiding," "abetting," "comforting," "concurring," "approbating," "encouraging," "consenting," "assenting," "countenancing," are to be found in the authorities. . . . All the words abovementioned are, I think, instances of one general idea, that the person charged as a principal in the second degree is in some way linked in purpose with the person actually committing the crime, and is by his words or conduct doing something to bring about, or rendering more likely, such commission. . . . Now in the circumstances of this case I think that an absence of dissent or of a real dissent by the accused might well "show assent" to the wife's action in drowning herself and their children. The jury may well have considered the woman was desperate and distracted or angry and thought that there was no way but this to end her troubles. One of the influences which would lead her to this would be the fact that her husband did not care what became of her or of her and the children, and that this was shown by his non-interference. In such a case a husband and father doing nothing, or nothing effective, to prevent a tragedy may well be taken as showing his assent to what he contemplated as likely to happen. . . .

For the reasons I have given, I think the verdicts on all three counts should stand. . . .

NOTES ON THE CONDUCT REQUIRED FOR COMPLICITY

1. **Questions and Comments on *Russell*.** The liability of a secondary participant in criminal activity is determined by reference to the conduct and culpability required for complicity. Consideration of the conduct component of complicity raises in a new context the familiar issue of how much conduct is enough. How much aid or encouragement must the accomplice give? How much must the accomplice's conduct contribute to the perpetration of the crime? Think about this issue as you study the *Russell* opinion and consider the following questions and comments.

(i) **Accomplice Liability.** How important is it to the result in *Russell* that the defendant was husband and father to the victims of the drowning? Would the same rule of assent by silence apply to someone who had no legal responsibility towards the persons involved? At one point, the opinion seems to emphasize the defendant's familial relationship as the basis of a duty on his part to take steps to prevent the suicide [a] of the wife and the murder of the children. Is it clear that a relationship of this sort would be necessary for an on-looker's silence to "show assent" to the criminal scheme? Might not a lover or friend, or even the wife's lawyer, also be found to be "comforting," "encouraging," or "countenancing" the wife's scheme by standing by and doing nothing? Should such a person be held guilty of homicide on the authority of this case?

(ii) **Independent Liability.** Consider the possibility that the defendant in *Russell* could have been convicted as a principal in the first degree rather than as a secondary party. Given that he had a legal duty to care for his wife and children, could his failure to do so be an independent basis of liability for homicide? [b] This possibility was raised but rejected in an opinion in the same case by Justice Mann.

----

[a] Suicide was a felony at common law. The major consequences of treating suicide as a felony were (i) forfeiture of goods and ignominious burial of the successful suicide; (ii) applicability of attempt sanctions for the unsuccessful suicide; and (iii) applicability of traditional complicity doctrines to one who aided or abetted another's suicide. Thus, the court in *Russell* was following established law in assuming that the defendant could be punished as an accomplice to his wife's suicide. For further elaboration of the common-law tradition on this point and the response of many modern statutes, see ALI, Model Penal Code and Commentaries, § 210.5, pp. 91–107 (1980).

[b] Recall the materials on omissions, pages 107–11, supra.

After citing cases involving starvation of a child or ward through neglect of a parent or guardian, he said:

> "These cases may be regarded as defining the legal sanctions which the law attaches to the moral duty of a parent to protect his children of tender years from physical harm. If applicable to the present case, those authorities would point to the accused's being guilty of what I may call an independent crime of murder. The outstanding difference between the facts of such cases as I have cited and the facts of the present case is the interposition in the latter of a criminal act of a third person which is the immediate cause of death, and the difficulty in such a case is in saying, in the absence of express authority, that the inaction of the accused has caused the death of the children, within the meaning of the criminal law."

Causation in the criminal law is covered in Chapter VI of this book at pages 923–32, infra. It is important to note here, however, that many secondary participants in homicide cases might plausibly be said to have "caused" the forbidden result of death of another by aiding or encouraging the primary actor. In such cases the secondary participant arguably should be held directly and independently liable for criminal homicide. The law, however, has not developed in this way. Traditionally, the courts have refused to find a remote actor liable for "causing" death of another where the chain of causation involves independent criminal participation by a responsible person. Justice Mann's argument against independent liability for criminal homicide on the facts of *Russell* thus reflects the settled understanding on this point.

There is one situation, however, in which the liability of a secondary participant for the primary actor's conduct or the result of that conduct is measured by the concept of causation. Where the remote actor acts through an innocent agent, i.e., a duped or irresponsible participant, he or she may be held liable as a principal in the first degree for "causing" the conduct of the agent. Thus, for example, if Russell had tricked his wife into administering poison to their children, he could have been punished for "causing" their deaths by means of an innocent agent. This is the situation contemplated by Model Penal Code Section 2.06(2)(a), which provides that one person is accountable for the conduct of another when, "acting with the kind of culpability that is sufficient for the commission of the offense, he *causes* an innocent or irresponsible person to engage in such conduct." (Emphasis added.)

For these reasons, the issue in *Russell* was whether the defendant "aided or abetted" his wife in causing the deaths and thereby became liable as an accomplice. The answer to this question depends on how much conduct is required to support liability for aiding, abetting, or encouraging another to commit a crime.

2. ***State v. Walden.*** Compare with *Russell* the very similar facts presented in State v. Walden, 306 N.C. 466, 293 S.E.2d 780 (1982). The defendant was charged with aiding and abetting a felonious assault on her one-year-old son. The child was beaten with a leather belt by one

"Bishop" Hoskins. The belt had a metal buckle, and the child was seriously injured. The mother was present during the beating. She did not participate, but neither did she do anything to prevent the assault. The trial court ruled that no affirmative action by the mother was necessary to her liability. Specifically, the jury was instructed that the defendant should be found guilty if she "was present with the reasonable opportunity and duty to prevent the crime and failed to take reasonable steps to do so." The resulting conviction was reversed by the intermediate appellate court but reinstated by the North Carolina Supreme Court. That court observed:

> "[W]e find our holding today to be consistent with our prior cases regarding the law of aiding and abetting. It remains the law that one may not be found to be an aider and abettor, and thus guilty as a principal, solely because he is present when a crime is committed. It will still be necessary, in order to have that effect, that it be shown that the defendant said or did something showing his consent to the criminal purpose and contribution to its execution. But we hold that the failure of a parent who is present to take all steps reasonably possible to protect the parent's child from an attack by another person constitutes an act of omission by the parent showing the parent's consent and contribution to the crime being committed.

> "Thus, we hold that the trial court properly allowed the jury in the present case to consider a verdict of guilty of assault with a deadly weapon inflicting serious injury, upon a theory of aiding and abetting, solely on the ground that the defendant was present when her child was brutally beaten by Hoskins but failed to take all steps reasonable to prevent the attack or otherwise protect the child from injury . . . ."

Is the decision correct? Does it rest on the same ground as the result in *Russell,* or are the two cases distinguishable?

3. *McGhee v. Virginia.* Also compare with *Russell* the case of McGhee v. Virginia, 221 Va. 422, 270 S.E.2d 729 (1980). Defendant was convicted as an accessory before the fact to the murder of her husband, and sentenced to a term of 20 years. The husband and two co-workers were killed by defendant's lover and his brother. The evidence showed that the defendant had urged the lover to kill her husband and had informed him of the logging site where the husband could be found. There was no evidence that the defendant was involved in planning the details of the killings or knew the precise date thereof.

The Supreme Court of Virginia affirmed the conviction. The court noted that Virginia law defined an accessory as "one not present at the commission of the offense, but who is in some way concerned therein, either before or after, as [a] contriver, instigator or advisor, or as a receiver or protector of the perpetrator." Applying this definition to the facts of the case at hand, the court said:

> "In the trial of an accessory before the fact, the Commonwealth must establish the accused was a 'contriver, instigator *or* advisor' of the crime committed by the principal. An instigator

of a crime is an accessory before the fact even though he or she did not participate in the planning of the crime or even though unaware of the precise time or place of the crime's commission or of the precise method employed by the principal. A contrary holding would allow instigators to escape liability for their actions by removing themselves from the planning of crimes they have incited."

One justice dissented.

Is this result sound? Does the court's opinion set forth an adequate standard for imposing accessorial liability? If not, how should that issue have been addressed?

4. *State* v. *Tally.* In this connection consider the famous old case of State ex rel. Attorney General v. Tally, Judge, 102 Ala. 25, 15 So. 722 (1894). An impeachment proceeding was brought against Judge Tally for his role in the murder of one Ross. Ross had seduced Tally's sister-in-law, Annie Skelton. Fearing retaliation by her kinsmen, Ross set out from Scottsboro to Stevenson, where he meant to catch a train to Chattanooga. A group of Skeltons followed Ross to Stevenson, where they ambushed and killed him.

Judge Tally remained in Scottsboro. After the Skeltons left town, he stationed himself at the telegraph office to prevent any warning to Ross. When a relative of Ross did send a warning, Judge Tally wired to his friend Huddleston, the telegraph operator in Stevenson, the following message: "Do not let the party warned get away. . . . Say nothing." Huddleston received both messages and immediately went to look for Ross. Not finding him, Huddleston returned to his office. He then saw a hack coming from the direction of Scottsboro with a man whom he correctly supposed to be Ross. This time, however, Huddleston made no effort to deliver the warning, and Ross was killed shortly thereafter.

The court found that these facts made Tally an accomplice in the murder of Ross. The basis for that determination was explained as follows:

> "We are therefore clear to the conclusion that, before Judge Tally can be found guilty of aiding and abetting the Skeltons to kill Ross, it must appear that his vigil at Scottsboro to prevent Ross from being warned of his danger was by preconcert with them, or at least known to them, whereby they would naturally be incited, encouraged, and emboldened—given confidence—to the deed, or that he aided them to kill Ross, contributed to Ross' death, in point of physical fact, by means of the telegram he sent to Huddleston. The assistance given, however, need not contribute to the criminal result in the sense that but for it the result would not have ensued. It is quite sufficient if it facilitated a result that would have transpired without it. It is quite enough if the aid merely rendered it easier for the principal actor to accomplish the end intended by him and the aider and abettor, though in all human probability the end would have been attained without it. If the aid in homicide can be shown to have

put the deceased at a disadvantage, to have deprived him of a single chance of life which but for it he would have had, he who furnishes such aid is guilty, though it cannot be known or shown that the dead man, in the absence thereof, would have availed himself of that chance; as, where one counsels murder, he is guilty as an accessory before the fact, though it appears to be probable that murder would have been done without his counsel . . . .

"[The evidence shows] that Tally's standing guard at the telegraph office in Scottsboro to prevent Ross being warned of the pursuit of the Skeltons was not by preconcert with them, and was not known to them. It is even clear and more certain that they knew neither of the occasion nor the fact of the sending of the message by him to Huddleston; and hence they were not, and could not have been, aided in the execution of their purpose to kill by the keeping of this vigil, or by the mere fact of the forwarding of the message to Stevenson, since these facts in and of themselves could not have given them any actual, substantial help, as distinguished from incitement and encouragement, and they could not have aided them by way of incitement and encouragement, because they were ignorant of them; and so we are come to a consideration of the effect, if any, produced upon the situation at Stevenson by the message of Judge Tally to Huddleston. . . .

"It is inconceivable to us after the maturest consideration, reflection, and discussion, but that Ross' predicament was rendered infinitely more desperate, his escape more difficult, and his death of much more easy and certain accomplishment by the withholding from him of the message [of warning] . . . ."

Is *Tally* a difficult case? As the court saw it, Tally made the killing of Ross "of much more easy and certain accomplishment." Given this conclusion, should it matter that the primary actors did not know of Tally's assistance?

A more difficult issue is posed where the accomplice's "aid" is entirely ineffective. Suppose, for example, that Tally had posted himself at the telegraph office in order to intercept a warning to Ross, but no such warning had ever been sent. In such a case his conduct, although intended to assist the Skeltons, would have had no impact on the course of events. Would Tally properly have been liable on those facts?

5. **Describing the Proscribed Conduct: Modern Statutes and the Common Law.** The opinion in *Russell* is typical of the common-law tradition in the proliferation of terminology used to define the actus reus of accomplice liability. A principal in the second degree typically was described as one who "aids and abets" the primary actor, but various other terms were also used. An accessory before the fact usually was defined as one who "counsels or procures" the criminal conduct, but "aids," "commands," and "encourages" were also used. However many such words may be strung together, they provide no

very precise guidance as to the kinds of conduct that may render one liable as an accomplice.

Modern statutes tend to pare the verbiage of the common law, but it may be doubted whether they achieve any great advance in specificity. Many states simply substitute a somewhat shortened list of verbs. The New York statute, for example, provides that one person is criminally liable for the conduct of another when, acting with the required culpability, he or she "solicits, requests, commands, importunes, or intentionally aids such person to engage in such conduct." N.Y. Penal Code § 20.00. The Model Penal Code formulation is more elaborate. It declares that a person is liable as an accomplice of another person if:

> "with the purpose of promoting or facilitating the commission of the offense, he
>
> > (i) solicits such other person to commit it; or
> >
> > (ii) aids or agrees or attempts to aid such other person in planning or committing it; or
> >
> > (iii) having a legal duty to prevent the commission of the offense, fails to make proper effort so to do . . . ."

MPC § 2.06(3)(a). See also Tex. Penal Code § 7.02. The Model Code formulation has the advantage of making clear what the drafters envisioned for a case such as *Russell*. Inaction is a basis for accomplice liability, but only for persons having a legal duty to act. For others, some affirmative aid or assistance would be required. Would the same conclusion be reached under the New York statute? Should it be so construed?

In this connection, also reconsider the hypothetical based on *Tally* posed at the end of the preceding note. If the actor attempted to aid another in a criminal endeavor but in fact made absolutely no contribution to the outcome of events, what would be the standard of liability under the Model Penal Code? Under the New York law?

6. **A Problem and an Analogy.** As the preceding note illustrates, the Model Penal Code proposes an exceedingly broad formulation of the conduct necessary for liability as an accomplice. The provision covers not only one who aids another in the commission of an offense, but also one who "agrees or attempts to aid such other person in planning or committing it." The drafters justified the reach of this proposal on the grounds that there is no risk to the innocent where a purpose to further or facilitate is required and that there is no reason, therefore, to inquire into the precise effect of the actor's conduct on the commission of the offense. MPC § 2.04, Comment at 26 (Tent.Draft No. 1, 1953). Is this explanation persuasive? Are you satisfied that so long as proof of a purpose to facilitate is required, there is no risk of convicting the innocent? In other contexts, the criminal law requires proof of purpose but also undertakes an independent inquiry into the sufficiency of the actor's conduct. Why is there no need to ask in the context of accomplice liability how much conduct is enough to justify the imposition of penal sanctions?

Compare the law of attempt. Attempt requires proof of the actor's purpose to complete the underlying offense. Yet the law does not rest liability entirely on proof of purpose. It also mandates an independent inquiry into the sufficiency of the actor's conduct. In the phraseology of the common law, this is the distinction between a criminal attempt and mere preparation. Under the Model Penal Code and derivative statutes, this issue is addressed through the requirement of "an act or omission constituting a substantial step in a course of conduct planned to culminate in [the] commission of the crime." MPC § 5.01(1)(c). This standard is elaborated further by examples and by the general specification that it must be conduct "strongly corroborative of the actor's criminal purpose." MPC § 5.01(2). Why is not the same concern present in the context of accomplice liability? Indeed, why should not the Model Code approach to this question in the law of attempt be adapted for inclusion in the law of complicity? Might it not be profitable to inquire, for example, whether the actor's "aid," or, as in *Russell* and *Walden*, inaction in the face of a duty to act, was sufficiently corroborative of culpability to support liability as an accomplice?

One answer might be that the Model Code formulation ("aids . . . or attempts to aid") requires either actual aid, in which case the actor's culpability is corroborated by the fact of assistance in a criminal endeavor, or an attempt to aid, in which case the standards of Section 5.01 should be applied. Is this a sufficient response? Or is there some other reason in this context to discount the value of an independent inquiry into the act requirement and to trust more fully the jury's inquiry into state of mind?

SUBSECTION B: THE CULPABILITY REQUIRED FOR COMPLICITY

UNITED STATES v. PEONI

United States Court of Appeals for the Second Circuit, 1938.
100 F.2d 401.

L. HAND, CIRCUIT JUDGE. Peoni was indicted in the Eastern District of New York upon three counts for possessing counterfeit money . . . . The jury convicted him on all counts, and the only question we need consider is whether the evidence was enough to sustain the verdict. It was this. In the Borough of the Bronx Peoni sold counterfeit bills to one, Regno; and Regno sold the same bills to one, Dorsey, also in the Bronx. All three knew the bills were counterfeit, and Dorsey was arrested while trying to pass them in the Borough of Brooklyn. The question is whether Peoni was guilty as an accessory to Dorsey's possession. . . .

The prosecution's argument is that, as Peoni put the bills in circulation and knew that Regno would be likely, not to pass them himself, but to sell them to another guilty possessor, the possession of the second buyer was a natural consequence of Peoni's original act, with which he might be charged. If this were a civil case, that would be true; an innocent buyer from Dorsey could sue Peoni and get judgment against him for his loss. But the rule of criminal liability is not the same; since Dorsey's possession was not de facto Peoni's, and since Dorsey was not Peoni's agent, Peoni can be liable only as an accessory to Dorsey's act of possession. The test of that must be found in the appropriate federal statute. [Section 550 of Title 18, predecessor of the current 18 U.S.C. § 2, provided punishment as a principal for anyone who "aids, abets, counsels, commands, induces, or procures" the commission of any offense against the United States.]

It will be observed that all these definitions have nothing whatever to do with the probability that the forbidden result would follow upon the accessory's conduct; and that they all demand that he in some sort associate himself with the venture, that he participate in it as in something that he wishes to bring about, that he seek by his action to make it succeed. All the words used—even the most colorless, "abet"— carry an implication of purposive attitude towards it. So understood, Peoni was not an accessory to Dorsey's possession; his connection with the business ended when he got his money from Regno, who might dispose of the bills as he chose; it was of no moment to him whether Regno sold them to a second possible passer. His utterance of the bills was indeed a step in the causal chain which ended in Dorsey's possession, but that was all .   .   ..

Conviction reversed; accused discharged.

BACKUN v. UNITED STATES

United States Court of Appeals for the Fourth Circuit, 1940.
112 F.2d 635.

PARKER, CIRCUIT JUDGE. This is an appeal from a conviction and sentence under an indictment charging the appellant Backun and one Zucker with the crime of transporting stolen merchandise of a value in excess of $5,000 in interstate commerce, knowing it to have been stolen, in violation of the National Stolen Property Act, 18 U.S.C. § 415. Zucker pleaded guilty and testified for the prosecution. There was evidence to the effect that he was apprehended at a pawnshop in Charlotte, N.C. in possession of a large quantity of silverware, a portion of which was shown to have been stolen a short while before. He testified that he purchased all of the silverware from Backun in New York; that the purchase was partly on credit; that Backun had the silverware concealed in a closet and in the cellar of his residence; that there was no sale for second-hand silverware in New York but a good market for it in the South; that Backun knew of Zucker's custom to travel in the South and was told by Zucker that he wished to take the silverware on the road with him; and that Backun sold to him for $1,400 silverware which was shown by other witnesses to be of a much greater value. A part of the silverware was wrapped in a laundry bag which was identified by means of a laundry ticket as having been in the possession of Backun. . . .

There is no serious controversy as to the evidence being sufficient to show that Backun sold the property to Zucker knowing it to have been stolen. It is contended, however . . . that there is no evidence that Backun had anything to do with the transportation in interstate commerce.

. . . [I]t is to be noted that the case presented is not that of a mere seller of merchandise, who knows that the buyer intends to put it to an unlawful use, but who cannot be said in anywise to will the unlawful use by the buyer. It is the case of a sale of stolen property by a guilty possessor who knows that the buyer will transport it in interstate commerce in violation of law and who desires to sell it to him for that reason. The stolen property was not salable in New York. Backun knew that Zucker could dispose of it on his visits to the Southern pawnbrokers and would take it with him on his trips to the South. The sale was made at a grossly inadequate price and Zucker was credited for a part even of that. While there was no express contract that Zucker was to carry the property out of the state, Backun knew that he would do so; and, by making the sale to him, caused the transportation in interstate commerce just as certainly as if that transportation had been a term of the contract of sale. As his will thus contributed to the commission of the felony by Zucker, he would have been guilty at common law as an accessory before the fact to the commission of the felony. His guilt as a principal is fixed by 18 U.S.C. § 550, which provides that one who "aids, abets, counsels, commands, induces, or procures" the commission of an offense is guilty as a principal . . . .

Whether one who sells property to another knowing that the buyer intends to use it for the commission of a felony renders himself criminally liable as aiding and abetting in its commission, is a question as to which there is some conflict of authority. It must be remembered, however, that guilt as accessory before the fact has application only in cases of felony; and since it is elementary that every citizen is under moral obligation to prevent the commission of felony, if possible, and has the legal right to use force to prevent its commission and to arrest the perpetrator without warrant, it is difficult to see why, in selling goods which he knows will make its perpetration possible with knowledge that they are to be used for that purpose, he is not aiding and abetting in its commission within any fair meaning of those terms. Undoubtedly he would be guilty, were he to give to the felon the goods which make the perpetration of the felony possible with knowledge that they would be used for that purpose; and we cannot see that his guilt is purged or his breach of social duty excused because he receives a price for them. In either case, he knowingly aids and assists in the perpetration of the felony.

Guilt as an accessory depends, not on "having a stake" in the outcome of the crime . . . but on aiding and assisting the perpetrators; and those who make a profit by furnishing to criminals, whether by sale or otherwise, the means to carry on their nefarious undertakings aid them just as truly as if they were actual partners with them, having a stake in the fruits of their enterprise. To say that the sale of goods is a normally lawful transaction is beside the point. The seller may not ignore the purpose for which the purchase is made if he is advised of that purpose, or wash his hands of the aid that he has given the perpetrator of a felony by the plea that he has merely made a sale of merchandise. One who sells a gun to another knowing that he is buying it to commit a murder, would hardly escape conviction as an accessory to the murder by showing that he received full price for the gun; and no difference in principle can be drawn between such a case and any other case of a seller who knows that the purchaser intends to use the goods which he is purchasing in the commission of felony. In any such case, not only does the act of the seller assist in the commission of the felony, but his will assents to its commission, since he could refuse to give the assistance by refusing to make the sale. . . .

But even if the view be taken that aiding and abetting is not to be predicated [on] an ordinary sale made with knowledge that the purchaser intends to use the goods purchased in the commission of felony, we think that the circumstances relied on by the government here are sufficient to establish the guilt of Backun. The sale here was not of a mere instrumentality to be used in the commission of felony, but of the very goods which were to be feloniously transported. Backun knew not only that the commission of felony was contemplated by Zucker with respect to such goods, but also that the felony could not be committed by Zucker unless the sale were made to him. The sale thus made possible the commission of the felony by Zucker; and, if Zucker is to be believed, the commission of the felony was one of the purposes which Backun had in mind in making the sale. After testifying that he had told Backun that he wished to go on the road with the silverware (i.e., transport it in interstate commerce), he says "He (Backun) knew that. That is the reason he wanted to sell it to me." There can be no question, therefore, but that the evidence sustains the view that the felony committed by Zucker flowed from the will of Backun as well as from his own will, and that Backun aided its commission by making the sale. There was thus evidence of direct participation of Backun in the criminal purpose of Zucker; and whatever view be taken as to the case of a mere sale, certainly such evidence is sufficient to establish guilt . . . . .

[Conviction reversed on other grounds.]

NOTES ON THE CULPABILITY REQUIRED FOR COMPLICITY

1. **Culpability Required for Conduct: Knowledge vs. Stake in the Venture.** The *Peoni* and *Backun* decisions are the most famous entries in the continuing debate on the culpability required for complicity. Of course, everyone agrees that the accomplice must have some culpability (probably knowledge) with respect to the conduct that con-

stitutes aid or assistance. That is to say, the accomplice must be aware of his or her own conduct. Not surprisingly, that aspect of the required culpability is so rarely put in issue that it is virtually never discussed.

The issue that engenders dispute is the accomplice's required culpability with respect to the conduct of the primary actor. More specifically, the question is whether the accomplice must actually intend to promote the criminal venture in the sense of being interested in its success or whether it suffices that he or she knowingly assist criminal activity by another. Judge Learned Hand took the view that complicity should require a true purpose to promote the commission of the offense. Judge Parker, by contrast, believed that knowing assistance to another's criminal endeavor should suffice, even if the accomplice had no stake in the success of the venture. Situations where the distinction matters were suggested by the drafters of the Model Penal Code:

> "A lessor rents with knowledge that the premises will be used to establish a bordello. A vendor sells with knowledge that the subject of the sale will be used in commission of a crime. A doctor counsels against an abortion but, at the patient's insistence, refers her to a competent abortionist. A utility provides telephone or telegraph service, knowing it is used for bookmaking. An employee puts through a shipment in the course of his employment though he knows the shipment is illegal. A farm boy clears the ground for setting up a still, knowing that the venture is illicit."

MPC § 2.04, Comment at 27–28 (Tent. Draft No. 1, 1953).

How do you think these situations should be resolved? Would you approve a rule that made sellers of goods or services liable as accomplices whenever they knew of a customer's criminal purpose? Should the sale of marijuana paraphernalia, or radar detectors, be punished on this ground? On the other hand, might it go too far to require that an accomplice actually be interested in the success of the crime? Would you allow one who knowingly aided a would-be assassin simply to ignore the consequences of that act?

The drafters of the Model Penal Code had some difficulty coming to rest on this point. The tentative draft provision on complicity included the following language:

> "A person is an accomplice of another person in commission of a crime if . . . acting with knowledge that such other person was committing or had the purpose of committing the crime, he knowingly, substantially facilitated its commission."

MPC § 2.04 (Tent. Draft No. 1, 1953). The drafters defended this proposal on the ground that knowing assistance should suffice for liability whenever such assistance substantially facilitated the criminal scheme. Under this approach, a vendor in the ordinary course of business probably would not be liable as an accomplice to a customer's crime, even if the criminal purpose were known at the time of sale. On the other hand, a vendor of highly specialized goods (e.g., unregistered firearms or an obscure poison) or one who sells outside the ordinary course of business (e.g., through special credit arrangements to an otherwise uncreditworthy purchaser) perhaps would be covered. Evidently, the wisdom of this approach came to be doubted, for the quoted provisions were deleted by vote of the American Law Institute after a floor debate in which both Judge Hand and Judge Parker were participants. As finally approved, the Model Penal Code imposes liability as an accomplice only where the aider has "the purpose of promoting or facilitating the commission of the offense." What reasons support this change? Is it justified? [a]

2. **Compromise Solutions and the Offense of Facilitation.** Some have sought to resolve the choice between knowledge and a stake in the venture by compromise solutions. One such effort was the original Model Penal Code proposal to punish knowing assistance as complicity, but only where it substantially facilitated commission of the offense. Another idea is to treat knowing assistance as a basis for complicity in serious offenses, but to require a stake in the venture for minor crimes. Although the courts seldom articulate a distinction of this sort, a review of the cases suggests that the gravity of the offense involved does affect the readiness to predicate accomplice liability on knowing aid.

The most ambitious attempt to compromise between requiring an intent to promote and punishing knowing assistance comes from the revised penal code of New York. The New York provision on complicity requires that the accomplice "intentionally aid" the criminal conduct of another. N.Y. Penal Code § 20.00. As the accompanying commentary explains, this formulation was intended to preclude liability as an accomplice for knowing aid rendered "without having any specific intent . . . to commit or profit from the crime." N.Y. Penal Code § 20.00, Practice Commentaries at 44. Additionally, however, the New York Code includes an entirely new offense called "criminal facilitation." It provides in pertinent part as follows:

> "A person is guilty of criminal facilitation . . . when, believing it probable that he is rendering aid to a person who intends to commit a crime, he engages in conduct which provides such person with means or opportunity for the commission thereof and which in fact aids such person to commit a felony."

N.Y. Penal Code § 115.00. [b] Although this provision punishes some instances of knowing assistance to criminal activity by another, it stops far short of a comprehensive acceptance of knowledge as sufficient for complicity. For one thing, the facilitation offense requires that the aid or assistance provide the principal actor "with means or opportunity for

[a] For a general treatment of this issue, see Westerfield, The Mens Rea Requirement of Accomplice Liability in American Criminal Law—Knowledge or Intent, 51 Miss.L.J. 155 (1980). The involved but interesting history of the issue in California is analyzed in Carpenter, Should the Court Aid and Abet the Unintending Accomplice: The Status of Complicity in California, 24 Santa Clara L.Rev. 343 (1984).

[b] The provision quoted actually defines the offense of facilitation in the second degree. It applies to facilitation of all felonies save the most serious category. Facilitation of these very serious crimes is covered in a related provision as facilitation in the first degree. See N.Y. Penal Law § 115.05.

the commission" of the crime. This specification of the quantum of assistance required has no parallel in the New York complicity provision. It is reminiscent of the original Model Code proposal, which emphasized the substantiality of facilitation as a criterion of liability. Moreover, the New York facilitation offense is limited to conduct which in fact aids another to commit a *felony*. By this limitation, knowing assistance to minor offenses is excluded. Finally, facilitation is graded less severely than the underlying offense. Thus, under the New York scheme, facilitation of very serious felonies (murder, forcible rape, etc.) is itself a lesser felony, while facilitation of all other felonies is punished as a misdemeanor.

Do you approve of this innovation? Would you recommend its inclusion in the penal laws of your state? [c]

3. **Culpability Required for Results.** The most controverted issue in the culpability required for complicity is the choice between intent to promote and knowing assistance, but this is not the only issue in the culpability of complicity. In fact, it seems clear, although the cases seldom so state, that the entire debate between intent to promote and knowing assistance is directed chiefly, if not exclusively, to the accomplice's state of mind with respect to the *conduct* elements of the underlying offense. In other words, the focus of disagreement is on what mental attitude the accomplice must have with respect to the acts done by the principal that complete the crime.

A different approach has been used for assessing the accomplice's culpability with respect to the *results* of that conduct. The following hypothetical presents the issue:

> *A* entertains *B* in her home. *A* has promised to drive *B* home but at the end of the evening she is too tired. *A* therefore lends *B* her car, even though she knows that *B* is quite drunk and unable to drive safely. On his way home, *B* veers onto the wrong side of the road and crashes into *C*, who dies instantly.[d]

Clearly *B* is liable for some form of criminal homicide. The question is whether and on what basis *A* may be liable as an accomplice to that offense.

Unlike most prior statutes, the Model Penal Code contains an explicit provision on the mens rea that an accomplice must have with respect to the results caused by the primary actor's conduct. Section 2.06(4) states:

> "When causing a particular result is an element of an offense, an accomplice in the conduct causing such result is an accomplice in the commission of that offense, if he acts with the kind of culpability, if any, with respect to that result that is sufficient for the commission of the crime."

[c] See Carpenter, Should the Court Aid and Abet the Unintending Accomplice: The Status of Complicity in California, 24 Santa Clara L.Rev. 343, 363–70 (1984), for an argument in favor of a facilitation statute and an analysis of its application in specific contexts.

[d] The hypothetical is based on People v. Marshall, 362 Mich. 170, 106 N.W.2d 842 (1961), where the court ruled against liability of the secondary party. But see, e.g., Story v. United States, 16 F.2d 342 (D.C.Cir. 1926).

What solution would the Model Code achieve in the hypothetical posed above? What issues would the jury have to resolve if *A* were charged with complicity in manslaughter under Sections 2.06 and 210.3? With complicity in negligent homicide under Sections 2.06 and 210.4? Does this approach seem sound? Note, in this connection, that although the Model Code is far more explicit, it basically accords with the common law in its resolution of the culpability required of an accomplice with respect to the results of a primary actor's homicidal conduct. On the other hand, it generalizes the principle so that it applies to all offenses containing a result component.

4. **Culpability Required for Circumstances.** In contrast to the explicit treatment of conduct and results, even modern penal codes fail to specify the state of mind required of an accomplice with respect to the attendant *circumstances* of the criminal conduct. There are two obvious possibilities. One is to require that the accomplice know that the circumstance element exists.[e] The alternative is to carry over to the accomplice the level of culpability required of the primary actor by the definition of the offense. The difference between these formulations is posed by the following hypothetical:

> *A* is asked by his friend *B* to assist in the latter's seduction of *C*, a mutual acquaintance. Specifically, *B* wants to borrow *A*'s apartment, which is fully equipped with soft lights and appropriate music. *A* agrees, and the seduction is accomplished. To the surprise of both *A* and *B*, *C* turns out to be underage.

Under traditional laws against "statutory rape," *B* is strictly liable with respect to the age of his sexual partner. Thus, he may be criminally punished for consensual sexual intercourse with an underage person even if he honestly and reasonably believed *C* to be over the age of consent. The issue here is whether *A* may be held liable on the same basis or whether a special mens-rea requirement of knowledge should be imposed for complicity.

Current law on this question is problematic. Some statutes can be read to embrace the view that no special mens rea is required,[f] but most are ambiguous on the point. The absence of any settled common-law understanding is probably due to the infrequency with which the question has been litigated. Obviously, the situation of the accomplice in the hypothetical described above is far less likely to excite prosecutorial interest than is the case of a secondary participant in criminal homicide. Perhaps for that reason, there seems to be no clear rule on the point. That is not to say, of course, that the issue cannot arise or that its resolution is unimportant, but only that the practical conse-

---

[e] Knowledge is the most that could be required, since it is in any event not meaningful to speak of a true purpose to promote the existence of attendant circumstances. See MPC § 2.02(2)(a)(ii), discussed at page 239, supra.

[f] See, e.g., N.Y. Penal Code § 20.00, which reads in its entirety as follows:

"When one person engages in conduct which constitutes an offense, another person is criminally liable for such conduct when, *acting with the mental culpability required for the commission thereof*, he solicits, requests, commands, importunes or intentionally aids such person to engage in such conduct." [Emphasis added.]

quence of resolving the question one way or the other may not be very great. How should this issue be resolved? Is the discussion of the analogous issue in the law of attempt, see pages 346–48, supra, helpful?

PEOPLE v. DURHAM

Supreme Court of California, 1969.
70 Cal.2d 171, 74 Cal.Rptr. 262, 449 P.2d 198.

SULLIVAN, JUSTICE. A jury found defendants Gilbert Lee Durham and Edgar Leonard Robinson guilty of murder in the first degree. After a penalty trial the same jury fixed the punishment of Durham at life imprisonment and the punishment of Robinson at death, and sentences were rendered accordingly. Durham appeals from the judgment and from the denial of his motion for a new trial. . . .

On October 16, 1966, about 4:00 a.m., Los Angeles Police Officers Treutlein and Du Puis, engaged in routine patrol duties, were driving westward on Pico Boulevard in a marked patrol car. They noticed a beige Thunderbird automobile travelling in the same direction in the lane nearest the curb; it bore Ohio license plates and was occupied by two male Negroes. As the Thunderbird proceeded down the boulevard it swerved slightly to the right at two intersecting streets as if making a right turn into them; on each occasion however it continued westward on Pico. The officers followed the vehicle and at the same time radioed headquarters to ascertain if it had been stolen. Before their radio call was answered, the Thunderbird again made a slight swerving motion to the right at an intersection and the officers decided to stop it and question its occupants. They moved into the curb lane behind the Thunderbird, activated their red light, sounded their horn, and directed their spotlight at the rear window. The vehicle stopped near a streetlight, and the patrol car stopped about six feet behind it.

Defendant Durham, the driver of the Thunderbird, got out and walked back toward the patrol car but his passenger, defendant Robinson, remained seated in the vehicle. The officers, who were in uniform, unsnapped the retaining straps on their holsters and alighted from the patrol car. Officer Treutlein asked Durham for his driver's license and the latter produced what appeared to be a plastic credit card. Officer Du Puis asked Durham the name of his passenger; Durham in reply gave a short name. Office Du Puis then went to the passenger side of the Thunderbird and, using the name which Durham had given him, asked Robinson to come to the rear where Durham and Officer Treutlein were standing.

Robinson complied, and Officer Du Puis asked him to raise his hands so as to check him for weapons. Instead, Robinson sprang to a position between the two vehicles and drew a gun from a concealed holster under his shirt. He pointed the weapon at the two officers and ordered them not to move. Officer Du Puis reached for his own revolver and Robinson fired a shot at him, hitting him in the mouth. As he fell Officer Du Puis, who had apparently succeeded in getting his gun free of the holster, fired at Robinson. At this point, Officer Treutlein, who had also drawn his gun, fired at Robinson and hit him. The latter stumbled backward and fell into the street where he lay face up with his gun still in his hand.

Officer Treutlein then directed his attention to Durham, who was crouched on one knee with his hands half raised and his palms spread at about shoulder level. The officer ordered him not to move. Then, keeping Durham covered with the gun, he stepped to the passenger side of the patrol car and reported the shooting on his radio. At one point during the radio call Durham began to lower his hands and Officer Treutlein again commanded him to keep them raised. Durham obeyed. At this point Robinson, who was still in the same position, began to raise his gun toward Officer Treutlein; the latter commanded him to drop it. Robinson did not do so, and the officer then fired a shot which struck the pavement close to Robinson's head. Robinson then dropped the gun.

Officer Treutlein ordered both defendants to lie face down on the pavement. Within a few minutes other officers arrived and took them into custody. A search of Durham produced a knife and sheath from his coat pocket.

Eleven days later, on October 27, 1966, Officer Du Puis died as a proximate result of the gunshot wound inflicted upon him.

Evidence of the foregoing facts, the substantiality of which is not here disputed, was admitted at trial. There was also admitted, over the strenuous objection of defendants, a considerable volume of evidence regarding the joint activities of defendants during some three weeks preceding the incident of October 16, 1966. This evidence showed in substance: (i) that on the day of the homicide both defendants were on parole under felony sentences from the state of Ohio; that defendant Robinson was at that time subject to arrest in Ohio for violation of the terms of his parole; and that the presence of defendants in California under the circumstances obtaining involved several violations of the terms of parole relating to each of them; (ii) that on October 5, 1966, eleven days prior to the incident, defendants robbed an A&P store in Toledo, Ohio, of $648; and that in the course of this robbery, Robinson exhibited a pistol similar to that used by him on October 16; (iii) that on October 8, 1966, eight days prior to the incident, defendants robbed the Hinky-Dinky Grocery Store in Omaha, Nebraska, of $2,815; that in the course of this robbery Robinson again exhibited a pistol similar to that used by him on October 16; and that he threatened to shoot a cashier in the store if she did not comply with his demands and Durham told the cashier that he (Robinson) "meant it"; (iv) that after defendants' departure from the Hinky-Dinky Store the manager ran out to the sidewalk in front of the store after them, and, although he saw neither defendant, he noticed a white car parked in an alley across from the store and heard a loud report which he assumed to be a backfire; that the rear window of a car then driving past the market was shattered by a bullet and an occupant of the car was injured by flying glass; that the bullet was found under the seat of that car, and a cartridge casing was found near the position of the lone car which the manager had noticed in the alley; and that scientific examination and tests had determined that the cartridge casing found in the Omaha alley was ejected from the same gun which Robinson used to kill Officer Du Puis; and (v) that the Thunderbird automobile in which defendants were riding on October 16, 1966, had been stolen from a San Francisco automobile agency on or about October 12, and it bore California license plates at that time. . . .

In the frequently cited case of People v. Villa, 156 Cal.App.2d 128, 318 P.2d 828 (1957), the court set forth the following principles relevant in the case before us:

"To be an abettor the accused must have *instigated or advised* the commission of the crime *or been present for the purpose of assisting in its commission.* He must share the criminal intent with which the crime was committed. . . . [W]hile mere presence alone at the scene of the crime is not sufficient to make the accused a participant, and while he is not necessarily guilty if he does not attempt to prevent the crime through fear, such factors may be circumstances that can be considered by the jury with the other evidence in passing on his guilt or innocence. *One may aid or abet in the commission of a crime without having previously entered into a conspiracy to commit it. Moreover, the aider and abettor in a proper case is not only guilty of the particular crime that to his knowledge his confederates are contemplating committing, but he is also liable for the natural and reasonable or probable consequences of any act that he knowingly aided or encouraged. Whether the act committed was the natural and probable consequence of the act encouraged and the extent of defendant's knowledge are questions of fact for the jury.*"

In the instant case the prosecution, in support of its sole theory of guilt as to Durham, sought to show that he "instigated or advised the commission of the crime" in that he was a party to a compact of criminal conduct which included within its scope the forcible resistance of arrest *and that he was also* "present for the purposes of assisting in its commission" in that his conduct at the scene of the incident, viewed in its totality, was wholly consistent with such purposes. The jury determined that the evidence produced supported the prosecution theory and accordingly found Durham guilty. The evidence supports the finding. . . .

[After a review of several precedents in which the rule as stated above had been applied, the court continued as follows.]

In view of the evidence in the instant case which we have outlined above the jury could reasonably have found that defendants for some time prior to October 16, 1966, had been engaged in a joint expedition which involved the commission of robberies as they moved westward across the country and which included among its purposes the forcible resistance to arrest; that Durham was fully aware of the fact that Robinson both had exhibited his pistol in the commission of said robberies and had actually fired it at one who had sought to apprehend them in the act of escaping; that at the very time they were stopped by Officers Treutlein and Du Puis, defendants were further engaged in the commission of a crime, namely, the driving of an automobile stolen by them; that Durham knew that Robinson was armed when they emerged from the car; and that in the totality of circumstances Robinson's act was, and was known by Durham to be, a reasonable and probable consequence of the continuing course of action undertaken by the defendants. The finding of such facts would be sufficient to support the finding of Durham's guilt as an aider and abettor under the principles we have above set forth. Since the jury was adequately instructed in the premises, we must conclude that the indicated findings were made—and that the evidence is therefore sufficient to support the verdict as to Durham. . . .

[Judgment affirmed.]

NOTE ON THE RULE OF NATURAL AND PROBABLE CONSEQUENCES

The rule of natural and probable consequences extends the liability of an accomplice beyond planned offenses. The rule as traditionally stated is that the liability of an accomplice includes the natural and probable consequences of the criminal endeavor that the accomplice meant to aid or encourage. This rule is applied chiefly where the principal actor engages in some act of violence not expressly endorsed by the accomplice. The decisive factor in such cases is often whether the accomplice knew that the principal was armed. Glanville Williams summarized the law on this point as follows:

> "The knowledge on the part of one criminal that his companion is carrying a weapon is strong evidence of a common intent to use violence, but is not conclusive. Nevertheless, it seems that a common intent to threaten violence is a common intent to use violence, for the one so easily leads to the other. [V]iolence with a weapon should be regarded as something different in kind from violence without a weapon, in the sense that a person should not be involved in the use by his companion of a weapon which he was not known to be carrying, when this weapon inflicts an injury beyond the scope of the common purpose."

G. Williams, Criminal Law: The General Part 397–98 (2d ed. 1961).

What is the impact of the rule of natural and probable consequences on the culpability required for complicity? Under the analysis of *Durham*, for example, what state of mind must the secondary party be found to have had in order to be held liable for the conduct of the principal actor? What state of mind would the primary actor be required to have had? What is the justification for imposing liability on the secondary participant on the *Durham* basis?

The rule of natural and probable consequences is still good law in many jurisdictions. It has been abandoned, however, in most states that have adopted comprehensive revisions of their penal laws. This, at least, is the implication of those statutes, such as Model Penal Code Section 2.06(3)(a), that expressly require that the accomplice have "the purpose of promoting or facilitating the commission of the offense" by the principal actor. See, e.g., Haw.Rev.Stat. § 702–222; Cons.Penn.Stat.Ann. tit. 18, § 306(c); Or.Rev.Stat. § 161.155. Such provisions presumably preclude liability as an accomplice where the particular purpose to promote or facilitate the principal's conduct cannot be proved. Note, however, that a few jurisdictions with recently revised penal codes expressly continue the older rule. Thus, for example, Kan.Stat.Ann. § 21–3205(2) provides that an accomplice to one offense "is also liable for any other crime committed in pursuance of the intended crime if reasonably foreseeable by him as a probable consequence of committing or attempting to commit the crime intended." Cf. Wis.Stat.Ann. § 939.05 (virtually identical). Which type of statute states the better rule? [a]

SUBSECTION C: GUILT OF THE PRINCIPAL

REGINA v. COGAN AND LEAK
Court of Appeal, 1975.
[1976] 1 Q.B. 217.

LAWTON, LORD JUSTICE read the following judgment of the court. The defendants appeal against their conviction of rape . . . .

The victim of the conduct which the prosecution submitted was rape by both defendants was Leak's wife . . . .

[On July 10, 1974] Leak came home at about 6 p.m. with Cogan. Both had been drinking. Leak told his wife Cogan wanted to have sexual intercourse with her and that he, Leak, was going to see she did. She was frightened of him and what he might do . . . . He made her go upstairs where he took her clothes off and lowered her on to a bed. Cogan then came into the room. Leak asked him twice whether he wanted sexual intercourse with her. On both occasions he said he did not. Leak then had sexual intercourse with her in the presence of Cogan. When he had finished, Leak again asked Cogan if he wanted sexual intercourse with his wife. This time Cogan said he did. He asked Leak to leave the room but he refused to do so. Cogan then had sexual intercourse with Mrs. Leak. Her husband watched. While all this was going on for most of the time, if not all, Mrs. Leak was sobbing. She did not struggle while Cogan was on top of her but she did try to turn away from him. When he had finished, he left the room. Leak then had intercourse with her again and behaved in a revolting fashion

---

[a] The rule of natural and probable consequences and the analogous approach to criminal conspiracy under the *Pinkerton* doctrine, see pp. 473–80 infra, are examined in Robinson, Imputed Criminal Liability, 93 Yale L.J. 609, 657–58, 665–68 (1984).

to her. When he had finished he joined Cogan and the pair of them left the house to renew their drinking. Mrs. Leak dressed. She went to a neighbour's house and then to the police. The two defendants were arrested about three-quarters of an hour later. Both defendants made oral and written statements. . . .

Leak's statement amounted to a confession that he had procured Cogan to have sexual intercourse with his wife. He admitted that while Cogan was having sexual intercourse with her she was "sobbing on and off not all the time." There was ample evidence from the terms of his statement that she had not consented to Cogan having intercourse with her. The whole tenor of this statement was that he had procured Cogan to do what he did in order to punish her for past misconduct. He intended that she should be raped and that Cogan's body should provide the physical means to that end.

Cogan, in his written statement, admitted that he had had sexual intercourse with Mrs. Leak at Leak's suggestion and that while he was on top of her she had been upset and had cried. At the trial Cogan gave evidence that he thought Mrs. Leak had consented. The basis for his belief was what he had heard from her husband about her. The drink he had seems to have been a reason, if not the only one, for mistaking her sobs and distress for consent. . . .

[In accord with the law as it then stood, the trial court instructed the jury to find Cogan guilty of rape, notwithstanding that he believed Mrs. Leak had consented, if his belief was unreasonable. The jury returned a verdict of guilty, reporting by special verdict that Cogan believed that she was consenting but that he had no reasonable grounds for his belief. Subsequently, the House of Lords ruled in Regina v. Morgan, [1976] A.C. 182, that even an unreasonable belief that the victim consented precluded conviction for rape. Cogan's conviction was therefore quashed.]

Leak's appeal against conviction was based on the proposition that he could not be found guilty of aiding and abetting Cogan to rape his wife if Cogan was acquitted of that offence as he was deemed in law to have been when his conviction was quashed . . . . The only case which [Leak's counsel] submitted had a direct bearing upon the problem of Leak's guilt was Walters v. Lunt, [1951] 2 All E.R. 645. In that case the respondents had been charged, under Section 33(1) of the Larceny Act 1916, with receiving from a child aged seven years, certain articles knowing them to have been stolen. In 1951, a child under eight years was deemed in law to be incapable of committing a crime: it followed that at the time of receipt by the respondents the articles had not been stolen and that the charge had not been proved. That case is very different from this because here one fact is clear—the wife had been raped. Cogan had had sexual intercourse with her without her consent. The fact that Cogan was innocent of rape because he believed that she was consenting does not affect the position that she was raped.

Her ravishment had come about because Leak had wanted it to happen and had taken action to see that it did by persuading Cogan to use his body as the instrument for the necessary physical act. In the language of the law the act of sexual intercourse without the wife's consent was the actus reus: it had been procured by Leak who had the appropriate mens rea, namely, his intention that Cogan should have sexual intercourse with her without her consent. In our judgment it is irrelevant that the man whom Leak had procured to do the physical act himself did not intend to have sexual intercourse with the wife without her consent. . . .

Appeals against conviction dismissed.

NOTES ON LIABILITY OF A SECONDARY PARTY WHERE THERE IS NO PRINCIPAL

1. **Questions on *Cogan and Leak*.** The *Lunt* case, relied on by Leak's counsel, involved a husband and wife who were charged with receiving a stolen tricycle from their minor child, aged seven. They were held not guilty on the ground that the child was legally incapable of stealing and therefore that the tricycle received by them was not "stolen." [a]

Is the opinion in *Cogan and Leak* persuasive in distinguishing *Lunt*? In what sense was it clear, as Lord Justice Lawton asserted, that "the wife had been raped"? Was it not equally clear, in *Lunt*, that the tricycle had been stolen? To put the same question the other way around, how can Mrs. Leak have been "raped" or the tricycle in *Lunt* have been "stolen" if in each case the primary actor lacked the mens rea to be guilty of the crime?

2. ***Dusenberry* v. *Commonwealth*: A Contrary View.** That the conclusion reached in *Cogan and Leak* is not everywhere accepted is shown by Dusenberry v. Commonwealth, 220 Va. 770, 263 S.E.2d 392 (1980), where the court unanimously overturned the defendant's conviction for rape on the following facts:

"At approximately 10:30 p.m. on September 16, 1978, T____ M____ and J____ G____, both 16 years of age, parked their car in a secluded area and partially undressed in preparation for sexual intercourse. Defendant, a part-time security guard wearing a uniform, badge, handcuffs, and a holstered pistol, appeared at the window with a flashlight, ordered the couple to get out, and demanded identification. Defendant told them that he would take them to the authorities or report their conduct to their parents unless they finished what they had started and allowed him to watch. The couple entered the back seat of the car, discussed the options, and agreed to attempt to perform the act in defendant's presence. Defendant watched as the couple undressed and the boy assumed the superior position. Complaining that the boy had not penetrated the girl, defendant

---

[a] Cf. the comparable hypothetical posed by Glanville Williams, page 358, supra, in connection with a charge of attempted receipt of stolen property and the defense of "impossibility".

thrust his head and shoulders through the open window, seized the boy's penis, and forced it 'partially in' the girl's vagina.

"Defendant contends that the evidence is insufficient to support his conviction under Va. Code § 18.2–61 because 'the evidence is clear that [he] did not "carnally know" the alleged victim' within the meaning of that statute.

"In felony cases, principals in the second degree and accessories before the fact are accountable 'in all respects as if a principal in the first degree.' But, by definition, there can be no accessory without a principal. Although *conviction* of a principal in the first degree is not a condition precedent to conviction of an accessory, 'before the accessory to a crime can be convicted as such, it must be shown that the crime has been committed by the principal.' Since the evidence fails to show that J_____ G_____ committed rape, defendant cannot be convicted as a principal in the second degree. The question remains whether the evidence is sufficient to prove that defendant committed that crime as a principal in the first degree.

"With respect to certain crimes, the law regards a person who acts through an innocent agent as a principal in the first degree. In some jurisdictions, this rule has been applied in rape cases where the accused forced an innocent third party to have carnal knowledge of an unwilling victim. But the 'innocent agent' rule cannot be applied here, for it is antithetical to the construction this court has placed upon Virginia's rape statute.

"Our prior decisions establish that one element of rape is the penetration of the female sexual organ by the sexual organ of the principal in the first degree. Whether Dusenberry's conduct constituted an offense other than rape is not a question before us on appeal. We hold only that the evidence is insufficient to prove that defendant carnally knew the prosecutrix within the intendment of Section 18.2–61 as construed by this court, and the judgment must be reversed. . . ."

Does *Dusenberry* or *Cogan and Leak* state the better view? Would you have been troubled if *Yoman*, had been punished for rape despite the fact that he neither committed the offense personally nor aided anyone else to become guilty of that crime?

3. **The Abandonment of Derivative Liability?** Whatever the merits of the matter, it seems that the position adopted in *Cogan and Leak* is becoming the prevailing view. As articulated by Professors Smith and Hogan, the modern view holds that the mens rea of the primary actor is irrelevant to the liability of a secondary participant in criminal conduct: "The true principle, it is suggested, is that where the principal has caused an actus reus, the liability of each of the secondary parties should be assessed according to his own mens rea." J. Smith & B. Hogan, Criminal Law 134 (4th ed. 1978). Under this approach, one looks to the primary actor only for the actus reus of the offense. If it exists, a secondary participant may be prosecuted and punished according to his or her own mens rea and without regard to the primary

actor's culpability or the lack thereof.[b] Thus, a person may be convicted as a secondary participant where the primary actor has committed no offense. Obviously, this amounts to a wholesale rejection of the common-law tradition of regarding the liability of secondary parties as derivative from the guilt of the primary actor.[c]

4. **The Theory of the Excusable Wrong.** A variation on the theory of *Cogan and Leak* has been suggested by George Fletcher in Rethinking Criminal Law 664–67 (1978). Fletcher distinguishes between justification and excuse. Justified conduct is by definition not wrongful. Excused conduct, by contrast, is wrongful, but liability is excused on some compassionate grounds, such as infancy or duress. The significance of this distinction for what Glanville Williams has called the problem of "accessories to a ghostly crime" (that is, accessories to a crime that did not occur) is the suggestion that excuses are always personal to the actor. On this view, a secondary actor can be held liable for aiding or abetting conduct that is wrongful, even though the primary actor may be excused. The question then becomes not whether the primary actor committed the actus reus of the offense, as *Cogan and Leak* put it, but whether the primary actor occasioned the wrong that the law aims to prevent. The characteristic that will acquit some secondary actors and convict others is that not every actus reus committed by the primary actor will entail a wrong in this sense.

In The Theory of Excuses, 1982 Crim.L.Rev. 732, Glanville Williams wrote to draw attention to Fletcher's theory of the excusable wrong and to suggest some difficulties with it. Williams focused on the case of Thornton v. Mitchell, [1940] 1 All E.R. 339. There a bus driver was backing the bus under the direction of a conductor standing in the rear. The conductor gave negligent directions, with the consequence that one pedestrian was injured and another died. The driver was found not guilty of careless driving on the ground that he had reasonably relied on the conductor. The conductor's conviction as an accomplice was quashed on the ground that he could not be convicted of abetting an offense that had not taken place. On Fletcher's theory, said Williams, the driver's conduct could be treated as an excusable wrong, for which the conductor could be held secondarily liable, but this result seemed to Williams unsound: "But, even so, how could a charge against the conductor be framed? To charge him with abetting an act of careless driving by the bus driver would assert an untruth, and would be an unjust slur on the driver."

Is it clear how the theory of the excusable wrong differs from the approach of *Cogan and Leak?* Is the difference justified? How, on these two theories, should *Thornton v. Mitchell* be analyzed? What is the right result in the two cases?

---

[b] If the conduct of the primary actor does not complete the actus reus of the offense, the secondary participant may become an accomplice in an attempt. This possibility is illustrated at page 411, infra.

[c] This view of the matter has not gone unchallenged. See Kadish, Complicity, Cause and Blame: A Study in the Interpretation of Doctrine, 73 Cal.L.Rev. 323 (1985).

5. Perjury: A Hypothetical. A useful way to explore these issues may be to pose the following hypothetical.[d] Suppose that *A* tells *B* a lie in the belief and with the purpose that *B* will repeat that statement on the witness stand. If *B* does so without knowledge of the falsity, *B* commits no perjury. The question then is whether *A* may be held liable as an accomplice to perjury or for subornation of perjury.

How should such a case be analyzed? Has the wrong at which the crimes of perjury and subornation of perjury are aimed occurred? It has occurred if these crimes are designed to prevent the miscarriage of justice that may result from false testimony on the witness stand. But it has not occurred if the wrong at which these crimes are aimed is the punishment of one who believes that a lie is being told on the stand. Should *A*'s liability as an accessory turn on such an inquiry? If you conclude that *B* did not commit the wrong condemned by these crimes, *A* would not be guilty under the "excusable wrong" theory. Would *A* be guilty under the theory used in *Cogan and Leak?* Which approach is preferable?

6. *Regina* v. *Richards* and Degrees of Liability. A similar problem is posed where a secondary party is charged with a higher degree of criminal liability than the principal. Thus, the question arises whether an accomplice who has the mens rea required for murder may be punished for that crime if the principal actor kills in a sudden heat of passion and is therefore liable only for manslaughter. The traditional answer of English authorities seems to have been "yes." See 1 M. Hale, Pleas of the Crown *438. It should be emphasized, however, that Hale's position on this point does not reflect general abandonment of the traditional common-law conception of derivative liability. Rather, it reflects a special rule based on the characterization of murder and manslaughter as two forms of the more generic offense of criminal homicide and applicable only to the distinction between those two offenses. The reluctance of the common law to extend this principle to other offenses is illustrated by Regina v. Richards, [1974] 1 Q.B. 776.

Mrs. Richards hired Bryant and Squires to beat up her husband. As she later admitted, "I told them I wanted them to beat him up bad enough to put him in the hospital for a month." On the date of the assault, Mrs. Richards gave the agreed signal when her husband left for work. Shortly thereafter, he was attacked in an alley by Bryant and Squires. As it turned out, they inflicted injuries rather less serious than his wife had contemplated, and no hospitalization was required.

The three defendants were charged with violating Sections 18 and 20 of the Offences Against the Person Act, 1961. Both provisions require unlawful wounding. Section 18 further requires a specific intent to do grievous bodily harm and is punished as a felony. Section

[d] The hypothetical comes from Williams, The Theory of Excuses, 1982 Crim.L.Rev. 732, 737. It is analyzed in Taylor, Complicity and Excuses, 1983 Crim.L.Rev. 656, 660–62.

20 requires no such intent and is a misdemeanor. At trial, both Bryant and Squires were acquitted of the more serious offense and convicted of the misdemeanor. Mrs. Richards, however, was convicted as a secondary party to the felony offense. She appealed on the ground set forth below:

"Mr. Alpin's submissions [for the accused] are brief. He says that looking at the facts of this case the defendant is in the position of one who aided and abetted, or counselled and procured, to use the old language, the other two to commit the offence, and that she cannot be guilty of a graver crime than the crime of which the two co-accused were guilty. There was only one offence that was committed by the co-accused, an offence under Section 20, and therefore there is no offence under Section 18 of the Act of which his client can properly be found guilty on the facts of this case. . . .

"That is the short point in the case as we see it. If there is only one offence committed, and that is the offence of unlawful wounding, then the person who has requested that offence to be committed, or advised that that offence be committed, cannot be guilty of a graver offence than that in fact which was committed."

In Complicity, Cause and Blame: A Study in the Interpretation of Doctrine, 73 Cal.L.Rev. 323, 388–89 (1985), Sanford Kadish defends the result in *Richards:*

"[T]he decision is supportable, it would seem, on the ground that Mrs. Richards did not *cause* the actions of the men. . . . She made no misrepresentation to the men she hired. They were not her unwitting instruments, but freely chose to act as they did. Hence their actions, as such, could not be attributed to Mrs. Richards. The innocent-agency doctrine is inapplicable because she did not cause their action.

"It is a further question whether Mrs. Richards *should* be liable for assault with intent to do grievous injury, even if I am right that existing doctrine precludes that result. Surely the strongest argument for liability is that the culpability of her hirelings is irrelevant to *her* culpability. But that argument proves too much. If her hirelings committed no assault, but instead went to the police, it is incontrovertible that Mrs. Richards could not be found liable for any assault, let alone an aggravated assault. Yet whether her hirelings chose to do as she bade them or to go to the police is also irrelevant to her culpability. The point would be that however culpable her intentions she could not be blamed for an assault that did not take place. The same retort is applicable on the facts of the case: an actual assault took place (and Mrs. Richards is liable for it) but an aggravated assault did not take place. It did not take place because those committing the assault did not intend to inflict grievous bodily harm. She could properly be held liable for solicitation to commit an aggravated assault, not for aggravated assault."

Is this analysis persuasive? Does it suggest the appropriate way to deal with such situations? Does your answer depend on how the crime of solicitation to commit an aggravated assault is graded?

7. **The Model Code and Modern Statutes.** Legislation based on the Model Penal Code goes far beyond elimination of many of the common-law doctrines governing the relationship between principals and accessories. Instead, these newer provisions abandon the common-law categories altogether. In their place, elaborate rules are stated for determining when one person may be held liable for the conduct of another. Section 2.06(1) of the Model Penal Code, for example, begins by providing that: "A person is guilty of an offense if it is committed by his own conduct or by the conduct of another person for which he is legally accountable, or both." Subsection (2) then describes three circumstances under which one person is legally accountable for the conduct of another: (i) the innocent agency situation; (ii) cases where the criminal law makes special provision (see, e.g., § 230.1(3)); and (iii) cases where the defendant is an "accomplice." Subsection (3) then elaborates on what it means to be an "accomplice" of another.

The text of the Model Code does not clearly state whether the liability of an "accomplice" depends upon the guilt of the primary actor. How would *Cogan and Leak* be decided under its provisions? How would *Dusenberry, Thornton v. Mitchell,* and *Richards* be decided? The commentary to § 2.06 does not directly address this issue. How should the Model Penal Code be interpreted on this point? Is § 5.01(3) relevant to your answer?

8. **Study Problems.** A good way to test your understanding of complicity is to consider the following problems.[e] For each situation, assume that *A* initiated the criminal endeavor by suggesting to *B* that they cooperate in the burglary of a store. *B*, who is related to the store owner, fakes acquiescence in order to trap *A*, and the following variations occur.

(i) *A* and *B* go to the store at midnight. *A* helps *B* enter the store and waits outside for *B* to hand out the loot. As per prior arrangement with *B*, the police intervene, and *A* is arrested.

(ii) *A* and *B* go to the store at midnight. *A* brings to the store various implements designed to facilitate surreptitious entry. *A* assists *B* to use these implements to pick the lock of the store's back door. Before either *A* or *B* gain entry to the store, the police intervene, and *A* is arrested.

(iii) Finally, suppose that *B* purports to agree with *A*'s scheme but goes directly to the police without taking any action toward fulfillment of the plan. The police find *A* at home, and *A* is arrested.

What is *A*'s liability in each of these situations at common law? Under the Model Penal Code?

---

[e] The fact situation is based on State v. Hayes, 105 Mo. 76, 16 S.W. 514 (1891).

SUBSECTION D: LIMITS OF ACCOMPLICE LIABILITY

REGINA v. TYRRELL

Court for Consideration of Crown Cases Reserved, 1893.
[1891–4] All E.R. 1215.

On September 15, 1893, Jane Tyrrell was arraigned before the Central Criminal Court, and pleaded not guilty to an indictment containing counts charging (i) that being a girl above the age of 13 years and under the age of 16 years she aided and abetted the commission upon herself of the offence of carnal knowledge, contrary to Section 5 of the Criminal Law Amendment Act, 1885; [a] and (ii) that she solicited and incited the commission of such offence upon her. The evidence for the prosecution proved that the defendant, who was under the age of 16, aided and abetted and solicited and incited Thomas Froud to have unlawful carnal connection with her, for which offence the defendant was convicted. . . . [A]t the request of defendant's counsel, the following question was reserved for the opinion of the court: Whether it was an offence for a girl between 13 years and 16 years of age, to aid and abet a male person in the commission of the misdemeanour of having unlawful carnal connection with her, or to solicit and incite a male person to commit that misdemeanour.

LORD COLERIDGE, C. J. I believe that I am expressing the opinion of my learned brothers when I say that this conviction must be quashed. What was intended by the legislature in passing the Act of 1885 was to protect girls against themselves, and it cannot be said that an act which says nothing at all about the girl inciting or anything of that kind, and the whole object of which is to protect women against men, is to be construed so as to render a girl against whom an offence is committed equally liable with the man by whom the offence is committed. In my opinion this conviction cannot be sustained, and must therefore be quashed.

MATHEW, J. I am of the same opinion. I fail to see how this argument on the construction of the statute can be supported. The consequences of upholding this conviction would, as has been pointed out in the course of the argument, be most serious, there being scarcely a section in the act which would not, upon the construction sought to be put upon the act, support a criminal prosecution against a girl. There is no trace anywhere in the act of any intention on the part of the legislature to deal with the woman as a criminal, and I am of the

---

[a] The statute in question provided as follows:

"[A]ny person who unlawfully and carnally knows, or attempts to have unlawful carnal knowledge of any girl being of or above the age of 13 years, and under the age of 16 years . . . shall be guilty of a misdemeanour. . . ."

This provision was reenacted in substantially the same form as Section 6 of the Sexual Offences Act, 1956. [Footnote by eds.]

opinion that the act does not create the offence alleged in the indictment. . . .

Conviction quashed.

NOTES ON THE LIMITS OF ACCOMPLICE LIABILITY

1. **Implied Exemption.** What do you take to be the precise basis of decision in *Tyrrell*? Are you persuaded by the lack of direct evidence of legislative intention to criminalize the girl's conduct? Would you expect to find, in the text or history of a particular criminal offense, explicit legislative attention to the potential scope of generally applicable principles of accomplice liability? If not, is there something about the context of this offense that makes the legislative silence informative?

In this connection, note the Model Penal Code effort to generalize on the limits of accomplice liability. Section 2.06(6) provides as follows:

"[U]nless otherwise provided by the Code or by the law defining the offense, a person is not an accomplice in an offense committed by another person if:

(a) he is a victim of that offense; or

(b) the offense is so defined that his conduct is inevitably incident to its commission. . . ."

Is the rationale for this provision clear? What reasons would you give to support an exception to accomplice liability for the victims of crime? What additional exemption is achieved by the further reference to persons whose conduct is "inevitably incident" to the commission of the offense? Is this exemption warranted?

2. **Withdrawal.** Note also that Section 2.06(6) of the Model Penal Code codifies the defense of withdrawal or abandonment as it applies to complicity. Specifically, the provision states that a person is not liable as an accomplice to the offense of another if "he terminates his complicity prior to the commission of the offense and (i) wholly deprives it of effectiveness in the commission of the offense; or (ii) gives timely warning to the law-enforcement authorities or otherwise makes proper effort to prevent commission of the offense." The role of withdrawal or abandonment in the law of complicity is analogous to the similar issue in the law of attempt. The chief differences are, first, that the defense is more widely recognized in the context of complicity, and, second, that most formulations of withdrawal from complicity require that the accomplice make affirmative efforts to give timely warning or otherwise to prevent the commission of the offense. Do you see why such a requirement is necessary in the context of complicity, but not for the crime of attempt? [a]

---

[a] For a discussion of this issue, see Smith, Withdrawal from Criminal Liability for Complicity and Inchoate Offences, 12 Anglo-Am. L.Rev. 200 (1983).

SECTION 2: VICARIOUS LIABILITY

COMMONWEALTH v. KOCZWARA

Supreme Court of Pennsylvania, 1959.
397 Pa. 575, 155 A.2d 825.

COHEN, JUSTICE. This is an appeal from the judgment of the Court of Quarter Sessions of Lackawanna County sentencing the defendant to three months in the Lackawanna County Jail, a fine of $500 and the costs of prosecution, in a case involving violations of the Pennsylvania Liquor Code.

[Defendant was the licensee and operator of a tavern. He was convicted of permitting minors to frequent the premises without parental supervision and of permitting the sale of beer to minors.]

Defendant raises two contentions, both of which, in effect, question whether the undisputed facts of this case support the judgment and sentence imposed by the Quarter Sessions Court. Judge Hoban found as fact that "in every instance the purchase [by minors] was made from a bartender, not identified by name, and service to the boys was made by the bartender. There was *no* evidence that the defendant was present on any one of the occasions testified to by [the] witnesses, nor that he had any personal knowledge of the sales to them or to other persons on the premises." We, therefore, must determine the criminal responsibility of a licensee of the Liquor Control Board for acts committed by his employees upon his premises, without his personal knowledge, participation, or presence, which acts violate a valid regulatory statute passed under the Commonwealth's police power.

While an employer in almost all cases is not criminally responsible for the unlawful acts of his employees, unless he consents to, approves, or participates in such acts, courts all over the nation have struggled for years in applying this rule within the framework of "controlling the sale of intoxicating liquor." At common law, any attempt to invoke the doctrine of respondeat superior in a criminal case would have run afoul of our deeply ingrained notions of criminal jurisprudence that guilt must be personal and individual. In recent decades, however, many states have enacted detailed regulatory provisions in fields which are essentially non-criminal, e.g., pure food and drug acts, speeding ordinances, building regulations, and child labor, minimum wage and maximum hour legislation. Such statutes are generally enforceable by light penalties, and although violations are labelled crimes, the considerations applicable to them are totally different from those applicable to true crimes, which involve moral delinquency and which are punishable by imprisonment or another serious penalty. Such so-called statutory crimes are in reality an attempt to utilize the machinery of criminal administration as an enforcing arm for social regulations of a purely civil nature, with the punishment totally unrelated to questions of moral wrongdoing or guilt. It is here that the social interest in the general well-being and security of the populace has been held to outweigh the individual interest of the particular defendant. The penalty is imposed despite the defendant's lack of a criminal intent or mens rea. . . .

In the instant case, the defendant has sought to surround himself with all the safeguards provided to those within the pale of criminal sanctions. He has argued that a statute imposing criminal responsibility should be construed strictly, with all doubts resolved in his favor. While the defendant's position is entirely correct, we must remember that we are dealing with a statutory crime within the state's plenary police power. In the field of liquor regulation, the legislature has enacted a comprehensive code aimed at regulating and controlling the use and sale of alcoholic beverages. The question here raised is whether the legislature *intended* to impose vicarious criminal liability on the licensee-principal for acts committed on his premises without his presence, participation or knowledge.

[On the basis of an extensive review of state law,] we find that the intent of the legislature in enacting this code was not only to eliminate the common-law requirement of mens rea, but also to place a very high degree of responsibility upon the holder of a liquor license to make certain that neither he nor anyone in his employ commit any of the prohibited acts upon the licensed premises. . . .

Can the legislature, consistent with the requirements of due process, thus establish absolute criminal liability? Were this the defendant's first violation of the code, and the penalty solely a minor fine of from $100–$300, we would have no hesitation in upholding such a judgment. Defendant, by accepting a liquor license, must bear this financial risk. Because of a prior conviction for violations of the code, however, the trial judge felt compelled under the mandatory language of the statute, Section 494(a), to impose not only an increased fine of $500, but also a three-month sentence of imprisonment. Such sentence to imprisonment in a case where liability is imposed vicariously cannot be sanctioned by this court consistently with the law-of-the-land clause of the Constitution of the Commonwealth of Pennsylvania, Art. I, Sec. 9.[7]

The courts of the Commonwealth have already strained to permit the legislature to carry over the civil doctrine of respondeat superior and to apply it as a means of enforcing the regulatory scheme that covers the liquor trade. We have done so on the theory that the Code established petty misdemeanors involving only light monetary fines. It would be unthinkable to impose vicarious criminal responsibility in cases involving true crimes. Although to hold a principal criminally liable might possibly be an effective means of enforcing law and order, it would do violence to our more sophisticated modern-day concepts of justice. Liability for all true crimes, wherein an offense carries with it a jail sentence, must be based exclusively upon personal causation. It can be readily imagined that even a licensee who is meticulously careful in the choice of his employees cannot supervise every single act

---

[7] Sec. 9 ". . . nor can he be deprived of his life, liberty or property, unless by the judgment of his peers or the law of the land."

of the subordinates. A man's liberty cannot rest on so frail a reed as whether his employee will commit a mistake in judgment. . . .

This court is very mindful of its duty to maintain and establish the proper safeguards in a criminal trial. To sanction the imposition of imprisonment here would make a serious change in the substantive criminal law of the Commonwealth, one for which we find no justification. We have found *no* case in any jurisdiction which has permitted a *prison term* for a vicarious offense. . . .

In holding that the punishment of [imprisonment deprives the defendant of due process of law under these facts, we are not declaring that Koczwara must be treated as a first offender under the code. He has clearly violated the law for a second time and must be punished accordingly. Therefore, we are only holding that so much of the judgment as calls for imprisonment is invalid, and we are leaving intact the $500 fine imposed by Judge Hoban under the subsequent offense section. . . .

Judgment, as modified, is affirmed.

MUSMANNO, JUSTICE (dissenting) . . . . The majority of this court is doing something which can find no justification in all the law books which ornament the libraries and enlighten the judges and lawyers in this commonwealth. It sustains the conviction of a person for acts admittedly not committed by him, not performed in his presence, not accomplished at his direction, and not even done within his knowledge. It is stigmatizing him with a conviction for an act which, in point of personal responsibility, is as far removed from him as if it took place across the seas. The majority's decision is so novel, so unique, and so bizarre that one must put on his spectacles, remove them to wipe the lenses, and then put them on again in order to assure himself that what he reads is a judicial decision proclaimed in Philadelphia, the home of the Liberty Bell, the locale of Independence Hall, and the place where the fathers of our country met to draft the Constitution of the United States, the Magna Charta of the liberties of Americans and the beacon of hope of mankind seeking justice everywhere.

The decision handed down in this case throws a shadow over that Constitution, applies an eraser to the Bill of Rights, and muffles the Liberty Bell which many decades ago sang its song of liberation from monarchial domination over man's inalienable right to life, liberty, and the pursuit of happiness. . . .

The majority introduces into its discussion a proposition which is shocking to contemplate. It speaks of "vicarious criminal liability." Such a concept is as alien to American soil as the upas tree. There was a time in China when a convicted felon sentenced to death could offer his brother or other close relative in his stead for decapitation. The Chinese law allowed such "vicarious criminal liability." I never thought that Pennsylvania would look with favor on anything approaching so revolting a barbarity. . . .

The majority opinion finds the imprisonment part of the sentence contrary to law. . . . But if the majority cannot sanction the incarceration of a person for acts of which he had no knowledge, how can it sanction the imposition of a fine? How can it sanction a conviction at all? . . . If it is wrong to send a person to jail for acts committed by another, is it not wrong to convict him at all? There are those who value their good names to the extent that they see as much harm in a degrading criminal conviction as in a jail sentence. The laceration of a man's reputation, the blemishing of his good name, the wrecking of his prestige by a criminal-court conviction may blast a person's chances for honorable success in life to such an extent that a jail sentence can hardly add much to the ruin already wrought to him by the conviction alone. . . . .

NOTES ON VICARIOUS LIABILITY

1. **Background.** Vicarious liability is related to, but distinct from, complicity. Both vicarious liability and complicity result in the punishment of one person for the conduct of another. Under ordinary principles of complicity, however, guilt is based on culpable involvement by the accomplice in the criminal conduct. Vicarious liability, by contrast, usually rests on some sort of status relationship between the accused and the primary actor. The most common basis of vicarious liability is the employment relationship. Under a wide variety of modern statutes, an employer may be liable for the conduct of an employee without proof of assistance, encouragement, or any other participation in the forbidden act. Moreover, vicarious liability is usually strict liability. As a result, the employer may be liable for the conduct of the employee without proof that the employer knew of such conduct, and, indeed, even in the face of evidence that the employee acted in disregard of the employer's wishes.

The history of this doctrine is set forth in Sayre, Criminal Responsibility for the Acts of Another, 43 Harv.L.Rev. 689 (1930). Vicarious liability was unknown to the common law. Unlike modern principles of complicity, it did not evolve from the common-law notions of parties to crime. Instead, vicarious liability was a relatively recent importation from the law of torts, specifically the doctrine of respondeat superior. Originally, the master was responsible in money damages for the acts of a servant only where the master had expressly commanded or authorized the tortious conduct. In time, however, the employer became liable for any act committed by an employee acting in the "course of business" or within the "scope of employment." *Koczwara* illustrates the modern transplantation of this doctrine to the field of criminal law under the name of vicarious liability.

Of course, the considerations governing compensatory damages and those surrounding the imposition of penal sanctions traditionally have been thought quite different. For that reason, the courts have been slow to engraft respondeat superior onto the doctrinal structure of the penal law. With few and unimportant exceptions, the initial inroads of vicarious liability were made not by courts, but by legislatures. Thus it is that today the issue of vicarious liability arises chiefly where the legislature has declared, or is understood by the courts to have intended, that one person should be held criminally responsible for the conduct of another. Not surprisingly, liability of this sort is used most frequently as an adjunct to some scheme of government regulation, and the penalties applicable to violations of such laws more nearly resemble civil fines than the distinctly penal sanctions authorized for "true" crimes.

2. **The Relevance of the Sanction.** The *Koczwara* court found great relevance in the nature of the sanction. Justice Musmanno's protest notwithstanding, the majority affirmed the judgment below insofar as it involved a fine and overturned only the sentence of imprisonment. This resolution of the case is consistent with the view that vicarious liability may be acceptable if strictly confined to the realm of minor offenses. Sayre defended this position in the concluding paragraph of his study of the question:*

"What, then, shall be said of the problem of vicarious criminal liability in the case of petty misdemeanors involving merely regulatory offenses? In such cases, there is no question of moral wrongdoing. The objective of the law is not to cure or change the mental processes of the defendant. There is no thought of social treatment or rehabilitation. The law's aim is not reformatory, but almost exclusively deterrent, to prevent future repetitions of similar offenses. To hold the master liable if he fails to prevent his servant from committing the prohibited conduct will have a powerful deterrent effect. On the other hand, to require from the state actual and positive proof of specific authorization or actual knowledge and acquiescence in a matter lying peculiarly within the secret knowledge of the two concerned in the offense, will effectually block most convictions and open the way for successful evasion through secret instructions and covert understandings. The protection of important social interests may thus be sacrificed to a too-zealous concern for individual interests of only trifling importance. Since in such cases deterrence is the essential objective, the present tendency of the law to hold the master criminally liable even for the unauthorized and unknown acts of his servant seems justified, and indicates a direction of sound growth. As long as courts are careful not to permit respondeat superior to creep into the true crime cases, masters and principals should be held criminally liable for the petty misdemeanors of their servants and agents which involve no moral delinquency or severe punishment and which are committed in the course of the master's business."

Are you persuaded? Does the efficiency justification for vicarious responsibility of some sort necessarily make the case for criminal liability? Is the objective of social control and regulation especially well served by reliance on criminal conviction and punishment? If so, why?

3. ***Iowa City* v. *Nolan.*** With the excerpt from Sayre, compare the opinions in Iowa City v. Nolan, 239 N.W.2d 102 (Iowa 1976). The defendant appealed three parking violations that resulted in total fines of $20. He challenged the constitutionality of a municipal ordinance that made the registered owner of an illegally parked vehicle "prima-facie responsible" where the operator could not be identified. The majority upheld the ordinance on the ground that, "[not only may public-welfare legislation dispense with a mens rea or scienter requirement, it may, and frequently does, impose a vicarious 'criminal' liability for the acts of another." *United States* v. *Dotterweich*, discussed at page 293, supra, and *United States* v. *Park*, reprinted at page 295, supra, were relied on to support the constitutionality of such legislation. Justice McCormick filed a lengthy dissent, from which the following excerpts are taken:

"In *Lambert* [v. *California*, reprinted at page 308, supra] the Supreme Court quoted with approval the following statement from Holmes, The Common Law, 'A law which punished conduct which would not be blameworthy in the average member of the community would be too severe for that community to bear.' I believe that the construction given [the] ordinance by the majority in this case puts it in this category.

"Under the majority construction of the ordinance an automobile owner is guilty of a crime when his car is illegally parked in Iowa City unless he proves the car was being operated without his consent on the occasion involved. Although the record does not show what maximum penalty is possible for such crimes in Iowa City, the conduct is a misdemeanor and may include misdemeanor penalties, a maximum fine of $100 or jail sentence of 30 days. . . .

"If an illegal parking violation is not a 'true crime,' as maintained in the majority opinion, it should not be called a crime nor should it carry criminal penalties. If it is a 'true crime,' vicarious strict liability is unreasonable and denies substantive due process of law. 'Where the offense is in the nature of a true crime, that is, where it involves moral delinquency or is punishable by imprisonment or a serious penalty, it seems clear that the doctrine of respondeat superior must be repudiated as a foundation for criminal liability. For it is of the very essence of our deep-rooted notions of criminal liability that guilt be personal and individual.' Sayre, Criminal Responsibility for the Acts of Another, 43 Harv.L.Rev. 689, 717 (1930).

"Municipal parking regulations like those involved here utilize the machinery of criminal administration as an enforcement tool for social regulations purely civil in nature. Due process does not permit the city to have it both ways. The right not to be labeled a criminal for conduct acknowledged not to amount to a true crime is cherished and constitutionally protected. [The ordinance], as construed by the majority, deprives those convicted under it of that basic right. It thereby violates the due process clause of the 14th amendment of the United States Constitution."

Do you agree with this analysis? Would you characterize the parking ordinances involved in this case as "true crimes"? Should the resolution of this case turn on that distinction? If not, what other basis for decision would you give?

SECTION 3: CORPORATE CRIMINALITY

COMMONWEALTH v. BENEFICIAL FINANCE CO.

Supreme Judicial Court of Massachusetts, 1971.
360 Mass. 188, 275 N.E.2d 33.

SPIEGEL, JUSTICE. [Representatives of various finance companies operating in Massachusetts joined in an illicit scheme to secure favorable treatment from the state regulatory authorities. Both individual participants and the corporations for which they worked were convicted of bribery and conspiracy to commit bribery. The relationships between corporate and individual defendants were as follows. Beneficial Finance Co. was held criminally responsible for the acts of two individuals, one an employee and the other the vice-president of a wholly owned subsidiary. Household Finance Corp. was held liable for the conduct of employees who were neither officers nor directors. Liberty Loan Corp. was convicted for the acts of an executive vice-president and director. Only portions of the opinion dealing with the liability of the corporate defendants are included in the excerpts that follow.]

The defendants and the commonwealth have proposed differing standards upon which the criminal responsibility of a corporation should be predicated. The defendants argue that a corporation should not be held criminally liable for the conduct of its servants or agents unless such conduct was performed, authorized, ratified, adopted or tolerated by the corporations' directors, officers or other "high managerial agents" who are sufficiently high in the corporate hierarchy to warrant the assumption that their acts in some substantial sense reflect corporate policy. This standard is that adopted by the American Law Institute Model Penal Code, approved in May, 1962. Section 2.07 of the code provides that, except in the case of regulatory offences and offences consisting of the omission of a duty imposed on corporations by law, a corporation may be convicted of a crime if "the commission of the offence was authorized, requested, commanded, performed or recklessly tolerated by the board of directors or by a high managerial agent acting in behalf of the corporation within the scope of his office or employment." This section proceeds to define "high managerial agent" as "an officer of a corporation . . . or any other agent . . .

having duties of such responsibility that his conduct may fairly be assumed to represent the policy of the corporation."[55]

The commonwealth, on the other hand, argues that the standard applied by the judge in his instructions to the jury was correct. These instructions, which proscribe a somewhat more flexible standard than that delineated in the Model Penal Code, state in part, as follows:

"[T]he commonwealth must prove beyond a reasonable doubt that there existed between the guilty individual or individuals and the corporation which is being charged with the conduct of the individuals, such *a relationship that the acts and the intent of the individuals were the acts and intent of the corporation.*
. . .

"How is that to be shown? How is the jury to determine whether the commonwealth has proved that? First let me say that the commonwealth does not have to prove that the individual who acted criminally was expressly requested or authorized in advance by the corporation to do so, nor must the commonwealth prove that the corporation expressly ratified or adopted that criminal conduct on the part of that individual or those individuals. *It does not mean that the commonwealth must prove that the individual who acted criminally was a member of the corporation's board of directors, or that he was a high officer in the corporation, or that he held any office at all.* . . . The commonwealth must prove that the individual for whose conduct it seeks to charge *the corporation criminally was placed in a position by the corporation where he had enough power, duty, responsibility and authority to act for and in behalf of the corporation to handle the particular business or operation or project of the corporation in which he was engaged at the time that he committed the criminal act, with power of decision as to what he would or would not do while acting for the corporation, and that he was acting for the corporation, and that he was acting for and in behalf of the corporation in the accomplishment of that particular business or operation or project, and that he committed a criminal act while so acting.* . . .

"*Now, this test doesn't depend upon the power, duty, the responsibility, or the authority which the individual has with reference to the entire corporation business. The test should be applied to his position with relation to the particular operation or project in which he is serving the corporation.*" [Emphasis by the court.]

The difference between the judge's instructions to the jury and the Model Penal Code lies largely in the latter's reference to a "high managerial agent" and in the code requirement that to impose corpo-

---

[55] Section 2.07 of the Model Penal Code was materially amended between 1955 (Tentative Draft No. 4) and its adoption in 1962 (Proposed Official Draft) by adding the . . . words "or recklessly tolerated." These words seem to expand corpo-

rate criminal liability to include at least cases where high managerial officers shut their eyes to (or try to remain aloof from and apparently unaware of) criminal activity by subordinates undertaken for the corporation's benefit. . . .

rate criminal liability, it at least must appear that its directors or high managerial agent "authorized . . . or recklessly tolerated" the allegedly criminal acts. The judge's instructions focus on the authority of the corporate agent in relation to the *particular* corporate business in which the agent was engaged. The code seems to require that there be authorization or reckless inaction by a corporate representative having some relation to framing corporate policy, or one "having duties of such responsibility that his conduct may fairly be assumed to represent the policy of the corporation." Close examination of the judge's instructions reveals that they preserve the underlying "corporate policy" rationale of the code by allowing the jury to infer "corporate policy" from the position in which the corporation placed the agent in commissioning him to handle the particular corporate affairs in which he was engaged at the time of the criminal act. . . .

It may also be observed that the judge's standard is somewhat similar to the traditional common-law rules of respondeat superior. However, in applying this rule to a criminal case, the judge added certain requirements not generally associated with that common-law doctrine. He further qualified the rule of respondeat superior by requiring that the conduct for which the corporation is being held accountable be performed *on behalf of the corporation*. This factor is noted as important in the commentary to Section 2.07(1) of the Model Penal Code. It may well be that there is often little distinction between an act done *on behalf of a principal* and an act done *within the scope of employment*, which is the traditional requirement of the doctrine of respondeat superior. Nevertheless, in the circumstances of this case it might reasonably be concluded that the explicit instruction of the judge that the jury look to the authority vested in the agent by the corporation to act within the particular sphere of corporate affairs relating to the criminal act, together with the explicit instruction that such act be performed on behalf of the corporation, required, in effect, the type of evidence which would support an inference that the criminal act was done as a matter of corporate policy. We deem this to be a valid conclusion, especially in view of the quantum of proof required in a criminal case in order to prove guilt beyond a reasonable doubt. . . . .

[The court then reviewed a number of Massachusetts precedents, including a line of cases holding that criminal liability of a master for the acts of a servant under the doctrine of respondeat superior requires that the master actually participate in, or approve of, the servant's criminal act.]

The thrust of each of the cases cited above involving a human principal is that it is fundamental to our criminal jurisprudence that for more serious offenses guilt is personal and not vicarious. "One is punished for his own blameworthy conduct, not that of others." Commonwealth v. Stasiun, 349 Mass. 38, 48, 206 N.E.2d 672, 679 (1965), citing Sayre, Criminal Responsibility for the Acts of Another, 43 Harv.L.Rev. 689 (1930). Professor Sayre's article is heavily relied on by Beneficial for the proposition that the considerations imposed by Sayre apply with equal weight to corporations. However, we do not think that the Sayre article, or the rule in the master-servant cases, is helpful to these corporations. The essence of Sayre's discussion is that, as to certain crimes, a theory of vicarious liabilty is an inadequate basis for imposing criminal liability on a natural person who can suffer imprisonment or ignominy for the acts of his agents. . . .

As alluded to by Professor Sayre, and pointed out by the commonwealth in its brief, the very nature of a corporation as a "person" before the law renders it impossible to equate the imposition of vicarious liability on a human principal with the imposition of vicarious liability on a corporate principal. "A corporation can only act through its agents. . . . [C]orporate criminal liability is necessarily vicarious." Note, Criminal Liability of Corporations for Acts of Their Agents, 60 Harv.L.Rev. 283 (1946). Since a corporation is a legal fiction, comprised only of individuals, it has no existence separate and distinct from those whom it has clothed with authority and commissioned to act for it whether such individuals are directors, officers, shareholders or employees. . . . For the foregoing reasons, despite the strenuous urging of the defendants, we are unconvinced that the standard for imposing criminal responsibility on a human principal adequately deals with the evidentiary problems which are inherent in ascribing the acts of individuals to a corporate entity.

Since we have exhausted our review of Massachusetts cases in point, we turn to cases in other jurisdictions discussing the problem of corporate criminal responsibility. . . .

We treat first with the case of New York Central & Hartford R.R. v. United States, 212 U.S. 481 (1909), a case relied upon by both the judge and the commonwealth. There, the Supreme Court of the United States upheld the constitutionality of a statute which specifically made corporations liable for the acts of their officers, agents or employees acting within the scope of their employment. . . .

In the often cited case of Egan v. United States, 137 F.2d 369, 379 (8th Cir. 1943), . . . the court said: "The test of corporate responsibility for the acts of its officers and agents, whether such acts be criminal or tortious, is whether the agent or officer in doing the thing complained of was engaged in 'employing the corporate powers actually authorized' for the benefit of the corporation 'while acting within the scope of his employment in the business of the principal.' . . . ."

Another federal case applying the above standard is C.I.T. Corp. v. United States, 150 F.2d 85 (9th Cir. 1945). This case is significant in that a large national money-lending corporation was held criminally responsible for the criminal acts of a minor branch manager. The corporation was convicted of conspiracy to make false credit-statement applications to the Federal Housing Administration, a crime which under the statute specifically required the element of knowledge. On appeal, the corporation argued that the branch manager was too low in the corporate hierarchy and that he had no corporate power to commit the acts complained of with the criminal intent imputable to the corporate entity. In refuting this argument the court said: "We do not agree. It is the function delegated to the corporate officer or agent which determines his power to engage the corporation in a criminal transaction." . . .

The standard applied in the above cases clearly focused on the scope of authority of the agents to act in the narrow sphere of corporate business relating to the criminal act. This essential consideration was succinctly set forth in somewhat different terms in the case of United States v. Nearing, 252 F. 223, 231 (S.D.N.Y.1918), wherein Judge Learned Hand stated that "the criminal liability of a corporation is to be determined by *the kinship of the act to the powers of the officials, who commit it*" (emphasis supplied). . . .

Household argues that in applying the foregoing standard of corporate criminal responsibility, we are merely applying the rule of respondeat superior as it is applied in civil cases . . . . It may be that the theoretical principles underlying this standard are, in general, the same as embodied in the rule of respondeat superior. Nevertheless, as we observed at the outset, the judge's instructions, as a whole and in context, required a greater quantum of proof in the practical application of this standard than is required in a civil case. In focusing on the "kinship" between the authority of an individual and the act he committed, the judge emphasized that the jury must be satisfied "beyond a reasonable doubt" that the act of the individual "*constituted*" the act of the corporation. Juxtaposition of the traditional criminal-law requirement of ascertaining guilt beyond a reasonable doubt (as opposed to the civil-law standard of the preponderance of the evidence), with the rule of respondeat superior, fully justifies application of the standard enunciated by the judge to a criminal prosecution against a corporation for a crime requiring specific intent.

The foregoing is especially true in view of the particular circumstances of this case. In order to commit the crimes charged in these indictments, the defendant corporation either had to offer to pay money to a public official or conspire to do so. The disbursal of funds is an act peculiarly within the ambit of corporate activity. These corporations by the very nature of their business are constantly dealing with the expenditure and collection of moneys. It could hardly be expected that any of the individual defendants would conspire to pay, or would pay, the substantial amount of money here involved, namely $25,000, out of his own pocket. The jury would be warranted in finding that the disbursal of such an amount of money would come from the corporate treasury. A reasonable inference could therefore be drawn that the payment of such money by the corporations was done as a matter of corporate policy and as a reflection of corporate intent, thus comporting with the underlying rationale of the Model Penal Code, and probably with its specific requirements.

Moreover, we do not think that the Model Penal Code standard really purports to deal with the evidentiary problems which are inherent in establishing the quantum of proof necessary to show that the directors or officers of a corporation authorize, ratify, tolerate, or participate in the criminal acts of an agent when such acts are apparently performed on behalf of the corporation. Evidence of such authorization or ratification is too easily susceptible of concealment. As is so trenchantly stated by the judge: "Criminal acts are not usually made the subject of votes of authorization or ratification by corporate boards of directors; and the lack of such votes does not prevent the act from being the act of the corporation."

It is obvious that criminal conspiratorial acts are not performed within the glare of publicity, nor would we expect a board of directors to meet officially and record on the corporate records a delegation of authority to initiate, conduct or conclude proceedings for the purpose of bribing a public official. Of necessity, the proof [of] authority to so act must rest on all the circumstances and conduct in a given situation and the reasonable inferences to be drawn therefrom. . . .

Considering everything we have said above, we are of opinion that the quantum of proof necessary to sustain the conviction of a corporation for the acts of its agents is sufficiently met if it is shown that the corporation has placed the agent in a position where he has enough authority and responsibility to act for and in behalf of the corporation in handling the *particular* corporate business, operation or project in which he was engaged at the time he committed the criminal act. The judge properly instructed the jury to this effect and correctly stated that this standard does not depend upon the responsibility or authority which the agent has with respect to the entire corporate business, but only to his position with relation to the particular business in which he was serving the corporation. . . .

All judgments affirmed.

NOTES ON CORPORATE CRIMINAL RESPONSIBILITY

1. **Liability for the Acts of an Agent.** As the main case illustrates, the liability of a corporation for the acts of its agents does not depend on the generally applicable principles of complicity. As the court noted, a corporation can act only through its agents. The test for attributing to the corporation the conduct and culpability of its agents is, therefore, the central issue in the field of corporate criminal liability. Obviously, the *Beneficial Finance* decision and the Model Penal Code take different approaches to this problem. Which is the better view?

Note that the scope of this dispute is somewhat narrower than might at first appear. For one thing, it is well settled that a corporation is criminally responsible for the acts of its agents and employees whenever the legislature so declares. That is the lesson of the *New York Central & Hartford R.R.* case discussed in the principal opinion. Additionally, there is widespread agreement that a corporation may be held liable on the basis of respondeat superior for the commission by its employees of so-called regulatory or public-welfare offenses. This result is endorsed by Model Penal Code Section 2.07(2), which states as a rule of construction that a legislative purpose to hold the corporation criminally responsible for the acts of its agents is to be assumed whenever the offense is one of strict liability. For such offenses, the corporation is liable whenever the criminal conduct is "performed by an agent of the corporation acting in behalf of the corporation within the scope of his office or employment." The disagreement between the *Beneficial Finance* approach and the Model Code solution therefore reduces to the context of "true" crimes—i.e., offenses of some seriousness that ordinarily require mens rea and conviction of which usually carries some stigma. Does this focus affect your view of the merits of the question?

Whatever the right answer to this question as a matter of policy, it seems clear that the trend is toward the broader liability endorsed in *Beneficial Finance*. As one authority noted: "To the question whether a corporation justifiably may be held accountable for the conduct of employees who have neither substantial authority over a particular aspect of the business nor broad responsibility within the company, the overwhelming response from the federal bench has . . . been affirmative." 1 K. Brickey, Corporate Criminal Liability 54–55 (1984). The test seems increasingly to be simply whether the agent has been authorized to act for the corporation in the matter at hand. Under this approach, the corporation may be held criminally liable for an agent who violates company policy and even for an agent who violates specific instructions not to do the very thing that is criminal. Despite some authority to the contrary, that position is said to represent "the clear weight of federal authority today." Id. at 63.

2. **Corporate Criminality and the Problem of Sanctions.** An underlying issue is whether the criminal law is a suitable instrument for the control of corporate misbehavior. Enforcement of criminal laws against corporations involves special problems. Perhaps the most pressing of these is the need to devise an effective array of sanctions applicable to corporations. The following excerpt from the commentary to the American Bar Association Standards for Criminal Justice suggests the range of considerations involved in that task: *

"[In recent years] the problem of corporate misconduct has come to the forefront of public attention. Watergate, illegal political contributions, foreign bribes, and alleged violations of penal laws protecting the environment, the consumer, and the worker—all of these highly publicized incidents underscore the public interest in achieving a sentencing system capable of deterring the organizational offender. . . .

"A number of unique factors, however, both distinguish and complicate the context of organizational crime and in balance make it essential that specially tailored remedies be available to the sentencing court in such cases.

"(i) Most obviously, the corporation cannot be incarcerated. Thus, normal fine schedules established primarily as a supple-

* Copyright © 1980 by the American Bar Association. Reprinted with permission.

mentary penalty for individual offenders are likely to be inadequate. . . .

"(ii) Recurrently, costs of compliance with many statutes applicable to organizations exceed the maximum penalties authorized by the law. This pattern is most prevalent in the area of safety and environmental regulation, where compliance may entail substantial expenditures. In such instances, not only does crime pay, but management may also misperceive a modest penalty as amounting to only a nuisance tax on the activity in question rather than a 'true' criminal prohibition. Unsubstantial fines also remove the incentive for shareholders to hold management accountable for the corporation's loss through the medium of the derivative suit.

"(iii) Although the need for special fine schedules in the case of organizations is thus clear, complete reliance cannot be placed on such a remedy alone. Where exemplary fines are used, the incidence of such penalties falls ultimately on persons who generally may be described as innocent: stockholders, creditors, consumers, and employees of the corporation. Thus, the Model Penal Code counsels restraint in the use of punitive fines to deter corporate misbehavior, because such a policy can amount to imposition of 'vicarious criminal liability' on a 'group ordinarily innocent of criminal conduct.' The dilemma, then, is that for adequate deterrence to be achieved through fines, it may be necessary to increase penalties in a manner that is inversely proportional to the culpability of those who bear them.

"(iv) An alternative policy focusing on the individual decision maker within the organization also encounters unique problems. First, it is a common pattern in many forms of organization crime that the actual decision maker cannot be reliably identified. This may be because no conscious decision to violate the law was ever made. Information often flows poorly within hierarchial organizations, and adverse information in particular may fail to be transmitted upward to those capable of acting on it. As a result, toxic chemicals may be released into a river, workers exposed illegally to harmful substances, or consumers sold a product that test reports suggested had dangerous design defects—all without any senior official being aware of the total pattern of the corporation's activities. . . .

"(v) A pattern of 'corporate recidivism' has characterized a number of corporations. Although this phrase may seem overly dramatic and the evidence cited by some commentators points more to venial sins than to serious crimes, examples can nonetheless be given of corporations that have recurrently run afoul of the antitrust laws, others that have regularly been found guilty of fraudulent activities, and still others whose products or methods of production have repeatedly brought prosecution to health and safety charges. In such cases, to 'rehabilitate' the organization, it becomes essential that an effective internal monitoring system be established by which both the court and the corporation's senior management can be apprised of impending developments. Deterrence is only one means to the law's primary goal of crime prevention, and in cases where illegal behavior was either tolerated or ignored as a result of organizational dysfunction, the court is justified in imposing incapacitative restraints.

"These complexities have been stressed to demonstrate both the absence of a single optimal sanction for organizational crime and the general inadequacy of the remedies currently available to the sentencing court. There is an unfortunate irony to the contrast existing today between civil and criminal remedies. For example, if a corporation were civilly held liable for creating an actionable nuisance, the court would have available to it a panoply of equitable remedies, including both injunctions and receivership. Yet, if the same corporation were tried and convicted on a criminal charge growing out of the same conduct, then, notwithstanding the higher burden of proof that would have been satisfied, the court would basically lose its ability to impose an equitable remedy and could only order a fine up to the limit authorized by the legislature. . . ."

3 Am. Bar Ass'n, Standards for Criminal Justice 18.164–69 (2d ed. 1980). The commentary then reviews a variety of sentencing options that could be adopted for use in dealing with corporate criminality. These include (i) special fine schedules applicable to corporate offenders; (ii) a criminal remedy of restitution to persons who have suffered loss as a result of criminal misconduct; (iii) notice of conviction in order to facilitate restitution; (iv) disqualification of certain individuals from corporate office; and (v) provisions for continuing judicial oversight of corporate activity.

Modern penal-code revisions typically include at least some of the sentencing options listed above. Special fine schedules for organizational offenders are the most widespread. A good example of this approach is contained in the proposed federal criminal code passed by the Senate in 1978. Under that proposal, the maximum fine for commission of a felony by an individual is $100,000; for an organization the maximum is $500,000. Both figures are considerably higher than the range of fines typical of current federal statutes. Of equal importance, the proposed code would also authorize an alternative fine schedule to be computed as follows: "[A] defendant who has been found guilty of an offense through which pecuniary gain was directly or indirectly derived, or by which bodily injury or property damage or other loss was caused, may be sentenced to pay a fine that does not exceed twice the gross gain derived or twice the gross loss caused, whichever is the greatest." S.1437, 95th Cong., 2d Sess. § 2201(c) (1978). This provision would apply equally to individuals and organizations, but it probably would be invoked most often against corporate offenders.[a]

It should be obvious that provisions of this sort increase the disparity between the mechanisms of the criminal law as applied to corporations and those traditionally invoked against individuals. The two contexts are distinguished by a number of facts. They include the irrelevance to corporations of the distinctively criminal sanction of incarceration, the uncertain impact on corporations of the stigma of criminal conviction, the increasing reliance for corporations on special fine schedules and other penalties not authorized for individuals, and the increasing interest (derived chiefly from concern with corporate misbehavior) in assessing criminal penalties based on a dollar evaluation of the quantum of gain derived or loss inflicted by the criminal misconduct. In light of these differences, it is fair to ask whether corporate misconduct should continue to be dealt with under the rubric of the criminal law at all. Might not the objectives of social control of organizational behavior be served as effectively through a system of civil regulation? What are the advantages of using the criminal law in this context? What are the costs? On balance, is reliance on the criminal law to control corporations sound social policy?[b]

3. **RICO.** Enforcement of the criminal law against corporations is increasingly dominated by federal statutes. Among the statutes used to police corporate misconduct are the Securities Act of 1933 and the Securities Exchange Act of 1934; the mail fraud statute, now codified at 18 U.S.C. § 1341; the parallel provision governing wire fraud, 18 U.S.C. § 1343; the Foreign Corrupt Practices Act of 1977, 15 U.S.C. §§ 78dd–1, et seq.; and many others. Perhaps most important of all is RICO, the Racketeer Influenced and Corrupt Organizations Act, enacted as Title IX of the Organized Crime Control Act of 1970 and now codified at 18 U.S.C. §§ 1961–68.

RICO is by any reckoning an innovative statute. It proscribes investment in, acquiring an interest in or maintaining control of, or participation in the conduct of an enterprise affecting interstate commerce, where such activity is related to a pattern of racketeering activity or collection of an unlawful debt. The key concept is that of the "enterprise," which plainly includes corporations and other business entities. Involvement in an enterprise violates the statute where it is related to a "pattern" of "racketeering activity" or unlawful debt collection.

[a] For the intriguing suggestion that corporate crime could be better controlled if fines were levied not in cash but in the equity securities of the offending corporation, as well as for a number of other innovative suggestions, see Coffee, Making the Punishment Fit the Crime: The Problem of Finding an Optimal Corporation Criminal Sanction, 1 N.Ill.U.L.Rev. 3 (1980).

[b] The suggestion that corporate criminal sanctions should be replaced by a system of civil liability is refuted in Fisse, Reconstructing Corporate Criminal Law: Deterrence, Retribution, Fault, and Sanctions, 56 So.Cal.L.Rev. 1141 (1983). A radically different perspective is taken in Braithwaite, Enforced Self-Regulation: A New Strategy for Corporate Crime Control, 80 Mich.L.Rev. 1466 (1982).

"Racketeering activity" encompasses a large number of federal offenses, including bribery, offenses concerning counterfeit obligations or securities, embezzlement, extortionate credit transactions, mail fraud, wire fraud, and various forms of obstruction of justice. Additionally, racketeering activity also includes eight categories of state crimes: "any act or threat involving murder, kidnapping, gambling, arson, robbery, bribery, extortion, or dealing in narcotic or other dangerous drugs, which is chargeable under state law and punishable by imprisonment for more than one year." 18 U.S.C. § 1961(1)(A).

A "pattern" of racketeering activity exists where two predicate offenses are committed within 10 years. Where such a pattern of racketeering activity can be shown, the very serious sanctions authorized by RICO come into play, and they can be imposed in addition to state or federal liability for any underlying offenses. Additionally, RICO authorizes civil enforcement by the government and treble damage actions by persons injured in their persons or property by violations of the statute.

The upshot is a sprawling and uncertainly defined criminalization of a broad range of actions that constitute a pattern of racketeering activity or unlawful debt collection in connection with an enterprise affecting interstate commerce. The issues raised by this legislation are technically complicated and politically controversial, and there is a growing body of case law and academic commentary on the subject. For a useful treatment of RICO, with comprehensive citations to recent decisions, see 1 K. Brickey, Corporate Criminal Liability §§ 7:01–7:30, pp. 229–358 (1984). Prominent among the many articles addressing one or another aspect of RICO is the very helpful analysis by Craig Bradley in Racketeering, Congress and the Courts: An Analysis of RICO, 65 Iowa L.Rev. 837 (1980).

4. **Partnerships and Other Unincorporated Associations.** Whether a partnership, as distinct from the partners individually, is criminally responsible for the acts of agents is in significant respects unsettled. One thing that is clear is that a partnership or other unincorporated association may be held criminally liable for the acts of its agents whenever the legislature so directs. Thus, for example, in United States v. A. & P. Trucking Co., 358 U.S. 121 (1958), the Supreme Court of the United States ruled that a partnership could be prosecuted for violation of federal penal statutes that explicitly provided for the liability of such organizations. The issue in such a case is simply the search for legislative intent. On the same rationale, a partnership may be held criminally liable for its failure to perform some duty imposed by law on the partnership itself, rather than on the partners as individuals. Both of these situations are recognized in Model Penal Code Section 2.07(3), which provides that a partnership or other unincorporated association may be convicted of a criminal offense whenever "(a) the offense is defined by a statute . . . which expressly provides for the liability of such an association . . .; or (b) the offense consists of an omission to discharge a specific duty of affirmative performance imposed on associations by law."

The unsettled question is whether a partnership or other unincorporated association may be criminally responsible for the acts of its agents where a legislative purpose to impose such liability is not evident. The standard answer is "no." This conclusion is based on the traditional view that a partnership, unlike a corporation, has no independent existence as a legal entity apart from its partners. In some jurisdictions, however, partnerships have been allowed to sue and be sued in their own names. One may expect that jurisdictions that have moved toward treating partnerships as independent legal entities in civil litigation will take the analogous step of recognizing partnerships as independent legal entities for criminal liability as well. This conclusion seems especially likely for limited partnerships organized under the Uniform Limited Partnership Act, the general effect of which is to treat limited partnerships very much like corporations. In such a case there may be strong pressure to abandon the traditional rule against partnership liability and to assimilate at least some partnerships and unincorporated associations to corporations for purposes of the rules governing organizational criminal liability for the acts of an agent.

5. **Bibliography.** The subject of corporate criminal liability has drawn increasing scholarly attention. No attempt is made here to provide a comprehensive list of references, but a few sources may be cited for those who desire an introduction to the field.

Among the most useful sources is Kathleen F. Brickey's three-volume treatise on Corporate Criminal Liability, which has been previously cited. It is comprehensive and up-to-date and analyzes a broad range of subjects related to corporate criminal liability, including the major federal statutes in the field. Another good general source on the subject is Developments in the Law, Corporate Crime: Regulating Corporate Behavior through Criminal Sanctions, 92 Harv.L.Rev. 1227 (1979).

The question of appropriate sanctions for corporate criminality has elicited a considerable literature. Making the Punishment Fit the Crime: The Problem of Finding an Optimal Corporation Sanction, 1 N.Ill.U.L.Rev. 3 (1980), by John C. Coffee, Jr., has already been noted. For a more elaborate work by the same author, see "No Soul to Damn, No Body to Kick": An Unscandalized Inquiry into the Problem of Corporate Punishment, 79 Mich.L.Rev. 386 (1981). Responses to some of Professor Coffee's ideas may be found in Morris, Commentary: The Interplay Between Corporate Liability and the Liability of Corporate Officers, 1 N.Ill.U.L.Rev. 36 (1980), and Crane, Commentary: The Due Process Considerations of the Imposition of Corporate Liability, 1 N.Ill. U.L.Rev. 48 (1980).

Professor Coffee also participated in an interesting symposium on "White Collar Crime," published in the American Criminal Law Review. Among the notable articles in that volume are Judge Posner's article on Optimal Sentences for White-Collar Criminals, 17 Am.Crim. L.Rev. 409 (1980); Professor Coffee's response in Corporate Crime and Punishment: A Non-Chicago View of the Economics of Criminal Sanctions, 17 Am.Crim.L.Rev. 419 (1980); and Leonard Orland's thoughtful comments on overcriminalization of corporate behavior in Reflections on Corporate Crime: Law in Search of Theory and Scholarship, 17 Am. Crim.L.Rev. 501 (1980).

Finally, there is a growing literature on the somewhat specialized question of the intra-enterprise corporate conspiracy. Criminal conspiracy ordinarily requires a plurality of actors. Application of this doctrine to corporate misconduct raises a number of related questions, e.g., whether a corporate agent and the corporation itself constitute a plurality for purposes of criminal conspiracy, whether several agents for the same corporation meet that requirement, and whether related corporations can be held liable for conspiracy based on the acts of a single agent. Issues of this sort are thoughtfully analyzed by Sarah N. Welling in Intracorporate Plurality in Criminal Conspiracy Law, 33 Hastings L.J. 1155 (1982), and by Kathleen Brickey in Conspiracy, Group Danger and the Corporate Defendant, 52 Cin.L.Rev. 431 (1983).

NOTE ON INDIVIDUAL RESPONSIBILITY
FOR CORPORATE ACTS

The preceding materials focus on the liability of a corporation for the acts of its agents. A related question is whether the individual agent may also be punished. This issue has several aspects.

First, it is clear that an individual who personally engages in criminal misconduct cannot evade liability by acting through, or in the name of, a corporation. Thus, for example, there is no doubt that a corporate executive who falsifies a corporate tax return is personally guilty of a crime. The controlling principle is recognized explicitly in Section 2.07(6)(a) of the Model Penal Code:

"A person is legally accountable for any conduct he performs or causes to be performed in the name of the corporation or an unincorporated association or in its behalf to the same extent as if it were performed in his own name or behalf."

This common-sense proposition is not very controversial. It may be expected to be applied even where there is no statute on point.

A second proposition, also well settled, is that a corporate officer or director is not, simply by virtue of that status, criminally responsible for acts or omissions done by others on behalf of the corporation. The doctrine of respondeat superior, whatever its scope in fixing the liability of the corporation, ordinarily does not apply against individuals. At least in the absence of express legislative declaration, the liability of individuals for the conduct of another depends on generally applicable principles of complicity. For example, the corporate superior of one who falsifies a corporate tax return is not automatically liable therefor. Criminal responsibility of the supervisor would depend on proof that the supervisor knowingly or purposefully aided, commanded, or encouraged the criminal act of the subordinate. The organizational connection between the executive and the subordinate might well have evidentiary significance in establishing complicity, but it would not provide an independent basis for criminal conviction and punishment of an individual.

A third and somewhat special situation arises where a criminal statute imposes on the corporation as an entity, but not on corporate managers as individuals, an affirmative duty to act. Often such duties are imposed on the corporation in its capacity as taxpayer or licensee. Thus, for example, a corporation may incur criminal liability for failure to file a required report with government regulators. Typically, the individual executive whose responsibility it was to file the report has no legal duty to do so. Therefore, that individual cannot be held directly liable for the omission. It is possible that the executive could be prosecuted as an accomplice to the offense of the corporation, but this route is likely to encounter evidentiary obstacles. The courts may be unwilling to find the requisite aid or assistance in the executive's inaction. Moreover, the prosecution would have to prove that the executive "acted" with knowledge or purpose of promoting the offense by the corporation. Thus, where an affirmative legal duty is owed only by the corporation as an entity, there may be no way to punish personally the individual agent who is responsible for the corporate default. The Model Penal Code attempts to close this gap in coverage by a provision specifically addressed to this situation. Section 2.07(6)(b) states:

> "Whenever a duty to act is imposed by law upon a corporation or an unincorporated association, any agent of the corporation or association having primary responsibility for the discharge of the duty is legally accountable for a reckless omission to perform the required act to the same extent as if the duty were imposed by law directly upon himself."

The effect is to extend criminal liability for corporate defaults to the responsible individuals, but only on a showing of reckless omission.

The most difficult problem in this field arises when the statute imposing criminal liability for an omission is construed to apply directly to corporate agents as well as to the corporation itself. The effect is to obviate the need to resort to generally applicable principles of complicity in order to hold the agent liable for the corporate default. An excellent example is *United States* v. *Park,* reprinted at pages 295–304, supra. The Federal Food, Drug & Cosmetic Act authorizes criminal penalties for "[a]ny person" who does or causes to be done any act violative of its provisions. The particular "act" complained of in *Park* was the storage of food held for sale in a warehouse accessible to rodents. Although the statute purports to punish only affirmative acts, the real focus of the prosecution, as the *Park* Court clearly recognized, was the failure to take effective steps against rodent infestation. The Supreme Court took the view, in line with earlier precedents, that the corporation's chief executive officer was personally and directly liable for causing to be done the "act" proscribed by law. Of course, the proof that he personally caused the rat infestation consisted entirely of evidence that he failed to exercise his authority as chief executive officer to prevent that evil. By this construction, therefore, Mr. Park was held liable for failure to supervise. This comes very close indeed to the imposition of criminal liability on an individual solely by reason of his corporate office. The only limitation was the assertion by the Supreme Court that only those corporate agents with a "responsible relation" to the violation of law could be held personally liable therefor. For a consideration of the merits of this result, review *Park* and the accompanying materials on strict liability at pages 295–308, supra.

SECTION 4: CONSPIRACY

INTRODUCTORY NOTES ON THE LAW OF CONSPIRACY

1. **Background.** The law of conspiracy has at least four distinct functions. First, at common law an act which an individual might do with impunity could become a criminal conspiracy if two or more persons agreed to do it. Criminal conspiracy thus serves, or at least used to serve, to enlarge the scope of the penal law. Second, conspiracy is an inchoate offense punishing agreement in advance of action. In this respect, conspiracy is analogous to attempt. Third, conspiracy usually carries sanctions heavier than, or additional to, those that could be imposed for the same misconduct by an individual acting alone. Thus, conspiracy can function as a ground for aggravation of penalties. Finally, conspiracy is often a way of holding one person liable for the completed conduct of another. In this aspect, conspiracy serves as an alternative to complicity.

Each of these four functions of the law of conspiracy is dealt with fully in the materials that follow. Also covered are certain subsidiary matters having to do with the scope and duration of a conspiracy and the limitations imposed on prosecution for conspiracy by the definition of certain substantive offenses. Preliminarily, however, there are three procedural aspects to the law of conspiracy that must also be taken into account. They are developed in the following notes.

2. **The Co-Conspirator's Exception to the Hearsay Rule.** The hearsay rule is a limitation on the admissibility of evidence. It forbids a witness from testifying to the out-of-court statements of another person (the declarant) where such testimony is offered to prove the truth of those statements. The rationale is that the declarant should be required to take the stand and submit to cross-examination in order to provide a fair opportunity for the veracity of the statement to be tested. Thus, for example, if *A* hears *B* say "I saw *C* rob a bank," the hearsay rule would forbid *A* from repeating *B*'s statement in a robbery prosecution against *C.* The rule would insist that *B* take the stand so that *C*'s attorney would have the opportunity to probe the accuracy of *B*'s observation, memory, and sincerity through cross-examination.

The hearsay rule is riddled with exceptions. One is an admission by a party, as where *A* hears *B* say "I robbed a bank last week" and *A* is called to repeat the statement in the trial of *B*. A closely related, and perhaps derivative, exception is that for the declarations of co-conspirators. Under this rule, a statement against interest by one co-conspirator is admissible against all members of the conspiracy. Thus, if a conspiracy between *B* and *C* is established, *B*'s out-of-court statement that the two of them robbed a bank could be repeated in court by *A* and admitted against both *B* and *C*.[a]

The administration of the co-conspirator's exception is a matter of some difficulty. The premise for holding the statement of one person admissible against another is the conspiracy between them. It is necessary, therefore, that the existence of the conspiracy be established by some independent evidence before the hearsay becomes admissible against the co-conspirator. Ideally, the independent evidence should be offered before any hearsay is admitted, and many courts attempt to follow this practice. As a practical matter, however, complete segregation may be impossible. The resulting situation was aptly described by Mr. Justice Jackson in a famous essay on the law of conspiracy in his concurring opinion in Krulewitch v. United States, 336 U.S. 440, 453 (1949):

"When the trial starts, the accused feels the full impact of the conspiracy strategy. Strictly, the prosecution should first establish prima facie the conspiracy and identify the conspirators, after which evidence of acts and declarations of each in the course of its execution are admissible against all. But the order of proof of so sprawling a charge is difficult for a judge to control. As a practical matter, the accused often is confronted with a hodgepodge of acts and statements by others which he may never have authorized or intended or even known about, but which help to persuade the jury of existence of the conspiracy itself. In other words, a conspiracy often is proved by evidence that is admissible only upon assumption that conspiracy existed. The naive assumption that prejudicial effects can be overcome by instructions to the jury, all practicing lawyers know to be unmitigated fiction."

Although many courts have adopted procedures that avoid or mitigate this problem, the situation described by Justice Jackson is difficult to resolve in all cases and still poses perplexing problems in a conspiracy trial. For an extended discussion of the operation of the hearsay rule in conspiracy trials, see P. Marcus, The Prosecution and Defense of Criminal Conspiracy Cases, pp. 5–1 to –72 (1978), and the materials cited therein.

3. **Joint Trial.** Economy in the use of judicial resources may argue for joint trial whenever several defendants are to be prosecuted for crimes arising from the same series of events. In a conspiracy case

---

[a] A short account of the hearsay rule and the co-conspirator's exception appears in G. Lilly, An Introduction to the Law of Evidence 157–69, 204–06, 374–76 (1978). For a comprehensive analysis of the subject, see Mueller, The Federal Co-conspirator Exception: Action, Assertion, and Hearsay, 12 Hofstra L.Rev. 323 (1984).

the necessity of showing that the participants acted in concert creates an especially strong justification for proceeding against all conspirators at once.

From the defendant's point of view, joint trial may have several disadvantages. For one thing, the number of peremptory challenges to prospective jurors may have to be divided among the several co-defendants. Moreover, the practical value of an individual's right to counsel may be compromised. The lawyer who wishes to pursue an independent trial strategy may be hindered by the presence in the courtroom of other lawyers pursuing different and perhaps inconsistent lines of defense. Perhaps most important of all is the risk that an arguably innocent defendant who is tried together with patently guilty ones may be prejudiced by the forced association. Again, Mr. Justice Jackson made the point in *Krulewitch*:

> "A co-defendant in a conspiracy trial occupies an uneasy seat. There generally will be evidence of wrongdoing by somebody. It is difficult for the individual to make his own case stand on its own merits in the minds of jurors who are ready to believe that birds of a feather are flocked together. If he is silent, he is taken to admit it and if, as often happens, co-defendants can be prodded into accusing or contradicting each other, they convict each other."

4. **Venue.** Under both state and federal law, the possible locations for a criminal trial are limited by the requirements of venue. Normally, venue lies where the actus reus of the offense is alleged to have occurred. For conspiracy, however, venue lies not only where the agreement was concluded but also where any act in furtherance of the agreement was performed. In the words of Mr. Justice Jackson:

> "[T]he crime is considered so vagrant as to have been committed in any district where any one of the conspirators did any one of the acts, however innocent, intended to accomplish its object. The government may, and often does, compel one to defend at a great distance from any place he ever did any act because some accused confederate did some trivial and by itself innocent act in the chosen district."

5. **Pervasive Issues.** It is important to keep these procedural consequences in mind as you study the materials that follow. They often influence the resolution of substantive questions. Indeed, in some cases, the chief reason that an issue of conspiracy law is raised is that it has a procedural ramification of some practical importance. You should also reflect on the more general questions that pervade these materials—in particular, whether the variety of substantive and procedural issues comprehended by the law of conspiracy can sensibly be addressed through a unitary doctrine and whether any of the four distinct substantive functions of the law of conspiracy justifies the existence of the offense.

———

SUBSECTION A: THE OBJECTIVES THAT MAKE CONSPIRACY CRIMINAL

COMMONWEALTH v. DONOGHUE

Court of Appeals of Kentucky, 1933.
250 Ky. 343, 63 S.W.2d 3.

STANLEY, COMMISSIONER. The opinion deals with the sufficiency of an indictment charging the common-law offense of conspiracy, and relates to what are popularly referred to by the invidious and iniquitous term of "loan sharks." . . . We shall abridge the indictment by omitting terms and words usually regarded as essential to technical sufficiency. The instrument charges M. Donoghue, W. T. Day, and Vernon L. Buckman with the offense of criminal conspiracy, committed as follows: That they unlawfully and corruptly conspired with one another and others, to the grand jury unknown, "to engage in the business of lending money in small amounts to poor and necessitous wage earners at excessive, exorbitant and usurious rates of interest and to prevent the recovery of such interest paid by said borrowers"; that while the conspiracy existed and in pursuance and furtherance thereof they "operated a money-lending business under the trade name of Boone Loan Company, with its office in Kenton County, Kentucky"; that the accused or one or more of them, with the advice, consent, and acquiescence of the others, acting in concert and in furtherance of the conspiracy and in the operation of the business, did lend to hundreds of poor and necessitous wage-earners small sums of money in amounts ranging from $5 to $50, at high, excessive, exorbitant, illegal, and usurious rates of interest, to wit, from 240 to 360 per cent per annum. . . . Only Donoghue was before the court. The trial court sustained a demurrer to the indictment and dismissed it. The commonwealth has appealed. . . .

The comprehensiveness and indefiniteness of the offense of conspiracy has made an exact definition a very difficult one, as has been often stated. But the broad definition or description everywhere accepted is that conspiracy is a combination between two or more persons to do or accomplish a criminal or unlawful act, or to do a lawful act by criminal or unlawful means. . . .

According to the overwhelming weight of authority the objects of the conspiracy need not be an offense against the criminal law for which an individual could be indicted or convicted, but it is sufficient if the purpose be unlawful. . . . "The proper rule undoubtedly is that all such acts as have the necessary tendency to prejudice the public or to injure or oppress individuals by unjustly subjecting them to the power of the conspirators are sufficiently tainted with the quality of the unlawfulness to satisfy the requirements as to conspiracy." . . .

So it may be said that within the contemplation of the offense of criminal conspiracy are the acts which by reason of the combination have a tendency to injure the public, to violate public policy, or to injure, oppress, or wrongfully prejudice individuals collectively or the public generally. . . .

With this abstract understanding as to what may be the subject matter of a criminal conspiracy, we may direct our consideration to the subject of usurious demands and collections.

Now, the occupation of a usurer has been bitterly denounced in all ages of the civilized world, and in most Christian countries there have been laws to suppress it. The implications and inferences to be drawn from the indictment, coupled with general knowledge of the rapaciousness, the audacious and unconscionable practices of this class of usurious money lenders to be found in every city, suggest the application of the following extravagant phillipic of St. Basil, one of the most learned theologians and illustrious orators of the early Christian church . . . . [The opinion then quotes, in condemnation of usury, not only St. Basil, but also Lord Bacon, Chancellor Kent, and the Holy Bible.]

Time and space forbid further travel in this alluring path of general history. It suffices to say that the business of the usurer has always called for vigorous condemnation and has ever been regarded as against public welfare and public policy. . . .

Our current statutes merely declare that the portions of contracts calling for payment of interest in excess of six per cent are void, authorize the recovery of the excess, and require the lender in an action to avoid payment to bear the entire costs of the proceeding. No subterfuge, device, or trick will be permitted to avoid this law. While in a degree this penalizes the usurer, the statute is remedial and cannot be regarded as making the act a criminal offense.

Turning our attention again to the indictment now before us. It is *much more* than merely a charge that the accused conspired to collect usury. The accusation is a conspiracy to carry on the business of lending money in small amounts from $5 to $50, to poor and necessitous wage-earners at rates of interest ranging from 240 to 360 per cent per annum, and then to prevent the recovery of the usury paid by such borrowers. . . .

The indictment does not charge the accused with the mere exaction of usury, or of isolated instances of collecting slight excesses over the legal rate of interest. The objects of the conspiracy were not incidents to a legitimate business. If that were all, it might be doubted whether it could be regarded as an offense or an unlawful act within the meaning of that term in its relation to conspiracy. It charges *a nefarious plan for the habitual exaction of gross usury*, that is, in essence, the operation of the business of extortion. The import of the indictment is to charge systematic preying upon poor persons, of taking an unconscionable advantage of their needy conditions, of oppressing them, of extorting money from them through the disguise of interest, and, as an intrinsic part of the plan, to prevent restitution by obstructing public justice and the administration of the law. If ever there was a violation of public policy as reflected by the statutes and public conscience, or a combination opposed to the common weal, it is that sort of illegitimate business. It was extortioners of this class, called money changers, whom the Christ drove from the Temple on two occasions. . . .

The amicus curiae filing brief on the appellee's side submits that the common-law offense of conspiracy of the sort charged is so indefinite and uncertain that it should not be recognized by the court. He would assimilate the view to the attitude of the courts under which is held invalid statutory laws that are so indefinite and uncertain as to be incapable of rational understanding or enforcement. We think the better comparison or analogy is to look upon the offense and the law as fraud, deceit, cheating, and kindred wrongs are viewed. They are not capable of exact definition or delineation in the abstract, but when it comes to concrete considerations the courts have pretty well hammered the nebulous character of those wrongs into such shape as to make an offense recognizable. So, although in the abstract conspiracy of this sort must be loosely defined, an enlightened conscience should have no difficulty in recognizing a wrong as being embraced within its wide compass.

Measuring the indictment by the foregoing considerations, the court is of the opinion that it states a public offense.

Wherefore, the judgment is reversed.

CLAY, JUSTICE (dissenting). I am unable to concur in the majority opinion. However indefensible the exaction of usury may be, it is a matter that should be regulated by the legislature and not by the courts. Already the conspiracy doctrine has been worked overtime, and should not be extended unless plainly required. When a court on the theory of conspiracy declares an act to be a crime, which was not recognized as a crime at the time it was done, its decision savors strongly of an ex post facto law. Briefly stated a criminal conspiracy is a combination of two or more persons by concerted action to accomplish some criminal or unlawful purpose, or to accomplish some purpose not in itself criminal or unlawful, by criminal or unlawful means. Stripped of surplusage, the indictment alleges a conspiracy to charge usury . . . . At common law, as adopted in Kentucky, it was not a crime to charge usury, and it has never been made so by statute. Therefore, it was essential to a good indictment to allege that the defendants charged usury by criminal or unlawful means. That, of course, has reference to the method of obtaining the loan . . . . It was not alleged that the defendants, for the purpose of effecting the loans, resorted to force, threats, intimidation, or fraud. On the contrary, the case is one where the borrowers were not imposed upon in any way, but willingly and freely entered into the arrangement. In the circumstances, the indictment does not allege facts showing that the defendants resorted to unlawful means.

The necessity of protecting the public, and particularly the laboring man, is much stressed, but that alone will not authorize the court to hold an indictment good. Moreover, it is not perceived how prosecutions like the one in question may help the situation, as separate individuals may still continue the business of lending money at exorbitant rates without being subject to punishment.

The decision not only presents a strained application of the conspiracy doctrine, but its chief danger lies in the fact that for all time to come it will be the basis for the creation of new crimes never dreamed of by the people.

NOTES ON THE OBJECTIVES THAT MAKE CONSPIRACY CRIMINAL

1. **Rationale for the Common-Law Rule**. *Donoghue* states the common-law rule on the objectives that render conspiracy criminal. Under this view, two persons may be prosecuted and punished for agreeing to do an act that would not be criminal if done by either individually. What is the rationale for this position? Does it make sense that the criminality of given conduct should depend on the number of participants? Consider Mr. Justice Frankfurter's comment in Callanan v. United States, 364 U.S. 587, 593 (1961), on the special danger of group criminality:

> "[C]ollective criminal agreement—partnership in crime—presents a greater potential threat to the public than individual delicts. Concerted action both increases the likelihood that the criminal object will be successfully attained and decreases the probability that the individuals involved will depart from their path of criminality. Group association for criminal purposes often, if not normally, makes possible the attainment of ends more complex than those which one criminal could accomplish. Nor is the danger of a conspiratorial group limited to the particular end toward which it embarked. Combination in crime makes more likely the commission of crimes unrelated to the original purpose for which the group was formed. In sum, the danger which a conspiracy generates is not confined to the substantive offense which is the immediate aim of the enterprise."

In context, this reasoning was advanced to support cumulative punishment for conspiracy and for the completed offense that was its object. Does the same rationale or some extension of it also apply where the object of the agreement is not itself a crime? Are there, as the *Donoghue* court declared, "acts *which by reason of the combination* have a tendency to injure the public," etc.? Or does the rationale for punishing conspiracy as an offense extend only to combinations dedicated to acts that would be punished if done by an individual?

2. **The Principle of Legality**. According to *Donoghue*, the objectives of criminal conspiracy include acts having a tendency "to injure the public, to violate public policy, or to injure, oppress, or wrongfully prejudice individuals collectively or the public generally." As another court phrased it, conspiracy is a crime "if the acts contemplated are corrupt, dishonest, fraudulent, or immoral, and in that sense illegal." State v. Kemp, 126 Conn. 60, 78, 9 A.2d 63, 72 (1939). Presumably, it

falls to the judges to say what these standards mean. Is such authority consistent with the principle of legality? Is there reason to regard judicial declaration of the objectives that make conspiracy a crime any differently from judicial crime creation for individual misconduct? Recall the cases with which this book began. *Rex* v. *Manley* involved the misdemeanor of effecting a public mischief. *Shaw* v. *D. P. P.* concerned a *conspiracy* to corrupt public morals. Does the fact of combination or agreement differentiate the two cases? Or do the concerns of the legality concept apply equally to each?

In this country the legality ideal is made operational chiefly through the constitutional vagueness doctrine. In this connection, consider the California conspiracy law, Cal. Penal Code § 182. It punishes two or more persons who conspire:

"1. To commit any crime.

"2. Falsely and maliciously to indict another for any crime, or to procure another to be charged or arrested for any crime.

"3. Falsely to move or maintain any suit, action or proceeding.

"4. To cheat and defraud any person of any property, by any means which are in themselves criminal, or to obtain money or property by false pretenses or by false promises with fraudulent intent not to perform such promises.

"5. To commit any act injurious to the public health, to public morals, or to pervert or obstruct justice, or the due administration of the laws.

"6. To commit any crime against the person of the President or Vice President of the United States, the governor of any state or territory, any United States justice or judge, or the secretary of any of the executive departments of the United States. . . ."

Obviously, Subdivision 5 of this provision codifies in slightly different language the common-law rule reflected in *Donoghue*. Is this provision constitutional? Would conviction under this law be permissible under the vagueness doctrine?

The Supreme Court of the United States had occasion to consider this question in Musser v. Utah, 333 U.S. 95 (1948). That case involved a vagueness challenge to the Utah version of Subdivision 5 of the California statute. Specifically, an agreement to advise and practice polygamy had been found to constitute a conspiracy "to commit [an] act injurious . . . to public morals" under the Utah law. The Supreme Court noted that, standing by itself, this provision "would seem to be warrant for conviction for agreement to do almost any act which a judge and jury might find at the moment contrary to his or its notions of what was good for health, morals, trade, commerce, justice or order." The Court also found, however, that the issue had not been adequately presented to the courts below and remanded for reconsideration. On remand, the Supreme Court of Utah held that the provision in question was not susceptible to any narrowing construction and was therefore void for vagueness. State v. Musser, 118 Utah 537, 223 P.2d 193 (1950). The same conclusion was reached with respect to the analogous Arizona provision in State v. Bowling, 5 Ariz.App. 436, 427 P.2d 928 (1967). The United States Supreme Court has not had a subsequent occasion to address the issue.

3. **Conspiracy to Defraud the United States.** At least partially for fear of constitutional infirmity, criminal conspiracy today is invoked only rarely against combinations aimed at non-criminal objectives. The older tradition of treating conspiracy as an independent basis for declaring acts criminal can still be seen, however, in federal law. The general conspiracy statute, 18 U.S.C.A. § 371, punishes two or more persons who conspire "either to commit any offense against the United States, or to defraud the United States, or any agency thereof in any manner or for any purpose." Since there is no general substantive offense against defrauding the United States, concerted action to obtain that objective may be punished as criminal, even where parallel conduct by an individual acting alone would be no crime.

Moreover, the conspiracy-to-defraud provision has been given an expansive construction strongly reminiscent of the common-law approach to defining the objectives of criminal conspiracy. Because "defraud the United States" first appeared in a conspiracy statute dealing primarily with taxation, its meaning was originally confined to tax fraud. Early on, however, the Supreme Court abandoned this limitation, and in Haas v. Henkel, 216 U.S. 462 (1910), the Court held that conspiracy to defraud the United States need not induce or contemplate any pecuniary loss to the government. The facts of that case involved cotton speculators who bribed a Department of Agriculture employee in order to receive pre-publication reports of the state of the cotton crop. This information was used to make money in the futures market, with no resulting loss to the government. The Supreme Court nevertheless upheld an indictment charging conspiracy to defraud the United States on the ground that the scheme would impair the government's function of "promulgating fair, impartial and accurate reports concerning the cotton crop." It was not necessary, said the Court, that the United States should suffer loss. Instead, it sufficed that the conspiracy was "for the purpose of impairing, or obstructing, or defeating the lawful function of any department of government."

This expansive interpretation was reiterated some years later in Hammerschmidt v. United States, 265 U.S. 182, 188 (1924), where the Court said:

> "To conspire to defraud the United States means primarily to cheat the government out of property or money, but it also means to interfere with or obstruct one of its lawful governmental functions by deceit, craft, trickery, or at least by means that are dishonest. It is not necessary that the government shall be subjected to property or pecuniary loss by the fraud, but only that its legitimate official action and purpose shall be defeated by misrepresentation, chicane or the over-reaching of those charged with carrying out the governmental intention."

Prosecutors have exploited the liberality of this formulation to reach a wide variety of interference with governmental functions. Thus, for example, Section 371 has been invoked successfully against federal prosecutors who solicited bribes for refusing to proceed in liquor cases; against persons who arranged sham marriages with aliens in order to avoid immigration quotas; against savings-and-loan officials who sought to use illicit influence in order to avoid pending indictments; against corporate officers for conspiring to obstruct the collection of revenue through false and inconsistent statements; against county-council members who sought kickbacks from the architect of a federally financed project; against labor-union officials who falsely denied Communist affiliation in affidavits before the National Labor Relations Board; against persons who tried to sell gold in quantities greater than those permitted by government regulations; against one person who impersonated another in a civil service examination in order to enable the other to qualify as a letter carrier; and, finally, in United States v. Haldeman, 559 F.2d 31 (D.C.Cir. 1976), against various government officials for using deceit, craft, and trickery to interfere with the lawful functions of the F.B.I., the C.I.A., and the Department of Justice.[a] No doubt most of these activities could have been prosecuted successfully under more narrowly drawn substantive provisions of federal law. Nevertheless, the frequent resort to the general conspiracy statute suggests something about the utility to prosecutors of the traditionally open-ended approach to the objectives that make conspiracy a crime.

As construed by the courts, the provision against conspiracy to defraud the United States has been subject to criticism on at least two grounds. First, no reason appears why the criminality of such conduct should be made to depend on the participation of two or more actors. Second, the elasticity of the offense has given rise to fears of inadequate notice to potential offenders and of unconstrained discretion in law enforcement. The National Commission on Reform of Federal Criminal Laws (also known as the Brown Commission) proposed to meet both criticisms by eliminating defrauding the United States from the general conspiracy statute. This change would conform the scope of criminal conspiracy to the law applicable to individuals and would require federal prosecutors to proceed through more narrowly drawn substantive offenses. Subsequent versions of the proposed federal criminal code, however, have not followed this lead. Instead, they delete defrauding the United States from the general conspiracy provision but make it the basis for a new substantive offense. A recent version of the bill, S. 1722, 96th Cong., 2d Sess., § 1031 (1980), proposes a new generic offense of obstructing a government function by fraud. The substantive portion of this provision reads as follows:

"A person is guilty of an offense if he intentionally obstructs or impairs a government function by defrauding the government

---

[a] These examples are taken from the Senate Judiciary Committee Report on the Criminal Code Reform Act of 1979, S. 1722, 96th Cong., 2d Session, pp. 272–75 (1980). A comprehensive treatment of the history of this provision is available in Goldstein, Conspiracy to Defraud the United States, 68 Yale L.J. 405 (1959).

through misrepresentation, chicanery, trickery, deceit, craft, overreaching, or other dishonest means."

The obvious intention is to resolve the disparity between conspiracy and individual offenses, but at the same time to perpetuate and endorse the body of precedent described above. Do you approve of this solution? Do you think it successfully answers the criticisms directed against the present Section 371?

4. **Modern State Statutes**. Revised state penal codes are virtually unanimous in curtailing the traditional reach of the law of conspiracy. They follow Section 5.03 of the Model Penal Code in expressly limiting the objectives that make combination criminal to acts that are in themselves criminal offenses. Under this approach, the scope of criminal conspiracy is determined solely by the content of the penal law and not by reference to other legal obligations or to concepts of public policy or morals. Except, therefore, for the unusual case where the underlying substantive offense requires more than one participant (e. g., riot), the reach of the criminal law is the same for both group and individual misconduct.

5. **The *Powell* Doctrine**. As has been noted, the common law regarded an intention to achieve a corrupt or immoral, though not criminal, objective as sufficient for the crime of conspiracy. An apparent offspring of this approach is the view that a corrupt motive is not only sufficient, but is also necessary, for liability for conspiracy. This is called the "corrupt motive" or *Powell* doctrine, after People v. Powell, 63 N.Y. 88 (1875). In that case, defendants were charged with conspiracy to violate a law requiring municipal officers to advertise for bids before letting contracts. The defendants were excused on the ground that they were honestly ignorant of the existence of the statute in question. The court reasoned that a requirement of corrupt motive was implicit in the word "conspiracy" and that no such motive could be shown where the object offense was not in itself immoral and the actors were not aware of the legal prohibition. Some version of this doctrine was once the law in most American jurisdictions, although the modern trend is towards its abandonment.

The curious thing is that the *Powell* doctrine carries no implication that ignorance of the law will excuse the completed substantive offense. On the contrary, the defense plainly applies only to conspiracy. Does this make sense? Are there reasons why ignorance of the law should preclude conviction for a charge of conspiracy, even where it would not excuse the completed object offense?

———

SUBSECTION B: CONSPIRACY AS AN INCHOATE OFFENSE

PEOPLE v. BURLESON

Appellate Court of Illinois, Fourth District, 1977.
50 Ill.App.3d 629, 8 Ill.Dec. 776, 365 N.E.2d 1162.

REARDON, JUSTICE. The defendant, Charles Edward Burleson, was charged in a two-count information filed December 8, 1975, with conspiracy to commit armed robbery and attempt[ed] armed robbery, violations of Sections 8–2(a) and 8–4(a) of the Criminal Code of 1961. The two offenses were alleged to have occurred on September 16, 1975. On April 21, 1976, a third count was added to the information charging the defendant with participating in a second conspiracy to commit armed robbery on September 13, 1975, another violation of Section 8–2(a) of the Code.

After being tried before a Logan County jury, the defendant was found guilty on all three counts contained in the information and judgments were entered on the three verdicts. . . . [T]he defendant was sentenced to a one- to five-year sentence for the attempt of September 16, 1975, to run concurrently with a one- to three-year sentence for the conspiracy of September 13, 1975.

The facts pertinent to this appeal are reflected in the trial testimony of defendant's alleged co-conspirator, Bruce Brown. Brown testified that he and the defendant agreed to rob the Middletown State Bank. Pursuant to that agreement, the two "cased" the bank on September 11, 1975. They decided to use two cars in the robbery. One would be left on a rural road near Middletown with a change of clothing for each conspirator. From that location, the two would proceed to the bank wearing nylon stockings and stocking caps over their heads. The defendant agreed to secure a shotgun for use in the robbery and Brown agreed to secure the disguises and a container for the money they expected to remove from the bank. They also decided to commit the crime on Saturday, September 13, 1975.

On September 13, 1975, the conspirators initiated their plan, but decided not to rob the bank on that day because they noticed too many people in town and around the bank. Instead, they made a practice run of their approach to and escape from the bank after agreeing that they would try again on Tuesday, September 16, 1975.

On September 16, 1975, the defendant and Brown again parked their cars along a rural road, changed clothing and drove into the town of Middletown in a single car with a white suitcase, shotgun and disguises consisting of the nylon stockings and stocking caps. When they arrived in town, they drove to the Middletown State Bank, exited from the car and approached the bank's front door. Brown carried the suitcase and the defendant carried the shotgun. As the duo neared the front door, however, a man bolted the door from the inside. Thereafter, the defendant and Brown scrambled back into the car and returned to their second car which was still parked along the rural road where they had commenced their escapade. Within minutes, Brown was arrested after being chased by the police. The defendant was arrested a few days later.

On appeal, the defendant raises a single issue for our review: whether his conviction for the September 13, 1975, conspiracy to commit armed robbery should be vacated because the alleged conspiracy arose from the same course of conduct that formed the basis for his attempt[ed] armed-robbery conviction.

Section 8–2(a) of the Criminal Code of 1961 provides in pertinent part:

"A person commits conspiracy when, with intent that an offense be committed, he *agrees* with another to the commission of that offense. No person may be convicted of conspiracy to commit an offense unless an *act in furtherance* of such agreement is alleged and proved to have been committed by him or by a co-conspirator." (Emphasis added.) [a]

Section 8–4(a) of the Code provides:

"A person commits an attempt when, with intent to commit a specific offense, he does any act which constitutes a substantial step toward the commission of that offense." [b]

Both of the quoted sections are contained in that part of the code which concerns inchoate or anticipatory offenses. Another of those sections, Section 8–5 of the Code provides that "[n]o person shall be convicted of both the inchoate and the principal offense."

In Illinois, in order for a defendant to be convicted for the offense of conspiracy, the state must establish three elements beyond a reasonable doubt: (i) that the defendant intended to commit an offense; (ii) that the defendant and another person entered into an agreement to commit the offense; and (iii) that one of the co-conspirators committed an act in furtherance of the agreement. In order for a defendant to be convicted for the offense of attempt, the state must only establish two elements beyond a reasonable doubt: (i) that the defendant intended to commit an offense; and (ii) that the defendant took a "substantial step" toward committing that offense. In comparing these two sections of our Criminal Code, we note that the conspiracy provision requires a lesser step to fulfill the act requirement, while the attempt provision requires a "substantial step" toward the commission of the offense. In each situation, as in situations involving other inchoate offenses, the law makes possible some preventive action by the police and courts before a defendant has come dangerously close to committing the intended crime.

Although Section 8–4(a) does not define "substantial step," Illinois courts have attempted to make the term more precise. [The discussion

[a] The maximum term for conspiracy to commit armed robbery was imprisonment for three years. [Footnote by eds.]

[b] The maximum term for attempt to commit armed robbery was imprisonment for five years. [Footnote by eds.]

of Illinois precedents on the distinction between preparation and attempt has been omitted.]

Analysis of these cases would seemingly lead one to suspect that the "substantial step" requirement, in order to amount to more than mere preparation, requires some sort of entry into an enclosure or structure for the purpose of committing a crime. We note, however, that Section 5.01(2) of the Model Penal Code contains a list of behavior constituting a "substantial step" which is strongly corroborative of the actor's criminal purpose. Noted on that list is:

"possession . . . of materials to be employed in the commission of the crime, at or near the place contemplated for its commission, where such possession . . . serves no lawful purpose of the actor under the circumstances."

Here, the defendant and Brown did not enter the bank building on September 16, 1975, although they were in possession of a shotgun, suitcase and disguises which were in place when they approached the bank building. We find these acts sufficient to constitute a "substantial step" toward the commission of an armed robbery in the bank.

In this case, the defendant was also charged with membership in two conspiracies having as their objects the armed robbery of the Middletown State Bank on two separate dates, September 13 and 16, 1975. . . .

Although other courts have [held] that an agreement to violate the same or different statutes on different occasions constitutes a single conspiracy [citing cases], we distinguish those decisions on the ground that the instant defendant entered two separate conspiracies, each of which was composed of the three elements set forth in Section 8–2(a) of the Criminal Code of 1961. On September 11, 1975 the defendant and Brown, having the necessary intent, agreed to rob the bank on September 13, 1975. In furtherance of this agreement, they committed the overt acts of "casing" the bank, procuring a weapon and disguises, and going to the bank on September 13, 1975, to commit the crime. This first conspiracy was abandoned when the conspirators observed a large number of persons in and around the bank. Thereafter, the same conspirators, with the necessary intent, agreed to rob the bank on September 16, 1975, after which they committed the overt acts of preserving the disguises, participating in a practice escape from the bank and in approaching the bank on September 16, 1975. The latter act also constituted the "substantial step" necessary to establish the offense of attempt[ed] armed robbery, of which the second conspiracy was a lesser included offense. . . .

We, therefore, hold that a person charged with multiple conspiracies cannot be convicted of more than a single conspiracy if he has with the necessary intent entered into a single agreement to commit a crime even if multiple overt acts are committed in furtherance of that agreement. We further hold, however, that a person charged with multiple conspiracies can be convicted of those multiple conspiracies if, with the necessary intent, he entered into multiple, although partially overlapping agreements to commit crimes so long as overt acts are

committed in furtherance of those agreements. It is this latter situation that is presented in the instant case.

As previously noted, Section 8–5 of the Code prohibits a defendant's
conviction for an inchoate offense and the principal offense. Here,
however, the defendant has been convicted for two inchoate offenses
and not for a principal offense. Recently, our supreme court stated
that when more than one offense arises from a single series of closely
related acts and when the offenses, by definition, are not lesser included offenses, convictions [for both offenses] may be entered. Lesser
included offenses are defined in Section 2–9 of the Code as an offense
which:

> "(a) Is established by proof of *the same or less than all of the
> facts* or a less culpable mental state (or both), than that which is
> required to establish the commission of the offense charged, or (b)
> Consists of an attempt to commit the offense charged or an
> offense included therein." (Emphasis added.)

Here, as already mentioned, the inchoate offenses of attempt and
conspiracy require some act for criminal liability to attach to the actor.
For an attempt to be committed, "a substantial step" in furtherance of
the criminal objective must occur. For a conspiracy to exist, some act
amounting to at least a lesser step is required. In the instant case,
however, the state has not relied on the same conduct of the defendant
to establish the conspiracy to rob the bank on September 13, 1975, and
the attempt to rob which was committed on September 16, 1975. We
do not view the conspirators' actions in terms of a single course of
conduct. Rather, the conspirators' actions originate in separate agreements or impulses to rob the bank on separate dates. With their
attempt to rob the bank on September 13, 1975, the conspirator's first
agreement to rob the bank came to an end. The attempt of September
16, 1975, was not the result of the original agreement, but of a fresh
agreement which was entered into after the attempt of September 13,
1975. Since we have held that the aforementioned offenses arise from
separate courses of conduct, we, accordingly, affirm the defendant's
convictions for the conspiracy of September 13, 1975, and for the
attempted armed robbery of September 16, 1975. In addition, we
reverse defendant's conviction for the conspiracy of September 16, 1975,
because it is a lesser included offense of attempt. . . .

Affirmed in part. Reversed in part.

NOTES ON CONSPIRACY AS AN INCHOATE OFFENSE

1. **Introduction.** The specific focus of the *Burleson* decision is the
number of offenses: Was there one conspiracy or two? Ultimately, this
is a question of the scope and duration of a conspiracy. These issues
are covered at pages 480–500, infra. For the moment, it is sufficient to
treat *Burleson* as a useful context for general consideration of conspiracy as an inchoate offense.

As *Burleson* illustrates, one of the principal functions of the law of conspiracy is to fix criminal liability for anticipatory or inchoate behavior. In this respect, conspiracy supplements attempt. Analytically, at least, the two offenses are closely parallel. Both confront the same range of problems in assigning criminal liability for uncompleted conduct. The best way to study conspiracy as an inchoate offense is, therefore, to contrast it with the law of attempt. In what ways does conspiracy differ from attempt, and are those differences justified? Does the inchoate offense of conspiracy provide a needed adjunct to the law of attempt, or does it produce unwarranted extensions of penal liability? These and other questions are considered in the following notes.

2. **Actus Reus: The Necessity of Agreement**. The traditional definition of conspiracy is an agreement between two or more persons to do an unlawful act or to do a lawful act by unlawful means. Modern formulations, typified by the Illinois statute quoted in *Burleson*, restrict the offense to agreement to do an act which is itself a crime. In either event, the objective need not be achieved for the offense to be made out; it is the agreement itself which is the essence of conspiracy.

At common law, no additional conduct was needed. Many statutes, however, also require that there be an overt act in furtherance of the conspiracy. Under the prevailing view, an act done by any one of the conspirators suffices for all. This requirement is imposed by the general federal conspiracy statute, 18 U.S.C.A. § 371,[a] and by many of the recently revised state penal codes.[b] The significance of the overt-act requirement, however, may well be doubted. Unlike attempt, the law of conspiracy has never elaborated doctrinal tests to determine what kind of act suffices. Instead, the courts have held that virtually any act committed by a conspirator in furtherance of the conspiracy will do. The result is that the independent requirement of an overt act, even where imposed, tends not to be very important. The actus reus of the offense is essentially the act of agreement.

The necessity of proving agreement raises questions both evidentiary and substantive. On the evidentiary side, it is clear that direct proof of criminal agreement is rarely to be had. As is often noted, "[a] conspiracy is seldom born of 'open covenants openly arrived at.'" Instead, the fact of agreement usually must be inferred from circumstantial evidence. Moreover, as a substantive matter, the agreement need never have been made express; a tacit, mutual understanding is enough. The upshot is that conspiracy requires agreement, but the agreement may be highly informal and its existence may be inferred without direct proof.

a Note, however, that other federal conspiracy statutes do not require an overt act. See, e. g., the general narcotics provision, 21 U.S.C.A. § 846, which bases liability for conspiracy exclusively on agreement.

b Note also the somewhat curious position advanced in Section 5.03(5) of the Model Penal Code. This provision requires proof of an overt act for conspiracy to commit lesser crimes but allows the agreement standing alone to suffice for conspiracy to commit a felony of the first or second degree. This approach has not been widely followed.

The danger here is that a rule of evidence may subsume a rule of law. The risk, in other words, is that the unavoidable reliance on circumstantial evidence may lead the trier of fact to find agreement where in reality there was nothing more than concurrent conduct. This issue typically arises as a question of the sufficiency of the evidence, and since that inquiry is inherently fact-specific, generalization on the subject is especially difficult. Certainly many appellate courts are at pains to require substantial evidence of an actual agreement—"an agreement understood by the defendant, to which the defendant was a party, and to which he meant to be a party." But many defense attorneys nevertheless believe that the substantive necessity of agreement may be lost sight of amidst a welter of evidence that a defendant was somehow involved in criminal activity. For a general discussion of this problem and comments on its practical implications, see Marcus, Conspiracy: The Criminal Agreement in Theory and in Practice, 65 Geo.L.J. 925, 952–57 (1977).

3. **Actus Reus: The Sufficiency of Agreement**. By focusing on agreement, the law of conspiracy allows intervention and punishment at a very early stage in a course of conduct designed to culminate in commission of a crime. Indeed, perhaps the chief justification for the offense of conspiracy is that it punishes some instances of inchoate misconduct that could not be reached under the law of attempt. The question therefore arises: Is the act of agreeing to commit a crime, standing alone or in connection with an overt act in furtherance of the agreement, a sufficient basis in conduct to support penal liability? Are the underlying concerns of the act requirement adequately protected by this rule?

Perhaps the best defense of agreement as a sufficient basis for criminal punishment was offered by the drafters of the Model Penal Code: *

> "The act of agreeing with another to commit a crime, like the act of soliciting, is concrete and unambiguous; it does not present the infinite degrees and variations possible in the general category of attempts. The danger that truly equivocal behavior may be misinterpreted as preparation to commit a crime is minimized; purpose must be relatively firm before the commitment involved in agreement is assumed. . . .

> "In the course of preparation to commit a crime, the act of combining with another is significant both psychologically and practically, the former since it crosses a clear threshold in arousing expectations, the latter since it increases the likelihood that the offense will be committed. Sharing lends fortitude to purpose. The actor knows, moreover, that the future is no longer governed by his will alone; others may complete what he has had a hand in starting, even if he has a change of heart."

ALI, Model Penal Code § 5.03, Comment at 97 (Tent. Draft No. 10, 1960).

This position is criticized in Johnson, The Unnecessary Crime of Conspiracy, 61 Calif.L.Rev. 1137, 1161–64 (1973).** In Professor Johnson's view, reliance on conspiracy to reach very preliminary conduct made sense when the crime of attempt was limited by strict notions of proximity. According to Johnson, however, the justification for an independent inchoate offense of conspiracy has been substantially vitiated by the modern reformulation of attempt to focus on dangerousness of the actor rather than the proximity of his conduct to the completed offense. Johnson describes the Model Penal Code approach to attempt and examines its relevance to the law of conspiracy as follows:

"Pursued to its logical conclusion, the modern approach [to distinguishing preparation from attempt] would permit the conviction of anyone shown to have had a firm intention to commit a crime, whether or not he had taken any steps towards its commission. The limiting factor, however, is our reluctance to put so much trust in either the omniscience or benevolence of those who administer the law. It is difficult to determine what someone intends to do before he does it, or at least prepares to do it. Even when an individual has plainly said what he intends to do, there remains the question of how serious or definite his intent is. . . .

"For this reason the modern codes retain the requirement that a defendant go beyond merely planning or contemplating a crime before he can be convicted of an attempt. He must engage in conduct that is a sufficiently substantial step towards completion of the crime to indicate his firm criminal intent, and to identify him as a dangerous individual who would probably have gone on to complete the crime if his design had not been frustrated. . . .

"Under the conspiracy sections of the Model Penal Code and proposed Federal Criminal Code, however, the act of agreement *is* the forbidden conduct whether or not it strongly corroborates the existence of a criminal purpose. In justifying this per se rule, the Model Penal Code commentary relied heavily on the argument . . . that the act of agreeing is so decisive and concrete a step towards the commission of a crime that it ought always to be regarded as a 'substantial step.' Whether this point is sense or nonsense depends upon how restrictively one defines the term 'agreement.' Hiring a professional killer to commit murder is an agreement, and surely few would doubt that it is a substantial step toward accomplishing the killing. But the language of the conspiracy sections of both the Model Penal Code and the proposed Federal Criminal Code is broad enough to reach conduct far less dangerous or deserving of punishment than letting a contract for murder. As the Model Penal Code commentary concedes, one may be liable for agreeing with another that *he* should commit a particular crime, although this agreement might be insufficient to establish complicity in the completed offense.   Furthermore, neither code would change the well-established rule that the agreement may be tacit or implied as well as as express, and that it may be proved by circumstantial evidence.   In short, the term 'agreement' may connote anything from firm commitment to engage in criminal activity oneself to reluctant approval of a criminal plot to be carried out entirely by others.   To be sure, the Model Penal Code also requires that one enter into the agreement with the purpose of promoting or facilitating the crime, but the existence of that purpose need not be substantiated by any conduct beyond the express or implied agreement and performance in some cases of a single overt act by any party to it.   .   .   .

"In summary, insofar as conspiracy adds anything to the attempt provisions of the reform codes under discussion, it adds only overly broad criminal liability.   .   .   .   [The use of an independent crime of conspiracy to punish inchoate crimes turns out to be unnecessary.   .   .   ."

Who do you think has the better side of this debate?   Does punishment of conspiracy as an inchoate offense lead to unwarranted extensions of penal liability, or are you persuaded that the act of agreeing with another is sufficiently informative to support the imposition of penal sanctions?

Although Professor Johnson's suggestion is simply to eliminate conspiracy as an inchoate offense, an alternative response to the same concern is to elaborate the conduct required for that offense.   A few American jurisdictions have supplemented the requirement of an overt act in conspiracy by analogizing to the law of attempt.   In Maine, Ohio, and Washington, conspiracy statutes explicitly require a "substantial step" in furtherance of the conspiracy.[c]   The Maine provision goes on to define "substantial step" in terms strongly reminiscent of the Model Penal Code standard for distinguishing preparation from attempt.   Under Maine law, there must be "conduct which, under the circumstances in which it occurs, is strongly corroborative of the firmness of the actor's intent to complete commission of the crime."   Do you think this improves the traditional formulation of the law of conspiracy, or is it merely an unnecessary complication?   Might this formulation bar conviction for conspiracy even in circumstances where the agreement itself is sufficiently corroborative of a dedicated intention to complete the crime?   Or should a "substantial step" in addition to agreement be required in every case?   Would the addition of a "substantial step" requirement make the crime of conspiracy entirely duplicative of attempt?   What independent function would conspiracy then serve?

For a useful discussion of these issues, see Note, Conspiracy: Statutory Reform Since the Model Penal Code, 75 Colum.L.Rev. 1122, 1153–

[c] Me.Rev.Stat.Ann.   § 151(4);   Ohio Rev.Code § 2923.01;   Rev.Code Wash.Ann. § 9A.28.040.

58 (1975), and Note, Developments in the Law: Criminal Conspiracy, 72 Harv.L.Rev. 920, 925–27 (1959).

4. **Actus Reus: Bilateral or Unilateral Agreement**. The definition of conspiracy as an agreement between two or more persons has given rise to a requirement of bilateralism. As the court explained in Regle v. Maryland, 9 Md.App. 346, 351, 264 A.2d 119, 122 (1970), "it must be shown that at least two persons had a meeting of the minds—a unity of design and purpose—to have an agreement."

The facts of that case reveal an interesting application of the traditional approach. The defendant invited a total of three other persons to participate in an armed robbery. One person was a police informer, and another an undercover agent, both of whom feigned the intention to go through with the crime. The four men planned the event, obtained a weapon, and drove to the scene of the intended robbery. At that point the undercover officer intervened and arrested the others. Of course, neither the undercover agent nor his informant could be charged with the crime. That left only the defendant and the fourth participant, a man named Fields. At his trial for conspiracy to commit armed robbery, the defendant showed that Fields had been insane at the time of the agreement. Therefore, said the court, the defendant could not be guilty of conspiracy:

> "By its nature, conspiracy is a joint or group offense requiring a concert of free wills, and the union of the minds of at least two persons is a prerequisite to the commission of the offense. The essence of conspiracy is, therefore, a mental confederation involving at least two persons . . .. [W]e hold that where only two persons are implicated in a conspiracy, and one is shown to have been insane at the time the agreement was concluded, and hence totally incapable of committing any crime, there is no punishable criminal conspiracy, the requisite joint criminal intent being absent."

Other courts take a different view. Among the best known explications of the so-called unilateral approach to the agreement of conspiracy is State v. St. Christopher, 305 Minn. 226, 232 N.W.2d 798 (1975), where the facts were as follows:

> "On March 16, 1974, defendant (who formerly was named Martin Peter Olson but legally changed his name to Daniel St. Christopher) stated to his cousin, Roger Zobel, that he wanted to kill his mother, Mrs. Marlin Olson, and that he wanted Zobel's help. He would pay him $125,000 over the years, money defendant would get from his father after his mother was dead. Zobel, the key witness against defendant at his trial on the charge of conspiracy, testified that at no time did he ever intend to participate in the murder but that he discussed the matter with defendant on that and subsequent occasions and acted as if he intended to participate in the plan. On March 18, Zobel contacted the police and told them of defendant's plan and they later told him to continue to cooperate with defendant. The plan, which became definite in some detail as early as March 20, was

for Zobel to go to the Olson farmhouse on Saturday, March 23, when defendant's father was at the weekly livestock auction. Since defendant's mother was Zobel's aunt, Zobel could gain entrance readily. The idea was for Zobel to break her neck, hide her body in his automobile trunk, and then attach bricks to it and throw it in a nearby river after dark. Later it developed that defendant's father might not go to the sale on Saturday, so a plan was developed whereby defendant would feign car trouble, call his father for help, then signal Zobel when the father was on his way. Police followed defendant on Saturday when he left his apartment and observed him make a number of telephone calls. In one of these he called his father and told him he was having car trouble and asked him to come and help him pay the bill. In a call to Zobel, which was taped, defendant told Zobel that his father was coming and that Zobel should proceed with the plan. Shortly thereafter, police arrested defendant."

In his subsequent prosecution for conspiracy to commit murder, the defendant contended that no conspiracy could be found where the only other party to the scheme had only feigned agreement. The court rejected that claim and construed the Minnesota law to punish one who conspires with another without regard to the other's actual state of mind. In the course of its opinion, the court surveyed the objections to the traditional rule:

"One criticism by a number of commentators of the rule followed in the cited cases is that the courts have reached their conclusion by using as a starting point the definition of conspiracy as an agreement between two or more persons, a definition which was framed in cases not involving the issue. As one commentator put if, 'if a conspiracy is arbitrarily defined as "an agreement of intentions and not merely of language (the intentions being unlawful)" the answer to the problem is undoubtedly that where there is no such agreement of intentions then there is no conspiracy.' Fridman, Mens Rea in Conspiracy, 19 Mod.L.Rev. 276, 278 (1956). In other words, the basis for the rule is a strict doctrinal approach toward the conception of conspiracy as an agreement in which two or more parties not only objectively indicate their agreement but actually have a meeting of the minds.

"Addressing the rule to be applied as a policy issue, a number of commentators have come to the conclusion that there should be no requirement of a meeting of the minds. Thus, Fridman points to cases holding that factual impossibility is no defense to a charge of attempt to commit a crime and argues that, because of close connections between the origins and purposes of the law of conspiracy and of attempt, a similar rule should obtain in conspiracy. Specifically, he argues that '[t]he fact that, unknown to a man who wishes to enter a conspiracy to commit some criminal purpose, the other person has no intention of fulfilling that purpose ought to be irrelevant as long as the first man does intend to fulfill it if he can' because 'a man who believes he is conspiring to commit a crime and wishes to conspire to commit a crime has a guilty mind and has done all in his power to plot the commission of an unlawful purpose.'

"Professor Glanville Williams makes a somewhat similar argument, basing his opinion on the fact that conspiracy, like attempt, is an inchoate crime and that it is the act of conspiring by a defendant which is the decisive element of criminality, for it makes no difference in logic or public policy that the person with whom the defendant conspires is not himself subject to prosecution. G. Williams, Criminal Law: The General Part 671–73 (2d ed. 1961).

"The draftsmen of the Model Penal Code take a slightly different approach. They recognize that conspiracy is not just an inchoate crime complementing the law of attempt and solicitation but that it is also a means of striking at the special dangers incident to group activity. In view of that recognition, it is probably not quite as easy to reject the approach taken by the cases cited, yet this is what the draftsmen have done. The provision which accomplishes this, Section 5.03(1) reads as follows:

'A person is guilty of conspiracy with another person or persons to commit a crime if with the purpose of promoting or facilitating its commission he:

(a) agrees with such person or persons that they or one or more of them will engage in conduct which constitutes such crime or an attempt or solicitation to commit such crime; or

(b) agrees to aid such other person or persons in the planning or commission of such crime or of an attempt or solicitation to commit such crime.'

"In comments explaining this provision, the reporters state as follows:[d]

'. . . The definition of the draft departs from the traditional view of conspiracy as an entirely bilateral or multilateral relationship, the view inherent in the standard formulation cast in terms of "two or more persons" agreeing or combining to commit a crime. Attention is directed instead to each individual's culpability by framing the definition in terms of the conduct which suffices to establish the liability of any given actor, rather than the conduct of a group of which he is charged to be a part—an approach which in this comment we have designated "unilateral."

'One consequence of this approach is to make it immaterial to the guilt of a conspirator whose culpability has

[d] This excerpt is taken from the commentary to the tentative draft version of the conspiracy offense. See A.L.I., Model Penal Code, § 5.03, Comment at 104–05 (Tent. Draft No. 10, 1960). [Footnote by eds.]

been established that the person or all of the persons with whom he conspired have not been or cannot be convicted. Present law frequently holds otherwise, reasoning from the definition of conspiracy as an agreement between two or more persons that there must be at least two guilty conspirators or none. The problem arises in a number of contexts. . . .

'Where the person with whom the defendant conspired secretly intends not to go through with the plan, . . . it is generally held that neither party can be convicted because there was no "agreement" between two persons. Under the unilateral approach of the draft, the culpable party's guilt would not be affected by the fact that the other party's agreement was feigned. He has conspired, within the meaning of the definition, in the belief that the other party was with him; apart from the issue of entrapment often presented in such cases, his culpability is not decreased by the other's secret intention. True enough, the project's chances of success have not been increased by the agreement; indeed, its doom may have been sealed by this turn of events. But the major basis of conspiratorial liability—the unequivocal evidence of a firm purpose to commit a crime—remains the same. The result would be the same under the draft if the only co-conspirator established a defense of renunciation under Section 5.03(6). While both the Advisory Committee and the Council supported the draft upon this point, it should be noted that the Council vote was 14–11, the dissenting members deeming mutual agreement on the part of two or more essential to the concept of conspiracy.' "

In consideration of these arguments, the court pronounced the "scholarly literature persuasive" and affirmed the conviction.

The position endorsed in *St. Christopher* may fairly be described as the modern trend. This is largely the result of a number of recently revised statutes that follow the Model Code in punishing one who agrees to commit a crime without regard to the actual intention of the supposed collaborator. Yet the unilateral approach is not without its critics. In particular, a sustained and elaborate rebuttal of the Model Code solution is advanced in P. Marcus, Prosecution and Defense of Criminal Conspiracy Cases, pp. 2–9 to –14 (1978). Professor Marcus argues that in a case such as *St. Christopher*, "[t]he defendant may have wanted to agree, may have intended to agree, and may have even believed he had agreed; but there was no agreement, no true planning by two or more persons, no meeting of the minds between the parties." Moreover, says Marcus, the requirement of bilateralism is not strictly doctrinal. Instead, it reflects the essential rationale for punishing conspiracy in the first place:

"The strongest proponents of conspiracy law argue that the reason the inchoate conspiracy offense is legitimate, and the reason the conspiracy offense can be punished wholly apart from the substantive offense, is that conspirators acting together are dangerous. Group activities, it is said, are more likely to lead to serious anti-social acts than the acts of a single criminal. Reasonable people may disagree on such a rationale, but it is the rationale which has been accepted by the courts and commentators. With the unilateral approach, however, this grave risk will likely be lessened considerably, or actually wholly eliminated. Under such circumstances the rationale for the crime is destroyed, for there is no group danger."

Do you agree? Would you say that the special danger of group criminality is the essential rationale for the inchoate offense of conspiracy? Would reliance on this rationale necessarily require bilateral agreement? Could the unilateral approach be viewed as also consistent with that rationale? Or were the drafters of the Model Penal Code emphasizing some other purpose for the law of conspiracy when they proposed their reformulation? Consideration of these questions may well be informed by the following notes on additional aspects of conspiracy as an inchoate offense.

5. **Mens Rea**. Analytically, it seems clear that the mens rea of the inchoate offense of conspiracy should parallel that of attempt. This kinship is suggested by the traditional designation of both conspiracy and attempt as specific-intent offenses. The label connotes some requirement of actual, subjective intention, but is otherwise not particularly informative. More elaborate formulations distinguish the intent to agree from the intent to accomplish the objective that makes agreement a crime. One may exist without the other. Assume for example, that A and B agree to remove certain property from the premises of C. A has the intent to agree, but if A believes that C has authorized the action, A plainly lacks the intent to commit theft. It is useful to distinguish these two intents chiefly in order to focus on the latter. The intent to agree is implicit in the requirement of agreement and therefore is rarely an issue independent of finding that the agreement exists. There remains the question of the actor's mens rea with respect to the underlying substantive offense that is the object of the conspiracy. The issue is what state of mind must the actor have with respect to the elements of the crime implicated by his agreement.

A partial answer is that the actor must have at least the level of culpability required by the definition of the underlying substantive crime. Certainly, the fact that the prosecution is for the inchoate offense of conspiracy is no reason to dilute the mens-rea component of the underlying offense. In the hypothetical noted above, for example, if theft requires an intention permanently to deprive another of his property, conspiracy to commit theft requires the same intention. Similarly, if perjury requires that the actor swear to a statement known to be false, conspiracy to commit perjury also requires awareness of the falsity of the statement agreed to. This much is well settled.

A more difficult issue is whether and to what extent the inchoate crime of conspiracy imposes mens-rea requirements beyond those of the underlying offense. The question, in other words, is whether conspiracy requires a higher level of culpability than would be necessary if the object offense were completed. Here the analogy to attempt is exact, and reference should be made to the materials on the mens rea of attempt at pages 317–27, supra. The arguments developed there will not be fully rehearsed here, but the following summary may facilitate consideration of the application of those arguments to the inchoate offense of conspiracy.

For conspiracy, as for attempt, it is useful to distinguish among conduct, result, and circumstance elements of the object offense:

(i) **Conduct**. The state of mind required by conspiracy for the conduct elements of the underlying substantive offense is rarely in dispute. An agreement to engage in certain conduct necessarily includes the intention that the conduct be completed. Thus, questions of the actor's mens rea with respect to the conduct elements of the underlying offense usually are subsumed in the requirement of agreement and rarely present any independent issue.

(ii) **Results**. Here the issue can arise, for it is possible to agree to engage in conduct that would cause a forbidden result without specifically intending that the result occur. Nevertheless, it is well settled that conspiracy requires an actual purpose to cause a proscribed result, even where the underlying substantive offense would allow conviction on proof of lesser culpability. A hypothetical may help frame the issue.

Assume that A and B agree to race their automobiles through an unlighted parking lot even though they are aware of a risk that other people may be present. Assume also that if someone were killed, the driver of the offending vehicle would be guilty of some variety of reckless homicide (probably manslaughter) since his conduct, under the circumstances, involved a substantial and unjustifiable risk of death to another. If the scheme were interrupted before any mishap occurred, on the other hand, there could be no prosecution for conspiracy to commit manslaughter. The reason is that A and B lack the state of mind required by the law of anticipatory offenses for result elements of the substantive crime. An actual purpose to cause that result is required, even where the completed offense would allow conviction for recklessness or negligence.[e]

(iii) **Circumstances**. The only real issue in this area is whether the inchoate offense of conspiracy imposes special mens-rea require-

---

[e] Sometimes the conclusion is drawn that there can be no conspiracy to commit an offense of recklessness or negligence. Strictly speaking, this statement may be wrong. In the hypothetical discussed above, there appears to be no reason why A and B could not be convicted of conspiracy to commit an offense of reckless (or negligent) operation of a motor vehicle. Each has agreed to engage in conduct that would constitute the actus reus of the completed offense, and each has the culpability (recklessness or negligence) required by that offense. The distinctive feature of the hypothetical discussed in text is that it involves a crime requiring recklessness or negligence *with respect to a result* of the contemplated conduct. There can be no crime of conspiracy recklessly or negligently to cause a result.

ments with respect to the attendant circumstances of an actor's conduct. A hypothetical from the law of theft presents the issue.

Assume that A and B agree to steal C's watch, which they believe to be worth about $100, to support their video-game habit. Suppose, however, that the watch in fact is worth $2000. Traditionally, the value of the property would be a strict liability component of the completed affense, and A and B would be guilty of grand larceny rather than petit larceny if they consummated the theft. But what if the scheme is interrupted before the theft occurs, and A and B are prosecuted for conspiracy to commit grand larceny? If conspiracy is graded at the same level as the offense one conspires to commit, of what grade is their offense, that of petit larceny or that of grand larceny? Is the value of the property still a strict-liability element, or does the law of conspiracy impose a mens-rea requirement where the underlying substantive offense has none?

One answer is suggested by Judge Learned Hand's famous comment in United States v. Crimmins, 123 F.2d 271, 273 (2d Cir. 1941):

"While one may, for instance, be guilty of running past a traffic light of whose existence one is ignorant, one cannot be guilty of conspiring to run past such a light, for one cannot agree to run past a light unless one supposes that there is a light to run past."

The implication is that conspiracy should require that the actor be aware of the attendant circumstances of the contemplated conduct, even where the completed offense would require no such awareness. An alternative answer is derived from the Model Penal Code approach to the mens rea of attempt. Under the approach reflected in Section 5.01, circumstance elements require only "the kind of culpability otherwise required for commission of the crime." [f] Which is the better view? How would the grand-larceny hypothetical discussed above be decided if the charge were an attempt to commit theft under Sections 5.01, 223.1, and 223.2 of the Model Penal Code? If the charge were conspiracy to commit theft under Sections 5.03, 223.1, and 223.2?

Perhaps it bears repeating at this point that the preceding comments on the mens rea of conspiracy as an inchoate offense are not designed to stand alone. They merely provide a convenient basis for reference to the more elaborate consideration of these issues in connection with the law of attempt at pages 317–27, supra. Any effort to understand the culpability structure of conspiracy as an anticipatory offense will be aided greatly by familiarity with those materials.

[f] An arguably special case of the mens rea required for attendant circumstances is presented by the jurisdictional ingredients of federal offenses. In many instances, federal statutes have been construed to require no mens rea with respect to the basis of federal jurisdiction—e.g., the fact that the person assaulted was a federal officer or that the property stolen belonged to the United States. For a long time the circuits were divided over the mens rea required with respect to such facts in a prosecution for conspiracy. Recently, the Supreme Court resolved the issue by holding that where a substantive offense requires no mens rea with respect to facts giving rise to federal jurisdiction, conspiracy to commit that offense also requires no mens rea with respect to such facts. United States v. Feola, 420 U.S. 671 (1975). Feola is excerpted at pages 470–72, infra.

6. **Impossibility.** The question of impossibility as a defense to the inchoate offense of conspiracy is arguably analogous to the impossibility issue in the law of attempt. See pages 328–41, supra. The law, however, has tended to treat the two crimes differently. Whereas the common law regarded impossibility (at least "legal" impossibility) as a defense to attempt, the authorities generally reject impossibility of any kind as a defense to conspiracy.

The issue arose in United States v. Thomas, 13 U.S.C.M.A. 278, 32 C.M.R. 278 (1962). Thomas and two others went into a bar. One of the three began to dance with a girl, who almost immediately collapsed into his arms. The three companions agreed to take the girl home and on the way took advantage of her unresisting condition to have sexual intercourse. When she did not revive, they became concerned and asked for help. Doctors subsequently agreed that she had died on the dance floor and was therefore not a living person at the time of the events described.

Defendants were convicted of attempted rape and of conspiracy to commit rape. On appeal they claimed that the girl's death prior to sexual intercourse made rape impossible and that the "impossibility" so described should be a defense to both attempt and conspiracy. The majority examined the authorities and concluded, in line with "the advanced and modern position," that impossibility was no defense on these facts. A dissenter, however, after an equally extensive review of the authorities, concluded that the impossibility involved here should be a defense to attempt:

> "[T]he barrier to consummation of the crime charged here is not factual but legal. Indeed, accused did everything they set out to do, but they admittedly could not commit the actual crime of rape because their victim was dead and thus outside the protection of the law appertaining to that offense. Because the objective of their loathsome attentions was no longer subject to being raped, it seems to me that there cannot be any liability for an attempt, for . . . a legal rather than a factual impediment existed to the offense's consummation."

Interestingly, the same judge concluded that impossibility should not be a defense to the charge of conspiracy:

> "Despite my position with respect to the charge of attempted rape, I would affirm the conviction of conspiracy to commit rape. Unlike criminal attempts, legal impossibility is not recognized as a defense to the charge of conspiracy. Although both crimes are, in a sense, inchoate offenses, their development has been some-what different. At common law, conspiracy consisted only of the agreement to do an unlawful act or a lawful act in an unlawful manner. Although [the relevant statute] requires proof of an overt act in addition to the agreement to commit an offense . . ., we have held that the heart of the crime remains the corrupt meeting of the minds. Here, the accused agreed to have intercourse with an unconscious girl against her will and while she was unable to resist. The averred overt act was also made

out. As what these two men thus subjectively agreed to be their objective constitutes in law the offense of rape, and as thereafter one of them performed an overt act, guilt of conspiracy is made out. My objection is simply to the action of my brothers in transferring the subjective approach in conspiracy to the objective questions involved in attempt."

What is the appropriate result on the facts of *Thomas*? Would you characterize the impossibility of rape as "factual" or "legal"? Is an attempt made out on these facts, or should the impossibility (of whatever sort) be a defense? And if impossibility is a defense to the charge of attempt, should it not also apply to conspiracy? Do you see any reason to differentiate the two offenses for this purpose?

7. **Renunciation and Withdrawal.** The role of conspiracy as an inchoate offense raises the question whether renunciation or abandonment should be a defense. The traditional position is that once agreement (or agreement plus an overt act) is reached, criminal conspiracy is complete, and no subsequent abandonment is a defense. The Model Penal Code, however, has proposed that renunciation be recognized as a defense to conspiracy on similar terms as it is for attempt. Section 5.03(6) of the Model Code provides a defense if "the actor, after conspiring to commit a crime, thwarted the success of the conspiracy, under circumstances manifesting a complete and voluntary renunciation of his criminal purpose."

Renunciation as a claim of defense to liability for conspiracy should be distinguished from the related issue of withdrawal as a means of terminating one's involvement in a conspiracy. Such withdrawal would not exculpate the actor from liability for the conspiracy, but it would limit the actor's liability for substantive offenses committed by co-conspirators after the actor's participation had ceased. Additionally, withdrawal of an individual from an on-going criminal enterprise starts the statute of limitations as against that individual. These aspects and other questions of withdrawal are illustrated by the materials on the scope and duration of conspiracy at pages 480–500, infra. For a discussion of both withdrawal and true renunciation, see Note, Conspiracy: Statutory Reform Since the Model Penal Code, 75 Colum.L.Rev. 1122 (1975).ᵍ

NOTE ON CONSPIRACY AND CUMULATIVE PUNISHMENT

In *Burleson* the court noted that Illinois law codified conspiracy as an inchoate offense and provided that "[n]o person shall be convicted of

ᵍ See also the decision in United States v. Read, 658 F.2d 1225 (7th Cir.1981), holding that the prosecution must disprove withdrawal beyond a reasonable doubt in order to convict of conspiracy. This conclusion is attacked in Note, Burden of Proof with Respect to the Defense of With-drawal from Conspiracy: *United States v. Read*, 4 Cardozo L.Rev. 151 (1982), and defended in Note, Withdrawal from Conspiracy: A Constitutional Allocation of Evidentiary Burdens, 51 Fordham L.Rev. 438 (1982).

both the inchoate and the principal offense." This rule has long been applied to attempt under the doctrine of merger. The attempt is said to merge into the completed offense, and the actor is therefore protected from punishment for both. At common law merger also applied to conspiracy, but today the majority rule is otherwise. Under federal law and the law of many states, conspiracy is treated as an independent wrong that does not merge into the completed crime that was its object. The result is that a person may be punished both for agreeing to commit a crime and for participation in the crime that was the object of the agreement. In this respect, conspiracy functions as an aggravation of penalties.[a] Cumulative punishment for conspiracy and for its object effectively extends the authorized maxima for substantive crimes whenever they are committed by two or more persons acting in concert.

What is the rationale for this result? The standard explanation was advanced by the Supreme Court in Callanan v. United States, 364 U.S. 587 (1961)—namely, that the special danger of concerted criminal activity warrants independent punishment. See page 451, supra. Are you persuaded? Consider the response made by the drafters of the Model Penal Code: "When a conspiracy is declared criminal because its object is a crime, we think it is entirely meaningless to say that the preliminary combination is more dangerous than the forbidden consummation; the measure of its danger is the risk of such a culmination." MPC § 5.03, Comment at 99 (Tent. Draft No. 10, 1960). Do you agree? Is the social danger of conspiracy adequately measured by the gravity of sanctions authorized for the completed offense, or is some aggravation of penalties appropriate?

A possible compromise position is that aggravation of penalties should be authorized in some, but by no means all, of the circumstances covered by the law of conspiracy. Modern statutes suggest ways to address this objective. The Model Penal Code, for example, bars cumulative punishment for conspiracy and the completed offense, Section 1.07(1)(b), but qualifies this position by special provisions for extended maximum terms where the defendant is "a professional criminal," Section 7.03(2), or where he is "a multiple offender whose criminality is so extensive that a sentence of imprisonment for an extended term is warranted." Section 7.03(4). Do provisions of this type meet the case for cumulative punishment of conspiracy and its object offense? Or is there some more generalized justification for continuing that tradition?

---

[a] A similar aggravation of penalties can result even where the object offense is not completed if, as is sometimes true, conspiracy carries a greater authorized penalty than does the completed offense. At one time the general federal conspiracy statute, 18 U.S.C. § 371, authorized imprisonment for up to five years and/or a fine of not more than $10,000 for conspiracy to commit any offense against the United States, including those carrying lesser sanctions. In 1948 the statute was amended to declare that conspiracy to commit a misdemeanor could not be punished more severely than the completed misdemeanor. For lesser felonies, however, it remains true that Section 371 authorizes heavier penalties for conspiracy than would be available for the completed offense.

SUBSECTION C: THE RELATION OF CONSPIRACY TO COMPLICITY

PEOPLE v. LAURIA

California Court of Appeal, Second District, 1967.
251 Cal.App.2d 471, 59 Cal.Rptr. 628.

FLEMING, ASSOCIATE JUSTICE. In an investigation of call-girl activity the police focused their attention on three prostitutes actively plying their trade on call, each of whom was using Lauria's telephone answering service, presumably for business purposes.

On January 8, 1965, Stella Weeks, a policewoman, signed up for telephone service with Lauria's answering service. Mrs. Weeks, in the course of her conversation with Lauria's office manager, hinted broadly that she was a prostitute concerned with the secrecy of her activities and their concealment from the police. She was assured that the operation of the service was discreet and "about as safe as you can get." It was arranged that Mrs. Weeks need not leave her address with the answering service, but could pick up her calls and pay her bills in person.

On February 11, Mrs. Weeks talked to Lauria on the telephone and told him her business was modelling and she had been referred to the answering service by Terry, one of the three prostitutes under investigation. She complained that because of the operation of the service she had lost two valuable customers, referred to as tricks. Lauria defended his service and said that her friends had probably lied to her about having left calls for her. But he did not respond to Mrs. Weeks' hints that she needed customers in order to make money, other than to invite her to his house for a personal visit in order to get better acquainted. In the course of his talk he said "his business was taking messages."

On February 15, Mrs. Weeks talked on the telephone to Lauria's office manager and again complained of two lost calls, which she described as a $50 and a $100 trick. On investigation the office manager could find nothing wrong, but she said she would alert the switchboard operators about slip-ups on calls.

On April 1 Lauria and the three prostitutes were arrested. Lauria complained to the police that this attention was undeserved, stating that Hollywood Call Board had 60 to 70 prostitutes on its board while his own service had only nine or 10, that he kept separate records for known or suspected prostitutes for the convenience of himself and the police. When asked if his records were available to police who might come to the office to investigate call girls, Lauria replied that they were whenever the police had a specific name. However, his service didn't "arbitrarily tell the police about prostitutes on our board. As long as they pay their bills we tolerate them." In a subsequent voluntary appearance before the grand jury Lauria testified he had always cooperated with the police. But he admitted he knew some of his customers were prostitutes, and he knew Terry was a prostitute because he had personally used her services, and he knew she was paying for 500 calls a month.

Lauria and the three prostitutes were indicted for conspiracy to commit prostitution, and nine overt acts were specified. Subsequently the trial court set aside the indictment as having been brought without reasonable or probable cause. The People have appealed, claiming that a sufficient showing of an unlawful agreement to further prostitution was made.

To establish agreement, the People need show no more than a tacit, mutual understanding between conspirators to accomplish an unlawful act. Here the People attempted to establish a conspiracy by showing that Lauria, well aware that his co-defendants were prostitutes who received business calls from customers through his telephone answering service, continued to furnish them with such service. This approach attempts to equate knowledge of another's criminal activity with conspiracy to further such criminal activity, and poses the question of the criminal responsibility of a furnisher of goods or services who knows his product is being used to assist the operation of an illegal business. Under what circumstances does a supplier become part of a conspiracy to further an illegal enterprise by furnishing goods or services which he knows are to be used by the buyer for criminal purposes?

The two leading cases on this point face in opposite directions. In United States v. Falcone, 311 U.S. 205 (1940), the sellers of large quantities of sugar, yeast, and cans were absolved from participation in a moonshining conspiracy among distillers who bought from them, while in Direct Sales Co. v. United States, 319 U.S. 703 (1943), a wholesaler of drugs was convicted of conspiracy to violate the federal narcotic laws by selling drugs in quantity to a co-defendant physician who was supplying them to addicts. The distinction between these two cases appears primarily based on the proposition that distributors of such dangerous products as drugs are required to exercise greater discrimination in the conduct of their business than are distributors of innocuous substances like sugar and yeast.

In the earlier case, *Falcone*, the sellers' knowledge of the illegal use of the goods was insufficient by itself to make the sellers participants in a conspiracy with the distillers who bought from them. Such knowledge fell short of proof of a conspiracy, and evidence on the volume of sales was too vague to support a jury finding that respondents knew of the conspiracy from the size of the sales alone.

In the later case of *Direct Sales*, the conviction of a drug wholesaler for conspiracy to violate federal narcotic laws was affirmed on a showing that it had actively promoted the sale of morphine sulphate in quantity and had sold codefendant physician, who practiced in a small town in South Carolina, more than 300 times his normal requirements of the drug, even though it had been repeatedly warned of the dangers of unrestricted sales of the drug. The court contrasted the restricted goods involved in *Direct Sales* with the articles of free commerce involved in *Falcone*: "All articles of commerce may be put to illegal ends," said the court. "But all do not have inherently the same susceptibility to harmful and illegal use. . . . This difference is important for two purposes. One is for making certain that the seller knows the buyer's intended illegal use. The other is to show that by the sale he intends to further, promote and cooperate in it. This intent, when given effect by overt act, is the gist of conspiracy. While it is not identical with mere knowledge that another purposes unlawful action, it is not unrelated to such knowledge. . . . The step from knowledge to intent and agreement may be taken. There is more than suspicion, more than knowledge, acquiescence, carelessness, indifference, lack of concern. There is informed and interested cooperation, stimulation, instigation. And there is also a 'stake in the venture' which, even if it may not be essential, is not irrelevant to the question of conspiracy."

While *Falcone* and *Direct Sales* may not be entirely consistent with each other in their full implications, they do provide us with a framework for the criminal liability of a supplier of lawful goods or services put to unlawful use. Both the element of *knowledge* of the illegal use of the goods or services and the element of *intent* to further that use must be present in order to make the supplier a participant in a criminal conspiracy.

Proof of *knowledge* is ordinarily a question of fact and requires no extended discussion in the present case. The knowledge of the supplier was sufficiently established when Lauria admitted he knew some of his customers were prostitutes and admitted he knew that Terry, an active subscriber of his service, was a prostitute. In the face of these admissions he could scarcely claim to have relied on the normal assumption an operator of a business or service is entitled to make, that his customers are behaving themselves in the eyes of the law. Because Lauria knew in fact that some of his customers were prostitutes, it is a legitimate inference he knew they were subscribing to his answering service for illegal business purposes and were using his service to make assignations for prostitution. On this record we think the prosecution is entitled to claim positive knowledge by Lauria of the use of his service to facilitate the business of prostitution.

The more perplexing issue in the case is the sufficiency of proof of *intent* to further the criminal enterprise. The element of intent may be proved either by direct evidence, or by evidence of circumstances from which an intent to further a criminal enterprise by supplying lawful goods or services may be inferred. Direct evidence of participation, such as advice from the supplier of legal goods or services to the user of those goods or services on their use for illegal purposes . . . provides the simplest case. When the intent to further and promote the criminal enterprise comes from the lips of the supplier himself, ambiguities of inference from circumstance need not trouble us. But in cases where direct proof of complicity is lacking, intent to further the conspiracy must be derived from the sale itself and its surrounding circumstances in order to establish the supplier's express or tacit agreement to join the conspiracy.

In the case at bench the prosecution argues that since Lauria knew his customers were using his service for illegal purposes but nevertheless continued to furnish it to them, he must have intended to assist them in carrying out their illegal activities. Thus through a union of knowledge and intent he became a participant in a criminal conspiracy. Essentially, the People argue that knowledge alone of the continuing use of his telephone facilities for criminal purposes provided a sufficient basis from which his intent to participate in those criminal activities could be inferred.

In examining precedents in this field we find that sometimes, but not always, the criminal intent of the supplier may be inferred from his knowledge of the unlawful use made of the product he supplies. Some consideration of characteristic patterns may be helpful.

(i) Intent may be inferred from knowledge, when the purveyor of legal goods for illegal use has acquired a stake in the venture. (United States v. Falcone, 109 F.2d 579, 581 (2d Cir., 1940)). For example, in Regina v. Thomas, 2 All E.R. 181, 342 (1957), a prosecution for living off the earnings of prostitution, the evidence showed that the accused, knowing the woman to be a convicted prostitute, agreed to let her have the use of his room between the hours of 9 p. m. and 2 a. m. for a charge of £3 a night. The Court of Criminal Appeal refused an appeal from the conviction, holding that when the accused rented a room at a grossly inflated rent to a prostitute for the purpose of carrying on her trade, a jury could find he was living on the earnings of prostitution.

In the present case, no proof was offered of inflated charges for the telephone answering services furnished the co-defendants.

(ii) Intent may be inferred from knowledge, when no legitimate use for the goods or services exists. The leading California case is People v. McLaughlin, 111 Cal.App.2d 781, 245 P.2d 1076 (1952), in which the court upheld a conviction of the suppliers of horse-racing information by wire for conspiracy to promote bookmaking, when it had been established that wire-service information had no other use than to supply information needed by bookmakers to conduct illegal gambling operations. . . . In such cases the supplier must necessarily have an intent to further the illegal enterprise since there is no known honest use for his goods.

However, there is nothing in the furnishing of telephone answering service which would necessarily imply assistance in the performance of illegal activities. Nor is any inference to be derived from the use of an answering service by women, either in any particular volume of calls, or outside normal working hours. Night-club entertainers, registered nurses, faith healers, public stenographers, photographic models, and free-lance substitute employees, provide examples of women in legitimate occupations whose employment might cause them to receive a volume of telephone calls at irregular hours.

(iii) Intent may be inferred from knowledge, when the volume of business with the buyer is grossly disproportionate to any legitimate demand, or when sales for illegal use amount to a high proportion of the seller's total business. In such cases an intent to participate in the illegal enterprise may be inferred from the quantity of the business done. For example, in *Direct Sales*, supra, the sale of narcotics to a rural physician in quantities 300 times greater than he would have normal use for provided potent evidence of an intent to further the illegal activity. In the same case the court also found significant the fact that the wholesaler had attracted as customers a disproportionately large group of physicians who had been convicted of violating the Harrison Act. . . .

No evidence of any unusual volume of business with prostitutes was presented by the prosecution against Lauria.

Inflated charges, the sale of goods with no legitimate use, sales in inflated amounts, each may provide a fact of sufficient moment from which the intent of the seller to participate in the criminal enterprise may be inferred. In such instances participation by the supplier of legal goods to the illegal enterprise may be inferred because in one way or another the supplier has acquired a special interest in the operation of the illegal [enterprise]. His intent to participate in the crime of which he has knowledge may be inferred from the existence of his special interest.

Yet there are cases in which it cannot reasonably be said that the supplier has a stake in the venture or has acquired a special interest in the enterprise, but in which he has been held liable as a participant on the basis of knowledge alone. Some suggestion of this appears in *Direct Sales*, supra, where both the knowledge of the illegal use of the drugs and the intent of the supplier to aid that use were inferred. In Regina v. Bainbridge, 3 W.L.R. 656 (C.C.A.1959), a supplier of oxygen-cutting equipment to one known to intend to use it to break into a bank was convicted as an accessory to the crime. In Sykes v. Director of Public Prosecutions, [1962] A.C. 528, one having knowledge of the theft of 100 pistols, four submachine guns, and 1960 rounds of ammunition was convicted of misprision of felony for failure to disclose the theft to the public authorities. It seems apparent from these cases that a supplier who furnishes equipment which he *knows* will be used to commit a serious crime may be deemed from that knowledge alone to have intended to produce the result. Such proof may justify an inference that the furnisher intended to aid the execution of the crime and that he thereby became a participant. For instance, we think the operator of a telephone answering service with positive knowledge that his service was being used to facilitate the extortion of ransom, the distribution of heroin, or the passing of counterfeit money who continued to furnish the service with knowledge of its use, might be chargeable on knowledge alone with participation in a scheme to extort money, to distribute narcotics, or to pass counterfeit money. The same result would follow the seller of gasoline who knew the buyer was using his product to make Molotov cocktails for terroristic use.

Logically, the same reasoning could be extended to crimes of every description. Yet we do not believe an inference of intent drawn from knowledge of criminal use properly applies to the less serious crimes

classified as misdemeanors.   The duty to take positive action to dissoci-
ate oneself from activities helpful to violations of the criminal law is far
stronger and more compelling for felonies than it is for misdemeanors
or petty offenses.   In this respect, as in others, the distinction between
felonies and misdemeanors, between more serious and less serious
crime, retains continuing vitality.   In historically the most serious
felony, treason, an individual with knowledge of the treason can be
prosecuted for concealing and failing to disclose it.   In other felonies,
both at common law and under the criminal laws of the United States,
an individual knowing of the commission of a felony is criminally liable
for concealing it and failing to make it known to proper authority.   But
this crime, known as misprision of felony, has always been limited to
knowledge and concealment of felony and has never extended to misdemeanor.   A similar limitation is found in the criminal liability of an
accessory [after the fact], which is restricted to aid in the escape of a
principal who has committed or been charged with a *felony*.   We
believe the distinction between the obligations arising from knowledge
of a felony and those arising from knowledge of a misdemeanor continues to reflect basic human feelings about the duties owed by individuals
to society.   Heinous crime must be stamped out, and its suppression is
the responsibility of all.   Venial crime and crime not evil in itself
present less of a danger to society, and perhaps the benefits of their
suppression through the modern equivalent of the posse, the hue and
cry, the informant, and the citizen's arrest, are outweighed by the
disruption to everyday life brought about by amateur law enforcement
and private officiousness in relatively inconsequential delicts which do
not threaten our basic security.   . . .

With respect to misdemeanors, we conclude that positive knowledge
of the supplier that his products or services are being used for criminal
purposes does not, without more, establish an intent of the supplier to
participate in the misdemeanors.   With respect to felonies, we do not
decide the converse, viz. that in all cases of felony knowledge of
criminal use alone may justify an inference of the supplier's intent to
participate in the crime.   The implications of *Falcone* make the matter
uncertain with respect to those felonies which are merely prohibited
wrongs.   But decision on this point is not compelled, and we leave the
matter open.

From this analysis of precedent we deduce the following rule: the
intent of a supplier who knows of the criminal use to which his supplies
are put to participate in the criminal activity connected with the use of
his supplies may be established by (i) direct evidence that he intends to
participate, or (ii) through an inference that he intends to participate
based on, (a) his special interest in the activity, or (b) the aggravated
nature of the crime itself.

When we review Lauria's activities in the light of this analysis, we
find no proof that Lauria took any direct action to further, encourage,
or direct the call-girl activities of his codefendants and we find an
absence of circumstances from which his special interest in their
activities could be inferred.   Neither excessive charges for standardized

services, nor the furnishing of services without a legitimate use, nor an unusual quantity of business with call girls, are present. The offense which he is charged with furthering is a misdemeanor, a category of crime which has never been made a required subject of positive disclosure to public authority. Under these circumstances, although proof of Lauria's knowledge of the criminal activities of his patrons was sufficient to charge him with that fact, there was insufficient evidence that he intended to further their criminal activities, and hence insufficient proof of his participation in a criminal conspiracy with his codefendants to further prostitution. Since the conspiracy centered around the activities of Lauria's telephone answering service, the charges against his codefendants likewise fail for want of proof.

In absolving Lauria of complicity in a criminal conspiracy we do not wish to imply that the public authorities are without remedies to combat modern manifestations of the world's oldest profession. Licensing of telephone answering services under the police power, together with the revocation of licenses for the toleration of prostitution, is a possible civil remedy. The furnishing of telephone answering service in aid of prostitution could be made a crime. Other solutions will doubtless occur to vigilant public authorities if the problem of call-girl activity needs further suppression.

The order is affirmed.

NOTES ON THE CONSPIRACY-COMPLICITY RELATIONSHIP

1. **The Conspiracy-Complicity Relationship.** As the principal case illustrates, conspiracy often functions as an alternative to complicity. Formally, of course, the doctrines are distinct. Complicity holds one person criminally responsible for the conduct of another. Depending on the law of the particular jurisdiction, such liability may require aid rendered to the primary actor with intent to promote the criminal venture, or it may rest on knowing assistance to the criminal activity of another. Conspiracy, on the other hand, imposes direct liability for the preliminary step of agreeing with another to commit an offense. A party to such agreement may be held criminally responsible for the object offense even though he or she did not personally complete the actus reus of that crime. In many situations, the choice between these two doctrinal characterizations is a matter of procedural convenience, for they are often functionally interchangeable.

Consider, for example, the facts of *Lauria*. As it happened, Lauria was prosecuted for conspiracy to commit prostitution. Obviously, this charge raises difficult questions about the liability of one who knowingly supplies goods or services to a criminal undertaking. Would these questions have been different if Lauria had been prosecuted for complicity in the acts of prostitution by his customers? Should the determinants of liability turn on which theory is used? In this connection, recall *United States* v. *Peoni* and *Backun* v. *United States*, which are excerpted in the materials on complicity at pages 411–14, supra. Would these cases have been resolved differently if conspiracy rather than complicity were the offense charged? Does your analysis of the issues involved depend on which doctrine is used? What reasons might induce the prosecutor to choose one theory rather than the other?

The fact that conspiracy and complicity overlap has two important implications. First, analysis of the law of conspiracy as an alternative to complicity largely replicates the range of issues dealt with under the doctrine of complicity. An understanding of that subject is, therefore, essential to critical evaluation of this aspect of criminal conspiracy. Second, it is important to remember that conspiracy functions not only as an alternative to prosecution for complicity but also as an inchoate offense and as a basis for aggravation of penalties. There is reason to doubt whether any unified statement of the law of conspiracy can deal coherently with such disparate subjects. The cases and notes that follow illustrate aspects of criminal conspiracy in its role as an alternative to complicity. In analyzing these materials, you should not only keep in mind the generally applicable principles of complicity as an essential frame of reference, but you should also ask whether the law of conspiracy as stated in these decisions could sensibly be applied in the context of inchoate behavior.[a]

2. *United States* v. *Feola.* Another aspect of the conspiracy-complicity relationship is illustrated by United States v. Feola, 420 U.S. 671 (1975). Feola and three others participated in what the Court termed "a classic narcotics 'rip-off' ":

> "Feola and his confederates arranged for a sale of heroin to buyers who turned out to be undercover agents for the Bureau of Narcotics and Dangerous Drugs. The group planned to palm off on the purchasers, for a substantial sum, a form of sugar in place of heroin and, should that ruse fail, simply to surprise their unwitting buyers and relieve them of the cash they had brought along for payment. The plan failed when one agent, his suspicions being aroused, drew his revolver in time to counter an assault upon another agent from the rear. Instead of enjoying the rich benefits of a successful swindle, Feola and his associates found themselves charged, to their undoubted surprise, with conspiring to assault, and with assaulting, federal officers."

Feola challenged the resulting conspiracy conviction on the claim that he lacked the required mens rea. In particular, he pointed out that he neither knew nor had reason to know that the targets of the scheme were federal agents. The United States Court of Appeals for the Second Circuit reversed the conspiracy conviction on this ground, despite its conclusion that the underlying crime of assaulting a federal officer (18 U.S.C. § 111) required *no* culpability with respect to the federal jurisdictional requirement of the victim's official identity. In other words, the court held that, even though the underlying substantive crime treated official identity as an element of strict liability, mens rea with respect to that fact would be required for conspiracy under 18 U.S.C. § 371. The basis for this conclusion was Crimmins v. United

---

[a] For a useful comparative analysis of the relation of conspiracy to complicity, see Lanham, Complicity, Concert, and Conspiracy, 4 Crim.L.J. 276 (1980).

States, 123 F.2d 271 (2d Cir. 1941), in which Judge Learned Hand had upheld a similar contention with the following comment:

"While one may, for instance, be guilty of running past a traffic light of whose existence one is ignorant, one cannot be guilty of conspiring to run past such a light, for one cannot agree to run past a light unless one supposes that there is a light to run past."

By analogy, the Court of Appeals concluded that Feola could not be guilty of agreeing to assault a federal officer without some awareness of his intended victim's official identity.

The Supreme Court reversed:

"Our analysis of the substantive offense . . . is sufficient to convince us that for the purpose of individual guilt or innocence, awareness of the official identity of the assault victim is irrelevant. We would expect the same to obtain with respect to the conspiracy offense unless one of the policies behind the imposition of conspiratorial liability is not served where the parties to the agreement are unaware that the intended target is a federal law-enforcement official.

"It is well settled that the law of conspiracy serves ends different from, and complementary to, those served by criminal prohibitions of the substantive offense. Because of this, consecutive sentences may be imposed for the conspiracy and for the underlying crime. Callanan v. United States, 364 U.S. 587 (1961). Our decisions have identified two independent values served by the law of conspiracy. The first is protection of society from the dangers of concerted criminal activity. That individuals know that their planned joint venture violates federal as well as state law seems totally irrelevant to that purpose of conspiracy law which seeks to protect society from the dangers of concerted criminal activity. Given the level of criminal intent necessary to sustain conviction for the substantive offense, the act of agreement to commit the crime is no less opprobrious and no less dangerous because of the absence of knowledge of a fact unnecessary to the formation of criminal intent. Indeed, unless imposition of an 'anti-federal' knowledge requirement serves social purposes external to the law of conspiracy of which we are unaware, its imposition here would serve only to make it more difficult to obtain convictions on charges of conspiracy, a policy with no apparent purpose.

"The second aspect is that conspiracy is an inchoate crime. This is to say, that, although the law generally makes criminal only anti-social conduct, at some point in the continuum between preparation and consummation, the likelihood of a commission of an act is sufficiently great and the criminal intent sufficiently well formed to justify the intervention of the criminal law. The law of conspiracy identifies the agreement to engage in a criminal venture as an event of sufficient threat to social order to permit the imposition of criminal sanctions for the agreement alone, plus an overt act in pursuit of it, regardless of whether the crime agreed upon actually is committed. Criminal intent has crystallized, and the likelihood of actual, fulfilled commission warrants preventive action.

"Again, we do not see how imposition of a strict 'anti-federal' scienter requirement would relate to this purpose of conspiracy law. Given the level of intent needed to carry out the substantive offense, we fail to see how the agreement is any less blameworthy or constitutes less of a danger to society solely because the participants are unaware which body of law they intend to violate. Therefore, we again conclude that imposition of a requirement of knowledge of those facts that serve only to establish federal jurisdiction would render it more difficult to serve the policy behind the law of conspiracy without serving any other apparent social purpose. . . ."

Is the Court's reasoning sound? Given that the underlying substantive offense requires no culpability with respect to the federal jurisdictional element of the offense, is there reason to impose such a requirement for conspiracy to commit that offense?

3. **Additional Note on Mens Rea.** The *Feola* decision concerns the mens rea required by the law of conspiracy with respect to those facts that would give rise to federal jurisdiction over the completed offense. Such jurisdictional facts are arguably only a special subset of the more general category of elements identifying the attendant circumstances of an actor's conduct. The issue of the mens rea required for attendant circumstances can be put by revisiting an earlier theft hypothetical. See page 459, supra. The hypothetical was that *A* and *B* agree to steal *C*'s watch to support their video-game habit. Assume in this instance that *A* steals the watch pursuant to the agreement and that, as before, it turns out to be worth $2000 rather than $100 as they thought. It is clear under traditional law that *A* is guilty of grand larceny based on the actual value of the property; strict liability is applied to the value of the property for purposes of grading. Of what level of offense should *B* be guilty? *B* may be prosecuted for complicity in the theft or for conspiracy to commit it. If conspiracy is the offense charged, what state of mind must *B* have had with respect to the value of the property? Does the strict liability of the underlying offense carry over, as in *Feola*, or is there some reason to impose a special mens-rea requirement as part of the law of conspiracy? Recall the argument, pages 322–23, supra, that for attendant circumstances attempt should require only the state of mind required by the underlying offense. Should the same position be taken for complicity? For conspiracy when it is performing the function of an inchoate offense? For conspiracy when it is performing the function of an alternative to complicity?

Now, make the same inquiry with respect to result elements. What state of mind should criminal conspiracy require for those elements of the underlying offense that identify results of the actor's conduct? Here again, it is instructive to recall the hypothetical discussed in the notes on conspiracy as an inchoate offense. See page 470, supra. *A* and *B* agree to race their cars through an unlighted parking lot. Each is aware of the risk that other people may be present. If *B* in fact kills someone, it was assumed that he would be guilty of some form of reckless homicide, since that conduct, under the circumstances, involved a substantial and unjustifiable risk of death to another. *A* may be prosecuted for complicity in *B*'s crime or for conspiracy to engage in the conduct that caused the forbidden result. Under generally applicable principles of complicity, *A* would be liable if he or she aided, counseled, or encouraged *B*'s course of conduct and was reckless with respect to death of another. If, in the circumstances where they overlap, conspiracy were to be construed to parallel the law of complicity, then conviction for conspiracy would rest on proof of *A*'s agreement to engage in the dangerous conduct in reckless disregard of risk of death of another. Yet the law of conspiracy rejects this result, presumably because of its obvious incompatibility with the role of conspiracy as an inchoate offense. If death of another did not actually occur, *B* could not be punished for attempt to commit reckless homicide. It also follows that *A* could not be punished for conspiracy to commit reckless homicide. In the context of an anticipatory offense, settled doctrine would require that the actor have a purpose to cause the forbidden result, even where the underlying offense allowed conviction for a lesser mens rea. The point, of course, is that conspiracy as an inchoate offense is functionally distinct from conspiracy as an alternative to complicity and that the same doctrinal formulations may not always serve both functions equally well.

PINKERTON v. UNITED STATES

Supreme Court of the United States, 1946.
328 U.S. 640.

MR. JUSTICE DOUGLAS delivered the opinion of the Court.

Walter and Daniel Pinkerton are brothers who live a short distance from each other on Daniel's farm. They were indicted for violations of the Internal Revenue Code. The indictment contained 10 substantive counts and one conspiracy count. The jury found Walter guilty on nine of the substantive counts and on the conspiracy count. It found Daniel guilty on six of the substantive counts and on the conspiracy count. Walter was fined $500 and sentenced generally on the substantive counts to imprisonment for 30 months. On the conspiracy count he was given a two-year sentence to run concurrently with the other sentence. Daniel was fined $1,000 and sentenced generally on the substantive counts to imprisonment for 30 months. On the conspiracy count he was fined $500 and given a two-year sentence to run concurrently with the other sentence. The judgments of conviction were affirmed by the Circuit Court of Appeals. . . .

It is contended that there was insufficient evidence to implicate Daniel in the conspiracy. But we think there was enough evidence for submission of the issue to the jury.

There is, however, no evidence to show that Daniel participated directly in the commission of the substantive offenses on which his conviction has been sustained, although there was evidence to show that these substantive offenses were in fact committed by Walter in furtherance of the unlawful agreement or conspiracy existing between the brothers. The question was submitted to the jury on the theory that each petitioner could be found guilty of the substantive offenses, if it was found at the time those offenses were committed petitioners were parties to an unlawful conspiracy and the substantive offenses charged were in fact committed in furtherance of it.

Daniel relies on United States v. Sall, 116 F.2d 745 (3d Cir. 1940). That case held that participation in the conspiracy was not itself enough to sustain a conviction for the substantive offense even though it was committed in furtherance of the conspiracy. The court held that, in addition to evidence that the offense was in fact committed in furtherance of the conspiracy, evidence of direct participation in the commission of the substantive offense or other evidence from which participation might fairly be inferred was necessary.

We take a different view. We have here a continuous conspiracy. There is here no evidence of the affirmative action on the part of Daniel which is necessary to establish his withdrawal from it. Hyde v. United States, 225 U.S. 347 (1912). As stated in that case,

> "[h]aving joined in an unlawful scheme, having constituted agents for its performance, scheme and agency to be continuous until full fruition be secured, until he does some act to disavow or defeat the purpose he is in no situation to claim the delay of the law. As the offense has not been terminated or accomplished he is still offending. And we think, consciously offending, offending as certainly, as we have said, as at the first moment of his confederation, and consciously through every moment of its existence."

And so long as the partnership in crime continues, the partners act for each other in carrying it forward. It is settled that "an overt act of one partner may be the act of all without any new agreement specifically directed to that act." Motive or intent may be proved by the acts or declarations of some of the conspirators in furtherance of the common objective. A scheme to use the mails to defraud, which is joined in by more than one person, is a conspiracy. Yet all members are responsible, though only one did the mailing. The governing principle is the same when the substantive offense is committed by one of the conspirators in furtherance of the unlawful project. The criminal intent to do the act is established by the formation of the conspiracy. Each conspirator instigated the commission of the crime. The unlawful agreement contemplated precisely what was done. It was formed for the purpose. The act done was in execution of the enterprise. The rule which holds responsible one who counsels, procures, or commands another to commit a crime is founded on the same principle. That principle is recognized in the law of conspiracy when the overt act of one partner in crime is attributable to all. An overt act is an essential ingredient of the crime of conspiracy under [18 U.S.C. § 371]. If that can be supplied by the act of one conspirator, we fail to see why the same or other acts in furtherance of the conspiracy are likewise not attributable to the others for the purpose of holding them responsible for the substantive offense.

A different case would arise if the substantive offense committed by one of the conspirators was not in fact done in furtherance of the conspiracy, did not fall within the scope of the unlawful project, or was merely a part of the ramifications of the plan which could not be reasonably foreseen as a necessary or natural consequence of the unlawful agreement. But as we read this record, that is not this case.

Affirmed.

MR. JUSTICE JACKSON took no part in the consideration or decision of this case.

MR. JUSTICE RUTLEDGE, dissenting in part.

The judgment concerning Daniel Pinkerton should be reversed. In my opinion it is without precedent here and is a dangerous precedent to establish.

Daniel and Walter, who were brothers living near each other, were charged in several counts with substantive offenses, and then a conspiracy count was added naming those offenses as overt acts. The proof showed that Walter alone committed the substantive crimes. There was none to establish that Daniel participated in them, aided and abetted Walter in committing them, or knew that he had done so. Daniel in fact was in the penitentiary, under sentence for other crimes, when some of Walter's crimes were done.

There was evidence, however, to show that over several years Daniel and Walter had confederated to commit similar crimes concerned with unlawful possession, transportation, and dealing in whiskey, in fraud of the federal revenues. On this evidence both were convicted of conspiracy. Walter also was convicted on the substantive counts on the proof of his committing the crimes charged. Then, on that evidence without more than the proof of Daniel's criminal agreement with Walter and the latter's overt acts, which were also the substantive offenses charged, the court told the jury they could find Daniel guilty of those substantive offenses. They did so. . . .

The court's theory seems to be that Daniel and Walter became general partners in crime by virtue of their agreement and because of that agreement without more on his part Daniel became criminally responsible as a principal for everything Walter did thereafter in the nature of a criminal offense of the general sort the agreement contemplated, so long as there was not clear evidence that Daniel had withdrawn from or revoked the agreement. Whether or not his commitment to the penitentiary had that effect, the result is a vicarious criminal responsibility as broad as, or broader than, the vicarious civil liability of a partner for acts done by a co-partner in the course of the firm's business.

Such analogies from private commercial law and the law of torts are dangerous, in my judgment, for transfer to the criminal field. Guilt there with us remains personal, not vicarious, for the more serious offenses. It should be kept so. The effect of Daniel's conviction in this case . . . is either to attribute to him Walter's guilt or to punish him twice for the same offense, namely, agreeing with Walter to engage in crime. Without the agreement Daniel was guilty of no crime on this record. With it and no more, so far as his own conduct is concerned, he was guilty of two. . . .

MR. JUSTICE FRANKFURTER . . . agrees in substance with the views expressed in this dissent.

———

NOTES ON THE *PINKERTON* RULE

1. **The Scope of Liability for Conspiracy.** *Pinkerton* is the most famous authority for the proposition that a member of a conspiracy is criminally responsible for substantive offenses committed by his co-conspirators in furtherance of their agreement. Of course, resort to *Pinkerton* is not necessary to find a conspirator liable for the particular crime covered by the agreement. The effect of this rule is, rather, to extend liability to include additional offenses that may not have been within the actor's contemplation but that were committed by his or her cohorts in the course of the criminal enterprise. The only limit on the scope of the conspirator's liability is that additional offenses must have been reasonably foreseeable consequences of the agreement.

The *Pinkerton* rule, as it is sometimes called, is probably the law in a majority of American jurisdictions. Typically, it is enforced without explicit statutory support. Some modern statutes, however, do codify the rule. Where this is done, the scope of a conspirator's liability for the substantive offenses of his or her colleagues is spelled out in the provision on complicity rather than in the section on conspiracy. An illustration of this approach comes from the law of Texas. Section 7.02 of the Texas Penal Code is entitled "Criminal Responsibility for the Conduct of Another." Subsection (a) sets forth the general requirements of complicity. Subsection (b) adds the following:

"If, in the attempt to carry out a conspiracy to commit one felony, another felony is committed by one of the conspirators, all conspirators are guilty of the felony actually committed, though having no intent to commit it, if the offense was committed in furtherance of the unlawful purpose and was one that should have been anticipated as a result of the carrying out of the conspiracy."

For other modern provisions to the same general effect, see N.J.Stat.Ann. § 2C:2–5 and Wis.Stat.Ann. § 939.05. The greater number of modern statutes do not include any explicit codification of the *Pinkerton* rule. In some of these jurisdictions, the effect is simply to continue unchanged the decisional authority on the subject. In others, however, the *Pinkerton* rule has been explicitly rejected. See, e.g., Code of Ala., §§ 13A–4–3(f), 13A–2–23; No.Dak.Cent. Code § 12.1–03–01; 17–A Me.Rev.Stat.Ann. § 151.

2. **Evaluating the *Pinkerton* Rule**. The impact of *Pinkerton* is not easy to assess. It seems likely that in most of the cases where the rule is invoked, generally applicable principles of complicity would authorize conviction in any event. That is not to say, however, that there are no circumstances where *Pinkerton* would extend liability, and logically it is on those cases that attention should focus. Two variables affect the dimensions of the issue. First, the impact of the *Pinkerton* rule depends in large measure on the question, "as compared to what?" If the otherwise applicable principles of complicity were tightly to restrict the liability of an accomplice to crimes which he or she had an actual purpose to aid or encourage, the effect of the *Pinkerton* approach to the scope of liability for conspiracy would be considerable. In such circumstances, *Pinkerton* would effectively dilute the mens-rea requirement from purpose to negligence whenever the primary and secondary actor are bound together by a criminal agreement. On the other hand, if the scope of an accomplice's liability were made to turn on the natural and probable consequences of the criminal endeavor that he meant to aid or encourage (as, for example, in *People* v. *Durham*, page 400, supra), the addition of *Pinkerton* would be a matter of little consequence. Thus, the practical impact of embracing the *Pinkerton* approach depends a great deal on the contours of the criminal liability that would otherwise exist.

A second variable concerns the approach taken to determining the size or scope of a single conspiracy. This is a matter considered in more detail in a later subsection of these materials, see pages 480–500, infra, but it is worth noting here that the consequence of *Pinkerton* depends in part on the scope of the activities for which an individual conspirator is thereby made criminally responsible. This, in fact, is the principal basis for opposition to *Pinkerton* by the drafters of the Model Penal Code. Consider the following comments made with respect to the tentative draft provision on complicity, MPC § 2.04, Comment at 20–21 (Tent. Draft No. 1, 1953): *

"The most important point at which the draft diverges from the language of the courts is that it does not make 'conspiracy,' as such, a basis of complicity in substantive offenses committed in furtherance of its aims. It asks, instead, . . . more specific questions about the behavior charged to constitute complicity, such as whether the defendant commanded, encouraged, aided or agreed to aid in the commission of the crime.

"The reason for this treatment is that there appears to be no other or no better way to confine within reasonable limits the scope of liability to which conspiracy may theoretically give rise. In People v. Luciano, 277 N.Y. 348, 14 N.E.2d 433 (1938), for example, Luciano and others were convicted of 62 counts of compulsory prostitution, each count involving a specific instance of placing a girl in a house of prostitution, receiving money for so doing or receiving money from the earnings of a prostitute, acts proved to have been done pursuant to a combination to control commercialized vice in New York City. The liability was properly imposed with respect to these defendants, who directed and controlled the combination; they commanded, encouraged and aided the commission of numberless specific crimes. But would so extensive a liability be just for each of the prostitutes or runners involved in the plan? They have, of course, committed their own crimes; they may actually have assisted others; but they exerted no substantial influence on the behavior of a hundred other girls or runners, each pursuing his or her own ends within the shelter of the combination. A court would and should hold that they all are parties to a single, large, conspiracy; this is itself, and ought to be, a crime. But it is one crime. Law would lose all sense of just proportion if in virtue of that one crime, each were held accountable for thousands of offenses that he did not influence at all."

3. **State v. Stein.** An interesting application of the *Pinkerton* rule is found in State v. Stein, 70 N.J. 369, 360 A.2d 347 (1976). Defendant Stein was a Trenton attorney with certain unsavory connections. One of them was Pontani, a "professional second-story man" in need of work. Pontani discussed with Stein the possibility of committing a burglary from which they both might benefit. Stein suggested the house of Dr. Arnold Gordon, a dentist who lived in Stein's neighborhood and was known to keep cash at home. At first nothing came of this suggestion, but about a year later two associates of Pontani gained entry to the Gordon home by impersonating policemen. They pulled pistols and demanded money and valuables. While they were tying up Dr. and Mrs. Gordon, a maid called the police. When the police arrived, the two robbers took Mrs. (Edith) Gordon and her 14-year-old daughter (Shelly) as hostages and attempted a getaway. A high-speed chase ensued, and the robbers were eventually captured when their car crashed into a police barrier, seriously wounding two police officers.

As a result of these events, a court sitting without a jury found Stein guilty not only of conspiracy to steal currency from the Gordon home, but also of armed robbery, assaults with an offensive weapon (against Edith and Shelly Gordon), kidnapping, kidnapping while armed, and assaults on a police officer. The intermediate appellate court affirmed the conspiracy and armed robbery convictions but reversed all the rest. The Supreme Court of New Jersey reached a different conclusion, as is explained in the excerpts that follow:

"The question as to the criminal responsibility of a conspirator for the commission by others of substantive offenses having some causal connection with the conspiracy but not in the contemplation of the conspirator has been a matter of considerable debate and controversy. Here there is no question but that Stein did not actually contemplate any criminal consequence of his 'tip' to Pontani beyond a burglary and theft of money from the Gordon home. . . .

"[T]he generally held rule, exemplified by the leading *Pinkerton* case [is] that so long as a conspiracy is still in existence 'an overt act of one partner may be the act of all without any new agreement specifically directed to that act,' provided the substantive act could 'be reasonably foreseen as a necessary or natural consequence of the unlawful agreement.'

"We regard the rule as just stated to be sound and viable. We hold it represents the law in this state.

"It remains to apply the rule to the instant fact situation. Ordinarily the matter of factual application of the rule would be submitted to the jury under appropriate instructions. Here the matter was for the trial judge in the first instance as fact-finder. The Appellate Division found correct the trial ruling that the armed robbery was within the scope of the conspiracy to steal currency from the Gordon home. We are in agreement. The robbery was a 'natural' or 'probable' consequence of the conspiracy. But the Appellate Division concluded that the assaults with an offensive weapon on the wife and daughter of Dr. Gordon were 'not connected with the robbery as such' but 'with the preliminary acts of taking the Gordons as hostages and the eventual kidnappings' and therefore 'not fairly . . . part of the conspiratorial agreement.' The assault convictions were therefore set aside.

"We are not in complete agreement with this last determination. The brandishing of handguns by the robbers when they first encountered Dr. and Mrs. Gordon in the house was clearly a foreseeable event in the course of an unlawful invasion of the house for criminal purposes by armed men. That assault on Mrs. Gordon did not merge with the armed robbery, as the Appellate Division suggested might be the case, since the robbery charged was of Dr. Gordon alone, not the members of his family assaulted. Thus the assault conviction as to Mrs. Gordon should not have been set aside as too remote from the conspiracy.

"As to the charge of assault with an offensive weapon on Shelly Gordon (daughter of the Gordons), since the evidence indicates that offense occurred only at the time of the attempted escape from the police, its disposition depends on the determination as to the other associated charges discussed next below.

"Liability of the defendant for the kidnapping, kidnapping while armed and assaults on a police officer presents a much closer question. The Appellate Division held that these substantive acts were 'offenses committed by the criminals effecting the conspiratorial specific crime after that crime had been committed, as part of a plan to flee when it became evident that they were about to be apprehended' and that defendant could not be charged therefor. On balance, we are satisfied that this is a correct result, particularly in relation to the kidnapping phases of the episode. This holding will also apply to the reversal by the Appellate Division of the conviction for assault with an offensive weapon on Shelly Gordon. However, we rest our concurrence with the Appellate Division not on the ground that the substantive offenses took place subsequent to the commission of the crime conspired or that the offenses were part of a plan to flee, but rather that it would be unreasonable for a fact-finder to find as a fact beyond a reasonable doubt that they were necessary, natural or probable consequences of the conspiracy, having in mind the unique fact-complex presented."

Do you follow this reasoning? Does Stein's liability for armed robbery depend on specific awareness by him that guns would be involved, or does it suffice that he agreed generally to some sort of theft? Would it matter if Stein had suggested that the house be burgled when the Gordons were away on vacation, or if he had explicitly directed Pontani not to create risk of bloodshed?

If, on the other hand, Stein properly is responsible for the armed robbery of Dr. Gordon and the assault of his wife, why should he not be held accountable for the other offenses as well? Is the taking of hostages or the assault of police officers really that remote from armed robbery? Would Stein have been liable for malicious wounding or some other aggravated assault offense if the robbers had shot and wounded Dr. Gordon in order to overcome his resistance? Would such an act be a natural and probable consequence of armed robbery? What if the robbers shot and wounded a police officer? Is that any less foreseeable? Can you think of any rationale for distinguishing Stein's liability according to the identity of the victim? If not, how should these issues be addressed? Are you tired of questions? If not, why not?

SUBSECTION D: SCOPE AND DURATION OF CONSPIRACY

BRAVERMAN v. UNITED STATES

Supreme Court of the United States, 1942.
317 U.S. 49.

MR. CHIEF JUSTICE STONE delivered the opinion of the Court.

[The question is whether] a conviction upon the several counts of an indictment, each charging conspiracy to violate a different provision of the Internal Revenue laws, where the jury's verdict is supported by evidence of but a single conspiracy, will sustain a sentence of more than two years' imprisonment, the maximum penalty for a single violation of the conspiracy statute [a] . . . .

------

[a] Section 37 of the Criminal Code, 18 U.S.C. § 88, at this time carried a maximum term of two-years' imprisonment. The general federal conspiracy statute has since been recodified as 18 U.S.C. § 371 and now carries a maximum term of five years in prison. [Footnote by eds.]

Petitioners were indicted, with others, on seven counts, each charging a conspiracy to violate a separate and distinct internal revenue law of the United States.[1] On the trial there was evidence from which the jury could have found that, for a considerable period of time, petitioners, with others, collaborated in the illicit manufacture, transportation, and distribution of distilled spirits, involving the violations of statute mentioned in the several counts of the indictment. At the close of the trial, petitioners renewed a motion which they had made at its beginning to require the government to elect one of the seven counts of the indictment upon which to proceed, contending that the proof could not and did not establish more than one agreement. In response the government's attorney took the position that the seven counts of the indictment charged as distinct offenses the several illegal objects of one continuing conspiracy, that if the jury found such a conspiracy it might find the defendants guilty of as many offenses as it had illegal objects, and that for each such offense the two-year statutory penalty could be imposed.

The trial judge submitted the case to the jury on that theory. The jury returned a general verdict finding petitioners "guilty as charged," and the court sentenced each to eight years' imprisonment. On appeal the Court of Appeals for the Sixth Circuit affirmed . . . .

Both courts below recognized that a single agreement to commit an offense does not become several conspiracies because it continues over a period of time and that there may be such a single continuing agreement to commit several offenses. But they thought that, in the latter case, each contemplated offense renders the agreement punishable as a separate conspiracy.

The question whether a single agreement to commit acts in violation of several penal statutes is to be punished as one or several conspiracies is raised on the present record, not by the construction of the indictment, but by the government's concession at the trial and here, reflected in the charge to the jury, that only a single agreement to commit the offenses alleged was proven. Where each of the counts of an indictment alleges a conspiracy to violate a different penal statute, it may be proper to conclude, in the absence of a bill of exceptions bringing up the evidence, that several conspiracies are charged rather than one, and that the conviction is for each. But it is a different matter to hold, as the court below appears to have done . . . that

---

[1] The seven counts respectively charged them with conspiracy, in violation of Section 37 of the Criminal Code, unlawfully (i) to carry on the business of wholesale and retail liquor dealers without having the special occupational tax stamps required by statute, 26 U.S.C. § 3253; (ii) to possess distilled spirits, the immediate containers of which did not have stamps affixed denoting the quantity of the distilled spirits which they contained and evidencing payment of all Internal Revenue taxes imposed on such spirits, 26 U.S.C. § 2803; (iii) to transport quantities of distilled spirits, the immediate containers of which did not have affixed the required stamps, 26 U.S.C. § 2803; (iv) to carry on the business of distillers without having given bond as required by law, 26 U.S.C. § 2833; (v) to remove, deposit and conceal distilled spirits in respect whereof a tax is imposed by law, with intent to defraud the United States of such tax, 26 U.S.C. § 3321; (vi) to possess unregistered stills and distilling apparatus, 26 U.S.C. § 2810; and (vii) to make and ferment mash, fit for distillation, on unauthorized premises, 26 U.S.C. § 2834.

even though a single agreement is entered into, the conspirators are guilty of as many offenses as the agreement has criminal subjects.

The gist of the crime of conspiracy as defined by the statute is the agreement or confederation of the conspirators to commit one or more unlawful acts "where one or more of such parties do any act to effect the object of the conspiracy." The overt act, without proof of which a charge of conspiracy cannot be submitted to the jury, may be that of only a single one of the conspirators and need not be itself a crime. But it is unimportant, for present purposes, whether we regard the overt act as part of the crime which the statute defines and makes punishable or as something apart from it, either an indispensable mode of corroborating the existence of the conspiracy or a device for affording a locus poenitentiae.

For when a single agreement to commit one or more substantive crimes is evidenced by an overt act, as the statute requires, the precise nature and extent of the conspiracy must be determined by reference to the agreement which embraces and defines its objects. Whether the object of a single agreement is to commit one or many crimes, it is in either case that agreement which constitutes the conspiracy which the statute punishes. The one agreement cannot be taken to be several agreements and hence several conspiracies because it envisages the violation of several statutes rather than one. . . .

The single agreement is the prohibited conspiracy, and however diverse its objects it violates but a single statute, Section 37 of the Criminal Code. For such a violation, only the single penalty prescribed by the statute can be imposed.

NOTES ON THE SCOPE OF CONSPIRACY—THE OBJECT DIMENSION

1. *Lievers* v. *State*. With *Braverman* compare the decision in Lievers v. State, 3 Md.App. 597, 241 A.2d 147 (1968). The evidence in that case showed that defendant Lievers was the ringleader of a bad check operation. The particular events on which prosecution was based arose from an effort by Lievers and several cohorts to cash a forged check made out in the fictitious name of Steven Thompson. For his part in that scheme, Lievers was convicted of (i) conspiracy to forge the check in question, (ii) conspiracy to utter the forged check, (iii) conspiracy to obtain money by false pretenses from the party who cashed the forged check, and (iv) conspiracy to hold and use a counterfeit Maryland chauffeur's license in the name of the fictitious payee. Lievers challenged the four convictions. He claimed that all of the object offenses were covered by a single agreement to pass bad checks and therefore constituted but one conspiracy. The Maryland Court of Appeals treated this claim as a question of cumulative punishment for the object offenses:

"In Tender v. State, 2 Md.App. 692, 237 A.2d 65 (1967), we held that a person should not be twice punished for the same acts whether the offenses charged by reason of such acts be deemed to be inconsistent, duplicitous, or to have merged. The true test of merger of offenses is whether one crime necessarily involves the other. Thus in Sutton v. State, 2 Md.App. 639, 236 A.2d 301 (1967), we held, on the facts of that case, that the substantive offense of uttering merged into the offense of false pretenses where the false representation consisted only of the uttering. It appears to us from the evidence in this case that the conspiracy to utter merged into the conspiracy to obtain money by false pretenses since no false representation independent of the uttering of the forged check itself is shown by the evidence."

This analysis led the court to vacate the conviction for the second offense on the ground that it had merged with the third. The three separate convictions for conspiracy to forge the check, conspiracy to obtain money by false pretenses, and conspiracy to use a counterfeit chauffer's license, however, were upheld as punishments for three distinct wrongs.

2. **Questions and Comments on *Braverman* and *Lievers*.** Are *Braverman* and *Lievers* consistent? If not, which states the better rule? The *Braverman* result is inconsistent, is it not, with the approach that would be followed in attempt? If Braverman and his cohorts had been prosecuted for attempt, they would have been subject to separate punishment for each offense attempted. Why should a different rule obtain for the inchoate offense of conspiracy? Is the penalty for agreeing to engage in criminal misconduct not properly related to the number of crimes contemplated? Is agreeing to commit a series of offenses no more serious than agreeing to commit one?

Is not *Braverman* also arguably incompatible with the role of conspiracy as an alternative to complicity? Should secondary participation in a plan to commit several crimes be punished more severely than a plan to commit only one? The law of complicity would so provide. Should conspiracy do likewise?

A different line of questions concerns the administrability of the rule of *Braverman*. In the context of an ongoing criminal enterprise, as is illustrated by the facts of both *Braverman* and *Lievers*, how realistic is it to inquire into the number of agreements? Such arrangements are unlikely to involve formal documentation and, indeed, may never have been precisely worked out by the parties themselves. Given that the agreement may be tacit and that it may evolve from collaborative effort rather than from any particular negotiation, how useful is it to ask whether the objectives of the combination were covered by one or more than one agreement? The risk, of course, is that the rule of *Braverman* is likely to turn less on underlying factual reality than on the characterizations imposed on the evidence, and the most influential factor in characterizing the evidence may be simply how the prosecutor chooses to frame the charges.

3. **The Model Code Approach.** Section 5.03(3) of the Model Penal Code addresses the *Braverman* issue explicitly:

"If a person conspires to commit a number of crimes, he is guilty of only one conspiracy so long as such multiple crimes are the object of the same agreement or continuous conspiratorial relationship."

Is this an improvement over the *Braverman* formulation? Why or why not?

Note that the drafters of this provision defended the limitation of liability on the basis of the possibility that conspiracy may be used to punish extremely inchoate behavior. See MPC § 5.03, Comment at 128 (Tent. Draft No. 10, 1960):

> "A rule treating the agreement as several crimes, equivalent in number and grade to the substantive crimes contemplated, might be unduly harsh in cases—uncommon though they may be— where the conspirators are apprehended in the very early stages of preparation. The grandiose nature of the scheme might be more indicative of braggadocio or foolhardiness than of the conspirators' actual abilities, propensities and dangerousness as criminals."

Are you persuaded? Is the *Braverman* question likely to be in issue when the conspirators "are apprehended in the very early stages of preparation"? In such a case, how would the prosecution prove the multiple objectives? That is not to suggest that the case put by the Model Code drafters cannot arise, but only that it is probably no accident that both *Braverman* and *Lievers* involved situations where conspiracy was used as an alternative to prosecution for complicity in completed conduct. It is cases of that sort in which the multiplicity of criminal objectives is likely to be made clear. Does the Model Code approach make sense in this context?

Today, most states continue to deal with the *Braverman* issue without explicit statutory authority. A number of modern code revisions, however, include provisions derived from the Model Code section quoted above. Most of these include the alternative formulation of "continuous conspiratorial relationship," but a few follow *Braverman* in focusing exclusively on the scope of the agreement. For a discussion of this issue and citations to several statutes, see Note, Conspiracy: Statutory Reform Since the Model Penal Code, 75 Colum.L.Rev. 1122, 1163–64 (1975).

UNITED STATES v. BRUNO

United States Court of Appeals for the Second Circuit, 1939.
105 F.2d 921.

PER CURIAM. Bruno and Iacono were indicted along with 86 others for a conspiracy to import, sell and possess narcotics; some were acquitted; others, besides these two, were convicted, but they alone appealed. They complain that if the evidence proved anything, it proved a series of separate conspiracies, and not a single one, as alleged in the indictment. . . .

The first point was made at the conclusion of the prosecution's case: the defendants then moved to dismiss the indictment on the ground that several conspiracies had been proved, and not the one alleged. The evidence allowed the jury to find that there had existed over a substantial period of time a conspiracy embracing a great number of persons, whose object was to smuggle narcotics into the Port of New York and distribute them to addicts both in this city and in Texas and Louisiana. This required the cooperation of four groups of persons; the smugglers who imported the drugs; the middlemen who paid the smugglers and distributed to retailers; and two groups of retailers—one in New York and one in Texas and Louisiana—who supplied the addicts. The defendants assert that there were, therefore, at least three separate conspiracies; one between the smugglers and the middlemen, and one between the middlemen and each group of retailers. The evidence did not disclose any cooperation or communication between the smugglers and either group of retailers, or between the two groups of retailers themselves; however, the smugglers knew that the middlemen must sell to retailers, and the retailers knew that the middlemen must buy of importers of one sort or another. Thus the conspirators at one end of the chain knew that the unlawful business would not, and could not, stop with their buyers; and those at the other end knew that it had not begun with their sellers. That being true, a jury might have found that all the accused were embarked upon a venture, in all parts of which each was a participant, and an abettor in the sense that the success of that part with which he was immediately concerned, was dependent upon the success of the whole. That distinguishes the situation from that in United States v. Peoni, 100 F.2d 401 (2d Cir. 1938) [see page 411, supra], where Peoni, the accused, did not know that Regno, his buyer, was to sell the counterfeit bills to Dorsey, and had no interest in whether he did, since Regno might equally well have passed them to innocent persons himself. It might still be argued that there were two conspiracies; one including the smugglers, the middlemen and the New York group, and the other, the smugglers, the middlemen and the Texas and Louisiana group, for there was apparently no privity between the two groups of retailers. That too would be fallacious. Clearly, quoad the smugglers, there was but one conspiracy, for it was of no moment to them whether the middlemen sold to one or more groups of retailers, provided they had a market somewhere. So too of any retailer; he knew that he was a necessary link in a scheme of distribution, and the others, whom he knew to be convenient to its execution, were as much parts of a single undertaking or enterprise as two salesmen in the same shop. We think therefore that there was only one conspiracy . . . .

NOTES ON THE SCOPE OF CONSPIRACY— THE PARTY DIMENSION

1. **Wheels and Chains**. Some of the most puzzling questions in conspiracy cases arise from the need to determine, in a wide variety of contexts, whether the relationships among participants in a large criminal enterprise constitute one or several conspiracies. Traditional-

ly, this issue is dealt with by superimposing on the evidence of conspiracy some visualization of its structure. The two most prominent shapes
accorded to conspiracies are the wheel and the chain. The wheel
conspiracy is based on a central figure (the hub) who deals separately
with various peripheral figures (the spokes) in a common undertaking.
Each of the spokes may be judged a member of the same conspiracy,
even though they have no direct relations with one another. The chain
conspiracy focuses on successive stages of cooperation, as, for example,
between *A* and *B*, *B* and *C*, *C* and *D*, and so forth. Again, a person at
one end of the chain may be found to have conspired with others with
whom that person had no direct dealings. Both types are illustrated by
the facts of *Bruno*. The progression from smugglers to middlemen to
retailers is a classic chain, while the two groups of retailers can be seen
as separate spokes of a wheel centered on the middlemen distributors.

Although this kind of categorization is standard, it is certainly open
to question whether visualizing the shape of a conspiracy is especially
helpful in determining its scope. The answer, of course, depends on the
functional consequence of making such determinations. Not surprisingly, the classification of wheels and chains is used to resolve a
number of different issues. Sometimes, as was apparently the case in
Bruno, the question is variance. Did the prosecution prove what the
indictment charged? If not, the conviction would be set aside, even
though the evidence would have supported conviction under a different
characterization of the facts. In other cases, the issue of single or
multiple conspiracies governs application of the statute of limitations.
Thus, for example, a member of a single, continuing conspiracy may be
prosecuted for that offense, even though prosecution based on his
personal participation in the enterprise would be barred by the passage
of time. In other situations, the scope of conspiracy is important
chiefly in resolving certain procedural issues—for example, whether
joint trial of several co-defendants is appropriate or whether out-of-
court statements of one person can be introduced against another under
the co-conspirator's exception to the hearsay rule. Finally, the issue of
single or multiple conspiracies may play a critical role in charting the
limits of an individual's liability under the *Pinkerton* rule for substantive crimes committed by co-conspirators. Obviously, these illustrations offer little in the way of conceptual unity, and it is doubtful
whether any classification of shapes can usefully address all these
questions in the same terms. Can you imagine, for example, that the
facts of *Bruno* would have been found to show only one conspiracy if
the issue had been the scope of the defendant's liability under the
Pinkerton rule?

2. **The Model Code Approach.** Under Section 5.03 of the Model
Penal Code, the scope of the offense is governed by the interaction of
Subsections (1) and (2). Subsection (1) declares a person guilty of
conspiracy with another to commit a crime if, with purpose to promote
that crime, he or she "agrees with such other person or persons that
they or one or more of them will engage in conduct which constitutes
such crime or an attempt or solicitation to commit such crime" or
"agrees to aid such other person or persons in the planning or commis-

sion of such crime or of an attempt or solicitation to commit such crime." Subsection (2) expands the party dimension of this liability as follows:

> "If a person guilty of conspiracy, as defined by Subsection (1) of this Section, knows that a person with whom he conspires to commit a crime has conspired with another person or persons to commit the same crime, he is guilty of conspiring with such other person or persons, whether or not he knows their identity, to commit such crime."

This formulation follows *Bruno* in allowing conviction for a single conspiracy of persons unknown to one another, but it departs from the approach of that case by requiring that all members share the same objective. Subsection (1) requires that the actor agree to promote or facilitate a particular object offense, and Subsection (2) extends the scope of the conspiracy only to those additional parties known to have conspired to commit the *same* crime.

How would this limitation affect the analysis in *Bruno*? Would persons involved in the New York retailing operation be subject to conviction for a single conspiracy with both the middlemen and the smugglers? Would the New York retailers also be guilty of conspiracy with the Texas and Louisiana retailers? What would the prosecution have to prove to sustain such charges?

3. *Kotteakos* v. *United States*. On the problem of variance between the number of conspiracies charged and the number proved by the evidence, see Kotteakos v. United States, 328 U.S. 750 (1946). In that case some 32 persons were charged with a single conspiracy to obtain loans by false and fraudulent applications to the Federal Housing Administration. Seven of those charged ultimately were convicted. The central figure in all of the transactions proved was one Simon Brown. Brown acted as a broker in procuring the illegal loans and charged each applicant a commission for his services. The applicants themselves, however, had no dealings with those on other loan applications. As the Court of Appeals noted, there were "at least eight, and perhaps more, separate and independent groups, none of which had any connection with any other, though all dealt independently with Brown as their agent." The court concluded that it therefore was error to convict the defendants of the single conspiracy charged in the indictment but nevertheless affirmed on the ground that the error was harmless. On review by the Supreme Court, the government admitted the variance but contended that the defendants had suffered no prejudice. The Supreme Court reversed:

> "The government's theory seems to be, in ultimate logical reach, that the error presented by the variance is insubstantial and harmless, if the evidence offered specifically and properly to convict each defendant would be sufficient to sustain his conviction, if submitted in a separate trial. For reasons we have stated and in view of the authorities cited, this is not and cannot be the test under Section 269 [which directs appellate courts to disregard "technical errors, defects, or exceptions which do not affect

the substantial rights of the parties"]. But in apparent support of its view the government argues that there was no prejudice here because the results show that the jury exercised discrimination as among the defendants whose cases were submitted to it. As it points out, the jury acquitted some, disagreed as to others, and found still others guilty. From this it concludes that the jury was not confused and, apparently, reached the same result as would have been reached or would be likely, if the convicted defendants had been or now should be tried separately.

"One difficulty with this is that the trial court itself was confused in the charge which it gave to guide the jury in deliberation. The court instructed:

'The indictment charges but one conspiracy, and to convict each of the defendants of a conspiracy the government would have to prove, and you would have to find, that each of the defendants was a member of that conspiracy. You cannot divide it up. It is one conspiracy, and the question is whether or not each of the defendants, or which of the defendants, are members of that conspiracy.'

"On its face, as the Court of Appeals said, this portion of charge was plainly wrong in application to the proof made; and the error pervaded the entire charge, not merely the portion quoted. The jury could not possibly have found, upon the evidence, that there was only one conspiracy. The trial court was of the view that one conspiracy was made out by showing that each defendant was linked to Brown in one or more transactions, and that it was possible on the evidence for the jury to conclude that all were in a common adventure because of this fact and the similarity of purpose presented in the various applications for loans.

"This view, specifically embodied throughout the instructions, obviously confuses the common purpose of a single enterprise with the several, though similar, purposes of numerous separate adventures of like character. It may be that, notwithstanding the misdirection, the jury actually understood correctly the purport of the evidence, as the government now concedes it to have been; and came to the conclusion that the petitioners were guilty only of the separate conspiracies in which the proof shows they respectively participated. But, in the face of the misdirection and in the circumstances of this case, we cannot assume that the lay triers of fact were so well informed upon the law or that they disregarded the permission expressly given to ignore that vital difference. . . .

"On those instructions, it was competent not only for the jury to find that all of the defendants were parties to a single common plan, design and scheme, where none was shown by the proof, but also for them to impute to each defendant the acts and statements of the others without reference to whether they related to one of the schemes proven or another, and to find an overt act affecting all in conduct which admittedly could only have affected some. True, the Court of Appeals painstakingly examined the evidence directly relating to each petitioner and concluded he had not been prejudiced in this manner. That judgment was founded largely in the fact that each was clearly shown to have shared in the fraudulent phase of the conspiracy in which he participated. Even so, we do not understand how it can be concluded, in the face of the instruction, that the jury considered and was influenced by nothing else. . . ."

Note that the original government theory of a single conspiracy was based on the analogy to a wheel. Simon Brown was the hub, and the various loan applicants were the spokes. Obviously, this analogy did not persuade the Supreme Court that there had been one conspiracy. In what ways does this version of the wheel conspiracy differ from the relation between the two groups of retailers in *Bruno*? Does *Kotteakos* reflect the view that the wheel configuration will never suffice, or are some wheels more unifying than others? Can you say what characteristics might cause a court to view a wheel as one conspiracy rather than several?

4. ***Blumenthal* v. *United States***. With *Kotteakos*, compare Blumenthal v. United States, 332 U.S. 539 (1947). Five individuals were convicted of a single conspiracy to sell whiskey at prices higher than those allowed by wartime price controls. Defendants Goldsmith and Weiss were, respectively, owner and sales manager of the Francisco Distributing Co., an authorized liquor dealer. Goldsmith and Weiss agreed to distribute under Francisco's name two carloads of whiskey owned by an unidentified person. Francisco handled the deliveries and collected from the ultimate purchasers a lawful price for the whiskey delivered to them. Defendants Blumenthal, Feigenbaum, and Abel acted as brokers for the illegal sales. They collected from the ultimate purchasers additional charges disallowed by law. Blumenthal, Feigenbaum, and Abel had no dealings with one another, and there was no evidence that they knew of the existence of, or the role played by, the unidentified owner of the whiskey. The claim before the Supreme Court was that the evidence showed not one conspiracy, but two: first, an agreement among Goldsmith, Weiss, and the unidentified owner to distribute the whiskey through Francisco; and second, a later agreement among the five named defendants to handle the illegal sales. The Supreme Court affirmed the convictions:

"We think that in the special circumstances of this case the two agreements were merely steps in the formation of the larger and ultimately more general conspiracy. In that view it would be a perversion of justice to regard the salesmen's ignorance of the unknown owner's participation as furnishing adequate ground for reversal of their convictions. The scheme was in fact the same scheme; the salesmen knew or must have known that others unknown to them were sharing in so large a project; and it hardly can be sufficient to relieve them that they did not know, when they joined the scheme, who those people were or exactly the parts they were playing in carrying out the common design and object of all. By their separate agreements, if such they were, they became parties to the larger common plan, joined together by their knowledge of its essential features and broad scope, though not of its exact limits, and by their common single goal.

"The case therefore is very different from the facts admitted to exist in the *Kotteakos* case. Apart from the much larger number of agreements there involved, no two of those agreements were tied together as stages in the formation of a larger all-inclusive combination, all directed to achieving a single unlawful end or result. On the contrary each separate agreement had its own distinct, illegal end. Each loan was an end in itself, separate from all others, although all were alike in having similar illegal objects. Except for Brown, the common figure, no conspirator was interested in whether any loan except his own went through. And none aided in any way, by agreement or otherwise, in procuring another's loan. The conspiracies therefore were distinct and disconnected, not parts of a larger general scheme, both in the phase of agreement with Brown and also in the absence of any aid given to others as well as in specific object and result. There was no drawing of all together in a single, over-all, comprehensive plan.

"Here the contrary is true. All knew of and joined in the overriding scheme. All intended to aid the owner, whether Francisco or another, to sell the whiskey unlawfully, though the two groups of defendants differed on the proof in knowledge and belief concerning the owner's identity. All by reason of their knowledge of the plan's general scope, if not its exact limits, sought a common end, to aid in disposing of the whiskey. True, each salesman aided in selling only his part. But he knew the lot to be sold was larger and thus that he was aiding in a larger plan. He thus became a party to it and not merely to the integrating agreement with Weiss and Goldsmith.

"We think therefore that in every practical sense the unique facts of this case reveal a single conspiracy of which the several agreements were essential and integral steps, and accordingly that the judgments should be affirmed."

Are you persuaded that *Kotteakos* is distinguishable? Were the salesmen in *Blumenthal* really more interested in the success of one another than were the loan applicants in *Kotteakos*? Was the role played by Goldsmith and Weiss substantially different from that played by Simon Brown? Finally, how would these cases come out under the Model Penal Code? Would the analysis proceed on the same terms as those reflected in the opinions, or would there be significant differences?

5. **United States v. Borelli**. Finally, consider the case of United States v. Borelli, 336 F.2d 376 (2d Cir. 1964). *Borelli* involved the importation and distribution of heroin over a period of several years.

Some participants were constant, but others came and went. The facts defy brief description, but the essential structure of the problem is suggested by the introductory comments of Judge Friendly:

"Appellants from conspiracy convictions too often remind us of Kotteakos v. United States, 328 U.S. 750 (1946), and of Mr. Justice Jackson's concurrence in Krulewitch v. United States, 336 U.S. 440 (1949), in instances where the reminder is inapposite. But a few facts will show in what degree the instant case gives point to Mr. Justice Jackson's description of conspiracy as 'that elastic, sprawling and pervasive offense,' whose development exemplifies, in Judge Cardozo's phrase, the 'tendency of a principle to expand itself to the limit of its logic'—and perhaps beyond.

"This indictment was filed August 15, 1962. The applicable statute of limitations is five years. The conspiracy is alleged to have begun in 1950 and to have lasted until 1959. The only acts of participation proved as to one appellant were in 1951. As to others there was no evidence of participation later than 1955. Two who first appear in 1958 were found to have been in 'partnership in crime,' Pinkerton v. United States, 328 U.S. 640 (1946), with those who, so far as the proof shows, left the stage seven and three years earlier. Tacitly recognizing inclusion of all the appellants in a single conspiracy to be something of a tour de force, the government contends in its able brief and argument that the convictions are buttressed by impressive authority and impeccable logic. The conspiracy, it says, was continuous as regards at least some of the principals; each participant is presumed to have been responsible for all that would ever go on, or that ever had; and he could terminate this responsibility only by making a clean breast to the authorities or by informing his colleagues—mostly unknown to him—that he was through. The appeal thus demands an examination of the application of the law of conspiracy to the long continued conduct of an illicit business."

The government argued that the facts thus outlined formed a classic "chain" conspiracy and relied on *United States* v. *Bruno*, page 497, supra, as authority. The Second Circuit, however, found this characterization inadequate to sustain a finding of a single conspiracy and remanded the case for retrial under instructions differentiating among the defendants. In reaching that conclusion, the court made the following comments on the nature and difficulties of determining the scope of a conspiracy:

"As applied to the long-term operation of an illegal business, the common pictorial distinction between 'chain' and 'spoke' conspiracies can obscure as much as it clarifies. The chain metaphor is indeed apt in that the links of a narcotics conspiracy are inextricably related to one another, from grower, through exporter and importer, to wholesaler, middleman, and retailer, each depending for his own success on the performance of all the others. But this simple picture tends to obscure that the links at either end are likely to consist of a number of persons who may have no reason to know that others are performing a role similar to theirs—in other words the extreme links of a chain conspiracy may have elements of the spoke conspiracy. Moreover, whatever the value of the chain concept where the problem is to trace a single operation from the start through its various phases to its successful conclusion, it becomes confusing when, over a long period of time, certain links continue to play the same role but with new counterparts, as where importers who regard their partnership as a single continuing one, having successfully distributed one cargo through *X* distributing organization, turn, years later, to moving another cargo obtained from a different source through *Y*. Thus, however reasonable the so-called presumption of continuity may be as to all the participants of a conspiracy which intends a single act, such as the robbing of a bank, or even as to the core of a conspiracy to import and resell narcotics, its force is diminished as to the outer links—buyers indifferent to their sources of supply and turning from one source to another, and suppliers equally indifferent to the identity of their customers.

"The basic difficulty arises in applying the 17th century notion of conspiracy, where the gravamen of the offense was the making of an *agreement* to commit a readily identifiable crime or series of crimes, such as murder or robbery, to what in substance is the conduct of an illegal business over a period of years. There has been a tendency in such cases 'to deal with the crime of conspiracy as if it were a group [of men] rather than an act' of agreement. Developments in the Law—Criminal Conspiracy, 72 Harv.L.Rev. 922, 934 (1959). Although it is usual and often necessary in conspiracy cases for the agreement to be proved by inference from acts, the gist of the offense remains the agreement, and it is therefore essential to determine what kind of agreement or understanding existed as to each defendant. It is a great deal harder to tell just *what* agreement can reasonably be inferred from the purchase, even the repeated purchase, of contraband, than from the furnishing of dynamite to prospective bank robbers or the exchange of worthless property for securities to be subsequently distributed. Purchase or sale of contraband may, of course, warrant the inference of an agreement going well beyond the particular transaction. A seller of narcotics in bulk surely knows that the purchasers will undertake to resell the goods over an uncertain period of time, and the circumstances may also warrant the inference that a supplier or a purchaser indicated a willingness to repeat. But a sale or a purchase scarcely constitutes a sufficient basis for inferring agreement to cooperate with the opposite parties for whatever period they continue to deal in this type of contraband, unless some such understanding is evidenced by other conduct which accompanies or supplements the transaction."

Judge Friendly's analysis suggests, does it not, that the whole pictorial approach to determining the scope of a conspiracy may be seriously flawed. Can you think of any better way to approach the problem? Why must such determinations be made in the first place? Would reformulation of the law of conspiracy obviate the need for such inquiries, or at least reduce their importance? Is this an important consideration, or is the scope of a conspiracy a question that safely can be left to more or less ad hoc resolution on the facts of each case?

GRUNEWALD v. UNITED STATES

Supreme Court of the United States, 1957.
353 U.S. 391.

MR. JUSTICE HARLAN delivered the opinion of the Court.

The three petitioners were convicted on count 1 of an indictment brought under 18 U.S.C. § 371 for conspiracy to defraud the United States with reference to certain tax matters. . . .

The proofs at trial presented a sordid picture of a ring engaged in the business of "fixing" tax-fraud cases by the use of bribes and improper influence. In general outline, the petitioners' scheme . . . was as follows:

In 1947 and 1948 two New York business firms, Patullo Modes and Gotham Beef Co., were under investigation by the Bureau of Internal Revenue for suspected fraudulent tax evasion. Through intermediaries, both firms established contact with Halperin, a New York attorney, and his associates in law practice. Halperin in turn conducted negotiations on behalf of these firms with Grunewald, an "influential" friend in Washington, and reported that Grunewald, for a large cash fee, would undertake to prevent criminal prosecution of the taxpayers. Grunewald then used his influence with Bolich, an official in the Bureau, to obtain "no prosecution" rulings in the two tax cases. These rulings were handed down in 1948 and 1949. Grunewald, through Halperin, was subsequently paid $60,000 by Gotham and $100,000 by Patullo.

Subsequent activities of the conspirators were directed at concealing the irregularities in the disposition of the Patullo and Gotham cases. Bolich attempted to have the Bureau of Internal Revenue report on the Patullo case "doctored," and careful steps were taken to cover up the traces of the cash fees paid to Grunewald. In 1951 a congressional investigation was started by the King Committee of the House of Representatives: the conspirators felt themselves threatened and took steps to hide their traces. Thus Bolich caused the disappearance of certain records linking him to Grunewald, and the taxpayers were repeatedly warned to keep quiet. In 1952 the taxpayers and the conspirators were called before a Brooklyn grand jury. Halperin attempted to induce the taxpayers not to reveal the conspiracy, and Grunewald asked his secretary not to talk to the grand jury. These attempts at concealment were, however, in vain. The taxpayers and some of Halperin's associates revealed the entire scheme, and petitioners' indictment and conviction followed.

The . . . question before us is whether the prosecution of these petitioners on count 1 of the indictment was barred by the applicable three-year statute of limitations.

The indictment in these cases was returned on October 25, 1954. It was therefore incumbent on the government to prove that the conspiracy, as contemplated in the agreement as finally formulated, was still in existence on October 25, 1951, and that at least one overt act in furtherance of the conspiracy was performed after that date. For where substantiation of a conspiracy charge requires proof of an overt act, it must be shown both that the conspiracy still subsisted within the three years prior to the return of the indictment, and that at least one overt act in furtherance of the conspiratorial agreement was performed within that period. Hence, in both of these aspects, the crucial question in determining whether the statute of limitations has run is the scope of the conspiratorial agreement, for it is that which determines both the duration of the conspiracy, and whether the act relied on as an overt act may properly be regarded as in furtherance of the conspiracy.

Petitioners, in contending that this prosecution was barred by limitations, state that the object of the conspiratorial agreement was a narrow one: to obtain "no prosecution" rulings in the two tax cases. When these rulings were obtained, in October 1948 in the case of Gotham Beef, and in January 1949 in the case of Patullo Modes, the criminal object of the conspiracy, petitioners say, was attained and the conspirators' function ended. They argue, therefore, that the statute of limitations started running no later than January 1949, and that the prosecution was therefore barred by 1954, when the indictment was returned.

The government counters with two principal contentions: First, it urges that even if the main object of the conspiracy was to obtain decisions from the Bureau of Internal Revenue not to institute criminal tax prosecutions—decisions obtained in 1948 and 1949—the indictment alleged, and the proofs showed, that the conspiracy also included as a subsidiary element an agreement to conceal the conspiracy to "fix" these tax cases, to the end that the conspirators would escape detection and punishment for their crime. Says the government, "from the very nature of the conspiracy . . . there had to be, and was, from the outset a conscious, deliberate, agreement to conceal . . . each and every aspect of the conspiracy . . . ." It is then argued that since the alleged conspiracy to conceal clearly continued long after the main criminal purpose of the conspiracy was accomplished, and since overt acts in furtherance of the agreement to conceal were performed well within the indictment period, the prosecution was timely.

Second, and alternatively, the government contends that the central aim of the conspiracy was to obtain for these taxpayers, not merely a "no prosecution" ruling, but absolute immunity from tax prosecution; in other words, that the objectives of the conspiracy were not attained until 1952, when the statute of limitations ran on the tax cases which these petitioners undertook to "fix." The argument then is that since the conspiracy did not end until 1952, and since the 1949–1952 acts of concealment may be regarded as, at least in part, in furtherance of the objective of the conspirators to immunize the taxpayers from tax prosecution, the indictment was timely.

For reasons hereafter given, we hold that the government's first contention must be rejected, and that as to the second . . . a new trial must be ordered.

I

We think that the government's first theory—that an agreement to conceal a conspiracy can, on facts such as these, be deemed part of the conspiracy and can extend its duration for the purposes of the statute of limitations—has already been rejected by this Court in Krulewitch v. United States, 336 U.S. 440 (1949), and in Lutwak v. United States, 344 U.S. 604 (1953).

In *Krulewitch* the question before the Court was whether certain hearsay declarations could be introduced against one of the conspirators. The declarations in question were made by one named in the indictment as a co-conspirator after the main object of the conspiracy (transporting a woman to Florida for immoral purposes) had been accomplished. The government argued that the conspiracy was not ended, however, since it included an implied subsidiary conspiracy to conceal the crime after its commission, and that the declarations were therefore still in furtherance of the conspiracy and binding on co-conspirators. The Court rejected the government's argument. It then stated:

"Conspirators about to commit crimes always expressly or implicitly agree to collaborate with each other to conceal facts in order to prevent detection, conviction and punishment. Thus the [government's] argument is that even after the central criminal objectives of a conspiracy have succeeded or failed, an implicit subsidiary phase of the conspiracy always survives, the phase which has concealment as its sole objective.

"We cannot accept the government's contention. . . . The rule contended for by the government could have far-reaching results. For under this rule plausible arguments could generally be made in conspiracy cases that most out-of-court statements offered in evidence tended to shield co-conspirators. We are not persuaded to adopt the government's implicit conspiracy theory which in all criminal conspiracy cases would create automatically a further breach of the general rule against the admission of hearsay evidence."

Mr. Justice Jackson, concurring, added:

"I suppose no person planning a crime would accept as a collaborator one on whom he thought he could not rely for help if he were caught, but I doubt that this fact warrants an inference of conspiracy for that purpose. . . .

"It is difficult to see any logical limit to the 'implied conspiracy,' either as to duration or means . . .. On the theory that the law will impute to the confederates a continuing conspiracy to defeat justice, one conceivably could be bound by another's unauthorized and unknown commission of perjury, bribery of a juror or witness, [etc.]. . . .

"Moreover, the assumption of an indefinitely continuing offense would result in an indeterminate extension of the statute of limitations. If the law implies an agreement to cooperate in defeating prosecution, it must imply that it continues as long as prosecution is a possibility, and prosecution is a possibility as long as the conspiracy to defeat it is implied to continue."

The *Krulewitch* case was reaffirmed in *Lutwak* v. *United States,* supra. Here again the question was the admissibility of hearsay declarations of co-conspirators after the main purpose of the conspiracy had been accomplished; again the government attempted to extend the life of the conspiracy by an alleged subsidiary conspiracy to conceal. Although in *Lutwak,* unlike in *Krulewitch,* the existence of a subsidiary conspiracy to conceal was charged in the indictment, the Court again rejected the government's theory, holding that no such agreement to conceal had been proved or could be implied.

The government urges us to distinguish *Krulewitch* and *Lutwak* on the ground that in those cases the attempt was to *imply* a conspiracy to conceal from the mere fact that the main conspiracy was kept secret and that overt acts of concealment occurred. In contrast, says the government, here there was an *actual* agreement to conceal the conspirators, which was charged and proved to be an express part of the initial conspiracy itself.

We are unable to agree with the government that, on this record, the cases before us can be distinguished on such a basis.

The crucial teaching of *Krulewitch* and *Lutwak* is that after the central criminal purposes of a conspiracy have been attained, a subsidiary conspiracy to conceal may not be implied from circumstantial evidence showing merely that the conspiracy was kept a secret and that the conspirators took care to cover up their crime in order to escape detection and punishment. . . .

A reading of the record before us reveals that on the facts of this case the distinction between "actual" and "implied" conspiracies to conceal, as urged upon us by the government, is no more than a verbal tour de force. True, in both *Krulewitch* and *Lutwak* there is language in the opinions stressing the fact that only an *implied* agreement to conceal was relied on. Yet when we look to the facts of the present cases, we see that the evidence from which the government here asks us to deduce an "actual" agreement to conceal reveals nothing beyond that adduced in prior cases. What is this evidence? First, we have the fact that from the beginning the conspirators insisted on secrecy. Thus the identities of Grunewald and Bolich were sedulously kept from the taxpayers; careful steps were taken to hide the conspiracy from an independent law firm which was also working on Patullo's tax problems; and the taxpayers were told to make sure that their books did not reflect the large cash payments made to Grunewald. Secondly, after the "no prosecution" rulings were obtained, we have facts showing that this secrecy was still maintained. Thus, a deliberate attempt was made to make the abovementioned independent law firm believe that it was *its* (quite legitimate) efforts which produced the successful ruling. Finally, we have the fact that great efforts were made to conceal the conspiracy when the danger of exposure appeared. For example, Bolich got rid of certain records showing that he had used Grunewald's hotel suite in Washington; Patullo's accountant was persuaded to lie to the grand jury concerning a check made out to an associate of the conspirators; Grunewald attempted to persuade his secretary not to talk to the grand jury; and the taxpayers were repeatedly told by Halperin and his associates to keep quiet.

We find in all this nothing more than what was involved in *Krulewitch*, that is, (i) a criminal conspiracy which is carried out in secrecy; (ii) a continuation of the secrecy after the accomplishment of the crime; and (iii) desperate attempts to cover up after the crime begins to come to light; and so we cannot agree that this case does not fall within the ban of those prior opinions. . . .

By no means does this mean that acts of concealment can never have a significance in furthering a criminal conspiracy. But a vital distinction must be made between acts of concealment done in furtherance of the *main* criminal objectives of the conspiracy, and acts of concealment done after these central objectives have been attained, for the purpose only of covering up after the crime. Thus the government argues in its brief that "in the crime of kidnapping, the acts of conspirators in hiding while waiting for ransom would clearly be planned acts of concealment which would be in aid of the conspiracy to kidnap. So here, there can be no doubt that . . . all acts of concealment, whether to hide the identity of the conspirators or the action theretofore taken, were unquestionably in furtherance of the initial conspiracy . . . ." We do not think the analogy is valid. Kidnappers in hiding, waiting for ransom, commit acts of concealment in furtherance of the objectives of the conspiracy itself, just as repainting a stolen car would be in furtherance of a conspiracy to steal; in both cases the successful accomplishment of the crime necessitates concealment. More closely analogous to our case would be conspiring kidnappers who cover their traces after the main conspiracy is finally ended—i.e., after they have abandoned the kidnapped person and then take care to escape detection. In the latter case, as here, the acts of covering up can by themselves indicate nothing more than that the conspirators do not wish to be apprehended—a concomitant, certainly, of every crime since Cain attempted to conceal the murder of Abel from the Lord.

We hold, therefore, that considering the main objective of the conspiracy to have been the obtaining of "no prosecution" rulings, prosecution was barred by the three-year statute of limitations, since no agreement to conceal the conspiracy after its accomplishment was shown or can be implied on the evidence before us to have been part of the conspiratorial agreement.

II

In view of how the case was submitted to the jury, we are also unable to accept the government's second theory for avoiding the statute of limitations. This theory is (i) that the main objective of the conspiracy was not merely to obtain the initial "no prosecution" rulings in 1948 and 1949, but to obtain *final immunity* for Gotham and Patullo from criminal tax prosecution; (ii) that such immunity was not obtained until 1952, when the statute of limitations had run on the tax-evasion cases which the petitioners conspired to fix; (iii) that the conspiracy therefore did not end until 1952, when this object was attained; (iv) that the acts of concealment within the indictment period were overt acts in furtherance of this conspiracy; and (v) that the prosecution was thus timely. In short, the contention is that the agreement to conceal was to protect the *taxpayers* rather than the *conspirators,* and as such was part of the main conspiracy rather than a subsidiary appendage to it, as under the government's first theory.

The Court of Appeals accepted this theory of the case in affirming these convictions. . . .

We find the legal theory of the Court of Appeals unexceptionable. If the central objective of the conspiracy was to protect the taxpayers from tax-evasion prosecution, on which the statute of limitations did not run until 1952, and if the 1948 and 1949 "no prosecution" rulings were but an "installment" of what the conspirators aimed to accomplish, then it is clear that the statute of limitations on the conspiracy did not begin to run until 1952, within three years of the indictment.

Furthermore, we agree with the Court of Appeals that there is evidence in this record which would warrant submission of the case to the jury on the theory that the central object of the conspiracy was not attained in 1948 and 1949, but rather was to immunize the taxpayers completely from prosecution for tax evasion and thus continued into 1952. . . .

If, therefore, the jury could have found that the aim of the conspiratorial agreement was to protect the taxpayers from tax prosecution, and that the overt acts occurring in the indictment period were in furtherance of that aim, we would affirm. We do not think, however, that we may safely assume that the jury so found, for we cannot agree with the Court of Appeals' holding that this theory of the case was adequately submitted to the jury. . . .

[Reversed and remanded for further proceedings consistent with this opinion.]

NOTES ON THE DURATION OF CONSPIRACY

1. **Duration Generally.** The duration of a conspiracy may be important for several reasons. As in *Grunewald,* it may control application of the statute of limitations. Or, as in *Krulewitch,* it may govern the admissibility of evidence under the co-conspirator's exception to the hearsay rule. Questions of duration also may arise in determining the extent of an individual's liability for the crimes of co-conspirators under *Pinkerton* and perhaps in other contexts as well.

The basic propositions in this area are set forth in Model Penal Code Section 5.03(7), which essentially codifies prior law. Paragraph (a) states the general rule that conspiracy is a continuing offense; it does not terminate with the agreement but continues until the objective is either accomplished or abandoned. Paragraph (b) of the Model Code provision imposes a limit on the continuing nature of a conspiracy by creating a presumption of abandonment where no overt act was committed during the applicable period of limitations. Thus, in most cases the defense will simply point to the prosecution's failure to prove an overt act occurring during the relevant time frame as proof that the conspiracy is over. Paragraph (c) deals with the somewhat special case of the individual who claims that the ongoing criminal enterprise is terminated as to that individual by withdrawal from participation. The Code provision makes such individual abandonment effective only where it is confirmed by notice to the other participants or by report to the authorities.

2. **Conspiracies to Conceal.** As *Grunewald* is sufficient to show, none of the propositions stated above is self-executing. In particular, identifying the objectives of an agreement is obviously crucial in determining whether they have been achieved or abandoned. The trilogy of *Krulewitch, Lutwak,* and *Grunewald* dealt with attempts by the prosecution to extend the duration of a conspiracy by focusing on the subsidiary objective, which surely must be implicit in every criminal agreement, to conceal the activities from the authorities. *Krulewitch* held that no conspiracy to conceal could be inferred from the fact of attempted concealment. *Lutwak* confirmed this result even though the conspiracy to conceal had been specifically alleged in the indictment. *Grunewald* applied the same rule despite the government's characterization of the agreement to conceal as "actual" rather than "implied." Are these results sound? Is it not true that most criminal conspiracies do in fact include an agreement to conceal? Should accomplishment or abandonment of the main objective terminate the conspiracy, even where affirmative and perhaps unlawful acts of concealment are done after that time? Why?

The *Grunewald* Court characterized the government's distinction between "actual" and implied" conspiracies to conceal as "no more than a verbal tour de force." And, in a portion of the opinion not here excerpted, the Court condemned the government's differentiation as "one of words rather than of substance." Is the Court's resolution of this case subject to the same objections? Recall that the Court remanded for a new trial to be conducted on the government's alternative theory that the agreement was not really to obtain "no prosecution" rulings, as was done in 1948 and 1949, but rather to obtain final immunity from tax prosecution, which was not accomplished until 1952. Is the difference between these two possibilities one of substance, or one of words only? Has not the government succeeded in accomplishing its objective through yet another "verbal tour de force"? Or do you see a purpose in the Court's decision?

SUBSECTION E: LIMITS ON LIABILITY FOR CONSPIRACY

GEBARDI v. UNITED STATES

Supreme Court of the United States, 1932.
287 U.S. 112.

MR. JUSTICE STONE delivered the opinion of the Court.

This case is here on certiorari to review a judgment of conviction for conspiracy to violate the Mann Act. Petitioners, a man and a woman, not then husband and wife, were indicted in the District Court for Northern Illinois, for conspiring together, and with others not named, to transport the woman from one state to another for the purpose of engaging in sexual intercourse with the man. At the trial without a jury there was evidence from which the court could have found that the petitioners had engaged in illicit sexual relations in the course of each of the journeys alleged; that the man purchased the railway tickets for both petitioners for at least one journey, and that in each instance the woman, in advance of the purchase of the tickets, consented to go on the journey and did go on it voluntarily for the specified immoral purpose. There was no evidence supporting the allegation that any other person had conspired. . . .

Section 2 of the Mann Act, violation of which is charged by the indictment here as the object of the conspiracy, imposes the penalty upon "[any person who shall knowingly transport or cause to be transported, or aid or assist in obtaining transportation for, or in transporting in interstate or foreign commerce . . . any woman or girl for the purpose of prostitution or debauchery or for any other immoral purpose . . . .."

The Act does not punish the woman for transporting herself; it contemplates two persons—one to transport and the woman or girl to be transported. For the woman to fall within the ban of the statute she must, at least, "aid or assist" someone else in transporting or in procuring transportation for herself. But such aid and assistance must . . . be more active then mere agreement on her part to the transportation and its immoral purpose. For the statute is drawn to include those cases in which the woman consents to her own transportation. Yet it does not specifically impose any penalty upon her, although it deals in detail with the person by whom she is transported. In applying this criminal statute we cannot infer that the mere acquiescence of the woman transported was intended to be condemned by the general language punishing those who aid and assist the transporter, any more than it has been inferred that the purchaser of liquor was to be regarded as an abettor of the illegal sale. The penalties of the statute are too clearly directed against the acts of the transporter as distinguished from the consent of the subject of the transportation. . . .

We come thus to the main question in the case, whether, admitting that the woman, by consenting, has not violated the Mann Act, she may be convicted of a conspiracy with the man to violate it. Section 37 of the Criminal Code [now 18 U.S.C. § 371] punishes a conspiracy by two or more persons "to commit any offense against the United States." The offense which she is charged with conspiring to commit is that perpetrated by the man, for it is not questioned that in transporting her he contravened Section 2 of the Mann Act. Hence we must decide whether her concurrence, which was not criminal before the Mann Act, nor punished by it, may, without more, support a conviction under the conspiracy section, enacted many years before.

[A]n agreement to commit an offense may be criminal, though its purpose is to do what some of the conspirators may be free to do alone. Incapacity of one to commit the substantive offense does not necessarily imply that he may with impunity conspire with others who are able to commit it.[5] . . .

But in this case we are concerned with something more than an agreement between two persons for one of them to commit an offense which the other cannot commit. There is the added element that the offense planned, the criminal object of the conspiracy, involves the agreement of the woman to her transportation by the man, which is the very conspiracy charged.

Congress set out in the Mann Act to deal with cases which frequently, if not normally, involve consent and agreement on the part of the woman to the forbidden transportation. In every case in which she is not intimidated or forced into the transportation, the statute necessarily contemplates her acquiescence. Yet this acquiescence, though an incident of a type of transportation specifically dealt with by the statute, was not made a crime under the Mann Act itself. Of this class of cases we say that the substantive offense contemplated by the statute itself involves the same combination or community of purpose of two persons only which is prosecuted here as conspiracy. If this were the only case covered by the Act, it would be within those decisions which hold, consistently with the theory upon which conspiracies are punished, that where it is impossible under any circumstances to commit

---

[5] So it has been held repeatedly that one not a bankrupt may be held guilty under Section 37 of conspiring that a bankrupt shall conceal property from his trustee. . . . In like manner, Chadwick v. United States, 141 F. 225 (6th Cir. 1905), sustained the conviction of one not an officer of a national bank for conspiring with an officer to commit a crime which only he could commit.

the substantive offense without cooperative action, the preliminary agreement between the same parties to commit the offense is not an indictable conspiracy, either at common law or under the federal statute. [Citing cases.] But criminal transportation under the Mann Act may be effected without the woman's consent, as in cases of intimidation or force (with which we are not now concerned). We assume therefore, for present purposes . . . that the decisions last mentioned do not in all strictness apply. We do not rest our decision upon the theory of those cases . . .. We place it rather upon the ground that we perceive in the failure of the Mann Act to condemn the woman's participation in those transportations which are effected with her mere consent, evidence of an affirmative legislative policy to leave her acquiescence unpunished. We think it a necessary implication of that policy that when the Mann Act and the conspiracy statute came to be construed together, as they necessarily would be, the same participation which the former contemplates as an inseparable incident of all cases in which the woman is a voluntary agent at all, but does not punish, was not automatically to be made punishable under the latter. It would contravene that policy to hold that the very passage of the Mann Act effected a withdrawal by the conspiracy statute of that immunity which the Mann Act itself confers.

It is not to be supposed that the consent of an unmarried person to adultery with a married person, where the latter alone is guilty of the substantive offense, would render the former an abettor or a conspirator, or that the acquiescence of a woman under the age of consent would make her a co-conspirator with the man to commit statutory rape upon herself. Compare Regina v. Tyrrell, [1894] 1 Q.B. 710. The principle, determinative of this case, is the same.

On the evidence before us the woman petitioner has not violated the Mann Act and, we hold, is not guilty of a conspiracy to do so. As there is no proof that the man conspired with anyone else to bring about the transportation, the convictions of both petitioners must be reversed.

MR. JUSTICE CARDOZO concurs in the result.

IANNELLI v. UNITED STATES
Supreme Court of the United States, 1975.
420 U.S. 770.

MR. JUSTICE POWELL delivered the opinion of the Court.

This case requires the Court to consider Wharton's Rule, a doctrine of criminal law enunciating an exception to the general principle that a conspiracy and the substantive offense that is its immediate end are discrete crimes for which separate sanctions may be imposed.

I

Petitioners were tried under a six-count indictment alleging a variety of federal gambling offenses. Each of the eight petitioners, along with seven unindicted coconspirators and six co-defendants, was charged, inter alia, with conspiring [1] to violate and violating 18 U.S.C. § 1955, a federal gambling statute making it a crime for five or more persons to conduct, finance, manage, supervise, direct, or own a gambling business prohibited by state law.[2] Each petitioner was convicted of both offenses, and each was sentenced under both the substantive and the conspiracy counts. The Court of Appeals for the Third Circuit affirmed . . ..

II

Wharton's Rule owes its name to Francis Wharton, whose treatise on criminal law identified the doctrine and its fundamental rationale:

> "When to the idea of an offense plurality of agents is logically necessary, conspiracy, which assumes the voluntary accession of a person to a crime of such a character that it is aggravated by a plurality of agents, cannot be maintained. . . . In other words, when the law says, 'a combination between two persons to effect a particular end shall be called, if the end be effected, by a certain name,' it is not lawful for the prosecution to call it by some other name; and when the law says, such an offense—e.g., adultery—shall have a certain punishment, it is not lawful for the prosecution to evade this limitation by indicting the offense as conspiracy." 2 F. Wharton, Criminal Law 1862 (12th ed. 1932).

The Rule has been applied by numerous courts, state and federal alike. It also has been recognized by this Court, although we have had no previous occasion carefully to analyze its justification and proper role in federal law.

The classic formulation of Wharton's Rule requires that the conspiracy indictment be dismissed before trial. . . . Federal courts earlier adhered to this literal interpretation and thus sustained demurrers to conspiracy indictments. More recently, however, some federal courts have . . . held that the Rule's purposes can be served equally

[1] The general conspiracy statute under which this action was brought, 18 U.S.C. § 371, provides in pertinent part:

"If two or more persons conspire either to commit any offense against the United States, or to defraud the United States, or any agency thereof in any manner or for any purpose, and one or more of such persons do any act to effect the object of the conspiracy, each shall be fined not more than $10,000 or imprisoned not more than five years, or both. . . ."

[2] Title 18 U.S.C. § 1955 provides in pertinent part:

"(a) Whoever conducts, finances, manages, supervises, directs, or owns all or part of an illegal gambling business shall be fined not more than $20,000 or im-

prisoned not more than five years, or both.

"(b) As used in this section—

(1) 'illegal gambling business' means a gambling business which—

(i) is a violation of the law of a state or political subdivision in which it is conducted;

(ii) involves five or more persons who conduct, finance, manage, supervise, direct, or own all or part of such business; and

(iii) has been or remains in substantially continuous operation for a period in excess of 30 days or has a gross revenue of $2,000 in any single day. . . ."

effectively by permitting the prosecution to charge both offenses and instructing the jury that a conviction for the substantive offense necessarily precludes conviction for the conspiracy.

Federal courts likewise have disagreed as to the proper application of the recognized "third-party exception," which renders Wharton's Rule inapplicable when the conspiracy involves the cooperation of a greater number of persons than is required for commission of the substantive offense. In the present case, the Third Circuit concluded that the third-party exception permitted prosecution because the conspiracy involved more than the five persons required to commit the substantive offense, a view shared by the Second Circuit. The Seventh Circuit reached the opposite result, however, reasoning that since Section 1955 also covers gambling activities involving more than five persons, the third-party exception is inapplicable.

The courts of appeals are at odds even over the fundamental question whether Wharton's Rule ever applies to a charge for conspiracy to violate 18 U.S.C. § 1955. The Seventh Circuit holds that it does. The Fourth and Fifth Circuits, on the other hand, have declared that it does not.

As this brief description indicates, the history of the application of Wharton's Rule to charges for conspiracy to violate 18 U.S.C. § 1955 fully supports the Fourth Circuit's observation that "rather than being a rule, [it] is a concept, the confines of which have been delineated in widely diverse fashion by the courts." . . .

III

Traditionally the law has considered conspiracy and the completed substantive offense to be separate crimes. . . . Thus, it is well recognized that in most cases separate sentences can be imposed for the conspiracy to do an act and for the subsequent accomplishment of that end. Indeed, the Court has even held that the conspiracy can be punished more harshly than the accomplishment of its purpose.

The consistent rationale of this long line of decisions rests on the very nature of the crime of conspiracy. This Court repeatedly has recognized that a conspiracy poses distinct dangers quite apart from those of the substantive offense [quoting Callanan v. United States, see page 451, supra, on the special dangers of group criminality].

The historical difference between the conspiracy and its end has led this Court consistently to attribute to Congress "a tacit purpose—in the absence of any inconsistent expression—to maintain a long established distinction between offenses essentially different; a distinction whose practical importance in the criminal law is not easily overestimated." Wharton's Rule announces an exception to this general principle. . . .

This Court's prior decisions indicate that the broadly formulated Wharton's Rule does not rest on principles of double jeopardy. Instead, it has current vitality only as a judicial presumption, to be applied in the absence of legislative intent to the contrary. The classic Wharton's

Rule offenses—adultery, incest, bigamy, duelling—are crimes that are characterized by the general congruence of the agreement and the completed substantive offense. The parties to the agreement are the only persons who participate in commission of the substantive offense,[15] and the immediate consequences of the crime rest on the parties themselves rather than on society at large. Finally, the agreement that attends the substantive offense does not appear likely to pose the distinct kinds of threats to society that the law of conspiracy seeks to avert. It cannot, for example, readily be assumed that an agreement to commit an offense of this nature will produce agreements to engage in a more general pattern of criminal conduct.

The conduct proscribed by Section 1955 is significantly different from the offenses to which the Rule traditionally has been applied. Unlike the consequences of the classic Wharton's Rule offenses, the harm attendant upon the commission of the substantive offense is not restricted to the parties to the agreement. Large-scale gambling activities seek to elicit the participation of additional persons—the bettors— who are parties neither to the conspiracy nor to the substantive offense that results from it. Moreover, the parties prosecuted for the conspiracy need not be the same persons who are prosecuted for commission of the substantive offense. An endeavor as complex as a large-scale gambling enterprise might involve persons who have played appreciably different roles, and whose level of culpability varies significantly. It might, therefore, be appropriate to prosecute the owners and organizers of large-scale gambling operations both for conspiracy and for the substantive offense but to prosecute the lesser participants only for the substantive offense. Nor can it fairly be maintained that agreements to enter into large-scale gambling activities are not likely to generate additional agreements to engage in other criminal endeavors.
. . . [T]he legislative history of Section 1955 provides documented testimony to the contrary.

Wharton's Rule applies only to offenses that *require* concerted criminal activity, a plurality of criminal agents. In such cases, a closer relationship exists between the conspiracy and the substantive offense because *both* require collective criminal activity. The substantive offense therefore presents some of the same threats that the law of conspiracy normally is thought to guard against, and it cannot automatically be assumed that the legislature intended the conspiracy and the substantive offense to remain as discrete crimes upon consummation of the latter. Thus, absent legislative intent to the contrary, the Rule supports a presumption that the two merge when the substantive offense is proved.

[15] An exception to the Rule generally is thought to apply in the case in which conspiracy involves more persons than are required for commission of the substantive offense. For example, while the two persons who commit adultery cannot normally be prosecuted both for that offense and for conspiracy to commit it, the third-party exception would permit the conspiracy charge where a "matchmaker"—the third party—had conspired with the principals to encourage commission of the substantive offense. The rationale supporting this exception appears to be that the addition of a third party enhances the dangers presented by the crime. Thus, it is thought that the legislature would not have intended to preclude punishment for a combination of greater dimension than that required to commit the substantive offense. . . .

But a legal principle commands less respect when extended beyond the logic that supports it. In this case, the significant differences in characteristics and consequences of the kinds of offenses that gave rise to Wharton's Rule and the activities proscribed by Section 1955 counsel against attributing significant weight to the presumption the Rule erects. More important, as the Rule is essentially an aid to the determination of legislative intent, it must defer to a discernible legislative judgment. We turn now to that inquiry.

IV

. . . In drafting the Organized Crime Control Act of 1970, Congress manifested its clear awareness of the distinct nature of a conspiracy and the substantive offenses that might constitute its immediate end. The identification of "special offenders" in Title X speaks both to persons who commit specific felonies during the course of a pattern of criminal activity and to those who enter into conspiracies to engage in patterns of criminal conduct. And Congress specifically utilized the law of conspiracy to discourage organized crime's corruption of state and local officials for the purpose of facilitating gambling enterprises.

But the Section 1955 definition of "gambling activities" pointedly avoids reference to conspiracy or to agreement, the essential element of conspiracy. Moreover, the limited Section 1955 definition is repeated in identifying the reach of Section 1511, a provision that specifically prohibits conspiracies. Viewed in this context, and in light of the numerous references to conspiracies throughout the extensive consideration of the Organized Crime Control Act, we think that the limited congressional definition of "gambling activities" in Section 1955 is significant. The Act is a carefully crafted piece of legislation. Had Congress intended to foreclose the possibility of prosecuting conspiracy offenses under Section 371 by merging them into prosecutions under Section 1955, we think it would have so indicated explicitly. It chose instead to define the substantive offense punished by Section 1955 in a manner that fails specifically to invoke the concerns which underlie the law of conspiracy.

Nor do we find merit to the argument that the congressional requirement of participation of "five or more persons" as an element of the substantive offense under Section 1955 represents a legislative attempt to merge the conspiracy and the substantive offense into a single crime. The history of the Act instead reveals that this requirement was designed to restrict federal intervention to cases in which federal interests are substantially implicated. The findings accompanying Title VIII would appear to support the assertion of federal jurisdiction over all illegal gambling activities. Congress did not, however, choose to exercise its power to the fullest. Recognizing that gambling activities normally are matters of state concern, Congress indicated a desire to extend federal criminal jurisdiction to reach only "those who are engaged in an illicit gambling business of major proportions." It accordingly conditioned the application of Section 1955 on a finding that the gambling activities involve five or more persons and that they remain substantially in operation in excess of 30 days or attain gross revenues of $2,000 in a single day. Thus, the requirement of "concerted activity" in Section 1955 reflects no more than a concern to avoid federal prosecution of small-scale gambling activities which pose a limited threat to federal interests and normally can be combated effectively by local law enforcement efforts.

Viewed in the context of this legislation, there simply is no basis for relying on a presumption to reach a result so plainly at odds with congressional intent. . . . We conclude, therefore, that the history and structure of the Organized Crime Control Act of 1970 manifest a clear and unmistakable legislative judgment that more than outweighs any presumption of merger between the conspiracy to violate Section 1955 and the consummation of that substantive offense. . . .

Affirmed.

MR. JUSTICE DOUGLAS, dissenting.

The eight petitioners in this case . . . were convicted both of participating in an "illegal gambling business," 18 U.S.C. § 1955, and of conspiring to commit that offense, 18 U.S.C. § 371. On both statutory and constitutional grounds, I would hold that the simultaneous convictions under both statutes cannot stand.

I

In my view the double-jeopardy clause forbids simultaneous prosecution under Sections 1955 and 371. Wharton's Rule in its original formulation was rooted in the double-jeopardy concern of avoiding multiple prosecutions. Carter v. McClaughry, 183 U.S. 365, 394–95 (1902), and later cases confine the double-jeopardy protection to prohibiting cumulative punishment of offenses that are absolutely identical, but I would not extend those cases so as to permit both convictions in this case to stand.

The evidence against petitioners consisted largely of conversations that involved gambling transactions. The government's theory of the case was that petitioner Iannelli was the central figure in the enterprise who, through other employees or agents, received bets, arranged payoffs, and parceled out commissions. The evidence established, in the government's view, "syndicated gambling," the kind of activity proscribed by Section 1955. The very same evidence was relied upon to establish the conspiracy—a conspiracy, apparently, enduring as long as the substantive offense continued, and provable by the same acts that established the violation of Section 1955. Thus the very same transactions among the defendants gave rise to criminal liability under both statutes.

Under these circumstances, I would require the prosecutor to choose between Section 371 and Section 1955 as the instrument for criminal punishment. . . .

II

Apart from my views of the double-jeopardy clause, I would reverse on the additional ground that Congress did not intend to permit simultaneous convictions under Section 371 and Section 1955 for the same acts. The rule that a conspiracy remains separable from the completed crime, thus permitting simultaneous conviction for both, rests on the assumption that the act of conspiring presents special dangers the legislature did not address in defining the substantive crime and that are not adequately checked by its prosecution. But the rule of separability is one of construction only, an aid to discerning legislative intent. Wharton's Rule teaches that where the substantive crime itself is aimed at the evils traditionally addressed by the law of conspiracy, separability should not be found unless the clearest legislative statement demands it. In my view this case fits the rationale of Wharton's Rule, and there is no legislative statement justifying the inference that Congress intended to permit multiple convictions. . . .

Conviction under Section 1955 satisfies, in my view, the social concerns that punishment for conspiracy is supposed to address. The provision was aimed not at the single unlawful wager but at "syndicated gambling." Congress viewed this activity as harmful because on such a scale it was thought to facilitate other forms of illicit activity, one of the reasons traditionally advanced for the separate prosecution of conspiracy. Where Section 1955 has been violated, the elements of conspiracy will almost invariably be found. The enterprises to which Congress was referring in Section 1955 cannot, as a practical matter, be created and perpetuated without the agreement and coordination that characterize conspiracy. Section 1955 is thus most sensibly viewed as a statute directed at conspiracy in a particular context. . . .

I would accordingly reverse these convictions.

MR. JUSTICE STEWART and MR. JUSTICE MARSHALL join Part II of this opinion.

MR. JUSTICE BRENNAN, dissenting.

In Bell v. United States, 349 U.S. 81 (1955), this Court held that in criminal cases: "When Congress leaves to the judiciary the task of imputing to Congress an undeclared will, the ambiguity should be resolved in favor of lenity." I agree with Mr. Justice Douglas that "[s]ection 1955 is . . . most sensibly viewed as a statute directed at conspiracy in a particular context," and that the statute is at best silent on whether punishment for both the substantive crime and conspiracy was intended. In this situation, I would invoke *Bell*'s rule of lenity. I therefore dissent.

NOTE ON *GEBARDI* AND *IANNELLI*

In *Gebardi* the Court relied on *Regina* v. *Tyrrell,* page 424, supra, as illustrative of the same general principle underlying the *Gebardi* decision. Is the citation apt? Does the *Tyrrell* rationale explain *Gebardi,* or does the result in *Gebardi* turn on something unique to the law of conspiracy? In particular, consider whether the *Tyrrell* rationale explains the *Gebardi* Court's reversal of the male defendant's conviction under the Mann Act. Given the *Gebardi* Court's conclusion that the terms of the Mann Act evidenced "an affirmative legislative policy" to leave the woman's participation unpunished, does it follow that in the circumstances of this case the man should also be set free? Is this result derived from the legislative history of the Mann Act or from the policies thought to underlie that legislation? If not, where does it come from?

Now consider the additional issues raised by *Iannelli.* Does *Iannelli* bear closer resemblance to that aspect of *Gebardi* that concerned the liability of the woman or to that which concerned the liability of the man? Are the two decisions consistent?

*

Chapter IV

JUSTIFICATION AND EXCUSE

INTRODUCTORY NOTE ON JUSTIFICATION
AND EXCUSE

The preceding chapters cover the central doctrines that shape the definition of criminal offenses. Chapter I deals with proscribed conduct, and Chapter II with required culpability. Chapter III covers the application of these principles in the context of group criminality. This chapter explores a body of defenses that are extrinsic to the definitions of specific crimes but that further elaborate the conditions of criminal liability. These defenses are usually grouped into the two general categories of justification and excuse.[a]

Justification defenses state exceptions to the prohibitions laid down by specific offenses. Thus, for example, an intentional homicide that would otherwise be murder is no crime at all if committed in self-defense. Similarly, conduct that would otherwise constitute criminal assault may be justified by a policeman's obligation to enforce the law. Self-defense and law enforcement are typical defenses of justification. They qualify, supplement, and refine the proscriptions of the penal law. The considerations that go into determining the scope of justification defenses are, therefore, essentially the same as those that govern the contours of particular offenses; both define the prohibitory content of the criminal law. Section 1 of this chapter elaborates the concepts of justification, both generally and in selected specific contexts.

The law also recognizes doctrines of excuse. These defenses accord exculpatory significance to claims by particular defendants that they cannot fairly be blamed for admittedly wrongful conduct. The defendant is excused not because his conduct was socially desirable, or even tolerable, but rather because the circumstances of the offense evoke the societal judgment that criminal conviction and punishment would be morally inappropriate. As Professor Sayre explained in Mens Rea, 45 Harv.L.Rev. 974, 1021 (1932), doctrines of excuse were a natural out-

---

[a] For recent analysis of the doctrinal structure of exculpatory defenses, see Robinson, Criminal Law Defenses: A Systematic Analysis, 83 Colum.L.Rev. 199 (1982), and Williams, Offences and Defences, 2 Leg.Stud. 233 (1982). For specific coverage of defensive doctrines, see P. Robinson, Criminal Law Defenses (1984) (2 vols.). For discussion of the significance of the distinction between justification and situational excuse, see G. Fletcher, Rethinking the Criminal Law, 759 et seq. (1978); Dressler, New Thoughts About the Concept of Justification in the Criminal Law: A Critique of Fletcher's Thinking and *Rethinking*, 32 UCLA L.Rev. 61 (1984); Greenawalt, The Perplexing Borders of Justification and Excuse, 84 Colum.L.Rev. 1897 (1984); Williams, The Theory of Excuses, [1982] Crim.L.Rev. 732.

growth of the early common-law insistence on moral guilt as the basis of criminal liability:

> "[T]he strong tendency of the early days to link criminal liability with moral guilt made it necessary to free from punishment those who perhaps satisfied the requirements of specific intent for particular crimes but who, because of some personal mental defect or restraint, should not be convicted of any crime. The person who lacked a normal intelligence because of mental disease, or who lacked discretion because of tender years, or who through fear of death lacked the power to choose his conduct—all these must escape punishment if criminality was to be based upon moral guilt. Thus, there developed certain well-recognized defenses in criminal law, affecting one's general capacity to commit crime. . . ."

At one time, theoretical coherence was attempted by characterizing all the various doctrines of excuse as defects of capacity. Insane persons, infants, and those acting under duress were all said to lack the capacity for criminal mens rea. Today, this unifying rubric has dissolved in the face of recognition that the various defects of "capacity" raise very different kinds of issues. In these materials, therefore, the topics of excuse are sorted into two categories. Section 2 of this chapter deals with variations of "situational excuse." This label is meant to suggest that an individual may be excused if the situation in which he finds himself overbears his otherwise normal abilities to conform his conduct to the requirements of law. In other words, the doctrines of situational excuse make allowance for abnormal situations, not abnormal persons. In such cases, the focus, as in the defenses of justification, is on the external realities of the actor's situation and the attitude of the actor concerning those realities. The problems of abnormal individuals—most notably immaturity and insanity—are dealt with in Chapter V under the rubric of "criminal responsibility."

SECTION 1: JUSTIFICATION

SUBSECTION A: THE GENERAL PRINCIPLE OF JUSTIFICATION

STATE v. WARSHOW
Supreme Court of Vermont, 1979.
138 Vt. 22, 410 A.2d 1000.

BARNEY, CHIEF JUSTICE. The defendants were part of a group of demonstrators that travelled to Vernon, Vermont, to protest at the main gate of a nuclear power plant known as Vermont Yankee. The plant had been shut down for repairs and refueling, and these protestors had joined a rally designed to prevent workers from gaining access to the plant and placing it on-line.

They were requested to leave the private premises of the power plant by representatives of Vermont Yankee and officers of the law. The defendants were among those who refused, and they were arrested and charged with unlawful trespass.

The issue with which this appeal of their convictions is concerned relates to a doctrine referred to as the defense of necessity. At trial the defendants sought to present evidence relating to the hazards of nuclear power plant operation which, they argued, would establish that defense. After hearing the defendants' offer of proof the trial court excluded the proffered evidence and refused to grant compulsory process for the witnesses required to present the defense. The jury instruction requested on the issue of necessity was also refused, and properly preserved for appellate review.

In ruling below, the trial court determined that the defense was not available. It is on this basis that we must test the issue.

The defense of necessity is one that partakes of the classic defense of "confession and avoidance." It admits the criminal act, but claims justification. It has a counterpart in civil litigation, recognized in Vermont in the case of Ploof v. Putnam, 81 Vt. 471, 71 A. 188 (1908).[a]

The doctrine is one of specific application insofar as it is a defense to criminal behavior. This is clear because if the qualifications for the defense of necessity are not closely delineated, the definition of criminal activity becomes uncertain and even whimsical. The difficulty arises when words of general and broad qualification are used to describe the special scope of this defense.

In the various definitions and examples recited as incorporating the concept of necessity, certain fundamental requirements stand out:

   (i) there must be a situation of emergency arising without fault on the part of the actor concerned;

   (ii) this emergency must be so imminent and compelling as to raise a reasonable expectation of harm, either directly to the actor or upon those he was protecting;

   (iii) this emergency must present no reasonable opportunity to avoid the injury without doing the criminal act; and

   (iv) the injury impending from the emergency must be of sufficient seriousness to outmeasure the criminal wrong. . . .

It is the defendants' position that they made a sufficient offer of proof to establish the elements of the necessity defense to raise a jury

---

[a] In *Ploof*, a ship captain sought to take refuge from a storm by mooring his ship to another's dock. The dock owner refused to permit the mooring and, as a result, the ship was destroyed in the storm. The Vermont Supreme Court held that if the ship captain had docked without consent, he would have had a defense of necessity in a civil action for trespass by the dock owner. Thus, since the captain had a right to dock there, the dock owner was obligated to tolerate the intrusion under the circumstances and was therefore liable for the damage to the ship that proximately resulted from his refusal of permission. [Footnote by eds.]

question. The trial court rejected this contention on the ground, among others, that the offer did not sufficiently demonstrate the existence of an emergency or imminent danger.

This ruling was sound, considering the offer. The defendants wished to subpoena witnesses to testify to the dangers of nuclear accidents and the effect of low-level radiation. It was conceded that there had been no serious accident at Vermont Yankee, but defendants contended that the consequences could be so serious that the mere possibility should suffice. This is not the law.

There is no doubt that the defendants wished to call attention to the dangers of low-level radiation, nuclear waste, and nuclear accident. But low-level radiation and nuclear waste are not the types of imminent danger classified as an emergency sufficient to justify criminal activity. To be imminent, a danger must be, or must reasonably appear to be, threatening to occur immediately, near at hand, and impending. We do not understand the defendants to have taken the position in their offer of proof that the hazards of low-level radiation and nuclear waste build-up are immediate in nature. On the contrary, they cite long-range risks and dangers that do not presently threaten health and safety. Where the hazards are long term, the danger is not imminent, because the defendants have time to exercise options other than breaking the law.

Nor does the specter of nuclear accident as presented by these defendants fulfill the imminent and compelling harm element of the defense. The offer does not take the position that they acted to prevent an impending accident. Rather, they claimed that they acted to foreclose the "chance" or "possibility" of accident. This defense cannot lightly be allowed to justify acts taken to foreclose speculative and uncertain dangers. Its application must be limited to acts directed to the prevention of harm that is reasonably certain to occur. Therefore the offer fails to satisfy the imminent danger element. The facts offered would not have established the defense.

These acts may be a method of making public statements about nuclear power and its dangers, but they are not a legal basis for invoking the defense of necessity. Nor can the defendants' sincerity of purpose excuse the criminal nature of their acts.

Since the offered evidence was insufficient to support any possible defense of necessity, we need not reach any of the other issues raised by this appeal, including the effect of declared legislative policy.

Judgment affirmed.

HILL, JUSTICE, concurring. . . . The convictions under review arose out of a peaceful anti-nuclear demonstration conducted on the property of Vermont Yankee Nuclear Power Station in Vernon on October 8, 1977. Although the power station had been shut down for six to eight weeks prior to the demonstration, it was about to be refueled and recommence operation. Based upon their belief that nuclear power presented real and substantial dangers, defendants blocked the entrance to the power station to prevent its further operation.

At trial defendants sought to raise the affirmative defense of necessity, arguing that they were faced with a choice of evils—either violate the literal terms of the law or comply with the law and allow the commission of a more egregious wrong, i.e., the proliferation of nuclear power—and that they chose the course which would result in the least harm to the public, even though it meant violating the criminal law. The trial court refused to allow the defendants to present the defense, stating that it was not available "in Vermont at this time."

Necessity has long been recognized at common law as a justification for the commission of a crime. And, although the defense has not been explicitly recognized in Vermont in the context of a criminal prosecution, it has been accepted in the law of torts. I see no reason why the defense should not be recognized in the criminal-law context. "The principle involved is one of general validity; . . .   and there is even greater need for its acceptance in the law of crime." Model Penal Code § 3.02, Comment 3 at 7 (Tent. Draft No. 8, 1958). Although this holding is implicit in the majority opinion, I would make it explicit.

The defense of necessity proceeds from the appreciation that, as a matter of public policy, there are circumstances where the value protected by the law is eclipsed by a superseding value, and that it would be inappropriate and unjust to apply the usual criminal rule. The balancing of competing values cannot, of course, be committed to the private judgment of the actor, but must, in most cases, be determined at trial with due regard being given for the crime charged and the higher value sought to be achieved.

Determination of the issue of competing values and, therefore, the availability of the defense of necessity is precluded, however, when there has been a deliberate legislative choice as to the values at issue. The common-law defense of necessity deals with imminent dangers from obvious and generally recognized harms. It does not deal with non-imminent or debatable harms, nor does it deal with activities that the legislative branch has expressly sanctioned and found not to be harms.

Both the state of Vermont and the federal government have given their imprimatur to the development and normal operation of nuclear energy and have established mechanisms for the regulation of nuclear power. Implicit within these statutory enactments is the policy choice that the benefits of nuclear energy outweigh its dangers.

If we were to allow defendants to present the necessity defense in this case we would, in effect, be allowing a jury to redetermine questions of policy already decided by the legislative branches of the federal and state governments. This is not how our system of government was meant to operate.

I express no opinion as to the relative merits or demerits of nuclear energy, nor do I question the sincerity of the defendants' beliefs. All that I would hold is that this court is not the proper forum to grant defendants the relief they seek. Defendants still have the right to try to induce those forums that have made the policy choices at issue today to reconsider their decisions. But until that time I feel constrained to follow the law as it is, not as some would like it to be.

In my opinion the majority puts the cart before the horse. It measures the offer made against the requisite elements of the defense of necessity and concludes that the defendants failed to show a likelihood of imminent danger; yet it reserves judgment on the legislative policy exception to the defense. It is illogical to consider whether the necessary elements of a defense have been shown before determining whether the defense is even available in the particular situation.

The dissent, on the other hand, assumes that defendants' offer was sufficient to show not only imminent danger but also a failure of the regulatory scheme. I cannot agree with this assumption because the offer failed to show a danger not contemplated by the legislative scheme. The legislative framework was set up to deal with the very situation defendants offered to prove "might" happen. But because neither the state legislature nor Congress acted to shut down the power plant based on speculative possibilities does not, in my opinion, give rise to the questionable inference that there was an emergency which the regulatory scheme failed to avert. . . .

BILLINGS, JUSTICE, dissenting. . . . The common law has recognized that an act done through the compulsion of an emergency situation where the peril of imminent danger exists is not a crime. . . .

Here the trial court prevented the introduction of any evidence on the issue of necessity in spite of the offer of proof. . . . The offer must be only specific and concrete enough to make apparent to the trial court the existence of facts, which, if proved, would make the evidence relevant to an issue in the case and otherwise admissible.

The majority states that the danger of low-level radiation and nuclear waste, which the defendants offer to prove, are "not the types of imminent danger classified as an emergency sufficient to justify criminal activity." Furthermore, the majority dismisses those portions of the proof dealing with the threat of a nuclear accident by characterizing them as mere "speculative and uncertain dangers." In doing so the majority has decided to so read the evidence as to give credibility only to that evidence offered on the effects of low-level radiation. . . . It is not for this court to weigh the credibility of the evidence in this manner where there is evidence offered on the elements of the defense. While this case might stand in a different posture if, at the close of the defendants' evidence, they had failed to introduce evidence, as offered, on each and every element of the defense sufficient to make out a prima-facie case, that situation is not before us. . . .

The defendants offered evidence on all the requisite elements of the defense of necessity. They stated as follows:

　　　"[They had] a feeling that there was a situation of an emergency or imminent danger that would have occurred with the

> start up of the reactor on October 8th the time of [their] alleged crime . . . the chance . . . of the nuclear power plant having a serious accident which would cause . . . great untold damage to property and lives and health for many generations."

The defendants also stated that "there was reasonable belief that it would have been an emergency had they started that reactor up . . . there was a very good chance of an accident there for which there is no insurance coverage or very little." Specifically, the defendants offered to show by expert testimony that there were defects in the cooling system and other aspects of the power plant which they believed could and would result in a meltdown within seven seconds of failure on the start up of the plant. In addition, the defendants went to great lengths to base their defense on the imminent danger that would result from the hazardous radiation emitted from the plant and its wastes when the plant resumed operations.

While the offer made by the defendants was laced with statements about the dangers they saw in nuclear power generally, it is clear that they offered to show that the Vermont Yankee facility at which they were arrested was an imminent danger to the community on the day of the arrests; that, if it commenced operation, there was a danger of meltdown and severe radiation damage to persons and property. In support of this contention, the defendants stated that they would call experts familiar with the Vermont Yankee facility and the dangerous manner of its construction, as well as other experts who would testify on the effects of meltdown and radiation leakage, on the results of governmental testing, and on the regulation of the Vermont Yankee facility. These witnesses were highly qualified to testify about the dangers at the Vermont Yankee facility based either on personal knowledge or on conditions the defendants offered to show existed at the time of the trespass.

Furthermore, the defendants offered to show that, in light of the imminent danger of an accident, they had exhausted all alternative means of preventing the start up of the plant and the immediate catastrophe it would bring. Under the circumstances of imminent danger arising from the start up of the plant, coupled with the resistance of Vermont Yankee and government officials, which the defendants offered to prove, nothing short of preventing the workers access to start up the plant would have averted the accident that the defendants expected.

Through this offer, it cannot be said, without prejudgment, that the defendants failed to set forth specific and concrete evidence, which, if proven, would establish the existence of an imminent danger of serious proportions through no fault of the defendants which could not be averted without the trespass. Whether the defendants' expectations and opportunities were reasonable under the circumstances of this case is not for the trial court to decide without hearing the evidence. From a review of the record, I am of the opinion that the offer here measured up to the standard required and that the trial court struck too soon in excluding the offered evidence.

I would also dissent from the concurring opinion in so far as it attempts to hide behind inferences that the legislature precluded the courts from hearing the defense of necessity in the instant case. . . . Even assuming that such inferences can be drawn from the regulatory schemes cited, they have no bearing on this case. We are asked to infer under the facts, which the defendants offered to prove (that they were acting to avert an imminent nuclear disaster), that the legislative branch of government would not permit the courts of this state to entertain the defense of necessity because it had legislatively determined nuclear power to be safe. Were the defense raised without any offer to show an imminent danger of serious accident, it might fail both because defendants did not offer evidence on imminent danger and on the basis of legislative preclusion. But, where, as here, the defendants offer to prove an emergency which the regulatory scheme failed to avert, the inference of preclusion is unwarranted. The defendants are entitled to show that although there is a comprehensive regulatory scheme, it had failed to such an extent as to raise for them the choice between criminal trespass and the nuclear disaster which the regulatory scheme was created to prevent. . . .

NOTES ON THE DEFENSE OF NECESSITY

1. **Common-Law Necessity and the *Warshow* Case.** Justice Hill's *Warshow* concurrence states that "[n]ecessity has long been recognized at common law as a justification for the commission of a crime." The opinions dispute the application of the defense to the facts of the case, but it seems to be common ground that, in a proper case, necessity (or choice of evils) may justify otherwise criminal conduct. At one level, the proposition is beyond dispute, for the unifying theme of all of the various defenses of justification is the necessity for making a choice among evils. Thus, defense of self and others, defense of property, the exercise of public authority, and law enforcement may all be viewed as doctrinal particularizations of the necessity principle.

Whether there remains a residual and otherwise undefined defense of necessity apart from such specific doctrines is not so clear. British authorities have disputed for years whether the common law recognizes a general necessity defense, and the prevailing view seems to be that it does not.[a] In this country, however, courts and commentators seem to agree that a general justification of necessity does exist at common law.[b] The uncertainty is no doubt due to the infrequency with which

---

[a] See Law Commission, Criminal Law Report on Defences of General Application 20 (1977): "[I]n no case has necessity been relied on successfully and we are very doubtful whether it at present provides a general defense at common law in this country." For the general debate, compare Williams, The Defence of Necessity, 6 Current Leg.Prob. 216 (1953), with Glazebrook, The Necessity Plea in English Criminal Law, 30 Camb.L.J. 87 (1972).

[b] See, e.g., W. LaFave & A. Scott, Criminal Law 381–88 (1972), and the authorities cited therein.

the issue is presented. Most claims of justification are handled under the more specific doctrines of self-defense, defense of others, etc., and only rarely is there need to consider whether any more general doctrine should be recognized. The facts of *Warshow* nonetheless provide a useful occasion for exploring the necessity concept and its place in the structure of justification defenses.

It should be noted that many modern decisions, like *Warshow,* assume the existence of a general common-law defense, while holding that the defendant's evidence is legally insufficient to raise it. *Warshow* is representative of many modern cases in another way as well. Claims of necessity or choice of evils have often been raised, usually unsuccessfully, in the context of politically controversial issues, first in protest against U.S. participation in the Vietnam War,[c] then in protest against the construction or operation of nuclear power plants,[d] and most recently by persons charged with trespass and other offenses committed on the premises of abortion clinics.[e] Typically the defendants have claimed in the abortion-clinic cases that by blocking the entrance and speaking to women arriving at the clinic, they sought to save the lives of unborn fetuses. Does this claim differ in any material respect from the claim raised in *Warshow?* Of what significance is the Supreme Court's ruling in Roe v. Wade, 410 U.S. 113 (1973), that state interference with a woman's decision to have an abortion during the early stages of pregnancy is constitutionally forbidden?

2. **Modern Statutory Formulations.** One of the significant innovations of the Model Penal Code was the proposed codification of a general choice-of-evils defense. Section 3.02 provides:

"(1) Conduct which the actor believes to be necessary to avoid a harm or evil to himself or to another is justifiable, provided that:

(a) the harm or evil sought to be avoided by such conduct is greater than that sought to be prevented by the law defining the offense charged; and

(b) neither the Code nor other law defining the offense provides exceptions or defenses dealing with the specific situation involved; and

(c) a legislative purpose to exclude the justification claimed does not otherwise plainly appear.

"(2) When the actor was reckless or negligent in bringing about the situation requiring a choice of harm or evils or in appraising the necessity for his conduct, the justification afforded by this Section is unavailable in a prosecution for any offense for

---

[c] See, e.g., United States v. Kroncke, 459 F.2d 697 (8th Cir.1972).

[d] In addition to *Warshow,* see, e.g., Commonwealth v. Capitolo, 508 Pa. 372, 498 A.2d 806 (1985); State v. Dorsey, 118 N.H. 844, 395 A.2d 855 (1978).

[e] See, e.g., Sigma Reproductive Health Center v. State, 297 Md. 660, 467 A.2d 483

(1983); City of St. Louis v. Klocker, 637 S.W.2d 174 (Mo.App.1982); Cleveland v. Municipality of Anchorage, 631 P.2d 1073 (Alaska 1981); People v. Krizka, 92 Ill.App. 3d 288, 48 Ill.Dec. 141, 416 N.E.2d 36 (1980); Gaetano v. United States, 406 A.2d 1291 (D.C.App.1979).

which recklessness or negligence, as the case may be, suffices to establish culpability."

This provision has been adopted in substance by approximately 10 American jurisdictions. The approach taken by the *Warshow* majority draws heavily on a similar New York provision, which has served as the model for legislation in about as many additional states. Section 35.05 of the New York Penal Code provides, in pertinent part:

"Unless otherwise limited by the ensuing provisions of this article defining justifiable use of physical force, or [by some other provision of law], conduct which would otherwise constitute an offense is justifiable and not criminal when: . . .

(2) Such conduct is necessary as an emergency measure to avoid an imminent public or private injury which is about to occur by reason of a situation occasioned or developed through no fault of the actor, and which is of such gravity that, according to ordinary standards of intelligence and morality, the desirability and urgency of avoiding such injury clearly outweigh the desirability of avoiding the injury sought to be prevented by the statute defining the offense in issue. The necessity and justifiability of such conduct may not rest upon considerations pertaining only to the morality and advisability of the statute, either in its general application or with respect to its application to a particular class of cases arising thereunder. Whenever evidence relating to the defense of justification under this [provision] is offered by the defendant, the court shall rule as a matter of law whether the claimed facts and circumstances would, if established, constitute a defense."

Would these formulations achieve different results as applied to the facts of *Warshow*? Are there significant differences between the two statutes? [d] Which is preferable?

3. **Illustrative Cases.** In connection with *Warshow* and the statutory formulations quoted above, consider the choice of evils issues presented in the following situations:

(i) **Deprogramming.** The Cramptons' 19-year-old daughter joined a religious sect and went to live at its headquarters in the state of Washington.[e] Because of their concern about her mental and emotional well-being, the Cramptons hired Theodore Patrick to remove her forcibly from Washington, to return her to California, and to "deprogram her." Patrick did so and was subsequently charged with kidnapping. Assume that these facts establish the elements of kidnapping by Patrick and conspiracy to commit kidnapping by the parents. Would either the parents or Patrick be entitled to a justification

---

[d] For commentary on modern statutory developments, see generally Tiffany & Anderson, Legislating the Necessity Defense in Criminal Law, 52 Denver L.J. 839 (1975); Note, Justification: The Impact of the Model Penal Code on Statutory Reform, 75 Colum.L.Rev. 914, 925–28 (1975).

[e] The facts are drawn from United States v. Patrick, 532 F.2d 142 (9th Cir.1976), and People v. Patrick, 541 P.2d 320 (Colo.App. 1975). For commentary on this problem, see Note, Cults, Deprogramming and the Necessity Defense, 80 Mich.L.Rev. 271 (1981).

instruction under either the Model Penal Code or the New York statute?　Is the harm or injury avoided "greater" than the harm occasioned by their conduct?　Who should decide this question, and by what criteria?

(ii) **Economic Necessity.**　An often cited choice-of-evils case is State v. Moe, 174 Wash. 303, 24 P.2d 638 (1933), which arose during the Depression.　The defendants tried, unsuccessfully, to persuade the chairman of the local Red Cross relief committee to increase their allowance of flour.　Having been advised that their demands would not be met, the defendants entered a local grocery store and helped themselves.　The Washington Supreme Court affirmed their convictions for grand larceny and riot and upheld the trial court's rejection of defendants' offer to prove their poverty in justification of their actions.　The court stated:

> "Economic necessity has never been accepted as a defense to a criminal charge.　The reason is that, were it ever countenanced, it would leave to the individual the right to take the law into his own hands.　In larceny cases, economic necessity is frequently invoked in mitigation of punishment, but has never been recognized as a defense."

The reach of this language has frequently been criticized on the ground that a defense might be appropriate in a case involving theft by a mother to feed her starving child, but no such case appears in the books.　However, an analogous claim of economic necessity was raised in State v. Mayfield.[f]　Mayfield was charged with fraudulently obtaining welfare assistance.　She admitted that she had filed reports which falsely stated that she was unemployed and that she had failed to report her earned income to her caseworker as she was legally required to do.　She claimed in defense that she needed the additional money to prevent irreparable harm to her children.　In support of her claim, she proffered the testimony of a physician and nurse who testified that the Mayfield children were suffering from nutritional deficiencies amounting to "starvation" in the medical sense.　In addition, she elicited testimony from the welfare department employees that the level of benefits granted to recipients was only 75 per cent of that computed in 1969 to be needed by a family of her size for a subsistence level of living, and proffered testimony by an economist who stated that the failure of the welfare department to adjust benefit levels between 1969 and 1974 (when the offenses occurred) had resulted in a 30 per cent loss of purchasing power.　Is this evidence legally sufficient to raise a necessity defense at common law?　Would Mayfield be entitled to a jury instruction under the Model Code or the New York statute?

(iii) **Medical Necessity.**　One of the issues discussed in *Warshow* is prior legislative resolution of the dangers of nuclear power.　A

---

[f] *Mayfield* is discussed in Sullivan, The Defense of Necessity in Texas: Legislative Invention Comes of Age, 16 Houston L.Rev. 333 (1979).　Ms. Mayfield's conviction was reversed on other grounds in Mayfield v. State, 585 S.W.2d 693 (Tex.Crim.App.1979).

comparable issue has been posed in connection with claims that medical necessity justifies violation of the drug laws.

Consider first the case of laetrile. Laetrile is a controversial compound claimed by its proponents to provide an effective cure for cancer. Pursuant to the Food, Drug and Cosmetic Act, the Food and Drug Administration (FDA) has classified it as a "new drug"—i.e., one not generally recognized by experts as safe and effective. The consequence of this classification is that it is illegal to transport laetrile in interstate commerce without FDA approval for experimental use of the drug under a "new drug" application. So far, approval has been withheld. Persons charged with illegal importation and distribution of laetrile have claimed in defense a medical necessity to provide the drug to terminally ill cancer patients. See, e.g., United States v. Richardson, 588 F.2d 1235 (9th Cir. 1978). Should this claim be entertained? Is it not clear that the controversy over laetrile is precisely the kind of dispute that the FDA was created to resolve? Would not the authority of the agency be undermined if its determinations could effectively be set aside by the contrary judgment of private individuals?

Now consider the case of *United States* v. *Randall*.[g] There the claim of "medical necessity" was advanced to justify the otherwise unlawful possession of marijuana plants. The trial court summarized the evidence offered in support of this defense as follows:

"Defendant testified that he had begun experiencing visual difficulties as an undergraduate in the late 1960's. In 1972 a local ophthalmologist, Dr. Benjamin Fine, diagnosed defendant's condition as glaucoma, a disease of the eye characterized by the excessive accumulation of fluid causing increased intraocular pressure, distorted vision, and ultimately, blindness. Dr. Fine treated defendant with an array of conventional drugs, which stabilized the intraocular pressure when first introduced but became increasingly ineffective as defendant's tolerance increased. By 1974, defendant's intraocular pressure could no longer be controlled by these medicines, and the disease had progressed to the point where defendant had suffered the complete loss of sight in his right eye and considerable impairment of vision in the left.

"Despite the ineffectiveness of traditional treatments, defendant during this period nonetheless achieved some relief through the inhalation of marijuana smoke. Fearing the legal consequences, defendant did not inform Dr. Fine of his discovery, but after his arrest defendant participated in an experimental program being conducted by ophthalmologist Dr. Robert Helper under the auspices of the United States government. Dr. Helper testified that his examination of the defendant revealed that treatment with conventional medications was ineffective, and also that surgery, while offering some hope of preserving the vision which remained to defendant, also carried significant risks

---

[g] The *Randall* case was decided by the Superior Court of the District of Columbia. It is reported in The Daily Washington Law Reporter for Dec. 28, 1976.

of immediate blindness. The results of the experimental program indicated that the ingestion of marijuana smoke had a beneficial effect on defendant's condition, normalizing intraocular pressure and lessening visual distortions."

In response to the defendant's claim of medical necessity, the government argued that the FDA had approved marijuana for medical use only in authorized experiments such as that run by Dr. Helper and that it was otherwise not legitimately available. Defendant's possession occurred outside the approved experimental program and therefore, so the argument ran, could not be justified by reference to the defendant's medical needs. Given these contentions, how should the court rule? Is *Randall* distinguishable from the laetrile cases? If so, on what ground? Are these cases harder or easier than *Warshow*? Do they present the same range of issues?

4. **Necessity as a Justification for Homicide:** *Dudley and Stephens.* The claim of necessity as a justification for intentional homicide arguably presents a special case. At common law, self-defense and other specific doctrines of justification authorized the necessary use of deadly force against a wrongdoer. The common law did not, however, permit a general plea of necessity to justify killing an innocent person in order to avoid some other evil. In contrast, most modern statutes, including both the Model Penal Code and the New York provision, seem to contemplate that a defense of necessity or choice of evils may be raised where one innocent person is killed in order to save others. This position was defended by the drafters of the Model Penal Code on the ground that "[i]t would be particularly unfortunate to exclude homicidal conduct from the scope of the defense," because "recognizing that the sanctity of life has a supreme place in the hierarchy of values, it is nonetheless true that conduct that results in taking life may promote the very value sought to be protected by the law of homicide." [h]

The issue of a limitation on necessity as a justification for intentional homicide is put by the famous case of Regina v. Dudley and Stephens, 14 Q.B.D. 273 (1884).[i] The facts as set forth by the jury in a special verdict, were as follows:

"[T]hat on July 5, 1884, the prisoners, Thomas Dudley and Edward Stephens, with one Brooks, all able-bodied English seamen, and the deceased also an English boy between 17 and 18 years of age, the crew of an English yacht, a registered English vessel, were cast away in a storm on the high seas 1600 miles from the Cape of Good Hope, and were compelled to put into an open boat belonging to the said yacht. That in this boat they had no supply of water and no supply of food, except two 1 lbs. tins of turnips, and for three days they had nothing else to

[h] ALI, Model Penal Code and Commentaries, § 3.02, p. 14 (1985).

[i] For a superb historical account of *Dudley and Stevens*, see A.W.B. Simpson, Cannabalism and the Common Law: The Story of the Tragic Last Voyage of the *Mignon-* *ette* and the Strange Legal Proceedings to Which It Gave Rise (1984). Simpson's book is insightfully reviewed in Chase, Fear Eats the Soul, 94 Yale L.J. 1253 (1985).

subsist upon. That on the fourth day they caught a small turtle, upon which they subsided for a few days, and this was the only food they had up to the 20th day when the act now in question was committed. That on the 12th day the remains of the turtle were entirely consumed, and for the next eight days they had nothing to eat. That they had no fresh water, except such rain as they from time to time caught in their oilskin capes. That the boat was drifting on the ocean, and was probably more than 1000 miles away from land. That on the 18th day, when they had been seven days without food and five without water, the prisoners spoke to Brooks as to what should be done if no succour came, and suggested that some one should be sacrificed to save the rest, but Brooks dissented, and the boy, to whom they were understood to refer, was not consulted. That on the 24th of July, the day before the act now in question, the prisoner Dudley proposed to Stephens and Brooks that lots should be cast who should be put to death to save the rest, but Brooks refused to consent, and it was not put to the boy, and in point of fact there was no drawing of lots. That on that day the prisoners spoke of their having families, and suggested it would be better to kill the boy that their lives should be saved, and Dudley proposed that if there was no vessel in sight by the morrow morning the boy should be killed. That next day, the 25th of July, no vessel appearing, Dudley told Brooks that he had better go and have a sleep, and made signs to Stephens and Brooks that the boy had better be killed. The prisoner Stephens agreed to the act, but Brooks dissented from it. That the boy was then lying at the bottom of the boat quite helpless, and extremely weakened by famine and by drinking sea water, and unable to make any resistance, nor did he ever assent to his being killed. The prisoner Dudley offered a prayer asking forgiveness for them all if either of them should be tempted to commit a rash act, and that their souls might be saved. That Dudley, with the assent of Stephens, went to the boy, and telling him that his time was come, put a knife into his throat and killed him then and there; that the three fed upon the body and blood of the boy for four days; that on the fourth day after the act had been committed the boat was picked up by a passing vessel, and the prisoners were rescued, still alive, but in the lowest state of prostration. That they were carried to the port of Falmouth, and committed for trial at Exeter. That if the men had not fed upon the body of the boy they would probably not have survived to be so picked up and rescued, but would within the four days have died of famine. That the boy, being in a much weaker condition, was likely to have died before them. That at the time of the act in question there was no sail in sight, nor any reasonable prospect of relief. That under these circumstances there appeared to the prisoners every probability that unless they then fed or very soon fed upon the boy or one of themselves they would die of starvation. That there was no appreciable chance of saving life except by killing someone for the others to eat. That assuming any necessity to kill anybody, there was no greater necessity for killing the boy than any of the other three men."

On the basis of these facts, the court found the defendants guilty of murder. The rejection of the claim of justification is explained in the following excerpt from the opinion of Lord Coleridge:

". . . Now, it is admitted that the deliberate killing of this unoffending and unresisting boy was clearly murder, unless the killing can be justified by some well-recognised excuse admitted by the law. It is further admitted that there was in this case no such excuse, unless the killing was justified by what has been called 'necessity.' But the temptation to the act which existed here was not what the law has ever called necessity. Nor is this to be regretted. Though law and morality are not the same, and many things may be immoral which are not necessarily illegal, yet the absolute divorce of law from morality would be of fatal consequence; and such divorce would follow if the temptation to murder in this case were to be held by law an absolute defence of it. It is not so. To preserve one's life is generally speaking a duty, but it may be the plainest and the highest duty to sacrifice it. War is full of instances in which it is a man's duty not to live, but to die. The duty, in case of shipwreck, of a captain to his crew, of the crew to the passengers, of soldiers to women and children, . . . these duties impose on men the moral necessity, not of the preservation, but of the sacrifice of their lives for others, from which in no country, least of all, it is to be hoped, in England, will men ever shrink, as indeed, they have not shrunk. It is not correct, therefore, to say that there is any absolute or unqualified necessity to preserve one's life. . . . It would be a very easy and cheap display of commonplace learning to quote from Greek and Latin authors, from Horace, from Juvenal, from Cicero, from Euripides, passage after passage, in which the duty of dying for others has been laid down in glowing and emphatic language as resulting from the principles of heathen ethics; it is enough in a Christian country to remind ourselves of the Great Example whom we profess to follow. It is not needful to point out the awful danger of admitting the principle which has been contended for. Who is to be the judge of this sort of necessity? By what measure is the comparative value of lives to be measured? Is it to be strength, or intellect, or what? It is plain that the principle leaves to him who is to profit by it to determine the necessity which will justify him in deliberately taking another's life to save his own. In this case the weakest, the youngest, the most unresisting, was chosen. Was it more necessary to kill him than one of the grown men? The answer must be 'No'—. . . It is not suggested that in this particular case the deeds were 'devilish,' but it is quite plain that such a principle once admitted might be made the legal cloak for unbridled passion and atrocious crime. There is no safe path for judges to tread but to ascertain the law to the best of their ability and to declare it according to their judgment; and if in any case the law appears to be too severe on individuals, to leave it to the sovereign to exercise that prerogative of mercy which the constitution has intrusted to the hands fittest to dispense it.

"It must not be supposed that in refusing to admit temptation to be an excuse for crime it is forgotten how terrible the temptation was; how awful the suffering; how hard in such trials to keep the judgment straight and the conduct pure. We are often compelled to set up standards we cannot reach ourselves, and to lay down rules which we could not ourselves satisfy. But a man has no right to declare temptation to be an excuse, though he might himself have yielded to it, nor allow compassion for the criminal to change or weaken in any manner the legal definition of the crime. It is therefore our duty to declare that the prisoners' act in this case was wilful murder, that the facts as stated in the verdict are no legal justification of the homicide; and to say that in our unanimous opinion the prisoners are upon this special verdict guilty of murder." [j]

Do you agree? On what ground? Should choice of evils never be allowed to justify intentional homicide, or is there some narrower principle on which the result in *Dudley and Stevens* can be defended? Would it matter if the person to be sacrificed had been chosen by lot?

5. **Necessity Created by Fault of the Actor.** The New York statute expressly limits the choice-of-evils defense to cases where the necessity is "occasioned or developed through no fault of the actor." Section 3.02(2) of the Model Penal Code imposes a similar limitation, as do most state statutes on the subject.[k] The application of this limitation is typically illustrated by the following hypothetical case: *A* becomes voluntarily intoxicated and, in an impaired condition, seriously injures *B*. Because *B* needs immediate medical assistance, *A* drives *B* to the hospital. If *A* is arrested for driving while intoxicated, *A* could not justify doing so by the necessity to seek help for *B*; the defect in the claim is that the situation requiring a choice of evils arose from *A*'s own fault. Do you see the logic of this position? Might there be cases in which denial of a necessity defense on this ground (assuming that the actor was aware of the law and acted accordingly) would encourage socially undesirable behavior? Can you think of situations where the necessity defense clearly should be denied because of the actor's fault in creating the occasion for his conduct?

6. **The Desirability of a General Defense of Necessity.** According to the drafters of the Model Penal Code, the choice-of-evils provision was predicated on "the view that a principle of necessity, properly conceived, affords a general justification for conduct that otherwise would constitute an offense" and "reflects the judgment that such a

[j] The court sentenced the defendants to death; however this sentence was afterwards commuted by the Crown to six months' imprisonment.

[k] For a thorough discussion of this limitation, see Robinson, Causing the Condi-tions of One's Own Defense: A Study in the Limits of Theory in Criminal Law Doctrine, 71 Va.L.Rev. 1 (1985).

qualification on criminal liability, like the general requirements of culpability, is essential to the rationality and justice of the criminal law."[l] This position is not universally accepted.

In 1974, a working party of the English Law Commission recommended statutory adoption of a general defense of necessity, provided that it could "be framed in terms which would obviate its being invoked in extravagant and inappropriate cases."[m] In support of this recommendation, the working party argued that it was unjust to impose criminal liability and punishment where the defendant avoided harm "all out of proportion to that actually caused by [his] conduct."

The members of the Law Commission were not persuaded. The Commission rejected this proposal and recommended instead that the parliament expressly abolish "any defence of necessity [which exists] at common law."[n] In support of this recommendation, the Commission observed first that the need for a general defense had not been shown:

> "From the record of reported cases, it seems to us fair to deduce that, while the state of the law may not in all respects be satisfactory, there has been no significant demand for or need of a general defence. The factors of sentencing or non-prosecution probably to some degree account for this situation. . . . It is probable also that the exceptions and qualifications provided in most statutes concerned with the major criminal offences . . . cover many situations in which a defence might otherwise be required. . . ."

The Law Commission then took note of the working party's view that "necessity would be relevant for the most part as a defence to relatively minor offenses":

> "At first sight, it certainly seems desirable that in situations such as that described in *Buckoke's* case, where without danger to others the crew of a fire-engine cross traffic-lights at red in order to deal with a nearby emergency, there should be a defence available. Analogous examples could be multiplied without difficulty; a boy under 17 years of age drives his seriously ill parent to hospital, or a man with a blood-alcohol concentration above the prescribed limit does the same for his wife, in each instance the conduct being the only means of saving life. In all these instances, a defence based upon the test of 'balance of harms' suggested by the working party, or of immediate danger to life suggested by some of those commenting on the working paper, might be expected to save the defendant from conviction. . . .
>
> "It would clearly be unfair for the defendants in the examples given above to be punished for their conduct, even though they have undoubtedly committed offences. But is it necessary to

---

[l] ALI, Model Penal Code and Commentaries, § 3.02, p. 9 (1985).

[m] See generally The Law Commission, Working Paper No. 55, Codification of the Criminal Law, General Principles, Defenses of General Application 20–39 (1974).

[n] The Law Commission, No. 83, Criminal Law, Report on Defenses of General Application 19–32 (1977).

construct a defence, unavoidably very elaborate, to avoid this outcome? It will be noted that, in the context of the example of the fire-engine crossing the traffic-lights to answer an emergency, Lord Denning remarked that the driver 'should not be *prosecuted.* He should be congratulated.' The inequity, in this and in the other examples postulated, lies, then, not in the conviction of the defendant, but in the absurdity of instituting proceedings in the first place in cases in which, whatever view is taken of the purposes which the penal process is intended to serve, no possible social benefit can ensue. We doubt whether any general defence, however elaborately contrived, would succeed in sifting out only those defendants to whom Lord Denning's remarks might deservedly be applied. At the same time, we are of the view that the proper exercise of a discretion in instituting proceedings in the field of minor offences would render such a general defence unnecessary."

The Commission then noted that the application of a general choice-of-evils defense to crimes against the person would raise serious "ethical problems." After laying aside the special case of necessity as a justification for intentional homicide, the Commission put the following case:

". . . 'An immediate blood transfusion must be made in order to save an injured person: the only one who has the same blood type as the injured [person] refuses to give blood. Can he be overpowered, and the blood taken from him?' The necessity defence advocated by the working party would by its terms almost certainly answer this in the affirmative. But one of those commenting on the working paper expressed doubts as to whether this would be regarded as a generally acceptable solution. We share these doubts. It is however, almost, if not entirely, impossible to devise any generalised exception which would exclude the availability of a general defence in this situation. It may, of course, be objected that such examples are mere academic puzzles, and are so unlikely to arise in practice that they may safely be ignored. That is not, we believe, an adequate rationalisation of this type of situation in a period in which the donation of rare blood-groups and bone marrows, and the making of organ transplants, is increasingly common; and if in the face of the multiplication of such examples no satisfactory general exception could, in legislative terms, be devised to cope with them, this provides evidence for the view that a general defence, as distinct from particular exceptions to specific offences, is not the right approach in the field of offences against the person.

"Any general defence ought, we think, to be capable of dealing with the exceptional and difficult case, and to apply to all offences save any to which, on rational and defensible grounds, an exception is thought to be desirable. . . ."

Finally, the Commission summarized its objections to a general choice-of-evils defense as follows:

"It is probable that situations where necessity may be in issue are so diverse as not to be readily classifiable; and in this respect the difference between, on the one hand, necessity and, on the other, duress and other defences applicable in more narrowly defined circumstances, such as self-defence, is perhaps more fundamental than the working party appreciated. Significantly, in our view, even some of those who, on the whole, were inclined to favour the creation of a general defence were in doubt as to how it would operate in relation to many offences. We are very doubtful whether a defence operating with such a degree of uncertainty ought to find a place in a code.

"Furthermore, even if a general defence were thought feasible there are a number of offences, among them the most serious of all, in relation to which, as we have seen, the operation of the defence would have to be excluded. Those exceptions, in particular those relating to murder and some serious offences against the person, would be necessary because of the unexplored implications the defence would have for sensitive questions of ethics and social responsibility, or because of the unacceptable results which might ensue from the application of the defence in special cases. Such exceptions, made necessary by expediency rather than principle, weigh further against the view that a general defence is desirable.

"We have indicated that any general defence might sometimes be uncertain in operation; that various qualifications would be needed to the generality of its operation; that, in respect of some important offenses, such as murder, exceptions to its application would be required, while, in respect of minor offenses, it would be preferable for no defence to be available; and, finally, that in respect of yet other offenses, there is probably little need for any defence. These considerations lead us to recommend that there should be no general defence of necessity in the Code. . . ."

Do you find these arguments persuasive? Does recognition of a general necessity defense introduce too many uncertainties into the penal law? Did the Law Commission adequately respond to the contention that recognition of a general justification is "essential to the rationality and justice of all penal prohibitions"? Are you comfortable with the reliance on prosecutorial discretion to "sift out" meritorious claims from unwarranted ones? Or would it be better to rely on the deliberations of a jury instructed on the general concept of justification by necessity?

SUBSECTION B: THE EFFECT OF MISTAKE

NOTES ON THE EFFECT OF MISTAKE IN CLAIMS OF JUSTIFICATION

1. **Introduction.** The effect of a mistaken belief in the existence of justificatory facts is conceptually analogous to the issue of mistake in the context of offenses. In order to examine the effect of mistake in claims of justification, it is desirable at the outset to assume a state of facts that would justify criminal conduct. For this purpose, assume a hypothetical case of self-defense. Suppose that *A* is accosted at the front door of her home by *B*, a neighbor who is angry because *A*'s dog is left out at night and, though fenced in the back yard, is keeping everyone awake by constant barking. *A* invites *B* to come in to discuss the matter, and closes the door. *B*, who is obviously distraught and irrational, then pulls a gun. *B* complains that he has not slept in weeks, that he has lost his job, that his wife is leaving him, and that his life is falling apart. He blames it all on *A*'s dog. He declares his intention to kill *A*, aims the gun at her, and seems ready to pull the trigger. At this point, *A* runs into the next room, dodges a bullet fired from *B*'s gun, grabs her own gun from a table on which she had just finished cleaning it, and, before *B* can fire again, shoots and kills him.

On the facts as stated, it is plain that *A* has a defense to a charge of criminal homicide. She intentionally caused the death of another, but did so in self-defense. The circumstances justify *A*'s effort to defend herself, even by the use of deadly force. Her otherwise criminal conduct is therefore no crime, and would not be punished as such by any American jurisdiction. Subsequent notes examine the effect of mistake by means of hypothetical variations of these basic facts.

2. **Reasonable Mistake.** Assume the facts are as stated above, with several crucial differences. *B* did not actually shoot at *A*, but appeared ready to do so, clearly threatened to do so, and chased *A* into the next room when she fled to get her gun, proclaiming that he was going to kill her. As before, *A* grabbed her gun and intentionally killed *B*. On this variation of the facts, however, *B*'s actual intention was only to frighten *A* into doing something about the dog, as is confirmed by *B*'s wife and another neighbor, who helped him formulate his plan, and by the fact that *B*'s gun was not loaded. In fact *B*'s wife was not leaving him, nor had he lost his job, yet *B* put on a good show and was all too successful in convincing *A* that *B*'s life was falling apart and that she, the cause of it all in his eyes, was in imminent danger of death.

On these facts, *A*'s response plainly satisfies the elements of criminal homicide: She intentionally caused the death of another human being. It is true that she acted in the belief that deadly force was necessary to protect herself against being killed, but the use of such force by her was in fact not necessary. *A* made a mistake—a reasonable mistake, you should assume—but it was a mistake nonetheless. The question is whether it should be a defense to a charge of criminal homicide that *A* honestly and reasonably believed in the existence of facts which, if true, would have justified her conduct.

The answer of the common law and of modern statutes is the same: An honest and reasonable belief in the existence of justificatory facts is ordinarily a defense, even if the belief turns out to have been mistaken.[a] The rationale for this position is not hard to see. The person who makes an honest and reasonable mistake in the apprehension of justificatory facts is not blameworthy. There is no basis in moral guilt to support the imposition of criminal liability. The actor is in the same position as the motorist who inadvertently and without fault hits a child who darts out from between parked cars. In both cases, the result of the actor's conduct is to be deplored, but it is not to be redressed by penal sanctions.

3. **Unreasonable Mistake.** But what if the defendant's mistaken perception is not reasonable? Suppose, for example, that *B* was unarmed. He was wild and abusive and repeatedly threatened to shoot *A* if she did not do something about that dog, but he showed no weapon. When *A* ran to the next room to get her gun, he followed her but made no move to draw a weapon. Nonetheless, *A* panicked, picked up her gun, and killed *B*. Suppose further that, having heard all the evidence, a jury concluded that *A* was in a genuine state of panic and that she formed an honest and sincere belief that *B* was going to kill her then and that the only way she could escape was to kill him first. The jury also concluded, however, that *A*'s belief was mistaken, and that most observers would have judged the mistake to have been decidedly unreasonable. What defensive significance should the mistake have in the face of such conclusions by the jury?

The common-law answer was "none." In this respect, the common-law approach to mistaken belief in the existence of justificatory facts was consistent with its approach to claims of mistake regarding elements of an offense that required general intent. In both cases, the general proposition was that mistake was exculpatory only if it was reasonable. This is the law today in most common-law jurisdictions and in more than a few states with recently revised penal statutes. The New York provision on defense of the person, N.Y. Penal Code § 35.15, is illustrative. It provides in part:

> "1. A person may . . . use physical force upon another person when and to the extent he reasonably believes such to be necessary to defend himself or a third person from what he reasonably believes to be the use or imminent use of unlawful physical force by such other person . . . .
>
> "2. A person may not use deadly physical force upon another person under circumstances specified in subdivision one unless:
>
> (a) He reasonably believes that such other person is using or about to use deadly physical force . . . or

---

[a] Actually, it is not clear that the common law uniformly recognized reasonable mistake as a defense for all doctrines of justification. The position stated in text, however, seems to have been firmly established for self-defense, which is the paradigm doctrine of justification and the principal context for litigation of such questions.

(b) He reasonably believes that such other person is committing or attempting to commit a kidnapping, forcible rape, forcible sodomy or robbery . . . .''

Note that the availability of the justification is made to depend not on objective reality but on the actor's belief in the existence of justificatory facts. Note also that the standard of belief is in every instance qualified by a requirement of reasonableness. If the belief is unreasonable, the justification is by its terms inapplicable, and the defendant is liable for whatever offense is made out by his or her conduct.

4. **Unreasonable Mistake and Imperfect Justification.** In many situations the limitation of such a defense to reasonable mistakes poses no particular problem. Where the offense charged is one of general intent, there may be no great disparity in making the defense of justification defeasible on proof of a form of negligence. Where, however, the offense requires a culpability substantially higher than ordinary negligence, an anomaly results. If, for example, "purpose" is the mens rea required for a given offense, the actor cannot be convicted for a merely negligent mistake regarding its elements; but a merely negligent mistake regarding the facts of a defense of justification will lead to a conviction. The disparity is most pronounced in criminal homicide. A person who intentionally kills another is ordinarily guilty of murder. If *A* intentionally kills *B* in the honest and reasonable, but mistaken, belief that deadly force is essential to *A*'s self-defense, *A* is guilty of no crime. But if *A*'s belief in the necessity of deadly force is unreasonable, *A* has no defense and is guilty of murder, even though liability for murder generally does not rest on proof of mere negligence.

In answer to this problem, many common-law jurisdictions have developed for the law of homicide a doctrine of "imperfect justification." Under this approach, an honest belief in the existence of justificatory facts, even if unreasonable, is said to negate the mens rea required for murder. The unreasonable mistake, however, provides no defense to the lesser charge of manslaughter. The effect is to recognize unreasonable mistake as a mitigation but not as a complete defense.[b] The law of criminal homicide lends itself to this solution because it traditionally has recognized murder and manslaughter as distinct offenses differentiated only by the actor's culpability. Most other crimes do not offer the same grading opportunity, and it is therefore no surprise that the common-law doctrine of "imperfect justification" has been confined primarily to criminal homicide.[c]

5. **The Model Penal Code.** The Model Penal Code generalizes the idea of imperfect justification. This is done by linking the kind of mistake deemed exculpatory with the kind of culpability required by

[b] Much the same result has been achieved under the New York Code by a reformulation of the traditional common-law mitigation of provocation to include most, if not all, of the factual situations likely to arise under a doctrine of imperfect justification. For a detailed discussion of the traditional rule of provocation, see the materials on criminal homicide at pages 882–904, infra. The New York provocation formula is set forth in Appendix B, page 8, infra.

[c] For a recent case holding that "imperfect self-defense" is a defense to assault with intent to murder, thereby reducing the crime to simple assault, see Faulkner v. State, 301 Md. 482, 483 A.2d 759 (1984).

the definition of the offense. Conceptually, the scheme is quite simple. A person who believes, however unreasonably, in the existence of justificatory facts has a defense to any crime requiring a culpability of purpose or knowledge. For a crime requiring only recklessness, however, the mistaken belief must be not only sincere but also non-reckless. And only a non-negligent belief would be a defense against a crime for which negligence was the required culpability.

Implementation of this scheme is technically elaborate. It is accomplished in two steps. First, each of the several justification defenses is defined in purely subjective terms. Thus, for example, § 3.04(1) provides that "the use of force upon or toward another person is justifiable when the actor *believes* that such force is immediately necessary for the purpose of protecting himself against the use of unlawful force by such other person on the present occasion" (emphasis added). Section 3.04(2)(b) further provides that the use of deadly force in self-defense is not justified "unless the actor *believes* that such force is necessary to protect himself against death, serious bodily harm, kidnapping or sexual intercourse compelled by force or threat . . ." (emphasis added). If these provisions were left unqualified, an honest belief in the necessity of using deadly force would be a defense to any charge of assault or homicide, no matter how reckless or negligent the actor might have been in forming that belief. Section 3.09(2) provides the second step:

> "When the actor believes that the use of force upon or toward the person of another is necessary for any of the purposes for which such belief would establish a justification . . . but the actor is reckless or negligent in having such belief or in acquiring or failing to acquire any knowledge or belief which is material to the justifiability of his use of force, the justification . . . is unavailable in a prosecution for an offense for which recklessness or negligence, as the case may be, suffices to establish culpability."

This scheme achieves a symmetry between the kind of belief recognized as a defense and the kind of culpability required by the definition of the crime. The rationale for this approach, however, is not merely aesthetic. The Model Code treatment of mistaken belief in the existence of justificatory facts is an essential feature of its general commitment to proof of subjective mens rea. Allowing only a reasonable mistake to be a defense would undercut the Model Code's general insistence on recklessness as the minimum culpability ordinarily required for criminal liability. Recognizing even an unreasonable mistake as to justification as a defense for crimes of recklessness eliminates a disparity that, given the Model Code definition of specific offenses, would otherwise be pervasive.

6. **Alternative Statutory Formulations.** The Model Penal Code position on mistaken belief in the existence of justificatory facts has been very influential. Not all statutes that follow the same policy, however, implement it in the same way.

Consider, for example, the following provisions of the proposed federal code drafted by the National Commission on Reform of the Federal Criminal Laws (the Brown Commission), Final Report at 45, 48, 52 (1970):

"Section 603.   Self-Defense

A person is justified in using force upon another person in order to defend himself against danger of imminent unlawful bodily injury, sexual assault or detention by such other person . . . .

"Section 607.   Limits on the Use of Force: Excessive Force; Deadly Force

(1) Excessive Force.   A person is not justified in using more force than is necessary and appropriate under the circumstances.

(2) Deadly Force.   Deadly force is justified . . . when used in lawful self-defense, or in lawful defense of others, if such force is necessary to protect the actor or anyone else against death, serious bodily injury, or the commission of a felony involving violence. . . .

"Section 608.   Excuse

(1) Mistake.   A person's conduct is excused if he believes the factual situation is such that his conduct is necessary and appropriate, for any of the purposes which would establish a justification . . . even though his belief is mistaken, except that, if his belief is negligently or recklessly held, it is not an excuse in a prosecution for an offense for which negligence or recklessness, as the case may be, suffices to establish culpability. . . ."

Does this formulation differ from that of the Model Code? In what way? Which approach seems preferable?

Study of this statute and of the Model Penal Code will be aided by attention to the following hypothetical. *B* starts a heated argument with *A*. *B* has a reputation for a quick and violent temper and is rumored to carry a knife. In the course of the quarrel, *B* suddenly reaches into a coat pocket. *A*, fearing that *B* is drawing a knife, hits *B* in the face and draws blood. It turns out that *B* had no knife, but was merely reaching for a pack of cigarettes. *A* is prosecuted for assault under Model Penal Code § 211.1(1)(a). On what determinations does *A*'s liability depend under the Model Code justification provisions? Under the Brown Commission provisions, if that code included an identically defined assault offense? Under the common law?

7. **Accidental Justification.** Should a defendant be entitled to acquittal for objectively justified conduct even if the reasons for his or her actions are not those that would justify them? Can conduct that violates the criminal law be justified by accident, so to speak? Although the question rarely arises, it has generated some theoretical interest. Suppose, for example, that *A* sees *B*, a long-time enemy, on the streets and suddenly punches *B* in the nose in repayment for what

A regards as a past pattern of insulting and abusive comments. Assume that *A* would be guilty of criminal assault but for the fact that, unknown to *A*, *B* had a gun, was about to shoot *A*, and would have done so if *A* had not acted first.

Professor Glanville Williams argues that *A* should be entitled to acquittal, Textbook of Criminal Law 457 (1978):

> "[T]he question is whether, to justify a conviction, all the external elements of defences must be absent, just as all the external elements of the definition [of the offense] must be present. . . . [A] crime requires the whole actus reus to be committed; and . . . the actus reus [should be seen to include] the negative of defences. If this is so, no crime is committed if the factual situation giving rise to the defence existed, even though the defendant did not know that it existed."

Is Professor Williams right? Do you see a basis for arguing that *A* should be convicted of assault? Would *A* be guilty of assault under the Model Penal Code? Under the Brown Commission proposal? Assuming that Professor Williams is correct and that *A* should not be guilty of the completed offense of assault under these circumstances, should *A* nonetheless be guilty of attempted assault?

8. **Mistake of Law in Claims of Justification.** The significance of mistakes of law in claims of justification is easily deduced from the basic policy of the criminal law regarding such mistakes. Recall the basic principle of ignorantia juris as it is stated in § 2.02(9) of the Model Code:

> "Neither knowledge nor recklessness or negligence as to whether conduct constitutes an offense or as to the existence, meaning or application of the law determining the elements of an offense is an element of such offense, unless the definition of the offense or the Code so provides."

In principle one would expect this policy to apply to the law defining justifications as well as to the law defining offenses, and that is exactly what the Model Code provides. According to § 1.13(9), "element of an offense" includes any conduct, circumstance, or result that "negatives an excuse or justification." Thus, by its terms, § 2.02(9) applies to mistakes regarding "the existence, meaning or application" of a defense of justification. In addition, § 3.09(1) states that the justifications for use of force are unavailable "when (a) the actor's belief in the unlawfulness of the force or conduct against which he employs protective force . . . is erroneous; and (b) his error is due to ignorance or mistake as to the provisions of the Code [or] any other provision of the criminal law. . . ." How would you expect such claims to be handled in a jurisdiction without an express statute on the subject?

Recall also that under § 2.04(1) of the Model Code, mistakes of law other than mistakes "as to the existence, meaning or application of law determining the elements of an offense" are assimilated to mistakes of fact. The same principle applies to mistakes of non-penal law regarding justifications. For example, suppose that *A* takes property from *B*.

B believes that the property is his or hers, and uses force to retrieve it from *A*. Section 3.06(1)(b), read together with § 2.04(1), makes clear that *B* is entitled to a defense even if the property in fact belongs to *A*. But if *B*'s mistake is reckless or negligent, *B* may be held liable for any offense for which recklessness or negligence, as the case may be, suffices. Whether the mistake arose from a misidentification of the property involved (mistake of fact) or from a misconstruction of one's rights in the property (mistake of law) would be immaterial. How would you expect the common law to treat mistakes of law in this context?

9. **Strict Liability in Claims of Justification.** It should be clear that when the law disregards a non-negligent, mistaken belief in the existence of justifying circumstances, it achieves, with respect to those circumstances, a result that is identical to the imposition of strict liability for circumstances in the definition of the underlying offense. The imposition of strict liability under doctrines of justification was not unknown at common law. Consider two illustrations.

First, suppose *A* uses deadly force to arrest *B* because *A* believes, upon reasonable grounds, that *B* has committed a felony. At common law, if *A* is a police officer, *A* is privileged in most jurisdictions to use deadly force if it is necessary to make such an arrest even if it turns out that a reasonable mistake was made about *B*'s guilt of a felony. However, if *A* is a private citizen, his or her assaultive conduct is privileged only if the felony has, in fact, been committed; *A*'s mistaken belief, however reasonable, has no legal significance.

Second, a person is justified, at common law, in using reasonable force against a police officer to resist and defend against a patently arbitrary or unreasonable arrest. However, if the arrest is lawful, the arrestee is liable for assaultive conduct regardless of the reasonableness and sincerity of the belief that it was unlawful, whether the mistake was based on a misperception of the facts or on a misunderstanding of the law of arrest.

In both of these situations, the limitation of the defense to conduct that is actually justified reflects policy judgments that the assaultive behavior should be strongly discouraged. Rather than withdrawing the privilege altogether, the law permits the individual to act, but only at the peril of being wrong. Not surprisingly, the recent trend is to withdraw the justification altogether in these situations. The Model Penal Code, for example, bars the use of deadly force by a private person in making arrests except when the person believes he or she is assisting a police officer. See § 3.07(2)(b). Similarly, § 3.04(2)(a)(i) of the Model Code and most recent authorities forbid forcible resistance to arrest and instead require the citizen to submit peaceably to an arrest by a person known to be a police officer.[d]

---

[d] For a recent decision abrogating the common-law privilege of resisting an unlawful arrest in favor of the Model Penal Code approach, see Commonwealth v. Moreira, 388 Mass. 596, 447 N.E.2d 1224 (1983).

SUBSECTION C: DEFENSE AGAINST AGGRESSION

CRAWFORD v. STATE

Court of Appeals of Maryland, 1963.
231 Md. 354, 190 A.2d 538.

BRUNE, CHIEF JUDGE. [Crawford was indicted for murder, tried before a court sitting without a jury, convicted of manslaughter, and sentenced to eight years' imprisonment. He claimed that he was defending himself and his home against an attack by the decedent Bobbie Ferrell, who was seeking to force his way into his home to beat and rob him.

[Crawford was a 42-year-old man, who had suffered from ulcers and nervous disorders, and was on relief for disability. He lived in a first-floor front room in a rooming house. A front outside door opened into a vestibule, and there was an inner door between the vestibule and a long hallway. This inner door could be secured by a spring lock, which seems to have been the only lock protecting Crawford's room. His room opened off the hallway just inside this inner door.

[The evidence showed that Ferrell, aged 23, and other young men had been in the habit of "hanging around" the front of the rooming house and going into Crawford's room whenever they pleased. On March 12, 1962, the day the shooting occurred, Crawford had complained about them to the police and the police had visited his home, finding none of the boys there at the time. Crawford stated that Ferrell and his friend Austin had come to his room shortly after the police left, accused him of being a "police snitcher," hit him in the face, asked him for money and left when he said he would have his welfare check later in the day.

[In order to keep the check away from Ferrell and Austin, Crawford met the postman about a block from his home, obtained his welfare check, cashed it, and left $45.00 of the proceeds with a neighbor. He then met the police officers who had visited his home earlier that day and told them that the boys had come to his home and demanded money. They told him to call the police if the boys returned. Crawford then went to a pawnshop to redeem a shotgun which he had pawned about a year before, and took it home "to scare them away."

[Crawford testified that Ferrell and Austin soon came back to his room for a second time and threatened him; then, he said, Austin, with a knife in his hand, threw an arm around his neck, rifled his pockets, and took about $7.00 from him. Crawford's testimony about the demand for money was generally corroborated by another boarder in the rooming house. The witness stated that Ferrell's parting remark, after the appellant had told him and Austin to leave, was "We're going out, but you better damn sight have the money when we get back."

However this witness did not confirm Crawford's claim that he was robbed at knifepoint.

[Ferrell and Austin soon returned a third time, Ferrell going to the front door and Austin to the rear door of the house. Crawford called to other boarders to get the police but they would not go out of the house for fear that they would be "jumped" by Ferrell or Austin. Ferrell entered the vestibule and was trying to get through the inner door; Crawford then picked up his gun, loaded it, and went into the front hall just inside this inner door. Ferrell, finding the inner door locked, kicked at the bottom of it and said, "I'm coming in to kick your ass." Crawford, holding the door with his feet, warned Ferrell to stay out and told him that he had the gun, but Ferrell said he did not care about the gun. Ferrell then knocked part of the door loose and reached inside to unlock it; as he did so, Crawford backed away from the door and fired the gun, hitting Ferrell in the face. Crawford testified that he backed away from the door because he was "scared" and Ferrell "was coming right in on me." He said he did not "aim for the head," that instead he fired at Ferrell's hand but the gun jerked up as he fired. He said that he did intend "for the gun to go off because the boys made me angry and I was scared they was coming in and hurt me."]

The trial court's comments at the end of the trial indicated that he accepted and believed these material parts of appellant's story: (i) that Ferrell had been in the appellant's room demanding and taking money; (ii) that Ferrell had warned that he would be back; (iii) that at the time of the shooting Ferrell was unlawfully forcing or attempting to force his way into the appellant's home; (iv) that the appellant did not deliberately fire at Ferrell's head. In addition, the court thought reasonable the appellant's explanation for not going outside to summon police help. But the court then found that "the defendant went further than the situation required," and entered a verdict of not guilty of murder but guilty of manslaughter.

. . . Most American jurisdictions in which the question has been decided have taken the view that if an assault on a dwelling and an attempted forcible entry are made under circumstances which would create a reasonable apprehension that it is the design of the assailant *to commit a felony* or to inflict on the inhabitants injury which may result in loss of life or great bodily harm, and that the danger that the design will be carried into effect is imminent, a lawful occupant of the dwelling may prevent the entry even by the taking of the intruder's life. [In] Pond v. People, 8 Mich. 150 (1860), . . . the court said that a man assaulted in his dwelling "may use such means as are absolutely necessary to repel the assailant from his house, or *to prevent his forcible entry*, even to the taking of life." (Emphasis added). . . .

There is also a generally accepted rule, which we think is correct, that a man faced with the danger of an attack upon his dwelling need not retreat from his home to escape the danger, but instead may stand his ground and, if necessary to repel the attack, may kill the attacker.
. . . .

Authorities elsewhere have recognized, correctly we think, that the rules regarding the defense of one's person and the rules regarding the defense of one's habitation are generally similar. . . . [I]n order to establish that a homicide is justifiable because committed in self defense the defendant must show (i) that he was not the aggressor, (ii) that he believed that he was in such immediate danger of losing his own life or suffering serious bodily harm that it was necessary to take the life of the deceased to save himself, and (iii) that the circumstances would warrant reasonable grounds for such belief in the mind of a man of ordinary reason.

The most difficult problem in this case is whether the force used by the appellant in resisting the intrusion was excessive. The authorities generally seem to agree that the force used must not be excessive. . . . [S]ee R. Anderson, 1 Wharton's Criminal Law and Procedure 453–55 (1957), where it is stated in part:

"It is a justifiable homicide to kill to prevent the commission of a felony by force or surprise.

"The crimes in prevention of which life may be taken are such and only such as are committed by forcible means, violence, and surprise, such as murder, robbery, burglary, rape, or arson. . . .

"It is also essential that killing is necessary to prevent the commission of the felony in question. If other methods could prevent its commission, a homicide is not justified; all other means of preventing the crime must first be exhausted." . . .

The material parts of the defendant's statements which the trial court accepted as true, which we have set forth above, and his acceptance of the appellant's explanation as to why he did not seek help from the police at the time of the attack lead us to conclude that the trial court was clearly in error in finding that the appellant used excessive force. One conclusion which the trial judge did not state, but which we think is a proper and, indeed, inescapable one to be drawn from the testimony which he did believe, is that Ferrell's purpose in seeking to break into the appellant's residence was to beat him and rob him. Robbery is a felony.

The appellant was in his home, and as we have already held, was under no duty to retreat therefrom. We might add that retreat seemed impossible with Ferrell at one door and Austin at the other. He defended his home first by locking the door, by warning the deceased to stay out, then by holding the door against the deceased, and finally, when it became apparent that the deceased would be able to force his way in, by backing away from the door and firing his shotgun at the deceased's hand. . . . We do not believe that the circumstances in this case show the use of unnecessary force by appellant, a man of 42 years of age with a history of illness and unable to work, in resisting the attack being actively made by a 23-year-old man with the cooperation of a youthful partner, when these two had previously had no apparent difficulty in overcoming appellant. "[T]he character and extent of the assault are important considerations." . . . Here important characteristics of the attack were that it was on the appellant's home and that its object was to beat and rob him. . . . The appellant had the burden of proving by a preponderance of the evidence that he acted reasonably in defense of his habitation against forcible entry. We think that he met this burden.[a]

Judgment reversed without a new trial.

NOTES ON DEFENSE OF SELF AND PROPERTY

1. **Introduction.** In general, one who is free from fault is privileged to use force to defend his or her person or property against harm threatened by the unlawful act of another if: (i) the person cannot avoid the threatened harm without using defensive force or giving up some right or privilege; and (ii) the force used for this purpose is not unreasonable or excessive in view of the harm which it is intended to prevent. This general principle has acquired contextual specificity through centuries of judicial development. Separate "defenses" are usually provided for use of force in defense of person, habitation, and property and in aid of law enforcement. Cutting across these doctrines is a set of limitations regarding the use of "deadly force" (force intended or likely to cause death or great bodily harm) as distinguished from non-deadly, or moderate, force. It is in this context, where one person kills another in defense of his own or her interests, that the most controversial issues arise.

2. **Common-Law Doctrines Justifying Deadly Force.** Several different but overlapping common-law "privileges" may be applicable to the *Crawford* situation:

(i) **Self-Defense.** The trial court in *Crawford* apparently found that the defendant, although afraid that the intruders would beat and rob him, did not fear for his life. Although some defensive force was undoubtedly necessary for Crawford to protect himself, the trial court found that, under the circumstances, deadly force was excessive in relation to the personal danger. On the other hand, as the appellate court observes, if Crawford had reasonably believed that Ferrell and Austin intended to kill him or cause him serious bodily harm, he would have been justified in using deadly force to defend himself. Statutory formulations on self-defense also typically provide that an innocent victim may use deadly force to protect himself against forcible sexual assault or kidnapping.

(ii) **Defense of Habitation.** The *Crawford* decision reflects the traditional common-law doctrine that a person is permitted to use

---

[a] In a substantial majority of states and in the federal courts, the prosecution bears the burden of disproving claims of self-defense, and most other claims of justification, beyond a reasonable doubt. See generally Jeffries & Stephan, Defenses, Presumptions, and Burden of Proof in The Criminal Law, 88 Yale L.J. 1325, 1329–31 (1979). As the *Crawford* court indicates, Maryland is one of the minority jurisdictions in which the defendant bears the burden of persuasion as well as the burden of production on self-defense claims. The constitutional issues raised by the minority approach are considered at pages 967–93, infra. [Footnote by eds.]

deadly force to prevent an entry into his or her home based on the reasonable belief that such force is necessary to prevent robbery, burglary, arson, or felonious assault, even if he or she is not fearful of death or great bodily injury. As a practical matter, of course, circumstances that would arouse a reasonable fear of such dangers would also be likely to arouse fear of death or serious injury. Nonetheless, the trial judge's finding that deadly force was not reasonably necessary to defend Crawford's life isolates the continuing vitality of this distinct "defense of habitation." According to Professors Perkins and Boyce, the trend has been in the direction of reaffirming this separate defense. R. Perkins & R. Boyce, Criminal Law 1148–54 (3d ed.1982).[a] It must be emphasized, however, that deadly force is not authorized to prevent a mere trespass or a non-felonious attack on the defender or another member of the household.

(iii) **Prevention of Dangerous Felonies.** At common law, every citizen was entitled to prevent any felony from being committed, regardless of whether he or she was being victimized. Today, the privilege of crime-prevention has a somewhat uncertain status. There are several reasons for this. First, many of the situations covered by the common-law defense are now covered by the separate privileges concerning defense of person, habitation, and property against unprovoked attack.[b] Second, the penal law now punishes as felonies a range of misconduct far wider than the predatory crimes so classified at common law. Third, all felonies were punishable by death at common law; today only the most serious homicides are subject to the capital sanction. Where crime prevention is still recognized as a separate defense, it justifies deadly force only to prevent "dangerous" felonies. As the court stated in State v. Harris, 222 N.W.2d 462, 466 (Iowa 1974): "[A] person may kill if he observes an atrocious, violent felony about to be or being committed—whether upon such person himself or not. . . . The law's rationale . . . is that such crimes themselves imperil human life or involve danger of great bodily harm." [c]

(iv) **Questions on *Crawford*.** Was *Crawford* correctly decided? Should Crawford be entitled to kill to prevent forcible entry into his

---

[a] For recent authority, see, e.g., State v. McCombs, 297 N.C. 151, 253 S.E.2d 906 (1979); Sledge v. State, 507 S.W.2d 726 (Tex.Cr.App.1974).

[b] At common law, the privilege of crime prevention permitted the victim of a felonious attack to resist with deadly force; this was said to be a "perfect" privilege because the actor had no obligation to retreat before employing deadly force. In contrast, the early common-law privilege of "self-defense" referred to an "imperfect" privilege for persons who found it necessary to defend themselves against an assault that was not felonious. For example, a person who was a party to a "sudden affray" or mutual combat—where no one was a culpable aggressor—could defend his life with deadly force only if he "retreated to the wall" before doing so. This retreat was said to be necessary to "perfect" his right to defend his life by killing his combatant.

In modern usage, the term self-defense refers to all situations involving personal defense, including the "sudden affray" as well as the clearly felonious assault. The scope of the requirement of retreat under modern law is explored at pages 559–63, infra.

[c] Many statutes accomplish the same result by including such a robbery in the list of offenses against which one may defend oneself or another by the use of deadly force. See, e.g., N.Y.Penal Code § 35.15(2)(b). Other similar statutes are collected in ALI, Model Penal Code and Commentaries, § 3.06, pp. 97–100 n. 49 (1985).

home? To prevent the robbery that was obviously about to occur? Even if he was not afraid that he would be killed or seriously harmed?

3. **Approaches to Defensive Use of Deadly Force.** What are the permissible occasions for defensive use of deadly force? What interests other than the preservation of life should justify killing the aggressor? On what basis should these fundamental questions be decided? As you think about these issues, consider the following comments:

(i) **The Law of Nature.** Blackstone found the well-springs of the common-law doctrines in human nature, 3 W. Blackstone, Commentaries 3–4 (Oxford, 1769); 4 id. at 180–81:

"[I]f the party himself, or any of . . . his relations, be forcibly attacked in his person or property, it is lawful for him to repel force by force; and the breach of the peace, which happens, is chargeable upon him only who began the affray. For the law, in this case, respects the passions of the human mind; and (when external violence is offered to a man himself, or those to whom he bears a near connection) makes it lawful in him to do himself that immediate justice to which he is prompted by nature, and which no prudential motives are strong enough to restrain. It considers that the future process of law is by no means an adequate remedy for injuries accompanied with force; since it is impossible to say to what wanton lengths of rapine or cruelty outrages of this sort might be carried, unless it were permitted a man immediately to oppose one violence with another. Self-defence, therefore, as it is justly called the primary law of nature, so it is not, neither can it be in fact, taken away by the law of society. In the English law particularly it is held an excuse for breaches of the peace, nay even for homicide itself; but care must be taken that the resistance does not exceed the bounds of mere defence and prevention, for then the defender would himself become an aggressor. . . .

"[S]uch homicide, as is committed for the *prevention* of any forcible and atrocious *crime*, is justifiable by the law of nature, and also by the law of England, as it stood so early as the time of Bracton, and as it is since declared by statute. If any person attempts a robbery or murder of another, or attempts to break open a house *in the night-time*, (which extends also to an attempt to burn it), and shall be killed in such attempt, the slayer shall be acquitted and discharged. This reaches not to any crime unaccompanied with force, as picking of pockets, or to the breaking open of any house *in the daytime*, unless it carries with it an attempt of robbery also.

". . . The English law [justifies] a woman, killing one who attempts to ravish her; and so too the husband or father may justify killing a man, who attempts a rape upon his wife or daughter; but not if he takes them in adultery by consent, for the one is forcible and felonious, but not the other. I make no doubt but the forcibly attempting a crime, of a still more detestable nature, may be equally resisted by the death of the unnatural aggressor. For the one uniform principle that runs through our own, and all other laws, seems to be this: that where a crime, in itself capital, is endeavored to be committed by force, it is lawful to repel that force by the death of the party attempting."

(ii) **Social Utility.** Professors Wechsler and Michael argue that the doctrines of justifiable homicide should be shaped with direct reference to their potential for achieving maximum protection for human life. In those terms, they find the common-law approach insufficiently restrictive. In Wechsler & Michael, A Rationale of the Law of Homicide I, 37 Colum.L.Rev. 701, 735–36, 740–41 (1937), they defended this position as follows: *

"It is obviously desirable to deter any act which is intended to kill and which under any circumstances may result in death, unless the act is itself a necessary means to preserving life or to some other end of greater social value than the preservation of life. . . .

"The most obvious case of homicidal behavior that serves the end of preserving life is that of the victim of a wrongful attack who finds it necessary to kill his assailant to save his own life. We need not pause to reconsider the universal judgment that there is no social interest in preserving the lives of aggressors at the cost of those of their victims. Given the choice that must be made, the only defensible policy is one that will operate as a sanction against unlawful aggression. . . .

"[The difficult question is] what ends, if any, *other than the preservation of life*, can justify intentional homicide. Such an end, it seems clear, must be one the achievement of which by common agreement is almost indispensable if life is to be worth living. For the most part it is possible to achieve and protect the conditions of worthwhile living by other means than homicide. But precisely as homicide is sometimes a necessary means to the preservation of life, it is sometimes a necessary means to the prevention of physical and psychic injuries that usually prove to be permanent and seriously impair the human capacities of those who suffer them. . . . There remains, of course, the difficult problem of determining what physical and psychic injuries so gravely impair the capacity to function that the value of life itself is seriously impaired. It is doubtful, indeed, whether a legislator can profitably do more than articulate a formula couched in these terms and leave to administrators the task of giving it a content that is consonant with the conditions and ideals of the community. Implicit in what has been said, however, is a condemnation of the common-law formula in so far as it includes within the ambit of 'violent felonies' crimes against property when threatened under circumstances involving little or no danger of serious personal injury."

* Reprinted with permission of Professor
Wechsler and the Columbia Law Review.

(iii) **Accommodating Autonomy and Proportionality.** Recent academic commentary suggests that the contemporary network of doctrines discussed earlier may be seen in terms of an evolving accommodation of values of personal autonomy and proportionality. Professor Kadish has summarized this point of view in Respect for Life and Regard for Rights in the Criminal Law, 64 Cal.L.Rev. 871, 886–88 (1976). According to the principle of personal autonomy, Professor Kadish says, "no one may be used as the mere instrument of another." It follows that a person has a "right to resist threats to [himself] or interests closely identified therewith. . . ." However, he emphasizes, the right to resist aggression derived from the principle of autonomy has no intrinsic limitation; the victim of aggression is entitled to use whatever force is necessary, including deadly force, to protect any of his "interests of personality." Instead, Professor Kadish argues, the principle of autonomy is limited by the concept of proportionality: "[T]he moral right to resist threats is subject to the qualification that the actions necessary to resist the threat must not be out of proportion to the nature of the threat." It is the tension between these two principles, Professor Kadish concludes, that "underlies the perennial controversy and changing shape of the law with respect to defining the interests for whose protection one may kill." He explains: *

". . . The proportionality principle is widely in evidence. It is strongly seen in the reform efforts of recent years, such as the proposals of the Model Penal Code, to confine the right to kill generally to cases where killing is necessary to avoid a danger to life. It is also evidenced in more settled provisions of the law which, while not so strictly defining proportionality, draw the line at some point on what interests deadly force may be used to protect—for example, the various restraints on killing to protect property . . . and even the denial of a right to kill to prevent an unaggravated battery. At the same time, however, the autonomy principle [continues to have] its influence. Even under recent statutes one may kill to protect one's property where the threat occurs through a forcible entry of one's dwelling. . . . Moreover, despite efforts to confine the use of deadly force to prevent felonies threatening the life of the person, the law of most states continues to permit its use in a much wider range of situations, such as whenever any degree of force is used by the aggressor.

"Now it may be argued that these latter rules are reflections not of the autonomy principle, but of varying judgments of what interests are proportional to taking the life of the aggressor. The argument has force in cases of killing to prevent crimes like kidnapping and rape, for one may plausibly argue that the interests protected are comparable to that of the victim's life. But one cannot say the same of the interest in remaining where one is, or in protecting one's property from an intruder into one's home, or in preventing any felony whenever some force is used.

* Copyright ©, 1976, California Law Review, Inc. Reprinted by Permission.

The strong current of sentiment behind such rules can be understood best as a reflection of the autonomy principle, which extends the right to resist aggression broadly to cover threats to the personality of the victim. It is hard to see from where the force behind the elevation of these distinctly lesser interests can come other than from the moral claim of the person to autonomy over his life."

(iv) **Questions and Comments.** As these comments indicate, the controversy has focused mainly on the legitimacy of permitting defensive use of deadly force to repel intrusions into the home. The permissibility of killing to prevent rape or kidnapping is rarely questioned even when there is no present threat to life itself. How would you formulate the relevant considerations? Would it matter that the United States Supreme Court has ruled that the death penalty is a constitutionally excessive punishment for the crime of rape, however aggravated? See Coker v. Georgia, 433 U.S. 584 (1977), reproduced as a main case at page 1004, infra.

4. **Modern Statutory Provisions.** Prior to the generation of statutes inspired by the Model Penal Code, most American criminal codes left the definition of general justifications to the courts. However, the drafters of most recent codifications have attempted to identify the values underlying these common-law doctrines and to integrate them in a coherent way. In some areas, such as self-defense, modern codes generally restate and rationalize the common-law rules, typically with greater specificity than the traditional formulations. In other respects, however, the new codes reflect judgments of policy significantly different from those underlying the common-law rules. This is especially true in the provisions governing the use of deadly force. In general, modern codes permit the use of life-threatening force only to prevent serious aggression against the person.

The Model Penal Code illustrates the modern trend toward greater specificity and more restrictive definition of the circumstances justifying the use of deadly force. At this point you should review §§ 3.04 to 3.08 of the Model Code. As you do so, consider how these provisions would apply to *Crawford*. Specifically, would Crawford be entitled to acquittal under § 3.04, governing defense of self? Under § 3.06(3)(d), governing use of deadly force for the protection of property? Under § 3.07(5), governing use of force to prevent commission of crime?

5. **Excessive Use of Defensive Force.** In general, a person who responds to unlawful aggression with excessive force is guilty of the assaultive offense applicable to his or her conduct. Although the provoking circumstances undoubtedly will influence prosecutorial charging and plea-bargaining decisions, the fact that a person who uses excessive force was defending against unlawful aggression is technically immaterial to the grade of the offense. However, as *Crawford* demonstrates, the initial provocation does have grading significance in homicide cases. Thus, a person who kills an aggressor whose conduct justified only moderate force would not be liable for murder in most jurisdictions. Instead, the conviction would be for manslaughter. In

most cases, this would be because the actor responded in the "heat of passion" to the aggressor's provocation and therefore would be said to lack the "malice aforethought" required for a murder conviction.[d] It should be noted, however, that a disproportionate response to unlawful aggression that does not occur "on the sudden" may not be covered by the provocation doctrine and may constitute murder. To deal with this problem, some jurisdictions recognize an independent principle that whenever a defendant is privileged to use defensive force but exceeds the limits allowed by law, he or she is entitled to a verdict of manslaughter rather than murder.[e]

6. **Prevention of Escape.** Consider the following variation of the facts of *Crawford*. Suppose that Crawford's effort to resist the intrusion by Ferrell and Austin had failed, and that they had taken his money and threatened to kill him if he went to the police. Suppose, further, that Crawford had then gathered up all of his nerve and followed them down the hall, commanding them to stop, and had shot Ferrell as he ran away.

On these facts, the use of force would no longer be necessary for Crawford to defend himself, his habitation, or even his personal property against any present threat, since the harm already would have occurred. Although Crawford would be privileged to use reasonable force to recapture his personal property in fresh pursuit of the thief, it is clear that he would not be justified in using deadly force merely to recover his property. Nor would the assailant's threat to harm him in the future provide a present necessity to defend himself.[f]

However, another justification might be available to Crawford in this situation. Although deadly force was never permitted for the purpose of apprehending a misdemeanant or preventing his escape from custody, the common law was clearly otherwise for fleeing felons: "If a felony be committed and the felon fly from justice . . . it is the duty of every man to use his best endeavours for preventing an escape; and if in the pursuit the felon be killed, where he cannot otherwise be overtaken, the homicide is justifiable." 1 E. East, Pleas of the Crown 298 (1806). Although some states continue to authorize private citizens to use deadly force to prevent the escape of a person

---

[d] The concept of provocation is explored at pages 882–904, infra.

[e] For a full discussion of the technical aspects of this grading problem, see Palmer v. Regina, 1 All E.R. 1077, 55 Crim.App. 223 (1971), and the commentary on this decision in Leigh, Manslaughter and the Limits of Self Defense, 34 Crim.L.Rev. 685 (1971), and G. Williams, Textbook of Criminal Law 497–500 (1978).

[f] The traditional approach to the concept of necessity in the doctrine of self-defense was summarized by Professor Beale in an influential article, Homicide in Self-Defense, 3 Colum.L.Rev. 526, 528–31 (1903):

"In order to excuse homicide on the ground of self-defense, the danger must not only be threatened or prospective; it must be pressing and urgent. The killer cannot act on his fear of future death, no matter how well justified; there must be a present danger, caused by some act or demonstration of the deceased. . . .

"As the defendant cannot kill until the danger appears imminent, so he cannot kill after the immediate danger is past; the right of self-defense, which begins only when the necessity begins, ends with the necessity also. If the defendant followed his retreating adversary and killed him as he retreated, the law will not excuse the . . . homicide. . . ."

believed to have committed a violent felony, the modern trend is to permit deadly force to be used in such circumstances only by law-enforcement officers and those aiding them.[g]

Should Crawford's use of deadly force in the hypothetical described above be justified on the ground that it was necessary to effect Ferrell's arrest or to prevent his escape? If not, should the victim ever be permitted to use deadly force to prevent the escape of a felonious attacker? If the attacker had just killed or raped a family member? Does the instinct for revenge have anything to do with your answer? Should it?

How would this hypothetical be analyzed under the Model Penal Code? Would Crawford be entitled to acquittal under Section 3.07(1) and (2), governing use of deadly force to effect an arrest? Under Section 3.07(5), governing use of deadly force to prevent the "consummation" of a crime? Under 3.06(3)(d), governing use of deadly force to prevent "consummation" of robbery? Do the Model Penal Code provisions reflect a consistent approach?

NOTES ON THE REQUIREMENT OF RETREAT

1. **The Retreat Rule.** Suppose *A*, himself free from fault, is placed in actual peril of deadly attack by *B*, who is wielding a knife. Should *A* be privileged "to stand his ground and resort to deadly force *there* merely because he is where he has a right to be, or must he take advantage of an obviously safe retreat if one is available"? Perkins, Self-Defense Re-examined, 1 U.C.L.A.L.Rev. 133, 145 (1954). This has been one of the most hotly contested questions in the law of self-defense.

The dispute regarding the requirement of retreat, usually called the "retreat rule," was summarized by the New Jersey Supreme Court in State v. Abbott, 36 N.J. 63, 69–72, 174 A.2d 881, 884–86 (1961):

> "The question whether one who is neither the aggressor nor a party to a mutual combat must retreat has divided the authorities. Self-defense is measured against necessity. From that premise one could readily say there was no necessity to kill in self-defense if the use of deadly force could have been avoided by retreat. The critics of the retreat rule do not quarrel with the theoretical validity of this conclusion, but rather condemn it as unrealistic. The law of course should not denounce conduct as criminal when it accords with the behavior of reasonable men. Upon this level, the advocates of no-retreat say the manly thing is to hold one's ground, and hence society should not demand what smacks of cowardice. Adherents of the retreat rule reply it is better that the assailed shall retreat than that the life of

[g] See the statutes cited in ALI, Model Penal Code and Commentaries, § 3.07, p. 117 n. 26 (1985). Because the contemporary significance of the so-called defense of law enforcement lies mainly in the authority it reposes in the police, it is addressed in the materials on public authority at pages 581–91, infra.

another be needlessly spent. They add that not only do right-thinking men agree, but further a rule so requiring may well induce others to adhere to that worthy standard of behavior. There is much dispute as to which view commands the support of ancient precedents.[a] . . .

"Other jurisdictions are closely divided upon the retreat doctrine. . . . The Model Penal Code embraces the retreat rule while acknowledging that on numerical balance a majority of the precedents oppose it.

"We are not persuaded to depart from the principle of retreat. We think it salutary if reasonably limited. Much of the criticism goes not to its inherent validity but rather to unwarranted applications of the rule. For example, it is correctly observed that one can hardly retreat from a rifle shot at close range. But if the weapon were a knife, a lead of a city block might be well enough. Again, the rule cannot be stated baldly, with indifference to the excitement of the occasion. As Mr. Justice Holmes cryptically put it, '[d]etached reflection cannot be demanded in the presence of an uplifted knife.' Brown v. United States, 256 U.S. 335, 343 (1921). Such considerations, however, do not demand that a man should have the absolute right to stand his ground and kill in any and all situations. Rather, they call for a fair and guarded statement of appropriate principles. . . .

"We believe the following principles are sound:

"1. The issue of retreat arises only if the defendant resorted to a deadly force. It is deadly force which is not justifiable when an opportunity to retreat is at hand. . . .

"Hence it is not the nature of the force defended against which raises the issue of retreat, but rather the nature of the force which the accused employed in his defense. If he does not resort to a deadly force, one who is assailed may hold his ground whether the attack upon him be of a deadly or some lesser character.

"2. What constitutes an opportunity to retreat which will defeat the right of self-defense? As [§ 3.04(2)(b)(ii)] of the Model Penal Code states, deadly force is not justifiable 'if the actor *knows* that he can avoid the necessity of using such force *with complete safety* by retreating. . . .' We emphasize 'knows' and 'with complete safety.' One who is wrongfully attacked need not risk injury by retreating, even though he could escape with something less than serious bodily injury. It would be unreal to require nice calculations as to the amount of hurt, or to ask him to endure any at all. And the issue is not whether in retrospect it can be found the defendant could have retreated unharmed. Rather the question is whether he knew the opportunity was

---

[a] Compare Perkins, Self-Defense Re-examined, 1 U.C.L.A.L.Rev. 133 (1954), with Beale, Retreat From a Murderous Assault, 16 Harv.L.Rev. 567 (1903). [Footnote by eds.]

there, and of course in that inquiry the total circumstances including the attendant excitement must be considered. . . ."

Professor Glanville Williams has argued, contrary to the view taken in *Abbott* and the Model Penal Code, that the retreat rule should be abolished. G. Williams, Textbook of Criminal Law 462–63 (1978). Although Professor Williams concedes that the privilege of self defense should ordinarily be "limited to circumstances of necessity," he argues that the requirement of necessity is not unqualified. He illustrates his point with the following hypothetical: If *A* says to *B* "If you don't do as I tell you, I will kill you," *B* is entitled to refuse to obey the order and to resist any attack thereafter initiated by *A* even though *B* could have avoided the necessity of self-defense by complying with the order in the first instance. Similarly, Professor Williams argues, the requirement of necessity should "not generally imply a duty to run away." Even though "many courageous people would rather run away than shed blood," the law should not impose such a duty. To the contrary, he concludes, "one who prefers to stand his ground and then act in necessary self-defence should be allowed to do so, unless he was the initial aggressor."

Do you agree with Professor Williams? Should there be no obligation to take advantage of an avenue of safe retreat before resisting a serious attack with deadly force? If you agree with Professor Williams' position, would you favor the following jury instruction?

> "In determining whether it was necessary for the defendant to defend himself with deadly force, you should not consider the alternative of retreating. A person who is being wrongfully attacked and is in reasonable fear of death or serious bodily harm has a right to defend himself there, where he has a right to be, when it becomes necessary to do so."

If you do not agree with Professor Williams, do you favor the Model Penal Code approach? Do you see a middle ground?

2. **The Wisdom of Rules.** As the *Abbott* court notes, the majority of states reject the retreat rule. However, they also reject the "right to stand one's ground" preferred by Professor Williams. Instead, the preponderant view seems to be the one endorsed by the United States Supreme Court in Brown v. United States, 256 U.S. 335, 343 (1921), that "the failure to retreat is a circumstance to be considered with all the others in order to determine whether the defendant went farther than he was justified in doing; not a categorical proof of guilt." This approach is reflected in the Texas statute, Penal Code § 9.32(2), which provides that a person is justified in using deadly force against another only "if a reasonable person in the actor's situation would not have retreated."

The debate regarding the retreat rule illustrates one of the generic issues in the formulation of doctrines of personal defense: To what extent should the norms governing the use of defensive force, especially deadly force, be specified by rule rather than be left to particularized applications of standards of "reasonableness" and "necessity." The typical formulation of the retreat rule has been criticized because of its inflexibility: "For the law to attempt a detailed formulation of rights and duties in cases of self-defence would be both futile and unjust—futile because no one can foresee all the possible circumstances in which self-defence might be raised, and unjust insofar as the result of failure to legislate for a particular type of situation might be the absence of rights on a most worthy occasion." Ashworth, Self-Defence and the Right to Life, 34 Camb.L.J. 282, 292 (1975). On the other hand, the "open-textured" standard of reasonableness—reflected in the majority view that the availability of an avenue of retreat is merely one of the circumstances taken into account in assessing the reasonableness of the defendant's use of deadly force—may be criticized on the grounds that it gives inadequate protection to human life and that it leaves too much room for inconsistent administration of the law.

Do you see the operational differences—in ruling on sufficiency of the evidence, in framing jury instructions, and in the role of appellate courts—between these two approaches to the retreat problem? Which approach do you prefer—the "open-textured" approach reflected in *Brown* v. *United States* or the rule-and-exception approach of the Model Penal Code endorsed in *Abbott*? Do you think that the outcomes of jury deliberations on self-defense claims are likely to depend on which of these instructions is given?

3. **The "Castle" Exception.** Even jurisdictions that have adopted the requirement of retreat recognize an exception for a person attacked in his or her own home. Recall, in this connection, the *Crawford* court's observation that "a man faced with the danger of an attack on his dwelling need not retreat . . . but . . . if necessary to repel the attack, may kill the attacker." The rationale for the so-called "castle" doctrine was reviewed by Judge Cardozo in People v. Tomlins, 213 N.Y. 240, 243–44, 107 N.E. 496, 497–98 (1914), a case in which a father killed his 22-year-old son, who had attacked him in the family home:

> "It is not now and never has been the law that a man assailed in his own dwelling, is bound to retreat. If assailed there, he may stand his ground and resist the attack. He is under no duty to take to the fields and the highways, a fugitive from his own home. More than 200 years ago it was said by Lord Chief Justice Hale (1 M. Hale, Pleas of the Crown 486): In case a man is assailed in his own house, he 'need not flee as far as he can as in other cases of se defendendo, for he hath the protection of his house to excuse him from flying, as that would be to give up the protection of his house to his adversary by his flight.' Flight is for sanctuary and shelter, and shelter, if not sanctuary, is in the home. That there is, in such a situation, no duty to retreat is, we think, the settled law in the United States as in England. . . .
> The rule is the same whether the attack proceeds from some other occupant or from an intruder. It was so adjudged in Jones v. State, 76 Ala. 8, 14 (1884). 'Why,' it was there inquired, 'should one retreat from his own house, when assailed by a partner or cotenant, any more than when assailed by a stranger

who is lawfully upon the premises? Whither shall he flee, and
how far, and when may he be permitted to return?' We think
that the conclusion there reached is sustained by principle, and
we have not been referred to any decision to the contrary.
. . ."

If such a doctrine is to be embraced, questions obviously will arise as
to what constitutes a "castle" and whether any other places aside from
a dwelling should qualify. The Model Penal Code, which requires
retreat if it can be accomplished "with complete safety" incorporates
the traditional exception and does not require retreat from a person's
"dwelling or place of work, unless [the actor] was the initial aggressor
or is assailed in his place of work by another person whose place of
work the actor knows it to be." Section 3.04(2)(b)(ii)(1). Do you agree
with the scope of these exceptions to the retreat rule? Why did the
drafters fail to require retreat in the workplace if it can be accomplished with complete safety? Why should it make any difference that
the assailant and the victim work in the same place? If this makes a
difference, why did the drafters fail to require a person to retreat from
his home when the assailant also lives there? Can rules of this detail
sensibly be prescribed in legislation?

STATE v. WANROW

Washington Supreme Court, 1977.
88 Wash.2d 221, 559 P.2d 548.

UTTER, ASSOCIATE JUSTICE. Yvonne Wanrow was convicted by a jury
of second-degree murder and first-degree assault. . . .

We order a reversal of the conviction [because of] error committed
by the trial court in improperly instructing the jury on the law of self-
defense as it related to the defendant.

On the afternoon of August 11, 1972, defendant's two children were
staying at the home of Ms. Hooper, a friend of defendant. Defendant's
son was playing in the neighborhood and came back to Ms. Hooper's
house and told her that a man tried to pull him off his bicycle and drag
him into a house. Some months earlier, Ms. Hooper's seven-year-old
daughter had developed a rash on her body which was diagnosed as
venereal disease. Ms. Hooper had been unable to persuade her daughter to tell her who had molested her. It was not until the night of the
shooting that Ms. Hooper discovered it was William Wesler (decedent)
who allegedly had violated her daughter. A few minutes after the
defendant's son related his story to Ms. Hooper about the man who
tried to detain him, Mr. Wesler appeared on the porch of the Hooper
house and stated through the door, "I didn't touch the kid, I didn't
touch the kid." At that moment, the Hooper girl, seeing Wesler at the
door, indicated to her mother that Wesler was the man who had
molested her.

Joseph Fah, Ms. Hooper's landlord, saw Wesler as he was leaving
and informed Shirley Hooper that Wesler had tried to molest a young

boy who had earlier lived in the same house, and that Wesler had previously been committed to the Eastern State Hospital for the mentally ill. Immediately after this revelation from Mr. Fah, Ms. Hooper called the police who, upon their arrival at the Hooper residence, were informed of all the events which had transpired that day. Ms. Hooper requested that Wesler be arrested then and there, but the police stated, "We can't, until Monday morning." Ms. Hooper was urged by the police officer to go to the police station Monday morning and "swear out a warrant." Ms. Hooper's landlord, who was present during the conversation, suggested that Ms. Hooper get a baseball bat located at the corner of the house and "conk him over the head" should Wesler try to enter the house uninvited during the weekend. To this suggestion, the policeman replied, "Yes, but wait until he gets in the house." (A week before this incident Shirley Hooper had noticed someone prowling around her house at night. Two days before the shooting someone had attempted to get into Ms. Hooper's bedroom and had slashed the window screen. She suspected that such person was Wesler.)

That evening, Ms. Hooper called the defendant and asked her to spend the night with her in the Hooper house. At that time she related to Ms. Wanrow the facts we have previously set forth. The defendant arrived sometime after 6 p. m. with a pistol in her handbag. The two women ultimately determined that they were too afraid to stay alone and decided to ask some friends to come over for added protection. The two women then called the defendant's sister and brother-in-law, Angie and Chuck Michel. The four adults did not go to bed that evening, but remained awake talking and watching for any possible prowlers. There were eight young children in the house with them. At around 5 a. m., Chuck Michel, without the knowledge of the women in the house, went to Wesler's house, carrying a baseball bat. Upon arriving at the Wesler residence, Mr. Michel accused Wesler of molesting little children. Mr. Wesler then suggested that they go over to the Hooper residence and get the whole thing straightened out. Another man, one David Kelly, was also present, and together the three men went over to the Hooper house. Mr. Michel and Mr. Kelly remained outside while Wesler entered the residence.

The testimony as to what next took place is considerably less precise. It appears that Wesler, a large man who was visibly intoxicated, entered the home and when told to leave declined to do so. A good deal of shouting and confusion then arose, and a young child, asleep on the couch, awoke crying. The testimony indicates that Wesler then approached this child, stating "My what a cute little boy," or words to that effect, and that the child's mother, Ms. Michel, stepped between Wesler and the child. By this time Hooper was screaming for Wesler to get out. Ms. Wanrow, a 54 woman who at the time had a broken leg and was using a crutch, testified that she then went to the front door to enlist the aid of Chuck Michel. She stated that she shouted for him and, upon turning around to re-enter the living room, found Wesler standing directly behind her. She testified to being gravely startled by this situation and to having then shot Wesler in what amounted to a reflex action. . . .

[In] Instruction No. 10, setting forth the law of self-defense, [the trial court] incorrectly limited the jury's consideration of acts and circumstances pertinent to respondent's perception of the alleged threat to her person. . . .

In the opening paragraph of Instruction No. 10, the jury, in evaluating the gravity of the danger to the respondent, was directed to consider only those acts and circumstances occurring "at or immediately before the killing. . . ." [7] This is not now, and never has been, the law of self-defense in Washington. On the contrary, the justification of self-defense is to be evaluated in light of *all* the facts and circumstances known to the defendant, including those known substantially before the killing.

In State v. Ellis, 30 Wash. 369, 70 P. 963 (1902), this court reversed a first-degree murder conviction obtained under self-defense instructions quite similar to that in the present case. The defendant sought to show that the deceased had a reputation and habit of carrying and using deadly weapons when engaged in quarrels. The trial court instructed that threats were insufficient justification unless " 'at the time of the alleged killing the deceased was making or immediately preceding the killing had committed some overt act. . . .' " This court found the instruction "defective and misleading," stating "the apparent facts should all be taken together to illustrate the motives and good faith of the defendant. . . ." [We said in *Ellis*:]

> "[I]t is apparent that a man who habitually carries and uses such weapons in quarrels must cause greater apprehension of danger than one who does not bear such reputation. . . . The vital question is the reasonableness of the defendant's apprehension of danger. . . . The jury [is] entitled to stand as nearly as practicable in the shoes of defendant, and from this point of view determine the character of the act."

Thus, circumstances predating the killing by weeks and months were deemed entirely proper, and in fact essential, to a proper disposition of the claim of self-defense. . . .

State v. Tribett, 74 Wash. 125, 132 P. 875 (1913), is in accord. There this court approved an instruction which twice directed the jury to

---

[7] Instruction No. 10 reads:

"To justify killing in self-defense, there need be no actual or real danger to the life or person of the party killing, but there must be, or reasonably appear to be, at or immediately before the killing, some overt act, or some circumstances which would reasonably indicate to the party killing that the person slain, is, at the time, endeavoring to kill him or inflict upon him great bodily harm.

"However, when there is no reasonable ground for the person attacked to believe that his person is in imminent danger of death or great bodily harm, and it appears to him that only an ordinary battery is all that is intended, and all that he has reasonable grounds to fear from his assailant, he has a right to stand his ground and repel such threatened assault, yet he has no right to repel a threatened assault with naked hands, by the use of a deadly weapon in a deadly manner, unless he believes, and has reasonable grounds to believe, that he is in imminent danger of death or great bodily harm."

evaluate the reasonableness of the defendant's actions in defense of himself " 'in the light of all the circumstances.' " Such circumstances included those existing and known long before the killing, such as the reputation of the place of the killing for lawlessness. This court stated with reference to the self-defense instruction:

> "All of these facts and circumstances should have been placed before the jury, to the end that they could put themselves in the place of the appellant, get the point of view which he had at the time of the tragedy, and view the conduct of the [deceased] with all its pertinent sidelights as the appellant was warranted in viewing it. In no other way could the jury safely say what a reasonably prudent man similarly situated would have done."

The rule firmly established by these cases has never been disapproved and is still followed today. "It is clear the jury is entitled to consider *all* of the circumstances surrounding the incident in determining whether [the] defendant had reasonable grounds to believe grievous bodily harm was about to be inflicted."

[I]nstruction No. 10 erred in limiting the acts and circumstances which the jury could consider in evaluating the nature of the threat of harm as perceived by respondent. Under the well-established rule, this error is presumed to have been prejudicial. Moreover, far from affirmatively showing that the error was harmless, the record demonstrates the limitation to circumstances "at or immediately before the killing" was of crucial importance in the present case. Respondent's knowledge of the victim's reputation for aggressive acts was gained many hours before the killing and was based upon events which occurred over a period of years. Under the law of this state, the jury should have been allowed to consider this information in making the critical determination of the " 'degree of force which . . . a reasonable person in the same situation . . . seeing what [s]he sees and knowing what [s]he knows, then would believe to be necessary.' " . . .

The second paragraph of Instruction No. 10 contains an equally erroneous and prejudicial statement of the law. That portion of the instruction reads:

> "However, when there is no reasonable ground for the person attacked to believe that *his* person is in imminent danger of death or great bodily harm, and it appears to *him* that only an ordinary battery is all that is intended, and all that *he* has reasonable grounds to fear from *his* assailant, *he* has a right to stand *his* ground and repel such threatened assault, yet *he* had no right to repel a threatened assault with naked hands, by the use of a deadly weapon in a deadly manner, unless *he* believes, *and has reasonable grounds* to believe, that *he* is in imminent danger of death or great bodily harm."

(Italics ours.) In our society women suffer from a conspicuous lack of access to training in and the means of developing those skills necessary to effectively repel a male assailant without resorting to the use of deadly weapons. [Another instruction given by the trial court] does indicate that the "relative size and strength of the persons involved" may be considered; however, it does not make clear that the defendant's actions are to be judged against her own subjective impressions and not those which a detached jury might determine to be objectively reasonable. The applicable rule of law is clearly stated in [our earlier cases]:

> "If the appellants, at the time of the alleged assault upon them, as reasonably and ordinarily cautious and prudent men, honestly believed that they were in danger of great bodily harm, they would have the right to resort to self-defense, and their conduct is to be judged by the condition appearing to them at the time, not by the condition as it might appear to the jury in the light of testimony before it."

The second paragraph of Instruction No. 10 not only establishes an objective standard, but through the persistent use of the masculine gender leaves the jury with the impression the objective standard to be applied is that applicable to an altercation between two men. The impression created—that a 54 woman with a cast on her leg and using a crutch must, under the law, somehow repel an assault by a 62 intoxicated man without employing weapons in her defense, unless the jury finds her determination of the degree of danger to be objectively reasonable—constitutes a separate and distinct misstatement of the law . . . . The portion of the instruction above quoted misstates our law in creating an objective standard of "reasonableness." It then compounds that error by utilizing language suggesting that the respondent's conduct must be measured against that of a reasonable male individual finding himself in the same circumstances.

We conclude that the instruction here in question contains an improper statement of the law on a vital issue in the case . . . .

[T]he conviction [is] reversed and the case remanded for a new trial.

NOTES ON THE REQUIREMENT OF "REASONABLE" BELIEF

1. **Introduction.** Whatever else Ms. Wanrow and her friends had to fear from Mr. Wesler, the objective evidence strongly suggests that neither Ms. Wanrow nor anyone else was actually in imminent danger of death, sexual assault, or serious bodily harm at his hands. However, acquittal on grounds of self-defense has never depended upon actual necessity. Instead, the common law framed the inquiry as one of "reasonably apparent necessity," thereby allowing the defendant to act on the reasonable perception of danger. It is the meaning of this requirement on which most litigated claims of self-defense turn.

The rationale for the traditional position was explained by Professors Wechsler and Michael in their classic article, A Rationale of the Law of Homicide I, 37 Colum.L.Rev. 701, 736 (1937): *

---

* Reprinted with permission of Professor
Wechsler and the Columbia Law Review.

"[M]en sometimes believe that they are being attacked, that their lives are in immediate peril and that it is necessary to kill to save themselves when such is not the case. So long as the belief is reasonable, it seems quite clear, however, that the [defense must be recognized]. Men must act on the basis of their appraisal of the situation in which they find themselves, if they are to act at all. Their behavior must accordingly be evaluated on the basis of what was known or could have been known to them at the moment of action, not at some later time. To concede a privilege to kill only in cases of actual necessity is to lay down a rule that must either be disregarded or else must operate to deny freedom of action even in cases where the necessity exists and not merely in those where it does not. On the other hand, no such onerous limitation on freedom of action is imposed by requiring that men exercise the degree of care to appraise the facts correctly which is appropriate to the situation. It is desirable to deter men from acting without exercising such care; unless such care is taken, death is not a justifiable means even to the preservation of their own lives."

What "degree of care" in appraising the facts is "appropriate to the situation" in cases such as *Wanrow*? This question, which is a pervasive and important one in the law of personal defense, is explored in the following notes.

2. **The Traditional Objective Standard.** The law has long recognized the need to assess the reasonableness of the innocent defender's perceptions and reactions from the perspective of an ordinary person "in the same circumstances." [a] These circumstances clearly include the suddenness of the provoking event and the psychological impact of previous interactions between the defendant and the perceived aggressor. As one court has said: "Ordinarily the question how far a party may properly go in self-defense is a question for the jury, not to be judged very nicely, but with due regard to the infirmity of human impulses and passions." Monize v. Bagazo, 190 Mass. 87, 89, 76 N.E. 460, 461 (1906). In a similar vein, Professor Ashworth has noted the "need for flexibility when making legal judgments about 'instinctive' human reactions to danger." It must be remembered, he says, that many victims of apparent aggression have no time to weigh possible courses of action, and that "fear, panic and surprise can bring about physiological changes which literally take a person out of his normal self." Ashworth, Self Defence and the Right to Life, 34 Camb.L.J. 282, 299 (1975).

a But see Regina v. Machekequonabe, 28 Ont.Rep. 309 (1897). Machekequonabe was a member of a tribe of Canadian Indians who believed in the existence of an evil spirit, called a wendigo, which would appear in human form and eat people. In response to a reported spotting of a wendigo in the neighborhood of the tribe's camp, armed sentries were placed at strategic locations. One night Machekequonabe was on sentry duty and saw what he believed to be the wendigo running in the distance, whereupon he and the other guard gave chase. After calling out three times for the figure to identify himself and receiving no answer, Machekequonabe fired a fatal shot at the supposed wendigo, who turned out to be his own foster father. His manslaughter conviction was affirmed on appeal.

Nonetheless, it must be emphasized that under the traditional approach the relevant criterion is the ordinary person. A still-cited article by Professor Beale, Homicide in Self-Defense, 3 Colum.L.Rev. 526, 528 (1903), describes the common law as follows:

"The question is not generally held to be, was the apprehension reasonable in such a man as the defendant, but, was it such fear as a reasonable man would have felt under the circumstances; and therefore the jury cannot consider the peculiarities of the defendant, as that he was a coward, or of immature judgment, or of a nervous temperament, nor can they consider the fact that he was drunk, and acted under a drunkard's imperfect apprehension."

The traditional approach to assessments of "reasonably apparent necessity" was applied in State v. Bess, 53 N.J. 10, 247 A.2d 669 (1968). In this case, the defendant, age 18, was employed as a bartender at a tavern. Grunden, a patron, complained about the price of drinks, claiming that the owner charged only 50 cents instead of the 60 cents charged by Bess. Grunden then hit the bar with his fist and said "I will come back there and take my drink." When he was almost to the entrance to the bar, the defendant took a pistol from behind the cash register and said "Don't come back here. I mean it." Grunden replied that "that gun don't scare me" and entered the rear of the bar. The two men slowly walked toward each other until they met. Grunden nudged the defendant with his elbow and the defendant stepped back, discharging the gun. Grunden died.

At his trial, Bess, who was 125 pounds lighter than Grunden, testified that he was "bewildered" when Grunden said he was coming behind the bar because he had never heard anyone say that before. When Grunden told him the gun would not stop him, Bess said he became afraid: "[M]y stomach had arose to my throat and seemed like it was choking." A psychologist testified that Bess, who had an IQ of 66 according to his school records, was "an emotionally unstable, immature individual whose thinking is often childish" and that "he can become confused and almost disorganized with pressure." Additional testimony by the psychologist that Bess would tend to overreact to protect himself was excluded. Bess was convicted of second-degree murder.

On appeal, Bess argued that the jury should have been permitted to consider what appeared reasonable and necessary to him, "not [to] the theoretical reasonable man," at the time of the shooting in order to protect himself or to prevent a robbery. He also argued that the additional psychological testimony should not have been excluded. The court responded as follows:

"Justification for a killing in self defense or to prevent a robbery, however, depends on the jury's determination of what they think a reasonable man would have done under the circumstances. This objective test, rather than a subjective exploration of Bess's psyche has been the standard for justifiable homicide consistently applied in this state. . . .

"The jury, as the representative of society, and not the defendant, determines what is reasonable under the circumstances. This is so because society has a vital interest in maintaining minimal standards of behavior for the protection of human life. . . ." [b]

3. **Subjective Standards of Reasonableness.** The *Wanrow* court holds that the trial judge's instruction erroneously directed the jury to apply an "objective standard of 'reasonableness' " in determining whether the defendant's mistaken apprehension of imminent danger was reasonable. Does this mean that the court meant to adopt a "subjective standard of reasonableness?" What criterion would a subjective standard of reasonableness establish? How would you formulate the inquiry to distinguish it from an objective standard of reasonableness on the one hand and from a purely subjective culpability requirement on the other? [c]

The court says the jury must consider the fact that the defendant was a small woman on crutches. Does this mean the jury should ask how an ordinary very-frightened-small-woman-on-crutches would have perceived and reacted to the situation? If so, what does it mean to say the inquiry is an objective one? Should the prosecution be permitted to introduce testimony tending to prove that the defendant's misperceptions were not shared by others, including women, in the same room? Would this be relevant? Would it be permissible for the prosecution to ask the jury, in a closing argument, whether a reasonably prudent

[b] However, the court reduced Bess' sentence from 10-to-15 years to two-to-five years, saying:

"Defendant's pre-sentence report indicates that he has no prior criminal record, and comes from a good family. The school principal testified as to Bess's good citizenship. Defendant, a young man, was confronted with a situation he did not seek. He was in charge of the place and was suddenly met with the unusual behavior of the deceased, presenting a challenge unfamiliar to him. Defendant reacted to the shooting by immediately summoning the police, and he cooperated fully with the investigation. Although the killing came within the ambit of second-degree murder, as the jury found, yet the degree of moral culpability is tempered by the above facts, and they as well reflect upon a sentence suitable for the punitive and rehabilitative objectives involved."

[c] Ohio appears to employ a purely subjective approach. In Nelson v. State, 42 Ohio App. 252, 181 N.E. 448 (1932), the court stated:

"[I]t seems now to be finally determined that guilt is personal, and that the conduct of any individual is to be measured by that individual's equipment mentally and physically. He may act in self-defense, not only when a reasonable person would so act, but when one with the particular qualities that the individual himself has would so do. A nervous, timid, easily frightened individual is not measured by the same standard that a stronger, calmer, and braver man might be. . . ."

This approach was recently applied in State v. Thomas, 13 Ohio App.3d 211, 468 N.E.2d 763 (1983), where the court reversed the conviction of a woman who killed a former lover during an argument and claimed that she had acted in self-defense. The court noted that the defendant's liability turned solely on whether "she had a bona fide belief that she was in imminent danger of death or great bodily harm and that her only means of escape" was to use deadly force. Accordingly, the court held, the trial court should not have excluded psychiatric testimony that the defendant had a "paranoid personality," and that she "viewed everything negatively" because this testimony was relevant to show why she "might interpret the danger presented by an advancing individual differently than an ordinary person would interpret such danger."

person, with due regard for the rights and interest of others, would have panicked and shot without looking?

How would *Bess* be decided in a jurisdiction employing the *Wanrow* standard? Would it be relevant that Bess was "an emotionally unstable, immature individual whose thinking is often childish [and who] can become confused and almost disorganized with pressure"? Are *Wanrow* and *Bess* distinguishable under the *Wanrow* court's approach? If so, how? If not, does the *Wanrow* approach unduly personalize the standards of criminal liability?

4. **The Case for a Subjective Approach.** Fright and panic are, of course, universally experienced; but, as *Wanrow* and *Bess* suggest, individuals differ markedly in their reactions to stress and in their susceptibility to panic. Is it possible to identify, or to expect the jury to identify, a community standard to which Crawford, Wanrow, Bess, and others in similar situations should be required to conform? Does the difficulty of formulating such a standard suggest that an "objective" standard of culpability is inappropriate in the context of instinctive acts of self-preservation by persons who mistakenly perceive themselves in imminent and sudden danger of deadly attack? Professor Glanville Williams defends a subjective approach in his Textbook of Criminal Law 452 (1978). He argues that the reasonableness requirement is designed to encourage people to verify their beliefs before acting and to compel compliance with well-known rules of prudence. But given that people must act instantly and instinctively, he continues, "are we not inflicting injustice on [them] without utilitarian purpose" if they are punished for acting according to their own perceptions? Do you agree? Should the law exonerate on the basis of subjective perceptions alone?

5. **The Model Penal Code.** Recall the discussion of mistaken justification on pages 530–36, supra. How would cases such as *Wanrow* and *Bess* be analyzed under the Model Penal Code? Has the Model Code partially accepted Professor Williams' argument in its "grading" solution to the problem of unreasonable mistakes, i.e., by reducing any conviction based on negligent error to an offense for which negligence is otherwise the required culpability? Recall also that the Model Code uses the deliberately ambiguous term "situation" in its definition of both recklessness and negligence in § 2.02. See pages 240–41, supra. Is it clear that Ms. Wanrow could be convicted of negligent homicide under the Model Penal Code? Should she be?

STATE v. KELLY

Supreme Court of New Jersey, 1984.
97 N.J. 178, 478 A.2d 364.

WILENTZ, C.J. . . . On May 24, 1980, defendant, Gladys Kelly, stabbed her husband, Ernest, with a pair of scissors. He died shortly thereafter. . . .

Ms. Kelly was indicted for murder. At trial, she did not deny stabbing her husband, but asserted that her action was in self-defense.

To establish the requisite state of mind for her self-defense claim, Ms. Kelly called Dr. Lois Veronen as an expert witness to testify about the battered-woman's syndrome. After hearing a lengthy voir dire examination of Dr. Veronen, the trial court ruled that expert testimony concerning the syndrome was inadmissible on the self-defense issue under State v. Bess, 53 N.J. 10, 247 A.2d 669 (1968). Apparently the court believed that the sole purpose of this testimony was to explain and justify defendant's perception of the danger rather than to show the objective reasonableness of that perception. Ms. Kelly was convicted of reckless manslaughter. . . .

The Kellys had a stormy [seven-year] marriage. Some of the details of their relationship, especially the stabbing, are disputed. The following is Ms. Kelly's version of what happened—a version that the jury could have accepted and, if they had, a version that would make the proffered expert testimony not only relevant, but critical.

The day after the marriage, Mr. Kelly got drunk and knocked Ms. Kelly down. Although a period of calm followed the initial attack, the next seven years were accompanied by periodic and frequent beatings, sometimes as often as once a week. During the attacks, which generally occurred when Mr. Kelly was drunk, he threatened to kill Ms. Kelly and to cut off parts of her body if she tried to leave him. Mr. Kelly often moved out of the house after an attack, later returning with a promise that he would change his ways. Until the day of the homicide, only one of the attacks had taken place in public.

[On the morning of the stabbing, Mr. Kelly] left for work. Ms. Kelly next saw her husband late that afternoon at a friend's house. She had gone there with her daughter, Annette, to ask Ernest for money to buy food. He told her to wait until they got home, and shortly thereafter the Kellys left. After walking past several houses, Mr. Kelly, who was drunk, angrily asked "What the hell did you come around here for?" He then grabbed the collar of her dress, and the two fell to the ground. He choked her by pushing his fingers against her throat, punched or hit her face, and bit her leg.

A crowd gathered on the street. Two men from the crowd separated them, just as Gladys felt that she was "passing out" from being choked. Fearing that Annette had been pushed around in the crowd, Gladys then left to look for her. . . .

After finding her daughter, Ms. Kelly then observed Mr. Kelly running toward her with his hands raised. Within seconds he was right next to her. Unsure of whether he had armed himself while she was looking for their daughter, and thinking that he had come back to kill her, she grabbed a pair of scissors from her pocketbook. She tried to scare him away, but instead stabbed him.[1] . . .

---

[1] This version of the homicide—with a drunk Mr. Kelly as the aggressor both in pushing Ms. Kelly to the ground and again in rushing at her with his hands in a threatening position after the two had been separated—is sharply disputed by the State. The prosecution presented testimony intended to show that the initial scuffle was started by Gladys; that upon disentanglement, while she was restrained by bystanders, she stated that she intended to kill Ernest; that she then chased after him, and upon catching up with him stabbed him . . . .

In the past decade social scientists and the legal community began to examine the forces that generate and perpetuate wife beating and violence in the family.[2] What has been revealed is that the problem affects many more people than had been thought . . . .

Due to the high incidence of unreported abuse (the FBI and other law enforcement experts believe that wife abuse is the most unreported crime in the United States), estimates vary of the number of American women who are beaten regularly by their husband, boyfriend, or the dominant male figure in their lives. One recent estimate puts the number of women beaten yearly at over one million. The state police statistics show more than 18,000 *reported* cases of domestic violence in New Jersey during the first nine months of 1983, in 83% of which the victim was female. It is clear that the American home, once assumed to be the cornerstone of our society, is often a violent place.

While common-law notions that assigned an inferior status to women, and to wives in particular, no longer represent the state of the law as reflected in statutes and cases, many commentators assert that a bias against battered women still exists, institutionalized in the attitudes of law enforcement agencies unwilling to pursue or uninterested in pursuing wife-beating cases. See Comment, The Battered Wife's Dilemma: Kill or be Killed, 32 Hastings L.J., 895, 897–911 (1981).

Another problem is the currency enjoyed by stereotypes and myths concerning the characteristics of battered women and their reasons for staying in battering relationships. Some popular misconceptions about battered women include the beliefs that they are masochistic and actually enjoy their beatings, that they purposely provoke their husbands into violent behavior, and, most critically, as we shall soon see, that women who remain in battering relationships are free to leave their abusers at any time. See L. Walker, The Battered Woman at 19–31 (1979). . . .

As the problem of battered women has begun to receive more attention, sociologists and psychologists have begun to focus on the effects a sustained pattern of physical and psychological abuse can have on a woman. The effects of such abuse are what some scientific observers have termed "the battered-woman's syndrome," a series of common characteristics that appear in women who are abused physically and psychologically over an extended period of time by the dominant male figure in their lives. . . .

According to Dr. [Lenore] Walker, relationships characterized by physical abuse tend to develop battering cycles. Violent behavior directed at the woman occurs in three distinct and repetitive stages that vary both in duration and intensity depending on the individuals involved.

---

[2] The works that comprise the basic study of the problem of battered women are all relatively recent. See, e.g., R. Langley & R. Levy, Wife Beating: The Silent Crisis (1979); D. Martin, Battered Wives (1976); L. Walker, The Battered Woman (1979); R. Gelles, The Violent Home: A Study of Physical Aggression between Husbands and Wives (1971); Battered Women: A Psychosociological Study of Domestic Violence (M. Roy ed. 1977).

Phase one of the battering cycle is referred to as the "tension-building stage," during which the battering male engages in minor battering incidents and verbal abuse while the woman, beset by fear and tension, attempts to be as placating and passive as possible in order to stave off more serious violence.

Phase two of the battering cycle is the "acute battering incident." At some point during phase one, the tension between the battered woman and the batterer becomes intolerable and more serious violence inevitable. The triggering event that initiates phase two is most often an internal or external event in the life of the battering male, but provocation for more severe violence is sometimes provided by the woman who can no longer tolerate or control her phase-one anger and anxiety.

Phase three of the battering cycle is characterized by extreme contrition and loving behavior on the part of the battering male. During this period the man will often mix his pleas for forgiveness and protestations of devotion with promises to seek professional help, to stop drinking,[5] and to refrain from further violence. For some couples, this period of relative calm may last as long as several months, but in a battering relationship the affection and contrition of the man will eventually fade and phase one of the cycle will start anew.

The cyclical nature of battering behavior helps explain why more women simply do not leave their abusers. The loving behavior demonstrated by the batterer during phase three reinforces whatever hopes these women might have for their mate's reform and keeps them bound to the relationship. R. Langley & R. Levy, Wife Beating: The Silent Crisis 112–14 (1977).

Some women may even perceive the battering cycle as normal, especially if they grew up in a violent household. Battered Women, A Psychosociological Study of Domestic Violence 60 (M. Roy ed. 1977); D. Martin, Battered Wives, 60 (1981). Or they may simply not wish to acknowledge the reality of their situation. T. Davidson, Conjugal Crime, at 50 (1978) ("The middle-class battered wife's response to her situation tends to be withdrawal, silence and denial . . . ").

Other women, however, become so demoralized and degraded by the fact that they cannot predict or control the violence that they sink into a state of psychological paralysis and become unable to take any action at all to improve or alter the situation. There is a tendency in battered women to believe in the omnipotence or strength of their battering husbands and thus to feel that any attempt to resist them is hopeless.

In addition to these psychological impacts, external social and economic factors often make it difficult for some women to extricate themselves from battering relationships. A woman without indepen-

[5] Alcohol is often an important component of violence toward women. Evidence points to a correlation between alcohol and violent acts between family members. In one British study, 44 of 100 cases of wife abuse occurred when the husband was drunk. Gayford, "Wife Battering: A Preliminary Survey of 100 Cases," British Medical Journal 1:194–197 (1975). . . .

dent financial resources who wishes to leave her husband often finds it difficult to do so because of a lack of material and social resources.

Even with the progress of the last decade, women typically make less money and hold less prestigious jobs than men, and are more responsible for child care. Thus, in a violent confrontation where the first reaction might be to flee, women realize soon that there may be no place to go. Moreover, the stigma that attaches to a woman who leaves the family unit without her children undoubtedly acts as a further deterrent to moving out.

In addition, battered women, when they want to leave the relationship, are typically unwilling to reach out and confide in their friends, family, or the police, either out of shame and humiliation, fear of reprisal by their husband, or the feeling they will not be believed.

Dr. Walker and other commentators have identified several common personality traits of the battered woman: low self-esteem, traditional beliefs about the home, the family, and the female sex role, tremendous feelings of guilt that their marriages are failing, and the tendency to accept responsibility for the batterer's actions.

Finally, battered women are often hesitant to leave a battering relationship because, in addition to their hope of reform on the part of their spouse, they harbor a deep concern about the possible response leaving might provoke in their mates. They literally become trapped by their own fear. Case histories are replete with instances in which a battered wife left her husband only to have him pursue her and subject her to an even more brutal attack.

The combination of all these symptoms—resulting from sustained psychological and physical trauma compounded by aggravating social and economic factors—constitutes the battered-woman's syndrome. Only by understanding these unique pressures that force battered women to remain with their mates, despite their long-standing and reasonable fear of severe bodily harm and the isolation that being a battered woman creates, can a battered woman's state of mind be accurately and fairly understood.

The voir dire testimony of Dr. Veronen . . . conformed essentially to this outline of the battered-woman's syndrome. Dr. Vernonen . . . documented, based on her own considerable experience in counseling, treating, and studying battered women, and her familiarity with the work of others in the field, the feelings of anxiety, self-blame, isolation, and, above all, fear that plagues these women and leaves them prey to a psychological paralysis that hinders their ability to break free or seek help. . . .

Dr. Veronen described the various psychological tests and examinations she had performed in connection with her independent research. These tests and their methodology, including their interpretation, are, according to Dr. Veronen, widely accepted by clinical psychologists. Applying this methodology to defendant (who was subjected to all of the tests, including a five-hour interview), Dr. Veronen concluded that defendant was a battered woman and subject to the battered-woman's syndrome.

In addition, Dr. Veronen was prepared to testify as to how, as a battered woman, Gladys Kelly perceived her situation at the time of the stabbing, and why, in her opinion, defendant did not leave her husband despite the constant beatings she endured.

Whether expert testimony on the battered-woman's syndrome should be admitted in this case depends on whether it is relevant to defendant's claim of self-defense, and, in any event, on whether the proffer meets the standards for admission of expert testimony in this state. We examine first the law of self-defense and consider whether the expert testimony is relevant. . . .

While it is not imperative that *actual* necessity exist, a valid plea of self-defense will not lie absent an actual (that is, honest) belief on the part of the defendant in the necessity of using force. [Further,] even when the defendant's belief in the need to kill in self-defense is conceded to be sincere, if it is found to have been unreasonable under the circumstances, such a belief cannot be held to constitute complete justification for a homicide. As with the determination of the existence of the defendant's belief, the question of the reasonableness of this belief "is to be determined by the jury, not the defendant, in light of the circumstances existing at the time of the homicide." . . .

Gladys Kelly claims that she stabbed her husband in self-defense, believing he was about to kill her. The gist of the state's case was that Gladys Kelly was the aggressor, that she consciously intended to kill her husband, and that she certainly was not acting in self-defense.

The credibility of Gladys Kelly is a critical issue in this case. If the jury does not believe Gladys Kelly's account, it cannot find she acted in self-defense. The expert testimony offered was directly relevant to one of the critical elements of that account, namely, what Gladys Kelly believed at the time of the stabbing, and was thus material to establish the honesty of her stated belief that she was in imminent danger of death.[10] . . .

As can be seen from our discussion of the expert testimony, Dr. Veronen would have bolstered Gladys Kelly's credibility. Specifically, by showing that her experience, although concededly difficult to comprehend, was common to that of other women who had been in similarly abusive relationships, Dr. Veronen would have helped the jury understand that Gladys Kelly could have honestly feared that she would suffer serious bodily harm from her husband's attacks, yet still remain with him. This, in turn, would support Ms. Kelly's testimony

---

[10] The factual contentions of the parties eliminated any issue concerning the duty to retreat. If the state's version is accepted, defendant is the aggressor; if defendant's version is accepted, the possibility of retreat is excluded by virtue of the nature of the attack that defendant claims took place. We do not understand that the state claims defendant breached that duty under any version of the facts. If, however, the duty becomes an issue on retrial, the trial court will have to determine the relevancy of the battered-woman's syndrome to that issue. Without passing on that question, it appears to us to be a different question from whether the syndrome is relevant to defendant's failure to leave her husband in the past.

about her state of mind (that is, that she honestly feared serious bodily harm) at the time of the stabbing. . . .

We also find the expert testimony relevant to the reasonableness of defendant's belief that she was in imminent danger of death or serious injury. We do not mean that the expert's testimony could be used to show that it was understandable that a battered woman might believe that her life was in danger when indeed it was not and when a reasonable person would not have so believed, for admission for that purpose would clearly violate the rule set forth in *State v. Bess.* Expert testimony in that direction would be relevant solely to the honesty of defendant's belief, not its objective reasonableness. Rather, our conclusion is that the expert's testimony, if accepted by the jury, would have aided it in determining whether, under the circumstances, a reasonable person would have believed there was imminent danger to her life.

At the heart of the claim of self-defense was defendant's story that she had been repeatedly subjected to "beatings" over the course of her marriage. While defendant's testimony was somewhat lacking in detail, a juror could infer from the use of the word "beatings," as well as the detail given concerning some of these events (the choking, the biting, the use of fists), that these physical assaults posed a risk of serious injury or death. When that regular pattern of serious physical abuse is combined with defendant's claim that the decedent sometimes threatened to kill her, defendant's statement that on this occasion she thought she might be killed when she saw Mr. Kelly running toward her could be found to reflect a reasonable fear; that is, it could so be found if the jury believed Gladys Kelly's story of the prior beatings, if it believed her story of the prior threats, and, of course, if it believed her story of the events of that particular day.

The crucial issue of fact on which this expert's testimony would bear is why, given such allegedly severe and constant beatings, combined with threats to kill, defendant had not long ago left decedent. Whether raised by the prosecutor as a factual issue or not, our own common knowledge tells us that most of us, including the ordinary juror, would ask himself or herself just such a question. And our knowledge is bolstered by the experts' knowledge, for the experts point out that one of the common myths, apparently believed by most people, is that battered wives are free to leave. To some, this misconception is followed by the observation that the battered wife is masochistic, proven by her refusal to leave despite the severe beatings; to others, however, the fact that the battered wife stays on unquestionably suggests that the "beatings" could not have been too bad for if they had been, she certainly would have left. The expert could clear up these myths, by explaining that one of the common characteristics of a battered wife is her *inability* to leave despite such constant beatings; her "learned helplessness"; her lack of anywhere to go; her feeling that if she tried to leave, she would be subjected to even more merciless treatment; her belief in the omnipotence of her battering husband; and sometimes her hope that her husband will change his ways.

Unfortunately, in this case the state reinforced the myths about battered women. On cross-examination, when discussing an occasion when Mr. Kelly temporarily moved out of the house, the state repeatedly asked Ms. Kelly: "You wanted him back, didn't you?" The implication was clear: domestic life could not have been too bad if she wanted him back. In its closing argument, the state trivialized the severity of the beatings, saying:

> I'm not going to say they happened or they didn't happen, but life isn't pretty. Life is not a bowl of cherries. [E]ach and every person who takes a breath has problems. Defense counsel says bruised and battered. Is there any one of us who hasn't been battered by life in some manner or means?

Even had the state not taken this approach, however, expert testimony would be essential to rebut the general misconceptions regarding battered women. . . .

Since a retrial is necessary, we think it advisable to indicate the limit of the expert's testimony on this issue of reasonableness. It would not be proper for the expert to express the opinion that defendant's belief on that day was reasonable, not because this is the ultimate issue, but because the area of *expert* knowledge relates, in this regard, to the reasons for defendant's failure to leave her husband. Either the jury accepts or rejects that explanation and, based on that, credits defendant's stories about the beatings she suffered. No expert is needed, however, once the jury has made up its mind on those issues, to tell the jury the logical conclusion, namely, that a person who has in fact been severely and continuously beaten might very well reasonably fear that the imminent beating she was about to suffer could be either life-threatening or pose a risk of serious injury. What the expert could state was that defendant had the battered-woman's syndrome, and could explain that syndrome in detail, relating its characteristics to defendant, but only to enable the jury better to determine the honesty and reasonableness of defendant's belief. Depending on its content, the expert's testimony might also enable the jury to find that the battered wife, because of the prior beatings, numerous beatings, as often as once a week, for seven years, from the day they were married to the day he died, is particularly able to predict accurately the likely extent of violence in any attack on her. That conclusion could significantly affect the jury's evaluation of the reasonableness of defendant's fear for her life.[13]

---

[13] At least two other courts agree that expert testimony about the battered-woman's syndrome is relevant to show the reasonableness as well as the honesty of defendant's fear of serious bodily harm.

. . .

Defendant's counsel at oral argument made it clear that defendant's basic contention was that her belief in the immediate need to use deadly force was both honest and reasonable; and that the evidence concerning the battered-woman's syndrome was being offered solely on that issue. We therefore are not faced with any claim that a battered woman's honest belief in the need to use deadly force, even if objectively unreasonable, constitutes justification so long as its unreasonableness results from the psychological impact of the beatings. The effect of cases like State v. Sikora, 44 N.J. 453, 210 A.2d 193 (1965) (opinion of psychiatrist that acts of defendant, admittedly sane, were predetermined by interaction of events and his abnormal character held inadmissible on issue of premeditation, and State v. Bess, 53 N.J. 10,

Having determined that testimony about the battered-woman's syndrome is relevant, we now consider whether Dr. Veronen's testimony satisfies the limitations placed on expert testimony by Evidence Rule 56(2) and by applicable case law. . . .

As previously discussed, a battering relationship embodies psychological and societal features that are not well understood by lay observers. Indeed, these features are subject to a large group of myths and stereotypes. It is clear that this subject is beyond the ken of the average juror and thus is suitable for explanation through expert testimony.

The second requirement that must be met before expert testimony is permitted is a showing that the proposed expert's testimony would be reliable. The rationale for this requirement is that expert testimony seeks to assist the trier of fact. An expert opinion that is not reliable is of no assistance to anyone.

[J]udicial opinions thus far have been split concerning the scientific acceptability of the syndrome and the methodology used by the researchers in this area. [T]he record before us reveals that the battered woman's syndrome has a sufficient scientific basis to produce uniform and reasonably reliable results. . . . The numerous books, articles and papers referred to earlier indicate the presence of a growing field of study and research about the battered woman's syndrome and recognition of the syndrome in the scientific field. However, while the record before us could require such a ruling, we refrain from conclusively ruling that Dr. Veronen's proffered testimony about the battered-woman's syndrome would satisfy New Jersey's standard of acceptability for scientific evidence. This is because the state was not given a full opportunity in the trial court to question Dr. Veronen's methodology in studying battered women or her implicit assertion that the battered-woman's syndrome has been accepted by the relevant scientific community. . . .

Ms. Kelly also contends that the sentence imposed—five years in state prison—was excessive. She asserts that imprisonment would result in a serious injustice that overrides the need to deter such conduct by others, and that she should instead be granted probation or entry into a release program. She cites several mitigating factors, including her abuse at the hands of Mr. Kelly and her children's need to have their mother at home.

The presumptive sentence for [reckless manslaughter] is seven years. In ordering a sentence of five years, the trial court agreed with defendant that there was a preponderance of mitigating factors, allowing it to sentence her to a minimum term for [this] crime. Although we appreciate the hardship that would result from defendant's incarceration, she is not the truly extraordinary defendant whose

247 A.2d 669 (1968) (reasonableness of belief in need for deadly force not measured by what would appear "reasonable" to abnormal defendant) is not before us. Nor is there any claim that the battering provocation might have some legal effect beyond the potential reduction of defendant's culpability to manslaughter, or that something other than an "immediate" need for deadly force will suffice. See State v. Felton, 110 Wis.2d 485, 329 N.W.2d 161 (1983), (battered wife stabs sleeping husband).

imprisonment would represent the "serious injustice" envisioned by the Criminal Code [as a basis for withholding a sentence of imprisonment].[23]

[The Court reversed the conviction and remanded for a new trial.]

HANDLER, J., concurring in part and dissenting in part. . . . The court in this case takes a major stride in recognizing the scientific authenticity of battered women's syndrome and its legal and factual significance in the trial of certain criminal cases. My difference with the court is quite narrow. I believe that defendant Gladys Kelly has demonstrated at her trial by sufficient expert evidence her entitlement to the use of the battered women's syndrome in connection with her defense of self-defense. I would therefore not require this issue—the admissibility of the battered women's syndrome—to be tried again. . . .

NOTES ON DOMESTIC VIOLENCE AND THE LAW OF SELF–DEFENSE

1. **Questions and Comments on** *Kelly* **and the Battered Woman Syndrome.** The issue raised in *Kelly* has been widely litigated in recent years. Most courts have ruled, as a matter of law, that testimony concerning the battered woman syndrome should be admitted in this context if offered by a qualified expert witness, although at least one court has ruled that the evidence should not be admitted.[a] In *Kelly*, the New Jersey Supreme Court took a middle position, leaving it to the trial judge to assess the reliability of the testimony on a case-by-case basis.[b] Which is the best approach?

[23] We note that under the Code even if it is certain that the actor's life will soon be threatened, the actor may not use deadly defensive force until that threat is imminent. If he or she does, the crime in most cases would presumably be murder or manslaughter, the last exposing the actor to a sentence of ten years in prison with a five-year discretionary parole ineligibility term or, if a firearm is used, a three-year mandatory parole ineligibility term. The requirement that the use of deadly force, in order to be justifiable, must be immediately necessary, has as its purpose the preservation of life by preventing the use of deadly force except when its need is beyond debate. The rule's presumed effect on an actor who reasonably fears that her life will soon be endangered by an imminent threat is to cause her to leave the danger zone, especially if, because of the circumstances, she knows she will be defenseless when that threat becomes imminent. The rule, in effect, tends to protect the life of both the potential aggressor and victim. If, however, the actor is unable to remove herself from the zone of danger (a psychological phenomenon common to battered women, according to the literature),

the effect of the rule may be to prevent her from exercising the right of self-defense at the only time it would be effective. Instead she is required by the rule to wait until the threat against her life is imminent before she responds, at which time she may be completely defenseless.

There is, of course, some danger that any attempt to mitigate what may be undeserved punishment in these cases (by some further statutory differentiation of criminal responsibility) might weaken the general deterrent effect of our homicide laws. That is a matter the legislature might wish to examine.

[a] State v. Thomas, 66 Ohio St.2d 518, 423 N.E.2d 137 (1981).

[b] This approach was also taken in Ibn-Tamas v. United States, 407 A.2d 626 (D.C. App.1979). On remand, the trial court excluded the evidence on the ground "that defendant failed to establish a general acceptance by the [scientific community] of the methodology used in the expert's study of 'battered women'". Ibn-Tamas v. United States, 455 A.2d 893, 894 (D.C.App. 1983).

Much of the dispute regarding testimony on the battered woman syndrome has focused on its scientific merit.[c] If the debate is resolved in favor of the scientific accuracy of such evidence, the critical legal question then becomes how the testimony relates (or ought to relate) to the law of self-defense. Do you agree with the court's conclusion in *Kelly* that the testimony is relevant to the issues that must be resolved by the jury under New Jersey law? Is it relevant only on the defendant's subjective assessment of the need for protective action, or should it also be taken into account in framing the objective standard against which the defendant's conduct is to be judged?

Assuming that the testimony is otherwise relevant to the legal test for self-defense, and that it satisfies the criteria for expert evidence, the case for admitting it would appear to be strong. As the *Kelly* court notes, admission of the testimony seems necessary to afford the defendant a fair adjudication of her self-defense claim. Consider, however, the opposing views expressed by James Acker and Hans Toch, Battered Women, Straw Men, and Expert Testimony: A Comment on State v. Kelly, 21 Crim.L.Bull. 125 (1985). Acker and Toch argue that the probative value of the testimony is outweighed by its tendency to expand the scope of self-defense beyond the bounds of lawful justification:

> "In defining the defendant as a battered woman, the expert would necessarily identify the deceased as a battering husband and highlight the years of abuse which the accused suffered at her spouse's hands. Both the character and the conduct of the deceased would be described, interpreted, and defined through the vehicle of scientific testimony. The jury's attention would in this manner be deflected from the *responses* of the *accused* at the *time of the homicide* to the general bad character and repeated acts of misconduct *of the deceased* at times *far removed* from the homicide. . . .

> "When the prior bad acts (the repeated beatings) and the bad character ('battering husband') of the deceased are made principal issues, this through the supportive testimony of an expert witness, the classic defense stratagem of 'blaming the victim' for his own demise has been interjected before the jury. This 'defense' has been dignified by the 'syndrome' concept which draws attention to the prevalence of domestic victimization in society, and which makes the victim and the deceased examples of this problem. The killing of a battering husband could be 'justified' in the jurors' minds not because it was necessary that a battered woman act with responsive deadly force when she was threatened with death or serious bodily injury by her mate but because it was a fitting act of retribution directed at a member of a sadistic fraternity who had finally reaped his just deserts. . . .

[c] See generally, J. Monahan and L. Walker, Social Science in Law: Cases and Materials 336–58 (1984).

"This conclusion, it must be stressed, is suggested . . . *independently* of the condition of lawful justification which demands that a homicide committed in self-defense be motivated by the apparent necessity to resort to deadly force in the face of an imminent lethal assault. The subtle conversion worked in the argument is that self-defense need not be limited to force applied under the strict demands of defensive necessity. The self-defense concept instead shades into and subsumes retributive acts committed by victims against their long-term tormentors, not because the violence was necessary in the short run but because it was deserved, or 'just,' in the long run."

Is this a persuasive argument? Note that the risk of distortion described by Acker and Toch can exist even without the expert testimony. Ms. Kelly clearly was entitled to testify, and introduce corroborative evidence, about her husband's prior acts of violence against her. Moreover, on the facts presented, she clearly was entitled to an instruction on self-defense. Does the expert testimony tend to shift the focus too much toward a trial of Mr. Kelly? Or is this concern offset by the need to be fair to Ms. Kelly in assessing her claim of self-defense?

2. **Self-Defense by a Battered Child:** *Jahnke v. State.* Issues analogous to those presented in *Kelly* have also been raised in cases involving defendants charged with patricide who seek to introduce expert testimony regarding the so-called "battered child syndrome." The relation between this evidentiary question and the substantive doctrine of self-defense was discussed at length by a court in Jahnke v. State, 682 P.2d 991 (Wyo.1984). Richard John Jahnke, then 16, killed his father with a shotgun in the driveway of their home as his mother and father were returning from dinner. The court described the killing as follows:

"[Earlier in the evening defendant] had been involved in a violent altercation with his father, and he had been warned not to be at the home when the father and mother returned. During the absence of his parents the [defendant] made elaborate preparation for the final confrontation with his father. He changed into dark clothing and prepared a number of weapons which he positioned at various places throughout the family home that he selected to serve as 'backup' positions in case he was not successful in his first effort to kill his father. These weapons included two shotguns, three rifles, a .38 caliber pistol and a Marine knife. In addition, he armed his sister, Deborah, with a .30 caliber M–1 carbine which he taught her how to operate so that she could protect herself in the event that he failed in his efforts. . . . He then waited inside the darkened garage in a position where he could not be seen but which permitted him to view the lighted driveway on the other side of the garage door. Shortly before 6:30 p.m. the parents returned, and the [defendant's] father got out of the vehicle and came to the garage door. The [defendant] was armed with a 12-gauge shotgun loaded with slugs, and when he could see the head and shoulders of his father through the spacing of the slats of the shade covering the windows of the garage door, he blew his R.O.T.C. command-sergeant-major's whistle for courage, and he opened fire. All six cartridges in the shotgun were expended, and four of them in one way or another struck the father. . . . "

Jahnke was charged with first-degree murder. In support of his self-defense plea, he sought to introduce evidence that his father had beaten him, his sister, and his mother over many years, and proffered psychiatric testimony that he was a battered child who believed himself to be in immediate danger of death or serious harm when he shot his father. Although the jury was instructed on the law of self-defense, the expert testimony was excluded. Jahnke was convicted of voluntary manslaughter and sentenced to a 5-to-15 year term of imprisonment. The Wyoming Supreme Court affirmed the conviction and sentence. The majority explained its ruling on the evidentiary issue as follows:

"It is clear that self-defense is circumscribed by circumstances involving a confrontation, usually encompassing some overt act or acts by the deceased, which would induce a reasonable person to fear that his life was in danger or that at least he was threatened with great bodily harm. . . . Although many people, and the public media, seem to be prepared to espouse the notion that a victim of abuse is entitled to kill the abuser, that special justification defense is antethetical to the mores of modern civilized society. It is difficult enough to justify capital punishment as an appropriate response of society to criminal acts even after the circumstances have been carefully evaluated by a number of people. To permit capital punishment to be imposed upon the subjective conclusion of the individual that prior acts and conduct of the deceased justified the killing would amount to a leap into the abyss of anarchy. [If expert testimony] has any role at all, it is in assisting the jury to evaluate the reasonableness of the defendant's fear in a case involving the recognized circumstances of self-defense which include a confrontation or conflict with the deceased not of the defendant's instigation. . . .

"[The] record contained no evidence that [defendant] was under either actual or threatened assault by his father at the time of the shooting. Reliance upon the justification of self-defense requires a showing of an actual or threatened imminent attack by the deceased. Absent [such a showing] the reasonableness of [the defendant's] conduct at the time was not an issue in the case, and the trial court, at the time it made its ruling, properly excluded the testimony sought to be elicited from the forensic psychiatrist."

Two judges dissented in lengthy opinions. Justice Rose stated:

"This case concerns itself with what happens—or can happen—and did happen when a cruel, ill-tempered, insensitive man roams, gun in hand, through his years of family life as a battering bully—a bully who, since his two children were babies, beat both of them and his wife regularly and unmercifully. Particularly, this appeal has to do with a 16-year-old boy who could stand his father's abuse no longer—who could not find solace or friendship in the public services which had been established for the purpose of providing aid, comfort and advice to abused family members—and who had no place to go or friends to help either him or his sister for whose protection he felt responsible and so—in fear and fright, and with fragmented emotion, Richard Jahnke shot and killed his father one night in November of 1982. [S]ince the jury was given a self-defense instruction, it must be conceded that the trial judge recognized this as a viable defense theory under the evidence adduced at trial. . . .

"Denied the explanatory assistance of a qualified expert witness, it is as though Richard Jahnke had not been permitted to defend himself at all. Since the necessity to defend oneself or others from perceived imminent danger is a subjective consideration for the defendant but one which is an objective concern of the jury, how could this young boy structure an understandable defense when—even though the record discloses that since age two he had been bullied, battered, frightened and emotionally traumatized—he was, nevertheless, denied the opportunity to have explained to his jury how abused people reasonably handle their fears and anxieties—what their apprehensions are—how, in the dark moments of their aloneness, they perceive the imminence of danger—and how, in response, they undertake to assert their right of self-defense? . . .

"Denied this opportunity, the [defendant] was forced to submit his case to the jury with what consequently presents itself as a ridiculous, unbelievable, outrageous defense. Without medical input, what possible sense could it make to a lay juror or any other nonprofessional person for the citizen accused to urge self-defense where the evidence is that, even though the recipient of untold battering and brutalizing by the victim, the defendant nevertheless contemplated the possibility of the use of deadly force as he lay in wait, gun in hand, for his father's return? How could any jury be receptive to such a defense on an informed basis if its members are not to be permitted to hear from those who understand how brutalized people—otherwise "reasonable" in all respects—entertain what, for them, is a belief that they are in imminent danger from which there is no escape and how they, with their embattled psyche, responsively behave?

"[C]ontrary to the holding of the majority, [it is not] necessary that the perceived danger must in fact be present and imminent—it need only to 'have appeared to be so under the circumstances.' In this case, therefore, the appearance of imminent danger must have been present in the mind of the defendant, not the trial court or this court. . . .

"[In] the *ordinary* self-defense situation where there are no psychiatric implications and where the jury is permitted to know what the accused knew about the violent character of his victim, there need be no expert testimony touching upon the reasonableness of the defendant's behavior. In normal circumstances, these are things that jurors can fathom for themselves. However, when the beatings of 14 years have—or may have—caused the accused to harbor types of fear, anxiety and apprehension with which the nonbrutalized juror is unfamiliar and which result in the taking of unusual defensive measures which, in the ordinary circumstances, might be thought about as premature, excessive or lacking in escape efforts by those who are uninformed about the fear and anxiety that permeate the world of the brutalized— then expert testimony is necessary to explain the battered-person syndrome and the way these people respond to what they understand to be the imminence of danger and to explain their propensity to employ deadly force in their self-defensive conduct. Given this information, the jury is then qualified to decide the reasonableness of a self-defense defendant's acts at the time and place in question."

Was *Jahnke* correctly decided? Even if the expert testimony was improperly excluded in *Kelly*, does it follow that it should have been admitted in *Jahnke*? [d]

PEOPLE v. YOUNG

New York Supreme Court, Appellate Division, 1961.
12 A.D.2d 262, 210 N.Y.S.2d 358.

BREITEL, JUSTICE. The question is whether one is criminally liable for assault in the third degree [a] if he goes to the aid of another who he mistakenly, but reasonably, believes is being unlawfully beaten, and thereby injures one of the apparent assaulters. In truth, the seeming victim was being lawfully arrested by two police officers in plain clothes. Defendant stands convicted of such a criminal assault, for which he received a sentence of 60 days in the workhouse, the execution of such sentence being suspended.

[d] One week after the court's decision, the Governor commuted Jahnke's sentence to three years.

[a] At the time of the *Young* case, the New York penal law defined three degrees of assault. According to Section 240, a person "who, with an intent to kill a human being or to commit a felony upon the person or property of the one assaulted, or of another, assaults another with [deadly force] is guilty of assault in the first degree." According to Section 242, a person who "wilfully and wrongfully wounds or inflicts grievous bodily harm upon another, either with or without a weapon" or who "wilfully and wrongfully assaults another by the use of a weapon or other instrument or thing likely to produce grievous bodily harm . . . is guilty of assault in the second degree." Finally, Section 244 provided that a person who "commits an assault, or an assault and battery" that is not specified in Sections 240 or 242 "is guilty of assault in the third degree." In its opinion, the court occasionally refers to assault in the third degree as "simple assault." [Footnote by eds.]

Defendant, aged 40, regularly employed, and with a clean record except for an $8 fine in connection with a disorderly conduct charge 19 years before in Birmingham, Alabama, observed two middle-aged men beating and struggling with a youth of 18. This was at 3:40 p. m. on October 17, 1958 in front of 64 West 64th Street in Manhattan. Defendant was acquainted with none of the persons involved; but believing that the youth was being unlawfully assaulted, and this is not disputed by the other participants, defendant went to his rescue, pulling on or punching at the seeming assailants. In the ensuing affray one of the older men got his leg locked with that of defendant and when defendant fell the man's leg was broken at the kneecap. The injured man then pulled out a revolver, announced to defendant that he was a police officer, and that defendant was under arrest. It appears that the youth in question had played some part in a street incident which resulted in the two men, who were detectives in plain clothes, seeking to arrest him for disorderly conduct. The youth had resisted, and it was in the midst of this resistance that defendant came upon the scene.

At the trial the defendant testified that he had known nothing about what had happened before he came upon the scene; that he had gone to his aid because the youth was crying and trying to pull away from the middle-aged men; and that the older men had almost pulled the trousers off the youth. The only detective who testified stated, in response to a question from the court, that defendant did not know and had no way of knowing, so far as he knew, that they were police officers or that they were making an arrest.

Two things are to be kept sharply in mind in considering the problem at hand. The first is that all that is involved here is a criminal prosecution for simple assault, and that the court is not concerned with the incidence of civil liability in the law of torts as a result of what happened on the street. Second, there is not here involved any question of criminal responsibility for interfering with an arrest where it is known to the actor that police officers are making an arrest, but he mistakenly believes that the arrest is unlawful.

Assault and battery is an ancient crime cognizable at the common law. It is a crime in which an essential element is intent. Of course, in this state the criminal law is entirely statutory. But, because assault and battery is a "common-law" crime, the statutory provisions, as in the case of most of the common-law crimes, do not purport to define the crime with the same particularity as those crimes which have a statutory origin initially. One of the consequences, therefore, is that while the provisions governing assault, contained in the Penal Law, refer to various kinds of intent, in most instances the intent is related to a supplemental intent, in addition to the unspecified general intent to commit an assault, in order to impose more serious consequences upon the actor. In some instances, of course, the intent is spelled out to distinguish the prohibited activity from what might otherwise be an innocent act or merely an accidental wrong.

It is in this statutory context that it was held in People v. Katz, 290 N.Y. 361, 49 N.E.2d 482 (1943), that in order to sustain a charge of assault in the second degree, based upon the infliction of grievous bodily harm, not only must there be a general intent to commit unlawful bodily harm but there must be a "specific intent," i.e., a supplemental intent to inflict grievous bodily harm. The case therefore does provide an interesting parallel analysis forwarding the idea that assault is always an intent crime even when the statute omits to provide expressly for such general intent, as is the case with regard to assault in the third degree. . . .

With respect to intent crimes, under general principles, a mistake of fact relates as a defense to an essential element of the crime, namely, to the mens rea. The development of the excuse of mistake is a relatively modern one and is of expanding growth. . . .

Mistake of fact, under our statutes, is a species of excuse rather than a matter of justification. Consequently, reliance on Section 42 [1] of the Penal Law which relates exclusively to justification is misplaced. Section 42 would be applicable only to justify a third party's intervention on behalf of a victim of an unlawful assault, but this does not preclude the defense of mistake which is related to subjective intent rather than to the objective ground for action. . . . While the distinctions between excuse and justification are often fuzzy, and more often fudged, in the instance of Section 42 its limited application is clear from its language.

It is in the homicide statutes in which the occasions for excuse or justification are made somewhat clearer; but the distinction is still relevant with respect to most crimes. In homicide it is made explicitly plain that the actor's state of mind, if reasonable, is material and controlling.[b] It does not seem rational that the same reasonable misapprehension of fact should excuse a killing in seeming proper defense of a third person in one's presence but that it should not excuse a lesser personal injury.

In this state there are no discoverable precedents involving mistake of fact when one intervenes on behalf of another person and the prosecution has been for assault, rather than homicide. (The absence of precedents in this state and many others may simply mean that no enforcement agency would prosecute in the situations that must have occurred.) No one would dispute, however, that a mistake of fact would

---

[1] The section reads as follows:

"§ 42. Rule when act done in defense of self or another.

"An act, otherwise criminal, is justifiable when it is done to protect the person committing it, or another whom he is bound to protect, from inevitable and irreparable personal injury, and the injury could only be prevented by the act, nothing more being done than is necessary to prevent the injury."

[b] Section 1055 provided, in relevant part, as follows:

"Homicide is . . . justifiable when committed:

1. In the lawful defense of the slayer, or of his or her husband, wife, parent, child, brother, sister, master or servant, or of any person in his presence or company, when there is reasonable ground to apprehend a design on the part of the person slain to commit a felony, or to do some great personal injury to the slayer, or to any such person, and there is imminent danger of such design being accomplished. . . ."

[Footnote by eds.]

provide a defense if the prosecution were for homicide. This divided approach is sometimes based on the untenable distinction that mistake of fact may negative a "specific" intent required in the degrees of homicide but is irrelevant to the general intent required in simple assault, or, on the even less likely distinction, that the only intent involved in assault is the intent to touch without consent or legal justification (omitting the qualification of unlawfulness). . . .

There have been precedents elsewhere among the states. There is a split among the cases and in the jurisdictions. Most hold that the rescuer intervenes at his own peril, but others hold that he is excused if he acts under mistaken but reasonable belief that he is protecting a victim from unlawful attack. Many of the cases which hold that the actor proceeds at his peril involve situations where the actor was present throughout, or through most, or through enough of the transaction and, therefore, was in no position to claim a mistake of fact. Others arise in rough situations in which the feud or enmity generally to the peace officer is a significant factor. Almost all apply unanalytically the rubric that the right to intervene on behalf of another is no greater than the other's right to self-defense, a phrasing of ancient but questionable lineage going back to when crime and tort were not yet divided in the common law—indeed, when the right to private redress was not easily distinguishable from the sanction for the public wrong. . . .

The modern view, as already noted, is not to impose criminal responsibility in connection with intent crimes for those who act with good motivation, in mistaken but reasonable misapprehension of the facts. . . .

More recently in the field of criminal law the American Law Institute in drafting a model penal code has concerned itself with the question in this case. Under Section 3.05 of the Model Penal Code the use of force for the protection of others is excused if the actor behaves under a mistaken belief.

The comments by the reporters on the Model Penal Code are quite appropriate. After stating that the defense of strangers should be assimilated to the defense of oneself the following is said:

> "In support of such a ruling, it may perhaps be said that the potentiality for deterring the actor from the use of force is greater where he is protecting a stranger than where he is protecting himself or a loved one, because in the former case the interest protected is of relatively less importance to him; moreover the potential incidence of mistake in estimating fault or the need for action on his part is increased where the defendant is protecting a stranger, because in such circumstances he is less likely to know which party to the quarrel is in the right. These arguments may be said to lead to the conclusion that, in order to minimize the area for error or mistake, the defendant should act at his peril when he is protecting a stranger. This emasculates the privilege of protection of much of its content, introducing a liability without fault which is indefensible in principle. The

cautious potential actor who knows the law will, in the vast majority of cases, refrain from acting at all. The result may well be that an innocent person is injured without receiving assistance from bystanders. It seems far preferable, therefore, to predicate the justification upon the actor's belief, safeguarding if thought necessary against abuse of the privilege by the imposition of a requirement of proper care in evolving the belief. Here, as elsewhere, the latter problem is dealt with by the general provision in Section 3.09."

Apart from history, precedents, and the language distinctions that may be found in the statutes, it stands to reason that a man should not be punished criminally for an intent crime unless he, indeed, has the intent. Where a mistake of relevant facts is involved the premises for such intent are absent. . . .

It is a sterile and desolate legal system that would exact punishment for an intentional assault from one like this defendant, who acted from the most commendable motives and without excessive force. Had the facts been as he thought them, he would have been a hero and not condemned as a criminal actor. The dearth of applicable precedents— as distinguished from theoretical generalizations never, or rarely, applied—in England and in most of the states demonstrates that the benevolent intervenor has not been cast as a pariah. It is no answer to say that the policeman should be called when one sees an injustice. Even in the most populous centers, policemen are not that common or that available. Also, it ignores the peremptory response to injustice that the good man has ingrained. Again, it is to be noted, in a criminal proceeding one is concerned with the act against society, not with the wrong between individuals and the right to reparation, which is the province of tort.

Accordingly, the judgment of conviction should be reversed, on the law, and the information dismissed. . . .

VALENTE, JUSTICE (dissenting) . . . . I dissent and would affirm the conviction because the intent to commit a battery was unquestionably proven; and, since there was no relationship between defendant and the person whom the police officers were arresting, defendant acted at his peril in intervening and striking the officer. Under well established law, defendant's rights were no greater than those of the person whom he sought to protect; and since the arrest was lawful, defendant was no more privileged to assault the police officer than the person being arrested.

Under our statutes a *specific* intent is necessary for the crimes of assault in the first and second degrees. Generally, the assaults contemplated by those sections were known as "aggravated" assaults under the common law. However, assault in the third degree is defined by Section 244 of the Penal Law as an assault and battery not such as is specified in Sections 240 and 242. No specific intent is required under Section 244. All that is required is the knowledgeable doing of the act. "It is sufficient that the defendant voluntarily intended to commit the unlawful act of touching."

In the instant case, had the defendant assaulted the officer with the specific intent of preventing the lawful apprehension of the other person he would have been subject to indictment [for] assault in the second degree. But the inability to prove a specific intent does not preclude the People from establishing the lesser crime of assault in the third degree which requires proof only of the general intent "to commit the unlawful act of touching," if such exists.

There is evidently no New York law on the precise issue on this appeal. However, certain of our statutes point to the proper direction for solution of the problem. Section 42 of the Penal Law provides:

> "An act, otherwise criminal, is justifiable when it is done to protect the person committing it, or another whom he is bound to protect, from inevitable and irreparable personal injury. . . ."

Similarly, Section 246, so far as here pertinent, provides:

> "To use or attempt, or offer to use, force or violence upon or towards the person of another is not unlawful in the following cases: . . .

> "3. When committed either by the party about to be injured or by another person in his aid or defense, in preventing or attempting to prevent an offense against his person, or a trespass or other unlawful interference with real or personal property in his lawful possession, if the force or violence used is not more than sufficient to prevent such offense."

These statutes represent the public policy of this state regarding the areas in which an assault will be excused or rendered "not unlawful" where one goes to the assistance of another. They include only those cases in which the other person is one whom the defendant "is bound to protect" or where the defendant is "preventing or attempting to prevent an offense against" such other person. Neither statute applies to the instant case since the other person herein was one unlawfully resisting a legal arrest—and hence no offense was being committed against his person by the officer—and he was not an individual whom defendant was "bound to protect."

It has been held in other states that one who goes to the aid of a third person acts at his peril, and his rights to interfere do not exceed the rights of the person whom he seeks to protect. We need not consider to what extent that rule is modified by Section 42 of the Penal Law since there is no question here but that the person being arrested was not in any special relation to defendant so that he was a person whom defendant was "bound to protect." It follows then that there being no right on the part of the person, to whose aid defendant came, to assault the officer—the arrest being legal—defendant had no greater right or privilege to assault the officer.

The conclusion that defendant was properly convicted in this case comports with sound public policy. It would be a dangerous precedent for courts to announce that plain-clothes police officers attempting lawful arrests over wrongful resistance are subject to violent interference by strangers ignorant of the facts, who may attack the officers with impunity so long as their ignorance forms a reasonable basis for a snap judgment of the situation unfavorable to the officers. Although the actions of such a defendant, who acts on appearances, may eliminate the specific intent required to convict him of a felony assault, it should not exculpate him from the act of aggressive assistance to a law breaker in the process of wrongfully resisting a proper arrest.

I do not detract from the majority's views regarding commendation of the acts of a good Samaritan, although it may be difficult in some cases to distinguish such activities from those of an officious intermeddler. But opposed to the encouragement of the "benevolent intervenor" is the conflicting and more compelling interest of protection of police officers. In a city like New York, where it becomes necessary to utilize the services of a great number of plain-clothes officers, the efficacy of their continuing struggle against crime should not be impaired by the possibility of interference by citizens who may be acting from commendable motives. It is more desirable—and evidently up to this point the legislature has so deemed it—that in such cases the intervening citizen be held to act at his peril when he assaults a stranger, who unknown to him is a police officer legally performing his duty. In this conflict of interests, the balance preponderates in favor of the protection of the police rather than the misguided intervenor.

The majority points to the recommendations of the American Law Institute in drafting a Model Penal Code which make the use of force justifiable to protect a third person when the actor believes his intervention is necessary for the protection of such third person. Obviously these are recommendations which properly are to be addressed to a legislature and not to courts. The comments of the reporters on the Model Penal Code, from which the majority quotes, indicate that in the United States the view is preserved in much state legislation that force may not be used to defend others unless they stand in a special relationship to their protector. The reporters state: "The simple solution of the whole problem is to assimilate the defense of strangers to the defense of oneself, and this the present section does." If this be so, then even under the Model Penal Code, since the stranger, who is being lawfully arrested, may not assault the officers a third person coming to his defense may not do so. In any event, the Model Penal Code recognizes that the law as it now stands requires the conviction of the defendant herein. Until the legislature acts, the courts should adhere to the well-established rules applicable in such cases. Such adherence demands the affirmance of the conviction herein.

PEOPLE v. YOUNG

Court of Appeals of New York, 1962.
11 N.Y.2d 274, 183 N.E.2d 319.

PER CURIAM.

Whether one, who in good faith aggressively intervenes in a struggle between another person and a police officer in civilian dress attempting to effect the lawful arrest of the third person, may be properly convicted of assault in the third degree is a question of law of first impression here.

The opinions in the court below in the absence of precedents in this state carefully expound the opposing views found in other jurisdictions. The majority in the Appellate Division have adopted the minority rule in the other states that one who intervenes in a struggle between strangers under the mistaken but reasonable belief that he is protecting another who he assumes is being unlawfully beaten is thereby exonerated from criminal liability. The weight of authority holds with the dissenters below that one who goes to the aid of a third person does so at his own peril.

While the doctrine espoused by the majority of the court below may have support in some states, we feel that such a policy would not be conducive to an orderly society. We agree with the settled policy of law in most jurisdictions that the right of a person to defend another ordinarily should not be greater than such person's right to defend himself. Subdivision 3 of Section 246 of the Penal Law does not apply as no offense was being committed on the person of the one resisting the lawful arrest. Whatever may be the public policy where the felony charged requires proof of a specific intent and the issue is justifiable homicide, it is not relevant in a prosecution for assault in the third degree where it is only necessary to show that the defendant knowingly struck a blow.

In this case there can be no doubt that the defendant intended to assault the police officer in civilian dress. The resulting assault was forceful. Hence motive or mistake of fact is of no significance as the defendant was not charged with a crime requiring such intent or knowledge. To be guilty of third-degree assault "[i]t is sufficient that the defendant voluntarily intended to commit the unlawful act of touching." Since in these circumstances the aggression was inexcusable the defendant was properly convicted.

Accordingly, the order of the Appellate Division should be reversed and the information reinstated.

[The dissenting opinion of Judge Froessel is omitted.]

NOTE ON DEFENSE OF OTHERS

The opinions in the *Young* litigation adequately canvass the policy arguments usually made on both sides of the question raised. How should that question be resolved? How would it be resolved under the current New York law, quoted at page 543, supra? Under the Model Penal Code? Is the case for ignoring a reasonable mistake, i.e., for strict liability, stronger in *Young* than it would be in *Wanrow*?

Do you understand the relevance of the distinction between general and specific intent to the reasoning in *Young*? Why is Young not equally guilty of aggravated assault if he seriously injures the victim?

SUBSECTION D: PUBLIC AUTHORITY

INTRODUCTORY NOTE ON PUBLIC AUTHORITY

From the earliest times, the common law regarded as justifiable otherwise criminal acts, including homicide, which were performed in execution of the law or in furtherance of justice. By the 13th century, according to Pollock and Maitland, some homicides were regarded as "absolutely justifiable." They offer two examples: "One such case is the execution of a lawful sentence of death. Another—and this is regarded as a very similar case—is the slaying of an outlaw or a hand-having thief or other manifest felon who resists capture." 2 F. Pollock & F. Maitland, The History of English Law 478 (2d ed. 1899).

It is clear that police and corrections officers have special authority to arrest, search, imprison, assault, and even kill to enforce and execute the law, and that this authority supersedes the norms otherwise defined by the law of crimes and torts. These subjects are too complex and wide-ranging to be given comprehensive coverage in basic materials on the substantive criminal law. Instead, the scope of official authority will be addressed in a single context—the authority of the police to use deadly force against a fleeing felon. The next main case addresses this issue.

The remainder of this subsection is devoted to an entirely different issue, one that cuts across all public-authority justifications—the problem of mistake regarding the existence of the claimed authority, either by a public official or by a private citizen who complies with an official request for assistance. The problem is illustrated in an unusual and controversial substantive context—the scope of the president's authority to authorize warrantless searches and seizures in the interests of "national security."

TENNESSEE v. GARNER
Supreme Court of the United States, 1985.
__ U.S. __.

JUSTICE WHITE delivered the opinion of the Court.

This case requires us to determine the constitutionality of the use of deadly force to prevent the escape of an apparently unarmed suspected felon. We conclude that such force may not be used unless it is necessary to prevent the escape and the officer has probable cause to believe that the suspect poses a significant threat of death or serious physical injury to the officer or others.

I

At about 10:45 p.m. on October 3, 1974, Memphis Police Officers Elton Hymon and Leslie Wright were dispatched to answer a "prowler inside call." Upon arriving at the scene they saw a woman standing on her porch and gesturing toward the adjacent house. She told them she had heard glass breaking and that "they" or "someone" was breaking in next door. While Wright radioed the dispatcher to say that they were on the scene, Hymon went behind the house. He heard a door slam and saw someone run across the back yard. The fleeing suspect . . . Edward Garner, stopped at a 6-feet-high chain link fence at the edge of the yard. With the aid of a flashlight, Hymon was able to see Garner's face and hands. He saw no sign of a weapon, and, though not certain, was "reasonably sure" and "figured" that Garner was unarmed. He thought Garner was 17 or 18 years old and about 5′5″ or 5′7″ tall.[2] While Garner was crouched at the base of the fence, Hymon called out "police, halt" and took a few steps toward him. Garner then began to climb over the fence. Convinced that if Garner made it over the fence he would elude capture, Hymon shot him. The bullet hit Garner in the back of the head. Garner was taken by ambulance to a hospital, where he died on the operating table. Ten dollars and a purse taken from the house were found on his body.

In using deadly force to prevent the escape, Hymon was acting under the authority of a Tennessee statute and pursuant to police department policy. The statute provides that "[i]f, after notice of the intention to arrest the defendant, he either flee or forcibly resist, the officer may use all the necessary means to effect the arrest." Tenn. Code Ann. § 40–7–108 (1982).[5] The department policy was slightly more restrictive than the statute, but still allowed the use of deadly force in cases of burglary. The incident was reviewed by the Memphis Police Firearm's Review Board and presented to a grand jury. Neither took any action.

[Garner's father brought a civil action for damages under 42 U.S.C. § 1983, alleging violation of Garner's constitutional rights. Named as defendants were Officer Hymon, the police department, the city of Memphis, and various city officials. The district court dismissed the action on the ground that Hymon's conduct was authorized by the Tennessee statute, which was found to be constitutional. The court of appeals ultimately reversed that determination, and the state of Tennessee intervened to defend the statute. The issue before the Supreme Court, therefore, was the constitutionality of the Tennessee law.[a]]

[2] In fact, Garner, an eighth-grader, was 15. He was 5′4″ tall and weighed somewhere around 100 or 110 pounds.

[5] Although the statute does not say so explicitly, Tennessee law forbids the use of deadly force in the arrest of a misdemeanant. See Johnson v. State, 173 Tenn. 134, 114 S.W.2d 819 (1938).

[a] It should be noted that Officer Hymon was no longer involved in the case by the time it reached the Supreme Court. The Court of Appeals affirmed the dismissal of the case as to him, on the ground that he had acted in good-faith reliance on the Tennessee statute and was therefore entitled to immunity from personal damage liability. This judgment was not appealed. The other city officials were also no longer involved in the case. The state of Tennessee, moreover, was not subject to damages liability; it had intervened only to defend the validity of the statute. The remaining liability question concerned whether the police department and/or the city of Memphis could be compelled to pay damages for the alleged constitutional violation. Whether either could be required to do so, even if—as the Supreme Court was to hold—the Tennessee statute was unconstitutional as applied to these facts, was not determined by the Supreme Court in this case, but was left to further litigation on

II

Whenever an officer restrains the freedom of a person to walk away, he has seized that person. While it is not always clear just when minimal police interference becomes a seizure, there can be no question that apprehension by the use of deadly force is a seizure subject to the reasonableness requirement of the fourth amendment.[b]

A

A police officer may arrest a person if he has probable cause to believe that person committed a crime. [Defendants] argue that if this requirement is satisfied the fourth amendment has nothing to say about *how* that seizure is made. This submission ignores the many cases in which this Court, by balancing the extent of the intrusion against the need for it, has examined the reasonableness of the manner in which a search or seizure is conducted. To determine the constitutionality of a seizure "[w]e must balance the nature and quality of the intrusion on the individual's fourth amendment interests against the importance of the governmental interests alleged to justify the intrusion." Because one of the factors is the extent of the intrusion, it is plain that reasonableness depends on not only when a seizure is made, but also how it is carried out. . . .

B

The same balancing process . . . demonstrates that, notwithstanding probable cause to seize a suspect, an officer may not always do so by killing him. The intrusiveness of a seizure by means of deadly force is unmatched. The suspect's fundamental interest in his own life need not be elaborated upon. The use of deadly force also frustrates the interest of the individual, and of society, in judicial determination of guilt and punishment. Against these interests are ranged governmental interests in effective law enforcement. It is argued that overall violence will be reduced by encouraging the peaceful submission of suspects who know that they may be shot if they flee. Effectiveness in making arrests requires the resort to deadly force, or at least the meaningful threat thereof. . . .

Without in any way disparaging the importance of these goals, we are not convinced that the use of deadly force is a sufficiently productive means of accomplishing them to justify the killing of nonviolent suspects. The use of deadly force is a self-defeating way of apprehending a suspect and so setting the criminal justice mechanism in motion. If successful, it guarantees that that mechanism will not be set in motion. And while the meaningful threat of deadly force might be thought to lead to the arrest of more live suspects by discouraging

remand. Determination of this issue raises a series of complex questions concerning the meaning of 42 U.S.C. § 1983 that are beyond the scope of the materials in this book. [Footnote by eds.]

[b] The fourth amendment guarantees the "right of the people to be secure in their persons, houses, papers, and effects, against unreasonable searches and seizures . . . ." [Footnote by eds.]

escape attempts, the presently available evidence does not support this thesis. The fact is that a majority of police departments in this country have forbidden the use of deadly force against nonviolent suspects. If those charged with the enforcement of the criminal law have abjured the use of deadly force in arresting nondangerous felons, there is a substantial basis for doubting that the use of such force is an essential attribute of the arrest power in all felony cases. [Defendants] have not persuaded us that shooting nondangerous fleeing suspects is so vital as to outweigh the suspect's interest in his own life.

The use of deadly force to prevent the escape of all felony suspects, whatever the circumstances, is constitutionally unreasonable. It is not better that all felony suspects die than that they escape. Where the suspect poses no immediate threat to the officer and no threat to others, the harm resulting from failing to apprehend him does not justify the use of deadly force to do so. It is no doubt unfortunate when a suspect who is in sight escapes, but the fact that the police arrive a little late or are a little slower afoot does not always justify killing the suspect. A police officer may not seize an unarmed, nondangerous suspect by shooting him dead. The Tennessee statute is unconstitutional insofar as it authorizes the use of deadly force against such fleeing suspects.

It is not, however, unconstitutional on its face. Where the officer has probable cause to believe that the suspect poses a threat of serious physical harm, either to the officer or to others, it is not constitutionally unreasonable to prevent escape by using deadly force. Thus, if the suspect threatens the officer with a weapon or there is probable cause to believe that he has committed a crime involving the infliction or threatened infliction of serious physical harm, deadly force may be used if necessary to prevent escape, and if, where feasible, some warning has been given. As applied in such circumstances, the Tennessee statute would pass constitutional muster.

III

It is insisted that the fourth amendment must be construed in light of the common-law rule, which allowed the use of whatever force was necessary to effect the arrest of a fleeing felon, though not a misdemeanant. . . .

It has been pointed out many times that the common-law rule is best understood in light of the fact that it arose at a time when virtually all felonies were punishable by death. "Though effected without the protections and formalities of an orderly trial and conviction, the killing of a resisting or fleeing felon resulted in no greater consequences than those authorized for punishment of the felony of which the individual was charged or suspected." A.L.I. Model Penal Code § 3.07, Comment 3, p. 56 (Tent. Draft No. 8, 1958). Courts have also justified the common-law rule by emphasizing the relative dangerousness of felons.

Neither of these justifications makes sense today. Almost all crimes formerly punishable by death no longer are or can be. See Enmund v.

Florida, 458 U.S. 782 (1982); Coker v. Georgia, 433 U.S. 584 (1977).
And while in earlier times "the gulf between the felonies and the minor
offences was broad and deep," 2 F. Pollock & F. Maitland, The History
of English Law 467 (1895), today the distinction is minor and often
arbitrary. Many crimes classified as misdemeanors, or nonexistent, at
common law are now felonies. These changes have undermined the
concept, which was questionable to begin with, that use of deadly force
against a fleeing felon is merely a speedier execution of someone who
has already forfeited his life. . . .

There is an additional reason why the common-law rule cannot be
directly translated to the present day. The common-law rule developed
at a time when weapons were rudimentary. Deadly force could be
inflicted almost solely in a hand-to-hand struggle during which, necessarily, the safety of the arresting officer was at risk. Handguns were
not carried by police officers until the latter half of the last century.
Only then did it become possible to use deadly force from a distance as
a means of apprehension. As a practical matter, the use of deadly force
under the standard articulation of the common-law rule has an altogether different meaning—and harsher consequences—now than in
past centuries. . . .

In short, though the common law pedigree of Tennessee's rule is
pure on its face, changes in the legal and technological context mean
the rule is distorted almost beyond recognition when literally applied.

In evaluating the reasonableness of police procedures under the
fourth amendment, we have also looked to prevailing rules in individual jurisdictions. The rules in the states are varied. Some 19 states
have codified the common-law rule, though in two of these the courts
have significantly limited the statute. Four states, though without a
relevant statute, apparently retain the common-law rule. Two states
have adopted the Model Penal Code's provision verbatim. Eighteen
others allow, in slightly varying language, the use of deadly force only
if the suspect has committed a felony involving the use or threat of
physical or deadly force, or is escaping with a deadly weapon, or is
likely to endanger life or inflict serious physical injury if not arrested.
Louisiana and Vermont, though without statutes or case law on point,
do forbid the use of deadly force to prevent any but violent felonies.
The remaining states either have no relevant statute or case-law or
have positions that are unclear.

It cannot be said that there is a constant or overwhelming trend
away from the common-law rule. In recent years, some states have
reviewed their laws and expressly rejected abandonment of the common-law rule. Nonetheless, the long-term movement has been away
from the rule that deadly force may be used against any fleeing felon,
and that remains the rule in less than half the states.

This trend is more evident and impressive when viewed in light of
the policies adopted by the police departments themselves. Overwhelmingly, these are more restrictive than the common-law rule.
. . . Overall, only 7.5% of departmental and municipal policies

explicitly permit the use of deadly force against any felon; 86.8% explicitly do not. . . .

Actual departmental policies are important for an additional reason. We would hesitate to declare a police practice of long standing "unreasonable" if doing so would severely hamper effective law enforcement. But the indications are to the contrary. There has been no suggestion that crime has worsened in any way in jurisdictions that have adopted, by legislation or departmental policy, rules similar to that announced today. . . .

Nor do we agree with [defendants] that the rule we have adopted requires the police to make impossible, split-second evaluations of unknowable facts. We do not deny the practical difficulties of attempting to assess the suspect's dangerousness. However, similarly difficult judgments must be made by the police in equally uncertain circumstances. Nor is there any indication that in states that allow the use of deadly force only against dangerous suspects, the standard has been difficult to apply or has led to a rash of litigation involving inappropriate second-guessing of police officers' split-second decisions. Moreover, the highly technical felony/misdemeanor distinction is equally, if not more, difficult to apply in the field. An officer is in no position to know, for example, the precise value of property stolen, or whether the crime was a first or second offense. Finally, as noted above, this claim must be viewed with suspicion in light of the similar self-imposed limitations of so many police departments.

IV

. . . The dissent argues that the shooting was justified by the fact that Officer Hymon had probable cause to believe that Garner had committed a nighttime burglary. While we agree that burglary is a serious crime, we cannot agree that it is so dangerous as automatically to justify the use of deadly force. The FBI classifies burglary as a "property" rather than a "violent" crime. Although the armed burglar would present a different situation, the fact that an unarmed suspect has broken into a dwelling at night does not automatically mean he is physically dangerous. This case demonstrates as much. In fact, the available statistics demonstrate that burglaries only rarely involve physical violence. During the 10-year period from 1973–1982, only 3.8% of all burglaries involved violent crime. Bureau of Justice Statistics, Household Burglary, p. 4 (1985).[23]

[23] The dissent points out that three-fifths of all rapes in the home, three-fifths of all home robberies, and about a third of home assaults are committed by burglars. These figures mean only that if one knows that a suspect committed a rape in the home, there is a good chance that the suspect is also a burglar. That has nothing to do with the question here, which is whether the fact that someone has committed a burglary indicates that he has committed, or might commit, a violent crime.

The dissent also points out that this 3.8% adds up to 2.8 million violent crimes over a 10-year period, as if to imply that today's holding will let loose 2.8 million violent burglars. The relevant universe is, of course, far smaller. At issue is only that tiny fraction of cases where violence has taken place and an officer who has no other means of apprehending the suspect is unaware of its occurrence.

V

. . . We hold that the statute is invalid insofar as it purported to give Hymon the authority to act as he did. . . . The judgment of the Court of Appeals is affirmed, and the case is remanded for further proceedings consistent with this opinion.

JUSTICE O'CONNOR, with whom THE CHIEF JUSTICE and JUSTICE REHNQUIST join, dissenting. . . .

Although the circumstances of this case are unquestionably tragic and unfortunate, our constitutional holdings must be sensitive both to the history of the fourth amendment and to the general implications of the Court's reasoning. By disregarding the serious and dangerous nature of residential burglaries and the longstanding practice of many states, the Court effectively creates a fourth amendment right allowing a burglary suspect to flee unimpeded from a police officer who has probable cause to arrest, who has ordered the suspect to halt, and who has no means short of firing his weapon to prevent escape. I do not believe that the fourth amendment supports such a right, and I accordingly dissent.

I

. . . The precise issue before the Court deserves emphasis, because both the decision below and the majority obscure what must be decided in this case. The issue is not the constitutional validity of the Tennessee statute on its face or as applied to some hypothetical set of facts. Instead, the issue is whether the use of deadly force by Officer Hymon under the circumstances of this case violated Garner's constitutional rights. . . . The question we must address is whether the Constitution allows the use of such force to apprehend a suspect who resists arrest by attempting to flee the scene of a nighttime burglary of a residence.

II

For purposes of fourth amendment analysis, I agree with the Court that Officer Hymon "seized" Garner by shooting him. Whether that seizure was reasonable and therefore permitted by the fourth amendment requires a careful balancing of the important public interest in crime prevention and detection and the nature and quality of the intrusion upon legitimate interests of the individual. . . .

The public interest involved in the use of deadly force as a last resort to apprehend a fleeing burglary suspect relates primarily to the serious nature of the crime. Household burglaries represent not only the illegal entry into a person's home, but also "pos[e] real risk of serious harm to others." Solem v. Helm, 463 U.S. 277, 315–316 (1983) (Burger, C.J., dissenting). According to recent Department of Justice statistics, "[t]hree-fifths of all rapes in the home, three-fifths of all home robberies, and about a third of home aggravated and simple assaults are committed by burglars." Bureau of Justice Statistics

Bulletin, Household Burglary 1 (January 1985). During the period 1973–1982, 2.8 million such violent crimes were committed in the course of burglaries. Victims of a forcible intrusion into their home by a nighttime prowler will find little consolation in the majority's confident assertion that "burglaries only rarely involve physical violence." Moreover, even if a particular burglary, when viewed in retrospect, does not involve physical harm to others, the "harsh potentialities for violence" inherent in the forced entry into a home preclude characterization of the crime as "innocuous, inconsequential, minor, or 'nonviolent.' " Solem v. Helm, supra, at 316 (Burger, C.J., dissenting).

Because burglary is a serious and dangerous felony, the public interest in the prevention and detection of the crime is of compelling importance. Where a police officer has probable cause to arrest a suspected burglar, the use of deadly force as a last resort might well be the only means of apprehending the suspect. With respect to a particular burglary, subsequent investigation simply cannot represent a substitute for immediate apprehension of the criminal suspect at the scene. Indeed, the captain of the Memphis police department testified that in his city, if apprehension is not immediate, it is likely that the suspect will not be caught. Although some law enforcement agencies may choose to assume the risk that a criminal will remain at large, the Tennessee statute reflects a legislative determination that the use of deadly force in prescribed circumstances will serve generally to protect the public. Such statutes assist the police in apprehending suspected perpetrators of serious crimes and provide notice that a lawful police order to stop and submit to arrest may not be ignored with impunity.

The Court unconvincingly dismisses the general deterrence effects by stating that "the presently available evidence does not support [the] thesis" that the threat of force discourages escape and that "there is a substantial basis for doubting that the use of such force is an essential attribute to the arrest power in all felony cases." There is no question that the effectiveness of police use of deadly force is arguable and that many states or individual police departments have decided not to authorize it in circumstances similar to those presented here. But it should go without saying that the effectiveness or popularity of a particular police practice does not determine its constitutionality. Moreover, the fact that police conduct pursuant to a state statute is challenged on constitutional grounds does not impose a burden on the state to produce social science statistics or to dispel any possible doubts about the necessity of the conduct. This observation, I believe, has particular force where the challenged practice both predates enactment of the Bill of Rights and continues to be accepted by a substantial number of the states.

Against the strong public interests justifying the conduct at issue here must be weighed the individual interests implicated in the use of deadly force by police officers. The majority declares that "[t]he suspect's fundamental interest in his own life need not be elaborated upon." This blithe assertion hardly provides an adequate substitute for the majority's failure to acknowledge the distinctive manner in which the suspect's interest in his life is even exposed to risk. For purposes of this case, we must recall that the police officer, in the course of investigating a nighttime burglary, had reasonable cause to arrest the suspect and ordered him to halt. The officer's use of force resulted because the suspected burglar refused to heed this command and the officer reasonably believed that there was no means short of firing his weapon to apprehend the suspect. Without questioning the importance of a person's interest in his life, I do not think this interest encompasses a right to flee unimpeded from the scene of a burglary. The legitimate interests of the suspect in these circumstances are adequately accommodated by the Tennessee statute: to avoid the use of deadly force and the consequent risk to his life, the suspect need merely obey the valid order to halt.

A proper balancing of the interests involved suggests that use of deadly force as a last resort to apprehend a criminal suspect fleeing from the scene of a nighttime burglary is not unreasonable within the meaning of the fourth amendment. . . .

NOTES ON THE USE OF DEADLY FORCE

1. **Questions and Comments on *Garner*.** The issue in *Garner* has been controversial for many years. On one level, *Garner* resolves that controversy, for it is now a violation of the federal constitution for a state official to follow the common-law rule. Instead, state officials must follow a more restrictive approach such as that outlined in Model Penal Code § 3.07(2)(b).

What is your view on this question? Does the majority or the dissent have the better argument? Is it surprising that the issue is addressed as a question of fourth-amendment law? Are the considerations the Court identifies as relevant to the fourth-amendment inquiry different from those you would use to resolve the issue as a matter of policy? Is this a question you think the Court should resolve as a matter of constitutional law? Consider also the impact of the Court's constitutional ruling on the content of the criminal law. The Court did not suggest, nor is it likely that it would, that it is unconstitutional for a state to give a police officer in such a context a defense to a charge of assault or homicide. But does the Court's ruling suggest that states should formulate the law so that a police officer in such a context would be guilty of a crime? Would you recommend that your state do so?

2. **The Authority of Private Citizens.** Perhaps half of the states specifically authorize private citizens to make felony arrests under some circumstances. However, many states expressly prohibit citizens from employing deadly force to effect an arrest or to prevent an escape. The modern trend is reflected in Section 3.07(2)(b)(ii) of the Model Penal Code, which permits citizens to use deadly force only if they are assisting a police officer. In those jurisdictions that still permit citizens to employ deadly force to effect an arrest or to prevent an escape, it is

clear that this privilege is confined to cases involving "dangerous" felonies and many of these jurisdictions apparently recognize the defense only if the felony was actually committed.

Commonwealth v. Chermansky, 430 Pa. 170, 242 A.2d 237 (1968), illustrates the restricted scope of the common-law privilege in jurisdictions that have not abolished it altogether. Chermansky was charged with murder. His testimony was summarized by the court as follows:

> "Chermansky testified that, while sleeping in his home, he was awakened by a noise; that he found a set of double doors on the side of his house pushed in about eight inches and kept from opening completely by an attached chain; that, upon looking out a window, he saw an unknown individual come out of an alleyway adjacent to his home and proceed to a house across the street, where 'he started fixing around the windows'; that the individual then ran into an alleyway as an automobile came down the street; that shortly thereafter he saw this same individual '. . . monkeying around the windows' of another house across the street; that he sent his son out the back door of his home to notify the police; that he secured his rifle, opened the front door and went out on the doorstep, intending to restrain the prowler until the police arrived; that the prowler then started to run and he yelled 'Halt or I'll shoot'; that, when the prowler continued to run, he fired a shot in the direction of a tree, intending not to kill or injure the prowler, but only to frighten him. . . ."

After noting that the common-law rule permitting the use of deadly force by a private citizen to apprehend any escaping felon is "manifestly inadequate for modern law," the court stated the governing legal principles:

> ". . . We [hold that] the use of deadly force by a private person in order to prevent the escape of one who has committed a felony or has joined or assisted in the commission of a felony is justified only if the felony committed is treason, murder, voluntary manslaughter, mayhem, arson, robbery, common-law rape, common-law burglary, kidnapping, assault with intent to murder, rape or rob, or a felony which normally causes or threatens death or great bodily harm. We also note that for the use of deadly force to be justified it remains absolutely essential, as before, that one of the enumerated felonies has been committed and that the person against whom the force is used is the one who committed it or joined or assisted in committing it. . . .
> If the private citizen acts on suspicion that such a felony has been committed, he acts at his own peril. For the homicide to be justifiable, it must be established that his suspicion was correct."

The court affirmed Chermansky's conviction on the ground that the jury had been properly instructed and could have found that Chermansky had failed to show that the victim in fact had committed one of the enumerated felonies.

In light of the issues raised in *Garner* regarding use of deadly force by the police, what criteria ought to govern use of deadly force by private citizens to apprehend fleeing felons? Is it socially desirable for private citizens to use deadly force to apprehend persons suspected of committing serious crimes? Even if this be regarded as undesirable, and hence unjustified, does it follow that penal liability should be imposed in such cases?

PROBLEM BASED ON UNITED STATES v. EHRLICHMAN

United States Court of Appeals for the District of Columbia Circuit, 1976.
546 F.2d 910.

[This problem and the following one are based on the facts of a prosecution associated with the Watergate scandal. In the actual case, John Ehrlichman was convicted of conspiring to violate the civil rights of Dr. Louis J. Fielding in violation of Section 241 of Title 18 of the United States Code. However, it will simplify the issues without changing the basic problem presented by the case if you assume instead that Ehrlichman was convicted, as in fact he might have been, of conspiracy to commit burglary.[a]

[The material reproduced below is excerpted from the unanimous decision affirming Ehrlichman's conviction. It has been modified only to take into account the assumption just made regarding the offense charged.]

WILKEY, CIRCUIT JUDGE. . . . The publication of the "Pentagon Papers" in the summer of 1971 spurred the President to form a "Special Investigations" or "Room 16" unit within the White House, whose purpose was to investigate the theft of the Pentagon Papers and prevent other such security leaks. Defendant Ehrlichman, who was the Assistant to the President for Domestic Affairs, exercised general supervision over the unit; Egil Krogh and David Young were charged with its operation. At the time, Krogh was an assistant to Ehrlichman; Young worked with the National Security Council. They sought, and received, Ehrlichman's approval to add G. Gordon Liddy, a former F.B.I. agent, and E. Howard Hunt, a former C.I.A. agent, to the unit.

. . . The unit's principal enterprise seemed to be the acquisition of all files and source material on Daniel Ellsberg. There was a generalized concern over his motives for releasing classified materials (the Pentagon Papers). Young and Krogh instructed the CIA to do a psychological profile on Ellsberg. Since Dr. Fielding had refused an interview by the FBI on the ground of doctor/patient confidentiality, Hunt suggested examining Dr. Fielding's file on Ellsberg, and further suggested a "black bag job" (surreptitious entry) while noting that the FBI no longer engaged in such activities. When Young reviewed the

---

[a] Assume that the offenses are defined as they are in Sections 5.03 and 221.1 of the Model Penal Code. Assume further that the unauthorized copying of confidential patient information from a psychiatrist's file is a criminal offense.

psychological assessment on Ellsberg prepared by the CIA, he determined that it was superficial, and recommended that a "covert operation be undertaken to examine all the medical files held by Ellsberg's psychoanalyst." The exhibit reflects Ehrlichman's approval of the recommendation with his addition: "Provided that it is not traceable back to the White House."

The members of the unit were clear that the "covert operation" in question would be a surreptitious entry into Dr. Fielding's office. Ehrlichman's primary defense at trial, however, was that he was not apprised of, and thus did not authorize, such an entry. He testified that he thought he had approved only a conventional private investigation, involving no surreptitious search of Dr. Fielding's office. Considerable evidence was introduced on both sides of the question. The jury's guilty verdict . . . reflected a finding that Ehrlichman had in fact authorized the search.

Krogh and Young insisted that no one employed by the White House was to effect the actual entry into Fielding's office. Hunt traveled to Miami in mid-August 1971 to enlist the assistance of Bernard Barker, who had worked under Hunt during the Bay of Pigs operation. Hunt was widely known and respected in Miami's Cuban-American community as a government agent who had been a leader in the fight to liberate Cuba. He did not identify the object of the search, but told Barker only that the operation involved a traitor who had been passing information to the Soviet Embassy. On the basis of this information Barker recruited two men, Eugenio Martinez and Felipe de Diego, for the operation.

Hunt and Liddy met Barker, Martinez, and de Diego in Los Angeles on 2 September 1971. The Miamians were informed their mission was to enter Dr. Fielding's office, that Dr. Fielding was not himself the subject of the investigation, but that they were to photograph the file of one of his patients (they were not told Ellsberg's name until minutes before the break-in) and return the file to its place. On 3 September Barker and de Diego, dressed as deliverymen, delivered a valise containing photographic equipment to Dr. Fielding's office, enabling them at the same time to unlock the door to facilitate subsequent entry. Later that evening they and Martinez, contrary to expectations, found both the building and Dr. Fielding's office locked. The Miamians forced their way into the building, broke the lock on the office door, and used a crowbar on Dr. Fielding's file cabinets. As instructed if this became necessary, they spilled pills and materials about the office to make it appear that the break-in was the work of a drug addict. Throughout the operation surgical gloves were used to avoid fingerprint detection. In spite of all efforts, Ellsberg's records eluded them.

After relating the details of the entry and their lack of success to Hunt, Barker, Martinez, and de Diego returned to Miami. Hunt and Liddy returned to Washington, where they reported the failure of the operation to Krogh and Young. Krogh relayed that information to Ehrlichman.

White House involvement in the break-in remained unknown for almost two years. When the facts about the operation began to surface, however, on 14 March 1973 Ehrlichman was called before the grand jury to testify about his knowledge of the affair. He stated that he had not been aware prior to the break-in that the Room 16 unit was looking for information with which to compose a psychological profile of Ellsberg, and had had no advance knowledge that an effort was to be made to get such information from Dr. Fielding. One year later he was indicted, subsequently tried and convicted, for his role in authorizing the break-in and for his efforts to conceal his involvement by lying to the grand jury.

[Ehrlichman challenged his conspiracy conviction on two grounds. First, he claimed that the break-in was justified because it was undertaken pursuant to the president's constitutional prerogative to authorize such a search, for national-security reasons, without first obtaining a judicial warrant. Thus, since the burglary itself was justified, he could not be guilty of conspiracy to commit it. Second, he claimed that even if the warrantless search was unconstitutional—and the burglary was therefore unjustified—his reasonable belief to the contrary should excuse him from criminal liability.

[The question of actual authority requires an interpretation of the fourth amendment.[b] According to settled construction, this constitutional provision bars warrantless searches of private property "except in certain carefully defined classes of cases." Camara v. Municipal Court, 387 U.S. 523 (1967). Ehrlichman sought to rely on a so-called "national-security" exception to the warrant requirement. The court rejected his claim as follows:]

Ehrlichman claimed that the . . . entry was undertaken pursuant to an authorized "foreign-affairs" or "national-security" operation. Since 1940 the "foreign-affairs" exception to the prohibition against wiretapping has been espoused by the executive branch as a necessary concomitant to the president's constitutional power over the exercise of this country's foreign affairs, and warrantless electronic surveillance has been upheld by lower federal courts on a number of occasions. No court has ruled that the president does not have this prerogative in a case involving foreign agents or collaborators with a foreign power. The Supreme Court, in a number of decisions requiring officials to obtain a warrant before engaging in electronic surveillance, has been careful to note that its rulings do not reach such cases.

Hoping to fall within this as yet not fully defined exception, Ehrlichman urges that in September 1971 "in a matter affecting national security and foreign-intelligence gathering" the absence of a judicially approved warrant did not render unlawful "a search and seizure authorized by a presidential delegate pursuant to a broad presidential mandate of power given to that delegate."

[b] The fourth amendment provides that "the right of the people to be secure in their persons, houses, papers, and effects, against unreasonable searches and seizures, shall not be violated; and no warrants shall issue, but upon probable cause, supported by oath or affirmation, and particularly describing the place to be searched, and the persons or things to be seized."

Ehrlichman further argues [in his brief] that no specific authorization by the president or the attorney general was required:

"Implicitly, an instruction to accomplish an end carries with it the duty of performing all lawful acts necessary to accomplish that end. In the instant case, the president delegated the power, to sworn officials of the executive branch, including Ehrlichman, to prevent and halt leaks of vital security information. To contend that the president must specifically chart out the methods of employing the power each and every time he delegates power is absurd."

The district court ruled as a matter of law that the national security exemption did not excuse the failure to obtain a judicial warrant for a physical search of Dr. Fielding's office either because there is no exemption for physical searches or because the exemption can only be invoked by the president or the attorney general in a particular case.

. . .

[Whether or not the national-security exemption extends beyond wiretapping to physical searches,] the district court was unquestionably correct in its ruling that in any event the "national-security" exemption can only be invoked if there has been a specific authorization by the president, or by the attorney general as his chief legal advisor, for the particular case.

Neither Ehrlichman nor any of his co-defendants [has] alleged that the attorney general gave his approval to the Fielding operation; and none has attempted to refute former President Nixon's assertion that he had no prior knowledge of the break-in and, therefore, could not and did not authorize the search.[66] . . . No court has ever in any way indicated, nor has any presidential administration or attorney general claimed, that any executive officer acting under an inexplicit presidential mandate may authorize warrantless searches of foreign agents or collaborators, much less the warrantless search of the offices of an American citizen not himself suspected of collaboration. . . .

As a constitutional matter, if presidential approval is to replace judicial approval for foreign intelligence gathering, the personal authorization of the President—or his alter ego for these matters, the attorney general—is necessary to fix accountability and centralize responsibility for insuring the least intrusive surveillance necessary and preventing zealous officials from misusing the presidential prerogative.

[The court then concluded that "under the circumstances of this case, the law is clear" that the warrantless burglary of Dr. Fielding's office exceeded Ehrlichman's constitutional authority and was therefore unjustified. The court then considered Ehrlichman's contention

[66] Indeed, for Ehrlichman to argue that the President gave his express authorization to a surreptitious entry and search of Dr. Fielding's office would have been patently inconsistent with Ehrlichman's primary defense at trial. Such authorization would have been transmitted to the "Room 16" unit through Ehrlichman, and he claimed not to have known the unit planned a surreptitious entry and search. The trial judge, however, put the question of Ehrlichman's prior knowledge of the break-in squarely to the jury and they found him guilty as charged.

that his reasonable belief in the legality of the search of Dr. Fielding's office should defeat criminal liability. Noting that mistake of law is generally no excuse, the court found "no support for Ehrlichman's position in any of the recognized common-law exceptions to the mistake-of-law doctrine." In particular, the court observed, "Ehrlichman cannot and does not argue that he should be allowed a defense based upon his reasonable reliance on an apparently valid statute or judicial decision. . . ." Nor, the court concluded, was he relying on a misleading assertion of authority by the president or the attorney general, even if that would establish an excuse. "He simply asserts that it was his belief that the break-in was lawful notwithstanding the absence of any such specific defense."]

For the foregoing reasons, the district-court judgment is

Affirmed.

NOTES ON MISTAKES BY PUBLIC OFFICIALS REGARDING THEIR OWN AUTHORITY

1. ***Ehrlichman* and Ignorantia Juris.** A mistake regarding the justifiability of otherwise criminal conduct ordinarily comes within the traditional principle of ignorantia juris. Applying this principle, the *Ehrlichman* court concluded that the defendant's mistake regarding the scope of his constitutional authority, however reasonable, was without exculpatory significance. Was this a correct application of the ignorantia-juris principle? Ehrlichman's mistake concerned the meaning of the fourth amendment rather than the meaning of the conspiracy or burglary statutes. Is it clear that his mistake pertained, in the language of Section 2.02(9) of the Model Penal Code, to the "existence, meaning or application of the law determining the elements of an offense"?

2. **Special Rules for Official Mistakes of Law.** Many modern criminal codes expressly provide a defense, under some circumstances, for officials who exceed their authority. For example, Section 939.45 of the Wisconsin Penal Code affords a "defense of privilege . . . when the actor's conduct is in good faith and is an apparently authorized and reasonable fulfillment of any duties of a public office." Section 35.05 of the New York Penal Code, which has been the model for many other states, provides that "conduct which would otherwise constitute an offense is justifiable [if] such conduct is required or authorized by law or by a judicial decree or is performed by a public servant in the reasonable exercise of his official powers, duties or functions." Do these provisions differ in important respects? Would the evidence in *Ehrlichman* support a jury instruction under either statute? Would Ehrlichman have a defense under Section 3.03 of the Model Penal Code?

3. **The Debate on Official Mistake.** In 1973, the Judiciary Committee of the United States Senate considered two proposed federal criminal code bills. Each of the bills included an official mistake provision. One of the bills provided a defense if "the defendant

reasonably believed that the conduct charged was required or authorized by law . . . to carry out his duty as a public servant." Inclusion
of this provision was vigorously criticized by the American Civil Liberties Union and other witnesses on the ground that it would encourage
official abuses of power. One witness summarized the argument in the
following terms: [a]

"[I]f enacted, this section would seriously dilute the power of
the law to deal with criminal conduct on the part of federal
officers. The public-duty defense would permit federal officials
to use their position of public trust to defend against criminal
prosecutions brought against them for violating that trust.
Rather than focusing on the legality of specific actions, rather
than considering whether those actions were in fact called for by
the individual's public duty, this section would focus the court's
attention on whether the official reasonably believed his conduct
was legal. If an official simply convinces a jury that he reasonably believed his actions were authorized or required by law, his
crime would be excused. . . .

"Whenever a federal official believes he can convince a jury
that his conduct, though perhaps unlawful in retrospect, was
guided by honest and praiseworthy motives and therefore reasonable, he will not be deterred from engaging in that conduct. The
public servant is thereby given a free rein in the shadowy no-
man's land of activities which are on the borderline of illegality.
Rather than steering clear of the legally dubious, the public
servant can chart a course significantly nearer criminal conduct
with the assurance that his only burden is to persuade a jury
that it was a gray area, that the lawfulness of his conduct was in
his eyes, unclear, and that he was motivated by a sense of public
duty rather than criminal malice. . . ."

Proponents of such a provision claim that a general mistake defense
is necessary to take into account the uncertain scope of many official
duties and obligations. It is said that "public officials . . . who act
in accordance with a reasonable belief that their actions are lawful
should not be treated as criminals and cannot be so treated if we expect
our laws to be enforced with the vigor required for successful implementation." [b] One opponent responded to these contentions as
follows: [c]

"[T]he public servant should not be protected from legal
consequences of acts which are in the twilight zone of legality.
Because the public servant exercises individual discretion, because he can always refuse or resign, because he carries with his
office substantial social responsibility and public trust, because

[a] Reform of the Federal Criminal Laws,
Hearings on S. 1 and S. 1400 before the
Subcommittee on Criminal Laws and Pro-
cedures of the Committee on the Judiciary,
United States Senate, 94th Cong., 1st Sess.,
Part XI, 8018–19 (Statement of Gregory
Craig) (1974).

[b] Id. at 8053 (Statement of John C. Ken-
ney).

[c] Id. at 8020 (Statement of Gregory
Craig).

the public servant invokes all the might and majesty of the state when he acts, the public servant should, at the very least, be held to the same standard of conduct applied to the ordinary citizen. One would hope, if anything, that a higher standard would be expected in the conduct of a public official."

Which is the better position? Should public officials such as Ehrlichman be acquitted if they persuade a jury that they "reasonably believed" that their criminal conduct was authorized by law? Would recognition of such a defense encourage abuse of official authority? Alternatively, do you think application of the ignorantia-juris principle in this context would make public officials unduly timid? Even apart from the impact of the alternative approaches on official behavior, do you think a public servant's "good motives" should be irrelevant to the question of penal liability?

PROBLEM BASED ON UNITED STATES v. BARKER
United States Court of Appeals for the District of Columbia Circuit, 1976.
546 F.2d 940.

WILKEY, CIRCUIT JUDGE. Two of the "footsoldiers" of the Watergate affair, Bernard Barker and Eugenio Martinez, are with us again.[a] They haven't been promoted, they are still footsoldiers. They come before us this time to challenge their convictions . . . for their parts in the 1971 burglary of the office of Dr. Lewis J. Fielding.

[As in *United States* v. *Ehrlichman,* supra, the defendants were convicted under 18 U.S.C. § 241 of conspiracy to violate Dr. Fielding's civil rights. You should assume, however, that they were convicted of burglary as defined in Section 221.1 of the Model Penal Code. After describing the circumstances surrounding the creation of the "Room 16" unit, detailed in *United States* v. *Ehrlichman,* supra, Judge Wilkey summarized the evidence concerning the recruitment of Barker and Martinez by Howard Hunt:]

Hunt had been a career agent in the CIA before his employment by the White House. One of his assignments was as a supervising agent for the CIA in connection with the Bay of Pigs invasion, and as "Eduardo," he was well known and respected in Miami's Cuban-American community. A fact destined to be of considerable importance later, he had been Bernard Barker's immediate supervisor in that operation. When the "Room 16" unit determined that it would be best if the actual entry into Dr. Fielding's office were made by individuals not in the employ of the White House, Hunt recommended enlisting the assistance of some of his former associates in Miami.

Hunt had previously re-established contact with Barker in Miami in late April 1971, and he met Martinez at the same time. He gave Barker an unlisted White House number where he could be reached by

a Judge Wilkey was referring to the efforts of Barker and Martinez to withdraw their guilty pleas in the case involving the burglary of the Democratic National Committee headquarters in the Watergate Office Building. [Footnote by eds.]

phone and wrote to Barker on White House stationery. On one occasion Barker met with Hunt in the Executive Office Building. By August 1971 Hunt returned to Miami and informed Barker that he was working for an organization at the White House level with greater jurisdiction than the FBI and the CIA. He asked Barker if he would become "operational" again and help conduct a surreptitious entry to obtain national-security information on "a traitor to this country who was passing . . . classified information to the Soviet Embassy." He stated further that "the man in question . . . was being considered as a possible Soviet agent himself."

Barker agreed to take part in the operation and to recruit two additional people. He contacted Martinez and Felipe de Diego. Barker conveyed to Martinez the same information Hunt had given him, and Martinez agreed to participate. Like Barker, Martinez had begun working as a covert agent for the CIA after Castro came to power in Cuba. Although Barker's formal relationship with the CIA had ended in 1966, Martinez was still on CIA retainer when he was contacted.

Both testified at trial that they had no reason to question Hunt's credentials. He clearly worked for the White House and had a well known background with the CIA. During the entire time they worked for the CIA, neither Barker nor Martinez was ever shown any credentials by their superiors. Not once did they receive written instructions to engage in the operations they were ordered to perform. Nevertheless, they testified, their understanding was always that those operations had been authorized by the government of the United States. That they did not receive more detail on the purpose of the Fielding operation or its target was not surprising to them; Hunt's instructions and actions were in complete accord with what their previous experience had taught them to expect. They were trained agents, accustomed to rely on the discretion of their superiors and to operate entirely on a "need-to-know" basis.

On 2 September 1971 Hunt and Liddy met Barker, Martinez and de Diego at a hotel in Beverly Hills, California. Hunt informed the defendants that they were to enter an office, search for a particular file, photograph it, and replace it. The following day the group met again. Hunt showed Barker and Martinez identification papers and disguises he had obtained from the CIA. That evening the defendants entered Dr. Fielding's office. Contrary to plan, it was necessary for them to use force to effect the break-in. As instructed in this event, the defendants spilled pills on the floor to make it appear the break-in had been a search for drugs. No file with the name Ellsberg was found.

The next day Barker and Martinez returned to Miami. The only funds they received from Hunt in connection with the entry of Dr. Fielding's office were reimbursement for their living expenses, the costs of travel, and $100.00 for lost income. . . .

[At their trial, the district court refused proffered jury instructions setting forth the defendants' theory of the case—that they should be found not guilty if they reasonably relied on Hunt's apparent authority.

Instead the court specifically instructed the jury that a mistake as to the legality of the operation was *not* a defense.]

The primary ground upon which defendants Barker and Martinez rest their appeal is the refusal of the district court to allow them a defense based upon their good faith, reasonable reliance on Hunt's apparent authority.

. . . A defendant's error as to his *authority* to engage in particular activity, if based upon a mistaken view of legal requirements (or ignorance thereof), is a mistake of *law*. Typically, the fact that he relied upon the erroneous advice of another is not an exculpatory circumstance.

[A]lthough the basic policy behind the mistake-of-law doctrine is that, at their peril, all men should know and obey the law, in certain situations there is an overriding societal interest in having individuals rely on the authoritative pronouncements of officials whose decisions we wish to see respected.

For this reason, a number of exceptions to the mistake-of-law doctrine have developed where its application would be peculiarly unjust or counterproductive. Their recognition in a particular case should give the defendant a defense [if his mistake] is *objectively reasonable* under the circumstances. The mistake of a government agent in relying on a magistrate's approval of a search can be considered virtually per se reasonable. . . . Similarly, if a private person is summoned by a police officer to assist in effecting an unlawful arrest, his reliance on the officer's authority to make the arrest may be considered reasonable as a matter of law. The citizen is under a legal obligation to respond to a proper summons and is in no position to second-guess the officer's determination that an arrest is proper. Indeed, it is society's hope in recognizing the reasonableness of a citizen's mistake in this situation to encourage unhesitating compliance with a police officer's call.[25]

Other situations in which a government official enlists the aid of a private citizen to help him perform a governmental task are not so obviously reasonable on their face. If the official does not *order* the citizen to assist him, but simply asks for such assistance, the citizen is not under a legal compulsion to comply. Also, if the circumstances do not require immediate action, the citizen may have time to question the lawfulness of the planned endeavor. Nevertheless, the public policy of encouraging citizens to respond ungrudgingly to the request of officials for help in the performance of their duties remains quite strong. Moreover, the gap (both real and perceived) between a private citizen and a government official with regard to their ability and authority to judge the lawfulness of a particular governmental activity is great. It would appear to serve both justice and public policy in a situation where an individual acted at the behest of a government official to allow the individual a defense based upon his reliance on the official's

[25] This common-law exception to the mistake-of-law doctrine is codified in Section 3.07(4)(a) of the Model Penal Code. . . .

authority—*if* he can show that his reliance was *objectively reasonable* under the particular circumstances of his case.

. . . I think it plain that a citizen should have a legal defense to a criminal charge arising out of an unlawful arrest or search which he has aided in the reasonable belief that the individual who solicited his assistance was a duly authorized officer of the law. It was error for the trial court to bar this defense in the admission of evidence and instructions to the jury, and the convictions must accordingly be

Reversed.

LEVENTHAL, CIRCUIT JUDGE (dissenting). . . . This [case] calls, I think, for an opening exclamation of puzzlement and wonder. Is this judicial novelty, a bold injection of mistake of law as a valid defense to criminal liability, really being wrought in a case where defendants are charged with combining to violate civil and constitutional rights? Can this extension be justified where there was a deliberate forcible entry, indeed a burglary, into the office of a doctor who was in no way suspected of any illegality or even impropriety, with the force compounded by subterfuge, dark of night, and the derring-do of "salting" the office with nuggets to create suspicion that the deed was done by addicts looking for narcotics?

Judge Wilkey begins to cast his spell by describing Barker and Martinez as "footsoldiers" here in court again. Of course, they are here this time for an offense that took place the year before the notorious 1972 Watergate entry that led them to enter pleas of guilty to burglary. Every violation of civil rights depends not only on those who initiate, often unhappily with an official orientation of sorts, but also on those whose active effort is necessary to bring the project to fruition. To the extent appellants are deemed worthy of sympathy, that has been provided by the probation. To give them not only sympathy but exoneration, and absolution, is to stand the law upside down, in my view, and to sack legal principle instead of relying on the elements of humane administration that are available to buffer any grinding edge of law. That this tolerance of unlawful official action is a defense available for selective undermining of civil-rights laws leads me to shake my head both in wonder and despair. . . .

I do not discount defendants' claims that their background, and particularly their previous relations with the CIA and Hunt explain their good-faith reliance on Hunt's apparent authority and their consequent failure to inquire about the legality of the activities they were to undertake on his request. I feel compassion for men who were simultaneously offenders and victims, and so did the trial judge when it came to sentencing. But testing their special circumstances against analogies they rely on to project a mistake-of-law defense, leads me to reject their claim to be relieved of personal accountability for their acts.

Appellants invoke the acceptance of good-faith reliance defenses in the Model Penal Code. However, the American Law Institute carefully limited the sections cited to persons responding to a call for aid from a police officer making an unlawful arrest,[34] and to obeying unlawful military orders,[35] and specifically rejected the defense for other mistake-of-law contexts.[36] In both instances, the A.L.I. recognizes limited curtailment of the doctrine excluding a mistake-of-law defense on the ground that the actor is under a duty to act—to help a police officer in distress to make an arrest when called upon, or to obey military orders. In each case, society has no alternative means available to protect its interest short of imposing a duty to act without a correlative duty to inquire about the legality of the act.[38] Punishing an individual for failure to inquire as to the lawful basis for the officer's request would frustrate the effective functioning of the duly constituted police (and military) forces and in its operation on the individual would compel a choice between the whirlpool and the rock. . . .

Barker and Martinez were under no tension of conflicting duties comparable to that experienced by a soldier or citizen responding to orders. They had and claim no obligation to aid Hunt. Nor did they have a belief of fact rendering their voluntary assistance lawful within Section 3.07(4). . . . Nor is there a compelling social interest to be served in allowing private citizens to undertake extra-legal activities, acting simply on the word of a government official. The purposes of the law in rejecting such a defense are underscored by the very kinds of extra-governmental, outside-normal-channels conduct that Barker and Martinez engaged in here. Government officials who claim to be seeking to implement the ends of government by bypassing the agencies and personnel normally responsible and accountable to the public transmit a danger signal. Barker and Martinez acted to help Hunt on his explanation that he sought their recruitment because the FBI's "hands were tied by Supreme Court decisions and the Central Intelligence Agency didn't have jurisdiction in certain matters." There is reason for the law to carve out limited exceptions to the doctrine negating defenses rooted in mistake of law, but the pertinent reasons have minimal weight, and face countervailing policies, when they are invoked for situations that on their face are outside the basic channels of law and government—in this case, requests for surreptitious or, if necessary, forcible entry and clandestine files search. These are plainly crimes, malum in se, unless there is legal authority. Citizens may take action in such circumstances out of emotions and motives that they deem lofty, but they must take the risk that their trust was misplaced, and that they will have no absolution when there was no authority for the request and their response. If they are later to avoid

---

[34] See, e.g., Model Penal Code § 3.07(4). . . .

[35] See Model Penal Code § 2.10. . . .

[36] When Section 3.07(4) does not specifically apply, Section 3.09(1) withdraws any justification defense to the use of improper force where the actor's "error is due to ignorance or mistake as to the provisions of the Code, any other provision of the criminal law or the law governing the legality of an arrest or search." The commentary explained that provision as dealing with a "body of law [which] is not stated in the Code and may not appear in the form of penal law at all. It seems clear, however, that the policy which holds mistake of penal law to be immaterial applies with no less force to the law of arrest or search." . . .

[38] A similar rationale underlies the exception for reliance on government authority when acting under a public duty. See Model Penal Code § 3.03.

the consequences of criminal responsibility, it must be as a matter of discretion. To make the defense a matter of right would enhance the resources available to individual officials bent on extra-legal government behavior. The purpose of the criminal law is to serve and not to distort the fundamental values of the society. . . .

The ultimate point is that appellants' mistake of law, whether or not it is classified as reasonable, does not negative legal responsibility, but at best provides a reason for clemency on the ground that the strict rules of law bind too tight for the overall public good. . . .

But sympathy for defendants, or the possibility that their mistake might be considered "reasonable" given their unique circumstances, must not override a pragmatic view of what the law requires of persons taking this kind of action. I come back—again and again, in my mind—to the stark fact that we are dealing with a breaking and entering in the dead of night, both surreptitious and forcible, and a violation of civil-rights statutes. This is simply light years away from the kinds of situations where the law has gingerly carved out exceptions permitting reasonable mistake of law as a defense—cases like entering a business transaction on the erroneous advice of a high responsible official or district attorney, or like responding to an urgent call for aid from a police officer. I dissent.

NOTES ON CITIZEN RELIANCE ON APPARENT OFFICIAL AUTHORITY

1. **Introduction.** Barker and Martinez did not claim that they believed that the search of Dr. Fielding's office had been authorized by a magistrate pursuant to normal procedures for obtaining a warrant. Nor did they claim that they had been misled into believing that the president or the attorney general had personally authorized the break-in. Instead, they testified that they believed that some White House official—Hunt, Krogh or, at best, Ehrlichman—had authorized it. Their mistake was in assuming that this constituted lawful authority; and, as Judges Wilkey and Leventhal seem to agree, this is a mistake of law regarding the justifiability of the defendants' conduct. The question is whether, and under what circumstances, a citizen's otherwise criminal conduct should be excused because he or she acted at the request or direction of a public official who exceeded his or her authority. Should a mistake regarding the lawfulness of the request or direction exculpate the citizen even though it would be insufficient to exculpate the public official?

2. **Compliance With Official Orders or Requests.** In ordinary social relationships there is no overriding societal interest in reflexive obedience to, and respect for, authority. Thus, suppose *A* orders a business subordinate, *B*, to do an illegal act. If *B* subsequently claims that she did not know it was illegal, the mistake is no defense; or if *B* subsequently claims she had no choice but to comply because she was pressured, afraid, or fearful of losing her job, her fear of the conse-

quences will be ignored. The subordinate is expected to retain the capacity for free and independent judgment.

In some situations, however, there is a societal interest in unquestioning obedience. This is most obviously true in the military setting, and the common law has long recognized a defense for soldiers who obey superior orders, so long as they are not "palpably illegal." [a] Section 2.10 of the Model Penal Code codifies this defense. (It should be emphasized that the "superior-orders" defense has not been applied outside the military context.) Common-law precedents also afford a defense to citizens who assist the police to make arrests that turn out to be unlawful. [b] This rule is codified in § 3.07(4)(a) of the Model Penal Code and appears in most modern statutes.

The relationship between Hunt and the Cuban defendants resembles the relationship between police officers and ordinary citizens. Judge Wilkey concluded that the similarity was close enough to warrant a defense for reasonable reliance on Hunt's apparent authority. Judge Leventhal disagreed. Who is right? Do you favor a defense for citizens who assist public officials in reasonable reliance on their apparent authority? Would this depend on whether you favor a similar defense for the public official who exceeds his or her authority? Would recognition of such a defense increase the likelihood of official abuse of power? On the other hand, is it just to punish a person who comes to the aid of a public official who appears to be acting within his or her authority?

Judge Leventhal points out that the *Barker* defendants invoked the "good-faith-reliance defenses" of the Model Penal Code. In response, he says that the defenses in the Code are "carefully limited . . . to persons responding to a call for aid from a police officer making an unlawful arrest and to obeying unlawful military orders." Is he right?

[a] See, e.g., United States v. Calley, 46 C.M.R. 1131, 1179–84 (1973); United States v. Kinder, 14 C.M.R. 742 (1954). In the *Calley* case, the defendant, a platoon leader, was convicted of three counts of murder arising out of a military operation in the Vietnamese hamlet of My Lai. During this operation, Calley directed and participated in the killing of approximately 70 unarmed villagers. He claimed, inter alia, that he did so in obedience to the orders of his superiors. The members of the court martial considered this claim under the following instruction, which was subsequently upheld by the Court of Military Review:

"A determination that an order is illegal does not, of itself, assign criminal responsibility to the person following the order for acts done in compliance with it. Soldiers are taught to follow orders, and special attention is given to obedience of orders on the battlefield. Military effectiveness depends upon obedience to others. On the other hand, the obedi-

ence of a soldier is not the obedience of an automaton. A soldier is a reasoning agent, obliged to respond, not as a machine, but as a person. The law takes these factors into account in assessing criminal responsibility for acts done in compliance with illegal orders.

"The acts of a subordinate done in compliance with an unlawful order given him by his superior are excused and impose no criminal liability upon him unless the superior's order is one which a man of ordinary sense and understanding would, under the circumstances, know to be unlawful, or if the order in question is actually known to the accused to be unlawful."

[b] Some statutes impose a duty on the citizen to aid a police officer under some circumstances; failure to obey would itself be a criminal offense. In these situations, the citizen has a public duty that justifies otherwise criminal conduct. See Model Penal Code § 3.03(1)(a).

Examine Section 3.03(3)(b) of the Model Code. Does Barker's claim raise a defense under this section? [c]

SECTION 2: SITUATIONAL EXCUSE

INTRODUCTORY NOTES ON THE DEFENSE OF DURESS

1. **Duress and Involuntariness.** The law has traditionally recognized a defense of duress where *A* commits a crime because *B* holds a gun to *A*'s head and forces *A* to do so. It is important to emphasize, however, that this defense has usually been restrictively defined. It is not, for example, normally available for intentionally killing another person. Moreover, the defendant typically bears the burden of proving the elements of the defense to the satisfaction of the jury.

The materials in this section explore the nature of the duress defense. It is important at the outset, however, to note the analytical distinction between the defense of duress and the "voluntary act" doctrine considered at pages 152–58, supra. It would do no violence to the English language to characterize as "involuntary" *A*'s act of committing a crime under duress. Indeed, *A*'s claim might appear, at first blush, to be functionally similar to the claim that could be raised by *A* if, with intent to injure *C, B* shoved *A* into *C,* thereby knocking *C* into the path of an oncoming car. However, the law draws a distinction between bodily movements that are within the conscious control of the actor and those that are not.

In 2 A History of the Criminal Law of England 102 (1883), Sir James Fitzjames Stephen described this distinction as follows:

> "A criminal walking to execution is under compulsion if any man can be said to be so, but his motions are just as much voluntary actions as if he [were] going to leave his place of confinement and regain his liberty. He walks to his death because he prefers it to being carried."

As a matter of legal definition, an act which the actor feels constrained to commit is regarded as "voluntary" for purposes of establishing that the actus reus of the offense has been committed. The involuntary-act doctrine covers cases where the actor makes no choice at all, not those where he or she is forced by circumstances to make a "hard choice."

The duress defense is the main device by which the law takes into account external constraints on a person's capacity to choose to comply with the law.[a] It must be emphasized, however, that the task of determining when a "hard choice" should have exculpatory significance

---

[c] For discussions of *Barker,* see Comment, United States v. Barker: Misapplication of the Reliance on an Official Interpretation of the Law Defense, 66 Calif.L.Rev. 809 (1978); Note, Reliance on Apparent Authority as a Defense to Criminal Prosecution, 77 Colum.L.Rev. 775 (1977).

[a] The impact of a person's abnormal mental condition on his or her capacity to conform to the law is explored in connec-

requires a judgment of degree. As Glanville Williams has noted, "[f]ear of violence does not differ in kind from fear of economic ills, fear of displeasing others, or any other determinant of choice." Criminal Law: The General Part 751 (2d ed. 1961). Under what circumstances should it be said that a person was "compelled" to commit a crime, that he or she could not have chosen to do otherwise? Stephen concluded that the law should never give exculpatory significance to hard choices, even those produced by threats of death. In a famous passage opposing the duress defense, 2 A History of the Criminal Law of England 107–08 (1883), Stephen argued as follows:

> "Criminal law is itself a system of compulsion on the widest scale. It is a collection of threats of injury to life, liberty, and property if people do commit crimes. Are such threats to be withdrawn as soon as they are encountered by opposing threats? The law says to a man intending to commit murder, if you do it I will hang you. Is the law to withdraw its threat if someone else says, if you do not do it, I will shoot you?
>
> "Surely it is at the moment when temptation to crime is strongest that the law should speak most clearly and emphatically to the contrary. It is, of course, a misfortune for a man that he should be placed between two fires, but it would be a much greater misfortune for society at large if criminals could confer impunity upon their agents by threatening them with death or violence if they refused to execute their commands. If impunity could be so secured a wide door would be opened to collusion, and encouragement would be given to associations of malefactors, secret or otherwise. No doubt the moral guilt of a person who commits a crime under compulsion is less than that of a person who commits it freely, but any effect which is thought proper may be given to this circumstance by a proportional mitigation of the offender's punishment.
>
> "These reasons lead me to think that compulsion by threats ought in no case whatever to be admitted as an excuse for crime, though it may and ought to operate in mitigation of punishment in most though not in all cases. . . ."

Professor Williams has observed that Stephen's view "would now be regarded as over-severe." In some cases, he continues, "justice demand[s] not merely a mitigation of punishment but no punishment at all. . . ." G. Williams, Criminal Law: The General Part 755 (2d ed. 1961). The drafters of the Model Penal Code responded to Stephen's argument as follows:

> "[L]aw is ineffective in the deepest sense, indeed . . . it is hypocritical, if it imposes on the actor who has the misfortune to confront a dilemmatic choice, a standard that his judges are not prepared to affirm that they should and could comply with if their turn to face the problem should arise. Condemnation in such a case is bound to be an ineffective threat; what is,

tion with the insanity defense at pages
686–720, infra.

however, more significant is that it is divorced from any moral base and is unjust. Where it would be both 'personally and socially debilitating' to accept the actor's cowardice as a defense, it would be equally debilitating to demand that heroism should be the standard of legality." [b]

2. **Elements of the Defense.** According to the traditional formulation, the duress defense is available if the defendant can show "a present, immediate and impending threat of such a nature as to induce a well founded fear of death or serious bodily injury if the criminal act is not done; the actor must have been so positioned as to have had no reasonable chance of escape." Commonwealth v. Robinson, 415 N.E.2d 805, 812 (Mass.1981). Thus, threats to destroy property or reputation do not suffice, although most courts have concluded that a threat to the life or safety of a loved one can exert as much coercive force as a threat to the actor's own life, and therefore can provide a basis for the defense.

The most frequently litigated aspect of duress is the requirement that the threat be present, immediate, and impending. An example is State v. Toscano, 74 N.J. 421, 378 A.2d 755 (1977). Dr. Toscano, a chiropractor, was convicted of conspiring with one William Leonardo and others to obtain money by false pretenses. Specifically, Toscano signed a false medical report for use by Leonardo in an insurance fraud scheme. Toscano claimed that he "just had to do it" in order to protect himself and his family from bodily harm threatened by Leonardo. Leonardo allegedly made several phone calls insisting that Toscano file the false report and sounded "vicious" and "desperate." Leonardo said, among other things: "Remember you just moved into a place that has a very dark entrance and you live there with your wife. . . . You and your wife are going to jump at shadows when you leave that dark entrance." Defendant finally agreed to Leonardo's demand and made out a single false medical report. He later moved to another house and changed his telephone number to avoid future contact with Leonardo. What he did not do was call the police.

The trial court refused to instruct on duress. The court reasoned that defendant's evidence, even if believed, would not show a "present, imminent and impending" threat of harm. Because Leonardo was not in a position to act immediately, Toscano had ample opportunity to call the police.

The Supreme Court of New Jersey held the evidence of duress sufficient to go to the jury and reversed Toscano's conviction. That court relied on Section 2.09 of the Model Penal Code and the then proposed (and subsequently enacted) New Jersey statute, both of which explicitly reject the common-law requirement of a threat of imminent harm; under these provisions, the immediacy of the danger is merely one of the circumstances to be considered in determining whether the threatened use of force was such that "a person of reasonable firmness in [the defendant's] situation would have been unable to resist."

[b] ALI, Model Penal Code and Commentaries, § 2.09, pp. 374–75 (1985).

Which approach is preferable? Is it fair to expect a person in Toscano's situation to contact the police rather than commit the crime? Even if he or she believes the police will be unable to provide effective protection? Does the Model Penal Code approach unduly compromise the deterrent effect of the law? Does it permit a terrorist to confer standing immunity on others to do his or her bidding? On the other hand, does the traditional approach require punishment of those who cannot fairly be blamed for their unwillingness to take risks in the face of intimidation?

3. **Duress as a Defense to Murder.** A widely discussed issue concerning the defense is whether it should be recognized as a defense to intentional homicide. The common law rejected such a claim, and many modern codes perpetuate the common law on this point. The drafters of the Model Penal Code, on the other hand, swept away this limitation as well. Can you sketch the arguments on either side of this controversy? c Which position do you favor?

Recent English precedents appear to support the proposition that duress may be raised as a defense by a person charged with being an accomplice to murder but not by the principal actor. In Director of Public Prosecutions for Northern Ireland v. Lynch, [1975] A.C. 653, the Appellate Committee of the House of Lords held, by a three-to-two majority, that an accomplice to murder could raise duress as a defense. In that case, the defendant drove several members of the I.R.A. on an expedition in which they shot and killed a Belfast policeman. In his defense, he claimed that he was not a member of the I.R.A. and that he drove the vehicle only because he feared that the leader of the group would shoot him if he disobeyed. However in Abbott v. The Queen, [1976] 3 All E.R. 140, the Judicial Committee of the Privy Council, sitting on an appeal from Trinidad, distinguished *Lynch* and held that the defense of duress is not available to a "principal in the first degree."

The evidence in *Abbott* showed that the defendant was pressed into the service of a man named Malik who had a reputation for violence. Malik had set up a commune in Trinidad and insisted that Abbott join it. A week later, Malik directed Abbott and others to kill the mistress of another member of the commune and outlined the plan for doing so. When Abbott objected, Malik said that if he did anything to endanger the others, Abbott and his mother would be killed. After Malik left, Abbott and the others began to dig a hole as they had been instructed. When the victim arrived, Abbott pushed her into the hole and held her while another person stabbed her. Because she was struggling, only minor wounds were inflicted and Abbott called to another of the group for help. This person then jumped into the hole and inflicted a major wound in the victim's lung. The four men, including Abbott, then buried her while she was still alive and still struggling. The Lords sitting in *Abbott* distinguished *Lynch* on the ground that this evidence supported the conclusion that Abbott was guilty as "a princi-

c In some jurisdictions an otherwise valid duress claim can reduce murder to manslaughter. For discussion of comparable issues in the grading of intentional homicides, see pages 882–904, infra.

pal in the first degree in that he took an active and indeed leading part in the killing." Does the line drawn between accomplices and principal actors represent a sensible distinction?

4. **Voluntary Exposure to Duress.** One final limitation on the traditional concept of duress should be taken into account. It is illustrated by the provision in § 2.09(2) of the Model Penal Code that the defense "is unavailable if the actor recklessly placed himself in a situation in which it was probable that he would be subjected to duress." Why was such a provision regarded as desirable? Is it a departure from the general grading principles underlying the Model Code? Recall, for example, that a person who mistakenly believes in the necessity of self-defense can be convicted only of an offense for which recklessness is the required culpability if the mistake was made recklessly, and only of an offense for which negligence is the required culpability if the mistake was made negligently.[d] Compare also the provision in § 3.02(2). Does the duress defense present a special situation justifying departure from this principle? Does § 2.09 represent a departure?

Consider in this regard the following comments by the English Law Commission, No. 83, Criminal Law: Report on Defences of General Application 13–14 (1977):

"It was clear to us that a person who had voluntarily, and with knowledge of its nature, joined a criminal association which he knew might bring pressure to bear on him to commit an offence, and was an active member when he was put under pressure to commit an offence, should not be entitled to avail himself of the defence. It was also clear to us that a person who had joined a criminal association without knowledge of its criminal nature, but which he only discovers when forced by a member to commit an offence, should not be precluded from relying on the defence. The cases for which it is not easy to lay down an explicit rule are those which fall between these two: where, for example, a person joined such an association in the full knowledge of its nature, but later repented and dissociated himself from it, or where, having joined innocently, he later discovers the association's true nature and takes no further part in its activities until he is forced by the association to commit some offence.

"In our view the vital issue in these types of cases—and it is an issue of fact for a jury—is whether, at the time of the threat which induces him to do the act required of him, the defendant has voluntarily put himself in a situation in which he knows that he will or may be subjected to duress to do such an act. . . .

"[W]e recommend that the defence of duress should not apply where, when the relevant threat is made, the defendant is voluntarily and without reasonable cause in a situation in which

---

[d] The Model Code provides in Section 2.09(2) that the defense "is also unavailable if he was negligent in placing himself in such a situation, whenever negligence suffices to establish culpability for the offense charged." Section 2.09(2) is thus consistent with the grading judgments expressed elsewhere in the Model Code.

he knows he will or may be subjected to duress to induce him to commit the offence with which he is charged, or an offence of the same or similar character."

Does the concern of the Law Commission adequately explain why § 2.09 of the Model Code contains a recklessness exclusion? Does it justify the exclusion? [e]

UNITED STATES v. BAILEY

Supreme Court of the United States, 1980.
444 U.S. 394.

MR. JUSTICE REHNQUIST delivered the opinion of the Court.

In the early morning hours of August 26, 1976, respondents Clifford Bailey, . . . Ronald C. Cooley, and Ralph Walker, federal prisoners at the District of Columbia jail, crawled through a window from which a bar had been removed, slid down a knotted bed sheet, and escaped from custody. Federal authorities recaptured them after they had remained at large for a period of time ranging from one month to three-and-one-half months. Upon their apprehension, they were charged with violating 18 U.S.C. § 751(a), which governs escape from federal custody.[1] At their [trial], each of the respondents adduced . . . evidence as to various conditions and events at the District of Columbia jail, but each was convicted by the jury. The Court of Appeals for the District of Columbia Circuit reversed the convictions by a divided vote, holding that the district court had improperly precluded consideration . . . of respondents' tendered evidence. We granted certiorari, and now reverse the judgments of the court of appeals. . . .

Respondents' defense of duress or necessity centered on the conditions in the jail during the months of June, July, and August 1976, and on various threats and beatings directed at them during that period. In describing the conditions at the jail, they introduced evidence of frequent fires in "Northeast One," the maximum-security cellblock occupied by respondents prior to their escape. Construed in the light most favorable to them, this evidence demonstrated that the inmates of Northeast One, and on occasion the guards in that unit, set fire to trash, bedding, and other objects thrown from the cells. According to the inmates, the guards simply allowed the fires to burn until they went out. Although the fires apparently were confined to small areas and posed no substantial threat of spreading through the complex, poor ventilation caused smoke to collect and linger in the cellblock.

[e] For criticism of the Model Code approach, see Robinson, Causing the Conditions of One's Defense: a Study in the Limits of Theory in Criminal Law Doctrine, 71 Va.L.Rev. 1 (1985).

[1] Title 18 U.S.C. § 751(a) provides:

"Whoever escapes or attempts to escape . . . from an institution or facility in which he is confined by direction of the Attorney General . . . shall, if the custody or confinement is by virtue of . . . conviction of any offense, be fined not more than $5,000 or imprisoned not more than five years or both. . . ."

Respondents Cooley and Bailey also introduced testimony that the guards at the jail had subjected them to beatings and to threats of death. Walker attempted to prove that he was an epileptic and had received inadequate medical attention for his seizures.

Consistently during the trial, the district court stressed that, to sustain their defenses, respondents would have to introduce some evidence that they attempted to surrender or engaged in equivalent conduct once they had freed themselves from the conditions they described. But the court waited for such evidence in vain. Respondent Cooley, who had eluded the authorities for one month, testified that his "people" had tried to contact the authorities, but "never got in touch with anybody." He also suggested that someone had told his sister that the FBI would kill him when he was apprehended.

Respondent Bailey, who was apprehended on November 19, 1976, told a similar story. He stated that he "had the jail officials called several times," but did not turn himself in because "I would still be under the threats of death." Like Cooley, Bailey testified that "the FBI was telling my people that they was going to shoot me."

Only respondent Walker suggested that he had attempted to negotiate a settlement. Like Cooley and Bailey, Walker testified that the FBI had told his "people" that they would kill him when they recaptured him. Nevertheless, according to Walker, he called the FBI three times and spoke with an agent whose name he could not remember. That agent allegedly assured him that the FBI would not harm him, but was unable to promise that Walker would not be returned to the D.C. jail.[2] Walker testified that he last called the FBI in mid-October. He was finally apprehended on December 13, 1976.

At the close of all the evidence, the district court rejected respondents' proffered instruction on duress as a defense to prison escape. The court ruled that respondents had failed as a matter of law to present evidence sufficient to support such a defense because they had not turned themselves in after they had escaped the allegedly coercive conditions. After receiving instructions to disregard the evidence of the conditions in the jail, the jury convicted Bailey, Cooley, and Walker of violating § 751(a). . . .

By a divided vote, the court of appeals reversed each respondent's conviction and remanded for new trials. The majority concluded that the district court should have allowed the jury to consider the evidence of coercive conditions in determining whether the respondents had formulated the requisite intent to sustain a conviction under § 751(a). According to the majority, § 751(a) required the prosecution to prove that a particular defendant left federal custody voluntarily, without permission, and "with an intent to avoid confinement." The majority then defined the word "confinement" as encompassing only the "normal aspects" of punishment prescribed by our legal system. Thus,

---

[2] On rebuttal, the prosecution called Joel Dean, the FBI agent who had been assigned to investigate Walker's escape in August 1976. He testified that, under standard Bureau practice, he would have been notified of any contact made by Walker with the FBI. According to Dean, he never was informed of any such contact.

where a prisoner escapes in order to avoid "non-confinement" conditions such as beatings or homosexual attacks, he would not necessarily have the requisite intent to sustain a conviction under § 751(a). . . .

Turning to the applicability of the defense of duress or necessity, the majority assumed that escape as defined by § 751(a) was a "continuing offense" as long as the escapee was at large. Given this assumption, the majority agreed with the district court that, under normal circumstances, an escapee must present evidence of coercion to justify his continued absence from custody as well as his initial departure. Here, however, respondents had been indicted for "flee[ing] and escap[ing]" "[o]n or about August 26, 1976," and not for "leaving *and staying away from custody.*" Similarly, "[t]he trial court's instructions when read as a whole clearly give the impression that [respondents] were being tried only for leaving the jail on August 26, and not for failing to return at some later date." . . .

As relevant to the charges against Bailey, Cooley, and Walker, § 751(a) required the prosecution to prove that (i) they had been in the custody of the attorney general, (ii) as the result of a conviction, and (iii) that they had escaped from that custody. . . . Although § 751(a) does not define the term "escape," courts and commentators are in general agreement that it means absenting oneself from custody without permission.

Respondents have not challenged the District Court's instructions on the first two elements of the crime defined by § 751(a). It is undisputed that, on August 26, 1976, respondents were in the custody of the attorney general as the result of . . . conviction. As for the element of "escape," we need not decide whether a person could be convicted on evidence of recklessness or negligence with respect to the limits on his freedom. A court may someday confront a case where an escapee did not know, but should have known, that he was exceeding the bounds of his confinement or that he was leaving without permission. Here, the district court clearly instructed the [jury] that the prosecution bore the burden of proving that respondents "knowingly committed an act which the law makes a crime" and that they acted "knowingly, intentionally, and deliberately. . . ." At a minimum, the [jury] had to find that respondents knew they were leaving the jail and that they knew they were doing so without authorization. The sufficiency of the evidence to support the [jury's] verdicts under this charge has never seriously been questioned, nor could it be.

The majority of the court of appeals, however, imposed the added burden on the prosecution to prove as part of its case-in-chief that respondents acted "with an intent to avoid confinement." [T]he majority left little doubt that it was requiring the government to prove that the respondents acted with the purpose—that is, the conscious objective—of leaving the jail without authorization. In a footnote explaining their holding, for example, the majority specified that an escapee did not act with the requisite intent if he escaped in order to avoid " 'non-confinement' conditions" as opposed to "normal aspects of 'confinement.' "

We find the majority's position quite unsupportable. Nothing in the language or legislative history of § 751(a) indicates that Congress intended to require either such a heightened standard of culpability or such a narrow definition of confinement. As we stated earlier, the cases have generally held that, except in narrow classes of offenses, proof that the defendant acted knowingly is sufficient to support a conviction. Accordingly, we hold that the prosecution fulfills its burden under § 751(a) if it demonstrates that an escapee knew his actions would result in his leaving physical confinement without permission. Our holding in this respect comports with [the definition] of the crime of escape . . . in the Model Penal Code [§ 242.6] . . . .

Respondents also contend that they are entitled to a new trial because they presented . . . sufficient evidence of duress or necessity to submit such a defense to the jury. The majority below did not confront this claim squarely, holding instead that, to the extent that such a defense normally would be barred by a prisoner's failure to return to custody, neither the indictment nor the jury instructions adequately described such a requirement.

Common law historically distinguished between the defenses of duress and necessity. Duress was said to excuse criminal conduct where the actor was under an unlawful threat of imminent death or serious bodily injury, which threat caused the actor to engage in conduct violating the literal terms of the criminal law. While the defense of duress covered the situation where the coercion had its source in the actions of other human beings, the defense of necessity, or choice of evils, traditionally covered the situation where physical forces beyond the actor's control rendered illegal conduct the lesser of two evils. Thus, where *A* destroyed a dike because *B* threatened to kill him if he did not, *A* would argue that he acted under duress, whereas if *A* destroyed the dike in order to protect more valuable property from flooding, *A* could claim a defense of necessity.

Modern cases have tended to blur the distinction between duress and necessity. In the court below, the majority discarded the labels "duress" and "necessity," choosing instead to examine the policies underlying the traditional defenses. In particular, the majority felt that the defenses were designed to spare a person from punishment if he acted "under threats or conditions that a person of ordinary firmness would have been unable to resist," or if he reasonably believed that criminal action "was necessary to avoid a harm more serious than that sought to be prevented by the statute defining the offense." The Model Penal Code redefines the defenses along similar lines. See Model Penal Code § 2.09 (duress) and § 3.02 (choice of evils).

We need not speculate now, however, on the precise contours of whatever defenses of duress or necessity are available against charges brought under § 751(a). Under any definition of these defenses one principle remains constant: If there was a reasonable, legal alternative to violating the law, "a chance both to refuse to do the criminal act and also to avoid the threatened harm," the defenses will fail. Clearly, in the context of prison escape, the escapee is not entitled to claim a defense of duress or necessity unless and until he demonstrates that, given the imminence of the threat, violation of § 751(a) was his only reasonable alternative.

In the present case, the government contends that respondents' showing was insufficient on two grounds. First, the government asserts that the threats and conditions cited by respondents as justifying their escape were not sufficiently immediate or serious to justify their departure from lawful custody. Second, the government contends that, once the respondents had escaped, the coercive conditions in the jail were no longer a threat and respondents were under a duty to terminate their status as fugitives by turning themselves over to the authorities.

Respondents, on the other hand, argue that the evidence of coercion and conditions in the jail was at least sufficient to go to the jury as an affirmative defense to the crime charged. As for their failure to return to custody after gaining their freedom, respondents assert that this failure should be but one factor in the overall determination whether their initial departure was justified. According to respondents, their failure to surrender "may reflect adversely on the bonafides of [their] motivation" in leaving the jail, but should not withdraw the question of their motivation from the jury's consideration.

We need not decide whether such evidence as that submitted by respondents was sufficient to raise a jury question as to their initial departures. This is because we decline to hold that respondents' failure to return is "just one factor" for the jury to weigh in deciding whether the initial escape could be affirmatively justified. On the contrary, several considerations lead us to conclude that, in order to be entitled to an instruction on duress or necessity as a defense to the crime charged, an escapee must first offer evidence justifying his continued absence from custody as well as his initial departure and that an indispensable element of such an offer is testimony of a bona fide effort to surrender or return to custody as soon as the claimed duress or necessity had lost its coercive force.

[W]e think it clear beyond peradventure that escape from federal custody as defined in § 751(a) is a continuing offense and that an escapee can be held liable for failure to return to custody as well as for his initial departure.

. . . As for the alleged failure of the district court to elaborate for the benefit of the jury on the continuing nature of the charged offense, we believe that such elaboration was unnecessary where, as here, the evidence failed as a matter of law in a crucial particular to reach the minimum threshold that would have required an instruction on their theory of the case generally.

The Anglo-Saxon tradition of criminal justice, embodied in the United States Constitution and in federal statutes, makes jurors the judges of the credibility of testimony offered by witnesses. It is for them, generally, and not for appellate courts, to say that a particular witness spoke the truth or fabricated a cock-and-bull story. An escapee who flees from a jail that is in the process of burning to the ground may well be entitled to an instruction on duress or necessity, " 'for he is not to be hanged because he would not stay to be burnt.' " United States v. Kirby, 74 U.S. [7 Wall.] 482, 487 (1868). And in the federal system it is the jury that is the judge of whether the prisoner's account of his reason for flight is true or false. But precisely because a defendant is entitled to have the credibility of his testimony, or that of witnesses called on his behalf, judged by the jury, it is essential that the testimony given or proffered meet a minimum standard as to each element of the defense so that, if a jury finds it to be true, it would support an affirmative defense—here that of duress or necessity.

We therefore hold that, where a criminal defendant is charged with escape and claims that he is entitled to an instruction on the theory of duress or necessity, he must proffer evidence of a bona-fide effort to surrender or return to custody as soon as the claimed duress or necessity had lost its coercive force. We have reviewed the evidence examined elaborately in the opinions below, and find the case not even close, even under respondents' versions of the facts, as to whether they either surrendered or offered to surrender at their earliest possible opportunity. Since we have determined that this is an indispensable element of the defense of duress or necessity, respondents were not entitled to any instruction on such a theory. Vague and necessarily self-serving statements of defendants or witnesses as to future good intentions or ambiguous conduct simply do not support a finding of this element of the defense.[11] . . .

This case presents a good example of the potential for wasting valuable trial resources. In general, trials for violations of § 751(a) should be simple affairs. The key elements are capable of objective demonstration; the mens rea . . . will usually depend upon reasonable inferences from those objective facts. Here, however, the jury heard five days of testimony. It was presented with evidence of every unpleasant aspect of prison life from the amount of garbage on the cellblock floor to the meal schedule to the number of times the inmates were allowed to shower. Unfortunately, all this evidence was present-

[11] Contrary to the implication of Mr. Justice Blackmun's dissent describing the rationale of the necessity defense as "a balancing of harms," we are construing an Act of Congress, not drafting it. The statute itself, as we have noted, requires no heightened mens rea that might be negated by any defense of duress or coercion. We nonetheless recognize that Congress in enacting criminal statutes legislates against a background of Anglo-Saxon common law, and that therefore a defense of duress or coercion may well have been contemplated by Congress when it enacted § 751(a). But since the express purpose of Congress in enacting that section was to punish escape from penal custody, we think that some duty to return, a duty described more elaborately in the text, must be an essential element of the defense unless the congressional judgment that escape from prison is a crime be rendered wholly nugatory. Our principal difference with the dissent, therefore, is not as to the existence of such a defense but as to the importance of surrender as an element of it. And we remain satisfied that, even if credited by the jury, the testimony set forth at length in Mr. Justice Blackmun's dissenting opinion could not support a finding that respondents had no alternatives but to remain at large until recaptured anywhere from one to three-and-one-half months after their escape. To hold otherwise would indeed quickly reduce the overcrowding in prisons that has been universally condemned by penologists. But that result would be accomplished in a manner quite at odds with the purpose of Congress when it made escape from prison a federal criminal offense.

ed in a case where the defense's reach hopelessly exceeded its grasp. Were we to hold, as respondents suggest, that the jury should be subjected to this potpourri even though a critical element of the proffered defenses was concededly absent, we undoubtedly would convert every trial under § 751(a) into a hearing on the current state of the federal penal system.

Because the juries below were properly instructed on the mens rea required by § 751(a), and because the respondents failed to introduce evidence sufficient to submit their defenses of duress and necessity to the juries, we reverse the judgments of the Court of Appeals.

Reversed.

MR. JUSTICE MARSHALL took no part in the consideration or decision of this case.

[The concurring opinion by MR. JUSTICE STEVENS has been omitted.]

MR. JUSTICE BLACKMUN, with whom MR. JUSTICE BRENNAN joins, dissenting.

The Court's opinion, it seems to me, is an impeccable exercise in undisputed general principles and technical legalism: The respondents were properly confined in the District of Columbia jail. They departed from that jail without authority or consent. They failed promptly to turn themselves in when, as the Court would assert by way of justification, the claimed duress or necessity "had lost its coercive force." Therefore, the Court concludes, there is no defense for a jury to weigh and consider against the respondents' prosecution for escape violative of 18 U.S.C. § 751(a).

It is with the Court's assertion that the claimed duress or necessity had lost its coercive force that I particularly disagree. The conditions that led to respondents' initial departure from the D.C. jail continue unabated. If departure was justified—and on the record before us that issue, I feel, is for the jury to resolve as a matter of fact in the light of the evidence, and not for this Court to determine as a matter of law—it seems too much to demand that respondents, in order to preserve their legal defenses, return forthwith to the hell that obviously exceeds the normal deprivations of prison life and that compelled their leaving in the first instance. The Court, however, requires that an escapee's action must amount to nothing more than a mere and temporary gesture that, it is to be hoped, just might attract attention in responsive circles. But life and health, even of convicts and accused, deserve better than that and are entitled to more than pious pronouncements fit for an ideal world.

The Court, in its carefully structured opinion, does reach a result that might be a proper one were we living in that ideal world, and were our American jails and penitentiaries truly places for humane and rehabilitative treatment of their inmates. Then the statutory crime of escape could not be excused by duress or necessity, by beatings, and by guard-set fires in the jails, for these would not take place, and escapees would be appropriately prosecuted and punished.

But we do not live in an ideal world "even" (to use a self-centered phrase) in America, so far as jail and prison conditions are concerned. The complaints that this Court, and every other American appellate court, receives almost daily from prisoners about conditions of incarceration, about filth, about homosexual rape, and about brutality are not always the mouthings of the purely malcontent. The Court itself acknowledges that the conditions these respondents complained about do exist. It is in the light of this stark truth, it seems to me, that these cases are to be evaluated. . . .

I

The atrocities and inhuman conditions of prison life in America are almost unbelievable; surely they are nothing less than shocking. The dissent in the *Bailey* case in the court of appeals acknowledges that "the circumstances of prison life are such that at least a colorable, if not credible, claim of duress or necessity can be raised with respect to virtually every escape." And the government concedes: "In light of prison conditions that even now prevail in the United States, it would be the rare inmate who could not convince himself that continued incarceration would be harmful to his health or safety."

A youthful inmate can expect to be subjected to homosexual gang rape his first night in jail, or, it has been said, even in the van on the way to jail. Weaker inmates become the property of stronger prisoners or gangs, who sell the sexual services of the victim. Prison officials either are disinterested in stopping abuse of prisoners by other prisoners or are incapable of doing so, given the limited resources society allocates to the prison system. Prison officials often are merely indifferent to serious health and safety needs of prisoners as well.

Even more appalling is the fact that guards frequently participate in the brutalization of inmates. The classic example is the beating or other punishment in retaliation for prisoner complaints or court actions.

The evidence submitted by respondents in this case fits that pattern exactly. Respondent Bailey presented evidence that he was continually mistreated by correctional officers during his stay at the D.C. jail. He was threatened that his testimony in [a pending] case would bring on severe retribution. Other inmates were beaten by guards as a message to Bailey. An inmate testified that on one occasion three guards displaying a small knife told him that they were going "to get your buddy, that nigger Bailey. We are going to kill him." The threats culminated in a series of violent attacks on Bailey. Blackjacks, mace, and slapjacks (leather with a steel insert) were used in beating Bailey.

Respondent Cooley also elicited testimony from other inmates concerning beatings of Cooley by guards with slapjacks, blackjacks, and flashlights. There was evidence that guards threatened to kill Cooley.

It is society's responsibility to protect the life and health of its prisoners. . . . Deliberate indifference to serious and essential medical needs of prisoners constitutes "cruel and unusual punishment violative of the eighth amendment." Estelle v. Gamble, 429 U.S. 97, 104 (1976):

> "An inmate must rely on prison authorities to treat his medical needs. . . . In the worst [case], such a failure may actually produce physical 'torture or a lingering death' . . . . In less serious cases, denial of medical care may result in pain and suffering which no one suggests would serve any penological purpose. . . . The infliction of such unnecessary suffering is inconsistent with contemporary standards of decency."

It cannot be doubted that excessive or unprovoked violence and brutality inflicted by prison guards upon inmates violates the eighth amendment. The reasons that support the Court's holding in *Estelle* v. *Gamble* lead me to conclude that failure to use reasonable measures to protect an inmate from violence inflicted by other inmates also constitutes cruel and unusual punishment. Homosexual rape or other violence serves no penological purpose. Such brutality is the equivalent of torture, and is offensive to any modern standard of human dignity. Prisoners must depend, and rightly so, upon the prison administrators for protection from abuse of this kind.

There can be little question that our prisons are badly overcrowded and understaffed and that this in large part is the cause of many of the shortcomings of our penal systems. This, however, does not excuse the failure to provide a place of confinement that meets minimal standards of safety and decency. . . .

II

The real question presented in this case is whether the prisoner should be punished for helping to extricate himself from a situation where society has abdicated completely its basic responsibility for providing an environment free of life-threatening conditions such as beatings, fires, lack of essential medical care, and sexual attacks. To be sure, Congress in so many words has not enacted specific statutory duress or necessity defenses that would excuse or justify commission of an otherwise unlawful act. The concept of such a defense, however, is "anciently woven into the fabric of our culture." J. Hall, General Principles of Criminal Law 416 (2d ed. 1960). And the government concedes that "it has always been an accepted part of our criminal justice system that punishment is inappropriate for crimes committed under duress because the defendant in such circumstances cannot fairly be blamed for his wrongful act."

Although the Court declines to address the issue, it at least implies that it would recognize the common-law defenses of duress and necessity to the federal crime of prison escape, if the appropriate prerequisites for assertion of either defense were met. Given the universal acceptance of these defenses in the common law, I have no difficulty in concluding that Congress intended the defenses of duress and necessity to be available to persons accused of committing the federal crime of escape.

I agree with most of the Court's comments about the essential elements of the defenses. I, too, conclude that intolerable prison conditions are to be taken into account through affirmative defenses of duress and necessity, rather than by way of the theory of intent espoused by the court of appeals. . . .

I also agree with the Court that the absence of reasonable less-drastic alternatives is a prerequisite to successful assertion of a defense of necessity or duress to a charge of prison escape. One must appreciate, however, that other realistic avenues of redress seldom are open to the prisoner. Where prison officials participate in the maltreatment of an inmate, or purposefully ignore dangerous conditions or brutalities inflicted by other prisoners or guards, the inmate can do little to protect himself. Filing a complaint may well result in retribution, and appealing to the guards is a capital offense under the prisoners' code of behavior.[6] In most instances, the question whether alternative remedies were thoroughly "exhausted" should be a matter for the jury to decide.

I, too, conclude that the jury generally should be instructed that, in order to prevail on a necessity or duress defense, the defendant must justify his continued absence from custody, as well as his initial departure. I agree with the Court that the very nature of escape makes it a continuing crime. But I cannot agree that the only way continued absence can be justified is evidence "of a bona-fide effort to surrender or return to custody." The Court apparently entertains the view, naive in my estimation, that once the prisoner has escaped from a life- or health-threatening situation, he can turn himself in, secure in the faith that his escape somehow will result in improvement in those intolerable prison conditions. While it may be true in some rare circumstance that an escapee will obtain the aid of a court or of the prison administration once the escape is accomplished, the escapee, realistically, faces a high probability of being returned to the same prison and to exactly the same, or even greater, threats to life and safety.

The rationale of the necessity defense is a balancing of harms. If the harm caused by an escape is less than the harm caused by remaining in a threatening situation, the prisoner's initial departure is justified. The same rationale should apply to hesitancy and failure to return. A situation may well arise where the social balance weighs in favor of the prisoner even though he fails to return to custody. The escapee at least should be permitted to present to the jury the possibility that the harm that would result from a return to custody outweighs the harm to society from continued absence.

Even under the Court's own standard, the defendant in an escape prosecution should be permitted to submit evidence to the jury to demonstrate that surrender would result in his being placed again in a

---

[6] The alleged facts in this case appear to be typical. Respondent Bailey filed suit in the Superior Court of the District of Columbia to "stop the administrators from threatening my life." Bailey testified that the suit caused the guards to threaten him in an attempt to persuade him to withdraw the action, to beat him, and to transfer him to the mental ward. Bailey's suit subsequently was dismissed with prejudice.

life- or health-threatening situation. The Court requires return to custody once the "claimed duress or necessity had lost its coercive force." Realistically, however, the escapee who reasonably believes that surrender will result in return to what concededly is an intolerable prison situation remains subject to the same "coercive force" that prompted his escape in the first instance. It is ironic to say that that force is automatically "lost" once the prison wall is passed. . . .

Finally, I of course must agree with the Court that use of the jury is to be reserved for the case in which there is sufficient evidence to support a verdict. I have no difficulty, however, in concluding that respondents here did indeed submit sufficient evidence to support a verdict of not guilty, if the jury were so inclined, based on the necessity defense. Respondent Bailey testifies that he was in fear for his life, that he was afraid he would still face the same threats if he turned himself in, and that "[t]he FBI was telling my people that they was going to shoot me." Respondent Cooley testified that he did not know anyone to call, and that he feared that the police would shoot him when they came to get him. Respondent Walker testified that he had been in "constant rapport," with an FBI agent, who assured him that the FBI would not harm him, but who would not promise that he would not be returned to the D.C. jail. Walker also stated that he had heard through his sister that the FBI "said that if they ran down on me they was going to kill me."

Perhaps it is highly unlikely that the jury would have believed respondents' stories that the FBI planned to shoot them on sight, or that respondent Walker had been in constant communication with an FBI agent. Nevertheless, such testimony, even though "self-serving," and possibly extreme and unwarranted in part, was sufficient to permit the jury to decide whether the failure to surrender immediately was justified or excused. This is routine grist for the jury mill and the jury usually is able to sort out the fabricated and the incredible.

[If] respondents' allegations are true, society is grossly at fault for permitting these conditions to persist at the D.C. jail. The findings of researchers and government agencies, as well as the litigated cases, indicate that in a general sense these allegations are credible. The case for recognizing the duress or necessity defenses is even more compelling when it is society, rather than private actors, that creates the coercive conditions. In such a situation it is especially appropriate that the jury be permitted to weigh all the factors and strike the balance between the interests of prisoners and that of society. In an attempt to conserve the jury for cases it considers truly worthy of that body, the Court has ousted the jury from a role it is particularly well-suited to serve.

NOTES ON DURESS AND SITUATIONAL COMPULSION

1. **Relation of Duress and Necessity.** As Justice Rehnquist observed in *Bailey,* the defenses of necessity (or choice of evils) and

duress have traditionally been distinguished according to the origin of the threatened harm. If *A* destroys a dike in order to prevent the greater harm that would be caused by a flood, *A*'s conduct is justified by necessity. In contrast, the concept of duress has usually been limited to cases involving human threats rather than those posed by natural forces. Notwithstanding this distinction, however, some commentators regard claims of duress as a subset of the general choice-of-evils defense. According to this view, duress is recognized only when the evil avoided (death or bodily harm to the defendant or a loved one) is greater than the harm occasioned by the offense. In the *Toscano* case (page 606, supra), for example, physical injury to the defendant or his wife could be said to be a greater evil than the defendant's commission of insurance fraud. In this sense, his conduct could be regarded as justified because violation of the penal law under these circumstances was the right thing to do.

By contrast, much contemporary thinking on the nature and scope of the defense of duress draws on the ethics of excuse. The Model Penal Code explicitly endorses this view. Under the Model Code, the general principle of justification (§ 3.02, discussed at pages 519–20, supra) covers all cases where one believes the conduct to be necessary to avoid an evil to oneself or another that is greater than the evil sought to be prevented by the law defining the offense charged. The commentary to § 3.02 explicitly indicates that the drafters meant to include cases involving coercive threats in that formulation. Duress as treated in § 2.09, on the other hand, deals only with cases where the actor cannot justify his or her conduct as a choice of the lesser evil, as when the choice involves an equal or greater evil than that threatened but the intimidation was so great that the actor cannot fairly be blamed for choosing to commit the crime. As the passage from the drafters' commentary quoted at pages 605–06, supra, indicates, the Model Code duress provision represents an explicit concession to the weakness of ordinary people in the face of overwhelming coercive pressure.[a]

When duress is viewed as an excuse, rather than as a justification, the harm occasioned by the defendant's crime remains relevant; it will be taken into account in determining whether a "person of reasonable firmness" would have committed the offense rather than suffer the threatened harm. However, the ultimate focus of the inquiry is not the weighing of evils, but the attribution of blame.

---

[a] See also The Law Commission, Report No. 83, Criminal Law Report on Defences of General Application 7 (1977):

"The main [argument for the defense] is that the law should not insist upon condemning a person who acts under compulsion which he is unable to resist; that in doing so it would be making excessive demands on human nature and imposing penalties in circumstances where they are unjustified as retribution and irrelevant as a deterrent. The law must recognize that the instinct and perhaps the duty of self-preservation is powerful and natural, and that it would be 'censorious and inhumane [if it] did not recognize the appalling plight of a person who perhaps suddenly finds his life in jeopardy unless he submits and obeys.' This argument . . . convinces us that it would be quite unjust that a person who has committed an offence only because of threats which he could not withstand (subject to qualifications as to the nature of the threats) should face trial and conviction with the obloquy inherent therein.'"

2. **Questions and Comments on *Bailey*.** The availability of a defense to escaping prisoners based on intolerable prison conditions has been frequently litigated in recent years. Many courts have rejected the proposed defense altogether, while others have held that it is available under limited circumstances. Decisions recognizing the defense have usually required, as did the Supreme Court in *Bailey*, that the defendant surrender soon after the successful escape.

What is the basis for Justice Blackmun's dissent in *Bailey?* Is he disagreeing with the majority on anything more significant than an evidentiary point—i.e., on whether the defendants' testimony, however implausible, was sufficient to raise a jury question on the surrender issue? If the disagreement is more fundamental, how would you describe it?

Justice Rehnquist seems to acknowledge that an escaping federal prisoner might have a defense under some circumstances. He mentions the case of the prisoner who flees a burning jail, and appears to concede that the defendants' claims concerning threats of serious bodily harm and sexual assault would have raised a jury question on the defense of "duress or necessity" if they had surrendered after the escape. What would be the moral basis for such a defense? Would the escape be justified or excused?

(i) **Justification.** Many courts have viewed the proposed defense as a choice-of-evils problem. The evils have been weighed at two levels—at the level of social policy and at the level of individual choice. Under a social-policy analysis, a recognition of the defense would permit those who escape successfully to avoid harms suffered in the prison and would also establish institutional pressure for improvement of poor, and possibly unconstitutional, prison conditions. On the other hand, recognition of the defense could undermine prison discipline and threaten the public safety since such a defense would be particularly susceptible to manipulation by shrewd escapees. Courts that have analyzed the issue in this manner have uniformly concluded that the evils of prison life are outweighed by the evils which would be occasioned by recognition of the defense.

Some courts have focused on the individual prisoner's choice; they have asked whether the harm or threatened harm suffered by the individual prisoner is sufficiently serious that society would prefer that he or she escape rather than suffer it. The effect of this analysis has been to focus judicial attention on the precise evils being avoided in each case and on the availability of avenues of avoidance other than escape. These courts have typically concluded that the defense should be recognized, but only in cases involving fear of immediate life-threatening assault or forcible sexual attack. This approach was described by the court in People v. Lovercamp, 43 Cal.App.3d 823, 831, 118 Cal.Rptr. 110, 115 (4th Dist.1975), as follows:

"A limited defense of necessity is available if the following conditions exist:

(i) The prisoner is faced with a specific threat of death, forcible sexual attack or substantial bodily injury in the immediate future;

(ii) There is no time for a complaint to the authorities or there exists a history of futile complaints which make any result from such complaints illusory;

(iii) There is no time or opportunity to resort to the courts;

(iv) There is no evidence of force or violence used towards prison personnel or other 'innocent' persons in the escape; and

(v) The prisoner immediately reports to the proper authorities when he has attained a position of safety from the immediate threat."

Is choice-of-evils analysis adequate to the task in these cases? Is it sensible to weigh the social values of prison discipline and public security on the same scale with the life and personal safety of the inmate? If the inmate's effort to avoid suffering or death can justify an escape, why does the threat need to be imminent, especially if the inmate cannot assume that the opportunity to escape will be readily available when the danger arises? Moreover, why should the defense be limited to threats of death or sexual assault? Why should the defense be unavailable, for example, if the inmate is exposed to unsanitary prison conditions?

(ii) **Excuse.** Even if socially beneficial results would not be achieved if prisoners were permitted to escape to avoid oppressive prison conditions, does it follow that the defense should not be allowed? Could a person of reasonable firmness exposed to the conditions described by the defendants in *Bailey* fairly be expected to remain in prison if an opportunity to escape arose? Should escaping prisoners be entitled to a jury determination on this question? If so, should they also be entitled to have the jury decide whether they fairly can be blamed for remaining at large?

3. **A General Principle of Situational Compulsion**? Under traditional principles, the *Bailey* defendants could not rely on the duress defense. As usually formulated, that defense would have been available only if someone threatened them with death or bodily harm *in order to force them to escape.* Indeed, if *Bailey* is analyzed as a problem of excuse, rather than as a choice of evils, it seems to fall in a moral gap between the traditional defenses of duress and necessity: Neither the common law nor most modern codes provide a defense in situations where the defendant's choice is constrained, however severely, by circumstances other than personal threats of harm—unless the harm occasioned by the offense is less than that which would have otherwise occurred. It has been suggested that the law should recognize a general principle of situational compulsion to rectify this situation. Do you agree? Specifically, should the law recognize an exculpatory doctrine that takes into account a defendant's claim that criminal conduct was responsive to coercive situational pressures rather than to

defects of character and that a person of reasonable firmness in the defendant's situation would have responded similarly? [b] Should such a defense be available on the *Bailey* facts?

Would consideration of such a defense be appropriate in *Regina* v. *Dudley and Stephens*, considered at pages 523–26, supra? In that case two members of a shipwrecked crew were charged with murder for killing and eating a dying cabin boy after several days without food in order to preserve their own lives. Assuming that the killing of an innocent person under these circumstances is not morally justified as a choice of evils, is it not still possible to argue that the homicide should be excused? Even if Dudley and Stephens acted wrongfully, can they fairly be blamed for having succumbed to the overwhelming pressures that confronted them? Does their behavior manifest a defect of character or the weakness of ordinary persons? Surely it is fair to expect that the threshold for giving in—and taking an innocent life—will be high, but is it fair to say that there is no point at which such action should be excused? How much fortitude can fairly be expected of persons in that situation?

Should the principle of situational compulsion be generalized beyond coercive circumstances involving demonstrable threats to the actor's life and safety? Are there other unusual circumstances that can propel the ordinary person toward criminal conduct, even though they may not be as coercive as those involved in *Dudley and Stephens*?

Consider, for example, the recurrent cases of mercy killings. In one publicized case, a 23-year-old man shot his dearly-loved elder brother who had been paralyzed, irreversibly, below the neck in a motorcycle accident. The victim, who was in severe pain, begged his brother to kill him. Three days after the accident, the defendant walked into the hospital and asked his brother if he was still in pain, and his brother nodded that he was. The defendant then said: "Well, I'm here today to end your pain. Is that all right with you?" His brother nodded and the defendant said: "Close your eyes, George. I'm going to kill you." He then placed his shotgun against his brother's temple and pulled the trigger.[c]

Anglo-American law has never regarded mercy killing as justifiable homicide, although the matter has not been free of moral controversy. Should the law recognize a claim of situational excuse in such a case?

Finally, consider the situation presented in *State v. Warshow*, at pages 512–18, supra. In that case the defendants trespassed on the

[b] Compare, for example, § 25 of the Criminal Code of Queensland, Australia:

"Subject to the express provisions of this Code relating to acts done upon compulsion or provocation or in self-defence, a person is not criminally responsible for an act or omission done or made under such circumstances of sudden or extraordinary emergency that an ordinary person possessing ordinary power of self-control could not reasonably be expected to act otherwise."

Although no comparable statute appears to have been enacted in this country, several duress statutes could be read to reach dangers to life or personal safety not stemming from human threats. See ALI Model Penal Code and Commentaries, § 2.09, pp. 383–84 n. 59 (1985).

[c] This case is described in P. Mitchell, Act of Love: The Killing of George Zygmanik (1976).

property of a nuclear utility in order to prevent the start-up of a nuclear power plant which they feared was unsafe. Assuming that their conduct is not justified as a choice of evils, would it make sense to entertain a claim of excuse based on the strength and sincerity of their belief that the public was being placed at grave risk? Should the law take into account compulsion of conscience in the assessment of individual blameworthiness?

4. **Situational Excuse and Mens Rea.** Recall that the Court of Appeals in *Bailey* held that an "intent to avoid confinement" was the required mens rea for the federal escape offense, and further defined "confinement" to mean only the "normal" aspects of punishment. Thus, it followed that if the defendants sought only to avoid the prison conditions of which they complained, but were not seeking to avoid confinement altogether, they would be entitled to an acquittal independent of any claim of justification or excuse. Do you see why the Supreme Court unanimously rejected this construction of the federal statute?

Consider also, in a more general sense, whether evidence of duress or other forms of situational compulsion can establish that a defendant lacked mens rea. The answer may be of some practical importance because the burden of proof for duress is typically placed on the defendant, whereas the prosecutor of course must establish any required mens rea.

It seems clear that knowledge, recklessness, and negligence cannot be negated by evidence of duress. A defendant forced to do something knows, by definition, what he or she is doing, and this knowledge will satisfy any recklessness or negligence that would otherwise suffice (see Model Penal Code § 2.02(5)). Is it so clear, however, that purpose cannot be negated by evidence of duress? Recall, for example, the "stake in the venture" formula for determining when a defendant is guilty of complicity (pages 395–97, supra). Would a defendant who is coerced have a stake in the venture? But is that what "purpose" means under the Model Penal Code? If complicity (§ 2.06), attempt (§ 5.01), or conspiracy (§ 5.03) were charged under the Model Penal Code, could the defendant claim to have lacked mens rea because he or she was forced to act at the point of a gun? Is motive generally relevant to the existence of mens rea?

5. **Brainwashing or Coercive Persuasion.** Patricia Hearst was kidnapped and held in captivity by the Symbionese Liberation Army. She reported that she was confined in a closet—tied and blindfolded—for almost two months, and was subjected to persistent interrogation, and to physical, emotional, and sexual abuse, by her captors. See *United States v. Hearst,* 563 F.2d 1331 (9th Cir.1977). Two-and-one-half months after her capture, she participated in a bank robbery with her abductors and was subsequently arrested and charged with bank robbery and weapons offenses. She raised two intertwined defensive claims: On the one hand, she claimed that she was forced to participate in the robbery by threats of death—a traditional duress claim; on the other hand, she claimed that after the robbery, her involvement in

other criminal activity and her continuing relationship with her captors was attributable to the "brainwashing" or "coercive persuasion" to which she had been subjected. In essence, her claim was that her captors had succeeded in inducing a profound alteration in her character, displacing her attitudes, beliefs and values with their own.

"Coercive persuasion" was first raised as a defense, unsuccessfully, by American prisoners of war in Korea who were charged in the 1950's with collaborating with the enemy.[d] The phenomenon attracted considerable clinical and scientific interest, which was revived in the wake of the Hearst trial.[e] Contemporary legal commentators are divided on whether the law should recognize "coercive persuasion" as a ground of exculpation.[f] What do you think? Assuming that sensory deprivation, social isolation, and persistent indoctrination actually can induce a drastic alteration of a captive's character and values, is it morally appropriate to punish the defendant, once he or she has been restored to "normal," for conduct engaged in while "brainwashed?" If so, would recognition of the defense undermine the social control functions of the law? Consider, in this connection, the argument that the brainwashed individual's claim is morally indistinguishable from that of a defendant whose attitudes and values were shaped by the experience of growing up in a deviant subculture. If the two claims are morally indistinguishable, should both or neither be adopted as forms of situational excuse that would exonerate for crime? Or would you permit one claim but not the other? How would you draft a law that recognized one or both claims as a defense?

NOTES ON THE DEFENSE OF ENTRAPMENT

1. **The Entrapment Defense**. The defense of entrapment, which is recognized in every United States jurisdiction, is generally covered in courses in criminal procedure. The main reason is that the defense is designed primarily to establish limitations on police investigative practices. The idea is that the police should not use tactics that improperly induce citizens to commit crimes for which they are then arrested. In this sense, the defense of entrapment, though it is not constitutionally based, is similar to other rules—many of them constitutional in origin—that are designed to limit the zeal with which the police enforce the law. Under one conception of the defense, regulation of police behavior is its sole concern. However, there is a competing view that the scope of the defense should be determined in part by considerations of situational excuse. The two approaches are explored in the following case.

[d] See, e.g., United States v. Batchelor, 19 L.M.R. 452 (1955).

[e] See generally, Davis, Brainwashing: Fact, Fiction and Criminal Defense, 44 UK MCLR 438 (1976).

[f] Lunde and Wilson, Brainwashing as a Defense to Criminal Liability: Patty Hearst Revisited, 13 Crim.L.Bull. 341 (1977); Delgado, Assumption of Criminal States of Mind: Towards a Defense Theory for the Coercively Persuaded ("Brainwashed") Defendant, 63 Minn.L.Rev. 1 (1978); Dressler, Professor Delgado's "Brainwashing" Defense: Courting a Determinist Legal System, 3 Minn.L.Rev. 335 (1979); Alldridge, Brainwashing as a Criminal Law Defense [1984] Crim.L.Rev. 726.

(i) ***People* v. *Barraza*.**   In People v. Barraza, 23 Cal.3d 675, 153 Cal.Rptr. 459, 591 P.2d 947 (1979), the defendant was charged with two counts of selling heroin to a female undercover agent.   He denied that the first sale had occurred but claimed he had been entrapped into committing the second.   The court summarized the evidence concerning the second transaction as follows:

"[Both the] agent and the defendant testified that the agent tried to contact defendant by telephoning the [drug abuse detoxification center] where he worked as a patient-care technician, several times during the three weeks between the dates of the two alleged heroin sale transactions.   On September 11, the agent finally succeeded in speaking to defendant and asked him if he had 'anything'; defendant asked her to come to the detoxification center.   The two then met at the center and talked for some time—a few minutes according to the agent, more than an hour by the defendant's account.

"The agent's version of this encounter described defendant as hesitant to deal because 'he had done a lot of time in jail and he couldn't afford to go back to jail and   .   .   .   he had to be careful about what he was doing.'   She further testified that after she convinced defendant she 'wasn't a cop,' he gave her a note, to present to a woman named Stella, which read: 'Saw Cheryl [the agent].   Give her a pair of pants [Bargot for heroin].   [signed] Cal.'   The agent concluded her testimony by stating that she then left defendant, used the note to introduce herself to the dealer Stella, and purchased an orange balloon containing heroin.

"Defendant described a somewhat different pattern of interaction with the agent at their September 11th meeting.   He related that he had asked her to come and see him because he was 'fed up with her' and wanted her to quit calling him at the hospital where he worked because he was afraid she would cause him to lose his job.   He insisted he told her during their conversation that he did not have anything; that he had spent more than 23 years in prison but now he had held a job at the detoxification center for four years, was on methadone and was clean, and wanted the agent to stop 'bugging' him.   He testified that the agent persisted in her efforts to enlist his aid in purchasing heroin, and that finally—after more than an hour of conversation—when the agent asked for a note to introduce her to a source of heroin he agreed to give her a note to 'get her off   .   .   .   [his] back.'   According to the defendant, he told the agent that he did not know if Stella had anything, and gave her a note which read: 'Saw Cheryl.   If you have a pair of pants, let her have them.'   .   .   ."

The trial judge refused to instruct the jury on entrapment, and Barraza was convicted.   His conviction was reversed by the California Supreme Court.

(ii) **Approaches to the Defense.** The *Barraza* court's opinion summarized the competing approaches to the entrapment defense as follows:

"Though long recognized by the courts of almost every United States jurisdiction,[1] the defense of entrapment has produced a deep schism concerning its proper theoretical basis and mode of application. The opposing views have been delineated in a series of United States Supreme Court decisions. The Court first considered the entrapment defense in Sorrells v. United States, 287 U.S. 435 (1932). The majority held that entrapment tended to establish innocence, reasoning that Congress in enacting the criminal statute there at issue could not have intended to punish persons otherwise innocent who were lured into committing the proscribed conduct by governmental instigation. This focus on whether persons were 'otherwise innocent' led the majority to adopt what has become known as the subjective or origin-of-intent test under which entrapment is established only if (i) governmental instigation and inducement overstep the bounds of permissibility, and (ii) the defendant did not harbor a pre-existing criminal intent. Under the subjective test a finding that the defendant was predisposed to commit the offense would negate innocence and therefore defeat the defense. Finally, because entrapment was viewed as bearing on the guilt or innocence of the accused, the issue was deemed proper for submission to the jury.

"Justice Roberts wrote an eloquent concurring opinion, joined by Justices Brandeis and Stone, in which he argued that the purpose of the entrapment defense is to deter police misconduct. He emphatically rejected the notion that the defendant's conduct or predisposition had any relevance: 'The applicable principle is that courts must be closed to the trial of a crime instigated by the government's own agents. No other issue, no comparison of equities as between the guilty official and the guilty defendant, has any place in the enforcement of this overruling principle of public policy.' Because he viewed deterrence of impermissible law enforcement activity as the proper rationale for the entrapment defense, Justice Roberts concluded that the defense was inappropriate for jury consideration: 'It is the province of the court and of the court alone to protect itself and the government from such prostitution of the criminal law.'

"In Sherman v. United States, 356 U.S. 369 (1958), the majority refused to adopt the 'objective' theory of entrapment urged by Justice Roberts, choosing rather to continue recognizing as relevant the defendant's own conduct and predisposition. The court

---

[1] The defense appears to have first been asserted by Eve, who complained, when charged with eating fruit of the tree of knowledge of good and evil: "The serpent beguiled me, and I did eat." Genesis 3:13. Though Eve was unsuccessful in asserting the defense, it has been suggested that the defense was unavailable to her because the entrapping party was not an agent of the punishing authority. Groot, The Serpent Beguiled Me and I (Without Scienter) Did Eat—Denial of Crime and the Entrapment Defense, 1973 U.Ill.L.F. 254.

held that 'a line must be drawn between the trap for the unwary innocent and the trap for the unwary criminal.' Justice Frankfurter, writing for four members of the Court in a concurring opinion, argued forcefully for Justice Roberts' objective theory: 'The courts refuse to convict an entrapped defendant, not because his conduct falls outside the proscription of the statute, but because, even if his guilt be admitted, the methods employed on behalf of the government to bring about conviction cannot be countenanced.' He reasoned that 'a test that looks to the character and predisposition of the defendant rather than the conduct of the police loses sight of the underlying reason for the defense of entrapment. No matter what the defendant's past record and present inclinations to criminality, or the depths to which he has sunk in the estimation of society, certain police conduct to ensnare him into further crime is not to be tolerated by an advanced society. . . . Permissible police activity does not vary according to the particular defendant concerned. . . .' 'Human nature is weak enough,' he wrote 'and sufficiently beset by temptations without government adding to them and generating crime.' Justice Frankfurter concluded that guidance as to appropriate official conduct could only be provided if the court reviewed police conduct and decided the entrapment issue.

"The United States Supreme Court recently reviewed the theoretical basis of the entrapment defense in United States v. Russell, 411 U.S. 423 (1973), and once again the court split five votes to four in declining to overrule the subjective theory adopted in *Sorrells*."

It was noted in a dissent in *Barraza* that the test in the federal courts and in all but seven states is the "predisposition" or subjective standard. The *Barraza* court nonetheless adopted the minority view on the ground that the defense should be granted in order to deter objectionable police behavior even if the defendant was predisposed to commit the crime. This is also the approach codified in Section 2.13 of the Model Penal Code.[a]

(iii) **Questions on the Defense.** Traditionally, the entrapment defense has been limited to cases involving inducements by the police. There is no defense of "private entrapment." To the extent that entrapment implies a lack of blameworthiness, why should it matter whether the defendant was entrapped by the police? On the other hand, the law's failure to recognize private entrapment tends to confirm the idea that the defense is designed mainly to deter unacceptable police behavior. If so, does it follow that the subjective test should be abandoned in favor of a test focusing squarely on the propriety of the official conduct? Does it follow, in other words, that considerations of individual blameworthiness should be irrelevant to the application of the defense? If so, why should a defendant who was predisposed to commit the crime be acquitted simply because the "ordinary" law-

[a] The two approaches to entrapment are skillfully contrasted in Park, The Entrap- ment Controversy, 60 Minn.L.Rev. 163 (1976).

abiding person would also have been induced by the police tactics? Conversely, should a defendant who proves that *he* was induced by the police, and would not otherwise have committed the crime, be deprived of the defense because the jury concludes that a hypothetical law-abiding person would not have been induced?

On the other hand, can it be argued that the entrapment defense represents an anomaly from the standpoint of the substantive policies of the penal law? Can it be sensibly argued that the ordinary law-abiding citizen should have the fortitude to resist inducements to criminal behavior, whether by the police or by anyone else? Is a person induced to commit a criminal act by the clever manipulations of undercover agents or informants any less blameworthy than a person who is induced to provide criminal assistance to an employer who threatens to fire him or disclose a sorry episode from his past? Or a person who is induced to provide illegal aid to a loved one who has become enmeshed in criminal activity? Short of duress, does sympathy, friendship, or fear provide an excuse for criminal behavior? Even if a jury were to find that Barraza was not otherwise predisposed to deal heroin and wanted to return to a law-abiding path, is it unfair to hold him criminally liable for giving in to Cheryl's persistent entreaties? Laying aside the question of deterring undesirable police practices, would you think it sensible to abolish the entrapment defense?

2. *Cox* v. *Louisiana.* In Cox v. Louisiana, 379 U.S. 559 (1965), the defendant was convicted of violating a statute punishing one who "pickets or parades . . . near a building housing a [state] court." The defendant's contention is revealed in the following excerpt from the decision reversing the conviction:

"Thus, the highest police officials of the city, in the presence of the sheriff and mayor, in effect told the demonstrators that they could meet where they did, 101 feet from the courthouse steps, but could not meet closer to the courthouse. In effect, appellant was advised that a demonstration at the place it was held would not be one 'near' the courthouse within the terms of the statute.

"In Raley v. Ohio, 360 U.S. 423 (1959), this Court held that the due process clause prevented conviction of persons refusing to answer questions of a state investigating commission when they relied upon assurances of the commission, either express or implied, that they had a privilege under state law to refuse to answer, though in fact this privilege was not available to them. The situation presented here is analogous to that in *Raley*, which we deem to be controlling. As in *Raley*, under all the circumstances of this case, after the public officials acted as they did, to sustain appellant's later conviction for demonstrating where they told him he could 'would be to sanction an indefensible sort of entrapment by the state—convicting a citizen for exercising a privilege which the state had clearly told him was available to him.' The due-process clause does not permit convictions to be obtained under such circumstances."

What was the basis for the *Cox* decision? Is "entrapment" the best description for the idea the Court had in mind? Was the Court aiming to deter objectionable police behavior? Or did the Court conclude that the defendants could not fairly be blamed for violating the law under these circumstances? On the other hand, if *Cox* is a case of situational excuse, is it consistent with the ignorantia-juris principle studied at pages 257–68, supra?

How would *Cox* be decided under the Model Penal Code? Would the defendants be entitled to a defense based on official misstatement of the law under § 2.04(3)(b)(iv)? Should the existence of the defense depend upon whether the "highest police officials" were present? Consider also § 2.13(1)(a). Should the existence of the defense depend upon whether the police made "knowingly false" statements designed to induce the defendants to violate the law?

In connection with *Cox*, consider *United States* v. *Barker*, reproduced at pages 597–602, supra. That case involved the "foot-soldiers" of the burglary of the office of Daniel Ellsberg's psychiatrist. The defendants claimed that they believed the break-in had been legally authorized by top White House aides. It turned out, however, that the aides did not have the authority to order a warrantless search. Can the defendants fairly be blamed for unquestioning obedience in this situation? Should a citizen's reasonable reliance on apparent official authority constitute a defense when it turns out that the officials exceeded their authority? Does *Cox* have any bearing on these questions?

Chapter V

CRIMINAL RESPONSIBILITY

INTRODUCTORY NOTE ON CRIMINAL RESPONSIBILITY

In contemporary usage, the term "mens rea" usually denotes the specific states of mind defined as "elements" of particular criminal offenses. The language is no longer meant to convey the idea of general malevolence characteristic of early common-law usage. However, the idea of a "guilty mind," in a more generalized moral sense, has continuing significance in relation to what the commentators have referred to as "the general conditions of criminal responsibility." The two most important of these conditions are maturity and sanity. Early on, the common-law courts developed the "defenses" of infancy and insanity (including "idiocy" and "lunacy") to exclude from criminal punishment those who lacked the "capacity" to have a "morally accountable and punishable mind." [a]

Definition of the conditions that establish irresponsibility or incapacity has been the subject of continuing debate since the middle of the 19th century. The materials presented below address the significance of age and mental abnormality in contemporary terms. It must be emphasized at the outset, however, that the concept of "responsibility" is not congruent with the technical requirements of culpability studied in Chapter II. As Professor Kadish has noted: [b]

> "In requiring mens rea in [its] special sense the law [absolves a person who] has shown himself . . . to be no different than the rest of us, or not different enough to justify the criminal sanction. In requiring . . . legal responsibility, the law absolves a person precisely because his deficiencies of temperament, personality or maturity distinguish him so utterly from the rest of us to whom the law's threats are addressed that we do not expect him to comply."

It is sometimes said that the "tests" of responsibility aim to identify those persons whose immaturity or mental aberration deprives them of the capacity to have criminal intent or mens rea. However, this is not an accurate statement of prevailing doctrine if the term mens rea is used in its technical sense. It is true, of course, that small infants lack the capacity to form a conscious purpose, to have a conscious awareness of the environment, or even to be conscious of making any choices at all. Elderly adults suffering from severe deterioration of brain func-

[a] Ballentine, Criminal Responsibility of the Insane and Feebleminded, 9 J.Crim.L. & Criminology 485, 493 (1919).

[b] Kadish, The Decline of Innocence, 26 Camb.L.J. 273, 275 (1968).

631

tion also might lack such capacities. However, the defenses of infancy and insanity have never been limited to such persons; the law has also withheld criminal liability from children and mentally disordered adults who clearly had the capacity to entertain the purposes, intentions, beliefs, or perceptions that would establish mens rea in its technical sense. As one commentator observed, "insane persons . . . may have intent to kill, to set fire to houses, to steal, to rape, to defraud; but the great question is whether [such a person] is a responsible moral agent." [c]

The materials in this chapter explore the factors that are taken into account in determining whether children and mentally disordered adults are "responsible moral agents" subject to criminal liability and punishment. Section 1 covers the common-law defense of infancy and its contemporary applications in the context of juvenile justice. Section 2 covers the defense of insanity and other doctrines that determine the significance of mental abnormality in the penal law.

SECTION 1: IMMATURITY

INTRODUCTORY NOTES ON THE INFANCY DEFENSE AND THE JUVENILE COURT

1. **The Common-Law Presumptions.** As the requirement of blameworthiness began to take shape in the criminal law, the idea soon developed—by the end of the 13th century—that children of tender years could not have a guilty mind and, accordingly, were not punishable. Although older children could be convicted if the circumstances of the offense demonstrated an "understanding discretion," royal pardons apparently spared many such children from execution. Sayre notes that the defense of infancy had "taken definite form" by the 16th century:

> ". . . An infant's guilt depended upon his mental state; but in a day when the defendant accused of felony was not allowed to take the stand, the determination of his mental capacity and discretion was naturally sought through legal presumptions and through the consequent drawing of somewhat arbitrary age lines when infants would be conclusively presumed to possess or to lack the necessary 'discretion.' " [a]

The lines marking the operation of these presumptions were somewhat unsettled until the 17th century, when the works of Coke and Hale fixed seven and 14 as the critical ages for determining the criminal responsibility of children. According to Hale,[b] an infant

---

[c] Ballentine, Criminal Responsibility of the Insane and Feebleminded, 9 J.Crim.L. & Criminology 485, 492 (1919).

[a] Sayre, Mens Rea, 45 Harv.L.Rev. 974, 1009 (1932).

[b] 1 M. Hale, The History of the Pleas of the Crown 25–27 (Philadelphia 1847) (1st ed. 1736). On the development of the common-law presumptions, see generally Ke-

younger than seven could not "be guilty of felony" because "for them a felonious discretion is almost an impossibility in nature"; the presumption of incapacity was irrebuttable. However, adolescents older than 14 were subject to criminal liability on the same terms as adults, for it was presumed that "they are doli capaces and can discern between good and evil." A child between seven and 14 could be convicted only if it was proved by "strong and pregnant evidence" that "he understood what he did"; in these cases the presumption of incapacity applied, but it was rebuttable. These common-law presumptions were received intact in the United States.

2. **Antecedents of the Juvenile Court.**[c] The determination that a youth was criminally liable did not necessarily mean that he was punished on the same terms as an adult. Historians who have researched early English records and colonial American practices have concluded that the death penalty generally was not imposed on youthful offenders. Also, during the colonial and post-colonial era, convicted children often were bound to masters for lengthy apprenticeships instead of suffering the normal penal consequences of conviction. Nonetheless, it does appear that many youthful offenders were confined with adults in local jails or almshouses and, eventually, in the penitentiaries that most states established during the first half of the 19th century.

A major 19th-century development was the creation of separate "houses of refuge," or reformatories, for children charged with, or convicted of, criminal offenses. One of the first such institutions was established in Pennsylvania in 1826 with statutory authority to "receive . . . such children who shall be taken up or committed as vagrants, or upon any criminal charge, or duly convicted of criminal offenses, as may . . . be deemed proper objects." [d] By the turn of the century, most states had established such institutions. Although some states prohibited confinement of youthful offenders in penitentiaries, assignment to the reformatories usually was discretionary. As a result, juvenile offenders frequently were confined in local jails with adults, both before trial and after conviction. Also, juveniles convicted of serious crimes—usually those punishable by life imprisonment—customarily were regarded as unfit subjects for correction in the houses of refuge and usually were imprisoned in the penitentiary.

The placement of juvenile offenders in reformatories represented an important dispositional reform, but it left the substantive criminal law unchanged. Children older than seven were still subject to conviction and punishment for criminal offenses. However, a concurrent statutory development had more far-reaching substantive significance. Nine years after establishing its House of Refuge, the Pennsylvania legislature authorized the institution to admit children who had not been charged with or convicted of crime, but who had been found by justices of the peace to be incorrigible or beyond parental authority.[e] In so

an, The History of the Criminal Liability of Children, 53 L.Q.Rev. 364 (1937).

[c] The development of the juvenile court is traced in A. Platt, The Child Savers (1960).

[d] Act of March 23, 1826, quoted in Ex parte Crouse, 4 Whart. 9, 10 (Pa.1839).

[e] Act of April 10, 1835, quoted in Ex parte Crouse, 4 Whart. 9, 10 (Pa.1839).

doing, the state was invoking its power as parens patriae or "common guardian of the community." The opinion of the Supreme Court of Pennsylvania rejecting a constitutional challenge to the commitment procedure reveals the animating spirit of these early laws:

"The House of Refuge is not a prison, but a school. Where reformation, and not punishment, is the end, it may indeed be used as a prison for juvenile convicts who would else be committed to a common gaol; and in respect to these, the constitutionality of the act which incorporated it, stands clear of controversy. It is only in respect of the application of its discipline to subjects admitted on the order of the court, a magistrate or the managers of the Almshouse, that a doubt is entertained. The object of the charity is reformation, by training its inmates to industry; by imbuing their minds with principles of morality and religion; by furnishing them with means to earn a living; and, above all, by separating them from the corrupting influence of improper associates. To this end may not the natural parents, when unequal to the task of education, or unworthy of it, be superseded by the parens patriae, or common guardian of the community? It is to be remembered that the public has a paramount interest in the virtue and knowledge of its members, and that of strict right, the business of education belongs to it. That parents are ordinarily intrusted with it is because it can seldom be put into better hands; but where they are incompetent or corrupt, what is there to prevent the public from withdrawing their faculties, held, as they obviously are, at its sufferance? . . . As to abridgment of indefeasible rights by confinement of the person, it is no more than what is borne, to a greater or less extent, in every school; and we know of no natural right to exemption from restraints which conduce to an infant's welfare. Nor is there a doubt of the propriety of their application in the particular instance. The infant has been snatched from a course which must have ended in confirmed depravity; and, not only is the restraint of her person lawful, but it would be an act of extreme cruelty to release her from it." [f]

Following Pennsylvania's lead, most states authorized summary commitment of incorrigible, ungovernable, or neglected children to the reformatories, and this practice was routinely upheld by the courts. Although data are not available, it seems likely that those youths who lacked criminal responsibility for otherwise criminal acts by operation of the common-law infancy defense were committed to Houses of Refuge through this separate "civil" process.

3. **The Juvenile-Court Movement.** The next step was the creation of the juvenile court, a reform predicated upon a wholesale repudiation of the premises and methods of the criminal law and an equally sweeping assertion of the state's parens-patriae authority. Jurisdiction over "delinquent" children below a designated age—usually

[f] Ex parte Crouse, 4 Whart. 9, 11 (Pa. 1839).

16 or 18—was vested exclusively in the juvenile court. The declared purpose of the intervention was therapeutic rather than punitive; the judge's task was to diagnose the child's problem and to order appropriate treatment. Illinois generally is credited with enacting the first juvenile-court law in 1899, and by 1917 all but three states had passed such laws. The attitudes and beliefs leading to creation of the juvenile court have been much discussed by legal and social historians. It is enough to note here that the juvenile court "represents the most important and ambitious effort yet undertaken by our law to give practical expression to the rehabilitative ideal." [g] The philosophy underlying the new court is captured in the following excerpt from H. Lou, Juvenile Courts in the United States 2 (1927): [*]

"What was lacking [before the juvenile court] was the conception that a child [who] broke the law was to be dealt with by the state not as a criminal but as a child needing care, education, and protection. Whatever solicitude for the welfare of children had been professed in these early laws, children who came into conflict with the law were tried for the commission of a specific crime and were treated as adults with all the formalities of the criminal law and constitutional safeguards in order to vindicate the dignity and majesty of the state. There was no constructive work which would make the individualization of treatment possible. The courts before which the children's cases were tried were courts of general criminal jurisdiction. Despite the various beneficent efforts in a number of states to save offending children, numberless children in the country as a whole were indicted, prosecuted, and tried as ordinary criminals and imprisoned in reformatories and penitentiaries. . . .

"[The] principles upon which the juvenile court acts are radically different from those of the criminal courts. In place of judicial tribunals, restrained by antiquated procedure, saturated in an atmosphere of hostility, trying cases for determining guilt and inflicting punishment according to inflexible rules of law, we have now juvenile courts, in which the relations of the child to his parents or other adults and to the state or society are defined and are adjusted summarily according to the scientific findings about the child and his environments. In place of magistrates, limited by the outgrown custom and compelled to walk in the paths fixed by the law of the realm, we have now socially-minded judges, who hear and adjust cases according not to rigid rules of law but to what the interests of society and the interests of the child or good conscience demand. In place of juries, prosecutors, and lawyers, trained in the old conception of law and staging dramatically, but often amusingly, legal battles, as the necessary paraphernalia of a criminal court, we have now probation officers, physicians, psychologists and psychiatrists, who search for

[g] F. Allen, The Borderland of Criminal Justice 48–49 (1964).

[*] From Juvenile Courts in the United States by Herbert H. Lou. Copyright 1927

The University of North Carolina press. Reprinted by permission of the publisher.

the social, physiological, psychological, and mental backgrounds of the child in order to arrive at reasonable and just solutions of individual cases. In other words, in this new court we tear down primitive prejudice, hatred, and hostility toward the lawbreaker in that most hidebound of all human institutions, the court of law, and we attempt, as far as possible, to administer justice in the name of truth, love, and understanding."

Challenges to the constitutionality of the procedures employed in juvenile proceedings were quickly and uniformly rejected. The courts typically emphasized the benevolent purposes of the intervention, as did the Supreme Court of Pennsylvania in 1905:

"To save a child from becoming a criminal, or from continuing in a career of crime, to end in maturer years in public punishment and disgrace, the legislature surely may provide for the salvation of such a child . . . by bringing it into one of the courts of the state without any process at all. . . .

"[T]he act is not for the trial of a child charged with a crime but is mercifully to save it from such an ordeal, with the prison or penitentiary in its wake, if the child's own good and the best interests of the state justify such salvation. . . .

"The design is not punishment nor the restraint imprisonment any more than is the wholesome restraint which a parent exercises over his child." [h]

4. **Contemporary Reform of Juvenile Justice.** By the 1960's, it was widely recognized that the juvenile-justice system had fallen far short of the aspirations of the child-savers described by Lou. The criticisms, which extended both to the premises and methods of the juvenile court, were summarized in 1967 by an influential government report, The President's Commission on Law Enforcement and Administration of Justice, Task Force Report: Juvenile Delinquency and Youth Crime 7–9 (1967):

"[T]he great hopes originally held for the juvenile court have not been fulfilled. It has not succeeded significantly in rehabilitating delinquent youth, in reducing or even stemming the tide of juvenile criminality, or in bringing justice and compassion to the child offender. . . .

"One reason for the failure of the juvenile courts has been the community's continuing unwillingness to provide the resources— the people and facilities and concern—necessary to permit them to realize their potential and prevent them from taking on some of the undesirable features typical of lower criminal courts in this country. In few jurisdictions, for example, does the juvenile-court judgeship enjoy high status in the eyes of the bar, and while there are many juvenile-court judges of outstanding ability and devotion, many are not. One crucial presupposition of the juvenile-court philosophy—a mature and sophisticated judge,

---

[h] Commonwealth v. Fisher, 213 Pa. 48, 53–56, 62 A. 198, 200–01 (1905). For a review of the early judicial decisions up-

holding the juvenile court procedures, see Mack, The Juvenile Court, 23 Harv.L.Rev. 104 (1909).

wise and well versed in law and the science of human behavior—
has proved in fact too often unattainable. A recent study of
juvenile-court judges . . . revealed that half had not received
undergraduate degrees; . . . a fifth were not members of the
bar. . . . [J]udicial hearings often are little more than attenuated interviews of 10 or 15 minutes' duration. . . .

"Other resources are equally lacking. The survey of juvenile-
court judges reveals the scarcity of psychologists and psychiatrists—over half a century after the juvenile-court movement set
out to achieve the coordinated application of the behavorial and
social sciences to the misbehaving child. Where clinics exist,
their waiting lists usually are months long and frequently they
provide no treatment but only diagnosis. And treatment, even
when prescribed, is often impossible to carry out because of the
unavailability of adequate individual and family casework, fos-
ter-home placement, treatment in youth institutions. . . .

"The dispositional alternatives available even to the better
endowed juvenile courts fall far short of the richness and the
relevance to individual needs envisioned by the court's founders.
In most places, indeed, the only alternatives are release outright,
probation, and institutionalization. Probation means minimal
supervision at best. A large percentage of juvenile courts have
no probation services at all, and in those that do, caseloads
typically are so high that counseling and supervision take the
form of occasional phone calls and perfunctory visits instead of
the careful, individualized service that was intended. Institutionalization too often means storage—isolation from the outside
world—in an overcrowded, understaffed, high-security institution
with little education, little vocational training, little counseling
or job placement or other guidance upon release. Programs are
subordinated to everyday control and maintenance. . . .

"But it is of great importance to emphasize that a simple
infusion of resources into juvenile courts and attendant institutions would by no means fulfill the expectations that accompanied the court's birth and development. There are problems that
go much deeper. The failure of the juvenile court to fulfill its
rehabilitative and preventive promise stems in important measure from a grossly over-optimistic view of what is known about
the phenomenon of juvenile criminality and of what even a fully
equipped juvenile court could do about it. Experts in the field
agree that it is extremely difficult to develop successful methods
for preventing serious delinquent acts through rehabilitative
programs for the child. . . .

"[O]fficial action . . . may do more harm than good.
Official action may actually help to fix and perpetuate delinquency in the child through a process in which the individual begins
to think of himself as delinquent and organizes his behavior
accordingly. The process itself is further reinforced by the effect
of the labeling upon the child's family, neighbors, teachers, and

peers, whose reactions communicate to the child in subtle ways a kind of expectation of delinquent conduct. The undesirable consequences of official treatment are heightened in programs that rely on institutionalizing the child. The most informed and benign institutional treatment of the child, even in well designed and staffed reformatories and training schools, thus may contain within it the seeds of its own frustration and itself may often feed the very disorder it is designed to cure.

". . . While statutes, judges, and commentators still talk the language of compassion, help, and treatment, it has become clear that in fact the same purposes that characterize the use of the criminal law for adult offenders—retribution, condemnation, deterrence, incapacitation—are involved in the disposition of juvenile offenders too. These are society's ultimate techniques for protection against threatening conduct; it is inevitable that they should be used against threats from the young as well as the old when other resources appear unavailing. As Professor Francis Allen has acutely observed:

'In a great many cases the juvenile court must perform functions essentially similar to those exercised by any court adjudicating cases of persons charged with dangerous and disturbing behavior. It must reassert the norms and standards of the community when confronted by seriously deviant conduct, and it must protect the security of the community by such measures as it has at its disposal, even though the available means may be unsatisfactory when viewed either from the standpoint of the community interest or of the welfare of the delinquent child.'

"The difficulty is not that this compromise with the rehabilitative ideal has occurred, but that it has not been acknowledged. Juvenile-court laws and procedures that can be defended and rationalized solely on the basis of the original optimistic theories endure as if the vitality of those theories were undiluted. Thus, for example, juvenile courts retain expansive grounds of jurisdiction authorizing judicial intervention in relatively minor matters of morals and misbehavior, on the ground that subsequent delinquent conduct may be indicated, as if there were reliable ways of predicting delinquency in a given child and reliable ways of redirecting children's lives. Delinquency is adjudicated in informal proceedings that often lack safeguards fundamental for protecting the individual and for assuring reliable determinations, as if the court were a hospital clinic and its only objective were to discover the child's malady and to cure him. As observed by Mr. Justice Fortas, speaking for the Supreme Court in Kent v. United States, 383 U.S. 541, 546 (1966), 'there may be grounds for concern that the child receives the worst of both worlds: that he gets neither the protections accorded to adults nor the solicitous care and regenerative treatment postulated for children.'

"What emerges then, is this: In theory the juvenile court was to be helpful and rehabilitative rather than punitive. In fact the distinction often disappears, not only because of the absence of facilities and personnel but also because of the limits of knowledge and technique. In theory the court's action was to affix no stigmatizing label. In fact a delinquent is generally viewed by employers, schools, the armed services—by society generally—as a criminal. In theory the court was to treat children guilty of criminal acts in non-criminal ways. In fact it labels truants and runaways as junior criminals.

"In theory the court's operations could justifiably be informal, its findings and decisions made without observing ordinary procedural safeguards, because it would act only in the best interest of the child. In fact it frequently does nothing more nor less than deprive a child of liberty without due process of law—knowing not what else to do and needing, whether admittedly or not, to act in the community's interest even more imperatively than the child's. In theory it was to exercise its protective powers to bring an errant child back into the fold. In fact there is increasing reason to believe that its intervention reinforces the juvenile's unlawful impulses.

". . . What is required is . . . a revised philosophy of the juvenile court based on the recognition that in the past our reach exceeded our grasp. The spirit that animated the juvenile-court movement was fed in part by a humanitarian compassion for offenders who were children. That willingness to understand and treat people who threaten public safety and security should be nurtured, not turned aside as hopeless sentimentality, both because it is civilized and because social protection itself demands constant search for alternatives to the crude and limited expedient of condemnation and punishment. But neither should it be allowed to outrun reality. The juvenile court is a court of law, charged like other agencies of criminal justice with protecting the community against threatening conduct. Rehabilitating offenders through individualized handling is one way of providing protection, and appropriately the primary way in dealing with children. But the guiding consideration for a court of law that deals with threatening conduct is nonetheless protection of the community. The juvenile court, like other courts, is therefore obliged to employ all the means at hand, not excluding incapacitation, for achieving that protection. What should distinguish the juvenile from the criminal courts is greater emphasis on rehabilitation, not exclusive preoccupation with it."

Doubts about the benevolent purposes and effects of delinquency adjudication have led to sweeping contemporary reforms designed to conform the juvenile-justice process more closely to the criminal process. Generally speaking, the doctrines governing the definition of criminal conduct and the procedures required for its proof now apply fully to the definition and proof of delinquent acts. In a series of decisions beginning with In re Gault, 387 U.S. 1 (1967), the Supreme Court of the United States held that, aside from trial by jury, a juvenile charged with a delinquent act is constitutionally entitled to virtually all of the procedural protections afforded to a defendant in a criminal prosecution.

The administration of juvenile justice has been reshaped. As the following materials make apparent, however, no consensus has emerged regarding the theoretical underpinnings of delinquency adjudication. Ultimately, the question is whether juvenile justice should be framed on a model of control and treatment or on a model of punishment.

IN RE DAVIS

Maryland Court of Appeals, 1973.
17 Md.App. 98, 299 A.2d 856.

ORTH, CHIEF JUDGE. Under the common law there is a presumption of criminal incapacity on the part of an infant below the age of 14, which is conclusive prior to the age of seven and rebuttable thereafter. When the presumption of doli incapax is rebuttable, the burden of rebutting it is on the state.[1]

Bryan Garland Davis, born 30 June 1959, would like to invoke the doli incapax rule in juvenile proceedings. He was found to be a delinquent child in the Circuit Court of Baltimore City, Division of Juvenile Causes, on 20 June 1972 and placed on probation. The petition against Davis, filed by the state's attorney, alleged that he was a delinquent child for the reason that on 20 May 1972, he, "in company with Allen Lorenzo Floyd, unlawfully did, or attempt to, steal, take and carry away the goods, chattels, moneys and property of Master John O'Grady, to wit: by attempting to force the right front vent [of a 1965 Buick] with a brick. . . ."

A declared purpose of the Juvenile Causes Act is "to remove from children committing delinquent acts the taint of criminality and the consequences of criminal behavior, and to substitute therefor a program of treatment, training, and rehabilitation consistent with the protection of the public interest." The Act shall be liberally construed to effectuate its purposes. A child means a person who has not reached his 18th birthday.[2] A delinquent child means a child who commits a delinquent act and who requires supervision, treatment or rehabilitation. A delinquent act includes an act which would be a crime if done by a person who is not a child. Thus the statute is more lenient than the common law with respect to an infant who commits a crime, for under

----

[1] "It is generally held that the presumption of doli incapax is 'extremely strong at the age of seven and diminishes gradually until it disappears entirely at the age 14 . . . .' Since the strength of the presumption of incapacity decreases with the increase in the years of the accused, the quantum of proof necessary to overcome the presumption would diminish in substantially the same ratio." Adams v. State, 8 Md.App. 684, 688–89, 262 A.2d 69, 72 (1970).

[2] In determining the jurisdiction of a juvenile court over persons alleged to be delinquent children, the age of the child at the time the alleged delinquent act was committed is controlling.

it, a person up to the age of 18 years may be protected from the taint of criminality. So the statute bestows on a juvenile court exclusive original jurisdiction over persons alleged to be delinquent children, with certain exemptions. . . .

What Davis urges is that because he was 12 years of age at the time he committed the delinquent act, and because that act, which was the basis of the finding that he was a delinquent child, would be a crime if done by a person not a child, the burden was on the state to rebut the presumption of his criminal incapacity before he could be found to be a delinquent child. He claims error for the reason that, over his objection, the state did not meet this burden.

. . . When a juvenile court has exclusive original jurisdiction over a person alleged to be a delinquent child and does not waive that jurisdiction, the result, stated in terms of the common law, is that the age under which a person is *conclusively presumed* to be incapable of committing a crime has been raised from seven to 18. The transgression by the child is not a crime at all, but a different kind of misdeed known as a "delinquent act." This is in accord with the previous holdings of the court of appeals and this court, that juvenile proceedings are of a special nature designed to meet the problems peculiar to the adolescent; that the proceedings of a juvenile court are not criminal in nature and its dispositions are not punishment for crime; that the juvenile law has as its underlying concept the protection of the juvenile, so that judges, in making dispositions in juvenile cases, think not in terms of guilt, but of the child's need for protection or rehabilitation. No disposition of any juvenile proceedings with respect to a child shall be deemed a conviction of crime or impose any civil disabilities ordinarily resulting from such a conviction. No child shall be committed or transferred to a penal institution or other facility used primarily for the execution of sentences of persons convicted of a crime. The proceedings with reference to a child in the juvenile court shall not be admissible as evidence against him in any criminal proceeding, other than a charge of perjury, except after conviction in proceedings to determine his sentence.

It being clear that the finding in a juvenile proceeding that a child is delinquent is not the equivalent of a determination arrived at in a criminal proceeding that he has committed a crime, it follows that it is not a prerequisite to a finding that a person is a delinquent child that the state show under the common-law rule that the child had such maturity in fact as to have a guilty knowledge that he was doing wrong, that is the capacity to commit crime. Under the statute, by its purpose and the very principles it advances, the child under the jurisdiction of a juvenile court is conclusively presumed doli incapax. The child is delinquent, not because he committed a crime, but because he committed an *act* which would be a crime if committed by a person who is not a child, and because he requires supervision, treatment or rehabilitation. He must be doli capax to commit a crime, but not to commit a delinquent act. The raison d'etre of the Juvenile Causes Act is that a child does not commit a crime when he commits a delinquent act and therefore is not a criminal. He is not to be punished but afforded supervision and treatment to be made aware of what is right and what is wrong so as to be amenable to the criminal laws.

We hold that the common-law rule concerning presumption of criminal incapacity is not applicable to juvenile proceedings with respect to the determination of delinquency vel non. . . .

[Affirmed.]

NOTES ON MENS REA AND RESPONSIBILITY IN DELINQUENCY PROCEEDINGS

1. **Mens Rea and Delinquency.** The *Davis* court concludes that a child within the jurisdiction of the juvenile court is conclusively presumed to lack the capacity to commit a crime, and that proof of such capacity therefore is not required in delinquency proceedings. Recall the court's statement that "the child is delinquent not because he committed a crime, but because he committed an *act* which would be a crime if committed by a person who is not a child, and because he requires supervision, treatment or rehabilitation." Does the court mean that proof of mens rea—even in its special technical sense—is not required as a predicate for a delinquency determination? Recall Lady Wootton's proposal to eliminate the emphasis of the law on mens rea and to establish instead a preventive system of social hygiene in lieu of a system of punishment, described and discussed at pages 385–92, supra. Does the juvenile-justice system implement the theory underlying her proposal? Are the objections raised to her approach less applicable in this context than in the administration of the criminal law?

The language in the *Davis* opinion may have been broader than the court intended. Most courts probably would hold that the state must prove both the actus reus and mens rea of the offense to establish the predicate for delinquency intervention, but that it is not required to prove that the child appreciated the wrongfulness of his conduct. That is, adjudication of delinquency requires the proof of mens rea in its special sense but not in the general sense of responsibility. This was the holding of the Supreme Court of Rhode Island in In re Michael, 423 A.2d 1180 (R.I. 1981). In that case, Michael, a 12-year-old boy was found "not innocent" of assaulting a five-year-old girl and was committed to a training school for one year. The evidence was summarized by the court:

> "The young girl testified that as she was walking home, a boy joined her. He asked her to go into the park with him to look for birds' eggs. Alone inside the park, he asked her to lie down, which she did. The boy then pulled up her dress and pulled down her underwear. The young girl had difficulty discussing exactly what happened after this. It is clear that she did scream at one point.

"As the two youngsters left the wooded area of the park, they met Patrolman George Bassett of the Providence police department, who was investigating screams he had heard. Michael told Patrolman Bassett that they were searching for birds' eggs. The girl's version was quite different. She told the officer that Michael had taken her up there to look for birds' eggs, but that he had been knocking her down and hurting her.

"The examining physician testified that the girl's vagina and perineal areas were very reddened and painful to the touch. The girl also had bruises on her cheek and on both knees."

Citing *Davis*, the court held that "the age under which a person is conclusively presumed to be incapable of committing a crime has been raised from seven to 15" and that, accordingly, "there is no necessity of finding that the juvenile had such maturity that he or she knew that what he or she was doing was wrong." However, the court also emphasized that:

"[A]ny adjudication of delinquency . . . must rest upon a finding beyond a reasonable doubt that the juvenile had formed whatever criminal intent or mens rea was an element of the offense that gave rise to his being before the Family Court.

. . .

"Here, even though Michael might be immune from criminal prosecution because of his age, there is ample evidence that he intended to do the proscribed act, that the act was unlawful, and that it was not done inadvertently. Michael's invitation to 'catch birds' eggs,' the five-year-old's testimony, the screams heard by the police officer, and the findings of the five-year-old's physical examination provided proof beyond a reasonable doubt that an assault had occurred and that Michael was the assaulter."

2. **The Relevance of Statutory Purpose.** *Davis* and *Michael* state the prevailing view that the common-law infancy defense does not apply to delinquency proceedings. Do you agree that the imposition of delinquency liability should not be predicated upon proof that the offender appreciated the wrongfulness of his or her conduct? Does the *Davis* court's recitation of the benevolent purposes of the juvenile-justice system provide a persuasive rationale?

Consider whether the result would be different if the Maryland legislature had explicitly abandoned the rehabilitative model of juvenile justice. In Minnesota, for example, the juvenile-court legislation provides that "[t]he purpose of the laws relating to children alleged or adjudicated to be delinquent is to promote the public safety and reduce juvenile delinquency by maintaining the integrity of the substantive law prohibiting certain behavior and by developing individual responsibility for lawful behavior." [a] Similarly the Washington legislature

a Minn.Stat.Ann. § 260.011. Before the amendment the sole declared purpose of the juvenile code had been to secure "for each minor . . . the care and guidance, preferably in his own home, as will serve the . . . welfare of the minor and the best interests of the state . . . and when the minor is removed from his own family, to secure for him custody, care and discipline as nearly as possible equivalent to that which should have been given by his parents." No distinction in purpose

declared that the purposes of delinquency adjudication included "mak[ing] the juvenile offender accountable for his or her criminal behavior; [and] provid[ing] for punishment commensurate with the age, crime, and criminal history of the juvenile offender." [b] How would you decide *Davis* and *Michael* if you were a judge in Minnesota or Washington?

3. *In re Gladys R.* One of the few cases holding the infancy presumption fully applicable to delinquency adjudication is In re Gladys R., 1 Cal.3d 855, 83 Cal.Rptr. 671, 464 P.2d 127 (1970). In that case a juvenile court found that Gladys R., a 12-year-old girl, had committed an act proscribed by the penal code (annoying or molesting a child under 18) and declared her to be a ward of the court under the delinquency provision (Section 602) of the juvenile-court law. The Supreme Court of California reversed the decision, holding that "in order to become a ward of the court under [the delinquency provision], clear proof must show that a child under the age of 14 years at the time of committing the act appreciated its wrongfulness." The court explained that the common-law infancy defense, which had been codified in Section 26 of the California Penal Code, "provides the kind of fundamental protection to children charged under Section 602 which this court should not lightly discard." The court continued:

> "If a juvenile court finds a lack of clear proof that a child under 14 years at the time of committing the act possessed knowledge of its wrongfulness . . . the court might well declare the child a ward under Section 600 [dependent children] or 601 [ungovernable children]. These latter provisions carry far less severe consequences for the liberty and life of the child. After all, it is the purpose of the Welfare and Institutions Code to 'insure that the rights or physical, mental or moral welfare of children are not violated or threatened by their present circumstances or environment.' Strong policy reasons cast doubt upon the placement of a child who is unable to appreciate the wrongfulness of his conduct [in] an institution where he will come into contact with many youths who are well versed in criminality. . . . We cannot condone a decision which would expose the child to consequences possibly disastrous to himself and society as a whole.

> "Other sections may possibly be invoked to provide for a wardship for this child with no injurious potentials. Section 601 provides that a child who disobeys the lawful orders of his parents or school authorities, who is beyond the control of such persons, or who is in danger of leading an immoral life may be adjudged a ward of the court. Section 601 might clearly cover younger children who lacked the age or experience to understand the wrongfulness of their conduct. If the juvenile court considers

was drawn before the amendment between delinquency proceedings and "dependency-and-neglect" proceedings. As a result of the 1980 amendment, the declaration of exclusively benevolent purposes applies only to dependency-and-neglect jurisdiction.

[b] Rev.Wash.Code Ann. § 13.40.010(2)(c), (d).

Section 601 inappropriate for the particular child, he may be covered by the even broader provisions of Section 600.

"Section 602 should apply only to those who are over 14 and may be presumed to understand the wrongfulness of their acts and to those under the age of 14 who clearly appreciate the wrongfulness of their conduct. In the instant case we are confronted with a 12-year-old girl of the social and mental age of a seven-year-old. Section 26 stands to protect her and other young people like her from the harsh strictures of Section 602. Only if the age, experience, knowledge, and conduct of the child demonstrate by clear proof that he has violated a criminal law should he be declared a ward of the court under Section 602."

Although Gladys R. may not be subject to control as a delinquent, the court strongly hints that she would be committable under the less precise dependency and ungovernability provisions. How do you suppose the Supreme Court of California would characterize the justifying purposes of intervention under Sections 600 and 601 on the one hand and Section 602 on the other? Is it likely to matter to Gladys R. whether she was committed under one section or another? Does anything turn on the court's distinction?

4. **Minimum Age for Delinquency Jurisdiction.** Even if the common-law infancy presumptions do not apply to delinquency proceedings, should there be a minimum age for delinquency jurisdiction? A few states specify such minimum age limits ranging from seven to 10 years of age. However, one commentator has noted that "even in the absence of a minimum age in the statute, there are no reported cases involving an attempt to charge delinquency against a child under the common-law immunity age of seven." [c] The Juvenile Justice Standards promulgated by the Institute of Judicial Administration and the American Bar Association recommend that delinquency liability be precluded for juveniles younger than 10.[d]

The designation of a minimum age for delinquency intervention could be based on a utilitarian judgment that any of the available dispositions would be more detrimental to the child's development than leaving his or her discipline and care to parents, schools, and other nongovernmental institutions of social control. However, the rationale for the common-law immunity, which is endorsed by the IJA–ABA standards, is that children below some level of maturity cannot fairly be blamed for their wrongful acts. What hypotheses about cognitive, social, and moral development underlie this judgment? Would it be important to know when children conform to social norms because they understand the reasons for the norms rather than because they fear the hand of authority figures? Researchers appear to agree that this phase of moral development does not ordinarily occur until at least six.[e] What other factors should be taken into account in determining when a

[c] S. Fox, Juvenile Courts in a Nutshell 18 (1971).

[d] IJA–ABA, Standards Relating to Juvenile Delinquency and Sanctions § 2.1(A) (1980).

[e] See generally Moral Development and Behavior: Theory, Research and Social Issues (T. Lickona ed., 1976).

person is sufficiently mature to be held responsible as a delinquent for wrongful acts?

IN RE DAHL
Supreme Court of Minnesota, 1979.
278 N.W.2d 316.

SCOTT, JUSTICE. This is an appeal from an order of a three-judge panel of the Ninth Judicial District affirming the Beltrami County Court's referral of a juvenile to district court for adult prosecution. . . .

On April 8, 1978, the dead body of Ricky Alan McGuire, who had been missing since November 17, 1977, was found in a remote area of Beltrami County. A witness described the frontal section of his head as "just disappeared, gone." A cap found near the body had a hole in it about the size of a half dollar. Three expended shotgun cartridges were also found lying near the body. In a petition filed on April 10, 1978, in Beltrami County Court, appellant was charged with delinquency for the first-degree murder of Ricky Alan McGuire. The petition alleged that appellant admitted that he shot McGuire on November 17, 1977, and planned to return to the scene in the spring to conceal the body; that witnesses are fearful of their safety and lives if appellant is freed during the pendency of the proceedings; that appellant was using a considerable amount of marijuana; and that appellant had recently authored a note stating that certain local persons must be "terminated." In addition, the petition requested that the court enter an order referring appellant for prosecution as an adult pursuant to Minn.Stat.Ann. § 260.125.[a]

Appellant was born on March 2, 1960, and therefore was 17 years old at the time of the alleged offense and 18 years old at the time the delinquency petition was filed. His parents described him as a respectful, obedient, and trustworthy child. Appellant stated that he had good relationships with his parents and younger brothers, and denied that he had any emotional problems.

At the time of the alleged wrongful conduct, appellant was a senior in high school, maintaining about a B average. He plans to attend Bemidji State University upon his graduation from high school. He participated in interscholastic track and cross-country running and in

---

[a] Section 260.125 then provided:

"(1) When a child is alleged to have violated a state or local law or ordinance after becoming 14 years of age the juvenile court may enter an order referring the alleged violation to the appropriate prosecuting authority for action under laws in force governing the commission of and punishment for violations of statutes or local laws or ordinances. . . .

"(2) The juvenile court may order a reference only if

(a) A petition has been filed . . .

(b) Notice has been given . . . .

(c) A hearing has been held . . .

(d) The court finds that the child is not suitable to treatment or that the public safety is not served under the provisions of the law relating to juvenile courts."

[Footnote by eds.]

intramural basketball. He once received a two day in-school suspension for swearing and kicking his locker. This conduct apparently occurred upon appellant's discovery that his expensive watch had been stolen. Appellant was employed since the fall of 1976 by a local restaurant. Prior to that time he worked as a stock boy and carryout boy at a local grocery store and as a trap setter at a local gun club. He was a steady and industrious worker.

Appellant's only prior contact with the juvenile court involved a charge of reckless driving which was eventually dismissed at the completion of a 45-day suspension of his driver's license. Accordingly, the county court observed that:

"[I]t is clearly apparent that the juvenile is not the typical delinquent seen by the juvenile court. This offense [first-degree murder], if he is guilty of it, appears to be an isolated delinquent act rather than an outcropping pattern of behavior normally associated with the classification of juvenile delinquent."

. . . A reference study by the county probation officer at the order of the court . . . recommended that appellant be referred for prosecution as an adult because of the lack of treatment programs for the serious juvenile offender who has reached the age of 18, and because the public safety is not served by the security measures taken at juvenile treatment centers. No psychological or psychiatric information concerning appellant was obtained.

[After a hearing] the [juvenile] court rendered its decision, referring appellant for prosecution as an adult for both non-amenability to treatment and public safety grounds. [A] three-judge panel of the Ninth Judicial District Court affirmed the decision of the [juvenile] court. . . .

The question before us is whether the . . . juvenile court, has met the required standards in ordering this juvenile referred to the adult authorities for prosecution. . . . Since [Section] 2(d) is phrased in the alternative, a finding of either non-amenability to treatment or harm to public safety is sufficient to refer a juvenile for prosecution as an adult. . . . In the instant case, the juvenile court found that both criteria . . . were satisfied, and thus referred appellant for prosecution as an adult.

The decision to refer a juvenile for prosecution as an adult, of course, is of tremendous consequence to both the involved juvenile and society in general. Unfortunately, the standards for referral adopted by present legislation are not very effective in making this important determination. . . .

[The opinion at this point refers to studies indicating that behaviorial scientists are unable to predict future behavior and tend to over-predict future violence. It then continues:]

Due to these difficulties in making the waiver decision, many juvenile-court judges have tended to be over-cautious, resulting in the referral of delinquent children for criminal prosecution on the erroneous, albeit good-faith, belief that the juveniles pose a danger to the public. Accordingly, a re-evaluation of the existing certification process may be in order. . . .

[However,] until changed, the statutory scheme for reference must be followed.

In this case, appellant was referred for prosecution as an adult primarily because the juvenile court determined that appellant could not be successfully treated within the period of time remaining before the juvenile court's jurisdiction of this matter is terminated.[2] This is a proper basis for concluding that a juvenile is unsuitable for treatment; however, the court's finding is not reasonably supported by the evidence. Although requested by the juvenile, no mental testing of appellant was performed, and consequently the record is devoid of any psychological or psychiatric data which could conceivably support the juvenile court's observation. Nor does the evidence disclose any negative information regarding the juvenile's background prior to the present act. On the contrary, the record shows that appellant has an exemplary background and is not the typical chronic offender who is usually subject to reference. In making its decision the juvenile court relied on the serious nature of the offense involved, appellant's age, "social adjustment," and maturity level. These considerations, in the absence of supporting psychological data or a history of misconduct, are insufficient to support the court's finding that appellant could not be successfully treated within the remaining three years the juvenile could be under the control of the juvenile-court system.

. . . The [juvenile and district] courts, in making their decisions, may very well have been using equitable reasoning and common sense based upon complete and sound logic in viewing a factual situation where an individual shot another three times, killing him; where . . . an adult jury would probably convict; and where in the eyes of the public, if he is convicted, a sentence for more than three years should be served. This attitude seems to be reflected by the record. But no matter how pragmatic such reasoning may be, it is a mistaken interpretation of the statutory intent of the legislature.

The legislature did not single out certain crimes for reference to adult prosecution, although it had that specific opportunity. The law does not say that all petitions filed in juvenile court alleging first-degree murder are automatically subject to certification, nor does the statute provide that 17-year-old violators are automatically referred for adult prosecution. . . . It appears in this case that reference was made because of age and seriousness of the crime, neither of which meets the statutory requirements.

The state argues that the juvenile court's determination, relative to public safety, is reasonable when the considerations set out in State v. Hogan, 297 Minn. 430, 438, 212 N.W.2d 664, 669 (1973),[6] are applied to

---

[2] Minn.Stat.Ann. § 260.181(4) states that the juvenile court's jurisdiction continues until the child reaches the age of 21, unless the court terminates its jurisdiction before that time. Thus, at the time of the court's decision, appellant could have been under the jurisdiction of the juvenile court for a little less than three years.

[6] In *Hogan*, we stated that: "[I]n determining if the public safety would be threatened, among the relevant factors to be considered are: (i) the seriousness of the

the facts of this case. Although this contention has some superficial appeal, when we apply all of the relevant evidence there is nothing in the record to show that the public safety will suffer in the future, or has done so in the time between the act and the arrest. No psychological information is contained in the record which might support this finding, nor does the juvenile's exemplary background indicate that he is a threat to the public safety. The record must reflect more reasons portending future danger; otherwise appellant would be referred solely on the basis of the offense in question. As discussed above, the existing statutory framework does not authorize referral based on the specific crime charged. Accordingly, this court did not intend the application of the *Hogan* factors to result in the referral of a juvenile solely because of the alleged offense. Rather, as stated in *Hogan*, the criteria we listed in that decision are only "*among* the relevant factors to be considered." . . . The record must contain direct evidence that the juvenile endangers the public safety for the statutory reference standard to be satisfied.

The present [delinquency] petition may make one shudder in reflecting upon the alleged event, but the record fails to show that this juvenile is "not suitable" to treatment or that the "public safety" will suffer. We therefore remand to the [juvenile] court with instructions to examine properly admissible evidence to be submitted at a further hearing for the purpose of determining whether, in light of this opinion, the statutory reference criteria are satisfied. If the record's substance is not materially altered as a result of this additional evidence, reference to adult court is not justified and thus the proceedings should continue in juvenile court.

The reference order is vacated and the matter is remanded for further proceedings consistent with this opinion.

NOTES ON TRANSFER OF JUVENILES
TO CRIMINAL COURT

1. **Introduction.** *In re Davis* and the previous notes dealt with the minimum level of maturity necessary for the imposition of delinquency liability. As *In re Gladys R.* suggests, the issue may also be characterized as the definition of the boundary between delinquency liability and "non-punitive" methods of coercive intervention for children. *In re Dahl* and the following notes address the other boundary of juvenile-court jurisdiction—the boundary between delinquency and criminal conviction.

offense in terms of community protection; (ii) the circumstances surrounding the offense; (iii) whether the offense was committed in an aggressive, violent, premeditated, or willful manner; (iv) whether the offense was directed against persons or property; (v) the reasonably foreseeable consequences of the act; and (vi) the absence of adequate protective and security facilities available to the juvenile treatment system."

At the extremes, the offender's age is the sole determinant of the jurisdictional question.[a] On the one hand, criminal prosecution of a person younger than 14 is absolutely barred in all but four states; the juvenile court's jurisdiction over such offenders is exclusive regardless of the offense charged. On the other hand, most states set the outer limit of juvenile-court jurisdiction at the 18th birthday; if the act charged occurred after the offender's 18th birthday, the criminal court's jurisdiction is exclusive.

The offender's age is not the sole jurisdictional criterion if the offender was older than the minimum (usually 14 or 15) and younger than the maximum (usually 18) at the time of the alleged offense. If the older adolescent is charged with a serious offense, the juvenile court is permitted or required in most states to waive its jurisdiction and to transfer the case to the criminal court. The statutes reflect two general approaches to transfer. Under the individualized approach used in most states, the juvenile-court judge retains or waives jurisdiction according to whether he finds, after a transfer hearing, that the offender is or is not "amenable to treatment" in the juvenile system. The Minnesota statute construed in *Dahl* is representative of statutes of this type. The other approach is a statute requiring mandatory transfer of a juvenile older than the designated age if the court finds probable cause to believe that the offender committed one of several specified serious offenses. These statutes are sometimes characterized as "legislative-waiver" provisions, as contrasted with the "judicial-waiver" provisions described above. It should be noted, however, that even in "legislative-waiver" states, the prosecutor's charging decision may determine which court has jurisdiction. Indeed, some states explicitly repose discretionary authority in the prosecutor to initiate either juvenile or criminal proceedings in cases involving the most serious offenses.

2. **The Responsibility of Older Adolescents.** The jurisdiction of juvenile courts over adolescents charged with homicide and other serious offenses has been a subject of continuing controversy since these courts were established. Many of the early statutes excluded murder and other serious offenses from juvenile-court jurisdiction, although subsequent legislation generally removed barriers to delinquency adjudication in such cases. The New Jersey experience is illustrative. Statutes passed in 1903 and 1912 expressly excluded murder and manslaughter from the juvenile court's jurisdiction; in these cases, the young offender's criminal liability continued to be determined by operation of the common-law infancy presumptions. However, the jurisdictional exclusion was deleted in 1929, and the legislature expressly provided in 1935 that "a person under the age of 16 is deemed incapable of committing a crime" and could be tried only in the juvenile court for any offense which, if committed by an adult, would constitute a crime. The Supreme Court of New Jersey subsequently held that the juvenile court had exclusive jurisdiction in a case involv-

a The statutes are summarized in IJA–ABA, Standards Relating to Transfer Between Courts 17–18 (1980).

ing a 15-year-old who participated with his father in a robbery during which his father killed two persons. State v. Monahan, 15 N.J. 34, 104 A.2d 21 (1954). However, this decision provoked a vigorous dissent:

"The constituents of a criminal offense are an evil intention and an unlawful act, so that the effect of the legislative declaration . . . is that any infant who is mentally capable of forming an evil intent and commits the overt act of homicide is not guilty or cannnot be found guilty of the highest crime against nature, because he is incapable of a criminal intent merely because of his age. . . .

"Man, including children, is a rational animal, a psychophysical being capable of rational thought and free will. Unless he is mentally incompetent and thus irrational, there comes a point in the life of each when he becomes capable of distinguishing between right and wrong. This is in the nature of man himself, although the point at which it is reached depends upon the type of society or civilization in which he lives and will also vary somewhat with each individual.

"At the common law and in this state, isofar as a crime is concerned, the inability to form a criminal intent is a matter of defense. [The opinion then reviews the common-law presumptions and continues:] These rules are consistent with the nature of man and the natural use of his faculties of intellect and will, and his freedom to acquire the necessary knowledge to make the distinction between right and wrong. They are rules to determine the ultimate fact of the ability of an individual to distinguish between right and wrong. The point in life when a person is capable of making this distinction may vary, but once it is reached that person, whether it be an adult or a child, is capable of criminal intent. . . .

"The views expressed here were of sufficient moment to induce the legislatures in many states to remove the charge of murder from the field of juvenile delinquency. . . .

"Whether in the matter of punishment of murder the legislature feels it desirable to place children in a different classification is purely a matter of public policy and within the legislature's power. But insofar as guilt for the commission of the crime of murder is concerned I cannot disregard the enormity of the offense . . . and agree that it can be treated as mere juvenile delinquency."

The dissenting judge in *Monahan* was objecting to what he regarded as an irrational legislative "finding" that persons under 16 are not sufficiently mature to be regarded as responsible for their acts, at least in cases involving a charge of murder. Was the 1935 amendment necessarily based upon such a finding? What else might the legislature have had in mind?

Transfer was not possible in *Monahan* because 16 was the minimum age for criminal-court jurisdiction under New Jersey law. However, transfer of a 15-year-old homicide defendant to criminal court is permitted in most jurisdictions. As was indicated in the previous note, the transfer decision generally turns on a predictive inquiry—whether the offender is amenable to treatment. Is that the right question? Should the transfer decision turn on the question asked in the *Monahan* dissent? Instead of asking whether the older adolescent is a "fit subject" for juvenile court disposition, would it be better to ask whether he is a "fit subject" for criminal punishment?

3. **The Contemporary Debate.** The individualized, predictive approach to transfer is under wholesale attack. Some critics take the view that 15, 16, or 17 year-olds who commit serious offenses are no less deserving of punishment than older offenders; the transfer decision, they argue, should be governed by the policies of the criminal law rather than the therapeutic assumptions of the juvenile court. Other critics argue that the individualized approach is objectionable regardless of the governing assumption about responsibility and punishment. The problem, they argue, is that the question whether a particular juvenile is dangerous or amenable to treatment cannot be answered reliably. The jurisdictional decision, therefore, should be predicated upon the application of more objective criteria. Professor Feld summarized the argument in Juvenile Court Legislative Reform and the Serious Young Offender: Dismantling the "Rehabilitative Ideal," 65 Minn.L.Rev. 167, 177–84 (1980): *

"Legislation instructing a court to determine a youth's amenability to treatment presupposes the existence of treatment programs that will systematically improve the social adjustment of some juvenile offenders, classification systems that will differentiate the rehabilitative responsiveness of various youths, and the availability of validated and reliable diagnostic tools and indicators that will enable a clinician or juvenile-court judge to determine in which class a particular youth belongs. These are all problematic assumptions. . . .

"There are no clinical factors . . . that indicate with certainty whether a particular youth will continue to engage in criminal behavior. . . .

"The lack of reliable psychological or clinical indicators to predict dangerousness almost invariably results in over-predicting and erroneously classifying as dangerous many young offenders who ultimately do not commit further offenses.

"[T]ypical waiver statutes, couched in terms of 'amenability to treatment' or 'dangerousness,' are in effect broad, standardless grants of discretion. . . . While appellate courts have been singularly unresponsive to various constitutional challenges to juvenile-waiver statutes, such as 'void for vagueness,' the empirical reality is that judges are not capable of consistent, even-handed administration of these discretionary statutes. Evidence exists that a juvenile's race may influence waiver decisions and

* Reprinted with the permission of the author and the Minnesota Law Review.

that waiver statutes are inconsistently interpreted and applied within a jurisdiction."

Despite these objections, the traditional individualized approach was endorsed by the Joint Commission on Juvenile Justice Standards of the Institute of Judicial Administration and the American Bar Association.[b] The Commission took the position that persons under 18 should be presumptively subject to juvenile-court jurisdiction; transfer is appropriate, the Commission said, only when a juvenile charged with a serious "class one" juvenile offense[c] "has demonstrated a propensity for violent attacks against other persons and, on the basis of personal background, appears unlikely to benefit from any disposition available in juvenile court." The Commission did not endorse any single rationale in support of its preference for juvenile-court jurisdiction. While it claimed that the "rehabilitative argument for the juvenile court" has "great moral force," the Commission nonetheless acknowledged that "recent research urges skepticism about the efficacy of existing rehabilitative methods." The Commission also noted the argument that persons below 18 are "in some moral sense less responsible for their acts and more deserving of compassion than are adults." In the final analysis, however, the Commission relied on the argument that delinquency intervention represents the lesser of two evils:

"[T]he criminal justice system is so inhumane, so poorly financed and staffed and so generally destructive that the juvenile court cannot do worse. Perhaps it can do better." [d]

4. **Questions on *In re Dahl*.** The *Dahl* court noted its uneasiness with the individualized predictive approach to the transfer decision and invited the Minnesota legislature to reconsider the statutory criteria for transfer. What are the proper criteria for determining the boundary between delinquency and criminal liability? Would you prefer a jurisdictional scheme based on age alone? On some combination of age, offense charged, and prior record of delinquency? Or do you favor the traditional individualized assessment of amenability to treatment? To what extent does your choice depend upon ideological assumptions about the respective purposes of juvenile and criminal processes? Or does your choice depend primarily on dispositional considerations?

As you think about these questions, consider the Minnesota legislature's response to *In re Dahl*. The criteria specified in Section 260.125(2)(d) still govern the transfer decision. However, subsequent amendments provide that the prosecutor establishes a "prima-facie case that the public safety is not served or that the child is not suitable for treatment" if the child was at least 16 years of age at the time of the alleged offense and if the child:

"(1) Is alleged by delinquency petition to have committed an aggravated felony against the person and (a) in committing the

---

[b] IJA–ABA, Standards Relating to Transfer Between Courts 3–7, 37 (1980).

[c] The Commission defined a class one juvenile offense as: "Those criminal offenses for which the maximum sentence for adults would be death or imprisonment for life or a term in excess of 20 years."

[d] For a criticism of the Commission's position, see In Re Seven Minors, 644 P.2d 947 (Nev.1983).

offense, the child acted with particular cruelty or disregard for the life or safety of another; or (b) the offense involved a high degree of sophistication or planning by the juvenile; or

"(2) Is alleged by delinquency petition to have committed murder in the first degree; or

"(3) Has been found by the court . . . to have committed an offense within the preceding 24 months, which would be a felony if committed by an adult, and is alleged by delinquency petition to have committed murder in the second or third degree, manslaughter in the first degree, criminal sexual conduct in the first degree or assault in the first degree; or

"(4) Has been found by the court . . . to have committed two offenses, not in the same behavioral incident, within the preceding 24 months which would be felonies if committed by an adult, and is alleged by delinquency petition to have committed manslaughter in the second degree, kidnapping, criminal sexual conduct in the second degree, arson in the first degree, aggravated robbery, or assault in the second degree; or

"(5) Has been found by the court . . . to have committed two offenses, not in the same behavioral incident, within the preceding 24 months, one or both of which would be the felony of burglary of a dwelling if committed by an adult, and the child is alleged by the delinquency petition to have committed another burglary of a dwelling . . .; or

"(6) Has been found by the court . . . to have committed three offenses, none in the same behavioral incident, within the preceding 24 months which would be felonies if committed by an adult, and is alleged by delinquency petition to have committed any felony other than those described in clauses (2), (3) or (4)"

Is this a better approach? What is its underlying rationale concerning the respective purposes of the juvenile and criminal processes? Would you expect transfer practices to change? [e]

SECTION 2: MENTAL ABNORMALITY

INTRODUCTORY NOTES ON THE INSANITY DEFENSE

1. **Introduction.** No area of the substantive criminal law has received more scholarly attention during the 20th century than the relation between mental abnormality and criminal responsibility. Although insanity has been an acknowledged ground of acquittal for many centuries, contemporary opinion reflects continuing disagreement about the type of mental incapacity that should suffice and, indeed,

---

[e] For an empirical study of the impact of these amendments on transfer practices, see Osbun and Rode, Prosecuting Juveniles as Adults: The Quest for Objective Decisions, 22 Criminology 187 (1984).

about desirability of any insanity defense at all. The dimensions of the dispute can readily be seen in any representative sample of commentary on the subject.[a] The reader will find proposals to broaden the exculpatory reach of the defense side-by-side with proposals to abolish it. While proponents of the defense argue that humanitarian morality demands exculpation of the mentally ill, abolitionists assert that a decent respect for the dignity of such persons requires that they be held accountable for their wrongdoing.

The insanity defense is a difficult subject. In large measure this is because the causal links between body, mind, and behavior continue to defy scientific understanding. Most of the clinician's operating assumptions about mental abnormality are not susceptible to empirical validation. Moreover, the prevailing clinical understanding is not easily translated into concepts of interest to the criminal law, mainly because scientific study of the human mind is fundamentally unconcerned with questions of blameworthiness and responsibility.

Another difficulty arises from the diversity of perspectives employed by the mental health disciplines in the study of human behavior and in the treatment of mental, emotional, and behavioral problems. One perspective draws on the traditional medical concept of "disease" to describe and explain abnormal mental phenomena; this view rests on the assumption that there are categorical differences, with probable biological underpinnings, between individuals having and not having the "disease." From another perspective, behavioral scientists have tried to identify and measure various dimensions of the human personality that differentiate one person from another—features that fall along a spectrum of degree and, at some point, can be characterized as abnormal. From yet a third perspective, clinicians study human motivation, aiming to identify the biological, psychological, and social forces that shape behavior, both normal and abnormal.

Although each of these three perspectives is undoubtedly required for a complete understanding of abnormal behavior, the heterogeneous, and often conflicting approaches employed by mental health practitioners can befuddle the efforts of legal institutions to shape and administer a doctrine of responsibility. Of particular concern is the fluid and often imprecise nature of clinical concepts of abnormality. Lines are not easily drawn between mental "illness" or "disease" and other conditions characterized by maladaptive behavior or emotional distress. Yet the law is in an important sense faced with an either/or choice: Questions of degree can be taken into account in grading and sentencing, but the imposition of criminal liability must be predicated upon a categorical determination of blameworthiness.

There is yet another overarching problem. The criminal law's response to the mentally disordered offender is shaped by preventive

[a] E.g., A. Goldstein, The Insanity Defense (1967); J. Feinberg, Doing and Deserving: Essays in the Theory of Responsibility (1970); H. Fingarette and A. Hasse, Mental Disabilities and Criminal Responsibility (1979); N. Morris, Madness and the Criminal Law (1982); D.H.J. Hermann, The Insanity Defense: Philosophical, Historical and Legal Perspectives (1983); M. Moore, Law and Psychiatry: Rethinking the Relationship (1984); S. Morse, The Jurisprudence of Craziness (1986).

concerns as well as retributive ones. The imposition of criminal punishment on culpable offenders serves the preventive ends of the penal law, including the incapacitation of those who are dangerous. If abnormal offenders are beyond the reach of the penal law, the preventive function must be performed by alternative mechanisms of social control, such as civil commitment.

The subject of mental abnormality and criminal responsibility is further complicated by questions of implementation. In much of the contemporary commentary, evidentiary questions about the proper scope of expert testimony by psychiatrists and other mental-health professionals [b] are superimposed on the substantive questions regarding the legal significance of mental abnormality. Although the limits of psychiatric expertise and the special risks associated with expert testimony merit independent attention, the materials in this book focus primarily on the substantive issues concerning the exculpatory or mitigating significance of mental abnormality rather than on the evidentiary questions associated with the proof of such conditions.

Despite these difficulties, the criminal law traditionally has included special doctrines for mentally disordered offenders. From the earliest times, the courts and legislatures have coupled unique dispositional provisions with exculpatory "tests" of criminal responsibility. The following notes introduce the major tests of responsibility as they were developed at common law and as they have since been modified. These notes are followed by a series of problems, notes, and cases designed to highlight the clinical realities of mental disorder and to identify the major policy questions that must be addressed by contemporary courts and legislators. As you study these introductory notes, you should focus particularly on the criteria of responsibility stated by the various "tests" and ask yourself: (i) how the specified criteria relate to other doctrines of exculpation previously studied; (ii) whether it seems appropriate to exculpate mentally disordered offenders who fit these criteria; and (iii) why it seems appropriate to do so. These questions will be explored in depth in the remaining materials in this section.

2. **Early History.** Before the 12th century, mental disease, as such, apparently had no legal significance.[c] However, as criminal liability came to be predicated upon general notions of moral blameworthiness, "madness" was recognized as an excusing condition. At first, insanity (like self-defense) was not a bar to criminal liability but only a recognized ground for granting a royal pardon; while the records are fragmentary, it appears that the king would remand the person to some

---

[b] In most jurisdictions, opinion testimony concerning a person's mental condition may be offered by psychologists as well as psychiatrists. For convenience of reference, these materials will use "psychiatric testimony" to refer to testimony by any qualified mental-health professional.

[c] For general background on the common-law history of the insanity defense,

see N. Walker, Crime and Insanity in England (1968); H. Crotty, The History of Insanity as a Defense to Crime in English Criminal Law, 12 Calif.L.Rev. 105 (1924); Platt and Diamond, The Origins of the "Right and Wrong" Test of Criminal Responsibility and Its Subsequent Development in the United States: An Historical Survey, 54 Calif.L.Rev. 1227 (1966).

form of indefinite custody in lieu of execution. The first recorded case of outright acquittal by reason of insanity occurred in 1505.[d]

The only commentator to give sustained attention to the subject before the 19th century was Lord Hale, whose treatise was published posthumously in 1736. According to Hale:[e]

> "Man is naturally endowed with these two great faculties, understanding and liberty of will. . . . The consent of the will is that which renders human actions either commendable or culpable. . . . And because the liberty or choice of the will presupposeth an act of understanding to know the thing or action chosen by the will, it follows that, where there is a total defect of the understanding, there is no free act of the will. . . ."

Hale distinguished between "total defect of understanding" due to insanity and "partial" madness involving those who "discovered their defect in excessive fears and griefs and yet are not wholly destitute of the use of reason." Conceding that "it is very difficult to define the indivisible line that divides perfect and partial insanity," Hale sought to identify that level of "understanding" necessary for criminal liability by assimilating insanity to infancy: "Such a person as labouring under melancholy distempers hath yet ordinarily as great understanding, as ordinarily a child of 14 years hath, is such a person as may be guilty of . . . felony."

Hale's approach failed to take hold.[f] Instead, as Sayre notes, 18th century courts "hark[ed] back strongly to the old ethical basis of criminal responsibility and [made] the test one of capacity to intend evil. Could the defendant at the time of the offense 'distinguish good from evil'?"[g] An often-cited example is Justice Tracy's charge to the jury in Arnold's Case, 16 How.St.Tr. 695, 764 (1724), which involved a known madman who killed a nobleman in the delusion that the victim had "bewitched him" and was "the occasion of all the troubles in the nation." After summarizing the evidence, Justice Tracy said that the only question was "whether this man had the use of his reason and senses." He continued:

> "[I]t is not every kind of frantic humour or something unaccountable in a man's actions, that points him out to be such a madman as is to be exempted from punishment; it must be a man that is totally deprived of his understanding and memory, and doth not know what he is doing, no more than an infant, than a brute, or a wild beast, such a one is never the object of punishment; therefore I must leave it to your consideration, whether the condition this man was in . . . doth shew a man, who knew what he was doing, and was able to distinguish

[d] N. Walker, Crime and Insanity in England 26 (1968). Apparently the offender was set free.

[e] 1 M. Hale, The History of Pleas of the Crown 14–15 (Philadelphia 1847) (1st ed. 1736).

[f] Sir James Stephen criticized Hale's comparison of infancy and insanity: "The

one is healthy immaturity, the other diseased maturity and between these there is no sort of resemblance." 2 A History of the Criminal Law of England 150–51 (1883).

[g] Sayre, Mens Rea, 45 Harv.L.Rev. 974, 1006 (1932).

whether he was doing good or evil, and understood what he did
. . . ."

As late as 1840, no appellate court in England or the United States
had had occasion to state the law on the defense of insanity. However,
the subject received a great deal of attention on both sides of the
Atlantic during the middle third of the century. One important development was the publication of Isaac Ray's treatise on the Medical
Jurisprudence of Insanity in 1838, signifying the first efforts of the
infant science of psychiatry to influence the development of the law.
Another major development was the trial, in 1843, of Daniel
M'Naghten.

3. ***M'Naghten's* Case.** The modern formulations of the insanity
defense derive from the "rules" stated by the House of Lords in Daniel
M'Naghten's Case, 10 Cl. & F. 200, 8 Eng. Rep. 718 (H.L.1843).[h]
M'Naghten was indicted for shooting Edward Drummond, secretary to
Robert Peel, the Prime Minister of England. According to M'Naghten's
statements to the police, he came to London for the purpose of shooting
Peel. However, Drummond was riding in Peel's carriage that day, and
M'Naghten shot Drummond in error. M'Naghten described his motive
as follows:

"The tories in my native city have compelled me to do this.
They follow and persecute me wherever I go, and have entirely
destroyed my peace of mind. . . . I cannot sleep at night in
consequence of the course they pursue towards me. . . . They
have accused me of crimes of which I am not guilty; they do
everything in their power to harass and persecute me; in fact
they wish to murder me."

The thrust of the medical testimony was that M'Naghten was
suffering from what would today be described as delusions of persecution symptomatic of paranoid schizophrenia. One of the medical witnesses concluded that:

"The act with which he is charged, coupled with the history of
his past life, leaves not the remotest doubt on my mind of the
presence of insanity sufficient to deprive the prisoner of all self-
control. I consider the act of the prisoner in killing Mr. Drummond to have been committed whilst under a delusion; the act
itself I look upon as the crowning act of the whole matter—as the
climax—as a carrying out of the pre-existing idea which had
haunted him for years."

The expert testimony was summarized in the official reports as follows:

"That persons of otherwise sound mind, might be affected by
morbid delusions; that the prisoner was in that condition; that a

---

[h] The history of the *M'Naghten* case is
reviewed, and the relevant documents collected, in D. West and A. Walk, Daniel
McNaughton: His Trial and the Aftermath
(1977), and R. Moran, Knowing Right from
Wrong (1981).

M'Naghten's name has been spelled at
least 12 different ways. Apparently, the

traditional spelling—the one used in this
book—is the only one that cannot be reconciled with the defendant's own signature.
See B. Diamond, On the Spelling of Daniel
M'Naghten's Name, 25 Ohio St. L.J. 84
(1964). According to Professor Moran, the
correct spelling is probably "McNaugh-
tan."

person so labouring under a morbid delusion might have a moral perception of right and wrong, but that in the case of the prisoner it was a delusion which carried him away beyond the power of his own control, and left him no such perception; and that he was not capable of exercising any control over acts which had connexion with his delusion; that it was of the nature of the disease with which the prisoner was affected, to go on gradually until it had reached a climax, when it burst forth with irresistible intensity; that a man might go on for years quietly, though at the same time under its influence, but would all at once break out into the most extravagant and violent paroxysms."

In his charge to the jury, Chief Justice Tindal practically directed a verdict of not guilty by reason of insanity. He observed "that the whole of the medical evidence is on one side and that there is no part of it which leaves any doubt on the mind," and then instructed the jury that the verdict should turn on the answer to the following question:

> "[W]hether . . . at the time the act was committed [M'Naghten] had that competent use of his understanding as that he knew that he was doing, by the very act itself, a wicked and a wrong thing. If he was not sensible at the time he committed that act, that it was a violation of the law of God or of man, undoubtedly he was not responsible for that act, or liable to any punishment whatever flowing from that act. . . . But if . . . you think the prisoner capable of distinguishing between right and wrong, then he was a responsible agent. . . ."

The jury returned a verdict of not guilty by reason of insanity.[j] This verdict became the subject of considerable "popular alarm," and was regarded with particular concern by Queen Victoria.[k] As a result, the House of Lords asked the judges of that body to give an advisory opinion regarding the answers to five questions "on the law governing such cases." The combined answers to two of these questions have come to be known as *M'Naghten's* rules:

> "[E]very man is to be presumed to be sane . . . . [T]o establish a defence on the ground of insanity, it must be clearly proved that, at the time of the committing of the act, the party accused was labouring under such a defect of reason, from disease of the mind, as not to know the nature and quality of the act he was doing; or if he did know it, that he did not know he was doing what was wrong."

4. **Other Common-Law Formulations.** *M'Naghten* quickly became the prevailing approach to the insanity defense in England and in

[j] Most commentary on the *M'Naghten* case proceeds on the assumption that he was mentally ill and that his crime was related to his delusions. However, a recent book by Professor Richard Moran presents strong evidence in support of the proposition that M'Naghten was not delusional and that his attempt to assassinate the Tory Prime Minister was "a purposeful act of political criminality." R. Moran, Knowing Right From Wrong (1981).

[k] She had been the target of assassination attempts three times in the preceding two years, and one of her attackers, Oxford, had also had won an insanity acquittal.

the United States. However, the test was subjected to criticism almost as soon as it was uttered. Nineteenth-century authorities offered two alternative formulations:

(i) **The Product Test.** The "intellectualist" approach of the 18th- and 19th-century English judges was criticized by Isaac Ray[1] and his followers because it failed to comprehend the more subtle forms of mental illness. The prevailing judicial ideas about idiocy and lunacy were derived, Ray argued, from "those wretched inmates of the madhouses whom chains and stripes, cold and filth, had reduced to the stupidity of the idiot or exasperated to the fury of a demon." The law failed to recognize "those nice shades of the disease" which can influence behavior and ought to have exculpatory significance. Accordingly, Ray argued, the insanity defense should turn on whether "the mental unsoundness . . . embraced the act within the sphere of its influence."

The New Hampshire Supreme Court accepted Ray's view. In State v. Pike, 49 N.H. 399 (1870), the court severely criticized the *M'Naghten* rules; the next year, in State v. Jones, 50 N.H. 369 (1871), the court stated its own rule, commonly known as the "product" test:

> "No man shall be held accountable, criminally, for an act which was the offspring and product of mental disease. Of the soundness of this proposition there can be no doubt. . . . No argument is needed to show that to hold that a man may be punished for what is the offspring of disease would be to hold that he may be punished for disease. Any rule which makes that possible cannot be law."

Although the New Hampshire formulation was applauded by many medical and legal commentators during the early part of the 20th century, it failed to win support in the courts.[m]

(ii) **The Control Test.** Although the notion of "irresistible impulse" was much discussed during the decades after the *M'Naghten* rules were announced,[n] it is not altogether clear whether the early proponents viewed it as an elaboration of *M'Naghten* or as an independent ground of exculpation. Some state courts employed the concept simply to acknowledge that an "insane impulse" could be so strong as to "dethrone reason" and thereby deprive the offender of the capacity to know that what he was doing was wrong.[o] However, the phrase ultimately came to denote an independent exculpatory doctrine. The central proposition was that the inability of a person to control his

---

[1] I. Ray, A Treatise on the Medical Jurisprudence of Insanity (1838).

[m] The product test was adopted by the United States Court of Appeals for the D.C. Circuit in Durham v. United States, 214 F.2d 862 (D.C. Cir. 1954), but was abandoned in favor of the Model Penal Code test (discussed at pages 658–59, infra) in United States v. Brawner, 471 F.2d 969 (D.C. Cir. 1972).

[n] See generally S. Glueck, Mental Disorder and the Criminal Law (1925); Waite,

Irresistible Impulse and Criminal Liability, 23 Mich.L.Rev. 443 (1925).

[o] See, e.g., Commonwealth v. Rogers, 48 Mass. (7 Metc.) 500, 41 Am.Dec. 458 (1844). For a review of the early decisions, see Hall, Psychiatry and Criminal Responsibility, 65 Yale L.J. 761 (1956); Keedy, Irresistible Impulse as a Defense in the Criminal Law, 100 U.Pa.L.Rev. 956 (1952).

behavior, as a result of mental disease, ought to excuse him even though he might be aware that his act was wrong. The focus of this doctrine is on mental disease that deprives the individual of the capacity to exercise his will, the capacity to choose whether or not to engage in proscribed behavior. It is therefore frequently referred to as a "volitional" or "control" inquiry, to be contrasted with the focus of the *M'Naghten* rules on the "cognitive" capacities of the defendant.

Sir James Stephen became a leading proponent of a control test. In 1883 he stated: "If it is not, it ought to be the law of England that no act is a crime if the person who does it is at the time . . . prevented either by defective mental power or by any disease affecting his mind from controlling his own conduct, unless the absence of the power of control has been produced by his own default."[P] The first unequivocal appellate endorsement of the control formulation as a supplement to *M'Naghten* is found in Parsons v. State, 81 Ala. 577, 596, 2 So. 854 (1886):

> "[D]id he know right from wrong, as applied to the particular act in question? . . . If he did have such knowledge, he may nevertheless not be legally responsible if the two following conditions concur: (i) If, by reason of the duress of such mental disease, he had so far lost the *power to choose* between the right and wrong, and to avoid doing the act in question, as that his free agency was at the time destroyed; (ii) and if, at the same time, the alleged crime was so connected with such mental disease, in the relation of cause and effect, as to have been the product of it *solely*."

Although several other courts endorsed this view during the next decade, most states rejected it. The predominant attitude of the common-law judges was graphically stated by a Canadian judge in 1908:

> "The law says to men who say they are afflicted with irresistible impulses: 'If you cannot resist an impulse in any other way, we will hang a rope in front of your eyes, and perhaps that will help.' No man has a right under our law to come before a jury and say to them, 'I did commit that act, but I did it under an uncontrollable impulse,' leave it at that and then say, 'now acquit me.' "[q]

The formative era of the modern insanity defense was completed by the end of the 19th century. Notwithstanding the persistent barrage of unfavorable commentary by forensic psychiatrists and academic lawyers, the law remained essentially unchanged for the first half of the 20th century. By the time the Model Penal Code was being drafted in 1955, the *M'Naghten* test still constituted the exclusive criterion of exculpation on ground of insanity in about two-thirds of the states.

5. **The Model Penal Code.** The Model Code formulation of the insanity defense (Section 4.01) provides:

> "A person is not responsible for criminal conduct if at the time of such conduct as a result of mental disease or defect he

---

P 2 J. Stephen, A History of the Criminal Law of England 168 (1883).

q King v. Creighton, 14 Can. Cr. Cases 349, 350 (1908) (Riddell, J.).

L., J. & B.Cs.Crim.Law 2nd Ed. UCB—16

lacks substantial capacity either to appreciate the criminality [wrongfulness] of his conduct or to conform his conduct to the requirements of law."

Two points should be noted about the Model Code formulation. First, in its joint focus on the capacity to appreciate criminality and the capacity to conform one's conduct to the requirements of law, the Model Code formulation includes both cognitive and volitional criteria. The drafters thus accepted the major criticism of *M'Naghten* that the exclusive focus on cognitive capacity was too narrow. The Model Code formulation accords *independent* exculpatory significance to volitional impairment.[r] Second, the Model Code "substantial capacity" formulation explicitly acknowledges that there is no bright line between the sane and the insane. Professor Herbert Wechsler, who inspired the Model Code language, explained:[*]

> "[O]ur judgment was that no test is workable that calls for the complete impairment of ability to know or to control; and that the extremity of these conceptions, as applied in court, posed the largest difficulty . . . . Disorientation, we were told, might be extreme and still might not be total; what clinical experience revealed was closer to a graded scale with marks along the way. Hence, an examiner confronting a person who had performed a seemingly purposive act might helpfully address himself to the extent of awareness, understanding and control. If, on the other hand, he must speak to utter incapacity vel non, he could testify meaningfully only as to delusional psychosis, when the act would not be criminal if the facts were as they deludedly were thought to be, although he knew that there were other situations in which the disorder was extreme. To meet this aspect of the difficulty, it was thought that the criterion should ask if there was, as a result of disease or defect, a deprivation of 'substantial capacity' to know or to control, meaning thereby the reduction of capacity to the vagrant and trivial dimensions characteristic of the most severe afflictions of the mind."[s]

The Model Penal Code test was very influential. By 1980, it had been adopted—by legislation or judicial ruling—in more than half the

[r] It should also be noted that the cognitive branch of the Model Code formulation asks only one of the *M'Naghten* questions. Section 4.01 omits reference to the capacity of the defendant to "know the nature and quality" of the act he was doing. One reason is that the significance of a person's mistake regarding the nature of his act lies, ultimately, in the fact that it prevents him from knowing it is wrong; thus, this prong of the test is theoretically superfluous. Another reason is that this aspect of the *M'Naghten* formula is primarily directed to the capacity of the defendant to form mens rea. As will be developed at pages 742–59, infra, the admissibility of evidence of mental abnormality on mens rea issues

is itself a controversial question. Since the Model Code resolves the controversy (in Section 4.02) in favor of admissibility, there is no need to include cognition as to the nature of the defendant's behavior as part of the insanity formulation. The effect of Section 4.01, therefore, is to supplement what remains of the *M'Naghten* formula with the volitional or control inquiry.

[*] Reprinted with the permission of the author and the Columbia Law Review.

[s] Wechsler, Codification of the Criminal Law in the United States: The Model Penal Code, 68 Colum.L.Rev. 1425, 1443 (1968).

states; and, in the absence of congressional action, formulations based on the Model Code were adopted by all the federal courts of appeal.

6. **The Hinckley Case.** Signs of dissatisfaction with the prevailing approach to insanity began to emerge in the late 1970's. One major factor was public concern about premature release of dangerous defendants acquitted by reason of insanity. During this period, several states narrowed the insanity criteria or introduced a new verdict of "guilty but mentally ill" to supplement the traditional alternatives of conviction or acquittal. One state, Montana, abolished the insanity defense in 1979. The simmering debate about the law of insanity took on national proportions in the aftermath of the trial of John W. Hinckley, Jr.

On March 30, 1981, Hinckley shot and wounded President Ronald Reagan and three other people as the President was walking from the Washington Hilton to his waiting limousine. The shooting was observed by scores of eyewitnesses and seen by millions of others on television. Hinckley was indicted for 13 offenses, including an attempt to assassinate the President. His claim of insanity was adjudicated under the Model Penal Code test then utilized in the federal courts for the District of Columbia. Hinckley's trial began on May 4, 1982, and lasted seven weeks. The prosecution and defense experts disagreed on the nature and severity of Hinckley's mental disorder and on his ability to appreciate the wrongfulness of his behavior and conform to the requirements of the law. On June 21, after deliberating for three days, the jury returned a verdict of not guilty by reason of insanity on each of the 13 counts.

According to media accounts and opinion surveys, the Hinckley acquittal shocked and angered the American public. Three days after the verdict, the New York Times referred to a "national reaction of stunned surprise" and a "cascade of public outrage." The verdict catalyzed latent public discomfort with the insanity defense and its administration, and triggered legislative activity throughout the country. The American Bar Association, the American Psychiatric Association, and the National Conference of Commissioners on Uniform State Laws recommended a narrowing of the insanity defense by eliminating its volitional prong. The American Medical Association recommended abolition of the defense. During the ensuing three years, half of the states and the Congress modified the law of insanity in some significant respect.

7. **Current Law.** As a result of the post-Hinckley reforms—all of which restricted the prevailing insanity test in the jurisdictions that changed their law—the Model Code no longer represents the prevailing approach in the United States. As of the summer of 1985, the sole criterion in about half the states was whether the defendant was unable to "know" or "appreciate" the nature or wrongfulness of the conduct; in these states volitional impairment was not an independent basis of exculpation. Twenty states retained the Model Code formula, and three states used *M'Naghten* and some variation of the "irresistible impulse" test. Only New Hampshire continued to use the "product"

test. Three states—Montana, Idaho, and Utah—abolished the insanity defense.[t]

Another feature of the law of insanity prominently featured in public discussion after the Hinckley verdict was the burden of proof. All states place the burden of producing sufficient evidence to raise the defense on the defendant. However, in two-thirds of the states recognizing the defense, the defendant bears the burden of persuasion, usually by a preponderance of the evidence;[u] in the remaining states, the prosecution bears the burden of disproving the defendant's claim of insanity beyond a reasonable doubt.

Congress has also modified the federal law governing the insanity defense. Until 1984, no statute governed the subject. Although the Supreme Court had ruled, in 1895, that the government bore the burden of persuasion on insanity claims in federal prosecutions, the Court had never prescribed a substantive test of insanity for the federal courts. As noted above, however, each of the federal circuits had adopted tests based on the Model Penal Code. The 1984 legislation eliminated the volitional prong of the defense and requires the defendant to establish an insanity claim by clear and convincing evidence. The new federal statute, codified at 18 U.S.C. § 20, provides:

"(a) Affirmative Defense.—It is an affirmative defense to a prosecution under any federal statute that, at the time of the commission of the acts constituting the offense, the defendant as a result of a severe mental disease or defect, was unable to appreciate the nature and quality or the wrongfulness of his acts. Mental disease or defect does not otherwise constitute a defense.[v]

"(b) Burden of Proof.—The defendant has the burden of proving the defense of insanity by clear and convincing evidence."

SUBSECTION A: THE INSANITY DEFENSE AND MAJOR MENTAL DISORDER

THE CASE OF JOY BAKER

[The following material presents the facts from a real case involving Joy Baker, a 31-year-old woman who was indicted for the murder of her aunt (Trevah) and pleaded not guilty by reason of insanity. It is

---

[t] The statutes in these states are discussed in the notes on abolition of the insanity defense on pages 771–72, infra.

Twelve states have supplemented the insanity defense with a separate verdict of "guilty but mentally ill." These statutes are considered at pages 750–52, infra.

[u] The constitutionality of placing the burden of persuasion on the defendant has been upheld in Leland v. Oregon, 343 U.S.

790 (1952), and Rivera v. Delaware, 429 U.S. 877 (1976). For a general discussion of the constitutionality of burden-shifting defenses, see pages 967–93, infra.

[v] In United States v. Lyons, 731 F.2d 243, 739 F.2d 994 (5th Cir. 1984) (en banc), the Fifth Circuit anticipated the eventual congressional action by abandoning the volitional prong of the Model Penal Code test.

designed to provide a basis for exploring the relationship between criminal responsibility and major mental disorder and for analyzing the meanings of the various "tests" of insanity reviewed in the preceding notes.   After a summary of Joy Baker's testimony concerning her background, the material includes a transcript of her own statements concerning the offense.   As you read this material, you should consider how you would apply the various tests of insanity to her case.   The notes following the case will explore the issues raised and will include relevant excerpts from expert testimony supporting her insanity claim.

Mrs. Baker testified that her mother had a history of psychiatric hospitalization and that, due to her mother's emotional instability, she was raised by her grandparents until the age of 10.   She then lived with her mother for three years and with Aunt Trevah for two.   After an unsuccessful attempt to rejoin her mother, she lived briefly in a foster home before returning to her grandparents.

Upon graduation from high school at 18, Mrs. Baker married.   The marriage ended in divorce six years later with Mrs. Baker retaining custody of the two children.   A year later she married her present husband, Curtis Baker.   According to Mrs. Baker's account, the marriage was a stressful one from the outset.   Her husband was often violent, especially when he had been drinking, and frequently assaulted her; the most recent episode was about a month before the offense. She stated that her husband told her that she was "jinxed" and that she brought him bad luck.   He also frequently accused her of having extramarital affairs, allegations that she denied.

Mrs. Baker's description of the offense and the preceding three-day period is excerpted below.   A transcription of her words obviously cannot convey the intensity with which she delivered this account; however, the transcript does fairly reflect the coherence and detail of her presentation, qualities which are atypical in such cases.   During the course of this testimony, Mrs. Baker refers to her two children— Danny (age 11) and Betty (age 9).

Q: What do you remember about the night of the shooting?

A: I know that about three days before that . . . I had gone out to take care of my cats and I noticed that the dog outside had a rope wrapped around her paw, and her paw was swollen and out like this and I put her on the back porch.   I took the kitten that had an infected ear to the vet and I drove back. . . .   When I got home, for some reason I felt . . . I had to dump all the dirty things in the house outside the house—anything that was bad, like alcohol, or stale food, leftover foods.   I put it all in garbage bags and I got rid of the garbage and—

Q: You said you felt you had to do that?

A: I felt like I *had* to, that I *had* to get these things out because something bad was going to happen.

Q: If you didn't take them out.

A: Yes, take all these things out.   And I felt like I had to get the house clean, the house had to be very, very clean.   Then—I can't keep the days straight, I think it was the next day—my husband decided to stay home, was going to stay home with me for a while.

Q: Why was he going to stay home?

A: He was just going to go in to work late that day for some reason. And over a long period of time—we've been living there about five and one-half years—he'd been asking me who I'd been with, who'd I seen, and where did I go, what did I do. He would accuse me of running around and I went ahead and told him about this one guy that I have talked to before, gave him his name, where he worked and he got angry; he said to write his name down. I wrote his name down on a card and he stormed out of the house. He said he was going to find him and he was going to kill him.

Q: Do you remember when that happened in relationship to the night of the shooting.

A: I think that was the day before the shooting. . . .

Q: Let me repeat this and correct me if I'm wrong. It's my understanding that you had had feelings that something bad was going to happen to you that day. That's why you didn't want to go down the highway [to pick the children up at school]. Is that right?

A: I went down. . . . .

Q: But you went anyway.

A: Yes. Well I left the dog out at the school grounds and then I felt like if I leave the dog there she's going to bite the children. I was trying to get the dog in, but I didn't want to put the dog back in the car because I was afraid she'd bite me, but my son started hollering and crying that he wanted his dog Brownie.

Q: Does the dog bite?

A: No, but she didn't want to come to me and I had trouble getting her in so I drove on up the road. I thought that maybe if I drove slow she would follow us.

Q: You say she didn't want to come to you? Is that not like her, or usually she comes to you?

A: Usually she comes to me, but she didn't want to come to me that day.

Q: Wonder why that was?

A: I don't know, but I drove on down to the main highway and I parked the car and I told the children to stay in the car and I felt like that I had to walk down the highway. I felt that sometime during my walk through that field Brownie was going to come up behind me or in front of me and just grab me around the throat and kill me and I stood out there waiting for her to do this and she never came and I turned around for her to do this and she never came and I turned around and started walking back. I remember I was scared and I started walking back to the car and when I got to the door I just jerked the door real quick and jumped in and I started taking off. Danny started hollering that he wanted Brownie and sometime on the way down the road towards the house, Brownie was following us, so I let Brownie in the car from the other side and I told Betty to hold her. I didn't want her near me because I was afraid she'd bite me.

I got home. That afternoon the children were upstairs in their room playing checkers and I was up there and Curtis came up there and he was angry and he had a gun in his hand and he said, "Come with me," and I said, "Well, what about the children?" He said "Leave the children here, they'll be all right." He told me to get in the truck and it was about 4:30, sometime in the afternoon. And I said "Where will we be going?" He says "We're going for a drive."

We drove all over the place, Centerville and everywhere possible. We went to that man's mother's house and several other places. Somebody else's house, I don't know whose and everytime we stopped somewhere he'd say "I want you to meet my wife, the adultress." And we stopped at this store. Curtis got out and was talking to this elderly man who ran the store and when he got ready to get back into the truck I asked the man if he had a telephone. I wanted to call somebody and tell them that Curtis was acting silly, you know, because he kept the gun between us on the truck seat and kept screaming at me about who I went with and what I had done, that I should be ashamed of myself and God is going to get me for this. He demanded I throw my rings out of the window and I threw them out because he was getting angry.

It was late when I got home and we had to knock on the door several times and my daughter came to the door and opened it. The whole time that I was riding around in the truck I thought the dog was going to bite my kids before I could get back home. When I got home I felt sick. I was tired, I hadn't eaten, the children hadn't eaten. I had to get them up at three and I was trying to fix something for them to eat at three o'clock in the morning.

And Brownie was in the house and it looked like everywhere I went, that dog was following me. If I had any food in my hand, she kept trying to get it out of my hands. Then, I fixed bacon. I figured I would throw the bacon real quick to the dog so she'd eat that and be busy eating that so I could give my children something to eat because I felt that she was going to bother them.

And that black dog of Curtis'—when we got back from the ride, that truck ride, he sat down at the table and we were arguing and I saw Curtis make sort of a sneer with his mouth and when he did that then that dog of his growled each time he pulled his lip up. The dog would growl, the black dog. And then Curtis got up, he kind of kicked the chair over and he says, "Make up the bed, I'm going to bed." And he made up the bed. He put the gun on the nightstand and that worried me. I took the gun. He asked me where I was going with it and I put it under the bed. I couldn't sleep. I was upset. I felt like if I went to sleep he was going to kill me. That night I just felt like Curtis didn't act right and I thought well I can't trust him and nobody. So I stayed up and it was about 7:30 when I went to bed because I was just too tired.

Q: 7:30?

A: The next morning. And I guess I slept 'til around 10.

Q: That was the morning of the shooting, is that right?

A: Yes.

Q: What happened that day. You got up?

A: I had a headache again. I felt bad, I was tired and when I got up Curtis wasn't there. I didn't see Curtis and I walked around the house three times and I called him three times and I didn't get any answer. The last time, after I walked through the bedroom and I got right into the living room, he says, "Yeah, what do you want?" I turned around and he was sitting on the bed. That kind of scared me because I hadn't seen him.

And I went ahead and took a bath. I thought maybe that would make me feel better. And I took a bath and then I tried to fix breakfast and everything I did that morning went wrong. I burned the bacon. I tried to clean the house. It seemed like when I cleaned the house I was making more of a mess than I was doing anything else. I tried to wash the dishes and I didn't feel like washing dishes cause when I did it, it just looked like there were that many more dishes to wash.

I tried to clean out my rabbit cage and I felt like if I put my hand in there that rabbit's going to bite me. I felt like my rabbit and my dog had rabies and my yellow cat. As I was putting the dog outside later that morning, she had, well, I don't know, she just looked like she had foam all around her mouth and when I saw that I thought "Oh my God, that dog's got rabies," and I wouldn't let her in and I looked at my yellow cat and he was panting and I said, well the dog has probably bitten the cat and I can't let him in.

Q: Were they vaccinated?

A: Yes.

Q: So even though they were vaccinated you had that feeling they had rabies.

A: Then, Curtis said he was going to the grocery store. I asked him not to leave me in the house in the first place because I was scared and that I was afraid something was going to happen, and he said nothing is going to happen.

Q: What did you think was going to happen?

A: I just felt like somebody was out to get me or those animals were going to attack me or something. When he left I shut the doors and well, really, I thought that the neighborhood—what they call it is God's country, they call that area God's country and for some reason I kind of thought it was funny because I thought to myself this is not God's country, this is Devil's land or something—and I thought like those people round there are witches and I felt like sooner or later they're going to get me. They're either going to kill me or they're going to do something to me and if they don't get to me, my dogs are going to break into the house and they are going to tear me to pieces and for a few minutes, I even thought my children were possessed by demons or a devil, or something.

Q: Had you ever had feelings like this before that day?

A: No, I have never been through anything like this before. I have never felt like I was going to be—[pause]—"slaughtered" is the word for it. I just felt like they were going to do anything and everything they could to destroy me. And my animals—I've never been afraid of my animals except for Midnight. Now I don't particularly like Midnight, the black dog.

Q: That's Curtis' dog.

A: Yeah, he has taught her to jump up and she'd put her teeth around your arm, like this, and she plays rough and when I came back from that ride the day I went to the school, I heard her barking on the back porch and she started growling. Well I was scared to go in there . . . but I had to in order to get in the house because the front door was shut. And to keep the dog from biting me I kept watching her and holding my pocketbook in front of her face because I just felt like she would bite me. And I even asked Curtis several times to get her off the back porch and take and put her back outside because I couldn't get out on the back porch to hang up clothes or anything else because she was out there.

Q: So then what happened?

A: So anyway, sometime or other I found the gun under the bed where I had laid it.

Q: Whose gun was it?

A: It's Curtis' gun.

Q: Does he have a lot of guns at home?

A: Well, he had another one that was hidden, that my aunt had hidden in the trunk, and he wanted that back so I got it back and gave it to him. He used to have a German type gun and he's bought another one since then, I don't know what type it is, it's a smaller one, and this one is a Western style. It's about so long and got a handle on it like this.

Q: Are you experienced with firearms? Do you shoot a lot?

A: No, he said sometime before this happened he said I ought to learn how to load a gun, and he had loaded it and then he says, "Now you try it." And I put the bullet in the slot but I was afraid to push this thing that slides out because I was afraid if I pushed it in and then turned it I might go too far and it might go off or something, so he said, "Well, here let me do it and I'll do it." So he put the two bullets back in the gun.

Q: So there were only the two bullets in the gun?

A: That's all he put in there.

Q: Was there anything special about keeping two bullets in the gun?

A: No, it was just bullets and . . .

Q: So he had that loaded, that gun was loaded then all the time in the house with the two bullets.

A: Yes, it was loaded with those two and he had mentioned something about he had ordered me a gun cause he thought I needed one to protect myself at the house at night and I might need it, being there by myself. Well I don't know anything about guns. The only gun I ever shot was a .22 rifle of my brother's when I was 17 and I just took two shots at a target out on the farm and from then on I had never bothered with guns.

Q: So this day you said you found the gun. It was under the bed. Is that right? You had put it under—

A: It's where I put it the night before and I got scared and I ran into the bedroom and I pulled the gun out and my children, I don't know, I kept telling my children that I felt something was going to happen. Something was wrong and that somebody was going to kill me and I upset them and they were sitting on the couch and I kept thinking "Are you against me too?"

Q: These feelings that everyone was against you were stronger as the day went on; they got worse?

A: Yes, I even demanded my children to tell me which one was against me and if they knew what was going on, that they better tell me. And finally I felt upset because I felt like I was getting so close to shooting my children—you know, I felt that I was going to kill my children—that I told both of them to get up real quick and go in the other room and get a Bible apiece and then go back to the sofa and sit down and turn to the 23rd Psalm and just keep reading it and reading it and not stop reading, because I felt like as long as they were reading that Bible—I said, "God would protect you from me because I am sick and I'm scared and I don't know what's going on and somebody is going to hurt me."

And I held that gun just like this because I didn't want to use it on my children. And I was just like this and while I was standing there I could see through my living room curtains and my aunt's car came flying down the hill. She looked like she was speeding. Well I didn't expect Trevah. I hadn't even called Trevah and she came up to the front porch and started knocking and calling me and I didn't answer her. I just figured she would go away and she'll leave me alone. But I felt like somebody was going to kill me, or was trying to hurt me and I wouldn't answer that door for her because I felt like, well, she's the one, it's going to be her. So she left the steps and she went around the house and I went through the living room to the back.

Q: Did you see her physically?

A: I could see her shadow through the curtains and I could hear her voice.

Q: You couldn't see her face clearly or you could see her face clearly?

A: Not at the front door.

Q: Not at the front. Okay.

A: And she went around the back and I had to go out and that black dog was there and that dog bothered me cause I thought, "Well if I get out there that thing is going to jump on me." So I took my foot and was kind of kicking the dog away and pushing the dog away with my other hand, and Trevah came around the corner of the back screen door and I told her to stay away and just stay right where she was and to leave me alone, that I didn't want to be bothered.

Q: When you said that to her through the screen door did you see her?

A: I could see her face.

Q: You could see her, and did it look like her or did it look different?

A: She didn't look happy. I mean she looked angry, was how she looked to me. She just looked angry and I said "Trevah get away from me and leave me alone." I said, "You're not going to hurt me, you're the devil, you're a demon or something is wrong, but you stay away from me and don't you come near me."

Q: Have you ever seen her look like that before?

A: Yes, when she's been angry.

Q: Does she look exactly like she looks when she looked angry or did she look different?

A: She looked angry. The expression on her face looked like she was angry and yet I kept telling her to leave me alone. I thought she'd just go on and leave me alone, get away from me.

Q: Were you hearing voices at this time, do you remember?

A: I wasn't hearing any voices. I felt like, right then I felt like "Okay, you're here and if you get your hands on me, you're going to kill me, or those kids are going to kill me, or that dog in front of me is going to jump me," and I was worried about Midnight and my aunt. I had my aunt over there and this black dog over here, and both of them were bothering me and I didn't know what to do with either one of them and I thought well maybe if I could holler at Trevah or get her away from me, she'd leave me alone, and she said, "No, I'm not leaving you alone." She says, "I'm coming in that door," and I said, "You better not, you better get away from me" and she says, "No, I'm not," and she took her hands and she started opening the door knobs off the screen, I think. She took her hands to get the edge of the door and started opening it, and that got on my nerves because I told her to leave me alone. And then I had that black dog in front of me and she turned around and I was trying to kick the dog and Trevah was coming in the door and I just took my hands and I just went like this—right through the screen.

Q: What happened?

A: I shot her.

Q: Then what happened after you shot her?

A: When I shot her she went backwards and she fell in the mud on her back and the dog kept coming near me and I pushed the door open real quick and got the dog out of the way and I, just—I don't know—I just stood there. I started crying and I felt like tearing up, I felt like tearing up everything in that back porch. I felt like taking something heavy and just smashing that red washing machine all to pieces. That's how I felt like. I just felt like I hated everybody and everything that minute, and I was hurting and I was mixed up and I felt sick and I was angry at Curtis for leaving me and I was angry because I had shot my aunt and I just felt like—

Q: Did you know that was your aunt when she came?

A: I know it was Trevah.

Q: Other times, you have said you had feelings that it was something else.

A: No, I knew that that was Trevah, but I felt like she and Curtis, and several of the people in the neighborhood were witches or had given their souls to the devil and they were all out to do some harm to me because they were against me. I just, that's how I felt and I felt like if Trevah got hold of me she was going to kill me because she was with everybody else. And I felt like Curtis was against me because he told me himself when he started taking me around in that truck ride—he says "I'm going to teach you a lesson you'll never forget." And . . .

Q: It was a pretty upsetting experience. . . .

A: So, I talked to my aunt a few minutes, right after I shot her and she said "Joy why?" and I said, "Trevah," I said, "You're the devil," and I said, "You came here to hurt me didn't you?" and she said, "Honey, no, I came to help you." And I started crying and then she said she was hurting and I don't know why I did this—but I guess because I felt that I was the reason for her bleeding to death—I took the gun and shot her again just to relieve the pain she was having because she said she hurt. And that was it. [Witness cries]

Q: What are you feeling now, Mrs. Baker?

A: Hurt. [Witness cries] [Long pause]

You know, sometimes you wonder, I've wondered, if I was going to do something like that, why did I have to hit her to kill

her? You know, some people you read about, they shoot people
and they hurt them in the arm. I feel like why in the world
couldn't I have hit her in the arm and I know I hit her here [in
the head] because I saw all that blood coming out of her chest.

Mrs. Baker's husband and children corroborated those portions of her
account about which they had direct knowledge.

NOTES ON THE INSANITY DEFENSE AND
MAJOR MENTAL DISORDER

1. **Introduction.** Some commentators claim that the medical
model of disease should not be applied to "crazy behavior" in the
absence of a verified causal link between neurobiology and the relevant
aberrant behavior. According to this view, "mental illness" is only a
label used to denote some forms of deviant behavior. Such a descriptive label, it is said, should not serve as a predicate either for attribution of cause or for ascription of legal consequences. Obviously, this
perspective leaves no room for an exculpatory doctrine of insanity.
However, from the earliest times, the common law has reflected a less
skeptical view; and the responsibility doctrines of the criminal law rest
on the widely shared belief that mental illness does exist and that it
"causes" crazy behavior.

To say that mental illness "exists" says nothing, of course, about
what it is or when it ought to have exculpatory significance. Indeed,
the vagueness of the concept and the imprecise relationship between
psychic abnormality and criminal behavior have troubled generations
of courts and commentators. However, before considering the gray
areas of mental abnormality, one should focus first on a case that does
not lie at the boundary. Joy Baker's case involves a claim of aberrant
mental functioning well within the layman's common-sense understanding of "insanity."

2. **Joy Baker's Credibility.** Because an insanity claim is based
largely on what a defendant says was going on in his or her mind—
mental events that cannot be verified by, or tested against, the experiences of ordinary people in the same circumstances—administration of
the defense involves a considerable risk of fabrication. Does Joy
Baker's testimony give you any reason to doubt the veracity of her
account of her feelings and thoughts at the time of the offense? Is it
relevant that she had no previous history of disordered behavior or
psychiatric treatment? Would your assessment of her credibility depend on whether the prosecution introduced any evidence suggesting a
"motive" for the killing other than the one described by the defendant?
Would your assessment be different if she had shot her husband instead
of her aunt?

3. **The Existence of Mental Disease.** Assume that the defendant's testimony is credible and that she has accurately described the
feelings and thoughts that she experienced before and during the
shooting. (In fact, everyone who interviewed her or heard her testimo-

ny believed she was telling the truth.) Does this evidence demonstrate that she had a "defect of reason from disease of the mind," as *M'Naghten* requires, or the "mental disease or defect" required under the Model Penal Code formulation?

The purpose and scope of the "mental-disease" requirement is explored in some detail in the materials that follow; however, several points should be noted here. First, the concept of mental disease is a threshold condition; abnormal psychological functioning at the time of a crime has exculpatory significance only if it can be attributed to the effects of a "mental disease." Obviously this excludes those aberrations in human behavior that are attributable to defects of character, intoxication, or emotional upheaval due to anger, panic, or grief. Second, while the boundaries of the concept are unclear, it plainly comprehends "psychotic" conditions, i.e., those abnormal mental conditions involving "gross impairment of reality testing" and often evidenced by hallucinations or delusions.[a] Indeed, a psychosis is widely regarded as the only type of mental disorder that can have exculpatory significance under *M'Naghten*.[b] Third, mental disease is *not* confined to those abnormalities associated with observable dysfunction of the brain, customarily labeled organic brain syndromes. If the concept were restricted to "organic" disorders, it would exclude a substantial proportion of persons whose contact with reality is severely impaired by what clinicians call "functional" psychoses—those for which the presence of a specific organic factor has not been established. The major types of "functional" psychoses are the schizophrenic and paranoid disorders and the major affective disorders (e.g., manic depressive disorder).

In Joy Baker's case, "direct evidence" of psychotic mental phenomena, including delusions, was presented in her own testimony and the corroborative testimony of her husband and children. Should the

[a] The glossary of the third edition of the Diagnostic and Statistical Manual of the American Psychiatric Association (DSM-III) defines psychotic as:

"A term indicating gross impairment in reality testing . . . . When there is gross impairment in reality testing, the individual incorrectly evelutes the accuracy of his or her perceptions and thoughts and makes incorrect inferences about external reality, even in the face of contrary evidence. The term psychotic does not apply to minor distortions of reality that involve matters of relative judgment. For example, a depressed person who underestimated his achievements would not be described as a psychotic, whereas one who believed he had caused a natural catastrophe would be so described.

"Direct evidence of psychotic behavior is the presence of either delusions or hallucinations without insight into their pathological nature. The term psychotic is sometimes appropriate when an individual's behavior is so grossly disorganized that a reasonable inference can be made that reality testing is disturbed. Examples include markedly incoherent speech without apparent awareness by the person that the speech is not understandable, and the agitated, inattentive, and disoriented behavior [often associated with alcohol withdrawal]."

[b] Many commentators—whether they support *M'Naghten* or oppose it—have taken the position that the phrase "defect of reason" is substantially equivalent to psychosis. According to Waelder, for example, the threshold condition for an insanity claim is one "in which the sense of reality is crudely impaired, and inaccessible to the corrective influence of experience—for example, when people are confused or disoriented or suffer from hallucinations or delusions." Waelder, Psychiatry and the Problem of Criminal Responsibility, 101 U.Pa.L.Rev. 378, 384 (1952). See also Livermore & Meehl, The Virtues of *M'Naghten*, 51 Minn.L.Rev. 789, 802–04 (1967).

defendant also be required to introduce expert psychiatric testimony to carry her burden of producing evidence that she was suffering from a "mental disease"?   Most courts have said "no," ruling that, in a jury trial, testimony by the defendant or by lay witnesses who have observed the defendant's behavior can be sufficient to raise a jury question on the issue of insanity.   In practice, of course, most insanity claims are predicated chiefly, if not entirely, on expert testimony.   As you review the following excerpt from the expert testimony offered in Mrs. Baker's case, consider whether it would influence your assessment regarding whether she had a "mental disease" at the time of the offense:

Q: Doctor, in your professional opinion, was the defendant suffering from a mental disease at the time of the offense?

A: When Mrs. Baker killed Trevah she was, in my professional opinion, suffering from an acute episode of paranoid schizophrenia.   This is an example of a major psychotic disorder; that is, a condition during which the person loses the ability to distinguish between what is outside herself, or what is "real," and what is inside herself, and in that sense, "not real."

Q: Doctor, could you explain how a person who has no previous history of mental illness would suddenly have an acute psychotic episode?

A: Mrs. Baker has a predisposition for psychiatric disease not only hereditarily via her mother's history of schizophrenia, but also with the chaotic nature of her early home environment.   It appears that prior to the shooting, there was a great deal of domestic stress in the Baker home.   The stresses which most of us can normally tolerate may become psychologically intolerable for a person with a predisposition for psychiatric disease.   The stress precipitates a disintegration of the personality, a deterioration which affects the person's thinking and emotions.   Any of us could become acutely psychotic under enough stress.   In Mrs. Baker's case, the stress to which she was exposed is readily apparent and this was enough to tip the psychic balance.

   4. **Mental Disorder and Criminal Responsibility.**   Even if Mrs. Baker was psychotic—was suffering from a major form of mental illness—at the time of the offense, she nonetheless might be found to have been criminally responsible for the homicide.   This is because mental disease is a necessary condition, but not a sufficient one, for exculpation on grounds of insanity.   Each of the prevailing insanity tests requires proof of two "elements": The defendant must have had (i) a mental disease (ii) that had specified incapacitating effects at the time of the offense.   The various tests differ, of course, in their definitions of those incapacities that have exculpatory significance.   Would you support a test that asked simply whether the defendant was mentally ill (or "insane") at the time of the offense?

   A partial answer to this question is that the criminal act may have been entirely unrelated to a person's sickness.   Thus, even a psychotic person usually has some grasp of reality.   Depending on the nature and severity of the person's condition, he may be capable of governing at least some of his actions in accord with "normal" human desires or emotions. For example, a person whose interactions with other people are shaped by clearly paranoid thinking and other schizophrenic symptoms may nonetheless take a radio which he knows to belong to someone else simply because he wants it and believes he will not be caught. His schizophrenic symptoms may be entirely unrelated to his "reasons" for engaging in the criminal act. It should be noted, however, that this observation does not provide a complete answer to the question posed above; it demonstrates only that the question should be reformulated to ask whether the symptoms of the defendant's mental illness (or "insanity") were related to the offense. This is precisely what the New Hampshire Supreme Court said when it endorsed the so-called "product" test in State v. Jones, 50 N.H. 369, 398 (1871):

> "Whether the defendant had a mental disease . . .
> seems to be as much a question of fact as whether he had a
> bodily disease; and whether the killing of his wife was the
> product of that disease, [is] also as clearly a matter of fact as
> whether thirst and a quickened pulse are the product of fever.
> That it is a difficult question does not change the matter at
> all. [Various] symptoms, phases, or manifestations of the
> disease . . . are all clearly matters of evidence to be
> weighed by the jury upon the question whether the act was
> the offspring of insanity: if it was, a criminal intent did not
> produce it; if it was not, a criminal intent did produce it, and
> it was crime. . . ."

Is this a sensible approach? Is it preferable to the other tests described earlier? Consider, in this connection the New Hampshire Supreme Court's criticism of the *M'Naghten* and "irresistible-impulse" tests. These tests, the court said, are misguided because they give conclusive significance to particular "symptoms, phases or manifestations of the disease," such as the capacity to distinguish right from wrong or to resist an insane impulse, instead of looking at the full impact of the disease as a clinical phenomenon. This observation was echoed 80 years later by Judge David Bazelon in a short-lived decision adopting the New Hampshire test: "In attempting to define insanity in terms of a symptom, the courts have assumed an impossible role, not merely one for which they have no special competence." Durham v. United States, 214 F.2d 862, 872 (D.C.Cir. 1954).

Do the tests of criminal responsibility purport to identify "symptoms" of insanity and therefore to establish a legal "test" for what is really a medical question? Sir James Stephen insisted, to the contrary, that definition of "[t]he mental elements of responsibility . . . is and must be a legal question. It cannot be anything else, for the meaning of responsibility is liability to punishment; and if criminal law does not determine who are to be punished under given circumstances, it determines nothing." 2 A History of the Criminal Law of England 183 (1883). Are you satisfied with Stephen's response? You should keep this issue in mind as you study the following notes.

5. **Applying the *M'Naghten* Test to Joy Baker.** Application of the *M'Naghten* test requires the fact-finder to reconstruct the defendant's "knowledge" at the time of the offense. The test has two prongs—knowledge of the "nature and quality" of the act and knowledge of its wrongfulness. The task of probing the defendant's psyche and applying these tests—difficult enough in any case—is complicated in Joy Baker's case by the apparent difference in her motivation for the two shots.

(i) **Knowledge of the Act.** The first prong of *M'Naghten* obviously overlaps analytically with the technical concept of mens rea. Did Mrs. Baker have the mens rea for some form of criminal homicide? It could be argued that she lacked the mens rea for murder at the time of her first shot because she did not intend to kill a "human being." At common law, this claim would probably be characterized as a mistake of fact. Since the mistake was obviously an unreasonable one, however, Mrs. Baker most likely would be guilty of some form of homicide if ordinary mens-rea principles were applied. It might also be argued that Mrs. Baker's first shot would have been justified if her delusional beliefs had been true since she would have been acting in self-defense. Again, the application of ordinary common-law culpability principles would indicate that she was unreasonably mistaken as to the existence of justificatory facts (the necessity for killing to protect herself) and her defense would fail, although the grade of the offense might be reduced to manslaughter. For present purposes, therefore, it can be assumed that Mrs. Baker would be guilty of some form of homicide—at least manslaughter—unless she is entitled to exculpation on grounds of insanity.[c]

It seems clear that Mrs. Baker was aware that she was pulling the trigger of a gun and that the bullet would kill or seriously injure the victim. But did she "know" that the intended victim was a "human being" when she fired the first shot? In this sense, did she know the nature and quality of her act?

In any event, the defendant's testimony shows that she "knew" at the time of the second shot that her aunt was not demonically possessed; her perceptual capacities appear to have been intact at this point. Remember that she observed that her aunt "hurt" and that killing her would put her out of her pain. Does this imply that she "knew" the nature and quality of the act of pulling the trigger the second time?

(ii) **Knowledge of Wrongfulness.** Even if Joy Baker was sufficiently aware of the physical characteristics of her conduct to be said to have "known" the "nature and quality" of her act, did she "know" that it was wrong? Undoubtedly, she knew, as an abstract matter, that killing another person without justification is wrong. However, Mrs. Baker claimed to have believed at the time of the first shot that she was in imminent peril of annihilation at the hands of the devil. Would

[c] The general relationship between mens rea and mental abnormality is explored at the end of this section on pages 752–70, infra, and is explored again in the specific context of homicide offenses on pages 841–43, infra.

such a "defect of reason" prevent her from knowing that her act was wrong? Is it wrong to shoot the devil?[d]

The second shot, unlike the first, was not motivated by Mrs. Baker's delusion. Her motive was to relieve her aunt's suffering. Was the second shot legally justified? If not, did her mental disease prevent her from "knowing" that her act was "wrong"? In what way?

Some courts permit exculpation only if, as a result of mental disease, the defendant was disabled from knowing that the act was *legally* wrong. The leading case to the contrary is People v. Schmidt, 216 N.Y. 324, 110 N.E. 945 (1915), involving a defendant who claimed that he killed a woman after hearing the voice of God calling upon him to do so as a sacrifice and atonement. In an opinion by Judge Cardozo, the Court of Appeals held "that there are times and circumstances in which the word 'wrong' . . . ought not to be limited to legal wrong." In particular, if a person has "an insane delusion that God has appeared to [him] and ordained the commission of a crime, we think it cannot be said of the offender that he knows the act to be wrong."[e] What is left of the right-wrong "test" under Judge Cardozo's approach? Does this mean that if a mentally ill person thinks, according to his own lights, that he is doing the "right" thing, then he is not criminally responsible even if he "knew" that his act was a crime? Is there any other possible meaning of "wrong"? How, in any event, should the right-wrong branch of *M'Naghten* be applied to Joy Baker?

(iii) **The Value of Expert Testimony.** Would your task of applying either branch of *M'Naghten* be aided materially by expert

[d] The *M'Naghten* decision contained another "rule" that might have been applicable to the first shot fired by Mrs. Baker. One of the questions posed by the House of Lords was: "If a person under an insane delusion as to existing facts commits an offense in consequence thereof, is he thereby excused?" The judges responded:

"[M]aking the assumption . . . that he labours under such partial delusion only, and is not in other respects insane, we think he must be considered in the same situation as to responsibility as if the facts with respect to which the delusion exists were real. For example, if, under the influence of his delusion, he supposes another man to be in the act of attempting to take away his life, and he kills that man, as he supposes, in self-defense, he would be exempt from punishment. If his delusion was that the deceased had inflicted a serious injury to his character and fortune, and he killed him in revenge for such supposed injury, he would be liable to punishment. . . ."

This "insane delusion" ground of exculpation has been discarded as a separate test in modern formulations of *M'Naghten* on the ground that it is but a specific application of the "nature-and-quality" and "right-wrong" branches of the *M'Naghten* test and is thus redundant as a separate rule.

[e] The drafters of the Model Penal Code took no position on this question, leaving it to the courts and legislatures to choose whether the test should include the term "wrongfulness" or "criminality." Jurisdictions adopting the Model Code test have divided evenly on the question.

For a recent case following *Schmidt*, see State v. Cameron, 100 Wn.2d 520, 674 P.2d 650 (en banc 1983). Cameron stabbed and killed his stepmother, believing that she was a satanic agent and that he was doing God's will, even though he knew that he was committing a crime. The jury was instructed that "the terms 'right and wrong' refer to knowledge of a person at the time of committing an act that he was acting contrary to law." The Washington Supreme Court overturned the conviction, holding that this instruction was erroneous.

psychiatric testimony?   The relevant portion of the opinion offered in
Joy Baker's case is excerpted below:

Q: At the time of the offense, did the defendant know she was
shooting her aunt?

A: In her psychotic state she was not able to draw the boundary
between her internal chaotic reality (her fear of annihilation)
and the external reality of her environment, and the two became
fused.   As she talks about that evening she states that she saw
her aunt coming towards the back door and she "knew" that this
person was her aunt.   It is essential here to understand what the
word "know" means in the context of Mrs. Baker's psychiatric
illness.   It is true that Mrs. Baker was able to recognize the form
which approached her home as that of her aunt.   This particular
perceptual mechanism seemed to remain intact.   However, Mrs.
Baker's interpretation of this perception is what was so profoundly affected by her psychotic state.   Her interpretation of her aunt
approaching her home was entirely out of touch with the reality
of the situation.   Mrs. Baker firmly believed that her aunt was a
witch and was afraid her aunt would annihilate her.   It was this
affective state, or emotional tone, which set the stage for Mrs.
Baker's actions.   She was unable at the time of the shooting,
with her abnormal intellectual functions, to recognize how invalid her interpretations were.   This is, of course, a result of her
psychotic state.   In other words, at the time of the shooting, Mrs.
Baker was unable, in my professional opinion, to understand the
difference between her own feelings and the events which were
occurring in the world around her.   She did not appreciate the
nature and consequences of her acts and acted purely from the
instinct of self-preservation.

Q: What about the second shot, Doctor?

A: Persons in a psychotic state have extreme polarization of emotions.   One moment they may feel intense love, the next moment
intense hate.   One moment they may feel intensely threatened
and the next moment they may feel intensely secure and so
forth.   In addition these polar feelings may switch very rapidly
and will not appear to be connected to one another because of the
chaotic state of that person's thinking.   In Mrs. Baker's psychotic
state she experienced these rapid disjointed changes in feelings.
This enabled her to feel threatened and fearful in one moment
and yet to feel concern and desire to help her wounded aunt in
the next.

Thus, the first shot removed the threat of her own imminent
destruction and generated feelings of relief.   This, in turn
"shocked" her and triggered a "jump" in her perceptual modalities.   Her perceptive focus shifted from her preoccupation with
the threats to herself to a recognition of her aunt's condition.
Now she was preoccupied with her desire to "stop the suffering."
To Mrs. Baker the immediate way to do this was to shoot her
aunt again.   In her "regressed" state, she was still not sufficient-

ly in touch with reality to call into play mature, normal responses to her aunt's condition. A person in a psychotic state cannot connect logically chains of events. Hence she did not make the rational connection between the act of shooting her aunt to stop her suffering and the finality of death. Thus, it is my professional opinion that a full appreciation of the nature and consequences of the second shot could not have existed in Mrs. Baker's mind.

Does this testimony help? Should Mrs. Baker be convicted in a *M'Naghten* jurisdiction?

6. **The Meaning of "Knowing."** The *M'Naghten* formulation has been subject to the persistent criticism that it requires conviction of psychotic offenders who are not blameworthy. According to the critics, only a handful of seriously ill offenders fail to "know" in a purely intellectual sense enough about what they are doing to know that it is punishable. Yet, because a mentally ill person's "intellectual" knowledge may not be assimilated by the whole personality, such a person may lack an emotional appreciation of the significance of conduct. In other words, the term "knowledge" is clinically meaningful, the critics say, only if it is given an "affective" or emotional meaning. The expert testimony offered in Joy Baker's case illustrates this clinical interpretation of "knowledge."

Perhaps the most famous statement of the clinical objection to *M'Naghten* appeared in Zilboorg, Misconceptions of Legal Insanity, 9 Am.J. Orthopsychiat. 540, 552–53 (1939):*

> "The crux of the question revolves around the word 'know.' The law automatically assumes that a child committing a felony does not know the nature and quality of the act and does not know that it is wrong. Yet a child of moderate brightness will say that he hit his sister on the head, that she bled and then she fell; he will even admit that she died or that he killed her and will perhaps say that he was wrong to kill his sister. The criminal code does not accept this knowledge as valid; without knowing it the law itself recognizes here a fundamental medicopsychological distinction between the purely verbal knowledge which characterizes the child and the other type of knowledge which characterizes the adult. The fundamental difference between verbal or purely intellectual knowledge and the mysterious other kind of knowledge is familiar to every clinical psychiatrist; it is the difference between knowledge divorced from affect and knowledge so fused with affect that it becomes a human reality.
> . . .
>
> "Therefore 'defect of reason' which the law stresses may not and, with the exception of cases of mental defectives, does not lie within the field of reason at all, but within the field of emotional appreciation. This emotional appreciation is a

very complex phenomenon. It is based on a series of intricate psychological mechanisms, the most potent of which is that of identification. What makes it possible for a civilized, mentally healthy human being to resist a murderous impulse is not the cold detached reasoning that it is wrong and dangerous but the automatic emotional, mostly unconscious identification with the prospective victim, an identification which automatically inhibits the impulse to kill and causes anxiety ('It is dangerous') which in turn produces the reflection: 'It is wrong, the same may and should happen to me.' Unless this identification is present the impulse breaks through and fear of the law and sense of wrong is paled, devoid of its affective component; it becomes a verbal, coldly intellectual, formal, childish, infantile psychological presentation."

In his definitive work on the insanity defense, Professor Abraham Goldstein concluded that, in practice, the *M'Naghten* formula has been interpreted and applied in a much less restrictive fashion than its critics have assumed. See A. Goldstein, The Insanity Defense 49–51 (1967):*

"The assertion that 'know' is narrowly defined has been made so often and so insistently that it comes as a surprise to find that very few appellate courts have imposed the restrictive interpretation. Indeed, most of the courts which have addressed themselves to the question have favored a rather broad construction. In [many] states, the jury is told that an accused 'knows' only if he 'understands' enough to enable him to judge of 'the nature, character and consequence of the act charged against him,' or if he has the 'capacity to appreciate the character and to comprehend the probable or possible consequences of his act.' . . . In this view, the word 'appreciate' draws most psychoses under the *M'Naghten* rules, because it addresses itself to the defendant's awareness of 'the true significance of his conduct.' . . . .

"The phrase 'nature and quality of the act' is [typically] either stated to the jury without explanation or treated as adding nothing to the requirement that the accused know his act was wrong. [However, one] court has held that 'nature and quality' gives 'important emphasis' to the realization of the wrongfulness of an act. It marks the distinction between 'vaguely . . . [realizing] that particular conduct is forbidden' and 'real insight into the conduct.' This construction illustrates the close connection between the definition of 'know' and that of 'nature and quality.' The broader meaning of 'nature and quality' carries with it the broader construction of 'know' and vice versa. To know the quality of an act, with all its social and emotional implications, requires more than an abstract purely intellectual knowledge. Like-

* Reprinted with the permission of the author and Yale University Press.

wise, to talk of appreciating the full significance of an act means that 'nature and quality' must be understood as including more than the physical nature of the act."

This broader reading of the word "knowledge" as it appears in the *M'Naghten* formulation is, as Professor Goldstein indicated, typically achieved by emphasizing that the actor must "appreciate" the nature and quality of the conduct and that it was wrong. Indeed, "appreciate" has become a kind of code-word for this "affective" reading of "knowledge"; the defendant must have sufficient understanding of the nature and consequences of the conduct to be said to "appreciate" its social and moral significance. Without such understanding, the defendant lacks the rudimentary tools by which "normal" responsible people govern their conduct. Use of the word "appreciate" in the reformulation of the *M'Naghten* test in Section 4.01 of the Model Penal Code is intended to embrace this broader notion of what it means to "know" something is wrong.

The trend in favor of an "affective" meaning of knowledge, however, has not been without its critics. Professor Glanville Williams is one of them. In Criminal Law: The General Part 491–92 (2d ed. 1961), he stated:

> "The tendency to widen the exemption . . . by referring it to some deeper kind of metaphysical insight is . . . found among American psychiatrists. The question, on this view, is not merely . . . whether the accused knew he was killing a human being, but whether he had any 'real appreciation' or 'understanding' of his act, or of its 'enormity, its significance or its implications.' This is metaphysical rather than scientific language and it may be permissible to doubt whether any citizen, sane or not, can be credited with the transcendental insight of the mystic. The formula of 'real nature' is used indulgently to give a general exemption on the ground of [mental illness]."

Does Professor Williams have a point? Should a mere "intellectual knowledge" be sufficient to establish criminal responsibility even if the defendant lacked a "true appreciation" of the significance of his conduct?

7. **The Significance of Cognitive Impairment.** The preceding notes have used the facts of the Joy Baker case to explore the meaning of the *M'Naghten* test and the analogous language in the Model Penal Code. Now, it is useful to return to the fundamental question raised at the outset, i.e., whether these tests identify proper critiera for assessing criminal responsibility.

To the extent that "nature and quality" of the act refers only to its physical character, the first prong of *M'Naghten* is, in the words of Lord Devlin, "practically obsolete."[f] No one who squeezes a person's neck really thinks he is squeezing lemons. Also, as Professor Goldstein

[f] Devlin, Criminal Responsibility and Punishment: Functions of Judge and Jury, [1954] Crim.L.Rev. 661, 678–79.

noted, an emphasis on the moral "quality" of the act makes this prong of the test functionally equivalent to its right-wrong prong. Thus, under either *M'Naghten* or the analogous language in the Model Penal Code, the real significance of cognitive impairment lies in whether the defendant knew or appreciated the "wrongfulness" of the act. Is this the right question to ask? The liability of a sane person does not turn on having a "mind bent on wrongdoing" or full appreciation or understanding of the legal or moral significance of conduct. Why should the liability of an "insane" person turn on such an inquiry?

Glanville Williams discussed this issue in Criminal Law: The General Part 495–96 (2d ed. 1961):

> "Why, precisely, does knowledge of wrong enter into a consideration of responsibility? . . . The exemption . . . may perhaps be regarded as dictated by the object of punishment [because] a psychotic who does not know that his act is wrong is not likely to be deterred by the legal prohibition. Yet the same is true of a sane person who does not know that his act is wrong. Why is not the rule ignorantia juris non excusat applied to the insane? Perhaps it is because the rule presupposes a mind capable of knowing right. But on this interpretation the question should be not: 'Did the accused know it was wrong' but 'Was he capable of knowing that it was wrong?' For if it once be admitted that some psychotics know right from wrong, it may be a mere accident of education (such as may befall a sane person) that this particular psychotic did not know the particular act to be wrong. What must be shown is that his ignorance was the result of his mental disease. . . ."

Professor Williams' point can be illustrated by the second shot in Joy Baker's case. This shot was not motivated by her delusional beliefs. Under the circumstances as she correctly perceived them, her conduct constitutes murder, for euthanasia has never been recognized as justifiable or excusable homicide under Anglo-American law. Perhaps Joy Baker did not know this, although it is more likely that she acted spontaneously and gave no thought to the legality of her conduct. Yet, if a sane person had shot an injured and suffering Aunt Trevah under similar circumstances, ignorance of (or emotional indifference to) the governing law of homicide would be legally irrelevant. Why should a different rule obtain for Joy Baker?

Questions of this nature have led some commentators to suggest that the *M'Naghten* formulation should be discarded altogether. The real basis for exculpation of the insane, they argue, lies not in a lack of a capacity to know or appreciate the wrongfulness of the conduct, but in a lack of capacity for rational control of behavior in relation to the criminal act.[g] Consider, for example, the position taken by Professor

---

[g] See, e.g., H. Fingerette and A. Haase, Mental Disabilities and Criminal Responsibility (1979); J. Feinberg, Doing and De- serving: Essays in the Theory of Responsibility 272–92 (1970).

Michael Moore.[h] Professor Moore argues that a "pattern of irrational action" is the "primary symptom of the mental capacities we label mental illness." By referring to a person as being irrational, "we mean . . . that some significant portion of his actions pursue irrational ends, are predicated on beliefs themselves irrational, or are not based on desire/belief sets at all." He continues: [*]

"Rationality is one of the fundamental properties by which we understand ourselves as persons, that is, as creatures capable of adjusting our actions as reasonably efficient means to rational ends. Being mentally ill means being incapacitated from acting rationally in this fundamental sense.

"There are obviously degrees of irrationality. How irrational must one be to be mentally ill in the popular understanding? Psychiatry in this century has doubtless influenced the popular understanding of the concept of mental illness. We are all to some degree irrational in our conduct; we are thus tempted to say that we are all a little bit crazy.

"Yet side by side with this sophisticated, educated view there exists our ancient paradigm of mental illness: It is not manifested by the occasional irrationality we all exhibit. It is reserved for those gross deviations from intelligibility we still capture with the more severe statements, 'He is crazy,' or 'He is insane,' or 'He is mad.' Those idioms capture the essential notion of the ancient conception of mental illness as madness: that mentally ill people are different from us in ways that we find hard to understand. . . .

Professor Moore suggests that the legal definition of insanity should draw on the "popular moral notion of mental illness" rather than on medical classification. From this perspective, he observes:

"One is a moral agent only if one is a rational agent. Only if we can see another being as one who acts to achieve some rational end in light of some rational beliefs will we understand him in the same fundamental way that we understand ourselves and our fellow persons in everyday life. We regard as moral agents only those beings we can understand in this way. . . .

"The proper definition of legal insanity is one that utilizes this moral criterion. . . . The only question appropriate to juries is thus one appealing to their moral paradigm of mental illness: Is the accused so irrational as to be nonresponsible? . . ."

Do you understand how Professor Moore's approach differs from the traditional criteria of cognitive impairment? Does the criterion of irrationality adequately distinguish between the tasks of identifying symptoms of mental illness and defining criteria of criminal responsibility?

[h] Moore, Law and Psychiatry: Rethinking the Relationship 197–98, 244–45 (1984).

[*] Reprinted with the permission of the author and Cambridge University Press.

8. **Applying Control Tests to Psychotic Defendants.** The control test provides an independent basis for exculpation in more than a third of the states. Proponents of such a test traditionally have claimed that a psychotic person who is "driven" by intrapsychic forces may be incapacitated from restraining his behavior even though he may know what he is doing and that it is wrong. This "psychological compulsion" is therefore thought to be a morally relevant feature of severe mental disorder.

How would the control formulas apply to Joy Baker? Would you find that she acted on an "irresistible impulse"? That she lacked "substantial capacity to conform her conduct to the requirements of law"? Do you need further information to apply these tests?

Obviously, the task of applying control tests requires speculation about whether the defendant "could" have acted otherwise than she did, and whether her mental illness prevented her from having the power of choice that she "normally" would have had. Since the only evidence available is her actual behavior—the defendant shot her aunt (twice)—how would you go about deciding whether she "could" have acted otherwise? Would expert testimony help? Consider these excerpts from the testimony offered in Mrs. Baker's case:

Q: Doesn't Mrs. Baker's effort to protect her children, only moments before the killing, indicate that she had the mental power to resist her homicidal impulses?

A: No, I don't think so. When Mrs. Baker ordered the children to read the 23rd Psalm, she was trying to assure that they would not be the ones to attack her; in this sense, putting the Bible in their hands was an act of self-defense. When the victim drove up, Mrs. Baker did everything she could to prevent her aunt from coming in the house. However, once her aunt put her hand through the door, Mrs. Baker had no options left, psychologically speaking. She was in a state of extreme anxiety and was fearful of imminent attack. The impulse for protective action was, if you will, irresistible.

Q: Defendant's own testimony would suggest that she did not feel threatened at the time of the second shot; indeed, her testimony indicates that she was acting from a rational motive—to stop her aunt's suffering. Doesn't this suggest that her capacity to make choices had returned?

A: It is probably true that she was less influenced by her delusional thinking; because her level of intense anxiety had been reduced, she was able to see the victim as her aunt. Her perceptual and interpretive capacities had been restored to some extent. But this doesn't mean her functioning was intact by any means. She still lacked insight and judgment. She saw that her aunt was in pain; the immediate issue was how to stop the pain, and she responded in a regressed, child-like way. She acted impulsively.

Q: Suppose a policeman, or perhaps the rescue squad, had pulled into the driveway after the first shot. As you understand her condition, what do you think she would have done?

A: This is speculation, of course. But I think she would have taken advantage of the alternative way to get help for her aunt. The problem, in fact, was that there were no visible options and in her compromised psychological condition she was unable to think about alternatives that were not visibly apparent.

The desirability of a control test of responsibility has been one of the most hotly debated issues in the criminal law for more than a century. In recent years the debate has focused chiefly on disorders other than psychoses. This dimension of the controversy is covered in the next section, immediately below. However, it should be emphasized that the early proponents of the "irresistible impulse" test argued that the *M'Naghten* formula was an inadequate measure of the morally significant features of psychotic deterioration. Moreover, many psychiatrists have opposed recent efforts to eliminate the volitional criterion on the same basis. In response, many of the commentators who support proposals to narrow the defense have argued that a broad, affective reading of the "knowledge" or "appreciation" test makes the control test superfluous in cases involving psychotic defendants.[i] Do you agree? Is Joy Baker's case for exculpation any stronger under a test of volitional impairment than it would be if cognitive impairment were the only inquiry?

———

SUBSECTION B: THE INSANITY DEFENSE AND THE CONTROL INQUIRY

———

THE CASE OF FRANCIS POLLARD

[The following case is designed to provide a factual context for exploring the meaning and desirability of a control test of criminal responsibility. The facts are based on the reported case of Pollard v. United States, 282 F.2d 450 (6th Cir. 1960), reversing United States v. Pollard, 171 F.Supp. 474 (E.D.Mich.1959). Following a summary of the evidence, excerpts are presented from a psychiatric report and from the arguments of counsel. You should consider how the various insanity formulations would apply to *Pollard* and what the policy of the criminal law should be in such cases. The notes following the case will explore these issues.]

Francis Pollard, age 29, has been charged with three counts of attempted bank robbery. He has pleaded not guilty by reason of insanity and has introduced psychiatric testimony in support of his defense. Throughout the relevant period, defendant was a member of

i See, e.g., J. Hall, General Principles of Criminal Law 486–500 (1960).

the city police department. He has no prior criminal arrests or convictions and no prior history of psychological difficulties.

The facts concerning his alleged criminal conduct are undisputed. The prosecution's evidence shows that on May 21 at about 11:00 a.m., defendant entered the 24th Branch of the City Bank & Trust Company. He paused for a few moments to look over the bank and then proceeded to an enclosure where a bank official was working. He told the official, whom he believed to be the manager, that he wanted to open a savings account. He then walked through a swinging gate into the enclosure, sat down at the desk, pulled out a gun, pointed it at the official, and ordered him to call a teller. When the teller arrived, the defendant handed him a brown paper grocery bag and told him to fill it with money. While it was being filled, defendant kept the gun pointed at the bank official. The teller filled the bag with money and turned it over to the defendant. Thereupon, defendant ordered the bank official to accompany him to the exit. As both the defendant and bank official approached the exit, the official suddenly wrapped his arms around the defendant, who then dropped the bag and fled from the bank and escaped.

About 4:00 p.m., on the same day, Pollard entered the East Branch of the Bank of the Commonwealth and walked to a railing behind which a bank employee was sitting. He pointed his gun at the man and told him to sit quietly. However, the employee did not obey this order, raising an alarm instead, whereupon the defendant ran from the bank and again escaped.

After the abortive attempts to rob the two banks, he decided to rob a third bank and actually proceeded on the same day to an unnamed bank he had selected. However, he decided not to make the attempt when he discovered that the bank was "too wide open"—had too much window area so that the possibility of apprehension was enhanced.

On June 3, at about 3:00 p.m., the defendant entered the Woodrow Wilson Branch of the Bank of the Commonwealth and went directly to an enclosure behind which a male and female employee were sitting at desks facing each other. Defendant held his gun under a jacket which he carried over his right arm. He ordered the woman employee to come out from behind the railing. In doing so, she grasped the edge of her desk. Defendant, in the belief that she may have pushed an alarm button, decided to leave but ordered the woman to accompany him out of the bank. When they reached the street, he told her to walk ahead of him, but not to attract attention. Defendant noticed a police car approaching the bank and waited until it passed him, then ran across an empty lot to his car and again escaped.

On June 11, Pollard attempted to hold up a grocery market. He was thwarted in the attempt when the proprietor screamed and he fled. In so doing, he abandoned his automobile in back of the market where he had parked it during the holdup attempt. This car was placed under surveillance and later when the defendant, dressed in his police officer's uniform, attempted to get in it, he was arrested by local detectives.

After his apprehension, the defendant initially denied his guilt; however, after five hours of interrogation, he confessed to the three robbery attempts for which he is being tried as well as to 11 other robberies or attempted robberies. In his written confession, he explained his motivation as follows:

> "On May 21, 1958, I was reflecting about the hard life that my first wife and I had led in attempting to achieve financial security. Inasmuch as I was about to marry my second wife on May 22, I decided that I would not lead the same type of financially insecure life that I led with my first wife. I needed about $5,000 in order to buy a house. My only purpose in deciding to rob a bank was to obtain $5,000 and, if I obtained the money, I did not intend to continue robbing."

Testimony introduced on behalf of the defendant established that he had a normal childhood and adolescence, and was married at the age of 19, having three sons and a daughter over the next four years. At the age of 22, defendant joined the police department and was a well liked officer with a good performance record. Then, two years before the robbery attempts, when the defendant was 27, his wife and infant daughter were brutally killed in an unprovoked attack by a drunken neighbor.

The defendant called three of his fellow police officers to testify about his behavior during the two-year period between the murders and the robbery attempts. They testified that after the murders, Pollard's behavior changed. He frequently seemed to be overcome by fatigue, would stare off into space and would cry for as long as 20 minutes at a time.

They testified that Pollard occasionally seemed to be lost in thought or forgetful. Sometimes a week would pass and he would seem all right; but then he would do something out of the ordinary. On one day he would insist upon enforcing the law and issue loitering tickets for violation of ordinances, and the next day, he would express an opinion that he did not see anything wrong with such conduct. When he would be asked a question by his fellow policemen, while driving with them in a scout car, he would sometimes be silent for about 10 minutes, and then answer the question as though he had just been asked. Sometimes when he came to work with a fellow officer, they might talk to each other normally. Other times he would sit for two hours at a time and say nothing. This was a change from his prior general demeanor, when he had always been very lively and talkative.

Once when he drove the scout car, he constantly beat on the steering wheel with his fist for approximately half an hour. When, on this occasion, he was asked if anything was wrong, he acted as though he didn't know he was doing it, and would continue. When he responded to roll call at police headquarters, he was almost always late, contrary to his prior punctuality; he would come in and appear sleepy all of the time. He would act lifeless and the police officers, as one of them stated, all started worrying about him. Shortly before he remarried, on occasion, he would attend a party and appear jovial, eating, dancing, and talking, and then would quickly change. He would suddenly sit down, stop dancing, refrain from eating with the others, and become very quiet.

On cross-examination, each of the officers admitted that they did not find Pollard's conduct or moods to be of such consequence that they believed it necessary to report him to a superior officer. One of them stated that they couldn't report every person that acts out of the ordinary.

The government called defendant's supervising lieutenant as a rebuttal witness. He testified that the defendant's police work, during the relevant period, as evidenced by his efficiency rating and his written duty reports, was, if anything, more effective than his service prior to the death of his wife.

The defendant also introduced testimony by his second wife, who stated that on two occasions defendant suddenly, and for no reason apparent to her, lapsed into crying spells and that he talked to her once or twice about committing suicide. She also testified that during one such period of depression he pointed a gun at himself; that she became frightened and called the police; that the police came, relieved him of his gun, and took him to the precinct police station; and that after his release he appeared jovial and acted as if nothing had happened. Defendant also called his brother-in-law, who stated that the defendant had always been a very happy person but that he became noticeably despondent after the death of his wife and child and expressed a desire to commit suicide because he now no longer had a reason for living.

Defendant also introduced testimony by three psychiatrists who had examined him. The experts' testimony was similar in all material respects and may be adequately summarized by quoting the written report prepared by the city's forensic clinic at the court's request.

After describing the "personality and performance changes" noted by Pollard's fellow officers and the "suicidal ideation" observed by his second wife, the report continued:

> "The onset and progressive intensification of Mr. Pollard's symptoms following the death of his wife and daughter demonstrates an almost classical form of depressive neurosis. (The diagnosis under DSM III [a] would probably be 'dysthymic disorder.') This form of mental illness is precipitated by deprivations and frustrations which exceed the limits of individual tolerance. Some individuals are especially prone to developing such a severe reaction because of their prior life experiences. Such a person will be especially vulnerable to anything that destroys or seriously threatens the satisfaction of deep dependency needs and/or lessens his or her self-esteem. On clinical assessment and a review of personal history, Mr. Pollard clearly exhibits these traits.

[a] American Psychiatric Association, Diagnostic and Statistical Manual of Mental Disorders (3d ed. 1980).

"Factors or events which commonly precipitate such a reaction in a vulnerable individual include: (i) loss of love or emotional support, (ii) personal or economic failures, and (iii) new responsibilities or the threat of new responsibilities. In Mr. Pollard's situation, the symtomatic deterioration was triggered by the traumatic death of his wife and child. The deaths set in motion unconscious emotional conflicts involving his strong feelings of loss and guilt. The feelings of guilt, which are a normal part of grieving, were aggravated in Pollard's situation by his belief that he was responsible for their deaths. He felt that by being absent from home, he left them exposed to the actions of the crazed, drunken neighbor.

"When a person is experiencing these unconscious conflicts of such severity, and they precipitate a clinically significant neurotic depression, one of the symptoms of such a condition is a partial regression. By regression is meant a return to earlier, and most often maladaptive, mechanisms for attempted problem or conflict resolution. The regressed individual functions as though he or she were a child, invoking childish 'solutions' to conflict and guilt-laden situations. A child does not have mental capacity to process complex emotional responses in a mature and constructive manner. Instead, he or she will 'act out' some type of 'conflict resolution'—which is, in effect, an externalization of intrapsychic conflict into the environment. Usually such 'acting out' behavior attracts the attention of others and calls forth some type of response or sanction which satisfies the intrapsychic need for punishment and control. Childhood and adolescent depression is, to a significant degree, characterized by negative, maladaptive behavior which appears designed to invite social sanctions against the individual. The regressed adult responds, psychologically, in approximately the same way.

"All of Mr. Pollards' symptoms, which became progressively more serious in the months before the offense, illustrate this regressive phenomenon. He unconsciously 'needed' to demonstrate what a 'bad' person he was and thereby to invite censure and punishment. For a policeman, criminal acts such as robbery would be perfectly suited for such a self-degrading purpose. Indeed, Pollard needed to confirm his belief that he was not fit to be a policeman at all since he had failed to prevent the murders of his wife and daughter.

"To review the clinical formulation, then, Mr. Pollard's psychiatric history clearly establishes the diagnosis of a depressive neurosis or dysthymic disorder. His symptoms, which appeared soon after the death of his wife and daughter, derived from deep feelings of guilt, resentment and a sense of lost emotional contact with two persons whom he loved. These conflicts were so intense that any conscious attention to them would be exceedingly painful. Thus, in order to avoid the pain and maintain some reasonable level of emotional homeostasis, Pollard's mind 'repressed' the memories and feelings associated with the unresolved conflicts—that is, it removed them from the level of conscious awareness. However, the psychological 'price' of repression of such powerful conflicts is 'regression,' the phenomenon of returning to earlier child-like patterns of adaptation described earlier.

"It became increasingly important for Mr. Pollard to find some form of punitive response from his environment that would 'punish' him for not preventing the death of his wife and daughter. It is significant that the initial series of robberies took place on the day before his second marriage. The imminent prospect of marriage intensified the unconscious feelings of guilt and the derivative 'need' for self-punishment. How could he—the survivor, the bad person who failed to rescue his wife and daughter—enter into and enjoy a new marriage?

"This interpretation and explanation of Mr. Pollard's anti-social behavior is strongly evidenced by the bizarre and childish manner in which the robberies were executed. His unconscious objective was self-punishment rather than financial gain. He was driven to do something punishable until he got caught.

"The question arises, of course, why he tried to evade detection, why he refused to confess and why, upon confessing, he said his motive was financial gain. Two explanations may be offered. First, this behavior is simply another sign of regression. The child who acts out, also seeks on a conscious level, to avoid detection, and if caught in a lie will often persist in denying his guilt in the face of overwhelming evidence to the contrary. Second, when it became necessary to dissemble and confess, Pollard was psychologically unable to 'admit' that he might have been 'sick' and in need of psychiatric help; and the only available explanation was the one he offered. This process is characterized in clinical terms, as rationalization."

After presenting this clinical formulation, the report concluded as follows:

"It is our clinical opinion that Mr. Pollard is not now and was not at the time of the offense, psychotic or in need of psychiatric hospitalization. During the period in question, Mr. Pollard was intellectually capable of knowing right from wrong and was consciously aware of the nature and wrongfulness of his actions. Indeed, on an unconscious level, the wrongfulness of his actions provided his very 'reason' for doing them. However, our findings, and the evidence summarized above, lead us to conclude that his actions during this time were probably not consciously activated. Instead his behavior was governed by unconscious drives which propelled

him toward anti-social behavior and compromised his normal
capacity to conform his behavior to the requirements of the
law."

After the introduction of the evidence just summarized, the government presented its closing argument. Excerpts follow:

"The defendant's psychiatrists testified that the defendant
suffered from severe feelings of depression and guilt; and that
in their opinion he was propelled to commit criminal acts by
an unconscious desire to be punished; and that he geared his
behavior to the accomplishment of this end. However, his
entire pattern of conduct during the period of his criminal
activities militates against this conclusion. His conscious
desire not to be apprehended and punished was demonstrably
greater than his unconscious desire to the contrary. After his
apprehension, despite searching interrogation for over five
hours by police detectives, he denied any participation in
criminal conduct of any kind. It was only after he was
positively identified by bank personnel that he finally admitted that he did attempt to perpetrate the bank robberies.

"I asked one of the psychiatrists to explain this apparent
inconsistency on cross-examination. In answer to my question, he stated that although the defendant had an unconscious desire to be apprehended and punished, when the
possibility of apprehension became direct and immediate, the
conscious mind required acts at least superficially consistent
with the desire for self-preservation. This explanation may
have merit if applied to individual acts. However, the validity of a theory that attempts to explain the behavior of a
person must be determined in light of that person's entire
behavioral pattern and not with reference to isolated acts
which are extracted from that pattern. The defendant's
pattern of behavior of May 21, discloses that the desire for
self-preservation was not fleeting and momentary but continuing, consistent and dominant.

"What, then, becomes of the theory of irresistible impulse
or substantial volitional impairment? Looking to the events
of that day, this court is asked to believe, first, that the
defendant, acting pursuant to an irresistible impulse, selected
a bank site to rob, entered the bank to accomplish that end,
purposely failed in the attempt and when the end he sought,
apprehension, was in view, escaped because of the dominance,
at the moment of ultimate accomplishment, of the stronger
drive for self-preservation. The court must then believe that
when the defendant knew he was apparently free from detection, his compulsive state reasserted itself and that he again
went through the steps of planning, abortive attempt and
escape. And if the court does acquiesce in this theory, what
other psychiatric theory explains his subsequent conduct—his
plan to rob a third unnamed bank and the rejection of that

plan because of his subjective belief that the possibility of apprehension would be too great? If the theory remains the same, then it appears that in the latter case, the fear of apprehension and punishment tipped 'the scales enough to make resistible an impulse otherwise irresistible.' It is a logical inference that, in reality, the other robbery attempts were made as the result of impulses that the defendant did not choose voluntarily to resist because, to him, the possibility of success outweighed the likelihood of detection which is in essence a motivation for all criminal conduct. The impulse being resistible, the defendant is accountable for his criminal conduct.

"Psychiatrists admit that the line between irresistible impulse and acts which are the result of impulses not resisted is not easy to trace. To the extent that the line may be traced, the distinguishing motivation of the action, whether the act is performed to satisfy an intrinsic need or is the result of extrinsic provocation, is a determining factor. Admittedly, motivations may be mixed. However, all the facts have clearly established that defendant's criminal activity was planned to satisfy an extrinsic need by a reasoned but anti-social method. The defendant had financial problems of varying degrees of intensity throughout his life. He was now embarking upon a second marriage. He was about to undertake the responsibility of supporting not only a wife and himself, but also four children, three of them the product of his first marriage. Defendant's entire pattern of conduct was consistent with his expressed motivation—his need for money.

"Life does not always proceed on an even keel. Periods of depression, feelings of guilt and inadequacy are experienced by many of us. His feelings of despondency and depression induced by the brutal killing of his wife and infant daughter were not unnatural. However, his conduct throughout this crucial period did not cause any significant concern among his colleagues. It is also important to note that his present wife married him on May 22, after a year of courtship. Although she knew he was despondent over his wife's murder, she apparently did not think he was mentally ill.

"This court should find that the defendant committed the acts for which he is now charged and that when he committed them he was legally sane."

The defendant's closing argument, which responded to some of these points, is excerpted below:

"The government has argued that Pollard's conduct was rationally motivated by his conscious desire for financial security and his desire not to be apprehended and punished. The evidence shows, to the contrary, that the defendant's behavior was not rational and, indeed, was senseless in terms of any normal reasoning. For this reason, his so-called 'conscious motivation,' as reflected in his confession, is nothing more than a rationalization for behavior Pollard neither understood nor could control.

"The evidence indicates that the attempted robberies by Pollard were bizarre and ineffectively planned and executed; that when he tried to leave one bank, he ordered a bank official to follow behind and barely escaped after a struggle, during which he dropped the paper bag of money he had collected; that on the various occasions of his attempted robberies, he would suddenly enter a bank that he had never seen before, without prior knowledge of the arrangement of the premises, or of the personnel. Taken in consideration with all of the other factors, such conduct, on the part of a highly intelligent police officer with a knowledge of how crimes are committed, has about it nothing of sanity.

"It is emphasized by the government that Pollard was motivated to attempt the bank robberies because of his need for financial security. This, the government claims, is shown by the confession he signed. But, the claimed motivation seems pointless. Pollard, during his first marriage, had been receiving the regular salary of a policeman with promotions, of approximately $450 a month. His first wife, at that time, was receiving about $300 a month as a clerk with the Unemployment Compensation Commission. Their joint income was almost twice what a regular policeman's salary would be. His second wife, at the time of her marriage to him, had money of her own—enough to pay her own bills, and take care of her daughter with the money which was paid for support by her former husband. She had previously held a position for six years with the Bell Telephone Company. She considered herself to be relatively comfortable financially. Between the time of Pollard's arrest on June 11, and his trial, she had, herself, paid off about $700 in bills that he had owed. Pollard's financial condition could not be considered a reasonable motivation for his attempted bank robberies. As far as income went, he was much better off than most other policemen and if such a financial condition could be considered a reasonable motivation for Pollard's attempted robberies, every other policeman in the department would have had twice the motivation to commit such crimes as Pollard had.

"The real explanation for the defendant's behavior is the one suggested by the expert witnesses. His behavior can only be understood in terms of intrapsychic processes triggered by the murder of his first wife and daughter. It must be emphasized that the robbery attempts do not stand alone as evidence of his mental illness. Pollard was clearly suffering from a serious, albeit undiagnosed, depression for many months.

"The government has argued that the evidence shows that Pollard's conduct throughout the period following the murder of his wife and child by a drunken neighbor did not cause any concern among his colleagues, and that, in their opinion, he was sane. However, this testimony supports exactly the opposite conclusion. From all of the evidence of the lay witnesses, the court must conclude that Pollard was suffering from a serious mental disorder. Obviously, as a result of the murder of his wife and child while he was absent from his home, he was suffering from some grave disorder, and that disorder was, in the opinion of all the psychiatric and medical experts, a depression related to an unresolved grief reaction. This disorder ultimately resulted in Pollard's commission of the acts charged."

NOTES ON VOLITIONAL CRITERIA OF RESPONSIBILITY

1. **Relation of Control Inquiry to Other Doctrines.** The central issue in the contemporary debate about the insanity defense is whether impairment of volitional capacity should have independent exculpatory significance. Opponents of control tests argue that significant impairment of cognitive functioning—whether or not measured in affective terms—should be required for the defense. On the other hand, proponents of a more expansive approach argue that persons whose abnormal mental condition compromises their ability to control behavior—even if reality-testing is intact—cannot fairly be blamed for acts that are beyond their capacity for self-restraint.

The debate over the volitional dimension of the insanity defense intersects two other doctrines of the penal law. The first is the requirement of the voluntary act, discussed at pages 152–58, supra. According to this doctrine, some acts are regarded as involuntary because they are not within the conscious, physical control of the actor. An opportunity for choosing to act or not to act establishes the minimum link between body and mind necessary for criminal liability. Although a mentally abnormal offender may be said to be driven to act by intra-psychic forces, the technical requirement of a voluntary act is virtually always met if the person is conscious at the time of the offense.[a]

The second intersecting doctrine might be called environmental or situational compulsion. Sometimes, people may have conscious, physical control over their bodily movements, but nonetheless feel that they have no "real" choice at all. The classic case is duress: *A* takes *B*'s

-----

[a] Indeed, evidence of mental abnormality is routinely rejected when offered to support an involuntary-act defense. The historical reason for this result, and for the continued conceptual separation of the voluntary-act doctrine and the insanity defense, undoubtedly is closely tied to the dispositional consequences of the two doctrines. Typically, as is discussed at pages 733–52, infra, an acquittal by reason of insanity leads to some form of commitment of the defendant for treatment of the underlying mental disorder. An involuntary-act acquittal, on the other hand, has no such consequence. This factor has considerable explanatory power as to why the voluntary-act doctrine is generally conceived in relatively narrow terms.

money because *C* is holding a gun to *A*'s head and threatening to shoot if *A* does not do so. The reach of the concept of situational compulsion is explored at pages 604–30, supra. For present purposes, the important point is that a person with normal strength of character who is confronted with such coercive circumstances will not be held criminally liable for "choosing" to violate the penal law. Even if the choice is not justifiable, the actor may be excused if blame would be unfair for conduct that is, morally speaking, "beyond control."

The case for the volitional prong of the insanity defense rests on the empirical proposition that mental abnormalities can compromise a person's capacity to choose to comply with the penal law, and on the moral proposition that such a person cannot fairly be blamed for criminal acts that are psychologically compelled. It should be noted, however, that acts "compelled" by psychic pathology stand on a very different footing from those "compelled" by external pressure. In the latter case, the incapacity is simply the frailty of the ordinary person; in the former, the defendant's claim to exculpation is pressed precisely because the strengths of the ordinary person are lacking.

2. **The Control Tests: Criticism and Defense.** Few would dispute the moral predicate for the control test—that persons who really "cannot help" doing what they did are not blameworthy. However, as Professors Wechsler and Michael observed in their classic article, A Rationale of the Law of Homicide I, 37 Colum.L.Rev. 701, 754 (1937), a cognitive formulation cannot cover the whole population of those who are beyond the deterrent influence of the penal law "*if* there are persons who, even though they are aware of the potentialities of their acts and of the threat of punishment, are nevertheless incapable of choosing to avoid the act in order to avoid the punishment. There is no reason to doubt that such persons exist." Although some skeptics do, in fact, doubt that "such persons exist," most opponents of the control formulation have concentrated their criticism on the difficulty of administering such a test in light of present knowledge.

The opponents of volitional criteria of responsibility argue that there is no scientific basis for measuring a person's capacity for self-control or for calibrating the impairment of such capacity.[b] There is, in short, no objective basis for distinguishing between offenders who were undeterrable and those who were merely undeterred, between the impulse that was irresistible and the impulse not resisted, or between substantial impairment of capacity and some lesser impairment. Whatever the precise terms of the volitional test, the critics assert that the question is unanswerable—or can be answered only by "moral guesses." To ask it at all, they say, invites fabricated claims, undermines equal administration of the penal law, and compromises its deterrent effect.

Sheldon Glueck observed in Mental Disorder and the Criminal Law 233, 430, 433 (1925), that the 19th-century effort to establish irresistible impulse as a defense met judicial resistance because "much less than

[b] See generally Morse, Crazy Behavior, Morals and Science: An Analysis of Mental Health Law, 51 So.Cal.L.Rev. 527 (1978).

we know today was known of mental disease." He predicted "that with the advent of a more scientific administration of the law—especially with the placing of expert testimony upon a neutral, unbiased basis and in the hands of well-qualified experts—much of the opposition to judicial recognition of the effect of disorders of the . . . impulses should disappear." Further, he said, "expert, unbiased study of the individual case will aid judge and jury to distinguish cases of pathological irresistible impulse from those in which the impulse was merely unresisted."

Despite these optimistic sentiments, Wechsler and Michael observed, in 1937, that "except in the clearest cases, such as kleptomania, any effort to distinguish deterrable from non-deterrable persons must obviously encounter tremendous difficulty in the present state of knowledge." Advances in clinical understanding of mental illness in the 1940's inspired a new era of optimisim about a "modern" doctrine of responsibility, including a control dimension. One example was the evolution of the Model Penal Code, which was drafted during the 1950's. Another was the Report of the Royal Commission on Capital Punishment, issued in 1953, which recommended that *M'Naghten* be abandoned in favor of a broadened formulation also permitting claims of volitional impairment. Many commentators, however, expressed doubt that medical science had progressed far enough to overcome the difficulties of administration. Lord Devlin observed, in Criminal Responsibility and Punishment: Functions of Judge and Jury, [1954] Crim.L.Rev. 661, 682–84:*

"If a case can be made out for saying that a man with such a disease is wholly incapable of preventing himself from committing the crime, and thus wholly irresponsible, it is prima facie a proper matter of substantive defence for the jury. The Royal Commission has come to the conclusion that medical opinion is now sufficiently certain to be able to say that there may be such cases. . . .

"I think that this is a problem that ought to be solved empirically rather than theoretically. If the door is opened, a multitude will try to enter through it. Many will be cases in which men and women, abnormal, but not in any ordinary sense mad, have failed to exercise proper control over their emotions. There will be many cases of gross mental abnormality where nevertheless it cannot be said that the prisoner was wholly irresponsible. There will be some cases—and I suspect they will be in a small minority—where the disease made the accused wholly irresponsible. If a sharp dividing line could be drawn between complete and partial irresponsibility, it would be right both in theory and practice that the question should be submitted to the jury. But it does not appear at present that a sharp line can be drawn, and unless [a satisfactory rule can be framed for the jury, the doctrine cannot be accepted]. Medical science

* Reprinted with the permission of Lord Devlin, the Criminal Law Review, and Sweet and Maxwell Ltd.

has advanced far enough to say that there ought to be an addition to the *McNaghten* rules, but not, I think, to formulate a satisfactory one. There must have been a period . . . when the law fumbled over mens rea, and when conceptions of deliberate intent and recklessness and foreseeable consequences had not been worked out with sufficient detail to give the juryman of the day something he could grasp: no doubt, the new concept was introduced gradually. The wider notion of emotional irresponsibility is still, I think, as novel as mens rea was six or seven hundred years ago. I am not myself satisfied that it is yet sufficiently clarified to be delivered over to the deliberation of a jury. If this meant that prisoners who suffered from emotional disorders, must either be acquitted or hanged, there would be an urgency about it, which could not wait for careful formulation. But that is not the question. The question is simply whether the time is ripe to take the matter out of the province of sentence and let it follow mens rea into the control of the jury."

Lord Devlin's observations are echoed in the comments of contemporary critics of the control test.[c] Professor Bonnie's views are illustrative. In The Moral Basis of the Insanity Defense, 69 A.B.A.J. 194, 196–97 (1983), he said:

"The Model Penal Code has had an extraordinary impact on criminal law. For this we should be thankful, but I believe the Code approach to criminal responsibility should be rejected. Psychiatric concepts of mental abnormality remain fluid and imprecise, and most academic commentary within the last ten years continues to question the scientific basis for assessment of volitional incapacity.

"The volitional inquiry probably would be manageable if the insanity defense were permitted only in cases involving psychotic disorders. When the control test is combined with a loose or broad interpretation of the term 'mental disease,' however, the inevitable result is unstructured clinical speculation regarding the 'causes' of criminal behavior in any case in which a defendant can be said to have a personality disorder, an impulse disorder, or any other diagnosable abnormality.

"For example, it is clear enough in theory that the insanity defense is not supposed to be a ground for acquittal of persons with weak behavior controls who misbehave because of anger, jealousy, fear, or some other strong emotion. These emotions may account for a large proportion of all homicides and other assaultive crimes. Many crimes are committed by persons who are not acting 'normally' and who are emotionally disturbed at the time. It is not uncommon to say that they are temporarily 'out of their minds.' But this is not what the law means or should mean by 'insanity.' Because the control test, as now

[c] See, e.g., Hermann, The Insanity Defense: Philosophical, Historical and Legal Perspectives (1983); Morse, Failed Explanations and Criminal Responsibility: Experts and the Unconscious, 68 Va.L.Rev. 971 (1982).

construed in most states, entitles defendants to insanity instructions on the basis of these claims, I am convinced that the test involves an unacceptable risk of abuse and mistake.

"It might be argued, of course, that the risk of mistake should be tolerated if the volitional prong of the defense is morally necessary. The question may be put this way: Are there clinically identifiable cases involving defendants whose behavior controls were so pathologically impaired that they ought to be acquitted although their ability to appreciate the wrongfulness of their actions was unimpaired? I do not think so. The most clinically compelling cases of volitional impairment involve the so-called impulse disorders—pyromania, kleptomania, and the like. These disorders involve severely abnormal compulsions that ought to be taken into account in sentencing, but the exculpation of pyromaniacs would be out of touch with commonly shared moral intuitions."

Not surprisingly, many of the same objections outlined above have also been raised against the cognitive prong of the insanity defense. However, most opponents of the volitional test do not favor abolition of the cognitive test of responsibility. They argue that the institutional risks are considerably different in the two contexts. Lady Barbara Wootton's observations are illustrative, Book Review of A. Goldstein, The Insanity Defense (1967), 77 Yale L.J. 1019, 1026–27 (1968):*

"What . . . has been insufficiently appreciated is that a volitional test raises practical difficulties far more formidable even than those involved in a purely cognitive formula. I am not suggesting that the *M'Naghten* test, interpreted (as most laymen would surely understand it) in strictly cognitive terms is free from ambiguities, or that it is an adequate instrument for distinguishing between the sane and the mentally disordered. But it is clear that in certain circumstances the limits of a man's knowledge and understanding can be convincingly demonstrated. Thus, if I am asked to translate a passage from Japanese into English it is indisputable that this is beyond my powers: everyone knows that merely trying harder will not make me any more successful. But if I assert that I have an uncontrollable impulse to break shop windows, in the nature of the case no proof of uncontrollability can be adduced. All that is known is that the impulse was not in fact controlled; and it is perfectly legitimate to hold the opinion that, had I tried a little harder, I might have conquered it. It is indeed apparent that some people, such as sadistic sexual perverts, suffer from temptations from which others are immune. But the fact that an impulse is unusual is no proof that it is irresistible. In short, it is not only difficult to devise a test of volitional competence the validity of which can be objectively established: it is impossible."

* Reprinted by permission of the author, B. Rothman & Company from The Yale The Yale Law Journal Company, and Fred   Law Journal, Vol. 77, pp. 1026–27.

A similar assessment of the utility of clinical expertise was recently presented by the American Psychiatric Association in the course of an official statement on the insanity defense: [d]

". . . Many psychiatrists . . . believe that psychiatric information relevant to determining whether a defendant understood the nature of his act, and whether he appreciated its wrongfulness, is more reliable and has a stronger scientific basis than, for example, does psychiatric information relevant to whether a defendant was able to control his behavior. The line between an irresistible impulse and an impulse not resisted is probably no sharper than that between twilight and dusk. Psychiatry is a deterministic discipline that views all human behavior as, to a good extent, 'caused.' The concept of volition is the subject of some disagreement among psychiatrists. Many psychiatrists therefore believe that psychiatric testimony (particularly that of a conclusory nature) about volition is more likely to produce confusion for jurors than is psychiatric testimony relevant to a defendant's appreciation or understanding."

Even if Lady Wootton and the other critics are right about the imprecise and speculative nature of the inquiry into volitional impairment, there is nevertheless an argument that the inquiry should be retained. In The Limits of the Criminal Sanction 132–33 (1968), Herbert Packer said:

"We must put up with the bother of the insanity defense because to exclude it is to deprive the criminal law of its chief paradigm of free will. . . . There must be some recognition of the generally held assumption that some people are, by reason of mental illness, significantly impaired in their volitional capacity. [I]t is not too important whether this is in fact the case. Nor is it too important how discriminating we are about drawing some kind of line to separate those suffering volitional impairment from the rest of us. The point is that some kind of line must be drawn in the face of our intuition, however wrongheaded it may be, that mental illness contributes to volitional impairment."

Should the volitional inquiry be retained? Would exclusion of claims of volitional impairment deprive the criminal law of its "chief paradigm of free will" or undermine its "moral integrity," so long as it recognizes claims of cognitive impairment? Should the difficulty of administering the control test be decisive?

3. **Responsibility and Unconscious Motivation.** The ongoing debate about the control inquiry has been carried on against the backdrop of changing scientific ideas about the human mind. One of the distinctive schools of contemporary psychology emphasizes the role of unconscious psychological processes in shaping human behavior. According to the "psychodynamic" school of psychology, a person's behavior may "really" be explained and "caused" by unconscious

[d] American Psychiatric Association, Statement on the Insanity Defense (December, 1982).

processes even though the person "thinks," at a conscious level, that action is being taken for other reasons. Many examples may be drawn from normal events in everyday life—e.g., slips of the tongue, sudden lapses of memory, etc. Psychiatrists and other mental-health professionals who find clinical value in a psychodynamic perspective also believe that some types of abnormal behavior are best understood as manifestations or symptoms of a "neurotic process." According to the psychiatric diagnostic manual, DSM-III, the neurotic process involves, in sequence: "unconscious conflict between opposing desires or wants or between desires and prohibitions, which causes unconscious perception of anticipated danger or dysphoria, which leads to the use of so-called defense mechanisms that result in either symptoms, personality disturbance or both."

In Pollard's case, the psychiatric experts concluded that Pollard's behavior was "caused" by a neurotic process. He was, at the time of the offenses, suffering from a neurotic condition involving a complex of depressive symptoms and unconscious turmoil even though his "reality testing" (conscious perceptual and integrative capability) was intact. The unconscious desire for self-punishment was so powerful that Pollard's mind suspended his otherwise "normal" understanding of the social and moral dimensions of his behavior in order to "permit him to act in accord with his unconscious desires." None of this, of course, was apparent to Pollard himself, who "thought" he had chosen to rob banks because he needed money. This, according to the experts, was simply a rationalization for behavior that he himself could not adequately explain.

Pollard is obviously guilty if his "real" reasons for the robbery attempts were those expressed in his confession, and if the psychiatric explanation for his behavior is regarded as implausible. However, if Pollard's behavior was, in fact, governed or propelled by unconscious forces, as the experts concluded, the question arises whether this explanation should have any legal significance. More generally, the question is whether psychodynamic explanations of criminal behavior should be considered in assessments of criminal responsibility.

The view that responsibility should be assessed at the conscious level was put forcefully by Chief Justice Weintraub of the New Jersey Supreme Court in State v. Sikora, 44 N.J. 453, 475–79, 210 A.2d 193, 205–07 (1965):

"[The] cause-and-effect thesis dominates the psychiatrist's view of his patient. He traces a man's every deed to some cause truly beyond the actor's own making, and says that although the man was aware of his action, he was unaware of assembled forces in his unconscious which decided his course. Thus the conscious is a puppet, and the unconscious the puppeteer. . . .

"Under this psychiatric concept no man could be convicted of anything if the law were to accept the impulses of the unconscious as an excuse for conscious misbehavior. . . .

"What then shall we do with our fellow automaton whose unconscious directs such anti-social deeds? For one thing, we could say it makes no difference. We could say that in punishing an evil deed accompanied by an evil-meaning mind, the law is concerned only with the existence of a will to do the evil act and it does not matter precisely where within the mind the evil drive resides.

"Or we could . . . require an evil-meaning unconscious. The possibilities here are rich. It would be quite a thing to identify the unconscious drive and then decide whether it is evil for the purpose of criminal liability. For example, if we somehow were satisfied that a man murdered another as an alternative to an unconscious demand for suicide or because the unconscious believed it had to kill to avoid a full-blown psychosis, shall we say there was or was not a good defense? Shall we indict for murder a motorist who kills another because, although objectively he was negligent at the worst, the psychoanalyst assures us that the conscious man acted automatically to fulfill an unconscious desire for self-destruction? All of this is fascinating but much too frothy to support a structure of criminal law.

"Finally, we could amend our concept of criminal responsibility by eliminating the requirement of an evil-meaning mind. That is the true thrust of this psychiatric view of human behavior, for while our criminal law seeks to punish only those who act with a sense of wrongdoing and hence excuses those who because of sickness were bereft of that awareness, the psychiatrist rejects a distinction between the sick and the bad. To him no one is personally blameworthy for his make-up or for his acts. To him the law's distinction between a defect of the mind and a defect of character is an absurd invention. . . .

"The subject of criminal blameworthiness is so obscure that there is an understandable disposition to let anything in for whatever use the jury may wish to make of it. But it will not do merely to receive testimony upon the automaton thesis, for the jury must be told what its legal effect may be. Specifically, the jury must be told whether a man is chargeable with his unconscious drives.

"It seems clear to me that the psychiatric view . . . is simply irreconcilable with the basic thesis of our criminal law, for while the law requires proof of an evil-meaning mind, this psychiatric thesis denies there is any such thing. To grant a role in our existing structure to the theme that the conscious is just the innocent puppet of a non-culpable unconscious is to make a mishmash of the criminal law, permitting—indeed requiring—each trier of the facts to choose between the automaton thesis and the law's existing concept of criminal accountability. It would be absurd to decide criminal blameworthiness upon a psychiatric thesis which can find no basis for personal blame. [Criminal blameworthiness] must be sought and decided at the level of conscious behavior."

Chief Justice Weintraub implies that the law should take an all-or-nothing view of unconscious motivation. Is he right? Is it possible to formulate a "control" test of responsibility that would permit the fact-finder to absolve Pollard but would not open the gates to unbounded psychological determinism?

In an article on Responsibility and the Unconscious, 53 So.Cal.L.Rev. 1563 (1980), Professor Michael Moore has argued that Weintraub's concern is misplaced; the problem, he suggests, is not the deterministic premise of psychodynamic psychology but rather the meaning of the concept of compulsion, as applied to specific cases. Professor Moore acknowledges at the outset that many psychiatrists think that "unconscious [motivations] cause bad behavior and that causation is an excuse," and, he agrees with Chief Justice Weintraub that this " 'puppeteer' view of human' beings" has unacceptable implications for ideas of responsibility:*

"[I]f Pollard is to be excused simply because his behavior was caused by unconscious mental states, why are all actions not similarly excused? If all conscious mental life is determined by unconscious mental states, as many psychoanalysts believe, why is everyone not excused for all of his actions, seemingly the product of his conscious decisions but in fact determined by his unconscious mental states?"

Professor Moore's answer is that compulsion, not causation, is the legally relevant concept: an action is not "compelled" simply because it is "caused" by unconscious forces; this, he says, "makes it sound as if one's unconscious, in effect, orders one around in the same way as does a gunman with a gun at one's head; both compel one to do what 'they demand.' " However, the analogy is not apt, Moore says:

"Everyone is undoubtedly caused to act as they do by a myriad of environmental, physiological, or psychological factors. Yet to say that any actions are caused, for example, by an unhappy childhood, a chemical imbalance, or a belief that it is raining, is not to say the actions are compelled. One must point to something other than causation to make out the excuse of compulsion. . . ."

Instead, Moore concludes, the legal significance of unconscious motivation must be determined by assessing, in each case, whether it "compelled" the criminal act. He illustrates the point in the context of the Pollard case as follows:

"Suppose Pollard did unconsciously feel guilty at the death of his first wife and child. He may have felt guilty because he had not been there; alternatively, he may have felt guilty because he had unconsciously wished to kill them himself. In either case, could such unconscious guilt *compel* Pollard to do an act for

---

* The excerpts below are reprinted with
the permission of the author and the
Southern California Law Review.

which he would be punished? If one can discover unconscious emotions, cases such as Pollard's would [seem to be like cases involving hard choices made under the influence of powerful emotions or cravings] . . ..

"An unconscious emotion in general, or an unconscious but passionately felt sense of guilt in particular, can be understood in the sense in which an actor does consciously experience or feel something, but does not know the object of his emotion. One may feel angry or afraid without knowing the object of such anger or fear; one may experience the uneasy and tensed craving characteristic of compulsive desires without knowing what one craves. . . .

"The sense in which one can speak of the actor yielding to such unconscious but passionately felt desires should be evident. The kleptomaniac feels compelled and knows that he yields to compulsion when he steals; yet he does not know the object of his passionate desire. He knows only that he feels that he must steal. He is compelled by an indefinite craving for some unknown object or objective. A few thefts readily tell him it is not the stolen objects themselves.

"Pollard presents a less convincing example of compulsion than does the kleptomaniac or the obsessional neurotic, probably because one is less inclined to believe the explanation proposed for his behavior. . . . Pollard had a perfectly intelligible, conscious motive for acting. In such circumstances one is often more reluctant to accept as a factual matter that some unconscious emotion really explains his behavior. But if one does believe the psychiatrists in this case, then Pollard's action of robbing the banks may also be compelled. If his unconscious guilt and consequent need to be punished truly explain his action of robbing the banks, then it may have been very difficult for him to act in any way but to alleviate this guilt feeling."

Moore goes on to emphasize that compulsion is a matter of degree and that a person "can be more or less compelled depending upon the severity of the constraints upon choice or upon the strength of the emotions on which one acts." Nonetheless, his argument implies that cases such as Pollard's are within the conceptual boundaries of the insanity defense and that the law should recognize that pathologically strong emotions, albeit unconscious, can compromise or constrain choices. The question then becomes: "How much constraint is enough to warrant exculpation?"

Do you agree with Professor Moore or with Chief Justice Weintraub? How should Pollard's case be decided? Does the clinical evidence demonstrate—in Model Penal Code terms—that Pollard lacked "substantial capacity" to conform his conduct to the laws against attempted bank robbery?

4. **Illustrative Claims of Insanity.** The preceding notes have explored the arguments for and against a control test of insanity in a single clinical context. However, a full appreciation of the complexities

of the volitional inquiry requires familiarity with the variety of clinical explanations that can be given for criminal behavior. The following cases are representative of the range of claims that have been raised in jurisdictions recognizing volitional impairment as an independent basis for exculpation on grounds of insanity. The factual summaries also fairly represent the expert testimony presented on the defendant's behalf. As you study these cases, you should consider whether each defendant should be entitled to an insanity instruction in a jurisdiction that uses a control test. If not, on what basis would you distinguish between those cases in which you would support such an instruction and those in which you would not?

(i) ***Barnes.***[e] James Barnes, age 18, was charged with six counts of arson and three counts of murder in connection with one of the fires, which had been set in an apartment building. He pleaded not guilty by reason of insanity. The expert witness testified that the defendant was suffering from a disorder of impulse control (pyromania) and schizoid personality disorder. According to the expert, Barnes' earliest childhood memory was watching a neighbor burn trash in the backyard. He began setting fires around his own home at the age of eight. During high school he set fires to student lockers on four occasions and periodically set fires at his part-time jobs, usually in trash containers in alleys. Despite the frequency of his firesetting, he was rarely caught and never punished for his actions.

Barnes' father was absent from home for extended periods until Barnes was 12. During adolescence, he and his father argued frequently; he felt his father viewed him as an ineffectual person, someone who "could not make it on his own."

At 16, Barnes began calling for emergency assistance from rescue squads in each of the surrounding counties by pretending to be suffocating. This practice continued for more than a year and occurred about 30 times. Barnes described a great sense of satisfaction from being cared for by the emergency crews on these occasions. Soon he became a member of his local rescue squad and felt secure as being part of a "team." He felt especially close to Carson, an older member of the squad. Along with other men of the rescue squad, Barnes and Carson spent their off-hours together.

Within a few months however, Carson married and left the rescue squad to become a fireman. During the same period, Barnes left home and moved into an apartment because of increasing tension with his father. His sense of isolation and loneliness increased soon thereafter, and he had fantasies of being rescued by Carson during a fire. In this fantasy Carson would carry him out of a burning building and would take care of him and ensure his continued safety. He also described feelings of sexual arousal in seeing firemen, particularly Carson, in their rubberized firefighting clothes.

Barnes soon began to set fires, reporting them in the hope that Carson would arrive. In this manner he would see Carson and would

---

[e] This fact situation is based on an unreported case. For a similar case, see Briscoe v. United States, 248 F.2d 640 (D.C.Cir. 1957).

be either praised for his assistance in fighting the fire or would possibly be "rescued." It was during this period that he committed the acts for which he was indicted. The last involved an apartment building.

The expert testified that, in his opinion, Barnes' drives and needs were so strong that they were able to override his generally intact judgment and his sense of social responsibility. Acknowledging that Barnes was able to delay his impulse to start a fire until the circumstances were favorable and the likelihood of his being caught was reduced, the expert nonetheless concluded that he exhibited an "extremely strong need to bring himself into close contact with Carson even though that required him to commit socially irresponsible and illegal actions." Moreover, the expert testified, Barnes' "need to start the fire in order to bring himself and Carson together was so strong that he unconsciously was able to keep from his awareness the possibility that others might be hurt or that extensive property damage might occur."

(ii) ***Chester.***[f] Jack Chester was charged with murder in the killing of Beatrice Fishman and pleaded not guilty by reason of insanity. The evidence shows that the defendant and the victim met as teenagers and became engaged while he was in the armed forces. Upon being discharged, he obtained a job in a factory in another state and plans were made for the wedding in July of that year. For a variety of reasons, the wedding was repeatedly postponed over the next four months. In October the defendant was "very perturbed" and decided that he and Beatrice "were through." He told her she could keep all that he had given her except the wedding ring.

Between October and the following April, the defendant was depressed. Although he dated other girls, none of them could replace Beatrice. He tried to bring about a reconciliation, but Beatrice seemed indifferent, although she still failed to return the wedding ring. He started to drink heavily and to use marijuana. Sometime before April, he bought a pistol.

The defendant decided to visit Beatrice one April weekend. When packing his bag for the trip he put in the pistol. Upon arriving, he went directly to the Fishman home and was told by her parents that she was "out on a date." After talking with them for a while, he left. On the following day the defendant went to the Fishman home and talked with Beatrice and her mother. Beatrice told him that he had been away so long "she didn't know [him] any more," but if he returned to Boston to live they "could get reacquainted." The defendant asked Beatrice to return the ring, and she told him it was in a safe deposit vault, and he could have it Monday. After further conversation, he became very upset; he later said that he felt that he had become entangled in an "utterly hopeless and impossible situation" and that he wanted to kill Beatrice. But he "fought this emotion down," kissed her goodbye, and walked out of the house.

[f] This case is based on Commonwealth v. Chester, 337 Mass. 702, 150 N.E.2d 914 (1958).

The defendant, according to his testimony at the trial, went to a bar, had "two shots of bourbon," and smoked two marijuana cigarettes, becoming slightly "high." But he said that this had no effect on his behavior; he admitted that he knew what he was doing. In about half an hour he returned to the Fishman house in an angry mood. He "figured it out [that he] couldn't live with her and [he] couldn't live without her and it did not make any difference." His intent was to "blow her head off." He went to the front door with his pistol in his pocket and rang the doorbell. As Beatrice opened the door he had the pistol in his hand. Seeing it, she hesitated and then closed the door. Thereupon the defendant started pulling the trigger and kept pulling it until he had fired nine shots through the door. Three of these entered the victim's body causing wounds from which she died within an hour. Shortly thereafter the defendant asked a policeman to arrest him as he had "just murdered someone."

According to the expert testimony introduced in support of Chester's insanity defense, his father died when the defendant was about five years old. His father's death was due to a head injury caused by a fall on the ice, suffered while running after the defendant after the defendant left the house without his hat. The defendant thereafter had guilt feelings because he thought he had caused his father's death. During his boyhood, without a father, he was difficult to control and there was considerable friction between him and his mother. As a result of one dispute with his mother, the defendant, then aged 12, drank a bottle of iodine. At 15 he sustained a serious injury to his eye from an air rifle. The injury affected his appearance, and as a consequence he became self-conscious.

While in the service, the defendant became despondent because of his relations with Beatrice and at one time considered suicide. He was unusually combative and frequently got into fights with other soldiers. Because two airplane pilots lost their lives in the crash of planes on which he had done mechanical work, he felt responsible for their deaths. He felt that he was "no good," that everything he did would turn out badly, and that he would die young.

The defendant's experts concluded that defendant had suffered, since the age of 12 from a "personality disorder characterized by passive obstructionism and by a tendency toward overt, aggressive, uncontrolled outbursts or giving vent to one's feelings with vigorous physical action toward others." He also had an obsession with guilt and strong feelings of worthlessness. While conceding that many people have such traits, the expert stated that Chester had them to a marked degree. "Most of the time the defendant has been able to repress his strong feelings of anger. However, when these feelings have become more intense due to an intolerably frustrating situation, he swings into impulsive violent action over which he momentarily has no conscious control." At the time of the offense, according to the expert, Chester was driven by twin motivations: uncontrollable anger at both himself and the victim, and strong feelings of guilt and worthlessness.

(iii) **Ellingwood.**[g] Sonny Ellingwood, a carpenter with no history of criminal behavior, was charged with criminal homicide in the second degree. The testimony adduced at trial revealed that the defendant shot two people with virtually no provocation and with no discernible motive. He pleaded not guilty by reason of insanity.

The evidence shows that on the day of the shooting the defendant was upset about various minor problems arising at home and on the job. During the morning he had corrected an erroneous estimate he had made on a construction project. Apparently his work had deteriorated somewhat in the weeks preceding the shooting.

At about noon of this day he returned home with two six-packs of beer. He drank some at that time. His wife chided him for drinking during the day. He complained about being pushed around by people and declared he wanted to quit his job and leave the state. Later he left his house trailer, taking with him his rifle and two bottles of beer. One of these bottles he put down and shot with his rifle. His wife came out of the trailer and reprimanded him for his action. He walked away toward a nearby gravel pit.

At the pit the defendant found James Hunter and his daughter, Jacqueline, removing some loam from the pit. The owner of the pit had requested that the defendant keep watch over it. The defendant confronted this pair demanding to know by what right they were removing soil from the pit. James Hunter countered by asking what business it was to the defendant. After this brief interchange the defendant turned his back to them, put down the remaining beer bottle, and turned again, aiming the rifle at James Hunter.

He sighted the rifle on James Hunter for a few seconds. The victim pointed at the defendant and ordered him to put down the gun. The defendant then shot, hitting James Hunter in the chest. Jacqueline Hunter heard the defendant prepare his rifle for a second shot. She looked at him and ordered him to put down the gun. He shot her in the face.

The defendant's wife drove into the pit and picked up the defendant, who then told her his life was over, that he should shoot himself because he had just killed two people. They then drove to a nearby house where the police were called at the defendant's request.

Police officers described the defendant as blubbering, babbling, and crying. Although he admitted the shooting in general terms at that time, he was never able to recall the events in detail.

The defendant introduced expert testimony to support his insanity plea. The psychiatrist testified that the defendant had an underlying obsessive-compulsive and hysterical personality disorder. Symptoms of this condition include "failure to admit feelings; being overly conscientious; being over-controlled; an inability to relax easily; a feeling of personal inadequacy; a chronic tendency to swallow difficulties without objection." The witness testified that during the days before the

[g] This case is based on State v. Ellingwood, 409 A.2d 641 (Me.1979).

offense, the defendant was experiencing substantial anxiety as a result of accumulating stress and that he could not control his exaggerated retributive feelings when confronted with the intruders in the pit. According to the expert, the defendant was probably aware of his actions at the time of the shooting but probably believed, "at some primitive level of psychological functioning, that he was acting in self-defense."

(iv) *Murdock.*[h] Murdock was one of three black patrons at a hamburger shop called the Little Tavern. At about 3:00 a.m., a white woman and five white U.S. Marine lieutenants, in white dress uniforms, entered the shop and ordered food. After Murdock had walked out, an argument developed between one of the whites and Alexander, one of Murdock's associates. Apparently one of the whites used a racial epithet, and Alexander drew a gun. Murdock then came back into the shop with his own gun drawn and fired, killing several of the Marines. Alexander and Murdock were charged with murder. Murdock pleaded not guilty by reason of insanity.

Murdock testified that he pulled his gun as a reflex and fired because he thought the Marines, who he said were moving toward him, would kill him. On cross-examination, he admitted that he did not see any weapons, that he emptied his fully loaded revolver at them in the restaurant and that he fired three shots from Alexander's gun from the window of the car as they drove away. In support of his insanity claim Murdock introduced psychiatric testimony that he is "strongly delusional, though not hallucinating or psychotic." In particular, he is "greatly preoccupied with the unfair treatment of negroes in this country and believes that racial war is inevitable." The witness stated that this behavior reflects compulsiveness, emotional immaturity and some psychopathic traits, and that his emotional disorder had its roots in his childhood. His father had deserted his mother and he grew up in the Watts section of Los Angeles in a large family with little love or attention. (As his attorney put it in the closing argument, Murdock had a "rotten social background.") Since Murdock's emotional difficulties are strongly tied to his sense of racial oppression, the witness said, "it is probable that when the Marine called him a 'black bastard,' Murdock had an irresistible impulse to shoot."

NOTES ON THE BOUNDARIES OF CRIMINAL RESPONSIBILITY

1. **The Significance of Mental Disease.** The concept of "mental disease or defect" is a necessary threshold for the insanity defense under all of the existing tests. Since the concept of irresistible impulse was first recognized, the courts have said the defense is limited to persons whose volition is impaired by mental disease. It has never covered a "normal" person who acts under the influence of strong

[h] This case is based on United States v. Alexander and Murdock, 471 F.2d 923 (D.C.Cir. 1973).

emotion, nor a person whose weakness of will is attributable to a defect of character.[a] Did Pollard have a mental disease? Clinicians would probably agree that Pollard had a clinically significant depression (or dysthymic disorder) during the two-year period after the murders and that he would have benefited from treatment. But should depression or other neurotic disorders be regarded as mental diseases for purposes of the insanity defense? Should a jury question be raised whenever a mental-health professional testifies that the defendant had a diagnosable mental disorder?[b] Would it make sense to rule as a matter of law that Pollard or any of the other defendants in the cases previously discussed did not have a "mental disease" and thereby close the door to their insanity claims? As you think about these questions, consider the following approaches to the issue:

(i) **Restrictive Definition.** Those who are dubious about volitional impairment as an independent ground of exculpation naturally insist on a narrow definition of mental disease, one limited to psychoses. See, e.g., Livermore and Meehl, The Virtues of *M'Naghten*, 51 Minn.L.Rev. 789, 831–32 (1967). However, even some advocates of the volitional inquiry have regarded a narrow definition of mental disease as an essential feature of the test. For example, the Royal Commission on Capital Punishment recommended revision of the "intellectualist" approach of *M'Naghten* in order to encompass affective and volitional considerations in a responsibility defense. However, the Commission also recommended that mental disease be defined restrictively, Royal Commission on Capital Punishment, Report 73 (1953):

> "[M]ental disease . . . broadly corresponds to what are often called major diseases of the mind, or psychoses; although it may also arise in cases, such as those of epilepsy and cerebral tumour, which are not ordinarily regarded by doctors as psychotic. Among the psychoses are the conditions known as schizophrenia, manic-depressive psychoses, and organic disease of the brain. Other conditions, not included under this term, are the minor forms of mental disorder—the neurotic reactions, such as neurasthenia, anxiety states and hysteria—and the disorders of development of the personality."

[a] E.g., Parsons v. State, 81 Ala. 577, 594, 2 So. 854, 865 (1886) ("[a mere moral or emotional insanity, so-called, unconnected with disease of the mind, or irresistible impulse resulting from mere moral obliquity, or wicked propensities and habits, is not recognized as a defense to crime in our courts"); Bell v. State, 120 Ark. 530, 555, 180 S.W. 186, 196 (1915), ("[it] must be remembered that one who is otherwise sane will not be excused from a crime he has committed while his reason is temporarily dethroned not by disease, but by anger, jealousy, or other passion").

agnostic manual, DSM-III, provides, in part:

"[A mental disorder is] . . . a clinically significant behavioral or psychologic syndrome or pattern that occurs in an individual and that typically is associated with either a painful symptom (distress) or impairment in one or more areas of functioning (disability). In addition, there is an inference that there is a behavioral, psychologic, or biologic dysfunction, and that the disturbance is not only in the relationship between the individual and society."

[b] The definition of "mental disorder" in the American Psychiatric Association's di-

A similar approach has been recommended by the American Psychiatric Association: [c]

"Another major consideration in articulating standards for the insanity defense is the definition of mental disease or defect. . . . Allowing insanity acquittals in cases involving persons who manifest primarily 'personality disorders' such as antisocial personality disorder (sociopathy) does not accord with modern psychiatric knowledge or psychiatric beliefs concerning the extent to which such persons do have control over their behavior. Persons with antisocial personality disorders should, at least for heuristic reasons, be held accountable for their behavior. The American Psychiatric Association, therefore, suggests that any revision of the insanity defense standards should indicate that mental disorders potentially leading to exculpation must be *serious*. Such disorders should usually be of the severity (if not always of the quality) of conditions that psychiatrists diagnose as psychoses."

The APA went on to endorse the definition of insanity proposed by Professor Bonnie in The Moral Basis of the Insanity Defense, 69 ABAJ 194, 197 (1983). Professor Bonnie recommended that mental disease should be defined to "include only those severely abnormal mental conditions that grossly and demonstrably impair a person's perception or understanding of reality. . . . " [d]

(ii) **Intermediate Position.** The drafters of the Model Penal Code rejected the idea that mental disease should be limited to psychoses; they clearly intended to permit neuroses or impulse disorders (kleptomania was the example always used) to have exculpatory significance if they "substantially" affected the defendant's volitional capacity. On the other hand, the drafters contemplated that the courts would exclude some disorders of character or personality even though clinicians might regard these conditions as "mental disorders." This intention is reflected in Subsection (2) of Section 4.01: "As used in this Article, the terms 'mental disease or defect' do not include an abnormality manifested only by repeated criminal or otherwise anti-social conduct." It is clear that the drafters meant specifically to exclude offenders who were characterized by clinicians as "psychopaths." The diagnostic label for such a condition has since been changed to "sociopathy" and later to "anti-social personality disorder."

In McDonald v. United States, 312 F.2d 847, 851 (D.C.Cir. 1962), the Court of Appeals for the District of Columbia Circuit defined mental disease or defect as "any abnormal condition of the mind which substantially affects mental or emotional processes and substantially impairs behavior controls." At the time, the court used the "product" test of insanity. However, when the court adopted the Model Penal Code test in United States v. Brawner, 471 F.2d 969 (D.C.Cir. 1972), it retained this definition and endorsed the so-called "caveat paragraph"

---

[c] American Psychiatric Association, Statement on the Insanity Defense (December, 1982).

[d] See also Morse, Excusing the Crazy: The Insanity Defense Reconsidered, 58 So. Cal.L.Rev. 777 (1985).

of Section 4.01(2) as a guideline for the judge rather than as a basis for instructing the jury.[e]

(iii) **Abandonment of the Requirement.** In a concurring opinion in *United States* v. *Brawner*, Judge Bazelon took the view that the mental-disease requirement should be abandoned.

> "At no point in its opinion does the court explain why the boundary of a legal concept—criminal responsibility—should be marked by medical concepts, especially when the validity of the 'medical model' is seriously questioned by some eminent psychiatrists. . . . How many psychiatrists must be convinced that a particular condition is 'medical' in nature before a defendant will be permitted, within the confines of the 'medical model,' to predicate a responsibility defense on such a condition? . . .

> "Our instruction to the jury should provide that a defendant is not responsible *if at the time of his unlawful conduct his mental or emotional processes or behavior controls were impaired to such an extent that he cannot justly be held responsible for his act.* This test would ask the psychiatrist a single question: What is the nature of the impairment of the defendant's mental and emotional processes and behavior controls? It would leave for the jury the question whether that impairment is sufficient to relieve the defendant of responsibility for the particular act charged."

(iv) **Questions on the Mental-Disease Requirement.** Which of these approaches do you favor? Would you limit the mental-disease concept to psychoses and expect trial judges to refuse jury instructions on insanity unless the defendant's evidence crosses that threshold of legal sufficiency? Would you let the defendant put his claim to the jury in every case while instructing the jury on the mental-disease requirement? Or would you adopt Judge Bazelon's approach and abandon the requirement altogether? Does his approach invite unstructured inquiries regarding the determinants of every defendant's criminal behavior? Do you suppose the courtroom experience under the Bazelon approach would differ substantially from the existing practice under the Model Penal Code or *Brawner* formulations? What would you expect to happen in the federal courts under the 1984 statute, which makes the insanity defense available only if the defendant has a "severe" mental disease or defect?

---

e "The judge will be aware that the criminal and antisocial conduct of a person—on the street, in the home, in the ward—is necessarily material information for assessment by the psychiatrist. On the other hand, rarely if ever would a psychiatrist base a conclusion of mental disease solely on criminal and anti-social acts. Our pragmatic solution provides for reshaping the rule, for application by the court, as follows: The introduction or proffer of past criminal and anti-social actions is not admissible as evidence of mental disease unless accompanied by expert testimony, supported by a showing of the concordance of a responsible segment of professional opinion, that the particular characteristics of these actions constitute convincing evidence of an underlying mental disease that substantially impairs behavioral controls."

Brawner v. United States, 471 F.2d 969, 994 (D.C.Cir. 1972).

2. **Compulsive Gambling:** *United States v. Torniero.* Torniero, a jewelry store manager, was charged with 10 counts of interstate transportation of jewelry allegedly stolen from his employer. He filed notice of his intent to rely on the insanity defense and to introduce expert testimony showing that he suffered from "pathological gambling disorder," [f] which led him to accumulate debts that, in turn, led him to steal. The government's motion to "exclude any expert testimony regarding the defendant's alleged mental disorder 'compulsive gambling'" was granted by Judge Cabranes in United States v. Torniero, 570 F.Supp. 721 (D.Conn.1983). Judge Cabranes concluded that Torniero's compulsion to gamble, even if it existed, did not have a sufficiently "direct bearing" on the charged criminal acts to establish the legal predicate for an insanity defense.

Judge Cabranes also noted his doubts "whether compulsive gambling disorder ought even to be the basis for an insanity defense when the offense charged is gambling." He thought it "questionable whether [this] disorder, characterized more by repeated engagement in a particular activity than by any derangement of one's mental faculties, amounts to a mental disease as that concept has long been understood by the criminal law." In a more general observation, Judge Cabranes suggested that the insanity defense "can and should be limited to instances where a jury could find that the defendant's mind was truly alienated from ordinary human experience at the time of the commission of the acts with which he is charged and where that mental condition had a direct bearing on the commission of those acts."

At Torniero's subsequent trial, the government showed that he took jewelry valued at approximately $750,000 from New Haven to the "diamond district" of Manhattan and sold it for cash. Notwithstanding the exclusion of the expert testimony concerning "compulsive gambling

---

[f] "Pathological gambling disorder" is described in DSM III as follows:

"[A] chronic and progressive failure to resist impulses to gamble and gambling behavior that compromises, disrupts, or damages personal, family, or vocational pursuits. The gambling preoccupation, urge, and activity increase during periods of stress. Problems that arise as a result of the gambling lead to an intensification of the gambling behavior. Characteristic problems include loss of work due to absences in order to gamble, defaulting on debts and other financial responsibilities, disrupted family relationships, borrowing money from illegal sources, forgery, fraud, embezzlement, and income tax evasion.

"Commonly these individuals have the attitude that money causes and is also the solution to all their problems. As the gambling increases, the individual is usually forced to lie in order to obtain money and to continue gambling, but hides the extent of the gambling. There is no serious attempt to budget or save money. When borrowing resources are strained, antisocial behavior in order to obtain money for more gambling is likely. Any criminal behavior—e.g., forgery, embezzlement, or fraud—is typically nonviolent. There is a conscious intent to return or repay the money."

DSM III also provides criteria for diagnosing pathological gambling. These include:

"A. The individual is chronically and progressively unable to resist impulses to gamble.

"B. Gambling compromises, disrupts, or damages family, personal, and vocational pursuits, as indicated by at least three of the following:

[Here the criteria mention seven effects of excessive gambling, including "arrest for forgery, fraud, embezzlement, or income tax evasion due to attempts to obtain money for gambling."]

"C. The gambling is not due to antisocial personality disorder."

disorder," Torniero relied on the insanity defense. In support of his claim, he presented two psychiatrists who testified that he suffered from paranoia, depression and a narcissistic personality, as a result of which, in their opinion, he lacked responsibility under the then-applicable Model Penal Code insanity test. After deliberating for less than one hour, the jury convicted Torniero and the judge sentenced him to a three-year prison term, to be followed by five years' probation and an ongoing duty to pay restitution to his former employer.

On appeal, the Second Circuit upheld the trial judge's decision to exclude the evidence concerning Torniero's alleged compulsive gambling disorder. It affirmed the conviction in United States v. Torniero, 735 F.2d 725 (2d Cir.1984). After reviewing the evolution of the insanity defense in the federal courts, and taking note of the controversy aroused by the *Hinckley* acquittal two years earlier, Judge Kaufman turned to the question raised by Torniero's appeal:

"To put in issue the defense of criminal insanity under the prevailing [Model Code] test in effect in this Circuit, Torniero must make a showing that compulsive gambling is a mental disease or defect. He must also demonstrate that the infirmity could have prevented him from appreciating that theft was wrongful, or could have deprived him of the ability to restrain himself from the criminal act. Torniero does not urge that his condition could have rendered him incapable of appreciating the illegality of transporting stolen goods. He contends only that under the volitional prong of the [Model Code] test, the compulsion to gamble rendered him unable to resist becoming a thief and stealing to support his habit. . . .

"This principle on which Torniero relies is a novel one. The disorder of pathological gambling was not included in the American Psychiatric Association Diagnostic and Statistical Manual of Mental Disorders until publication in 1980 of the third edition. . . . Where, as here, a defendant contends that evidence of a newly-recognized disorder would be relevant to an insanity defense, there must be a showing that respected authorities in the field share the view that the disorder is a mental disease or defect that could have impaired the defendant's ability to desist from the offense charged or to appreciate the wrongfulness of his conduct. We state no iron-clad mathematical rule, but we do not believe that an hypothesis subscribed to by only a small number of professionals establishes that a proposed defense can carry the day on relevance.

"At the same time, we recognize that unanimity on mental health issues is rare and we suggest no requirement of universal or even majority professional acceptance. In fashioning its preliminary decision on relevance, a court must make a discretionary determination that the hypotheses relied upon have substantial acceptance in the discipline, as a basis for a finding that the disorder is relevant to the insanity defense.

"The first hurdle Torniero's proposed insanity defense must traverse is that the alleged disorder constitutes a mental disease or defect as the term is used in the [Model Code] definition. We are convinced that persuasive evidence was adduced at the pretrial hearing to justify a conclusion that members of the mental health profession hold seriously contradicting views in this regard. [A psychiatrist] who helped draft DSM–III testified that the clinical definition of compulsive gambling as a 'failure to resist' rather than an 'inability to resist' the urge to wager was a deliberate effort to distinguish this disorder from those defects of the mind appropriate for an insanity defense. Another psychiatrist testified before Judge Cabranes in support of the argument that compulsive gambling is not a mental disease or defect as defined by the [Model Code] rule. Several mental health and social work professionals testified on the debilitating effects of the compulsion to gamble and stated for the record that they believed the pathology should be considered a mental disease or defect. One of these witnesses, however, conceded that 'pathological gambling has not ever been considered a serious disorder' within the profession.

"The trial court stated no conclusion on the issue, nor are we called upon to rule that compulsive gambling can never constitute a mental disease or defect. We need not rest, however, on the ground that the proffered gambling defense was not shown to be a mental disease or defect. Assuming without deciding, that it did cross that threshold of the [Model Code] test, there is still ample basis for the trial court's conclusion that Torniero's compulsive gambling disorder is not relevant to the insanity defense. The trial judge correctly noted that the relevance standard requires that the pathology alleged have 'a direct bearing on [the] commission of the acts with which [the defendant] is charged.' In sum, a compulsion to gamble, even if a mental disease or defect, is not, ipso facto, relevant to the issue whether the defendant was unable to restrain himself from non-gambling offenses such as transporting stolen property.

"Although several of Torniero's witnesses expressed the opinion that compulsive gamblers they have treated or observed were unable to resist the impulse to steal as a result of the gambling pathology, this view was vigorously contradicted by the government's experts. Moreover, not one of the experts stated that the connection between compulsive gambling and the impulse to steal for purposes of the insanity defense has substantial acceptance in the profession. While we cannot agree with the trial court that no evidence whatsoever on the volitional nexus between gambling and stealing was adduced, we are of the view that there is ample basis in the record to warrant the conclusion that the trial judge did not abuse his discretion in finding the connection between the two was not satisfactorily established. In the absence of such evidence the proffered defense cannot be deemed relevant to the insanity defense. . . .

"As the psychiatric and psychological professions refine their understanding of impulse disorders such as pathological gambling, courts are called upon to make difficult and delicate decisions under the volitional prong of the insanity test. We rule today that when evidence of an impulse disorder is offered in support of an insanity defense, the trial judge must first determine that the evidence is relevant. We do not foreclose admissibility of compulsive gambling in all circumstances, nor do we speculate on the desirability of the [proposals to eliminate the volitional prong] now being considered by Congress.

"The insanity defense has never been free from controversy, criticism, and revision. No rule designed to embody societal values will ever be sacrosanct. As our understanding of the intricacies of the fathomless human mind continues to evolve, legal rules must respond to changed conceptions of the nature of moral culpability, and to advances in the science of mental illness. The fundamental question will always be an inquiry into how best to embody society's sense of what conduct is appropriate for punishment by criminal sanctions. The district court's exclusion of the compulsive gambling defense proposed here accords with accepted notions of criminal responsibility. . . . Accordingly, we affirm the judgment of conviction."

Although it affirmed the district court's decision to exclude the evidence proffered by Torniero, the circuit court refused to foreclose the admissibility of such evidence "in all circumstances." Should similar evidence be admissible in a prosecution for illegal gambling? Of what significance is the fact that chronic and progressive inability to resist impulses to gamble is one of the criteria for the diagnosis under DSM III? If the expert testimony would be admitted in a prosecution for illegal gambling, why should it be excluded in a theft prosecution if the defendant's experts are prepared to testify that the defendant's capacity to refrain from stealing was substantially impaired? Do you agree with the circuit court's decision? With Judge Kaufman's rationale? [g]

3. **Drug-Dependence:** *United States* v. *Moore*. The boundaries of criminal responsibility in the related context of drug dependence were explored in United States v. Moore, 486 F.2d 1139 (D.C.Cir. 1973). Raymond Moore was charged with possession of heroin. He claimed, in defense, that he was an opiate-dependent person with an overpowering need to use heroin. He sought to introduce supporting testimony on the ground that, due to his abnormal psychological condition, he lacked substantial capacity to conform his behavior to the laws prohibiting

[g] For decisions reaching the same result on similar grounds, see United States v. Gould, 741 F.2d 45 (4th Cir.1984), and United States v. Lewellyn, 723 F.2d 615 (8th Cir.1983).

At least one defendant has successfully relied upon pathological gambling disorder in a theft prosecution. The defendant was acquitted by reason of insanity, despite having embezzled more than $300,000 from

his employer, in State v. Lafferty, 192 Conn. 571, 472 A.2d 1275 (1984). The Connecticut General Assembly subsequently amended its insanity statute to preclude exculpation in such cases by excluding "pathological or compulsive gambling" from the definition of "mental disease or defect." Conn. Penal Code § 53a–13(c) (1985 Supp.).

possession of heroin. The government, though conceding that Moore was dependent on heroin, objected to the admissibility of this evidence on the ground that it was insufficient, as a matter of law, to establish that Moore lacked criminal responsibility for his acts. Moore was convicted and sentenced to prison. A closely divided (five to four) court of appeals, sitting en banc, affirmed the conviction, rejecting Moore's claim that he was entitled to raise a "common-law defense" of addiction. The court also rejected Moore's argument that his conviction was barred by the eighth amendment as interpreted in *Robinson* v. *California* and *Powell* v. *Texas,* reprinted on pages 158–82, supra.

Judge Wright's dissenting opinion observed that the eighth amendment, as construed in *Powell* v. *Texas,* "provides only the floor and not the ceiling for development of common-law notions of criminal responsibility" and argued that Moore's claim should be reached by evolving doctrines of volitional impairment:

"The concept of criminal responsibility is, by its very nature, 'an expression of the moral sense of the community.' . . . [T]here has historically been a strong conviction in our jurisprudence that to hold a man criminally responsible, his actions must have been the product of a 'free will.' . . . Thus criminal responsibility is assessed only when through 'free will' a man elects to do evil, and if he is not a free agent, or is unable to choose or to act voluntarily, or to avoid the conduct which constitutes the crime, he is outside the postulate of the law of punishment.

"Despite this general principle, however, it is clear that our legal system does not exculpate all persons whose capacity for control is impaired, for whatever cause or reason. Rather, in determining responsibility for crime, the law assumes 'free will' and then recognizes known deviations 'where there is a broad consensus that free will does not exist' with respect to the particular condition at issue. The evolving nature of this process is amply demonstrated in the gradual development of such defenses as infancy, duress, insanity, somnambulism and other forms of automatism, epilepsy and unconsciousness, involuntary intoxication, delirium tremens, and chronic alcoholism.

"A similar consensus exists today in the area of narcotics addiction. . . . The World Health Organization has ranked heroin addiction as the most intensive form of drug dependence, far more severe than alcoholism. Indeed, the primary element of the most widely accepted definition of opiate addiction is 'an *overpowering* desire or need to continue taking the drug,' and Congress has repeatedly defined as an addict any individual who is 'so far addicted to the use of narcotic drugs as to have *lost the power of self-control* with reference to his addiction.' Thus it can no longer seriously be questioned that for at least some addicts the 'overpowering' psychological and physiological need to possess and inject narcotics cannot be overcome by mere exercise of 'free will.' . . .

"The genius of the common law has long been its responsiveness to changing times, its ability to reflect new knowledge and developing social and moral values. . . . I conclude that imposition of criminal liability on the non-trafficking addict possessor is contrary to our historic common-law traditions of criminal responsibility. This being so, it is clear that a defense of "addiction" must exist for these individuals unless Congress has expressly and unequivocally manifested its intent to preclude such a defense. [Judge Wright concluded that recognition of the defense had not been precluded by congressional action.]"

The majority of the court rejected this view. Judge Leventhal responded directly to Judge Wright in his concurring opinion:

"Appellant's key defense concepts are impairment of behavioral control and loss of self-control. These have been considered by this court most fully in discussion of the insanity defense, and the philosophy of those opinions is invoked, although appellant disclaims the insanity defense as such. . . .

"Appellant's presentation rests, in essence, on the premise that the 'mental disease or defect' requirement of *McDonald* and *Brawner* is superfluous. He discerns a broad principle that excuses from criminal responsibility when conduct results from a condition that impairs behavior control. . . .

"It does not follow that because one condition (mental disease) yields an exculpatory defense if it results in impairment of and lack of behavioral controls the same result follows when some other condition impairs behavior controls. . . .

"The legal conception of criminal capacity cannot be limited to those of unusual endowment or even average powers. A few may be recognized as so far from normal as to be entirely beyond the reach of criminal justice, but in general the criminal law is a means of social control that must be potentially capable of reaching the vast bulk of the population. Criminal responsibility is a concept that not only extends to the bulk of those below the median line of responsibility, but specifically extends to those who have a realistic problem of substantial impairment and lack of capacity due, say, to weakness of intellect that establishes susceptibility to suggestion; or to a loss of control of the mind as a result of passion, whether the passion is of an amorous nature or the result of hate, prejudice or vengeance; or to a depravity that blocks out conscience as an influence on conduct.

"The criminal law cannot 'vary legal norms with the individual's capacity to meet the standards they prescribe, absent a disability that is both gross and verifiable, such as the mental disease or defect that may establish irresponsibility. The most that it is feasible to do with lesser disabilities is to accord them proper weight in sentencing.'

"Only in limited areas have the courts recognized a defense to criminal responsibility, on the basis that a described condition establishes a psychic incapacity negativing free will in the broader sense. These are areas where the courts have been able to respond to a deep call on elemental justice, and to discern a demarcation of doctrine that keeps the defense within verifiable bounds that do not tear the fabric of the criminal law as an instrument of social control. . . .

"[A]ppellant disclaims any direct reliance on the insanity defense. He agrees with our rulings that heroin dependence may have probative value, along with other evidence of mental disease, but is not by itself evidence of 'mental disease or defect' sufficient to raise the insanity issue, unless so protracted and extensive as to result in unusual deterioration of controls.

"Our opinion in *Brawner* declined to accept the suggestion that it 'announce' a standard exculpating anyone whose capacity for control is insubstantial, for whatever cause or reason, and said, disclaiming an 'all-embracing unified field theory,' that we would discern the appropriate rule 'as the cases arise in regard to other conditions.'

"In our view, the rule for drug addiction should not be modeled on the rule for mental disease because of crucial distinctions between conditions. The subject of mental disease, though subject to some indeterminacy, and difficulty of diagnosis when extended to volitional impairment as well as cognitive incapacity, has long been the subject of systematic study, and in that framework it is considered manageable to ask psychiatrists to address the distinction, all-important and crucial to the law, between incapacity and indisposition, between those who can't and those who won't, between the impulse irresistible and the impulse not resisted. These are matters as to which the court has accepted the analysis of medicine, medical conditions and symptoms, and on the premise that they can be considered on a verifiable basis, and with reasonable dispatch, the courts have recognized a defense even in conditions not as obvious and verifiable as those covered in the older and limited test of capacity to know right from wrong.

"[T]here is considerable difficulty of verification of the claim of a drug user that he is unable to refrain from use. . . .

"The difficulty of the verification problem of lack of capacity to refrain from use is sharpened on taking into account that the issue comprehends the addict's failure to participate in treatment programs. This raises problems of the addict's personal knowledge, disposition, motivation, as well as extent of community programs, that may usefully be assessed by someone considering what program to try now or next, but would irretrievably tangle a trial.

"The feature that narcotic addiction is not a stable condition undercuts any approach patterned on the mental disease, where there is a reasonable projection that subsequent analysis of particular incidents over time may delineate an ascertainable condition. It is unrealistic to expect the addict himself to supply accurate information on the nature and extent of addiction at the time of the offense, particularly as to 'psychic dependence.'

"The difficulty is sharpened by the appreciable number of narcotic 'addicts' who do abandon their habits permanently, and much larger number who reflect their capacity to refrain by ceasing use for varying periods of time. The reasons are not clear but the phenomenon is indisputable. . . .

"There is need for reasonable verifiability as a condition to opening a defense to criminal responsibility. The criminal law cannot gear its standards to the individual's capacity 'absent a disability that is both gross and verifiable, such as the mental disease or defect that may establish irresponsibility.' . . .

"Reliability and validity of a legal defense require that it can be tested by criteria external to the actions which it is invoked to excuse. And so the Model Penal Code's caveat paragraph rejects an insanity defense based on an abnormality manifested only by repeated criminal or otherwise anti-social conduct. This approach was followed in *Brawner*. The defense of drug dependence to a charge of drug use cannot clear the hurdle of circularity."

Do you agree with Judge Leventhal or Judge Wright? Do you think the reasons given by Judge Leventhal for rejecting the addiction defense would also apply to the volitional prong of the insanity defense? Does the "mental-disease" requirement really limit the defense to conditions that are "gross and verifiable"? Do you now have a deeper appreciation for the concerns expressed by the plurality in *Powell* v. *Texas*, pages 168–82, supra?

SUBSECTION C: THE INSANITY DEFENSE AND INTOXICATION

PEOPLE v. KELLY

Supreme Court of California, 1973.
10 Cal.3d 565, 111 Cal.Rptr. 171, 516 P.2d 875.

SULLIVAN, J. Defendant Valerie Dawn Kelly was charged in count one of an information with assault with a deadly weapon with intent to commit murder, in count two thereof with attempted murder, and in count three with assault with a deadly weapon and by means of force likely to produce great bodily injury. Defendant pleaded not guilty and not guilty by reason of insanity to all counts. Trial by jury was waived, counts one and two were dismissed by the court on the People's motion on the ground of insufficiency of evidence, and the court found defendant guilty of assault with a deadly weapon. The court thereafter found that defendant was legally sane at the time the offense was committed. Imposition of sentence was suspended and defendant was granted probation for a period of five years under specified terms and conditions. She appeals from the judgment of conviction.

Defendant has used drugs ever since she was 15 years old.[2] In the fall of 1970, when she was 18 years old, she began taking mescaline and LSD, using those drugs 50 to 100 times in the months leading up to the offense. On December 6, 1970, her parents received a telephone call that defendant was being held at the police substation located at the Los Angeles International Airport after being found wandering about the airport under the influence of drugs. In response to the call, her parents picked up defendant at the airport and drove her back to their home in San Diego. Although they recognized that she was not acting normally, at defendant's request they drove her to her own apartment where she spent the night.

On the next morning, December 7, defendant telephoned her mother and asked to be driven to her parents' home. Mrs. Kelly did so but noticed that defendant "wasn't there"; she seemed to be "[j]ust wandering" and told her mother that she heard "a lot of noises, and a lot of people talking . . .".[3] Mrs. Kelly made defendant change into pajamas and lie down, and then went into the kitchen to prepare defendant's breakfast. Shortly thereafter, defendant entered the kitchen and, while Mrs. Kelly was turned toward the stove, repeatedly stabbed her mother with an array of kitchen knives. The police were called, defendant was arrested, and eventually charged as already indicated.

On December 14, 1971, the case proceeded to trial before the court sitting without a jury.[4] The parties waived their right to a bifurcated trial on the separate issues of guilt and insanity and agreed that the court upon receiving evidence at a single trial, could separately decide the two issues after allowing counsel to argue as to each. . . .[a]

[2] In 1968, following a call by her parents to the police, defendant, then just 16 years old, was taken into custody for being under the influence of drugs. She spent three weeks in a ward of the county mental-health clinic for abuse of habit-forming drugs and was released on two-years' probation. In December 1968, she voluntarily entered Patton State Hospital, after again being found under the influence of drugs. Two months later, she ran away from the hospital but refrained from using drugs until the period preceding the instant offense. In November 1970, about a month before the offense here involved, defendant was again taken into custody for drug abuse and spent several days in the county mental health clinic after which she was released.

[3] In a psychiatric report made after the attack and introduced into evidence, defendant described her hallucinations at this time. She thought that her parents "were with the devils." She would talk to her parents "but not out loud." Her mother "told" her that "they had devils," and defendant "realized that something was going to die—that they were going to kill me."

[4] Before defendant could be tried, the trial court, doubting her competency, ordered a hearing to determine whether she was presently sane. The court found that defendant was insane and ordered her committed to Patton State Hospital. . . . She remained there for nine months and was released in September 1971, after being certified as sane and able to stand trial.

. . .

[a] A defendant in California may plead both "not guilty" and "not guilty by reason of insanity." When a defendant enters both pleas, the case is tried in two phases. During the first phase of the bifurcated trial, the defendant is presumed to be sane, and the issue of "guilt or innocence" of the crime is decided. If the defendant is convicted, the trial moves into a second phase, during which the defendant's "legal sani-

Much of the evidence presented at the trial consisted of the reports and testimony of seven psychiatrists. Since there was substantial agreement among them, we briefly summarize their testimony. . . .

Defendant suffered from personality problems—according to one witness an underlying schizophrenia—but was normally a sane person.[5] However, her voluntary and repeated ingestion of drugs over a two-month period had triggered a legitimate psychosis so that on the day of the attack, defendant was unable to distinguish right from wrong. Nevertheless, defendant was conscious in that she could perceive the events that were taking place.

The trial court heard considerable testimony that defendant was not acting simply as a person who, after ingesting drugs or alcohol, is unable to perceive reality and reason properly. Rather, the drug abuse was deemed the indirect cause of a legitimate, temporary psychosis that would remain even when defendant was temporarily off drugs. Finally, there was general agreement that defendant, although still a "brittle" person with latent schizophrenic tendencies, was sane at the time of trial.

At the conclusion of all the evidence, the prosecutor and defense counsel presented their arguments to the court on the guilt phase of the case. The court then in essence found that defendant did the acts constituting an assault with a deadly weapon, that at such time she was not in a state of unconsciousness, and that defendant was "guilty as charged."

After a recess, counsel for both parties then presented their arguments on the sanity phase of the case. At the conclusion of the arguments the court found that while defendant was indeed psychotic both before and after the attack, and "was not capable of understanding that her act was wrong," her insanity was no defense because it "was not of a settled and permanent nature, and, in addition, was produced by the voluntary ingestion of hallucinatory drugs." Accordingly the court found that defendant was legally sane at the time the offense was committed.

Defendant contends (i) that the evidence before the court established a defense of unconsciousness and (ii) that insanity, however caused, was a defense to [assault with a deadly weapon], a general-intent crime.

In support of her first contention, defendant argues that the evidence showed her to be psychotic at the time of her actions. She relies on the court's findings that there was no evidence she was fully aware of what she was doing on the day of the assault but was shown to have been intermittently aware of her actions. . . . She urges that the

ty" at the time of the crime is adjudicated. Although one of the objectives of the bifurcated trial is to defer evidence of mental abnormality to the second phase, this aim may be frustrated if the defendant is permitted to introduce such evidence to disprove mens rea during the first phase. This problem is addressed at pages 769–70, infra. [Footnote by eds.]

[5] The testimony of several psychiatrists showed that defendant had underlying personality defects accompanied by a "schizoid personality," which denotes a tendency to withdraw from reality but is not as severe as schizophrenia. "She was not overtly schizophrenic. . . . Normally sane, but she did have a character disorder [even before her period of drug abuse."

only determination to be made by the trial court was whether she was in fact unconscious at the time of her acts and that the fact that such unconsciousness was the product of drug intoxication voluntarily induced should not negate the defense.

[U]nconsciousness caused by voluntary intoxication is only a partial defense to a criminal charge—that is, it may serve to negate the specific intent or state of mind requisite to the offense. . . . It follows, therefore, that unconsciousness caused by voluntary intoxication is *no* defense to a general-intent crime—by definition a crime in which no specific intent is required. Assault with a deadly weapon is such a crime, and we have held that the requisite general intent therefor may not be negated through a showing of voluntary intoxication. Thus, if there was substantial evidence to support the trial court's conclusion, defendant's argument that she was not guilty because of unconsciousness must fail. . . .[b]

We turn to defendant's second contention which relates to the sanity phase of her trial. She claims that the court erred in finding her legally sane at the time of the offense on the basis that, although she did not know that what she was doing was wrong, her insanity was drug-induced and not of a settled and permanent nature. . . . She argues that insanity, however caused, is a defense to a criminal charge.

It is fundamental to our system of jurisprudence that a person cannot be convicted for acts performed while insane. . . . Insanity, under the California *M'Naghten* test, denotes a mental condition which renders a person incapable of knowing or understanding the nature and quality of his act, or incapable of distinguishing right from wrong in relation to that act.[c] . . . This is a factual question to be decided by the trier of fact. . . .

In this case the trial court found that defendant "was not capable of understanding that her act was wrong." We can only construe this finding to mean that defendant was insane under the aforementioned test. Despite this finding, the trial court adjudged defendant legally sane because her psychosis was "not of a settled and permanent nature, and, in addition, was produced by the voluntary ingestion of hallucinatory drugs." In so ruling, the trial court misinterpreted the rules regarding the defense of insanity and committed prejudicial error.

As we have already stated, voluntary intoxication by itself is no defense to a crime of general intent such as assault with a deadly weapon. . . . However, we have repeatedly held that "when insanity is the result of long continued intoxication, it affects responsibility in the same way as insanity which has been produced by any other cause." . . . .

Policy considerations support this distinction in treatment between voluntary intoxication resulting in unconsciousness and voluntary in-

---

[b] Compare the *Majewski* case and the accompanying notes, pages 274–83, supra. [Footnote by eds.]

[c] The California Supreme Court subsequently abandoned the *M'Naghten* test and adopted the Model Penal Code formulation in People v. Drew, 22 Cal.3d 333, 149 Cal.Rptr. 275, 583 P.2d 1318 (1978). A popular initiative restored the *M'Naghten* test in 1982. [Footnote by eds.]

toxication which causes insanity. The former encompasses those situations in which mental impairment does not extend beyond the period of intoxication. . . .

When long-continued intoxication results in insanity, however, the mental disorder remains even after the effects of the drug or alcohol have worn off. The actor is "legally insane," and the traditional justifications for criminal punishment are inapplicable because of his inability to conform, intoxicated or not, to accepted social behavior. . . . He is, of course, subject to commitment in a mental institution. In the instant case, the trial court appears to have confused these separate rules. The proper rule of law was early established. . . . "[S]ettled insanity produced by a long-continued intoxication affects responsibility in the same way as insanity produced by any other cause. *But it must be 'settled insanity,' and not merely a temporary mental condition produced by recent use of intoxicating liquor."* Thus it is immaterial that voluntary intoxication may have caused the insanity, as long as the insanity was of a settled nature and qualifies under the *M'Naghten* test as a defense.

The trial court carried this distinction too far, however, for it required proof that defendant's insanity was both settled and *permanent.* Such a requirement violates the rule that "[t]emporary insanity, as a defense to crime, is as fully recognized by law as is permanent insanity." . . . Thus, if defendant at the time of the offense was insane under the California *M'Naghten* test, it makes no difference whether the period of insanity lasted several months, as in this case, or merely a period of hours. . . .

We have reviewed the record in the instant case and we find substantial evidence to support the trial court's finding that defendant was psychotic at the time of the offense. This finding is amply supported by the testimony of psychiatrists. Substantial evidence also supports the finding that the psychosis was a product of voluntary ingestion of drugs. Finally, the trial court found that defendant "was not capable of understanding that her act was wrong," a finding supported by considerable psychiatric testimony that defendant could not distinguish right from wrong at the time of her offense.

As already pointed out, if defendant was insane at the time of the offense, it is immaterial that her insanity resulted from repeated voluntary intoxication, as long as her insanity was of a settled nature. The trial court made a compound finding that defendant's insanity "was not of a settled and permanent nature"; however, we have pointed out that insanity need not be permanent in order to establish a defense. The trial court also found that defendant suffered from a "temporary psychosis" that "was operating on this defendant from some time in November, at least through December and beyond the date of December 7." We hold that such a temporary psychosis which was not limited merely to periods of intoxication . . . and which rendered defendant insane under the *M'Naghten* test constitutes a settled insanity that is a complete defense to the offense here charged.

The judgment is reversed and the cause is remanded to the trial court with directions to enter a judgment of not guilty by reason of insanity and to take such further proceedings as are required by law.

NOTES ON THE INSANITY DEFENSE
AND INTOXICATION

1. **Introduction.** It is often said that voluntary intoxication is not a defense to criminal liability. This position is reflected in both the voluntary-act doctrine and the insanity defense: Voluntary intoxication is not an excuse even if the defendant's mental functioning was so impaired by the acute effects of alcohol or other drugs that he would otherwise have an "unconsciousness" defense or would satisfy the criteria of the insanity test. In cases of incapacitating voluntary intoxication, the law finds the governing moral criterion in the culpable origin of the incapacity rather than in its severity. As Hale said, a person who commits a crime while drunk "shall have no privilege by this voluntary contracted madness, but shall have the same judgment as if he were in his right senses."[a] However, Hale identified two situations in which the madness induced by intoxication would not be contracted voluntarily and therefore would have exculpatory significance:

> "[First,] if a person by the unskillfulness of his physician, or by the contrivance of his enemies, eat or drink such a thing as causeth such a temporary or permanent phrenzy, . . . this puts him into the same condition, in reference to crimes, as any other phrenzy, and equally excuseth him. [Second,] although the *simplex* phrenzy occasioned immediately by drunkenness excuse not in criminals, yet if by one or more such practices, an *habitual* or fixed phrenzy be caused, though this madness was contracted by the vice and will of the party, yet this habitual and fixed phrenzy thereby caused puts the man into the same condition in relation to crimes, as if the same were contracted involuntarily at first."

Each of these two propositions now represents settled law in the United States.

2. **Non-Culpable Intoxication.** The first of the principles mentioned by Hale, typically labeled "involuntary intoxication," covers a variety of cases in which the person cannot fairly be blamed for becoming intoxicated. Cases of intoxication under duress or by contrivance (*A* puts LSD in *B*'s coffee) simply do not appear in the books. Most of the reported cases involve psychoactive side effects of medically-prescribed substances, typically arising in connection with automobile offenses.

The leading case is Minneapolis v. Altimus, 306 Minn. 462, 238 N.W.2d 851 (1976). The defendant was charged with careless driving

---

[a] 1 M. Hale, The History of the Pleas of the Crown 32 (Philadelphia 1847) (1st ed. 1736).

and a "hit and run" offense. The evidence showed that he made an illegal left turn from a right-hand lane, crashed into another vehicle, and then continued driving. He was arrested by a policeman who had observed the accident. In his defense, he testified that three days before the incident he started taking Valium (a psychoactive, anti-anxiety drug with muscle-relaxing effects) for back pain pursuant to a physician's prescription. He said that he began experiencing mental confusion and disorientation while driving and remembered nothing about either the accident or the arrest. He also introduced expert testimony regarding the effects of Valium. The court instructed the jury on voluntary intoxication but refused to instruct on "involuntary intoxication." The Minnesota Supreme Court reversed, holding that defendant's evidence that "at the time he committed the acts in question he was intoxicated and unaware of what he was doing due to an unusual and unexpected reaction to drugs prescribed by a physician" was sufficient "to raise the defense of temporary insanity due to involuntary intoxication."

How should the jury be instructed on remand? The court's language suggests that the test has two elements: first, the intoxication must be "involuntary," which means the effect must have been both atypical and "unexpected" by Altimus; and the unexpected impairment must amount to "insanity," which in Minnesota is defined according to the *M'Naghten* test. Are these the correct criteria? Compare § 2.08 of the Model Penal Code. Does the Model Penal Code formulation differ from the court's test in *Altimus*? How? Is the Model Code approach sound?

3. **Alcohol-Related Insanity.** The second principle to which Hale referred was the exculpatory effect of the "fixed phrenzy" produced by chronic intoxication. The clinical predicate for this universally recognized doctrine is that chronic use of alcohol can result in organic brain pathology. Although chronic alcohol use can contribute to the development of "dementia,"[b] a condition sometimes associated with aging, the most relevant disorder for present purposes is "alcohol withdrawal delirium" (also called delirium tremens, or "DT's"), which is precipitated by a cessation or reduction of alcohol consumption after heavy use for many years. This condition usually involves delusions, vivid hallucinations, and agitated behavior. A related condition is alcoholic hallucinosis, involving vivid and usually unpleasant auditory hallucinations without the clouding of consciousness characteristic of delirium. Usually this disorder lasts only a few hours or days but can involve significant danger if the individual responds to hallucinatory threats. This condition can occur after a long period of "spree" drinking.

A famous case involving delirium tremens is Beasley v. State, 50 Ala. 149 (1874). Beasley was charged with murder. The evidence showed that the defendant had shot himself in the head, partially paralyzing his left side, 19 years before the offense, and had been chronically drunk for several years before the killing. He frequently

---

[b] Dementia is the general term for an organic brain syndrome characterized by intellectual deficits and impaired memory and often by impaired judgment and impulse control.

experienced hallucinations and had an attack of delirium tremens three weeks before the killing. He testified that he was seeing devils and witches before and during the day of the shooting and that he "imagined that men were after him to kill him." Prosecution evidence showed that the killing was brutal and unprovoked. The trial court refused to instruct on insanity saying, instead, that "drunkenness, in itself, was no palliation or excuse." Beasley was convicted of second-degree murder. On appeal the conviction was reversed because the intoxication charge failed to distinguish between the "immediate effects of the defendant's drunkenness" and the effects of "mental unsoundness brought on by excessive drinking which remains after the intoxication has subsided." The appellate court held that the jury should have been instructed on insanity.

It is often said that delirium tremens and alcoholic hallucinosis exculpate to the same degree as any other psychotic disorder, notwithstanding the fact that these conditions were "caused" by the defendant's own excessive drinking. In these situations, the law looks not to the original source of the impairment but to its effect. In sum, the defendant's pattern of voluntary decisions loses its moral significance when behavior "ripens" into a pathological condition no longer subject to voluntary control.

What is the basis for this distinction? Why does the idiom of moral discourse shift from voluntariness to involuntariness when one moves from the unanticipated and uncontrollable effects of an acute episode of intoxication to the unanticipated and uncontrollable effects of a pattern of intoxication? What is the crucial moral variable? The chronicity of the condition? The psychotic character of the impairment? The remote connection between a psychotic condition and individual instances of intoxication? Consider the suggestion of Monrad Paulsen in Intoxication as a Defense to Crime, 1961 U.Ill.L.F. 1, 22–23:

> ". . . In a sense it is true that an actor, who by drinking destroys his powers of perception or self-control, bears responsibility for his ultimate state. Does it follow that mental disorder produced by long-term alcoholic behavior should be given a different effect in the law from insanity not produced by 'voluntary' behavior? The law is clear. Lack of responsibility can be shown by 'settled' insanity without regard to the chain of causation. To give the genesis of mental disorder a legal effect is to put upon the processes of litigation an impossible task. If the full exculpatory effect of mental disease were denied to those illnesses which are related to unwise choices in life, many cases other than those of the alcoholics would be involved. We need only recall that general paresis [a type of dementia] was a not-uncommon consequence of syphilis."

Are you persuaded? Is it really an "impossible" task to determine whether the defendant's disorder is attributable to once voluntary choices? Or does the law rest on a moral judgment that a person cannot fairly be said to have voluntarily assumed the risk of becoming "mentally ill"?

Hale emphasized the "fixed" nature of the "phrenzy" and, as *Kelly* demonstrates, the courts have typically said that an alcohol-related condition must be "settled" to have exculpatory significance. However, recent commentary has taken note of the clinical reality that both delirium and hallucinosis linked to cessation of drinking usually involve temporary impairment incidental to chronic and heavy use. Although the person's heavy drinking has probably caused organic brain damage, the "phrenzy" is in fact not "fixed." This has led one court to note that "the distinction, notwithstanding the language of the cases, is not so much between temporary and permanent insanity as it is one between the direct results of drinking, which are voluntarily sought after, and its remote and undesired consequences." Parker v. State, 7 Md.App. 167, 179, 254 A.2d 381, 388 (1969). Should this be the governing principle? Is there not an increased risk of fabrication associated with claims of "temporary" insanity due to drinking? Does this concern you?

4. Insanity Related to Use of Other Drugs. It is well known, of course, that alcohol intoxication impairs perception and judgment and, in doing so, loosens behavioral controls. However, alcohol use is not generally associated with psychotic symptoms, such as delusions or hallucinations, except in relation to the two "withdrawal syndromes" described above. Thus, to the extent that the law's conception of insanity requires psychotic symptoms, the distinction reflected in *Beasley* between the effects of intoxication and the effects of "disease" conforms to clinical realities.

This doctrinal picture became considerably blurred by the patterns of psychoactive drug use that emerged in the 1960's. Many of these drugs can affect cognitive functioning in profound ways that bear no resemblance to the effects of alcohol. As one court noted in 1968, "we anticipate . . . that the demands of due process may require adjustment and refinement in traditional and 'stock' instructions on the subject of criminal responsibility in view of the frightening effects of the hallucinatory drugs."[c] Three distinct clinical situations are explored below.

(i) **Psychoactive Effects of Intoxication.** Hallucinogenic drugs such as LSD have sometimes been called "psychotomimetic" drugs because the acute effects of ordinary doses "mimic" psychotic symptoms. The perceptual changes include subjective intensification of perceptions, depersonalization, illusion, and visual hallucinations. The direct effects of the intoxication usually last about six hours. Users of high doses of amphetamines and other stimulant drugs may experience delusions or hallucinations; and users of phencyclidine (PCP) and related substances may experience hallucinations and paranoid ideation.

The question is whether the hallucinogenic effects of these drugs warrant any qualification of the rule that voluntary intoxication is no defense regardless of the nature and severity of the impairment. The

[c] Pierce v. Turner, 402 F.2d 109, 112 (10th Cir. 1968).

courts have uniformly rejected this claim. Consider, for example, State v. Hall, 214 N.W.2d 205 (Iowa 1974). Hall was charged with the fatal shooting of his driving companion during the course of a trip from Oregon to Chicago. He testified that before the shooting he had taken a pill (presumably LSD) which he had been told was a "little sunshine" and would make him feel "groovy." He said he drove all the way to Iowa without rest, took the pill at Des Moines and began experiencing hallucinations. The victim, who was sleeping, appeared to make growling sounds and turn into a rabid dog like one he saw his father kill when he was a child. In panic, he seized the victim's gun and shot him three times. The trial court refused an insanity instruction, and the jury convicted defendant of first-degree murder despite an instruction that his intoxication could be considered in connection with the issue of intent. The appellate court affirmed, holding that the acute, psychotomimetic effects of LSD do not justify a departure from the traditional rule that "a temporary mental condition caused by voluntary intoxication . . . does not constitute a complete defense." Three judges dissented, arguing, inter alia:

". . . The fallacy in the majority's position is that it puts the issue on a *time* basis rather than an *effect* basis. It says the use of drugs is no defense unless mental illness resulting from long-established use is shown because that's what we have said of alcoholic intoxication. But we have said that about alcohol because ordinarily the use of alcohol produces no mental illness except by long-continued excessive use. On the other hand, that same result can be obtained overnight by the use of modern hallucinatory drugs like LSD."

Is there merit to the view expressed in the *Hall* dissent?

(ii) **Precipitation of a "Functional" Psychosis.** As the testimony in *Kelly* indicates, use of hallucinogenic or stimulant drugs can precipitate psychotic deterioration in a predisposed individual, even though the person has never previously had an acute psychotic episode.[d] How should a case such as *Kelly* be decided under the principles thus far reviewed? Should *Hall* or *Beasley* control? Should the applicable rule be determined by the pathological nature of the impairment or by the role of voluntary drug use in causing it?

The exculpatory approach taken by the *Kelly* court seems to represent the prevailing judicial view. In a factually similar case, State v. Maik, 60 N.J. 203, 287 A.2d 715 (1972), the Supreme Court of New Jersey reached the same result. Chief Justice Weintraub wrote for a unanimous court:

"[The defendant claimed] that the drugs [LSD], acting upon [an] underlying illness, triggered or precipitated a psychotic state which continued after the direct or immediate influence of the drug had dissipated, and that it was the psychosis, rather than

[d] See, e.g., Vandy and Kay, LSD Psychosis or LSD-Induced Schizophrenia? A Multimethod Inquiry, 40 Arch. Gen. Psychiatry 877 (1983); Fairman and Fairman, Phencyclidine Abuse and Crime: A Psychiatric Perspective, 10 Bull.Amer. Acad. of Psychiatry and Law 171 (1982).

the drug, which rendered defendant unable to know right from wrong at the time of the killing. In other words, defendant urges that when a psychosis emerges from a fixed illness, we should not inquire into the identity of the precipitating event or action. Indeed, it may be said to be unlikely that the inquiry would be useful, for when, as here, the acute psychosis could equally be triggered by some other stress, known or unknown, which the defendant could not handle, a medical opinion as to what did in fact precipitate the psychosis is not apt to rise above a speculation among mere possibilities.

"We think it compatible with the philosophical basis of [the insanity defense] to accept the fact of a schizophrenic episode without inquiry into its etiology."

What principle emerges from these cases? Was an exculpatory defense allowed because the defendants were mentally ill *before* taking the drugs?[e] Or because they were mentally ill *after* taking the drugs? Neither court alludes to the fact that the defendant's possession and use of LSD were criminal acts. Should that make any difference?

(iii) **Toxic Psychosis.** Assume that both *Hall* and *Kelly* are correctly decided. In other words, assume (i) that a defendant is not entitled to an insanity instruction if the claimed mental impairment is directly attributable to the intoxicating effects of the drug—i.e., those effects which result from the direct action of the drug on the central nervous system during the period when it is pharmacologically active, but (ii) that a predisposed defendant who experiences a "functional" psychosis triggered by drug use may invoke the insanity defense. Which principle should control in the case of a "normal" person who uses an hallucinogenic drug and experiences a so-called "toxic psychosis"—i.e., a transient dysfunction of the brain which is directly attributable to the toxic effects of the drug but which outlasts the period of intoxication?

A toxic psychosis (or "delusional disorder") may vary in effect and length depending on the drug, the dose, the person's psychological status or "set," and the setting of use. For example, a single dose of LSD can induce a psychotic episode ranging from a transient "panic reaction" to a long-lasting disorder.[f] A single dose of PCP (phencyclidine) can cause a condition characterized by paranoid delusions and violent behavior lasting from several days to several weeks.[g]

---

[e] One court has said: "[I]f the pre-existing condition of mind of the accused is not such as would render him legally insane in and of itself, then the recent use of intoxicants causing stimulation or aggravation of the pre-existing condition to the point of insanity cannot be relied upon as a defense. . . ." Evilsizer v. State, 487 S.W.2d 113, 116 (Tex.Cr.App.1972).

[f] See generally, Jones, Mental Illness and Drugs: Pre-existing Psychopathology and Response to Psychoactive Drugs, in National Commission on Marihuana and Drug Abuse, Drug Use in America: Prob-

lem in Perspective, Appendix Vol. I, 373, 393 (1973).

[g] During the 1960's, PCP was studied experimentally in "normal" volunteers. The major finding of these studies was "that PCP had no equal in its ability to produce brief psychoses nearly indistinguishable from schizophrenia." Generally, these episodes began immediately after ingestion of the drug but lasted for several hours. They were often characterized by violently paranoid behavior. Recent clinical experience with PCP users experiencing toxic psychoses indicates that they

While a single dose of amphetamines would be unlikely to induce a toxic psychosis, a person who has used moderate or high doses of amphetamines for a long period may develop a disorder, characterized by delusions of persecution, indistinguishable from schizophrenia.

Should a toxic psychosis be regarded as within the range of risk voluntarily assumed by a user of hallucinogenic drugs? Or should such a condition have exculpatory significance despite the fact that the "insanity" is both temporary and unrelated to any pre-existing psychopathology?

5. **Pathological Intoxication: The Problem of Unanticipated Effects.** Section 2.08(4) of the Model Penal Code provides that intoxication resulting in substantial cognitive or volitional incapacity is a defense if it is not self-induced or if it "is pathological." Paragraph 5(c) defines "pathological intoxication" as "intoxication grossly excessive in degree, given the amount of the intoxicant, to which the actor does not know he is susceptible."

According to the psychiatric diagnostic manual, DSM-III, the essential feature of pathological intoxication (now called "alcohol idiosyncratic intoxication") is "marked behavioral change—usually to aggressiveness—that is due to the recent ingestion of alcohol insufficient to induce intoxication in most people."[h] This response, which may appear to involve loss of contact with reality, is a direct effect of the intoxication itself; the person will return to normal as the blood alcohol level falls. The disorder is thought to be associated with predisposing brain pathology as a result of which the individual may lose "tolerance" for alcohol.

Standing alone, this particular clinical condition is not especially important; it is extemely rare and has arisen in litigation only a handful of times.[i] However, it may be useful to ask whether the quoted provision in Section 2.08 stands for a more general proposition. Note that pathological intoxication represents the single instance in which the drafters of the Model Code endorsed a claim of excuse based on the direct effects of intoxication by a person who knowingly and voluntarily ingests an intoxicating substance in order to experience its intoxicating properties. In this sense, the provision qualifies the definition of self-induced intoxication. Consider a general statement of this principle:

can last considerably longer and that the nature and severity of the symptoms varies widely among individuals. See generally Luisada, The Phencyclidine Psychosis: Phenomenology and Treatment, in R. Petersen and R. Stillman (eds.), Phencyclidine (PCP) Abuse: An Appraisal 241 (1978).

[h] American Psychiatric Association, Diagnostic and Statistical Manual of Mental Disorders 132 (3d ed. 1980).

[i] For a case involving a successful claim of pathological intoxication, see Leggett v. State, 21 Tex.App. 382, 17 S.W. 159 (1886). For a recent case in which the claim was rejected, see Kane v. United States, 399 F.2d 730 (9th Cir. 1968). Kane was convicted of manslaughter in the killing of his wife. His condition was diagnosed as pathological intoxication by three of four expert psychiatrists and his medical history was strongly supportive of the diagnosis. Kane had suffered three head injuries, including one several months before the shooting. However, in dictum, the court observed that Kane's testimony showed that he had become aware, after the second injury, of the fact that a modest amount of alcohol would cause him to black out and experience amnesia, and that these effects intensified after the third injury.

"An extreme mental impairment which could not reasonably have been anticipated will not be regarded as self-induced even though the individual was aware of the tendency of the substance to cause intoxication." Would you favor such a provision?

Professor Jerome Hall made a similar proposal in General Principles of Criminal Law 554–56 (2d ed. 1966):*

"[T]he inexperienced inebriate . . . [should not] be held criminally liable for a harm committed under gross intoxication [e]sewhere defined as severe blunting of the capacity to understand the moral quality of the act in issue combined with a drastic lapse of inhibition. For such persons, there can be no valid reliance on the drinking to support liability, because, though 'voluntary,' it was quite innocent. . . .

"[S]ince drinking alcoholic liquor is not usually followed by gross intoxication and such intoxication does not usually lead to the commission of serious injuries, it follows that persons who commit them while grossly intoxicated should not be punished unless, at the time of sobriety and the voluntary drinking, they had such prior experience as to anticipate their intoxication and that they would become dangerous in that condition."

The commentators generally have been unenthusiastic about Professor Hall's proposal. They have emphasized the practical difficulties involved, and have argued that awareness of the dangers of gross intoxication does not depend on personal experience. Professor Paulsen's reaction was typical: "Our culture does not fail to give warning about drunkenness. The risks involved are so widely advertised that few can claim surprise and be believed." Does the "culture" give adequate warning to naive users of the potpourri of psychoactive drugs now so widely used? The dissenting judges in the *Hall* case did not think so:

". . . There is nothing to indicate [that Hall] knew [the drug] could induce hallucinations or lead to the frightening, debilitating effects of mind and body to which the doctors testified. The majority nevertheless holds [that the defendant's resulting drug intoxication was voluntary. I disagree. . . .

"[The term] voluntary as here used should relate to a knowledgeable acceptance of the danger and risk involved. . . ."

Do you agree? What is the Model Penal Code solution to such a case?

---

* Reprinted with the permission of the author and Bobbs-Merrill Co., Inc.

SUBSECTION D: DISPOSITION OF MENTALLY DISORDERED OFFENDERS

INTRODUCTORY NOTES ON THE DISPOSITION OF MENTALLY DISORDERED OFFENDERS

1. **Background.** The insanity defense is successfully raised in fewer than one per cent of all criminal cases. Moreover, persons acquitted by reason of insanity (NGI's) represent a very small proportion—less than 10 per cent—of those criminal defendants who eventually are placed in institutions for the mentally disordered. The great majority of persons sent to such institutions either have been committed after being found incompetent to stand trial or have been placed there after conviction to serve their sentences. The latter group is by far the larger.[a]

2. **Commitment of Persons Incompetent to Stand Trial.** Every Anglo-American jurisdiction forbids trial of a person who, as a result of mental disease or mental retardation, is incapable of understanding the proceedings or of assisting in the defense. Because this long-standing practice is regarded as "fundamental to an adversary system of justice," the United States Supreme Court has held that a judge is constitutionally required to request a competency determination whenever there is a bona fide doubt about the defendant's competency to proceed. See Drope v. Missouri, 420 U.S. 162 (1975).

If a person is found incompetent to stand trial, the criminal proceedings are suspended while he or she is committed for treatment. In the past, the incompetency commitment mooted the issue of criminal responsibility in most cases because these defendants were held indefinitely and the criminal proceedings were rarely revived. However, in Jackson v. Indiana, 406 U.S. 715 (1972), the Supreme Court held that a defendant committed solely on account of incapacity to stand trial "cannot be held more than a reasonable period of time necessary to determine whether there is a substantial probability that he will attain that capacity in the foreseeable future." If there is no substantial probability that the defendant will be restored to competency within the foreseeable future, or if the treatment provided does not succeed in advancing the defendant toward that goal, the state must either institute civil-commitment proceedings or release the defendant. Most states now require such a definitive determination within 18 months. The average length of hospitalization for incompetency commitments is now about six months.

The incompetency commitment still functions, in practice, as a substitute for insanity adjudication in many cases. Empirical studies have shown that most persons found incompetent to stand trial are not prosecuted for the criminal offenses that triggered their commitments.

[a] See generally J. Monahan & H. Steadman (eds.), Mentally Disordered Offenders: Perspectives from Law and Social Sciences (1981).

The charges against these defendants are routinely dropped when they are released. Only if the charges are especially serious are they likely to be prosecuted; in most of these cases, the insanity defense is then raised.

3. **Special Sentencing Provisions.** In the vast majority of cases, the criminal law defers consideration of the psychological dimensions of the offender's conduct until sentencing. At that time, judges in most states are empowered to take into account the defendant's dangerousness and amenability to treatment, as well as any claim of diminished responsibility, in choosing the type or severity of sentence.[b] In some states, the court's customary sentencing options are augmented by special "mentally disordered offender" provisions that permit the defendant to be confined in special institutions and that may extend the otherwise authorized period of confinement.[c] In a recent development, at least 12 states now permit or require defendants found "guilty but mentally ill" to be placed in secure psychiatric hospitals, in lieu of ordinary correctional facilities, for some portion of the term of imprisonment.[d] Finally, it should also be noted that most states permit mentally disordered prisoners to be transferred from prisons to psychiatric hospitals in the absence of a special verdict.

4. **Commitment of Persons Acquitted by Reason of Insanity.** Historically, persons acquitted by reason of insanity have been subject to special procedures requiring commitment to institutions for the "criminally insane" until such time as they "recovered their sanity." However, little systematic attention was given to the procedures or criteria governing these decisions, or to the conditions in the institutions for the criminally insane, until the early 1970's, when the traditional restrictive approach was challenged on both constitutional and therapeutic grounds. It was argued that the substantial disparity between "ordinary" civil commitment procedures and the NGI[e] procedures was constitutionally unjustified. Moreover, the mental health community argued that advances in pharmacological treatment had reduced the therapeutic need for long-term hospitalization in most cases. In response to the numerous judicial rulings on the subject, every state has revised its NGI dispositional statute. Although the initial trend was to make the NGI statutes less restrictive, and bring them into congruence with ordinary "civil" commitment statutes, increased public concern about premature release of dangerous insanity acquittees led to a second generation of reforms in many states.

This flurry of legislative and judicial activity has left the current generation of NGI dispositional statutes in considerable disarray.[f] In some states, insanity acquittees are subject to the same criteria and

[b] The significance of mental disorder in sentencing is discussed in N. Morris, Madness and the Criminal Law (1982), and Morse, Justice, Mercy, and Craziness, 36 Stan.L.Rev. 1485 (1984).

[c] These statutes are discussed in G. Dix, Special Dispositional Alternatives for Abnormal Offender: Developments in the Law (1981).

[d] The "guilty but mentally ill" verdict is considered at pages 750–52, infra.

[e] The term "NGI" is commonly used to refer to defendants found not guilty by reason of insanity.

[f] The statutes are surveyed and discussed in German and Singer, Punishing the Not Guilty: Hospitalization of Persons Acquitted by Reason of Insanity, 29 Rutgers

procedures governing civil commitment of the mentally ill. In most states, the procedures, though similar to those governing civil commitment, vary in a few significant respects. For example, while a civilly committed patient may be hospitalized for emergency evaluation for only a short period—up to one week, perhaps—NGI's may be committed for evaluation for up to 90 days. In addition, whereas a civilly committed patient is entitled to be discharged without judicial approval whenever the medical staff determines that hospitalization is no longer necessary, statutes governing insanity acquittees typically require a judicial order authorizing discharge. Finally, in a third group of states, the procedures differ substantially from those governing civil commitment. Typically, the statutes provide for automatic, indefinite commitment of the insanity acquittee and place the burden on the acquittee to prove that he or she is no longer committable. Even in these states, however, the acquittee is usually entitled to periodic administrative and judicial review of his or her status and the burden of proof may shift to the state if the hospital authorities recommend discharge.

The ongoing debate about the desirability and scope of the insanity defense is inextricably linked to the controversy concerning the proper disposition of insanity acquittees. This controversy is explored in the next case and its accompanying notes.

IN RE TORSNEY

New York Court of Appeals, 1979.
47 N.Y.2d 667, 420 N.Y.S.2d 192, 394 N.E.2d 262.

JASEN, JUDGE. In a tragic incident occurring on Thanksgiving Day, November 25, 1976, appellant Robert Torsney, a New York City police officer, shot and killed a 15-year-old black youth. He was indicted and charged with second-degree murder. . . .[a]

[The defendant pleaded not guilty by reason of insanity. The prosecution called the five police officers who were with Torsney when he shot the victim. They testified that they responded to a radio call indicating that a man with a gun had been seen at an address in Brooklyn. When they arrived, they discovered that the difficulty involved a family dispute and went up to the apartment. Torsney unlocked his gun from his holster as he was climbing the stairs. After dealing with the disputants, the officers began to descend. As they were doing so, the victim walked up to Torsney and asked if the police had come from apartment 7–D. Torsney responded "damn right" and shot the boy point blank in the forehead. He then walked to his car, unloaded the spent shell, inserted a new bullet, and reholstered the gun. None of the officers reported seeing a gun or any other metal in

L.Rev. 1011 (1976); Morris, Dealing Responsibly with the Criminally Irresponsible, 1982 Ariz.St.L.J. 855; Note, Rules for an Exceptional Class: The Commitment and Release of Persons Acquitted of Violent Offenses by Reason of Insanity, 57 N.Y.U.L.Rev. 281 (1982); Note, Commit-

ment Following an Insanity Acquittal, 94 Harv.L.Rev. 605 (1981).

[a] The following summary of the evidence is based on the trial transcript. [Footnote by eds.]

the victim's possession. Other witnesses said the victim's hands were at his side when he was shot.

[After Torsney got in the car, one of his fellow officers asked him "what the fuck did you do?" He reportedly responded: "I don't know, Matty, what did I do?" He was apparently calm. At the stationhouse, his commanding officer asked him what happened and he said "what difference does it make? You're guilty anyway."

[Torsney testified that he remembered having his hand on his unlocked gun, seeing the victim pull out a silver object that looked like a gun, and firing. He said he did not remember hearing the noise of the shot and that "everything after the shot went to blur." He remembered walking back to the car in a daze. Other evidence indicated that this was the first time Torsney had fired his gun while on duty.

[Defendant's expert witness, Dr. Schwartz, testified that he concluded that Torsney had psychomotor epilepsy at the time of the offense which he admitted was "a very uncertain diagnosis to make." He explained that the stress of the situation and his memories of cruelty at the hands of his father could have triggered a psychomotor seizure. He said he was 70 per cent certain of his diagnosis. The prosecution's expert witness, Dr. Spiegel, concluded that there was no evidence of psychosis and that a seizure disorder was clinically inconsistent with the evidence; in particular, he said, a total amnesia is a necessary symptom of a psychomotor seizure and any violent behavior during a seizure would not be purposeful. Instead, Dr. Spiegel testified, Torsney had a "neurotic character disorder with difficulty in controlling his impulses, especially under stress, and a proneness to hysterical disassociation." In short, he said, Torsney panicked. He concluded that this condition was not a mental disease. The jury returned a verdict of not guilty by reason of insanity.[b]

On that same date, Torsney was ordered committed to the custody of the Commissioner of the Department of Mental Hygiene, pursuant to Section 330.20 of the Criminal Procedure Law.[c] After initial commit-

---

[b] Section 30.05(1) of the New York Penal Law then provided:

"A person is not criminally responsible for conduct if at the time of such conduct, as a result of mental disease or defect, he lacks substantial capacity to know or appreciate either:

    (a) The nature and consequence of such conduct; or

    (b) That such conduct was wrong."

[Footnote by eds.]

[c] Section 330.20 of The New York Criminal Procedure Law then provided, in relevant part:

"(1) Upon rendition of a verdict of acquittal by reason of mental disease or defect, the court must order the defendant to be committed to the custody of the commissioner of mental hygiene to

be placed in an appropriate institution . . . .

"(2) If the commissioner of mental hygiene is of the opinion that a person committed to his custody . . . may be discharged or released on condition without danger to himself or to others, he must make application for the discharge or release of such person in a report to the court by which such person was committed. . . . The court may then appoint up to two qualified psychiatrists . . . to examine such person [and] report . . . their opinion as to his mental condition. . . .

"(3) If the court is satisfied that the committed person may be discharged or released on condition without danger to himself or others, the court must order his discharge, or his release on such conment to Mid-Hudson Psychiatric Center, Torsney was transferred to Creedmoor Psychiatric Center on March 3, 1978. Shortly thereafter, a recommendation was made to the director of Creedmoor that inasmuch as Torsney was not dangerous or mentally ill, he should be released. On May 19, 1978, a special release committee was convened for the purpose of examining Torsney to determine his suitability for release. After the special release committee agreed with the staff's findings and recommendations, in which the then director of Creedmoor, Dr. Werner, concurred, the findings and recommendations were reported to the commissioner. The commissioner thereupon convened an independent review panel, which also concurred in the recommendation.

Thereafter, on July 20, 1978 . . . the commissioner petitioned the committing court for an order discharging Torsney from his custody. The court ordered a full evidentiary hearing [and] sustained the petition and ordered Torsney released . . . upon the following conditions: (i) that he not be permitted to carry a gun; (ii) that he not be a police officer or peace officer; (iii) that he continue as an outpatient at Creedmoor for a period of five years on conditions to be imposed as determined by Creedmoor Psychiatric Center; and (iv) if within five years after the conditional release the court should determine after a hearing that for the safety of Mr. Torsney or of others the conditional release should be revoked, the court must recommit him. On cross appeals taken by the district attorney and by the commissioner and Torsney, the appellate division reversed and ordered that Torsney be recommitted to the custody of the Commissioner of Mental Hygiene.

On this appeal, two issues are presented for our review. The threshold issue is whether the appellate division properly construed the standard for release of persons held in the custody of the Commissioner of the Department of Mental Hygiene. . . . Contingent upon resolution of this issue is the second issue: namely, whether evaluated under the proper standard for release the weight of the credible evidence presented at the hearing requires the detainee's continued confinement, discharge or release on condition. . . .

The purpose of automatic commitment after acquittal of a crime by reason of mental disease or defect is a narrow one: to determine the mental condition of the person committed on the date of acquittal. Notwithstanding the literal terms of Section 330.20, automatic commitment of persons acquitted of crimes by reason of mental disease or defect is constitutionally permissible only for a reasonable period of time—that is, sufficient time to permit an examination and report as to the detainee's sanity. Moreover, a prompt hearing must be held on this

ditions as the court determines to be necessary. If the court is not so satisfied, it must promptly order a hearing to determine whether such person may safely be discharged or released. . . . The commissioner of mental hygiene must make suitable provision for the care and supervision by the department of mental hygiene of persons released conditionally under this section.

"(4) If within five years after the conditional release of a committed person, the court shall determine, after a hearing, that for the safety of such person or the safety of others his conditional release should be revoked, the court must forthwith order him recommitted to the commissioner of mental hygiene . . .."

[Footnote by eds.].

issue, a hearing at which a person committed under Section 330.20—like any other involuntarily committed patient seeking release from custody—is entitled to a jury trial. . . .

The purpose of this hearing, characterized as a civil proceeding, is to determine whether the detainee "may be discharged or released on condition without danger to himself or others." The appellate division equated the standard of dangerousness under Section 330.20 with the standard of dangerousness for involuntary civil commitment under the Mental Hygiene Law. Specifically, the court incorporated by reference the standard for involuntary admission contained in Section 9.37 of the Mental Hygiene Law, which provides for the admission of

"any person who, in the opinion of the director of community services or his designee, has a mental illness for which immediate inpatient care and treatment in a hospital is appropriate and which is likely to result in serious harm to himself or others; 'likelihood of serious harm' shall mean:

"1. substantial risk of physical harm to himself as manifested by threats of or attempts at suicide or serious bodily harm or other conduct demonstrating that he is dangerous to himself, or

"2. a substantial risk of physical harm to other persons as manifested by homicidal or other violent behavior by which others are placed in reasonable fear of serious physical harm."

In adopting this definitional standard, however, the appellate division, although noting that this section requires as a condition precedent to application of the "likelihood of serious harm" test that the patient suffer a mental illness requiring immediate inpatient care and treatment, expressly held that a detainee under Section 330.20 need not satisfy this [criterion] to preclude his discharge. In that court's view, "[a] dangerous detainee [can] be confined even if not mentally ill or in need of immediate treatment, under Section 330.20." We disagree.
. . . .

Unquestionably, the unique status of persons acquitted of a crime by reason of mental disease or defect permits the state to treat this "exceptional class" somewhat differently from other individuals believed suffering from mental disease or defect. Because such persons have demonstrated past anti-social behavior, the state is permitted to engage in what may be broadly termed a presumption that the causative mental illness or defect continues beyond the date of the criminal conduct to the date of acquittal. . . . Of course, the flaw in viewing this principle as a true presumption is readily apparent: namely, the possibility that years may have intervened between commission of the crime charged and the date of acquittal. The significance of this contingency is further buttressed when consideration is given to the fact that in New York . . . an acquittal predicated on [insanity] indicates only that the People failed to prove beyond a reasonable doubt that the defendant was criminally responsible for his act and not that the jury found by a preponderance of the evidence that he was suffering from a mental disease or defect on the date of the commission of the crime charged. . . .

Thus, it may be said more accurately that the presumption flowing from an acquittal by reason of mental disease or defect does not presume that a person so acquitted presently suffers from mental disease or defect, but, rather, posits merely that having raised this defense and having previously engaged in anti-social behavior, he has demonstrated sufficient grounds for further examination to determine his present need for treatment and confinement as opposed to immediate release. . . . It is for this purpose only—a prompt examination and report as to sanity—that such a person may be automatically committed to the custody of the commissioner of mental hygiene upon acquittal. . . .

Beyond automatic commitment of persons found not guilty by reason of mental disease or defect for a reasonable period to determine their present sanity, justification for distinctions in treatment between persons involuntarily committed under the Mental Hygiene Law and persons committed under Section 330.20 draws impermissibly thin. Clearly, the Mental Hygiene Law requires for involuntary civil commitment that the patient be mentally ill and in need of immediate inpatient treatment. Absent such a finding, a dangerous propensity is, in itself, insufficient to permit involuntary commitment. In our view, to permit commitment of a person acquitted of a crime by reason of mental disease or defect on a lesser substantive predicate would run afoul of the constitutional guarantees to due process and equal protection of the laws. . . .

In the present case, we deal with an individual [who] has been charged with a crime, has stood trial, and has been acquitted by reason of mental disease or defect. That equal protection mandates that he be afforded the same procedural rights governing his release from custody as any other involuntarily committed person is settled. Similarly, in our view, appellant's petition for release must be measured by the same substantive standards governing involuntary civil commitment of any other individual. . . . Thus, we interpret Section 330.20 [to require] a detainee's release unless it is found that he is presently dangerous to himself or others by reason of a mental disease or defect. . . .

With this constitutionally mandated interpretation of Section 330.-20 in mind, we proceed to the second issue in this case: whether the weight of the credible evidence presented at the hearing requires continued confinement or release of the detainee on condition. Torsney committed the crime for which he was acquitted by reason of mental illness or defect on November 25, 1976. . . .

Of course, the question whether on [the evidence at trial] the People failed to demonstrate beyond a reasonable doubt that Torsney was criminally responsible for his act is not now material. Suffice it to say that upon the testimony produced at trial Torsney was acquitted on November 30, 1977, of the crime charged by reason of mental illness or defect. Thereupon he was admitted to Mid-Hudson Psychiatric Center on December 6, 1977, pursuant to the automatic-commitment procedure contained in Section 330.20.

[During the eight-month period between his commitment and the filing of the release petition, Torsney was examined by at least 12 different psychiatrists, including the two review panels specially convened to evalute his present condition. These examiners unanimously concluded that he suffered from no present mental illness, that he had adjusted well to his living conditions, and that no psychiatric justification existed for his continued confinement. The two psychiatrists appointed by the trial court under Section 330.20 filed reports agreeing with these findings. At the hearing, 18 witnesses testified to this same effect. After reviewing this evidence in detail, the court continued:]

Integrating the testimony elicited at the hearing with the proper standard for discharge or release on condition under Section 330.20, we conclude that the weight of the credible evidence mandates that the order of the hearing court be reinstated. One thing is abundantly clear: Every opinion offered at the hearing substantiated Torsney's claim that he is neither suffering from a mental illness or defect nor dangerous to himself or others. We reject as constitutionally suspect the interpretation of Section 330.20 given by the appellate division, which would permit a detainee's continued institutionalization on a vague concept of dangerousness unrelated to mental illness or defect and for which no immediate in-patient treatment is required. . . .

An individual's liberty cannot be deprived by "warehousing" him in a mental institution when he is not suffering from a mental illness or defect and in no need of in-patient care and treatment [6] on a ground which amounts to a presumption of a dangerous propensity flowing from, as in this case, an isolated, albeit tragic, incident occurring years ago. Were this the standard for involuntary institutionalization, logical extension would require that anyone convicted of a violent crime should upon completion of his sentence similarly be required to demonstrate that he or she is not dangerous before his release into the community. Whatever its label, confinement on a showing of mere propensity amounts to nothing more than preventive detention, a concept foreign to our constitutional order. . . .

The friction between the operation of a perhaps theoretically subjective rule permitting acquittals on something less than uniform notions of mental disease or defect and the cry of due process for objective criteria upon which to predicate continued institutionalization is amply illustrated in the case at bar. Perhaps resolution of this conflict lies in re-evaluation of the scope and applicability of the insanity defense. . . . Given the unsettled state of the law in this area, we do not suggest that in a proper case a "personality disorder" which resulted in a finding of dangerousness and which required treatment would not be

[6] We do not suggest . . . that a person suffering from a mental disease or defect which is "untreatable" and who constitutes a danger to himself and society as a result of this disease or defect may not be institutionalized. In such instances it is obvious that the individual is in need of treatment. The stark reality that an effective mode of treatment has at a given point in time remained elusive does not dictate a contrary result.

sufficient to preclude a detainee's discharge or release on condition. Suffice it to say, on the present record it is clear that Torsney suffers from neither a mental illness or defect nor a personality disorder which renders him dangerous to himself or others. He should, therefore, be released pursuant to the conditions properly imposed by the hearing court.

Accordingly, the order of the appellate division should be reversed.
. . .

WACHTLER, JUDGE (dissenting). The court holds today that a man committed to a psychiatric institution because he shot and killed a young boy should be released despite expert psychiatric testimony that under similar circumstances he would be prone to act again with the same uncontrolled violence. I cannot agree with such a result and therefore dissent. The record offers insufficient proof that the appellant, Robert Torsney, no longer suffers from the very symptoms and personality disorder that precipitated the tragic killing of Randolph Evans. Releasing Torsney at this time would not only deprive him of the opportunity for rehabilitation offered in a psychiatric institution, but would also subject the public to the danger that Torsney might again be overcome by uncontrollably destructive impulses. . . .

I would hold that the detention of a person committed to a mental institution in accordance with Section 330.20 should continue unless he proves that he no longer suffers from the symptomatology which made him dangerous. . . .

The verdict of not guilty by reason of mental disease or defect presumably resulted from a finding by the jury that the defendant at the time of the wrongful act suffered from symptoms which substantially limited his appreciation of "[t]he nature and consequence of such conduct" or "[t]hat such conduct was wrong." The purpose for institutionalizing someone acquitted for this reason is twofold: to protect society from the threat that, because of a mental disorder, the detainee might again commit acts of violence . . . and to rehabilitate him so that he may be released into society without the risk of further harm. Should the symptoms of the mental disorder disappear, both justifications for continued confinement disappear as well. . . . It is therefore logical that to secure his release the detainee should have to prove that he no longer suffers from the symptomatology associated with the wrongful act. . . .

But I cannot agree with the plurality that a dangerous detainee must be released if he does not suffer from a "mental disease or defect" which fits into a psychiatric category and has a particular psychiatric label. Over the years the definition of mental illness has shifted according to the prevailing doctrine of psychological thought. In addition, there is often a lack of agreement among psychiatrists as to whether a given mode of unusual or deviant behavior constitutes a "mental illness" at all. We would therefore be unwise to bind our legal determinations to psychiatric theories which are not only undergoing constant reexamination and modification, but which are designed to deal with medical rather than legal problems. Our primary concern must be to protect the public from those who, for psychological reasons, have caused and are likely in the future to cause serious harm to others. To release such a person merely because his symptoms elude classification is indefensible.

. . . Because a person cannot be civilly committed unless he is "mentally ill," [it is argued] that a person who has been acquitted of a killing by reason of mental disease or defect must be released unless he too is "mentally ill," despite the absence of any such requirement in Section 330.20. The equation fails because there is a critical distinction between the two classes; the person acquitted of a violent crime by reason of mental defect has necessarily demonstrated by his own hand that he is a menace to society, whereas the person sought to be civilly committed has not. The state may not ignore the greater threat posed by the acquitted person. The compelling state interest to shield the public from this threat justifies that the two classes be dealt with somewhat differently.

. . . When [the] trial evidence is compared to the testimony presented at the hearing, it becomes all too apparent that Torsney's condition has never changed substantially and that he remains as dangerous today as he was on the day he shot Randolph Evans.

At the [Brelease] hearing, Dr. Stanley Portnow, one of the two independent court-appointed psychiatrists, noted that Torsney was not suffering from a classical form of psychosis or neurosis but rather labeled Torsney's condition a "personality disorder." Dr. Portnow further stated: "My diagnosis would have been constant throughout the entire spectrum of events and that diagnosis would read 'impulsive or explosive personality.'" "Stress," according to Dr. Portnow, "is frequently the trigger by which the impulsive personality fires off." He also expressed his belief that Torsney should face stress in small quantities to be reasonably sure that another catastrophe would not occur. Explaining why he recommended a gradual release procedure the doctor said: "I attempted to protect both Mr. Torsney and the community by recommending a pre-release procedure to minimize the severity of the stress upon this impulsive personality which already, on one occasion, has exploded, the result having been a catastrophe." The other court-appointed psychiatrist, Dr. Milton Hollar, agreed that Torsney is "impulsive," "volatile" and "explosive." Dr. Hollar also feared that under stressful circumstances Torsney might erupt again. Nevertheless the doctor recommended Torsney's release because as a nonpsychotic patient, Torsney's institutionalization was not medically warranted.

During the period that Torsney was detained in the Mid-Hudson Psychiatric Center his principal therapist was Dr. Mark Vandenbergh who conducted five to eight sessions with Torsney of about one hour each. Dr. Vandenbergh stated that Torsney was susceptible to hysterical dissociative reactions under stress. It was such a reaction that precipitated the slaying of Evans, and according to Dr. Vandenbergh a violent explosion could occur again under similar circumstances. In view of these findings, Dr. Vandenbergh's conclusion that Torsney was neither mentally ill nor in need of treatment are of little moment. Likewise, Dr. Alan Halpern, a staff psychologist at Mid-Hudson who examined Torsney only once, found some evidence of a neurotic character disorder—an hysterical personality. Dr. Halpern also observed that Torsney consistently seemed to lose his emotional control when faced with emotionally laden test situations. . . .

It is most important to remember that in analyzing this testimony, the trier of the facts need not accept the ultimate conclusions of expert witnesses regarding a patient's dangerousness or the propriety of his continued confinement, for the underlying facts as attested to by the witnesses may support contrary conclusions. . . . Hence although several psychiatrists testified that Torsney should be released, I would agree with the view expressed by the appellate division that their testimony strongly indicates the need for his further confinement.

The hearing testimony overwhelmingly demonstrates that Torsney has remained as volatile and explosive as he was on the date of the killing. The evidence shows that his explosiveness is a manifestation of a personality disorder [and] an hysterical dissociative reaction, the same diagnosis offered by Dr. Spiegel at the murder trial. According to these experts it was this disorder that impelled Torsney to kill Randolph Evans, and according to the same experts it is this disorder that could drive Torsney to commit a similar act of violence in the future. Clearly Torsney's condition has not changed. Indeed he has not received individualized treatment at either Mid-Hudson or Creedmoor.

. . . I agree, of course, that hospital confinement should never be abused to deprive someone of his liberty unfairly. However, when a person, driven by an explosive personality disorder, has proven by an act of senseless violence that he is a menace to others, so long as the psychological condition persists it is our obligation to protect the public from further acts of violence that he may commit.

Accordingly, I would affirm the order of the appellate division.

NOTES ON THE DISPOSITION OF PERSONS
ACQUITTED BY REASON OF INSANITY

1. **The Statutory Response to *Torsney*.** The year after *Torsney* was decided by the Court of Appeals, the New York legislature overhauled the statutory provisions governing commitment and release of insanity acquittees. In general, the legislation was designed to assure continuing long-term judicial control of insanity acquittees within the framework announced by the Court of Appeals in *Torsney* and earlier decisions. Under the complicated new statute, the acquittee may be held for up to 30 days for the purpose of psychiatric evaluation of his or her present condition. The court must then hold a commitment hearing to decide which of three statutory categories is applicable.

If the court determines [a] that the acquittee has a "dangerous mental disorder," [b] it must issue an order committing the acquittee to a secure mental health facility. The order is valid for six months, after which the acquittee is entitled to another hearing. If the court finds that the acquittee continues to have a "dangerous mental disorder," it must issue a retention order which is valid for up to one year. Second and subsequent retention orders may be issued for up to two years. Whenever the court determines that the acquittee no longer suffers from a dangerous mental disorder, the acquittee is subject to a mandatory three-year period of conditional release.

If the court determines that the acquittee does not have a "dangerous mental disorder" but is "mentally ill," [c] the acquittee is committed to state custody to be treated in the same manner as involuntarily committed "civil" patients, except that the acquittee is subject to an "order of conditions" issued by the court. If, during the effective period of this order, the acquittee is found to have a "dangerous mental disorder," commitment under the provisions previously described must follow.

Finally, if the court determines that the acquittee does not have a "dangerous mental disorder" and is not "mentally ill," the acquittee must be released from confinement. However, the court is authorized to issue an order of conditions even in this category of cases, and the acquittee may thereafter be committed if he or she is found to have a "dangerous mental disorder."

2. **State v. Gebarski.** Although procedural questions regularly arise under NGI commitment statutes, *Torsney* is one of the few cases focusing squarely on the substantive criteria for commitment and release of insanity acquittees. It should be contrasted with State v. Gebarski, 90 Wis.2d 754, 280 N.W.2d 672 (1979). Gebarski lived next door to his estranged wife and her parents. On the day of the offense, he suddenly appeared at an upstairs window of his house and began firing a rifle at his wife and her family. After killing his wife and her 12-year-old sister, he said "John, there is one for you" and shot a family friend. He made a similar remark before firing at his wife's mother. After a jury trial, he was found not guilty of the murders and assaults by reason of insanity, based upon psychiatric testimony that he was

---

[a] The statute is not explicit about the level of proof. In People v. Escobar, 61 N.Y.2d 431, 462 N.E.2d 1171 (1984), the Court of Appeals held that the state is required to prove the applicable commitment criteria by a preponderance of the evidence.

[b] Under § 330.20(2)(c) of the Criminal Procedure Law, the acquittee has a dangerous mental disorder if he or she "currently suffers from a 'mental illness'" and "because of such condition, currently constitutes a physical danger to himself or others." The definition of "mental illness," incorporated by reference from the Mental Hygiene Law, is "an affliction with

a mental disease or mental condition which is manifested by a disorder or disturbance in behavior, feeling, thinking, or judgment to such an extent that the person afflicted requires care, treatment and rehabilitation."

[c] Under § 330.20(2)(d) of the Criminal Procedure Law, a person is "mentally ill" for this purpose who "suffers from a mental illness for which care and treatment as a patient in the in-patient services of a psychiatric center . . . is essential to [the person's] welfare" and whose "judgment is so impaired that [the person] is unable to understand the need for such care and treatment . . . ."

suffering an "acute psychotic reaction" at the time of the crimes. He was subsequently committed for treatment.

Three years later, Gebarski petitioned for re-examination under the applicable Wisconsin statutes and requested a jury trial. The psychiatric witnesses all testified that his condition had been successfully treated and that he was not currently psychotic; the witnesses also indicated that he appeared to be safe, although they all conceded that they could not be certain that he would not experience another psychotic episode if exposed to sufficient stress. Gebarski submitted a proposed jury instruction to the effect that he was entitled to be released unless the jury found both (i) that he was presently mentally ill and a proper subject for treatment and (ii) that he was dangerous to himself or others. He based the proposed instruction on the Wisconsin statutes governing civil commitment of the mentally ill. The trial court instead charged the jury that the state had to prove only that he was dangerous. A finding of present mental illness was not required. The Supreme Court of Wisconsin affirmed. After holding that the legislature "did not intend to [apply] the civil-commitment standards" to proceedings for release of NGI's, the court rejected the constitutional arguments accepted by the *Torsney* majority.

3. **Questions on *Torsney* and *Gebarski*.** *Torsney* and *Gebarski* raise many difficult questions. Should the criteria of commitment and release be the same for insanity acquittees as for civil patients? If so, are you prepared to permit defendants such as Joy Baker, Torsney and Gebarski to be released soon after the NGI verdict? If not, on what basis can you justify different criteria, and what should those criteria be? Should a person be confined despite the fact that symptoms of a major mental illness are no longer present? Despite the fact that the illness has been successfully treated and is "in remission"? Should the concept of "mental illness" or "mental disease" be defined to encompass personality disorders for purposes of NGI dispositional statutes even if they are not encompassed by normal civil commitment statutes? Should this depend on the definition of "mental disease" used for the insanity defense? Should dangerousness alone be a sufficient predicate for confinement as the *Gebarski* court held?

Regardless of the definition of mental illness, how should "dangerousness" be defined? Should the acquittee be entitled to release in the absence of a determination of imminent danger to oneself or others (the normal civil commitment standard)? If the predicted danger need not be imminent, within what time frame should the prediction be made? Does the occurrence of the criminal act have evidentiary significance in assessing the potential for dangerous conduct in the future? If so, does the criminal act lose its predictive value at some point? After the initial commitment, who should bear the burden of proof on the dangerousness issue? What must be proved? Should the acquittee be required to prove that future violence is unlikely? Would Torsney or Gebarski ever be entitled to release under such a standard? How should these issues be resolved if the offense with which the defendant was charged involved no violence or threat of violence?

4. *Jones v. United States.* Although NGI dispositional statutes were first exposed to intensive constitutional scrutiny in the early 1970's, the Supreme Court did not address the subject until Jones v. United States, 463 U.S. 354 (1983). Michael Jones was charged with attempting to steal a jacket from a department store on September 19, 1975. He pleaded insanity and the government did not contest the plea. After the court found him not guilty by reason of insanity, Jones was automatically committed to St. Elizabeth's hospital. Under the District of Columbia NGI commitment statute, Jones was entitled 50 or more days thereafter to request a "release hearing" at which he bore the burden of proving that he was no longer mentally ill or dangerous. At Jones' first release hearing on May 25, 1976, the court found that he was not entitled to release. A second release hearing was held on February 22, 1977. Jones' counsel requested at this hearing that he be released or civilly committed, on the ground that his cumulative hospital confinement had exceeded the one-year maximum period of incarceration for the offense charged. The court denied the request and continued Jones' commitment under the NGI statute. The District of Columbia Court of Appeals affirmed, en banc, with three judges dissenting.

In a 5–4 decision, the Supreme Court affirmed. The Court addressed two questions: whether the District's automatic commitment procedure after an insanity acquittal violated the due process clause; and, if his initial commitment was constitutional, whether he was entitled to be released or civilly committed upon expiration of the one-year maximum term prescribed for the offense of attempted petit larceny.

(i) **Automatic Commitment of Insanity Acquittees.** In the District of Columbia, as is the case in most states, the defendant bears the burden of proving an insanity defense by a preponderance of the evidence. The question before the Court was whether the findings underlying Jones' insanity verdict established a constitutionally adequate basis for his commitment. Justice Powell, writing for the Court, said it did:

> "[An insanity verdict] establishes two facts: (i) The defendant committed an act that constitutes a criminal offense, and (ii) he committed the act because of mental illness. Congress has determined that these findings constitute an adequate basis for hospitalizing the acquittee as a dangerous and mentally ill person. . . . We cannot say that it was unreasonable and therefore unconstitutional for Congress to make this determination.

> "The fact that a person has been found, beyond a reasonable doubt, to have committed a criminal act certainly indicates dangerousness. . . . Indeed, the concrete evidence generally may be at least as persuasive as any predictions about dangerousness that might be made in a civil commitment proceeding. . . .

> "Nor can we say that it was unreasonable for Congress to determine that the insanity acquittal supports an inference of

continuing mental illness. It comports with common sense to conclude that someone whose mental illness was sufficient to lead him to commit a criminal act is likely to remain ill and in need of treatment. . . . Because a hearing is provided within 50 days of the commitment, there is assurance that every acquittee has a prompt opportunity to obtain release if he has recovered. . . .

"We hold that when a criminal defendant establishes by a preponderance of the evidence that he is not guilty of a crime by reason of insanity, the Constitution permits the government, on the basis of the insanity judgment, to confine him to a mental institution until such time as he has regained his sanity or is no longer a danger to himself or society. This holding accords with the widely and reasonably held view that insanity acquittees constitute a special class that should be treated differently from other candidates for commitment. . . . "

Justice Brennan's dissenting opinion concluded that the insanity verdict did not provide "a constitutionally adequate basis for involuntary, indefinite commitment" and that the government should be required to prove the commitment criteria, in a post-verdict hearing, by clear and convincing evidence.

Does this aspect of the Court's holding in *Jones* have any bearing on the issues resolved by the New York Court of Appeals in *Torsney*? Recall that under the law in effect at the time of Torsney's trial, the prosecution was required to disprove his claim of insanity beyond a reasonable doubt.[d] Did his insanity verdict establish a constitutionally adequate substantive predicate for commitment? Recall also that the *Torsney* court concluded that the substantive standards governing commitment and release of insanity acquittees should be equivalent to those governing involuntary civil commitment of any other individual; unlike the *Gebarski* court, the New York Court of Appeals thought this conclusion to be "constitutionally mandated." Does *Jones* shed any light on this question?

Finally, consider the matter of release. Even if a state may presume that an insanity acquittee continues to be mentally ill and dangerous, shifting the burden to the acquittee to prove eligibility for release, how long may this presumption remain in force? Indefinitely? Should the state be required at some point to prove that the acquittee continues to be mentally ill and dangerous? How does this question relate to the criteria for commitment and release? How does it relate to the second issue raised in *Jones*?

(ii) **Commitment and Proportionality.** The Supreme Court also addressed Jones' contention "that an acquittee's hypothetical maximum sentence provides the conditional limit for his commitment." He argued that a comparison of the NGI and civil-commitment procedures demonstrated that an NGI commitment is inescapably based on "puni-

[d] In 1984, the New York legislature modified its insanity defense to place the burden of persuasion on the defendant by a preponderance of the evidence. See New York Penal Law § 40.15 (1984 Supp.).

tive" considerations and that, accordingly, the justification for the special procedures lapses after expiration of the maximum sentence authorized for the offense that triggered the commitment. This contention had been accepted by three judges on the District of Columbia Court of Appeals. They reasoned:

"[NGI] acquittees are not confined to mental institutions for medical reasons alone. They are confined there in part because society is unwilling to allow those who have committed crimes to escape without paying for their crimes. The intent of the statute is partially punitive, and thus the [stricter procedures governing commitment and release of NGI's] reflect this added burden on the defendant. Because of this punitive purpose, the maximum statutory period of confinement becomes relevant, for at that point society no longer has a valid interest in continued confinement on the basis of a shortcut procedure. . . . Society's right to punish Michael Jones for his first offense, a misdemeanor— [attempting to steal] a coat—has long since expired. . . . Michael Jones should be released unless civilly committed."

The Supreme Court rejected this analysis. Writing for the majority, Justice Powell explained:

"A particular sentence of incarceration is chosen to reflect society's view of the proper response to commission of a particular criminal offense, based on a variety of considerations such as retribution, deterrence, and rehabilitation. The state may punish a person convicted of a crime even if satisfied that he is unlikely to commit further crimes.

"Different considerations underlie commitment of an insanity acquittee. As he was not convicted, he may not be punished. His confinement rests on his continuing illness and dangerousness. Thus, under the District of Columbia statute, no matter how serious the act committed by the acquittee, he may be released within 50 days of his acquittal if he has recovered. In contrast, one who committed a less serious act may be confined for a longer period if he remains ill and dangerous. There simply is no necessary correlation between severity of the offense and length of time necessary for recovery. The length of the acquittee's hypothetical criminal sentence therefore is irrelevant to the purposes of his commitment."

In dissent, Justice Brennan took the view that since Jones' commitability had not been proved by clear and convincing evidence, he could not be held beyond the maximum sentence for attempted petit larceny. Justice Brennan did appear to concede, however, that indefinite hospitalization would be permissible if the commitment were predicated upon constitutionally adequate proof.

Did Justice Powell accurately characterize the underlying purpose of NGI commitment? Is it so clear that an NGI commitment does not have a "partially punitive" purpose, as claimed by the dissenting judges on the Court of Appeals? Does it have a punitive effect? Assuming that the justifying purpose is therapeutic restraint rather than punishment for an offense, does it follow that the seriousness of the triggering offense should be irrelevant in determining the length of an NGI commitment?   In determining the criteria and procedures governing release?

5. **Relation Between Automatism and Insanity Defenses.**   One of the underlying difficulties in the *Torsney* case is the fact that virtually all of the other clinical examiners disagreed with the defense psychiatrist who testified that Torsney was suffering from epilepsy at the time of the offense and that the shooting occurred during a psychomotor seizure.   According to all subsequent examiners, Torsney exhibited no signs of epilepsy; essentially they agreed with the prosecution's trial expert who had testified that Torsney probably had panicked when he saw what he erroneously thought was a gun in the victim's hand.

If Torsney in fact had epilepsy, was he entitled to outright acquittal rather than acquittal on grounds of insanity?   Recall the discussion of the voluntary-act requirement, pages 152–58, supra.   Muscular contractions occurring during an epileptic seizure are beyond the control of the individual and are typically said to be involuntary acts, thereby negating the actus reus of the offense.   If Torsney's act of drawing and shooting his gun had really occurred during an epileptic seizure, would he have been entitled to an "automatism" instruction had he requested one?

Consider in this connection Bratty v. Attorney-General for Northern Ireland, [1961] 3 All E.R. 523.   Bratty was charged with killing a young girl, a passenger in his car, by strangling her with her own stocking. He testified that a "blackness" came over him and that "I didn't know what I was doing; I didn't realize anything."   He produced medical testimony that he might have been suffering from psychomotor epilepsy at the time of the offense and requested instructions on both insanity and automatism.   The automatism instruction was refused and he appealed.   The House of Lords unanimously affirmed, holding that epilepsy should be regarded as a "disease of the mind" for purposes of the insanity defense.   Lord Denning explained:

"The major mental diseases, which the doctors call psychoses, such as schizophrenia, are clearly diseases of the mind.   But in Regina v. Charlson, [1955] 1 W.L.R. 317, Barry, J., seems to have assumed that other diseases such as epilepsy or cerebral tumour are not diseases of the mind, even when they are such as to manifest themselves in violence.   I do not agree with this.   It seems to me that any mental disorder which has manifested itself in violence and is prone to recur is a disease of the mind. At any rate it is the sort of disease for which a person should be detained in hospital rather than be given an unqualified acquittal."

Similarly, in Regina v. Kemp, [1957] 1 Q.B. 399, the defendant claimed that the violent act was committed during a period of unconsciousness arising from arteriosclerosis and that this condition should be regarded as a physical disease, not a mental disease. Lord Devlin rejected the argument, saying:

"It does not matter, for the purposes of the law, whether the defect of reason is due to a degeneration of the brain or to some other form of mental derangement. That may be a matter of importance medically, but it is of no importance to the law, which merely has to consider the state of mind in which the accused is, not how he got there."

Lord Devlin's position has been criticized on the ground that if it were applied "without qualification of any kind [it] would have some surprising consequences." In Regina v. Quick, [1973] 3 Q.B. 910, Lawton, L. J., elaborated:

"Take the not uncommon case of the rugby player who gets a kick on the head early in the game and plays on to the end in a state of automatism. If, while he was in that state, he assaulted the referee, it is difficult to envisage any court adjudging that he was not guilty by reason of insanity. Another type of case which could occur is that of the dental patient who kicks out while coming round from an anaesthetic. The law would be in a defective state if a patient accused of assaulting a dental nurse by kicking her while regaining consciousness could only excuse himself by raising the defence of insanity."

This line of cases has led to the distinction between "insane automatism," which, like epilepsy, arises from a continuing abnormal brain condition, and "non-insane automatism," like concussion, which arises from an acuʲe incapacitation involving some external force and is unlikely to reflect a settled or permanent condition.[e] Does this distinction make sense? Does it draw a defensible line, in analytical terms, between an actus reus "defense" and the defense of insanity? Is the distinction sensible in dispositional terms?[f]

NOTE ON THE VERDICT OF GUILTY BUT MENTALLY ILL

At least 12 states have established a separate verdict of "guilty but mentally ill" (GBMI) as an optional verdict in cases in which the

[e] This distinction was reaffirmed by the House of Lords in Regina v. Sullivan [1984] 1 A.C. 156, [1983] 2 All E.R. 673. In *Sullivan*, the evidence clearly established that the defendant was experiencing a psychomotor seizure when he kicked and injured an elderly friend. At the close of the evidence, the judge ruled that he would instruct the jury that if they accepted the evidence, they should return a verdict of not guilty by reason of insanity. The defendant then changed his plea to guilty of assault causing bodily harm. He appealed on the ground that the defense of non-insane automatism should have been left to the jury. The House of Lords affirmed the trial judge's ruling.

[f] Although the relation between automatism and insanity has been much discussed in England and other Commonwealth jurisdictions, it has not been the subject of much litigation in this country. Two recent cases discussing the issue are People v. Grant, 71 Ill.2d 551, 17 Ill.Dec. 814, 377 N.E.2d 4 (1978), reversing 46 Ill.App.3d 125, 4 Ill.Dec. 696, 360 N.E.2d 809 (1977), and Fulcher v. State, 633 P.2d 142 (Wyo. 1981).

defendant pleads insanity.[a] The GBMI concept, as adopted in these states, should be distinguished from two other concepts to which this or similar terminology may refer. First, the GBMI verdict is available in conjunction with, rather than in lieu of, the verdict of "not guilty by reason of insanity"; this procedure should therefore be distinguished from proposals to abolish the insanity defense and to establish, in its stead, a special dispositional procedure for guilty but mentally ill defendants. Second, the consequence of a GBMI verdict is conviction and a criminal sentence; the procedure should therefore be distinguished from proposals to rename the insanity verdict ("guilty but insane" rather than "not guilty by reason of insanity") without altering its dispositional consequences—i.e., subjecting the defendant only to therapeutic restraint under a civil commitment statute.

Procedures under GBMI legislation vary significantly from state to state. However, the statutes typically provide that upon entry of the verdict, the trial judge must impose a criminal sentence. The defendant is then evaluated by correctional or mental health authorities for the purpose of determining his or her suitability for psychiatric treatment. If the evaluators conclude that psychiatric treatment is needed, the person is hospitalized and, upon discharge, is returned to prison to serve the remainder of the sentence. In effect, whether the prisoner will actually be placed in a mental health facility is typically a discretionary determination.

The GBMI verdict is predicated upon different findings in different states. Under most of the statutes, the dispositive finding is that the defendant was "mentally ill" (though not legally insane) at the time of the offense; the definition of "mental illness" is typically drawn from the state's civil commitment statute. In Michigan, for example, mental illness is defined as "a substantial disorder of thought or mood which significantly impairs judgment, behavior, capacity to recognize reality, or ability to cope with the ordinary demands of life."

In a few states, the required finding is linked to criteria of criminal responsibility. In Delaware, for example, the exclusive criterion of insanity is "lack of substantial capacity to appreciate wrongfulness," whereas the GBMI verdict can be based on volitional impairment (that the defendant suffered from a "psychiatric disorder" which "left [him] with insufficient will-power to choose whether he would do the act or refrain from doing it. . . . "). In Alaska, the exclusive criterion of exculpation is that the defendant was "unable . . . to appreciate the nature and quality of his conduct," whereas the criteria for the GBMI verdict are derived from the Model Penal Code insanity test.

The debate about GBMI legislation focuses in part on its dispositional consequences. Its proponents claim that it is designed to establish a procedure other than the NGI verdict to facilitate psychiatric treat-

---

[a] For general commentary on the GBMI verdict, see Slobogin, The Guilty But Mentally Ill Verdict: An Idea Whose Time Should Not Have Come, 53 G.W.L.Rev. 494 (1985); McGraw, Farthing-Capowich, and Keilitz, The Guilty But Mentally Ill Verdict & Current State of Knowledge, 30 Vill. L.Rev. 117 (1984); Slovenko, Commentaries on Psychiatry and Law: Guilty But Mentally Ill, 10 J.Amer.Acad.Psychiatry and L. 541 (1982).

ment of mentally disordered offenders who would otherwise be untreated. Critics respond that the procedure is misleading because it does not, in fact, assure treatment; further, they argue, a separate verdict is unnecessary to accomplish dispositional objectives because all states either operate psychiatric hospitals within the correctional system or have well-established procedures for transferring prisoners to secure mental health facilities. Finally, the critics say, a jury verdict based on evidence of past mental condition is an awkward device for triggering placement decisions based on the defendant's mental condition at the time of sentence.

As these observations suggest, the impact of the GBMI procedure on the sentencing and correctional process is ancillary to its effect on the adjudication of criminal responsibility. What is the intended effect of the optional verdict? Is it designed to subvert the insanity defense by offering juries a compromise verdict in cases in which an insanity acquittal would otherwise be proper? Or is it designed to establish a criterion of diminished responsibility to take into account psychological impairments that do not meet the criteria for insanity? Regardless of the legislative purpose, what is the likely effect of the GBMI procedure on the frequency of NGI pleas and acquittals? [b]

SUBSECTION E: MENTAL ABNORMALITY AND MENS REA

INTRODUCTORY NOTE ON THE MEANING OF DIMINISHED RESPONSIBILITY

The terms "diminished capacity" and "diminished responsibility" [a] appear frequently in judicial opinions and scholarly commentary. The terms have no generally recognized meanings, however, and have been used interchangeably to refer to two distinct concepts:

(i) **Rule of Logical Relevance.** In this country, courts usually use the terms "diminished capacity" and "diminished responsibility" to refer to the following rule of evidence: "Evidence of mental abnormality is admissible whenever it is logically relevant to disprove the existence of a mental state required by the definition of an offense or by its grading." As is developed in more detail in the next two main cases

---

[b] For empirical studies of the GBMI procedure, see National Center for State Courts, The Guilty But Mentally Ill Verdict: An Empirical Study (1985); Smith and Hall, Evaluating Michigan's Guilty But Mentally Ill Verdict: An Empirical Study, 16 Mich.J.L.Reform 77 (1982).

[a] For discussion of the different meanings of diminished responsibility, see Morse, Undiminished Confusion in Diminished Capacity, 75 J.Crim.L. and Criminol-

ogy 1 (1984); Mandiberg, Protecting Society and Defendants Too: The Constitutional Dilemma of Mental Abnormality and Intoxication Defenses, 53 Ford.L.Rev. 221 (1984); Morse, Diminished Capacity: A Moral and Legal Conundrum, 2 Int'l J. of Law & Psychiatry 271 (1979); Arenella, The Diminished Capacity and Diminished Responsibility Defenses: Two Children of a Doomed Marriage, 77 Colum.L.Rev. 827 (1977).

and the notes accompanying them, many courts do not always follow this rule of evidence. They either exclude evidence of mental abnormality altogether or restrict its admissibility short of its full logical import, based on doubts as to its reliability and fear that its use will undermine the social-control functions of the criminal law.

The labels "diminished capacity" and "diminished responsibility" apparently have been used to refer to this evidentiary proposition because the legal effect of admitting such evidence normally is to permit a serious offense to be reduced in grade to a less serious offense, thereby "diminishing" the offender's legal responsibility for criminal conduct. For example, the premeditation and deliberation required for first-degree murder may be rebutted in a particular case by evidence of mental abnormality, but the defendant may still be guilty of second-degree murder or manslaughter. Use of the terms "diminished capacity" or "diminished responsibility" to describe this result is misleading, however, because the terms carry the implication that "diminished capacity" or "diminished responsibility" can be proved by showing a "partial" incapacity in contrast to the "total" incapacity of insanity. As the materials on the insanity defense have demonstrated, however, mens rea requirements in the definition of criminal offenses may not be directly related to the criteria of non-responsibility used by the insanity defense. In particular, defendants found legally insane typically have the state of mind required for conviction of the most serious offense charged. On the other hand, in some instances, a mentally abnormal person shown to lack the required mens rea may not satisfy the requirements of the insanity defense.

In any event, the question raised by American cases decided under the "diminished capacity" rubric, simply put, is whether and under what circumstances evidence of mental abnormality should be admissible on mens rea issues. This is the question to which the cases and notes in this subsection are addressed.

(ii) **Partial Responsibility.** The term "diminished responsibility" is sometimes—and perhaps more appropriately—used to refer to the idea that the law should recognize that some offenders are not fully responsible for their crimes even though they are not entitled to exculpation and even though they had the mens rea required for conviction. Those who are only "partly responsible" in this sense would be entitled to a formal mitigation of their crime to a lesser offense. When used in this way, "diminished responsibility" refers to a substantive limitation on criminal liability rather than an evidentiary rule. Thus, a person found to be legally sane and to have had the requisite intent might nonetheless be regarded as being only partly responsible for the crime because of the disabling effects of mental abnormality. If an intermediate or partial degree of cognitive or volitional impairment is to have independent grading significance, this will call for a "test" of diminished responsibility to supplement the test of insanity.

No American jurisdiction has explicitly adopted this approach to the grading of any criminal offense, including homicide.[b] However, it is reflected in the criteria used in several states for the verdict of "guilty but mentally ill," [c] and in the current generation of capital sentencing statutes.[d] It is discussed in these materials in those contexts.

REGINA v. STEPHENSON
Court of Appeal, 1979.
[1979] 1 Q.B. 695.

GEOFFREY LANE, LORD JUSTICE. [The] appellant was found guilty by the jury of arson, contrary to Section 1(1) and (3) of the Criminal Damage Act 1971,[a] and pleaded guilty to another count of burglary. He was made the subject of a probation order for three years with a condition of medical treatment. He now appeals against his conviction on the charge of arson. . . .

The facts giving rise to the charge of arson were as follows. On November 28, 1977, the appellant went to a large straw stack in a field near Ampleforth, made a hollow in the side of the stack, crept into the hollow and tried to go to sleep. He felt cold, so he lit a fire of twigs and straw inside the hollow. The stack caught fire and damage of some £3,500 in all resulted. The appellant was stopped by the police soon afterwards. He first of all maintained that the fire had been caused by his smoking a cigarette. However, the next day he admitted what he had done. He said: "I kept putting bits of straw on the fire. Then the lot went up. As I ran away I looked back and saw the fire. Then getting bigger. I ran off down the road, that's when I was picked up. I'm sorry about it, it was an accident."

On those facts without more no jury would have had any difficulty in coming to the certain conclusion that the appellant had damaged the straw stack and had done so being reckless as to whether the stack would be damaged or not, whatever the true definition may be of the word "reckless."

However, the appellant did not give evidence, and the only witness called on behalf of the defence was Dr. Hawkings, a very experienced consultant psychiatrist. His evidence was to the effect that the appellant had a long history of schizophrenia. This, he said, would have the effect of making the appellant quite capable of lighting a fire to keep himself warm in dangerous proximity to a straw stack without having

---

[b] In England, a finding of diminished responsibility reduces murder to manslaughter. The English doctrine and related features of the law of homicide in this country are explored at pages 903–04, infra.

[c] See, for example, the provisions of the GBMI statutes in Alaska and Delaware quoted at page 751, supra.

[d] The criteria of diminished responsibility as used in modern capital sentencing statutes are discussed at pages 841–43, infra.

[a] Criminal Damage Act 1971, § 1: "(1) A person who without lawful excuse . . . damages any property belonging to another . . . being reckless as to whether any such property would be . . . damaged shall be guilty of an offence . . . (3) An offence committed under this section by . . . damaging property by fire shall be charged as arson." [Footnote by eds.]

taken the danger into account. In other words he was saying that the appellant may not have had the same ability to foresee or appreciate risk as the mentally normal person.

The guilt or innocence of the appellant turned on the question whether the jury were satisfied so as to feel sure that he had been reckless when he lit the fire. The judge gave the following direction to the jury:

"The prosecution say to you, though, that he set fire to it in a situation and a frame of mind which amounted to recklessness as to whether the straw stack would be damaged. . . . [A] man is reckless if he realises that there is a risk, but nevertheless presses on regardless. . . . [A] man is reckless when he carried out a deliberate act knowing or closing his mind to the obvious fact that there is some risk of damage. First you perhaps want to ask yourselves whether in lighting the fire the accused carried out a deliberate act, and the answer to that one thinks must be yes, because he has said that he lit the fire. Secondly, you may want to ask yourselves whether you regard it or not as an obvious fact that there was some risk of damage and when the act is the act of lighting a fire inside a straw stack, you may have little difficulty in dealing with the question whether it is an obvious fact that there is some risk of damage. Did he then do that knowing or closing his mind to the obvious fact, in the case from which these words are taken, as I say the reason advanced or the reason found for the man closing his mind to the obvious fact was that he was so angry that he pressed on regardless, and there may be . . . all kinds of reasons which make a man close his mind to the obvious fact—among them may be schizophrenia, that he is a schizophrenic." . . .

What then must the prosecution prove in order to bring home the charge of arson in circumstances such as the present? They must prove that (i) the defendant deliberately committed some act which caused the damage to property alleged or part of such damage; (ii) the defendant had no lawful excuse for causing the damage; these two requirements will in the ordinary case not be in issue; (iii) the defendant either (a) intended to cause the damage to the property, or (b) was reckless as to whether the property was damaged or not. A man is reckless when he carries out the deliberate act appreciating that there is a risk that damage to property may result from his act. It is however not the taking of every risk which could properly be classed as reckless. The risk must be one which it is in all the circumstances unreasonable for him to take.

Proof of the requisite knowledge in the mind of the defendant will in most cases present little difficulty. The fact that the risk of some damage would have been obvious to anyone in his right mind in the position of the defendant is not conclusive proof of the defendant's knowledge, but it may well be and in many cases doubtless will be a matter which will drive the jury to the conclusion that the defendant himself must have appreciated the risk. The fact that he may have been in a temper at the time would not normally deprive him of knowledge or foresight of the risk. If he had the necessary knowledge or foresight and his bad temper merely caused him to disregard it or put it to the back of his mind not caring whether the risk materialised, or if it merely deprived him of the self-control necessary to prevent him from taking the risk of which he was aware, then his bad temper will not avail him. This was the concept which the court in Regina v. Parker, [1977] 1 W.L.R. 600, 604, was trying to express when it used the words "or closing his mind to the obvious fact that there is some risk of damage resulting from that act. . . ." We wish to make it clear that the test remains subjective, that the knowledge or appreciation or risk of some damage must have entered the defendant's mind even though he may have suppressed it or driven it out. . . .

How do these pronouncements affect the present appeal? The appellant, through no fault of his own, was in a mental condition which might have prevented him from appreciating the risk which would have been obvious to any normal person. When the judge said to the jury "there may be . . . all kinds of reasons which make a man close his mind to the obvious fact—among them may be schizophrenia—" we think he was guilty of a misapprehension, albeit possibly an understandable misapprehension. The schizophrenia was on the evidence something which might have prevented the idea of danger entering the appellant's mind at all. If that was the truth of the matter, then the appellant was entitled to be acquitted. That was something which was never left clearly to the jury to decide.

We should add this. The mere fact that a defendant is suffering from some mental abnormality which may affect his ability to foresee consequences or may cloud his appreciation of risk does not necessarily mean that on a particular occasion his foresight or appreciation of risk was in fact absent. In the present case, for example, if the matter had been left to the jury for them to decide in the light of all the evidence, including that of the psychiatrist, whether the appellant must have appreciated the risk, it would have been open to them to decide that issue against him and to have convicted. As it is, we are of the view that, for the reasons indicated, the conviction for arson . . . must be quashed. . . .

Appeal against conviction for arson allowed.

NOTES ON MENTAL ABNORMALITY AND MENS REA

1. **The Rule of Relevance.** The *Stephenson* decision reflects the view that evidence of mental abnormality should be taken into account whenever it is logically relevant to the existence of the mental state required for conviction, irrespective of whether the defendant enters an insanity plea.[a] Section 4.02(1) of the Model Penal Code adopts the

[a] The student at this point should reread the note on mens rea and mental abnormality at pages 290–91, supra, for a summary of the historical background on this issue. The reform that led to cases like *Stephenson* was initiated in the law of homicide, where the subject still receives special attention. For that reason, this

same approach: "Evidence that the defendant suffered from a mental disease or defect is admissible whenever it is relevant to prove that the defendant did or did not have a state of mind which is an element of the offense."

Proponents of this position typically argue that it is illogical and unfair to define mens rea in subjective terms but then to preclude defendants from introducing otherwise competent evidence to support the claim that they in fact did not have the required state of mind. This view has been summarized by Bonnie and Slobogin, The Role of Mental Health Professionals in the Criminal Process: The Case For Informed Speculation, 66 Va.L.Rev. 427, 477 (1980):

> "In a criminal case involving subjective mens-rea requirements, the prosecution usually has no direct evidence concerning the defendant's state of mind; it must rely on 'common sense' inferences drawn from the defendant's conduct. This has the practical effect of shifting the burden to the defendant to demonstrate that he did not perceive, believe, expect, or intend what an ordinary person would have perceived, believed, expected, or intended under the same circumstances. Restriction of clinical testimony on mens rea thus compromises the defendant's opportunity to present a defense on an issue concerning which he, in reality, bears the burden of proof. The factfinder is likely to view with considerable skepticism the defendant's claim that he did not function as would a normal person under the circumstances. The defendant must establish the plausibility of his claim of abnormality. By precluding the defendant from offering relevant expert testimony, the law unduly enhances the prosecution's advantage on this issue. For this reason, we believe the only limitations on admissibility of mens-rea testimony by mental-health professionals should be relevance and the normal requirements for expert opinion."

Can you think of reasons that might justify exclusion of the type of evidence admitted in *Stephenson* even if it is relevant? Recall that all jurisdictions restrict the admissibility of intoxication evidence considerably short of its logical import, although most jurisdictions do admit such evidence to negate purpose, knowledge, or "specific intent." Would it make sense to treat evidence of intoxication and evidence of mental abnormality on the same terms, admitting the evidence to negate "specific intent" but not otherwise? Some jurisdictions that admit evidence of intoxication to negate specific intent nonetheless exclude evidence of mental abnormality in cases where evidence of intoxication would be admitted. Can you think of arguments in favor of this approach? The proponents of the Model Penal Code find it indefensible:

> "Neither logic nor justice can tolerate a jurisprudence that defines the elements of an offense as requiring a mental state

section of the book deals in general terms with mental abnormality and mens rea, and the subject is revisited in the chapter on homicide, pages 841–43 and 903–04, infra.

such that one defendant can properly argue that his voluntary drunkenness removed his capacity to form the specific intent but another defendant is inhibited from a submission of his contention that an abnormal mental condition, for which he was in no way responsible, negated his capacity to form a particular specific intent, even though the condition did not exonerate him from all criminal responsibility." [b]

The modern trend is clearly in the direction of the rule of relevance stated in the Model Penal Code. Of the states that have addressed the issue by statute or decision, about one third have adopted provisions similar to § 4.02(1) and now admit evidence of mental abnormality in any case involving a subjective mens-rea inquiry. Another third admit such evidence whenever the offense requires "specific intent." In the remaining jurisdictions, however, evidence of mental abnormality is excluded altogether unless it is offered in support of an insanity plea.

2. **The Case for Exclusion.** In Bethea v. United States, 365 A.2d 64 (D.C.App.1976), the Court of Appeals for the District of Columbia stated the case for excluding expert psychiatric testimony on mens-rea issues. The court's argument can usefully be presented in three stages. First, the court offers a conceptual defense of the categorical approach of the common law to evidence of mental abnormality:

"In the abstract, evidence of a mental disease or defect may be as relevant to the issue of mens rea as proof of intoxication or epilepsy, and the logic of consistency could compel a similar evidentiary rule for all such incapacitating conditions. However, recognizing the unique position of the concept of insanity in the framework of criminal responsibility, and considering the substantial problems which would accrue from the adoption of the diminished-capacity doctrine, we conclude that the argument of logical relevance is insufficient to warrant [its adoption]. . . .

"It is true, of course, that the existence of the required state of mind is to be determined subjectively in the sense that the issue must be resolved according to the particular circumstances of a given case. However, this fact may not be allowed to obscure the critical difference between the legal concepts of mens rea and insanity. The former refers to the existence in fact of a 'guilty mind'; insanity, on the other hand, connotes a presumption that a particular individual lacks the capacity to possess such a state of mind. It is upon this distinction that the 'logic' of the diminished-capacity doctrine founders.

"The concept of mens rea involves what is ultimately the fiction of determining the actual thoughts or mental processes of the accused. It is obvious that a certain resolution of this issue is beyond the ken of scientist and laymen alike. Only by inference can the existence of intent—or the differentiation between its forms, such as general or specific—be determined. The law presumes that all individuals are capable of the mental processes

b United States v. Brawner, 471 F.2d 969, 999 (D.C.Cir. 1972).

which bear the jurisprudential label 'mens rea'; that is, the law presumes sanity. Moreover, for the sake of administrative efficiency and in recognition of fundamental principles of egalitarian fairness, our legal system further presumes that each person is equally capable of the same forms and degrees of intent. The concept of insanity is simply a device the law employs to define the outer limits of that segment of the general population to whom these presumptions concerning the capacity for criminal intent shall not be applied. The line between the sane and the insane for the purposes of criminal adjudication is not drawn because for one group the actual existence of the necessary mental state (or lack thereof) can be determined with any greater certainty, but rather because those whom the law declares insane are demonstrably so aberrational in their psychiatric characteristics that we choose to make the assumption that they are incapable of possessing the specified state of mind. Within the range of individuals who are not 'insane,' the law does not recognize the readily demonstrable fact that as between individual criminal defendants the nature and development of their mental capabilities may vary greatly. . . .

"By contradicting the presumptions inherent in the doctrine of mens rea, the theory of diminished capacity inevitably opens the door to variable or sliding scales of criminal responsibility. . . ."

Next the *Bethea* court responds to the argument that restrictions on psychiatric evidence concerning mental impairment are illogical. To the contrary, the court argues, sound evidentiary policies underlie an exclusionary rule:

"We recognize that there are exceptions to the basic principle that all individuals are presumed to have a similar capacity for mens rea. The rule that evidence of intoxication may be employed to demonstrate the absence of specific intent figure[s] prominently in the [argument for admissibility] of expert evidence of mental impairment. The asserted analogy is flawed, however, by the fact that there are significant evidentiary distinctions between psychiatric abnormality and the recognized incapacitating circumstances. Unlike the notion of partial or relative insanity, conditions such as intoxication, medication, epilepsy, infancy, or senility are, in varying degrees, susceptible to quantification or objective demonstration, and to lay understanding. . . .

"While the rationale for . . . diminished capacity rest[s] heavily upon the concept of logical relevance, [attention must be paid] to the other general prerequisites to the admissibility of evidence, i.e., its reliability and the balance between its probative value and its potential impact upon the other interests which are critical to the adjudicatory mechanism. . . .

"[T]he degree of sophistication of the psychiatric sciences and the validity and reliability of its evidentiary product are not beyond dispute. In Wahrlich v. Arizona, 479 F.2d 1137, 1138 (9th Cir. 1973), the [court] concluded:

'[T]he state of the developing art of psychiatry is such that we are not convinced that psychiatric testimony directed to a retrospective analysis of the subtle gradations of specific intent has enough probative value to compel its admission. . . .'

"The potential impact of psychiatric evidence in an area so critically close to the ultimate issue of responsibility cannot be minimized. . . . There is no reason to suppose that the problem will be any less acute where the issue is the subtle distinction between mental states such as those reflecting specific and general intent, as opposed to the question whether there existed a mental abnormality of sufficient magnitude to be labeled insanity. . . .

"[Moreover] we are not satisfied that the rule [of admissibility can logically be limited to cases of specific intent]. Assuming the competency of experts to testify as to an accused's capacity for specific intent, we see no logical bar to their observations as to the possible existence or lack of malice or general intent. Moreover, it does not appear to us that the balance between the evidentiary value of medical testimony and its potential for improper impact upon the trier would vary sufficiently as between the various degrees of mens rea to warrant such an artificial distinction."

Finally, the court argues that the dispositional consequences of "unrestrained application" of the rule of logical relevance would be unacceptable:

"While there may be superficial appeal to the idea that the standards of criminal responsibility should be applied as subjectively as possible, the overriding danger of the disputed doctrine is that it would discard the traditional presumptions concerning mens rea without providing for a corresponding adjustment in the means whereby society is enabled to protect itself from those who cannot or will not conform their conduct to the requirements of the law.

"Under the present statutory scheme, a successful plea of insanity avoids a conviction, but confronts the accused with the very real possibility of prolonged therapeutic confinement. If, however, psychiatric testimony were generally admissible to cast a reasonable doubt upon whatever degree of mens rea was necessary for the charged offense, thus resulting in outright acquittal, there would be scant reason indeed for a defendant to risk such confinement by arguing the greater form of mental deficiency. Thus, quite apart from the argument that the diminished capacity doctrine would result in a considerably greater likelihood of acquittal for those who by traditional standards would be held responsible, the future safety of the offender as well as the community would be jeopardized by the possibility that one who is genuinely dangerous might obtain his complete freedom merely by applying his psychiatric evidence to the threshold issue of intent.

"[It has been argued] that the statutory procedures governing civil commitment would 'provide a shield against danger from persons with abnormal mental condition.' We do not share [this view]. While confinement as a result of either a plea of insanity or a civil petition turns upon the existence of a similar degree of mental impairment, there exist significant procedural differences. . . . The difference between the burden and standards of proof has been justified on the quite logical ground that under normal circumstances civil commitment is directed toward a potential threat to an individual or the community, while in the context of the criminal defense, harm in fact has occurred, and the commission of the act is tacitly acknowledged. We see no justification for thwarting the legitimate policy objectives of the mandatory commitment provisions [for persons acquitted by reason of insanity] by reopening the gap between the civil and criminal structures. In our view, to do so would 'tear the fabric of the criminal law as an instrument of social control.' . . ."

The *Bethea* court asserts that the rule of relevance must "founder" on the conceptual distinction between insanity and mens rea. Is the court's argument persuasive? What does the court mean when it says that mens rea "ultimately [involves] the fiction of determining the actual thoughts or mental processes of the accused"? Is the court suggesting that the law is unconcerned with actual mental functioning of persons presumed to be sane and that the idea of mens rea is not as subjective as the proponents of the rule of relevance assume? Do you agree?

The court rejects the "asserted analogy" to intoxication on the ground that evidence of mental abnormality is less objective and reliable than evidence of "intoxication, medication, epilepsy, infancy or senility." Do you agree? How objective and reliable is evidence regarding the effects of intoxication, medication, etc.?

The court also asserts that the logical argument for admissibility applies to all mens-rea inquiries, including "malice or general intent," and that any distinction among specific- and general-intent offenses would be "artificial." Is the court right? Can you envision any acceptable ground for drawing such a distinction? Is evidence of mental abnormality relevant to general intent? Does any of the rationales offered for the traditional restriction on evidence of intoxication apply in this context?

Finally, the court observes that acquittal of a person who lacks mens rea because of mental abnormality would undermine the social-control functions of the criminal law. Is this a legitimate concern? If it is, does it suggest that the distinction between specific- and general-intent offenses would not be "artificial?" If no such line were drawn and a mentally abnormal defendant could win acquittal, can you think of appropriate ways to deal with the problem as a dispositional matter?

3. ***People* v. *Wetmore*.** The tension between subjective criteria of culpability and the social interest in control of dangerous persons is illustrated by the decision of the California Supreme Court in People v. Wetmore, 22 Cal.3d 318, 149 Cal.Rptr. 265, 583 P.2d 1308 (1978). Wetmore was charged with burglary. The evidence was summarized by the Supreme Court:

> "[Joseph Cacciatore, the victim of the burglary] testified that he left his apartment on March 7, 1975. When he returned three days later, he discovered defendant in his apartment. Defendant was wearing Cacciatore's clothes and cooking his food. The lock on the front door had been broken; the apartment lay in a shambles. Cacciatore called the police, who arrested defendant for burglary. Later Cacciatore discovered that a ring, a watch, a credit card, and items of clothing were missing.[1]

> "The psychiatric reports submitted to the court explain defendant's long history of psychotic illness, including at least 10 occasions of hospital confinement for treatment. According to the reports, defendant, shortly after his last release from [a V.A. hospital], found himself with no place to go. He began to believe that he 'owned' property and was 'directed' to Cacciatore's apartment. When he found the door unlocked he was sure he owned the apartment. He entered, rearranged the apartment, destroyed some advertising he felt was inappropriate, and put on Cacciatore's clothes. When the police arrived, defendant was shocked and embarrassed, and only then understood that he did not own the apartment. . . ."

Wetmore argued that the psychiatric evidence showed that as a result of mental illness he lacked the specific intent required for conviction of burglary. The trial court acknowledged that the evidence might negate specific intent but concluded that, under the controlling precedents, "if a defendant's mental capacity which would preclude the forming of a specific intent is that of insanity," evidence of such a mental condition "is not admissible to establish . . . lack of specific intent due to diminished capacity." The court was also concerned that there was no lesser offense under California law for which Wetmore could be convicted if he were acquitted of burglary. It accordingly found Wetmore guilty of burglary as charged. Pursuant to California's bifurcated trial procedure, the court then considered the question of insanity and found Wetmore not guilty by reason of insanity. At a subsequent hearing, the trial court found that Wetmore "had not recovered his sanity" and ordered him committed.

The Supreme Court of California unanimously reversed the judgment:

> "The state bears the burden of proving every element of the offense charged; defendant cannot logically or constitutionally be denied the right to present probative evidence rebutting an

"[1] At the preliminary hearing defendant appeared wearing one of Cacciatore's shirts. . . ."

element of the crime merely because such evidence also suggests insanity.   Defendant's evidence established that he entered an apartment under a delusion that he owned that apartment and thus did not enter with the intent of committing a theft or felony.   That evidence demonstrated that defendant lacked the specific intent required for a conviction of burglary; the trial court's refusal to consider the evidence at the guilt phase of the trial therefore constituted prejudicial error.

"We reject the suggestion that we sustain the trial court by holding that a defense of diminished capacity cannot be raised whenever, owing to the lack of a lesser included offense, it might result in the defendant's acquittal.   A defendant who, because of diminished capacity, does not entertain the specific intent required for a particular crime is entitled to be acquitted of that crime.   If he cannot be convicted of a lesser offense and cannot safely be released, the state's remedy is to institute civil commitment proceedings, not to convict him of a specific-intent crime which he did not commit."

The court elaborated on its rejection of the argument that civil commitment provided inadequate social protection:

"A defendant whose criminal activity arises from mental disease or defect usually requires confinement and special treatment.   [The penal code provides for] such confinement and treatment for persons found not guilty by reason of insanity.   A defendant acquitted because, as a result of diminished capacity, he lacked the specific intent required for the crime cannot be confined pursuant to [those] sections, yet often he cannot be released without endangering the public safety.

"The same danger may arise, however, when a diminished-capacity defense does not result in the defendant's acquittal, but in his conviction for a lesser-included offense.   A defendant convicted of a lesser-included misdemeanor, for example, will be confined for a relatively short period in a facility which probably lacks a suitable treatment program, and may later, having served his term, be released to become a public danger.   The solution to this problem thus does not lie in barring the defense of diminished capacity when the charged crime lacks a lesser included offense, but in providing for the confinement and treatment of defendants with diminished capacity arising from mental disease or defect.

"[California law] provides for the civil commitment of any person who, 'as a result of mental disorder, [is] a danger to others, or to himself, or gravely disabled.' . . . [I]f evidence adduced in support of a successful diminished capacity defense indicates to the trial judge that the defendant is dangerous, the court is not compelled to foist the defendant upon the public; it may, instead, initiate procedures for civil commitment.

"The attorney general points out that a person who commits a crime against property, such as defendant Wetmore, might not be [civilly] commitable . . . unless he were 'gravely disabled.' A more serious omission lies in the act's failure to provide for long-term commitment of persons dangerous to others; unless found 'gravely disabled,' a person 'who, as a result of mental disorder, presents an imminent threat of substantial physical harm to others' cannot be confined beyond the initial 90-day post-certification treatment period unless 'he has threatened, attempted, or actually inflicted physical harm to another during his period of post-certification treatment.' If the [civil-commitment statute] does not adequately protect the public against crimes committed by persons with diminished mental capacity, the answer lies either in amendment to that act or in the enactment of legislation that would provide for commitment of persons acquitted by virtue of a successful diminished capacity defense in the same manner as persons acquitted by reason of insanity are presently committed. It does not lie in judicial creation of an illogical—and possibly unconstitutional [c]—rule denying the defense of diminished capacity to persons charged with crimes lacking a lesser included offense."

Has the court properly resolved the tension between subjective criteria of culpability and the social interest in control over mentally disordered persons who have committed anti-social acts? Has the court simply shifted the tension to the civil commitment process? The *Wetmore* court rejected the "illogical" suggestion that evidence of mental abnormality should be inadmissible "whenever, owing to the lack of a lesser-included offense, it might result in the defendant's acquittal." In common-law terms, the rejected approach would preclude the use of such evidence to negate "general intent" and would also preclude its use in cases such as *Wetmore* that involve specific-intent crimes with no lesser-included general-intent offense. How would you implement such an approach in a jurisdiction with a culpability structure based on the Model Penal Code? Would this approach be entirely illogical? Does it represent a useful compromise?

UNITED STATES v. BRIGHT

United States Court of Appeals for the Second Circuit, 1975.
517 F.2d 584.

GURFEIN, CIRCUIT JUDGE. Catherine Bright appeals from a judgment of conviction entered on . . . three counts of possession of [checks stolen from the mail].[a] [She] received a six-month suspended sentence and six-months probation.

c The court's suggestion that denying the defense might be unconstitutional is derived from the cases considered at pages 967–93, infra. [Footnote by eds.]

a The statute involved, 18 U.S.C. § 1708, provides in pertinent part: "Whoever . . . unlawfully has in his possession . . . any . . . mail . . . which has been . . . stolen, . . . knowing the same to have been stolen, . . . [s]hall be fined . . . or imprisoned . . . .." [Footnote by eds.]

Appellant presses two points on this appeal. First, she argues that the district court committed error in failing to permit the defense to introduce psychiatric evidence to negate her knowledge that the checks were stolen, although no insanity defense was tendered. Second, she argues that the district court committed reversible error in its charge to the jury with respect to the element of knowledge required under 18 U.S.C. § 1708. We affirm the district court on the first of these contentions, but reverse on the charge to the jury.

It is uncontested that appellant had been in possession of some nine welfare checks at various dates during 1972, and that these checks had been stolen from the mail. The checks had been in the possession of one Fred Scott, an acquaintance of appellant's "boyfriend" Leslie; Scott gave Bright the checks to cash for him on the pretense that he had no bank account of his own. Appellant admitted at trial that she had cashed or deposited the checks in question in the two accounts she had at her bank, but swore that she had not known that they were stolen. She testified that Scott had told her that he had received the checks in payment for debts or rent owed to him.

She testified that on one occasion, when a check she had cashed had been returned unpaid and her account charged accordingly, she confronted Scott who made good on the loss. After that incident, she cashed three more checks for Scott. The three counts of her conviction are based on her cashing the latter three checks.

At trial, the appellant's defense was based upon her purported lack of knowledge that the checks had been stolen and her naive belief that everything Scott told her was true. Appellant testified in her own behalf accordingly.

In support of her contention that she did not know the checks were stolen, appellant sought to introduce testimony by Dr. Norman Weiss, a psychiatrist who examined appellant on August 21, 1974 before trial. The trial court excluded the proffered testimony and appellant assigns the exclusion as reversible error . . . .

Though Dr. Weiss examined appellant only once, he was prepared to testify, as indicated in a letter he addressed to defense counsel, that "though I do not consider Mrs. Bright to have been suffering mental illness, I believe that her dependent, childlike character structure unconsciously 'needed' to believe that these men would never involve her in illegal activities and that Leslie [her boyfriend] could do no wrong. I believe that at the time of the alleged crime, because of this unconscious 'need,' she did not think that the checks had been stolen."

He later suggested, "I do not believe that she knew that the checks that she allegedly possessed were stolen as a result of her need to deny the possibility that the men involved would in any way take advantage of her. This passive-dependent personality disorder rendered her incapable of understanding this."

Appellant argues that the proffered psychiatric testimony should have been admitted for the purpose of showing her inability to know that the checks had been stolen, a requisite element under Section

1708. [Appellant's trial counsel] specifically disavowed the assertion of an insanity defense . . .. We hold the trial court did not err in rejecting the testimony.

The proffered testimony was a weak reed. The hurried diagnosis prepared for an advocate for purposes of trial would simply tender an opinion by the psychiatrist, not that appellant was suffering from mental disease, or that she lacked substantial capacity either to appreciate the wrongfulness of her conduct or to conform her conduct to the requirements of law, but that, on the basis of this single examination, the psychiatrist was of the opinion that appellant had a "passive-dependent personality disorder." . . . Couched in simpler language he was prepared to testify that appellant was a gullible person but a person unaffected either by psychosis or neurosis.

Nor was the proffered testimony to show that appellant did not have the capacity to form a specific intent to commit the crime. Concededly she was quite capable of the mental responsibility required to cash a stolen check and to recognize circumstances that would lead to the suspicion that it was stolen. The interposition by Dr. Weiss was simply that this particular man, Leslie, was in such a relationship to the passive-dependent personality on trial that she had to believe him when he told her the checks were not stolen.

In dealing with forensic psychiatry, we must be humble rather than dogmatic. The mind and motivation of an accused who is not on the other side of the line [drawn by the insanity defense] is, by the judgment of experience, left to the jury to probe. The complexity of the fears and long-suppressed traumatic experiences of a lifetime is in the personality of all of us. All humankind is heir to defects of personality.

To transmute the effect of instability, of undue reliance on another, of unrequited love, of sudden anger, of the host of attitudes and syndromes that are a part of daily living, into opinion evidence to the jury for exculpation or condemnation is to go beyond the boundaries of current knowledge. The shallower the conception the deeper runs the danger that the jury may be misled. . . .

In short, appellant asks us to go beyond the boundaries of conventional psychiatric opinion testimony. We think the testimony offered was not sufficiently grounded in scientific support to make us reach or, indeed, cross the present frontier of admissibility. On the instant appeal we need decide no more than that [the trial judge] did not abuse her discretion in rejecting the opinion evidence.

[The court next considered the jury instruction on the meaning of knowledge. After an elaborate analysis, it concluded that the absence of several words from the instruction insufficiently emphasized the entirely subjective nature of the inquiry. It then reversed the conviction on this ground.]

———

NOTES ON THE BOUNDARIES OF PSYCHIATRIC TESTIMONY ON MENS REA

1. **Introduction.** The *Bright* court held that the trial judge had not abused her discretion in excluding the proffered testimony by Dr. Weiss. The court does not appear to take the position that evidence of mental abnormality is categorically excluded in the absence of an insanity plea. What, then, was the ground for excluding the testimony? To what extent is the ruling based on the same substantive policies of the penal law articulated in *Bethea*? To what extent is the ruling based, instead, on general policies of the law of evidence concerning expert-opinion testimony—in this case the proper scope of opinion testimony by psychiatrists and other mental-health professionals? Three possible bases for the court's ruling are explored in the following notes.

2. **Lack of Capacity vs. Actual State of Mind.** The *Bright* court observes that the expert testimony was not offered to show that the defendant "did not have the capacity to form a specific intent to commit the crime," but only that in fact she did not have the requisite knowledge at the time of the offense. Does this imply that expert testimony concerning mental abnormality is admissible *only* to show lack of capacity to entertain the required mental state? This approach is followed in many jurisdictions. Is this a proper basis for determining the admissibility of expert testimony and for instructing a jury on the relevance of such testimony? [a]

The capacity requirement is omitted in modern statutes and judicial decisions adopting the rule of logical relevance. The typical formulation is that of the Model Penal Code—evidence of mental disease or defect is admissible whenever it is relevant to show the absence of mens rea at the time of the offense. Would the *Bright* evidence be admissible under the Model Penal Code? Would the *Stephenson* evidence be admissible in a jurisdiction following the *Bright* court's approach?

3. **The Significance of Mental Disease.** The *Bright* court observes that the proffered testimony did not purport to show that the defendant was "suffering from a mental disease   . . . but that [she] had a 'passive-dependent personality disorder.' " Clearly the defendant had no "mental disease or defect" in the sense ordinarily required for the insanity defense. But should admissibility of expert testimony concerning mens rea be dependent upon the presence of mental disease? If so, should the threshold of legal significance for clinically significant psychological "abnormalities" be the same in the mens-rea context as it is in the context of the insanity defense? Do the policies underlying the mental-disease requirement for the insanity defense apply to mens-rea inquiries?

The case against the mental-disease limitation has been made by Bonnie and Slobogin in The Role of Mental Health Professionals in the

---

[a] Courts divide in a similar way on the significance of evidence of intoxication. See pages 283–90, supra.

Criminal Process: The Case for Informed Speculation, 66 Va.L.Rev. 427, 477–81 (1980). They argue that "the only limitations on admissibility of mens-rea testimony by mental-health professionals should be relevance and the normal requirements for expert opinion." They illustrate the theoretical bases for this position with an elaborated version of the *Bright* situation:

"The defense proffers expert testimony by a psychiatrist to the effect that Ms. *B*'s personality is marked by a high degree of passivity and dependency. Because she is highly dependent on others to satisfy her emotional needs, she is compliant and characteristically avoids situations of conflict that could threaten the stability of her emotional attachments. In this particular situation, her dependence on her boyfriend and desire to please him led her to want to please his good friend Scott. As is characteristic of persons with her personality traits, Ms. *B* relies on the ego defense mechanisms of 'denial' and 'repression' to keep anxiety-provoking thoughts out of her consciousness, in order to maintain her emotional equilibrium. Doubts about Scott's honesty—and, by inference, about her boyfriend's character and relationship with her—would have generated intense anxiety and psychological conflict. Thus, she denied and repressed the doubts, which never rose to the level of consciousness.

"This formulation, if believed, tends to support Ms. *B*'s claim that she did not 'knowingly' possess stolen checks. However, it does not show that she suffered from a mental disease or defect— or even a substantial behavioral abnormality—that would deprive her of the capacity to know that the checks were stolen. Instead, it draws on theories of personality and [psychodynamic psychology] to explain the way she functions as a person, and adds some plausibility to the notion that under the described circumstances she could have been 'abnormally gullible.'

"Let us assume that this testimony satisfies the governing evidentiary criteria for expert opinion but that it is nonetheless excluded because a claim of mental disease or defect is a prerequisite for admissibility of expert opinion testimony on mens rea. This exclusion compromises Ms. *B*'s ability to persuade the factfinder not to draw inferences about her beliefs on the basis of what a normal person would have believed under the circumstances. Because Ms. *B* carries a de-facto burden of proof on this issue, the exclusion of expert testimony in effect holds her to the standards of a normally suspicious person, selectively redefining the offense to apply objective standards to her and subjective standards to everyone else."

Why do you think many courts disagree with this line of argument? What position would you take?

4. **Proper Subjects for Expert Testimony.** As Bonnie and Slobogin note, otherwise relevant opinion testimony by psychiatrists and other mental-health professionals may properly be excluded if the

proffered opinion fails to satisfy the normal criteria for expert testimony. In particular, the subject of the testimony must be based on the specialized knowledge of the expert. As the *Bethea* opinion suggests, the traditional exclusionary approach to evidence of mental abnormality may be linked as much to skepticism about psychiatric testimony as it is to policies of the penal law. Any residual limitations, such as the mental-disease requirement, may also be predicated on evidentiary concerns rather than substantive ones.

Doubts about the scientific basis of the proffered testimony are also reflected in the *Bright* opinion. The court observes that the expert testimony proffered by the defendant goes "beyond the boundaries of current knowledge" and is insufficiently "grounded in scientific support" to be admissible. Do you share the court's concern? Is psychiatric opinion about the defendant's personality traits and about the "dynamic" of her psychological functioning too speculative to warrant consideration? Insufficiently grounded in scientific support? Are you any less skeptical about the scientific basis for the testimony offered in Joy Baker's case and the other cases considered in connection with the insanity defense? Do limitations on the insanity defense, such as the allocation of the burden of proof and the dispositional consequences, justify different treatment of the issue in that context?

A final point should be made regarding expert testimony. Even if a defendant's mental functioning is a proper subject for expert-opinion testimony, the trial court must rule on the qualifications of the individual witness to offer such an opinion in the particular case. Would careful scrutiny of the training of the witness and the quality of his evaluation provide an adequate safeguard against unreliable psychiatric testimony in cases like *Bright*? If you were the trial judge, would you have admitted Dr. Weiss' testimony?

NOTE ON BIFURCATION OF INSANITY AND MENS REA

Cases involving insanity pleas are sometimes tried in two phases. Under this bifurcated procedure, the issues of "guilt or innocence" and "insanity" are tried in successive stages with separate verdicts. Although bifurcation is permitted in many states, the procedure is required by statute only in California and a handful of others.[a]

In a jurisdiction that excludes evidence of mental abnormality from the guilt stage, the bifurcated trial can have decided advantages. By deferring psychiatric testimony to the second stage, it avoids confusing the jury and reduces the risk of compromise verdicts. Also, in many cases it helps protect the defendant's privilege against self-incrimination. If the insanity issue were tried simultaneously with the "guilt" issue, many defendants would be forced to make a strategic choice

[a] In many states, the trial judge has the discretion to bifurcate the trial but is not required to do so. In some states, bifurcation is required upon the defendant's request. Some states forbid the procedure altogether.

between contesting the issue of guilt or admitting the elements of the offense and attempting to prove insanity. This is because the defendant's own statements are often an integral part of a defense based on his mental condition at the time of the offense. Thus, the bifurcated trial permits the defendant to remain silent during the guilt phase, thereby assuring that the prosecution bears the burden of proving the elements of the offense without the defendant's assistance. If the prosecution is successful, the defendant is then permitted to put on an insanity defense and may choose to testify at that time.

Obviously the advantages of a bifurcated trial are diminished if the defendant is permitted to introduce evidence of mental abnormality to negate mens rea at the guilt stage while the "insanity" issue is deferred; such a trial can become highly cumbersome and redundant since it also bifurcates the expert testimony. For this reason, a judge sitting in a jurisdiction which does not require bifurcation might decide to hold a unified proceeding. However, what is the correct response if bifurcation is required by statute? On the one hand, the California Supreme Court has taken the position that the defendant cannot fairly be precluded from introducing relevant evidence of mental abnormality at the guilt stage even though the insanity issue will be tried separately. This led the court to recommend that the legislature abandon the bifurcated procedure in favor of a unified trial. People v. Wetmore, 22 Cal.3d 318, 331, 149 Cal.Rptr. 265, 274, 583 P.2d 1308, 1317 (1978). On the other hand, the Wisconsin Supreme Court has concluded that the advantages of the bifurcated trial procedure provide another reason, in addition to those presented by the *Bethea* court, for excluding evidence of mental abnormality on mens-rea issues. See Steele v. State, 97 Wis.2d 72, 294 N.W.2d 2 (1980).

SUBSECTION F: ABOLITION OF THE INSANITY DEFENSE

NOTES ON ABOLITION OF THE INSANITY DEFENSE

1. **Approaches to Abolition.** Proposals to abolish the insanity defense have been made with some regularity since the latter part of the 19th century. These proposals have taken two forms:

(i) **The Sentencing Approach.** Some abolitionists recommend that all evidence regarding the defendant's mental abnormality be excluded from the "guilt stage" of the criminal proceeding and that such evidence be taken into account only at the sentencing stage. This approach, which was widely discussed during the early years of this century [a] was actually enacted by the state of Washington in 1909:

"It shall be no defense to a person charged with the commission of a crime that at the time of its commission he was unable, by reason of his insanity, idiocy or imbecility, to comprehend the nature and quality of the act committed, or to understand that it was wrong; or that he was afflicted with a morbid propensity to commit prohibited acts; nor shall any testimony or other proof thereof be admitted in evidence."

The statute also provided that the trial judge could order a convicted defendant to be committed to a state hospital or confined in the psychiatric unit of the penitentiary if he determined that the defendant was insane. This scheme was declared unconstitutional by the Supreme Court of Washington in State v. Strasburg, 60 Wash. 106, 110 P. 1020 (1910). The court concluded that the statute precluded the defendant from offering evidence to negate the constitutionally required predicate for criminal liability:

"[T]he sanity of the accused, at the time of committing the act charged against him, has always been regarded as much a substantive fact, going to make up his guilt, as the fact of his physical commission of the act. It seems to us the law could as well exclude proof of any other substantive fact going to show his guilt or innocence. If he was insane at the time to the extent that he could not comprehend the nature and quality of the act— in other words, if he had no will to control the physical act of his physical body—how can it in truth be said that the act was his act? To take from the accused the opportunity to offer evidence tending to prove this fact is in our opinion as much a violation of his constitutional right of trial by jury as to take from him the right to offer evidence before the jury tending to show that he did not physically commit the act or physically set in motion a train of events resulting in the act."

(ii) **The Mens-Rea Approach.** Concerns such as those expressed by the *Strasburg* court have inspired a less sweeping abolitionist proposal. Under this approach, evidence of mental abnormality would be excluded unless relevant to the mens rea of the offense charged; criteria of criminal responsibility extrinsic to the definition of the offense would be abandoned.

The mens-rea variant of the abolitionist proposals has been especially popular in recent years. It has significant support in the academic literature [b] and has been adopted in Montana, Idaho, and Utah. Section 46–14–201 of Mont.Rev.Codes Ann. provides, in relevant part:

"(1) Evidence of mental disease or defect is not admissible in a trial on the merits unless the defendant . . . files a writ-

---

[a] See, e.g., Wilbur, Should the Insanity Defense to a Criminal Charge be Abolished?, 8 A.B.A.J. 631 (1922); Rood, Abolition of the Defense of Insanity in Criminal Cases, 9 Mich.L.Rev. 126 (1910). More recent endorsements include H.L.A. Hart,

Punishment and Responsibility 186–205 (1968).

[b] See, e.g., Goldstein & Katz, "Abolish the Insanity Defense"—Why Not?, 72 Yale L.J. 853 (1963); Morris, Psychiatry and the

ten notice of his purpose to rely on a mental disease or defect to prove that he did not have a particular state of mind which is an essential element of the offense charged. . . .

"(2) When the defendant is found not guilty of the charged offense or offenses or any lesser included offense for the reason that due to a mental disease or defect, he could not have a particular state of mind that is an essential element of the offense charged, the verdict and judgment shall so state."

Assessing the merits of the mens-rea approach to mental abnormality is aided by consideration of three questions: (i) Would the outcomes of criminal trials under the mens-rea scheme differ significantly from those that would occur under the existing responsibility tests? (ii) How would the dispositional consequences of the mens-rea approach differ from those that now obtain? (iii) To the extent that some defendants now acquitted under the insanity tests would be convicted under the mens-rea approach, are these results morally acceptable? Each of these issues is addressed in the following notes.

2. **Effect on Case Outcome.** In theory, it seems clear that some claims that now fit within the various insanity tests would not be exculpatory under the mens-rea approach. First, claims of volitional impairment would have no exculpatory significance outside the narrow confines of the voluntary-act doctrine. Second, claims of cognitive impairment would have exculpatory significance only (i) if the defendant were charged with an offense requiring a subjectively defined level of culpability, and (ii) if the impairment so distorted the defendant's perceptual capacities that the physical nature and consequences of the alleged criminal acts were not perceived or foreseen. Stephenson and Wetmore might be acquitted, but Joy Baker would not.

As a practical matter, however, it is possible that case outcomes would remain much the same as they are now. If the expert testimony is admitted on mens-rea issues, judges and juries may behave as many observers believe they do now—they may ignore the technical aspects of the legal formulae and decide, very simply, whether the defendant was crazy. If judges and juries do in fact respond to psychiatric evidence in this blunt way, one might be led to expect, as Professor Dershowitz has asserted, Abolishing the Insanity Defense, 9 Crim.L.Bull. 434, 438–39 (1973), that "nothing much will change":

"The clash of experts testifying about the defendant's state of mind will continue, as it has for more than a century. The battlefield may shift from the issue of right versus wrong to the equally troublesome issue of intent, but the jurors will hear testimony not substantially different—or more informative— from what they hear today.

"In the last analysis, it is the jury that decides whether an accused is to be convicted or acquitted. No matter how the law reads, it is a deeply entrenched human feeling that those who are grossly disturbed—whether they are called 'madmen,' 'lunatics,'

Dangerous Criminal, 41 So.Cal.L.Rev. 514 (1968). Professor Morris reiterated and elaborated on his views in Madness and the Criminal Law (1982).

'insane,' or 'mentally ill'—should not be punished like ordinary criminals. This feeling, which is as old as recorded history, is unlikely to be rooted out by new legislation."

It is also possible that courts will soften the impact of abolition of the responsibility inquiries by reinterpreting the elements of the offense. For example, the concepts of knowledge, purpose, and specific intent, might be given "affective" or qualitative meanings in order to achieve exculpatory results in cases where criminal liability seems morally offensive. Moreover, the voluntary-act doctrine might be broadened to permit the jury to consider claims of volitional impairment now considered under the various insanity tests.[c]

3. **Dispositional Considerations.** Concerns about the need for control of dangerous persons figure prominently in the controversies over commitment of persons acquitted by reason of insanity and the relationship between mental abnormality and mens-rea. What are the dispositional implications of proposals to abolish the insanity defense in favor of a mens-rea approach? Two separate issues should be considered: First, how would the abolitionists deal with mentally disordered defendants who would have been acquitted by reason of insanity but would now be convicted? Second, how would they deal with persons who are acquitted because they lack the mens-rea for any form of criminal liability?

(i) **Sentencing the Mentally Disordered Offender.** Many proponents of abolition have argued that insanity tests mistakenly focus attention on backward-looking "moral guesses" about the person's blameworthiness at the time of the offense when the real issue is what ought to be done now to prevent further harm. Other abolitionists argue that considerations of responsibility are relevant but should be taken into account in mitigation of punishment rather than exculpation. Both views lead to the conclusion that evidence of mental abnormality should be taken fully into account at sentencing. Consider, in this connection, the relevant provisions of the Montana statute abolishing the insanity defense:

"Section 46–14–311. Consideration of mental disease or defect in sentencing. Whenever a defendant is convicted on a verdict or a plea of guilty and he claims that at the time of the commission of the offense . . . he was suffering from a mental disease or defect which rendered him unable to appreciate the criminality of his conduct or to conform his conduct to

---

[c] In 1916, the American Institute of Criminal Law and Criminology recommended abolition of the traditional insanity formulations in favor of a mens-rea proposal strikingly similar to the Montana statute quoted in the text:

"No person shall hereafter be convicted of any criminal charge when at the time of the act or omission alleged against him he was suffering from mental disease and by reason of such mental disease he did not have the particular state of mind that must accompany such act or omission to constitute the crime charged."

Professor Edwin Keedy, the architect of the proposal, asserted that it would not abolish the defense of irresistible impulse because "volition is a necessary element of every crime." He concluded that "It is almost inconceivable that any court of last resort in this country would refuse to allow as a defense a clearly established case of insane impulse." Keedy, Insanity and Criminal Responsibility, 30 Harv.L.Rev. 535, 546–48, 550–51 (1917).

the requirements of law, the sentencing court shall consider any relevant evidence presented at the trial and shall require such additional evidence as it considers necessary for the determination of the issue including examination of the defendant and a report thereof. . . .

"Section 46–14–312. Sentence to be imposed. (1) If the court finds that the defendant at the time of the commission of the offense of which he was convicted did not suffer from a mental disease or defect as described in Section 46–14–311, it shall sentence him [pursuant to otherwise applicable sentencing provisions].

"(2) If the court finds that the defendant at the time of the commission of the offense suffered from a mental disease or defect as described in Section 46–14–311, any mandatory minimum sentence prescribed by law for the offense need not apply and the court shall sentence him to be committed to the custody of the director of the department of institutions to be placed in an appropriate institution for custody, care, and treatment for a definite period of time not to exceed the maximum term of imprisonment that could be imposed under Subsection (1). . . .

"(3) A defendant whose sentence has been imposed under Subsection (2) may petition the sentencing court for review of the sentence if the [responsible mental-health professional] certifies that the defendant has been cured of the mental disease or defect. The sentencing court may make any [otherwise authorized order] except that the length of confinement or supervision must be equal to that of the original sentence. The [responsible mental-health professional] shall review the defendant's status each year.

"Section 46–14–313. Discharge of defendant from supervision. At the expiration of the period of commitment or period of treatment specified by the court under Section 46–14–312(2), the defendant must be discharged from custody and further supervision, subject only to the law regarding the civil commitment of persons suffering from serious mental illness."

Do you understand how the dispositional consequences of this scheme differ from those that would obtain if the insanity defense had not been "abolished"?[d] To what extent is the Montana scheme predicated on retributive considerations in addition to purely dispositional considerations?

(ii) **Disposition of Persons Lacking Mens Rea Due to Mental Disease.** One of the arguments against admitting evidence of mental

[d] Idaho and Utah have similar provisions. These schemes are unusual because they were adopted in lieu of an insanity defense. It should be recalled, however, that at least 12 states have *combined* a similar sentencing scheme with the insanity defense: in those states, a verdict of not guilty by reason of insanity leads to commitment while a "guilty but mentally ill" verdict leads to special sentencing procedures similar to those in Montana. See, e.g., Mich.Comp.Laws Ann. § 768.36. The GBMI verdict is discussed at pages 750–52, supra.

abnormality whenever it is relevant to mens rea is that this could result in release of dangerous persons. The fear is that the procedures for civil commitment of the mentally ill afford inadequate social protection. Not surprisingly, proponents of the mens-rea alternative to the insanity defense usually provide for a separate commitment procedure for persons who lack mens rea due to mental disease. Thus, the same questions concerning the proper criteria for commitment of such persons that arise in a jurisdiction that admits evidence on mens rea in addition to the insanity defense would also have to be resolved under the mens-rea alternative to the defense.

Consider for example, the applicable Montana provisions.[e] After a person "is acquitted on the ground that due to a mental disease or defect he could not have a particular state of mind that is an essential element of the offense charged," the court is required to commit him to the mental-health department "for custody, care and treatment." The person is entitled to a hearing within 50 days to "determine his present mental condition and whether he may be discharged or released without danger to others." The burden of proof is placed on the defendant to prove "that he may be safely released." The person is committed indefinitely until a court finds that he "may be discharged or released on condition without danger to himself or others." Would this commitment scheme be acceptable if the subjects were persons acquitted by reason of insanity? Do they provide a more or less acceptable basis for committing persons, such as Stephenson or Wetmore, found to lack the mens rea required for criminal liability?

4. **Blameworthiness Considerations.** The proposals to abolish the insanity defense implicate fundamental moral concerns. The central question may be put as follows: To the extent that the mens-rea approach in fact would reduce the exculpatory significance of mental abnormality, would it require criminal conviction of "a class of persons who, on any common-sense notion of justice, are beyond blaming and ought not to be punished"?[f]

The proponents of the mens-rea approach respond that it would not. They argue that the only meaningful line between the blameless and the blameworthy is that represented by mens rea. Although they concede that responsibility may otherwise be diminished by mental disability, they argue that such factors should be taken into account in sentencing, together with other social and psychological information relevant to the offender's responsibility for his behavior. This argument was developed by Professor Norval Morris in Psychiatry and the Dangerous Criminal, 41 So.Cal.L.Rev. 514, 520–21 (1968): [*]

"[T]he moral issue remains central—whether we should include as criminally responsible . . . those whose freedom to

[e] Mont.Rev.Stat.Ann. §§ 46–14–301, et seq. Unlike Montana, Idaho and Utah did not enact special dispositional procedures for mens-rea acquittees. In Idaho and Utah, these individuals are subject to the generally applicable civil commitment statutes.

[f] Kadish, The Decline of Innocence, 26 Camb.L.J. 273, 283 (1968).

[*] The excerpts below are reprinted with the permission of the author and the Southern California Law Review.

choose between criminal and lawful behavior was curtailed by mental illness. It too often is overlooked that one group's exculpation from criminal responsibility confirms the inculpation of other groups. Why not permit the defense of dwelling in a Negro ghetto? Such a defense would not be morally indefensible. Adverse social and subcultural background is statistically *more* criminogenic than is psychosis; like insanity, it also severely circumscribes the freedom of choice which a non-deterministic criminal law . . . attributes to accused persons. True, a defense of social adversity would politically be intolerable; but that does not vitiate the analogy for my purposes. [It will be argued] that insanity destroys, undermines, diminishes man's capacity to reject what is wrong and to adhere to what is right. So does the ghetto—more so. But surely, [it will be replied,] I would not have us punish the sick. Indeed I would, if [society insists] on punishing the grossly deprived. To the extent that criminal sanctions serve punitive purposes, I fail to see the difference between these two defenses. To the extent that they serve rehabilitative, treatment, and curative purposes I fail to see the need for the difference.

" . . . It seems clear that there *are* different degrees of moral turpitude in criminal conduct and that the mental health or illness of an actor is relevant to an assessment of that degree—as are many other factors in a crime's social setting and historical antecedents. This does not mean, however, that we are obliged to quantify these pressures for purposes of a moral assessment . . . leading to conclusions as to criminal responsibility.

"In a few cases moral non-responsibility is so clear that it would be purposeless to invoke the criminal process. Accident, in its purest and least subconscious, accident-prone form, is a situation where there is little utility in invoking the criminal process. The same is true where a person did not know what he was doing at the time of the alleged crime. But in these situations there is no need for [responsibility] rules, because they clearly fall within general criminal law exculpatory rules. The actor simply lacks the mens rea of the crime. It thus seems to me that, within the area of criminal responsibility and psychological disturbance, all that we need is already achieved with existing, long-established rules of intent and crime; I would allow either sane or insane mens rea to suffice for guilt."

Professor Sanford Kadish has responded, in The Decline of Innocence, 26 Camb.L.J. 273, 284 (1968),* as follows:

"[Professor Morris argues] that we convict and punish persons daily whose ability to conform is impaired by a variety of circumstances—by youthful neglect, by parental inadequacy, by

* The excerpts below are reprinted with the permission of the author and the Cambridge University Press.

the social and psychical deprivations of growing up in a grossly underprivileged minority subculture, or by countless other contingencies of life. This is perfectly true, but I fail to see that it supports eliminating the insanity defence. First, the argument logically is an argument for extension of the defence of lack of responsibility, not for its abolition. It is never a reason for adding to injustice that we are already guilty of some. Second, confining the defence to patent and extreme cases of irresponsibility is not a whimsical irrationality. There may well be an injustice in it, but it rests upon the practical concern to avoid vitiating the deterrent impact of the criminal law upon those who are more or less susceptible to its influences. . . . We may accept as a necessary evil—necessary, that is, given our commitment to a punishment system—the criminal conviction of persons whose ability to conform is somewhat impaired and still protest that it is unacceptable for a society to fail to make a distinction for those who are utterly and obviously beyond the reach of the law."

It is noteworthy that Professors Morris and Kadish join issue most clearly on whether a qualitative line can be drawn through claims of volitional impairment. Does agreement with Professor Morris on this issue necessarily entail abolition of the cognitive prong of the insanity defense as well?

The exchange between Professors Morris and Kadish also highlights another dimension of the controversy. Professor Morris argues that persons who are supposedly held blameless on grounds of insanity in fact are punished under the present system of commitment:

"[It is said that] the criminal justice system is a . . . stigmatizing . . . system which should not be used against the mentally ill. They are mad not bad, sick not wicked; it is important that we should not misclassify them.

"The rebuttal to this defense of the [insanity defense] is the fact of 'double stigmatization.' . . . Prison authorities regard their inmates in the facilities for the psychologically disturbed as both criminal and insane, bad and mad; mental hospital authorities regard their inmates who have been convicted—or only arrested and charged with crime—as both insane and criminal, mad and bad. . . .

"[T]he defense of insanity is neither essential to the morality of punishment nor effective at present to reduce social stigma. Nor is it a necessary or effective principle around which to mobilize clinical resources for the rational treatment of the psychologically disturbed criminal actor."

Professor Kadish responds as follows:

"The criminal law as we know it today does associate a substantial condemnatory onus with conviction for a crime. So long as this is so a just and humane legal system has an obligation to make a distinction between those who are eligible for this condemnation and those who are not. It is true, as [Professor Morris has] argued, that a person adjudicated not guilty but insane suffers a substantial social stigma. It is also true that this is hurtful and unfortunate, and indeed, unjust. But it results from the misinterpretation placed upon the person's conduct by people in the community. It is not, like the conviction of the irresponsible, the paradigmatic affront to the sense of justice in the law which consists in the deliberative act of convicting a morally innocent person of a crime, of imposing blame when there is no occasion for it."

Professors Kadish and Morris disagree on where the line must be drawn to separate the blameless from the blameworthy. They also disagree on the meaning of "punishment." Who is right? Should the insanity defense be abolished? [g]

[g] Professor Morris recently reaffirmed his position in Madness and the Criminal Law (1982). His view was endorsed by the American Medical Association in 251 J.Am.Med.Ass'n 2967 (1984). The abolitionist position is criticized in Morse, Excusing the Crazy: The Insanity Defense Reconsidered, 58 So.Cal.L.Rev. 777 (1985); Hermann, Book Review: Madness and the Criminal Law, 51 G.W.L.Rev. 329 (1983); Arenella, Reflections on Current Proposals to Abolish or Reform the Insanity Defense, 8 Am.J.Leg.Med. 271 (1982).

Chapter VI

HOMICIDE: A PROBLEM OF CULPABILITY AND GRADING

INTRODUCTORY NOTES ON THE HISTORY OF CRIMINAL HOMICIDE

The term "homicide" refers to any conduct that causes the death of another. The task of the criminal law is two-fold: (i) to distinguish those homicides that should be criminal from those that should not; and (ii) to grade those homicides punished as crimes. The issue of criminalization is governed by the general doctrines explored in Chapters I, II, IV, and V. This chapter is devoted mainly to a study of the gradations drawn by the law among criminal homicides.

Because the intentional taking of human life is widely regarded as among the most heinous of criminal offenses, the penalties prescribed for criminal homicide include the most severe sanctions known to the law. An enormous range of human conduct can result in criminal homicide, however, and it is necessary to take account of less egregious forms of the offense in establishing the penalty structure. As a result, penalties authorized for homicidal behavior span the entire range of penal sanctions.

The problem of grading criminal homicides—of matching appropriate sanctions to patterns of homicidal behavior—presents a number of difficult questions with which the law has never come comfortably to rest. Chapter VI is designed to highlight several of the more important of these questions in some detail, at the cost of more summary treatment of others. The following historical summary provides background and context for the materials that follow.[a]

1. **The Early Law.** From a modern perspective, the most important aspect of early English law was the development of the separate offenses of murder and manslaughter. Prior to 1496, murder was the only homicide offense, and the penalty was death. For those who could come within its terms, however, benefit of clergy was available to avoid the death penalty. By the late 15th century, the categories of offenders who could claim this mitigation had expanded to include virtually all literate persons.

A series of statutes enacted between 1496 and 1547 led to the development of manslaughter as a distinct and lesser homicide offense.

---

[a] The information contained in this summary is elaborated in more detail in ALI, Model Penal Code and Commentaries, §§ 210.0 to .6, pp. 1–171 (1980). Additional sources are cited in the Model Code commentary. Among the more useful of those sources are Royal Comm'n on Capital Punishment, Report, CMND. No. 8932 (1953); 3 J. Stephen, A History of the Criminal Law of England 1–107 (1883); Wechsler & Michael, A Rationale of the Law of Homicide, 37 Colum.L.Rev. 701, 1261 (1937).

The effect of these statutes was to exclude certain of the more serious forms of murder from the benefit of clergy. Those convicted of the excluded offenses thus became subject to the death penalty, unless they could obtain a royal pardon. As the law matured, the dividing line between murder and manslaughter came to be the concept of "malice prepense" or "malice aforethought." In time, murder came to include all homicides committed with "malice aforethought," and manslaughter all criminal homicides committed without "malice aforethought." As the law evolved, to paraphrase Stephen, the judges allocated criminal homicides between murder and manslaughter—and gave meaning to the determinative term "malice aforethought"—according to which offenders deserved to be hanged.[b] This initial effort at grading criminal homicide offenses thus used the definition of murder as the device for isolating those homicides for which the death penalty was imposed.[c]

2. **The Distinction Between Murder and Manslaughter.** The remaining common-law history of murder and manslaughter principally concerns the content assigned to the two categories as they expanded in scope. Murder came to encompass four types of cases: (i) those where the actor intended to kill or knew that death would result from his conduct; (ii) those where the actor intended to inflict grievous bodily harm or knew that such harm would result from his conduct; (iii) those where the actor manifested reckless indifference to death—a state of mind described in relatively modern usage as a "depraved mind," an "abandoned and malignant heart," or "wickedness of disposition, hardness of heart, cruelty, recklessness of consequences, and a mind regardless of social duty"; and (iv) those where the death occurred while the actor was engaged in the commission of a felony. Malice aforethought became a term of art, if not, as Glanville Williams has said, a term of deception,[d] that encompassed all of these various circumstances and states of mind. The term was thus a token, an arbitrary symbol, used to collect under a single label a wide variety of cases having no more in common than that they were at one time or another deemed appropriate situations for imposition of the death penalty.

Manslaughter, defined only as all homicide that on the one hand was committed without malice aforethought and on the other lacked any justification or excuse, came to include a similarly broad range of conduct. Common-law manslaughter encompassed three distinct types of offenses: (i) those where the actor intended to kill but committed the offense in a sudden heat of passion engendered by adequate provoca-

---

[b] See Royal Comm'n on Capital Punishment, CMND. No. 8932, at 28 (1953). What Stephen actually said (in 1866), was that "the loose term 'malice' was used, and then when a particular state of mind came to their notice the judges called it 'malice' or not according to their view of the propriety of hanging particular people. That is, in two words, the history of the definition of murder."

[c] The traditional definition of murder, as paraphrased from Coke's rendition in the 17th century, was: "When a man of sound memory and of the age of discretion unlawfully kills any reasonable creature in being and under the King's peace, with malice aforethought, either express or implied by the law, the death taking place within a year and a day." See 3 Coke, Institutes * 47; Royal Comm'n on Capital Punishment, CMND. No. 8932, at 28 (1953).

[d] G. Williams, Textbook of Criminal Law 208 (1978).

tion; (ii) those where the actor engaged in reckless or negligent behavior that was insufficiently culpable to constitute murder but more culpable than ordinary civil negligence; and (iii) those where the death occurred while the actor was engaged in the commission of an unlawful act not amounting to a felony. The term "voluntary manslaughter" refers to the first category. The term "involuntary manslaughter" refers to the second and third categories. The distinction between voluntary and involuntary manslaughter had no significance at common law, although modern statutes frequently use these terms to describe different grading categories.[e]

3. **The Premeditation-Deliberation Formula.** The common-law structure has survived to this day in England, although grading provisions designed to restrict use of the death penalty were adopted in 1957 and the death penalty was abandoned altogether in 1965. In the United States, the common-law structure still prevails in many states, though in most it has been modified by statute.

The earliest significant change occurred in a Pennsylvania statute adopted in 1794, which introduced a distinction between "first-degree" and "second-degree" murder. That statute provided:

> "[A]ll murder, which shall be perpetrated by means of poison, or by lying in wait, or by any other kind of wilful, deliberate and premeditated killing, or which shall be committed in the perpetration or attempt to perpetrate any arson, rape, robbery, or burglary, shall be deemed murder in the first degree; and all other kinds of murder shall be deemed murder in the second degree."

The purpose of this legislation was to confine the capital sanction, which remained the mandatory penalty,[f] to first-degree murder. The statute proved enormously influential. The majority of American jurisdictions adopted similar provisions early in the 19th century. By 1959, the statutes in 34 jurisdictions were closely derived from the original Pennsylvania formula.

By far the most litigated issue under this statute was the meaning of the phrase "by any other kind of wilful, deliberate and premeditated killing." It clearly referred to an intentional killing, but the question was whether it was meant to include all intentional killings or to be limited to an intent to kill formed in a particular manner.[g]

(i) **The Pennsylvania Construction.** In his article, History of the Pennsylvania Statute Creating Degrees of Murder, 97 U.Pa.L.Rev.

[e] See, e.g., the Virginia statutes reproduced in Appendix B, pages 1–5, infra.

[f] All states retained the mandatory death penalty for the most serious form of murder until 1838, when Tennessee adopted the first discretionary death penalty statute. Twenty-three American jurisdictions followed suit by the turn of the century, and by 1962 all American jurisdictions had adopted this modification of the common-law system.

[g] Note that the statute begins with the words "all murder," then describes those forms of "murder" that fall into the first-degree category, and concludes by classifying "all other kinds of murder" as of the second degree. The statute thus built upon the common-law definition of murder. Any form of common-law murder not included in the first-degree category fell into the residual second-degree category.

759, 771–73 (1949), Professor Keedy concluded that the Pennsylvania legislature originally intended the words "deliberate" and "premeditated" to be read literally. Nevertheless, the Pennsylvania courts did not construe the language in this manner: "Soon after the statute was enacted the judges began to nullify its requirements by refusing to give effect to the meaning of the words 'deliberate' and 'premeditated,' and by announcing the proposition that killing with an intent to kill constitutes first-degree murder." As early as 1794, the year the degree statute was enacted, a Pennsylvania trial judge adopted this construction. Later pronouncements of the Pennsylvania courts were to the same effect. In Keenan v. Commonwealth, 44 Pa. 55, 56 (1862), the Pennsylvania Supreme Court summarized prior decisions with the comment that "our reported jurisprudence is very uniform in holding that the true criterion of the first degree is the intent to take life."

Modern Pennsylvania decisions have reaffirmed this interpretation. In Commonwealth v. Carroll, 412 Pa. 525, 526, 194 A.2d 911, 915 (1963), the court said:

> "The specific intent to kill which is necessary to constitute . . . murder in the first degree may be found from a defendant's words or conduct or from the attendant circumstances together with all reasonable inferences therefrom, and may be inferred from the intentional use of a deadly weapon on a vital part of the body of another human being. . . . 'Whether the intention to kill and the killing, that is, the premeditation and the fatal act, were within a brief space of time or a long space of time is immaterial if the killing was in fact intentional, wilful, deliberate and premeditated.' "

This approach, moreover, is by no means limited to Pennsylvania. Professors Wechsler and Michael, in their classic article, A Rationale of the Law of Homicide I, 37 Colum.L.Rev. 701, 707–09 (1937),* summarized the general state of American law as follows:

> "The most striking phase of the development of the English law was the reduction of 'malice aforethought' to a term of art signifying neither 'malice' nor 'aforethought' in the popular sense. Strikingly analogous in the judicial development of the American law of homicide is the narrow interpretation of 'deliberation' and 'premeditation' to exclude the two elements which the words normally signify: a determination to kill reached (i) calmly and (ii) some appreciable time prior to the homicide. The elimination of these elements leaves, as Judge Cardozo pointed out, nothing precise as the critical state of mind but intention to kill. Such a result creates particular difficulty in a jurisdiction like New York where 'design' to kill is, by statute, the distinguishing feature of second-degree murder.[h] The trial judge must solemnly distinguish in his charge between the two degrees in terms which frequently render them quite indistinguishable, a

---

* Reprinted with permission of Professor Wechsler and the Columbia Law Review.

[h] The New York statute in effect at this time is reproduced in Appendix B, pages 6–7, infra. [Footnote by eds.]

procedure which obviously confers on the jury a discretion to follow one aspect of the charge or the other, if not a valid excuse for neglecting the charge entirely. The statutory scheme was apparently intended to limit administrative discretion in the selection of capital cases. As so frequently occurs, the discretion which the legislature threw out the door was let in through the window by the courts." [i]

The reference to Judge Cardozo in the preceding excerpt was to a lecture given to the Academy of Medicine in 1928, subsequently published in Law and Literature 97–101 (1931).* Judge Cardozo said:

"The difficulty arises when we try to discover what is meant by the words deliberate and premeditated. A long series of decisions, beginning many years ago, has given to these words a meaning that differs to some extent from the one revealed upon the surface. To deliberate and premeditate within the meaning of the statute, one does not have to plan the murder days or hours or even minutes in advance, as where one lies in wait for one's enemy or places poison in his food or drink. The law does not say that any particular length of time must intervene between the volition and the act. The human brain, we are reminded, acts at times with extra-ordinary celerity. All that the statute requires is that the act must not be the result of immediate or spontaneous impulse. 'If there is hesitation or doubt to be overcome, a choice made as the result of thought, however short the struggle between the intention and the act,' there is such deliberation and premeditation as will expose the offender to the punishment of death. . . .

"I think the distinction [between murder in its two degrees] is much too vague to be continued in our law. There can be no intent unless there is a choice, yet by the hypothesis, the choice without more is enough to justify the inference that the intent was deliberate and premeditated. The presence of a sudden impulse is said to mark the dividing line, but how can an impulse be anything but sudden when the time for its formation is measured by the lapse of seconds? Yet the decisions are to the effect that seconds may be enough. . . . I think the students of the mind should make it clear to the law-makers that the statute is framed along the lines of a defective and unreal psychology. If intent is deliberate and premeditated whenever there is choice, then in truth it is always deliberate and premeditated, since choice is involved in the hypothesis of the intent. What we have is merely a privilege offered to the jury to find the lesser degree, when the suddenness of the intent, the vehemence of the passion,

[i] The early New York cases as well as those of four states that patterned their law on the New York model are analyzed in Knudson, Murder by the Clock, 24 Wash.U.L.Q. 305 (1939). The results confirm the general conclusions advanced by Professors Wechsler and Michael. [Footnote by eds.]

* From Law and Literature by Benjamin Cardozo, copyright 1931 by Harcourt Brace Jovanovich, Inc.; renewed 1959 by First National Trust Co. Reprinted by permission of the publishers.

seems to call irresistibly for the exercise of mercy. I have no objection to giving them this dispensing power, but it should be given to them directly and not in a mystifying cloud of words. The present distinction is so obscure that no jury hearing it for the first time can fairly be expected to assimilate and understand it. . . . Upon the basis of this fine distinction with its obscure and mystifying psychology, scores of men have gone to their death. . . . "

(ii) *People v. Anderson.* A few courts have given the formula a more literal meaning. Consider, for example, People v. Anderson, 70 Cal.2d 15, 73 Cal.Rptr. 550, 447 P.2d 942 (1968). Anderson was convicted of the first-degree murder of a 10-year old girl and sentenced to death. He had been living with the girl's mother for about eight months prior to the homicide. On the morning of the murder, the mother went to work, leaving Anderson at home alone with the girl. Anderson had not worked for two days and had been drinking heavily. The girl's nude body was discovered in her bedroom by her brother that evening after the mother returned from work. More than 60 knife wounds, some severe and some superficial, were found on her body, including the partial amputation of her tongue and a post-mortem cut extending from the rectum through the vagina. There was no evidence of sexual molestation prior to the death. Blood was found in every room of the house.

The court held that there was insufficient evidence of premeditation and deliberation and that the killing therefore should be reduced to murder in the second degree. It began by noting that it was "well established that the brutality of a killing cannot in itself support a finding that the killer acted with premeditation and deliberation." The court continued:

"[W]e find no indication that the legislature intended to give the words 'deliberate' and 'premeditated' other than their ordinary dictionary meanings. Moreover, we have repeatedly pointed out that the legislative classification of murder into two degrees would be meaningless if 'deliberation' and 'premeditation' were construed as requiring no more reflection than may be involved in the mere formation of a specific intent to kill.

"Thus we have held that in order for a killing with malice aforethought to be first- rather than second-degree murder, ' "[t]he intent to kill must be . . . formed upon a *pre-existing* reflection" [and must have] been the subject of actual deliberation or *forethought*.' We have therefore [required that the killer act] 'as a result of careful thought and weighing of considerations; as a *deliberate* judgment or plan; carried on cooly and steadily, [especially] according to a *preconceived design*.' "

The court then held that evidence of premeditation and deliberation generally fell into three patterns: evidence of "planning" activity, evidence of "motive," and evidence as to the "manner" of the killing that showed a preconceived design to kill. Most first-degree verdicts that it had sustained, the court said, contained evidence of all three types, though some had consisted of the second in conjunction with one of the other two. But Anderson's case, the court concluded, "lacks evidence of any of the three types." There was no evidence of planning or motive. And "the only inference" which the evidence as to the manner of the killing supports "is that the killing resulted from a 'random,' violent, indiscriminate attack rather than from deliberately placed wounds inflicted according to a preconceived design." [j]

(iii) **Modern Utility of the Formula.** A number of states still retain the premeditation-deliberation language to describe the highest category of criminal homicide. Most recently drafted statutes, however, have followed the Model Penal Code in abandoning that formula. In states where the phrase had been interpreted to include every intentional killing, deleting the language in favor of a phrase such as "intent to kill" merely clarifies the inquiry the jury is expected to undertake. In states where the formula had been taken more literally, the legislatures have been convinced that it does not accurately separate the more heinous forms of murder from the less heinous, regardless of whether the most serious class of offenses is punishable by death. They have concluded, in essence, that the formula does not ask the right question—that it does not reflect an intelligible policy for the grading of criminal homicides. The point was put nicely by Sir James Fitzjames Stephen in 3 A History of the Criminal Law of England 94 (1883):

> "As much cruelty, as much indifference to the life of others, a disposition at least as dangerous to society, probably even more dangerous, is shown by sudden as by premeditated murders. The following cases appear to me to set this in a clear light. A man passing along the road, sees a boy sitting on a bridge over a deep river and, out of mere wanton barbarity, pushes him into it and so drowns him. A man makes advances to a girl who repels him. He deliberately but instantly cuts her throat. A man civilly asked to pay a just debt pretends to get the money, loads a rifle and blows out his creditor's brains. In none of these cases is there premeditation unless the word is used in a sense as unnatural as 'aforethought' in 'malice aforethought,' but each represents even more diabolical cruelty and ferocity than that which is involved in murders premeditated in the natural sense of the word."

Quite apart from concerns about capital punishment, do you see any modern utility for the premeditation-deliberation formula? Should

---

[j] Compare Washington v. Bingham, 40 Wn.App. 553, 699 P.2d 262 (1985), where the court said:

"[R]eview of [prior Washington] cases reveals that in each one where the evidence has been found sufficient, there has been some evidence beyond time from which a jury could infer the fact of deliberation. This evidence has included, inter alia, motive, acquisition of a weapon, and planning directly related to the killing.

"Unless evidence of both time for and fact of deliberation are required, premeditation could be inferred in any case where the means of effecting death requires more than a moment in time. For all practical purposes, it would merge with intent; proof of intent would become proof of premeditation. However, the two elements are separate. Premeditation cannot be inferred from intent."

Anderson be included in the highest category of murder? Even if the California court was right that there was insufficient evidence of premeditation and deliberation?

SECTION 1: CAPITAL HOMICIDE

INTRODUCTORY NOTE ON USE OF
THE DEATH PENALTY

Capital punishment was an established feature of American law at the time the Constitution and the Bill of Rights were adopted, as well as when the 14th amendment was ratified following the Civil War. Although a movement to abolish the death penalty surfaced during the 1830's, only a few states (Michigan in 1847, Rhode Island in 1852, and Wisconsin in 1853) eliminated the capital sanction before the Civil War. Thereafter, occasional surges of abolitionist sentiment led to a gradual reduction of offenses punishable by death.

Abolitionist sentiment emerged on a broad scale after World War II, provoking widespread debate and occasional legislative action; seven state legislatures eliminated capital punishment between 1957 and 1965, bringing to 10 the number of abolitionist states. Meanwhile, the penalty was carried out with declining frequency: the average annual number of executions gradually dropped from 167 during the 1930's to less than 50 during the late 1950's and early 1960's.

Notwithstanding these trends, public opinion was divided on the issue, and most states defeated abolitionist proposals. In the early 1960's, death penalty opponents began to focus their attention on the courts. Although the constitutionality of capital punishment had traditionally been regarded as well settled, there was reason to believe that the Supreme Court would be receptive to the abolitionist cause. The Court had recently shown its willingness—in the school desegregation and reapportionment cases—to use constitutional litigation as a mechanism for changing social and political institutions. Moreover, the claim that the death penalty had been administered in a racially discriminatory fashion [a] implicated one of the central concerns of the Warren Court.

Litigation challenging the constitutionality of various features of capital sentencing proceedings gradually proceeded through the federal courts under the direction of lawyers associated with the NAACP Legal Defense and Educational Fund.[b] In 1968, the Supreme Court invalidated procedures that permitted the prosecution to exclude "for cause" any jurors who had "conscientious scruples" against the death penalty.

---

[a] Of the 3,859 persons executed between 1930 and 1968, 2,066 were black. Of the 455 executed for rape during this period, 405 were black. Of the 2,306 persons executed in the South during these years, 72 per cent were black.

[b] An insider's account of the death penalty litigation, culminating in the Supreme Court's decision in *Furman v. Georgia*, is presented in M. Meltsner, Cruel and Unusual: The Supreme Court and Capital Punishment (1973).

The Court held, in Witherspoon v. Illinois, 391 U.S. 510 (1968), that the exclusion of jurors for cause should be limited to those who were unequivocally opposed to the death penalty in all cases; exclusion of jurors with more ambiguous attitudes, the Court ruled, tended to produce a "hanging jury." The *Witherspoon* decision had the effect of invalidating most death sentences that were pending at the time. A de facto moratorium on executions then took hold as the abolitionist litigants pressed other claims calling into question the constitutionality of the death penalty itself.

Over the next decade, a closely divided Court decided a series of cases that significantly altered the constitutional landscape. Although the Court eventually upheld the constitutionality of capital punishment, it restricted the offenses for which the death penalty may be imposed and restructured the procedures by which capital sentencing must be administered. In response to these decisions, the great majority of states have revised their death penalty statutes.[c] The first execution under this contemporary generation of statutes was carried out in 1977 and, by the end of 1985, more than 50 persons had been executed and about 1600 prisoners were awaiting execution.

It is evident that the death penalty continues to command substantial political support in the United States. For that reason it is likely that there will continue to be executions for the foreseeable future. It is also evident, however, that the debate concerning the merits of capital punishment will continue and that administration of the penalty will be subject to ongoing constitutional scrutiny. Although full coverage of this complex subject is not feasible in these materials, this section is designed, first, to provide an overview of the Supreme Court's decisions and, second, to survey the basic issues that arise under modern capital sentencing statutes.

INTRODUCTORY NOTE ON THE EFFICACY AND MORALITY OF THE DEATH PENALTY

At the outset, it may be useful to review the traditional arguments made for and against the efficacy and morality of the death penalty. The literature on the subject is voluminous,[a] and often polemical. The major arguments on both sides of the controversy are summarized in

[c] Thirty-seven states had capital sentencing statutes in force on January 1, 1985. Statutes on the books in two other states, New York and Massachusetts, had been declared unconstitutional by the highest courts in those states.

[a] The Model Penal Code Commentaries, quoted below, summarize the literature as of its publication. More recent entries in the debate include W. Bowers, Legal Homicide: Death as Punishment in America, 1864–1982 (1984); E. Vanden Haag & J. Conrad, The Death Penalty: A Debate (1983); H. Bedau, The Death Penalty in America (3d ed. 1982); R. Berger, Death Penalties: The Supreme Court's Obstacle Course (1982); S. Dike, Capital Punishment in the U.S.: A Consideration of the Evidence (1982); C. Black, Capital Punishment: The Inevitability of Caprice and Mistake (1981); T. Sellin, The Penalty of Death (1980); W. Berns, For Capital Punishment: Crime and Morality of the Death Penalty (1979); Lempert, Desert and Deterrence: An Assessment of The Moral Basis for Capital Punishment, 79 Mich.L.Rev. 1177 (1981). See also the symposium published in 18 U.C.Davis L.Rev. 865 (1985).

the following excerpt from ALI, Model Penal Code and Commentaries, § 210.6, pp. 111–17 (1980): *

"[A] broad societal consensus on the issue of capital punishment seems as elusive as ever. Debate continues, and the literature on the subject grows more and more abundant. Although this commentary makes no attempt to resolve the matter, it may be useful to describe the dimensions of the controversy. Abolitionist sentiment often reflects a profound moral distaste for 'official murder.' For some, the death penalty is simply an unacceptable contradiction of the intrinsic worth of a human being. As Mr. Justice Brennan made the point, 'the calculated killing of a human being by the state involves, by its very nature, a denial of the executed person's humanity.' For others, death is a fitting penalty for one who takes another's life and an appropriate expression of societal outrage at such conduct. In any event, judgments of this sort do not readily yield to reasoned support or refutation, at least not in terms within the special competence of lawyers. The debate, therefore, has tended to shift to other grounds.

"Chief among them is the efficacy of the death penalty as a deterrent. In a monograph prepared for the [American Law Institute,] Professor Thorsten Sellin collected data on actual imposition of the death penalty and attempted to assess the relationship, if any, between homicide rates and the authorization of death as a possible sanction for murder.[9] Sellin selected clusters of neighboring states with similar social and economic conditions. Within each cluster he compared the experience of abolitionist and retentionist jurisdictions and found no significant or systematic difference between them: 'The inevitable conclusion is that executions have no discernible effect on homicide death rates. . . . '

"Sellin concluded that a sentence of death is executed in a trivial fraction of the cases in which it might legally be imposed and that there is no quantitative evidence that either its availability or its imposition has noticeable influence upon the frequency of murder. The latter conclusion is not surprising when it is remembered that murders are, upon the whole, either crimes of passion, in which a calculus of consequences has small psychological reality, or crimes of such depravity that the actor reveals himself as doubtfully within the reach of influences that might be especially inhibitory in the case of an ordinary man. These factors, therefore, leave room for substantial doubt that any solid case can be maintained for the death penalty as a deterrent to murder, at least as it is employed in the United States. If this conclusion is correct, it would seem that the social need for

---

* Copyright © 1980 by the American Law Institute. Reprinted with permission.

[9] "T. Sellin, The Death Penalty (ALI 1959), also printed at MPC § 201.6, p. 221 (Tent.Draft No. 9, 1959). See Sellin, Capital Punishment, 25 Fed.Probation, Part 3, at 3 (1961); Sellin, Homicides in Retentionist and Abolitionist States, in Capital Punishment (T.Sellin ed. 1967)."

grievous condemnation of the act can be met, as it is met in abolition states, without resorting to capital punishment.

"Sellin's work proved extremely influential for almost 15 years. It survived without major challenge until Professor Isaac Ehrlich's efforts to test implications of general deterrence theory in the context of capital punishment.[11] Ehrlich looked at the relationship between the homicide rate in the nation as a whole and the 'execution risk,' that is, the fraction of convicted murderers who are actually put to death. He tried to hold other factors constant by the technique of multiple regression analysis. From experience in the United States from 1933 through 1967 Ehrlich drew the tentative conclusion that execution of an offender tended on the average to deter eight homicides. This finding prompted a storm of controversy that has not yet begun to abate. Sellin's work and Ehrlich's analysis have been attacked and defended on methodological grounds,[13] and each has been tested by replication.[14] These disputes of methodology and statistical technique are largely beyond the competence of those without special training in the field. Further research may clarify the matter, but at present the verdict must be that the existence of a significant deterrent effect from retention of the death penalty has been neither proved nor disproved.

"Apart from the efficacy of the death penalty as a deterrent, its possible imposition exerts a discernible and baneful effect on the administration of criminal justice. A trial where life is at stake becomes inevitably a morbid and sensational affair, fraught with risk that public sympathy will be aroused for the defendant without reference to guilt or innocence of the crime charged. In the rare cases where a capital sentence is imposed, this unwholesome influence carries through the period preceding execution, reaching a climax when sentence is carried out.

"The special sentiment associated with judgment of death is reflected also in the courts, lending added weight to claims of error in the trial and multiplying and protracting the appellate processes, including post-conviction remedies. As astute and realistic an observer as Mr. Justice Jackson observed to the Chief

[11] "Ehrlich, The Deterrent Effect of Capital Punishment: A Question of Life or Death, 65 Am.Econ.Rev. 397 (1975); Ehrlich, The Deterrent Effect of Capital Punishment: A Question of Life or Death (Working Paper No. 18, Center for Economic Analysis of Human Behavior and Social Institutions, 1973)."

[13] "See, e.g., Zeisel, Deterrent Effect of the Death Penalty: Facts v. Faiths, 1976 Sup.Ct.Rev. 317 (1976); Baldus & Cole, A Comparison of the Work of Thorsten Sellin and Isaac Ehrlich on the Deterrent Effect of Capital Punishment, 85 Yale L.J. 170 (1975); Bowers & Pierce, The Illusion of Deterrence in Isaac Ehrlich's Research on Capital Punishment, 85 Yale L.J. 187

(1975); Ehrlich, Deterrence: Evidence and Inference, 85 Yale L.J. 209 (1975); Peck, The Deterrent Effect of Capital Punishment: Ehrlich and his Critics, 85 Yale L.J. 356 (1976); Ehrlich, Rejoinder, 85 Yale L.J. 368 (1976)."

[14] "W. Bowers, Executions in America 137–47 (1974); Bailey, Murder and the Death Penalty, 65 J.Crim.L.C. & P.S. 416, 421 (1974); Passel, The Deterrent Effect of the Death Penalty: A Statistical Test, 28 Stan.L.Rev. 61 (1975); Passel & Taylor, The Deterrent Effect of Capital Punishment: Another View 9–11 (Discussion Paper 74–7509, Columbia Univ. Dept. of Economics, Feb. 1975)."

Reporter [b] shortly prior to his death that he opposed capital punishment because of its deleterious effects on the judicial process and stated that he would appear and urge the Institute to favor abolition.

"Beyond these considerations, it is obvious that capital punishment is the most difficult of sanctions to administer with even rough equality. A rigid legislative definition of capital murders has proved unworkable in practice, given the infinite variety of homicides and possible mitigating factors. A discretionary system thus becomes inevitable, with equally inevitable differences in judgment depending on the individuals involved and other accidents of time and place.[15] Yet most dramatically when life is at stake, equality is, as it is generally felt to be, a most important element of justice.

"Sellin's data showed a total of 3096 civilian executions for murder in the United States during the years 1930–57. This number represents only a small fraction of all murder convictions. The annual number of executions declined noticeably across this time period. The decline resulted in part from a decreasing homicide rate and in part from the removal of mandatory death sentences in a few jurisdictions, but it also reflects a growing reluctance by judges and juries to impose the ultimate sanction. Subsequent experience confirms the point that imposition of the death penalty is an increasingly rare occurrence. The average annual rate of execution dropped from 128 in the 1940's to 72 in the 1950's to 31 in the years 1960–65. These figures give rise to the argument that the death penalty is actually carried out so rarely that its imposition in any particular case must be arbitrary. As Mr. Justice Stewart captured the thought in a constitutional context, 'death sentences are cruel and unusual in the same way that being struck by lightning is cruel and unusual.' Discomfort with the discretionary aspects of the system is aggravated, moreover, by a suspicion that the grounds for differentiating among individuals may include illegitimate factors such as race.[20] Finally, there is the point that erroneous convictions are inevitable and beyond correction in the light of newly discovered evidence when a capital sentence has been carried out.

"These, then, are the major arguments against capital punishment for murder. The arguments on the other side may well begin with crediting some deterrent efficacy to the threat of death as punishment, given the weight that such a threat ap-

---

[b] The reference is to Professor Herbert Wechsler, Chief Reporter for the Model Penal Code. [Footnote by eds.]

[15] "Even when a capital sentence is imposed, the speed as well as the certainty of its execution may depend primarily upon the resignation of the individual or his disposition to pursue appellate and collateral proceedings which may carry on for years. Indeed, as recent experience has shown, even the resignation of the individual to execution will not necessarily bring litigation to an end. See Gilmore v. Utah, 429 U.S. 1012 (1976)."

[20] "More than half the persons executed in the years 1930–57 were non-white. . . . "

pears to have on introspection. However one evaluates the studies by Sellin and Ehrlich, reported homicide rates per 100,000 of population may be too crude an instrument to reflect all the cases where the threat has been effective; and it may be regarded as sufficient to justify the means that some innocent lives *may* be preserved.

"Many would argue, further, that it is appropriate for a society to express its condemnation of murder by associating the offense with the highest sanction that the law can use, however much considerations of humanity should temper the exaction of the penalty when there are extenuations. And some communities may still have cause to fear the greater evil of resort to private violence as reprisal, if the law excludes the possibility that the murderer may lose his life. The problem of equality, to which attention has been drawn, will not appear to all to be dispositive. Arguments based on the discretionary character of the death penalty and the infrequency of its imposition may call for reform and review of the discretionary system rather than abolition of the punishment. And it may be thought enough that the capital penalty is merited in any case in which it actually is imposed. Finally, these arguments may be regarded as outweighing the costs of the penalty to the administration of justice, given the difficulty of measuring the effect of such factors on the deterrence and the condemnation points.

"Whatever the merits of the debate, in any event, capital punishment continues to command substantial political support within the American system.[22] It is as clear today as it was when the Model Code was drafted that many jurisdictions will continue to authorize the death penalty for at least some offenses for a considerable time to come. Those jurisdictions that elect to retain the penalty must confront the special need to provide a fair and rational system of administration and to meet recently developed constitutional standards. . . ."

---

[22] "As of 1976, 10 states had abolished the death penalty for all crimes: Alaska (1957), Hawaii (1957), Iowa (1965), Maine (1887), Michigan (1847), Minnesota (1911), Oregon (1964), South Dakota (1976), West Virginia (1965), and Wisconsin (1853). Popular support for the death penalty, as indicated by the Gallup polls, declined consistently from 62 per cent in 1936 to 42 per cent in 1966. After 1966, however, the trend reversed and by 1969 the approval rating had risen to 51 per cent. A nationwide Harris survey conducted in 1973 showed that 59 per cent of the American people supported the death penalty for murder while 31 per cent opposed it. The reaction to the *Furman* decision by the national and state legislatures . . . and to the 1976 death-penalty decisions . . . is further evidence of the substantial political support the death penalty commands."

SUBSECTION A: THE SUPREME COURT AND CAPITAL PUNISHMENT

INTRODUCTORY NOTES ON THE SUPREME COURT AND CAPITAL PUNISHMENT

1. **Background.** As opponents of capital punishment prepared to take their challenge to the Supreme Court in the 1960's, 40 states authorized (but did not require) the death penalty for the highest form of murder. Kidnapping was a capital offense in two-thirds of the states, and treason and rape were punishable by death in about half. In trials for capital offenses, juries in most states typically returned a sentence recommendation (often binding) together with the verdict of guilt. No additional criteria or standards were spelled out in the instructions to explain how the jury's discretion should be exercised. Moreover, because the jury decisions on guilt and sentence were made at the same time, no evidence beyond that admissible on the question of guilt was directed specifically to the propriety of a capital sentence. Since evidence concerning the defendant's character, personal background, and prior criminal record is normally inadmissible to determine guilt, the jury was required in many cases to make its sentencing decision without such information.[a]

Constitutional attacks against the death penalty proceeded along two lines. One focused on the capital sanction itself: it was argued that the death penalty contravened "evolving standards of decency in a civilized society" and therefore constituted a cruel and unusual punishment forbidden by the eighth amendment.[b] Second, it was argued that even if death is a constitutionally permissible punishment for some offenses, the existing capital sentencing procedures were unfair. The following notes summarize the Supreme Court decisions that responded to these arguments.

2. *McGautha v. California.* The first major decision focused explicitly on the procedural challenge and seemed to represent a significant defeat for those who were seeking constitutional reform. In McGautha v. California, 402 U.S. 183 (1971), the Court considered two claims that called into question the constitutionality of every capital sentencing statute then in use. First, the challengers contended that the practice of leaving the sentencing decision to unguided jury discretion was fundamentally unfair because it invited arbitrary and ad-hoc determinations.[c] Second, they argued that the practice of submitting

---

[a] This information could be considered by the judge, however, in states where the jury recommendation was not binding.

[b] The quotation, indicating that the eighth amendment has an evolving meaning, is from Chief Justice Warren's plurality opinion in Trop v. Dulles, 356 U.S. 86 (1958) (holding denationalization to be a cruel and unusual punishment).

[c] In McGautha's trial, the jury had been instructed that "the law itself provides no standard for the guidance of the jury in the selection of the penalty, but . . . commits the whole matter . . . to the judgment, conscience, and absolute discretion of the jury."

the guilt and punishment issues to the jury in a single proceeding excluded relevant sentencing information from the jury and thereby deprived the defendant of a fair sentencing hearing.[d] In a 6–3 decision, the Court held that discretionary jury sentencing, even in a single proceeding, did not violate due process.[e]

3. ***Furman v. Georgia.*** Shortly thereafter, the situation changed dramatically. One month after *McGautha* was decided, the Court granted certiorari in four cases to decide whether "the imposition and carrying out of the death penalty [in these cases] constitutes cruel and unusual punishment in violation of the eighth and 14th amendments."[f] The cases involved two death sentences for rape and one each for felony murder and murder by a person previously convicted of murder. A year later, a 5–4 majority set aside the death sentences in all four cases. The result was announced in a short per curiam opinion without supporting explanation. Furman v. Georgia, 408 U.S. 238 (1972). Each member of the Court wrote separately in opinions occupying more than 230 pages in the United States Reports.

The opinions fall into three categories. Justices Brennan and Marshall concluded that the death penalty was unconstitutional no matter what offenses were punished by death and no matter what procedures were used to administer the sanction. Justices Douglas, Stewart, and White concurred on narrower grounds. They seemed to be concerned with the risk that unguided jury discretion would degenerate into unacceptably inconsistent judgments. Chief Justice Burger and Justices Blackmun, Powell, and Rehnquist dissented. The views of each group of Justices are summarized below.

(i) **Brennan and Marshall.** Justice Brennan found the death penalty to be incompatible with evolving conceptions of human dignity for four reasons. First, he argued that the death penalty is so extreme in its severity and so degrading in its character as to be equivalent to the "barbaric punishments condemned by history," such as the rack, the thumbscrew, and the iron boot. Second, he thought that capital punishment, as it is administered, is incompatible with the principle that the state "must not arbitrarily inflict a severe punishment." Third, he concluded that the infrequency with which executions actually occurred demonstrated that capital punishment had become morally unacceptable to contemporary society. Finally, Justice Brennan canvassed the various purposes of punishment and concluded that, as it is being administered, the death penalty "serves no penal purpose more effectively than a less severe punishment." With respect to deterrence, he observed that "whatever the speculative validity of the assumption

---

[d] Although California was one of the few states with a bifurcated sentencing process, *McGautha* had been consolidated for decision with an Ohio case in which the death penalty had been imposed in a unitary proceeding.

[e] The majority opinion was written by Justice Harlan, who was joined by Chief Justice Burger and Justices Stewart, White, and Blackmun and, in large part, by Justice Black. Justices Douglas, Brennan, and Marshall dissented.

[f] As students of constitutional law will know, the eighth amendment in terms applies only to the federal government. The Court had previously held, however, that the cruel-and-unusual-punishment clause of the eighth amendment applied to the states through the 14th amendment.

that the threat of death is a superior deterrent, there is no reason to believe that as currently administered, the punishment of death is necessary to deter the commission of capital crimes." As for retribution, he said:

> "Obviously concepts of justice change; no immutable moral order requires death for murderers and rapists. The claim that death is a just punishment necessarily refers to the existence of certain public beliefs. The claim must be that for capital crimes death alone comports with society's notion of proper punishment. As administered today, however, the punishment of death cannot be justified as a necessary means of exacting retribution from criminals. When the overwhelming number of criminals who commit capital crimes go to prison, it cannot be concluded that death serves the purpose of retribution more effectively than imprisonment. The asserted public belief that murderers and rapists deserve to die is flatly inconsistent with the execution of a random few. . . . "

Justice Marshall reasoned that the average American citizen, if fully informed on the issue, would find the death penalty "shocking to his conscience and sense of justice." He also argued that the death penalty was unconstitutionally excessive because it made no measurable contribution to legitimate legislative objectives. He concluded that "retribution for its own sake is improper" and that the available statistical evidence demonstrated that the death penalty had no significant deterrent effect.

(ii) **Douglas, Stewart, and White.** Justices Douglas, Stewart, and White concluded that the sentencing procedures then in use were constitutionally defective. Justice Douglas noted that discretionary capital sentencing statutes are, in operation, "pregnant with discrimination" against poor, black defendants. Justice Stewart observed that the death penalty is "wantonly and freakishly imposed" and that "death sentences are cruel and unusual in the same way that being struck by lightning is cruel and unusual." Justice White concluded that "there is no meaningful basis for distinguishing the few cases in which [the death penalty] is imposed from the many cases in which it is not."

(iii) **The Dissenters.** In response to Justices Brennan and Marshall, the dissenters argued that it was institutionally inappropriate for the Supreme Court to foreclose use of the death penalty. They noted that capital punishment was widely used when the Constitution and the Bill of Rights were adopted; that it had been in continuous use since then; and that the declining frequency of imposition indicated that the penalty was being reserved for the most extreme cases, not that it was no longer socially acceptable. As for the argument that the death penalty does not serve valid penological objectives, the dissenters concluded that the Court should defer to rational legislative judgments regarding its retributive and deterrent value. Having concluded that the penalty of death was constitutionally permissible, at least for some offenses, the dissenters also concluded that the procedures by which it was administered did not violate the eighth amendment.   Chief Justice Burger specifically noted that "all of the arguments and factual contentions accepted [by Justices Douglas, Stewart, and White] were considered and rejected by the Court one year ago" in *McGautha*.

4. **The Aftermath of *Furman*.**   The meaning of *Furman* was obscure even to the practiced eye.   As Chief Justice Burger had observed, the heart of the objection by Justices Douglas, Stewart, and White seemed to be precisely the argument that had failed to command a majority in *McGautha*.   It now appeared that the states were not constitutionally permitted to commit the sentencing decision to unguided jury discretion.   Since all states followed that procedure, the effect of the decision was to invalidate every death penalty statute then in force.

Thirty-five states responded to *Furman* by reformulating their capital sentencing provisions to restrict sentencing discretion in a way that would meet the objections of at least one of the three Justices whose views had been pivotal in *Furman*.[g]   Two approaches seemed plausible, and the states were evenly divided on which would succeed.   Eighteen states attempted to eliminate sentencing discretion altogether by making death the mandatory punishment for conviction of a capital crime.[h]   The remaining 17 states rejected the mandatory approach but attempted to structure and control the exercise of sentencing discretion.   Fifteen adopted statutes, more or less patterned after the Model Penal Code, that provided for bifurcated proceedings and required consideration of specified aggravating and mitigating factors.   Two specified aggravating and mitigating factors but did not require bifurcated proceedings.

5. **The 1976 Decisions.**   The Court considered a representative group of these statutes in five cases decided in 1976.[i]   The Court was again badly divided.   Justices Brennan and Marshall adhered to their view that the death penalty was unconstitutional in all cases.   The Chief Justice and Justices Blackmun and Rehnquist adhered to their *Furman* dissents.   Justice White joined them in voting to sustain all of the statutes, holding that the defect in the *Furman* generation of statutes could be remedied either by making the death penalty mandatory or by requiring consideration of specified aggravating and mitigating circumstances.   Two Justices thus voted to hold all five statutes unconstitutional, and four to sustain them.   The three remaining Justices—Stewart, Powell and Stevens (who had succeeded Douglas)—voted to invalidate the mandatory statutes but to uphold the statutes that specified criteria to structure the exercise of discretion.

[g] Citations to these provisions can be found in the summary of *Furman* and subsequent decisions contained in ALI, Model Penal Code and Commentaries § 210.6, pp. 153–67 (1980).

[h] Although most of these states restricted the death penalty to a narrowed range of homicides, two (New Mexico and North Carolina) provided that death would be the mandatory punishment for all cases of first-degree murder as traditionally defined.

[i] Gregg v. Georgia, 428 U.S. 153 (1976); Proffitt v. Florida, 428 U.S. 242 (1976); Jurek v. Texas, 428 U.S. 262 (1976); Woodson v. North Carolina, 428 U.S. 280 (1976); Roberts v. Louisiana, 428 U.S. 325 (1976). The statutes involved in these five decisions are reproduced in Appendix B, pages 12–19, infra.

Together, the various opinions in these five cases occupy 210 pages in the United States Reports.

The net result was that a 7–2 majority affirmed the constitutionality of three statutes (Georgia, Florida and Texas) that attempted to structure the exercise of discretion. The Court thereby definitively rejected the view that the death penalty was unconstitutional per se, at least as applied to homicide offenses.[j] However, a 5–4 majority struck down those statutes (North Carolina and Louisiana) that prescribed death as a mandatory penalty, even for a narrow class of homicides.[k]

Because the votes of Justices Stewart, Powell and Stevens were determinative of the outcome, their views are generally understood to state the governing constitutional principles. The concluding portion of their joint opinion upholding the Georgia statute explained their rationale:

> "The basic concern of *Furman* centered on those defendants who were being condemned to death capriciously and arbitrarily. Under the procedures before the Court in that case, sentencing authorities were not directed to give attention to the nature or circumstances of the crime committed or to the character or record of the defendant. Left unguided, juries imposed the death sentence in a way that could only be called freakish. The new Georgia sentencing procedures, by contrast, focus the jury's attention on the particularized nature of the crime and the particularized characteristics of the individual defendant. While the jury is permitted to consider any aggravating or mitigating circumstances, it must find and identify at least one statutory aggravating factor before it may impose a penalty of death. In this way the jury's discretion is channeled. No longer can a jury wantonly and freakishly impose the death sentence; it is always circumscribed by the legislative guidelines. In addition, the review function of the Supreme Court of Georgia affords additional assurance that the concerns that prompted our decision in *Furman* are not present to any significant degree in the Georgia procedure applied here."

In the course of its opinion, the plurality rejected two major arguments against the Georgia system. The first was that the prosecutor in charging and plea bargaining, the jury in convicting the defendant of a non-capital form of criminal homicide, and the governor in exercising his pardoning power can all exercise a kind of unfettered discretion that is inconsistent with the concerns of *Furman*. The plurality responded that:

j The Court ruled one year later that the death penalty is an unconstitutionally excessive punishment for the crime of rape. Coker v. Georgia, 433 U.S. 584 (1977). This decision appears as a main case at page 1004, infra.

k Subsequently, the Court has held unconstitutional all mandatory death penalty statutes brought before it. See, in addition to the cases discussed in text, Roberts v. Louisiana, 431 U.S. 633 (1977), striking down a mandatory death penalty for murder of an on-duty policeman. However, the Court has repeatedly reserved decision on whether a state may make the death penalty mandatory for a murder committed by a person serving a life sentence.

"Nothing in any of our cases suggests that the decision to afford an individual defendant mercy violates the Constitution. *Furman* held only that, in order to minimize the risk that the death penalty would be imposed on a capriciously selected group of offenders, the decision to impose it had to be guided by standards so that the sentencing authority would focus on the particularized circumstances of the crime and the defendant."

The second argument was that the standards adopted by the Georgia statute were so broad and vague as to provide no meaningful guidance and thus to permit the kind of arbitrary decisions at which *Furman* was aimed. The plurality did not reject this argument out of hand, but held that in context, particularly given the reviewing function exercised by the Georgia Supreme Court, the provisions were not unacceptably vague. In effect, the plurality was unwilling to construe *Furman* as requiring that all possibility of arbitrary action be eliminated. A reasonable effort to guide and control the discretion of the jury was all that could be expected. A more rigid approach would have the effect of outlawing capital punishment altogether. This the plurality was unwilling to do.

By contrast, the plurality held the mandatory North Carolina statute unconstitutional for three reasons. The first was based on history, and the judgment that contemporary values as reflected in a proper interpretation of the cruel-and-unusual-punishment clause were offended by mandatory imposition of the death penalty. The second and third arguments are reflected in the following excerpt:

"A separate deficiency of North Carolina's mandatory death-sentence statute is its failure to provide a constitutionally tolerable response to *Furman's* rejection of unbridled jury discretion in the imposition of capital sentences. Central to the limited holding in *Furman* was the conviction that the vesting of standard-less sentencing power in the jury violated the eighth and 14th amendments. It is argued that North Carolina has remedied the inadequacies of the death-penalty statutes held unconstitutional in *Furman* by withdrawing all sentencing discretion from juries in capital cases. But when one considers the long and consistent American experience with the death penalty in first-degree murder cases, it becomes evident that mandatory statutes enacted in response to *Furman* have simply papered over the problem of unguided and unchecked jury discretion.

"[T]here is general agreement that American juries have persistently refused to convict a significant portion of persons charged with first-degree murder of that offense under mandatory death-penalty statutes. [A]s a matter of historic fact, juries operating under discretionary sentencing statutes have consistently returned death sentences in only a minority of first-degree murder cases. In view of the historic record, it is only reasonable to assume that many juries under mandatory statutes will continue to consider the grave consequences of a conviction in reaching a verdict. North Carolina's mandatory death-penalty statute provides no standards to guide the jury in its inevitable exercise of the power to determine which first-degree murderers shall live and which shall die. And there is no way under the North Carolina law for the judiciary to check arbitrary and capricious exercise of that power through a review of death sentences. Instead of rationalizing the sentencing process, a mandatory scheme may well exacerbate the problem identified in *Furman* by resting the penalty determination on the particular jury's willingness to act lawlessly. While a mandatory death-penalty statute may reasonably be expected to increase the number of persons sentenced to death, it does not fulfill *Furman's* basic requirement by replacing arbitrary and wanton jury discretion with objective standards to guide, regularize, and make rationally reviewable the process for imposing a sentence of death.

"A third constitutional shortcoming of the North Carolina statute is its failure to allow the particularized consideration of relevant aspects of the character and record of each convicted defendant before the imposition upon him of a sentence of death. In *Furman*, members of the Court acknowledged what cannot fairly be denied—that death is a punishment different from all other sanctions in kind rather than degree. A process that accords no significance to relevant facets of the character and record of the individual offender or the circumstances of the particular offense excludes from consideration in fixing the ultimate punishment of death the possibility of compassionate or mitigating factors stemming from the diverse frailties of humankind. It treats all persons convicted of a designated offense not as uniquely individual human beings, but as members of a faceless, undifferentiated mass to be subjected to the blind infliction of the penalty of death.

"This Court has previously recognized that '[f]or the determination of sentences, justice generally requires consideration of more than the particular acts by which the crime was committed and that there be taken into account the circumstances of the offense together with the character and propensities of the offender.' Consideration of both the offender and the offense in order to arrive at a just and appropriate sentence has been viewed as a progressive and humanizing development. While the prevailing practice of individualizing sentencing determinations generally reflects simply enlightened policy rather than a constitutional imperative, we believe that in capital cases the fundamental respect for humanity underlying the eighth amendment requires consideration of the character and record of the individual offender and the circumstances of the particular offense as a constitutionally indispensable part of the process of inflicting the penalty of death.

"This conclusion rests squarely on the predicate that the penalty of death is qualitatively different from a sentence of imprisonment, however long. Death, in its finality, differs more from life imprisonment than a 100-year prison term differs from one of only a year or two. Because of that qualitative difference, there is a corresponding difference in the need for reliability in the determination that death is the appropriate punishment in a specific case."

6. **Lockett and Eddings.** In striking down the mandatory death penalty statutes, Justices Stewart, Powell, and Stevens emphasized that an individualized determination of the death penalty question is "constitutionally indispensable." The Court has elaborated on the individualization theme in two subsequent cases.

Sandra Lockett was waiting in a car when an accomplice committed a homicide during the course of a pawn shop robbery.[1] She was convicted of murder under the ordinary rules of complicity. She wanted to argue in mitigation that she was a secondary participant in the offense, that she had not previously committed any major crimes, and that her youth (she was 21) should be taken into account. Under the Ohio statute, the judge was required to impose the death penalty unless the defendant proved one of three mitigating circumstances— that the victim had induced or facilitated the offense; that the defendant was "under duress, coercion or strong provocation"; or that the offense was "primarily the product of psychosis or mental deficiency." Because Lockett's mitigating claims did not fall within the factors specified by the statute, the trial judge said he had "no alternative" but to impose a death sentence.

In Lockett v. Ohio, 438 U.S. 586 (1978), the Supreme Court struck down her death sentence by a 7–1 vote. (Justice Brennan did not participate.) The plurality opinion by Chief Justice Burger, joined by Justices Stewart, Powell, and Stevens, held that the Ohio statute violated the principle of individualization:

"The eighth and 14th amendments require that the sentencer, in all but the rarest kind of capital case, not be precluded from considering, *as a mitigating factor*, any aspect of a defendant's character or record and any of the circumstances of the offense that the defendant proffers as a basis for a sentence less than death." [m]

[1] The person who actually fired the fatal shot pleaded guilty to a non-capital murder charge and was the chief prosecution witness. Lockett twice refused to plead guilty to a reduced charge which would have been punishable by a mandatory life sentence.

[m] Justice Marshall concurred in the result, adhering to his view that the death penalty is always unconstitutional. Justice Blackmun concurred on the narrow ground that the death penalty could not constitutionally be imposed on a defendant who aided and abetted a murder without considering the degree of the defendant's involvement and the mens rea for the homicide. Justice White also concurred,

but would have rested the decision on the principle that the death penalty is unconstitutionally excessive absent a finding that the defendant had a conscious purpose to kill the victim.

Lockett is commonly understood to stand for the principle stated by the plurality. However, the Court subsequently accepted the principle on which Justice White relied in his concurring opinion. In Enmund v. Florida, 458 U.S. 782 (1982), the Court ruled, 5–4, that the eighth amendment does not permit imposition of the death penalty on a person "who aids and abets a felony in the course of which a murder is committed by others but who does not himself kill, attempt to kill or intend that a

Justice Rehnquist's dissent argued that the effect of the plurality decision was to resurrect the discretionary sentencing practices—and the risk of arbitrariness—that *Furman* was designed to eliminate.

In Eddings v. Oklahoma, 455 U.S. 104 (1982), a 5–4 majority relied on *Lockett* to strike down a death sentence imposed on a 16-year-old defendant for killing a police officer. Although the Court had granted certiorari to consider whether imposition of the death penalty on a minor was forbidden by the eighth amendment, it did not reach this question. Instead, it ruled that the sentencing judge had failed to consider evidence of Eddings' "turbulent family history, of beatings by a harsh father and of severe emotional disturbance." Justice Powell explained in the opinion for the majority that "the sentencer [and the appellate court] may determine the weight to be given relevant mitigating evidence. But they may not give it no weight by excluding such evidence from their consideration" as a matter of law. Chief Justice Burger dissented, joined by Justices White, Blackmun and Rehnquist. He questioned the majority's assumption that the mitigating evidence was ignored by the trial judge and concluded that "it is clearly the choice of the Oklahoma courts—a choice not inconsistent with *Lockett* or any other decision of this Court—to accord relatively little weight to Eddings' family background and emotional problems as balanced against the circumstances of his crime and his potential for future dangerousness."

7. ***Zant v. Stephens.*** As Justice Rehnquist noted in his *Lockett* dissent, there is considerable tension between two themes that underlie the death penalty cases—that capital sentencing decisions must be structured so as to promote consistency and reduce the risk of arbitrariness; and that the states may not either eliminate discretion or structure it in such a way as to compromise the defendant's right to an individualized determination of sentence. In Zant v. Stephens, 462 U.S. 862 (1983), the Court addressed this tension. The case involved an allegedly unconstitutional application of the Georgia statute that required the Court to address two features of the Georgia system: the jury was permitted to consider evidence in aggravation beyond the statutory list of aggravating factors; and the jury was permitted to exercise unconstrained discretion in determining whether the death penalty should be imposed after a statutory aggravating circumstance was found to be satisfied.

In the course of his opinion for the Court, Justice Stevens summarized the governing constitutional imperatives in the administration of capital sentencing statutes:

"The [Court's] approval of Georgia's capital sentencing procedure [in *Gregg*], rested primarily on two features of the scheme: that the jury was required to find at least one valid statutory aggravating circumstance and to identify it in writing, and that the state supreme court reviewed the record of every death

killing take place or that lethal force will be employed." The opinions in *Enmund* are summarized at pages 1020–28, infra.

penalty proceeding to determine whether the sentence was arbitrary or disproportionate. These elements, the opinion concluded, adequately protected against the wanton and freakish imposition of the death penalty. This conclusion rested . . . on the
fundamental requirement that . . . an aggravating circumstance must genuinely narrow the class of persons eligible for the
death penalty and must reasonably justify the imposition of a
more severe sentence on the defendant compared to others found
guilty of murder. . . .

"Our cases indicate, then, that the statutory aggravating
circumstances play a constitutionally necessary function at the
stage of legislative definition; they circumscribe the class of
persons eligible for the death penalty. But the Constitution does
not require the jury to ignore other possible aggravating factors
in the process of selecting, from among that class, those defendants who will actually be sentenced to death. What is important at the selection stage is an *individualized* determination on
the basis of the character of the individual and the circumstances
of the crime.

"The Georgia scheme provides for categorical narrowing at
the definition stage, and for individualized determination and
appellate review at the selection stage. We therefore remain
convinced, as we were in 1976, that the structure of the statute is
constitutional. . . . "

GODFREY v. GEORGIA

Supreme Court of the United States, 1980.
446 U.S. 420.

MR. JUSTICE STEWART announced the judgment of the Court and
delivered an opinion, in which MR. JUSTICE BLACKMUN, MR. JUSTICE
POWELL, and MR. JUSTICE STEVENS joined.

Under Georgia law, a person convicted of murder may be sentenced
to death if it is found beyond a reasonable doubt that the offense "was
outrageously or wantonly vile, horrible or inhuman in that it involved
torture, depravity of mind, or an aggravated battery to the victim." In
Gregg v. Georgia, 428 U.S. 153 (1976), the Court held that this statutory
aggravating circumstance (Subsection (b)(7)) is not unconstitutional on
its face.[a] Responding to the argument that the language of the provision is "so broad that capital punishment could be imposed in any
murder case," the joint opinion said:

"It is, of course, arguable that any murder involves depravity of
mind or an aggravated battery. But this language need not be
construed in this way, and there is no reason to assume that the
Supreme Court of Georgia will adopt such an open-ended construction." (opinion of Stewart, Powell, and Stevens, JJ.).

---

[a] The Georgia statute before the Court in   Appendix B, pages 12–15, infra. [Footnote
Gregg and again in *Godfrey* is reprinted in   by eds.]

Nearly four years have passed since the *Gregg* decision, and during that time many death sentences based in whole or in part on Subsection (b)(7) have been affirmed by the Supreme Court of Georgia. The issue now before us is whether, in affirming the imposition of the sentences of death in the present case, the Georgia Supreme Court has adopted such a broad and vague construction of the Subsection (b)(7) aggravating circumstance as to violate the eighth and 14th amendments to the United States Constitution.[2]

I

On a day in early September in 1977, the petitioner and his wife of 28 years had a heated argument in their home. During the course of this altercation, the petitioner, who had consumed several cans of beer, threatened his wife with a knife and damaged some of her clothing. At this point, the petitioner's wife declared that she was going to leave him, and departed to stay with relatives. That afternoon she went to a justice of the peace and secured a warrant charging the petitioner with aggravated assault. A few days later, while still living away from home, she filed suit for divorce. Summons was served on the petitioner, and a court hearing was set on a date some two weeks later. Before the date of the hearing, the petitioner on several occasions asked his wife to return to their home. Each time his efforts were rebuffed. At some point during this period, his wife moved in with her mother. The petitioner believed that his mother-in-law was actively instigating his wife's determination not to consider a possible reconciliation.

In the early evening of September 20, according to the petitioner, his wife telephoned him at home. Once again they argued. She asserted that reconciliation was impossible and allegedly demanded all the proceeds from the planned sale of their house. The conversation was terminated after she said that she would call back later. This she did in an hour or so. The ensuing conversation was, according to the petitioner's account, even more heated than the first. His wife reiterated her stand that reconciliation was out of the question, said that she still wanted all the proceeds from the sale of their house, and mentioned that her mother was supporting her position. Stating that she saw no further use in talking or arguing, she hung up.

At this juncture, the petitioner got out his shotgun and walked with it down the hill from his home to the trailer where his mother-in-law lived. Peering through a window, he observed his wife, his mother-in-law, and his 11-year-old daughter playing a card game. He pointed the shotgun at his wife through the window and pulled the trigger. The charge from the gun struck his wife in the forehead and killed her

---

[2] The other statutory aggravating circumstances upon which a death sentence may be based after conviction of murder in Georgia are considerably more specific or objectively measurable than Subsection (b)(7). . . .

In [a prior decision], the Supreme Court of Georgia held unconstitutional the portion of the first statutory aggravating circumstance encompassing persons who have a "substantial history of serious assaultive criminal convictions" because it did not set "sufficiently 'clear and objective standards.' "

instantly. He proceeded into the trailer, striking and injuring his fleeing daughter with the barrel of the gun. He then fired the gun at his mother-in-law, striking her in the head and killing her instantly.

The petitioner then called the local sheriff's office, identified himself, said where he was, explained that he had just killed his wife and mother-in-law, and asked that the sheriff come and pick him up. Upon arriving at the trailer, the law-enforcement officers found the petitioner seated on a chair in open view near the driveway. He told one of the officers that "they're dead, I killed them" and directed the officer to the place where he had put the murder weapon. Later the petitioner told a police officer: "I've done a hideous crime, . . . but I have been thinking about it for eight years . . . I'd do it again."

The petitioner was subsequently indicted on two counts of murder and one of aggravated assault. He pleaded not guilty and relied primarily on a defense of temporary insanity at his trial. The jury returned verdicts of guilty on all three counts.

The sentencing phase of the trial was held before the same jury. No further evidence was tendered, but counsel for each side made arguments to the jury. Three times during the course of his argument, the prosecutor stated that the case involved no allegation of "torture" or of an "aggravated battery." When counsel had completed their arguments, the trial judge instructed the jury orally and in writing on the standards that must guide them in imposing sentence. Both orally and in writing, the judge quoted to the jury the statutory language of the Subsection (b)(7) aggravating circumstance in its entirety.

The jury imposed sentences of death on both of the murder convictions. As to each, the jury specified that the aggravating circumstance they had found beyond a reasonable doubt was "that the offense of murder was outrageously or wantonly vile, horrible and inhuman."

In accord with Georgia law in capital cases, the trial judge prepared a report in the form of answers to a questionnaire for use on appellate review. One question on the form asked whether or not the victim had been "physically harmed or tortured." The trial judge's response was "No, as to both victims, excluding the actual murdering of the two victims." [4]

The Georgia Supreme Court affirmed the judgments of the trial court in all respects. With regard to the imposition of the death sentence for each of the two murder convictions, the court rejected the petitioner's contention that Subsection (b)(7) is unconstitutionally vague. The court noted that Georgia's death-penalty legislation had been upheld in *Gregg* and cited its prior decisions upholding Subsection (b)(7) in the face of similar vagueness challenges. As to the petitioner's argument that the jury's phraseology was, as a matter of law, an inadequate statement of Subsection (b)(7), the court responded by simply observing that the language "was not objectionable." The court found no evidence that the sentence had been "imposed under the

---

[4] Another question on the form asked the trial judge to list the mitigating circumstances that were in evidence. The judge noted that the petitioner had no significant history of prior criminal activity.

influence of passion, prejudice, or any other arbitrary factor," held that the sentence was neither excessive nor disproportionate to the penalty imposed in similar cases, and stated that the evidence supported the jury's finding of the Subsection (b)(7) statutory aggravating circumstance. Two justices dissented.

II

In Furman v. Georgia, 408 U.S. 238 (1972), the Court held that the penalty of death may not be imposed under sentencing procedures that create a substantial risk that the punishment will be inflicted in an arbitrary and capricious manner. *Gregg* reaffirmed this holding:

"[W]here discretion is afforded a sentencing body on a matter so grave as the determination of whether a human life should be taken or spared, that discretion must be suitably directed and limited so as to minimize the risk of wholly arbitrary and capricious action." (opinion of Stewart, Powell, and Stevens, JJ.).

A capital-sentencing scheme must, in short, provide a "meaningful basis for distinguishing the few cases in which [the penalty] is imposed from the many cases in which it is not."

This means that if a state wishes to authorize capital punishment it has a constitutional responsibility to tailor and apply its law in a manner that avoids the arbitrary and capricious infliction of the death penalty. Part of a state's responsibility in this regard is to define the crimes for which death may be the sentence in a way that obviates "standardless [sentencing] discretion." It must channel the sentencer's discretion by "clear and objective standards" that provide "specific and detailed guidance," and that "make rationally reviewable the process for imposing a sentence of death." As was made clear in *Gregg*, a death-penalty "system could have standards so vague that they would fail adequately to channel the sentencing decision patterns of juries with the result that a pattern of arbitrary and capricious sentencing like that found unconstitutional in *Furman* could occur."

In the case before us, the Georgia Supreme Court has affirmed a sentence of death based upon no more than a finding that the offense was "outrageously or wantonly vile, horrible and inhuman." There is nothing in these few words, standing alone, that implies any inherent restraint on the arbitrary and capricious infliction of the death sentence. A person of ordinary sensibility could fairly characterize almost every murder as "outrageously or wantonly vile, horrible and inhuman." Such a view may, in fact, have been one to which the members of the jury in this case subscribed. If so, their preconceptions were not dispelled by the trial judge's sentencing instructions. These gave the jury no guidance concerning the meaning of any of Subsection (b)(7)'s terms. In fact, the jury's interpretation of Subsection (b)(7) can only be the subject of sheer speculation.

The standardless and unchanneled imposition of death sentences in the uncontrolled discretion of a basically uninstructed jury in this case was in no way cured by the affirmance of those sentences by the

Georgia Supreme Court. Under state law that court may not affirm a judgment of death until it has independently assessed the evidence of record and determined that such evidence supports the trial judge's or jury's finding of an aggravating circumstance.

In past cases the state supreme court has apparently understood this obligation as carrying with it the responsibility to keep Subsection (b)(7) within constitutional bounds. Recognizing that "there is a possibility of abuse of [the Subsection (b)(7)] statutory aggravating circumstance," the court has emphasized that it will not permit the language of that subsection simply to become a "catchall" for cases which do not fit within any other statutory aggravating circumstance. Thus, in exercising its function of death-sentence review, the court has said that it will restrict its "approval of the death penalty under this statutory aggravating circumstance to those cases that lie at the core."

When *Gregg* was decided by this Court in 1976, the Georgia Supreme Court had affirmed two death sentences based wholly on Subsection (b)(7). The homicide in [the first case] was "a horrifying torture-murder." There, the victim had been beaten, burned, raped, and otherwise severely abused before her death by strangulation. The homicide in [the second case] was of a similar ilk. In that case, the convicted murderer had choked two seven-year-old boys to death after having forced each of them to submit to anal sodomy.

[Subsequent decisions] suggest that the Georgia Supreme Court had by 1977 reached three separate but consistent conclusions respecting the Subsection (b)(7) aggravating circumstance. The first was that the evidence that the offense was "outrageously or wantonly vile, horrible or inhuman" had to demonstrate "torture, depravity of mind, or an aggravated battery to the victim." The second was that the phrase, "depravity of mind," comprehended only the kind of mental state that led the murderer to torture or to commit an aggravated battery before killing his victim. The third . . . was that the word, "torture," must be construed in pari materia with "aggravated battery" so as to require evidence of serious physical abuse of the victim before death. Indeed, the circumstances proved in a number of the Subsection (b)(7) death-sentence cases affirmed by the Georgia Supreme Court have met all three of these criteria.

The Georgia courts did not, however, so limit Subsection (b)(7) in the present case. No claim was made, and nothing in the record before us suggests, that the petitioner committed an aggravated battery upon his wife or mother-in-law or, in fact, caused either of them to suffer any physical injury preceding their deaths. Moreover, in the trial court, the prosecutor repeatedly told the jury—and the trial judge wrote in his sentencing report—that the murders did not involve "torture." Nothing said on appeal by the Georgia Supreme Court indicates that it took a different view of the evidence. The circumstances of this case, therefore, do not satisfy the criteria laid out by the Georgia Supreme Court itself in [the prior] cases. In holding that the evidence supported the jury's Subsection (b)(7) finding, the state Supreme Court simply asserted that the verdict was "factually substantiated."

Thus, the validity of the petitioner's death sentences turns on whether, in light of the facts and circumstances of the murders that Godfrey was convicted of committing, the Georgia Supreme Court can be said to have applied a constitutional construction of the phrase "outrageously or wantonly vile, horrible or inhuman in that [they] involved . . . depravity of mind. . . . " [15] We conclude that the answer must be no. The petitioner's crimes cannot be said to have reflected a consciousness materially more "depraved" than that of any person guilty of murder. His victims were killed instantaneously.[16] They were members of his family who were causing him extreme emotional trauma. Shortly after the killings, he acknowledged his responsibility and the heinous nature of his crimes. These factors certainly did not remove the criminality from the petitioner's acts. But . . . it "is of vital importance to the defendant and to the community that any decision to impose the death sentence be, and appear to be, based on reason rather than caprice or emotion."

That cannot be said here. There is no principled way to distinguish this case, in which the death penalty was imposed, from the many cases in which it was not. Accordingly, the judgment of the Georgia Supreme Court insofar as it leaves standing the petitioner's death sentences is reversed, and the case is remanded to that court for further proceedings.

It is so ordered.

MR. JUSTICE MARSHALL, with whom MR. JUSTICE BRENNAN joins, concurring in the judgment.

I continue to believe that the death penalty is in all circumstances cruel and unusual punishment forbidden by the eighth and 14th amendments. In addition, I agree with the plurality that the Georgia Supreme Court's construction of the provision at issue in this case is unconstitutionally vague under Gregg v. Georgia, 428 U.S. 153 (1976). I write separately, first, to examine the Georgia Supreme Court's application of this provision, and second, to suggest why the enterprise on which the Court embarked in *Gregg* increasingly appears to be doomed to failure.

I

. . . The Court's conclusion in *Gregg* was . . . expressly based on the assumption that the Georgia Supreme Court would adopt a narrowing construction that would give some discernible content to Subsection (b)(7). In the present case, no such narrowing construction was read to the jury or applied by the Georgia Supreme Court on

---

[15] The sentence of death in this case rested exclusively on Subsection (b)(7). Accordingly, we intimate no view as to whether or not the petitioner might constitutionally have received the same sentences on some other basis. Georgia does not, as do some states, make multiple murders an aggravating circumstance, as such.

[16] In light of this fact, it is constitutionally irrelevant that the petitioner used a shotgun instead of a rifle as the murder weapon, resulting in a gruesome spectacle in his mother-in-law's trailer. An interpretation of Subsection (b)(7) so as to include all murders resulting in gruesome scenes would be totally irrational.

appeal. As it has so many times in the past, that court upheld the jury's finding with a simple notation that it was supported by the evidence. The premise on which *Gregg* relied has thus proved demonstrably false. . . .

In addition I think it necessary to emphasize that even under the prevailing view that the death penalty may, in some circumstances, constitutionally be imposed, it is not enough for a reviewing court to apply a narrowing construction to otherwise ambiguous statutory language. The jury must be instructed on the proper, narrow construction of the statute. The Court's cases make clear that it is the *sentencer's* discretion that must be channeled and guided by clear, objective, and specific standards. To give the jury an instruction in the form of the bare words of the statute—words that are hopelessly ambiguous and could be understood to apply to any murder—would effectively grant it unbridled discretion to impose the death penalty. Such a defect could not be cured by the post hoc narrowing construction of an appellate court. The reviewing court can determine only whether a rational jury might have imposed the death penalty if it had been properly instructed; it is impossible for it to say whether a particular jury would have so exercised its discretion if it had known the law. . . .

II

The preceding discussion leads me to what I regard as a more fundamental defect in the Court's approach to death-penalty cases. In *Gregg*, the Court rejected the position, expressed by my Brother Brennan and myself, that the death penalty is in all circumstances cruel and unusual punishment forbidden by the eighth and 14th amendments. Instead it was concluded that in "a matter so grave as the determination of whether a human life should be taken or spared," it would be both necessary and sufficient to insist on sentencing procedures that would minimize or eliminate the "risk that [the death penalty] would be inflicted in an arbitrary and capricious manner." (opinion of Stewart, Powell, and Stevens, JJ.). Contrary to the statutes at issue in *Furman,* under which the death penalty was "infrequently imposed" upon "a capriciously selected random handful," (Stewart, J., concurring), and "the threat of execution [was] too attenuated to be of substantial service to criminal justice," (White, J., concurring), it was anticipated that the Georgia scheme would produce an evenhanded, objective procedure rationally " 'distinguishing the few cases in which [the death penalty] is imposed from the many cases in which it is not.' " (White, J., concurring).

For reasons I expressed in *Furman* and *Gregg*, I believe that the death penalty may not constitutionally be imposed even if it were possible to do so in an evenhanded manner. But events since *Gregg* make that possibility seem increasingly remote. Nearly every week of every year, this Court is presented with at least one petition for certiorari raising troubling issues of non-compliance with the strictures of *Gregg* and its progeny. On numerous occasions since *Gregg*, the Court has reversed decisions of state supreme courts upholding the imposition of capital punishment, [citing 14 cases over a three-year period], frequently on the ground that the sentencing proceeding allowed undue discretion, causing dangers of arbitrariness in violation of *Gregg* and its companion cases. These developments, coupled with other pervasive evidence,[6] strongly suggest that appellate courts are incapable of guaranteeing the kind of objectivity and evenhandedness that the Court contemplated and hoped for in *Gregg*. The disgraceful distorting effects of racial discrimination and poverty continue to be painfully visible in the imposition of death sentences.[7] And while hundreds have been placed on death row in the years since *Gregg*,[8] only three persons have been executed.[9] Two of them made no effort to challenge their sentence and were thus permitted to commit what I have elsewhere described as "state-administered suicide." The task of eliminating arbitrariness in the infliction of capital punishment is proving to be one which our criminal justice system—and perhaps any criminal justice system—is unable to perform. In short, it is now apparent that the defects that led my Brothers Douglas, Stewart, and White to concur in the judgment in *Furman* are present as well in the statutory schemes under which defendants are currently sentenced to death.

The issue presented in this case usefully illustrates the point. The Georgia Supreme Court has given no real content to Subsection (b)(7) in by far the majority of the cases in which it has had an opportunity to do so. In the four years since *Gregg,* the Georgia court has *never* reversed a jury's finding of a Subsection (b)(7) aggravating circumstance. With considerable frequency the Georgia court has, as here, upheld the imposition of the death penalty on the basis of a simple conclusory statement that the evidence supported the jury's finding under Subsection (b)(7). Instances of a narrowing construction are difficult to find, and those narrowing constructions that can be found have not been adhered to with any regularity. In no case has the Georgia court required a narrowing construction to be given to the jury—an indispensable method for avoiding the "standardless and unchanneled imposition of death sentences." Genuinely independent review has been exceedingly rare. . . .

[6] See generally Dix, Appellate Review of the Decision To Impose Death, 68 Geo.L.J. 97 (1979). Professor Dix's meticulous study of the process of appellate review in Georgia, Florida, and Texas since 1976 demonstrates that "objective standards" for the imposition of the death penalty have not been achieved and probably are impossible to achieve, and concludes that *Gregg* and its companion cases "mandate pursuit of an impossible goal."

[7] On April 20, 1980, for example, over 40 per cent of the persons on death row were Negroes.

[8] See NAACP Legal Defense and Educational Fund, Death Row, U.S.A. (April 20, 1980) (642 people on death row); U.S. Department of Justice, Capital Punishment 1978, p. 1 (1979) (445 people on death row as of December 31, 1978).

[9] In *Furman,* my Brothers Stewart and White concurred in the judgment largely on the ground that the death penalty had been so infrequently imposed that it made no contribution to the goals of punishment. Mr. Justice Stewart stated that "the petitioners are among a capriciously selected random handful upon whom the sentence of death has in fact been imposed." Mr. Justice White relied on his conclusion that "the penalty is so infrequently imposed that the threat of execution is too attenuated to be of substantial service to criminal justice." These conclusions have proved to be equally valid under the sentencing schemes upheld in *Gregg*.

The Georgia court's inability to administer its capital-punishment statute in an evenhanded fashion is not necessarily attributable to any bad faith on its part; it is, I believe, symptomatic of a deeper problem that is proving to be genuinely intractable. Just five years before *Gregg,* Mr. Justice Harlan stated for the Court that the tasks of identifying "before the fact those characteristics of criminal homicides and their perpetrators which call for the death penalty, and [of] express[ing] these characteristics in language which can be fairly understood and applied by the sentencing authority, appear to be . . . beyond present human ability." McGautha v. California, 402 U.S. 183, 204 (1971). From this premise, the Court in *McGautha* drew the conclusion that the effort to eliminate arbitrariness in the imposition of the death penalty need not be attempted at all. In *Furman,* the Court concluded that the arbitrary infliction of the death penalty was constitutionally intolerable. And in *Gregg,* the Court rejected the premise of *McGautha* and approved a statutory scheme under which, as the Court then perceived it, the death penalty would be imposed in an evenhanded manner.

There can be no doubt that the conclusion drawn in *McGautha* was properly repudiated in *Furman,* where the Court made clear that the arbitrary imposition of the death penalty is forbidden by the eighth and 14th amendments. But I believe that the Court in *McGautha* was substantially correct in concluding that the task of selecting in some objective way those persons who should be condemned to die is one that remains beyond the capacities of the criminal justice system. For this reason, I remain hopeful that even if the Court is unwilling to accept the view that the death penalty is so barbaric that it is in all circumstances cruel and unusual punishment forbidden by the eighth and 14th amendments, it may eventually conclude that the effort to eliminate arbitrariness in the infliction of that ultimate sanction is so plainly doomed to failure that it—and the death penalty—must be abandoned altogether.

Mr. Chief Justice Burger, dissenting.

After murdering his wife and mother-in-law, petitioner informed the police that he had committed a "hideous" crime. The dictionary defines hideous as "morally offensive," "shocking," or "horrible." Thus, the very curious feature of this case is that petitioner himself characterized his crime in terms equivalent to those employed in the Georgia statute. For my part, I prefer petitioner's characterization of his conduct to the plurality's effort to excuse and rationalize that conduct as just another killing. The jurors in this case, who heard all relevant mitigating evidence obviously shared that preference; they concluded that this "hideous" crime was "outrageously or wantonly vile, horrible and inhuman" within the meaning of Subsection (b)(7).

More troubling than the plurality's characterization of petitioner's crime is the new responsibility that it assumes with today's decision— the task of determining on a case-by-case basis whether a defendant's conduct is egregious enough to warrant a death sentence. . . . I am convinced that the course ⟨th⟩e plurality embarks on today is sadly mistaken . . . .

MR. JUSTICE WHITE, with whom MR. JUSTICE REHNQUIST joins, dissenting. . . .

The question [is] whether the facts of this case bear sufficient relation to Subsection (b)(7) to conclude that the Georgia Supreme Court responsibly and constitutionally discharged its review function. I believe that they do.

[P]etitioner, in a coldblooded executioner's style, murdered his wife and his mother-in-law and, in passing, struck his young daughter on the head with the barrel of his gun. The weapon, a shotgun, is hardly known for the surgical precision with which it perforates its target. The murder scene, in consequence, can only be described in the most unpleasant terms. Petitioner's wife lay prone on the floor. Mrs. Godfrey's head had a hole described as "[a]pproximately the size of a silver dollar" on the side where the shot entered, and much less decipherable and more extensive damage on the side where the shot exited. Pellets that had passed through Mrs. Godfrey's head were found embedded in the kitchen cabinet.

It will be remembered that after petitioner inflicted this much damage, he took out time not only to strike his daughter on the head, but also to reload his single-shot shotgun and to enter the house. Only then did he get around to shooting his mother-in-law, Mrs. Wilkerson, whose last several moments as a sentient being must have been as terrifying as the human mind can imagine. The police eventually found her face down on the floor with a substantial portion of her head missing and her brain, no longer cabined by her skull, protruding for some distance onto the floor. Blood not only covered the floor and table, but dripped from the ceiling as well.

The Georgia Supreme Court held that these facts supported the jury's finding of the existence of statutory aggravating circumstance Subsection (b)(7). A majority of this Court disagrees. But this disagreement, founded as it is on the notion that the lower court's construction of the provision was overly broad, in fact reveals a conception of this Court's role in backstopping the Georgia Supreme Court that is itself overly broad. Our role is to correct genuine errors of constitutional significance resulting from the application of Georgia's capital sentencing procedures; our role is not to peer majestically over the lower court's shoulder so that we might second-guess its interpretation of facts that quite reasonably—perhaps even quite plainly—fit within the statutory language.[2]

---

[2] The plurality opinion states that "[A]n interpretation of Subsection (b)(7) so as to include all murders resulting in gruesome scenes would be totally irrational" and that the fact that both "victims were killed instantaneously" makes the gruesomeness of the scene irrelevant. This view ignores the indisputable truth that Mrs. Wilkerson did not die "instantaneously"; she had many moments to contemplate her impending death, assuming that the stark terror she must have felt permitted any contemplation. More importantly, it also ignores the obvious correlation between gruesomeness and "depravity of mind," between gruesomeness and "aggravated battery," between gruesomeness and "horrible," between gruesomeness and "vile," and between gruesomeness and "inhuman." Mere gruesomeness, to be sure,

Who is to say that the murders of Mrs. Godfrey and Mrs. Wilkerson were not "vile," or "inhuman," or "horrible"? In performing his murderous chore, petitioner employed a weapon known for its disfiguring effects on targets, human or other, and he succeeded in creating a scene so macabre and revolting that, if anything, "vile," "horrible," and "inhuman" are descriptively inadequate.

And who among us can honestly say that Mrs. Wilkerson did not feel "torture" in her last sentient moments. Her daughter, an instant ago a living being sitting across the table from Mrs. Wilkerson, lay prone on the floor, a bloodied and mutilated corpse. The seconds ticked by; enough time for her son-in-law to reload his gun, to enter the home, and to take a gratuitous swipe at his daughter. What terror must have run through her veins as she first witnessed her daughter's hideous demise and then came to terms with the imminence of her own. Was this not torture? And if this was not torture, can it honestly be said that petitioner did not exhibit a "depravity of mind" in carrying out this cruel drama to its mischievous and murderous conclusion? I should have thought, moreover, that the Georgia court could reasonably have deemed the scene awaiting the investigating policemen as involving "an aggravated battery to the victim[s]."

The point is not that, in my view, petitioner's crimes were definitively vile, horrible, or inhuman, or that, as I assay the evidence, they beyond *any* doubt involved torture, depravity of mind, or an aggravated battery to the victims. Rather, the lesson is a much more elementary one, an instruction that, I should have thought, this Court would have taken to heart long ago. Our mandate does not extend to interfering with factfinders in state criminal proceedings or with state courts that are responsibly and consistently interpreting state law, unless that interference is predicated on a violation of the Constitution. No convincing showing of such a violation is made here, for, as Mr. Justice Stewart has written in another place, the issue here is not what *our* verdict would have been, but whether "any rational factfinder" could have found the existence of aggravating circumstance Subsection (b)(7). Faithful adherence to this standard of review compels our affirmance of the judgment below. . . .

Under the present statutory regime, adopted in response to *Furman,* the Georgia Supreme Court has responsibly and consistently performed its review function pursuant to the Georgia capital-sentencing procedures. The state reports, that at the time its brief was written, the Georgia Supreme Court had reviewed some 99 cases in which the death penalty has been imposed. Of these, 66 had been affirmed, five had been reversed for errors in the guilt phase; and 22 had been reversed for errors in the sentencing phase. This reversal rate of over 27 per cent is not substantially lower than the historic reversal rate of state supreme courts. See Courting Reversal: The Supervisory Role of State Supreme Courts, 87 Yale L.J. 1191, 1198, 1209 (1978), where it is

would not itself serve to establish the existence of Subsection (b)(7). But it certainly fares sufficiently well as an indicator of this particular aggravating circumstance to signal to a reviewing court the distinct possibility that the terms of the provision, upon further investigation, might well be met in the circumstances of the case.

indicated that 16 state supreme courts over a 100-year period, in deciding 5,133 cases, had a reversal rate of 38.5 per cent; for criminal cases, the reversal rate was 35.6 per cent. To the extent that the reversal rate is lower than the historic level, it doubtless can be attributed to the great and admirable extent to which discretion and uncertainty have been removed from Georgia's capital-sentencing procedures since our decision in *Furman* and to the fact that review is mandatory.

The Georgia Supreme Court has vacated a death sentence where it believed that the statutory sentencing procedures, as passed by the legislature, were defective; it has held that jurors must be instructed that they can impose a life sentence even though they find the existence of a statutory aggravating circumstance; it has reversed the imposition of the death penalty where the prosecutor made an improper comment during his argument to the jury in the sentencing phase; it has reversed a trial court's decision limiting the type of mitigating evidence that could be presented; it has set aside a death sentence when jurors failed to specify which aggravating circumstances they found to exist; it has reversed a death sentence imposed on a partial finding of an aggravating circumstance; it has disapproved a death penalty because of errors in admitting evidence; it has reversed a capital sentence where a co-defendant received only a life sentence; and it has held a statutory aggravating circumstance to be unconstitutional.

The Georgia Supreme Court has also been responsible and consistent in its construction of Subsection (b)(7). The provision has been the exclusive or nonexclusive basis for imposition of the death penalty in over 30 cases. In one excursus on the provision's language, the court in effect held that the section is to be read as a whole, construing "depravity of mind," "torture," and "aggravated battery" to flesh out the meaning of "vile," "horrible," and "inhuman." I see no constitutional error resulting from this understanding of the provision. . . . And the court has noted that it would apply the provision only in "core" cases and would not permit Subsection (b)(7) to become a "catchall."

Nor do the facts of this case stand out as an aberration. A jury found Subsection (b)(7) satisfied, for example, when a child was senselessly and ruthlessly executed by a murderer who, like petitioner, accomplished this end with a shotgun. The Georgia Supreme Court affirmed. The court has also affirmed a jury's finding of Subsection (b)(7) where, as here, there was substantial disfigurement of the victim, and where, as arguably with Mrs. Wilkerson, there was torture of the victim.

The majority's attempt to drive a wedge between this case and others in which Subsection (b)(7) has been applied is thus unconvincing, as is any suggestion that the Georgia Supreme Court has somehow failed overall in performance of its review function.

In the circumstances of this case, the majority today endorses the argument that I thought we had rejected in *Gregg*: namely, "that no matter how effective the death penalty may be as a punishment, government, created and run as it must be by humans, is inevitably incompetent to administer it." The Georgia Supreme Court, faced with a seemingly endless train of macabre scenes, has endeavored in a responsible, rational, and consistent fashion to effectuate its statutory mandate as illuminated by our judgment in *Gregg*. Today, a majority of this Court, its arguments shredded by its own illogic, informs the Georgia Supreme Court that, to some extent, its efforts have been outside the Constitution. I reject this as an unwarranted invasion into the realm of state law, for, as in *Gregg*, "I decline to interfere with the manner in which Georgia has chosen to enforce [its] laws" until a genuine error of constitutional magnitude surfaces.

I would affirm the judgment of the Supreme Court of Georgia.

NOTES ON *GODFREY*

1. **The Constitutional Defect in Godfrey's Death Sentence.** Although the Supreme Court held that Godfrey's death sentence was unconstitutional, the rationale for the decision is somewhat elusive. Did the Court hold that subsection (b)(7) is void for vagueness? If not, how would you state the holding of the case?

The plurality and dissenting opinions appear to view the outcome in Godfrey's case through different lenses. Justice White asserts that the case does not "stand out as an aberration" when compared with other cases in which death sentences had been imposed under subsection (b) (7). In contrast, Justice Stewart observes that "there is no meaningful way to distinguish [Godfrey's] case in which the death penalty was imposed from the many cases in which it was not." Which is the right question to ask? How did Justice Stewart know about the cases in which the death penalty had not been imposed?

2. **The Proper Role of the Supreme Court.** The *Godfrey* opinions reflect continuing disagreement about the proper role of the Supreme Court in this area. The plurality appears willing to pursue a relatively aggressive role in supervising state administration of capital sentencing. This approach is flanked on one side by the more passive position of White, Rehnquist, and Burger who object, in White's words, to the plurality's effort to "backstop" the Georgia Supreme Court and to the Court's "unwarranted invasion into the realm of state law." The plurality is flanked on the other side by Marshall and Brennan, who assert that "the effort to eliminate arbitrariness" in the administration of the death penalty is "so plainly doomed to failure" that capital punishment should be declared unconstitutional. What position should the Court take? Why?

3. **Subsequent History.** After Godfrey's case was remanded to the Georgia courts, the prosecution again sought the death penalty. This time another statutory circumstance was advanced to establish the predicate for a death sentence—that the murder "was committed while the offender was engaged in the commission of another capital felony."

The jury found that this circumstance had been proved and recommended death sentences for each murder. On appeal, the Georgia Supreme Court affirmed. Godfrey v. State, 248 Ga. 616, 284 S.E.2d 422 (1981). The court held that Godfrey's retrial and the reimposition of the death sentences did not violate the double jeopardy provisions of the state or federal Constitutions. The court also rejected Godfrey's contention that the particular aggravating circumstance had been improperly applied:

> "[Godfrey] argues that since both murders were separate in time, although only moments apart, and each was instantaneous, one could not have occurred while in the commission of another. However, this argument has been raised before and decided in a manner contrary to Godfrey's position [citing a 1981 case]. Furthermore, under the plain meaning of the statute, multiple murders are included as 'another capital felony.' "

Is Godfrey's second death sentence constitutional?

4. **The Structure of Modern Capital Sentencing Statutes: An Overview.** The Supreme Court has established certain conditions that must be met by capital sentencing procedures if they are to survive constitutional scrutiny. Within these boundaries the legislatures have considerable flexibility. Thus, while the Supreme Court's death penalty decisions provide an essential foundation for further study, a complete understanding of the place of the death penalty in the modern law of homicide requires attention to the formulation and administration of contemporary capital sentencing statutes. The next section considers these questions in some detail. The following overview illustrates the questions raised.

(i) **Criteria of Inclusion.** The Supreme Court appears to have ruled that the death penalty may not be imposed in the absence of proof that the defendant "intended that a killing take place or that lethal force be used." [a] In addition, the line of decisions culminating in *Zant v. Stephens,* summarized at pages 800–01, supra, stands for the proposition that the state is required to establish additional substantive criteria so as to "genuinely narrow the class of persons eligible for the death penalty." The state may provide such criteria in the definition of the elements of capital homicide, as has been done in Texas and Virginia, or in the definition of aggravating circumstances that must be proved at the sentencing stage, as has been done in Georgia and Florida. It may be useful at this point to review § 210.6 of the Model Penal Code and the capital sentencing statutes of Texas, Virginia, Georgia, and Florida reprinted in Appendix B. These statutes reflect varying judgments concerning appropriate criteria of inclusion. Have they specified substantive predicates for imposition of the death penalty in a way that "genuinely narrows the class" of intentional homicides to those for which the ultimate sanction is reasonably justified?

(ii) **Criteria of Exclusion.** Section 210.6(1)(d) of the Model Penal Code precludes imposition of the death penalty on a person who

---

a Enmund v. Florida, 458 U.S. 782 (1982), discussed at pages 1020–28, infra.

was under 18 years of age at the time of the homicide. At least 10 states have enacted a similar limitation. What is the basis for this legislative judgment? Is it correct? Can you think of other factors that should preclude imposition of the death penalty for an intentional homicide otherwise properly punishable as a capital offense?

(iii) **Criteria of Mitigation and Selection.** Once the legislature has defined the class of intentional homicides for which the death penalty is permissible, what additional criteria should be considered? The Supreme Court has made it clear that the death sentence cannot be mandatory and that the sentencer is constitutionally required to "consider" any evidence proffered by the defendant in mitigation. Within this framework, should the sentencer's discretion be subject to normative constraint or guidance? In this connection, compare the Model Penal Code and the Georgia and Florida statutes reproduced in Appendix B. Under the Georgia statute, the sentencer's discretion "to recommend" a death sentence for a death-eligible offender is unconstrained by normative criteria. In contrast, the Model Penal Code provides that the sentencing court is permitted to consider a death sentence only if it (or the jury) finds that "there are no mitigating circumstances sufficiently substantial to call for leniency." Even in the absence of such a finding, moreover, it appears that the court has residual discretion to impose a life sentence. The Florida statute appears to tip the scale in the other direction, requiring a death sentence to be imposed if "there are insufficient mitigating circumstances to outweigh the aggravating circumstances." Are these variations significant? In what way? Which one do you prefer? Why?

(iv) **Comparative Review.** Appellate review serves the same functions in capital cases as in any other case—assuring, for example, that the trial court has properly interpreted and applied the governing law and that the evidence is legally sufficient to establish the necessary substantive predicates for the disposition of the case below. In addition to the standard functions, however, appellate courts in most states also have a unique responsibility in capital cases—conducting "comparative review" of each death sentence to determine whether the imposition of the capital sanction is consistent with the sentences imposed in similar cases. Although the Supreme Court has held that comparative review is not constitutionally required, Pulley v. Harris, 465 U.S. 37 (1984), most state statutes include provisions, modeled on the Georgia statute, which direct the appellate court to determine "whether the sentence of death is excessive or disproportionate to the penalty imposed in similar cases, considering both the crime and the defendant." Comparative review is designed to promote consistency in the administration of the death penalty in each state and thereby to respond to the concerns underlying the Supreme Court's decision in *Furman*. Do you think it can work for this purpose? On what data should the comparisons be based? Are any two offenses likely to be identical in *all* relevant respects? What kinds of variations are tolerable?

In a general sense, these questions go to the heart of the constitutional issue raised by *Furman*. The Supreme Court has apparently determined that the *Furman* defect is adequately remedied, from a constitutional standpoint, if the state statute "genuinely narrows the class" of death-eligible offenders. The risk of arbitrary selection within the class is apparently tolerable as a constitutional matter. Is the Court right? Even if the risk is not of constitutional magnitude, what should state appellate courts do to reduce it?

SUBSECTION B: ADMINISTRATION OF MODERN CAPITAL SENTENCING STATUTES

STATE v. MOOSE

Supreme Court of North Carolina, 1984.
310 N.C. 482, 313 S.E.2d 507.

MEYER, JUSTICE. [The defendant was convicted of first-degree murder for killing Ransom Connelly and was sentenced to death.]

. . . . Phillip Kincaid, a surviving eye-witness to the murder, testified that he and Ransom Connelly were driving down Zion Road at about 10:30 p.m. on the night of 26 March 1982. As they crossed the intersection of Zion Road and Settlemyer Road, they noticed a pickup truck. The truck followed them for a distance of 1.3 miles to the intersection of Zion Road and Highway 64–70. The truck followed Connelly's Pontiac Bonneville very closely, repeatedly honking its horn, and bumping the back of the car as it came to a stop at the 64–70 intersection. Although there was no traffic and the pickup truck had numerous opportunities to pass, it did not. The pickup truck continued to follow Connelly's car as it turned left on 64–70, at which point Connelly and Kincaid became alarmed and decided to pull off the road into the parking lot of the Drexel Discount Drug Store. Kincaid watched as the pickup truck drove up along the driver's side of the car, and the barrel of a shotgun emerged from the window on the passenger side of the truck. Kincaid testified that the shotgun remained pointed at them for approximately five seconds before the blast which shattered the driver's window of the Pontiac and killed Ransom Connelly.

The defendant testified on his own behalf to the effect that he and two women, Lynn Whisnant and Carolyn Bradshaw Chapman, left the American Legion Hut on Settlemyer Road in defendant's pickup truck. He and Whisnant were living together at the home of Whisnant's father in Morganton. Defendant had been drinking beer and liquor all day. He pulled up behind a vehicle on Zion Road and attempted to pass it twice. He blew his horn when he reached the stop sign at the 64–70 intersection. He followed the car as it turned left on 64–70 because he was going to visit a friend in Valdese. He attempted to pass the car again, but it veered to the middle of the road. He was carrying two shotguns in the cab of his truck. He asked Whisnant to pass him one of the guns because "Well, we were sitting there at the stop sign and there were several cars coming by, and he was taking longer than he should to be turning, and stuff, and I, you know, got a little irritated sitting there behind him, and after we turned, you know, the idea struck me to fire over him and scare him."

The defendant placed the shotgun "across the upper part of the door frame, where the window rolls down, inside there. It was laid across that and my leg, with my hand on it." Defendant testified that he remembered being off the road and "the doorpost of the truck being approximately even with the front window of the car." He then testified, "I thought somebody hollered at me, but anyway, I had the impression that I was about to hit something and I swerved to the left, as instinct, to get the truck turned as fast as I could, and as I started to turn, I brought my right hand up to grab for the wheel and the shotgun went off." He maintained that he did not bring the truck to a complete stop, did not aim the shotgun at anyone, and did not know that he had shot anyone until after he was arrested. Nevertheless, immediately after the blast, defendant fled the scene, colliding with another automobile as he entered highway 64–70. He drove his truck into the M & C Auto Parts Store lot, located a short distance down the road, and began to repair a broken fuel line "busted during the impact." Shortly afterwards the defendant and Whisnant were apprehended. Carolyn Bradshaw disappeared before the police arrived. She would not testify at trial.

Lynn Whisnant testified that as they drove down Zion Road defendant did follow a car which she knew to be occupied by two black men. Although she and the defendant had decided to go to Morganton after leaving the American Legion Hut, when they reached the intersection of 64–70, rather than turning right to Morganton as she had asked him to do, the defendant turned left. He continued to follow the Pontiac until it pulled into the Drexel Discount Drug parking lot. The truck pulled up nearly parallel to the car. She remembered the blast of the shotgun and hearing glass shatter.

Ronnie Glenn Bowen testified for the state. Bowen occupied the same jail cell with the defendant in the Burke County jail and the two discussed the murder of Ransom Connelly. Moose described to Bowen the events leading up to the murder, repeatedly referred to the victim as an "old man" or a "nigger," expressed no regret for his actions, and said he wished that he had shot one of the arresting officers.

[The jury found Moose guilty of a "willful, deliberate and premeditated killing." A separate verdict was returned on sentence. Under North Carolina's capital sentencing statute, the jury is instructed that it may recommend the death penalty if it finds that one or more statutory aggravating circumstances exist, that the aggravating circumstances are sufficiently substantial to call for the death penalty, and that the aggravating circumstances outweigh the mitigating circumstances. The jury found two aggravating circumstances: that "the murder was especially heinous, atrocious or cruel" and that "the defendant knowingly created a great risk of death to more than one person by means of a weapon or device which would normally be hazardous to the lives of more than one person." The jury also found, as mitigating factors, that the defendant had "exhibited good behavior" while in jail and that he had a "history of alcohol abuse." [a] Based on its judgment that the aggravating circumstances outweighed the mitigating circumstances, the jury recommended a death sentence. Moose sought to set aside his death sentence on a variety of grounds.]

Defendant first contends that the evidence . . . was insufficient to support a finding . . . that the murder was especially heinous, atrocious, or cruel.

[T]he state argued that because the victim was "stalked" for a period of time prior to the murder, he suffered psychological torture in excess of that normally present in a first-degree murder case. We agree . . . that where the facts . . . support a finding that a victim is stalked and during the stalking the victim is aware of it and in fear that death is likely to result, the issue of whether the murder is especially heinous, atrocious, or cruel may be properly submitted for jury consideration.

Thus the issue before us is whether, as a matter of law, there is sufficient evidence to submit the issue to the jury. . . .

[T]he state was permitted to present the testimony of Phillip Kincaid for the purpose of [proving] that through a continuing and escalating course of events culminating in the murder, the victim became increasingly fearful for his life, and thereby underwent psychological torture. Kincaid testified that shortly after the defendant appeared behind them, he discovered that he and Mr. Connelly were not being pursued by a police car and informed Connelly of the fact. They "were asking each other, wondering who was that behind us." The vehicle behind them continued to bump them and at the intersection they thought the truck was going to pull around them. Connelly then said, "Well, maybe we can make it on to Fender's." They continued to wonder "who was that behind us blowing the horn." As they turned into the Drexel Discount Drug Connelly said, "I'll just pull off here, maybe whoever it is will go on by." Kincaid's testimony concluded with:

Q. Was there anything stated about the ability to make it to Fender's?

A. Well, we thought we would have been safe if we got to Fender's.

Q. Was there anything said by Ransom Connelly when the shotgun came out the window and during the time that it was pointed at him and you?

A. He said "Oh God, what are they going to do?"

Q. What conversation during the entire time, beginning from Zion Road and coming on down No. 64–70 what, if anything,

---

[a] The trial judge had submitted a list of other factors in mitigation which the jury apparently rejected. These included two statutory factors (that "the defendant has no significant history of prior criminal activity" and that his "capacity to appreciate the criminality of his conduct or to conform his conduct to the requirements of the law was impaired.") and several other factors proposed by the defense concerning the defendant's relationship with his mother and children. [Footnote by eds.]

did Ransom Connelly say about wanting the vehicle behind to go on and pass to leave you alone?

A. Yeah, he said I wish they'd go ahead and pass and leave us alone.

Kincaid's testimony before the jury essentially paralleled that given during the voir dire hearing. He did state before the jury, however, that they "drove up the road frightened" and that he [Kincaid] "was beginning to get more frightened after [the defendant] wouldn't pass" and "after we pulled off the road, and after the shotgun came out of the window I just froze."

It seems then that although there was a considerable amount of "wondering" about the intentions of their pursuer, and some very legitimate concern and apprehension engendered by defendant's inexplicable behavior, there is no evidence that either Kincaid or Connelly believed that the ultimate result of the pursuit would be death—at least not until the shotgun appeared. In fact, Connelly's final utterance, "Oh God, what are they going to do?" suggests that even then, the controlling factor was as much incredulity as it was fear.

We do not consider this evidence sufficient to support the state's theory that Ransom Connelly suffered excessive psychological torture as he was being "stalked for the kill." . . .

Defendant [also] contends that the evidence was insufficient to support the aggravating circumstance that "[t]he defendant knowingly created a great risk of death to more than one person by means of a weapon or device which would normally be hazardous to the lives of more than one person." This court has not previously spoken to this particular aggravating circumstance . . .

The aggravating factor requires a showing that defendant (i) knowingly created a great risk of death to more than one person, (ii) by means of a weapon or device which would normally be hazardous to the lives of more than one person. This factor thus addresses essentially two considerations: a great risk of death knowingly created and the weapon by which it is created. We therefore address ourselves to both the risk and the weapon.

With regard to the risk element, the evidence is certainly sufficient to support a jury finding that the defendant knew there were two people in the front seat of Connelly's car. While much of the evidence is conflicting, it is clear that defendant's passenger, Mrs. Whisnant, testified that she knew there were two men in the victim's car and that they were black, and said in a statement given three days after the incident that the driver was wearing a hat and the passenger was not. The defendant . . . drove right on the bumper of the victim's car for . . . 1.3 miles and . . . bumped it at least twice. The defendant stopped his car in the parking lot within several feet of the victim's car and . . . fired the shotgun into the occupied vehicle within two or three feet of the victim and his passenger. . . . It cannot be said that the defendant did not knowingly create the risk.

When a shotgun is fired at close range into the passenger compartment of an automobile, the risk created is not simply a risk of injury but a risk of death. The risk of death to Connelly and Kincaid was "great" and not merely negligible. The risk did not exist as to only one of the occupants but to both. The fact that only one of the occupants was killed does not refute the fact that both were placed at risk of death.

As to the weapon, the crucial consideration . . . is its potential to kill more than one person . . . . The focus must be upon the destructive capabilities of the weapon or device. Whether used for sporting purposes against game birds, water fowl and animals, or as a weapon against man, the shotgun is selected for the very reason that it is capable of firing more than one, and in fact, many projectiles in a pattern over a wide impact area rather than a specifically aimed single projectile such as from a rifle or pistol. It is used by law enforcement officers and the military alike for its widespread destructive power in close places or at close range. It is axiomatic that a shotgun is a weapon which would normally be hazardous to more than one person if it is fired into a group of two or more persons in close proximity to one another.

. . . We note [that the shell used] would have contained . . . approximately 253 pellets . . . . We further note that only approximately 40 pellets were recovered from the victim's body.

We hold that a shotgun falls within the category of weapon envisioned in [the statute] and that there was sufficient evidence from which the jury could conclude that the defendant knowingly created a great risk of death to Ransom Connelly and Phillip Kincaid by means of a weapon or device which would normally be hazardous to the lives of more than one person. The jury's finding of this factor is supported by the evidence.

Defendant [next] contends that the trial judge erred when he refused to submit, as a mitigating factor, that the defendant was under the influence of mental or emotional disturbance at the time of the offense. The basis for the submission of this factor was the testimony of Dr. Bruce Berg, a forensic psychiatrist, who conducted a pretrial evaluation of the defendant. Dr. Berg testified that defendant had a history of repeated alcohol abuse and had a "mixed personality disorder" which was manifested by his inability to deal adequately with frustrations which led to outbursts of temper. On the other hand, the state's characterization of defendant was, in short, "a man of average intelligence with a penchant for alcohol and a hot temper."

We agree that this evidence falls short of that necessary to support the submission of [the mitigating circumstance] that the defendant was under the influence of mental or emotional disturbance when he murdered Ransom Connelly. The inability to control one's drinking habits or one's temper is neither a mental disturbance nor an emotional disturbance as contemplated by this mitigating factor. In State v. Brown, 306 N.C. 151, 293 S.E.2d 569 (1982), we reiterated this court's

position with respect to the definition of mitigating circumstances
. . . . That definition and the policy it represents bears repeating:

"A definition of mitigating circumstance approved by this Court
is a fact or group of facts which do not constitute any justification or excuse for killing or reduce it to a lesser degree of the
crime of first-degree murder, *which may be considered as extenu-
ating, or reducing the moral culpability of killing or making it
less deserving of the extreme punishment than other first-degree
murders.*" (emphasis added).

[I]n *Brown* . . . we stated that " 'voluntary intoxication by alcohol or
narcotic drugs at the time of the commission of a murder is not within
the meaning of a mental or emotional disturbance under [this paragraph of the statute]. Voluntary intoxication, to a degree that it affects
defendant's ability to understand and to control his actions . . . is
properly considered under the provision for impaired capacity.' " In
the present case the trial judge submitted and the jury failed to find as
a mitigating factor that "[t]he capacity of the defendant to appreciate
the criminality of his conduct or to conform his conduct to the requirements of the law was impaired."

The burden was on the defendant to prove in mitigation that he was
under the influence of mental or emotional disturbance. Here he failed
to come forward with any evidence other than that his temper controlled his reason, particularly when he consumed alcohol. Furthermore, the trial judge submitted and the jury found as an additional
factor in mitigation that the defendant had a history of alcohol abuse.
The submission of [this circumstance] thus would have been duplicative
with respect to defendant's alcohol abuse. The assignment of error is
overruled. . . .

Defendant additionally asserts that the state impermissibly appealed to racial fears and biases when [the prosecution] argued that the
murder was racially motivated. We held in [upholding the conviction]
that arguments relating to the racially motivated character of this
murder were supported by the evidence and relevant to refute defendant's contention that he did not intend to harm Mr. Connelly. Likewise, this evidence and the argument based thereon was relevant at
sentencing to illustrate the depravity of defendant's character. . . .

In the guilt phase we find no error. The case is remanded to the
Superior Court, Burke County, for resentencing.

MARTIN, JUSTICE, dissenting in part. [I] respectfully dissent from the
remanding of the case for a new sentencing hearing. The majority
finds the evidence insufficient to submit the issue to the jury of
whether the capital crime was especially heinous, atrocious, or cruel.
In this finding I cannot concur. I do concur in that portion of the
majority opinion concerning whether the shotgun in this case was a
weapon within the meaning of [the statute].

This blatant murder in cold blood of a black man by this white
defendant was racially motivated. A racially motivated murder evi-

dences abnormal brutality and depravity not found in other murders. It is especially heinous, atrocious, or cruel.

The majority concedes that for the purpose of evaluating the prosecution's jury argument, the evidence supports a finding that the murder was racially motivated. The deceased, Ransom Connelly, was a 62-year-old black man driving his car through a white community in the night-time. He was accompanied by another black man, the witness Phillip Kincaid. When defendant and his women friends, Lynn Whisnant and Carolyn Bradshaw, left the American Legion hut, they intended to go to Morganton. However, after following Connelly and Kincaid on Zion Hill Road for 1.3 miles, defendant changed his mind. Even though Lynn asked him to turn right on highway 64–70 toward Morganton, defendant turned left and continued to follow his intended victims. All during this travel, defendant had repeatedly honked the car horn, followed Connelly's Pontiac car very closely, and bumped the rear of the car at least twice.

The testimony of Ronnie Bowen supports a finding that defendant murdered Connelly for racial reasons. Bowen was in jail with defendant for about two months after the murder and before the trial. He testified that he talked with defendant several times about defendant's case and:

Q. State whether or not you told him what you were charged with and if he told you about things he was charged with.

A. Yes sir, I told him I was charged with forgery and he was in there for shooting a nigger, is what he told me. . . . He told me that he had followed a dude, that he followed a nigger into, down the road into a parking lot drug store and pulled up beside of him, that he shot the man with a shotgun out of the window, was rolled down on the truck. . . . Yes sir, he said something about it wasn't on his conscience and that he had killed the nigger, but since he was in jail he regreted it, but that it didn't bother him, though. . . .

Q. By what names did he refer to the person that he told you that he had shot; what did he call that person?

A. Old man. Nigger; most of all nigger. . . .

Q. And did you tell me in that statement the names, or three different names that he referred to the dead man by? What he called the dead man.

A. Nigger. Old man and damn nigger. [H]e told me that he did kill the damn nigger . . . .

Q. Has he ever said that he was sorry that he shot the man?

A. Naw, he ain't never said that. He was sorry. He said that he wished it hadn't happened, but he never said that he was sorry.

This testimony as to what the defendant said evidences on his part a hatred for black people, a feeling of his superiority to them, and a cruel indifference to their fate. He was not sorry that he murdered the black man, it was not on his conscience. He only regretted being in jail. There is no other cause for this murder except defendant's racist attitude toward black people in general and toward Ransom Connelly in particular. Such evidence indicates abnormal brutality and depravity in the commission of the capital crime and is sufficient to submit the issue of especially heinous, atrocious, or cruel to the jury.

In analyzing this assignment of error, the majority only discusses the evidence that defendant stalked the deceased prior to the killing, thereby causing psychological torture to him. Contrary to the majority, I also find the evidence sufficient on this theory to submit the issue to the jury. Although the surviving witness failed to testify that Ransom Connelly was in panic because of the conduct of defendant in following Connelly's car, the evidence is sufficient to support a finding by the jury that Connelly suffered psychological torture during this period of time. When defendant failed to turn right on U.S. 64 toward Morganton as he had planned to do, it demonstrated an intent on his part to further inflict psychological torture on Connelly. The most potent evidence supporting this theory is that of the defendant ordering one of the women to hand him the shotgun, directing that the window be rolled down on the passenger side of his pickup truck, and coolly pointing the shotgun at Ransom Connelly's head for a period of five seconds before blowing him away. Five seconds is a short time in most circumstances, but when looking into the muzzle of a shotgun, it can be as an eternity. Ransom Connelly's remarks during the drive and as he faced the shotgun manifest the mental torture he was suffering. He said he wished they would go ahead and pass and leave us alone; maybe we could make it on to Fender's store; we will be safe if we can get to Fender's; I'll just pull in here (at the Drexel Discount Drugstore) and maybe whoever it is will go on by. Finally, as the gun was levelled at his head, Connelly said, "Oh God, what are they going to do?" The majority characterizes the last statement as being one of incredulity. I find it to be a despairing prayer. Just as the hunter stalks his frightened and cornered prey, defendant stalked Connelly for the kill.

Further, the conduct of defendant after the murder, which I will not repeat, also supports a finding of depravity on the part of defendant within the holding of State v. Oliver, 309 N.C. 326, 307 S.E.2d 304 (1983).[b]

The majority correctly states the rule to be applied in determining the sufficiency of the evidence to submit an aggravating circumstance to the jury. Upon applying the rule to the evidence in this case, I find

[b] In *Oliver*, two defendants were sentenced to death in connection with two murders committed in the course of an armed robbery of a convenience store. The Court upheld the "heinous, atrocious or cruel" finding against one of defendants on the following basis:

"[T]he evidence justifies a conclusion that the murder [of the store attendant], committed in total disregard for the value of human life, was a senseless murder, executed in cold blood as the victim pleaded 'please don't shoot me'; and that the defendant showed no remorse. In fact, [the defendant] later laughingly boasted to his fellow inmates that he pointed the gun at [the victim] who begged not to be shot and offered the defendant more money, and that the defendant 'kind of liked the idea of it.'" [Footnote by eds.]

it sufficient to support the issue on the theories that (i) defendant stalked his victim, causing him to suffer psychological torture; (ii) the conduct of defendant was abnormally depraved under *Oliver*; and (iii) the capital crime was a racially motivated murder. The evidence was sufficient to submit the aggravating circumstance of especially heinous, atrocious, or cruel to the jury for its determination.

I am authorized to state that JUSTICES COPELAND and MITCHELL join in this dissenting opinion.

_____

NOTES ON SUBSTANTIVE PREDICATES FOR IMPOSITION OF THE DEATH PENALTY

1. **Questions and Comments on *Moose*.** As noted below, creating a risk of death to more than one person is a fairly common criterion of inclusion in modern death penalty statutes. According to the court's interpretation, the circumstance is established whenever the intended victim is in the company of one other person and the offender uses a shotgun. Thus, the offense would not have been punishable by death if Ransom Connelly had been driving alone or if Moose had used a rifle in a context where only one person was endangered. Should the imposition of the death penalty hinge on such considerations? Does the Court's intepretation "reasonably justify" the imposition of a death sentence? Does it establish a "meaningful difference" between those homicides that are punishable by death and those that are not?

Assume that the North Carolina statute had not included the aggravating factor discussed above. On this state of the law, Moose's offense would be punishable by death in North Carolina only if the offense had been properly found to be "heinous, atrocious or cruel." Although a majority of the court ruled that the evidence was not legally sufficient to establish this circumstance, Justice Martin argued in dissent that three dimensions of the case were sufficient to establish that the offense was "heinous, atrocious or cruel": (i) that Moose caused his victim "psychological torture" by "stalking" him; (ii) that the killing was "racially motivated"; and (iii) that Moose's conduct after the murder (his failure to express remorse) demonstrated "abnormal depravity." Is any of these three factors, standing alone, a proper predicate for a death sentence? Would it matter if the legislature had specified intentionally placing the victim in mortal fear, racial antipathy, or failure to express remorse as aggravating factors? If none of these factors is regarded as independently sufficient, do you agree with Justice Martin's view that, taken together, they should be regarded as sufficient to support a finding that Moose's offense was "heinous, atrocious or cruel"? Would such a determination survive constitutional scrutiny under *Godfrey v. Georgia*?

2. **Statutory Criteria of Inclusion.** What criteria should be used to define the class of homicides punishable by death? The statutes now in force reveal a number of common legislative judgments about the

characteristics of the offense or of the defendant that are regarded as sufficient to support a death sentence. They are summarized below.

(i) **Identity of the Victim.** Under most modern statutes, an intentional killing is punishable by death if the victim falls within certain specified categories. A basis for the death penalty is established in most states [a] if the victim is a law enforcement officer or a correctional officer. In addition, many states make a killing punishable by death if the victim is a fireman, a judge, a prosecutor, a witness, or an elected official, or, in a smaller number of states, a kidnap victim, a hostage, or a shield. On what rationale do these provisions rest? Are they justified?

(ii) **Accompanying Criminal Offenses.** In most states, an intentional killing is punishable by death if it occurred while the defendant was committing, attempting to commit, or fleeing after committing, a variety of specified felonies—usually rape, robbery, burglary, arson and kidnapping. About a third of the states make multiple murders punishable by death, and a few make a killing capital if the defendant committed other crimes of violence against persons other than the murder victim at the same time or in the same course of conduct. What is the rationale for these provisions? To the extent that a killing is punishable by death solely because it occurred during the course of a robbery or burglary, or because the defendant assaulted or injured more than one person, has the class of death-eligible offenses been "genuinely narrowed"?

(iii) **Hazardous Conduct.** As *Moose* illustrates, many state statutes make intentional homicide punishable by death if the defendant "knowingly created a great risk of death to many persons" or if the defendant "knowingly created a great risk of death to more than one person in a public place by means of a weapon or device which would normally be hazardous to the lives of more than one person." In other states, a killing is capital if it is committed by use of explosives. What policy underlies these provisions? Did the drafters have in mind offenders such as Moose?

(iv) **Pecuniary Motive.** About half the states make murder punishable by death if the defendant was hired to commit it or hired someone else to do so; in a few other states, only the hired killer is punishable by death. Under a related provision in several states, a killing is death-eligible if the defendant caused or directed another to commit it or committed it as the agent or employee of another. In a number of additional states, the standard is more broadly defined: a killing is punishable by death if "it was committed . . . for the purpose of receiving anything of monetary value" or "for pecuniary gain." Why is pecuniary motivation so widely accepted as a sufficient predicate for a death sentence? Is the person who kills for life insurance proceeds more or less deserving of a death sentence than a person who is motivated by sexual arousal or racial bigotry?

a The reference here, and below, is limited to those states that retain capital punishment.

(v) **Hindrance of Law Enforcement.** A large number of statutes make a killing capital if it was committed to avoid or prevent arrest or to effect escape, and a few others make a killing punishable by death if it was committed for the purpose of disrupting or hindering law enforcement or governmental functions. What is the rationale for such provisions? Should the degree of hindrance of law enforcement matter?

(vi) **Unusual Cruelty or Depravity.** In about three-quarters of the states a killing is capital if it is "especially heinous, atrocious or cruel" or "unwantonly vile, horrible or inhuman in that it involved torture, depravity of mind or aggravated battery to the victim" or especially cruel by some similar epithetical description. In a few additional states, a killing is capital if it involves torture. These criteria have a catch-all quality, requiring interpretation and application in a manner that provides some objective basis for distinguishing between killings that are punishable by death and those that are not. In light of the difficulties explored in connection with *Godfrey* and *Moose,* should these provisions be invalidated?

(vii) **In Custody.** In most states, an intentional killing is punishable by death if it is committed by a person who is either confined in a correctional institution or is "in custody" at the time of the offense. On what policy is this criterion based? Should it be restricted, as a few states do, to cases in which the defendant was serving a life sentence? A felony sentence?

(viii) **Prior Criminal Conduct.** In most states, an intentional killing is punishable by death if the offender has previously been convicted of murder. In about half of the states, the predicate for a death sentence is established if the defendant has previously been convicted of any felony involving the use or threat of violence. In a few additional states, it is sufficient if the defendant has a "substantial history of serious assaultive convictions" or a significant history of "criminal activity." What is the basis for these provisions? To what extent do they "genuinely narrow the class" of death-eligible offenders to those for whom the death penalty is reasonably justified?

(ix) **Prediction of Future Criminal Conduct.** The "prior criminal record" provisions discussed above should be contrasted with the unusual provisions found in Oklahoma and Idaho, which make an intentional killing punishable by death if the sentencer finds that there is a "probability that the defendant would commit criminal acts of violence that would constitute a continuing threat to society."[b] These provisions rest explicitly on an incapacitative rationale. Is the death penalty reasonably justified on purely incapacitative grounds? Is this criterion of inclusion defined with adequate specificity? Would it make any difference if the courts interpreted the provision to require one or more previous convictions for violent offenses as a necessary predicate for the prediction of future dangerousness? Typical problems with the

[b] In two other states, Virginia and Texas, such a finding constitutes an aggravating circumstance but is not sufficient, in itself, to establish the substantive predicate for a death sentence for an intentional killing.

prediction of future dangerousness are errors of over-inclusion. Should that be a concern here?

3. **Relevance of the Premeditation-Deliberation Formula.** Under the contemporary generation of capital sentencing statutes, the premeditation-deliberation formula no longer provides a sufficient substantive basis for imposing a death sentence; other factors relating to the offender and the offense, reviewed in the preceeding notes, are now required. However, even though the formula no longer establishes a legally sufficient predicate for a capital sentence, the statutes of at least 20 states, including North Carolina, still retain it in the definition of capital homicide. In these states, the formula remains a necessary predicate for imposition of the death penalty in cases not involving torture, lying in wait, or felony murder.

Abandonment of the original mandatory approach to the capital punishment of premeditated killings indicates that lawmakers concluded long ago that the formula does not isolate a class of homicide offenders all of whom should be executed. The question remains, however, whether the formula is nonetheless useful as a screening device. Does it accurately sort intentional homicides into a class for which the death penalty should be foreclosed and a class for which the death penalty should be considered if other criteria are met? Reconsider the discussion of the meaning of the formula summarized at pages 781–86, supra. Does its utility depend on what it means? Should Anderson (page 784, supra) be excluded from the death penalty because there was no evidence that he "deliberated" and "premeditated" before he killed a 13-year-old girl by inflicting some 60 knife wounds? Did Moose "premeditate and deliberate" before shooting his victim? Should it matter?

STATE OF ALABAMA v. JUDITH ANN NEELLEY

Circuit Court of DeKalb County, Alabama, April 18, 1983.

Sentencing Order

DONALD L. COLE, CIRCUIT JUDGE. The defendant was charged by indictment with the murder of Lisa Ann Millican during a kidnapping in the first degree, a capital offense. A jury returned a verdict on March 22, 1983, finding the defendant guilty of the capital offense, whereupon the court adjudged the defendant guilty in accordance with the jury's verdict.

Following the adjudication of guilt, a separate sentence hearing was conducted before the same jury, and the jury returned a recommendation that the defendant be sentenced to life without parole.[a]

The court has ordered and received a written pre-sentence investigation report and has conducted an additional sentence hearing pursuant

---

[a] The vote was ten jurors for life without parole and two for death. [Footnote by eds.]

to Ala.Code § 13A–5–47. At the sentence hearing, the state, through its district attorney, urged that the court fix the defendant's punishment at death. The defendant, through her counsel, argued that the court should fix her punishment, in accordance with the jury's recommendation, at life in prison without parole.

FINDING OF FACTS SUMMARIZING THE CRIME AND THE DEFENDANT'S PARTICIPATION IN IT

The body of Lisa Ann Millican, age 13, was found in a gorge known as Little River Canyon near Fort Payne on September 29, 1982. Lisa was a resident of the Ethel Harpst Home, a Methodist home for neglected children located in Cedartown, Georgia.

Lisa and five other girls from the home were taken by a house parent on an outing to Riverbend Mall in Rome, Georgia on September 25, 1982. While at the mall, Lisa became separated from the others. During this separation, she was abducted by the defendant, who asked Lisa to go "riding around." Lisa hesitated at first, but then agreed. The events which followed the abduction led to the death of Lisa when the defendant shot her in the back on September 28, 1982, and threw her body into the canyon.

The abduction of Lisa Ann Millican was part of a bizarre scheme whereby the defendant attempted to lure girls and young women into the car with her for the ultimate purpose of making them available to her husband, Alvin Neelley, for sex with him. For several days immediately prior to Lisa's abduction, the defendant and Alvin drove up and down Rome streets in separate automobiles looking for girls who would be suitable. When Alvin would see one who appealed to him, he would communicate with the defendant by C–B radio, and the defendant would invite the girl to go riding around with her. Numerous girls refused the defendant's invitation; her first successful pick-up was Lisa Ann Millican.

The defendant took Lisa to a motel in Franklin, Georgia, where she tried to persuade Lisa to submit to sex with Alvin, but Lisa resisted. Finally, Alvin told Lisa that if she did not submit to sex, the defendant would kill her. Following this threat, Alvin engaged in sex with Lisa, and later that night, Lisa was handcuffed to the bed to prevent her escape.

The next day, the defendant and Alvin, traveling in two cars, took Lisa with them to Cleveland, Tennessee, where they picked up their two-year-old twins who were being cared for by Alvin's mother. Later that day, they travelled to Scottsboro, Alabama where they rented a motel room. Shortly after their arrival at the motel, the defendant hit Lisa in the head several times with a slapjack in an attempt to render her unconscious, but she was unsuccessful in achieving that result. Alvin then had sex with Lisa, and afterward Lisa slept overnight on the floor, unclothed, and handcuffed to the bed.

The following day, Alvin had sex with Lisa twice more despite her cries and pleas that he stop: The defendant was present during these sexual encounters and at one point during the day, she handcuffed Lisa to the plumbing in the bathroom and interrogated her about a man she had appeared to know at a dairy bar near the motel.

The next morning, Lisa was taken to Little River Canyon by the defendant where the defendant instructed Lisa to lie face down and place her hands around a tree. The defendant then handcuffed Lisa's hands. She explained to Lisa that she was going to give her a shot that would make her fall asleep and that when she waked up, Lisa would be free to go. Using a needle and syringe, the defendant injected Lisa in the neck with liquid drain cleaner. When Lisa did not die in five minutes, the defendant injected her again in the neck. She injected Lisa four additional times, twice in the arms and twice in the buttocks, waiting about five minutes after each injection for Lisa to die. Twice during the infliction of these injections, Lisa requested to get up and "use the bathroom" in the woods. She was allowed to do so, and each time she returned and resumed her position on the ground with her hands around the tree.

Following the last injection, the defendant instructed Lisa to walk around for awhile to hasten the work of the poison in her body. When it finally appeared that Lisa was not going to die from the drain cleaner, the defendant marched Lisa to the rim of the canyon to shoot her in the back in a manner that would cause her body to fall into the canyon. Lisa begged to go back to the Harpst Home and promised not to tell what had happened. The defendant told Lisa to be quiet and then shot her in the back. Lisa fell backward toward the defendant instead of falling into the canyon. The defendant picked up the body and, using her knee, propelled it into the canyon.

During the defendant's trial testimony, she testified that Alvin was present at the canyon directing her every action. However, in an out-of-court statement made shortly after her arrest, the defendant stated that Alvin was not present at the canyon.

Five days after the death of Lisa Ann Millican, the defendant picked up a young woman named Janice Chapman and her common-law husband, John Hancock, from a street in Rome. Later that night, the defendant shot John Hancock in the back and left him for dead. He survived, however, and was present at the trial to testify to the incident.

The defendant and Alvin took Janice Chapman to a motel in Rome where Alvin engaged in sex with Janice. The next day, the defendant killed Janice Chapman, shooting her once in the back and twice in the chest. During the defendant's trial testimony, she testified that Alvin was present during the shooting of John Hancock and Janice Chapman and that he directed her to shoot them; however, in her out-of-court statement given shortly after her arrest, she stated that Alvin was present when she shot John Hancock but that he was not present when she killed Janice Chapman.

On October 9, 1982, the day before the defendant's arrest, she picked up another young woman in Nashville, Tennessee, who was present with the defendant and Alvin in a motel room in Murfreesboro, Tennessee, on October 10, 1982, when the defendant was arrested on a bad check charge. Later, this woman was released by Alvin unharmed.

Alvin was arrested in Murfreesboro on October 13, 1982, also on a bad check charge. While the defendant and Alvin were in custody on the bad check charges, additional charges were placed against them arising from the murders of Lisa Ann Millican and Janice Chapman, and the shooting of John Hancock.

FINDINGS CONCERNING THE EXISTENCE OR NON-EXISTENCE OF AGGRAVATING CIRCUMSTANCES

In compliance with the requirements of the law that the trial court shall enter specific findings concerning the existence or non-existence of each aggravating circumstance enumerated by statute, the court finds that none of the aggravating circumstances enumerated by statute [was] proved beyond a reasonable doubt in the proceedings before this court except the following, which the court finds were proved beyond a reasonable doubt:

1. The capital offense was committed while the defendant was engaged in kidnapping. The jury's verdict establishes the existence of this aggravating circumstance, and the verdict is supported by the evidence.

2. The capital offense was especially heinous, atrocious and cruel compared to other capital offenses. The court reaches the conclusion that this aggravating circumstance exists based upon uncontroverted evidence of the following:

   a. The victim of the crime was a child, age 13.

   b. Repeatedly, the child was abused and violated sexually causing her enormous fright and pain. While the evidence is insufficient to establish that the defendant participated in sex acts upon the child, she was an accomplice to the sexual abuse perpetrated upon the child by Alvin Neelley.

   c. The defendant inflicted pain and suffering upon the child by hitting her on the head with a slapjack in an attempt to knock her unconscious.

   d. The defendant physically restrained the child much of the time following her abduction by the use of handcuffs.

   e. The defendant made the child lie on the ground with her hands handcuffed around a tree while the defendant injected her six times with liquid drain cleaner.

   f. The defendant marched the child to the rim of the deep canyon, with the child begging to be released, where the defendant shot her in the back.

By any standard acceptable to civilized society, this crime was extremely wicked and shockingly evil. It was perpetrated with a design to inflict a high degree of pain with utter indifference to the suffering of the victim. The court recognizes that all capital offenses are heinous, atrocious and cruel to some extent, but the degree of heinousness, atrociousness and cruelty which characterizes this offense exceeds that which is common to all capital offenses.

FINDINGS CONCERNING THE EXISTENCE OR NON–EXISTENCE OF MITIGATING CIRCUMSTANCES

I.

In compliance with the statutory requirement that the trial court enter specific findings concerning the existence or non-existence of each mitigating circumstance enumerated by statute, the court finds that none of the following mitigating circumstances [existed] in this case:

1. That the defendant has no significant history of prior criminal activity. The defendant testified to a significant history of criminal conduct. When she was 16 years of age, she robbed a woman of her purse at gunpoint. As a result of this offense, she was committed to the Georgia Youth Development Center, and her husband, Alvin, who was an accomplice to the robbery, was sentenced to a term in the Georgia State Penitentiary.

The defendant was released from the Georgia Youth Development Center in December, 1981, and Alvin was released from the penitentiary several months later. The defendant testified that upon Alvin's release, he was obsessed with the notion that she had been sexually abused by employees at the Youth Development Centers in Rome and Macon. To avenge the alleged wrong, Alvin and the defendant set out to kill or terrorize employees of the YDC. Pursuant to this objective, they shot into the house of one employee and attempted to firebomb the automobile of another in Rome. In Macon, the defendant attempted to lure YDC employees to a motel room where Alvin was prepared to kill them. The defendant was unsuccessful in luring any employees to the motel, and none [was] harmed.

Additional criminal activity by the defendant, according to her own testimony, includes writing bad checks, raising the amounts on money orders, stealing checks from post office boxes and cashing them with false identification, and stealing from convenience stores where Alvin was employed.

2. That the capital offense was committed while the defendant was under the influence of extreme mental or emotional disturbance. When the defendant was arraigned on December 17, 1982, her counsel requested that the defendant be committed to Bryce Hospital for psychiatric examination and evaluation. The court granted the request, and the defendant thereafter underwent psychiatric examination and evaluation at Bryce Hospital. Dr. Alexander Salillas, a staff psychiatrist at Taylor Hardin Secure Medical Facility and a consultant at Bryce, testified that as a result of his examination of the defendant, he found no mental disease or defect and that, in his opinion, she knew right from wrong at the time of the offense and that she acted with deliberation and premeditation.

While the court recognizes that this mitigating circumstance contemplates a disturbance of the mind which might exist separate and apart from a mental disease or defect, and that the testimony of the psychiatrist is, by no means, conclusive, the court finds from a consideration of all the evidence that the defendant was not under the influence of extreme mental or emotional disturbance.

3. That the victim was a participant in the defendant's conduct or consented to it. There is no support for this mitigating circumstance. Although Lisa Ann Millican initially agreed to go with the defendant when the defendant picked her up at the mall in Rome, the fact that Lisa was less than 16 years old and that the Harpst Home, which had legal custody of her, had not acquiesced to her being taken by the defendant, makes any consent given by Lisa legally ineffectual. Any consent given by the child to the acts of violence and abuse committed upon her was the result of threats or false promises and provides no support for this mitigating circumstance.

4. That the defendant was an accomplice in the capital offense committed by another person and her participation was relatively minor. The evidence is uncontroverted that the defendant abducted Lisa Ann Millican, that the defendant injected her six times with liquid drain cleaners, and that the defendant shot her in the back and threw her body into the canyon. Although there is evidence that the defendant's husband, Alvin, was also involved in this criminal conduct, there is no support for a finding that the defendant's participation was relatively minor.

5. That the defendant acted under extreme duress or under the substantial [domination] of another person. The defendant's primary contention throughout the trial and the sentence hearings was that she had become completely submissive to the will of her husband, Alvin, and that he exercised total control over her. Perhaps the strongest support for this contention is found in the following:

a. testimony by Alvin's former wife that Alvin dominated their relationship and imposed his will upon her;

b. evidence, including pictures of the defendant's bruised body, that Alvin beat the defendant frequently;

c. letters written by Alvin while he was incarcerated in the penitentiary which portray him as a vile and dominant husband; and

d. the fact that the defendant had no record of criminal activity prior to her association with Alvin Neelley.

The evidence cited above, together with the defendant's testimony, convinces the court that the defendant was substantially influenced by her husband, but the court concludes that the husband's influence did not constitute extreme duress or substantial domination.

The defendant is an intelligent person capable of making independent choices. The evidence is substantial that she made a willing choice to follow her husband's influence rather than to depart from it. There were numerous opportunities for the defendant to break with her husband and seek help had she felt the need or been so inclined. These opportunities were enhanced by the fact that the defendant was armed and traveling in a separate vehicle during most of their exploits. Ultimately, the defendant chose, rather than to make the break or turn on her husband, to brutally murder Lisa Ann Millican.

The court finds that the defendant was not brainwashed and that she retained her will and her capacity to make independent choices.

6.   That the capacity of the defendant to appreciate the criminality of her conduct or to conform her conduct to the requirements of law was substantially impaired.   The defendant entered a plea of not guilty by reason of mental disease or defect.   With regard to this defense, the court instructed the jury that a person is not responsible for criminal conduct if at the time of such conduct, as a result of mental disease or defect, such person lacks substantial capacity to appreciate the criminality of his conduct or to conform his conduct to the requirements of law.   By its verdict of guilt, the jury found the evidence insufficient to support the plea of insanity, and the jury's finding is supported by the evidence.   While the court recognizes that this mitigating circumstance contemplates impaired capacity which might exist separate and apart from a mental disease or defect, the court finds from a consideration of Dr. Salillas' testimony and the evidence as a whole that this mitigating circumstance does not exist.

II.

The court finds that the following mitigating circumstance enumerated by statute does exist in this case:

1.   The age of the defendant at the time of the crime.   The defendant was 18 years of age at the time she committed the capital offense of which she is convicted.   While the court finds the defendant's age to be a mitigating circumstance, the court considers the weight to be given this circumstance lessened by the fact that the defendant, since a much earlier age, had adopted the lifestyle of an adult.   She commenced a marital relationship with Alvin Neelley when she was age 15, and gave birth to twins when she was age 16.   The criminal activity in which the defendant engaged was less akin to the behavior of a teenager and more akin to the conduct of a seasoned criminal.

III.

The court finds two additional mitigating circumstances not enumerated by the statute:

1.   The defendant was substantially influenced by her husband. Although the court has heretofore found that the husband's influence did not constitute extreme duress or substantial domination, it seems appropriate that such influence should be given weight as a mitigating circumstance.

2.   The defendant voluntarily and intentionally set in motion the events which led to her arrest and the arrest of her husband, thus ending the reign of terror which they had perpetrated throughout three states.   The defendant did this while at her mother's house in Murfreesboro by instructing her mother to notify the police that she was in

the area and could be arrested on bad check charges pending against her. In the defendant's testimony, she could not explain what prompted her to give her mother these instructions, but it is fair to infer that conscience had a hand in it.

CONCLUSION

The court has carefully weighed the aggravating and mitigating circumstances which it finds to exist in this case, and has given consideration to the recommendation of the jury contained in its advisory verdict. While the mitigating circumstances and the jury's recommendation of life without parole have weighed heavily in the court's consideration, it is the judgment of this court that they are outweighed by the aggravating circumstances of this horrible crime. Accordingly, it is ordered, adjudged, and decreed that the defendant shall be punished by death.

A formal sentencing entry shall be made by separate order.

NEELLEY v. STATE

Court of Criminal Appeals of Alabama, 1985.
—— So.2d ——

BOWEN, PRESIDING JUDGE. . . . In reviewing any case in which the death penalty has been imposed, this Court must follow the guidelines set out in § 13A–5–53.[a]

In accordance with § 13A–5–53(a), we have reviewed the entire record . . . for any error adversely affecting the rights of the defendant and have found no error.

The trial court properly found the existence of two aggravating circumstances: "The capital offense was committed while the defendant was engaged . . . in . . . kidnapping" and that it was "espe-

---

[a] Section 13A–5–53 provides in relevant part:

"(a) In any case in which the death penalty is imposed, in addition to reviewing the case for any error involving the conviction, the Alabama Court of Criminal Appeals, subject to review by the Alabama Supreme Court, shall also review the propriety of the death sentence. This review shall include the determination of whether any error adversely affecting the rights of the defendant was made in the sentence proceedings, whether the trial court's findings concerning the aggravating and mitigating circumstances were supported by the evidence, and whether death was the proper sentence in the case. . . .

"(b) In determining whether death was the proper sentence in the case the Alabama Court of Criminal Appeals, subject to review by the Alabama Supreme Court, shall determine:

(1) Whether the sentence of death was imposed under the influence of passion, prejudice, or any other arbitrary factor;

(2) Whether an independent weighing of the aggravating and mitigating circumstances at the appellate level indicates that death was the proper sentence; and

(3) Whether the sentence of death is excessive or disproportionate to the penalty imposed in similar cases, considering both the crime and the defendant.

"(c) The Court of Criminal Appeals shall explicitly address each of the three questions specified in subsection (b) of this section in every case it reviews in which a sentence of death has been imposed. . . . "

[Footnote by eds.]

cially heinous, atrocious and cruel compared to other capital offenses." Even a cursory reading of the record and the trial judge's reasons for finding these two aggravating circumstances reveals that his findings are supported by the evidence.

The trial judge stated his reasons for finding the nonexistence of statutory mitigating circumstances identified in § 13A–5–51(1) through (6). The only statutory mitigating circumstance found to exist was the age of the defendant at the time of the crime (§ 13A–5–51(7)).

The trial judge did find the existence of two nonstatutory mitigating circumstances. Although he found that the offense was not committed while the defendant was under the influence of extreme mental or emotional disturbance, he did find, as a nonstatutory mitigating circumstance, that the "defendant was substantially influenced by her husband." As a second nonstatutory mitigating circumstance, the trial judge considered the fact that Mrs. Neelley "voluntarily and intentionally set in motion the events which led to her arrest and the arrest of her husband." The judge's findings concerning the statutory and nonstatutory mitigating circumstances are supported by the evidence.

The following findings are in compliance with § 13A–5–53(b). First, despite the shocking nature of the criminal acts involved, the record reveals no evidence that the sentence of death was imposed under the influence of passion, prejudice, or any other arbitrary factor. In this dramatic trial, there is no evidence of prejudicial sensationalism. . . . .

Second, our independent weighing of the aggravating and mitigating circumstances indicates that death was the proper sentence. This Court has read and reread the testimony of clinical psychologist Margaret Nichols. At the hearing on the motion for new trial, she testified that Mrs. Neelley "probably fits the battered women's syndrome to the most severe extent that [she had] seen." She stated that Alvin's mental state was substituted for hers so that Mrs. Neelley "had no intents of her own." This Court is not insensitive to Mrs. Neelley's defense.[b] However, the Court is also aware of the trial testimony of psychiatrist Alexander Salillas that Mrs. Neelley's actions were not those "of a crazy person, but a demented person," and that, if Mrs. Neelley had been beaten and abused to the extent she testified, she would "probably be dead by now and so disfigured and mentally impaired as to be unable to do anything else at this point in time. . . . She would probably have every bone broken in her body."

[b] In an omitted portion of the opinion, the Court described Mrs. Neelley's defense as a "combination of duress and coercive persuasion":

"The defense was that Alvin had subjected Mrs. Neelley to such violent and gross mental, emotional, physical, and sexual abuse that she would have done anything, and did do everything he asked. A picture was painted, in the terminology used at trial, of Alvin as 'Frankenstein' and Mrs. Neelley as 'the Bride of Frankenstein.' The jury was exposed to accounts of 'putrid, pornographic, degrading, disgusting sex' as Mrs. Neelley testified how she had been dominated, manipulated, and trained like an animal. She described herself as feeling like a 'piece of meat' and it was argued that she had been reduced to a nonhuman."

[Footnote by eds.]

There are four conceivable legal issues upon which evidence of the abuse suffered by Mrs. Neelley might have been relevant, namely: (i) duress, (ii) insanity, (iii) diminished capacity, and (iv) mitigation of punishment.[c]

The first, duress, is unavailable as a defense to Mrs. Neelley. Alabama Code § 13A–3–30 provides that duress is no defense "in a prosecution for murder or any killing of another under aggravated circumstances."

While the second, insanity, has been used as a defense in other cases dealing with battered women . . . there was absolutely no evidence— expert or lay—presented by the defense that Mrs. Neelley was legally insane. . . . The following observation by the court in McKinnon v. State, 405 So.2d 78 (Ala.Crim.App.1981), applies with equal force here:

> "Insanity which will excuse a crime, even under the new criminal code test, must be the result of a 'mental disease or defect.' Emotional insanity or temporary mania, not associated with a disease of the mind, does not constitute insanity. . . . "

The third legal theory, diminished capacity, is not recognized as a defense in Alabama. Some commentators have suggested an additional defense for crimes committed by those who suffer from the kind of abuse alleged by Mrs. Neelley. "One researcher suggests that the psychological effects of the battered spouse syndrome can be compared to classic brainwashing," see Steinmetz, Wife Beating: A Critique and Reformulation of Existing Theory, 6 Amer. Acad. of Psych. & Law Bull. 322, 327 (1978) (quoted in Comment, The Battered Spouse Syndrome as a Defense to a Homicide, 26 Vill.L.Rev. 105, 111 (1980)). See also Delgado, Ascription of Criminal States of Mind: Toward A Defense Theory For The Coercively Persuaded ("Brainwashed") Defendant, 63 Minn.L.Rev. 1 (1978). The "brainwashing" defense has not achieved acceptance in any jurisdiction, see Dressler, Professor Delgado's "Brainwashing" Defense: Courting A Determinist Legal System, 63 Minn.L. Rev. 335 (1979).

Finally, the only legal theory upon which Mrs. Neelley's alleged treatment by her husband was relevant was the one the jury properly considered—mitigation of sentence. While the factfinders determined Mrs. Neelley guilty of the crime charged, they apparently considered the evidence of her abuse as indicative of one or more of the following mitigating circumstances outlined in Ala.Code § 13A–5–51:

> "(2) The capital offense was committed while the defendant was under the influence of extreme mental or emotional disturbance;" . . .

> "(5) The defendant acted under extreme duress or under the substantial domination of another person;

> "(6) The capacity of the defendant to appreciate the criminality of his conduct or to conform his conduct to the requirements of law was substantially impaired."

[c] The relevance of the "battered wife syndrome" to claims of self-defense is con- sidered in these materials at pages 559–70, supra. [Footnote by eds.]

The brutal reality of the cruel abuse and calculated murder of 13-year old Lisa Ann Millican stands in stark contrast to Mrs. Neelley's allegations of her own abuse and mental condition. This Court agrees with the trial court that "[w]hile the mitigating circumstances and the jury's recommendation of life without parole have weighed heavy in the court's consideration, . . . they are outweighed by the aggravating circumstances of this horrible crime."

Finally, the sentence of death in this case is neither excessive nor disproportionate to the penalty imposed in similar cases, considering both the crime and the defendant. The death sentence for a murder/kidnapping was imposed in [two other cases]. Although a factor to consider, the fact that Alvin Neelley has not been prosecuted for his involvement in Miss Millican's murder does not render Mrs. Neelley's death sentence disproportionate.

Mrs. Neelley's own defense counsel described her as the "Bride of Frankenstein." Her actions were overwhelmingly demonic and savagely inhuman, generating fear, horror, and shock.

After careful review and consideration, this court concludes that Judith Ann Neelley received a fair trial and that the sentence of death is proper under the laws of Alabama and of the United States. The judgment of the circuit court is affirmed.

Affirmed.

All Judges Concur.

NOTES ON CRITERIA OF MITIGATION AND SELECTION IN CAPITAL CASES

1. **Questions on *Neelley*.** There can be little doubt about the sufficiency of the substantive predicate for Mrs. Neelley's death sentence.[a] Her case calls attention, instead, to the procedures and criteria for deciding which offenders within the death-eligible class should be sentenced to death. Was the trial judge correct that aside from Mrs. Neelley's youthfulness, none of the statutory criteria in mitigation had been demonstrated? Would it have mattered if the jury had made a specific finding that she had acted under the "substantial domination" of her husband? Should any of Mrs. Neelley's claims in mitigation, if believed, have precluded imposition of the death penalty?

Under Alabama law, the ultimate sentencing determination turned on a "weighing" of the aggravating and mitigating circumstances. Ten of the 12 jurors apparently concluded that the mitigating evidence was compelling enough to outweigh the aggravating circumstances. Should the judge have had the authority to override the jury's decision?[b] What is the proper role of the appellate court in such a case?

[a] Indeed, a review of current statutes indicates that the evidence probably would have established a proper statutory predicate in most death penalty states.

[b] In most death penalty states, a jury's rejection of a death sentence is final. In only three states (Alabama, Florida, and Indiana) is a judge authorized to override a

2. **Statutory Mitigating Circumstances.** Of the 37 states with capital punishment statutes in force on January 1, 1985, 29 specify a list of mitigating circumstances. Typically, they are based on § 210.6 of the Model Penal Code. In most instances, these criteria of mitigation reflect judgments about reduced culpability and proportionate punishment that parallel the defenses considered in earlier chapters of this book.

It is important to remember that the statutory lists of mitigating factors are not exclusive. The Supreme Court held, in *Lockett v. Ohio*, summarized at pages 799–800, supra, that a capital defendant is entitled to offer any evidence concerning character, record, or the circumstances of the offense as a basis for mitigation. Moreover, in several states the trial judge is required to include in the jury instructions any mitigating claims raised by the evidence, whether or not they are included in the statutory list. In short, evidence that does not satisfy the criteria of mitigation specified in the statutes is still entitled to consideration in sentencing.

Note that § 210.6 of the Model Code does not give determinative significance to the statutory mitigating criteria. Instead it is left to the judge or jury to determine whether any of the mitigating factors is "sufficiently substantial to call for leniency." Should the death penalty be precluded, as a matter of law, if one of these statutory mitigating criteria exists? [c] Is the death penalty morally appropriate in *any* such case, regardless of the degree of aggravation? Suppose that Judge Cole had found one of the circumstances in the Alabama statute (other than the defendant's youthfulness) to have been proved in *Neelley*. In that event, could you articulate the moral justification for imposing the death penalty in her case? Or should such a finding have required the imposition of a life sentence?

The following notes address mitigating criteria commonly specified in capital sentencing statutes. Keeping in mind that these criteria are neither preclusive nor exclusive, should they play a significant role in the administration of the death penalty?

3. **Youth.** At least 10 states, following the lead of the Model Penal Code, preclude execution of a defendant who was younger than 18 at the time of the offense. In the remaining states, youthfulness does not foreclose imposition of a death sentence on any offender who is properly within the jurisdiction of the criminal courts.[d] Although it has been argued that the eighth amendment forbids the execution of juveniles, no court to date has so held.[e]

jury's recommendation of a life sentence. In four other states, the sentencing process is conducted solely by the judge, with no jury participation. In Spaziano v. Florida, 468 U.S. 447 (1984), the Supreme Court held that jury sentencing in capital cases is not constitutionally required and also upheld Florida's jury-override procedure.

[c] Alabama, like many states, directs the decision-maker to determine whether the mitigating factors outweigh the aggravating factors, or vice-versa. Only one state, Connecticut, precludes a death sentence if one of the statutory mitigating criteria exists.

[d] The doctrines governing the respective jurisdictions of the juvenile justice and criminal justice systems are discussed at pages 632–54, supra.

[e] The most extensive treatment of the issue at this writing appears in Trimble v.

In the absence of a categorical exclusion, the significance of the defendant's youthfulness is considered on a case-by-case basis. All except two of the states with statutory lists of mitigating circumstances include the "age" or "youth" of the defendant. But why should youthfulness matter? Should Mrs. Neelley's age (18) be regarded as a mitigating factor? Is youthfulness significant because the offender does not bear the full measure of responsibility for criminal conduct? Because younger defendants have better prospects for rehabilitation? Compare the following two cases to *Neelley* in this respect.

(i) *State v. Valencia.* Frank Valencia, age 16, was convicted of first-degree murder for ambushing and shooting a woman in a parking garage in the course of a robbery attempt. He was also convicted for kidnapping, robbing, and raping another victim at gunpoint. He was sentenced to death. Death sentences imposed by the trial judge (juries are not involved in capital sentencing in Arizona) were twice set aside by the Arizona Supreme Court, and the case was remanded for resentencing. A third death sentence was imposed by another judge. Finally, on the third appeal, the Arizona Supreme Court reversed the death sentence, holding that the defendant's age was a mitigating factor "sufficiently substantial" to call for leniency. State v. Valencia, 132 Ariz. 248, 645 P.2d 239 (1982). The Court explained that "while we do not hold that age alone will always [preclude a death sentence] in every case of first-degree murder, it is a substantial and relevant factor which must be given great weight." The Court did not elaborate.

(ii) *Trimble v. State.* A different result was reached in Trimble v. State, 300 Md. 387, 478 A.2d 1143 (1984). Trimble was convicted of raping the victim, assaulting her with a baseball bat, and then killing her by slitting her throat. He was 17 at the time of the offense. Prosecution and defense experts agreed that he met the criteria for antisocial personality disorder, had a history of substance abuse, and was mildly mentally retarded (64 IQ). The defense expert testified that it was possible that Trimble had experienced temporary organic psychosis as a result of his drug use. The trial judge sentenced him to death. The Court of Appeals affirmed the sentence, making the following observations concerning the significance of Trimble's youthfulness:

> "Even though society's interest in retribution is focused mainly on the crime, not the defendant, we do not believe that consideration of the defendant's age is irrelevant. Society's 'moral outrage' may be tempered somewhat by the youthful age of the perpetrator; hence the alternate 'response' of treatment in the juvenile system. Nevertheless, society's interest in retribution is by no means inapplicable in juvenile cases. In extreme cases, the benign goals of the juvenile system are subordinated to the more broad-based and immediate interest in retribution. In short, a particularly heinous act can take the juvenile outside of the protective umbrella of the juvenile system.

State, 300 Md. 387, 478 A.2d 1143 (1984). The United States Supreme Court granted certiorari to consider this issue in *Eddings* *v. Oklahoma*, but did not reach the question. See page 800, supra.

"We believe that such a crime was committed here. Trimble's crime was not a youthful prank; it was a cold, brutal act of repeated and sadistic violence. The trial judge was presented with psychiatric testimony indicating that Trimble's prospects of rehabilitation were bleak. Thus, the one factor that could temper society's justifiable moral outrage was noticeably absent. In these circumstances, the death penalty is not an unjustified response solely because the perpetrator of these acts was four months shy of his 18th birthday. . . .

"[W]hile the youthful age of the offender is a relevant mitigating factor, it alone does not end the weighing process. Here, the sentencing authority had before it a wealth of information about Trimble's character. Trimble was expelled from school while in the 10th grade after several suspensions. At the time of the offense, he had been steadily employed at an airport for seven months. He maintained a steady relationship with a girlfriend. In addition to his low intelligence, he was diagnosed as having antisocial personality, possible temporary organic psychosis, and possible schizophrenia but nevertheless criminally responsible. These characteristics were exacerbated by his drug and alcohol abuse.

"According to the psychiatric testimony, his criminal behavior was part of his lifestyle (he regarded Charles Manson as a role model) and a matter of choice. Trimble freely admitted his involvement in 10 breaking and entering crimes, a handgun violation, an assault, and several drug arrests. He further admitted a pattern of sadistic behavior toward his girlfriend and animals. The psychiatrists determined his prospects for rehabilitation to be bleak because he had no respect for the rights of others. In our view, the trial judge who sentenced him to death could reasonably conclude that Trimble was an adult beyond repair rather than a juvenile in need of treatment."

4. **Degree of Participation.** Under the law of complicity, more than one person may be liable for a single murder. However, the capital sentencing statutes of a number of states permit a death sentence only for the person who actually caused the victim's death. Moreover, even in the remaining death penalty states, a death sentence is constitutionally permissible for an accomplice only if the accomplice intended the victim's death.[f] Within these boundaries, an accomplice otherwise within the death-eligible class may seek to establish, under the typical formulation, that "his participation was relatively minor."

5. **Duress or Domination By Another.** Mrs. Neelley claimed that her will was subordinated to that of her husband. Alabama's statute, like those of most other states, recognizes the mitigating significance of a claim that the defendant acted under duress or under the "substantial influence" or "domination" of another person. As the Alabama Supreme Court notes, this factor takes into account actual

---

[f] See Enmund v. Florida, summarized at pages 1020–28, infra.

coercive threats which do not provide a defense in homicide cases. In People v. Gleckler, 82 Ill.2d 145, 44 Ill.Dec. 483, 411 N.E.2d 849 (1980), for example, the Illinois Supreme Court determined that a death sentence was excessive for a defendant "with no criminal history, the personality of a doormat, and a problem with alcohol" who succumbed to an accomplice's threats when he fatally shot two robbery victims who had already been wounded by the accomplice.

The mitigating significance of this factor explicitly extends beyond coercive threats in a substantial number of states. In State v. McIlvoy, 629 S.W.2d 333 (Mo.1982), a closely divided (4–3) court set aside a death sentence imposed on a defendant who had been recruited by one Nicki Williams to kill her husband. The Court explained that McIlvoy "appears to be a person with only minimal juvenile criminal record, limited education (9th grade) and limited intelligence (81 IQ), substantial alcohol problems, and appears to [have been] a weakling and follower in executing the murder scheme perpetrated by Nicki Williams."

Gleckler and *McIlvoy* both reflect the moral judgment that the death penalty is not appropriate for psychologically weak and vulnerable offenders who are used as instruments for achieving the criminal ambitions of others. In this sense, the factor represents a particular dimension of diminished responsibility.

6. **Diminished Responsibility.** Evidence of mental abnormality plays a somewhat complicated role in the administration of the death penalty and, more generally, in the law of homicide. Recall the two meanings of "diminished responsibility" or "diminished capacity" explored at pages 752–54, supra. One refers to a rule of evidence; testimony concerning mental abnormality is admissible whenever it is logically relevant to the existence of a mental state determinative of the fact or grade of criminal liability. The other refers to a substantive concept denoting an "intermediate" degree of cognitive or volitional impairment falling short of insanity but entitling the defendant to reduction of the grade of the offense or mitigation of the punishment.

Historically, evidence of mental abnormality was pressed upon the courts with greatest frequency in homicide cases. A review of the extensive literature on the question between 1880 and 1950 demonstrates that proponents of broader rules of admissibility were aiming primarily at capital prosecutions. It was the image of the executioner that drove the engines of reform. However, the courts were slow to accept such evidence for any purpose beyond the insanity defense. In 1925, Professor Glueck summarized the law regarding what he called "partial responsibility":

> "Does mental disease, though not of sufficient degree to excuse entirely from criminal responsibility, ever operate to *reduce the degree* of the criminal offense? For example, a person is charged with murder: Is it possible that, though he can not be acquitted entirely, yet, by reason of his mental abnormality he cannot be said to have had the 'malice aforethought' or deliberation or premeditation, or any other condition of mind which must

be proved . . . ? Can evidence of some degree of mental unsoundness reduce to murder in the second degree or manslaughter a crime which, had the defendant been perfectly sound mentally, would have been first-degree murder? Is there room in the law for the 'semi-responsible' in this sense of the term? As a general rule, no." [g]

Today, in a majority of jurisdictions the answer is "yes," at least when the evidence is offered on a charge of first-degree murder. The logical relevance of mental abnormality to such a charge is readily apparent. It can, for example, negate an intent to kill, which all states require as a prerequisite to the first-degree offense. In those states that also require actual reflection and deliberation, expert testimony can shed light on whether the defendant consciously thought about the homicide before it occurred and whether the required reflection took place. Most states today give evidence of mental abnormality its full logical import when relevant to the issues involved in a first-degree murder prosecution.

More importantly for present purposes, evidence of mental abnormality is virtually unrestricted in capital sentencing proceedings. The statutes of most states include provisions, based on the Model Penal Code, which accord mitigating significance to claims of diminished or partial responsibility. The two pertinent provisions of § 210.6(4) of the Model Code are:

"(b) the murder was committed while the defendant was under the influence of extreme mental or emotional disturbance. . . . ; and

"(g) at the time of the murder, the capacity of the defendant to appreciate the criminality [wrongfulness] of his conduct or to conform his conduct to the requirements of law was impaired as a result of mental disease or defect or intoxication."

Most capital sentencing statutes include formulations based on Subsections (4)(b) and (4)(g). These provisions reflect a virtually unanimous legislative judgment that the presence of mens rea for capital homicide and a determination that the defendant is legally sane, however these concepts are defined, do not exhaust the significance of mental abnormality in determining the moral propriety of the death penalty. Unhinged from the technical concepts of malice, premeditation, deliberation, and insanity, the evidence of mental abnormality is measured explicitly by criteria of diminished responsibility.

(i) **Extreme Mental or Emotional Disturbance.** The concept of provocation, recognized in § 210.3(1)(b) of the Model Code, is dealt with in the next section of these materials. For present purposes, it is sufficient to note that it permits mitigation of murder to manslaughter based on provoking circumstances, and that its scope is restricted by an objective inquiry into whether the defendant's homicidal reaction was a "reasonable" (or at least understandable) response to the provoking event. The language of § 210.6(4)(b) resembles the language of

[g] S. Glueck, Mental Disorder and the Criminal Law 199–200 (1925).

§ 210.3(b), but with an important difference. Section 210.6(4)(b) does not include the limitation "for which there is a reasonable explanation or excuse." Does this mean that virtually any psychiatric evidence of "extreme mental or emotional disturbance" can establish this basis for mitigation? Was this circumstance proved in *Godfrey?* Did Judge Cole correctly rule that it had not been proved in *Neelley?* Would it be appropriate for a court to instruct a jury that a claimed mental disturbance does not have mitigating significance under this standard if it is attributable to voluntary intoxication? A few states have omitted the word "extreme" from their formulations of this criterion. Is this a significant omission?

(ii) **Impaired Capacity for Appreciation or Control.** Section 210.6(4)(g) is derived from the Model Code insanity defense, provided in § 4.01(1). Note the two key differences. First, subsection (4)(g) encompasses impairments attributable to intoxication as well as mental disease. Impairment due to voluntary intoxication, no matter how extreme, is without significance under the insanity test unless it is related to an independent mental disease. Under subsection (4)(g), however, a lesser impairment affecting behavioral controls would have mitigating significance. Second, the Model Code insanity test focuses on whether defendants lack "substantial" capacity to appreciate the criminality of their conduct or conform their behavior to the requirements of law. The question asked in a capital-sentencing proceeding is whether the offender's cognitive or volitional capacity was sufficiently impaired by mental disease or intoxication to warrant some penalty other than death even though it was not so substantially impaired as to require exculpation.

What is the purpose of the "mental disease or defect" requirement in subsection (4)(g)? Is it undermined by the provisions of subsection (4)(b)? Of the states that include a criterion of impaired capacity, about half omit the threshold condition of "mental disease or defect or intoxication." However, many of these states require instead that the defendant's capacity be "substantially" impaired, and some require that it be "significantly" impaired. It has been observed that deletion of the "mental disease" threshold is not a "minor editorial omission" since "the concept of mitigating mental abnormality has been detached from the medical model [opening the door] to the full spectrum of explanations that may be offered."[h] Do you agree with this modification? Alabama is one of the states which has deleted the mental disease requirement. Did Judge Cole properly interpret the provision when he determined that Mrs. Neelley had not established the mitigating circumstance?

7. **The Double-Edged Sword.** The tension between subjective criteria of blameworthiness and the incapacitative functions of the penal law has been highlighted frequently in these materials. The problem is raised most vividly in the administration of capital punishment because the most compelling claims of diminished responsibility

[h] Bonnie, Psychiatry and the Death Penalty: Emerging Problems in Virginia, 66 Va.L.Rev. 167, 184 (1980).

often arise in cases presenting the most demonstrable need for incapacitation. Consider, in this connection, Miller v. State, 373 So.2d 882 (Fla. 1979).

After being released one morning from jail, where he had been incarcerated for possession of a concealed weapon (a fishing knife), Miller wandered around Ft. Myers and bought a fishing knife similar to the one which had been taken from him by the police. An employee in the store where the weapon was purchased stated that Miller was "wild looking" and was mumbling angrily to himself. This employee called the police and followed Miller to two nearby bars. Eventually, when he saw Miller leaving in a taxicab with a woman driver, he contacted the taxi company to inform them of the apparent danger. The woman taxi driver was found murdered soon thereafter. She had been stabbed nine times, and had been raped when she was dead or dying. When Miller was arrested at the bus station that evening, his pants were still covered with blood. Blood-soaked money, some of which had been taken from the taxi driver, was found in his pockets.

Soon after his arrest, Miller was found incompetent to stand trial and was committed to a state mental hospital. Two-and-a-half years later, his mental illness was regarded as sufficiently controlled by medication to render him competent to stand trial. He was convicted of first-degree murder. The jury recommended a death sentence, which the judge imposed. The Florida Supreme Court affirmed the conviction but reversed the sentence on the ground that the trial judge should have granted a continuance to permit the defendant to present psychiatric testimony at the sentencing hearing. On remand, a new jury recommended another death sentence and the trial judge once again followed the jury's recommendation.

Undisputed psychiatric testimony presented at the sentencing hearing indicated that Miller was suffering from paranoid schizophrenia, had been committed to mental hospitals on several previous occasions, and had a long history of drug abuse. The evidence showed that Miller had been raised primarily by his mother, who had been married four times. For many years prior to this crime, Miller's mother had refused any contact with him. On several previous occasions, Miller had experienced hallucinations in which he saw his mother in the faces of other persons. He had once assaulted a woman while experiencing such an hallucination. Miller testified that he hated his mother and had planned to kill her after his release from jail on the day of the murder. He also testified that at the time of the murder, he saw his mother's face on this 56-year-old woman taxi driver, in a "yellow haze," and proceeded to stab her to death.

The trial court found that three statutory aggravating circumstances had been proved: (i) the defendant had previously been convicted of a felony involving the threat of violence to another person; (ii) the murder was committed while the defendant was engaged in the commission of or attempt to commit robbery, and was thus committed for pecuniary gain; and (iii) the murder was especially heinous, atrocious, and cruel.

The trial court also found, as mitigating circumstances, that (i) the murder was committed while the defendant was under the influence of extreme mental disturbance; (ii) the defendant acted under mental duress; (iii) due to mental sickness, the defendant's capacity and ability to conform his conduct to the requirements of law were substantially impaired. However, the trial court concluded that the defendant could and did appreciate the criminality of his conduct.

Having made these findings, the trial judge explained:

"[In] weighing the aggravating and mitigating factors, I [take into account] the reality of Florida law [that] life imprisonment . . . doesn't mean life imprisonment and there is a substantial chance he could be released into society. And the testimony overwhelmingly establishes that the mental sickness or illness that he suffers from is such that he will never recover [and that] it will only be repressed by the use of drugs. . . .

"If the law in Florida were such that life imprisonment meant the ability to live in a prison environment for the entire remainder of one's life, I would [reach] the conclusion that there would be sufficient mitigating factors to offset the aggravating factors, and allow him to live in prison. But since this is not the case, the reality is that life imprisonment does not mean that, I conclude in this case that the aggravating factors heavily outweigh the mitigating factors. . . . "

The Florida Supreme Court unanimously reversed:

"It is clear [that the trial judge] considered as an aggravating factor the defendant's alleged incurable and dangerous mental illness. The use of this nonstatutory aggravating factor as a controlling circumstance tipping the balance in favor of the death penalty was improper. The aggravating circumstances specified in the statute are exclusive, and no others may be used for that purpose. This court [has] stated: 'We must guard against any unauthorized aggravating factor going into the equation which might tip the scales of the weighing process in favor of death.'

"Strict application of the sentencing statute is necessary because the sentencing authority's discretion must be 'guided and channeled' by requiring an examination of specific factors that argue in favor of or against imposition of the death penalty, thus eliminating total arbitrariness and capriciousness in its imposition. The trial judge's use of the defendant's mental illness, and his resulting propensity to commit violent acts, as an aggravating factor favoring the imposition of the death penalty appears contrary to the legislative intent set forth in the statute. The legislature has not authorized consideration of the probability of recurring violent acts by the defendant if he is released on parole in the distant future. To the contrary, a large number of the statutory mitigating factors reflect a legislative determination to mitigate the death penalty in favor of a life sentence for those persons whose responsibility for their violent actions has been substantially diminished as a result of a mental illness, uncontrolled emotional state of mind, or drug abuse.

"It appears likely that at least one of the aggravating circumstances proven at the sentencing hearing, the heinous nature of the offense, resulted from the defendant's mental illness. This court has previously recognized in other capital cases that those mitigating circumstances involved in the present case may be sufficient to outweigh the aggravating circumstances involved even in an atrocious crime. . . . In [another case], this court . . . stated:

> 'Our decision here is based on the causal relationship between the mitigating and aggravating circumstances. The heinous and atrocious manner in which this crime was perpetrated, and the harm to which the members of [the defendant's] family were exposed, were the direct consequence of his mental illness, so far as the record reveals.'

"In light of the trial court's findings that the defendant was suffering from mental illness at the time he committed this crime, the motivating role the defendant's mental illness played in this crime, and the apparent causal relationship between the aggravating circumstances and his mental illness, it was reversible error for the trial court to consider as an additional aggravating circumstance, not enumerated by the statute, the possibility that Miller might commit similar acts of violence if he were ever to be released on parole. Whether a defendant who is convicted of a capital crime and receives a life sentence should be allowed a chance of parole after 25 years is a policy determination for the legislature or the parole authorities rather than for the courts. Therefore, the sentence of death is vacated and the cause remanded to the trial court for resentencing in a manner not inconsistent with this opinion."

Suppose the defendant's propensity for violence had been specified as an aggravating circumstance, as it is in a few states. Or suppose that consideration of non-statutory aggravating factors is permissible, as it is in many states, so long as a statutory predicate for a death sentence has been properly established. Would Miller's death sentence then have been proper?[i]

[i] Compare State v. Gretzler, 135 Ariz. 42, 659 P.2d 1 (1983). The trial judge had found that Gretzler's "capacity to appreciate the wrongfulness of his conduct or to conform his conduct to the requirements of the law was significantly impaired." Gretzler argued that this finding should have precluded the imposition of the death penalty for kidnapping, robbing, and murdering a young couple. (This crime was only part of a spree of 17 aggravated murders committed by Gretzler and an accomplice.) The court rejected the claim:

"Incarceration is intended to serve the goal of isolation of dangerous individuals, but the prison system is a human enterprise, and thus it cannot serve this goal perfectly no matter how diligent the effort. This state has learned through sad experience that even after incarceration a violent person may become a menace to other prisoners or may escape and become a menace to the public at large. At some point a violent individual has caused so much harm and destruction of human life that society is entitled to foreclose the possibility of further deprivation."

8. **Limits on Mitigating Evidence.** As previously noted, the Supreme Court held in *Lockett v. Ohio* that a capital defendant is entitled to put before the sentencer "any aspect of [his or her] character or record, and any circumstances of the offense that [he or she] proffers as a basis for a sentence less than death." A statute restricting mitigating claims is unconstitutional, Chief Justice Burger said, because it "creates the risk that the death penalty will be imposed in spite of factors which may call for a less severe penalty." However, in a footnote, the Chief Justice cautioned that "nothing in this opinion limits the traditional authority of a court to exclude, as irrelevant, evidence not bearing on the defendant's character, prior record, or the circumstances of [his or her] offense."

Is it true that evidence not bearing on the defendant's character, prior record, or the circumstances of the offense is "irrelevant" to the propriety of a death sentence in a particular case? It has been argued that the defendant should be permitted to offer any evidence that might persuade the jury to preclude a death sentence, including evidence designed to call into question the morality or efficacy of the death penalty or designed to describe the process of execution.[j] Although no court has permitted defendants to introduce evidence on the desirability of the death penalty or on the mode by which it is carried out, some courts have admitted evidence calculated to arouse the jury's sympathy and compassion. For example, the Georgia Supreme Court has permitted the defense to elicit testimony from the defendant's grandfather that he did not want his grandson executed for killing his parents. Romine v. State, 251 Ga. 208, 305 S.E.2d 93 (1983).

What are the arguments favoring and opposing admissibility of evidence designed to dampen the jurors' retributive instincts or arouse their compassion, but which has no bearing on the defendant's blameworthiness or potential for rehabilitation? Should the defense be permitted to present testimony by members of the defendant's family regarding the impact on them of the defendant's execution?[k] Recall the *Godfrey* case. Should he have been permitted to introduce evidence showing that he continued to provide financial support for his children after killing their mother and grandmother? Should he have been permitted to introduce statistical evidence on the frequency with which death sentences have been imposed for domestic homicides?[l]

9. **Limits on Discretion to be Lenient.** Proper resolution of these evidentiary questions may depend on underlying substantive judgments about proper grounds for leniency. Specifically, should the sentencer's discretion to be lenient be unconstrained, or should leniency be permitted only for prescribed reasons? In Gregg v. Georgia, 428 U.S. 153 (1976), Justices Stewart, Powell and Stevens interpreted

---

[j] See, e.g., Ledewitz, The Requirement of Death: Mandatory Language in the Pennsylvania Death Penalty Statute, 21 Duq.L. Rev. 103 (1982).

[k] Compare Houston v. State, 593 S.W.2d 267 (Tenn.1980) (no), with Cofield v. State, 247 Ga. 98, 274 S.E.2d 530 (1981) (yes).

[l] The Georgia Supreme Court held that the evidence had been properly excluded. Godfrey v. Francis, 251 Ga. 652, 308 S.E.2d 806 (1982).

Furman to stand for the proposition that "where discretion is afforded a sentencing body on a matter so grave as the determination of whether a human life should be taken or spared, that discretion must be suitably directed and limited so as to minimize the risk of wholly arbitrary and capricious action." It has become clear, however, that discretion to *take* life and discretion to *spare* life are not constitutionally equivalent.[m]

Under Georgia's capital sentencing statute, the jury's discretion to be lenient is unconstrained by any normative criteria. The constitutionality of this feature of the Georgia statute was explicitly upheld by a majority of the Supreme Court in Zant v. Stephens, 462 U.S. 862 (1983). The Court held that the "mandate of *Furman* is [not] violated by a scheme that permits the jury to exercise unbridled discretion in determining whether the death penalty should be imposed after it has found that the defendant is a member of the class made eligible for the penalty by statute."

Statutes of about half of the death penalty states are similar to Georgia's in the sense that the sentencer has unfettered discretion to be lenient.[n] In the other states, however, the statutes seek to constrain the sentencer's discretion. Most of these states use a balancing formula which directs the sentencer to impose a death sentence if it finds that the aggravating circumstances outweigh the mitigating circumstances (or that the mitigating circumstances do not outweigh the aggravating circumstances). Some statutes, such as Pennsylvania's, explicitly require the jury to impose a death sentence if it finds at least one aggravating circumstance and no mitigating circumstances.

The constitutionality of statutory constraints on discretion to be lenient is not yet settled. Can you outline the arguments favoring and opposing the constitutionality of the Pennsylvania statute? How should the Supreme Court resolve this question? Note that the jury-override procedure invoked in *Neelley* is also designed to provide a check on jury discretion to be lenient. The constitutionality of this procedure was upheld in Spaziano v. Florida, 468 U.S. 447 (1984). Was *Spaziano* correctly decided?

10. **Intracase Disparity as a Basis for Leniency.** Consider the problem presented in Biondi v. State, 699 P.2d 1062 (Nev.1985). The facts were summarized in the court's opinion as follows:

"Timothy Smith, a parole officer, was stabbed in the parking lot of a Las Vegas bar in the early morning hours of February 4, 1981. Smith, who was off duty, arrived at the bar around 12:45 a.m. with a friend, Carl Blair. Appellant Biondi and his friends,

---

[m] The plurality opinion in *Gregg* had also stated that "[n]othing in any of the cases suggests that the decision to afford an individual defendant mercy violates the Constitution." 428 U.S. at 199.

[n] The statutes differ, however, on the conditions which must be satisfied before a death sentence may be imposed. In Georgia, one statutory aggravating circumstance is enough. In Mississippi, by comparison, a death sentence is permitted only if the jury finds that "sufficient aggravating factors exist," *and* that mitigating circumstances are insufficient to outweigh the aggravating circumstances. Even if these conditions are satisfied, however, the sentencer still has absolute discretion not to impose a death sentence.

including Michael Phillips, Ron and Becky Lacey, and Steve Izzi, were in the bar. They were drinking, and they were intoxicated. When in the bar Timothy Smith and Ron Lacey began an argument. They left the bar and went outside to "settle" the dispute. A fight ensued between Timothy Smith and Blair and Ron Lacey. Lacey cut the two men with a knife. After this fight had ended, four of those present saw Timothy Smith struggling with Biondi and Phillips between two parked cars. One of the witnesses, Becky Lacey, testified that Biondi and Phillips each stabbed Smith. Blair testified that only Biondi stabbed Smith. Izzy testified that Biondi held Smith while Phillips stabbed him. Biondi and Phillips fled the scene. Biondi discarded the knife he was carrying. The knife was not recovered. Smith had been stabbed in the chest. He suffered brain death from loss of blood. He was pronounced dead two days later."

Biondi and Phillips were both charged with first-degree murder. Phillips pleaded guilty and was sentenced to life in prison without parole. At Biondi's trial, the prosecution argued that Biondi was guilty of first-degree murder on either of two theories—that both Biondi and Phillips had stabbed Smith or that Biondi had aided and abetted Phillips by holding Smith while Phillips stabbed him. The jury found Biondi guilty of first-degree murder. At the penalty hearing, the jury returned a special verdict finding that Biondi had stabbed Smith, and found, as an aggravating circumstance, that Biondi had previously been convicted of a felony (armed robbery) involving the use of violence. The jury sentenced Biondi to death.

The Nevada Supreme Court affirmed the conviction but set aside the sentence. The court found the disparity between the sentences for Phillips and Biondi "strikingly significant":

"Biondi and Phillips each had one prior felony conviction for a violent crime; Biondi pleaded guilty to armed robbery in 1976; Phillips was convicted in 1977 or 1978 for assault with a deadly weapon. Biondi's participation in the murder was no more significant than Phillips'. In fact, one eyewitness testified that Biondi had held Smith while Phillips stabbed him. The state has provided no explanation for its decision to allow Phillips to plead guilty and be sentenced to life with the possibility of parole but to seek the death penalty for Biondi. Nor does any justification for this disparity appear in the record. This is a case where similar defendants were sentenced differently for the identical crime. For this reason, and for [other] reasons discussed above, we hold the death penalty imposed on Biondi is disproportionate."

Compare Miller v. State, 415 So.2d 1262 (Fla.1982). Ernest Miller and his step-brother William Jent were charged with first degree murder for the death of a young woman known only as "Tammy," and were tried before separate juries. Three eyewitnesses testified that during the course of a swimming party, at which the participants had been using drugs and drinking heavily, Jent and Miller had beaten

Tammy and transported her in the trunk of a car to Miller's home where four men raped her while their female companions watched. She was placed back in the trunk and taken to a game preserve where Jent and Miller poured gasoline on her and set her on fire. The medical examiner testified that she had been alive when ignited and that the burns caused her death.

The respective juries convicted Miller and Jent of first-degree murder, but Miller's jury recommended life imprisonment while Jent's recommended a death sentence. In a combined sentencing order, the trial judge imposed the death penalty on both defendants, based on his conclusion that the mitigating evidence offered in Miller's behalf did not outweigh the aggravating evidence and that following the recommendation of Miller's jury would result in an unwarranted disparity in sentences. The Florida Supreme Court affirmed, holding that the judge had properly overriden the jury's recommendation under the applicable standard (that "on the totality of the circumstances, no reasonable person would differ on the appropriateness of the death penalty"). Two Justices dissented. They found the different sentences to be justifiable in light of psychological testimony that Miller was a "follower" with a "weak ego" who tended to "go along with the group."

Recall that Judith Neelley's counsel had brought to the appellate court's attention the fact that Alvin Neelley had not been prosecuted for Lisa Ann Millican's death. Was this fact pertinent? Would it have been more pertinent if Alvin Neelley had been prosecuted, convicted of murder, and sentenced to life imprisonment?

INTRODUCTORY NOTE ON COMPARATIVE REVIEW OF DEATH SENTENCES

The Supreme Court's death penalty decisions have indicated that "meaningful appellate review" of death sentences by a court with statewide jurisdiction is an indispensable feature of a constitutional capital sentencing scheme. Many of the functions performed by appellate courts in capital cases merely extend to the sentencing phase the same form of review exercised with respect to adjudication of guilt. This includes review of trial court decisions concerning the admissibility of evidence in aggravation or mitigation, and the sufficiency of the evidence to prove aggravating circumstances. In addition, however, most appellate courts have a further responsibility of reviewing the correctness of the sentencer's decision to impose a death sentence in each case. That is, even if a legally adequate predicate for a death sentence was established, and even if the sentencing process was untainted by error, the appellate court has an independent obligation to review the correctness of the sentence. Capital sentence review takes two basic forms:

(i) **Case-by-Case Proportionality Review.** The appellate courts of most death penalty states have authority to set aside a death sentence adjudged to be excessive in the particular case. Proportionality review [a] in this sense refers to a qualitative judgment concerning the suitability of the punishment for a given offense or offender. A court might determine, for example, that the offense was not sufficiently aggravated to warrant the death penalty even though an adequate statutory predicate for the sentence was established. Or a court might set aside a sentence in light of factors relating to the reduced responsibility, character, or background of the offender.

(ii) **Comparative Review.** In a large number of states, appellate courts—normally because mandated to do so by statute, but in a few states in the absence of statutory directive—undertake an additional responsibility: to determine whether a defendant's death sentence is excessive in comparison with the penalty imposed in "similar" cases. The justifying premise for comparative review is that even if a death sentence does not strike the judicial mind as disproportionate when the case is viewed on its own terms, such a sentence is nonetheless objectionable if death sentences have not ordinarily been imposed in "similar" cases. Unlike case-by-case proportionality review, which is entirely qualitative in nature, judgments about "comparative excessiveness" have a quantitative dimension; the courts require a systematic method of compiling information regarding the characteristics and outcomes of a pool of "similar" cases.[b]

STATES v. YATES

Supreme Court of South Carolina, 1982.
280 S.C. 29, 310 S.E.2d 805.

PER CURIAM:

Appellant, Dale Robert Yates, was indicted and convicted of murder, armed robbery, assault and battery with intent to kill, and conspiracy. After being found guilty of murder, the jury recommended at the second phase of the bifurcated trial, that he should die by electrocution. From these convictions and sentence, he appeals. The basic issue involved in the appeal is whether the death sentence should be carried out.

On February 12, 1981, David Loftis (not on trial), Henry Davis (killed in the robbery), and appellant Yates talked about various places to rob and rode around in the car of Davis looking for a store which could be easily robbed. As a part of the plan, they borrowed a gun from the appellant's brother. On the following day, February 13, they continued to ride around, casing places to rob. The appellant and Davis left Loftis (who turned state's evidence) at a shopping mall and

[a] The Supreme Court has determined that a death sentence is constitutionally excessive for the crime of rape or for an accomplice to homicide if the defendant did not intend the victim's death. It has also determined that some non-death sentences can be constitutionally disproportionate. These cases are considered together at pages 1004–53, infra. As used here, the term "proportionality review" refers to case-by-case assessments by the state courts of the propriety of a death sentence.

[b] See generally, Baldus, Pulaski, Woodworth & Kyle, Identifying Comparatively Excessive Sentences of Death: A Quantitative Approach, 33 Stan.L.Rev. 1 (1980).

drove away with the pistol under the passenger's side of the front seat. The appellant and Davis subsequently entered Wood's rural store, by the appellant's own testimony, for the purpose of committing armed robbery. Appellant was armed with the pistol and Davis with a knife. They demanded and received approximately $3,000 from Willie Wood, who was alone and in charge of the store operation. When Willie Wood failed to cooperate to the satisfaction of the robbers, the appellant shot him, but not fatally. About that time, the mother of Willie Wood, who was the postmistress in the adjoining building, came upon the scene. The appellant ran out of the store, taking the money and the gun. Davis remained in the store, and stabbed Mrs. Wood to death with his knife. Willie Wood succeeded in obtaining a gun and killed Davis. After appellant waited in Davis' car and concluded that Davis had been caught, he drove off, hid the money and pistol in a wooded area, and was later apprehended.

The appellant testified in his own behalf. His testimony was not inconsistent with the facts recited above. It was his contention that he did not kill Mrs. Wood and that it was his intent all along to abandon the robbery without hurting anybody if the victims refused to cooperate.

[The prosecution's theory of liability was that "Yates and Davis were present aiding and abetting each other in the commission of a planned armed robbery and that the hand of one was the hand of all." The Court concluded that Yates "is equally responsible for the stabbing death of Mrs. Wood, even though he did not actually cast the fatal blows. [Yates] and Henry Davis entered the store armed and did commit a robbery. As a direct result of their joint actions in committing the armed robbery, Mrs. Wood was killed." The Court upheld Yates' conviction for murder and the jury's finding of the aggravating circumstance that the "murder was committed while in the commission of . . . robbery while armed with a deadly weapon."]

Appellant challenges the trial court's refusal to enjoin the solicitor from seeking the death penalty in his case. Appellant based this challenge on the prosecutor's record of handling previous death penalty cases involving triggermen and nontriggermen. . . . Appellant argues that the solicitor normally sought the death penalty only against the triggerman.

It would be error for the trial judge to tell a solicitor how to determine whether the death penalty should be sought. This is the prerogative of the solicitor. . . .

The appellant requested the trial judge to charge the jury as a mitigating circumstance: "That Dale Robert Yates did not kill the victim Helen Wood." . . . The judge very properly told counsel, in lieu of granting the request, "you may argue it [to the jury] all you wish to." Presumably, counsel did exactly that. The fact that Yates did not do the stabbing personally was one of the facts upon which counsel relied in hopes of obtaining a life sentence. Instead of charging the jury in the language suggested by counsel, the judge [charged]:

"[T]he defendant asks you to consider that [he] was an accomplice to the murder, committed by another person, and his participation was relatively minor. In other words, that embraces the theory that the defendant did not, himself, personally strike the fatal blow."

The charge, first orally and then in writing, to the jury, let it know that it should give consideration to the fact that Yates did not personally stab Mrs. Wood. The thought counsel wished the judge to convey was actually given to the jury, although not in the exact verbiage requested. . . .

The last questions raised . . . call upon this Court to perform the duty imposed upon it by § 16–3–25(C) of our Code[:]

"(C) With regard to the sentence, the court shall determine:

(1) Whether the sentence of death was imposed under the influence of passion, prejudice, or any other arbitrary factor, and

(2) Whether the evidence supports the jury's or judge's finding of a statutory aggravating circumstance as enumerated in § 16–3–20, and

(3) Whether the sentence of death is excessive or disproportionate to the penalty imposed in similar cases, considering both the crime and the defendant."

. . . We discussed the duty of the Court under the statutory requirements in the recent case of State v. Copeland, 278 S.C. 572, 300 S.E.2d 63 (1982), . . .[a] While the duty imposed is a difficult one because no two defendants and no two crimes are exactly alike, it is not an unsurmountable chore. Prior to imposition of sentence, the trial judge . . . made this finding:

"Mr. Yates, as the trial judge in the case just concluded in which you are indicted for the crime of murder, prior to imposing the death sentence upon you, I find as an affirmative fact beyond

---

[a] In *Copeland*, the court reviewed the United States Supreme Court's capital sentencing decisions and stated:

"[These decisions] encourage, while not mandating, an appellate review which accords priority to the particular and distinctive features of each defendant as well as the specific circumstances of the crime for which the death sentence has been imposed. The ultimate outcome, it is suggested by these decisions, should be the infliction of capital punishment upon only those individuals who have been culled from all other defendants by a process which highlights the unique attributes of their personalities and their crimes.

"From a logical standpoint, of course, that which is unique is also incommensurable. Herein lies the conflict between particularized sentencing (and review) and the notion of comparing 'similar cases.' Clearly, a comparative review cannot be permitted to diminish the particularized quality of sentencing, since the latter is now an absolute command of the U.S. Constitution. By the same token, the final resolution of a given appeal, if sentence is to be affirmed, should rest upon the unique correctness of the result in the given instance rather than its coarse resemblance to other cases. . . .

"In our view, the search for 'similar cases' can only begin with an actual conviction and sentence of death rendered by a trier of fact. . . . We consider such findings by the trial court to be a threshold requirement for comparative study and indeed the only foundation of 'similarity' consonant with our role as an appellate court."

[Footnote by eds.]

any reasonable doubt that the evidence warrants the imposition of the death penalty and that its imposition is not a result of prejudice, passion, or any other arbitrary factor."

The . . . record . . . supports the trial judge's finding. We agree that the evidence warrants the death penalty and our independent finding and conclusion is that the penalty was not the result of prejudice, passion or any other arbitrary factor.

The appellant [argues] that the sentence is disproportionate to penalties imposed in similar cases. He argues that he personally did not stab and cause the death of Mrs. Wood. He testified during the trial that at the time of her death he was not in the store but had departed to the getaway car.

[The Court first ruled that the death penalty was not unconstitutionally excessive under Enmund v. Florida, 458 U.S. 782 (1982),[b] because Yates intended for life to be taken: "[H]e failed to kill Willie Wood merely because his aim was less than perfect. It is of little significance that the life he intended to take and attempted to take was that of Willie Wood instead of his mother, who was actually stabbed."]

In determining whether . . . the sentence . . . is excessive or disproportionate in light of the crime and the defendant, this Court has reviewed the entire record. We have also considered the circumstances of State v. Gilbert, 277 S.C. 53, 283 S.E.2d 179 (1981) the only prior holding of this court suitable for comparison. In that case, the two defendants, Gilbert and Gleaton, spent a morning cruising in search of a target to rob. . . . In the instant case, appellant with Davis and Loftis apparently contemplated robbery for over a day, making a diligent search of Greenville County for just the right setting. Indeed, Loftis, one of the accomplices, withdrew from the enterprise before the actual robbery and testified to this lengthy prologue.

As in *Gilbert*, appellant and his cohort, Davis, found a solitary, apparently unarmed victim in Mr. Willie Wood. In almost every respect, the robbery unfolded as in the case of Gilbert and Gleaton with one assailant wielding a knife and the other a pistol. Mr. Wood was directed to lean over the store counter by Davis who appeared ready to stab him with the knife. At this point, however, the victim refused to obey. At Davis' command, the appellant fired two bullets at Wood from close range and fled. From this a jury could conclude beyond a reasonable doubt that appellant fully intended Wood's death, either by Davis' hand or his own, in the course of this armed robbery.

Hereafter the facts diverge from [*Gilbert*]. Mr. Wood did not die from his wound but instead seized his own gun and fought off Davis. Willie Wood's sixty-eight year-old mother then came upon the scene and was stabbed to death by Davis, who in turn was shot and killed by Wood. Although this outcome sets the instant case apart from previous capital sentences we have affirmed, it is sufficient for our purposes that the appellant displayed the same intent and followed the same pattern of preparation as Gilbert [and] Gleaton . . . before him.

b The holding in *Enmund* is summarized at pages 1020–28, supra.

In mitigation, appellant offered his own testimony and that of his mother. The jury learned that appellant had been a poor student in school, achieving basically a ninth grade education. In appellant's own words, he was more interested in "getting out and having fun, shooting pool." If given a life sentence, however, he intended to write a book, study, and improve the prison system. Appellant frankly conceded that he had not managed to do these things during ten previous periods of incarceration. Both appellant and his mother testified generally that he had some history of drug abuse and that, most importantly, he allowed himself to be influenced by Davis, the deceased accomplice. Appellant did not contend, however, that he was actually inebriated at the time of the robbery nor that Henry Davis forced him to participate.

The trial judge meticulously instructed the jury on the available mitigating circumstances under [the statute]. In addition, the trial court orally and in writing directed the jury to consider any other mitigating circumstances presented by the defendant.

In our view, the appellant had the benefit of every reasonable explanation for his acts. We are satisfied that the jury properly found the aggravating circumstance of robbery while armed with a deadly weapon and did so without any influence of passion, prejudice or other arbitrary factor. The testimony in mitigation is comparable to that in *Gilbert,* if not somewhat less impressive, given the claim of Gilbert and Gleaton that they had partaken of drugs and were acting solely on impulse. We are satisfied that the penalty here imposed is neither excessive nor disproportionate in light of this crime and this defendant. Given that we have upheld a comparable sentence in the comparable case of *State v. Gilbert,* we are confident that the finding of this jury represents consistent application of the ultimate sanction in this category of capital crime.

. . . The convictions and sentence of the appellant, Dale Robert Yates, are, accordingly,

Affirmed.

STATE v. YOUNG

Supreme Court of North Carolina, 1985.
312 N.C. 669, 325 S.E.2d 181.

After finishing a bottle of vodka in [a] parking lot, defendant, Presnell, and Jackson began to talk about how they might obtain more liquor. . . . Since the men had no money, defendant suggested that the three men go to [J.O.] Cooke's house, rob and kill him, and take money. Presnell and Jackson testified that they thought defendant was joking . . . . The three men left the . . . parking lot and began walking to Cooke's house. On the way defendant suggested that Jackson hold Cooke, defendant stab him, and Presnell "finish" him. When the men arrived at Cooke's house, Jackson knocked on the door and told Cooke that they wanted to buy liquor. Cooke let the men inside and went into the kitchen to get the liquor. When he returned with the vodka, defendant suddenly reached into his pants, pulled out a knife and stabbed Cooke twice in the chest. Cooke said "What are you doing?" and fell to the floor. Cooke was able to take the knife from his own chest, at which point defendant told Presnell to "finish him." Presnell stabbed the victim five or six times in the back.

Defendant searched through Cooke's pockets and wallet and divided the money he found among the three men. The men then searched the house for other valuables and found a coin collection which they divided. They left the house, and Jackson placed the knife in a nearby snowbank.

[D]efendant was charged with first-degree murder, first-degree burglary, and robbery with a dangerous weapon. At trial defendant offered no evidence. The jury found defendant guilty of first-degree murder, first-degree burglary, and robbery with a dangerous weapon.

In the sentencing phase of the trial, . . . the trial court submitted three aggravating circumstances: (i) whether the murder was committed while defendant was engaged in a commission of robbery with a dangerous weapon or first-degree burglary; (ii) whether the murder was committed for pecuniary gain; and (iii) whether the murder was especially heinous, atrocious, or cruel. The trial court submitted two mitigating circumstances for consideration by the jury: (i) the age (19) of defendant; and (ii) any other circumstance deemed to have mitigating value. The jury found . . . that the murder was committed while in the commission of a robbery or burglary and that it was committed for pecuniary gain. The jury found evidence of one or more mitigating circumstances, but found them insufficient to outweigh the aggravating circumstances. The jury recommended that defendant be sentenced to death and the trial court entered judgment accordingly. . . .

BRANCH, CHIEF JUSTICE. [The Court affirmed Young's conviction and held that the sentencing proceedings had been conducted in conformity with state and federal law.]

As a final matter in every capital case, we are directed by [statute] to review the record and determine (i) whether the record supports the jury's findings of any aggravating . . . circumstances upon which the sentencing court based its sentence of death; (ii) whether the sentence was imposed under the influence of passion, prejudice or any other arbitrary factor; and (iii) whether the sentence of death is excessive or disproportionate to the penalty imposed in similar cases, considering both the crime and the defendant.

[W]e find that the evidence supports the two aggravating factors found by the jury . . . We also conclude that there is nothing in the record which suggests that the sentence of death was influenced by passion, prejudice or any other arbitrary factor. We thus turn to our final statutory duty of proportionality review.

In determining whether the death sentence in this case is disproportionate to the penalty imposed in similar cases, we first refer to the now familiar "pool" of cases established [by a prior case]:

"In comparing 'similar cases' for purposes of proportionality review, we use as a pool for comparison purposes *all cases* arising since the effective date of our capital punishment statute, 1 June 1977, which have been tried as capital cases and reviewed on direct appeal by this court and in which the jury recommended death or life imprisonment or in which the trial court imposed life imprisonment after the jury's failure to agree upon a sentencing recommendation within a reasonable period of time."

. . . The pool "includes only those cases which have been affirmed by this court."

We have held that our task on proportionality review is to compare the case "with other cases in the pool which are roughly similar with regard to the crime and the defendant. . . . "

In conducting our proportionality review in this case, we have reviewed the approximately 28 robbery murder cases in the "pool." We note that in 23 of these cases, juries imposed sentences of life imprisonment rather than death. The death penalty was imposed in five cases. While we wish to make it *abundantly clear* that we do not consider this numerical disparity dispositive . . . , our careful examination of these cases has led us to the conclusion that although the crime here committed was a tragic killing, "it does not rise to the level of those murders in which we have approved the death sentence upon proportionality review." The facts presented by this appeal more closely resemble those cases in which the jury recommended life imprisonment than those in which the defendant was sentenced to death.

In this case, the evidence essentially reveals that defendant, a young man 19 years of age, and two companions went to the victim's home . . . They gained entry to Cooke's dwelling by trick. Defendant stabbed Cooke twice in the chest and his companion Presnell "finished him" by stabbing him several more times. Young and his two friends then stole the victim's money and some valuable coins and fled the scene. The pathologist testified that the victim died shortly after he was stabbed.

Although we have not in the past, and will not in the future "necessarily feel bound during [our] proportionality review to give a citation to every case in the pool of 'similar cases' used for comparison," we find it instructive to discuss several cases which impelled our conclusion that the death penalty is disproportionate in this case.

A case with facts similar to the murder here under review is State v. Whisenant, 308 N.C. 791, 303 S.E.2d 784 (1983). In *Whisenant,* the defendant, a 43-year-old male, discussed with several witnesses his intention to rob the Leonhardt home in Morganton, North Carolina. [He] went to the Leonhardt residence and shot and killed the owner, a 79-year-old male, and the housekeeper, a 66-year-old female. The jury found as aggravating circumstances that defendant had previously been convicted of a felony involving the use of violence against another person; the murder was committed while defendant was engaged in the commission of armed robbery; the murder was perpetrated for pecuniary gain; and the murder was committed while defendant was engaged in a course of conduct which included the commission of another crime of violence against another person. No mitigating circumstances were found. Despite the presence of four aggravating circumstances and the failure of the jury to find a single circumstance in mitigation of defendant's punishment, defendant was sentenced to consecutive life sentences after the jury was unable to agree upon the recommendation of punishment.

State v. Hunt, 305 N.C. 238, 287 S.E.2d 818 (1982) is another capital case in which the crime committed by the defendant was much worse than that committed by Phillip Young . . . .

In *Hunt*, the deceased, Walter Ray, lived alone in a trailer in Henderson, North Carolina. Ray operated an illegal bar in his residence. As Ray was closing the bar one night, defendant put on gloves, walked up behind the victim, grabbed him and put a knife against his throat. Defendant then forced Ray back to the bedroom where defendant searched a closet and removed approximately $400.00 and a pistol from it. As defendant prepared to shoot Ray with the pistol, Ray begged him not to kill him that way. Defendant agreed to employ another method.

After forcing Ray to drink beer and a pint of liquor, defendant slashed one of Ray's forearms near the wrist with a knife. He slashed him again and waited while the victim slowly bled to death. Defendant then left the trailer carrying the pistol and the money with him.

The jury found six aggravating circumstances, but specified no mitigating circumstances since they found that the aggravating circumstances were insufficient to support the death penalty.

Finally,[3] we agree with defendant's contention that this case is very similar to State v. Jackson, 309 N.C. 26, 305 S.E.2d 703 (1983) in which this Court overturned a death sentence as disproportionate to the penalty imposed in similar cases.

In *Jackson*, three men conspired to ambush and rob a 71-year-old ailing man. The trio faked car trouble and the elderly victim, George McAulay, stopped to offer aid. One of the three men told McAulay that they needed jumper cables. McAulay replied that he did not have any with him, but would give one of the men a ride to town. Defendant got into the car with him. When the victim refused to give Jackson money, Jackson murdered McAulay by shooting him twice in the head. Jackson took the money, met his companions and reported to them that he had killed McAulay because he had refused to relinquish the money.

The jury found as an aggravating circumstance that the crime was committed for pecuniary gain. They found as the sole mitigating circumstance that defendant had no significant history of prior criminal activity. In the instant case, the jury found the two aggravating circumstances earlier mentioned, that is, that the murder was committed while defendant was engaged in the commission of armed robbery

---

[3] By singling out these few cases for discussion, we do not mean to imply that these were the only cases reviewed by this court in conducting our proportionality review. We considered carefully each of the cases in the "pool" . . .

and that it was committed for pecuniary gain. The jury did not specify the mitigating circumstances they found.

In contrast to *Whisenant, Hunt, Jackson* and other cases [where the death penalty was either not imposed or set aside on appeal] are those armed robbery cases in which this Court affirmed the jury's recommendation of the death penalty . . . . We do not deem it necessary to discuss each of these cases; suffice it to say that we have carefully reviewed each of them and are convinced that defendant Young did not commit a crime as egregious as those committed by the defendants in [those cases]. In nearly all those cases, the jury found as an aggravating circumstance that the defendants were engaged in a course of conduct which included the commission of another crime of violence against another person. Furthermore, in [two of them], the jury found that the murder was especially atrocious, heinous or cruel. . . . In this case, however, the jury specifically found that this aggravating circumstance did *not* exist.

In conclusion, we hold as a matter of law that the death sentence imposed in this case is disproportionate . . . . We are therefore required by the statute to sentence defendant to life imprisonment in lieu of the death sentence. . . .

Guilt-Innocence Phase: No Error;

Sentencing Phase: Death Sentence Vacated, Sentence of Life Imprisonment Imposed.

VAUGHN, J., did not participate in the consideration or decision of this case.

NOTES ON COMPARATIVE REVIEW
OF DEATH SENTENCES

1. **Questions on *Yates* and *Young*.** The decisions in *Yates* and *Young* reflect polar extremes among the litigated cases in how courts should approach the task of comparative review. How would you characterize the differences between the two approaches? Which do you prefer? The South Carolina Supreme Court's earlier decision in *Gilbert* demonstrates that Yates' death sentence is not unprecedented, but does it show that such a sentence is "consistently" imposed in similar cases? By contrast, the North Carolina Supreme Court examines a broader base of cases. In light of the highly individualized nature of the sentencing inquiry, is it possible for the court to know which cases *Young* "more closely resembles?" Will it always be possible to find cases "worse" than the one being considered in which the death sentence was not imposed? One could interpret *Young* to indicate that a death sentence for robbery-murder is likely to be found comparatively excessive unless the offense was "heinous, atrocious or cruel." If this is what *Young* means, has the court rewritten the statute? Should it have done so?

2. **Methodology of Comparative Review: Defining the Universe of Relevant Cases.** The first question that must be resolved by

appellate courts conducting comparative review is how to define the universe of cases within which comparisons will be made. Courts in more than half the death penalty states limit their review to appealed cases, although most of these courts follow the approach taken by the North Carolina Supreme Court in *Young* (including appealed life sentences) rather than that taken by the South Carolina Supreme Court in *Yates* (including only appealed death sentences). The remaining states broaden the universe to include some portion of unappealed cases. The information in these states is typically provided by reports which must be filed by the trial court. Some of these states define the universe to include all cases in which a capital sentencing proceeding was held, thus excluding all those in which the death penalty was not sought by the prosecution; others include all convictions for capital crimes, thus including some cases in which the prosecution did not seek the death penalty; and one state, Louisiana, includes all cases initiated by indictments for capital crimes, encompassing cases in which the defendant was convicted of a non-capital murder and thereby reaching all exercises of prosecutorial discretion.[a]

Putting aside some of the less significant variations in these approaches, they reflect different responses to two basic questions. First, should comparative review be limited to cases in which death sentences have been imposed? Second, even if the pool is broadened to include life sentences, should it be limited to cases in which the prosecution sought the death sentence, i.e., to cases in which capital sentencing proceedings were held? These issues are addressed in turn below.

(i) **Should Comparison be Limited to Cases in Which Death Sentences Were Imposed?** The argument against a pool limited to appealed death sentences was stated by Justice Exum of the North Carolina Supreme Court: [b]

"The basic purpose of [comparative] review is to make sure that the death sentence in the case before us is not 'excessive' to sentences 'imposed in similar cases.' If we look for comparison only to cases in which the death penalty has been imposed, the sentence in the case under review could never be excessive because one death sentence never 'exceeds' another. It is only by comparing the case being reviewed in which a death sentence was imposed with other similar cases in which life was imposed that we can determine whether the death penalty in the case being reviewed is really excessive to the penalty being imposed in similar cases. For, to reiterate what the Supreme Court said in *Gregg v. Georgia*, if there are certain kinds of murder cases in which our juries are generally not recommending death, then an occasional death sentence imposed in those kinds of cases ought to be set aside by this court.

[a] Another unique feature of the Louisiana scheme is that the statute directs the court to compare only those cases arising in the same parish. In every other state, the review is statewide, and some courts occasionally consult cases arising in other states.

[b] State v. Pinch, 306 N.C. 1, 292 S.E.2d 203, 242–43 (1982) (Exum, J., dissenting). The North Carolina Supreme Court adopted Justice Exum's view in State v. Williams, 308 N.C. 47, 301 S.E.2d 335 (1983).

"We ought not limit ourselves only to cases where the death sentence was imposed and affirmed. To do so means that we only ask whether the case under review is as bad as the other death cases. The legislature intended us not only to make that determination but also to determine whether the case under review is more deserving of the death penalty than similar cases in which life sentences have been imposed. The statute's plain language requires that we make both kinds of comparisons. Of the two, the latter is the more meaningful and is probably constitutionally required."

The Supreme Court of South Carolina, which limits its pool to appealed death sentences, defended its approach against such criticisms as follows: [c]

"We recognize that [some feel] that the reviewing court should compare a given death sentence with a 'universe' of cases which includes sentences of life imprisonment, acquittals, reversals and even mere indictments and arrests. Under such a regime, the review court could only determine the size of its sample or 'universe' by some arbitrary device. Fact findings of the trial court [supporting a sentence of death], by contrast, provide a fundamental line of demarcation well recognized in and even exalted by our legal tradition. . . .

"To expand the notion of a 'universe' would also entail intolerable speculation by this court. Under the South Carolina statute, a jury is not required to state its reasons for failing to recommend a sentence of death. In a given case, the alleged aggravating circumstance may not have been proven to the satisfaction of the jury, while in another 'similar case' (expansively defined) the statutory mitigating circumstances or some mitigating factor 'otherwise authorized or allowed by law' may have deterred imposition of the death sentence.

"This Court would enter a realm of pure conjecture if it attempted to compare and contrast such verdicts with an actual sentence of death. They represent acts of mercy which have not yet been held to offend the United States Constitution. Moreover, they reflect the emphasis upon individualized sentencing mandated by the United States Supreme Court. We will not subject these verdicts to scrutiny in pursuit of phantom 'similar cases,' when a meaningful sample lies ready at hand in those cases where the jury has spoken unequivocally."

Does the disagreement between these two courts reflect a fundamental disagreement about the purpose of appellate review of death sentences? Which is more appropriate?

(ii) **Should Comparison be Limited to Cases in Which the Prosecution Sought a Death Sentence?** In Tichnell v. State, 297 Md. 1, 468 A.2d 1 (1983), the Maryland Court of Appeals concluded "that the legislatively intended inventory of cases from which 'similar

[c] State v. Copeland, 278 S.C. 572, 300 S.E.2d 63 (1982).

cases' are to be culled encompasses only those first-degree murder cases in which the state sought the death penalty . . . whether it was imposed or not." [d]

Three members of the court objected:

" '[D]eath eligible murder cases in which the prosecutor could have, but did not seek the death penalty' must be included in the inventory of relevant cases in order to achieve the goal of proportionality review—the consistent and fair application of the death penalty. . . .

"[T]his Court has before it data concerning the exercise of prosecutorial discretion in death penalty cases. This data dramatically demonstrates that the inventory of relevant cases for proportionality review must include all death-eligible murder cases—not only those in which the prosecutor sought the death penalty, but also those in which he did not.

"This data reveals that in Maryland prosecutors seek the death penalty in only 7.8 per cent of the death-eligible cases, whereas in 92.2 per cent of the death-eligible cases the death penalty is not sought. Consequently, this data establishes that Maryland prosecutors rarely seek the death penalty, a fact that is relevant, in and of itself, in determining whether the death penalty is disproportionate.

"More important, the purpose of proportionality review is to assure that a person is not sentenced to death unless the death penalty has been imposed generally in similar cases throughout the state. If this purpose is to be effectuated . . . a person sentenced to death must have his background and the nature and the circumstances of the crime committed compared to the sentence imposed on other persons in this state of similar background who committed a similar crime under similar circumstances. That prosecutors do not seek the death penalty in 92.2 per cent of death-eligible murder cases shows that unless all death-eligible cases are included in the inventory, a significant number of cases involving similar defendants and similar crimes would be excluded from proportionality review.

"In addition, the data [show] that in cases in which the death penalty has been sought juries in Garrett County have imposed the death penalty in 50 per cent of the cases, whereas juries in Baltimore City have imposed the death penalty in 33 per cent. This data suggests that in these two jurisdictions the death penalty has been imposed in a somewhat consistent manner. The data further reveals [that] there is a substantial variation in the exercise of prosecutorial discretion. In Garrett County prosecutors seek the death penalty in 100 per cent of the death-eligible

[d] The court noted, however, that "we do not preclude any defendant whose death sentence is under appellate review from presenting argument, with relevant facts, that designated non-capital murder cases are similar to the case then under scrutiny and should be taken into account in the exercise of our proportionality review function."

cases, whereas in Baltimore City, they seek that penalty in only 1.8 per cent. [J]uries in Garrett County have imposed the death penalty in 50 per cent of all the death-eligible cases, whereas juries in Baltimore City have imposed the death penalty in only .6 per cent. [I]n these two jurisdictions the death penalty has been imposed in an inconsistent manner. If death-eligible cases in which the death penalty has not been sought are excluded from the inventory, a person who has committed a crime in Garrett County is deprived of a realistic comparison of the treatment accorded to other persons of similar background who committed a similar crime under similar circumstances in Baltimore City and, indeed, throughout the state. . . .

"The data before this court for the first time provides facts concerning the exercise of prosecutorial discretion. This data demonstrates a substantial variation, ranging from 1.8 per cent to 100 per cent, in the percentage of cases in which the death penalty is sought, depending upon the identity of the prosecutor making the determination. Equally important, [the] data shows that there is a substantial variation in the standards employed by prosecutors in deciding in which cases to seek the death penalty. In six counties, the prosecutors exercise virtually no discretion; these prosecutors seek the death penalty whenever a single aggravating circumstance is present and mitigating circumstances are not taken into account. In six other counties and Baltimore City, prosecutors exercise considerable discretion. Such prosecutors weigh the aggravating circumstances against the mitigating circumstances in determining whether to seek the death penalty. There are many other variations in the standards employed by prosecutors. In some jurisdictions the strength of the case is evaluated. Sometimes the question whether a jury would impose the death penalty is considered. In Baltimore City the death penalty is sought if there is a substantial likelihood that the jury would impose death. In Montgomery County, the death penalty is sought if there is a reasonable possibility. In Charles County, the death penalty is sought unless it is very unlikely that the jury will impose that penalty. In two counties, the prosecutors take public sentiment with respect to the case into account, whereas in seven others, they do not. In five counties, prosecutors take the relationship between the accused and the victim into account, whereas in three others they do not. In one county, the prosecutor considers the burden of prosecuting a death penalty case upon the state attorney's office and the courts, whereas in seven other counties, they do not. A prosecutor in one county seeks the death penalty as a device to obtain a plea bargain, whereas the prosecutors in no other county engage in such a practice. In a single county, the prosecutor seeks the death penalty in felony-murder cases only when the aggravating circumstances are separate and distinct from the underlying felony, whereas no prosecutor in any other county has such a policy. . . .

". . . It is . . . apparent that the existence of such data raises the question whether the relevant inventory of cases must include those in which the death penalty was not sought in order for proportionality review to be constitutional. . . . "

Is it feasible for courts to broaden in this manner the universe of cases to be considered? Prosecutors are not required to articulate reasons for their decisions to negotiate plea arrangements, to reduce charges, or not to seek the death penalty. If the courts were to include such cases within the universe of comparative review, how would it be determined whether the evidence in the case would have been legally sufficient to support a death sentence? How would the court obtain other information relevant to the prosecutor's decision and, ultimately, to its own comparison?

Recall that Yates sought to "enjoin" the prosecution from seeking the death penalty because the prosecutor's normal policy was to seek the capital sanction only against the "triggerman." If this were the normal policy, would it demonstrate that the decision to seek the death penalty against Yates was arbitrary or unjustified? Does it matter that the "triggerman" was dead? Would it matter if Yates had more previous convictions for violent felonies than most of the other accomplices against whom the prosecutor decided not to seek a death sentence? Or that Yates' claims in mitigation were weaker? In the absence of adjudication of these issues, how could the court evaluate them?

3. **Methodology of Comparative Review: Selecting and Comparing "Similar" Cases.** Within the universe of cases available for comparative review, the court must develop a methodology for deciding which features make cases similar or dissimilar to one another and for determining whether the death sentence being reviewed is "comparatively excessive." Professor Baldus and his colleagues have recommended that courts develop quantitative approaches using statistical techniques for classifying cases and developing measures of comparative excessiveness. See Baldus, Pulaski, Woodworth, & Kyle, Comparative Review of Death Sentences: An Empirical Study of the Georgia Experience, 74 J.Crim.L. and Criminology 661 (1983). Is this feasible or desirable? No court has adopted a sophisticated quantitative methodology for conducting comparative review. The Supreme Court of North Carolina expressly refused to do so in State v. Williams, 308 N.C. 47, 301 S.E.2d 335 (1983):

"We do not propose to attempt to employ mathematical or statistical models involving multiple regression analysis or other scientific techniques, currently in vogue among social scientists, which have been described as having 'the seductive appeal of science and mathematics.' The factors to be considered and their relevancy during [comparative] review in a given capital case are not readily subject to complete enumeration and definition. Those factors will be as numerous and as varied as the cases coming before us on appeal. This truth is readily revealed by a comparison of the opinions of the Justices of the Supreme Court of the United States concerning the relevancy of certain factors as revealed in *Godfrey v. Georgia.* Even those with extensive training in data collection and statistical evaluation and analysis are unable to agree concerning the type of statistical methodology which should be employed if statistical or mathematical models are adopted for purposes of proportionality review. E.g., Baldus, Pulaski, Woodworth, and Kyle, Identifying Comparatively Excessive Sentences of Death: A Quantitative Approach, 33 Stan.L.Rev. 1 (1980); Dix, Appellate Review of the Decision to Impose Death, 68 Geo.L.J. 97 (1979). Additionally, the categories of factors which would be used in setting up any statistical model for quantitative analysis, no matter how numerous those factors, would have a natural tendency to become the last word on the subject of proportionality rather than serving as an initial point of inquiry. After making numerical determinations concerning the number of similar and dissimilar characteristics in the case before it and in other cases in which the death sentence was or was not imposed, a reviewing court might well tend to disregard the experienced judgments of its own members in favor of the 'scientific' evidence resulting from quantitative analysis. To the extent that a reviewing court allowed itself to be so swayed, it would tend to deny the defendant before it the constitutional right to 'individualized consideration' as that concept was expounded in *Lockett v. Ohio.* This is so because, a 'close reading of the actual records of cases identified as "similar" by a quantitative measure may reveal factual distinctions which make them legally dissimilar.' Baldus, Pulaski, Woodworth, and Kyle, Identifying Comparatively Excessive Sentences of Death: A Quantitative Approach, 33 Stan.L.Rev. 1, 68 (1980). Further, the reviewing court would still be required to rely upon a 'best estimate' of the factors that actually influenced the sentencing juries. Id. at 24–25. Therefore, this court will not attempt to engage in the systematic and scientific collection of statistical data or its evaluation and analysis through the theory of probability, multiple regression analysis, graphs or the other tools of statistical analysis which are of value to scientists engaged in the physical sciences and dealing with matters other than [comparative] review in capital cases."

Although the North Carolina Supreme Court rejected sophisticated statistical methodologies, it does appear to employ one of the quantitative techniques (the "salient factors method") described by Professor Baldus and his colleagues: in *Young,* it selected cases involving the same statutory aggravating circumstance (murder in the course of armed robbery) as the pool for comparison; within that group, it identified those features of the cases which appear to explain the variation in outcome between the five death sentences and the 23 life sentences; it then concluded that in the absence of these distinguishing characteristics, the death sentence in *Young* was comparatively excessive. Does this approach give undue emphasis to the characteristics of the offense? Is it possible that Young's case was dissimilar to the life-sentence cases in other respects, such as the absence of any compelling claim in mitigation? Is comparative review of individualized death sentences a self-contradiction?

4. *Godfrey* **Reconsidered.** As noted at pages 813–14, supra, Godfrey was sentenced to death a second time after the United States Supreme Court remanded the case to the Georgia courts. This time, the sentence rested on the jury's finding that the murder "was committed while the offender was engaged in the commission of another capital felony." On appeal, Godfrey argued that the sentence should have been set aside because death sentences for domestic murders are comparatively rare. In Godfrey v. State, 248 Ga. 616, 284 S.E.2d 422 (1981), the Georgia Supreme Court rejected his contention:

> "Appellant [argues] that the death penalty in domestic cases is such a rarity that, considering the mitigation, i.e., lack of prior criminal record and psychiatric history, the death penalty as applied to appellant is disproportionate and is also 'unusual' and therefore violates the eighth and 14th Amendments of the United States Constitution. In reviewing the death penalties in this case, we have considered the cases appealed to this court since January 1, 1970, in which a death or life sentence was imposed. Cases selected for comparison included those involving a death sentence or those involving a life sentence for domestic homicides, that is where the victim was a girlfriend, spouse, or ex-spouse of the perpetrator, or a relative of the girlfriend, spouse, or ex-spouse. As we [have previously noted,] 'although lesser sentences than death are frequently imposed in domestic murder cases, it does not follow that the death penalty would not be authorized for the murder of one spouse by another under any circumstances. Some of the more vile, horrible or inhuman homicides have been perpetrated by family members against one another.' Since January 1, 1970, juries throughout the state have given the death penalty in seven domestic murder cases. . . . Therefore, domestic murders are not a 'capriciously selected group of offenders.' In addition, multiple murder cases were selected for comparison . . . . In three of the seven cases in which the death penalty was returned, not only did defendant have no prior record, but also there was a history of prior psychiatric disorder, as in the instant case. Therefore, we find the appellant's sentence to death for murder is not excessive or disproportionate to the penalty imposed in similar cases considering both the crime and the defendant. . . . "

Was this a satisfactory response to Godfrey's argument? The court concludes that Godfrey's death sentence was not "capricious" because seven other domestic killers had received death sentences since 1970. Is the court's conclusion supported by the data upon which it relies?

5. ***Pulley v. Harris.*** Appellate courts in some death penalty states have no statutory obligation to conduct comparative review.[e] In Pulley v. Harris, 465 U.S. 37 (1984), the Supreme Court held that comparative review was not constitutionally required so long as the state's statutory scheme otherwise provides adequate safeguards against arbitrary application of the death penalty. The Court concluded that by limiting the death sentence to a "small sub-class of capital-eligible cases," and by specifying a statutory list of "relevant factors" to be considered by the jury at the penalty phase, California had adopted a facially constitutional statute notwithstanding the absence of a requirement for comparative review. Justice White concluded the Court's opinion with the following observations:

> "Any capital sentencing scheme may occasionally produce aberrational outcomes. Such inconsistencies are a far cry from the major systemic defects identified in *Furman.* As we have acknowledged in the past, 'there can be "no perfect procedure for deciding in which cases governmental authority should be used to impose death." ' As we are presently informed, we cannot say that the California procedures provided Harris inadequate protection against the evil identified in *Furman.*"

Justice Stevens wrote a separate concurring opinion, agreeing with the Court's conclusion that comparative review is not constitutionally required but emphasizing that "some form of meaningful appellate review is an essential safeguard against the arbitrary and capricious imposition of death sentences by individual juries and judges." Justices Brennan and Marshall dissented. They argued that comparative review should be constitutionally required because it "serves to eliminate some, if only a small part, of the irrationality that infects the current imposition of death sentences in the United States," and that judicial experience demonstrates "that such review can be administered without much difficulty. . . . "

6. **Efficacy of Comparative Review.** Although the courts of most states exercise comparative review, they have set aside very few death sentences on the basis of comparative excessiveness. It seems clear that by confining their review to appealed death sentences, some of these states have eliminated the most meaningful basis of comparison; instead, previously decided cases are invoked to demonstrate that the death penalty has been imposed in one or more cases similar to the one being reviewed. Not surprisingly, none of these states has reversed a death sentence on grounds of comparative excessiveness. The occasional reversals have been firmly grounded on a judgment that the death sentence is disproportionate to the seriousness of the crime in the

---

[e] The courts in some of these states do conduct a case-by-case proportionality review.

particular case. This restricted view of the appellate role is evident in the language routinely employed by the South Carolina Supreme Court:

"Cases tried in this state under the death penalty statute resulting in capital punishment heretofore involved factual situations, and accused persons, similarly atrocious to those involved in this case. It is our observation that a unanimous jury in South Carolina has ordered the death penalty in only those cases where the proof of facts is virtually undebatable and the nature of the wrongful killing is such as to shake the conscience of the community. The facts are not the same in any two cases and, accordingly, our review of the facts relate[s] largely to degree of culpability of the defendants and the viciousness of the killing. In the case at hand, there is no semblance of an excuse for the wrongful killing, nor does the record reveal any facts relative to the accused persons themselves that would warrant leniency." [f]

Although the universe of comparison used in the other states does encompass some cases in which the death penalty was not imposed, most of these courts have not yet held a sentence to be comparatively excessive. The experience of the Georgia Supreme Court is illustrative. Although the court had reached the issue of sentence review in more than 150 cases from 1973 to 1984, it had reversed only two sentences, and neither reversal was on grounds of comparative excessiveness.[g] Putting to one side cases involving different sentences for co-defendants convicted of the same crime, and focusing only on comparisons across cases, one finds that at this writing only North Carolina, Florida, Nevada, and Oklahoma have held sentences to be comparatively excessive.

How should this experience be interpreted? Does it show that comparative review cannot work? Does it show that comparative review is exercised deficiently by most courts? Or does it show that comparative review is superfluous in light of other safeguards against arbitrary sentences?

NOTES ON RACE AND THE DEATH PENALTY

1. **Introduction.** The arbitrariness concern expressed in *Furman* has two dimensions: (i) random or capricious decisions that make no

[f] State v. Gaskins, 284 S.C. 105, 130, 326 S.E.2d 132, 147 (1985).

[g] One reversal involved the special problem of intra-case disparity: the court reversed a defendant's death sentence because a co-defendant, the actual triggerman, had received a life sentence. The other case reversed a death sentence imposed on a defendant who had received a life sentence in a previous trial for the same offense.

The Georgia experience with comparative review has been assessed by a number of commentators. See, e.g., Baldus, Woodworth & Pulaski, Monitoring and Evaluating Contemporary Death Sentencing Systems: Lessons from Georgia, 18 U.C. Davis L.Rev. 1375 (1985); Barnett, Some Distribution Patterns for the Georgia Death Sentence, 18 U.C. Davis L.Rev. 1327 (1985); Liebman, Appellate Review of Death Sentences: A Critique of Proportionality Review, 18 U.C. Davis L.Rev. 1433 (1985); Baldus, Pulaski & Woodworth, Comparative Review of Death Sentences, 74 J.Crim. L. and Criminology 661 (1983).

effort rationally to justify differential outcomes; and (ii) "discriminatory" decisions that are based on impermissible factors. The preceding materials have focused mainly on the first dimension of *Furman*. These notes address the second in the context of racial discrimination.

Empirical studies conducted before *Furman* suggested two respects in which the death penalty may have been discriminatory: first, black defendants were more likely to receive the death penalty than white defendants in the South, although this finding was not consistently demonstrated elsewhere; and second, the death penalty was less likely to be imposed for homicides with black victims than for those with white victims.[a] In 1976, a majority of the Supreme Court expressed confidence that the contemporary generation of capital sentencing statutes had substantially reduced the risk of discrimination in the administration of the death penalty. Empirical investigations of sentencing patterns under post-*Furman* statutes have raised doubts about the Court's supposition. The two most sophisticated studies are described below.

2. **The Gross and Mauro Study.** Professors Gross and Mauro examined death sentencing patterns from 1976 through 1980 in eight states, using data obtained primarily from reports on homicide cases filed by local police agencies with the FBI. The FBI reports included data on: (i) the sex, age, and race of the victim(s); (ii) the sex, age, and race of the suspect(s); (iii) the date and place of the homicide; (iv) the weapon used; (v) the commission of any accompanying felony; and (vi) the relationship between the victim(s) and the suspected killer(s). The findings from this study are described and discussed in Gross and Mauro, Patterns of Death: An Analysis of Racial Disparities in Capital Sentencing and Homicide Victimization, 37 Stan.L.Rev. 27 (1984). The portions of this article summarized below pertain to the three states (Georgia, Florida, and Illinois) that had the highest number of death sentences.

First, Gross and Mauro presented their aggregate findings regarding the relation between outcome and the race of victim and suspect: [*]

"In each state a large proportion of homicide victims in this period were black: a majority in Georgia and Illinois (63.5 per cent and 58.6 per cent, respectively) and nearly half in Florida (43.3 per cent). This is consistent with the national pattern of homicides; blacks and other racial minorities are far more likely than whites to be the victims of homicides. . . . At the same time, the risk of a death sentence was far lower for those suspects charged with killing black people in Georgia, Florida, and Illinois than for those charged with killing whites. In Georgia, those who killed whites were almost ten times as likely to be sentenced to death as those who killed blacks; in Florida the ratio was about eight to one, and in Illinois about six to one.

[a] These studies are summarized in Kleck, Racial Discrimination in Criminal Sentencing: A Critical Evaluation of the Evidence with Additional Evidence on the Death Penalty, 46 Am.Soc.Rev. 783 (1981).

[*] The excerpts below are reproduced with permission of the authors and the Stanford Law Review.

"In Georgia and Florida, white homicide suspects were, on the whole, about twice as likely to get death sentences as black homicide suspects: 5.5 per cent versus 2.9 per cent in Georgia, 5.2 per cent versus 2.4 per cent in Florida. In Illinois, there was a similar but smaller difference. . . . In each state, however, the relationship between the suspect's race and the likelihood of a death sentence appears to be due entirely to the fact that black suspects were more likely to kill black victims and white suspects were more likely to kill white victims. Indeed, when we control for the race of the victim, blacks who killed whites were several times more likely to be sentenced to death than whites who killed whites in each state.

Next, Gross and Mauro turned to the relation between outcome and the nonracial variables included in the FBI data. They found that three of these factors had a strong aggregate effect on the likelihood of death sentences in each state: the commission of a homicide in the course of another felony, the killing of a stranger, and the killing of multiple victims.[b] They then sought to determine whether the race-of-victim disparities could be explained by any of these nonracial effects:

"(i) Felony circumstances. Although only a minority of all reported homicides in each state involved other felonies—17.5 per cent in Georgia, 18.1 per cent in Florida, and 27.1 per cent in Illinois—the great majority of death sentences fell in this category—over 80 per cent in Georgia and Florida, and about 75 per cent in Illinois. Among homicides with suspects over fourteen years old, the commission of a separate felony increased the likelihood of a death sentence by a factor of about twelve in Illinois, twenty-six in Georgia, and nearly twenty-four in Florida. . . . Nevertheless, the disparities in capital sentencing by race of victim persist when we control for the felony circumstance of the homicide. For both felony and nonfelony homicides, white-victim cases were far more likely to result in death sentences in each state[:]

TABLE 4

Percentage of Death Sentences by Felony Circumstance and Race of Victim

	Georgia		Florida		Illinois	
	Felony	Non-Felony	Felony	Non-Felony	Felony	Non-Felony
White Victim	35.0% (57/163)	1.9% (10/520)	27.5% (95/346)	1.5% (19/1272)	9.4% (24/256)	1.2% (11/890)
Black Victim	6.6% (7/106)	0.4% (5/1165)	7.0% (9/128)	0.3% (5/1468)	3.0% (10/330)	0% (0/1475)

[b] Two other factors (killing a female and using a gun) had less pronounced and less consistent aggregate effects on outcome. In addition, rural homicides were some- what more likely than urban homicides to result in death sentences in Georgia and Florida, but not in Illinois.

"Controlling for both the race of the suspect and felony circumstance does not dilute the capital sentencing disparities by race of victim, but it does change the race of suspect pattern seen in [the aggregated data]. When we consider felony and nonfelony homicides separately, there are no substantial differences in capital sentencing rates between blacks who kill whites and whites who kill whites in Florida; in Illinois there is a sizable difference between these two racial groups of suspects among nonfelony homicides, and essentially none among felony homicides; and in Georgia there are disparities between whites who kill whites and blacks who kill whites in both felony and nonfelony homicides . . .[:]

TABLE 5

Percentage of Death Sentences by Race of Suspect and
Victim and Felony Circumstance

	Georgia		Florida		Illinois	
	Felony	Non-Felony	Felony	Non-Felony	Felony	Non-Felony
Black Kills White	38.5% (30/78)	4.2% (2/48)	28.8% (32/111)	2.5% (2/79)	8.8% (10/114)	7.2% (6/83)
White Kills White	31.8% (27/85)	1.7% (8/472)	26.9% (63/234)	1.4% (17/1187)	10.2% (14/137)	0.6% (5/791)
Black Kills Black	6.3% (6/96)	0.4% (5/1146)	6.0% (7/116)	0.3% (4/1414)	3.1% (10/321)	0% (0/1429)
White Kills Black	11.1% (1/9)	0% (0/19)	18.2% (2/11)	1.9% (1/53)	0% (0/9)	0% (0/45)

"(ii) Relationship of victim to suspect. Relatively few homicide victims in these three states were killed by strangers—17 per cent in Georgia, 17 per cent in Florida, and 22 per cent in Illinois—but the majority of death sentences in each state were pronounced in those cases: over half in Florida, nearly two-thirds in Georgia, and about 70 per cent in Illinois. Those who killed strangers were far more likely to be sentenced to death than those who killed family members, friends, or acquaintances: ten times as likely in Georgia, four times as likely in Florida, and over six times as likely in Illinois.

"Controlling for the relationship of the suspect to the victim, however, does little to change the pattern of disparities in capital sentencing by the race of the victim. Those who killed whites were much more likely to be sentenced to death, in each state, regardless of their relationship to the victim[:]

TABLE 7

Percentage of Death Sentences by Race of Victim and Relationship of Victim to Suspect

	Georgia		Florida		Illinois	
	Strangers	Non-Strangers	Strangers	Non-Strangers	Strangers	Non-Strangers
White Victim	26.6% (47/177)	3.4% (20/591)	14.5% (68/469)	3.7% (46/1227)	5.8% (26/448)	1.2% (9/745)
Black Victim	3.1% (4/130)	0.7% (8/1207)	1.2% (3/257)	0.8% (11/1337)	1.5% (6/389)	0.3% (4/1450)

Controlling further for the race of the suspect does not alter this pattern. In addition, among both stranger and nonstranger homicides, blacks who killed whites were more likely to be sentenced to death in each state than whites who killed whites[:]

TABLE 8

Percentage of Death Sentences by Race of Victim and Suspect and Their Relationship

	Georgia		Florida		Illinois	
	Strangers	Non-Strangers	Strangers	Non-Strangers	Strangers	Non-Strangers
Black Kills White	28.6% (28/98)	6.6% (4/61)	19.3% (29/150)	6.5% (5/77)	8.4% (13/155)	5.6% (3/54)
White Kills White	24.1% (19/79)	3.0% (16/530)	12.3% (39/318)	3.6% (41/1146)	4.6% (13/285)	0.9% (6/678)
Black Kills Black	2.6% (3/115)	0.7% (8/1189)	1.3% (3/227)	0.6% (8/1302)	1.7% (6/360)	0/3% (4/1425)
White Kills Black	6.7% (1/15)	0% (0/18)	0% (0/29)	8.8% (3/34)	0% (0/29)	0% (0/24)

"(iii) Number of victims. Multiple homicides are quite rare; they accounted for only about two per cent of all homicides reported to the FBI from Georgia and Florida, and about four per cent from Illinois. Killing more than one victim increased the probability of a death sentence greatly in Georgia and Florida— by a factor of about six—and even more dramatically in Illinois— by a factor of more than eighteen. Despite the small proportion of multiple homicides in Illinois, 44 per cent of those sentenced to death in Illinois from 1976 through 1980 killed more than one victim. But the higher death sentencing rate for multiple homicides does not explain the racial disparities that we have observed. Disparities by race of victim persist in each state after we control for the number of victims; [and] among homicides with white victims, [black] suspects were more likely to be sentenced to death than white suspects[:]"

TABLE 10

Percentages of Death Sentences by Race of Victim and Number of Victims

	Georgia		Florida		Illinois	
	Multiple	Single	Multiple	Single	Multiple	Single
White Victim	27.6% (8/29)	7.9% (59/744)	20.4% (20/98)	5.5% (94/1705)	22.5% (16/71)	1.7% (19/1143)
Black Victim	6.3% (1/16)	0.8% (11/1329)	11.1% (3/27)	0.7% (11/1656)	6.8% (4/59)	0.3% (6/1807)

TABLE 11

Percentage of Death Sentences by Race of Victim and Defendant and Number of Victims

	Georgia		Florida		Illinois	
	Multiple	Single	Multiple	Single	Multiple	Single
Black Kills White	42.9% (3/7)	19.1% (29/152)	26.7% (4/15)	12.8% (30/234)	41.2% (7/17)	4.6% (9/196)
White Kills White	22.7% (5/22)	5.1% (30/592)	19.3% (16/83)	4.4% (64/1464)	16.7% (9/54)	1.1% (10/926)
Black Kills Black	6.3% (1/16)	0.8% (10/1294)	12% (3/25)	0.5% (8/1587)	6.8% (4/59)	0.3% (6/1750)
White Kills Black	—	2.9% (1/34)	0% (0/2)	4.5% (3/67)	—	0% (0/56)

Having determined that none of the nonracial variables, standing alone, could account for the observed racial disparities, Gross and Mauro turned to the possibility that the racial patterns are a byproduct of the *combined* effects of the other variables. They used two techniques to control simultaneously for the effects of nonracial variables. First, they constructed a scale of aggravation by scoring each homicide on a scale of zero to three, according to the number of major aggravating factors (felony circumstance, stranger victim, and multiple victims) present in the case. As their Table 21 shows, this score was a good predictor of the probability of a death sentence:

TABLE 21

Percentage of Death Sentences by Level of Aggravation

Number of Major Aggravating Circumstances

	0	1	2	3
Georgia	0.4% (6/1635)	7.7% (26/339)	31.6% (43/136)	57.1% (4/7)
Florida	0.6% (14/2295)	4.7% (41/874)	21.9% (62/283)	44.0% (11/25)
Illinois	0.1% (2/1924)	1.0% (7/711)	7.4% (29/392)	22.6% (7/31)

However, as their Table 23 shows, this aggregate measure of aggravation did not account for the race-of-victim effect in any state: at each level of aggravation, killers of white victims were substantially more likely to receive death sentences than killers of black victims: [c]

TABLE 23

Percentage of Death Sentences by Level of Aggravation and Race of Victim

Number of Major Aggravating Circumstances

	0	1	2–3
	Georgia		
White Victim	0.8% (4/499)	10.1% (18/179)	47.4% (45/95)
Black Victim	0.2% (2/1136)	5.0% (8/160)	4.2% (2/48)
	Florida		
White Victim	1.0% (10/1044)	7.0% (36/511)	28.2% (68/241)
Black Victim	0.3% (4/1251)	1.4% (5/363)	7.5% (5/67)
	Illinois		
White Victim	0.3% (2/646)	1.8% (6/329)	12.4% (27/218)
Black Victim	0% (0/1278)	0.3% (1/382)	4.4% (9/205)

The second technique used by Gross and Mauro to control simultaneously for all nonracial variables was "multiple regression analysis." This technique produces a mathematical model of the data that estimates the effect of each independent variable on the dependent variable (the outcome). Gross and Mauro summarized their findings as follows:

"In each state, the race of the victim had a sizable and statistically significant effect on the odds of a defendant receiving a death sentence. In Florida the overall odds of an offender receiving the death penalty for killing a white victim were 4.8 times greater than for killing a black victim. In Illinois the overall odds of an offender receiving the death penalty for killing a white were 4.0 times greater than for killing a black. In Georgia . . . the odds of receiving the death penalty for killing a white are approximately 7.2 times greater than the odds of receiving the death penalty for killing a black. . . .

[c] Controlling for the level of aggravation did eliminate any independent race-of-suspect effect.

"The magnitude of the racial effects . . . can also be described by comparing the predicted probabilities of receiving the death penalty generated by these models for hypothetical homicide cases that differ only in the race of the victim. In Table 25 these predicted probabilities are compared for hypothetical 'high aggravation' and 'low aggravation' homicides[:]

TABLE 25

Best Logistic Regression Models: Predicted Probability of
a Death Sentence in Hypothetical High and Low
Aggravation Cases, by Race of Victim

	Georgia	Florida	Illinois
High-Aggravation Case [a]			
White Victim	.653	.362	.352
Black Victim	.025	.107	.120
Low-Aggravation Case [b]			
White Victim	.0048	.010	.0020
Black Victim	.0006	.002	.0006

[a] Multiple homicide of at least one female during the course of a felony in which a gun was used; all victims were strangers to the offender.

[b] Single victim homicide of a male relative, friend, or acquaintance not committed with a gun; no other felonies involved.

". . . As Table 25 demonstrates, these regression analyses indicate substantial racial disparities in each of these three states at both ends of the continuum of aggravation. . . .

"Multiple logistic regression analysis reveals large and statistically significant race-of-victim effects on capital sentencing in Georgia, Florida, and Illinois. After controlling for the effects of all of the other variables in our data set, the killing of a white victim increased the odds of a death sentence by an estimated factor of four in Illinois, about five in Florida, and about seven in Georgia. This method of analysis reveals some evidence that the race of the suspect had an independent effect on capital sentencing in Illinois, but no evidence of independent race-of-suspect effects in Georgia or Florida." [d]

Gross and Mauro also anticipate the methodological objections that could be raised to their analysis. In particular, they focus on the possibility that information not included in the FBI files (concerning the strength of evidence or the suspects' prior record, for example) could account for the observed racial disparities. Although they concede that the inclusion of information on other variables would proba-

[d] Gross and Mauro also found that these racial patterns persisted when the analysis was restricted to affirmed death sentences in Georgia and Florida, thereby taking into account the effect of appellate review. They also found similar racial effects in the other five states that they studied although some of the findings were not statistically significant due to the low numbers of death sentences in those states.

bly affect the magnitude of the effects yielded by the regression analysis, they insist that there is little likelihood that the omitted variables would "substantially explain[ ]" the racial disparities. "In sum," they conclude, "we are aware of no plausible alternative hypothesis that might explain the observed racial patterns in capital sentencing in legitimate, nondiscriminatory terms." [e]

3. **The Baldus, Pulaski, and Woodworth Study.** Professor Baldus and his colleagues examined capital sentencing in Georgia, both before and after *Furman*.[f] One part of the study concerned approximately 2500 defendants arrested for homicides committed from 1973 to 1979 and subsequently convicted of murder or voluntary manslaughter. The study was based on a random stratified sample of 1066 of the 2500 cases, from which data were compiled on more than 400 variables, including details about the charges, plea bargaining, outcome, the defendant's characteristics and prior record, circumstances of the offense and any contemporaneous offenses, various aggravating and mitigating factors, the involvement of any co-defendant, and the strength of the prosecution's evidence of guilt.

The unadjusted figures show that death sentences were imposed in 11 per cent of the death-eligible cases involving white victims, but only in one per cent of the death-eligible cases involving black victims. When race of the defendant and the victim were simultaneously controlled, the figures showed that death sentences were imposed in 22 per cent of the black defendant/white victim cases, eight per cent of the white defendant/white victim cases, three per cent of the white defendant/black victim cases, and one per cent of the black defendant/black victim cases.

[e] The analysis leading to this conclusion is illustrated by their assessment of the possible significance of the suspect's prior record:

"[T]he criminal record of the suspect undoubtedly has an effect on the chances of a death sentence. Moreover, we know that black defendants in general are more likely to have serious criminal records than white defendants, and we can safely assume that this general relationship applies to the homicide suspects in our study. This association, however, explains very little. After controlling for level of aggravation, the race of the suspect is not a significant predictive variable, and the principal racial pattern that we did find—discrimination by race of victim—persisted when we controlled for the race of the suspect. Indeed, we were careful to make sure that the effect of the race of the victim could be determined separately from any possible race-of-suspect effect. To assert that the criminal records of the *suspects* might account for discrimination by the race of the *victim* one would have to suppose that, controlling for the nature of the homicide and for their relationship to the victims, the killers of whites, regardless of their own race, were more likely to have serious criminal records than the killers of blacks. We know of no empirical or logical basis for such a supposition, and it seems unlikely that any unforeseen effect of this type could be large enough and consistent enough to have the power to explain the racial patterns that we have reported."

[f] The findings from this study are reported in Discrimination and Arbitrariness in Georgia's Capital Charging and Sentencing System: A Preliminary Report, an unpublished document filed by the petitioner in McCleskey v. Zant, 580 F.Supp. 338 (N.D. Ga.1984). Some of the data have been published in Baldus, Woodworth & Pulaski, Monitoring and Evaluating Contemporary Death Sentencing Systems: Lessons From Georgia, 18 U.C. Davis L.Rev. 1375 (1985), and Baldus, Pulaski & Woodworth, Comparative Review of Death Sentences: An Empirical Study of the Georgia Experience, 24 J.Crim.L. and Criminology 661 (1983).

Professor Baldus and his colleagues used a variety of multiple regression techniques to control simultaneously for all the variables that could explain the disparity. Using one type of regression analysis ("weighted least squares") and controlling simultaneously for 230 factors, they found a .06 partial regression coefficient for race of victim, indicating that a white-victim crime was six percentage points more likely to result in a death sentence than a comparable black-victim crime. Using another type of regression analysis ("logistic"), which controlled simultaneously for the nine most significant non-racial variables, they found that the odds of receiving a death sentence were three times higher if the victim was white than if the victim was black.[g]

Both types of regression analysis were also conducted while controlling for the 20 legitimate variables most strongly associated with death sentences (e.g., prior record for serious felony, stranger-victim, multiple victims). In the weighted least squares analysis, the partial regression coefficient for race-of-victim was .09—an effect comparable in magnitude to that associated with occurrence of a contemporaneous felony. In the logistic analysis, the odds of receiving a death sentence were 4.3 times higher if the victim was white than if the victim was black. Baldus and his colleagues concluded that in each analysis "the race of victim coefficient suggests an effect which is stronger or comparable to a number of important aggravating and mitigating factors."

The data also showed that the racial disparity was particularly pronounced in cases involving the two statutory aggravating factors that establish the predicate(s) for a death sentence in most cases—contemporaneous felony and vileness.[h] Whereas the race-of-victim coefficient was .06 for all cases (when controlling for 230 variables in a weighted least squares analysis), it was .10 for the (b)(2) and (b)(7) cases. When a logistic analysis was used (controlling for 14 statistically significant non-racial factors), the average defendant's odds of receiving a death sentence were enhanced by a factor of 4.6 if the victim was white than if the victim was black in (b)(2) and (b)(7) cases.[i] In contrast, race-of-victim effects were not strongly apparent in analyses conducted separately for cases with the following statutory aggravating circumstances: murder for hire, killing to avoid arrest, risk of death to two or more in public, defendant a prisoner or escapee, and police-officer victim.

One other aspect of the analysis should be mentioned. The researchers used a multiple regression analysis to identify the 15 legitimate non-racial variables that best predicted the cases in which death sentences would be imposed. They then used these variables (and their respective regression coefficients) to rank the cases according to the

[g] Although the weighted least squares regression analysis also indicated that a black defendant was four percentage points more likely to receive a death sentence than a comparable white defendant, the race-of-defendant effect was only weakly evident in the logistic analysis.

[h] One or both of these factors was present in 89% of the death-sentenced cases.

The study refers to these two statutory aggravating circumstances by their statutory labels in Georgia—paragraphs (b)(2) and (b)(7) respectively.

[i] Again, the weighted least squares analysis also showed a statistically significant race-of-defendant effect (.10), but the logistic analysis did not.

estimated likelihood of a death sentence, and divided the cases into eight roughly equal groups in which the death sentencing rate ranged from zero to .39. For each of these eight subgroups, they calculated the racial disparities. Because the eighth subgroup accounted for 86 per cent of all death sentences, the racial disparities were most evident in these cases (the race-of-victim coefficient was .27). The researchers then selected the slice of cases (20 per cent) with the highest predicted likelihood of receiving a death sentence and subdivided them into eight subgroups in which the death sentencing rate ranged from zero to .88.

The data showed that the race-of-victim effect was least significant in the least aggravated and most aggravated cases, and was most significant in cases involving "intermediate" levels of aggravation. In general, white victim crimes at intermediate levels of aggravation were 20 percentage points more likely to receive the death penalty than equally aggravated black victim crimes. Baldus and his colleagues summarized their conclusions as follows: *

"[R]acial factors appear to play their largest role in cases the circumstances of which neither preclude a death sentence nor compel it. At the lowest levels of aggravation and sentencing risk there are virtually no death sentences imposed, and no racial disparities occur. Conversely, in the most aggravated cases, for which a death sentence is a virtual certainty, juries and prosecutors respond punitively to the circumstances of the case regardless of racial factors. In the intermediate groups of cases, however, the sentencing outcome is not clear; the facts allow the maximum exercise of discretionary judgment. Here is where one finds racial factors exerting the greatest impact.

"These circumstances support what is sometimes called the 'liberation hypothesis.' . . . The ambiguity of the situation in terms of the legitimate criteria 'liberate[s]' the decision-makers to consider other, possibly less appropriate factors. The [data] suggest that when the circumstances of capital cases included in our studies generate this 'liberating' effect, racial considerations have been a major influence.

"[The data] also demonstrate a classic interaction effect. [A]mong black defendant cases, death sentencing rates rise faster in the face of increasing levels of aggravation in white victim cases than they do in black victim cases. [A]mong white victim cases, death sentencing rates respond more sharply to increasing levels of aggravation in black defendant cases than in white defendant cases. These differing responses support the hypothesis that Georgia operates a dual system for processing homicide cases, one which tolerates higher levels of aggravation in black victim than in white victim cases before a death sentence is sought or imposed. And when processing white victim cases it is a system which tolerates more aggravation when the defendant is white."

---

* The excerpts below are reproduced with the permission of the authors.

4. ***McCleskey v. Zant.***   Extensive evidence based on the Baldus
study was presented at an evidentiary hearing in McCleskey v. Zant,
580 F.Supp. 338 (N.D.Ga.1984), in support of the claim that Georgia's
capital sentencing law is being administered in an unconstitutionally
discriminatory manner.   The district court rejected the claim.   That
ruling was affirmed, 9–3, in McCleskey v. Kemp, 753 F.2d 877 (11th Cir.
1985) (en banc).   The majority of the Court of Appeals was willing to
assume that the study was valid (i.e., that it accurately measured what
it purported to measure), but held that the proven racial disparities
were not substantial enough to establish a constitutional violation:

"The Baldus study revealed an essentially rational system in
which high aggravation cases were more likely to result in the
death sentence than low aggravation cases.   As one would expect
in a rational system, factors such as torture and multiple victims
greatly increased the likelihood of receiving the penalty. . . .
Although no single factor, or combination of factors, will irrefuta-
bly lead to the death sentence in every case, the system in
operation follows the pattern the legislature intended, which the
Supreme Court found constitutional in *Gregg,* and sorts out cases
according to levels of aggravation, as gauged by legitimate factors. . . .

"Taking the six per cent bottom line revealed in the Baldus
figures as true, this figure is not sufficient to overcome the
presumption that the statute is operating in a constitutional
manner.   In any discretionary system, some imprecision must be
tolerated, and the Baldus study is simply insufficient to support a
ruling, in the context of a statute that is operating much as
intended, that racial factors are playing a role in the outcome
sufficient to render the system as a whole arbitrary and capricious. . . .

"McCleskey's argument about the heightened influence of the
race-of-victim factor in the mid-range of cases requires a somewhat different analysis. . . . [Baldus'] testimony leaves this
court unpersuaded that there is a rationally classified, well-
defined class of cases in which it can be demonstrated that a
race-of-the-victim effect is operating with a magnitude approxi-
mating 20 per cent.

"Assuming arguendo, however, that the 20 per cent disparity
is an accurate figure, it is apparent that such a disparity only in
the mid-range cases, and not in the system as a whole, cannot
provide the basis for a systemwide challenge.   As previously
discussed, the system as a whole is operating in a rational
manner, and not in a manner that can fairly be labeled arbitrary
or capricious.   A valid system challenge cannot be made only
against the mid-range cases.   Baldus did not purport to define
the mid-range of cases; nor is such a definition possible.   It is
simply not satisfactory to say that the racial effect operates in
'close cases' and therefore that the death penalty will be set aside
in 'close cases.' . . .

"Viewed broadly, it would seem that the statistical evidence presented here, assuming its validity, confirms rather than condemns the system. In a state where past discrimination is well documented, the study showed no discrimination as to the race of the defendant. The marginal disparity based on the race of the victim tends to support the state's contention that the system is working far differently from the one which *Furman* condemned. In pre-*Furman* days, there was no rhyme or reason as to who got the death penalty and who did not. But now, in the vast majority of cases, the reasons for a difference are well documented. That they are not so clear in a small percentage of the cases is no reason to declare the entire system unconstitutional."

Three judges dissented. Judge Johnson explained why he regarded the Baldus findings as constitutionally significant:

"[T]he majority takes comfort in the fact that the level of aggravation powerfully influences the sentencing decision in Georgia. Yet this fact alone does not reveal a 'rational' system at work. The statistics not only show that the number of aggravating factors is a significant influence; they also point to the race of the victim as a factor of considerable influence. Where racial discrimination contributes to an official decision, the decision is unconstitutional even though discrimination was not the primary motive.

"Neither can the racial impact be explained away by the need for discretion in the administration of the death penalty or by any 'presumption that the statute is operating in a constitutional manner.' The discretion necessary to the administration of the death penalty does not include the discretion to consider race: the jury may consider any proper aggravating factors, but it may not consider the race of the victim as an aggravating factor. And a statute deserves a presumption of constitutionality only where there is real uncertainty as to whether race influences its application. Evidence such as the Baldus study, showing that the pattern of sentences can only be explained by assuming a significant racial influence, overcomes whatever presumption exists.

". . . In support of his contention that juries were more inclined to rely on race when other factors did not militate toward one outcome or another, Dr. Baldus noted that a more pronounced racial influence appeared in cases of medium aggravation (20 percent) than in all cases combined (six per cent). The majority states that racial impact in a subset of cases cannot provide the basis for a systemwide challenge. However, there is absolutely no justification for such a claim. The fact that a system mishandles a sizeable subset of cases is persuasive evidence that the entire system operates improperly. A system can be applied arbitrarily and capriciously even if it resolves the obvious cases in a rational manner. Admittedly, the lack of a precise definition of medium aggravation cases could lead to

either an overstatement or understatement of the racial influence. Accepting, however, that the racial factor is accentuated
to some degree in the middle range of cases, the evidence of
racial impact must be taken all the more seriously. . . .

"Thus, the Baldus study offers a convincing explanation of the
disproportionate effects of Georgia's death penalty system. It
shows a clear pattern of sentencing that can only be explained in
terms of race, and it does so in a context where direct evidence of
intent is practically impossible to obtain. It strains the imagina-
tion to believe that the significant influence on sentencing left
unexplained by 230 alternative factors is random rather than
racial, especially in a state with an established history of racial
discrimination. . . . "

In another dissenting opinion, Judge Clark noted the Supreme
Court's observation, in Rose v. Mitchell, 443 U.S. 545 (1979), that
"[d]iscrimination on the basis of race, odious in all aspects, is especially
pernicious in the administration of justice." He continued:

"If discrimination is especially pernicious in the administration of justice, it is nowhere more sinister and abhorrent than
when it plays a part in the decision to impose society's ultimate
sanction, the penalty of death. It is also a tragic fact that this
discrimination is very much a part of the country's experience
with the death penalty. [As] the majority points out, the new
post-*Furman* statutes have improved the situation but the Baldus
study shows that race is still a very real factor in capital cases in
Georgia. Some of this is conscious discrimination, some of it
unconscious, but it is nonetheless real and it is important that we
at least admit that discrimination is present.

"Finally, the state of Georgia also has no compelling interest
to justify a death penalty system that discriminates on the basis
of race. Hypothetically, if a racial bias reflected itself randomly
in 20 per cent of the convictions, one would not abolish the
criminal justice system. Ways of ridding the system of bias
would be sought but absent a showing of bias in a given case,
little else could be done. The societal imperative of maintaining
a criminal justice system to apprehend, punish, and confine
perpetrators of serious violations of the law would outweigh the
mandate that race or other prejudice not infiltrate the legal
process. In other words, we would have to accept that we are
doing the best that can be done in a system that must be
administered by people, with all their conscious and unconscious
biases.

"However, such reasoning cannot sensibly be invoked and
bias cannot be tolerated when considering the death penalty, a
punishment that is unique in its finality. The evidence in this
case makes a prima facie case that the death penalty in Georgia
is being applied disproportionately because of race. The percentage differentials are not de minimis. To allow the death penalty
under such circumstances is to approve a racial preference in the

most serious decision our criminal justice system must make. This is a result our Constitution cannot tolerate."

A case like *McCleskey* will eventually make its way to the Supreme Court. What should the Court do?

SECTION 2: GRADING OF NON–CAPITAL HOMICIDES

SUBSECTION A: INTENTIONAL HOMICIDE

FREDDO v. STATE

Supreme Court of Tennessee, 1913.
127 Tenn. 376, 155 S.W. 170.

WILLIAMS, J. The plaintiff in error, Raymond Freddo, was indicted . . . for the crime of murder in the first degree . . . and was found by the jury guilty of murder in the second degree; his punishment being fixed at 10 years imprisonment. [I]t is . . . urged . . . that the facts adduced did not warrant a verdict of guilty of a crime of degree greater than voluntary manslaughter, if guilt of any crime be shown.

[I]n the roundhouse department of the shops of the Nashville & Chattanooga Railway Company from 50 to 60 men were employed, among them being . . . Freddo and the deceased, Higginbotham. Freddo was at the time about 19 years of age; he had been from the age of four years an orphan; he had been reared thereafter in an orphanage, and yet later in the family of a Nashville lady, with result that he had been morally well trained. The proof shows him to have been a quiet, peaceable, high-minded young man of a somewhat retiring disposition. Due, perhaps, to the loss of his mother in his infancy, and to his gratitude to his foster mother, he respected womanhood beyond the average young man, and had a decided antipathy to language of obscene trend or that reflected on womanhood.

Deceased, Higginbotham, was about six years older than Freddo, [was taller than Freddo and outweighed him by about 30 pounds,] and was one of a coterie of the roundhouse employees, . . . given to the use . . . of the expression "son of a bitch"—meant to be taken as an expression of good fellowship or of slight deprecation. Deceased, prior to the date of the difficulty, had applied this epithet to . . . Freddo without meaning offense, but was requested by the latter to discontinue it, as it was not appreciated, but resented. It was not discontinued, but repeated, and Freddo so chafed under it that he again warned deceased not to repeat it; and the fact of Freddo's sensitiveness being noted by the mechanic, J.J. Lynch, under whom Freddo served as helper, Lynch sought out deceased in Freddo's behalf and warned him to desist. On

Lynch's telling deceased of the offense given to plaintiff in error, and that "he will hurt you some day," deceased replied, "The son of a bitch, he won't do nothing of the kind." [D]eceased is shown to have been habitually foul-mouthed, overbearing, and "nagging and tormenting" in language, and at times in conduct.

On the afternoon of the tragedy, Higginbotham and Freddo were engaged . . . in the packing of a locomotive cylinder . . . . Deceased, so engaged, was in a squatting posture, holding a pinch bar. It appears that some one, thought by deceased to have been Freddo, had spilled oil on deceased's tool box, and as he proceeded with his work the latter, in hearing of the crew, remarked: "Freddo, what in the hell did you want to spill that oil on that box for. If some one spilled oil on your box, you would be raising hell, wouldn't you, you son of a bitch?" Freddo asked Higginbotham if he meant to call the former a son of a bitch, and was replied to in an angry and harsh tone: "Yes, you are a son of a bitch." The plaintiff in error, standing to the left of and about eight feet away from deceased, seeing deceased preparing to rise or rising from his squatting posture, seized a steel bar, one yard long and one inch thick, lying immediately at hand, and advancing struck deceased a blow on the side of his head, above the left ear, and extending slightly to the front and yet more to the rear of the head, but not shown to have been delivered from the rear. Deceased in rising had not gained an erect posture, but is described as stooping at the time the blow was delivered.

Plaintiff in error testified that deceased, in rising, was apparently coming at him; that deceased made a gesture, and had his hand behind him all the time; that he (Freddo) believed that Higginbotham was going to strike; and that he struck because of anger at the epithet and to defend himself, but would not have struck but for deceased's movement. It appears, however, that deceased had not gained a position where he could strike the accused, and it does not appear that he had anything in his hand with which to attack; and the evidence preponderates against the prisoner on the point of deceased's having his hand behind him.

[W]e deem the facts sufficient to show that plaintiff in error killed deceased under the impulse of sudden heat of passion; but, no matter how strong his passionate resentment was, it did not suffice to reduce the grade of the crime from murder to voluntary manslaughter, unless that passion were due to a provocation such as the law deemed reasonable and adequate—that is, a provocation of such a character as would, in the mind of an average reasonable man, stir resentment likely to cause violence, obscuring the reason, and leading to action from passion rather than judgment.

While the testimony indicates that plaintiff in error was peculiarly sensitive in respect of the use by another, as applied to him, of the opprobrious epithet used by deceased, yet we believe the rule to be firmly fixed on authority to the effect that the law proceeds in testing the adequacy of the provocation upon the basis of a mind ordinarily constituted—of the fair average mind and disposition. . . .

The rule in this state is, as it was at common law, that the law regards no mere epithet or language, however violent or offensive, as sufficient provocation for taking life. . . .

It is contended, however, that while the use of such an epithet may not of itself be sufficient cause for provocation, yet that, looked to in connection with the conduct of the deceased at the time of its utterance, in rising from a squatting to a stooping posture, just reached as the blow was delivered, the epithet and the act in combination make a cause of adequate provocation.

The common-law rule appears to be that an assault, too slight in itself to be a sufficient provocation, may become such when accompanied by offensive language. [But the jury was correctly charged on the] proper definitions of and distinctions between murder in the second degree and manslaughter . . . . The stroke having been delivered by plaintiff in error at a moment when deceased may have been found by the jury not to have been in a position to assault him, and since the determination of the fact whether the provocation relied upon in such a case is adequate or reasonable is, under a proper charge, for the jury, we hold that the errors assigned and here treated of are not well taken.

. . .

Affirmed.

In view of the very good character of the young plaintiff in error, as disclosed in the record, and of the peculiar motive and the circumstances under which he acted, we feel constrained to and do recommend to the governor of the state that his sentence be commuted to such punishment as the executive may, in the light of this record and opinion, in his discretion think proper. To allow time for such application, execution of sentence is ordered stayed for 10 days from this date.

NOTES ON THE MITIGATION OF MURDER TO MANSLAUGHTER AT COMMON LAW

1. **The Provocation Formula.** As was pointed out in the introductory note to this chapter, the distinction between murder and manslaughter originally emerged as a device for isolating a class of offenders who would be subjected to capital punishment. Those convicted of murder received the mandatory death penalty; those convicted of manslaughter received a lesser sentence. It was in this context that the law of provocation first developed. When American jurisdictions narrowed the category of murder to which capital punishment applied, the law continued to recognize the distinction between murder and manslaughter as a grading device. Today, every state employs some variation of the provocation formula to distinguish between two distinct grades of non-capital criminal homicide.

The origins of the doctrine and its early meaning are summarized in the following excerpt from Ashworth, The Doctrine of Provocation, 35 Camb.L.J. 292, 293 (1976): *

"When in the 17th century the defence of provocation began to assume a recognisable form and function, it took its place within a rigidly structured law of homicide. Killings were presumed to proceed from malice aforethought: if there was no evidence of express malice, then the law would imply malice. Evidence of provocation came to be accepted in rebuttal of this implication of malice, the theory being that such evidence showed that the cause of the killing lay not in some secret hatred or design in the breast of the slayer but rather in provocation given by the deceased which inflamed the slayer's passions. Hale thus 'inquired, what is such a provocation, as will take off the presumption of malice in him that kills another,' and he discussed the various forms of provocation which the judges had ruled sufficient or insufficient for this purpose. These decisions were conveniently summarised by Lord Holt, C.J., in his judgment in Mawgridge, [1707] Kel. 119, where the categories of provocation are set forth. It was generally agreed that any striking of the accused would be sufficient provocation, and Lord Holt discussed four further types of provocation which had been legally sufficient to rebut the implication of malice: (i) angry words followed by an assault, (ii) the sight of a friend or relative being beaten, (iii) the sight of a citizen being unlawfully deprived of his liberty, and (iv) the sight of a man in adultery with the accused's wife. The categories of provocation insufficient to reduce murder to manslaughter were (i) words alone, (ii) affronting gestures, (iii) trespass to property, (iv) misconduct by a child or servant, and (v) breach of contract."

The rule applied in *Freddo* that "the law regards no mere epithet . . . as sufficient provocation" is thus consistent with early statements of the concept of provocation. The same rule would be applied with equal rigor by many courts today.

Beginning in the middle of the 19th century, however, another aspect of the provocation formula was developed. In Maher v. People, 10 Mich. 212, 220–22 (1862), provocation was described as follows:

"The principle involved . . . would seem to suggest as the true general rule, that reason should, at the time of the act, be disturbed or obscured by passion to an extent which *might render* ordinary men, of fair average disposition, *liable* to act rashly or without due deliberation or reflection, and from passion, rather than judgment. . . .

"In determining whether the provocation is sufficient or reasonable, *ordinary human nature*, or the average of men recognized as men of fair average mind and disposition, should be taken as the standard . . . .

* Reprinted with permission of the author and the Cambridge University Press.

"The judge, it is true, must, to some extent, assume to decide upon the sufficiency of the alleged provocation, when the question arises upon the admission of testimony, and when it is so clear as to admit of no reasonable doubt upon any theory, that the alleged provocation could not have had any tendency to produce such state of mind, in ordinary men, he may properly exclude the evidence; but, if the alleged provocation be such as to admit of any reasonable doubt, whether it might not have had such tendency, it is much safer, . . . and more in accordance with principle, to let the evidence go to the jury under the proper instructions. [T]he question of the reasonableness or adequacy of the provocation must depend upon the facts of each particular case. . . . The law can not with justice assume, by the light of past decisions, to catalogue all the various facts and combinations of facts which shall be held to constitute reasonable or adequate provocation. . . ."[a]

It seems clear that the *Maher* formulation, which implies that all of the old rules of exclusion should be discarded, goes considerably beyond what most American courts would traditionally have accepted. What has happened instead is that the reliance on the reasonable person has in most cases been merged with the old exclusions to produce a three-stage analysis: (i) the defendant must in fact have acted in a heat of passion based on sudden provocation; (ii) the events giving rise to the provocation must have been legally adequate, i.e., not one of the events, such as mere epithet, excluded from the mitigation even though it may in fact have provoked "heat of passion" in the defendant;[b] and (iii) the provocation must also have been of a sufficient degree to have excited the passions of a reasonable person. The existence of actual and legally sufficient provocation is not enough, in other words, since the jury must still pass on the reasonableness of the defendant's response to the provoking events. How many of these steps are reflected in the analysis in *Freddo?* Is the *Maher* approach to be preferred? The pre-19th century rule that ignores the third step?

2. **Rationale for the Provocation Formula.** These questions can be answered only by thinking about why the rule of provocation was developed and what its modern function should be. It is helpful to subdivide this inquiry into three separate questions corresponding to the three steps in the analysis suggested above.

(i) **Defendant in Fact Provoked.** Why should it matter that the defendant killed in the "heat of passion" produced by provoking events? The traditional answer to this question is that a killing which "is the result of temporary excitement" is substantially less blamewor-

[a] A comparable and contemporaneous development occurred in England. In Regina v. Welsh, 11 Cox C.C. 336 (1869), the court noted that "[t]he law contemplates the case of a reasonable man, and requires that the provocation shall be . . . that such a man might naturally be induced, in the anger of the moment, to commit the act."

[b] For a discussion of the various rules the courts have developed to test the "adequacy" of provocation, see Note, Manslaughter and the Adequacy of Provocation: The Reasonableness of the Reasonable Man, 106 U.Pa.L.Rev. 1021 (1958).

thy than a killing which is the result of "wickedness of heart or innate recklessness of disposition." [c] Glanville Williams had the same point in mind when he said in Provocation and the Reasonable Man, [1954] Crim.L.Rev. 740, 742, that:

> "Surely the true view of provocation is that it is a concession to 'the frailty of human nature' in those exceptional cases where the legal prohibition fails of effect. It is a compromise, neither conceding the propriety of the act nor exacting the full penalty for it."

Are you satisfied by this explanation? Is "heat of passion" more justified as a mitigation that excludes persons from the death penalty (as was its original function) than as a mitigation leading to different authorized terms of imprisonment (as is its modern function)?

(ii) **Legally Adequate Provocation.** The concept of "legally adequate" provocation has been abandoned by the Model Penal Code and by many American statutes that have followed its lead. England also abandoned it in the Homicide Act of 1957. The drafters of the Model Code defend this result on the ground that the central blameworthiness question "cannot be resolved successfully by categorization of conduct" and that the correct approach should be "to abandon preconceived notions of what constitutes adequate provocation and to submit that question to the jury's deliberation." [d] Is this the better approach? Does the concept of legally adequate provocation reduce the opportunity for individual ad hoc determinations by the jury and thus contribute to the fairness of the criminal process? Should it be retained for this reason? For any other reason?

(iii) **The Objective Standard.** Why should an objective standard be used for measuring the mitigating significance of the provocation to which the defendant reacted? If a reasonable person would have been provoked to the point of losing self-control, is it fair to punish the defendant at all? [e] If the defendant was in fact provoked and acted "in the heat of passion," should not the grade of the offense at least be reduced below that of unprovoked intent-to-kill murders, however confident we are that ordinary people would have remained calm in the face of the provocation? On the other hand, do arguments premised on deterrence suggest that provocation should not be recognized as a mitigation, no matter how reasonable or understandable the circum-

[c] State v. Gounagais, 88 Wash. 304, 311, 153 P. 9, 12 (1915).

[d] ALI, Model Penal Code and Commentaries, § 210.3, p. 61 (1980).

[e] Compare Williams, Provocation and the Reasonable Man, [1954] Crim.L.Rev. 740, 742:

"Plausible as this formulation may appear, it creates a serious problem. In the law of contract and tort, and elsewhere in the criminal law, the test of the reasonable man indicates an ethical standard; but it seems absurd to say that the reasonable man will commit a felony the possible punishment for which is imprisonment for life. To say that the 'ordinary' man will commit this felony is hardly less absurd. The reason why provoked homicide is punished is to deter people from committing the offence; and it is a curious confession of failure on the part of the law to suppose that, notwithstanding the possibility of heavy punishment, an ordinary person will commit it. If the assertion were correct, it would raise serious doubts whether the offense should continue to be punished. [H]ow can it be admitted that the paragon of virtue, the reasonable man, gives way to provocation?"

stances? As you think about these questions, consider the observations of Wechsler & Michael in A Rationale of the Law of Homicide II, 37 Colum.L.Rev. 1261, 1281–82 (1937): *

"Provocation may be greater or less, but it cannot be measured by the intensity of the passions aroused in the actor by the provocative circumstances. It must be estimated by the probability that such circumstances would affect most men in like fashion; although the passions stirred up in the actor were violent, the provocation can be said to be great only if the provocative circumstances would have aroused in most men similar desires of comparable intensity. Other things being equal, the greater the provocation, measured in that way, the more ground there is for attributing the intensity of the actor's passions and his lack of self-control on the homicidal occasion to the extraordinary character of the situation in which he was placed rather than to any extraordinary deficiency in his own character. While it is true, it is also beside the point, that most men do not kill on even the gravest provocation; the point is that the more strongly they would be moved to kill by circumstances of the sort which provoked the actor to the homicidal act, and the more difficulty they would experience in resisting the impulse to which he yielded, the less does his succumbing serve to differentiate his character from theirs. But the slighter the provocation, the more basis there is for ascribing the actor's act to an extraordinary susceptibility to intense passion, to an unusual deficiency in those other desires which counteract in most men the desires which impel them to homicidal acts, or to an extraordinary weakness of reason and consequent inability to bring such desires into play. Moreover, since the homicidal act does not always follow closely upon the provocative circumstances and since the passions which they arouse may in the meantime gain or lose in intensity, provocation must be estimated as of the time of the homicidal act and in the light of those additional circumstances which may have intensified or diminished the actor's passions."

Compare the observations in Ashworth, The Doctrine of Provocation, 35 Camb.L.J. 292, 307–09 (1976): **

"It is contended here that the doctrine of provocation as a qualified defence rests just as much on notions of justification as upon the excusing element of loss of self-control. The term 'partial justification' will be used for this, but the term does not necessarily imply a connection with the legal concept of justifiable force (i.e., in self-defence); its closest relationship is with the moral notion that the punishment of wrongdoers is justifiable. This is not to argue that it is ever morally right to kill a person who does wrong. Rather, the claim implicit in partial justification is that an individual is *to some extent* morally justified in

---

* Reprinted with permission of Professor Wechsler and the Columbia Law Review.   ** Reprinted with permission of the author and the Cambridge University Press.

making a punitive return against someone who intentionally causes him serious offence, and that this serves to differentiate someone who is provoked to lose his self-control and kill from the unprovoked killer. Whereas the paradigmatic case of murder might be an attack on an innocent victim, the paradigm of provocation generally involves moral wrongs by both parties. The victim plays an important role in provocation cases, either as instigator of the conflict or by doing something which the accused regards as a wrong against him. Ordinary language reflects this approach, with characteristic phrases such as 'he brought it on himself,' 'she asked for it' and 'it served him right.' Now the court which tries the accused's case is not standing in judgment upon the victim. But, [contrary to what some judges have said], it does not follow that the court 'is not concerned with blame here—the blame attaching to the dead man.' The complicity of the victim cannot and should not be ignored, for the blameworthiness of his conduct has a strong bearing on the court's judgment of the seriousness of the provocation and the reasonableness of the accused's failure to control himself. . . .

"The objective standard may also be supported by causal reasoning. The offender's responsibility for a provoked killing may be said to be reduced by the fact that the victim's wrongful action was the original cause of the offender's loss of self-control. [T]he objective standard might be defended on the basis that it distinguishes those cases in which the provocation was the substantial cause of the loss of self-control from those in which the provocation was so trivial that the loss of control is attributable rather to an abnormal weakness in the accused's temperament. The defence of provocation implies that the loss of self-control was *caused* by the provocation: if the provocation was objectively slight, this suggests that the substantial cause of the loss of control was not the provocation but rather some weakness (or wickedness) in the accused's character, and the case then becomes one of murder or mental abnormality—not provocation.

" 'When we plead . . . provocation, there is genuine uncertainty or ambiguity as to what we mean—is *he* partly responsible, because he roused a violent impulse or passion in me, so that it wasn't truly or merely me acting "of my own accord" (excuse)? Or is it rather that, he having done me such injury, I was entitled to retaliate (justification)?' [W]e have attempted here to defend the law's objective standard on the ground that it respects these elements in the concept of provocation. But, although legal commentators have tended to neglect the element of partial justification, its importance should not be over-emphasized. Standing alone, it would lead the courts to indulge those who take the law into their own hands and deliberately wreak vengeance upon those who insult or wrong them. Without the subjective condition of sudden loss of self-control, as judges have frequently observed, every divorce petitioner who killed the corespondent might be entitled to have his crime reduced from murder to manslaughter. But, [on the other hand], without the objective standard and its flavour of partial justification, everyone who killed another in a fit of temper or rage would be entitled to have his crime reduced to manslaughter upon provocation, irrespective of the seriousness of the provocation and irrespective of whether the substantial cause of his loss of self-control lay in the provocation received or in his own fault or mental abnormality."

Are you persuaded that an objective standard should be required? Does it help to think of the provocation mitigation as derived partially from concepts of excuse and partially from concepts of justification? [f]

3. **Cooling Time.** Any statement of the rule of provocation must also take account of the requirement that the killing be the result of sudden passion engendered by the provoking event and must occur before a sufficient interval has passed "to permit the passions to cool and to allow thought and reflection and reason to reassert itself." [g] Many courts have followed a three-step analysis of the cooling-time question similar to that employed for the main body of the provocation rule: (i) the defendant's passion must not in fact have abated; (ii) the passage of a period of time sufficient for reason to be restored will preclude the defense as a matter of law; and (iii) it is in any event a question for the jury whether a reasonable person would have cooled off in the interval between the provocation and the act of killing.

State v. Gounagias, 88 Wash. 304, 153 P. 9 (1915), is a dramatic illustration of the operation of the "cooling time" requirement. The defendant and the deceased lived in the same house. Defendant became quite drunk on the evening of April 19, 1914—so drunk that he fell helpless and almost unconscious on the floor. Deceased, after making many insulting remarks about defendant and his wife, committed sodomy on the defendant while he lay there. Deceased then left the house, and shortly moved to another dwelling. The next day, defendant confronted the deceased about the sodomy, but they parted after defendant asked the deceased not to tell anyone what had happened. The deceased spread the story widely, however, and defendant was continuously taunted by numerous acquaintances about the incident. On April 30, a revolver that defendant had ordered on April 18 arrived, and he placed it in the mattress of his bed. The continual taunting caused defendant severe emotional distress and frequent headaches.

---

[f] The ethical basis of the provocation mitigation is explored in Dressler, Rethinking Heat of Passion: A Defense in Search of a Rationale, 73 J.Crim.Law & Criminology 421 (1982). Professor Dressler concludes that the mitigation should be derived from the ethics of excuse, not the ethics of justification. See pages 511–12, supra. In particular, he argues that the provoked defendant is less blameworthy because his capacity for choice has been limited by the provoking situation. He also argues that under some circumstances—those "which would render the ordinarily reasonable and law-abiding person in the same situation liable to become so emotionally upset that he would be wholly incapable of controlling his conduct"—provocation should be a complete defense. For discussion of the exculpatory effect of situational excuse under present law, see the notes on duress and situational compulsion. See pages 619–25, supra.

[g] State v. Lee, 36 Del. 11, 19, 171 A. 195, 198 (1933). Compare the language of the Georgia statute reproduced in Appendix B, page 5, infra.

As a result, he stayed home from work on May 6. That evening, he entered a coffeehouse and was again taunted by about 10 of his acquaintances. He became so excited and enraged that, as he sought to testify, "he lost all control of his reason," and resolved to kill the deceased. He went home, picked up his gun and loaded it, went to the nearby house where the deceased lived, entered the house, found the deceased asleep, and, without waking him, emptied the revolver into the deceased's head. He then returned to his house, removed the discharged cartridges, put the gun back in his mattress, and went to bed. He was arrested shortly thereafter.

Evidence of provocation was excluded from the defendant's trial for murder, and he was convicted. On appeal, the Washington Supreme Court held the evidence properly excluded and affirmed the conviction. The court first reviewed the law on provocation and the cooling-time requirement, and then reasoned:

> "The offered evidence makes it clear that the appellant knew and appreciated for days before the killing the full meaning of the words, signs, and vulgar gestures of his [acquaintances] which, as the offer shows, he had encountered from day to day for about three weeks following the original outrage, wherever he went. The final demonstration in the coffeehouse was nothing new. It was exactly what the appellant, from his experience for the prior three weeks, must have anticipated. To say that it alone tended to create the sudden passion and heat of blood essential to mitigation is to ignore the admitted fact that the same thing had created no such condition on its repeated occurrence during the prior three weeks. To say that these repeated demonstrations, coupled with the original outrage, *culminated* in a sudden passion and heat of blood when he encountered the same character of demonstration in the coffeehouse on the night of the killing, is to say that sudden passion and heat of blood in the mitigative sense may be a cumulative result of repeated reminders of a single act of provocation occurring weeks before, and this, whether that provocation be regarded as the original outrage or the spreading of the story among appellant's associates, both of which he knew and fully realized for three weeks before the fatal night. This theory of the cumulative effect of reminders of former wrongs, not of new acts of provocation by the deceased, is contrary to the idea of sudden anger as understood in the doctrine of mitigation. In the nature of the thing *sudden* anger cannot be cumulative. A provocation which does not cause instant resentment, but which is only resented after being thought upon and brooded over, is not a provocation sufficient in law to reduce intentional killing from murder to manslaughter . . . .

> "The evidence offered had no tendency to prove sudden anger and resentment. On the contrary, it did tend to prove brooding thought, resulting in the design to kill. It was therefore properly excluded."

How should the passage of time between the provoking event and the killing be treated? Did the proffered evidence in *Gounagias* demonstrate that the defendant was *more* or *less* entitled to mitigation? Should "brooding thought, resulting in a design to kill" always be a disqualification?

4. **Characteristics of the Objective Standard.** Both the sufficiency of the original provocation and the passage of adequate time to cool down are measured by an objective standard. How objective should it be? Should it exclude all individual characteristics that may have made the defendant more or less excitable than the average person? The court in *Maher* took the position that "the average of men . . . . of fair average mind and disposition should be taken as the standard—*unless* . . . the person whose guilt is in question be shown to have some peculiar weakness of mind or infirmity of temper, not arising from wickedness of heart or cruelty of disposition."

At the other extreme is the holding in Bedder v. Director of Public Prosecutions, [1954] 2 All E.R. 801. The defendant was an 18-year-old youth who was sexually impotent and emotionally distressed by his condition. On the night of the offense, he saw a prostitute talking to another man, went up and spoke to her when the man left, and was led by her to a quiet court off the street nearby. There he attempted in vain to have intercourse with her. She responded by jeering at him and trying to get away. He tried to hold her, and she slapped him in the face and punched him in the stomach. He grabbed her shoulders and pushed her back, whereupon she kicked him in the groin. He then pulled a knife and stabbed her twice. Defendant testified that: "She kicked me in the privates. Whether it was her knee or foot, I do not know. After that I do not know what happened till she fell." She died from the knife wounds, and the defendant was prosecuted for murder. The trial judge instructed on the nature of the objective standard as follows:

> "The reasonable person, the ordinary person, is the person you must consider when you are considering the effect which any acts, any conduct, any words, might have to justify the steps which were taken in response thereto, so that an unusually excitable or pugnacious individual, or drunken one or a man who is sexually impotent is not entitled to rely on provocation which would not have led an ordinary person to have acted in the way which was in fact carried out."

Defendant argued on appeal that this instruction was wrong, but his conviction was affirmed. Lord Simonds reasoned in part that:

> "It would be plainly illogical not to recognize an unusually excitable or pugnacious temperament in the accused as a matter to be taken into account [as a prior case had established] but yet to recognize for that purpose some unusual physical characteristic, be it impotence or another. Moreover, the proposed distinction appears to me to ignore the fundamental fact that the temper of a man which leads him to react in such and such a way to provocation, is, or may be, itself conditioned by some physical

defect. It is too subtle a refinement for my mind or, I think, for that of a jury to grasp that the temper may be ignored but the physical defect taken into account."

Delores Donovan and Stephanie Wildman attack the ruthless objectivity of the "reasonable man" standard in Is the Reasonable Man Obsolete? A Critical Perspective on Self-Defense and Provocation, 14 Loyola of L.A.L.Rev. 435 (1981). Professors Donovan and Wildman conclude their article with a quotation from Anatole France: "The law in its majestic equality forbids the rich as well as the poor to sleep under bridges, to beg in the streets, and to steal bread." They argue that the law of provocation should take account of such factors as race, sex, socio-economic background, traumatic personal experiences, and other factors relevant to the "social reality" of the defendant's behavior. They would instruct the jury along the following lines in a case where provocation is asserted:

> "In determining whether the killing was done with malice aforethought, you must consider whether, in light of all the evidence in the case, the accused was honestly and understandably aroused to the heat of passion. In determining whether [he or she] was understandably aroused to the heat of passion, you must ask yourselves whether [he or she] could have been fairly expected to avoid the act of homicide."

This instruction does not, they insist, abandon the idea that an objective judgment must be made. What it does is convey that idea to the jury in terms that are more likely to produce just results.

Do you agree that the objectivity of the "reasonable man" standard should be moderated in the law of provocation? If not, how would you answer the argument that the mitigating claim of a black person enraged by repeated racial slurs cannot fairly be judged against the abstraction of the "reasonable man" who has not experienced discrimination? On the other hand, if you agree with the thrust of the argument by Professors Donovan and Wildman, have they put the right questions to the jury? Are you concerned that one jury's concept of what is "fair" may be different from another's? But how else could the inquiry be put? Is this an instance where asking the jury to "do justice in light of all the circumstances" is the only (and right) thing to do?

5. **The Relevance of Mistake.** In W. LaFave & A. Scott, Criminal Law 578 (1972), it is asserted that:

> "It would seem that the provocation is adequate to reduce the homicide to voluntary manslaughter if the killer reasonably believes that the injury to him exists, though actually he has not been injured. In other words, a man's passion directed against another person is reasonable if (i) he reasonably believes that he has been injured by the other, and (ii) a reasonable man who actually has suffered such an injury would be put in a passion directed against the other."

The leading American case for this proposition is State v. Yanz, 74 Conn. 177, 50 A. 37 (1901), where an instruction that "[i]f, in fact, no adultery was going on, and the husband is mistaken as to the fact, though the circumstances were such as to justify a belief . . . of adultery, the offense would not be reduced to manslaughter" was held to be reversible error. The court said that:

"The excitement is the effect of a belief, from ocular evidence, of the actual commission of adultery. It is the belief, so reasonably formed, that excites the uncontrollable passion. Such a belief, though a mistaken one, is calculated to induce the same emotions as would be felt were the wrongful act in fact committed."

One judge dissented, reasoning in part that when anger

"is provoked by the wrongful act of the person slain, who thus brings upon himself the fatal blow, given in the first outbreak of rage, caused by himself, the offense is manslaughter; not only because the voluntary act is, in a way, compelled by an ungovernable rage, but also because the victim is the aggressor; and his wrong, although it cannot justify, may modify, the nature of the homicide thus induced. The court therefore correctly told the jury that to make the offense manslaughter, the injury claimed as a provocation must in fact have been done. Our law of homicide recognizes no provocation as legally competent to so modify the cruelty of intentional, unlawful killing as to reduce the offense to manslaughter, except the provocation involved in an actual and adequate injury and insult."

In Provocation and the Reasonable Man, [1954] Crim.L.Rev. 740, 752–53,* Glanville Williams disagrees with LaFave and Scott and with both the majority and the dissent in *Yanz,* at least as to what the law ought to be:

"There seems to be no doubt that a mistaken belief in provocation is equivalent to actual provocation. The mistake is a defence to the same extent as if the facts supposed were true.

. . . .

"It is further submitted that there is no 'objective' test in respect of the mistake; in other words, the mistake need not be reasonable. As a general principle in criminal matters, a mistake entitles the accused to be treated on the basis that the facts he supposed existed, whether the mistake was reasonable or not; negligence is not generally a question in issue in criminal law. This is not a denial of the objective test of provocation, for the objective test operates only on the facts as they were believed by the accused to exist. The question asked by the objective test is whether, assuming the facts to be as the accused believed them to be, those facts would come within the legal categories of provocation, or would be provocation for an ordinary man. What the objective test discountenances is unusual deficiency of self-control, not the making of an error of observation or inference in point of fact.

---

* Reprinted with permission of the author and the Criminal Law Review.

"The chief practical importance of this is in connection with drunkenness, for a person under the influence of drink is particularly prone to mistake the intentions of another. (An extraordinary instance is that of Booth the actor—the brother of Lincoln's assassin—who on one occasion when he was playing Macbeth under the influence of liquor, refused to be killed, and chased Macduff murderously all through the stalls.) If the drunkard acts in supposed self-defence, he is entitled (on a charge involving intention or recklessness) to have the facts taken as he supposed them to be, however unreasonable the mistake; and if he acts under supposed provocation, the rule is the same."

What would you expect the law to be on these points? How should mistakes be treated in the context of provocation? Should mistakes induced by intoxication be treated differently?

6. **The Relevance of Mental Abnormality.** To what extent is evidence of mental abnormality logically relevant to the criteria governing the reduction of murder to manslaughter? There are two principal contexts in which this question has arisen:

(i) **Provocation.** Is evidence of mental abnormality relevant to the ordinary provocation inquiry? Clearly, such evidence can be probative as to one component of the mitigation—that the defendant in fact acted in the heat of passion generated by the provoking event. For this reason, several courts have admitted such evidence to show that the defendant actually was provoked. But unless the "reasonable man" is to be imbued with the peculiar mental characteristics of the defendant—a step which the courts uniformly have refused to take—the defendant's mental abnormality would not be relevant to whether the "reasonable man" would have been provoked under similar circumstances. Thus, the fact that the standard of adequate provocation requires the application of an objective measure of liability eliminates such evidence from consideration on this branch of the inquiry.

Since evidence of mental abnormality would be relevant on the subjective dimension of the inquiry but not the objective one, should the evidence be admitted or excluded? Do you think the admission of testimony about the defendant's abnormality could mislead and confuse a jury that is told to consider it for one purpose but ignore it for another? Could admission of such evidence push the inquiry too far in a subjective direction? On the other hand, is it fair to foreclose the defendant from a reliable source of evidence on one important aspect of the inquiry?

(ii) **"Imperfect" Justification.** A person charged with an intentional killing will be exonerated if it can be shown that the defendant believed that the killing was a necessary response to unlawful deadly force and if it can be shown that the response was reasonable under the circumstances. Moreover, many courts reduce the offense from murder to manslaughter if only the subjective component of this inquiry is met. As described on page 532, supra, the term "imperfect justification" is often used to describe the rule that permits such mitigation.

In jurisdictions that follow this rule, it seems plain that evidence of mental abnormality can be logically relevant to the subjective consideration that will suffice for mitigation of the offense to manslaughter. Such evidence was held admissible in People v. Wells, 33 Cal.2d 330, 202 P.2d 53 (1949), where the defendant was prosecuted under a statute that read: "Every person undergoing a life sentence in a state prison . . . who, with malice aforethought, commits an assault upon the person of another . . . by any means of force likely to produce great bodily injury, is punishable with death." The defendant sought to introduce evidence that he suffered from a condition that produced an abnormal fear for his own safety causing him to overreact to conduct which he perceived as threatening. He did not claim that he met the objective criterion for exoneration on the ground of self-defense. The court held that "malice aforethought" in the quoted statute had the same meaning as it would in a prosecution for murder, and that because such evidence would be admissible to negate the malice aforethought required for murder (reducing the offense to manslaughter), it was also logically relevant and admissible to negate an essential element of the offense charged.

Suppose Wells had also claimed self-defense and had sought to show that the objective component of that defense had been satisfied. Would the expert testimony be admissible for that purpose? If not, does this cast doubt on whether it should be admitted in a case where both the complete defense and the mitigation are claimed and the evidence is offered for the sole purpose of establishing the mitigation? Can the jury be expected to keep the two issues separate in this context? Is the provocation situation sufficiently different to suggest that the expert testimony might be excluded entirely in provocation cases but admitted for a limited purpose in a case where the defendant claims both complete and imperfect justification?

PEOPLE v. CASASSA

Court of Appeals of New York, 1980.
49 N.Y.2d 668, 427 N.Y.S.2d 769, 404 N.E.2d 1310.

JASEN, JUDGE. The significant issue on this appeal is whether the defendant, in a murder prosecution, established the affirmative defense of "extreme emotional disturbance" which would have reduced the crime to manslaughter in the first degree.

On February 28, 1977, Victoria Lo Consolo was brutally murdered. Defendant Victor Casassa and Miss Lo Consolo had been acquainted for some time prior to the latter's tragic death. They met in August, 1976 as a result of their residence in the same apartment complex. Shortly thereafter, defendant asked Miss Lo Consolo to accompany him to a social function and she agreed. The two apparently dated casually on other occasions until November, 1976 when Miss Lo Consolo informed defendant that she was not "falling in love" with him. Defendant claims that Miss Lo Consolo's candid statement of her feelings "devastated him."

Miss Lo Consolo's rejection of defendant's advances also precipitated a bizarre series of actions on the part of defendant which, he asserts, demonstrate the existence of extreme emotional disturbance upon which he predicates his affirmative defense. Defendant, aware that Miss Lo Consolo maintained social relationships with others, broke into the apartment below Miss Lo Consolo's on several occasions to eavesdrop. These eavesdropping sessions allegedly caused him to be under great emotional stress. Thereafter, on one occasion, he broke into Miss Lo Consolo's apartment while she was out. Defendant took nothing, but, instead, observed the apartment, disrobed and lay for a time in Miss Lo Consolo's bed. During this break-in, defendant was armed with a knife which, he later told police, he carried "because he knew that he was either going to hurt Victoria or Victoria was going to cause him to commit suicide."

Defendant's final visit to his victim's apartment occurred on February 28, 1977. Defendant brought several bottles of wine and liquor with him to offer as a gift. Upon Miss Lo Consolo's rejection of this offering, defendant produced a steak knife which he had brought with him, stabbed Miss Lo Consolo several times in the throat, dragged her body to the bathroom and submerged it in a bathtub full of water to "make sure she was dead." . . .

Defendant waived a jury and proceeded to trial before the County Court. . . . The defendant did not contest the underlying facts of the crime. Instead, the sole issue presented to the trial court was whether the defendant, at the time of the killing, had acted under the influence of "extreme emotional disturbance." Penal Law, § 125.25(1)(a).[a] The defense presented only one witness, a psychiatrist, who testified, in essence, that the defendant had become obsessed with Miss Lo Consolo and that the course which their relationship had taken, combined with several personality attributes peculiar to defendant, caused him to be under the influence of extreme emotional disturbance at the time of the killing.

In rebuttal, the People produced several witnesses. Among these witnesses was a psychiatrist who testified that although the defendant was emotionally disturbed, he was not under the influence of "extreme emotional disturbance" within the meaning of § 125.25(1)(a) of the Penal Law because his disturbed state was not the product of external factors but rather was "a stress he created from within himself, dealing mostly with a fantasy, a refusal to accept the reality of the situation."

The trial court in resolving this issue noted that the affirmative defense of extreme emotional disturbance may be based upon a series of events, rather than a single precipitating cause. In order to be entitled to the defense, the court held, a defendant must show that his reaction to such events was reasonable. In determining whether defendant's emotional reaction was reasonable, the court considered the appropriate test to be whether in the totality of the circumstances the finder of

---

[a] The applicable New York statutes are reproduced in Appendix B, pages 7–9, infra. [Footnote by eds.]

fact could understand how a person might have his reason overcome. Concluding that the test was not to be applied solely from the viewpoint of defendant, the court found that defendant's emotional reaction at the time of the commission of the crime was so peculiar to him that it could not be considered reasonable so as to reduce the conviction to manslaughter in the first degree. Accordingly, the trial court found defendant guilty of the crime of murder in the second degree. The Appellate Division affirmed, without opinion.

On this appeal defendant contends that the trial court erred in failing to afford him the benefit of the affirmative defense of "extreme emotional disturbance." It is argued that the defendant established that he suffered from a mental infirmity not arising to the level of insanity which disoriented his reason to the extent that his emotional reaction, from his own subjective point of view, was supported by a reasonable explanation or excuse. Defendant asserts that by refusing to apply a wholly subjective standard the trial court misconstrued § 125.25(1)(a) of the Penal Law. We cannot agree.

Section 125.25(1)(a) of the Penal Law provides that it is an affirmative defense to the crime of murder in the second degree where "[t]he defendant acted under the influence of extreme emotional disturbance for which there was a reasonable explanation or excuse." This defense allows a defendant charged with the commission of acts which would otherwise constitute murder to demonstrate the existence of mitigating factors which indicate that, although he is not free from responsibility for his crime, he ought to be punished less severely by reducing the crime upon conviction to manslaughter in the first degree.

In enacting § 125.25(1)(a) of the Penal Law, the Legislature adopted the language of the manslaughter provisions of the Model Penal Code (see § 210.3(1)(b). The only substantial distinction between the New York statute and the Model Penal Code is the designation by the legislature of "extreme emotional disturbance" as an "affirmative defense," thus placing the burden of proof on this issue upon defendant.[b] The Model Penal Code formulation, however, as enacted by the legislature, represented a significant departure from the prior law of this state.

The "extreme emotional disturbance" defense is an outgrowth of the "heat of passion" doctrine which had for some time been recognized by New York as a distinguishing factor between the crimes of manslaughter and murder. However, the new formulation is significantly broader in scope than the "heat of passion" doctrine which it replaced.

For example, the "heat of passion" doctrine required that a defendant's action be undertaken as a response to some provocation which prevented him from reflecting upon his actions. Moreover, such reaction had to be immediate. The existence of a "cooling off" period completely negated any mitigating effect which the provocation might otherwise have had. In People v. Patterson, 39 N.Y.2d 288, 303, 383

---

[b] The constitutionality of the burden-of-proof feature of this statute was upheld in Patterson v. New York, 432 U.S. 197 (1977). *Patterson* is reproduced as a main case on page 975, infra. [Footnote by eds.]

N.Y.S.2d 573, 582, 347 N.E.2d 898, 908 (1976) [c], aff'd sub nom. Patterson v. New York, 432 U.S. 197 (1977), however, this court recognized that "[a]n action influenced by an extreme emotional disturbance is not one that is necessarily so spontaneously undertaken. Rather, it may be that a significant mental trauma has affected a defendant's mind for a substantial period of time, simmering in the unknowing subconscious and then inexplicably coming to the fore." This distinction between the past and present law of mitigation, enunciated in *Patterson,* was expressly adopted by the trial court and properly applied in this case.

The thrust of defendant's claim, however, concerns a question arising out of another perceived distinction between "heat of passion" and "extreme emotional disturbance" which was not directly addressed in *Patterson,* to wit: whether, assuming that the defense is applicable to a broader range of circumstances, the standard by which the reasonableness of defendant's emotional reaction is to be tested must be an entirely subjective one. Defendant relies principally upon our decision in *Patterson* and upon the language of the statute to support his claim that the reasonableness of his "explanation or excuse" should be determined solely with reference to his own subjective viewpoint. Such reliance is misplaced.

In *Patterson,* this court was concerned with the question of whether the defendant could properly be charged with the burden of proving the affirmative defense of "extreme emotional disturbance." In deciding that the defendant could constitutionally be required to carry such a burden, we noted that "[t]he purpose of the extreme emotional disturbance defense is to permit the defendant to show that his actions were caused by a mental infirmity not arising to the level of insanity, and that he is less culpable for having committed them." We also noted that "[t]he differences between the present New York statute and its predecessor . . . can be explained by the tremendous advances made in psychology since 1881 and a willingness on the part of the courts, legislators, and the public to reduce the level of responsibility imposed on those whose capacity has been diminished by mental trauma." . . .

Defendant . . . would read *Patterson* as holding that all mental infirmity, short of insanity, must constitute "extreme emotional disturbance" if such infirmity causes the defendant to become emotionally disturbed and the defendant subjectively believed his disturbance had a reasonable explanation or excuse. While it is true that the court in *Patterson* recognized that "extreme emotional disturbance" as contemplated by the statute is a lesser form of mental infirmity than insanity, the court did not hold that all mental infirmities not arising to the level of insanity constitute "extreme emotional disturbance" within the meaning of the statute. This question was not presented to us in *Patterson* and we did not decide it. Defendant's attempt to further extend our holding in *Patterson* to support the proposition that the reasonableness of the explanation or excuse for defendant's emotional

---

[c] The New York Court of Appeals' decision in *Patterson* contains an extensive review of the history of provocation in the New York law of homicide. [Footnote by eds.]

disturbance must be tested from the subjective viewpoint of defendant is completely unavailing, for that case had nothing whatever to do with this issue.

Having determined that our decision in *Patterson* does not require that reasonableness be tested with a completely subjective standard, we must now determine whether the language of the statute or the legislative history of the statute indicates that such a standard is required.

Section 125.25(1)(a) of the Penal Law states it is an affirmative defense to the crime of murder that "[t]he defendant acted under the influence of extreme emotional disturbance for which there was a reasonable explanation or excuse, the reasonableness of which is to be determined from the viewpoint of a person in the defendant's situation under the circumstances as the defendant believed them to be." Whether the language of this statute requires a completely subjective evaluation of reasonableness is a question that has never been decided by this court. . . . Moreover, although several states have enacted identical or substantially similar statutes,[d] only one decision of the highest court of any of our sister states which has addressed this question has been called to our attention (State v. Elliott, 177 Conn. 1, 411 A.2d 3 (1979)) and that court expressly followed Justice Bentley Kassal's well-reasoned opinion in People v. Shelton, 88 Misc.2d 136, 385 N.Y.S.2d 708 (1976). . . .

Consideration of the comments to the Model Penal Code, from which the New York statute was drawn, are instructive. The defense of "extreme emotional disturbance" has two principal components—(i) the particular defendant must have "acted under the influence of extreme emotional disturbance," and (ii) there must have been "a reasonable explanation or excuse" for such extreme emotional disturbance, "the reasonableness of which is to be determined from the viewpoint of a person in the defendant's situation under the circumstances as the defendant believed them to be." The first requirement is wholly subjective—i.e., it involves a determination that the particular defendant did in fact act under extreme emotional disturbance, that the claimed explanation as to the cause of his action is not contrived or sham.

The second component is more difficult to describe—i.e., whether there was a reasonable explanation or excuse for the emotional disturbance. It was designed to sweep away "the rigid rules that have developed with respect to the sufficiency of particular types of provocation, such as the rule that words alone can never be enough," and "avoids a merely arbitrary limitation on the nature of the antecedent circumstances that may justify a mitigation." "The ultimate test, however, is objective; there must be 'reasonable' explanation or excuse for the actor's disturbance." In light of these comments and the necessity of articulating the defense in terms comprehensible to jurors,

[d] The court here cited statutes from eight other states. ALI, Model Penal Code and Commentaries § 210.3, p. 63 (1980), cites three additional statutes that have adopted the "extreme emotional disturbance" formula. [Footnote by eds.]

we conclude that the determination whether there was reasonable explanation or excuse for a particular emotional disturbance should be made by viewing the subjective, internal situation in which the defendant found himself and the external circumstances as he perceived them at the time, however inaccurate that perception may have been, and assessing from that standpoint whether the explanation or excuse for his emotional disturbance was reasonable, so as to entitle him to a reduction of the crime charged from murder in the second degree to manslaughter in the first degree.[2] We recognize that even such a description of the defense provides no precise guidelines and necessarily leaves room for the exercise of judgmental evaluation by the jury. This, however, appears to have been the intent of the draftsmen. "The purpose was explicitly to give full scope to what amounts to a plea in mitigation based upon a mental or emotional trauma of significant dimensions, with the jury asked to show whatever empathy it can." Wechsler, Codification of Criminal Law in the United States: The Model Penal Code, 68 Col.L.Rev. 1425, 1446 (1968).

By suggesting a standard of evaluation which contains both subjective and objective elements, we believe that the drafters of the code adequately achieved their dual goals of broadening the "heat of passion" doctrine to apply to a wider range of circumstances while retaining some element of objectivity in the process. The result of their draftsmanship is a statute which offers the defendant a fair opportunity to seek mitigation without requiring that the trier of fact find mitigation in each case where an emotional disturbance is shown—or as the drafters put it, to offer "room for argument as to the reasonableness of the explanations or excuses offered."

We note also that this interpretation comports with what has long been recognized as the underlying purpose of any mitigation statute. In the words of Mr. Justice Cardozo, referring to an earlier statute: "What we have is merely a privilege offered to the jury to find the lesser degree when the suddenness of the intent, the vehemence of the passion, seems to call irresistibly for the exercise of mercy. I have no objection to giving them this dispensing power, but it should be given to them directly and not in a mystifying cloud of words." B. Cardozo, Law and Literature 100–101.[e] In the end, we believe that what the legislature intended in enacting the statute was to allow the finder of fact the discretionary power to mitigate the penalty when presented with a situation which, under the circumstances, appears to them to have caused an understandable weakness in one of their fellows. Perhaps the chief virtue of the statute is that it allows such discretion without engaging in a detailed explanation of individual circumstances in which the statute would apply, thus avoiding the "mystifying cloud of words" which Mr. Justice Cardozo abhorred.[f]

[2] We emphasize that this test is to be applied to determine whether defendant's emotional disturbance, and not the act of killing, was supported by a reasonable explanation or excuse.

[e] The passage from which this quotation is taken is reproduced in context at pages 783–84, supra. [Footnote by eds.]

[f] In the *Shelton* case, referred to approvingly by the court on page 900, supra, Justice Kassal said of the New York statute: "In reviewing the present provisions, I

We conclude that the trial court, in this case, properly applied the statute. The court apparently accepted, as a factual matter, that defendant killed Miss Lo Consolo while under the influence of "extreme emotional disturbance," a threshold question which must be answered in the affirmative before any test of reasonableness is required. The court, however, also recognized that in exercising its function as trier of fact, it must make a further inquiry into the reasonableness of that disturbance. In this regard, the court considered each of the mitigating factors put forward by defendant, including his claimed mental disability, but found that the excuse offered by defendant was so peculiar to him that it was unworthy of mitigation. The court obviously made a sincere effort to understand defendant's "situation" and "the circumstances as defendant believed them to be," but concluded that the murder in this case was the result of defendant's malevolence rather than an understandable human response deserving of mercy. We cannot say, as a matter of law, that the court erred in so concluding. Indeed, to do so would subvert the purpose of the statute.

In our opinion, this statute would not require that the jury or the court as trier of fact find mitigation on any particular set of facts, but, rather, allows the finder of fact the opportunity to do so, such opportunity being conditional only upon a finding of extreme emotional disturbance in the first instance. In essence, the statute requires mitigation to be afforded an emotionally disturbed defendant only when the trier of fact, after considering a broad range of mitigating circumstances, believes that such leniency is justified. Since the trier of fact found that defendant failed to establish that he was acting "under the influence of extreme emotional disturbance for which there was a reasonable explanation or excuse," defendant's conviction of murder in the second degree should not be reduced to the crime of manslaughter in the first degree. . . .

Accordingly, the order of the Appellate Division should be affirmed.

COOKE, C.J., and GABRIELLI, JONES, WACHTLER, FUCHSBERG and MEYER, JJ., concur.

NOTES ON "EXTREME EMOTIONAL DISTURBANCE" AS A MITIGATION OF MURDER TO MANSLAUGHTER

1. **Questions and Comments on *Casassa*.** The Model Penal Code has led to a reformulation of the law of provocation in at least a dozen states. It is clear from the discussion in *Casassa* that it significantly broadens the common-law standard in a number of respects. Exactly how does it do so? Review the sequence of notes following the *Freddo* case, beginning at page 884, supra. How does the Model Code differ from the common-law provocation inquiry on the issues treated in those notes? If you were a trial judge sitting without a jury, how would you apply the Model Code to *Freddo* (page 882, supra), *Gounagias*

must agree with Professor Robert M. Byrn, who concludes that: 'All that has happened is that "one mystifying cloud of words" has been substituted for another.' Byrn, Homicide Under the Proposed New York Penal Law, 33 Fordham L.Rev. 173, 179 (1964)." [Footnote by eds.]

(page 890, supra), *Bedder* (page 892, supra), and *Yanz* (page 893, supra)? Does the Model Code reach more desirable results in these cases? Does it do a better job of stating the crucial inquiries? Or is it too permissive and not sufficiently protective of human life? The formulation in Oregon, reproduced in Appendix B, page 10, infra, is worded differently from the Model Code. Is it an improvement? [a]

Note that New York authorizes a maximum prison sentence of 25 years for a person whose offense is mitigated from murder to manslaughter by an "extreme emotional disturbance." The maximum in Oregon is 20 years. By contrast, the maximum in Virginia, which follows the traditional common-law provocation formula, is 10 years. See Appendix B, page 3. Does the formula you would be willing to embrace depend in part on the severity with which the offense can be punished? Is changing the label from murder to manslaughter under more relaxed standards more tolerable if the offense is still subject to severe punishments approaching those for murder?

2. **Diminished Responsibility in England.** In the Homicide Act, 1957, 5 & 6 Eliz. 2, c. 11, § 2, England amended the common-law homicide structure as follows:

> "Persons suffering from diminished responsibility.
>
> "(1) Where a person kills or is a party to the killing of another, he shall not be convicted of murder if he was suffering from such abnormality of mind (whether arising from a condition of arrested or retarded development of mind or any inherent causes or induced by disease or injury) as substantially impaired his mental responsibility for his acts and omissions in doing or being a party to the killing.
>
> "(2) On a charge of murder, it shall be for the defence to prove that the person charged is by virtue of this section not liable to be convicted of murder.
>
> "(3) A person who but for this section would be liable, whether as principal or as accessory, to be convicted of murder shall be liable instead to be convicted of manslaughter.
>
> "(4) The fact that one party to a killing is by virtue of this section not liable to be convicted of murder shall not affect the question whether the killing amounted to murder in the case of any other party to it."

The term "abnormality of mind" has since been defined in Regina v. Byrne, [1960] 2 Q.B. 396, 403, in the following terms:

> " 'Abnormality of mind,' which has to be contrasted with the time-honoured expression in the *M'Naghten* rules, 'defect of reason,' means a state of mind so different from that of ordinary human beings that the reasonable man would term it abnormal. It appears to us to be wide enough to cover the mind's activities in all its aspects, not only the perception of physical acts and

---

[a] The Oregon statute is extensively considered in State v. Ott, 297 Or. 375, 686 P.2d 1001 (1984).

matters and the ability to form a rational judgment whether an act is right or wrong, but also the ability to exercise will-power to control physical acts in accordance with that rational judgment."

The English statute was adopted as part of a package of legislation designed to limit the range of offenses for which the death penalty could be imposed. The death penalty itself was abolished in England in 1965, but the 1957 diminished-responsibility provisions were retained. Note that the effect of the 1957 legislation was to broaden the substantive criteria under which evidence of "abnormality of mind" could be considered as a mitigating factor to reduce murder to manslaughter. Functionally, therefore, it operates much as does the provocation mitigation. Like provocation, it provides the jury with a substantive basis for reducing the grade of the offense, and in so doing broadens the base of evidence that can be introduced for this purpose. Do you see how it makes evidence of mental abnormality relevant in ways not encompassed by the *M'Naghten* formulation of the insanity defense and also not encompassed by the provocation mitigation? Is this a desirable development?

3. **Diminished Responsibility Under the "Extreme Emotional Disturbance" Formulation.** In what ways does the "extreme emotional disturbance" formulation broaden the base of psychiatric testimony that can be considered for the purpose of reducing an offense from murder to manslaughter? If a defendant is not insane within the applicable definition used by a given jurisdiction for that defense, is it nonetheless desirable that evidence of mental abnormality be considered as a grading factor that will distinguish murder from manslaughter? Did the court so use such evidence in *Casassa*? Should it have? Do those states in which the Model Penal Code formulation is used now have a diminished responsibility basis for reducing murder to manslaughter analogous to the English concept discussed above? How is the Model Code formula different from the English concept? Which is the better approach?

4. **Burden of Persuasion.** Note that New York places the burden of persuasion on the defendant to prove "extreme emotional disturbance" by a preponderance of the evidence. The court in *Casassa* asserts that the Model Penal Code and the New York statute differ on this point. Did the court correctly interpret the Model Penal Code? As a matter of legislative policy,[b] on whom should the burden be placed on this issue? What factors should be taken into account in resolving this question?

---

b Constitutional questions posed by placing the burden of persuasion on this issue on the defendant are postponed in these materials to pages 967–93, infra. For now you should assume, as the United States Supreme Court held in the *Patterson* case, that the Constitution permits this issue to be resolved as a matter of legislative policy.

SUBSECTION B: UNINTENTIONAL HOMICIDE

ESSEX v. COMMONWEALTH

Supreme Court of Virginia, 1984.
228 Va. 273, 322 S.E.2d 216.

RUSSELL, J., delivered the opinion of the Court.

In this case of first impression, we must determine whether driving under the influence of alcohol, resulting in a fatal collision, can supply the requisite element of implied malice to support a conviction of second-degree murder. . . . A jury convicted Warren Wesley Essex of . . . three counts of second-degree murder . . . .

The collision occurred about 10:45 p.m. on November 20, 1981, at a point on State Route 28 south of its intersection with State Route 17. Essex, driving a Plymouth Duster automobile, entered Route 28, a two-lane, hardsurfaced highway, north of the intersection and headed south. Linda Bates, who was traveling south on Route 28, testified that the Duster entered the highway behind her, passed her across a solid center line, almost struck her car as it returned to the right lane, and ran onto the shoulder of the road, nearly striking a mailbox before it reentered the southbound lane. She said that the Duster passed another vehicle across a solid line and returned to the right lane just in time to avoid a northbound pickup truck. Later, it crossed double solid lines on a curve to pass yet another vehicle. For a distance of six miles, Mrs. Bates watched the car as it swerved from one lane to the other and off the edge of the hard surface.

Although there were "speed bumps" in the pavement north of the intersection, the Duster ran through a red traffic signal at a speed Mrs. Bates estimated at 55 m.p.h. A tractor-trailer truck moving through the intersection on Route 17 "nearly hit the back end of the Plymouth." A mile and a half south of the intersection, the Duster collided with a northbound pickup truck driven by John Gouldthorpe.

Gouldthorpe testified that "[t]he last thing I remember was seeing four headlights, one set in one lane and one in the other." State Trooper Donald Johnson, the investigating officer, testified that when he asked Essex what had happened, the defendant replied, "I was in his lane because my steering had gone . . . I had been having trouble with it all night." An expert mechanic who inspected the Duster at the officer's request testified that "there was nothing loose" and "no failures" in any part of the steering linkage, and that the only damage he found was a break in the steering column which he said was "due to the impact where the front end had been shoved back about a foot."

Debra Gouldthorpe and Nora Neale, passengers in the pickup, and James Carter, a passenger in the defendant's car, died from injuries sustained in the collision.

Essex was treated at Fauquier Hospital for "a large laceration on his knee" and "a small laceration of the tongue." Dr. Steven Von

Elton, the attending physician in the emergency room who examined Essex about 12:30 a.m., testified that Essex was in a "stuperous condition" and that although "the lady next to him was screaming very intensely . . . he was totally unaware of that." Because he could "very easily . . . smell the odor of alcohol . . . at that bedside," Dr. Elton ordered a blood alcohol content test. The test, conducted about two and a half hours after the collision, disclosed an alcohol content of .144 percent. [At this point, the court summarized additional evidence that Essex was intoxicated, primarily from persons who observed him at the scene of accident.]

Where death proximately results from the want of ordinary care as practiced by a reasonably prudent person, the causative negligence is actionable as a tort. If the negligence is so gross, wanton, and culpable as to show a reckless disregard of human life, a killing resulting therefrom, although unintentional, is both a tort and a crime, punishable as involuntary manslaughter.

Criminal homicides in Virginia are classified as follows:

1. Capital murder,

2. First-degree murder,

3. Second-degree murder,

4. Voluntary manslaughter, and

5. Involuntary manslaughter.[a]

Malice, a requisite element for murder of any kind, is unnecessary in manslaughter cases and is the touchstone by which murder and manslaughter cases are distinguished. Malice may be either express or implied by conduct. Whether the defendant acted with malice is a question for the trier of fact. "Express malice is evidenced when 'one person kills another with a sedate, deliberate mind, and formed design.' . . . . Implied malice exists when any *purposeful, cruel act* is committed by one individual against another without any, or without great provocation . . . ." Pugh v. Commonwealth, 223 Va. 663, 668, 292 S.E.2d 339, 341 (1982) (emphasis added).

The authorities are replete with definitions of malice, but a common theme running through them is a requirement that a wrongful act be done "wilfully or purposefully." This requirement of volitional action is inconsistent with inadvertence. Thus, if a killing results from negligence, however gross or culpable, and the killing is contrary to the defendant's intention, malice cannot be implied. In order to elevate the crime to second-degree murder, the defendant must be shown to

---

a Non-capital murder is defined in § 18.2–32 of the Virginia Code in terms similar to the original "premeditation-deliberation" statute in Pennsylvania, reproduced on page 781, supra. Murder in the first degree is a class 2 felony, punishable by life imprisonment or by imprisonment for not less than 20 years. Murder in the second degree is a class 3 felony, punishable by not less than five nor more than 20 years. Voluntary manslaughter is declared in § 18.2–35 to be a class 5 felony (punishable by not less than one nor more than 10 years, or by a local jail sentence), but is otherwise undefined by statute. Involuntary manslaughter is declared by § 18.2–36 to be a class 6 felony (punishable by not less than one nor more than five years, or by a local jail sentence), and is also undefined by statute. These statutes are set forth in Appendix B, pages 1–3, infra. [Footnote by eds.]

have wilfully or purposefully, rather than negligently, embarked upon a course of wrongful conduct likely to cause death or great bodily harm.

A motor vehicle, wrongfully used, can be a weapon as deadly as a gun or a knife. Circumstances can be imagined in which a killing caused by the wrongful use of a motor vehicle might fit any one of the five categories of homicide known to our law. We recognized in Harrison v. Commonwealth, 183 Va. 394, 401, 32 S.E.2d 136, 139–40 (1944), that the premeditated use of an automobile to kill can be first-degree murder. If such an act fits within the statutory categories of Code § 18.2–31, such a killing could be capital murder. A killing in sudden heat of passion, upon reasonable provocation, by the use of a motor vehicle, could be voluntary manslaughter. Killings caused by the grossly negligent operation of motor vehicles, showing a reckless disregard of human life, have frequently resulted in convictions of involuntary manslaughter.

We have not, heretofore, had occasion to review a second-degree murder conviction based upon the use of an automobile, but the governing principles are the same as those which apply to any other kind of second-degree murder: the victim must be shown to have died as a result of the defendant's conduct, and the defendant's conduct must be shown to be malicious. In the absence of express malice, this element may only be implied from conduct likely to cause death or great bodily harm, wilfully or purposefully undertaken. Thus, for example, one who deliberately drives a car into a crowd of people at a high speed, not intending to kill or injure any particular person, but rather seeking the perverse thrill of terrifying them and causing them to scatter, might be convicted of second-degree murder if death results. One who accomplishes the same result inadvertently, because of grossly negligent driving, causing him to lose control of his car, could be convicted only of involuntary manslaughter. In the first case the act was volitional; in the second it was inadvertent, however reckless and irresponsible.

What effect has the defendant's degree of intoxication, if any, upon the factfinder's determination? The defendant may negate the specific intent requisite for capital or first-degree murder by showing that he was so greatly intoxicated as to be incapable of deliberation or premeditation, Giarratano v. Commonwealth, 220 Va. 1064, 266 S.E.2d 94 (1980), but voluntary intoxication is no defense to the lesser degrees of homicide, or to any other crime. Chittum v. Commonwealth, 211 Va. 12, 17, 174 S.E.2d 779, 783 (1970).[b] Particularly, his state of intoxication, however great, will not repel an inference of malice, implied by the circumstances surrounding his conduct.

In some jurisdictions, drunken driving is held to be malum in se, and where death is the proximate result of any degree of negligence attributable to intoxication, malice may be inferred by the fact-finder. See, e.g., Shiflet v. State, 216 Tenn. 365, 392 S.W.2d 676 (1965). We do not follow that view because of our distinction between volitional and inadvertent conduct. Cf. Hamilton v. Com., 560 S.W.2d 539 (Ky.1977)

---

[b] See page 285, supra. [Footnote by eds.]

(statute penalizing as murder "wanton" conduct causing death, supports murder conviction for unintentional homicide). Other states have enacted vehicular homicide statutes, which create a statutory felony, more serious than manslaughter, covering deaths caused by the negligence of drunken drivers. Ga.Code Ann. § 40–6–393 (Supp.1984); N.C. Gen.Stat. § 20–141.4 (1983). Our General Assembly has not seen fit to adopt such legislation.

Indeed, Code § 18.2–33, enacted in 1975, provides: "The killing of one accidentally, contrary to the intention of the parties, while in the prosecution of some felonious act other than those specified in §§ 18.2–31 and 18.2–32, is murder of the second degree and is punishable as a Class 3 felony." We think it significant that the General Assembly elected not to expand the ambit of this statute so as to include killings occurring in the commission of drunken driving, a misdemeanor.

We therefore apply the common-law principles mentioned above and hold that the defendant's degree of intoxication, however great, neither enhances nor impairs the set of facts relied upon to establish implied malice. In making the determination whether malice exists, the factfinder must be guided by the quality of the defendant's conduct, its likelihood of causing death or great bodily harm, and whether it was volitional or inadvertent; not by the defendant's blood-alcohol level.

In Baker v. Marcus, 201 Va. 905, 114 S.E.2d 617 (1960), we considered, in a civil context, whether malice could be inferred from drunken driving so as to support an award of punitive damages. There we said: "One who knowingly drives his automobile on the highway under the influence of intoxicants, in violation of statute is, of course, negligent. It is a wrong, reckless and unlawful thing to do; but it is not necessarily a malicious act." A sober driver may be eminently malicious, while a drunken driver may be merely reckless.[3]

Even though the fact of the defendant's intoxication, and its degree, are irrelevant to the determination whether his conduct was volitional or inadvertent, and thus whether it was malicious or merely negligent, the question remains whether such evidence is relevant for any other purpose. Evidence which tends to establish the probability or improbability of any fact in issue is relevant.

Drunken driving is not only unlawful in itself, but it tends to make the defendant's dangerous conduct more dangerous. A sober but reckless driver may rely on his skill and prompt reflexes to extricate himself from any emergency created by his reckless driving. A drunken driver has dulled his perceptions, blunted his skill, and slowed his reflexes in advance. The same reckless driving is more dangerous at his hands than it would be if he were sober, and his conduct is therefore more culpable. Intoxication, therefore, is relevant as an aggravating factor, increasing with its degree, bearing upon the relative culpability

---

[3] Some courts reason that one who deliberately drives a car to a place remote from home for the purpose of drinking, knowing that he will have to drive home under the influence of alcohol, then, after becoming intoxicated, drives recklessly, thereby acts so wantonly, and with such a disregard of human life as to supply an inference of malice. See e.g. People v. Watson, 30 Cal. 3d 290, 637 P.2d 279, 179 Cal.Rptr. 43 (1981). We do not think the premises support the conclusion reached.

of the defendant's conduct, even though it is irrelevant to the determination of malice.

Intoxication is, accordingly, relevant to a determination of the degree of the defendant's negligence: whether ordinary, gross, or wanton. It may serve to elevate the defendant's conduct to the level of "negligence so gross, wanton, and culpable as to show a reckless disregard of human life," a requisite element for a conviction of involuntary manslaughter.

The defendant's degree of intoxication is also relevant to a determination of the appropriate quantum of punishment. In Virginia, the fact-finder, whether judge or jury, has the duty, if it convicts the defendant, of fixing his punishment, usually within wide limits. The principal criterion for the discharge of the responsibility must be the relative seriousness of the offense, within its grade. All aggravating and mitigating factors shown by the evidence must be taken into account. Voluntary intoxication, in the case of a driver, is an aggravating factor properly considered for this purpose.

Applying these principles to the record before us, we find the evidence, viewed in the light most favorable to the Commonwealth, insufficient to support a finding of implied malice. The defendant was intoxicated and guilty of an appalling degree of reckless driving. His multiple tortious acts conjoined as proximate causes of three tragic deaths, and clearly met the . . . standard for proof of involuntary manslaughter: an "accidental killing which, although unintended, is the proximate result of negligence so gross, wanton, and culpable as to show a reckless disregard of human life." The Commonwealth, however, has the burden of proving malice beyond a reasonable doubt. The jury could only speculate, upon this evidence, whether the defendant embarked upon his ill-fated course of conduct wilfully and with a malicious purpose. No facts were proved from which such a purpose can be inferred. The distinction is close but crucial.

"[T]he intent to do an act in wanton and wilful disregard of the *obvious likelihood* of causing death or great bodily injury is a malicious intent . . . . [A] motorist who attempts to pass another car on a "blind curve" may be acting with such criminal negligence that if he causes the death of another in a resulting traffic accident he will be guilty of manslaughter. And such a motorist may be creating fully as great a human hazard as one who shoots into a house or train "just for kicks," who is guilty of murder if loss of life results. The difference is that in the act of the shooter there is an element of *viciousness* —an extreme indifference to the value of human life—that is not found in the act of the motorist."

Blackwell v. State, 34 Md.App. 547, 553–54, 369 A.2d 153, 158 (1977) (emphasis added). Because the evidence was insufficient to support a finding of malice, it was error to instruct the jury that it might find the defendant guilty of second-degree murder. . . .

For the foregoing reasons, the convictions of second-degree murder will be vacated and the three homicide cases remanded for further proceedings, consistent with this opinion, wherein the Commonwealth may, if it be so advised, retry the defendant for offenses no greater than involuntary manslaughter. . . .

Reversed and remanded.

POFF, J., . . . dissenting . . . .

I disagree, . . . with the majority's view of the law of criminal homicide.

Negligence resulting in an accidental death may be a tort or a crime, or both. The character of such negligence is the determinative factor. Ordinary negligence, i.e., the want of ordinary care as practiced by a reasonably prudent person, is actionable as a tort. Negligence so gross as to manifest depravity of mind and a callous disregard for human safety is criminal negligence, and if death results, constitutes criminal homicide. Unlike violations of some statutory rules of the road, the offense of driving under the influence of intoxicants constitutes criminal negligence.

In Virginia, criminal homicide is divided into two major categories, murder and manslaughter. Malice is the element which distinguishes the two. Malice may be either express or implied by conduct, and "whether a defendant acted with malice is generally a question to be decided by the trier of fact."

The level of culpability of criminal negligence determines the grade of the offense. Between the class of deliberate deeds committed with premeditated intent to kill, which is the essence of murder of the first degree, and the type of negligence inherent in the definition of involuntary manslaughter there is a species of reckless behavior so willful and wanton, so heedless of foreseeable consequences, and so indifferent to the value of human life that it supplies the element of malice which distinguishes murder of the second degree from manslaughter. More than a century and a half ago, this court observed that a killing caused by "criminal carelessness" could constitute "murder in the second degree." Whiteford v. Commonwealth, 27 Va. (6 Rand.) 721, 724–25 (1828).

While, as the majority notes, we have never, until now, had occasion to review a second-degree murder conviction based upon malice inferred from the negligent operation of a motor vehicle, we have commented upon the question in rather unmistakable language:

"When men, while drunk or sober, drive automobiles along highways and through crowded streets recklessly, the killing of human beings is a natural and probable result to be anticipated. When a homicide follows as a consequence of such conduct, a criminal intent is imputed to the offender and he may be punished for his crime. The precise grade of such a homicide, whether murder or manslaughter, depends upon the facts of the particular case." Goodman v. Commonwealth, 153 Va. 943, 952, 151 S.E. 168, 171 (1930).

I acknowledge that the language in *Goodman* is dicta. But it is in harmony with the common law in most jurisdictions. The great weight of authority holds that a motorist's negligence may be so gross and culpable as to imply a malicious intent to kill and that, in determining whether the homicide is manslaughter or murder, intoxication is an aggravating factor.

The vehicular homicide statutes adopted by some states abandon the definitional differences the common law makes between manslaughter and murder and define homicide resulting from the criminal negligence of the driver of a motor vehicle as a unique offense, graded according to the nature and extent of the driver's negligence. See Traffic Laws Annotated § 11–903. See also Model Penal Code § 210.4. Virginia has no such statute, and as defined by the majority opinion, vehicular homicide is hereafter relegated to the lowest grade of criminal homicide. The degree of culpability is immaterial.

Reaffirming what we said in *Whiteford* and *Goodman* and adopting what appears to be the judicial consensus, I would hold that where the evidence is sufficient to show that the driver of a motor vehicle, whether drunk or sober, is guilty of criminal negligence which is the sole proximate cause of a homicide, such evidence raises a question of fact whether the offense is manslaughter or murder of the second degree. Unless the finding made by the trier of fact is plainly wrong or without evidence to support it, the finding should be upheld by this Court.

I am of opinion that the evidence of record in this case is fully sufficient to justify the jury's finding that the defendant's negligence was the sole proximate cause of three deaths and that such negligence was so willful and wanton, so heedless of foreseeable consequences, and so indifferent to the value of human life as to imply the element of malice charged in the homicide counts of the indictment.

THOMAS, J., joins in [the] dissenting opinion.

———————

NOTES ON THE GRADING OF UNINTENTIONAL HOMICIDE AT COMMON LAW

1. **The Degree of Culpability Sufficient for Murder.** Leaving aside the felony-murder doctrine, which is covered in the final section of this chapter, the common law recognized two kinds of unintentional homicide as murder. The first, illustrated by the charge but not the reasoning in *Director of Public Prosecutions v. Smith*, page 204, supra, was based on intent to inflict grievous bodily injury. The second, which effectively subsumes the first, was based on a theory of recklessness or negligence that reached a high degree of callousness or indifference to life.

(i) **Commonwealth v. Malone.** The second theory is illustrated by the well-known case of Commonwealth v. Malone, 354 Pa. 180, 47 A.2d 445 (1946). Malone, then 17 years old, engaged in a game of Russian Roulette with a 13-year-old friend. He loaded one chamber of a pistol that held five bullets and, with his friend's consent, held the gun to his friend's side and pulled the trigger three times. The gun fired on the third try and Malone's friend died from the wound two days later. Malone was convicted of second-degree murder.

The conviction was affirmed on appeal. The court reasoned that "the 'grand criterion' which 'distinguished murder from other killing' was malice on the part of the killer and this malice was not necessarily 'malevolent to the deceased particularly' but 'any evil design in general; the dictate of a wicked, depraved and malignant heart.' " The court continued:

> "When an individual commits an act of gross recklessness for which he must reasonably anticipate that death to another is likely to result, he exhibits that 'wickedness of disposition, hardness of heart, cruelty, recklessness of consequences, and a mind regardless of social duty' which proved that there was at that time in him 'the state or frame of mind termed malice.' This court has declared that if a driver 'wantonly, recklessly, and in disregard of consequences' hurls 'his car against another, or into a crowd' and death results from that act 'he ought . . . to face the same consequences that would be meted out to him if he had accomplished death by wantonly and wickedly firing a gun.'
> . . .
> "The killing . . . resulted from an act intentionally done . . . , in reckless and wanton disregard of the consequences . . . . The killing was, therefore, murder, for malice in the sense of a wicked disposition is evidenced by the intentional doing of an uncalled-for-act in callous disregard of its likely harmful effects on others. The fact that there was no motive for this homicide does not exculpate the accused. In a trial for murder proof of motive is always relevant but never necessary."

(ii) **Comments and Questions on *Essex* and *Malone*.** As both *Essex* and *Malone* reveal, American common law found the existence of malice in unintentional homicides—and distinguished between murder and manslaughter—on the basis of epithetical descriptions of the defendant's behavior. Did either Essex or Malone have a "wicked, depraved and malignant heart?" How is a jury to be expected to answer such a question? Is it clear that Malone's heart was more depraved than Essex's?

The court in *Essex* held that malice was not established by the proof in that case. Can you follow its reasoning? Can you articulate the difference between murder and manslaughter envisioned by the majority? By the dissent? Which opinion states the better view?

2. **The Degree of Culpability Sufficient for Involuntary Manslaughter.** Common law courts have also been imprecise in defining the difference between ordinary negligence sufficient for tort liability and that degree of negligence that will support a conviction of involuntary manslaughter.[a] Most agree that it takes "more" negligence than

---

[a] There is also a misdemeanor-manslaughter analogue to the felony murder rule, permitting a conviction for involuntary manslaughter in some cases where the defendant has caused a death while engaged in an unlawful act. This doctrine is considered at page 965, *infra*.

will suffice for an ordinary tort, but there is surprisingly little attention in common-law cases to how that additional ingredient can be formulated in a way that effectively communicates to juries the judgment to be made.[b] In addition to *Essex* on this point, consider the following cases. Can you understand the standard the court means to be applying? Would a jury?

(i) *Commonwealth v. Sostilio.* In Commonwealth v. Sostilio, 325 Mass. 143, 89 N.E.2d 510 (1949), the court said:

> "The question in this case is whether there is evidence of wanton or reckless conduct on the part of the defendant. Wanton or reckless conduct has been defined as 'intentional conduct, by way either of commission or omission where there is a duty to act, which conduct involves a high degree of likelihood that substantial harm will result to another.' Wanton or reckless conduct is the legal equivalent of intentional conduct. If by wanton or reckless conduct bodily injury is caused to another, the person guilty of such conduct is guilty of assault and battery. And since manslaughter is simply a battery that causes death, if death results he is guilty of manslaughter."

The court applied this standard to uphold the manslaughter conviction of a driver of midget race-cars who killed another competitor by causing a crash while trying to pass by fitting his four-foot car into a two-foot space.

(ii) *Commonwealth v. Agnew.* Contrast Commonwealth v. Agnew, 263 Pa.Super. 424, 398 A.2d 209 (1979). The defendant was a farmer who was driving his tractor home after disking a field. It was close to midnight and the road, a two-lane highway bounded by guard rails, was unlighted. The road was 33 feet wide from guard rail to guard rail, and the disk the farmer was towing behind his tractor was 17 feet, four inches wide. No lights were placed on the disk. An oncoming car travelling at about 55 miles per hour saw the tractor but not the disk, never slowed down, and hit the disk. The driver and his passenger were killed. The policeman who came to the scene testified that he was unable to see the disk, even with the aid of headlights, until he came to within 30 or 40 feet of the tractor.

The court reversed a conviction of involuntary manslaughter. It reasoned as follows:

> "The state of mind or mens rea which characterizes involuntary manslaughter is recklessness or gross negligence: a great departure from the standard of ordinary care evidencing a disregard for human life or an indifference to the possible consequences of the actor's conduct. . . .
>
> "We feel that the facts in the instant case . . . fail to show Agnew's indifference to the possible consequences of his actions. While the evidence shows that Agnew committed two summary

[b] For recent treatments of the largely unavailing efforts to solve this problem in Commonwealth countries, see Briggs, In Defence of Manslaughter, [1983] Crim.L. Rev. 764; Peiris, Involuntary Manslaughter in Commonwealth Law, 5 Legal Studies 21 (1985).

offenses under the Motor Vehicle Code [c] which were substantial factors in bringing about the accident, this in itself is not sufficient to sustain a charge of involuntary manslaughter. However, the commonwealth argues that since Agnew drove his tractor at night knowing that the unlighted extremeties of the towed disk would encroach upon the oncoming lane, the requisite mens rea was present. However, what must be shown is *disregard* for human life, and an *indifference* to consequences. Here the record shows that Agnew was quite aware of the risk he created and took positive steps to reduce the risk. He placed flashing yellow lights on the top of the tractor cab, placed warning signs on the tractor disk, and proceeded at a slow rate of speed. Obviously, as the opinion of the lower court concludes, '[t]he precautions were tragically inadequate.' Still, the fact that Agnew took these precautions negates the requisite *disregard* of human life. Additionally, when Agnew perceived the oncoming car, he took every possible step to avoid a collision, pulling his tractor over to the right so far as the guard rails would allow . . . , and slowing his tractor down to a stop. This is not indifference to potential consequences, but a conscientious attempt to reduce the risk of an accident. Unhappily, the [driver of the] oncoming car never saw the towed disk in his lane and drove into it at full speed. While a jury could find Agnew guilty of ordinary negligence and impose civil liability on him, we assume, his actions disprove the 'disregard of human life and indifference to consequences' mens rea necessary to support the criminal charge of involuntary manslaughter."

PEOPLE v. REGISTER
Court of Appeals of New York, 1983.
60 N.Y.2d 270, 469 N.Y.S.2d 599, 457 N.E.2d 704.

SIMONS, JUDGE. Defendant appeals from [a conviction] of murder in the second degree and two counts of assault in the first degree. The charges arose from a barroom incident in which defendant shot and killed one man and seriously injured two others. He alleges . . . that the trial court erred in refusing to instruct the jury that it could consider intoxication evidence to negate an element of the crime of depraved mind murder. . . .

The shootings occurred about 12:30 a.m. on January 15, 1977 in a crowded barroom in downtown Rochester. The evidence established that defendant and a friend, Duval, had been drinking heavily that day celebrating the fact that Duval, through an administrative mixup, would not have to spend the weekend in jail. Sometime between 7:00 p.m. and 8:00 p.m., the two men left home for the bar. Defendant took a loaded pistol with him and shortly after they arrived at the bar, he

---

[c] He violated prohibitions limiting the maximum width of farm equipment on a highway and requiring that one-half of the roadway be yielded to an oncoming vehicle. [Footnote by eds.]

produced it when he got into an argument with another patron over money owed him. Apparently the dispute ended without incident and defendant continued his drinking. After midnight another argument developed, this time between Duval and Willie Mitchell. Defendant took out the gun again, shot at Mitchell but mistakenly injured Lawrence Evans who was trying to stop the fight. He then stepped forward and shot Mitchell in the stomach from close range. At that, the 40 or 50 patrons in the bar started for the doors. Some of the bystanders tried to remove Mitchell to a hospital and while they were doing so, the decedent, Marvin Lindsey, walked by defendant. Lindsey was apparently a friend or acquaintance of defendant although that was the first time he had seen him that night. For no explained reason, defendant turned and fired his gun killing Lindsey.

Defendant did not contest the shootings. In defense, his counsel elicited evidence during the prosecution's case of defendant's considerable drinking that evening. . . . The jury acquitted defendant of intentional murder but convicted him of depraved mind murder and the two assault counts.

The murder conviction must be supported by evidence that defendant "[u]nder circumstances evincing a depraved indifference to human life . . . recklessly engage[d] in conduct which create[d] a grave risk of death to another person, and thereby cause[d] the death of another person" (Penal Law, § 125.25, subd. 2).[a] A person acts recklessly when he is aware of and consciously disregards a substantial and unjustifiable risk (Penal Law, § 15.05, subd. 3), but to bring defendant's conduct within the murder statute, the People were required to establish also that defendant's act was imminently dangerous and presented a very high risk of death to others and that it was committed under circumstances which evidenced a wanton indifference to human life or a depravity of mind. The crime differs from intentional murder in that it results not from a specific, conscious intent to cause death, but from an indifference to or disregard of the risks attending defendant's conduct.

. . . The jury's proper role . . . was to make a qualitative judgment whether defendant's act was of such gravity that it placed the crime upon the same level as the taking of life by premeditated design. It had to determine from the evidence if defendant's conduct, though reckless, was equal in blameworthiness to intentional murder.

The evidence in the record supports the verdict. Defendant's awareness of and indifference to the attendant risks was established by evidence that he entered a crowded bar with a loaded gun, he said that he was "going to kill somebody tonight," or similar words, several times, and he had brought the gun out in the bar once before during the evening only to be told to put it away. Ultimately, he fired the gun three times in the "packed" barroom, conduct which presented a grave

---

[a] The New York murder statute is printed in full in Appendix B, pages 7–9, infra. [Footnote by eds.]

risk of death and did in fact result in the death of Marvin Lindsey. His conduct was well within that defined by the statute.

At the conclusion of the evidence and after the charge, defendant requested the court to instruct the jury on the effect of intoxication. The court complied with the request when discussing the intentional murder and assault counts, but it refused to charge the jury that it could consider defendant's intoxication in determining whether he acted "[u]nder circumstances evincing a depraved indifference to human life" in causing the death of Marvin Lindsey. The court held that the mens rea required for depraved mind murder is recklessness and that subdivision 3 of § 15.05 of the Penal Law precludes evidence of intoxication in defense of reckless crimes because it provides that "[a] person who creates such a risk but is unaware thereof solely by reason of voluntary intoxication also acts recklessly." That ruling is assigned as error by defendant. He contends that depraved mind murder contains a different or additional element of mental culpability, namely "circumstances evincing a depraved indifference to human life," which elevates defendant's conduct from manslaughter to murder and that this additional element may be negatived by evidence of intoxication.

[T]he statutory definition of depraved mind murder includes both a mental element ("recklessly") and a voluntary act ("engaging in conduct which creates a grave risk of death to another person"). Recklessness refers to defendant's conscious disregard of a substantial risk and the act proscribed, the risk creating conduct, is defined by the degree of danger presented. Depraved mind murder resembles manslaughter in the second degree (a reckless killing which includes the requirement that defendant disregard a substantial risk [Penal Law, § 125.15, subd. 1; § 15.05, subd. 3]), but the depraved mind murder statute requires in addition not only that the conduct which results in death present a grave risk of death but that it also occur "[u]nder circumstances evincing a depraved indifference to human life." This additional requirement refers to neither the mens rea nor the actus reus. If it states an element of the crime at all, it is not an element in the traditional sense but rather a definition of the factual setting in which the risk creating conduct must occur—objective circumstances which are not subject to being negatived by evidence of defendant's intoxication.

[This] view is supported by an analysis of the statutory development of the crime. Because of an inability to quantify homicidal risks in precise terms, the legislature structured the degree of risk which must be present in nonintentional killings by providing that in a depraved mind murder the actor's conduct must present a grave risk of death whereas in manslaughter it presents the lesser substantial risk of death (see, also, Penal Law, § 15.05, subd. 4 [criminal negligence, a failure to perceive a substantial risk]). The phrase "[u]nder circumstances evincing a depraved indifference to human life" refers to the wantonness of defendant's conduct and converts the substantial risk present in manslaughter into a *very* substantial risk present in murder. The predecessor statute referred to "a depraved mind, regardless of human life" and the older cases, in attempting to explicate this factor, speak of a "depraved heart devoid of social duty and fatally bent on mischief." Such phrases, suggesting malice aforethought, have provoked statements that malice or intent is inferred in depraved mind murder.[1] However, the focus of the offense is not upon the subjective intent of the defendant, as it is with intentional murder (Penal Law, § 125.25, subd. 1), but rather upon an objective assessment of the degree of risk presented by defendant's reckless conduct (see, e.g., People v. Jernatowski, 238 N.Y. 188, 144 N.E. 497 (1924) [firing a bullet into a room defendant knew contained several people]; People v. Poplis, 30 N.Y.2d 85, 330 N.Y.S.2d 365, 281 N.E.2d 167 (1972) [defendant continually beat 3½-year-old infant over five-day period]; see, also, Hechtman, Practice Commentaries, McKinney's Cons.Laws of N.Y., Book 39, Penal Law, § 125.25 [depraved mind murder committed when one shoots into a crowd, places a time bomb in a public place or opens the door of a lion's cage in a zoo].

The present statute is derived from this conceptual base but it contains important differences. Thus, whereas the former penal statutes defined depraved mind murder by referring to defendant's conduct, i.e., "[w]hen perpetrated by any act imminently dangerous to others," etc., defined mens rea "as a depraved mind" and contained no references to recklessness, the present statute defines the crime by reference to the circumstances under which it occurs and expressly states that recklessness is the element of mental culpability required. The concept of depraved indifference was retained in the new statute not to function as a mens rea element, but to objectively define the circumstances which must exist to elevate a homicide from manslaughter to murder. . . .

Further evidence that "recklessness" is the mens rea, and the only mens rea, of the crime is to be found in other sections of article 15. Section 15.05, which was intended to "limit and crystalize" the culpable mental states involved in the criminal law includes recklessness as one of those culpable mental states but it does not list "depraved indifference." Moreover, subdivision 1 of § 15.15 provides that when an offense requires a particular culpable mental state, such mental state is designated by use of the terms found in § 15.05. When only one culpable mental state appears in a statute defining an offense, § 15.15 directs that the mental state is presumed to apply to every element of the offense. The only culpable mental state found in § 125.25 which defines depraved mind murder is recklessness; it is defined in subdivision 3 of § 15.05 (which prohibits evidence of intoxication to negative it) and the statute prescribes that it apply to every element of the offense.

The dissenter's concern that this decision will result in wholesale depraved mind murder prosecutions for what are essentially intentional murders is unwarranted. Our statutes have included a crime of depraved mind murder in its various forms and definitions for over 150 years. Its nature is "well understood," and the unusual settings

---

[1] Inferred intent is a legal fiction much like the transferred intent concept of felony murder. . . .

appropriate to it have been stated frequently. It is not and never has been considered as a substitute for intentional homicide. That intoxication evidence might under some unusual circumstances negative the intent of an intentional homicide although by virtue of the statute it would have no similar effect on the same act charged as done recklessly in a depraved mind murder should not alter the implementation of the statute. A similar alleged paradox exists presently for an act done under a mistaken belief of fact.

In sum, the statutory requirement that the homicide result from conduct evincing a depraved indifference to human life is a legislative attempt to qualitatively measure egregiously reckless conduct and to differentiate it from manslaughter. It does not create a new and different mens rea, undefined in the Penal Law, or a voluntary act which can be negatived by evidence of intoxication. If the objective circumstances under which the crime is committed constitute an element of it, they do so only in the sense that carrying a gun or acting in concert with another are elements of the crime of robbery or that the theft of more than $250 is an element of grand larceny. It is an element which elevates the severity of the offense but it is not an element subject to being negatived by evidence of intoxication as may intent or the physical capacity to act. . . .

The rationale [of the present statute] is readily apparent: the element of recklessness itself—defined as conscious disregard of a substantial risk—encompasses the risks created by defendant's conduct in getting drunk.

Ultimately, the only intended purpose in permitting the jury to consider intoxication in a reckless crime is to negate defendant's awareness and disregard of the risk. It is precisely that point—the inconsistency of permitting reckless and otherwise aggravating conduct to negate an aspect of the offense—that persuades us that intoxication evidence should be excluded whenever recklessness is an element of the offense. In utilitarian terms, the risk of excessive drinking should be added to and not subtracted from the risks created by the conduct of the drunken defendant for there is no social or penological purpose to be served by a rule that permits one who voluntarily drinks to be exonerated from failing to foresee the results of his conduct if he is successful at getting drunk.

Accordingly, the order of the Appellate Division should be affirmed.

JASEN, JUDGE (dissenting).

The majority holds that the element of "circumstances evincing a depraved indifference to human life" set forth in subdivision 2 of § 125.25 of the Penal Law is not part of the mens rea of murder in the second degree and that evidence of intoxication is, therefore, inadmissible to negate that element. Since I believe the legislature intended that a defendant's alleged intoxication could be used to negate that element of the crime, I respectfully dissent.

[Judge Jason first traced the evolution of New York murder statutes, concluding that "it should be clear beyond cavil that depraved 'indifference' was intended by the legislature to constitute a culpable state of mind which could be negated by proof that the actor was so intoxicated he was not aware of existing conditions or the risks inherent in his conduct." The opinion then continued:]

The construction which I would give the depraved mind murder statute is not only consistent with the legislature's intent, the history of the statute and precedent of this court, but is also in line with the basic underpinnings of our system of criminal justice. The rule announced by the majority today effectively eviscerates the distinction between manslaughter in the second degree and murder in the second degree with respect to the accused's state of mind. The majority holds that mere recklessness is a sufficient mens rea under the depraved mind murder statute if the objective circumstances surrounding the killing "presented a grave risk of death and did in fact result in the death" of another.

Historically, our criminal law is based upon a theory of "punishing the vicious will." It is a deep-rooted part of our jurisprudence that, in the ordinary case, only those offenders who consciously choose to do evil rather than good will be punished. Under the majority's rule, however, a person who possessed only a reckless state of mind when he caused the death of another could be convicted of depraved mind murder and sentenced to a term of 15 years to life imprisonment simply because objective circumstances surrounding the killing presented a "grave risk" of death even though the actor, due to intoxication, was unaware of those circumstances and could not appreciate the risks. The majority would also hold that another person who is fully aware of a "substantial and unjustifiable risk" and consciously disregards that risk can only be found guilty of manslaughter in the second degree and sentenced to as little as one and one-half years in jail. While there may be a technical distinction between a "grave" risk and a "substantial" one, the only real difference is about 15 years in prison. To accept this distinction as justification for the disparate penalties which the respective crimes carry defies basic principles of fairness and logic. I simply cannot agree that the legislature intended that convictions for murder as opposed to manslaughter would turn upon the nature of the objective surrounding circumstances regardless of whether or not the accused was aware of those circumstances or could appreciate the consequences of his conduct.

In my view, the legislature purposely distinguished between reckless manslaughter and depraved mind murder, intending that depraved indifference plus recklessness would connote a mens rea more culpable than recklessness alone and nearly as culpable as intent. The differences between the mental states set forth in the reckless manslaughter, depraved mind murder and intentional murder statutes are easily delineated, although somewhat difficult to apply. A person acts recklessly in causing the death of another when he is aware of and consciously disregards a substantial and unjustifiable risk. A person intentionally kills another when his "conscious objective" is to cause the death of the victim. A person acts with depraved indifference, however, when he engages in conduct whereby he does not intend to kill but is so indifferent to the consequences, which he knows with substantial certainty will result in the death of another, as to be willing to kill. It is at this point that reckless homicide becomes knowing homicide and the killing differs so little from an intentional killing that parity of punishment is required. This is so not because the surrounding circumstances happened to create a "grave" as opposed to a "substantial" risk, but because the accused has acted with greater culpability and a wickedness akin to that of one whose conscious objective is to kill.

By this approach, a person who acts without an awareness of the risks involved, due to intoxication or otherwise, will be punished for manslaughter, while a person who acts in a way which he knows is substantially certain to cause death, although not intending to kill, will be treated the same as a person who intentionally kills. It seems to me that this is the far more reasonable approach and the one intended by the legislature.

Additionally, I note that the majority's rationale appears to be inconsistent with the over-all legislative scheme manifest in article 125 of the Penal Law. In enacting subdivision 3 of § 15.05 of the Penal Law, the legislature declared that a reckless killer should not be permitted to hide behind a defense of intoxication. However, recognizing that a reckless killer, whether intoxicated or not, should not be punished as severely as a person who intentionally takes the life of another, the lawmakers categorized reckless homicide as manslaughter in the second degree . . ., rather than murder in the second degree . . . . It is, therefore, anomalous to say, as the majority does, that the legislature intended that an individual who had no awareness of the seriousness of his conduct or the circumstances surrounding his actions due to intoxication and had no intent to kill should be punished as severely as the intentional killer. Furthermore, as a result of the majority's interpretation of the statute, prosecutors will be able to obtain murder convictions simply by proving that the defendant acted recklessly in killing another. This is so because the simple fact that the defendant's conduct resulted in the victim's death will, with 20/20 hindsight, be proof enough to a jury that the circumstances existing at the time and place of the killing presented a "grave risk" of death and that the defendant, therefore, acted with depraved indifference to human life.[4] This result is clearly at odds with the legislative scheme set forth in article 125 of the Penal Law. . . .

Inasmuch as the legislative history of subdivision 2 of section 125.25 of the Penal Law, prior precedent of this court and basic notions of justice make clear that the element of "depraved indifference" should

---

[4] It is curious that the majority would opine that the depraved mind murder statute "is not and never has been considered as a substitute for intentional homicide" and that it would be an unusual case where intoxication would "negative the intent [element] of an intentional homicide [when] it would have no similar effect on the same act charged as done recklessly in a depraved mind murder." Indeed, this is precisely what happened in this case where defendant was acquitted of intentional murder yet the prosecutor was still able to obtain a murder conviction from the jury under the depraved mind murder statute.

be construed as a mental state more culpable than recklessness, evidence of defendant's intoxication should have been admitted, pursuant to § 15.25 of the Penal Law, to negate that element of the offense.

Accordingly, I would reverse the conviction and order a new trial.

JONES, WACHTLER and KAYE, JJ., concur with SIMONS, J.

JASEN, J., dissents and votes to reverse in a separate opinion in which COOKE, C.J., and MEYER, J., concur.

NOTES ON THE GRADING OF UNINTENTIONAL HOMICIDE UNDER MODERN STATUTES

1. **The Degree of Culpability Sufficient for Murder.** The New York statute at issue in *Register* is derived from § 210.2(1)(b) of the Model Penal Code. The Model Penal Code provision, in turn, is derived from the "depraved heart" formulation that constituted malice, and hence justified a murder conviction, at common law. What is the justification for grading this form of murder at the same level as intentional homicide? Consider the facts of *Malone* (page 911, supra), *Acevedo* (assuming that the defendant killed one or more people) (page 344, supra), and *Smith* (page 204, supra). Could findings be made in any of those cases that would justify grading the offense as the equal of an intentional homicide? Are the Model Code and New York formulations an improvement over the questions asked in common law jurisdictions?

In *Register,* the New York Court of Appeals rejected the claim that the defendant's intoxication was admissible to negate the degree of recklessness required for a murder conviction. As claimed by the dissent, does this holding undermine the justification for treating this form of recklessness as the moral equivalent of intentional homicide? Or did the majority get the right answer? How would you interpret the Model Penal Code on this point?

2. *Northington v. State.* The revised Alabama statute provides that a person commits murder if:

> "Under circumstances manifesting extreme indifference to human life, he recklessly engages in conduct which creates a grave risk of death to a person other than himself, and thereby causes the death of another person."

Northington v. State, 413 So.2d 1169 (Ala.Cr.App.1981), involved a mother convicted of murder for allowing her five-month old daughter to starve to death. The court reversed the conviction because it interpreted the statute to require "universal malice" and no such malice was shown in this case:

> "Under whatever name, the doctrine of universal malice, depraved heart murder, or reckless homicide manifesting extreme indifference to human life is intended to embrace those cases where a person has no deliberate intent to kill or injure any *particular* individual. 'The element of "extreme indifference to

human life," by definition, does not address itself to the life of the victim, but to human life generally.' People By and Through Russel v. District Court, 185 Colo. 78, [83,] 521 P.2d 1254, 1256 (1974). . . .

"The state presented no evidence that the defendant engaged in conduct 'under circumstances manifesting extreme indifference to human life' for, while the defendant's conduct did indeed evidence an extreme indifference to the life of her child, there was nothing to show that the conduct displayed an extreme indifference to human life generally. Although the defendant's conduct created a grave risk of death to another and thereby caused the death of that person, the acts of the defendant were aimed at the particular victim and no other. Not only did the defendant's conduct create a grave risk of death to only her daughter and no other, but the defendant's actions (or inactions) were directed specifically against the young infant. This evidence does not support a conviction of murder . . . . The function of this section is to embrace those homicides caused by such acts as driving an automobile in a grossly wanton manner, shooting a firearm into a crowd or a moving train, and throwing a timber from a roof onto a crowded street." [a]

The court concluded its opinion by noting that it was "extremely reluctant to reverse the conviction" because of "the revolting and heartsickening details of this case." [b] "Yet, because our system is one of law and not of men, we have no other choice." Can this be right? Is it consistent for the court to say, as it did in another part of its opinion, that the case would have been different if Northington had been convicted of intentional murder?

3. **The Degree of Culpability Sufficient for Manslaughter and Negligent Homicide.** Note that the Model Penal Code divides the former common law offense of involuntary manslaughter into two offenses. Section 210.3 punishes a homicide as manslaughter if "recklessly" committed and § 210.4 punishes a homicide as negligent homicide if "negligently" committed. Examine carefully the definitions of "recklessly" and "negligently" in § 2.02. It may help to reread pages 239–41, supra, and the note on negligence as the basis for criminal liability beginning on page 214, supra. Are the Model Code formulations an improvement over the common law inquiries illustrated by such cases as *Essex* (page 905, supra), *Sostilio* (page 913, supra), and *Agnew* (page 913, supra)? Do they justify the grading distinction reflected in the Model Code? For what offenses, if any, could Essex, Sostilio, and Agnew be convicted under the Model Penal Code? Finally, is the grading distinction in the Model Code between the form of

---

[a] The court quoted extensively from State v. Berge, 25 Wash.App. 433, 607 P.2d 1247 (1980), in support of this interpretation of the Alabama statute. *Berge,* in turn, identifies Darry v. People, 10 N.Y. 120 (1854), as the origin of the notion that "depraved mind" murder refers, as the court in *Darry* put it, to "general malice" and not "any affection of the mind having for its object a particular individual." [Footnote by eds.]

[b] The court's opinion did not elaborate on the facts beyond this cryptic statement.

recklessness that will suffice for murder and that which will suffice for manslaughter intelligible?   Desirable?

SECTION 3:   CAUSATION

PEOPLE v. KIBBE

Court of Appeals of New York, 1974.
35 N.Y.2d 407, 362 N.Y.S.2d 848, 321 N.E.2d 773.

GABRIELLI, JUDGE.   Subdivision 2 of Section 125.25 of the Penal Law provides, in pertinent part, that "[a] person is guilty of murder" when "[u]nder circumstances evincing a depraved indifference to human life, he recklessly engages in conduct which creates a grave risk of death to another person, and thereby causes the death of another person."

The factual setting of the bizarre events of a cold winter night of December 30, 1970, . . . reveal the following: During the early evening the defendants were drinking in a Rochester tavern along with the victim, George Stafford.   The bartender testified that Stafford was displaying and "flashing" $100 bills, was thoroughly intoxicated and was finally "shut off" because of his inebriated condition.   At some time between 8:15 and 8:30 p.m., Stafford inquired if someone would give him a ride to Canandaigua, New York, and the defendants, who, according to their statements, had already decided to steal Stafford's money, agreed to drive him there in Kibbe's automobile.   The three men left the bar and proceeded to another bar where Stafford was denied service due to his condition.   The defendants and Stafford then walked across the street to a third bar where they were served, and each had another drink or two.

After they left the third bar, the three men entered Kibbe's automobile and began the trip toward Canandaigua.   Krall drove the car while Kibbe demanded that Stafford turn over any money he had.   In the course of an exchange, Kibbe slapped Stafford several times, took his money, then compelled him to lower his trousers and to take off his shoes to be certain that Stafford had given up all his money; and when they were satisfied that Stafford had no more money on his person, the defendants forced Stafford to exit the Kibbe vehicle.

As he was thrust from the car, Stafford fell onto the shoulder of the rural two-lane highway on which they had been traveling.   His trousers were still down around his ankles, his shirt was rolled up towards his chest, he was shoeless and he had also been stripped of any outer clothing.   Before the defendants pulled away, Kibbe placed Stafford's shoes and jacket on the shoulder of the highway.   Although Stafford's eyeglasses were in the Kibbe vehicle, the defendants, either through inadvertence or perhaps by specific design, did not give them to Stafford before they drove away.   It was some time between 9:30 and 9:40 p.m. when Kibbe and Krall abandoned Stafford on the side of the road. The temperature was near zero, and although it was not snowing at the time, visibility was occasionally obscured by heavy winds which intermittently blew previously fallen snow into the air and across the highway; and there was snow on both sides of the road as a result of previous plowing operations. The structure nearest the point where Stafford was forced from the defendants' car was a gasoline service station situated nearly one half of a mile away on the other side of the highway. There was no artificial illumination on this segment of the rural highway.

At approximately 10:00 p.m. Michael W. Blake, a college student, was operating his pickup truck in the northbound lane of the highway in question. Two cars, which were approaching from the opposite direction, flashed their headlights at Blake's vehicle. Immediately after he had passed the second car, Blake saw Stafford sitting in the road in the middle of the northbound lane with his hands up in the air. Blake stated that he was operating his truck at a speed of approximately 50 miles per hour, and that he "didn't have time to react" before his vehicle struck Stafford. After he brought his truck to a stop and returned to try to be of assistance to Stafford, Blake observed that the man's trousers were down around his ankles and his shirt was pulled up around his chest. A deputy sheriff called to the accident scene also confirmed the fact that the victim's trousers were around his ankles, and that Stafford was wearing no shoes or jacket.

At the trial, the Medical Examiner of Monroe County testified that death had occurred fairly rapidly from massive head injuries. In addition, he found proof of a high degree of intoxication with a .25 per cent, by weight, of alcohol concentration in the blood.

For their acts, the defendants were convicted of murder, robbery in the second degree and grand larceny in the third degree. However, the defendants basically challenge only their convictions of murder, claiming that the People failed to establish beyond a reasonable doubt that their acts "caused the death of another," as required by the statute. As framed by the appellate division the only serious question raised by these appeals "is whether the death was caused by [the defendants'] acts." In answering this question, we are required to determine whether the defendants may be convicted of murder for the occurrences which have been described. They contend that the actions of Blake, the driver of the pickup truck, constituted both an intervening and superseding cause which relieves them of criminal responsibility for Stafford's death. There is, of course, no statutory provision regarding the effect of an intervening cause of injury as it relates to the criminal responsibility of one who sets in motion the machinery which ultimately results in the victim's death; and there is surprisingly little case law dealing with the subject. Moreover, analogies to causation in civil cases are neither controlling nor dispositive, since, as this court has previously stated: "A long distance separates the negligence which renders one criminally liable from that which establishes civil liability"; and this is due in large measure to the fact that the standard or measure of persuasion by which the prosecution must convince the trier of all the essential elements of the crime charged, is beyond a reasonable doubt. Thus, actions which may serve as a predicate for civil liability may not be sufficient to constitute a basis for the imposition of criminal sanctions because of the different purposes of these two branches of law. Stated another way, the defendants should not be found guilty unless their conduct "was a cause of death sufficiently direct as to meet the requirements of the *criminal,* and not the *tort,* law." However, to be a sufficiently direct cause of death so as to warrant the imposition of a criminal penalty therefor, it is not necessary that the ultimate harm be intended by the actor. It will suffice if it can be said beyond a reasonable doubt, as indeed it can be here said, that the ultimate harm is something which should have been foreseen as being reasonably related to the acts of the accused.

In People v. Kane, 213 N.Y. 260, 107 N.E. 655 (1915), the defendant inflicted two serious pistol shot wounds on the body of a pregnant woman. The wounds caused a miscarriage; the miscarriage caused septic peritonitis, and the septic peritonitis, thus induced, caused the woman's death on the third day after she was shot. Over the defendant's insistence that there was no causal connection between the wounds and the death and, in fact, that the death was due to the intervention of an outside agency, namely, the negligent and improper medical treatment at the hospital, this court affirmed the conviction "even though the medical treatment may also have had some causative influence."

We subscribe to the requirement that the defendants' actions must be a *sufficiently direct cause* of the ensuing death before there can be any imposition of criminal liability, and recognize, of course, that this standard is greater than that required to serve as a basis for tort liability. Applying these criteria to the defendants' actions, we conclude that their activities on the evening of December 30, 1970, were a sufficiently direct cause of the death of George Stafford so as to warrant the imposition of criminal sanctions. In engaging in what may properly be described as a despicable course of action, Kibbe and Krall left a helplessly intoxicated man without his eyeglasses in a position from which, because of these attending circumstances, he could not extricate himself and whose condition was such that he could not even protect himself from the elements. The defendants do not dispute the fact that their conduct evinced a depraved indifference to human life which created a grave risk of death, but rather they argue that it was just as likely that Stafford would be miraculously rescued by a good samaritan. We cannot accept such an argument. There can be little doubt but that Stafford would have frozen to death in his state of undress had he remained on the shoulder of the road. The only alternative left to him was the highway, which in his condition, for one reason or another, clearly forboded the probability of his resulting death.

Under the conditions surrounding Blake's operation of his truck (i.e., the fact that he had his low beams on as the two cars approached; that there was no artificial lighting on the highway; and that there was insufficient time in which to react to Stafford's presence in his lane), we do not think it may be said that any supervening wrongful act occurred to relieve the defendants from the directly foreseeable consequences of their actions. In short, we will not disturb the jury's determination that the prosecution proved beyond a reasonable doubt that their actions came clearly within the statute and "cause[d] the death of another person."

We also reject the defendants' present claim of error regarding the trial court's charge. Neither of the defendants took exception or made any request with respect to the charge regarding the cause of death. While the charge might have been more detailed, appellants' contention that the appellate division should have reversed for its claimed inadequacy in the interests of justice may not be here reviewed, for the intermediate appellate court's refusal to so reverse was exclusively within its discretion.[a]

The orders of the appellate division should be affirmed.

NOTES ON CAUSATION

1. **The Relevance of Causation.** Issues of causation arise in the criminal law whenever the definition of the offense specifies a result as an actus reus element. The causation inquiry, as *Kibbe* illustrates, concerns a relationship or linkage between the defendant's conduct and the result such that the defendant can properly be punished for the result. Offenses against the person are the predominate context where issues of causation arise, and homicide is the offense where most causation problems are litigated.

Both issues of grading and criminality vel non can turn on resolution of the question of causation. This point can be illustrated by assuming on the *Kibbe* facts that the court had found Blake's conduct to be "an intervening and superseding cause" of Stafford's death and therefore had concluded that Kibbe and Krall were not guilty of murder. The New York Penal Code includes two reckless-endangering offenses derived from Section 211.2 of the Model Penal Code. Section 120.25 of the New York Code establishes the offense of reckless endangering in the first degree as a class D felony (seven-year maximum) if, "under circumstances evincing a depraved indifference to human life," a person "recklessly engages in conduct which creates a grave risk of death to another person." Section 120.20 provides that the offense is of the second degree and a class A misdemeanor (one-year maximum) if the actor "recklessly engages in conduct which creates a substantial risk of serious physical injury to another person." Since the offense of

---

a The trial judge had not specifically charged the jury on the requirement of causation, as separate from the other elements of the offense. This fact led a divided court in Kibbe v. Henderson, 534 F.2d 493 (2d Cir.1976), to set aside Kibbe's conviction on habeas corpus as a violation of the due process requirement that proof of every element of a crime be established beyond a reasonable doubt. This conclusion was derived from In re Winship, 397 U.S. 358 (1970). The *Winship* decision and some of its progeny are discussed further at pages 967–1004, infra. In Henderson v. Kibbe, 431 U.S. 145 (1977), the Supreme Court reinstated Kibbe's conviction, holding that the omission of more complete instructions on the causation issue was not an error of constitutional dimension. [Footnote by eds.]

which Kibbe and Krall were actually convicted carried a maximum term of life imprisonment, a significant grading differential turns on the causation inquiry. Assuming that the culpability finding remains the same in both cases, the defendants would be subject to a life maximum if they caused the death and a seven-year maximum if they did not. If the jury found that the defendants did not cause the death but acted with the lesser culpability required by Section 120.20 of the New York Code, the grade of the offense would be reduced further.

Variation of the culpability finding still further illustrates the capacity of the causation inquiry to determine criminality vel non. If the jury found no causation and were prepared to find that Kibbe and Krall were only negligent as to the possibility of death or serious injury, there could be no criminal liability under the New York statutes. Like the Model Penal Code, the New York statutes include an offense of negligent homicide, but contain no counterpart offense of negligent endangering. Thus, a finding of negligence and causation in New York can result in conviction of a class E felony (four-year maximum) and a finding of negligence but no causation exonerates from criminal liability altogether.[a]

Why should causation have such significance in the criminal law? A closely related inquiry has been previously explored in connection with the *Thacker* and *Acevedo* cases, reproduced at pages 342–51, supra. In those cases, the defendants had engaged in conduct, to paraphrase the New York statute, that recklessly created a grave risk of death to another under circumstances evincing a depraved indifference to human life. No death resulted, however, and the question was whether they could be convicted of attempted murder. The conclusion that they were not guilty of attempt left them in much the same situation as the hypothetical variations of the *Kibbe* facts recited above. Can you defend a system under which Kibbe and Krall are guilty of murder because they "caused" a death, but Thacker and Acevedo are guilty only of a lesser offense because they did not? Who in your mind is the more blameworthy? The more dangerous? Was the fact that Stafford died any more or less fortuitous than the fact that Thacker's and Acevedo's "victims" did not? Should grading or criminality turn on such fortuities?

The most elaborate treatment of these issues in the literature can be found in Schulhofer, Harm and Punishment: A Critique of Emphasis on Results of Conduct in the Criminal Law, 122 U.Pa.L.Rev. 1497 (1974).[b] Professor Schulhofer concludes that "many problems associated with mens rea and the law of attempts have never been resolved satisfactorily, due to the absence of acceptable or coherent reasons for attributing significance to the harm caused; the entire field of causation in criminal law is utterly bankrupt for the same reason. Identifi-

---

[a] The New York statutes are not atypical in this regard. Indeed, Section 211.2 of the Model Penal Code (reckless endangering) was an innovation, extending criminal liability considerably beyond the former law in most jurisdictions. Thus, the New York statutes described above actually give *less* significance to the causation inquiry than was typical prior to statutory revisions inspired by the Model Code.

[b] A useful discussion can also be found in Note, Causation in the Model Penal Code, 78 Colum.L.Rev. 1249, 1252–60 (1978).

cation of the precise policies served by emphasis on results should provide a basis for more meaningful efforts to tackle these problems." Can you identify any "precise policies" that justify the emphasis of the criminal law on results?

2. **The Common-Law Approach to Causation.** Most descriptions of the common-law approach to causation divide the problem into two questions.[c] The first is one of factual causation, frequently measured by the so-called "but for" test. This inquiry states a necessary but not sufficient condition of liability, i.e., that the result would not have occurred "but for" the defendant's antecedent conduct. In the *Kibbe* case, this inquiry is easily satisfied; it is clear that Stafford would not have been killed if Kibbe and Krall had not left him on the highway. A simple illustration of when this test would not be satisfied would be a case where *A* inflicts a minor flesh wound on *B*, and *C*—acting independently—shoots *B* through the heart and kills *B* instantly. *A*'s conduct in this instance would plainly not be a "but for" cause of *B*'s death, even though *A* may have intended to kill *B*.

It is clear, however, that the law cannot stop by asking the "but for" question. Consider the following case. *D* attempts to kill his wife and fails, and as a result she leaves home, goes to live on a farm with her family, falls off a horse while riding in the woods, lands on a rattlesnake, and dies from the bite of the snake. In this case, *D*'s conduct is related to his wife's death in a "but for" sense; were it not for his attempt to kill her, she would not have left home, would not have been riding in the woods, would not have fallen off her horse, etc. But, although *D* is guilty of attempted murder for his initial conduct, it is clear that he could not be convicted of murder following her death.

The concept used by the common law to describe this conclusion is called "proximate" or "legal" cause. If the defendant's conduct is a "but for" cause of death, the second question that must be asked is whether it was also the "proximate cause" of the death. It is this inquiry that is ordinarily crucial and that is described in the *Kibbe* case as whether the defendants' conduct was a "sufficiently direct cause" of the death. The question usually asked in this context is whether some other cause "intervened" in the chain of events begun by the defendant's conduct such that the defendant should not be held responsible for the ultimate result. The common-law vocabulary for analyzing this question often used the terms "dependent intervening cause" to describe a more immediate causal factor that would not exculpate (e.g., the victim actually died from an infection that resulted from wounds inflicted by the defendant) and "independent intervening cause" to describe a causal factor that would exculpate (e.g., the wife's decision to go horseback riding in the hypothetical used above).

The difficulty with these terms is that they are merely labels that can be attached to conclusions reached on other grounds. They do not describe the process or the criteria by which one could reason to those conclusions. To say that Blake's conduct in *Kibbe* was a "dependent

---

[c] See, e.g., R. Perkins, Criminal Law 685–738 (2d ed. 1969).

intervening cause" is to announce the result that Kibbe and Krall are guilty. It does not explain why they should be guilty, nor does it establish the criteria that can be applied to the next case.

It should be noted, however, that the *Kibbe* court did not limit itself to a recitation of these conclusory terms. The court characterized Stafford's death as "directly foreseeable" and said that "to be a sufficiently direct cause of death so as to warrant the imposition of a criminal penalty, [i]t will suffice if it can be said . . . that the ultimate harm is something which should have been foreseen as being reasonably related to the acts of the accused." What does the court mean by this language? Does it mean that even though the statute requires an extreme form of recklessness, negligence is a sufficient level of culpability so long as the harm is "reasonably related" to the acts of the accused? Does this confuse the standard of culpability with the standard that should be used to measure causation? Does this reflect an insight or a confusion on the part of the court? You may want to reconsider this question after you have studied the Model Penal Code provisions on causation reproduced in the following note.

3. **The Model Code Approach.** It is said in H. Hart and A. Honore, Causation in the Law 353 (1959), that "[t]he most lucid, comprehensive, and successful attempt to simplify problems of 'proximate cause' in the criminal law is that contained in the . . . Model Penal Code prepared by the American Law Institute." The Model Code made a deliberate attempt "to cut loose from the 'encrusted precedents' of 'proximate cause.' " In doing so, it substituted a new vocabulary and discarded the old common-law terms for reasoning about the proximate-cause question.

The key to the Model Code analysis of causation is the recognition that the problem of proximate cause is not a problem of describing physical relationships, but one of assessing their legal significance. Moreover, the criteria against which their significance should be assessed are closely related to the criteria used for measuring responsibility in the criminal law. The question, in other words, is not quantitative, but qualitative; it turns on a judgment of blameworthiness and responsibility and should be thought of in those terms, not in terms of physical causation. Section 2.03 of the Model Code provides:

"(1) Conduct is the cause of a result when:

(a) it is an antecedent but for which the result in question would not have occurred; and

(b) the relationship between the conduct and result satisfies any additional causal requirements imposed by the Code or by the law defining the offense.

"(2) When purposely or knowingly causing a particular result is an element of an offense, the element is not established if the actual result is not within the purpose or the contemplation of the actor unless:

(a) the actual result differs from that designed or contemplated, as the case may be, only in the respect that a different person or different property is injured or affected or that the injury or harm designed or contemplated would have been more serious or more extensive than that caused; or

(b) the actual result involves the same kind of injury or harm as that designed or contemplated and is not too remote or accidental in its occurrence to have a [just] bearing on the actor's liability or on the gravity of his offense.

"(3) When recklessly or negligently causing a particular result is an element of the offense, the element is not established if the actual result is not within the risk of which the actor is aware or, in the case of negligence, of which he should be aware unless:

(a) the actual result differs from the probable result only in the respect that a different person or different property is injured or affected or that the probable injury or harm would have been more serious or more extensive than that caused; or

(b) the actual result involves the same kind of injury or harm as the probable result and is not too remote or accidental in its occurrence to have a [just] bearing on the actor's liability or on the gravity of his offense.

"(4) When causing a particular result is a material element of an offense for which absolute liability is imposed by law, the element is not established unless the actual result is a probable consequence of the actor's conduct."

How would the *Kibbe* case be decided if the Model Code standards of causation were applied? Do you agree with Hart and Honore that this is a more successful mode of analysis than was used by the common law?

4. **Problems With the Model Code.** The Model Code provisions on causation have not been received uncritically. Many recently revised codes have not included a comparable provision, at least partly on the ground that the Model Code provision is too complex. There have also been a number of substantive criticisms, among them the following:

(i) **Concurrent Causes.** In 1 Working Papers of the Nat'l Comm'n on Reform of Federal Criminal Laws 144–45 (1970), the Model Code reliance on "but-for" causation in § 2.03(1)(a) is criticized because it "ignores the cases in which ['but-for' causation] is not essential for liability." The example given is a case of concurrent causation:

"Even though all of the senators may have intended to kill Caesar and all of them stabbed him, under the Model Penal Code's formulation none would be criminally liable for his death since (so I shall assume) he would have died even though any one of them had held back his knife. Even a senator who stabbed Caesar through the heart would not be liable, since so Anthony tells us (act 3, scene 2) 'sweet Caesar's blood' was streaming from all the wounds."

Is this a likely situation? Is it adequately dealt with under the Model Code provisions?[d] What result under the Model Code if *A* inflicts a mortal wound on *B* with intent to kill, but *C* kills *B* before *A*'s wound can have its natural effect? Is *A* guilty of murder? Should *A* be?

    (ii) **Transferred Intent.** Consider the following situation. *A* shoots at *B* with intent to kill. Because it was aimed badly, the shot misses, richochets off a rock, and kills *C*. The common law would have resolved this case by using the fictional concept of "transferred intent"—by magically "transferring" *A*'s intent from *B* to *C* and holding *A* liable for murder. Under the Model Code, *A* would be liable for murder because *A* acted purposely with respect to the death of another and because the causation requirements of § 2.03(2)(a) would be satisfied; the actual result would have differed from the intended result "only in the respect that a different person . . . is injured."

It is argued in Note, Causation in the Model Penal Code, 78 Colum. L.Rev. 1249, 1267–72 (1978), that the common-law transferred-intent doctrine is a species of strict liability and that the Model Code resolution in effect continues that result and is thus inconsistent with its normal approach to strict liability:

> "A difference in victims is not simply a trivial variation in the manner in which harm occurs; the identity of the victim is apt to be of great significance both to the offender and to those affected by the killing. No one would suppose that an offender who fails to kill his intended victim has achieved his basic objective if he inadvertently kills someone else. Admittedly, the harm that ultimately results may be as great as that which would have occurred if the offender had accomplished his precise objective. But if the magnitude of resulting harm were the sole prerequisite for the imposition of liability, there would be no need for any proximity requirement."

The suggested solution is to treat the actor in the transferred-intent situation under the provisions of § 210.2(1)(b) of the Model Code, by adding a presumption of the required recklessness in cases where the death occurs during the attempted murder of another. Is this a better resolution? Does the Model Code embrace a form of strict liability in § 2.03(2)(a)? Is the transferred-intent situation properly treated as a causation problem?

    (iii) **Volitional Human Intervention.** A difficult class of causation problems is created when the defendant sets in motion a series of

---

[d] The membership of the American Law Institute debated this issue when the Proposed Official Draft of the Model Penal Code was under consideration at the May 1962 meeting. It adopted the following instruction to the Reporter: "The comment is to make clear why the Reporter considers the formulation [in § 2.03(1)] sufficient to include concurrent sufficient causes, and what language should be added if it is desired to deal with this problem explicitly." ALI, Model Penal Code 1 (P.O.D. July 1962). Is additional language necessary? Do you see how § 2.03(1) could be construed to cover the case of "concurrent sufficient causes?" Is it clear that it should be so construed?

events that is interrupted by the voluntary action of another person. Suppose on the *Kibbe* facts, for example, that it was clear that Blake could have stopped in time and that he was at least negligent in causing Stafford's death. Should Kibbe and Krall still be liable for murder? Would the *Kibbe* court have convicted them on these facts? Would it matter if Blake recognized Stafford sitting in the road and decided to kill him because he had raped Blake's sister?

The Model Code would resolve such a case by asking in § 2.03(3)(b) whether the actual result was "not too remote or accidental in its occurrence to have a [just] bearing on the actor's liability or the gravity of his offense." The words "remote or" were added to an earlier draft, partially in response to the criticism of Hart and Honore that the words "too accidental" put the crucial inquiry in this kind of case "in quite unfamiliar terms." Several states have responded to this problem by modification of the applicable standard. New Jersey, for example, adopts the basic Model Code structure but modifies § 2.03(3)(b) as follows: "the actual result must involve the same kind of injury or harm as the probable result and must not be too remote, accidental in its occurrence, or dependent on another's volitional act to have a just bearing on the actor's liability or on the gravity of his offense." N.J. Stat.Ann. § 2C:2–3(c) (1980 Pamphlet). Is the New Jersey statute an improvement on the Model Code? How should liability in this situation be measured?

SECTION 4: FELONY MURDER

INTRODUCTORY NOTES ON FELONY MURDER

1. **The Rule and its Traditional Limitations.** The original statement of the felony-murder rule was that a person who commits any felony and all accomplices in that felony are guilty of murder if a death occurs during the commission or attempted commission of the felony. Liability is strict, in the sense that no inquiry need be made into the culpability as to the death of any of the participants in the felony; their culpability for the underlying felony is sufficient. As the next main case puts the point, "the killer's malignant purpose is established by proof of the collateral felony." Thus, if two persons undertake to commit a robbery, they are both guilty of murder if a victim of the robbery is killed during the commission of the offense, whether or not either robber would have been guilty of murder by the application of the normal mens rea requirements for murder.

The history of felony murder is marked by judicial efforts to limit its scope. The premise of these efforts is that "any" felony should not trigger the rule, because not all felonies present a likelihood of danger to human life. The list of modern felonies includes offenses related to election returns and voting, securities and insurance violations, conflict of interest, fraud, and a wide variety of similar activity in which the prospect of violence or other life-endangering activity is at best remote. If the rationale of the rule is based on the tendency of certain felonies to threaten life, it follows that some limitation on the kinds of felonies that support application of the felony-murder rule is needed.

The courts have used essentially three devices for limiting the situations to which the rule applies: (i) a requirement that the felony be inherently dangerous, either in general or on the particular facts; (ii) a causation limitation, usually expressed as a requirement that the death be a "natural and probable result" of the felonious conduct; and (iii) a requirement that the felony be "independent" of the homicide, often stated to exclude lesser-included homicide and assault offenses from those felonies to which the rule applies. The first limitation is sometimes expressed as a requirement that the felony must be malum in se rather than malum prohibitum, though this is an obvious over generalization since not all malum in se offenses are dangerous to life. The third is sometimes stated as a rule of merger; an assault with intent to kill, for example, may be said to merge into a resulting homicide and thus not to be an "independent" felony that can result in a felony-murder conviction.

In many states, a form of the first limitation is required by statute. For example, those states that have followed the original Pennsylvania degree structure generally include a list of "inherently dangerous" felonies that will support a first-degree murder conviction. In most such states, however, second-degree murder consists of all other forms of murder at common law, and thus includes a residual category of felony-murder based on felonies not included on the first-degree list. Thus the need to address appropriate limitations on the unadorned felony-murder rule exists in states where the highest grade of murder encompasses homicides that occur during the commission of "any" felony,[a] as well as in those states in which a lower grade of murder includes a residual category composed of other homicides that would constitute "murder" at common law.[b]

2. **Rationale of the Rule.** The felony-murder rule has two principal consequences. First, it criminalizes behavior that absent the rule would not be an independent homicide offense. The defendant will be guilty of murder without proof that any traditional culpability standard, independent of that required for the felony that triggered the rule, was satisfied. Thus, an entirely accidental killing—one for which neither an intent to kill nor recklessness or negligence as to the death can be shown—may result in a conviction for murder if it occurs during the commission of a qualifying felony. Second, it upgrades homicidal behavior that otherwise might be classified as a lesser offense. A negligent killing, for example, might be punished as involuntary manslaughter under normal circumstances, but is upgraded to murder if committed during the course of a qualifying felony. Similarly, provocation that ordinarily might reduce an offense to manslaughter may not have that effect if the charge is felony murder.

---

[a] See, e.g., the Kansas statute quoted on p. 939, infra.

[b] See, e.g., the original Pennsylvania statute quoted on p. 781, supra.

Why has the law provided for these results? Given the general reluctance of the common-law system to rely on strict liability, why is strict liability used for one of the most serious criminal offenses? The usual answer is the one endorsed in the next main case: "The only rational function of the felony-murder rule is to furnish an added deterrent to the perpetration of felonies which, by their nature or by the attendant circumstances, create a foreseeable risk of death." A well-known defense, though not necessarily an endorsement, of the rule was offered by Oliver Wendell Holmes in The Common Law 59 (1881):

> "[I]f experience shows, or is deemed by the lawmaker to show, that somehow or other deaths which the evidence makes acciden-tal happen disproportionately often in connection with other felonies, or with resistance to officers, or if on any other ground of policy it is deemed desirable to make special efforts for the prevention of such deaths, the lawmaker may consistently treat acts which, under the known circumstances, are felonious, or constitute resistance to officers, as having a sufficiently danger-ous tendency to be put under a special ban. The law may, therefore, throw on the actor the peril, not only of the conse-quences foreseen by him, but also of consequences which, al-though not predicted by common experience, the legislator appre-hends."

It is often noted in response to this contention that there is little empirical evidence that homicides "which the evidence makes acciden-tal happen disproportionately often in connection with other felonies." In ALI, Model Penal Code and Commentaries, § 210.2, p. 38 (1980), statistics are reproduced which show that of 16,273 robberies in New Jersey in 1975, only 66 homicides (or homicides in .41 per cent of the cases) were committed. Similar figures are cited for other felonies and other jurisdictions. Do these statistics show that the felony-murder rule is unnecessary, or that it works? Is Holmes right in considering only those homicides "which the evidence makes accidental?" Are these the only homicides as to which a special rule may be needed?

A more recent defense of the felony-murder rule was advanced by David Crump and Susan Waite Crump in an article entitled In Defense of the Felony Murder Doctrine, 8 Harv.J.Law & Pub.Policy 359 (1985). They advance six modern rationales that could be used to justify the offense. First, they argue that the rule "reflects a societal judgment that an intentionally committed robbery that causes . . . death . . . is qualitatively more serious than an identical robbery that does not." The law often classifies offenses, they elaborate, on the basis of results. Murder and attempted murder, for example, may be committed with the same mens rea, yet attempted murder is usually graded less severely. The only factor that can account for this grading differential is that the murderer has caused a death. If it is not irrational to grade murder more seriously than attempted murder, they conclude, it is similarly not irrational to classify robbery-that-causes-a-death more seriously than robbery. Secondly, they argue that the "reinforcement of societal norms" associated with the function of condemnation supports placing the label "murder" on a death that occurs during certain felonies that are by their nature violent. They think this particularly appropriate when, as they argue is the case with felony murder, common social judgment coincides with the classification. Third, they argue that the "felony murder rule is just the sort of simple, common-sense, readily enforceable, and widely known principle that is likely to result in deterrence."

Their remaining arguments list advantages of the rule that cannot stand as independent justifications, but that ought to be considered, in their view, in any rational debate. Their fourth argument is that "the aim of consistent and predictable adjudication" is better served by the felony murder rule than by the convoluted rules that are often used to describe the mens rea of murder. Fifth, the "rule has beneficial allocative consequences because it clearly defines the offense, simplifies the task of judge and jury with respect to questions of law and fact, and thereby promotes efficient administration of justice." Finally, they argue that the rule reduces the incentive to commit perjury by removing defenses that can most readily be proved by the defendant's own testimony.

3. **Judicial Rejection of the Rule:** *People v. Aaron.* The felony-murder rule was rejected by the Michigan Supreme Court in People v. Aaron, 409 Mich. 672, 299 N.W.2d 304 (1980). The court first addressed the history of the doctrine, noting that "the rule is of questionable origin" and "the reasons for the rule no longer exist, making it an anachronistic remnant, 'a historic survivor for which there is no logical or practical basis for existence in modern law.'" As to its origins, the court referred to scholarship [c] suggesting that the 16th century cases commonly thought to have established the rule were misinterpreted by Lord Coke and some of the other early writers. As to its initial rationale, the court said:

> "The failure of the felony-murder rule to consider the defendant's moral culpability is explained by examining the state of the law at the time of the rule's inception. The concept of culpability was not an element of homicide at early common law. The early history of malice aforethought was vague. The concept meant little more than intentional wrongdoing with no other emphasis on intention except to exclude homicides that were committed by misadventure or in some otherwise pardonable manner. Thus, under this early definition of malice aforethought, an intent to commit the felony would itself constitute malice.[d] Furthermore, as all felonies were punished alike, it made little difference whether the felon was hanged for the felony or for the death.

[c] E.g., Kaye, The Early History of Murder and Manslaughter, Part II, 83 Quarterly Rev. 569 (1967); Recent Developments, Felony-Murder Rule—Felon's Responsibility for Death of Accomplice, 65 Colum.L. Rev. 1496 (1965); Note, Felony Murder as a First Degree Offense: An Anachronism Retained, 66 Yale L.J. 427 (1957).

[d] Compare the discussion by Sayre, pages 194–196, supra, and the issues in the *Faulkner* and *Cunningham* cases, pages 196–203, supra. [Footnote by eds.]

"Thus, the felony-murder rule did not broaden the concept of murder at the time of its origin because proof of the intention to commit a felony met the test of culpability based on the vague definition of malice aforethought governing at that time. Today, however, malice is a term of art. It does not include the nebulous definition of intentional wrongdoing. Thus, although the felony-murder rule did not broaden the definition of murder at early common law, it does so today. We find this enlargement of the scope of murder unacceptable, because it is based on a concept of culpability which is 'totally incongruous with the general principles of our jurisprudence' today."

The Michigan statute at issue in *Aaron* was based on the original Pennsylvania degree structure:

"Murder which is perpetrated by means of poison, lying in wait, or other wilful, deliberate, and premeditated killing, or which is committed in the perpetration or attempt to perpetrate [certain listed felonies], is murder in the first degree . . . ."

The court held that the purpose of the statute was only "to graduate punishment"; it "only serves to raise an already established *murder* to the first-degree level, not to transform a death, without more, into a murder." Thus, the "use of the term 'murder' in the . . . statute requires that a murder first be established before the statute is applied to elevate the degree."

The question, then, was what constituted a "murder" that could be elevated to "murder in the first degree" when committed in the course of one of the listed felonies. The prosecutor argued that the undefined term "murder" referred to the common law, and that the common law included a felony-murder rule that could trigger the statute. The court recognized the logic of this argument, but held that it was an unsound rule that was "no longer acceptable":

"Accordingly we hold today that malice is the intention to kill, the intention to do great bodily harm, or the wanton and wilful disregard of the likelihood that the natural tendency of the defendant's behavior is to cause death or great bodily harm. We further hold that malice is an essential element of any murder, as that term is judicially defined, whether the murder occurs in the course of a felony or otherwise. The facts and circumstances involved in the perpetration of a felony may evidence an intent to kill, an intent to cause great bodily harm, or a wanton and wilful disregard of the likelihood that the natural tendency of the defendant's behavior is to cause death or great bodily harm; however, the conclusion must be left to the jury to infer from all the evidence."

Finally, the court addressed the practical effect of its abolition of the felony-murder rule. It said:

"From a practical standpoint, the abolition of the category of malice arising from the intent to commit the underlying felony should have little effect on the result of the majority of cases. In many cases where the felony-murder rule has been applied, the use of the doctrine was unnecessary because the other types of malice could have been inferred from the evidence.

"Abrogation of this rule does not make irrelevant the fact that a death occurred in the course of a felony. A jury can properly *infer* malice from evidence that a defendant set in motion a force likely to cause death or great bodily harm. Thus, whenever a killing occurs in the perpetration or attempted perpetration of an inherently dangerous felony, in order to establish malice the jury may consider the 'nature of the underlying felony and the circumstances surrounding its commission.' If the jury concludes that malice existed, they can find murder and, if they determine that the murder occurred in the perpetration or attempted perpetration of one of the enumerated felonies, by statute the murder would become first-degree murder.

"The difference is that the jury may not find malice from the intent to commit the underlying felony alone. The defendant will be permitted to assert any of the applicable defenses relating to mens rea which he would be allowed to assert if charged with premeditated murder. The latter result is reasonable in light of the fact that felony murder is certainly no more heinous than premeditated murder. The prosecution will still be able to prove first-degree murder without proof of premeditation when a homicide is committed with malice, as we have defined it, and the perpetration or attempted perpetration of an enumerated felony is established. Hence, our first-degree statute continues to elevate to first-degree murder a *murder* which is committed in the perpetration or attempted perpetration of one of the enumerated felonies."

Two justices wrote separately to explain the rationale on which they agreed with the result reached by the court's opinion. There were no dissents.

4. **The Model Penal Code and Modern Statutes.** The Model Penal Code takes the position that the felony-murder rule is indefensible in principle because it bases the most severe sanctions known to the criminal law on strict liability. The Model Code suggests instead that ordinary principles of criminal homicide, causation, and complicity should be used for the prosecution of homicides that occur during the commission of a felony. It does, however, make one concession to the historical momentum of the rule. This is contained in the provisions of § 210.2(1)(b), which read as follows:

"[C]riminal homicide constitutes murder when . . . it is committed recklessly under circumstances manifesting extreme indifference to the value of human life. Such recklessness and indifference are presumed if the actor is engaged or is an accomplice in the commission of, or an attempt to commit, or flight after committing or attempting to commit robbery, rape or deviate sexual intercourse by force or threat of force, arson, burglary, kidnapping or felonious escape."

The effect of a presumption under the Model Code is dealt with in § 1.12(5). Is this an effective compromise? Is the point one that should be compromised?

ALI, Model Penal Code and Commentaries, § 210.2, pp. 40–42 (1980), reports that among the states in which recent penal-code revisions have been undertaken, only Hawaii and Kentucky have abolished the felony-murder rule completely,[e] and only New Hampshire has adopted the Model Penal Code solution. Delaware has also restricted the rule by requiring that the actor "recklessly cause the death of another person" in order to be guilty of first-degree murder under the felony-murder doctrine, and reduces the offense to second-degree murder if the actor is negligent.

Among the other states, the most important revision is New York's, which is reproduced in Appendix B, pages 8–9, infra. The Model Code commentary reports that the New York approach has been copied in at least seven enacted codes. Does the New York approach represent a more principled compromise of the felony-murder debate? Why do you think it has been copied in more states than the Model Penal Code? What explains the persistence of the felony-murder rule?

STATE v. GOODSEAL

Supreme Court of Kansas, 1976.
220 Kan. 487, 553 P.2d 279.

HARMAN, COMMISSIONER. . . . Appellant Goodseal . . . was convicted of murder in the first degree, done in the commission of a felony, unlawful possession of a firearm after a felony conviction. . . .

[Goodseal had been convicted on two counts of forcible rape. He served a term of imprisonment, from which he had been released slightly more than four years before the incident that led to the current charge. On the morning of the events in question, he met a woman named "Silky." They spent the day drinking together, and that night she went to work as a topless dancer in a nightclub. Hunter was a customer at the nightclub. At closing time, Silky and Hunter went outside to Hunter's car so that Silky could "turn a trick." Goodseal and Silky had previously agreed that Goodseal would pretend to be Silky's husband and pull her from the car so that Silky would not actually be required to have sexual relations with Hunter. At the appointed time, Goodseal approached the car and tapped the glass on the back window with the butt of a pistol. The following events then occurred.]

Silky unlocked the door and appellant opened the passenger side door. Hunter and Silky were in the back seat. Silky got out of the car immediately, pulling on her pants and asking appellant to get her shoes. Appellant asked Hunter what he was doing with his "wife" and

---

[e] England has also abolished the felony-murder rule. Homicide Act, 1957, 5 & 6 Eliz. II, c. 11, § 1.

Hunter replied he had paid her. Hunter then pulled on his pants, turned the pockets partially inside out and said, "Hey, she got my money." Appellant testified he remembered saying, "No wonder she wanted me to play this little trick so she could steal somebody's money." [a] Appellant further testified he then bent over to pick up Silky's shoes, he slipped in the snow, bumped into the door and the gun discharged. The bullet struck Hunter in the armpit beneath his right shoulder and penetrated the lung area, causing his death. Appellant's version was that the shooting was accidental and the only reason he took the gun was to scare Hunter with it. . . .

Appellant's principal point upon appeal is that . . . the offense of felonious possession of a firearm is not inherently dangerous to human life and therefore cannot be the basis for felony murder. [The statute] under which appellant was convicted provides:

> "*Murder in the first degree is the killing of a human being* committed maliciously, willfully, deliberately and with premeditation or *committed in the perpetration or attempt to perpetrate any felony.* . . . " (Emphasis supplied.)

Possession of a firearm with a barrel less than 12 inches long by a person who within five years has been released from imprisonment for a felony, is one form of unlawful possession of a firearm and is a class D felony. Here there is no question that appellant [was committing this felony] when a bullet from [the] weapon caused Hunter's death. . . .

Appellee [argues] that our present statute does not require that a felony be one inherently dangerous to human life in order to support a felony-murder conviction. We cannot agree. [P]rior to 1970, our felony-murder statute provided:

> "*Every murder* which shall be committed by means of poison or by lying in wait, or by any kind of willful, deliberate and premeditated killing, or *which shall be committed in the perpetration or an attempt to perpetrate any arson, rape, robbery, burglary, or other felony, shall be deemed murder in the first degree.*" (Emphasis supplied.)

[As originally enacted in 1970,] our new criminal code provided:

> "*Murder in the first degree is the malicious killing of a human being* committed willfully, deliberately and with premeditation or *committed in the perpetration or attempt to perpetrate any felony.*" (Emphasis supplied.)

Under the context of this statute it was possible to consider malice as a separate essential element of felony murder. In 1972, the statute was amended to its present form, as already quoted, to indicate that malice is not an essential element of felony murder, following [a case] in which we indicated that the effect of the felony-murder rule is to relieve the state of the burden of proving premeditation and malice when the victim's death is caused by the killer while he is committing

[a] Goodseal was acquitted of participation in a robbery. [Footnote by eds.]

another felony, the rationale being that the killer's malignant purpose is established by proof of the collateral felony.

In State v. Moffitt, 199 Kan. 514, 431 P.2d 879 (1967), we affirmed the rule that a homicide resulting from the commission of a felony inherently dangerous to human life constitutes felony murder or murder in the first degree. Although our statute has been twice amended since *Moffitt* we have adhered to the same ruling. In State v. Bey, 217 Kan. 251, 535 P.2d 881 (1975), we said: "[T]o support a conviction for felony murder all that is required is to prove that a felony was being committed which was inherently dangerous to human life, and that the homicide was a direct result of the commission of that felony."

In *Moffitt* we were dealing with the "other felony" clause of the then felony-murder statute and we concluded that to come within the clause such a felony must be one inherently dangerous to human life. Our present statute, and the one under which appellant is being prosecuted, uses the term "any felony." We see no significant distinction between the two expressions for purposes of determining the applicability of the felony-murder rule and no reason to depart from the traditional requirement that the felony must be one inherently or foreseeably dangerous to human life. This limitation has always been imposed even in the absence of specific statutory mention and we adhere to that requirement. To go further could lead to manifestly unjust and even absurd results. In reaching the same conclusion the Delaware Supreme Court in Jenkins v. State, 230 A.2d 262, 268–69 (Del. 1967), commented:

> ". . . The only rational function of the felony-murder rule is to furnish an added deterrent to the perpetration of felonies which, by their nature or by the attendant circumstances, create a foreseeable risk of death. This function is not served by application of the rule to felonies not foreseeably dangerous. The rule should not be extended beyond its rational function. Moreover, application of the rule to felonies not foreseeably dangerous would be unsound analytically because there is no logical basis for imputing malice from the intent to commit a felony not dangerous to human life."

The next question is whether unlawful possession of a firearm by an ex-felon is an offense inherently dangerous to human life. In *Moffitt* we said that it was. In reaching this conclusion we did not specifically state whether we were viewing the felony in the abstract or, as several courts have done, were considering both the nature of the felony and the circumstances of its commission. In *Moffitt* the facts were that the defendant, a convicted felon, fired a pistol while assaulting two pedestrians and inadvertently killed a woman sitting on a motorcycle some distance down the street. We did comment in *Moffitt* upon legislative recognition that persons who had once committed a felony were dangerous to society and should not have in their possession concealable weapons. Beyond this, where doubt may exist, we see nothing wrong in considering both the nature of the offense in the abstract and the circumstances of its commission in determining whether a particular felony was inherently dangerous to human life. Some felonies, such as aggravated robbery, viewed in the abstract alone, are of such nature as to be inherently dangerous to human life, while another which seems of itself not to involve any element of human risk may be committed in such a dangerous manner as to be of the same character.

Hence we hold that the nature of the felony and, where necessary for determination, the circumstances of its commission are relevant factors in considering whether the particular felony was inherently and foreseeably dangerous to human life so as to support a conviction of felony murder. These are questions for the trial court and jury to decide in appropriate cases. In the case at bar appellant's own testimony was that he used the pistol to scare the victim. However, there was no evidence he made any presentment of the pistol in an offer to do corporal hurt to the victim so as to amount to an assault constituting an integral part of a murder charge as prohibited by State v. Clark, 204 Kan. 38, 460 P.2d 586 (1969). Under appellant's undisputed admissions the trial court in effect correctly held as a matter of law that the collateral felony, unlawful possession of a firearm, was a sufficient basis for application of the felony-murder rule. . . .

The felony-murder rule represents a long-standing policy of this state. We have already indicated its rationale—to furnish an added deterrent to the perpetration of felonies which, by their nature or the attendant circumstances, create a foreseeable risk of death. "The legislature, acting in the exercise of the police power of the state, is empowered to enact measures in furtherance of the public welfare and safety, and its enactments in such areas are not to be judicially curtailed where they reasonably relate to the ends sought to be attained. Classifications honestly designed to protect the public from evils which might otherwise arise are to be upheld unless they are unreasonable, arbitrary or oppressive." The felony-murder rule, designed as it is to protect human life, represents sound public policy, is reasonably related to the end sought to be accomplished and is not constitutionally impermissible. . . .

Appellant [argues that] the trial court erred in refusing to instruct the jury on the lesser-included offenses of second-degree murder and involuntary manslaughter. In State v. Reed, 214 Kan. 562, 520 P.2d 1314 (1974), we noted that a trial court's duty to instruct on a lesser-included offense arises only where there is evidence under which the defendant might reasonably have been convicted of the lesser offense. As already indicated, under the felony-murder rule the felonious conduct itself is held tantamount to the elements of malice, deliberation and premeditation which are otherwise required for first-degree murder, and if proof is adduced during the trial that the accused was committing a felony inherently dangerous to human life and the homicide was a direct result of that felony, then the only possible conviction can be that of first-degree murder under the felony-murder rule. [I]n the recent case of State v. Bradford, 219 Kan. 336, 548 P.2d 812 (1976), . . . this court upheld a trial court's decision to instruct the jury on the lesser-included offense of second-degree murder even though the defendant was charged with felony murder. The court's rationale was as follows:

> ". . . Ordinarily, in a felony-murder case, where the evidence of the commission of the felony is clear and uncontroverted, no instruction on lesser degrees of homicide should be given. But where, as here, there is conflicting evidence as to the commission of the felony, and where the evidence will support a conviction of a lesser degree of homicide, instructions on appropriate lesser degrees should be given."

. . . Appellant's own testimony was that he used the pistol to scare the victim and all the evidence compels the conclusion he did in fact use the pistol in a menacing fashion as a weapon even though its discharge may have been accidental. Under these uncontroverted facts instructions on any lesser degree of homicide would have been improper.

Finally, appellant complains of the trial court's failure to permit the jury to fix the punishment to be assessed upon conviction. . . . Murder in the first degree is a class A felony. [The operative statute] provides:

> "For the purpose of sentencing, the following classes of felonies and terms of imprisonment authorized for each class are established:
>
> > (a) Class A, the sentence for which shall be death or imprisonment for life. If there is a jury trial the jury shall determine which punishment shall be inflicted. . . ."

The complaint has no merit. At the time of appellant's trial the death penalty in Kansas had been judicially abolished and a jury in a class A felony case no longer had any function or choice to perform in fixing the penalty upon conviction. The law fixed the only permissible punishment and its declaration was a matter for the trial court.

The judgment is affirmed.

Approved by the court.

KAUL, JUSTICE (concurring). I concur with the majority's disposition of this appeal, but feel compelled to record these observations. In *Moffitt*, a unanimous court firmly established that possession of a pistol after a felony conviction . . . constituted a felony inherently dangerous to human life. . . .

Moffitt was decided in 1967. I think it may be said, without dispute, that it is a matter of common knowledge that firearm homicides, committed by felons, have dramatically increased even since the *Moffitt* decision. Our legislature has examined our criminal code on several occasions and found no reason to alter the *Moffitt* rule. Under the circumstances, it appears to me that modification or reversal of our unanimous decision in *Moffitt* would be a grave mistake.

PRAGER, JUSTICE (dissenting): I respectfully dissent from that portion of the majority opinion which holds that mere possession of a firearm . . . may be used to convert an accidental or non-malicious killing to murder in the first-degree by application of the felony-murder rule. In the typical murder case in order for a defendant to be convicted of murder in the first degree it is incumbent upon the state to prove that the defendant killed his victim maliciously, willfully, and with deliberation and premeditation. Murder in the first degree is punishable by life imprisonment under our present statute. The majority opinion correctly points out that the felony-murder rule was designed to relieve the state of the burden of proving willfulness, premeditation, deliberation, and malice when the victim's death is caused by the killer while he is committing another felony. The rationale behind the felony-murder rule is that the killer's malignant purpose is established by proof of the collateral felony. The majority opinion correctly declares that all felonies are not sufficient to permit the application of the felony-murder rule. In order for the felony-murder rule to be applicable, the collateral felony must be one inherently or foreseeably dangerous to human life, and to sustain a conviction for murder in the first degree under that rule, it must be shown that the homicide committed was a direct causal result of the commission of such felony. At this point I am in complete agreement with the majority.

The basic issue presented in this case is whether or not the mere unlawful possession of a firearm by a convicted felon . . . is the type of felony which reasonably permits the application of the felony-murder rule to a killing which is accidental or non-malicious. I wish to emphasize in the beginning that the offense of unlawful possession of a firearm by a convicted felon is an important part of our criminal code. [The offense] is punishable by confinement in a penal institution for a variable minimum term of not less than one year nor more than three years and a maximum term of 10 years. The law is well designed to protect the public from the improper use of firearms by convicted felons. The majority opinion appears to concede that unlawful possession of a firearm in the abstract is not an inherently or foreseeably dangerous act unless the circumstances of its commission make it so. Such a rule is logically based upon the assumption that it is not the possession of the firearm which is inherently dangerous but it is rather the handling or the *use* which is made of the firearm which may be inherently dangerous so as to justify the application of the felony-murder rule.

The issue before us in this case was determined by the Supreme Court of California . . . in People v. Satchell, 6 Cal.3d 28, 98 Cal.Rptr. 33, 489 P.2d 1361 (1971). In that case the California court pointed out that the felony-murder rule is a highly artificial concept and warned that "it should not be extended beyond any rational function that it is designed to serve." The court further held that the determination as to whether a felony is inherently dangerous for purposes of the felony-murder rule must be based upon an assessment of that felony in the abstract and not on the particular facts of a case. It concluded that neither possession of a concealable firearm by a person who has previously been convicted of a felony nor possession by any person of a weapon such as a sawed-off shotgun is a felony inherently dangerous to human life for purposes of the felony-murder rule. It concluded that a person who perpetrates a homicide while engaged merely in the commission of the felony of possession of a firearm may not be convicted of murder unless the existence of the crucial mental state of malice aforethought is actually proved by the prosecution. It is important that we examine closely the rationale of the California court in *Satchell* where the court stated:

"It is manifest that the range of anti-social activities which are criminally punishable as felonies in this state is very wide indeed. Some of these felonies, such as certain well-known crimes against the person of another, distinctly manifest a propensity for acts dangerous to human life on the part of the perpetrator. Others . . . just as distinctly fail to manifest such a propensity. Surely it cannot be said that a person who has committed a crime in this latter category, when he arms himself with a concealable weapon, presents a danger to human life so significantly more extreme than that presented by a non-felon similarly armed as to justify the imputation of malice to him if a homicide should result. Accordingly, because we can conceive of such a vast number of situations wherein it would be grossly illogical to impute malice, we must conclude that [possession of a firearm] by one previously convicted of a felony is not itself a felony *inherently* dangerous to human life which will support a . . . felony-murder instruction. . . .

"Viewing the matter from the standpoint of inherent danger, we find it difficult to understand how any offense of mere passive possession can be considered to supply the element of malice in a murder prosecution. To be sure, if such possession is of an extremely reckless nature manifesting a conscious disregard for human life, malice may be imputed by means of basic murder principles. . . . Moreover, if passive possession ripens into a felonious *act* in which danger to human life is inherent, the purpose of the felony-murder rule is served by its application— for it is the deterrence of such acts by felons which the rule is designed to accomplish. However, mere possession *in itself*— ignoring the propensities and conduct of the possessor—is essentially neutral in its intentional aspect and should not serve as the basis for the imputation of malice."

The rule adopted by the majority in the case before us is not sound for several reasons. In the first place, in my judgment, it is a rule which would be impossible for the trial courts of this state to apply. The majority opinion states that where doubt exists as to whether in a particular case unlawful possession of a firearm is inherently dangerous, there is nothing wrong in considering both the nature of the offense in the abstract and the circumstances of its commission in determining whether the offense was inherently dangerous to human life in the particular case. The majority opinion has furnished no guidelines to assist the trial court in instructing the jury. This in my judgment places a difficult burden upon the district courts of this state in applying the rule adopted by the majority.

The rule of the majority opinion also may result in serious conflict with the established principle of law that in a first-degree murder prosecution the felony-murder rule may not properly be invoked when it is based upon a felony which is an integral part of the homicide. State v. Clark, 204 Kan. 38, 460 P.2d 586 (1969). The rule followed by the majority requires the trial court and the jury to consider not only the unlawful possession of a pistol in the abstract but also the manner in which the pistol is handled or used in determining whether the possession was inherently dangerous to human life. In the case now before us the majority relies upon the fact that the defendant had a gun in his hand in order to scare the deceased and thereby to coerce him into involuntary action. In order to avoid a conflict with the rule of *State v. Clark,* supra, the majority opinion emphasizes that there was no evidence the defendant made any presentment of the pistol in an offer to do corporal hurt to the victim so as to amount to an assault constituting an integral part of the murder charge as prohibited by *Clark.* The clear implication is that if the defendant had actually assaulted the deceased with a gun, then the felony-murder rule would not have been applicable since in that situation the assault would have been an integral part of the homicide. It would seem to follow that if a defendant unlawfully possessing a firearm does not commit an assault upon his victim but accidentally kills him, then he may be found guilty of felony-murder. If, however, he assaults his victim then the felony-murder rule cannot be applied and in order to convict the defendant of murder the state must prove that the defendant intentionally and with malice committed the homicide. The irrationality of this distinction is obvious on its face.

Furthermore, I wish to point out that the practical application of the rule approved by the majority can produce other absurd results. For example, let us assume that a defendant, having been previously convicted of felony . . . accidentally shoots another person. At the time defendant was in the possession of a firearm with a barrel 11 inches long. Applying the felony-murder rule the defendant would be guilty of felony murder and upon conviction a life sentence would be imposed. If the firearm involved in the case had a barrel 12 inches long the defendant would not be guilty of any criminal offense since the shooting was accidental and would fall into the category of an excusable homicide. It does not seem reasonable to impute malice to the defendant in the first situation and not to do so in the second situation; yet this absurd result would follow under the rule adopted by the majority of the court in this case.

[It is] irrational . . . to use the unlawful possession of a firearm as a basis for application of the felony-murder rule. I want to emphasize the fact that the California rule does not prevent prosecution for murder in cases such as the one now before us. *People v. Satchell,* supra, merely holds that malice may not be imputed from the passive act of possession of a weapon. The state may properly prove the basic elements of premeditated murder where the evidence establishes that the firearm was used by the convicted felon in such a manner as to show malice, willfulness, and premeditation. The jury could then properly convict the defendant of first-degree murder.

Assuming that the rule of the majority should be adopted, it would still be necessary to reverse this case and grant the defendant a new trial. As pointed out above the majority has taken the position that felony possession of a firearm in the abstract is not sufficient to justify the application of the felony-murder doctrine. For the felony-murder rule to be applied the possession of the firearm must be under such circumstances as to be inherently dangerous to human life. The majority rule would, of necessity, require an instruction to the jury that before the felony-murder rule should be applied it must find that the factual circumstances of the case made felony possession an inherently dangerous crime. Absent such a qualifying instruction the jury would be permitted to use a passive nondangerous type of possession of a firearm as sufficient basis to find the defendant guilty of felony murder. In this case the jury was instructed without qualification that if the defendant killed the deceased and if such killing was done in the commission of the felony of unlawful possession of a firearm he should be found guilty of murder in the first degree. They were not instructed to take into consideration the factual circumstances present in the case. Even the majority would appear opposed to this result. . . .

In view of the position that has been taken in this dissent, it would logically follow that *State v. Moffitt,* supra, should be overruled. *Moffitt* relies to a great extent on [a series of California cases]. Those . . . cases held that unlawful possession of a pistol by a convicted felon was capable of supporting a felony-murder instruction. The rationale of those cases was considered and rejected by the California Supreme Court in *People v. Satchell,* supra. *Moffitt* should be overruled by this court not only for the reason that it relied upon California decisions which are no longer the law but also because the basic rationale of the case is not legally sound and is inherently unjust.

For the reasons set forth above I would reverse this case with directions that a new trial be granted.

STATE v. UNDERWOOD

Supreme Court of Kansas, 1980.
228 Kan. 294, 615 P.2d 153.

FROMME, JUSTICE. Curtis Leon Underwood appeals from a jury conviction of felony murder. The underlying felony . . . used to classify the homicide as a felony murder is unlawful possession of a firearm . . . .

[Underwood had been convicted in 1974 for stealing a bicycle and had served a two-year period of probation. He was 18 at the time of that offense. In 1978, he got into a fist fight with one Brewer. After the fight ended, Brewer was handed a shotgun by a friend, after which he brandished the shotgun at Underwood. Underwood left, went home, changed clothes, obtained a pistol, gave it to his half-brother to bring along, and returned to the scene. The fight was resumed, joined by friends of both Underwood and Brewer. At least one person was stabbed. One of Brewer's friends retrieved the shotgun. Brewer and Underwood had been wrestling on the ground, but suddenly Brewer escaped, got up, and ran toward his friend with the shotgun. Underwood then ran for the pistol, obtained it, and fired four shots, one of which struck Brewer and killed him. Underwood's testimony was that he fired because he saw Brewer reaching for the shotgun, and feared for the lives of himself and his friends.]

This court is again confronted with the question decided in State v. Moffitt, 199 Kan. 514, 431 P.2d 879 (1967), and State v. Goodseal, 220 Kan. 487, 553 P.2d 279 (1976). . . . For the reasons set forth below a [4–3] majority of this court [a] has concluded that it was prejudicial error for the trial court to instruct the jury on the theory of felony murder. Accordingly we reverse the judgment. . . .

Under the literal wording of [our] statute any felony is sufficient to support a charge of felony murder if a causal relation exists. [We have held, however,] that the collateral felony [must be] inherently dangerous to human life. . . .

Theoretically the elements of malice, deliberation and premeditation which are required for murder in the first degree are deemed to be supplied by felonious conduct alone if a homicide results. It is not necessary for the prosecutor to prove these elements or for the jury to find such elements of the crime. They are established by proof of the collateral felony. Therefore, to support a conviction for felony murder all that is required is to prove that a felony was being committed, which felony was inherently dangerous to human life, and that the homicide which followed was a direct result of the commission of that felony.

The felony-murder rule has logic based on the theory of transferred intent. The malicious and premeditated intent of committing the inherently dangerous collateral felony is transferred to the homicide to supply the elements of malice and premeditation without further proof. Consistent with this thinking, most courts require that the collateral felony be inherently dangerous for the felony-murder rule to be applicable. . . .

The collateral felony we are dealing with in the present case is . . . a status crime in that it is limited to drunkards, drug addicts and ex-felons. It is malum prohibitum. The possession of the firearm is prohibited because a firearm in the possession of a habitual drunkard, a narcotics addict or an ex-felon is against the public policy of the state as declared by the legislature. The possession of the firearm when viewed in the abstract is not inherently dangerous to human life. This is true because it seems unlikely that mere possession, which has been defined as dominion and control over an object, and not its use, could be undertaken in so dangerous a manner that the prohibited possession would result in murder in the first degree. . . . It appears quite impossible to find an intent in this collateral felony encompassing

[a] *Goodseal* was also decided by a 4–3 margin. [Footnote by eds.]

malice, deliberation and premeditation so as to transfer these elements to the homicide and relieve the prosecution from proof of the same. If these elements are present in the use of the firearm they are not present in the possession of the firearm. They should then be proven as elements of premeditated first-degree murder by reason of the malicious and deliberate use of the gun.

We note that once the *use* of the firearm begins, a separate crime is committed; e.g., assault with a deadly weapon assuming the required intent is present. Aggravated assault is an integral part of the homicide and felony murder cannot be based thereon. State v. Clark, 204 Kan. 38, 460 P.2d 586 (1969). It follows that unlawful possession of a firearm, when viewed in the abstract, does not harbor the malice and premeditation for the transferred intent so as to make a homicide a felony-murder. . . .

Further injustice may occur in felony-murder cases because the charge of felony-murder may strip an accused of the normal defenses possible in a murder case. In the present case, for instance, appellant had no intent to violate the law by possessing the firearm. He believed his previous bicycle-theft conviction was automatically dismissed when he successfully completed his probation. He was in error and he possessed a firearm so under the felony-murder charge the defenses such as accident, lack of malice and heat of passion were not open to him for the possession establishing the underlying felony could not be disputed. When proof of the underlying felony is strong no instructions on lesser degrees of murder are required.

In addition, filing a charge under the felony-murder rule in most, if not all, cases removes any possibility of establishing the defense of self-defense. Under [Kansas law], a person is justified in the use of force against an aggressor when and to the extent it appears to him, and he reasonably believes, that such conduct is necessary to defend himself or another against the aggressor's imminent use of unlawful force. If two men are fighting, as in this case, and one grabs a shotgun he is then the aggressor and the other may defend himself by use of a gun, if he can find one in time. However, an instruction on self-defense is not available to a person who is committing a forcible felony, [the definition of which] includes treason, murder, voluntary manslaughter, rape, robbery, burglary, arson, kidnapping, aggravated battery, aggravated sodomy and *any other felony which involves the use or threat of physical force or violence against any person.* Unlawful possession of a firearm is not included in the forcible felonies enumerated nor does it fit within the catch-all phrase at the end of the definition.

Now, where does that leave the person who is confronted with the rule in *Moffitt* and *Goodseal* holding that possession of a pistol after conviction of a felony is inherently dangerous to human life? Logically under *Goodseal* it follows that the defendant when charged with felony murder is not entitled to an instruction on self-defense. If the court considers the use of the firearm to establish that the collateral felony is inherently dangerous to human life, the use also establishes that the collateral felony is a forcible felony. This takes away from the accused the defense of self-defense.

A majority of this court now are convinced that the logic, reasoning and rule urged by Mr. Justice Prager in the dissent in *Goodseal* should be adopted for Kansas. Accordingly, we hold that in determining whether a particular collateral felony is inherently dangerous to human life so as to justify a charge of felony-murder, the elements of the collateral felony should be viewed in the abstract, and the circumstances of the commission of the felony should not be considered in making the determination. [A]ll cases holding to the contrary are disapproved.

The unlawful possession of a firearm when considered in the abstract is not a felony inherently dangerous to human life and will not sustain a conviction for murder in the first degree under the felony-murder rule. The rule formerly stated and applied in *State v. Moffitt* and its progeny [including *Goodseal* and two subsequent cases] is disapproved and overruled.

Reversed.

NOTES ON FELONY MURDER

1. **Questions and Comments on *Goodseal* and *Underwood*.** Each of the traditional limitations on the felony-murder rule summarized in the introductory notes to this section has the effect of modifying the rule by importing some measure of culpability for the offender's conduct in relation to the victim's death—though not that normally associated with murder. The scope of the felony-murder rule in a given jurisdiction thus can be seen as an adjustment of the tension between the deterrent objectives of the rule and limitations based on individual blameworthiness. Comparisons of the sort made in the *Goodseal* dissent are frequently used to illustrate the anomalous results that can arise from such compromises. Do they indicate the fundamental unsoundness of the rule? Or are they inevitable byproducts of the need to draw lines in the implementation of a desirable legislative policy?

Consider also the following aspects of the opinions in *Goodseal* and *Underwood:*

(i) **Merger.** In the *Clark* decision, discussed in *Goodseal*, the felony that was the basis of the defendant's conviction was his assault with intent to kill the victim of the homicide. The court reversed the conviction, holding that where the felony on which application of the rule is predicated "directly results in or is an element of the homicide, the assault becomes merged with the killing and cannot be relied upon as an ingredient of felony murder. [I]f the rule were to be applied otherwise, . . . 'there could be no such thing as any lower degree of homicide than murder in the first degree.'"

The court's reasoning in *Clark* seems irrefutable in one respect: if there were no merger rule of any kind, every person guilty of any felonious grade of homicide would automatically be guilty of felony murder—in effect, for example, one who committed manslaughter would automatically be guilty of murder if the crime of manslaughter could supply the basis for a charge of felony murder. The absence of some merger doctrine thus would erase altogether the distinctions traditionally drawn in grading serious homicides. No court has refused to apply a version of the merger doctrine in this context.

The disputed issue in most decisions concerning the merger doctrine is whether application of the felony-murder rule can be predicated on a felonious assault. Resolution of this question would not seem to have much practical significance if the crime of assault relied upon as the predicate felony itself requires proof of "intent to kill," as was the case in *Clark*. In such a case, proof of "intent to kill" plus the resulting death could independently supply the culpability needed for a murder conviction; the prosecutor would not have to rely on the felony-murder theory. However, in most jurisdictions, intent to injure or recklessness concerning the risk of injury is sufficient to establish the mens rea for some form of felonious assault. What is the proper approach in this situation? Should the felony-murder rule be applied in such a case or should the assault be said to merge with the homicide?

Consider in this connection the decision of the Washington Supreme Court in State v. Wanrow, 91 Wash.2d 301, 588 P.2d 1320 (1978).[a] The Washington second-degree murder statute covered the killing of a human being, not justifiable or excusable, "committed with a design to effect the death of the person killed or of another, but without premeditation" (subsection (1)) or perpetrated during the commission of "a felony other than those enumerated" on the first-degree list (subsection (2)). Apparently, the prosecution theory was that the defendant committed a felonious assault when she "wilfully assault[ed]" the victim with a gun, and that this offense established the predicate felony for second-degree felony murder even if she did not intend to kill the victim. The defense argued that this construction of the statute would effectively eliminate the requirement of intent to kill as an element of second-degree murder, and that application of the merger doctrine was necessary to ameliorate the otherwise harsh application of the felony-murder rule.[b] The court rejected these arguments.[c] Did the court

[a] The *Wanrow* case involved the same defendant whose prior convictions for assault and second-degree murder had been reversed for errors in the self-defense instructions to the jury. See the opinion of the Washington Supreme Court reproduced on pages 551–55, supra. On remand from that decision, the prosecutor sought to retry her for the same offenses. She moved to dismiss the second-degree murder charge, which was based on the theory that her assault of the homicide victim constituted a felony that would support a charge of second-degree felony murder. Her motion was based on the argument that such an assault should "merge" into the homicide and thus should not be regarded as an "independent" felony that would support such a conviction. The trial judge denied

her motion, and the Washington Supreme Court then granted an interlocutory review before the commencement of her second trial.

[b] Ms. Wanrow also attacked the felony-murder rule on constitutional grounds. In rejecting her argument, the court noted that the Supreme Court of the United States had in effect upheld the constitutionality of the rule by its summary order in Thompson v. Washington, 434 U.S. 898 (1977).

[c] The court said that subsection (1) of the statute was not rendered meaningless by its decision

"because there are many conceivable circumstances in which an intent to kill is both present and clearly manifested. In

reach the proper result? [d]

(ii) **Determination of Inherent Dangerousness.** In *Underwood,* the court held that possession of a firearm could under no circumstances be an "inherently dangerous" felony that would support application of the felony-murder rule. The court thus expressed a preference for classifying felonies according to their general tendencies and ignoring the facts and circumstances of the particular offense. In *Goodseal,* a majority of the court had rejected this conclusion and held that "the nature of the felony and, where necessary for determination, the circumstances of its commission" were both relevant factors in determining which felonies would qualify for operation of the rule. Other courts have held that only the particular facts and circumstances should be considered. Which of these views states the preferable position? Do the purposes of the felony-murder rule suggest an answer? Which answer?

If the offense is to be classified in the abstract, as *Underwood* concludes, the question to be determined would appear to be one of law for the court. But if the circumstances of the offense are to be considered, should the question be determined by the court or the jury? How did the majority in *Goodseal* resolve this issue? What is its answer to the argument of the dissent on this point?

(iii) **Lesser-Included-Offense Instruction.** Was the court in *Goodseal* correct in refusing an instruction that would have permitted the jury to convict of a lesser homicide offense? What pressures does the absence of such an instruction place on the jury? In Beck v. Alabama, 447 U.S. 625 (1980), the Supreme Court held, in the context of a prosecution for capital murder, that the refusal to give a lesser-included-offense charge was an error of constitutional dimension:

"In the final analysis the difficulty with the Alabama statute is that it interjects irrelevant considerations into the factfinding process, diverting the jury's attention from the central issue of whether the state has satisfied its burden of proving beyond a reasonable doubt that the defendant is guilty of a capital crime. Thus, on the one hand, the unavailability of the . . . option of convicting on a lesser-included offense may encourage the jury to convict for an impermissible reason—its belief that the defendant is guilty of some serious crime and should be punished. On the other hand, the apparently mandatory nature of the death penalty may encourage it to acquit for an equally impermissible reason—that, whatever his crime, the defendant does not deserve

these circumstances the state may properly charge under subsection (1). In practice it may be that most second-degree murders are proved through subsection (2), but as long as clear cases of unpremeditated acts with a manifest intent to kill are conceivable, subsection (1) is not meaningless."

[d] The court in *Wanrow* cited decisions in four other states that had not adopted a merger rule in this context, but noted that at least seven states had adopted such a rule.

It should also be noted that the merger doctrine is applied in some jurisdictions only where the victim of the assault is also the victim of the homicide. Thus, where the defendant assaults one person and accidently kills another (as on the facts of the *Moffitt* case discussed in *Goodseal*), the merger doctrine does not apply and a felony-murder conviction becomes possible.

death. In any particular case these two extraneous factors may favor the defendant or the prosecution or they may cancel each other out. But in every case they introduce a level of uncertainty and unreliability into the factfinding process that cannot be tolerated in a capital case."

As is clear from the quoted excerpt, the Court restricted its holding to capital cases and did not mean to cast doubt in constitutional terms on the need for lesser-included-offense instructions in non-capital cases. But does the Court's reasoning nonetheless suggest concerns that ought to be taken into account in formulating the correct policy in a case like *Goodseal?* Is the fact that life imprisonment is the only sanction available for first-degree murder in Kansas relevant to your answer? Why do you think the defendant's lawyer argued on appeal that the jury should have fixed the punishment upon conviction? Why did the court reject the argument?

Finally, note the relationship between this issue and the rule of the *Clark* case. If Goodseal had assaulted Hunter, would he have been entitled to a lesser-included-offense instruction? Since he did not, is it right that he is either guilty of felony murder (with a life sentence) or of no homicide offense at all? Is this anomaly necessarily eliminated by the holding in *Underwood?*

(iv) **Defenses and Mitigations.** The court notes in *Underwood* that the "heat of passion" mitigation would not be open to a person charged under the felony-murder theory, and adds that it would follow also that the defense of self-defense would not be available under the applicable Kansas statutory provisions. Should the rule have these consequences? If it does, are these reasons, as the Michigan Supreme Court seemed to think in *Aaron,* why the rule should be regarded as producing unwarranted harshness? Or are they sound implications of a sensible policy?

2. **Distribution of Controlled Substances.** Recent litigation has focused on the applicability of the felony-murder rule in the context of deaths caused by the distribution of controlled substances. At least one state has addressed the question by statute. Section 782.04(1)(a)(3) of the Florida penal code provides that:

"The unlawful killing of a human being . . . which resulted from the unlawful distribution of opium or any synthetic or natural salt, compound, derivative, or preparation of opium by a person 18 years of age or older, when such drug is proven to be the proximate cause of the death of the user, is murder in the first degree and constitutes a capital felony . . . ." [d]

Does this statute establish a wise public policy? What does it mean by "proximate cause?"

In the absence of legislative guidance, the cases are divided on whether the traditional felony-murder rule should be applied in this

[d] The capital punishment aspect of this statute may well be unconstitutional under *Enmund* v. *Florida,* 458 U.S. 782 (1982), discussed at page 799 n.m, supra, and pages 1020–28, infra. *Enmund* does not speak, however, to when a non-capital sentence can be imposed for felony murder.

context. Consider, for example, the views expressed in three recent cases. Which states the better view?

(i) **Heacock v. Commonwealth.** The Virginia statutes contain a traditional category of first-degree felony murder based on the Pennsylvania model, and also provide that the "killing of one accidentally, contrary to the intention of the parties, while in the prosecution of some felonious act other than those specified [in the first-degree statute], is murder of the second degree." In Heacock v. Commonwealth, 228 Va. 397, 323 S.E.2d 90 (1984), the court applied this statute in its affirmance of the conviction of a person who supplied cocaine to the participants at a "drug party." The defendant, with another, "prepared the narcotic mixture in a spoon" prior to a fatal injection and was present at the time of the injection.

The court first rejected the "inherently dangerous felony" limitation, concluding that the statute applied to "all felonious acts" except those particularly named in the first-degree statute. The court then noted that even if it were prepared to accept that limitation, "which we are not," the evidence was that the defendant "knew, or should have known" that the dosage he helped prepare was inherently dangerous. It based this conclusion on the fact that another person had suffered a violent reaction to the same substance prior to the lethal injection, on medical testimony that "any amount" of cocaine could cause such a reaction in "anyone," and on the fact that the legislature had classified cocaine distribution as a very serious felony (40 years for the first offense; life imprisonment for a second). "Accordingly, we hold as a matter of law, that the unlawful distribution of cocaine is conduct potentially dangerous to human life."

The court then held that any proximate cause limitation that might apply to this class of homicide was satisfied here: "The underlying felony was distribution of cocaine, a drug the defendant should have known was inherently dangerous to human life; [the victim] ingested that drug and, as we have said, it is immaterial who made the injection; [the victim] died of 'acute intravenous cocainism'; thus cause and effect were proximately interrelated." The court accordingly concluded:

> "[W]e hold that where, as here, death results from ingestion of a controlled substance, classified in law as dangerous to human life, the homicide constitutes murder of the second degree . . . if that substance had been distributed to the decedent in violation of the felony statutes of this commonwealth."

(ii) **Sheriff, Clark County v. Morris.** By contrast, in Sheriff, Clark County v. Morris, 99 Nev. 109, 659 P.2d 852 (1983), the court carefully limited the circumstances that would support conviction of a drug-seller for second-degree felony murder:

> "First, it must be established by the evidence that the unauthorized sale and ingestion of [a controlled substance] in the quantities involved are inherently dangerous in the abstract, i.e., without reference to the specific victim. Second, there must be an immediate and causal relationship between the felonious conduct of the defendant and the death of the [victim]. By the

term 'immediate' we mean without the intervention of some other source or agency. Third, the causal relationship must extend beyond the unlawful sale of the drugs to an involvement by commission or omission in the ingestion of a lethal dosage by the decedent. This element of the rule would be satisfied by the unlawful selling or providing of the drugs and helping the recipient of the drugs to ingest a lethal dose or by unlawfully selling or dispensing the drugs and being present during the consumption of a lethal dose. Thus, absent more, the rule would not apply to a situation involving a sale only or a sale with a nonlethal dosage ingested in the defendant's presence. Although it may be cogently argued that an unlawful sale of drugs is inherently dangerous per se, and therefore an appropriate basis for a charge of murder when death occurs, we leave such a determination to the legislature."

(iii) **State v. Randolph.** Finally, the court in State v. Randolph, 676 S.W.2d 943 (Tenn.1984), declined to embrace a felony-murder theory, but suggested that ordinary principles of culpability could be used in some contexts to convict a drug-seller of second-degree murder or involuntary manslaughter for the death of a drug-purchaser. On the question of causation that such a prosecution would involve, the court said that "we are of the opinion that the act of the customer in injecting himself is not necessarily so unexpected, unforseeable or remote as to insulate the seller from criminal responsibility as a matter of law."

3. **Attempted Felony Murder.** In Amlotte v. Florida, 456 So.2d 448 (Fla.1984), the court held that "attempted felony murder is a crime in Florida" and that the "essential elements of the crime are the perpetration or attempt to perpetrate an enumerated felony, together with an intentional overt act, or the aiding and abetting of such an act, which could, but does not, cause the death of another." The court added: "Because the attempt occurs during the commission of a felony, the law, as under the felony-murder doctrine, presumes the existence of the specific intent required to prove attempt." The court made these statements in the context of an attempted robbery where two of the felons returned gunfire when a victim of the robbery tried to shoot them. Is this a sound extension of the felony-murder rule? [e]

PEOPLE v. ANTICK

Supreme Court of California, 1975.
15 Cal.3d 79, 123 Cal.Rptr. 475, 539 P.2d 43.

SULLIVAN, JUSTICE. [The defendant was charged with burglary, grand theft, assault with a deadly weapon, and murder. He was convicted on all counts and given consecutive sentences with a minimum term of 10 years. On September 28, 1973, a home was burglar-

[e] Note that Florida had previously held that where a specific intent was not required for a completed crime it was also not required for an attempt to commit that crime. See Gentry v. State, 437 So.2d 1097 (Fla.1983), discussed at page 350, supra.

ized of property that included an adding machine, a typewriter, a check writer, a stereo set, and a television so large that it required at least two people to carry it. The burglary occurred between 7 p.m. and 10 p.m. At about 9 p.m., two police officers on patrol spotted a car carrying what appeared to be furniture in a manner that blocked the rear view mirror. Two people were in the car. The officers lost the car in traffic for a short time, but then spotted it again parked on the side of the road with its motor off. The officers approached the car. Only the driver was inside, but a second person was seen about 30 feet away approaching a nearby house. When questioned by one of the officers, the driver, one Donald Bose, gave evasive answers and made a furtive movement that aroused the officer's suspicions. The officer ordered Bose out of the car to frisk him. Spotting a revolver and holster on the front seat of the car, the officer drew his own gun and ordered Bose to place his hands on the hood of the nearby police car. The other person was then seen by one of the officers approaching the car. Bose pulled a gun from his waist and fired at one of the officers. The officer returned the fire and Bose started running. Bose was ordered to stop, and when he kept running, one of the officers fired again. Bose staggered and fell, and later died of the gunshot wound. A search of the car revealed that it was carrying the items stolen in the burglary.

[The second person was not apprehended at the scene. Nor could either police officer identify the defendant as the person who was riding in the car when it was first spotted or the person who was nearby when the shooting occurred. Defendant was connected to the offense through a green sweater and keys to the defendant's car found in the car Bose was driving. Defendant had been living with Bose, and stolen items from another burglary were found in the defendant's room. The case against the defendant was highly circumstantial, but sufficient in the jury's view to identify him as the second person involved in the September 28 burglary. The murder prosecution was based on the theory, as charged in the information, that "during the perpetration of the [September 28] burglary [defendant's] co-partner in the burglary, Donald Joseph Bose, initiated a gun battle which was the direct and unlawful cause of the death of the said Donald Joseph Bose."

[The defendant appealed his conviction on all counts on the ground that certain evidence should not have been admitted. The court agreed that two such errors were made and reversed the convictions. It also addressed the defendant's argument that on no theory could he be guilty of murder based on Bose's death. The portion of the court's opinion responding to this contention is reproduced below:]

[D]efendant's conviction of first-degree murder may have been based upon either of two theories: (i) his participation in the commission of a burglary which resulted in the death of his accomplice, or (ii) his vicarious liability for the crimes of his accomplice. Defendant contends that on the present record he cannot be convicted of murder under either theory.

Our consideration of defendant's contention requires us at the start to briefly review the basic principles underlying the crime of murder, the felony-murder doctrine and the theory of accomplice liability. A defendant is not guilty of murder unless he is legally chargeable, either by virtue of his own conduct or that of an accomplice, with the two component elements of the crime: its actus reus, a homicide, and its mens rea, malice.[8] "Homicide is the killing of a human being by another human being." Malice is the state of mind of one who has "an intent to kill or an intent with conscious disregard for life to commit acts likely to kill."[9] In addition, "[t]he felony-murder doctrine ascribes malice . . . to the felon who kills in the perpetration of an inherently dangerous felony."[10]

The imputation of malice by application of the felony-murder doctrine has been limited by this court to those cases in which the actual killing is committed by the defendant or his accomplice.

> "When a killing is not committed by a robber or by his accomplice but by his victim, malice aforethought is not attributable to the robber, for the killing is not committed by him in the perpetration or attempt to perpetrate robbery. It is not enough that the killing was a risk reasonably to be foreseen and that the robbery might therefore be regarded as a proximate cause of the killing. Section 189 requires that the felon or his accomplice commit the killing, for if he does not, the killing is not committed to perpetrate the felony. Indeed, in the present case the killing was committed to thwart a felony. To include such killings within Section 189 would expand the meaning of the words 'murder . . . which is committed in the perpetration [of] robbery . . . ' beyond common understanding."

People v. Washington, 62 Cal.2d 777, 781, 44 Cal.Rptr. 442, 445, 402 P.2d 130, 133 (1965).

However, we have been careful to point out that this limitation upon the felony-murder doctrine does not shield a defendant from criminal liability for murder when the elements of the crime, a homicide plus malice, can be established without resort to this doctrine. Thus,

> "[w]hen the defendant or his accomplice, with a conscious disregard for life, intentionally commits an act that is likely to cause death, and his victim or a police officer kills in reasonable response to such act, the defendant is guilty of murder. In such a case, the killing is attributable, not merely to the commission of a felony, but to the intentional act of the defendant or his accomplice committed with conscious disregard for life. [T]he victim's self-defensive killing or the police officer's killing in the performance of his duty cannot be considered an independent

[8] Cal.Penal Code § 187 provides in pertinent part: "(a) Murder is the unlawful killing of a human being . . . with malice aforethought."

[9] Cal.Penal Code § 188 defines "malice" for purposes of murder: "Such malice may be express or implied. It is express when there is manifested a deliberate intention unlawfully to take away the life of a fellow creature. It is implied, when no considerable provocation appears, or when the circumstances attending the killing show an abandoned and malignant heart."

[10] Under Cal.Penal Code § 189, "[a]ll murder . . . which is committed in the perpetration of, or attempt to perpetrate, arson, rape, robbery, burglary, mayhem, or any act punishable under Section 288 [lewd or lascivious acts against children], is murder of the first degree. . . ."

intervening cause for which the defendant is not liable, for it is a reasonable response to the dilemma thrust upon the victim or the policeman by the intentional act of the defendant or his accomplice."

People v. Gilbert, 63 Cal.2d 690, 704–05, 47 Cal.Rptr. 909, 917, 408 P.2d 365, 373 (1965). Under these circumstances, "it is unnecessary to imply malice by invoking the felony-murder doctrine." *People v. Washington,* supra.

Where a murder committed in this manner is attributable not to the acts of the defendant himself, but rather to the acts of his accomplice, the defendant's vicarious liability for the killing is based upon "the rules defining principals and criminal conspiracies . . . . [For the defendant to] be so guilty, however, the accomplice must cause the death *of another human being* by an act committed in furtherance of the common design." *People v. Gilbert,* supra.

The operation of these principles can best be illustrated by the following example. Three persons agree to commit a robbery, and during its commission *one* of them initiates a gun battle in which the victim or a police officer in reasonable response to such act kills *another* of the robbers. Since the immediate cause of death is the act of the victim or the officer, the felony-murder rule is not applicable to convert the killing into a murder. Nevertheless, the robber initiating the gun battle and the third accomplice are guilty of murder. The former commits a homicide, since his conduct is the proximate cause of the death of another human being; the intervening act of the victim or police officer is not an independent superseding cause, eliminating responsibility for the killing. Furthermore, in initiating the shootout the robber acts with malice, having intentionally and with conscious disregard for life engaged in conduct likely to kill. That this malice is directed at someone other than his crime partner who as a proximate result of the robber's acts is eventually killed "does not prevent the killing from constituting the offense of murder [since] the law transfers the felonious intent from the original object of his attempt to the person killed and the homicide so committed is murder." Since in the posited situation the robber initiating the gun battle is acting in furtherance of the common design of all three participants, the third robber as well may be held vicariously liable for the murder.

On the other hand, neither the felony-murder doctrine nor the theory of vicarious liability may be used to hold a defendant guilty of murder solely because of the acts of an accomplice, if the accomplice himself could not have been found guilty of the same offense for such conduct. In People v. Ferlin, 203 Cal. 587, 265 P. 230 (1928), the defendant was charged with and convicted of the murder of one Skala, whom he had hired to burn insured property. Skala accidentally killed himself while perpetrating the arson and the defendant was charged with arson, destruction of insured property, and murder upon a theory of felony-murder. In holding as a matter of law that the crime of murder had not been established under any theory of the evidence, this court stated:

"It would not be seriously contended that one accidentally killing himself while engaged in the commission of a felony was guilty of murder. If the defendant herein is guilty of murder because of the accidental killing of his co-conspirator then it must follow that Skala was also guilty of murder, and if he had recovered from his burns, that he would have been guilty of an attempt to commit murder. . . . It cannot be said from the record in the instant case that defendant and deceased had a common design that deceased should accidentally kill himself. Such an event was not in furtherance of the conspiracy, but entirely opposed to it."

The *Ferlin* holding was aptly explained by the Court of Appeal in Woodruff v. Superior Court, 237 Cal.App.2d 749, 47 Cal.Rptr. 291 (1965): "We believe the rationale of that decision to be that § 189 was inapplicable because there was no killing by the accused felon and no killing of another by one for whose conduct the accused was vicariously responsible. [I]n *Ferlin* 'the co-conspirator killed himself while he alone was perpetrating the felony he conspired to commit' and 'it was held in substance and effect that inasmuch as [deceased] killed himself Ferlin could not be held criminally responsible for his death.' "

Similar reasoning compelled our recent decision in People v. Taylor, 12 Cal.3d 686, 117 Cal.Rptr. 70, 527 P.2d 622 (1974). There Taylor was convicted of the murder of his accomplice Smith who was shot and killed by the victims during a robbery at their liquor store. Smith and one Daniels entered the store while Taylor remained in the getaway car. Taylor was found guilty on a theory of vicarious liability for the acts of his confederate Daniels who by threatening the life of one of the victims had provoked in response their return fire which killed Smith. However, Daniels had been separately tried and acquitted of the murder charge.[a] Reversing Taylor's murder conviction but affirming his robbery conviction, we held that the doctrine of collateral estoppel precluded "the conviction of an accused based on his vicarious responsibility for the acts of a previously acquitted confederate." We reasoned that our decision was essential

"to prevent the compromising of the integrity of the judicial system . . . . Few things undermine the layman's faith in the integrity of our legal institutions more than the specter of a system which results in a person being punished for the acts of another, when the actor himself under identical charges had been previously exonerated from responsibility for those very acts. This is particularly so under the facts of the instant case when the People seek to punish defendant, who was not even present on the immediate scene, for the death of an accomplice

---

[a] Daniels was, however, convicted for the robbery. The court noted in *Taylor* that "[t]here is no indication that Daniels' acquittal [of murder] is based on anything other than a final determination [by the jury] that his and Smith's acts were not sufficiently provocative to support a finding of implied malice" and that Daniels had not relied on a defense, such as insanity, intoxication, or duress, designed to show his personal lack of culpability. [Footnote by eds.]

caused by the acts of another confederate who himself has been exonerated."

Applying these principles to the case at bench, we first observe that on the uncontradicted evidence defendant himself did not participate in the immediate events which preceded his accomplice's death. Under the People's version of the facts, which we accept as accurate for purposes of this discussion, Bose initiated a gun battle with the police in order to escape apprehension for a burglary which he and defendant had recently committed. The police officer responded by killing Bose. As the immediate cause of death was the act of the officer, it is clear that the felony-murder rule does not operate to convert the killing into a murder for which defendant may be liable by virtue of his participation in the underlying burglary.[11] *People v. Washington,* supra.

Nor may defendant be held legally accountable for Bose's death based upon his vicarious liability for the crimes of his accomplice. In order to predicate defendant's guilt upon this theory, it is necessary to prove that Bose committed a murder, in other words, that he caused the death of another human being [and] that he acted with malice.

It is well settled that Bose's conduct in initiating a shootout with police officers may establish the requisite malice. As we have noted on a number of occasions, a person who initiates a gun battle in the course of committing a felony intentionally and with a conscious disregard for life commits an act that is likely to cause death. However, Bose's malicious conduct did not result in the unlawful killing of *another* human being, but rather in Bose's own death. The only homicide which occurred was the justifiable killing of Bose by the police officer. Defendant's criminal liability certainly cannot be predicated upon the actions of the officer. As Bose could not be found guilty of murder in connection with his own death, it is impossible to base defendant's liability for this offense upon his vicarious responsibility for the crime of his accomplice.

In summary defendant's conviction of the murder of his accomplice Bose cannot be upheld either on the doctrine of felony-murder or on a theory of vicarious liability. We are therefore compelled to conclude that on the instant record defendant as a matter of law cannot be found guilty of murder and that the verdict of the jury to that effect is against the law and the evidence. . . .

The judgment is reversed.

———

FURTHER NOTES ON FELONY MURDER

1. **Homicide Committed by a Non-Participant.** Situations where the homicide is actually committed by the police or a victim have proved particularly troublesome in American litigation over the proper

---

[11] The People concede in their brief on appeal that the felony-murder instruction was erroneous and that the only possible legal basis for defendant's murder conviction is his vicarious liability for the consequences of Bose's act in initiating the shootout with the police officers.

scope of the felony-murder rule. Basically, two approaches have been taken. The first, sometimes called the "proximate-cause" theory, is illustrated by State v. Canola, 135 N.J.Super. 224, 343 A.2d 110 (1974). Four men were engaged in an armed robbery. One of them shot a victim of the offense, who in turn drew a weapon and shot his assailant. Both men died. The defendant was convicted of felony murder for *both* deaths, and his convictions were affirmed. The court said that "[t]he proximate-cause theory simply stated is that when a felon sets in motion a chain of events which were or should have been within his contemplation when the motion was initiated, the felon, and those acting in concert with him, should be held responsible for any death which by direct and almost inevitable consequences results from the initial criminal act."

Canola's conviction for the murder of his accomplice was reversed by the New Jersey Supreme Court, 73 N.J. 206, 374 A.2d 20 (1977). The court rejected the "proximate cause" theory and adopted instead the so-called "agency theory," applied in Commonwealth v. Redline, 391 Pa. 486, 137 A.2d 472 (1958). In *Redline,* the defendant and a co-felon were engaged in the commission of an armed robbery. They engaged in a gun battle with the police, during which the co-felon was killed by police bullets. The Pennsylvania Supreme Court held that "in order to convict for felony murder, the killing must have been done by the defendant or by an accomplice or confederate or by one acting in furtherance of the felonious undertaking." As described in *Canola,* "the [*Redline*] court held that in order to convict for felony murder the killing must have been done by defendant or someone acting in concert with him in furtherance of the felonious undertaking; that the death must be a consequence of the felony and not merely coincidental; and that a justifiable homicide could not be availed of to support a charge of murder."

What would be the result on the *Canola* facts under the line of California cases described in *Antick?* On the *Redline* facts? Does California adopt the "proximate cause" theory of felony murder or the "agency" theory? Can you think of reasons why one or the other of the two theories should be adopted?

2. ***People v. Washington.*** In connection with the last question, consider the arguments of Chief Justice Traynor in the *Washington* case, cited in *Antick.* In *Washington,* the defendant was convicted of felony murder for participating in a robbery in which his accomplice was killed by a victim of the robbery. In reversing the conviction, the court reasoned:

"The purpose of the felony-murder rule is to deter felons from killing negligently or accidentally by holding them strictly responsible for killings they commit. This purpose is not served by punishing them for killings committed by their victims.

"It is contended, however, that another purpose of the felony-murder rule is to prevent the commission of robberies. Neither the common-law rationale of the rule nor the penal code supports this contention. In every robbery there is a possibility that the victim will resist and kill. The robber has little control over such a killing once the robbery is undertaken. . . . To impose an additional penalty for the killing would discriminate between robbers, not on the basis of any difference in their own conduct, but solely on the basis of the response by others that the robber's conduct happened to induce. An additional penalty for a homicide committed by the victim would deter robbery haphazardly at best. To 'prevent stealing, [the law] would do better to hang one thief in every thousand by lot.' O. Holmes, The Common Law 58 (1881). . . .

"A defendant need not do the killing himself, however, to be guilty of murder. He may be vicariously responsible under the rules defining principals and criminal conspiracies. All persons aiding and abetting the commission of a robbery are guilty of first-degree murder when one of them kills while acting in furtherance of the common design. Moreover, when the defendant intends to kill or intentionally commits acts that are likely to kill with a conscious disregard for life, he is guilty of murder even though he uses another person to accomplish his objective.

"Defendants who initiate gun battles may also be found guilty of murder if their victims resist and kill. Under such circumstances, 'the defendant for a base, anti-social motive and with wanton disregard for human life, does an act that involves a high degree of probability that it will result in death' and it is unnecessary to imply malice by invoking the felony-murder doctrine. To invoke the felony-murder doctrine to imply malice in such a case is unnecessary and overlooks the principles of criminal liability that should govern the responsibility of one person for a killing committed by another.

"To invoke the felony-murder doctrine when the killing is not committed by the defendant or by his accomplice could lead to absurd results. Thus, two men rob a grocery store and flee in opposite directions. The owner of the store follows one of the robbers and kills him. Neither robber may have fired a shot. Neither robber may have been armed with a deadly weapon. If the felony-murder doctrine applied, however, the surviving robber could be convicted of first-degree murder, even though he was captured by a policeman and placed under arrest at the time his accomplice was killed.

"The felony-murder rule has been criticized on the grounds that in almost all cases in which it is applied it is unnecessary and that it erodes the relation between criminal liability and moral culpability. Although it is the law in this state, it should not be extended beyond any rational function that it is designed to serve. Accordingly, for a defendant to be guilty of murder under the felony-murder rule the act of killing must be committed by the defendant or by his accomplice acting in furtherance of their common design."

Is Chief Justice Traynor's opinion internally consistent? Why is the deterrent purpose of the felony-murder rule accomplished by punishing felons for accidental killings committed by them, but not for intentional or accidental killings committed by their victims? Does the *Canola* result extend the rule "beyond any rational function that it is designed to serve?"

3. **Relation to Principles of Causation.** Causation problems can arise in two distinct ways in connection with felony-murder situations:

(i) **Application of Felony-Murder Rule.** The first concerns the principles of causation that should control the operation of the felony-murder rule itself. The debate between the "proximate-cause" theory and the "agency" theory for analyzing cases where the homicide is committed by a victim or the police is illustrative. Are those courts which adopt the "agency" theory in effect applying narrower notions of proximate cause to the felony-murder rule than would otherwise be applicable in a prosecution for criminal homicide? If the answer is "yes," then it would seem that a special doctrine of causation is being applied to limit the scope of the felony-murder rule. On the other hand, if the answer is "no," then it would seem that courts adopting the "proximate cause" approach are creating a special doctrine of causation in order to extend the felony-murder rule beyond the limits that ordinary principles of criminal liability would suggest. Which is the more accurate answer to the question? Should special causation principles be applied to limit or to extend the scope of the felony-murder rule?

(ii) **Independent Prosecution for Murder.** The second way in which causation principles become relevant concerns the possibility of a murder prosecution without resort to the felony-murder rule. Consider the following hypothetical. If a single felon initiates a gun battle with intent to kill or in reckless disregard of human life, and if the victim returns the fire and accidentally kills a bystander, would normal principles of causation permit the felon's conviction of murder, the felony-murder rule aside? Is the action of the victim an "independent intervening cause" of the bystander's death? Would it matter if the victim intentionally killed a co-felon in order not to be killed? Would § 2.03 of the Model Penal Code permit a conviction of murder in either of these situations? Are they, as the court suggests in *Antick*, "transferred-intent" cases, with conviction proper under ordinary principles of liability for criminal homicide?

Note also the relationship between these two ways in which causation can be relevant. If an independent prosecution for murder is possible in those cases where the defendant is culpable as to death (albeit not necessarily the one that actually occurred), does this then make the use of narrower causation principles in connection with the operation of the felony-murder rule more justifiable? Should the felony-murder doctrine be discarded entirely in favor of such independent prosecutions for murder? What kinds of murder convictions would be excluded by such an approach? Is the loss significant to the deterrent purposes of the law?

4. **Relation to Principles of Accessorial Liability.** The felony-murder rule also intersects with problems of accessorial liability. It is again helpful in thinking about this relationship to focus separately on the operation of the felony-murder rule itself and the possibility of an independent prosecution for murder.

(i) **Application of Felony-Murder Rule.** As the foregoing materials indicate, one of the principal ways in which the felony-murder rule operates is as an independent basis for accomplice liability. Thus, even under the relatively narrow formulation adopted in *Antick,* the court described the felony-murder doctrine as embracing cases where "the actual killing is committed by the defendant *or his accomplice.*" Recall the facts of the *Taylor* case, discussed in *Antick.* There the defendant was sitting outside the scene of the robbery in a getaway car. If one of his co-felons had killed a victim of the robbery, the felony-murder rule as applied in California would make Taylor guilty of murder. Similarly, in *Canola* the defendant was convicted of murder even though he did not shoot either of the persons who died. This aspect of the felony-murder rule thus does not depend on the debate between the "agency" and "proximate cause" theory of felony-murder. Under any formulation of the rule, once its scope is determined, all participants in the felony are guilty of murder if any one of them commits an included homicide.

Does this aspect of the felony-murder rule represent an extension of the ordinary principles of accessorial liability that would otherwise determine responsibility for the acts of a confederate? Do the policies underlying the felony-murder rule suggest the need for a separate set of more inclusive principles of accomplice liability? Or is the felony-murder rule on this point simply redundant, i.e., does it lead to the result that ordinary principles of accomplice liability would otherwise accomplish in any event? [a]

(ii) **Independent Prosecution for Murder.** In situations to which the felony-murder rule does not apply, as in *Taylor* and *Antick* on the law as determined by the California Supreme Court, the way is nonetheless open for the prosecutor to rely on ordinary principles of accomplice liability in an effort to secure a murder conviction. Do you agree with the results of *Taylor* and *Antick* on this point? Are they proper applications of the principles of accomplice liability that ought to control in such situations? Given the possibility of an ordinary murder prosecution and conviction of accomplices under ordinary principles, is there any need for a special felony-murder rule for accomplices?

[a] The relationship of the felony-murder rule to principles of accessorial liability is further complicated by the possibility of a conspiracy charge. As developed in the materials on conspiracy at pages 463–80, supra, the liability of a conspirator for crimes committed by other conspirators is frequently measured by the law of conspiracy without reference to the law of accomplice liability. Thus, in felony-murder situations there are three possible bases of accomplice liability: (i) liability under ordinary complicity rules; (ii) liability as a co-conspirator; and (iii) liability under felony-murder rule. Precisely how these three doctrines overlap and when they are in effect congruent is a question rarely explored in the cases or the literature.

5. **Duration of the Felony.** Note that the information in *Antick* charged that Bose was killed "during the perpetration of the [September 28] burglary." Was the burglary still under way when Bose parked his car? Would it matter whether he was driving away from the house when apprehended? Whether the burglary had occurred two hours earlier or 10 minutes earlier? How far it was from the scene of the burglary to the place where Bose parked his car? What Antick had been doing in the interim between the offense and the killing?

These questions raise the general problem of determining the operative time span during which the felony-murder rule can be applied— when, in other words, the felony to which the rule attaches begins, and when it ends. The normal statement of the rule is that the felony-murder doctrine applies from the time when an attempt to commit the felony has occurred, through its actual commission, and through the period of immediate flight therefrom. One of the ways in which the felony-murder rule can be contracted or expanded is by tinkering with the time during which the felony can be said to be in process. Can you think of ways in which this problem can be intelligently addressed? Does the purpose of the felony-murder rule as you understand it suggest how lines of this sort should be drawn? As you think about these questions, consider the comments in Wechsler & Michael, A Rationale of the Law of Homicide I, 37 Colum.L.Rev. 701, 716–17 (1937):

> "The rule has . . . been restricted by the contraction of the period during which the felony can be said to be 'in the course of' commission. Thus, if a person in flight kills a policeman attempting to interfere with his escape, it is not felony-murder if he was not carrying away spoils. Conceding the ever present legislative necessity for reconciling extremes by drawing arbitrary lines the justice of which must be viewed from afar, the limits of intelligent casuistry have clearly been reached when the question whether judgment of death shall be imposed on a man who went no further than to participate in the planning of a robbery depends upon whether his accomplice shot the victim in his store or on the sidewalk outside."

6. **Modern Statutes.** As noted at page 938, supra, the New York felony-murder statute is the most widely copied of the modern statutory revisions. Note the language of the statute, quoted in Appendix B, pages 8–9, infra. How would it apply to a case where the victim of a felony killed one of the felons? How would it apply where the police killed a victim while trying to prevent the felony? Does the New York statute codify the California rule described in *Antick?*

Most statutes do not speak to the situations described in *Antick* and the preceding notes, and the courts are accordingly left to the development of common-law principles to decide such cases. An exception is § 782.04(3) of the Florida penal code, which provides:

> "When a person is killed in the perpetration of, or in the attempt to perpetrate, any [one of a series of enumerated felonies] by a person other than the person engaged in the perpetration of or attempt to perpetrate such felony, the person perpe-

trating or attempting to perpetrate such felony is guilty of murder in the second degree, . . . punishable by imprisonment for a term of years not exceeding life . . . ."

Does this statute permit conviction of a surviving felon if the police kill one of the co-felons in an attempt to prevent the felony? Does it permit conviction if the police kill a victim? If you were testifying before a legislative committee that was charged with recommending a choice between the New York and the Florida statutes, which would you defend and how would you structure your arguments?

NOTE ON MISDEMEANOR MANSLAUGHTER

As has been noted previously, manslaughter typically was defined at common law to encompass cases where death was caused by an unlawful act or by a lawful act committed in an unlawful manner. The second part of this definition is a reference to liability for recklessness or negligence, which has been dealt with at pages 905–14, supra. The first part is a reference to the so-called misdemeanor-manslaughter rule. This rule provides in effect that when a death occurs during the commission of or attempt to commit a misdemeanor, all participants in the offensive conduct are guilty of manslaughter. As it has been applied in some jurisdictions, the rule encompasses all "unlawful" behavior, i.e., it includes conduct that was not criminal but that only involved the breach of civil standards of liability. In most jurisdictions, however, the rule has been limited to misdemeanors, hence the derivation of the name by which the doctrine is normally called. As in the case of felony-murder, liability is strict as to death in those jurisdictions that follow the rule, and all participants are liable regardless of their culpability as to the death. Analytically, the problems of implementing the misdemeanor-manslaughter rule are directly analogous to problems encountered with felony murder.

The history of the misdemeanor-manslaughter rule also parallels the felony-murder rule. In the main, it consists of a series of judicially derived limitations on its reach. As summarized in Wechsler and Michael, A Rationale of the Law of Homicide I, 37 Colum.L.Rev. 701, 722–23 (1937): *

"Homicides resulting from unlawful acts were manslaughter, subject to the single qualification which early appeared, that the unlawful act be malum in se. In the course of time the same impetus was felt as in the case of felony murder, to narrow this category to cases where the unlawful act was dangerous to life. This was accomplished more successfully than in the case of felonies in similar ways, by defining malum in se so as to include misdemeanors dangerous to life or limb and exclude non-dangerous misdemeanors, or by introducing the factor of danger by means of a requirement of proximate causation. But the limita-

---

* Reprinted with permission of Professor
Wechsler and the Columbia Law Review.

tion has resulted in uncertainties similar to those created by efforts to limit the felony-murder rule. Is it sufficient that a misdemeanor involve some kind of behavior which is usually dangerous to life or limb, or must the particular instance of such behavior be dangerous to some serious degree? And if the former, is it also sufficient that the legislature has regarded behavior, such, for example, as driving an automobile at a speed in excess of a statutory limit, as generally dangerous and has therefore forbidden it, or is this legislative judgment open to re-examination by court and jury? And if the latter, is the degree of danger required the same or less than, and the state of mind required the same or different from, what would be required if the behavior were not a misdemeanor? Finally, does the answer to any of these questions vary with the technique employed to limit the rule by a particular court? These are issues which have not received definitive consideration in the cases, and remain for the most part unresolved."

The Model Penal Code does not include a counterpart to the misdemeanor-manslaughter rule. It is reported in ALI, Model Penal Code and Commentaries, § 210.3, p. 77 (1980), that 22 recently enacted codes and nine recently drafted proposals have agreed with the Model Code and abolished the rule in its entirety. Eleven recently revised codes and one proposal, on the other hand, have retained some form of the rule, and there are a number of jurisdictions that have not recently revised their penal codes and that still retain some version of the common-law rule. Is the Model Code solution the right one? Can you think of reasons why the Model Code recommendation with respect to misdemeanor manslaughter has been more sympathetically received in recent code revisions than the recommendation with respect to felony murder? Does strict liability become more defensible or less defensible as the penalty is increased?

Chapter VII

PROOF, PROPORTIONALITY, AND CRIMINALIZATION

SECTION 1: PROOF BEYOND A REASONABLE DOUBT

INTRODUCTORY NOTE ON *IN RE WINSHIP*

Proof beyond a reasonable doubt has long been thought fundamental to the American system of criminal justice. Only in 1970, however, did the Supreme Court make this standard a constitutional requirement. The issue arose under a New York statute that permitted adjudication of juvenile delinquency on a preponderance of the evidence. The Court declared that scheme unconstitutional in In re Winship, 397 U.S. 358 (1970). The opinion held first, that criminal conviction had to be based on proof beyond a reasonable doubt, and second, that the same standard applied to delinquency proceedings. The Court's conclusion was made unmistakably plain: "Lest there remain any doubt about the constitutional stature of the reasonable-doubt standard, we explicitly hold that the due-process clause protects the accused against conviction except upon proof beyond a reasonable doubt of every fact necessary to constitute the crime with which he is charged."

At first glance, this requirement was scarcely revolutionary. By the time of *Winship*, every American jurisdiction required that conviction of an adult be based on proof beyond a reasonable doubt. Aside from extending that standard to delinquency proceedings, therefore, *Winship* seemed to have little impact. It merely confirmed the status quo.

The issue lurking in *Winship*, however, was the scope of the reasonable-doubt requirement. What, exactly, would be included by the phrase "every fact necessary to constitute the crime . . . charged?" Should it cover only those facts formally made elements of the crime by the definition of the offense? Or should it also include facts technically extrinsic to the definition of the offense, e.g., a fact relevant only to a defense but nonetheless determinative of guilt or innocence? Or should the constitutional requirement of proof beyond a reasonable doubt perhaps be limited to those facts constitutionally necessary to constitute the crime charged? If so, what facts are constitutionally necessary?

These and other possible interpretations surfaced in the years following *Winship*. By the end of the decade, a constitutional pronouncement that originally had seemed largely symbolic in character had become the subject of intense and on-going debate. The essential problem is how to mesh a judicially enforced requirement of proof beyond a reasonable doubt with the tradition of legislative control over the substance of the penal law. The Supreme Court's efforts to resolve this issue are recounted in the cases that follow.

SUBSECTION A: MITIGATIONS AND DEFENSES

MULLANEY v. WILBUR
Supreme Court of the United States, 1975.
421 U.S. 684.

MR. JUSTICE POWELL delivered the opinion of the Court.

The State of Maine requires a defendant charged with murder to prove that he acted "in the heat of passion on sudden provocation" in order to reduce the homicide to manslaughter. We must decide whether this rule comports with the due-process requirement, as defined in In re Winship, 397 U.S. 358 (1970), that the prosecution prove beyond a reasonable doubt every fact necessary to constitute the crime charged.

I

In June 1966 a jury found respondent Stillman E. Wilbur, Jr., guilty of murder. The case against him rested on his own pretrial statement and on circumstantial evidence showing that he fatally assaulted Claude Hebert in the latter's hotel room. Respondent's statement, introduced by the prosecution, claimed that he had attacked Hebert in a frenzy provoked by Hebert's homosexual advance. The defense offered no evidence, but argued that the homicide was not unlawful since respondent lacked criminal intent. Alternatively, Wilbur's counsel asserted that at most the homicide was manslaughter rather than murder, since it occurred in the heat of passion provoked by the homosexual assault.

The trial court instructed the jury that Maine law recognizes two kinds of homicide, murder and manslaughter, and that these offenses are not subdivided into different degrees. The common elements of both are that the homicide be unlawful—i.e., neither justifiable nor excusable—and that it be intentional.[2] The prosecution is required to prove these elements by proof beyond a reasonable doubt, and only if they are so proved is the jury to consider the distinction between murder and manslaughter.

In view of the evidence the trial court drew particular attention to the difference between murder and manslaughter. After reading the

---

[2] The court elaborated that an intentional homicide required the jury to find "either that the defendant intended death, or that he intended an act which was calculated and should have been understood by [a] person of reason to be one likely to do great bodily harm and that death resulted."

statutory definitions of both offenses,[3] the court charged that "malice aforethought is an essential and indispensable element of the crime of murder," without which the homicide would be manslaughter. The jury was further instructed, however, that if the prosecution established that the homicide was both intentional and unlawful, malice aforethought was to be conclusively implied unless the defendant proved by a fair preponderance of the evidence that he acted in the heat of passion on sudden provocation. The court emphasized that "malice aforethought and heat of passion on sudden provocation are two inconsistent things"; thus, by proving the latter the defendant would negate the former and reduce the homicide from murder to manslaughter. The court then concluded its charge with elaborate definitions of "heat of passion" and "sudden provocation."

After retiring to consider its verdict, the jury twice returned to request further instruction. It first sought reinstruction on the doctrine of implied malice aforethought, and later on the definition of "heat of passion." Shortly after the second reinstruction, the jury found respondent guilty of murder.

Respondent appealed to the Maine Supreme Judicial Court, arguing that he had been denied due process because he was required to negate the element of malice aforethought by proving that he had acted in the heat of passion on sudden provocation. . . .

[The state court affirmed the conviction. There ensued a rather complicated series of proceedings resulting in a decision by the United States Court of Appeals for the First Circuit upholding Wilbur's constitutional contention. The First Circuit ordered that he be either released or retried. The state authorities then sought certiorari to review that judgment, and the Supreme Court granted that petition. After describing these proceedings, the Court resolved in Part II of its opinion a dispute about Maine law. It then undertook in Part III of its opinion to analyze Wilbur's federal constitutional claim.]

III

The Maine law of homicide, as it bears on this case, can be stated succinctly: Absent justification or excuse, all intentional or criminally reckless killings are felonious homicides. Felonious homicide is punished as murder—i.e., by life imprisonment—unless the defendant proves by a fair preponderance of the evidence that it was committed in the heat of passion on sudden provocation, in which case it is punished as manslaughter. . . . The issue is whether the Maine rule requir-

---

[3] The Maine murder statute, 17 Me.Rev.Stat.Ann. § 2651, provides:

"Whoever unlawfully kills a human being with malice aforethought, either express or implied, is guilty of murder and shall be punished by imprisonment for life."

The manslaughter statute, 17 Me.Rev.Stat.Ann. § 2551, in relevant part provides:

"Whoever unlawfully kills a human being in the heat of passion, on sudden provocation, without express or implied malice aforethought . . . shall be punished by a fine of not more than $1,000 or by imprisonment for not more than 20 years. . . ."

ing the defendant to prove that he acted in the heat of passion on sudden provocation accords with due process.

A

Our analysis may be illuminated if this issue is placed in historical context. At early common law only those homicides committed in the enforcement of justice were considered justifiable; all others were deemed unlawful and were punished by death. Gradually, however, the severity of the common-law punishment for homicide abated. Between the 13th and 16th centuries the class of justifiable homicides expanded to include, for example, accidental homicides and those committed in self-defense. Concurrently, the widespread use of capital punishment was ameliorated further by extension of the ecclesiastic jurisdiction. Almost any person able to read was eligible for "benefit of clergy," a procedural device that effected a transfer from the secular to the ecclesiastic jurisdiction. And under ecclesiastic law a person who committed an unlawful homicide was not executed; instead he received a one-year sentence, had his thumb branded and was required to forfeit his goods. At the turn of the 16th century, English rulers, concerned with the accretion of ecclesiastic jurisdiction at the expense of the secular, enacted a series of statutes eliminating the benefit of clergy in all cases of "murder of malice prepensed." Unlawful homicides that were committed without such malice were designated "manslaughter," and their perpetrators remained eligible for the benefit of clergy.

Even after ecclesiastic jurisdiction was eliminated for all secular offenses the distinction between murder and manslaughter persisted. It was said that "manslaughter, when voluntary, arises from the sudden heat of the passions, murder, from the wickedness of the heart." 4 W. Blackstone, Commentaries *190. Malice aforethought was designated as the element that distinguished the two crimes, but it was recognized that such malice could be implied by law as well as proved by evidence. Absent proof that an unlawful homicide resulted from "sudden and sufficiently violent provocation," the homicide was "presumed to be malicious." In view of this presumption, the early English authorities held that once the prosecution proved that the accused had committed the homicide, it was "incumbent upon the prisoner to make out, to the satisfaction of the court and jury all . . . circumstances of justification, excuse, or alleviation." Thus, at common law the burden of proving heat of passion on sudden provocation appears to have rested on the defendant.

In this country the concept of malice aforethought took on two distinct meanings: In some jurisdictions it came to signify a substantive element of intent, requiring the prosecution to prove that the defendant intended to kill or to inflict great bodily harm; in other jurisdictions it remained a policy presumption, indicating only that absent proof to the contrary a homicide was presumed not to have occurred in the heat of passion. In a landmark case, Commonwealth v. York, 50 Mass. (9 Met.) 93 (1845), Chief Justice Shaw of the Massachusetts Supreme Judicial Court held that the defendant was required to negate malice aforethought by proving by a preponderance of the evidence that he acted in the heat of passion. Initially, *York* was adopted in Maine as well as several other jurisdictions. In 1895, however, in the context of deciding a question of federal criminal procedure, this Court explicitly considered and unanimously rejected the general approach articulated in *York.* Davis v. United States, 160 U.S. 469 (1895). And, in the past half century, the large majority of states have abandoned *York* and now require the prosecution to prove the absence of the heat of passion on sudden provocation beyond a reasonable doubt.

This historical review establishes two important points. First, the fact at issue here—the presence or absence of the heat of passion on sudden provocation—has been, almost from the inception of the common law of homicide, the single most important factor in determining the degree of culpability attaching to an unlawful homicide. And, second, the clear trend has been toward requiring the prosecution to bear the ultimate burden of proving this fact.

B

Petitioners, the warden of the Maine Prison and the state of Maine, argue that despite these considerations *Winship* should not be extended to the present case. They note that as a formal matter the absence of the heat of passion on sudden provocation is not a "fact necessary to constitute the *crime*" of felonious homicide in Maine. This distinction is relevant, according to petitioners, because in *Winship* the facts at issue were essential to establish criminality in the first instance, whereas the fact in question here does not come into play until the jury already has determined that the defendant is guilty and may be punished at least for manslaughter. In this situation, petitioners maintain, the defendant's critical interests in liberty and reputation are no longer of paramount concern since, irrespective of the presence or absence of the heat of passion on sudden provocation, he is likely to lose his liberty and certain to be stigmatized. In short, petitioners would limit *Winship* to those facts which, if not proved, would wholly exonerate the defendant.

This analysis fails to recognize that the criminal law of Maine, like that of other jurisdictions, is concerned not only with guilt or innocence in the abstract but also with the degree of criminal culpability. Maine has chosen to distinguish those who kill in the heat of passion from those who kill in the absence of this factor. Because the former are less "blameworth[y]," they are subject to substantially less severe penalties. By drawing this distinction, while refusing to require the prosecution to establish beyond a reasonable doubt the fact upon which it turns, Maine denigrates the interests found critical in *Winship.*

The safeguards of due process are not rendered unavailing simply because a determination may already have been reached that would stigmatize the defendant and that might lead to a significant impairment of personal liberty. The fact remains that the consequences resulting from a verdict of murder, as compared with a verdict of manslaughter, differ significantly. Indeed, when viewed in terms of the potential difference in restrictions of personal liberty attendant to each conviction, the distinction established by Maine between murder and manslaughter may be of greater importance than the difference between guilt or innocence for many lesser crimes.

Moreover, if *Winship* were limited to those facts that constitute a crime as defined by state law, a state could undermine many of the interests that decision sought to protect without effecting any substantive change in its law. It would only be necessary to redefine the elements that constitute different crimes, characterizing them as factors that bear solely on the extent of punishment. An extreme example of this approach can be fashioned from the law challenged in this case. Maine divides the single generic offenses of felonious homicide into three distinct punishment categories—murder, voluntary manslaughter, and involuntary manslaughter. Only the first two of these categories require that the homicidal act either be intentional or the result of criminally reckless conduct. But under Maine law these facts of intent are not general elements of the crime of felonious homicide. Instead, they bear only on the appropriate punishment category. Thus, if petitioners' argument were accepted, Maine could impose a life sentence for any felonious homicide—even those that traditionally might be considered involuntary manslaughter—unless the *defendant* was able to prove that his act was neither intentional nor criminally reckless.[24]

Winship is concerned with substance rather than this kind of formalism. The rationale of that case requires an analysis that looks to the "operation and effect of the law as applied and enforced by the state," and to the interests of both the state and the defendant as affected by the allocation of the burden of proof.

In *Winship* the Court emphasized the societal interests in the reliability of jury verdicts:

> "The requirement of proof beyond a reasonable doubt has [a] vital role in our criminal procedure for cogent reasons. The accused during a criminal prosecution has at stake interests of immense importance, both because of the possibility that he may lose his liberty upon conviction and because of the certainty that he would be stigmatized by the conviction. . . .

> "Moreover, use of the reasonable-doubt standard is indispensable to command the respect and confidence of the community in applications of the criminal law. It is critical that the moral force of the criminal law not be diluted by a standard of proof that leaves people in doubt whether innocent men are being condemned."

The interests are implicated to a greater degree in this case than they were in *Winship* itself. Petitioner there faced an 18-month sentence, with a maximum possible extension of an additional four and one-half

---

[24] Many states impose different statutory sentences on different degrees of assault. If *Winship* were limited to a state's definition of the elements of a crime, these states could define all assaults as a single offense and then require the defendant to disprove the elements of aggravation—e.g., intent to kill or intent to rob. . . .

years, whereas respondent here faces a differential in sentencing ranging from a nominal fine to a mandatory life sentence. Both the stigma to the defendant and the community's confidence in the administration of the criminal law are also of greater consequence in this case, since the adjudication of delinquency involved in *Winship* was "benevolent" in intention, seeking to provide "a generously conceived program of compassionate treatment."

Not only are the interests underlying *Winship* implicated to a greater degree in this case, but in one respect the protection afforded those interests is less here. In *Winship* the ultimate burden of persuasion remained with the prosecution, although the standard had been reduced to proof by a fair preponderance of the evidence. In this case, by contrast, the state has affirmatively shifted the burden of proof to the defendant. The result, in a case such as this one where the defendant is required to prove the critical fact in dispute, is to increase further the likelihood of an erroneous murder conviction.   .   .   .

C

It has been suggested that because of the difficulties in negating an argument that the homicide was committed in the heat of passion the burden of proving this fact should rest on the defendant. No doubt this is often a heavy burden for the prosecution to satisfy. The same may be said of the requirement of proof beyond a reasonable doubt of many controverted facts in a criminal trial. But this is the traditional burden which our system of criminal justice deems essential.

Indeed, the Maine Supreme Judicial Court itself acknowledged that most states require the prosecution to prove the absence of passion beyond a reasonable doubt.[28] Moreover, the difficulty of meeting such an exacting burden is mitigated in Maine where the fact at issue is largely an "objective, rather than a subjective, behavioral criterion." In this respect, proving that the defendant did not act in the heat of passion on sudden provocation is similar to proving any other element of intent; it may be established by adducing evidence of the factual circumstances surrounding the commission of the homicide. And although intent is typically considered a fact peculiarly within the knowledge of the defendant, this does not, as this Court has long recognized, justify shifting the burden to him.

Nor is the requirement of proving a negative unique in our system of criminal jurisprudence. Maine itself requires the prosecution to prove the absence of self-defense beyond a reasonable doubt. Satisfying this burden imposes an obligation that, in all practical effect, is identical to the burden involved in negating the heat of passion on sudden provocation. Thus, we discern no unique hardship on the prosecution that would justify requiring the defendant to carry the burden of proving a fact so critical to criminal culpability.

---

[28] Many states do require the defendant to show that there is "some evidence" indicating that he acted in the heat of passion before requiring the prosecution to negate this element by proving the absence of passion beyond a reasonable doubt. Nothing in this opinion is intended to affect that requirement.

IV

Maine law requires a defendant to establish by a preponderance of the evidence that he acted in the heat of passion on sudden provocation in order to reduce murder to manslaughter. Under this burden of proof a defendant can be given a life sentence when the evidence indicates that it is *as likely as not* that he deserves a significantly lesser sentence. This is an intolerable result in a society where, to paraphrase Mr. Justice Harlan, it is far worse to sentence one guilty only of manslaughter as a murderer than to sentence a murderer for the lesser crime of manslaughter. In re Winship, 397 U.S. at 372 (concurring opinion). We therefore hold that the due-process clause requires the prosecution to prove beyond a reasonable doubt the absence of the heat of passion on sudden provocation when the issue is properly presented in a homicide case. Accordingly, the judgment below is

Affirmed.

MR. JUSTICE REHNQUIST, with whom THE CHIEF JUSTICE joins, concurring. . . .

I agree with the Court that In re Winship, 397 U.S. 358 (1970), does require that the prosecution prove beyond a reasonable doubt every element which constitutes the crime charged against a defendant. I see no inconsistency between that holding and the holding of Leland v. Oregon, 343 U.S. 790 (1953). In the latter case this Court held that there was no constitutional requirement that the state shoulder the burden of proving the sanity of the defendant.[a]

The Court noted in *Leland* that the issue of insanity as a defense to a criminal charge was considered by the jury only after it had found that all elements of the offense, including the mens rea, if any, required by state law, had been proved beyond a reasonable doubt. Although as the state court's instructions in *Leland* recognized, evidence relevant to insanity as defined by state law may also be relevant to whether the required mens rea was present, the existence or non-existence of legal insanity bears no necessary relationship to the existence or non-existence of the required mental elements of the crime. For this reason, Oregon's placement of the burden of proof of insanity on Leland, unlike Maine's redefinition of homicide, in the instant case, did not effect an unconstitutional shift in the state's traditional burden of proof beyond a reasonable doubt of all necessary elements of the offense. Both the Court's opinion and the concurring opinion of Mr. Justice Harlan in *In re Winship* stress the importance of proof beyond a reasonable doubt in a criminal case as "bottomed on a fundamental value determination of our society that it is far worse to convict an innocent man than to let a guilty man go free." Having once met that rigorous burden of proof that, for example, in a case such as this, the defendant not only killed a fellow human being, but did it with malice aforethought, the state could quite consistently with such a constitutional principle conclude that a defendant who sought to establish the defense of insanity, and thereby

---

[a] The Oregon statute at issue in *Leland* required the defendant to prove insanity beyond a reasonable doubt. [Footnote by eds.]

escape any punishment whatever for a heinous crime, should bear the laboring oar on such an issue.

PATTERSON v. NEW YORK

Supreme Court of the United States, 1977.
432 U.S. 197.

MR. JUSTICE WHITE delivered the opinion of the Court.

The question here is the constitutionality under the 14th amendment's due-process clause of burdening the defendant in a New York state murder trial with proving the affirmative defense [b] of extreme emotional disturbance as defined by New York law.

I

After a brief and unstable marriage, the appellant, Gordon Patterson, Jr., became estranged from his wife, Roberta. Roberta resumed an association with John Northrup, a neighbor to whom she had been engaged prior to her marriage to appellant. On December 27, 1970, Patterson borrowed a rifle from an acquaintance and went to the residence of his father-in-law. There, he observed his wife through a window in a state of semi-undress in the presence of John Northrup. He entered the house and killed Northrup by shooting him twice in the head.

Patterson was charged with second-degree murder. In New York there are two elements of the crime: (i) "intent to cause the death of another person"; and (ii) "caus[ing] the death of such person or of a third person." N.Y. Penal Law § 125.25. Malice aforethought is not an element of the crime. In addition, the state permits a person accused of murder to raise an affirmative defense that he "acted under the influence of extreme emotional disturbance for which there was a reasonable explanation or excuse." [c]

New York also recognizes the crime of manslaughter. A person is guilty of manslaughter if he intentionally kills another person "under circumstances which do not constitute murder because he acts under the influence of extreme emotional disturbance." Appellant confessed before trial to killing Northrup, but at trial he raised the defense of extreme emotional disturbance.

[b] "Affirmative defense" is used here to indicate a defense that shifts to the defendant both the burden of production (which means that the issue will be resolved against him if it is not raised by the evidence) and the burden of persuasion (which means that the issue will be resolved against him if, after considering the evidence, the trier of fact remains uncertain whether the required standard of proof has been met). An "affirmative defense" is thus distinguished from an ordinary "defense," which shifts to the defendant only the burden of production. This usage is increasingly widespread, but not uniform. See, e.g., MPC § 1.12, which uses the term "affirmative defense" even where there is no shift in the burden of persuasion. [Footnote by eds.]

[c] The New York homicide provisions are reprinted in Appendix B at pages 8–9, infra. [Footnote by eds.]

The jury was instructed as to the elements of the crime of murder. Focusing on the element of intent, the trial court charged:

"Before you, considering all of the evidence, can convict this defendant or anyone of murder, you must believe and decide that the People have established beyond a reasonable doubt that he intended, in firing the gun, to kill either the victim himself or some other human being. . . .

"Always remember that you must not expect or require the defendant to prove to your satisfaction that his acts were done without the intent to kill. Whatever proof he may have attempted, however far he may have gone in an effort to convince you of his innocence or guiltlessness, he is not obliged, he is not obligated to prove anything. It is always the People's burden to prove his guilt, and to prove that he intended to kill in this instance beyond a reasonable doubt."

The jury was further instructed, consistently with New York law, that the defendant had the burden of proving his affirmative defense by a preponderance of the evidence. The jury was told that if it found beyond a reasonable doubt that appellant had intentionally killed Northrup but that appellant had demonstrated by a preponderance of the evidence that he had acted under the influence of extreme emotional disturbance, it had to find appellant guilty of manslaughter instead of murder.

The jury found appellant guilty of murder. Judgment was entered on the verdict, and the appellate division affirmed. While appeal to the New York Court of Appeals was pending, this Court decided Mullaney v. Wilbur, 421 U.S. 684 (1975) . . . . In the court of appeals appellant urged that New York's murder statute is functionally equivalent to the one struck down in *Mullaney* and that therefore his conviction should be reversed.

The Court of Appeals rejected appellant's argument, holding that the New York murder statute is consistent with due process. The court distinguished *Mullaney* on the ground that the New York statute involved no shifting of the burden to the defendant to disprove any fact essential to the offense charged since the New York affirmative defense of extreme emotional disturbance bears no direct relationship to any element of murder. This appeal ensued. . . . We affirm.

II

It goes without saying that preventing and dealing with crime is much more the business of the states than it is of the federal government, and that we should not lightly construe the Constitution so as to intrude upon the administration of justice by the individual states. Among other things, it is normally "within the power of the state to regulate procedures under which its laws are carried out, including the burden of producing evidence and the burden of persuasion," and its decision in this regard is not subject to proscription under the due process clause unless "it offends some principle of justice so rooted in the traditions and conscience of our people as to be ranked as fundamental."   Speiser v. Randall, 357 U.S. 513 (1958).

In determining whether New York's allocation to the defendant of proving the mitigating circumstances of severe emotional disturbance is consistent with due process, it is therefore relevant to note that this defense is a considerably expanded version of the common-law defense of heat of passion on sudden provocation and that at common law the burden of proving the latter, as well as other affirmative defenses—indeed, "all . . . circumstances of justification, excuse or alleviation"—rested on the defendant.   This was the rule when the fifth amendment was adopted, and it was the American rule when the 14th amendment was ratified. . . .

III

We cannot conclude that Patterson's conviction under the New York law deprived him of due process of law.   The crime of murder is defined by the statute, which represents a recent revision of the state criminal code, as causing the death of another person with intent to do so.   The death, the intent to kill, and causation are the facts that the state is required to prove beyond a reasonable doubt if a person is to be convicted of murder.   No further facts are either presumed or inferred in order to constitute the crime.   The statute does provide an affirmative defense—that the defendant acted under the influence of extreme emotional disturbance for which there was a reasonable explanation—which, if proved by a preponderance of the evidence, would reduce the crime to manslaughter, an offense defined in a separate section of the statute.   It is plain enough that if the intentional killing is shown, the state intends to deal with the defendant as a murderer unless he demonstrates the mitigating circumstances.

Here, the jury was instructed in accordance with the statute, and the guilty verdict confirms that the state successfully carried its burden of proving the facts of the crime beyond a reasonable doubt.   Nothing in the evidence, including any evidence that might have been offered with respect to Patterson's mental state at the time of the crime, raised a reasonable doubt about his guilt as a murderer; and clearly the evidence failed to convince the jury that Patterson's affirmative defense had been made out.   It seems to us that the state satisfied the mandate of *Winship* that it prove beyond a reasonable doubt "every fact necessary to constitute the crime with which [Patterson was] charged."

In convicting Patterson under its murder statute, New York did no more than Leland v. Oregon, 343 U.S. 790 (1952), . . . permitted it to do without violating the due-process clause.   Under [that precedent] once the facts constituting a crime are established beyond a reasonable doubt, based on all the evidence including the evidence of the defendant's mental state, the state may refuse to sustain the affirmative defense of insanity unless demonstrated by a preponderance of the evidence.

The New York law on extreme emotional disturbance follows this pattern.   This affirmative defense, which the court of appeals described as permitting "the defendant to show that his actions were caused by a mental infirmity not arising to the level of insanity, and that he is less culpable for having committed them," does not serve to negative any facts of the crime which the state is to prove in order to convict of murder. It constitutes a separate issue on which the defendant is required to carry the burden of persuasion; and unless we are to overturn *Leland* . . ., New York has not violated the due-process clause, and Patterson's conviction must be sustained.

We are unwilling to reconsider *Leland.* . . . But even if we were to hold that a state must prove sanity to convict once that fact is put in issue, it would not necessarily follow that a state must prove beyond a reasonable doubt every fact, the existence or non-existence of which it is willing to recognize as an exculpatory or mitigating circumstance affecting the degree of culpability or the severity of the punishment. Here, in revising its criminal code, New York provided the affirmative defense of extreme emotional disturbance, a substantially expanded version of the older heat-of-passion concept; but it was willing to do so only if the facts making out the defense were established by the defendant with sufficient certainty. The state was itself unwilling to undertake to establish the absence of those facts beyond a reasonable doubt, perhaps fearing that proof would be too difficult and that too many persons deserving treatment as murderers would escape that punishment if the evidence need merely raise a reasonable doubt about the defendant's emotional state. It has been said that the new criminal code of New York contains some 25 affirmative defenses which exculpate or mitigate but which must be established by the defendant to be operative.[10] The due-process clause, as we see it, does not put New York to the choice of abandoning those defenses or undertaking to disprove their existence in order to convict of a crime which otherwise is within its constitutional powers to sanction by substantial punishment.

The requirement of proof beyond a reasonable doubt in a criminal case is "bottomed on a fundamental value determination of our society that it is far worse to convict an innocent man than to let a guilty man go free." The social cost of placing the burden on the prosecution to prove guilt beyond a reasonable doubt is thus an increased risk that the guilty will go free. While it is clear that our society has willingly chosen to bear a substantial burden in order to protect the innocent, it is equally clear that the risk it must bear is not without limits; and Mr. Justice Harlan's aphorism provides little guidance for determining

[10] The State of New York is not alone in this result:

"Since the Model Penal Code was completed in 1962, some 22 states have codified and reformed their criminal laws. At least 12 of these jurisdictions have used the concept of an 'affirmative defense' and have defined that phrase to require that the defendant prove the existence of an 'affirmative defense' by a preponderance of the evidence. Additionally, at least six proposed state codes and each of the four successive versions of a revised federal code use the same procedural device. Finally, many jurisdictions that do not generally employ this concept of 'affirmative defense' nevertheless shift the burden of proof to the defendant on particular issues."

Low & Jeffries, DICTA: Constitutionalizing the Criminal Law?, 29 Va. Law Weekly, No. 18, p. 1 (1977) (footnotes omitted). . . .

what those limits are.   Due process does not require that every conceivable step be taken, at whatever cost, to eliminate the possibility of convicting an innocent person.   Punishment of those found guilty by a jury, for example, is not forbidden merely because there is a remote possibility in some instances that an innocent person might go to jail.

It is said that the common-law rule [requiring the accused to prove heat of passion based on sudden provocation] permits a state to punish one as a murderer when it is as likely as not that he acted in the heat of passion or under severe emotional distress and when, if he did, he is guilty only of manslaughter.   But this has always been the case in those jurisdictions adhering to the traditional rule.   It is also very likely true that fewer convictions of murder would occur if New York were required to negative the affirmative defense at issue here.   But in each instance of a murder conviction under the present law, New York will have proved beyond a reasonable doubt that the defendant has intentionally killed another person, an act which it is not disputed the state may constitutionally criminalize and punish.   If the state nevertheless chooses to recognize a factor that mitigates the degree of criminality or punishment, we think the state may assure itself that the fact has been established with reasonable certainty.   To recognize at all a mitigating circumstance does not require the state to prove its non-existence in each case in which the fact is put in issue, if in its judgment this would be too cumbersome, too expensive, and too inaccurate.[11]

We thus decline to adopt as a constitutional imperative, operative countrywide, that a state must disprove beyond a reasonable doubt every fact constituting any and all affirmative defenses related to the culpability of the accused.   Traditionally, due process has required that only the most basic procedural safeguards be observed;   more subtle balancing of society's interests against those of the accused have been left to the legislative branch.   We therefore will not disturb the balance struck in previous cases holding that the due-process clause requires the prosecution to prove beyond a reasonable doubt all of the elements included in the definition of the offense of which the defendant is charged.   Proof of the non-existence of all affirmative defenses has never been constitutionally required;   and we perceive no reason to fashion such a rule in this case and apply it to the statutory defense at issue here.

---

[11] The drafters of the Model Penal Code would, as a matter of policy, place the burden of proving the non-existence of most affirmative defenses, including the defense involved in this case, on the prosecution once the defendant has come forward with some evidence that the defense is present.   The drafters recognize the need for flexibility, however, and would, in "some exceptional situations," place the burden of persuasion on the accused.

"Characteristically these are situations where the defense does not obtain at all under existing law and the Code seeks to introduce a mitigation.   Resistance to the mitigation, based upon the prosecution's difficulty in obtaining evidence, ought to be lowered if the burden of persuasion is imposed on the defendant.   Where that difficulty appears genuine and there is something to be said against allowing the defense at all, we consider it defensible to shift the burden in this way."

ALI, Model Penal Code § 1.13, Comment, p. 113 (Tent. Draft No. 4, 1955).   Other writers have recognized the need for flexibility in allocating the burden of proof in order to enhance the potential for liberal legislative reform.

This view may seem to permit state legislatures to reallocate burdens of proof by labeling as affirmative defenses at least some elements of the crime, now defined in their statutes. But there are obviously constitutional limits beyond which the states may not go in this regard. "[I]t is not within the province of a legislature to declare an individual guilty or presumptively guilty of a crime." McFarland v. American Sugar Rfg. Co., 241 U.S. 79, 86 (1916). The legislature cannot "validly command that the finding of an indictment, or mere proof of the identity of the accused, should create a presumption of the existence of all the facts essential to guilt." Tot v. United States, 319 U.S. 463, 469 (1943).

Long before *Winship*, the universal rule in this country was that the prosecution must prove guilt beyond a reasonable doubt. At the same time, the long-accepted rule was that it was constitutionally permissible to provide that various affirmative defenses were to be proved by the defendant. This did not lead to such abuses or to such widespread redefinition of crime and reduction of the prosecutor's burden that a new constitutional rule was required.[12] This was not the problem to which *Winship* was addressed. Nor does the fact that a majority of the states have now assumed the burden of disproving affirmative defenses—for whatever reasons—mean that those states that strike a different balance are in violation of the Constitution.

IV

It is urged that *Mullaney* necessarily invalidates Patterson's conviction. . . .

Mullaney's holding, it is argued, is that the state may not permit the blameworthiness of an act or the severity of punishment authorized for its commission to depend on the presence or absence of an identified fact without assuming the burden of proving the presence or absence of that fact, as the case may be, beyond a reasonable doubt.[15] In our view, the *Mullaney* holding should not be so broadly read. The concurrence of two justices in *Mullaney* was necessarily contrary to such a reading.

. . .

[12] Whenever due-process guarantees are dependent upon the law as defined by the legislative branches, some consideration must be given to the possibility that legislative discretion may be abused to the detriment of the individual. The applicability of the reasonable-doubt standard, however, has always been dependent on how a state defines the offense that is charged in any given case; yet there has been no great rush by the states to shift the burden of disproving traditional elements of the criminal offenses to the accused.

[15] There is some language in *Mullaney* that has been understood as perhaps construing the due-process clause to require the prosecution to prove beyond a reasonable doubt any fact affecting "the degree of criminal culpability." It is said that such a rule would deprive legislatures of any discretion whatsoever in allocating the burden of proof, the practical effect of which might be to undermine legislative reform of our criminal justice system. Carried to its logical extreme, such a reading of *Mullaney* might also, for example, discourage Congress from enacting pending legislation to change the felony-murder rule by permitting the accused to prove by a preponderance of the evidence the affirmative defense that the homicide committed was neither a necessary nor a reasonably foreseeable consequence of the underlying felony. The Court did not intend *Mullaney* to have such far-reaching effect.

Mullaney surely held that a state must prove every ingredient of an offense beyond a reasonable doubt, and that it may not shift the burden of proof to the defendant by presuming that ingredient upon proof of the other elements of the offense. This is true even though the state's practice, as in Maine, had been traditionally to the contrary. Such shifting of the burden of persuasion with respect to a fact which the state deems so important that it must be either proved or presumed is impermissible under the due process clause.

It was unnecessary to go further in *Mullaney*. The Maine Supreme Judicial Court made it clear that . . . a killing became murder in Maine when it resulted from a deliberate, cruel act committed by one person against another, "suddenly without any, or without a considerable provocation." . . . [M]alice, in the sense of the absence of provocation, was part of the definition of that crime. Yet malice, i.e., lack of provocation, was presumed and could be rebutted by the defendant only by proving by a preponderance of the evidence that he acted with heat of passion upon sudden provocation. In *Mullaney* we held that however traditional this mode of proceeding might have been, it is contrary to the due process clause as construed in *Winship*.

As we have explained, nothing was presumed or implied against Patterson; and his conviction is not invalid under any of our prior cases. The judgment of the New York Court of Appeals is affirmed.

MR. JUSTICE REHNQUIST took no part in the consideration or decision of this case.

MR. JUSTICE POWELL, with whom MR. JUSTICE BRENNAN and MR. JUSTICE MARSHALL join, dissenting.

In the name of preserving legislative flexibility, the Court today drains *In re Winship* of much of its vitality. Legislatures do require broad discretion in the drafting of criminal laws, but the Court surrenders to the legislative branch a significant part of its responsibility to protect the presumption of innocence.

I

An understanding of the import of today's decision requires a comparison of the statutes at issue here with the statutes and practices of Maine struck down by a unanimous Court just two years ago in Mullaney v. Wilbur, 421 U.S. 684 (1975).

A

Maine's homicide laws embodied the common-law distinctions along with the colorful common-law language. Murder was defined as the unlawful killing of a human being "with malice aforethought, either express or implied." Manslaughter was a killing "in the heat of passion, on sudden provocation, without express or implied malice aforethought." . . .

New York's present homicide laws had their genesis in lingering dissatisfaction with certain aspects of the common-law framework that this Court confronted in *Mullaney*. Critics charged that the archaic language tended to obscure the factors of real importance in the jury's decision. Also, only a limited range of aggravations would lead to mitigation under the common-law formula, usually only those resulting from direct provocation by the victim himself. It was thought that actors whose emotions were stirred by other forms of outrageous conduct, even conduct by someone other than the ultimate victim, also should be punished as manslaughterers rather than murderers. Moreover, the common-law formula was generally applied with strict objectivity. Only provocations that might cause the hypothetical reasonable man to lose control could be considered. And even provocations of that sort were inadequate to reduce the crime to manslaughter if enough time had passed for the reasonable man's passions to cool, regardless of whether the actor's own thermometer had registered any decline.

The American Law Institute took the lead in moving to remedy these difficulties. As part of its commendable undertaking to prepare a Model Penal Code, it endeavored to bring modern insights to bear on the law of homicide. The result was a proposal to replace "heat of passion" with the moderately broader concept of "extreme mental or emotional disturbance." . . .

At about this time the New York legislature undertook the preparation of a new criminal code, and the Revised Penal Law of 1967 was the ultimate result. The new code adopted virtually word for word the ALI formula for distinguishing murder from manslaughter. Under current New York law . . . the last traces of confusing archaic language have been removed. There is no mention of malice aforethought, no attempt to give a name to the state of mind that exists when extreme emotional disturbance is not present. . . .

B

Mullaney held invalid Maine's requirement that the defendant prove heat of passion. The Court today, without disavowing the unanimous holding of *Mullaney*, approves New York's requirement that the defendant prove extreme emotional disturbance. The Court manages to run a constitutional boundary line through the barely visible space that separates Maine's law from New York's. It does so on the basis of distinctions in language that are formalistic rather than substantive.

This result is achieved by a narrowly literal parsing of the holding in *Winship*: "[T]he due-process clause protects the accused against conviction except upon proof beyond a reasonable doubt of every fact necessary to constitute the crime with which he is charged." The only "facts" necessary to constitute a crime are said to be those that appear on the face of the statute as a part of the definition of the crime. Maine's statute was invalid, the Court reasons, because it "defined murder as the unlawful killing of a human being 'with malice aforethought, either express or implied.'" "[M]alice," the Court reiterates, "in the sense of the absence of provocation, was part of the definition of that crime." *Winship* was violated only because this "fact"—malice—was "presumed" unless the defendant persuaded the jury otherwise by showing that he acted in the heat of passion. New York, in form presuming no affirmative "fact" against Patterson, and blessed with a statute drafted in the leaner language of the 20th century, escapes constitutional scrutiny unscathed even though the effect on the defendant of New York's placement of the burden of persuasion is exactly the same as Maine's.

This explanation of the *Mullaney* holding bears little resemblance to the basic rationale of that decision. But this is not the cause of greatest concern. The test the Court today establishes allows a legislature to shift, virtually at will, the burden of persuasion with respect to any factor in a criminal case, so long as it is careful not to mention the non-existence of that factor in the statutory language that defines the crime. The sole requirement is that any references to the factor be confined to those sections that provide for an affirmative defense.

Perhaps the Court's interpretation of *Winship* is consistent with the letter of the holding in that case. But little of the spirit survives. Indeed, the Court scarcely could distinguish this case from *Mullaney* without closing its eyes to the constitutional values for which *Winship* stands. As Mr. Justice Harlan observed in *Winship*, "a standard of proof represents an attempt to instruct the factfinder concerning the degree of confidence our society thinks he should have in the correctness of actual conclusions for a particular type of adjudication." Explaining *Mullaney*, the Court says today, in effect, that society demands full confidence before a Maine factfinder determines that heat of passion is missing—a demand so insistent that this Court invoked the Constitution to enforce it over the contrary decision by the state. But we are told that society is willing to tolerate far less confidence in New York's factual determination of precisely the same functional issue. One must ask what possibly could explain this difference in societal demands. According to the Court, it is because Maine happened to attach a name—"malice aforethought"—to the absence of heat of passion, whereas New York refrained from giving a name to the absence of extreme emotional disturbance.

With all respect, this type of constitutional adjudication is indefensibly formalistic. A limited but significant check on possible abuses in the criminal law now becomes an exercise in arid formalities. What *Winship* and *Mullaney* had sought to teach about the limits a free society places on its procedures to safeguard the liberty of its citizens becomes a rather simplistic lesson in statutory draftsmanship. Nothing in the Court's opinion prevents a legislature from applying this new learning to many of the classical elements of the crimes it punishes.[8] It would be preferable, if the Court has found reason to reject the rationale of *Winship* and *Mullaney*, simply and straightforwardly to overrule those precedents.

[8] For example, a state statute could pass muster under the only solid standard that appears in the Court's opinion if it defined murder as mere physical contact between the defendant and the victim leading to the victim's death, but then set up an affirmative defense leaving it to the defendant to prove that he acted without culpable mens rea. The state, in other words, could be relieved altogether of responsibility for proving *anything* regarding the defendant's state of mind, provided only that the face of the statute meets the Court's drafting formulas. . . .

The Court understandably manifests some uneasiness that its formalistic approach will give legislatures too much latitude in shifting the burden of persuasion. And so it issues a warning that "there are obviously constitutional limits beyond which the states may not go in this regard." The Court thereby concedes that legislative abuses may occur and that they must be curbed by the judicial branch. But if the state is careful to conform to the drafting formulas articulated today, the constitutional limits are anything but "obvious." This decision simply leaves us without a conceptual framework for distinguishing abuses from legitimate legislative adjustments of the burden of persuasion in criminal cases.

II

It is unnecessary for the Court to retreat to a formalistic test for applying *Winship*. Careful attention to the *Mullaney* decision reveals the principles that should control in this and like cases. *Winship* held that the prosecution must bear the burden of proving beyond a reasonable doubt " 'the existence of every fact necessary to constitute the crime charged.' " In *Mullaney* we concluded that heat of passion was one of the "facts" described in *Winship*—that is, a factor as to which the prosecution must bear the burden of persuasion beyond a reasonable doubt. We reached that result only after making two careful inquiries. First, we noted that the presence or absence of heat of passion made a substantial difference in punishment of the offender and in the stigma associated with the conviction. Second, we reviewed the history, in England and this country, of the factor at issue. Central to the holding in *Mullaney* was our conclusion that heat of passion "has been, almost from the inception of the common law of homicide, the single most important factor in determining the degree of culpability attaching to an unlawful homicide."

Implicit in these two inquiries are the principles that should govern this case. The due-process clause requires that the prosecutor bear the burden of persuasion beyond a reasonable doubt only if the factor at issue makes a substantial difference in punishment and stigma. The requirement of course applies a fortiori if the factor makes the difference between guilt and innocence. But a substantial difference in punishment alone is not enough. It also must be shown that in the Anglo-American legal tradition the factor in question historically has held that level of importance. If either branch of the test is not met, then the legislature retains its traditional authority over matters of proof. But to permit a shift in the burden of persuasion when both branches of this test are satisfied would invite the undermining of the presumption of innocence, "that bedrock 'axiomatic and elementary' principle whose 'enforcement lies at the foundation of the administration of our criminal law.' "

I hardly need add that New York's provisions allocating the burden of persuasion as to "extreme emotional disturbance" are unconstitutional when judged by these standards. "[E]xtreme emotional disturbance" is . . . the direct descendant of the "heat of passion" factor considered at length in *Mullaney*. I recognize, of course, that the differences between Maine and New York law are not unimportant to the defendant; there is a somewhat broader opportunity for mitigation. But none of those distinctions is relevant here. The presence or absence of extreme emotional disturbance makes a critical difference in punishment and stigma, and throughout our history the resolution of this issue of fact, although expressed in somewhat different terms, has distinguished manslaughter from murder.

III

The Court beats its retreat from *Winship* apparently because of a concern that otherwise the federal judiciary will intrude too far into the substantive choices concerning the content of a state's criminal law. The concern is legitimate, but misplaced. *Winship* and *Mullaney* are no more than what they purport to be: decisions addressing the procedural requirements that states must meet to comply with due process. They are not outposts for policing the substantive boundaries of the criminal law.

The *Winship/Mullaney* test identifies those factors of such importance, historically, in determining punishment and stigma that the Constitution forbids shifting to the defendant the burden of persuasion when such a factor is at issue. *Winship* and *Mullaney* specify only the procedure that is required when a state elects to use such a factor as part of its substantive criminal law. They do not say that the state must elect to use it. For example, where a state has chosen to retain the traditional distinction between murder and manslaughter, as have New York and Maine, the burden of persuasion must remain on the prosecution with respect to the distinguishing factor, in view of its decisive historical importance. But nothing in *Mullaney* or *Winship* precludes a state from abolishing the distinction between murder and manslaughter and treating all unjustifiable homicide as murder.[13] In this significant respect, neither *Winship* nor *Mullaney* eliminates the substantive flexibility that should remain in legislative hands.

Moreover, it is unlikely that more than a few factors—although important ones—for which a shift in the burden of persuasion seriously would be considered will come within the *Mullaney* holding. With some exceptions, then, the state has the authority "to recognize a factor that mitigates the degree of criminality or punishment" without having "to prove its non-existence in each case in which the fact is put in

[13] Perhaps under other principles of due-process jurisprudence, certain factors are so fundamental that a state could not, as a substantive matter, refrain from recognizing them so long as it chooses to punish given conduct as a crime. . . . But substantive limits were not at issue in *Winship* or *Mullaney*, and they are not at issue here.

Even if there are no constitutional limits preventing the state, for example, from treating all homicides as murders punishable equally regardless of mitigating factors like heat of passion or extreme emotional disturbance, the *Winship/Mullaney* rule still plays an important role. The state is then obliged to make its choices concerning the substantive content of its criminal laws with full awareness of the consequences, unable to mask substantive policy choices by shifts in the burden of persuasion. The political check on potentially harsh legislative action is then more likely to operate. . . .

issue." New ameliorative affirmative defenses, about which the Court expresses concern, generally remain undisturbed by the holdings in *Winship* and *Mullaney*—and need not be disturbed by a sound holding reversing Patterson's conviction.

Furthermore, as we indicated in *Mullaney*, even as to those factors upon which the prosecution must bear the burden of persuasion, the state retains an important procedural device to avoid jury confusion and prevent the prosecution from being unduly hampered. The state normally may shift to the defendant the burden of production, that is, the burden of going forward with sufficient evidence "to justify [a reasonable] doubt upon the issue." If the defendant's evidence does not cross this threshold, the issue—be it malice, extreme emotional disturbance, self-defense, or whatever—will not be submitted to the jury.
. . .

To be sure, there will be many instances when the *Winship/ Mullaney* test as I perceive it will be more difficult to apply than the Court's formula. Where I see the need for a careful and discriminating review of history, the Court finds a brightline standard that can be applied with a quick glance at the face of the statute. But this facile test invites tinkering with the procedural safeguards of the presumption of innocence, an invitation to disregard the principles of *Winship* that I would not extend.

NOTES ON BURDEN OF PROOF FOR MITIGATIONS AND DEFENSES

1. **The Distinction Between *Mullaney* and *Patterson*.** Note that the *Patterson* majority purported to distinguish rather than to overrule *Mullaney*. Presumably, that means that *Mullaney* is still good law for certain situations. What are those situations? What is the dividing line between the continuing authority of *Mullaney* and the superseding rule of *Patterson*? Is the effort to distinguish them, as Mr. Justice Powell charged, "indefensibly formalistic?" Can you think of a rationale for *Mullaney* that does not apply with equal force to *Patterson*? If not, why do you suppose the Supreme Court tried to distinguish the two cases rather than to apply the same approach to both?

2. **The Procedural Interpretation of *Winship*.** If you conclude that *Mullaney* and *Patterson* are inconsistent, it necessarily follows that at least one of them is wrong. The question is which one. This issue has divided both courts and commentators and sparked a continuing controversy over the legitimate reach of *In re Winship*. For a time, at least, the prevailing reaction was that *Mullaney* was right and *Patterson* wrong. This position is founded on what may be called the procedural interpretation of *Winship*. Under this view, the constitutional commitment to proof beyond a reasonable doubt should extend to every fact determinative of criminal liability. The prosecution would be required to prove beyond a reasonable doubt not only every element of the offense charged but also the absence of justification, excuse, or

other grounds of defense or mitigation. This is termed the procedural interpretation of *Winship* because it sees the reasonable-doubt standard as a procedural requirement to be enforced without regard to the scope of legislative control over the substance of the penal law. In other words, the value of requiring proof beyond a reasonable doubt is thought to be entirely independent of the substantive issue of what must be proved.

The most articulate exponent of this view is Professor Barbara Underwood. In her article, The Thumb on the Scales of Justice: Burdens of Persuasion in Criminal Cases, 86 Yale L.J. 1299 (1977), she postulates two distinct purposes for requiring proof beyond a reasonable doubt: "First, the rule is meant to affect the outcome of individual cases, reducing the likelihood of an erroneous conviction. Second, the rule is meant to symbolize for society the great significance of a criminal conviction." The first function is, therefore, to reduce the chance of criminal conviction "by putting a thumb on the defendant's side of the scales of justice." This imbalance is designed to reflect what Mr. Justice Harlan termed "a fundamental value determination of our society that it is far worse to convict an innocent man than to let a guilty man go free." Underwood's second function for the reasonable-doubt requirement is "to single out criminal conviction as peculiarly serious among the adjudications made by courts" and thus to make a public affirmation of the "shared moral purpose" of protecting individual liberty.

In Professor Underwood's view, these considerations support an insistence on proof beyond a reasonable doubt even in the face of undoubted legislative authority over what must be proved. She denies that legislative power to eliminate altogether a ground of defense or mitigation should entail the lesser power to shift to the defendant the burden of establishing its existence. In her view, the fact that a defense is gratuitous—i.e., may be granted or withheld at the legislature's option—provides no basis for treating it as an exception to the reasonable-doubt requirement.

The result of this approach would be to force legislatures to extreme choices. Thus, under the procedural interpretation of *Winship*, a legislature could choose to require that the prosecution disprove a defense beyond a reasonable doubt, *or* it could choose to eliminate the defense entirely. But it could not adopt the compromise solution of recognizing the defense and requiring the defendant to establish its existence. In the following passage, Professor Underwood confronts these implications of her argument and explains why she regards the compromise solution as constitutionally inappropriate:*

"Broad application of the requirement of proof beyond a reasonable doubt operates to foreclose certain kinds of compromise in the formulation of criminal law policy. In general, compromise is a desirable and indeed essential part of the lawmaking process. If this reading of the constitutional require-

* Reprinted by permission of the author, The Yale Law Journal Company, and Fred   B. Rothman & Company from The Yale Law Journal, Vol. 86, pp. 1320, 1322.

ment [i.e., the procedural interpretation of *Winship*] seemed to foreclose sensible legislative options for no good reason, that would count heavily for a different and more felicitous reading. But the kind of compromise prohibited by the reasonable-doubt rule is less satisfactory than other forms of compromise that remain available, and therefore its loss is no ground for concern.

. . .

"A substantive disagreement about whether to recognize a defense amounts to a disagreement about whether the person with the proposed defense is less suitable than other offenders for specified criminal sanctions. By shifting the burden of persuasion to the defendant, a legislature limits the defense to those for whom the evidence is most abundant. That group, however, is not necessarily the least culpable, least harmful, or least deterrable. For there is no reason to think that the continuum of culpability, harm, or deterrability bears any relationship to the continuum of available evidence. The person for whom the evidence is strongest may not be the person whose claim, if believed, has the strongest relationship to the policies behind the defense. A disagreement about the proper scope of the substantive criminal law can be compromised by an intermediate definition of the facts that constitute crimes and defenses. Tinkering with the reasonable-doubt rule, which determines when to believe a defendant's version of the facts, requires an explanation in terms of the purposes of that rule. But those purposes are no less relevant to factfinding when a controversial gratuitous defense is at issue than they are to the determination of any other fact in a criminal case. Indeed, any controversy over the defense may enhance the threat to the values the reasonable-doubt rule was designed to protect.

". . . A legislature uncertain about the merits of a proposed defense might reasonably wish to change its assessment of the relative costs of errors. But a constitutional valuation of the relative costs of errors cannot be avoided by legislative fiat. So long as the factual determination has the function and consequences that characterize other issues in a criminal case, such as enhanced stigma and an increased period of potential incarceration, the reasons for the constitutional rule remain. The costs of erroneous convictions and erroneous acquittals are not different by virtue of the gratuitous character of the defense. . . ." [a]

Are you persuaded? Should the New York law on "extreme emotional disturbance" have been invalidated on the authority of *Mullaney*? Even if the shift in the burden of persuasion was an essential part of a legislative compromise to secure enactment of a broader formulation of the rule of provocation? Is there a tension between the requirement of

[a] Professor Underwood's defense of her position is far more elaborate than can be reflected here. In addition to the excerpts printed in the text, other aspects of her argument may be found in 86 Yale L.J. at 1316–20 and 1322–29. Rebuttal of these points is attempted in Jeffries & Stephan, Defenses, Presumptions, and Burden of Proof in the Criminal Law, 88 Yale L.J. 1325, 1348–52 (1979).

proof beyond a reasonable doubt and efficient deterrence? To the extent that weaker evidentiary support for a claimed defense or mitigation must be recognized as exculpatory, is the social-control function of the criminal law undermined? Is this a legitimate legislative concern? One that should be foreclosed by constitutional imperatives?

3. **Criticisms of the Procedural Approach.** The procedural interpretation of *Winship* has been attacked on a number of grounds. Representative criticisms are made in Jeffries & Stephan, Defenses, Presumptions, and Burden of Proof in the Criminal Law, 88 Yale L.J. 1325 (1979).[b] In their opinion, the rationales for the reasonable-doubt requirement demand that *something* be proved beyond a reasonable doubt, but "do not establish that *every* fact relevant to the imposition or grade of penal liability be subject to that standard." They focus squarely on the gratuitous defense. In their view, the constitutional insistence on proof beyond a reasonable doubt "no longer makes sense" when applied to a gratuitous defense. "Such a rule would purport to preserve individual liberty and the societal sense of commitment to it by forcing the government *either* to disprove the defense beyond a reasonable doubt *or* to eliminate the defense altogether." The government could cure the purported unconstitutionality *either* by proving more *or* by proving less, as it saw fit. "The latter solution results in an extension of penal liability despite the presence of mitigating or exculpatory facts. It is difficult to see this result as constitutionally compelled and harder still to believe that it flows from a general policy, whether actual or symbolic, in favor of individual liberty."

In addition to the theoretical criticism stated above, Jeffries and Stephan also attempt a practical evaluation of the procedural interpretation of *Winship*. The following excerpt describes their views and the basis for them: *

"The procedural interpretation of *Winship* would not only be illogical in concept; it would also be potentially pernicious in effect. It is at least plausible, indeed we think it likely, that a rule barring reallocation of the burden of proof would thwart legislative reform of the penal law and stifle efforts to undo injustice in the traditional law of crimes. Even if one were to believe that rigid insistence on proof beyond a reasonable doubt might in some purely symbolic sense reaffirm the 'presumption of innocence,' it would do so at the risk of a harsh and regressive expansion in the definition of guilt.

"This is a point of some importance, for, quite surprisingly, proponents of a procedural interpretation of *Winship* have made exactly the contrary argument. They assume that forcing legislatures to choose between proving more and proving less would

---

[b] See also the very able articles on this subject by Professor Ronald J. Allen. Allen, The Restoration of *In re Winship*: A Comment on Burdens of Persuasion in Criminal Cases After *Patterson* v. *New York*, 76 Mich.L.Rev. 30 (1977), and Allen, *Mullaney* v. *Wilbur*, The Supreme Court and the Substantive Criminal Law—An Examination of the Limits of Legitimate Intervention, 55 Tex.L.Rev. 269 (1977).

* The excerpts below are printed by permission of the authors, The Yale Law Journal Company, and Fred B. Rothman & Company from The Yale Law Journal, Vol. 88, pp. 1353–56.

produce good choices. In other words, they argue that a legislature required to abandon an affirmative defense would be likely to force the prosecution to disprove the existence of a ground of exculpation beyond a reasonable doubt rather than to eliminate it altogether. Popular pressure, it is asserted, would act as a check against untoward expansion of criminal liability. The net effect, therefore, of disallowing the intermediate solution of an affirmative defense would be a benign and progressive influence on the substance of the penal law.

"Aside from failing to demonstrate whether this supposition, even if true, would be sufficient basis for constitutional adjudication, advocates of the procedural approach fail to produce evidence to support the supposition. The best evidence of what legislatures would do if they were forced to abandon the affirmative defense is the catalogue of uses to which that device is currently put. If it were used to disguise harsh innovations in the law of crimes, one might reasonably infer that elimination of the procedural device would have an ameliorative effect on substance. In point of fact, however, the burden-shifting defense quite generally is employed to moderate traditional rigors in the law of crimes. There is, therefore, reason to believe that rejection of this device would result in abandonment of the underlying substantive innovations and reversion to older and harsher rules of penal liability.

"In order to test this proposition, we surveyed the practices of the 33 American states that have recently enacted comprehensive revisions of their penal laws. These are the jurisdictions that in modern times have had an occasion to confront the issues here under discussion. Eight of these states provide no statutory guidance on this point, and six more expressly require that the prosecution bear the burden of proof beyond a reasonable doubt for every fact needed to obtain conviction. However, 19 states have enacted revised codes that include burden-shifting defenses. Virtually all of these uses of the burden-shifting defense mark instances of benevolent innovation in the penal law. Thirteen states recognize an affirmative defense of renunciation for the crime of attempt. Nine permit reasonable mistake as to age as an affirmative defense to statutory rape. Eight create an affirmative defense to liability for felony murder, and six exonerate the accused if he can show reasonable reliance on an official misstatement of law. In each of these cases, the affirmative defense is used to introduce a new ground of exculpation, often in circumstances where an obligation to disprove its existence beyond a reasonable doubt would be especially onerous. None of the named defenses existed at common law, and none is a traditional feature of American statutes. A plausible conclusion is that shifting the burden of proof is often politically necessary to secure legislative reform. It seems quite possible, therefore, that disallowance of this procedural device would work to inhibit reform and induce retrogression in the penal law."

Are you persuaded? Would you agree with the implication of this argument that *Mullaney* is the case that should have come out the other way? Even though there was no indication that the shift in the burden of persuasion involved in *Mullaney* had anything to do with political compromise or legislative reform?

4. **An Alternative Reformulation of *Mullaney*: The *Patterson* Dissent.** The *Patterson* majority undertook to reinterpret *Mullaney* in order to avoid it. Interestingly, the author of that opinion undertook to reinterpret *Mullaney* in order to save it. Mr. Justice Powell's *Patterson* dissent does not take *Mullaney* at face value, but instead finds implicit in that decision two limiting criteria. First, "[t]he due-process clause requires that the prosecution bear the burden of persuasion beyond a reasonable doubt only if the factor at issue makes a substantial difference in punishment and stigma." Second, "[i]t must also be shown that in the Anglo-American legal tradition the factor in question historically has held that level of importance." Only where both conditions are met would burden-shifting be disallowed. But, as Mr. Justice Powell was at pains to point out, these criteria would not limit legislative authority over substance. Even where both criteria were met (and burden-shifting consequently forbidden), the legislature would remain free to eliminate altogether the mitigating or exculpatory effect of the fact in issue.

What do you think of this approach? It has the advantage, does it not, of reducing the risk of thwarting legislative reform? Few, if any, of the "benevolent innovations" described above would be barred by Powell's revised formulation. Yet he plainly would disallow the law in *Patterson*, which not only shifted to defendants the burden of persuasion but also broadened significantly the substantive criteria of mitigation. Should the loss of this kind of legislative opportunity be cause for concern?

One might also ask why the "Anglo-American legal tradition" should play so decisive a role in constitutional adjudication. Is there necessarily virtue in antiquity? Should the constitutionality of modern legislation depend on its consistency with the common law? And if history is to be decisive in limiting shifts in the burden of persuasion, why should it not also be decisive in limiting legislative power over the substance of the law? If the historic importance of provocation in the law of homicide precludes the legislature from shifting the burden of persuasion, why does it not also prevent the legislature from taking the much greater step of eliminating provocation altogether? Is not Justice Powell's reinterpretation of *Mullaney* subject to much the same criticism as the rigidly procedural approach that he abandoned? Or do you see something different in his scheme?

5. **Burden of Proof and Substantive Justice.** It seems clear that the underlying concern in much of the debate over burden of proof is not procedural regularity but substantive justice. This concern surfaces in the "horror stories" used to describe what a legislature might do if burden-shifting were allowed. Recall, for example, the *Patterson* footnote where Justice Powell speculates that a state might

define murder "as mere physical contact between the defendant and the victim leading to the victim's death, but then set up an affirmative defense leaving it to the defendant to prove that he acted without culpable mens rea." By this device, says Justice Powell, the prosecution "could be relieved altogether of responsibility for proving *anything* regarding the defendant's state of mind . . . ." Professor Underwood advances a similar concern over the rubric of "the slippery slope." What if, she asks, the legislature were to replace the entire range of homicide and assault offenses with the single crime of "personal attack?" Unless burden-shifting were disallowed, she continues, the legislature could authorize major penalties "on proof of a trivial assault, with the burden on the defendant to establish the mitigating defenses of the victim's survival, his freedom from injury, or the defendant's lack of intent to harm or injure." In both of these hypotheticals, serious punishment would be authorized on proof beyond a reasonable doubt of no more than trivial wrongdoing. The result would be the use of burden-shifting defenses to impose criminal penalties far out of proportion to any proven misconduct by the accused.

Do you follow this argument? Is it clear that the danger posed by these hypotheticals has any necessary connection with shifting the burden of proof? Consider the response of Jeffries & Stephan:

> "The trouble [with this argument] lies in the unspoken assumption that excessive punishment is somehow a product of shifting the burden of proof. In fact, use of a burden-shifting defense . . . does not necessarily result in excessive punishment, nor does excessive punishment necessarily involve reallocation of the burden of proof. Thus, to forbid burden-shifting devices *in order to* reduce disparity between proven fault and authorized penalties is a non sequitur. In point of fact, a constitutional stricture against shifting the burden of proof would not prevent the injustice of unwarranted or disproportionate criminal punishment. . . . The hypothetical legislature that would assign the fact of the victim's survival to an affirmative defense to a 'personal attack' charge just as easily could eliminate the victim's death as a grading factor for assaultive behavior. The state could simply authorize serious sanctions for any physical assault, whether fatal or trivial, and leave distinctions among cases to the sentencing stage. This scheme involves no reallocation of the burden of proof, but it is just as objectionable as Underwood's original hypothetical. Both schemes would authorize major felony sanctions on proof of nothing more than a trivial assault; both involve the infliction of punishment grossly disproportionate to any proven blameworthiness of the defendant."

The excerpt from Jeffries and Stephan also suggests their alternative construction of *In re Winship*. In their view, the constitutional insistence on proof beyond a reasonable doubt should extend only to facts constitutionally required to be proved. "In other words, *Winship* should be read to assert a constitutional requirement of proof beyond a reasonable doubt of a constitutionally adequate basis for imposing the punishment authorized." The state could shift to the defendant the burden of persuasion for any additional or gratuitous factor which it chose to take into account. The focus would be not on what the government invited the defendant to prove by way of mitigation or excuse, but rather on what the prosecution had to prove beyond a reasonable doubt in order to establish liability in the first instance. For Jeffries and Stephan, therefore, the question in both *Mullaney* and *Patterson* would be whether the facts required to be proved beyond a reasonable doubt established a constitutionally adequate basis for imposing the authorized maximum of life imprisonment. If so, "nothing would bar the state from going beyond the constitutional minimum to allow mitigation when the defendant can prove his claim to it." If not, the state would be required to establish a constitutionally adequate basis for life imprisonment by disproving heat of passion or extreme emotional disturbance beyond a reasonable doubt.[c]

It should be emphasized that no one disputes the applicability of the reasonable-doubt requirement within the sphere of constitutionally required facts. Professor Underwood, no less than Jeffries and Stephan, supports the insistence on proof beyond a reasonable doubt of facts constitutionally required for conviction or punishment. The dispute is limited to whether other facts—facts that the state may choose to recognize as exculpatory or mitigating or not, as it pleases—should also be subject to a constitutionally imposed standard of proof. In light of the several aspects of this problem developed in the notes above, what do you think is the best solution?

SUBSECTION B: PRESUMPTIONS

SANDSTROM v. MONTANA

Supreme Court of the United States, 1979.
442 U.S. 510.

MR. JUSTICE BRENNAN delivered the opinion of the Court.

The question presented is whether, in a case in which intent is an element of the crime charged, the jury instruction "the law presumes that a person intends the ordinary consequences of his voluntary acts,"

---

[c] Of course, specifying a constitutionally adequate basis for criminal punishment is no easy task. As Jeffries and Stephan confess, "the existence of constitutional constraints on the substantive criminal law is largely terra incognita." Their view, advanced only "to suggest a direction of analysis," is that the constitutional focus should be on three factors: (i) the requirement of an act; (ii) the requirement of culpability; and (iii) the requirement of

rough proportionality between the penalty authorized and the wrong done. With respect to the first factor, see *Robinson* v. *California* and the accompanying materials at pages 158–83, supra. With respect to the second, see the materials on strict liability, especially *Lambert* v. *California*, at pages 308–13, supra. On the issue of proportionality, see *Solem* v. *Helm* and the accompanying materials at pages 1028–53, infra.

violates the 14th amendment's requirement that the state prove every element of a criminal offense beyond a reasonable doubt.

I

On November 22, 1976, 18-year-old David Sandstrom confessed to the slaying of Annie Jessen. Based upon the confession and corroborating evidence, petitioner was charged on December 2 with "deliberate homicide," Rev. Code Mont. § 45–5–102, in that he "purposely or knowingly caused the death of Annie Jessen."[1] At trial, Sandstrom's attorney informed the jury that, although his client admitted killing Jessen, he did not do so "purposely or knowingly," and was therefore not guilty of "deliberate homicide" but of a lesser crime. The basic support for this contention was the testimony of two court-appointed mental health experts, each of whom described for the jury petitioner's mental state at the time of the incident. Sandstrom's attorney argued that this testimony demonstrated that petitioner, due to a personality disorder aggravated by alcohol consumption, did not kill Annie Jessen "purposely or knowingly."

The prosecution requested the trial judge to instruct the jury that "[t]he law presumes that a person intends the ordinary consequences of his voluntary acts." Petitioner's counsel objected, arguing that "the instruction has the effect of shifting the burden of proof on the issue of" purpose or knowledge to the defense, and that "that is impermissible under the federal Constitution, due process of law." He offered to provide a number of federal decisions in support of the objection, including this Court's holding in Mullaney v. Wilbur, 421 U.S. 684 (1975), but was told by the judge: "You can give those to the Supreme Court. The objection is overruled." The instruction was delivered, the jury found petitioner guilty of deliberate homicide, and petitioner was sentenced to 100 years in prison.

Sandstrom appealed to the Supreme Court of Montana, again contending that the instruction shifted to the defendant the burden of disproving an element of the crime charged, in violation of *Mullaney* v. *Wilbur*, supra, In re Winship, 397 U.S. 358 (1970), and Patterson v. New York, 432 U.S. 197 (1977). The Montana court conceded that these cases did prohibit shifting the burden of proof to the defendant by means of a presumption, but held that these cases "do not prohibit allocation of *some* burden of proof to a defendant under certain circumstances." Since in the court's view "[d]efendant's sole burden . . . was to produce *some* evidence that he did not intend the ordinary consequences of his voluntary acts, not to disprove that he acted

---

[1] The statute provides:

"45–5–101. Criminal homicide.

"(1) A person commits the offense of criminal homicide if he purposely, knowingly, or negligently causes the death of another human being.

"(2) Criminal homicide is deliberate homicide, mitigated deliberate homicide, or negligent homicide.

"45–5–102. Deliberate homicide.

"(1) Except as provided in 45–5–103(1), criminal homicide constitutes deliberate homicide if:

"(a) it is committed purposely or knowingly. . . ."

'purposely' or 'knowingly,' . . . the instruction does not violate due process standards as defined by the United States or Montana Constitution. . . ." [Emphasis added].

Both federal and state courts have held, under a variety of rationales, that the giving of an instruction similar to that challenged here is fatal to the validity of a criminal conviction. We granted certiorari to decide the important question of the instruction's constitutionality. We reverse.

II

The threshold inquiry in ascertaining the constitutional analysis applicable to this kind of jury instruction is to determine the nature of the presumption it describes. That determination requires careful attention to the words actually spoken to the jury, for whether a defendant has been accorded his constitutional rights depends upon the way in which a reasonable juror could have interpreted the instruction.

Respondent argues, first, that the instruction merely described a permissive inference—that is, it allowed but did not require the jury to draw conclusions about defendant's intent from his actions—and that such inferences are constitutional. These arguments need not detain us long, for even respondent admits that "it's possible" that the jury believed they were required to apply the presumption. Sandstrom's jurors were told that "[t]he law presumes that a person intends the ordinary consequences of his voluntary acts." They were not told that they had a choice, or that they might infer that conclusion; they were told only that the law presumed it. It is clear that a reasonable juror could easily have viewed such an instruction as mandatory.

In the alternative, respondent urges that, even if viewed as a mandatory presumption rather than as a permissive inference, the presumption did not conclusively establish intent but rather could be rebutted. On this view, the instruction required the jury, if satisfied as to the facts which trigger the presumption, to find intent *unless* the defendant offered evidence to the contrary. Moreover, according to the state, all the defendant had to do to rebut the presumption was produce "some" contrary evidence; he did not have to "prove" that he lacked the required mental state. Thus, "[a]t most, it placed a *burden of production* on the petitioner," but "did not shift to petitioner the *burden of persuasion* with respect to any element of the offense. . . ." [Emphasis added.] Again, respondent contends that presumptions with this limited effect pass constitutional muster.

We need not review respondent's constitutional argument on this point either, however, for we reject this characterization of the presumption as well. Respondent concedes there is a "risk" that the jury, once having found petitioner's act voluntary, would interpret the instruction as automatically directing a finding of intent. Moreover, the state also concedes that numerous courts "have differed as to the effect of the presumption when given as a jury instruction without further explanation as to its use by the jury," and that some have found it to shift more than the burden of production, and even to have conclusive effect. Nonetheless, the state contends that the only authoritative reading of the effect of the presumption resides in the Supreme Court of Montana. And the state argues that by holding that "[d]efendant's sole burden . . . was to produce *some* evidence that he did not intend the ordinary consequences of his voluntary acts, not to disprove that he acted 'purposely' or 'knowingly,'" (emphasis added), the Montana Supreme Court decisively established that the presumption at most affected only the burden of going forward with evidence of intent—that is, the burden of production.

The Supreme Court of Montana is, of course, the final authority on the legal weight to be given a presumption under Montana law, but it is not the final authority on the interpretation which a jury could have given the instruction. If Montana intended its presumption to have only the effect described by its Supreme Court, then we are convinced that a reasonable juror could well have been misled by the instruction given, and could have believed that the presumption was not limited to requiring the defendant to satisfy only a burden of production. Petitioner's jury was told that "the law *presumes* that a person intends the ordinary consequences of his voluntary acts." They were not told that the presumption could be rebutted, as the Montana Supreme Court held, by the defendant's simple presentation of "some" evidence; nor even that it could be rebutted at all. Given the common definition of "presume" as "to suppose to be true without proof," and given the lack of qualifying instructions as to the legal effect of the presumption, we cannot discount the possibility that the jury may have interpreted the instruction in either of two more stringent ways.

First, a reasonable jury could well have interpreted the presumption as "conclusive," that is, not technically as a presumption at all, but rather as an irrebuttable direction by the court to find intent once convinced of the facts triggering the presumption. Alternatively, the jury may have interpreted the instruction as a direction to find intent upon proof of the defendant's voluntary actions (and their "ordinary" consequences), unless *the defendant* proved the contrary by some quantum of proof which may well have been considerably greater than "some" evidence—thus effectively shifting the burden of persuasion on the element of intent. Numerous federal and state courts have warned that instructions of the type given here can be interpreted in just these ways. And although the Montana Supreme Court held to the contrary in this case, Montana's own Rules of Evidence expressly state that the presumption at issue here may be overcome only "by a preponderance of evidence contrary to the presumption." Montana Rule of Evidence 301(b)(2).[6] Such a requirement shifts not only the burden of produc-

---

[6] Rev. Code Mont. § 26–1–602 states:

"'[D]isputable presumptions' . . . may be controverted by other evidence. The following are of that kind: . . .

3. that a person intends the ordinary consequence of his voluntary act."

Montana Rule of Evidence 301 provides:

"(b)(2) All presumptions, other than conclusive presumptions, are disputable presumptions and may be controverted. A *disputable presumption may be overcome by a preponderance of evidence contrary to the presumption. Unless the presumption is overcome, the trier of fact must find the assumed fact in accordance*

tion, but also the ultimate burden of persuasion on the issue of intent.[7]

We do not reject the possibility that some jurors may have interpreted the challenged instruction as permissive, or, if mandatory, as requiring only that the defendant come forward with "some" evidence in rebuttal. However, the fact that a reasonable juror could have given the presumption conclusive or persuasion-shifting effect means that we cannot discount the possibility that Sandstrom's jurors actually did proceed upon one or the other of these latter interpretations. And that means that unless these kinds of presumptions are constitutional, the instruction cannot be adjudged valid.[8] It is the line of cases urged by the petitioner, and exemplified by In re Winship, 397 U.S. 358 (1970), that provides the appropriate mode of constitutional analysis for these kinds of presumptions.

III

In *Winship*, the Court stated:

"Lest there remain any doubt about the constitutional stature of the reasonable-doubt standard, we explicitly hold that the due process clause protects the accused against conviction except upon proof beyond a reasonable doubt of every *fact* necessary to constitute the crime with which he is charged." [Emphasis added.]

Accord, *Patterson* v. *New York*, supra. The petitioner here was charged with and convicted of deliberate homicide, committed purposely or knowingly . . . . It is clear that under Montana law, whether the crime was committed purposely or knowingly is a fact necessary to constitute the crime of deliberate homicide. Indeed, it was the lone element of the offense at issue in Sandstrom's trial, as he confessed to causing the death of the victim, told the jury that knowledge and purpose were the only questions he was controverting, and introduced evidence solely on those points. Moreover, it is conceded that proof of defendant's "intent" would be sufficient to establish this element. Thus, the question before this Court is whether the challenged jury instruction had the effect of relieving the state of the burden of proof

with the presumption." [Emphasis added.] . . .

We do not, of course, cite this Rule of Evidence to dispute the Montana Supreme Court's interpretation of its own law. It merely serves as evidence that a reasonable man—here, apparently, the drafter of Montana's own Rules of Evidence—could interpret the presumption at issue in this case as shifting to the defendant the burden of proving his innocence by a preponderance of the evidence.

[7] The potential for these interpretations of the presumption was not removed by the other instructions given at the trial. It is true that the jury was instructed generally that the accused was presumed innocent until proved guilty, and that the state had the burden of proving beyond a reasonable doubt that the defendant caused the death

of the deceased purposely or knowingly. But this is not rhetorically inconsistent with a conclusive or burden-shifting presumption. The jury could have interpreted the two sets of instructions as indicating that the presumption was a means by which proof beyond a reasonable doubt as to intent could be satisfied. For example, if the presumption were viewed as conclusive, the jury could have believed that although intent must be proved beyond a reasonable doubt, proof of the voluntary slaying and its ordinary consequences constituted proof of intent beyond a reasonable doubt. . . .

[8] Given our ultimate result in this case, we do not need to consider what kind of constitutional analysis would be appropriate for other kinds of presumptions.

enunciated in *Winship* on the critical question of petitioner's state of mind. We conclude that under either of the two possible interpretations of the instruction set out above, precisely that effect would result, and that the instruction therefore represents constitutional error.

We consider first the validity of a conclusive presumption. This Court has considered such a presumption on at least two prior occasions. In Morissette v. United States, 342 U.S. 246 (1952),[a] the defendant was charged with willful and knowing theft of government property. Although his attorney argued that for his client to be found guilty, "the taking must have been with felonious intent," the trial judge ruled that "[t]hat is presumed by his own act." After first concluding that intent was in fact an element of the crime charged, and after declaring that "[w]here intent of the accused is an ingredient of the crime charged, its existence is . . . a jury issue," *Morissette* held:

> "*It follows that the trial court may not withdraw or prejudge the issue by instruction that the law raises a presumption of intent from an act*. It often is tempting to cast in terms of a 'presumption' a conclusion which a court thinks probable from given facts.
> . . . [But we] think presumptive intent has no place in this case. *A conclusive presumption which testimony could not overthrow would effectively eliminate intent as an ingredient of the offense*. A presumption which would permit but not require the jury to assume intent from an isolated fact would prejudge a conclusion which the jury should reach of its own volition. A presumption which would permit the jury to make an assumption which all the evidence considered together does not logically establish would give to a proven fact an artificial and fictional effect. In either case, *this presumption would conflict with the overriding presumption of innocence with which the law endows the accused and which extends to every element of the crime*." [Emphasis added.]

Just last term in United States v. United States Gypsum Co., 438 U.S. 422 (1978),[b] we reaffirmed the holding of *Morissette*. In that case defendants, who were charged with criminal violations of the Sherman Act, challenged the following jury instruction:

> "The law presumes that a person intends the necessary and natural consequences of his acts. Therefore, if the effect of the

[a] *Morissette* concerned the interpretation of a federal statute punishing one who "embezzles, steals, purloins, or knowingly converts to his use" any property of the United States. The opinion is famous for a long discourse on the role of mens rea in the criminal law and for its refusal to construe the statute to impose strict liability in the context of a traditional, as distinct from regulatory or public welfare, offense. Excerpts on these points appear at pages 197–200 and 355–57, supra. The reference in text is to a portion of the *Morissette* opinion, not included in the excerpts reprinted elsewhere in this book, finding that the trial court could not presume intent to steal government property from the fact of taking. [Footnote by eds.]

[b] *United States Gypsum Co.* concerned the interpretation of the criminal provisions of the Sherman Anti-trust Act. The Court held that intent was a necessary element of the criminal offenses defined by that statute, even though it would not be required for the analogous civil violations. The reference in text is to a portion of the opinion disapproving a presumption of criminal intent from anti-competitive impact. [Footnote by eds.]

exchanges of pricing information was to raise, fix, maintain, and stabilize prices, then the parties to them are presumed, as a matter of law, to have intended that result."

After again determining that the offense included the element of intent, we held:

"[A] defendant's state of mind or intent is an element of a criminal anti-trust offense which . . . cannot be taken from the trier of fact through reliance on a legal presumption of wrongful intent from proof of an effect on prices. . . ."

As in *Morissette* and *United States Gypsum Co.*, a conclusive presumption in this case would "conflict with the overriding presumption of innocence with which the law endows the accused and which extends to every element of the crime," and would "invade [the] factfinding function" which in a criminal case the law assigns solely to the jury. The instruction announced to David Sandstrom's jury may well have had exactly these consequences. Upon finding proof of one element of the crime (causing death), and of facts insufficient to establish the second (the voluntariness and "ordinary consequences" of defendant's action), Sandstrom's jurors could reasonably have concluded that they were directed to find against defendant on the element of intent. The state was thus not forced to prove "beyond a reasonable doubt . . . every fact necessary to constitute the crime . . . charged," and defendant was deprived of his constitutional rights as explicated in *Winship*.

A presumption which, although not conclusive, had the effect of shifting the burden of persuasion to the defendant, would have suffered from similar infirmities. If Sandstrom's jury interpreted the presumption in that manner, it could have concluded that upon proof by the state of the slaying, and of additional facts not themselves establishing the element of intent, the burden was shifted to the defendant to prove that he lacked the requisite mental state. Such a presumption was found constitutionally deficient in Mullaney v. Wilbur, 421 U.S. 684 (1975). In *Mullaney* the charge was murder, which under Maine law required proof not only of intent but of malice. The trial court charged the jury that " 'malice aforethought is an essential and indispensable element of the crime of murder.' " However, it also instructed that if the prosecution established that the homicide was both intentional and unlawful, malice aforethought was to be implied unless the defendant proved by a fair preponderance of the evidence that he acted in the heat of passion on sudden provocation. As we recounted just two terms ago in *Patterson* v. *New York*, supra, "[t]his Court . . . unanimously agreed with the Court of Appeals that Wilbur's due process rights had been invaded by the presumption casting upon him the burden of proving by a preponderance of the evidence that he had acted in the heat of passion upon sudden provocation." And *Patterson* reaffirmed that "a state must prove every ingredient of an offense beyond a reasonable doubt, and . . . may not shift the burden of proof to the defendant" by means of such a presumption.

Because David Sandstrom's jury may have interpreted the judge's instruction as constituting either a burden-shifting presumption like that in *Mullaney*, or a conclusive presumption like that in *Morissette* and *United States Gypsum Co.*, and because either interpretation would have deprived defendant of his right to the due process of law, we hold the instruction given in this case unconstitutional. . . .

[The concurring opinion of Mr. Justice Rehnquist, with whom the Chief Justice joined, is omitted.]

NOTES ON BURDEN OF PROOF AND PRESUMPTIONS

1. **Introduction.** A presumption arises when the existence of one fact is "presumed" from proof of another. Unfortunately, this description covers a variety of evidentiary relationships, and, as noted by one authority, "the language used with reference to presumptions is exasperatingly indiscriminate." G. Lilly, An Introduction to the Law of Evidence 49 (1978). The *Sandstrom* Court's classification of conclusive presumptions, rebuttable presumptions, and permissive inferences provides a useful basis for discussion and analysis, but the reader should be aware that this usage is not uniformly adopted. Moreover, as the facts of *Sandstrom* illustrate, courts often identify "presumptions" without further specifying their procedural consequences. For these reasons it is important that any use of the label "presumption" be approached with caution and that care be taken to determine precisely what the term is used to designate. For an excellent survey, see G. Lilly, An Introduction to the Law of Evidence 48–62 (1978).

2. **Conclusive Presumptions.** The *Sandstrom* Court was concerned that the jury might have construed the instruction on intending the ordinary consequences of one's voluntary acts as creating a conclusive or mandatory presumption. Perhaps it might have been so understood, but in fact the true conclusive presumption is extremely rare in the criminal law. The effect of this device is, of course, simply to redefine the substantive law. If fact A is *conclusively* presumed from proof of fact B, B becomes sufficient, and A is rendered unnecessary and irrelevant. Thus, on the facts of *Sandstrom*, a conclusive presumption would have redefined the crime of murder to require not a subjective intent to kill, but an objective determination that death of another was an "ordinary consequence" of the defendant's voluntary acts.[a]

The *Sandstrom* Court declared that this construction would be unconstitutional. Do you see why? Do *Morissette* and *United States Gypsum Co.* support the Court's holding? Would a conclusive presumption of intent from proof of the ordinary consequences of one's voluntary acts "conflict with the overriding presumption of innocence"? Would it "invade the factfinding function" of the jury? Does the

---

[a] Cf. *Director of Public Prosecutions* v. *Smith*, page 204, supra, and the notes on this issue, pages 209–211, supra.

answer to these questions depend on whether Montana would have constitutional authority to base liability for the crime of "deliberate homicide" on proof of negligence? Do you understand *Sandstrom* to stand for the proposition that it would be unconstitutional to impose sanctions typically associated with murder on proof of merely negligent homicide? If not, what exactly is the discussion of conclusive presumptions designed to forbid?

3. **Rebuttable Presumptions.** A second possibility considered in *Sandstrom* is that the jury might have construed the instruction as creating a rebuttable or burden-shifting presumption. Under this interpretation, proof that death of another was an "ordinary consequence" of the defendant's voluntary acts would shift to him the obligation to disprove that he killed purposely or knowingly. The *Sandstrom* Court concluded that this kind of presumption would be constitutionally invalid under *Mullaney*. Is that conclusion sound? Does it depend on whether the state could constitutionally have imprisoned the defendant for 100 years merely on proof that he killed another by voluntary acts the ordinary consequence of which was death?

A different way to approach this issue is to ask whether the following hypothetical statute would be unconstitutional under the authority of *Sandstrom*:

"Section 101. Criminal homicide.

"(1) A person commits the offense of criminal homicide if he causes the death of another human being by voluntary acts the ordinary consequence of which is death of another.

"(2) Criminal homicide is aggravated criminal homicide [carrying a maximum term of life imprisonment] or simple criminal homicide carrying a maximum term of imprisonment for five years.

"(3) It is an affirmative defense to aggravated criminal homicide, but not to simple criminal homicide, that the actor did not kill purposely or knowingly."

Do you understand *Sandstrom* to stand for the invalidity of such a statute? If not, can the state of Montana achieve substantively the same result deemed unconstitutional by the Supreme Court simply by rephrasing its law to avoid use of the language of presumption? Is the message of *Sandstrom* merely to excise an offending vocabulary, or are there substantive rationales to support the decision? If an "affirmative defense" must be established by the defendant by a preponderance of the evidence, is Subsection (3) of the hypothetical statute unconstitutional?

4. **Shift in the Burden of Production.** Another possibility raised by the state's argument in *Sandstrom* is that a presumption might be construed to shift to the defendant only the burden of production. So construed, the presumption would not affect the prosecution's obligation to persuade the trier of fact beyond a reasonable doubt, but would place on the defendant the obligation to see that a particular issue is raised by the evidence. This is the functional description of a defense,

and most devices that shift to the defendant only the burden of production are called defenses. An example is self-defense. If the defendant wishes to claim self-defense, he bears the burden of raising the issue by producing some evidence to support his claim. If that burden of production is met, the prosecution must disprove self-defense beyond a reasonable doubt, and the jury is instructed accordingly. If the burden of production is not met, the issue of self-defense is simply not raised, and the jury is given no instruction on the subject. Whether many such devices would be labeled presumptions seems doubtful, but in any event, *Mullaney* and *Patterson* make clear that a device that shifts to the defendant only the burden of production is constitutionally permissible.

5. **Permissive Inferences.** The final possibility considered by the *Sandstrom* Court is that the trial judge's instruction only stated a permissive inference. Under this view, the jury would have been allowed, but not required, to consider the ordinary consequences of the defendant's voluntary acts in determining whether he killed purposely or knowingly, but would have been instructed to make the ultimate finding of purpose or knowledge beyond a reasonable doubt. Apparently, this sort of evidentiary device is constitutional, and presumably, there would have been no defect in the *Sandstrom* conviction if the trial court had explicitly couched the instruction in these terms. Is the basis for this conclusion clear? Do you see why the Supreme Court attaches so much importance to the explicit differentiation of presumptions and permissive inferences? Would you expect juries to make the distinction with equal care?

Professor Ronald Allen has argued that presumptions (of whatever sort) and permissive inferences are not so clearly different and that in fact both have a lot in common with other devices such as defenses, affirmative defenses, and comments on the evidence. Allen's conclusion is that all these devices should be constitutionally permissible so long as they are not used to undermine the state's obligation to prove beyond a reasonable doubt a constitutionally sufficient basis to support the punishment authorized. See Allen, Structuring Jury Decisionmaking in Criminal Cases: A Unified Constitutional Approach to Evidentiary Devices, 94 Harv.L.Rev. 321 (1980). Professor Charles Nesson, on the other hand, shares Allen's view that these various evidentiary devices are not readily distinguishable, but believes that they should generally be condemned as unconstitutional. See Nesson, Reasonable Doubt and Permissive Inferences: The Value of Complexity, 92 Harv.L.Rev. 1187 (1979). Both Allen and Nesson have written in rebuttal of the other's view. See Nesson, Rationality, Presumptions, and Judicial Comment: A Response to Professor Allen, 94 Harv.L.Rev. 1574 (1981), and Allen, More on Constitutional Process-of-Proof Problems in Criminal Cases, 94 Harv.L.Rev. 1795 (1981).

6. **Defenses, Presumptions, and Legislative Candor.** An argument occasionally advanced in the context of affirmative defenses, and more forcefully pressed in the context of presumptions, is that such devices should be declared unconstitutional in order to induce legisla-

tive candor. The contention is that legislatures use presumptions to disadvantage defendants in ways that the people would find unacceptable if they understood the legislative action. If presumptions are outlawed, the argument continues, the legislative intention will be forced out in the open and thus made amenable to popular control through the political process.

This argument was first developed in Ashford & Risinger, Presumptions, Assumptions, and Due Process in Criminal Cases: A Theoretical Overview, 79 Yale L.J. 165, 177–78 (1969). Their discussion was based on a hypothetical suggesting the following three statutes:

(i) "It shall be a crime for an individual to be present in a house where he knows narcotics are illegally kept."

(ii) "It shall be a crime for an individual to be present in a house where narcotics are illegally kept, whether or not he knows that the narcotics are so kept."

(iii) "It shall be a crime for an individual to be present in a house where he knows narcotics are illegally kept, but such knowledge may be presumed from the fact that the defendant was present in a house where narcotics were so kept."

In the first hypothetical statute, the legislature has made liability turn on three factors: presence of the individual, presence of narcotics in the house, and the defendant's knowledge. In the second statute, only two factors are made relevant to liability: presence of the individual and presence of narcotics in the house. In the view of Ashford and Risinger, the third statute is designed to look like the first but work like the second. The risk, therefore, is that the legislature might use a presumption to undermine the political process:

"If the legislature nominally recognizes knowledge as germane (as it did in the first statute) and further, as the type of germane issue to be proved by the state, and then arranges its processes so that most of those who lack knowledge are still sent to jail (as though the second statute had been passed), then those individuals are punished for a crime which has never undergone the political checks guaranteed by representative government. This, we believe, is a violation of due process."

Are you persuaded by this argument? Do you agree that the use of presumptions renders penal statutes obscure and inaccessible? Is that a reason for declaring such statutes unconstitutional? If so, should criminal statutes be declared unconstitutional whenever they use (or rely on the courts to use) obscure language? Arguably, this proposition might require that the entire mens-rea structure of the common law be declared unconstitutional. Would you expect, for example, that the political electorate would understand the meaning of "malice aforethought" or could successfully differentiate "specific" from "general" intent? Should the legislature be prohibited from using such formulations on the ground that the general public might not understand them? If not, what basis exists for invalidating presumptions for the reason suggested by Ashford & Risinger? Are presumptions fundamentally different?

SECTION 2: PROPORTIONALITY

SUBSECTION A: PROPORTIONALITY AND CAPITAL PUNISHMENT

COKER v. GEORGIA
Supreme Court of the United States, 1977.
433 U.S. 584.

MR. JUSTICE WHITE announced the judgment of the Court and filed an opinion in which MR. JUSTICE STEWART, MR. JUSTICE BLACKMUN, and MR. JUSTICE STEVENS, joined.

. . . Petitioner Coker was convicted of rape and sentenced to death. Both the conviction and the sentence were affirmed by the Georgia Supreme Court. Coker was granted a writ of certiorari limited to the single claim, rejected by the Georgia court, that the punishment of death for rape violates the eighth amendment, which proscribes "cruel and unusual punishments" and which must be observed by the states as well as the federal government. Robinson v. California, 370 U.S. 660 (1962).

I

While serving various sentences for murder, rape, kidnapping, and aggravated assault, petitioner escaped from the Ware Correctional Institution near Waycross, Ga., on September 2, 1974. At approximately 11 o'clock that night, petitioner entered the house of Allen and Elnita Carver through an unlocked kitchen door. Threatening the couple with a "board," he tied up Mr. Carver in the bathroom, obtained a knife from the kitchen, and took Mr. Carver's money and the keys to the family car. Brandishing the knife and saying "you know what's going to happen to you if you try anything, don't you," Coker then raped Mrs. Carver. Soon thereafter, petitioner drove away in the Carver car, taking Mrs. Carver with him. Mr. Carver, freeing himself, notified the police; and not long thereafter petitioner was apprehended. Mrs. Carver was unharmed.

Petitioner was [tried on charges of] escape, armed robbery, motor vehicle theft, kidnapping, and rape. . . . The jury returned a verdict of guilty, rejecting his general plea of insanity. A sentencing hearing was then conducted in accordance with the procedures dealt with at length in Gregg v. Georgia, 428 U.S. 153 (1976) . . . . The jury's verdict on the rape count was death by electrocution. . . .

II

[The Court's prior capital punishment decisions] make unnecessary the recanvassing of certain critical aspects of the controversy about the constitutionality of capital punishment. It is now settled that the death penalty is not invariably cruel and unusual punishment within the meaning of the eighth amendment; it is not inherently barbaric or an unacceptable mode of punishment for crime; neither is it always disproportionate to the crime for which it is imposed. . . .

In sustaining the imposition of the death penalty, however, the Court [has] firmly embraced the holdings and dicta from prior cases, to the effect that the eighth amendment bars not only those punishments that are "barbaric" but also those that are "excessive" in relation to the crime committed. Under *Gregg v. Georgia,* supra, a punishment is "excessive" and unconstitutional if it (i) makes no measurable contribution to acceptable goals of punishment and hence is nothing more than the purposeless and needless imposition of pain and suffering; or (ii) is grossly out of proportion to the severity of the crime. A punishment might fail the test on either ground. Furthermore, these eighth amendment judgments should not be, or appear to be, merely the subjective views of individual Justices; judgment should be informed by objective factors to the maximum possible extent. To this end, attention must be given to the public attitudes concerning a particular sentence—history and precedent, legislative attitudes, and the response of juries reflected in their sentencing decisions are to be consulted. In *Gregg,* after giving due regard to such sources, the Court's judgment was that the death penalty for deliberate murder was neither the purposeless imposition of severe punishment nor a punishment grossly disproportionate to the crime. But the Court reserved the question of the constitutionality of the death penalty when imposed for other crimes.

III

That question, with respect to rape of an adult woman, is now before us. We have concluded that a sentence of death is grossly disproportionate and excessive punishment for the crime of rape and is therefore forbidden by the eighth amendment as cruel and unusual punishment.[4]

A

As advised by recent cases, we seek guidance in history and from the objective evidence of the country's present judgment concerning the acceptability of death as a penalty for rape of an adult woman. At no time in the last 50 years have a majority of the states authorized death

[4] Because the death sentence is a disproportionate punishment for rape, it is cruel and unusual punishment within the meaning of the eighth amendment even though it may measurably serve the legitimate ends of punishment and therefore is not invalid for its failure to do so. We observe that in the light of the legislative decisions in almost all of the states and in most of the countries around the world, it would be difficult to support a claim that the death penalty for rape is an indispensable part of the states' criminal justice system.

as a punishment for rape. In 1925, 18 states, the District of Columbia, and the federal government authorized capital punishment for the rape of an adult female. By 1971 just prior to the decision in Furman v. Georgia, 408 U.S. 238 (1972), that number had declined, but not substantially, to 16 states plus the federal government. *Furman* then invalidated most of the capital-punishment statutes in this country, including the rape statutes, because, among other reasons, of the manner in which the death penalty was imposed and utilized under those laws.

With their death-penalty statutes for the most part invalidated, the states were faced with the choice of enacting modified capital-punishment laws in an attempt to satisfy the requirements of *Furman* or of being satisfied with life imprisonment as the ultimate punishment for *any* offense. Thirty-five states immediately reinstituted the death penalty for at least limited kinds of crime. This public judgment as to the acceptability of capital punishment, evidenced by the immediate, post-*Furman* legislative reaction in a large majority of the states, heavily influenced the Court to sustain the death penalty for murder in *Gregg v. Georgia*, supra.

But if the "most marked indication of society's endorsement of the death penalty for murder is the legislative response to *Furman*," it should also be telling datum that the public judgment with respect to rape, as reflected in the statutes providing the punishment for that crime, has been dramatically different. In reviving death-penalty laws to satisfy *Furman's* mandate, none of the states that had not previously authorized death for rape chose to include rape among capital felonies. Of the 16 states in which rape had been a capital offense, only three provided the death penalty for rape of an adult woman in their revised statutes—Georgia, North Carolina, and Louisiana. In the latter two states, the death penalty was mandatory for those found guilty, and those laws were invalidated by Woodson [v. North Carolina, 428 U.S. 280 (1976),] and Roberts [v. Louisiana, 428 U.S. 325 (1976)].[a] When Louisiana and North Carolina, responding to those decisions, again revised their capital punishment laws, they re-enacted the death penalty for murder but not for rape; none of the seven other legislatures that to our knowledge have amended or replaced their death penalty statutes since July 2, 1976, . . . included rape among the crimes for which death was an authorized punishment.

Georgia argues that 11 of the 16 states that authorized death for rape in 1972 attempted to comply with *Furman* by enacting arguably mandatory death-penalty legislation and that it is very likely that, aside from Louisiana and North Carolina, these states simply chose to eliminate rape as a capital offense rather than to *require* death for *each* and *every* instance of rape. The argument is not without force; but four of the 16 states did not take the mandatory course and also did *not* continue rape of an adult woman as a capital offense. Further, as we have indicated, the legislatures of six of the 11 arguably mandatory

[a] See pp. 795–799, supra. [Footnote by eds.]

states have revised their death-penalty laws since *Woodson* and *Roberts* without enacting a new death penalty for rape. And this is to say nothing of 19 other states that enacted nonmandatory, post-*Furman* statutes and chose not to sentence rapists to death.

It should be noted that Florida, Mississippi, and Tennessee also authorized the death penalty in some rape cases, but only where the victim was a child and the rapist an adult. The Tennessee statute has since been invalidated because the death sentence was mandatory. The upshot is that Georgia is the sole jurisdiction in the United States at the present time that authorizes a sentence of death when the rape victim is an adult woman and only two other jurisdictions provide capital punishment when the victim is a child.

The current judgment with respect to the death penalty for rape is not wholly unanimous among state legislatures, but it obviously weighs very heavily on the side of rejecting capital punishment as a suitable penalty for raping an adult woman.[10]

B

It was also observed in *Gregg* that "[t]he jury . . . is a significant and reliable objective index of contemporary values because it is so directly involved," and that it is thus important to look to the sentencing decisions that juries have made in the course of assessing whether capital punishment is an appropriate penalty for the crime being tried. Of course, the jury's judgment is meaningful only where the jury has an appropriate measure of choice as to whether the death penalty is to be imposed. As far as execution for rape is concerned, this is now true only in Georgia and in Florida; and in the latter state, capital punishment is authorized only for the rape of children.

According to the factual submissions in this Court, out of all rape convictions in Georgia since 1973—and that total number has not been tendered—63 cases had been reviewed by the Georgia Supreme Court as of the time of oral argument; and of these, six involved a death sentence, one of which was set aside, leaving five convicted rapists now under sentence of death in the state of Georgia. Georgia juries have thus sentenced rapists to death six times since 1973. This obviously is not a negligible number; and the state argues that as a practical matter juries simply reserve the extreme sanction for extreme cases of rape and that recent experience surely does not prove that jurors consider the death penalty to be a disproportionate punishment for every conceivable instance of rape, no matter how aggravated. Nevertheless, it is true that in the vast majority of cases, at least nine out of 10, juries have not imposed the death sentence.

[10] In Trop v. Dulles, 356 U.S. 86, 102 (1958), the plurality took pains to note the climate of international opinion concerning the acceptability of a particular punishment. It is thus not irrelevant here that out of 60 major nations in the world surveyed in 1965, only three retained the death penalty for rape where death did not ensue. United Nations, Department of Economic and Social Affairs, Capital Punishment 40, 86 (1968).

IV

These recent events evidencing the attitude of state legislatures and sentencing juries do not wholly determine this controversy, for the Constitution contemplates that in the end our own judgment will be brought to bear on the question of the acceptability of the death penalty under the eighth amendment. Nevertheless, the legislative rejection of capital punishment for rape strongly confirms our own judgment, which is that death is indeed a disproportionate penalty for the crime of raping an adult woman.

We do not discount the seriousness of rape as a crime. It is highly reprehensible, both in a moral sense and in its almost total contempt for the personal integrity and autonomy of the female victim and for the latter's privilege of choosing those with whom intimate relationships are to be established. Short of homicide, it is the "ultimate violation of self." It is also a violent crime because it normally involves force, or the threat of force or intimidation, to overcome the will and the capacity of the victim to resist. Rape is very often accompanied by physical injury to the female and can also inflict mental and psychological damage. Because it undermines the community's sense of security, there is public injury as well.

Rape is without doubt deserving of serious punishment; but in terms of moral depravity and of the injury to the person and to the public, it does not compare with murder, which does involve the unjustified taking of human life. Although it may be accompanied by another crime, rape by definition does not include the death of or even the serious injury to another person. The murderer kills; the rapist, if no more than that, does not. Life is over for the victim of the murderer; for the rape victim, life may not be nearly so happy as it was, but it is not over and normally is not beyond repair. We have the abiding conviction that the death penalty, which "is unique in its severity and irrevocability," is an excessive penalty for the rapist who, as such, does not take human life.

This does not end the matter; for under Georgia law, death may not be imposed for any capital offense, including rape, unless the jury or judge finds one of the statutory aggravating circumstances and then elects to impose that sentence. For the rapist to be executed in Georgia, it must therefore be found not only that he committed rape but also that one or more of the following aggravating circumstances were present: (i) that the rape was committed by a person with a prior record of conviction for a capital felony; (ii) that the rape was committed while the offender was engaged in the commission of another capital felony, or aggravated battery; or (iii) the rape "was outrageously or wantonly vile, horrible or inhuman in that it involved torture, depravity of mind, or aggravated battery to the victim." [b] Here, the

---

[b] The applicable Georgia statutes are reprinted in Appendix B of the Casebook, pp. 12–15. [Footnote by eds.]

first two of these aggravating circumstances were alleged and found by the jury.

Neither of these circumstances, nor both of them together, change our conclusion that the death sentence imposed on Coker is a disproportionate punishment for rape. Coker had prior convictions for capital felonies—rape, murder, and kidnapping—but these prior convictions do not change the fact that the instant crime being punished is a rape not involving the taking of life.

It is also true that the present rape occurred while Coker was committing armed robbery, a felony for which the Georgia statutes authorize the death penalty. But Coker was tried for the robbery offense as well as for rape and received a separate life sentence for this crime; the jury did not deem the robbery itself deserving of the death penalty, even though accompanied by the aggravating circumstance, which was stipulated, that Coker had been convicted of a prior capital crime.[16]

We note finally that in Georgia a person commits murder when he unlawfully and with malice aforethought, either express or implied, causes the death of another human being. He also commits that crime when in the commission of a felony he causes the death of another human being, irrespective of malice. But even where the killing is deliberate, it is not punishable by death absent proof of aggravating circumstances. It is difficult to accept the notion, and we do not, that the rapist, with or without aggravating circumstances, should be punished more heavily than the deliberate killer as long as the rapist does not himself take the life of his victim. The judgment of the Georgia Supreme Court upholding the death sentence is reversed, and the case is remanded to that court for further proceedings not inconsistent with this opinion.

So ordered.

MR. JUSTICE BRENNAN, concurring in the judgment.

Adhering to my view [c] that the death penalty is in all circumstances cruel and unusual punishment prohibited by the eighth and 14th amendments, I concur in the judgment of the Court setting aside the death sentence imposed under the Georgia rape statute.

MR. JUSTICE MARSHALL, concurring in the judgment.

. . . . I continue to adhere to [my previously expressed view [d] that the death penalty is a cruel and unusual punishment prohibited by the

---

[16] Where the accompanying capital crime is murder, it is most likely that the defendant would be tried for murder, rather than rape; and it is perhaps academic to deal with the death sentence for rape in such a circumstance. It is likewise unnecessary to consider the rape-felony murder—a rape accompanied by the death of the victim which was unlawfully but nonmaliciously caused by the defendant.

Where the third aggravating circumstance mentioned in the text is present—that the rape is particularly vile or involves torture or aggravated battery—it would seem that the defendant could very likely be convicted, tried, and appropriately punished for this additional conduct.

[c] See pp. 793–94, supra. [Footnote by eds.]

[d] See p. 794, supra. [Footnote by eds.]

eighth and 14th amendments] in concurring in the judgment of the Court in this case.

MR. JUSTICE POWELL, concurring in the judgment in part and dissenting in part.

I concur in the judgment of the Court on the facts of this case, and also in the plurality's reasoning supporting the view that ordinarily death is disproportionate punishment for the crime of raping an adult woman. Although rape invariably is a reprehensible crime, there is no indication that petitioner's offense was committed with excessive brutality or that the victim sustained serious or lasting injury. The plurality, however, does not limit its holding to the case before us or to similar cases. Rather, in an opinion that ranges well beyond what is necessary, it holds that capital punishment *always*—regardless of the circumstances—is a disproportionate penalty for the crime of rape.

The Georgia statute specifies [three] aggravating circumstances [for the crime of rape]: (i) the offense was committed by a person with a prior record of conviction for a capital felony; (ii) the offense was committed while the offender was engaged in another capital felony or in aggravated battery; and (iii) the offense was "outrageously or wantonly vile, horrible or inhuman in that it involved torture, depravity of mind, or an aggravated battery to the victim." Only the third circumstance describes in general the offense of aggravated rape, often identified as a separate and more heinous offense than rape. See, e.g., ALI, Model Penal Code § 213.1. That third circumstance was not submitted to the jury in this case, as the evidence would not have supported such a finding. It is therefore quite unnecessary for the plurality to write in terms so sweeping as to foreclose each of the 50 state legislatures from creating a narrowly defined substantive crime of aggravated rape punishable by death.[1] . . .

Today, in a case that does not require such an expansive pronouncement, the plurality draws a bright line between murder and all rapes—regardless of the degree of brutality of the rape or the effect upon the victim. I dissent because I am not persuaded that such a bright line is appropriate. "[There] is extreme variation in the degree of culpability of rapists." The deliberate viciousness of the rapist may be greater than that of the murderer. Rape is never an act committed accidentally. Rarely can it be said to be unpremeditated. There also is wide variation in the effect on the victim. The plurality opinion says that "[l]ife is over for the victim of the murderer; for the rape victim, life may not be nearly so happy as it was, but it is not over and normally is not beyond repair." But there is indeed "extreme variation" in the crime of rape. Some victims are so grievously injured physically or psychologically that life *is* beyond repair.

[1] It is not this Court's function to formulate the relevant criteria that might distinguish aggravated rape from the more usual case, but perhaps a workable test would embrace the factors identified by Georgia: the cruelty or viciousness of the offender, the circumstances and manner in which the offense was committed, and the consequences suffered by the victim. The legislative task of defining, with appropriate specificity, the elements of the offense of aggravated rape would not be easy, but certainly this Court should not assume that the task is impossible. . . .

Thus, it may be that the death penalty is not disproportionate punishment for the crime of aggravated rape. Final resolution of the question must await careful inquiry into objective indicators of society's "evolving standards of decency," particularly legislative enactments and the responses of juries in capital cases.[2] The plurality properly examines these indicia, which do support the conclusion that society finds the death penalty unacceptable for the crime of rape in the absence of excessive brutality or severe injury. But it has not been shown that society finds the penalty disproportionate for all rapes. In a proper case a more discriminating inquiry than the plurality undertakes well might discover that both juries and legislatures have reserved the ultimate penalty for the case of an outrageous rape resulting in serious, lasting harm to the victim. I would not prejudge the issue. To this extent, I respectfully dissent.

MR. CHIEF JUSTICE BURGER, with whom MR. JUSTICE REHNQUIST joins, dissenting.

In a case such as this, confusion often arises as to the Court's proper role in reaching a decision. Our task is not to give effect to our individual views on capital punishment; rather, we must determine what the Constitution permits a state to do under its reserved powers. In striking down the death penalty imposed upon the petitioner in this case, the Court has overstepped the bounds of proper constitutional adjudication by substituting its policy judgment for that of the state legislature. I accept that the eighth amendment's concept of disproportionality bars the death penalty for minor crimes. But rape is not a minor crime . . . .

(1)

On December 5, 1971, the petitioner, Ehrlich Anthony Coker, raped and then stabbed to death a young woman. Less than eight months later Coker kidnapped and raped a second young woman. After twice raping this 16-year-old victim, he stripped her, severely beat her with a club, and dragged her into a wooded area where he left her for dead. He was apprehended and pleaded guilty to offenses stemming from these incidents. He was sentenced by three separate courts to three life terms, two 20-year terms, and one eight-year term of imprisonment. Each judgment specified that the sentences it imposed were to run consecutively rather than concurrently. Approximately one and one-half years later, on September 2, 1974, petitioner escaped from the state prison where he was serving these sentences. He promptly raped another 16-year-old woman in the presence of her husband, abducted her from her home, and threatened her with death and serious bodily harm. It is this crime for which the sentence now under review was imposed.

[2] These objective indicators are highly relevant, but the ultimate decision as to the appropriateness of the death penalty under the eighth amendment . . . must be decided on the basis of our own judgment in light of the precedents of this Court.

The Court today holds that the state of Georgia may not impose the death penalty on Coker. In so doing, it prevents the state from imposing any effective punishment upon Coker for his latest rape. The Court's holding, moreover, bars Georgia from guaranteeing its citizens that they will suffer no further attacks by this habitual rapist. In fact, given the lengthy sentences Coker must serve for the crimes he has already committed, the Court's holding assures that petitioner—as well as others in his position—will henceforth feel no compunction whatsoever about committing further rapes as frequently as he may be able to escape from confinement and indeed even within the walls of the prison itself. To what extent we have left states "elbow-room" to protect innocent persons from depraved human beings like Coker remains in doubt.

(2)

My first disagreement with the Court's holding is its unnecessary breadth. The narrow issue here presented is whether the state of Georgia may constitutionally execute this petitioner for the particular rape which he has committed, in light of all the facts and circumstances shown by this record. The plurality opinion goes to great lengths to consider societal mores and attitudes toward the generic crime of rape and the punishment for it; however, the opinion gives little attention to the special circumstances which bear directly on whether imposition of the death penalty is an appropriate societal response to Coker's criminal acts: (i) On account of his prior offenses, Coker is already serving such lengthy prison sentences that imposition of additional periods of imprisonment would have no incremental punitive effect; (ii) by his life pattern Coker has shown that he presents a particular danger to the safety, welfare, and chastity of women, and on his record the likelihood is therefore great that he will repeat his crime at the first opportunity; (iii) petitioner escaped from prison, only a year and a half after he commenced serving his latest sentences; he has nothing to lose by further escape attempts; and (iv) should he again succeed in escaping from prison, it is reasonably predictable that he will repeat his pattern of attacks on women—and with impunity since the threat of added prison sentences will be no deterrent.

Unlike the plurality, I would narrow the inquiry in this case to the question actually presented: Does the eighth amendment's ban against cruel and unusual punishment prohibit the state of Georgia from executing a person who has, within the space of three years, raped three separate women, killing one and attempting to kill another, who is serving prison terms exceeding his probable lifetime and who has not hesitated to escape confinement at the first available opportunity? Whatever one's view may be as to the state's constitutional power to impose the death penalty upon a rapist who stands before a court convicted for the first time, this case reveals a chronic rapist whose continuing danger to the community is abundantly clear.

Mr. Justice Powell would hold the death sentence inappropriate in *this* case because "there is no indication that petitioner's offense was committed with excessive brutality or that the victim sustained serious or lasting injury." Apart from the reality that rape is inherently one of the most egregiously brutal acts one human being can inflict upon another, there is nothing in the eighth amendment that so narrowly limits the factors which may be considered by a state legislature in determining whether a particular punishment is grossly excessive. Surely recidivism, especially the repeated commission of heinous crimes, is a factor which may properly be weighed as an aggravating circumstance, permitting the imposition of a punishment more severe than for one isolated offense. . . . As a factual matter, the plurality opinion is correct in stating that Coker's "prior convictions do not change the fact that the instant crime being punished is a rape not involving the taking of life"; however, it cannot be disputed that the existence of these prior convictions makes Coker a substantially more serious menace to society than a first-time offender:[4]

> "There is a widely held view that those who present the strongest case for severe measures of incapacitation are not murderers as a group (their offenses often are situational) *but rather those who have repeatedly engaged in violent, combative behavior.* A well-demonstrated propensity for life-endangering behavior is thought to provide a more solid basis for infliction of the most severe measures of incapacitation than does the fortuity of a single homicidal incident." Packer, Making the Punishment Fit the Crime, 77 Harv.L.Rev. 1071, 1080 (1964). (Emphasis added.)

In my view, the eighth amendment does not prevent the state from taking an individual's "well-demonstrated propensity for life-endangering behavior" into account in devising punitive measures which will prevent inflicting further harm upon innocent victims. Only one year ago Mr. Justice White succinctly noted: "[D]eath finally forecloses the possibility that a prisoner will commit further crimes, whereas life imprisonment does not."

In sum, once the Court has held that "the punishment of death does not invariably violate the Constitution," it seriously impinges upon the state's legislative judgment to hold that it may not impose such sentence upon an individual who has shown total and repeated disregard for the welfare, safety, personal integrity, and human worth of others, and who seemingly cannot be deterred from continuing such conduct.[5] I therefore would hold that the death sentence here imposed is within

---

[4] This special danger is demonstrated by the very record in this case. After tying and gagging the victim's husband, and raping the victim, petitioner sought to make his getaway in their automobile. Leaving the victim's husband tied and gagged in his bathroom, Coker took the victim with him. As he started to leave, he brandished the kitchen knife he was carrying and warned the husband that "if he would get pulled over or the police was following him in any way that he would kill—he would kill my wife. *He said he didn't have nothing to lose—that he was in prison for the rest of his life, anyway.* . . . " Testimony of the victim's husband, App. 121 (emphasis added).

[5] Professor Packer addressed this:

"What are we to do with those whom we cannot reform, and, in particular, those who by our failure are thought to remain menaces to life? Current penal theories admit, indeed insist upon, the need for permanent incapacitation in such cases. Once this need is recognized, the death penalty as a means of incapacitation for the violent psychopath can hardly be objected to on grounds that will survive rational scrutiny, *if the use*

the power reserved to the state and leave for another day the question of whether such sanction would be proper under other circumstances. The dangers which inhere whenever the Court casts its constitutional decisions in terms sweeping beyond the facts of the case presented, are magnified in the context of the eighth amendment. In *Furman v. Georgia*, Mr. Justice Powell, in dissent, stated:

"[W]here, as here, the language of the applicable [constitutional] provision provides great leeway and where the underlying social policies are felt to be of vital importance, the temptation to read personal preference into the Constitution is understandably great. *It is too easy to propound our subjective standards of wise policy under the rubric of more or less universally held standards of decency.*" (Emphasis added.)

Since the Court now invalidates the death penalty as a sanction for all rapes of adults at all times under all circumstances, I reluctantly turn to what I see as the broader issues raised by this holding.

(3)

The plurality acknowledges the gross nature of the crime of rape. A rapist not only violates a victim's privacy and personal integrity, but inevitably causes serious psychological as well as physical harm in the process. The long-range effect upon the victim's life and health is likely to be irreparable; it is impossible to measure the harm which results. Volumes have been written by victims, physicians, and psychiatric specialists on the lasting injury suffered by rape victims. Rape is not a mere physical attack—it is destructive of the human personality. The remainder of the victim's life may be gravely affected, and this in turn may have a serious detrimental effect upon her husband and any children she may have. I therefore wholly agree with Mr. Justice White's conclusion as far as it goes—that "[s]hort of homicide, [rape] is the 'ultimate violation of self.' " Victims may recover from the physical damage of knife or bullet wounds, or a beating with fists or a club, but recovery from such a gross assault on the human personality is not healed by medicine or surgery. To speak blandly, as the plurality does, of rape victims who are "unharmed," or to classify the human outrage of rape, as does Mr. Justice Powell, in terms of "excessively brutal," versus "moderately brutal," takes too little account of the profound suffering the crime imposes upon the victims and their loved ones.

Despite its strong condemnation of rape, the Court reaches the inexplicable conclusion that "the death penalty . . . is an excessive penalty" for the perpetrator of this heinous offense. This, the Court holds, is true even though in Georgia the death penalty may be imposed only where the rape is coupled with one or more aggravating circumstances. The process by which this conclusion is reached is as startling as it is disquieting. It represents a clear departure from precedent by

of the death penalty in any situation is to be permitted. And its use in rape cases as a class, while inept, is no more so than its use for any other specific offense involving danger to life and limb." Making the Punishment Fit the Crime, 77 Harv.L.Rev. 1071, 1081 (1964). (Emphasis added.)

making this Court "under the aegis of the cruel and unusual punishments clause, the ultimate arbiter of the standards of criminal responsibility in diverse areas of the criminal law, throughout the country." This seriously strains and distorts our federal system, removing much of the flexibility from which it has drawn strength for two centuries.

The analysis of the plurality opinion is divided into two parts: (i) an "objective" determination that most American jurisdictions do not presently make rape a capital offense, and (ii) a subjective judgment that death is an excessive punishment for rape because the crime does not, in and of itself, cause the death of the victim. I take issue with each of these points.

(a)

The plurality opinion bases its analysis, in part, on the fact that "Georgia is the sole jurisdiction in the United States at the present time that authorizes a sentence of death when the rape victim is an adult woman." Surely, however, this statistic cannot be deemed determinative, or even particularly relevant. As the opinion concedes, two other states—Louisiana and North Carolina—have enacted death penalty statutes for adult rape since this Court's 1972 decision in *Furman v. Georgia.* If the Court is to rely on some "public opinion" process, does this not suggest the beginning of a "trend"?

More to the point, however, it is myopic to base sweeping constitutional principles upon the narrow experience of the past five years. Considerable uncertainty was introduced into this area of the law by this Court's *Furman* decision. A large number of states found their death-penalty statutes invalidated; legislatures were left in serious doubt by the expressions vacillating between discretionary and mandatory death penalties, as to whether this Court would sustain *any* statute imposing death as a criminal sanction. Failure of more states to enact statutes imposing death for rape of an adult woman may thus reflect hasty legislative compromise occasioned by time pressures following *Furman,* a desire to wait on the experience of those states which did enact such statutes, or simply an accurate forecast of today's holding.

In any case, when considered in light of the experience since the turn of this century, where more than one-third of American jurisdictions have consistently provided the death penalty for rape, the plurality's focus on the experience of the immediate past must be viewed as truly disingenuous. Having in mind the swift changes in positions of some members of this Court in the short span of five years, can it rationally be considered a relevant indicator of what our society deems "cruel and unusual" to look solely to what legislatures have *refrained* from doing under conditions of great uncertainty arising from our less than lucid holdings on the eighth amendment? Far more representative of societal mores of the 20th century is the accepted practice in a substantial number of jurisdictions preceding the *Furman* decision. "[The] problem . . . is the suddenness of the Court's perception of progress in the human attitude since decisions of only a short while ago."

However, even were one to give the most charitable acceptance to the plurality's statistical analysis, it still does not, to my mind, support its conclusion. The most that can be claimed is that for the past year Georgia has been the only state whose adult rape death penalty statute has not otherwise been invalidated; two other state legislatures had enacted rape death penalty statutes in the last five years, but these were invalidated for reasons unrelated to rape under the Court's decisions. . . . Even if these figures could be read as indicating that no other states view the death penalty as an appropriate punishment for the rape of an adult woman, it would not necessarily follow that Georgia's imposition of such sanction violates the eighth amendment.

The Court has repeatedly pointed to the reserve strength of our federal system which allows state legislatures, within broad limits, to experiment with laws, both criminal and civil, in the effort to achieve socially desirable results. Various provisions of the Constitution, including the eighth amendment and the due process clause, of course place substantive limitations on the type of experimentation a state may undertake. However, as the plurality admits, the crime of rape is second perhaps only to murder in its gravity. It follows then that Georgia did not approach such substantive constraints by enacting the statute here in question.

Statutory provisions in criminal justice applied in one part of the country can be carefully watched by other state legislatures, so that the experience of one state becomes available to all. Although human lives are in the balance, it must be remembered that failure to allow flexibility may also jeopardize human lives—those of the victims of undeterred criminal conduct. Our concern for the accused ought not foreclose legislative judgments showing a modicum of consideration for the potential victims.

Three state legislatures have, in the past five years, determined that the taking of human life and the devastating consequences of rape will be minimized if rapists may, in a limited class of cases, be executed for their offenses. That these states are presently a minority does not, in my view, make their judgment less worthy of deference. Our concern for human life must not be confined to the guilty; a state legislature is not to be thought insensitive to human values because it acts firmly to protect the lives and related values of the innocent. In this area, the choices for legislatures are at best painful and difficult and deserve a high degree of deference. Only last Term Mr. Justice White observed:

> "It will not do to denigrate these legislative judgments as some form of vestigial savagery or as purely retributive in motivation; for they are solemn judgments, reasonably based, that imposition of the death penalty will save the lives of innocent persons. This concern for life and human values and the sincere efforts of the states to pursue them are matters of the greatest moment *with which the judiciary should be most reluc-*

tant to interfere." Roberts v. Louisiana, 428 U.S., at 355 (dissenting opinion). (Emphasis added.)

The question of whether the death penalty is an appropriate punishment for rape is surely an open one. It is arguable that many prospective rapists would be deterred by the possibility that they could suffer death for their offense; it is also arguable that the death penalty would have only minimal deterrent effect. It may well be that rape victims would become more willing to report the crime and aid in the apprehension of the criminals if they knew that community disapproval of rapists was sufficiently strong to inflict the extreme penalty; or perhaps they would be reluctant to cooperate in the prosecution of rapists if they knew that a conviction might result in the imposition of the death penalty. Quite possibly, the occasional, well-publicized execution of egregious rapists may cause citizens to feel greater security in their daily lives; or, on the contrary, it may be that members of a civilized community will suffer the pangs of a heavy conscience because such punishment will be perceived as excessive.[13] We cannot know which among this range of possibilities is correct, but today's holding forecloses the very exploration we have said federalism was intended to foster. It is difficult to believe that Georgia would long remain alone in punishing rape by death if the next decade demonstrated a drastic reduction in its incidence of rape, an increased cooperation by rape victims in the apprehension and prosecution of rapists, and a greater confidence in the rule of law on the part of the populace.

In order for Georgia's legislative program to develop it must be given time to take effect so that data may be evaluated for comparison with the experience of states which have not enacted death penalty statutes. Today, the Court repudiates the state's solemn judgment on how best to deal with the crime of rape before anyone can know whether the death penalty is an effective deterrent for one of the most horrible of all crimes. . . . To deprive states of this authority as the Court does, on the basis that "[t]he current judgment with respect to the death penalty for rape . . . weighs very heavily on the side of rejecting capital punishment as a suitable penalty for raping an adult woman" is impermissibly rash. . . . Social change on great issues generally reveals itself in small increments, and the "current judgment" of many states could well be altered on the basis of Georgia's experience, were we to allow its statute to stand.

(b)

The subjective judgment that the death penalty is simply disproportionate to the crime of rape is even more disturbing than the "objective" analysis discussed supra. The plurality's conclusion on this point is based upon the bare fact that murder necessarily results in the physical death of the victim, while rape does not. However, no member

---

[13] Obviously I have no special competence to make these judgments, but by the same token no other member of the Court is competent to make a contrary judgment. This is why our system has, until now, left these difficult policy choices to the state legislatures, which may be no wiser, but surely are more attuned to the mores of their communities, than are we.

of the Court explains why this distinction has relevance, much less constitutional significance. It is, after all, not irrational—nor constitutionally impermissible—for a legislature to make the penalty more severe than the criminal act it punishes in the hope it would deter wrongdoing. . . .

It begs the question to state, as does the plurality opinion: "Life is over for the victim of the murderer; for the rape victim, life may not be nearly so happy as it was, but it is not over and normally is not beyond repair." Until now, the issue under the eighth amendment has not been the state of any particular victim after the crime, but rather whether the punishment imposed is grossly disproportionate to the evil committed by the perpetrator. As a matter of constitutional principle, that test cannot have the primitive simplicity of "life for life, eye for eye, tooth for tooth." Rather states must be permitted to engage in a more sophisticated weighing of values in dealing with criminal activity which consistently poses serious danger of death or grave bodily harm. If innocent life and limb are to be preserved I see no constitutional barrier in punishing by death all who engage in such activity, regardless of whether the risk comes to fruition in any particular instance.

. . . The clear implication of today's holding appears to be that the death penalty may be properly imposed only as to crimes resulting in death of the victim. This casts serious doubt upon the constitutional validity of statutes imposing the death penalty for a variety of conduct which, though dangerous, may not necessarily result in any immediate death, e.g., treason, airplane hijacking, and kidnapping. In that respect, today's holding does even more harm than is initially apparent. We cannot avoid taking judicial notice that crimes such as airplane hijacking, kidnapping, and mass terrorist activity constitute a serious and increasing danger to the safety of the public. It would be unfortunate indeed if the effect of today's holding were to inhibit states and the federal government from experimenting with various remedies—including possibly imposition of the penalty of death—to prevent and deter such crimes.

Some sound observations, made only a few years ago, deserve repetition:

> "Our task here, as must so frequently be emphasized and re-emphasized, is to pass upon the constitutionality of legislation that has been enacted and that is challenged. This is the sole task for judges. We should not allow our personal preferences as to the wisdom of legislative and congressional action, or our distaste for such action, to guide our judicial decision in cases such as these. The temptations to cross that policy line are very great. In fact, as today's decision reveals, they are almost irresistible." Furman v. Georgia, 408 U.S., at 411 (Blackmun, J., dissenting).

Whatever our individual views as to the wisdom of capital punishment, I cannot agree that it is constitutionally impermissible for a state legislature to make the "solemn judgment" to impose such penalty for the crime of rape. Accordingly, I would leave to the states the task of legislating in this area of the law.

NOTES ON PROPORTIONALITY AND CAPITAL PUNISHMENT

1. **Questions and Comments on *Coker*.** The *Coker* case should be approached on the Court's assumption that capital punishment is *sometimes* appropriate for *some* offenses. Obviously, one could take the view—as Justices Brennan and Marshall do—that capital punishment is always inappropriate. From this perspective, *Coker* is an easy case. It is a hard case, and worth talking about as a problem independent of the legitimacy of capital punishment in general, only if one is prepared to assume that the capital sanction is sometimes appropriate.

On this assumption, the case may be evaluated from at least two perspectives. The first concerns the Court's methodology. Justice White argues that the judgment involved "should not be, or appear to be, merely the subjective views of individual Justices; judgment should be informed by objective factors to the maximum possible extent." To what "objective factors" does he look? Does the Chief Justice disagree about what factors are relevant, or only about their application to the case at hand? Are the factors to which either opinion looks really "objective," or does the case in the end turn on "merely the subjective views of the individual Justices?"

Secondly, there is the question on the merits: whether rape in general, or Coker in particular, can appropriately be distinguished from those murders, or murderers, constitutionally punishable by death. Do you agree with Justice White's treatment of this issue? With the Chief Justice's? Or should Justice Powell's view—that some rapists may be executed but not Coker—prevail? [a]

The Court has also been asked to address the proportionality of capital punishment in other contexts. The following notes describe two recent cases in which the issue was raised.

2. ***Eddings* v. *Oklahoma*.** In Eddings v. Oklahoma, 455 U.S. 104 (1982), the Court granted certiorari limited to the question whether the death penalty for a 16-year-old constituted cruel and unusual punishment. Eddings and several other youths ran away from their Missouri home, leaving in a car owned by Eddings' brother. They drove without destination or purpose, eventually reaching a highway in Oklahoma. Eddings was driving when he momentarily lost control of the car, as a result of which he was signalled by a state trooper to pull over. Eddings did so, and when the trooper approached the car, Eddings stuck a loaded shotgun out of the window, pulled the trigger, and killed him.

[a] The constitutional and jurisprudential aspects of the issue presented in *Coker* are extensively examined in Radin, The Juris- prudence of Death: Evolving Standards for the Cruel and Unusual Punishments Clause, 126 U.Pa.L.Rev. 989 (1978).

Justice Powell, in a majority opinion joined by Justices Brennan, Marshall, Stevens, and O'Connor, reversed without deciding the question on which certiorari had been granted. The Court held that the sentence had been imposed without "the type of individualized consideration of mitigating factors" required by the *Lockett* decision.[b] The majority explicitly stated in a footnote that "we do not reach the question of whether—in light of contemporary standards—the eighth amendment forbids the execution of a defendant who was 16 at the time of the offense."

Chief Justice Burger dissented, joined by Justices White, Blackmun, and Rehnquist. The dissent disagreed with the *Lockett* ground of decision and argued that the Court should have addressed the question on which certiorari had been granted. The Chief Justice stated that he "would decide the sole issue on which we granted certiorari, and affirm the judgment." He did not elaborate.

3. ***Enmund* v. *Florida.*** The Court addressed the use of capital punishment for an accomplice to murder in Enmund v. Florida, 458 U.S. 782 (1982). Enmund planned the robbery of an elderly couple, Thomas and Eunice Kersey, who were known to keep large sums of cash in their home. He waited in a car some distance from the victims' house while two accomplices, Sampson and Jeanette Armstrong, approached the house on the pretense of asking for water for an overheated radiator. After Thomas Kersey retrieved a water jug in response to the request, Sampson Armstrong held a gun to him while Jeanette tried to get his wallet. Hearing her husband's cry for help, Eunice Kersey came around the side of the house with a gun and shot Jeanette Armstrong. Sampson, and perhaps Jeanette, returned Eunice's fire, killing both her and her husband. They then dragged the bodies into the kitchen, took what money they could find, and fled in the waiting car. Sampson Armstrong and Enmund were tried together, and both were sentenced to death. Jeanette Armstrong was tried separately. She was convicted of two counts of second-degree murder and one of robbery, and given three consecutive life sentences.

Under Florida law, the "felony-murder rule and the law of principals combine to make a felon generally responsible for the lethal acts of his co-felon." No findings were required as to whether Enmund planned the killings or actually anticipated that lethal force might be used. The imposition of capital punishment for felony murder was limited, however, by the requirement that the defendant be classified in common-law terms as a principal in the second degree rather than an accessory before the fact. The Florida courts held that Enmund satisfied this condition.[c]

[b] Described at pp. 799–800, supra.

[c] On this point, the Florida Supreme Court noted that "the presence of the aider and abetter need not have been actual, but it is sufficient if he was constructively present, provided the aider, pursuant to previous understanding, is sufficiently near and so situated as to abet or encourage, or render assistance to, the actual perpetrator in committing the felonious act or in escaping after its commission." Compare the discussion at pp. 379–80.

The Supreme Court set aside Enmund's death sentence. Justice White wrote for the majority, which included Justices Brennan, Marshall, Blackmun, and Stevens. Justice O'Connor wrote a dissent on behalf of herself, Chief Justice Burger, and Justices Powell and Rehnquist.

(i) **Debate About Indicators of Societal Judgment.** Justice White began his majority opinion by referring to the methodology of *Coker:*

"[I]t was stressed that our judgment 'should be informed by objective factors to the maximum possible extent.' Accordingly, the Court looked to the historical development of the punishment at issue, legislative judgments, international opinion, and the sentencing decisions juries have made before bringing its own judgment to bear on the matter. We proceed to analyze the punishment at issue in this case in a similar manner."

He began by undertaking a complex analysis of the felony-murder provisions of the 36 American jurisdictions that authorize the death penalty. Essentially, he divided the states into three categories: (i) nine states in which the death penalty is authorized "solely for participation in a robbery in which another robber takes life"; (ii) nine states in which conviction of a capital offense for unadorned felony murder is permissible, but in which various combinations of aggravating and mitigating circumstances must be satisfied before a capital sentence can be imposed; and (iii) the remainder of the states, in three of which felony murder is not a capital offense, in four of which Enmund could not have been convicted of a capital offense because of various limitations in the statutes, and in the remaining 11 of which some culpability as to the death must be proved in order to justify conviction of a capital crime. Justice White concluded from this review that:

"Thus only a small minority of jurisdictions—nine—allow the death penalty to be imposed solely because the defendant somehow participated in a robbery in the course of which a murder was committed. Even if the nine states are included where such a defendant could be executed for an unintended felony murder if sufficient aggravating circumstances are present to outweigh mitigating circumstances—which often include the defendant's minimal participation in the murder—only about a third of American jurisdictions would ever permit a defendant who somehow participated in a robbery where a murder occurred to be sentenced to die. Moreover, of the eight states which have enacted new death-penalty statutes since 1978, only one authorizes capital punishment in such circumstances. While the current legislative judgment with respect to imposition of the death penalty where a defendant did not take life, attempt to take it, or intend to take life is neither 'wholly unanimous among state legislatures,' nor as compelling as the legislative judgments considered in *Coker,* it nevertheless weighs on the side of rejecting capital punishment for the crime at issue."

Justice White then turned to the second "objective" factor relied upon in *Coker.* He asserted that "[s]ociety's rejection of the death penalty for accomplice liability in felony murders is also indicated by the sentencing decisions that juries have made. . . . The evidence is overwhelming that American juries have repudiated imposition of the death penalty for crimes such as petitioner's." Justice White cited in support of this conclusion a search by Enmund's lawyer of all reported appellate court decisions since 1954 involving defendants who were executed for homicide. The study showed that of 362 executions, the defendant personally committed the homicide in 339. In two cases, the defendant hired the killer, and in 16 others it could not be determined from the reported facts who committed the homicide:

> "The survey revealed only six cases out of 362 where a nontriggerman felony murderer was executed. All six executions took place in 1955. By contrast, there were 72 executions for rape in this country between 1955 and this Court's decision in *Coker v. Georgia* in 1977."

Justice White also cited a study by counsel of the nation's death row population as of October 1, 1981. There were then 796 inmates under a capital sentence for homicide. Of the 739 for whom the data were sufficient, only 41 did not actually participate in the fatal assault. Of this group of 41, only 16 were not present at the homicide, and 13 of these 16 either hired or solicited someone else to commit the offense or participated in a scheme designed to kill the victim. Thus only three offenders, including Enmund, did not take life themselves, attempt to take life, or intend to take life. Of the 45 felony murderers on Florida's death row, moreover, Enmund was the only one in this category.[d]

"[W]e are not aware," Justice White concluded, "of a single person convicted of felony murder over the past quarter century who did not kill or attempt to kill, and did not intend the death of the victim, who has been executed." And "only three persons in that category are presently sentenced to die."

Justice O'Connor's dissent accepted the premise that the factors to be examined were those identified by the *Coker* plurality. She concluded, however, that "the available data do not show that society has rejected conclusively the death penalty for felony murderers."

She first noted that historically—beginning with the English law from which the American tradition is derived—the death penalty was an accepted sanction for felony murder. She then examined Enmund's evidence as to contemporary attitudes: the study of reported appellate opinions since 1954, the examination of the prisoners currently on death row, and the conclusions drawn from current death penalty legislation. As to the first two points, she argued:

---

[d] Justice White added a footnote to this part of his discussion:

" 'The climate of international opinion concerning the acceptability of a particular punishment' is an additional consideration which is 'not irrelevant.' It is thus worth noting that the doctrine of felony murder has been abolished in England and India, severely restricted in Canada and a number of other Commonwealth countries, and is unknown in continental Europe. . . . "

"Impressive as these statistics are at first glance, they cannot be accepted uncritically. So stated, the data do not reveal the number or fraction of homicides that were charged as felony murders, or the number or fraction of cases in which the state sought the death penalty for an accomplice guilty of felony murder. Consequently, we cannot know the fraction of cases in which juries rejected the death penalty for accomplice felony murder.[e] Moreover, . . . much of these data classify defendants by whether they 'personally committed homicidal assault,' and do not show the fraction of capital defendants who were shown to have an intent to kill. While the petitioner relies on the fact that he did not pull the trigger, his principal argument is, and must be, that death is an unconstitutional penalty absent an intent to kill, for otherwise, defendants who hire others to kill would escape the death penalty. Thus, the data he presents are not entirely relevant. Even accepting the petitioner's facts as meaningful, they may only reflect that sentencers are especially cautious in imposing the death penalty, and reserve that punishment for those defendants who are sufficiently involved in the homicide, whether or not there was specific intent to kill."

With respect to the third point—the current status of state legislation authorizing the death penalty for felony murder—Justice O'Connor disagreed strongly with Justice White's characterization of the statutes. She divided the states into a different three categories: (i) 21 states that "permit imposition of the death penalty for felony murder even though the defendant did not commit the homicidal act, and even though he had no actual intent to kill"; she added three additional states to this category that do not require a purpose to take life, but do require some form of recklessness or negligence; (ii) seven states that "authorize the death penalty only if the defendant had the specific intent (or some rough equivalent) to kill the victim"; and (iii) three states that "restrict the application of the death penalty to those felony murderers who actually commit the homicide." Thus, she regarded the laws of 24 states as permitting an execution that would violate the principle underlying the majority opinion, whereas Justice White considered that only nine—or at most 18—would permit such an execution. Justice O'Connor concluded as follows:

"Thus, in nearly half the states, and in two-thirds of the states that permit the death penalty for murder, a defendant who neither killed the victim nor specifically intended that the victim die may be sentenced to death for his participation in the robbery-murder. Far from '[w]eighing very heavily on the side of

---

[e] Justice White responded to this argument as follows:

"The dissent criticizes these statistics on the ground that they do not reveal the percentage of homicides that were charged as felony murders or the percentage of cases where the state sought the death penalty for an accomplice guilty of felony murder. We doubt whether it is possible to gather such information, and at any rate, it would be relevant if prosecutors rarely sought the death penalty for accomplice felony murder, for it would tend to indicate that prosecutors, who represent society's interest in punishing crime, consider the death penalty excessive for accomplice felony murder." [Footnote by eds.]

rejecting capital punishment as a suitable penalty for felony murder, these legislative judgments indicate that our 'evolving standards of decency' still embrace capital punishment for this crime. For this reason, I conclude that the petitioner has failed to meet the standards in *Coker* . . . that the 'two crucial indicators of evolving standards of decency . . . —jury determinations and legislative enactments—*both point conclusively* to the repudiation' of capital punishment for felony murder. In short, the death penalty for felony murder does not fall short of our 'national standards of decency.'"

(ii) **Debate About "Ultimate" Judgment.** After his review of the "objective" indicators of society's judgment on the death penalty for persons in Enmund's situation, Justice White concluded his opinion for the Court as follows:

"Although the judgments of legislatures, juries and prosecutors [who may have contributed to the low death-row population of people in Enmund's situation by not seeking the death penalty] weigh heavily in the balance, it is for us ultimately to judge whether the eighth amendment permits imposition of the death penalty on one such as Enmund who aids and abets a felony in the course of which a murder is committed by others but who does not himself kill, attempt to kill, or intend that a killing take place or that lethal force will be employed. We have concluded, along with most legislatures and juries, that it does not.

"We have no doubt that robbery is a serious crime deserving serious punishment. It is not, however, a crime 'so grievous an affront to humanity that the only adequate response may be the penalty of death.' '[I]t does not compare with murder, which does involve the unjustified taking of human life. Although it may be accompanied by another crime, [robbery] by definition does not include the death of or even the serious injury to another person. The murderer kills; the [robber], if no more than that, does not. Life is over for the victim of the murderer; for the [robbery] victim, life . . . is not over and normally is not beyond repair.' Coker v. Georgia, 433 U.S. 584, 598 (1977). As was said of the crime of rape in *Coker,* we have the abiding conviction that the death penalty, which is 'unique in its severity and irrevocability,' is an excessive penalty for the robber who, as such, does not take human life.

"Here the robbers did commit murder; but they were subjected to the death penalty only because they killed as well as robbed. The question before us is not the disproportionality of death as a penalty for murder, but is rather the validity of capital punishment for Enmund's own conduct. The focus must be on *his* culpability, not on that of those who committed the robbery and shot the victims, for we insist on 'individualized consideration as a constitutional requirement in imposing the death sentence,' which means that we must focus on 'relevant facets of the character and record of the individual offender.' [f] Enmund himself did not kill or attempt to kill; and as construed by the Florida Supreme Court, the record before us does not warrant a finding that Enmund had any intention of participating in or facilitating a murder. . . .

"In Gregg v. Georgia, 428 U.S. 153, 183 (1976), the prevailing opinion observed that '[t]he death penalty is said to serve two principal social purposes: retribution and deterrence of capital crimes by prospective offenders.' Unless the death penalty when applied to those in Enmund's position measurably contributes to one or both of these goals, it 'is nothing more than the purposeless and needless imposition of pain and suffering,' and hence an unconstitutional punishment. We are quite unconvinced, however, that the threat that the death penalty will be imposed for murder will measurably deter one who does not kill and has no intention or purpose that life will be taken. Instead, it seems likely that 'capital punishment can serve as a deterrent only when murder is the result of premeditation and deliberation,' for if a person does not intend that life be taken or contemplate that lethal force will be employed by others, the possibility that the death penalty will be imposed for vicarious felony murder will not 'enter into the cold calculus that precedes the decision to act.'

"It would be very different if the likelihood of a killing in the course of a robbery were so substantial that one should share the blame for the killing if he somehow participated in the felony. But competent observers have concluded that there is no basis in experience for the notion that death so frequently occurs in the course of a felony for which killing is not an essential ingredient that the death penalty should be considered as a justifiable deterrent to the felony itself. ALI, Model Penal Code § 210.2, Comment at 38 & n. 96 (Official Draft and Revised Comments, 1980). This conclusion was based on three comparisons of robbery statistics, each of which showed that only about one-half of one per cent of robberies resulted in homicide.[g] The most recent national crime statistics strongly support this conclusion. In addition to the evidence that killings only rarely occur during robberies is the fact, already noted, that however often death occurs in the course of a felony such as robbery, the death penalty is rarely imposed on one only vicariously guilty of the murder, a fact which further attenuates its possible utility as an effective deterrent.

"As for retribution as a justification for executing Enmund, we think this very much depends on the degree of Enmund's

[f] The reference is to the individualization requirements of *Lockett* and *Bell*, which are summarized at pp. 799–800, supra. [Footnote by eds.]

[g] The cited discussion in the Model Penal Code Commentaries occurs in the context of whether there should be a felony-mur-der rule in the first place, not whether the death penalty should be authorized if there is to be such a rule. The Model Penal Code rejects the traditional formulation of the felony-murder rule. See pp. 937–38, supra. [Footnote by eds.]

culpability—what Enmund's intentions, expectations, and actions were. American criminal law has long considered a defendant's intention—and therefore his moral guilt—to be critical to 'the degree of [his] criminal culpability' and the Court has found criminal penalties to be unconstitutionally excessive in the absence of intentional wrongdoing. [Citing *Robinson v. California,* Casebook, p. 157, which held a statute unconstitutional under the eighth amendment because it punished an "illness which may be contracted innocently or involuntarily" and *Godfrey v. Georgia,* Casebook p. 789, which held a death sentence in violation of the eighth amendment because "the defendant's crime did not reflect 'a consciousness materially more "depraved" than that of any person guilty of murder.' "]

"For purposes of imposing the death penalty, Enmund's criminal culpability must be limited to his participation in the robbery, and his punishment must be tailored to his personal responsibility and moral guilt. Putting Enmund to death to avenge two killings that he did not commit and had no intention of committing or causing does not measurably contribute to the retributive end of ensuring that the criminal gets his just deserts. This is the judgment of most of the legislatures that have recently addressed the matter, and we have no reason to disagree with that judgment for purposes of construing and applying the eighth amendment."

Justice O'Connor's dissent also addressed the requirement of *Coker* that "the penalty imposed in a capital case be proportional to the harm caused and the defendant's blameworthiness." On this point, she concluded:

"Although the Court disingenuously seeks to characterize Enmund as only a 'robber,' it cannot be disputed that he is responsible, along with Sampson and Jeanette Armstrong, for the murders of the Kerseys. There is no dispute that their lives were unjustifiably taken, and that the petitioner, as one who aided and abetted the armed robbery, is legally liable for their deaths. Quite unlike the defendant in *Coker,* the petitioner cannot claim that the penalty imposed is 'grossly out of proportion' to the harm for which he admittedly is at least partly responsible.

"The Court's holding today is especially disturbing because it makes intent a matter of federal constitutional law, requiring this Court both to review highly subjective definitional problems customarily left to state criminal law and to develop an eighth amendment meaning of intent. . . . Although the Court's opinion suggests that intent can be ascertained as if it were some historical fact, in fact it is a legal concept, not easily defined. Thus, while proportionality requires a nexus between the punishment imposed and the defendant's blameworthiness, the Court fails to explain why the eighth amendment concept of proportionality requires rejection of standards of blameworthiness based on other levels of intent, such as, for example, the intent to commit an armed robbery coupled with knowledge that armed robberies involve substantial risk of death or serious injury to other persons. Moreover, the intent-to-kill requirement is crudely crafted; it fails to take into account the complex picture of the defendant's knowledge of his accomplice's intent and whether he was armed, the defendant's contribution to the planning and success of the crime, and the defendant's actual participation during the commission of the crime. Under the circumstances, the determination of the degree of blameworthiness is best left to the sentencer, who can sift through the facts unique to each case. Consequently, while the type of mens rea of the defendant must be considered carefully in assessing the proper penalty, it is not so critical a factor in determining blameworthiness as to require a finding of intent to kill in order to impose the death penalty for felony murder.

"In sum, the petitioner and the Court have failed to show that contemporary standards, as reflected in both jury determinations and legislative enactments, preclude imposition of the death penalty for accomplice felony murder. Moreover, examination of the qualitative factors underlying the concept of proportionality do not show that the death penalty is disproportionate as applied to Earl Enmund. In contrast to the crime in *Coker,* the petitioner's crime involves the very type of harm that this Court has held justifies the death penalty. Finally, because of the unique and complex mixture of facts involving a defendant's actions, knowledge, motives, and participation during the commission of a felony murder, I believe that the factfinder is best able to assess the defendant's blameworthiness. Accordingly, I conclude that the death penalty is not disproportionate to the crime of felony murder even though the defendant did not actually kill or intend to kill his victims." [h]

At this point, Justice O'Connor appended a footnote:

"The petitioner and the Court also contend that capital punishment for felony murder violates the eighth amendment because it 'makes no measurable contribution to acceptable goals of punishment.' In brief, the petitioner and the Court reason that since he did not specifically intend to kill the Kerseys, since the probability of death during an armed robbery is so low, and since the death penalty is so rarely imposed on nontriggermen, capital punishment could not have deterred him or anyone else from participating in the armed robbery. The petitioner and the Court also reject the notion that the goal of retribution might be served because his 'moral guilt' is too insignificant.

"At their core, these considerations are legislative judgment decisions regarding the efficacy of capital punishment as a tool in achieving retributive justice and deterring violent crime. Surely,

---

[h] Justice O'Connor went on to argue on other grounds, however, that the case should have been remanded for a new sentencing hearing. [Footnote by eds.]

neither the petitioner nor the Court has shown that capital punishment is ineffective as a deterrent for his crime; the most the Court can do is speculate as to its effect on other felony murderers and rely on 'competent observers' rather than legislative judgments. Moreover, the decision of whether or not a particular punishment serves the admittedly legitimate goal of retribution seems uniquely suited to legislative resolution. Because an armed robber takes a serious risk that someone will die during the course of his crime, and because of the obviousness of that risk, we cannot conclude that the death penalty 'makes no measurable contribution to acceptable goals of punishment.' "

(iii) **Questions on *Coker* and *Enmund*.** Is the effect of *Coker* and *Enmund* that the death penalty is no longer available for any offense other than intentional homicide? Are the states and the federal government constitutionally precluded from imposing the death penalty on persons convicted of kidnapping, airplane hijacking, and treason? Is it settled after *Enmund* that robbery, no matter how aggravated, cannot be punished by death if the victim is not killed? Suppose the victim is *un*intentionally killed during the course of a robbery. Is it constitutional to impose the death penalty on the killer? Is the death penalty always foreclosed in the context of felony murder, absent a finding of intent to kill by the defendant sentenced to death?

It is also helpful to think about *Enmund* from the same perspectives suggested above in connection with *Coker*. First, consider the Court's methodology. Is the Court's "objective" evidence of the societal attitude toward the death penalty for Enmund's crime stronger or weaker than it is for Coker's? Does Justice O'Connor disagree with Justice White about what factors are relevant, or only about their application to the case at hand? Which opinion has the better of this debate? Second, on the merits of the "ultimate" issue, are you persuaded by Justice White or by Justice O'Connor?

SUBSECTION B: PROPORTIONALITY AND IMPRISONMENT

SOLEM v. HELM

Supreme Court of the United States, June 28, 1983.
463 U.S. 277.

JUSTICE POWELL delivered the opinion of the Court.

The issue presented is whether the eighth amendment proscribes a life sentence without possibility of parole for a seventh nonviolent felony.

I

By 1975 the state of South Dakota had convicted respondent Jerry Helm of six nonviolent felonies. In 1964, 1966, and 1969 Helm was convicted of third-degree burglary.[a] In 1972 he was convicted of obtaining money under false pretenses.[b]

In 1973 he was convicted of grand larceny.[c] And in 1975 he was convicted of third-offense driving while intoxicated.[d] The record contains no details about the circumstances of any of these offenses, except that they were all nonviolent, none was a crime against a person, and alcohol was a contributing factor in each case.

In 1979 Helm was charged with uttering a "no account" check for $100.00.[5] The only details we have of the crime are those given by Helm to the state trial court:

"'I was working in Sioux Falls, and got my check that day, was drinking and I ended up here in Rapid City with more money than I had when I started. I knew I'd done something I didn't know exactly what. If I would have known this, I would have picked the check up. I was drinking and didn't remember, stopped several places.'"

After offering this explanation, Helm pleaded guilty.

Ordinarily the maximum punishment for uttering a "no account" check would have been five years imprisonment in the state penitentiary and a $50,000 fine. As a result of his criminal record, however, Helm was subject to South Dakota's recidivist statute:

"When a defendant has been convicted of at least three prior convictions [sic] in addition to the principal felony, the sentence for the principal felony shall be enhanced to the sentence for a Class 1 felony." S.D. Codified Laws § 22–7–8 (1979) (amended 1981).

The maximum penalty for a "Class 1 felony" was life imprisonment in the state penitentiary and a $25,000 fine. Moreover, South Dakota law explicitly provides that parole is unavailable . . . . The Governor is

---

[a] Third-degree burglary consisted, inter alia, of breaking or entering any building not used as a dwelling, with intent to commit larceny or any felony. It carried a maximum prison sentence of 15 years. [Footnote by eds.]

[b] The false pretense statute punished one who obtained any money or property by use of a false token or writing, or any other false pretense. The maximum prison sentence was three years. [Footnote by eds.]

[c] Larceny was defined as the taking of personal property by fraud or stealth with intent to deprive another thereof. It was classified as grand larceny if the taking was of property exceeding $50 in value, from the person, or of livestock. The maxi-

mum penalty for grand larceny was 10 years in prison. [Footnote by eds.]

[d] A third offense of driving while intoxicated was a felony carrying a maximum prison sentence of two years. [Footnote by eds.]

[5] The governing statute provides, in relevant part:

"Any person who, for himself or as an agent or representative of another for present consideration with intent to defraud, passes a check drawn on a financial institution knowing at the time of such passing that he or his principal does not have an account with such financial institution, is guilty of a Class 5 felony." S.D. Codified Laws § 22–41–1.2 (1979).

authorized to pardon prisoners, or to commute their sentences, but no other relief from sentence is available even to a rehabilitated prisoner.

Immediately after accepting Helm's guilty plea, the South Dakota Circuit Court sentenced Helm to life imprisonment under § 22–7–8. The court explained:

> " 'I think you certainly earned this sentence and certainly proven that you're an habitual criminal and the record would indicate that you're beyond rehabilitation and that the only prudent thing to do is to lock you up for the rest of your natural life, so you won't have further victims of your crimes, just be coming back before courts. You'll have plenty of time to think this one over.' "

The South Dakota Supreme Court, in a 3–2 decision, affirmed the sentence despite Helm's argument that it violated the eighth amendment.

After Helm had served two years in the state penitentiary, he requested the Governor to commute his sentence to a fixed term of years. Such a commutation would have had the effect of making Helm eligible to be considered for parole when he had served three-fourths of his new sentence. The Governor denied Helm's request in May 1981.

In November 1981, Helm sought habeas relief in the United States District Court for the District of South Dakota. Helm argued, among other things, that his sentence constituted cruel and unusual punishment under the eighth and 14th amendments. Although the District Court recognized that the sentence was harsh, it concluded that this Court's recent decision in Rummel v. Estelle, 445 U.S. 263 (1980), was dispositive. It therefore denied the writ.

The United States Court of Appeals for the Eighth Circuit reversed. 684 F.2d 582 (1982). The Court of Appeals noted that *Rummel v. Estelle* was distinguishable. Helm's sentence of life without parole was qualitatively different from Rummel's life sentence with the prospect of parole because South Dakota has rejected rehabilitation as a goal of the criminal justice system. The Court of Appeals examined the nature of Helm's offenses, the nature of his sentence, and the sentence he could have received in other states for the same offense. It concluded, on the basis of this examination, that Helm's sentence was "grossly disproportionate to the nature of the offense." It therefore directed the District Court to issue the writ unless the state resentenced Helm.

We granted certiorari to consider the eighth amendment question presented by this case. We now affirm.

II

The eighth amendment declares: "Excessive bail shall not be required, nor excessive fines imposed, nor cruel and unusual punishments inflicted." The final clause prohibits not only barbaric punishments, but also sentences that are disproportionate to the crime committed.

A

The principle that a punishment should be proportionate to the crime is deeply rooted and frequently repeated in common-law jurisprudence. In 1215 three chapters of Magna Carta were devoted to the rule that "amercements" [8] may not be excessive.[9] And the principle was repeated and extended in the First Statute of Westminster, 3 Edw. I, ch. 6 (1275). These were not hollow guarantees, for the royal courts relied on them to invalidate disproportionate punishments. See, e.g., Le Gras v. Bailiff of Bishop of Winchester, Y.B.Mich. 10 Edw. II, pl. 4 (C.P. 1316). When prison sentences became the normal criminal sanctions, the common law recognized that these, too, must be proportional. See, e.g., Hodges v. Humkin, 80 Eng.Rep. 1015, 1016 (K.B. 1615) (Croke, J.) ("imprisonment ought always to be according to the quality of the offence").

The English Bill of Rights repeated the principle of proportionality in language that was later adopted in the eighth amendment: "excessive Baile ought not to be required nor excessive Fines imposed nor cruell and unusuall Punishments inflicted." 1 W. & M., sess. 2, ch. 2 (1689). Although the precise scope of this provision is uncertain, it at least incorporated "the longstanding principle of English law that the punishment . . . should not be, by reason of its excessive length or severity, greatly disproportionate to the offense charged." R. Perry, Sources of Our Liberties 236 (1959); see also 4 W. Blackstone, Commentaries * 16–17 (in condemning "punishments of unreasonable severity," uses "cruel" to mean severe or excessive). Indeed, barely three months after the Bill of Rights was adopted, the House of Lords declared that a "fine of £ 30,000, imposed by the court of King's Bench upon the earl of Devon, was excessive and exorbitant, against magna carta, the common right of the subject, and against the law of the land." Earl of Devon's Case, 11 State Trials 133, 136 (1689).

When the framers of the eighth amendment adopted the language of the English Bill of Rights,[10] they also adopted the English principle of proportionality. Indeed, one of the consistent themes of the era was that Americans had all the rights of English subjects. Thus our Bill of Rights was designed in part to ensure that these rights were preserved. Although the Framers may have intended the eighth amendment to go beyond the scope of its English counterpart, their use of the language of the English Bill of Rights is convincing proof that they intended to

[8] An amercement was similar to a modern-day fine. It was the most common criminal sanction in 13th century England. See 2 F. Pollock & F. Maitland, The History of English Law 513–15 (2d ed. 1909).

[9] Chapter 20 declared that "[a] freeman shall not be amerced for a small fault, but after the manner of the fault; and for a great crime according to the heinousness of it." According to Maitland, "there was no clause in Magna Carta more grateful to the mass of the people. . . . " F. Maitland, Pleas of the Crown for the County of Gloucester XXXIV (1884). Chapter 21 granted the same rights to the nobility, and chapter 22 granted the same rights to the clergy.

[10] The eighth amendment was based directly on Art. I, § 9 of the Virginia Declaration of Rights (1776), authored by George Mason. He, in turn, had adopted verbatim the language of the English Bill of Rights. There can be no doubt that the Declaration of Rights guaranteed at least the liberties and privileges of Englishmen. . . .

provide at least the same protection—including the right to be free from excessive punishments.

B

The constitutional principle of proportionality has been recognized explicitly in this Court for almost a century.[11] In the leading case of Weems v. United States, 217 U.S. 349 (1910), the defendant had been convicted of falsifying a public document and sentenced to 15 years of "cadena temporal," a form of imprisonment that included hard labor in chains and permanent civil disabilities. The Court noted "that it is a precept of justice that punishment for crime should be graduated and proportioned to offense," and held that the sentence violated the eighth amendment. The Court endorsed the principle of proportionality as a constitutional standard and determined that the sentence before it was "cruel in its excess of imprisonment," as well as in its shackles and restrictions.

The Court next applied the principle to invalidate a criminal sentence in Robinson v. California, 370 U.S. 660 (1962). A 90-day sentence was found to be excessive for the crime of being "addicted to the use of narcotics." The Court explained that "imprisonment for 90 days is not, in the abstract, a punishment which is either cruel or unusual." Thus there was no question of an inherently barbaric punishment. "But the question cannot be considered in the abstract. Even one day in prison would be a cruel and unusual punishment for the 'crime' of having a common cold."

Most recently, the Court has applied the principle of proportionality to hold capital punishment excessive in certain circumstances. Enmund v. Florida, 458 U.S. 782 (1982); Coker v. Georgia, 433 U.S. 584 (1977). And the Court has continued to recognize that the eighth amendment proscribes grossly disproportionate punishments, even when it has not been necessary to rely on the proscription. Cf. Hutto v. Davis, 454 U.S. 370, 374, and n. 3 (1982) (recognizing that some prison sentences may be constitutionally disproportionate); Rummel v. Estelle, 445 U.S., at 274, n. 11 (1980) (same).

C

There is no basis for the state's assertion that the general principle of proportionality does not apply to felony prison sentences.[14] The

---

[11] In O'Neil v. Vermont, 144 U.S. 323 (1892), the defendant had been convicted of 307 counts of "selling intoxicating liquor without authority," and sentenced to a term of over 54 years. The majority did not reach O'Neil's contention that this sentence was unconstitutional [because, inter alia,] the eighth amendment "does not apply to the states." [Justice Field in] dissent, however, reached the eighth amendment question, observing that it "is directed . . . against all punishments which by their excessive length or severity are greatly disproportioned to the offences charged."

[14] According to *Rummel, "One could argue* without fear of contradiction by any decision of this Court that for crimes concededly classified and classifiable as felonies, that is, as punishable by significant terms of imprisonment in a state penitentiary, the length of sentence actually imposed is purely a matter of legislative prerogative." 445 U.S. at 274 (emphasis added). The Court did not adopt the standard proposed, but merely recognized that

constitutional language itself suggests no exception for imprisonment. We have recognized that the eighth amendment imposes "parallel limitations" on bail, fines, and other punishments, and the text is explicit that bail and fines may not be excessive. It would be anomalous indeed if the lesser punishment of a fine and the greater punishment of death were both subject to proportionality analysis, but the intermediate punishment of imprisonment were not. There is also no historical support for such an exception. The common-law principle incorporated into the eighth amendment clearly applied to prison terms. And our prior cases have recognized explicitly that prison sentences are subject to proportionality analysis.

When we have applied the proportionality principle in capital cases, we have drawn no distinction with cases of imprisonment. It is true that the "penalty of death differs from all other forms of criminal punishment, not in degree but in kind." Furman v. Georgia, 408 U.S. 238, 306 (1972) (Stewart, J., concurring). As a result, "our decisions [in] capital cases are of limited assistance in deciding the constitutionality of the punishment" in a non-capital case. *Rummel v. Estelle,* supra at 272. We agree, therefore, that, "[o]utside the context of capital punishment, *successful* challenges to the proportionality of particular sentences [will be] exceedingly rare." Ibid. (emphasis added). This does not mean, however, that proportionality analysis is entirely inapplicable in noncapital cases.

In sum, we hold as a matter of principle that a criminal sentence must be proportionate to the crime for which the defendant has been convicted. Reviewing courts, of course, should grant substantial deference to the broad authority that legislatures necessarily possess in determining the types and limits of punishments for crimes, as well as to the discretion that trial courts possess in sentencing convicted criminals.[16] But no penalty is per se constitutional. As the Court noted in *Robinson,* a single day in prison may be unconstitutional in some circumstances.

III

A

When sentences are reviewed under the eighth amendment, courts should be guided by objective factors that our cases have recognized.[17]

the argument was possible. To the extent that the state—or the dissent—makes this argument here, we find it meritless.

[16] Contrary to the dissent's suggestions, we do not adopt or imply approval of a general rule of appellate review of sentences. Absent specific authority, it is not the role of an appellate court to substitute its judgment for that of the sentencing court as to the appropriateness of a particular sentence; rather, in applying the eighth amendment the appellate court decides only whether the sentence under review is within constitutional limits. In view of the substantial deference that must

be accorded legislatures and sentencing courts, a reviewing court rarely will be required to engage in extended analysis to determine that a sentence is not constitutionally disproportionate.

[17] The dissent concedes—as it must— that some sentences of imprisonment are so disproportionate that they are unconstitutional under the cruel and unusual punishments clause. It offers no guidance, however, as to how courts are to judge these admittedly rare cases. We reiterate the objective factors that our cases have recognized. See, e.g., Coker v. Georgia, 433 U.S. 584, 592 (1977) (plurality opinion). As

First, we look to the gravity of the offense and the harshness of the penalty. In Enmund v. Florida, 458 U.S. 782 (1982), for example, the Court examined the circumstances of the defendant's crime in great detail. In *Coker* the Court considered the seriousness of the crime of rape, and compared it to other crimes, such as murder. In *Robinson* the emphasis was placed on the nature of the "crime." And in *Weems,* the Court's opinion commented in two separate places on the pettiness of the offense. Of course, a court must consider the severity of the penalty in deciding whether it is disproportionate.

Second, it may be helpful to compare the sentences imposed on other criminals in the same jurisdiction. If more serious crimes are subject to the same penalty, or to less serious penalties, that is some indication that the punishment at issue may be excessive. Thus in *Enmund* the Court noted that all of the other felony murderers on death row in Florida were more culpable than the petitioner there. The *Weems* Court identified an impressive list of more serious crimes that were subject to less serious penalties.

Third, courts may find it useful to compare the sentences imposed for commission of the same crime in other jurisdictions. In *Enmund* the Court conducted an extensive review of capital-punishment statutes and determined that "only about a third of American jurisdictions would ever permit a defendant [such as Enmund] to be sentenced to die." Even in those jurisdictions, however, the death penalty was almost never imposed under similar circumstances. The Court's review of foreign law also supported its conclusion. The analysis in *Coker* was essentially the same. And in *Weems* the Court relied on the fact that, under federal law, a similar crime was punishable by only two years' imprisonment and a fine.

In sum, a court's proportionality analysis under the eighth amendment should be guided by objective criteria, including (i) the gravity of the offense and the harshness of the penalty; (ii) the sentences imposed on other criminals in the same jurisdiction; and (iii) the sentences imposed for commission of the same crime in other jurisdictions.

B

Application of these factors assumes that courts are competent to judge the gravity of an offense, at least on a relative scale. In a broad sense this assumption is justified, and courts traditionally have made these judgments—just as legislatures must make them in the first instance. Comparisons can be made in light of the harm caused or threatened to the victim or society, and the culpability of the offender. Thus in *Enmund* the Court determined that the petitioner's conduct

the Court has indicated, no one factor will be dispositive in a given case. See *Rummel v. Estelle,* supra at 275–76. The inherent nature of our federal system and the need for individualized sentencing decisions result in a wide range of constitutional sentences. Thus no single criterion can identify when a sentence is so grossly dis-

proportionate that it violates the eighth amendment. See Jeffries & Stephan, Defenses, Presumptions, and Burden of Proof in the Criminal Law, 88 Yale L.J. 1325, 1376–77 (1979). But a combination of objective factors can make such analysis possible.

was not as serious as his accomplices' conduct. Indeed, there are widely shared views as to the relative seriousness of crimes. For example, as the criminal laws make clear, nonviolent crimes are less serious than crimes marked by violence or the threat of violence.

There are other accepted principles that courts may apply in measuring the harm caused or threatened to the victim or society. The absolute magnitude of the crime may be relevant. Stealing a million dollars is viewed as more serious than stealing a hundred dollars—a point recognized in statutes distinguishing petty theft from grand theft. Few would dispute that a lesser included offense should not be punished more severely than the greater offense. Thus a court is justified in viewing assault with intent to murder as more serious than simple assault. Cf. [cases saying armed robbery more serious than robbery and rape more serious than assault with intent to commit rape.] It also is generally recognized that attempts are less serious than completed crimes. Similarly, an accessory after the fact should not be subject to a higher penalty than the principal.

Turning to the culpability of the offender, there are again clear distinctions that courts may recognize and apply. In *Enmund* the Court looked at the petitioner's lack of intent to kill in determining that he was less culpable than his accomplices. Most would agree that negligent conduct is less serious than intentional conduct. South Dakota, for example, ranks criminal acts in ascending order of seriousness as follows: negligent acts, reckless acts, knowing acts, intentional acts, and malicious acts. A court, of course, is entitled to look at a defendant's motive in committing a crime. Thus a murder may be viewed as more serious when committed pursuant to a contract.

This list is by no means exhaustive. It simply illustrates that there are generally accepted criteria for comparing the severity of different crimes on a broad scale, despite the difficulties courts face in attempting to draw distinctions between similar crimes.

C

Application of the factors that we identify also assumes that courts are able to compare different sentences. This assumption, too, is justified. The easiest comparison, of course, is between capital punishment and noncapital punishments, for the death penalty is different from other punishments in kind rather than degree.[18] For sentences of imprisonment, the problem is not so much one of ordering, but one of line-drawing. It is clear that a 25-year sentence generally is more severe than a 15-year sentence,[19] but in most cases it would be difficult to decide that the former violates the eighth amendment while the latter does not. Decisions of this kind, although troubling, are not unique to this area. The courts are constantly called upon to draw similar lines in a variety of contexts.

[18] There is also a clear line between sentences of imprisonment and sentences involving no deprivation of liberty.

[19] The possibility of parole may complicate the comparison, depending upon the time and conditions of its availability.

[At this point, Justice Powell drew two parallels from the sixth amendment. The first concerned the necessity of making case-by-case determinations of how much delay can be tolerated before the accused is denied a speedy trial. He concluded that "the type of inquiry that a court should conduct to determine if a given sentence is constitutionally disproportionate is similar to the type of inquiry required by the speedy trial clause." The second concerned the right to a jury trial, which the amendment seems to require in literally "all" criminal prosecutions but which has been limited by decision to "serious" criminal cases. This standard has been held to require a jury in all cases where imprisonment for more than six months is authorized. The six-month standard, moreover, was selected in a case that "relied almost exclusively" on the fact that this was the criterion for requiring a jury trial in all American jurisdictions save New York City. Justice Powell quoted Justice White's opinion in that case to the effect that "[t]his near-uniform judgment of the nation furnishes us with the only objective criterion by which a line could ever be drawn. . . . " Justice Powell then concluded that this case "clearly demonstrates that a court properly may distinguish one sentence of imprisonment from another. It also supports our holding that courts properly may look to the practices in other jurisdictions in deciding where lines between sentences should be drawn."]

IV

It remains to apply the analytical framework established by our prior decisions to the case before us. We first consider the relevant criteria, viewing Helm's sentence as life imprisonment without possibility of parole. We then consider the state's argument that the possibility of commutation is sufficient to save an otherwise unconstitutional sentence.

A

Helm's crime was "one of the most passive felonies a person could commit." State v. Helm, 287 N.W.2d 497, 501 (S.D.1980) (Henderson, J., dissenting). It involved neither violence nor threat of violence to any person. The $100 face value of Helm's "no account" check was not trivial, but neither was it a large amount. One hundred dollars was less than half the amount South Dakota required for a felonious theft.[20] It is easy to see why such a crime is viewed by society as among the less serious offenses.

[20] If Helm had been convicted simply of taking $100 from a cash register, or defrauding someone of $100, or obtaining $100 through extortion, or blackmail, or using a false credit card to obtain $100, or embezzling $100, he would not be in prison today. All of these offenses would have been petty theft, a misdemeanor. Similarly, if Helm had written a $100 check against insufficient funds, rather than a nonexistent account, he would have been guilty of a misdemeanor. Curiously, under South Dakota law there is no distinction between writing a "no account" check for a large sum and writing a "no account" check for a small sum.

Helm, of course, was not charged simply with uttering a "no account" check, but also with being an habitual offender.[21] And a state is justified in punishing a recidivist more severely than it punishes a first offender. Helm's status, however, cannot be considered in the abstract. His prior offenses, although classified as felonies, were all relatively minor.[22] All were nonviolent and none was a crime against a person. Indeed, there was no minimum amount in either the burglary or the false pretenses statutes, and the minimum amount covered by the grand larceny statute was fairly small.[23]

Helm's present sentence is life imprisonment without possibility of parole.[24] Barring executive clemency, Helm will spend the rest of his life in the state penitentiary. This sentence is far more severe than the life sentence we considered in *Rummel*. Rummel was likely to have been eligible for parole within 12 years of his initial confinement,[25] a fact on which the Court relied heavily. Helm's sentence is the most severe punishment that the state could have imposed on any criminal for any crime. Only capital punishment, a penalty not authorized in South Dakota when Helm was sentenced, exceeds it.

We next consider the sentences that could be imposed on other criminals in the same jurisdiction. When Helm was sentenced, a South Dakota court was required to impose a life sentence for murder, and was authorized to impose a life sentence for treason, first-degree manslaughter, first-degree arson, and kidnapping. No other crime was punishable so severely on the first offense. Attempted murder,. placing an explosive device on an aircraft, and first-degree rape were only Class 2 felonies [25-year maximum]. Aggravated riot was only a Class 3 felony [15-year maximum]. Distribution of heroin and aggravated assault were only Class 4 felonies [10-year maximum].

Helm's habitual-offender status complicates our analysis, but relevant comparisons are still possible. Under § 22–7–7, the penalty for a second or third felony is increased by one class. Thus a life sentence was mandatory when a second or third conviction was for treason, first-degree manslaughter, first-degree arson, or kidnapping, and a life sentence would have been authorized when a second or third conviction

[21] We must focus on the principal felony—the felony that triggers the life sentence—since Helm already has paid the penalty for each of his prior offenses. But we recognize, of course, that Helm's prior convictions are relevant to the sentencing decision.

[22] Helm, who was 36 years old when he was sentenced, is not a professional criminal. The record indicates an addiction to alcohol, and a consequent difficulty in holding a job. His record involves no instance of violence of any kind. Incarcerating him for life without possibility of parole is unlikely to advance the goals of our criminal justice system in any substantial way. Neither Helm nor the state will have an incentive to pursue clearly needed treatment for his alcohol problem, or any other program of rehabilitation.

[23] As suggested at oral argument, the third-degree burglary statute covered entering a building with the intent to steal a loaf of bread. It appears that the grand larceny statute would have covered the theft of a chicken.

[24] Every life sentence in South Dakota is without possibility of parole. We raise no question as to the general validity of sentences without possibility of parole. The only issue before us is whether, in the circumstances of this case and in light of the constitutional principle of proportionality, the sentence imposed on this petitioner violates the eighth amendment.

[25] We note that Rummel was, in fact, released within eight months of the Court's decision in his case. See L.A. Times, Nov. 16, 1980, p. 1, col. 3.

was for such crimes as attempted murder, placing an explosive device on an aircraft, or first-degree rape. Finally, § 22–7–8, under which Helm was sentenced, authorized life imprisonment after three prior convictions, regardless of the crimes.

In sum, there were a handful of crimes that were necessarily punished by life imprisonment: murder, and, on a second or third offense, treason, first-degree manslaughter, first-degree arson, and kidnapping. There was a larger group for which life imprisonment was authorized in the discretion of the sentencing judge, including: treason, first-degree manslaughter, first-degree arson, and kidnapping; attempted murder, placing an explosive device on an aircraft, and first-degree rape on a second or third offense; and any felony after three prior offenses. Finally, there was a large group of very serious offenses for which life imprisonment was not authorized, including a third offense of heroin dealing or aggravated assault.

Criminals committing any of these offenses ordinarily would be thought more deserving of punishment than one uttering a "no account" check—even when the bad-check writer had already committed six minor felonies. Moreover, there is no indication in the record that any habitual offender other than Helm has ever been given the maximum sentence on the basis of comparable crimes. It is more likely that the possibility of life imprisonment under § 22–7–8 generally is reserved for criminals such as fourth-time heroin dealers, while habitual bad-check writers receive more lenient treatment.[26] In any event, Helm has been treated in the same manner as, or more severely than, criminals who have committed far more serious crimes.

Finally, we compare the sentences imposed for commission of the same crime in other jurisdictions. The Court of Appeals found that "Helm could have received a life sentence without parole for his offense in only one other state, Nevada," and we have no reason to doubt this finding. At the very least, therefore, it is clear that Helm could not have received such a severe sentence in 48 of the 50 States. But even under Nevada law, a life sentence without possibility of parole is merely authorized in these circumstances. We are not advised that any defendant such as Helm, whose prior offenses were so minor, actually has received the maximum penalty in Nevada. It appears that Helm was treated more severely than he would have been in any other state.

B

The state argues that the present case is essentially the same as *Rummel v. Estelle,* for the possibility of parole in that case is matched by the possibility of executive clemency here. The state reasons that the Governor could commute Helm's sentence to a term of years. We

---

[26] The state contends that § 22–7–8 is more lenient than the Texas habitual offender statute in *Rummel,* for life imprisonment under § 22–7–8 is discretionary rather than mandatory. Helm, however, has challenged only his own sentence. No one suggests that § 22–7–8 may not be applied constitutionally to fourth-time heroin dealers or other violent criminals. Thus we do not question the legislature's judgment. Unlike in *Rummel,* a lesser sentence here could have been entirely consistent with both the statute and the eighth amendment.

conclude, however, that the South Dakota commutation system is fundamentally different from the parole system that was before us in *Rummel.*

As a matter of law, parole and commutation are different concepts, despite some surface similarities. Parole is a regular part of the rehabilitative process. Assuming good behavior, it is the normal expectation in the vast majority of cases. The law generally specifies when a prisoner will be eligible to be considered for parole, and details the standards and procedures applicable at that time. Thus it is possible to predict, at least to some extent, when parole might be granted. Commutation, on the other hand, is an ad hoc exercise of executive clemency. A Governor may commute a sentence at any time for any reason without reference to any standards.

The Texas and South Dakota systems in particular are very different. In *Rummel,* the Court did not rely simply on the existence of some system of parole. Rather it looked to the provisions of the system presented, including the fact that Texas had "a relatively liberal policy of granting 'good time' credits to its prisoners, a policy that historically has allowed a prisoner serving a life sentence to become eligible for parole in as little as 12 years." A Texas prisoner became eligible for parole when his calendar time served plus "good conduct" time equaled one-third of the maximum sentence imposed or 20 years, whichever is less. An entering prisoner earned 20 days good-time per 30 days served, and this could be increased to 30 days good-time per 30 days served. Thus Rummel could have been eligible for parole in as few as 10 years, and could have expected to become eligible, in the normal course of events, in only 12 years.

In South Dakota commutation is more difficult to obtain than parole. For example, the board of pardons and paroles is authorized to make commutation recommendations to the Governor, but [the statute] provides that "no recommendation for the commutation of . . . a life sentence, or for a pardon . . . shall be made by less than the unanimous vote of all members of the board." In fact, no life sentence has been commuted in over eight years, while parole—where authorized—has been granted regularly during that period. Furthermore, even if Helm's sentence were commuted, he merely would be eligible to be considered for parole. Not only is there no guarantee that he would be paroled, but the South Dakota parole system is far more stringent than the one before us is *Rummel.* Helm would have to serve three-fourths of his revised sentence before he would be eligible for parole, and the provision for good-time credits is less generous.

The possibility of commutation is nothing more than a hope for "an ad hoc exercise of clemency." It is little different from the possibility of executive clemency that exists in every case in which a defendant challenges his sentence under the eighth amendment. Recognition of such a bare possibility would make judicial review under the eighth amendment meaningless.

V

The Constitution requires us to examine Helm's sentence to determine if it is proportionate to his crime. Applying objective criteria, we find that Helm has received the penultimate sentence for relatively minor criminal conduct. He has been treated more harshly than other criminals in the state who have committed more serious crimes. He has been treated more harshly than he would have been in any other jurisdiction, with the possible exception of a single state. We conclude that his sentence is significantly disproportionate to his crime, and is therefore prohibited by the eighth amendment.[32] The judgment of the Court of Appeals is accordingly

Affirmed.

CHIEF JUSTICE BURGER, with whom JUSTICE WHITE, JUSTICE REHNQUIST, and JUSTICE O'CONNOR join, dissenting.

The controlling law governing this case is crystal clear, but today the Court blithely discards any concept of stare decisis, trespasses gravely on the authority of the states, and distorts the concept of proportionality of punishment by tearing it from its moorings in capital cases. Only two Terms ago, we held in Rummel v. Estelle, 445 U.S. 263 (1980), that a life sentence imposed after only a *third* nonviolent felony conviction did not constitute cruel and unusual punishment under the eighth amendment. Today, the Court ignores its recent precedent and holds that a life sentence imposed after a *seventh* felony conviction constitutes cruel and unusual punishment under the eighth amendment. Moreover, I reject the fiction that all Helm's crimes were innocuous or nonviolent. Among his felonies were three burglaries and a third conviction for drunk driving. By comparison Rummel was a relatively "model citizen." Although today's holding cannot rationally be reconciled with *Rummel,* the Court does not purport to overrule *Rummel.* I therefore dissent.

I

A

The Court's starting premise is that the eighth amendment's cruel and unusual punishments clause "prohibits not only barbaric punishments, but also sentences that are disproportionate to the crime committed." What the Court means is that a sentence is unconstitutional if it is more severe than five justices think appropriate. In short, all

[32] Contrary to the suggestion in the dissent, our conclusion today is not inconsistent with *Rummel v. Estelle.* The *Rummel* Court recognized—as does the dissent—that some sentences of imprisonment are so disproportionate that they violate the eighth amendment. Indeed, Hutto v. Davis, 454 U.S., at 374, and n. 3, makes clear that *Rummel* should not be read to foreclose proportionality review of sentences of imprisonment. *Rummel* did reject a pro-portionality challenge to a particular sentence. But since the *Rummel* Court—like the dissent today—offered no standards for determining when an eighth-amendment violation has occurred, it is controlling only in a similar factual situation. Here the facts are clearly distinguishable. Whereas Rummel was eligible for a reasonably early parole, Helm, at age 36, was sentenced to life with no possibility of parole.

sentences of imprisonment are subject to appellate scrutiny to ensure that they are "proportional" to the crime committed.

The Court then sets forth three assertedly "objective" factors to guide the determination of whether a given sentence of imprisonment is constitutionally excessive: (i) the "gravity of the offense and the harshness of the penalty;" (ii) a comparison of the sentence imposed with "sentences imposed on other criminals in *the same* jurisdiction" (emphasis added); (iii) and a comparison of "the sentences imposed for commission of the same crime in *other* jurisdictions" (emphasis added). In applying this analysis, the Court determines that respondent

> "has received the penultimate sentence for *relatively minor* criminal conduct. He has been treated more harshly than other criminals in the state who have committed more serious crimes. He has been treated more harshly than he would have been in any other jurisdiction, . . . " (emphasis added).

Therefore, the Court concludes, respondent's sentence is "significantly disproportionate to his crime, and is . . . prohibited by the eighth amendment." This analysis is completely at odds with the reasoning of our recent holding in *Rummel,* in which, of course, Justice Powell dissented.

B

The facts in *Rummel* bear repeating. Rummel was convicted in 1964 of fraudulent use of a credit card; in 1969, he was convicted of passing a forged check; finally, in 1973 Rummel was charged with obtaining money by false pretenses, which is also a felony under Texas law. These three offenses were indeed nonviolent. Under Texas' recidivist statute, which provides for a mandatory life sentence upon conviction for a third felony, the trial judge imposed a life sentence as he was obliged to do after the jury returned a verdict of guilty of felony theft.

Rummel, in this Court, advanced precisely the same arguments that respondent advances here; we rejected those arguments notwithstanding that his case was stronger than respondent's. The test in *Rummel* which we rejected would have required us to determine on an abstract moral scale whether Rummel had received his "just deserts" for his crimes. We declined that invitation; today the Court accepts it. Will the Court now recall Rummel's case so five justices will not be parties to "disproportionate" criminal justice?

It is true, as we acknowledged in *Rummel,* that the "Court has on occasion stated that the eighth amendment prohibits imposition of a sentence that is grossly disproportionate to the severity of a crime." But even a cursory review of our cases shows that this type of proportionality review has been carried out only in a very limited category of cases, and never before in a case involving solely a sentence of imprisonment. In *Rummel,* we said that the proportionality concept of the capital punishment cases was inapposite because of the "unique nature of the death penalty. . . . " "Because a sentence of death differs in kind from any sentence of imprisonment, no matter how long, our decisions applying the prohibition of cruel and unusual punishments to capital cases are of limited assistance in deciding the constitutionality of the punishment meted out to Rummel."

The *Rummel* Court also rejected the claim that Weems v. United States, 217 U.S. 349 (1910), required it to determine whether Rummel's punishment was "disproportionate" to his crime. In *Weems,* the Court had struck down as cruel and unusual punishment a sentence of cadena temporal imposed by a Philippine court. This bizarre penalty, which was unknown to Anglo-Saxon law, entailed a minimum of 12 years' imprisonment chained day and night at the wrists and ankles, hard and painful labor while so chained, and a number of "accessories" including lifetime civil disabilities. In *Rummel* the Court carefully noted that "[*Weems*'] finding of disproportionality cannot be wrenched from the facts of that case."

The lesson the *Rummel* Court drew from *Weems* and from the capital punishment cases was that the eighth amendment did not authorize courts to review sentences of *imprisonment* to determine whether they were "proportional" to the crime. In language quoted incompletely by the Court, the *Rummel* Court stated:

> "Given the *unique nature* of the punishments considered in *Weems* and in the death penalty cases, one could argue without fear of contradiction by any decision of this Court that for crimes concededly classified and classifiable as felonies, that is, as punishable by significant terms of imprisonment in a state penitentiary, the *length of the sentence actually imposed is purely a matter of legislative perogative.*" 445 U.S. at 274. (Emphasis added).

Five Justices joined this clear and precise limiting language.

In context it is clear that the *Rummel* Court was not merely summarizing an argument, as the Court suggests [in footnote 14], but was stating affirmatively the rule of law laid down. This passage from *Rummel* is followed by an explanation of why it is permissible for courts to review sentences of death or bizarre physically cruel punishments as in *Weems,* but not sentences of imprisonment. The *Rummel* Court emphasized, as has every opinion in capital cases in the past decade, that it was possible to draw a "bright line" between "the punishment of death and the various other permutations and commutations of punishment short of that ultimate sanction"; similarly, a line could be drawn between the punishment in *Weems* and "more traditional forms of imprisonment imposed under the Anglo-Saxon system." However, the *Rummel* Court emphasized that drawing lines between different sentences of imprisonment would thrust the Court inevitably "into the basic line-drawing process that is pre-eminently the province of the legislature" and produce judgments that were no more than the visceral reactions of individual Justices.

The *Rummel* Court categorically rejected the very analysis adopted by the Court today. Rummel had argued that various objective criteria existed by which the Court could determine whether his life sentence was proportional to his crimes. In rejecting Rummel's contentions, the

Court explained why each was insufficient to allow it to determine in an *objective* manner whether a given sentence of imprisonment is proportionate to the crime for which it is imposed.

First, it rejected the distinctions Rummel tried to draw between violent and nonviolent offenses, noting that "the absence of violence does not always affect the strength of society's interest in deterring a particular crime or in punishing a particular individual." Similarly, distinctions based on the amount of money stolen are purely "subjective" matters of line drawing.

Second, the Court squarely rejected Rummel's attempt to compare his sentence with the sentence he would have received in other states—an argument that the Court today accepts. The *Rummel* Court explained that such comparisons are flawed for several reasons. For one, the recidivist laws of the various states vary widely. "It is one thing for a court to compare those states that impose capital punishment for a specific offense with those states that do not. . . . It is quite another thing for a court to attempt to evaluate the position of any particular recidivist scheme within Rummel's complex matrix." Another reason why comparison between the recidivist statutes of different states is inherently complex is that some states have comprehensive provisions for parole and others do not. Perhaps most important, such comparisons trample on fundamental concepts of federalism. Different states surely may view particular crimes as more or less severe than other states. Stealing a horse in Texas may have different consequences and warrant different punishment than stealing a horse in Rhode Island or Washington, D.C. Thus, even if the punishment accorded Rummel in Texas were to exceed that which he would have received in any other state,

> "that severity would hardly render Rummel's punishment 'grossly disproportionate' to his offenses or to the punishment he would have received in the other states. . . . *Absent a constitutionally imposed uniformity inimical to tradition notions of federalism, some state will always bear the distinction of treating particular offenders more severely than any other state.*" 445 U.S., at 281–282. (Emphasis added).

Finally, we flatly rejected Rummel's suggestion that we measure his sentence against the sentence imposed by Texas for other crimes:

> "Other crimes, of course, implicate other societal interests, making any such comparison inherently speculative. . . . Once the death penalty and other punishments different in kind from fine or imprisonment have been put to one side, there remains little in the way of objective standards for judging whether or not a life sentence imposed under a recidivist statute for several separate felony convictions not involving 'violence' violates the cruel and unusual punishment of the eighth amendment." 445 U.S., at 282–283, n. 27.

Rather, we held that the severity of punishment to be accorded different crimes was peculiarly a matter of legislative policy.

In short, *Rummel* held that the length of a sentence of imprisonment is a matter of legislative discretion; this is so particularly for recidivist statutes. I simply cannot understand how the Court can square *Rummel* with its holding that "a criminal sentence must be proportionate to the crime for which the defendant has been convicted." [2]

If there were any doubts as to the meaning of *Rummel*, they were laid to rest last Term in Hutto v. Davis, 454 U.S. 370 (1982) (per curiam). There a United States District Court held that a 40-year sentence for the possession of nine ounces of marijuana violated the eighth amendment. The District Court applied almost exactly the same analysis adopted today by the Court. Specifically, the District Court stated:

> "After examining the nature of the offense, the legislative purpose behind the punishment, the punishment in the [sentencing jurisdiction] for other offenses, and the punishment actually imposed for the same or similar offenses in Virginia, this court must necessarily conclude that a sentence of 40 years and twenty thousand dollars in fines is so grossly out of proportion to the severity of the crimes as to constitute cruel and unusual punishment in violation of the United States Constitution." Davis v. Zahradnick, 432 F.Supp. 444, 453 (W.D.Va.1977).

The Court of Appeals sitting en banc affirmed. We reversed in a brief per curiam opinion, holding that *Rummel* had disapproved each of the "objective" factors on which the District Court and en banc Court of Appeals purported to rely. It was therefore clear error for the District Court to have been guided by these factors, which, paradoxically, the Court adopts today.

Contrary to the Court's interpretation of *Davis*, the *Davis* Court did *not* hold that the District Court miscalculated in finding Davis' sentence disproportionate to his crime. It did *not* hold that the District Court improperly weighed the relevant factors. Rather, it held that the District Court clearly erred in even embarking on a determination whether the sentence was "disproportionate" to the crime. *Davis* makes crystal clear that under *Rummel* it is error for appellate courts to second-guess legislatures as to whether a given sentence of imprisonment is excessive in relation to the crime,[3] as the Court does today.

---

[2] Although [footnote 11 in] *Rummel* conceded that "a proportionality principle [might] come into play . . . if a legislature made overtime parking a felony punishable by life imprisonment," the majority has not suggested that respondent's crimes are comparable to overtime parking. Respondent's seven felonies are far more severe than Rummel's three.

[3] Both *Rummel* and *Davis* leave open the possibility that in extraordinary cases—such as a life sentence for overtime parking—it might be permissible for a court to decide whether the sentence is grossly disproportionate to the crime. I agree that the cruel and unusual punishments clause might apply to those rare cases where reasonable men cannot differ as to the inappropriateness of a punishment. In all other cases, we should defer to the legislature's line-drawing. However, the Court does not contend that this is such an extraordinary case that reasonable men could not differ about the appropriateness of this punishment.

I agree with what the Court stated only days ago, that "the doctrine of stare decisis, while perhaps never entirely persuasive on a constitutional question, is a doctrine that demands respect in a society governed by the rule of law." While the doctrine of stare decisis does not absolutely bind the Court to its prior opinions, a decent regard for the orderly development of the law and the administration of justice requires that directly controlling cases be either followed or candidly overruled.[4]

Especially is this so with respect to two key holdings only three years old.

II

Although historians and scholars have disagreed about the framers' original intentions, the more common view seems to be that the framers viewed the cruel and unusual punishments clause as prohibiting the kind of torture meted out during the reign of the Stuarts. Moreover, it is clear that until 1892, over 100 years after the ratification of the Bill of Rights, not a single Justice of this Court even asserted the doctrine adopted for the first time by the Court today. The prevailing view up to now has been that the eighth amendment reaches only the *mode* of punishment and not the length of a sentence of imprisonment.[6] In light of this history, it is disingenuous for the Court blandly to assert that "[t]he constitutional principle of proportionality has been recognized explicitly in this Court for almost a century." That statement seriously distorts history and our cases.

This court has applied a proportionality test only in extraordinary cases, *Weems* being one example and the line of capital cases another. The Court's reading of the eighth amendment as restricting legislatures' authority to choose which crimes to punish by death rests on the finality of the death sentence. Such scrutiny is not required where a

---

[4] I do not read the Court's opinion as arguing that respondent's sentence of life imprisonment without possibility of parole is so different from Rummel's sentence of life imprisonment with the possibility of parole as to permit it to apply the proportionality review used in the death penalty cases to the former although not the latter. Nor would such an argument be tenable. As was noted in [the plurality opinion in *Woodson*, see Casebook pp. 785–88],

"[T]he penalty of death is qualitatively different from a sentence of imprisonment. Death, in its finality, differs more from life imprisonment than a 100-year prison term differs from one of only a year or two. Because of that qualitative difference, there is a corresponding difference in the need for reliability in the determination that death is the appropriate punishment in a given case."

The greater need for reliability in death penalty cases cannot support a distinction between a sentence of life imprisonment

with possibility of parole and a sentence of life imprisonment without possibility of parole, especially when executive commutation is permitted as in South Dakota.

[6] In 1892, [Justice Field's] dissent in O'Neil v. Vermont, 144 U.S. 323, 339–340 (1892), argued that the eighth amendment "is directed . . . against all punishments which by their excessive length or severity are greatly disproportioned to the offenses charged." Before and after *O'Neil* most authorities thought that the eighth amendment reached only the mode of punishment and not the length of sentences. Even after *Weems* was decided in 1910, it was thought unlikely that the Court would extend proportionality analysis to cases involving solely sentences of imprisonment. Until today, not a single case of this Court applied the "excessive punishment" doctrine of *Weems* to a punishment consisting solely of a sentence of imprisonment, despite numerous opportunities to do so.

sentence of imprisonment is imposed after the state has identified a criminal offender whose record shows he will not conform to societal standards.

The Court's traditional abstention from reviewing sentences of imprisonment to ensure that punishment is "proportionate" to the crime is well founded in history, in prudential considerations, and in traditions of comity. Today's conclusion by five Justices that they are able to say that one offense has less "gravity" than another is nothing other than a bald substitution of individual subjective moral values for those of the legislature. Nor, as this case well illustrates, are we endowed with Solomonic wisdom that permits us to draw principled distinctions between sentences of different length for a chronic "repeater" who has demonstrated that he will not abide by the law.

The simple truth is that "[n]o neutral principle of adjudication permits a federal court to hold that in a given situation individual crimes are to trivial in relation to the punishment imposed." The apportionment of punishment entails, in Justice Frankfurter's words, "peculiarly questions of legislative policy." Legislatures are far better equipped that we are to balance the competing penal and public interests and to draw the essentially arbitrary lines between appropriate sentences for different crimes.

By asserting the power to review sentences of imprisonment for excessiveness the Court launches into uncharted and unchartable waters. Today it holds that a sentence of life imprisonment, without the possibility of parole, is excessive punishment for a seventh allegedly "nonviolent" felony. How about the eighth "nonviolent" felony? The ninth? The twelfth? Suppose one offense was a simple assault? Or selling liquor to a minor? Or statutory rape? Or price-fixing? The permutations are endless and the Court's opinion is bankrupt of realistic guiding principles. Instead, it casually lists several allegedly "objective" factors and arbitrarily asserts that they show respondent's sentence to be "significantly disproportionate" to his crimes. Must all these factors be present in order to hold a sentence excessive under the eighth amendment? How are they to be weighed against each other? Suppose several states punish severely a crime that the Court views as trivial or petty? I can see no limiting principle in the Court's holding.

There is a real risk that this holding will flood the appellate courts with cases in which equally arbitrary lines must be drawn. It is no answer to say that appellate courts must review criminal convictions in any event; up to now, that review has been on the validity of the judgment, not the sentence. The vast majority of criminal cases are disposed of by pleas of guilty, and ordinarily there is no appellate review in such cases. To require appellate review of all sentences of imprisonment—as the Court's opinion necessarily does—will "administer the coup de grace to the courts of appeal as we know them." This is judicial usurpation with a vengeance; Congress has pondered for decades the concept of appellate review of sentences and has hesitated to act.

III

Even if I agreed that the eighth amendment prohibits imprisonment "disproportionate to the crime committed," I reject the notion that respondent's sentence is disproportionate to his crimes for, if we are to have a system of laws, not men, *Rummel* is controlling.

The differences between this case and *Rummel* are insubstantial. First, Rummel committed three truly nonviolent felonies, while respondent, as noted at the outset, committed seven felonies, four of which cannot fairly be characterized as "nonviolent." At the very least, respondent's burglaries and his third-offense drunk driving posed real risk of serious harm to others. It is sheer fortuity that the places respondent burglarized were unoccupied and that he killed no pedestrians while behind the wheel. What would have happened if a guard had been on duty during the burglaries is a matter of speculation, but the possibilities shatter the notion that respondent's crimes were innocuous, inconsequential, minor, or "nonviolent." Four of respondent's crimes, I repeat, had harsh potentialities for violence. Respondent, far more than Rummel, has demonstrated his inability to bring his conduct into conformity with the minimum standards of civilized society. Clearly, this difference demolishes any semblance of logic in the Court's conclusion that respondent's sentence constitutes cruel and unusual punishment although Rummel's did not.

The Court's opinion necessarily reduces to the proposition that a sentence of life imprisonment with the possibility of commutation, but without possibility of parole, is so much more severe than a life imprisonment with the possibility of parole that one is excessive while the other is not. This distinction does not withstand scrutiny; a well-behaved "lifer" in respondent's position is most unlikely to serve for life.

It is inaccurate to say, as the Court does, that the *Rummel* holding relied on the fact that Texas had a relatively liberal parole policy. In context, it is clear that the *Rummel* Court's discussion of parole merely illustrated the difficulty of comparing sentences between different jurisdictions. However, accepting the Court's characterization of *Rummel* as accurate, the Court today misses the point. Parole was relevant to an evaluation of Rummel's life sentence because in the "real world," he was unlikely to spend his entire life behind bars. Only a fraction of "lifers" are not released within a relatively few years. In Texas, the historical evidence showed that a prisoner serving a life sentence could become eligible for parole in as little as 12 years. In South Dakota, the historical evidence shows that since 1964, 22 life sentences have been commuted to terms of years, while requests for commutation of 25 life sentences were denied. And, of course, those requests for commutation may be renewed.

In short, there is a significant probability that respondent will experience what so many "lifers" experience. Even assuming that at the time of sentencing, respondent was likely to spend more time in prison than Rummel,[8] that marginal difference is surely supported by respondent's greater demonstrated propensity for crime—and for more serious crime at that.

IV

It is indeed a curious business for this Court to so far intrude into the administration of criminal justice to say that a state legislature is barred by the Constitution from identifying its habitual criminals and removing them from the streets. Surely seven felony convictions warrant the conclusion that respondent is incorrigible. It is even more curious that the Court should brush aside controlling precedents that are barely in the bound volumes of United States Reports. The Court would do well to heed Justice Black's comments about judges overruling the considered actions of legislatures under the guise of constitutional interpretation:

> "Such unbounded authority in any group of politically appointed or elected judges would unquestionably be sufficient to classify our nation as a government of men, not the government of laws of which we boast. With a 'shock the conscience' test of constitutionality, citizens must guess what is the law, guess what a majority of nine judges will believe fair and reasonable. Such a test wilfully throws away the certainty and security that lies in a written constitution, one that does not alter with a judge's health, belief, or his politics." Boddie v. Connecticut, 401 U.S. 371, 393 (1971) (Black, J., dissenting).

NOTES ON PROPORTIONALITY AND IMPRISONMENT

1. **Pre-*Rummel* Decisions.** As the *Helm* opinions indicate, the centerpiece of the precedential dispute was the meaning of Rummel v. Estelle, 445 U.S. 263 (1980). A few courts, however, had faced the issue of unconstitutional disproportionality in sentences of imprisonment prior to *Rummel*. Most courts had rejected such claims, even when presented on what might be regarded as egregious facts. In McDougle v. Maxwell, 1 Ohio St.2d 68, 203 N.E.2d 334 (1964), for example, the Ohio Supreme Court held over only one dissent that a sentence of 20 years for operating a motor vehicle without the owner's consent was not unconstitutional, even though the legislature had subsequently amended the statute to provide for a maximum of six months' imprisonment for that offense. On the other hand, a few courts had vindicated such claims. In Downey v. Perini, 518 F.2d 1288 (6th Cir.1975), for example, the court held that a 60-year sentence for possession and sale

---

[8] No one will ever know if or when Rummel would have been released on parole since he was released in connection with a separate federal habeas proceeding in 1980. On October 3, 1980, a federal District Court granted Rummel's petition for a writ of habeas corpus on the grounds of ineffective assistance of counsel. Rummel v. Estelle, 498 F.Supp. 793 (W.D.Tex.1980). Rummel then plead guilty to theft by false pretenses and was sentenced to time served under the terms of a plea bargaining agreement. Two-Bit Lifer Finally Freed-After Pleading Guilty, Chicago Tribune, Nov. 15, 1980, at 2, col. 3.

of "very small" amounts of marijuana violated the eighth amendment. Similarly, in People v. Lorentzen, 387 Mich. 167, 194 N.W.2d 827 (1972), the court set aside as unconstitutional a mandatory minimum sentence of 20 years for a single unlawful sale of marijuana. And in the famous case of In re Lynch, 8 Cal.3d 410, 105 Cal.Rptr. 217, 503 P.2d 921 (1972), the California Supreme Court held that a life sentence for a second indecent-exposure conviction violated the California constitution.

Perhaps the most influential of the pre-*Rummel* decisions was Hart v. Coiner, 483 F.2d 136 (4th Cir.1973). In that case the Fourth Circuit invalidated a mandatory life sentence imposed under a recidivist statute. Hart had been convicted of perjury and received the life sentence because he had two prior convictions of offenses punishable by penitentiary sentences, one for writing a $50 bad check and one for transporting a $140 forged check across state lines. The life sentence was found to be "wholly disproportionate to the nature of the offenses" and hence violative of the eighth amendment. In reaching this judgment, the Fourth Circuit focused upon four factors: (i) the nature of the offense, (ii) the legislative purpose in prohibiting the proscribed conduct, (iii) the penalties authorized for similar misconduct in other jurisdictions, and (iv) the penalties authorized for misconduct of comparable severity in the sentencing jurisdiction. In subsequent cases, the same court employed these four factors to invalidate a 40-year sentence for possession of fewer than nine ounces of marijuana, Davis v. Davis, 601 F.2d 153 (4th Cir.1979), and to rule that a person could not receive a longer term for assault than was authorized for the more serious crime of assault with intent to murder, Roberts v. Collins, 544 F.2d 168 (4th Cir.1976).

2. ***Rummel v. Estelle.*** Whatever trend might have been indicated by these early cases seemed to have been cut short by the decision in *Rummel v. Estelle.* William James Rummel had been convicted in 1964 of fraudulent use of a credit card to obtain $80 worth of goods or services and in 1969 of passing a forged check in the amount of $28.36. Both of these crimes were felonies, and for both Rummel went to prison. In 1973 he was charged with obtaining $120.75 by false pretenses. He thereby became liable to prosecution under the Texas recidivist statute. The jury convicted Rummel of the third felony and found that he had twice before been convicted and imprisoned for felonies, thus bringing him within the statutory provision for a mandatory life sentence.

Rummel's federal habeas corpus petition was originally denied, but a divided panel of the Fifth Circuit held that the sentence was "so grossly disproportionate" to his offense that it violated the eighth amendment. That judgment was then vacated by the Fifth Circuit sitting en banc, with six judges dissenting. The majority relied particularly on the fact that Rummel would be eligible for parole within 12 years of his initial confinement. The Supreme Court then affirmed the denial of relief in an opinion written by Justice Rehnquist and joined by the Chief Justice and Justices Stewart, White, and Blackmun. The majority refused to follow the constitutional requirement of proportionality developed in the death-penalty cases, on the ground that the capital sanction is unique. *Weems* was distinguished on the ground that it involved the unusual regime of the cadena temporal. Additionally, the Court emphasized the absence of "objective" criteria by which to determine disproportionality and the difficulty of both intra- and interjurisdictional comparisons of relative sentence severity. With respect to the significance of parole, the Court said:

> "Texas, we are told, has a relatively liberal policy of granting 'good time' credits to its prisoners, a policy that historically has allowed a prisoner serving a life sentence to become eligible for parole in as little as 12 years. We agree with Rummel that his inability to enforce any 'right' to parole precludes us from treating his life sentence as if it were equivalent to a sentence of 12 years. Nevertheless, because parole is 'an established variation on imprisonment of convicted criminals,' a proper assessment of Texas' treatment of Rummel could hardly ignore the possibility that he will not actually be imprisoned for the rest of his life."

The possibility of parole proved to be an important factor by which the *Helm* Court distinguished *Rummel*. Does it provide a persuasive explanation for the difference in outcomes? Is it clear that Helm had been dealt with more harshly than Rummel?

3. ***Hutto v. Davis.*** In his *Rummel* dissent, Justice Powell relied on the Fourth Circuit's experience in *Hart v. Coiner* and its progeny to demonstrate that inquiry into the unconstitutional disproportionality of sentences of imprisonment was a feasible enterprise. One of the Fourth Circuit's cases reached the Supreme Court shortly after *Rummel*. Hutto v. Davis, 454 U.S. 370 (1982). Davis' convictions were based on possession and distribution of approximately nine ounces of marijuana (with a street value of about $200), although there were indications in the record that he may have been more heavily involved as a drug distributor. He was given two consecutive 20-year sentences. His sentence was set aside prior to *Rummel*, and that decision was affirmed by the Fourth Circuit sitting en banc in Davis v. Davis, 601 F.2d 153 (4th Cir.1979). The Supreme Court remanded for reconsideration in light of *Rummel*, after which the Fourth Circuit re-entered its prior judgment by an equally divided vote. The Supreme Court then reversed in a sharply worded per curiam order that held the rationale of *Rummel* controlling and reprimanded the lower court for not following applicable precedent:

> "In short, *Rummel* stands for the proposition that federal courts should be 'reluctan[t] to review legislatively mandated terms of imprisonment' and that 'successful challenges to the proportionality of particular sentences' should be 'exceedingly rare.' By affirming the District Court decision after our decision in *Rummel*, the Court of Appeals sanctioned an intrusion into the basic line-drawing process that is 'properly within the province of legislatures, not courts.' More importantly, however, the Court of Appeals could be viewed as having ignored, consciously or unconsciously, the hierarchy of the federal court system creat-

ed by the Constitution and Congress. Admittedly, the members of the Court decide cases 'by virtue of their commissions, not their competence.' And arguments may be made one way or the other whether the present case is distinguishable, except as to its facts, from *Rummel*. But unless we wish anarchy to prevail within the federal judicial system, a precedent of this Court must be followed by the lower federal courts no matter how misguided the judges of those courts may think it to be."

Justice Powell concurred in the judgment on the ground that *Rummel* was indistinguishable, even though he viewed the sentence as "unjust and disproportionate to the offense." Justices Brennan, Marshall, and Stevens dissented.

4. **Questions and Comments on *Solem v. Helm*.** After *Rummel* and *Davis,* one might well have thought that, absent a penalty so extravagantly ridiculous as to be unlikely ever to arise, no sentence of imprisonment would be set aside as unconstitutionally disproportionate. Indeed, that seems to have been the impression of the commentators, most of whom found *Rummel* objectionable.[a] Of course, *Solem v. Helm* "corrected" that misimpression. Is it clear on what ground? Note that Justice Powell, who had written a long dissent in *Rummel,* spoke for a majority in *Helm*. In the interim, Justice Stewart had been replaced by Justice O'Connor, but she voted with the dissenters, which is presumably how Justice Stewart would have voted. The Court's shift of direction cannot be explained, therefore, by the change of personnel; all of the other Justices who participated in *Rummel* were still on the Court at the time of *Helm*.

On what ground, therefore, can *Rummel* and *Helm* be reconciled? Was Helm's situation more like a life sentence for a parking violation than Rummel's? Did *Helm* in effect overrule *Rummel?* If so, which is the better decision? [b]

5. **Footnote on Proportionality and Sentencing.** Whatever the constitutional limits imposed by the principle of proportionality, it is clear that a wide range of options will remain open to legislatures and courts concerned with sentencing policy. When and whether long sentences should be imposed are only aspects of the complex issues involved. Additionally, the role that the concept of proportionality should play and how that concept should be implemented present questions both difficult and controversial.

As is discussed in the introduction on the purposes of punishment, pages 7–8, supra, the issue of proportionality must be faced at two

[a] See, e.g., Dressler, Substantive Criminal Law Through the Looking Glass of *Rummel v. Estelle:* Proportionality and Justice as Endangered Doctrines, 34 Sw.L. Rev. 1063 (1981) (extensively criticizing both the result and the opinion); Gardner, The Determinate Sentencing Movement and the Eighth Amendment: Excessive Punishment Before and After *Rummel v. Estelle,* 1980 Duke L.J. 1103 (arguing that the inflexibility of determinate sentencing leads to the risk of excessive punishment, which *Rummel* undermined the ability of the courts to prevent).

[b] For a thoughtful analysis of *Rummel, Davis,* and *Helm* and the implications of those decisions, see Baker and Baldwin, Eighth Amendment Challenges to the Length of a Criminal Sentence: "From Precedent to Precedent," 27 Ariz.L.Rev. 25 (1985).

different stages. First, the legislature establishes the relative severity of criminal offenses by providing the authorized terms of incarceration for each offense. Traditionally, American legislatures have discharged this function in terms that leave wide discretion to the courts in selecting sentences for particular cases. They have done so in part because of the inherent generality of any prospective categorization of offenses. All persons who commit robbery (or any other crime) do not do so for the same reasons or in the same manner or with the same consequences, and it is impossible to specify in the definition of the offense all of the factors that might rationally be taken into account in determining an appropriate sentence for a particular offender. Legislative grading has therefore traditionally been limited to fairly gross distinctions among offenses.

Under traditional schemes, the proportionality inquiry is also relevant at a second stage in the process, namely in the selection of particular punishments for individual cases. The distribution of sentencing authority after legislative grading presents issues of such complexity that the subject cannot be explored fully in these materials. The prosecutor (in charging and plea-bargaining decisions), the jury (in determining guilt and in some states in fixing the sentence), the trial judge (in most states in imposing sentence), the appellate courts (in reviewing convictions and, less commonly, in reviewing sentences), the parole authorities (in deciding whether to release an offender prior to the expiration of the sentence imposed), and the chief executive officer (in deciding whether to commute a sentence or grant a pardon)—all may participate in determining the punishment that actually is imposed. The concept of proportionality plays an important role, along with other factors related to the proper punishment for crime, in determinations made by each of these actors.

Today, sentencing policy is the subject of unprecedented ferment and debate. Abstracted from their details, there are essentially two opposing perspectives.[c] On the one side are those who endorse incremental reform. They urge that sentencing discretion should be controlled by such devices as the specification of criteria by legislation or by special sentencing commissions, the requirement that a judge give reasons for the particular sentence imposed, advance consultation among judges, and increased appellate review of sentences. On the other side are those who believe in more drastic change. They urge that parole should be abolished and the range of options open to the sentencing authority (usually the trial judge) drastically reduced. This so-called "just deserts" model of sentencing orients the sentence more to the nature of the offense than to characteristics of the individual offender, and in effect is designed in part to remove individualized proportionality judgments from the sentencing decision. Common to both camps is the belief that much is wrong with contemporary sen-

[c] The literature on this subject is voluminous. Two recent publications provide useful summaries of the debate as well as citations to other relevant materials. See ABA Standards for Criminal Justice, ch. 18 (2d ed. 1980); Perlman & Stebbins, Implementing an Equitable Sentencing System: The Uniform Law Commissioners' Model Sentencing and Corrections Act, 65 Va.L. Rev. 1175 (1979).

tencing—chiefly, unjustified disparity in the sentences imposed on comparably situated offenders, uncontrolled discretion by various participants in the sentencing process, and excessive reliance on vague and empirically questionable intuitions about the purposes of punishment.

SECTION 3: CRIMINALIZATION

INTRODUCTORY NOTE ON CRIMINALIZATION

For the most part, materials in earlier chapters do not focus directly on the behavioral content of a penal code—that is, on what conduct should, or should not, be punishable by criminal sanctions. Obviously, particular criminalization decisions require full understanding of the relevant social, economic, and psychological realities. It is possible, however, to explore several general questions: What considerations should be taken into account in deciding whether disapproved behavior should be prohibited by the criminal law? Should it be enough that a majority of lawmakers find the behavior morally objectionable? On the other hand, is it appropriate to criminalize socially undesirable behavior that has no moral significance? How should a lawmaker assess the utility of the criminal sanction in comparison with other legal mechanisms of social control? How does one know when the costs of criminalization outweigh its benefits? Of what significance is the difficulty of enforcement? Or the pervasiveness of the prohibited behavior? Is it appropriate to make conduct criminal with the expectation that the law will not be enforced or will be significantly under-enforced?

These questions have received considerable attention in recent academic commentary and official reports. A major contribution to this now-extensive literature is The Limits of the Criminal Sanction (1968), by Professor Herbert Packer. Many observers, including Packer, have concluded that the criminal law is seriously over-extended, especially in the area of the so-called "vice crimes" such as prostitution, homosexuality, drugs, and gambling. The following material is designed to present an overview of the factors that should influence legislative decisions concerning the reach of the criminal law in these as well as other areas.

JOHN STUART MILL, ON LIBERTY (1859) *

The object of this essay is to assert one very simple principle, as entitled to govern absolutely the dealings of society with the individual in the way of compulsion and control, whether the means used be physical force in the form of legal penalties, or the moral coercion of public opinion. That principle is, that the sole end for which mankind

* J. S. Mill, On Liberty 22–29, 156–62, 188–95 (Ticknor and Fields, Boston, 1863).

are warranted, individually or collectively, in interfering with the liberty of action of any of their number, is self-protection. That the only purpose for which power can be rightfully exercised over any member of a civilized community, against his will, is to prevent harm to others. His own good, either physical or moral, is not a sufficient warrant. He cannot rightfully be compelled to do or forbear because it will be better for him to do so, because it will make him happier, because, in the opinions of others, to do so would be wise, or even right. These are good reasons for remonstrating with him, or reasoning with him, or persuading him, or entreating him, but not for compelling him, or visiting him with any evil in case he do otherwise. To justify that, the conduct from which it is desired to deter him must be calculated to produce evil to some one else. The only part of the conduct of any one, for which he is amenable to society, is that which concerns others. In the part which merely concerns himself, his independence is, of right, absolute. Over himself, over his own body and mind, the individual is sovereign.

It is, perhaps, hardly necessary to say that this doctrine is meant to apply only to human beings in the maturity of their faculties. We are not speaking of children, or of young persons below the age which the law may fix as that of manhood or womanhood. Those who are still in a state to require being taken care of by others, must be protected against their own actions as well as against external injury.

. . . This, then, is the appropriate region of human liberty. It comprises, first, the inward domain of consciousness; demanding liberty of conscience, in the most comprehensive sense; liberty of thought and feeling; absolute freedom of opinion and sentiment on all subjects, practical or speculative, scientific, moral, or theological. The liberty of expressing and publishing opinions may seem to fall under a different principle, since it belongs to that part of the conduct of an individual which concerns other people; but, being almost of as much importance as the liberty of thought itself, and resting in great part on the same reasons, is practically inseparable from it. Secondly, the principle requires liberty of tastes and pursuits; of framing the plan of our life to suit our own character; of doing as we like, subject to such consequences as may follow: without impediment from our fellow creatures, so long as what we do does not harm them, even though they should think our conduct foolish, perverse, or wrong. Thirdly, from this liberty of each individual, follows the liberty, within the same limits, of combination among individuals; freedom to unite, for any purpose not involving harm to others: the persons combining being supposed to be of full age, and not forced or deceived.

No society in which these liberties are not, on the whole, respected, is free, whatever may be its form of government; and none is completely free in which they do not exist absolute and unqualified. The only freedom which deserves the name, is that of pursuing our own good in our own way, so long as we do not attempt to deprive others of theirs, or impede their efforts to obtain it. Each is the proper guardian of his own health, whether bodily, or mental and spiritual. Mankind are greater gainers by suffering each other to live as seems good to themselves, than by compelling each to live as seems good to the rest. . . .

I fully admit that the mischief which a person does to himself may seriously affect, both through their sympathies and their interests, those nearly connected with him, and in a minor degree, society at large. When, by conduct of this sort, a person is led to violate a distinct and assignable obligation to any other person or persons, the case is taken out of the self-regarding class, and becomes amenable to moral disapprobation in the proper sense of the term. If, for example, a man, through intemperance or extravagance, becomes unable to pay his debts, or, having undertaken the moral responsibility of a family, becomes from the same cause incapable of supporting or educating them, he is deservedly reprobated, and might be justly punished; but it is for the breach of duty to his family or creditors, not for the extravagance. . . . Whoever fails in the consideration generally due to the interests and feelings of others, not being compelled by some more imperative duty, or justified by allowable self-preference, is a subject of moral disapprobation for that failure, but not for the cause of it, nor for the errors, merely personal to himself, which may have remotely led to it. In like manner, when a person disables himself, by conduct purely self-regarding, from the performance of some definite duty incumbent on him to the public, he is guilty of a social offence. No person ought to be punished simply for being drunk; but a soldier or a policeman should be punished for being drunk on duty. Whenever, in short, there is a definite damage, or a definite risk of damage, either to an individual or to the public, the case is taken out of the province of liberty, and placed in that of morality or law.

But with regard to the merely contingent, or, as it may be called, constructive injury which a person causes to society, by conduct which neither violates any specific duty to the public, nor occasions perceptible hurt to any assignable individual except himself; the inconvenience is one which society can afford to bear, for the sake of the greater good of human freedom. If grown persons are to be punished for not taking proper care of themselves, I would rather it were for their own sake, than under pretence of preventing them from impairing their capacity of rendering to society benefits which society does not pretend it has a right to exact.

[T]he strongest of all the arguments against the interference of the public with purely personal conduct, is that when it does interfere, the odds are that it interferes wrongly, and in the wrong place. On questions of social morality, of duty to others, the opinion of the public, that is, of an overruling majority, though often wrong, is likely to be still oftener right; because on such questions they are only required to judge of their own interests, of the manner in which some mode of conduct, if allowed to be practised, would affect themselves. But the opinion of a similar majority, imposed as a law on the minority, on questions of self-regarding conduct, is quite as likely to be wrong as right; for in these cases public opinion means, at the best, some people's opinion of what is good or bad for other people; while very often it does not even mean that; the public, with the most perfect indifference, passing over the pleasure or convenience of those whose conduct they censure, and considering only their own preference. There are many who consider as an injury to themselves any conduct which they have a distaste for, and resent it as an outrage to their feelings; as a religious bigot, when charged with disregarding the religious feelings of others, has been known to retort that they disregard his feelings, by persisting in their abominable worship or creed. But there is no parity between the feeling of a person for his own opinion, and the feeling of another who is offended at his holding it; no more than between the desire of a thief to take a purse, and the desire of the right owner to keep it. And a person's taste is as much his own peculiar concern as his opinion or his purse. . . .

The right inherent in society, to ward off crimes against itself by antecedent precautions, suggests the obvious limitations to the maxim, that purely self-regarding misconduct cannot properly be meddled with in the way of prevention or punishment. Drunkenness, for example, in ordinary cases, is not a fit subject for legislative interference; but I should deem it perfectly legitimate that a person, who had once been convicted of any act of violence to others under the influence of drink, should be placed under a special legal restriction, personal to himself; that if he were afterwards found drunk, he should be liable to a penalty, and that if when in that state he committed another offence, the punishment to which he would be liable for that other offence should be increased in severity. The making himself drunk, in a person whom drunkenness excites to do harm to others, is a crime against others. So, again, idleness, except in a person receiving support from the public, or except when it constitutes a breach of contract, cannot without tyranny be made a subject of legal punishment; but if, either from idleness or from any other avoidable cause, a man fails to perform his legal duties to others, as for instance to support his children, it is no tyranny to force him to fulfill that obligation, by compulsory labour, if no other means are available.

Again, there are many acts which, being directly injurious only to the agents themselves, ought not to be legally interdicted, but which, if done publicly, are a violation of good manners, and coming thus within the category of offenses against others, may rightfully be prohibited. Of this kind are offences against decency; . . . they are only connected indirectly with our subject, the objection to publicity being equally strong in the case of many actions not in themselves condemnable, nor supposed to be so.

There is another question to which an answer must be found, consistent with the principles which have been laid down. In cases of personal conduct supposed to be blameable, but which respect for liberty precludes society from preventing or punishing, because the evil directly resulting falls wholly on the agent; what the agent is free to do, ought other persons to be equally free to counsel or instigate? This question is not free from difficulty. The case of a person who solicits another to do an act, is not strictly a case of self-regarding conduct. To give advice or offer inducements to any one, is a social act, and may, therefore, like actions in general which affect others, be supposed amenable to social control. But a little reflection corrects the first impression, by showing that if the case is not strictly within the definition of individual liberty, yet the reasons on which the principle of individual liberty is grounded, are applicable to it. If people must be allowed, in whatever concerns only themselves, to act as seems best to themselves at their own peril, they must equally be free to consult with one another about what is fit to be so done; to exchange opinions, and give and receive suggestions. Whatever it is permitted to do, it must be permitted to advise to do. The question is doubtful, only when the instigator derives a personal benefit from his advice; when he makes it his occupation, for subsistence or pecuniary gain, to promote what society and the state consider to be an evil. Then, indeed, a new element of complication is introduced; namely, the existence of classes of persons with an interest opposed to what is considered as the public weal, and whose mode of living is grounded on the counteraction of it. Ought this to be interfered with, or not? Fornication, for example, must be tolerated, and so must gambling; but should a person be free to be a pimp, or to keep a gambling-house? The case is one of those which lie on the exact boundary line between two principles, and it is not at once apparent to which of the two it properly belongs. There are arguments on both sides. On the side of toleration it may be said, that the fact of following anything as an occupation, and living or profiting by the practice of it, cannot make that criminal which would otherwise be admissible; that the act should either be consistently permitted or consistently prohibited; that if the principles which we have hitherto defended are true, society has no business, *as* society, to decide anything to be wrong which concerns only the individual; that it cannot go beyond dissuasion, and that one person should be as free to persuade, as another to dissuade. In opposition to this it may be contended, that although the public, or the state, are not warranted in authoritatively deciding, for purposes of repression or punishment, that such or such conduct affecting only the interests of the individual is good or bad, they are fully justified in assuming, if they regard it as bad, that its being so or not is at least a disputable question: That, this being supposed, they cannot be acting wrongly in endeavouring to exclude the influence of solicitations which are not disinterested, of instigators who cannot possibly be impartial—who have a direct personal interest on one side, and that side the one which the state believes to be wrong, and who confessedly promote it for personal objects only. There can surely, it may be urged, be nothing lost, no sacrifice of good, by so ordering matters that persons shall make their election, either wisely or foolishly, on their own prompting, as free as possible from the arts of persons who stimulate their inclinations for interested purposes of their own. Thus (it may be said) though the statutes respecting unlawful games are utterly indefensible—though all persons should be free to gamble in their own or each other's houses, or in any place of meeting established by their own subscriptions, and open only to the members and their visitors—yet public gambling-houses should not be permitted. It is true that the prohibition is never effectual, and that whatever amount of tyrannical power is given to the police, gambling-houses can always be maintained under other pretences; but they may be compelled to conduct their operations with a certain degree of secrecy and mystery, so that nobody knows anything about them but those who seek them; and more than this, society ought not to aim at. There is considerable force in these arguments. I will not venture to decide whether they are sufficient to justify the moral anomaly of punishing the accessary, when the principal is (and must be) allowed to go free; of fining or imprisoning the procurer, but not the fornicator, the gambling-house keeper, but not the gambler. Still less ought the common operations of buying and selling to be interfered with on analogous grounds. Almost every article which is bought and sold may be used in excess, and the sellers have a pecuniary interest in encouraging that excess; but no argument can be founded on this . . . because the class of dealers in strong drinks, though interested in their abuse, are indispensably required for the sake of their legitimate use. The interest, however, of these dealers in promoting intemperance is a real evil, and justifies the state in imposing restrictions and requiring guarantees, which but for that justification would be infringements of legitimate liberty.

A further question is, whether the state, while it permits, should nevertheless indirectly discourage conduct which it deems contrary to the best interests of the agent, whether, for example, it should take measures to render the means of drunkenness more costly, or add to the difficulty of procuring them, by limiting the number of the places of sale. On this as on most other practical questions, many distinctions require to be made. To tax stimulants for the sole purpose of making them more difficult to be obtained, is a measure differing only in degree from their entire prohibition; and would be justifiable only if that were justifiable. Every increase of cost is a prohibition, to those whose means do not come up to the augmented price; and to those who do, it is a penalty laid on them for gratifying a particular taste. Their choice of pleasures, and their mode of expending their income, after satisfying their legal and moral obligations to the state and to individuals, are their own concern, and must rest with their own judgment. These considerations may seem at first sight to condemn the selection of stimulants as special subjects of taxation for purposes of revenue. But it must be remembered that taxation for fiscal purposes is absolutely inevitable; that in most countries it is necessary that a considerable part of that taxation should be indirect; that the state, therefore, cannot help imposing penalties, which to some persons may be prohibitory, on the use of some articles of consumption. It is hence the duty of the state to consider, in the imposition of taxes, what commodities the consumers can best spare; and a fortiori, to select in preference those of which it deems the use, beyond a very moderate quantity, to be positively injurious. Taxation, therefore, of stimulants, up to the point which produces the largest amount of revenue (supposing that the state needs all the revenue which it yields) is not only admissible, but to be approved of. . . .

———

NOTES ON THE ENFORCEMENT OF MORALS

1. **Stephen's Response.** Mill's essay is the classic statement of the theoretical position that there are categorical limits on the purposes for which the government properly may interfere with the individual, and, in particular, that enforcement of the prevailing moral code is not, in itself, a sufficient reason for criminalization. In his famous essay, Mill argued that personal decisions within the "sphere of liberty" should be immune from official "moral coercion" as well as from "physical force" through the criminal law.

Mill's position was criticized, in theory and in application, by Sir James Fitzjames Stephen in Liberty, Equality, Fraternity (1874). "Complete moral tolerance," Stephen said, "is possible only when men have become completely indifferent to each other—that is to say, when society is at an end." The moral coercion of public opinion, he argued, "is the great engine by which the whole mass of beliefs, habits, and customs, which collectively constitute positive morality, are protected and sanctioned." Although Stephen acknowledged that the proper use of the criminal law to enforce positive morality is subject to restraints "independent of general considerations about liberty," he insisted that the penal law ought to prohibit "grossly immoral" or "unquestionably wicked" acts on that ground alone. He summarized his argument as follows:

> "[T]here is a sphere, none the less real because it is impossible to define its limits, within which law and public opinion are intruders likely to do more harm than good. To try to regulate the internal affairs of a family, the relations of love or friendship, or many other things of the same sort, by law or by the coercion of public opinion, is like trying to pull an eyelash out of a man's eye with a pair of tongs. They may put out the eye, but they will never get hold of the eyelash.

> "[T]he principal importance of what is done [in promoting virtue and restraining vice] by criminal law is that in extreme cases it brands gross acts of vice with the deepest mark of infamy which can be impressed upon them, and that in this manner it protects the public and accepted standard of morals from being grossly and openly violated. In short, it affirms in a singularly emphatic manner a principle which is absolutely inconsistent with and contradictory to Mr. Mill's—the principle, namely, that there are acts of wickedness so gross and outrageous that, self-protection apart, they must be prevented as far as possible at any cost to the offender, and punished, if they occur, with exemplary severity."

2. **The Wolfenden Report.** A modern version of Mill's position regarding the proper scope of the criminal law was endorsed in a 1957 report by an English Committee on Homosexual Offenses and Prostitution, generally known as the Wolfenden Report. According to the Committee:

"[T]he function of the criminal law . . . is to preserve public order and decency, to protect the citizen from what is offensive or injurious, and to provide sufficient safeguards against exploitation and corruption of others, particularly those who are specially vulnerable because they are young, weak in body or mind, inexperienced, or in a state of special physical, official or economic dependence.

"It is not, in our view, the function of the law to intervene in the private lives of citizens, or to seek to enforce any particular pattern of behavior, further than is necessary to carry out the purposes we have outlined.

". . . Unless a deliberate attempt is to be made by society, acting through the agency of the law, to equate the sphere of crime with that of sin, there must remain a realm of private morality and immorality which is, in brief and crude terms, not the law's business. To say this is not to condone or encourage private immorality."

The Wolfenden Committee's major recommendation was that private homosexual behavior between consenting adults should be decriminalized.[b]

The drafters of the Model Penal Code also took the position that "private immorality should be beyond the reach of the penal law" in the absence of a demonstrable secular justification, and specifically recommended that private sexual activity between consenting adults should be decriminalized. Accordingly, the Model Code does not prohibit adultery, fornication, or other forms of sexual relations between consenting adults. See ALI Model Penal Code and Commentaries, Part II, pp. 357–74 (Comment on Section 213.2 (Deviate Sexual Intercourse by Force or Imposition)) and 430–39 (Note on Adultery and Fornication) (1980).

The Wolfenden Report and the Model Penal Code renewed the controversy initiated by Mill and Stephen a century earlier. The leading figures in the contemporary debate are Lord Patrick Devlin, who criticizes the libertarian position advanced by Mill and the Wolfenden Committee, and Professor H.L.A. Hart, who defends a modified version of the libertarian position.[c] The following notes highlight several dimensions of this famous exchange.

3. **Lord Devlin's Response.** Lord Devlin takes issue with the Wolfenden Committee's central assertion that the enforcement of con-

[b] This recommendation was implemented in England in The Sexual Offenses Act, 1967, § 1(1).

[c] The debate between Lord Devlin and Professor Hart is fully developed in H.L.A. Hart, Law, Liberty and Morality (1963), P. Devlin, The Enforcement of Morals (1965), and Hart, Social Solidarity and the Enforcement of Morality, 35 U.Chi.L.Rev. 1

(1967). See also Dworkin, Lord Devlin and the Enforcement of Morals, 75 Yale L.J. 986 (1966); Williams, Authoritarian Morals and the Criminal Law, [1966] Crim.L.Rev. 132. The libertarian position is refined and defended by Joel Feinberg in Harm to Others (1984). This book is the first in a four-volume series entitled The Moral Limits of the Criminal Law.

ventional morality is not, in itself, a sufficient condition for criminalization. He develops his argument as follows: [d]

". . . What makes a society of any sort is community of ideas, not only political ideas but also ideas about the way its members should behave and govern their lives; these latter ideas are its morals. Every society has a moral structure as well as a political one: or rather, since that might suggest two independent systems, I should say that the structure of every society is made up both of politics and morals. . . .

"The institution of marriage is a good example for my purpose because it bridges the division, if there is one, between politics and morals. Marriage is part of the structure of our society and it is also the basis of a moral code which condemns fornication and adultery. The institution of marriage would be gravely threatened if individual judgements were permitted about the morality of adultery; on these points there must be a public morality. But public morality is not to be confined to those moral principles which support institutions such as marriage. People do not think of monogamy as something which has to be supported because our society has chosen to organize itself upon it; they think of it as something that is good in itself and offering a good way of life and that it is for that reason that our society has adopted it. . . . If men and women try to create a society in which there is no fundamental agreement about good and evil they will fail; if, having based it on common agreement, the agreement goes, the society will disintegrate. For society is not something that is kept together physically; it is held by the invisible bonds of common thought. If the bonds were too far relaxed the members would drift apart. A common morality is part of the bondage. The bondage is part of the price of society; and mankind, which needs society, must pay its price.

". . . [I]f society has the right to make a judgment and has it on the basis that a recognized morality is as necessary to society as, say, a recognized government, then society may use the law to preserve morality in the same way as it uses it to safeguard anything else that is essential to its existence. If therefore the first proposition is securely established with all its implications, society has a prima-facie right to legislate against immorality as such. . . .

"I think, therefore, that it is not possible to set theoretical limits to the power of the state to legislate against immorality. It is not possible to settle in advance exceptions to the general rule or to define inflexibly areas of morality into which the law is in no circumstances to be allowed to enter. Society is entitled by means of its laws to protect itself from dangers, whether from within or without. Here again I think that the political parallel

---

[d] Maccabaean Lecture in Jurisprudence, 45 Proceedings of The British Academy 136–49 (1959). This lecture is reproduced as Chapter 1 of Lord Devlin's book, The Enforcement of Morals (1965).

is legitimate. The law of treason is directed against aiding the king's enemies and against sedition from within. The justification for this is that established government is necessary for the existence of society and therefore its safety against violent overthrow must be secured. But an established morality is as necessary as good government to the welfare of society. Societies disintegrate from within more frequently than they are broken up by external pressures. There is disintegration when no common morality is observed and history shows that the loosening of moral bonds is often the first stage of disintegration, so that society if justified in taking the same steps to preserve its moral code as it does to preserve its government and other essential institutions. The suppression of vice is as much the law's business as the suppression of subversive activities; it is no more possible to define a sphere of private morality than it is to define one of private subversive activity. It is wrong to talk of private morality or of the law being concerned with immorality as such or to try to set rigid bounds to the part which the law may play in the suppression of vice. There are no theoretical limits to the power of the state to legislate against treason and sedition, and likewise I think there can be no theoretical limits to legislation against immorality. You may argue that if a man's sins affect only himself it cannot be the concern of society. If he chooses to get drunk every night in the privacy of his own home, is any one except himself the worse for it? But suppose a quarter or a half of the population got drunk every night, what sort of society would it be? You cannot set a theoretical limit to the number of people who can get drunk before society is entitled to legislate against drunkenness. The same may be said of gambling. The Royal Commission on Betting, Lotteries, and Gaming took as their test the character of the citizen as a member of society. They said: 'Our concern with the ethical significance of gambling is confined to the effect which it may have on the character of the gambler as a member of society. If we were convinced that whatever the degree of gambling this effect must be harmful we should be inclined to think that it was the duty of the state to restrict gambling to the greatest extent practicable.' "

Lord Devlin then goes on to consider what he characterizes as "practical" limits on the criminalization of immorality. First, he notes, "[t]here must be toleration of the maximum individual freedom that is consistent with the integrity of society." He continues as follows:

". . . Nothing should be punished by the law that does not lie beyond the limits of tolerance. It is not nearly enough to say that a majority dislike a practice; there must be a real feeling of reprobation. Those who are dissatisfied with the present law on homosexuality often say that the opponents of reform are swayed simply by disgust. If that were so it would be wrong, but I do not think one can ignore disgust if it is deeply felt and not manufactured. Its presence is a good indication that the bounds of toleration are being reached. Not everything is to be tolerated. No society can do without intolerance, indignation, and disgust; they are the forces behind the moral law, and indeed it can be argued that if they or something like them are not present, the feelings of society cannot be weighty enough to deprive the individual of freedom of choice. . . . Every moral judgement, unless it claims a divine source, is simply a feeling that no right-minded man could behave in any other way without admitting that he was doing wrong.[e] . . . There is, for example, a general abhorrence of homosexuality. We should ask ourselves in the first instance whether, looking at it calmly and dispassion-ately, we regard it as a vice so abominable that its mere presence is an offence. If that is the genuine feeling of the society in which we live, I do not see how society can be denied the right to eradicate it. Our feeling may not be so intense as that. We may feel about it that, if confined, it is tolerable, but that if it spread it might be gravely injurious; it is in this way that most societies look upon fornication, seeing it as a natural weakness which must be kept within bounds but which cannot be rooted out. It becomes then a question of balance, the danger to society in one scale and the extent of the restriction in the other. . . .

"The limits of tolerance shift. This is supplementary to what I have been saying but of sufficient importance in itself to deserve statement as a separate principle which law-makers have to bear in mind. I suppose that moral standards do not shift; so far as they come from divine revelation they do not, and I am willing to assume that the moral judgements made by a society always remain good for that society. But the extent to which society will tolerate—I mean tolerate, not approve—departures from moral standards varies from generation to generation. . . . Laws, especially those which are based on morals, are less easily moved. It follows as another good working principle that in any new matter of morals the law should be slow to act. By the next generation the swell of indignation may have abated and the law be left without the strong backing which it needs. But it is then difficult to alter the law without giving the impression that moral judgment is being weakened. This is now one of the factors that is strongly militating against any altera-tion to the law on homosexuality.

"[Another principle is that] as far as possible privacy should be respected. This is not an idea that has ever been made

[e] At another point in his lecture, Lord Devlin asks "How is the law-maker to as-certain the moral judgments of society?" He responds:

"It is surely not enough that they should be reached by the opinion of the majority; it would be too much to re-quire the individual assent of every citi-zen. [The law] regularly uses a standard which does not depend on the counting of heads. It is that of the reasonable man. He is not to be confused with the rational man. He is not expected to reason about anything and his judge-ment may be largely a matter of feeling. It is the viewpoint of the man in the street—or to use an archaism familiar to all lawyers—the man in the Clapham omnibus. . . ."

explicit in the criminal law. Acts or words done or said in public or in private are all brought within its scope without distinction in principle. But there goes with this a strong reluctance on the part of judges and legislators to sanction invasions of privacy in the detection of crime. . . .

"This indicates a general sentiment that the right to privacy is something to be put in balance against the enforcement of the law. Ought the same sort of consideration to play any part in the formation of the law? Clearly only in a very limited number of cases. When the help of the law is invoked by an injured citizen, privacy must be irrelevant; the individual cannot ask that his right to privacy should be measured against injury criminally done to another. But when all who are involved in the deed are consenting parties and the injury is done to morals, the public interest in the moral order can be balanced against the claims of privacy. The restriction on police powers of investigation goes further than the affording of a parallel; it means that the detection of crime committed in private and when there is no complaint is bound to be rather haphazard and this is an additional reason for moderation. [But these] considerations do not justify the exclusion of all private immorality from the scope of the law.

". . . Discussion among law-makers, both professional and amateur, is too often limited to what is right or wrong and good or bad for society. There is a failure to keep separate . . . the question of society's right to pass a moral judgement and the question of whether the arm of the law should be used to enforce the judgment. The criminal law is not a statement of how people ought to behave; it is a statement of what will happen to them if they do not behave; good citizens are not expected to come within reach of it or to set their sights by it, and every enactment should be framed accordingly.

". . . The line that divides the criminal law from the moral is not determinable by the application of any clear-cut principle. It is like a line that divides land and sea, a coastline of irregularities and indentations. . . . Adultery of the sort that breaks up marriage seems to me to be just as harmful to the social fabric as homosexuality or bigamy. The only ground for putting it outside the criminal law is that a law which made it a crime would be too difficult to enforce; it is too generally regarded as a human weakness not suitably punished by imprisonment. All that the law can do with fornication is to act against its worst manifestations; there is a general abhorrence of the commercialization of vice, and that sentiment gives strength to the law against brothels and immoral earnings. There is no logic to be found in this. The boundary between the criminal law and the moral law is fixed by balancing in the case of each particular crime the pros and cons of legal enforcement in accordance with the sort of considerations I have been outlining.

The fact that adultery, fornication, and lesbianism are untouched by the criminal law does not prove that homosexuality ought not to be touched. The error of jurisprudence in the Wolfenden Report is caused by the search for some single principle to explain the division between crime and sin. The Report finds it in the principle that the criminal law exists for the protection of individuals; on this principle fornication in private between consenting adults is outside the law and thus it becomes logically indefensible to bring homosexuality between consenting adults in private within it. But the true principle is that the law exists for the protection of society. It does not discharge its function by protecting the individual from injury, annoyance, corruption, and exploitation; the law must protect also the institutions and the community of ideas, political and moral, without which people cannot live together. Society cannot ignore the morality of the individual any more than it can his loyalty; it flourishes on both and without either it dies."

4. **Hart's Rejoinder.** Professor Hart defends the libertarian position against Lord Devlin's criticism in Immorality and Treason, 62 Listener 163 (1959),* as follows:

"No doubt we would all agree that a consensus of moral opinion on certain matters is essential if society is to be worth living in. Laws against murder, theft, and much else would be of little use if they were not supported by a widely diffused conviction that what these laws forbid is also immoral. So much is obvious. But it does not follow that everything to which the moral vetoes of accepted morality attach is of equal importance to society; nor is there the slightest reason for thinking of morality as a seamless web: one which will fall to pieces carrying society with it, unless all its emphatic vetoes are enforced by law. Surely even in the face of the moral feeling that is up to concert pitch—the trio of intolerance, indignation, and disgust—we must pause to think. We must ask a question at two different levels which Sir Patrick never clearly enough identifies or separates. First, we must ask whether a practice which offends moral feeling is harmful, independently of its repercussion on the general moral code. Secondly, what about repercussion on the moral code? Is it really true that failure to translate this item of general morality into criminal law will jeopardize the whole fabric of morality and so of society?

"We cannot escape thinking about these two different questions merely by repeating to ourselves the vague nostrum: 'This is part of public morality and public morality must be preserved if society is to exist.' Sometimes Sir Patrick seems to admit this, for he says in words which both Mill and the Wolfenden Report might have used, that there must be the maximum respect for individual liberty consistent with the integrity of society. Yet this, as his contrasting examples of fornication and homosexuali-

---

* Reprinted by permission of the author.

ty show, turns out to mean only that the immorality which the law may punish must be generally felt to be intolerable. This plainly is no adequate substitute for a reasoned estimate of the damage to the fabric of society likely to ensue if it is not suppressed.

"Nothing perhaps shows more clearly the inadequacy of Sir Patrick's approach to this problem than his comparison between the suppression of sexual immorality and the suppression of treason or subversive activity. Private subversive activity is, of course, a contradiction in terms because 'subversion' means over-throwing government, which is a public thing. But it is gro-tesque, even where moral feeling against homosexuality is up to concert pitch, to think of the homosexual behavior of two adults in private as in any way like treason or sedition either in intention or effect. We can make it *seem* like treason only if we assume that deviation from a general moral code is bound to affect that code, and to lead not merely to its modification but to its destruction. The analogy could begin to be plausible only if it was clear that offending against this item of morality was likely to jeopardize the whole structure. But we have ample evidence for believing that people will not abandon morality, will not think any better of murder, cruelty, and dishonesty, merely because some private sexual practice which they abominate is not punished by the law. . . .

"Sir Patrick's doctrine is also open to a wider, perhaps a deeper, criticism. In his reaction against a rationalist's morality and his stress on feeling, he has I think thrown out the baby and kept the bath water; and the bath water may turn out to be very dirty indeed. When Sir Patrick's lecture was first delivered *The Times* greeted it with these words: 'There is a moving and welcome humility in the conception that society should not be asked to give its reason for refusing to tolerate what in its heart it feels intolerable.' This drew from a correspondent in Cam-bridge the retort: 'I am afraid that we are less humble than we used to be. We once burnt old women because, without giving our reasons, we felt in our hearts that witchcraft was intolera-ble.'

"This retort is a bitter one, yet its bitterness is salutary. We are not, I suppose, likely, in England, to take again to the burning of old women for witchcraft or to punishing people for associating with those of a different race or colour, or to punish-ing people again for adultery. Yet if these things were viewed with intolerance, indignation, and disgust, as the second of them still is in some countries, it seems that on Sir Patrick's principles no rational criticism could be opposed to the claim that they should be punished by law. We could only pray, in his words, that the limits of tolerance might shift.

"It is impossible to see what curious logic has led Sir Patrick to this result. For him a practice is immoral if the thought of it makes the man on the Clapham omnibus sick. So be it. Still, why should we not summon all the resources of our reason, sympathetic understanding, as well as critical intelligence, and insist that before general moral feeling is turned into criminal law it is submitted to scrutiny of a different kind from Sir Patrick's? Surely, the legislator should ask whether the general morality is based on ignorance, superstition, or misunderstanding; whether there is a false conception that those who practise what it condemns are in other ways dangerous or hostile to society; and whether the misery to many parties, the blackmail and the other evil consequences of criminal punishment, especially for sexual offences, are well understood. It is surely extraordinary that among the things which Sir Patrick says are to be considered before we legislate against immorality these appear nowhere; not even as 'practical considerations,' let alone 'theoretical limits.' To any theory which, like this one, asserts that the criminal law may be used on the vague ground that the preservation of morality is essential to society and yet omits to stress the need for critical scrutiny, our reply should be: 'Morality, what crimes may be committed in thy name!'"

5. **Questions on the Hart-Devlin Debate.** Putting aside the "practical limits" on the reach of the criminal law to which Lord Devlin alludes, do you agree with his theoretical argument that the enforcement of morality, as such, should be a sufficient reason for criminalization? Or do you agree with Professor Hart, and the Wolfenden Committee, that criminalization should be predicated upon the existence of a demonstrable social impact independent of repercussions on the moral code? To the extent that you agree with Devlin, how does one assess the disintegrative effect of a proposal to decriminalize any particular conduct, such as adultery, homosexuality, bestiality, or incest between consenting adults? How does one determine what parts of the common morality are so essential to the existence of the society that they may legitimately be enforced by criminal sanctions? On the other hand, if you agree with Hart, what kind of social harm, and what type of empirical verification, are necessary to establish a sound predicate for criminalization? Can you defend prohibitions against incest between consenting adults, bestiality, cruelty to animals, or abuse of a corpse in terms that are compatible with the libertarian position? [f]

6. **Offenses Against Decency.** Recall that Mill acknowledged the legitimacy of punishing, as an "offense against decency," an act occurring in public that would be within the sphere of liberty if it occurred in private. Indeed, every penal code includes bans on public sexual activity, public nudity, and other forms of indecent conduct. See, for example, §§ 251.1 and 250.2 of the Model Penal Code. Section 251.1 prohibits "any lewd act which [the actor] knows is likely to be observed

[f] Prohibitions against cruelty to animals, especially as applied to scientific research, have attracted renewed interest. See T. Regan, The Case for Animal Rights (1983). Regan's book is reviewed in R. Dresser, Respecting and Protecting Nonhuman Animals; Regan's Case for Animal Rights, 1984 A.B.F.Res.J. 831. For a recent analysis of incest, see Hermann and Wilcox, An Economic Analysis of Incest: Prohibition, Behavior and Punishment, 25 St.L.U.L.J. 735 (1982).

by others who would be affronted or alarmed," and Section 250.2, prohibits, inter alia, the making of "unreasonable noise or offensively coarse utterance, gesture or display. . . ." What is the theoretical basis for these provisions? Lord Devlin argues in The Enforcement of Morals 120 (1965) that they must be grounded on the idea that it is legitimate for society to protect its citizens from conduct which they find offensive only because of prevailing moral sentiments:

> "[Why] do we object to the public exhibition of a false morality and call it indecency? If we thought that unrestricted indulgence in the sexual passions was as good a way of life as any other for those who liked it, we should find nothing indecent in the practice of it either in public or in private. It would become no more indecent than kissing in public. Decency as an objective depends on the belief in continence as a virtue which requires sexual activity to be kept within prescribed bounds."

It follows, Lord Devlin argues, that the prevention of morally offensive conduct, as such, is a sufficient reason for criminalizing acts occurring in public. Yet, if this is true, he asks, why should the same not be true for private actions? Professor Hart, in Law, Liberty and Morality 45–48 (1963), gives the following answer to this question: *

> "It may no doubt be objected that too much has been made . . . of the distinction between what is done in public and what is done in private. For offence to feelings, it may be said, is given not only when immoral activities or their commercial preliminaries are thrust upon unwilling eyewitnesses, but also when those who strongly condemn certain sexual practices as immoral learn that others indulge in them in private. Because this is so, it is pointless to attend to the distinction between what is done privately and what is done in public; and if we do not attend to it, then the policies of punishing men for mere immorality and punishing them for conduct offensive to the feelings of others, though conceptually distinct, would not differ in practice. All conduct strongly condemned as immoral would then be punishable.

> "It is important not to confuse this argument with the thesis . . . that the preservation of an existing social morality is itself a value justifying the use of coercion. The present argument invokes in support of the legal enforcement of morality not the values of morality but Mill's own principle that coercion may be justifiably used to prevent harm to others. Various objections may be made to this use of the principle. It may be said that the distress occasioned by the bare thought that others are offending in private against morality cannot constitute 'harm,' except in a few neurotic or hypersensitive persons who are literally 'made ill' by this thought. Others may admit that such distress is harm, even in the case of normal persons, but argue that it is too

slight to outweigh the great misery caused by the legal enforcement of sexual morality.

"Although these objections are not without force, they are of
subsidiary importance. The fundamental objection surely is that
a right to be protected from the distress which is inseparable
from the bare knowledge that others are acting in ways you
think wrong, cannot be acknowledged by anyone who recognises
individual liberty as a value. For the extension of the utilitarian
principle that coercion may be used to protect men from harm, so
as to include their protection from this form of distress, cannot
stop there. If distress incident to the belief that others are doing
wrong is harm, so also is the distress incident to the belief that
others are doing what you do not want them to do. To punish
people for causing this form of distress would be tantamount to
punishing them simply because others object to what they do;
and the only liberty that could coexist with this extension of the
utilitarian principle is liberty to do those things to which no one
seriously objects. Such liberty plainly is quite nugatory. Recognition of individual liberty as a value involves, as a minimum,
acceptance of the principle that the individual may do what he
wants, even if others are distressed when they learn what it is
that he does—unless, of course, there are other good grounds for
forbidding it. No social order which accords to individual liberty
any value could also accord the right to be protected from
distress thus occasioned.

"Protection from shock or offence to feelings caused by some
public display is, as most legal systems recognise, another matter. The distinction may sometimes be a fine one. It is so, in
those cases such as the desecration of venerated objects or
ceremonies where there would be no shock or offence to feeling,
if those on whom the public display is obtruded had not subscribed to certain religious or moral beliefs. Nonetheless the use
of punishment to protect those made vulnerable to the public
display by their own beliefs leaves the offender at liberty to do
the same thing in private, if he can. It is not tantamount to
punishing men simply because others object to what they do."

Hart uses the bigamy prohibition to demonstrate "the need to
distinguish between the immorality of a practice and its aspect as a
public offensive act or nuisance":

"In most common-law jurisdictions it is a criminal offence for
a married person during the lifetime of an existing husband or
wife to go through a ceremony of marriage with another person,
even if the other person knows of the existing marriage. The
punishment of bigamy not involving deception is curious in the
following respect. In England and in many other jurisdictions
where it is punishable, the sexual cohabitation of the parties is
not a criminal offence. If a married man cares to cohabit with
another woman—or even several other women—he may do so
with impunity so far as the criminal law is concerned. He may

set up house and pretend that he is married: he may celebrate his union with champagne and a distribution of wedding cake and with all the usual social ceremonial of a valid marriage. None of this is illegal; but if he goes through a ceremony of marriage, the law steps in not merely to declare it invalid but to punish the bigamist.

"Why does the law interefere at this point, leaving the substantial immorality of sexual cohabitation alone? Various answers have been given to this question. Some have suggested that the purpose of the legal punishment of bigamy is to protect public records from confusion, or to frustrate schemes to misrepresent illegitimate children as legitimate. The American Law Institute suggests in its commentary on the draft Model Penal Code that bigamous adultery, even where it does not involve deception, might call for punishment because it is a public affront and provocation to the first spouse, and also because cohabitation under the colour of matrimony is specially likely 'to result in desertion, non-support and divorce'. These, it is urged, are harms to individuals which the criminal law may properly seek to prevent by punishment.

"Some at least of these suggested grounds seem more ingenious than convincing. The harms they stress may be real enough; yet many may still think that a case for punishing bigamy would remain even if these harms were unlikely to result, or if they were catered for by the creation of specific offences which penalized not the bigamy but, for example, the causing of false statements to be entered into official records. Perhaps most who find these various justifications of the existing law unconvincing but still wish to retain it would urge that in a country where deep religious significance is attached to a monogamous marriage and to the act of solemnizing it, the law against bigamy should be accepted as an attempt to protect religious feelings from offence by a public act desecrating the ceremony. [The] question is whether those who think that the use of the criminal law for these purposes is in principle justified are inconsistent if they also deny that the law may be used to punish immorality as such.

"I do not think that there is any inconsistency in this combination of attitudes, but there is a need for one more important distinction. It is important to see that if, in the case of bigamy, the law intervenes in order to protect religious sensibilities from outrage by a public act, the bigamist is punished neither as irreligious nor as immoral but as a nuisance. For the law is then concerned with the offensiveness to others of his public conduct, not with the immorality of his private conduct, which, in most countries, it leaves altogether unpunished. In this case, as in the case of ordinary crimes which cause physical harm, the protection of those likely to be affected is certainly an intelligible aim for the law to pursue, and it certainly could not be said of this case that 'the function of the criminal law is to enforce a moral principle and nothing else.' . . ."

Lord Devlin was unpersuaded. In The Enforcement of Morals 138 (1965), he states:

"Bigamy violates neither good manners nor decency. It is therefore a difficult crime for Mill's disciples to deal with. When it is committed without deception it harms no one; yet in these days of easy divorce bigamists do not arouse sympathy as homosexuals do and no one is very enthusiastic about altering the law in their favour. A variety of reasons for leaving the law as it is have been put forward, but the one selected by Professor Hart seems to me to wound Mill's doctrine more sharply than any other. A marriage in a registry office is only in form a public act. Mill's exception is grounded not upon a formal distinction between public and private but upon the right of society not to have obnoxious conduct forced on its attention. No one with deep religious feelings is likely to attend in the registry office; and the chance of the happy couple as they leave the office running into a man who happens to combine deep religious feelings with the knowledge that one of the parties has been married before is remote."

Do you agree with Professor Hart or Lord Devlin on the theoretical basis for offenses against public decency? Do you think the bigamy prohibition is defensible in libertarian terms? [g]

7. **Paternalism in Health and Safety.** It is important to recall that Mill finds paternalism in matters of health and morals equally objectionable; he contends that coercion is permissible only to prevent direct harm to others and that the individual's "own good, either physical or moral, is not sufficient warrant." Do you think these grounds for intervention are theoretically distinguishable? Is the ethical basis for criminalization stronger in connection with consumption-related drug offenses, for example, than it is for consensual sex offenses?

The possibility of drawing a theoretical distinction between enforcement of morals and paternalism in matters of health or physical safety was debated by Lord Devlin and Professor Hart. Lord Devlin argues that the function of several criminal offenses "is simply to enforce a moral principle and nothing else," and includes among his examples the bans on euthanasia and duelling. In Law, Liberty and Morality 31–33 (1963),* Professor Hart responds as follows:

". . . The rules excluding the victim's consent as a defence to charges of murder or assault may perfectly well be explained as a piece of paternalism, designed to protect individuals against themselves. Mill no doubt might have protested against a paternalistic policy of using the law to protect even a consenting

[g] See generally Conway, Law, Liberty and Indecency, 49 Philos. 135 (1974).

1963 by the Board of Trustees of the Leland Stanford Junior University.

* Reprinted with the permission of the publishers, Stanford University Press. ©

victim from bodily harm nearly as much as he protested against laws used merely to enforce positive morality; but this does not mean that these two policies are identical. . . .

"Lord Devlin says of the attitude of the criminal law to the victim's consent that if the law existed for the protection of the individual there would be no reason why he should avail himself of it if he did not want it. But paternalism—the protection of people against themselves—is a perfectly coherent policy. . . . The supply of drugs or narcotics, even to adults, except under medical prescription is punishable by the criminal law, and it would seem very dogmatic to say of the law creating this offence . . . that the law was concerned not with the protection of the would-be purchasers against themselves, but only with the punishment of the seller for his immorality. If, as seems obvious, paternalism is a possible explanation of such laws, it is also possible in the case of the rule excluding the consent of the victim as a defence to a charge of assault. In neither case are we forced to conclude with Lord Devlin that the law's 'function' is 'to enforce a moral principle and nothing else.'

". . . Mill carried his protests against paternalism to lengths that may now appear to us fantastic. He cites the example of restrictions of the sale of drugs, and criticises them as interferences with the liberty of the would-be purchaser rather than with that of the seller. No doubt if we no longer sympathise with this criticism this is due, in part, to a general decline in the belief that individuals know their own interests best, and to an increased awareness of a great range of factors which diminish the significance to be attached to an apparently free choice or to consent. Choices may be made or consent given without adequate reflection or appreciation of the consequences; or in pursuit of merely transitory desires; or in various predicaments when the judgment is likely to be clouded; or under inner psychological compulsion; or under pressure by others of a kind too subtle to be susceptible of proof in a law court. . . .

"Certainly a modification in Mill's principles is required, if they are to accommodate the rule of criminal law under discussion or other instances of paternalism. But the modified principles would not abandon the objection to the use of the criminal law merely to enforce positive morality. They would only have to provide that harming others is something we may still seek to prevent by use of the criminal law, even when the victims consent to or assist in the acts which are harmful to them."

In The Enforcement of Morals 135–36 (1965), Lord Devlin responds that Hart tries to stake out a position as a "physical paternalist and a moral individualist" and that such a distinction is illogical:

"[If] there is an element of physical paternalism in the law that forbids masochism and euthanasia these crimes seem to me as good examples as any that could be selected to illustrate the difficulty in practice of distinguishing between physical and moral paternalism. Neither in principle nor in practice can a line be drawn between legislation controlling the individual's physical welfare and legislation controlling his moral welfare. If paternalism be the principle, no father of a family would content himself with looking after his children's welfare and leaving their morals to themselves. If society has an interest which permits it to legislate in the one case, why not in the other? If, on the other hand, we are grown up enough to look after our own morals, why not after our own bodies?"

The drug laws provide a useful vehicle for testing your views on the theoretical questions raised by Mill's essay and debated by Hart and Devlin. Are prohibitions against availability and use of psychoactive drugs ethically defensible? Does it provide "sufficient warrant" that the prevailing public opinion regards use of psychoactive drugs for purposes of "getting high" to be morally wrong? Is it "sufficient warrant" that society is protecting the individual from harming himself? Does the legitimacy of the prohibition depend upon the social impact of drug consumption? If so, does it depend upon a determination that the use of the particular drug is likely to cause disordered or violent behavior that could harm someone else? Or is criminalization permissible if use of the drug would impair the person's health or behavior in a way likely to burden the society's health-care and social-service systems? Would your ethical analysis differ according to whether the prohibition was limited to trafficking offenses or also included possession and use offenses?

NOTES ON THE EFFECTS OF CRIMINALIZATION

1. **Introduction.** Although Stephen and Devlin reject the libertarian effort to define theoretical limits on the reach of the criminal law, they both acknowledge that there are many practical arguments against the criminalization of private vice. In Liberty, Equality, Fraternity 159–61 (1874), Stephen emphasizes that "criminal law is at once by far the most powerful and by far the roughest engine which society can use for any purpose." He continues:

"It strikes so hard that it can be enforced only on the gravest occasions, and with every sort of precaution against abuse or mistake. Before an act can be treated as a crime, it ought to be capable of distinct definition and of specific proof, and it ought also to be of such a nature that it is worthwhile to prevent it at the risk of inflicting great damage, direct and indirect, upon those who commit it. These conditions are seldom, if ever, fulfilled by mere vices. It would obviously be impossible to indict a man for ingratitude or perfidy. Such charges are too vague for specific discussion and distinct proof on the one side, and disproof on the other. Moreover, the expense of the investigations necessary for the legal punishment of such conduct would be enormous. It would be necessary to go into an infinite number of delicate and subtle inquiries which would tear off all privacy from the lives of a large number of persons. These considerations are, I think, conclusive reasons against treating vice in general as a crime.

"The excessive harshness of criminal law is also a circumstance which very greatly narrows the range of its application. . . . A law which enters into a direct contest with fierce imperious passion, which the person who feels it does not admit to be bad, and which is not directly injurious to others, will generally do more harm than good; and this is perhaps the principal reason why it is impossible to legislate directly against unchastity, unless it takes forms which everyone regards as monstrous and horrible. . . ."

Surely Stephen is right when he observes that socially disapproved behavior should not be punished by criminal sanctions if this will "do more harm than good." The question arises, however, whether it is possible to identify more specific criteria for assessing the effects of criminalization and for determining, in a given case, whether its costs outweigh its benefits. Recent efforts to identify such criteria are summarized in the following notes.

2. **Assessing Benefits.** Empirical assessments of the benefits of any particular criminal prohibition are not easily made. Perhaps the main difficulty is the need to isolate the incremental preventive effects of any given scheme of criminalization beyond those that would be achieved in any event by non-criminal methods of legal regulation and other means of social control. Consider, for example, the utility of criminal sanctions to punish parents who physically abuse their children. What would be the prevalence of child abuse if this conduct were not criminally punishable? To what extent does the threatened imposition of criminal punishment supplement the preventive effect of civil schemes for state intervention and termination of parental rights? To what extent does any type of legal control, civil or criminal, shape parental behavior in this context when one takes into account personal pathology and the impact of community expectations and pressures? On the other hand, to what extent does criminalization reinforce and perpetuate proper parental attitudes regarding the use of violence to discipline and control their children? Obviously these questions are not easily researched.[a]

A second problem is presented by the need to quantify the behavioral impact of criminalization. Take the offense of driving while intoxicated (DWI) as an example. Initially it is necessary to determine the degree to which the precise scheme of criminalization being studied reduces the number of incidents of drunken driving.[b] However, as is the case with many criminal offenses, the DWI prohibition is designed

---

[a] For an illuminating discussion of this issue, see Rosenthal, Physical Abuse of Children by Parents: The Criminalization Decision, 7 Am.J.Crim.L. 141 (1979).

[b] As the materials at pages 8–30, supra, demonstrated, this preventive effect can be achieved in a variety of ways—by deterring potential offenders, by shaping and reinforcing beliefs and attitudes that are unfavorable to the objectionable conduct, and by affording a basis for preventing recidivism through the punishment of individual violators.

to prevent harm by reducing risk-creating conduct. Thus, a precise calculation of the social benefits of the scheme of criminalization requires a further determination regarding the degree to which it reduces the social costs associated with the harms ultimately feared—in the case of DWI, this would mean the health and welfare costs associated with accidents and fatalities that are attributable to drunken driving.

A third difficulty involved in assessing the social benefits of criminalization arises from the fact that "criminalization" is a variable that is itself subject to manipulation. For one thing, the behavioral effects obviously will depend on the precise definition of the prohibited conduct. For example, DWI can be defined as: (i) impaired driving due to intoxication; or (ii) driving while one's faculties are impaired by the effects of intoxicating substances; or (iii) having a designated level of alcohol in one's blood, a level which itself can be varied. In addition, the deterrent effect of any particular prohibition will depend upon the probability of apprehension and conviction and the magnitude of the anticipated penalty. As is noted in the materials on deterrence considered at pages 19–22, supra, it is generally believed that the deterrent effect of a prohibition can be affected by manipulating either of these variables.

It must be emphasized, of course, that the use of criminal sanctions for most of the behavior covered in any criminal code is not open to serious question; in these contexts, attention is focused mainly on the determination of the optimal combination of probability and severity of punishment. However, in some contexts, the conclusion that a criminal sanction is useful at all may depend on a set of assumptions about the level of enforcement and the severity of the effective penalty. Specifically, it might be determined that the optimal scheme of legal control will include some or all of the distinctive features of a criminal sanction *only* at a specified level of enforcement, and that otherwise the costs of criminalization will exceed its benefits.

3. **Assessing Costs.** Obviously the costs of any scheme of criminal sanctions will also depend directly on the level of enforcement and the characteristics of the penalties imposed on violators. Indeed, some of the distinctive costs of criminalization frequently mentioned in the literature arise only under certain conditions of enforcement and punishment. Also, several of the special problems associated with the criminal process are primarily ethical in nature and therefore defy quantitative measurement. These observations should be kept in mind while reviewing the following summary of the considerations usually regarded as relevant to the task of assessing the costs of criminalization.

(i) **Deterrence of Socially Valuable Behavior.** As is noted in the materials on obscenity at pages 80–90, supra, criminal prohibitions, like other types of legal regulation, can deter lawful behavior on the margins of the forbidden conduct. The magnitude of this effect will vary in relation to the indeterminacy of the prohibition and the instrumental nature of the prohibited behavior. In most situations, of course, the marginally lawful behavior will be without social value and its deterrence therefore will not constitute a cost of the prohibition. However, if the marginal behavior does have social value, its reduction must be counted as a cost of the prohibition.

(ii) **Enforcement Expenditures.** Although the level of enforcement can be varied, the costs of an existing or proposed criminal prohibition obviously include the resources devoted to the detection and punishment of violators. Although police departments, prosecutors, courts, and correctional agencies usually do not have line-item budgets linked to various offenses, it is possible to make general estimates of the costs incurred in enforcing a particular prohibition at any given time. It should be noted, however, that one cannot automatically conclude that these costs would be saved if the criminal prohibition were repealed or if the level of enforcement were reduced. This is because criminal-justice budgets typically do not vary with the number of offenses enforced, and most of the expenditure is attributable to the costs of maintaining the system itself. In any case, any resources identifiably related to enforcement of any particular offense are best seen as "opportunity costs"—resources that would otherwise have been spent in enforcing other penal laws.

(iii) **Effects on the Individual.** Not all of the "pains" of punishment are measurable in economic terms, or even in psychological ones. However, it is possible to describe the effects of arrest, prosecution, conviction, and sentence on individual offenders. These include reduced productivity attributable to stigmatization and confinement, adverse impact on dependents, and the psychic and physical harms that can occur as a result of imprisonment. Such effects must be taken into account in a comprehensive assessment of the social costs of any particular criminal prohibition. Obviously, these effects vary among individuals. They also are linked directly to the level of enforcement and the severity of the deprivations (both before and after conviction) that are experienced by the offender in connection with particular offenses.

(iv) **Effects on Privacy.** Stephen and Devlin both acknowledges the dangers of criminalizing behavior that occurs in private without direct injury to another. The problem is that enforcement of these laws requires the police to employ intrusive investigative techniques that offend widely-shared expectations of privacy. More recently, Professor Packer has observed, in The Limits of the Criminal Sanction 283–86 (1968), that any criminal prohibition that requires systematic use of decoys, undercover agents, residential searches, and electronic surveillance in order to detect violations "should be suspect." These techniques, he argues, "are so at odds with values of privacy and human dignity that we should resort to them only under the most exigent circumstances." Professor Packer finds the vice laws especially objectionable because they "thrust the police into the role of snoopers and harassers." The enforcement of laws against bribery, weapons transactions, and virtually all possessory offenses also require systematic use of intrusive investigative techniques. Should these offenses be "suspect" also?

(v) **Criminogenic Effects.** Some prohibitions have criminogenic consequences—that is, they create circumstances that increase the likelihood of criminal activity that would not have occurred in the absence of the prohibition. It has been clearly demonstrated, for example, that drug-dependent persons commit property crimes, or engage in prostitution or retail drug trafficking, to obtain money to buy illicit drugs at high prices—drugs that would cost very little if they were legitimately available. Also, prohibitions of drug use and homosexuality are thought to force persons who engage in such behavior into association with persons who engage in other criminal activities, thereby increasing the likelihood that they too will develop deviant lifestyles.

One of the most lively controversies in the recent criminology literature concerns the so-called "labeling" hypothesis. According to labeling theorists, official responses to deviance, especially through the stigmatizing processes of the criminal law, increase the likelihood of further deviance by individuals who did not already view themselves as "outsiders" before they were so labeled. To the extent that this phenomenon does occur, it has special implications for the criminalization of conduct, such as drug use and petty shoplifting, that is relatively prevalent among young and otherwise law-abiding persons. It should be noted, however, that the validity of the labeling theory is difficult to test because it requires proof that recidivist offenders would not have continued or diversified their deviant conduct in the absence of official intervention.

(vi) **Costs of Under-Enforcement.** Economic theory demonstrates that the optimal level of enforcement is something less than 100 per cent. Although relatively full enforcement is usually sought in connection with the most serious predatory offenses, the actual level of enforcement is determined by the allocation of investigative and prosecutorial resources as well as by the prevalence of the prohibited behavior. However, violations of some laws are so pervasive and difficult to detect that they will be significantly under-enforced no matter what the police choose to do. Moreover, to the extent that these laws are enforced at all, the conditions are established for arbitrariness in the administration of the penal law. The threat to the rule of law is aggravated even further if the criminal conduct is not uniformly condemned by the prevailing public morality.

The costs of under-enforcement are especially palpable in connection with laws proscribing various types of consensual sexual conduct. Professor Kadish elaborates this point in his article, The Crisis of Overcriminalization, 374 Annals 157, 159–60 (1967): *

"[Laws in many jurisdictions prohibit] extra-marital and abnormal sexual intercourse between a man and a woman. Whether or not Kinsey's judgment is accurate that 95 per cent of the

---

* Reprinted with permission from the Crisis of Overcriminalization by Sanford Kadish in volume no. 374 of The Annals of the American Academy of Political and Social Science. © 1967, by the American Academy of Political and Social Science.

population are made potential criminals by these laws, no one doubts that their standard of sexual conduct is not adhered to by vast numbers in the community . . .; nor is it disputed that there is no effort to enforce these laws. The traditional function of the criminal law, therefore—to curtail socially threatening behavior through the threat of punishment and the incapacitation and rehabilitation of offenders—is quite beside the point. Thurman Arnold surely had it right when he observed that these laws 'are unenforced because we want to continue our conduct, and unrepealed because we want to preserve our morals.'

"But law enforcement pays a price for using the criminal law in this way. First, the moral message communicated by the law is contradicted by the total absence of enforcement; for while the public sees the conduct condemned in words, it also sees in the dramatic absence of prosecution that it is not condemned in deed. Moral adjurations vulnerable to a charge of hypocrisy are self-defeating no less in law than elsewhere. Second, the spectacle of nullification of the legislature's solemn commands is an unhealthy influence on law enforcement generally. It tends to breed a cynicism and an indifference to the criminal-law processes which augment tendencies toward disrespect for those who make and enforce the law, a disrespect which is already widely in evidence. . . . Finally these laws invite discriminatory enforcement against persons selected for prosecution on grounds unrelated to the evil against which these laws are purportedly addressed. . . ." [c]

In Marijuana Use and Criminal Sanctions 31–35 (1980), Professor Bonnie emphasized the threat to the rule of law as a reason for decriminalizing possession of marijuana:

". . . No criminal law can be fairly or effectively enforced unless it commands a popular consensus. Yet, the consensus which supported the marijuana laws from 1915 to 1965 evaporated as soon as the prohibition encountered the rigors of public dialogue. This is not to say that the prohibition lacks the support of a numerical majority. The point is that utility or propriety of a criminal law is not measured in votes but in shared values. . . . [M]arijuana prohibition does not command the minimum amount of public support necessary to sustain and reinforce a criminal prohibition. [d]

[c] Compare ALI, Model Penal Code and Commentaries, Part II, 435 (1980) (Note on Fornication and Adultery):

"Like other dead-letter statutes, unenforced laws against fornication and adultery lend themselves to abuse. They may be invoked only in special circumstances, such as relations between persons of different races or liaisons involving a political figure. . . . Use of widely disregarded laws to reach a few individuals selected for reasons wholly unrelated to the conduct for which they are punished is obviously undesirable. It comes close to a de-facto delegation to law enforcement authorities of a power to decide for themselves who shall be subjected to penal sanctions and why."

[Footnote by eds.]

[d] Compare J. Stephen, Liberty, Equality, Fraternity 173–74 (1874):

"Legislation ought in all cases to be graduated to the existing level of morals in the time and country in which it is employed. You cannot punish anything

"As a result, the law suffers disobedience and ridicule. [M]illions of Americans use marijuana [and] the moral force of the criminal law wanes with each undetected or unenforced violation. . . . Since the larger society generally may not view its marijuana offenders, who are overwhelmingly young, as . . . deserving of punishment, the effort is now made to select from the near half-million persons who are arrested each year, those few who should continue to be processed through the system. . . .

"The net result is that the police, prosecutors and the courts aim to ameliorate the consequences of criminalization. The police respond unsystematically and inconsistently; the prosecutors decline to prosecute, sometimes with screening guidelines, most of the time without them; and the judges respond according to their own views of the offense and of their role as judges. Police, prosecutors and courts roam at large in a sea of discretion because the public doesn't want to punish but the legislature doesn't want to repeal. . . .

"To the extent that the mere existence of a criminal prohibition, credible or not, functions as a 'moralizing' preventive influence, it is conceivable that society could reap some of the benefits of criminalization, with little lost, simply by leaving the law on the books and failing to enforce it or enforcing it only sporadically. . . .

"However legitimate this use of the criminal law may be for behavior like adultery, which touches the core of our public morality, it has almost a comic quality in reference to marijuana use. Marijuana use is a matter of minor public consequence. . . . The law is no longer defended on the intensely moralistic grounds which characterized its days as a 'killer of youth' and a stepping stone to both heroin and a life of debauchery. Such a blatant insult to the rule of law should surely not be tolerated in the name of reinforcing norms whose moral supports have long since fallen away."

Many commentators have suggested that the penal law should not include offenses that will not be enforced, or will be enforced only sporadically. Do you agree? Is it appropriate to enact or retain a criminal prohibition simply to declare and symbolize the prevailing morality with no expectation that it will be enforced? Do you think the costs of under-enforcement are higher in connection with adultery or marijuana use? Why?

(vii) **The Crime Tariff.** Prohibitions against commercial activity in gambling, sex, pornography, and drugs clearly reduce the supply of the prohibited goods and services, but so long as there continue to be willing buyers, an illicit commercial market will develop. Of course,

which public opinion, as expressed in the common practice of society, does not strenuously and unequivocally condemn. To try to do so is a sure way to produce gross hypocrisy and furious reaction. To be able to punish, a moral majority must be overwhelming. . . ."

[Footnote by eds.]

the threat of criminal punishment will reduce the number of producers and sellers; and reduced competition, together with the suppliers' costs of avoiding detection, will drive up the price. As a result, the degree to which the prohibition actually reduces the undesired activity depends on the elasticity of demand—i.e., on the extent to which potential consumers are responsive to the increase in price. Whatever the size of the illegal market, the prohibition's main economic effect in any case is to establish what the economists call "barriers to entry" and to assure a high return for entrepreneurs who are willing to assume the risks of violating the law. Professor Packer referred to this economic effect as a "crime tariff."

What are the social consequences of the crime tariff? For one thing, the tremendous revenues generated by illegal trafficking in prohibited goods and services are untaxed. For another, black-market entrepreneurs obviously have strong incentives, and substantial capital, to take whatever measures are necessary to protect their investment and reduce the risk of punishment. Pervasive corruption of law enforcement officials is an all-too-frequent result. Moreover, high crime tariffs for commerce in drugs, sex, and gambling establish the economic conditions for large-scale criminal organizations to flourish. Finally, to the extent that the illicit good or service can vary in quality, society forgoes the benefits of regulation: prostitutes are not required to be examined and treated for venereal disease; gambling establishments are not monitored for fraudulent practices; and drugs are not tested for purity.

4. **Weighing Costs and Benefits.** As is apparent from the examples given in the preceding note, recent discussion of the costs and benefits of the criminal sanction has focused primarily on "vice" crimes such as adultery, prostitution, homosexuality, drug offenses, and gambling. Professor Junker has argued that the cost-benefit argument for decriminalization is really libertarianism in disguise, and that its proponents implicitly devalue the legitimacy and social benefits of the prohibitions they challenge. Junker, Criminalization and Criminogenesis, 19 U.C.L.A.L.Rev. 697 (1972). Do you agree? Doubts about the ethical legitimacy of criminalization in these contexts naturally will be reinforced by arguments concerning the costs of these prohibitions. However, how should these considerations affect a legislator who is convinced that criminalization of these behaviors is ethically permissible and socially beneficial? Do you know how to weigh costs and benefits in the context of vice crimes? In other contexts?

Professor Kadish concedes that his criticisms of criminal sanctions against the so-called vice crimes do not suggest a general principle "for determining how much of what costs are too much for what benefits." Kadish, More on Overcriminalization: A Reply to Professor Junker, 19 U.C.L.A.L.Rev. 719, 721 (1972). He nonetheless defends the cost-benefit approach as follows:

"The argument is not that any of these adverse consequences affords a sufficient reason for abandoning every criminal law whose use produces it. It is simply that in any use of the criminal law a particular adverse consequence may be so severe and so combined with other kinds of adverse consequences . . . that, considering the relative importance of the purposes of that law and the extent to which they are achieved, a prudential judgment would be to abandon it.

"[T]here is a big problem in this cost-benefit approach to deciding what to make criminal. The problem is that it is easier to state what the costs and benefits may be than to measure their quantity with any degree of accuracy or to assess them with reliability and objectivity."

NOTES ON DRUG OFFENSES: A CASE STUDY IN CRIMINALIZATION

1. **Background.** The penal codes of every state and the federal government prohibit production, distribution, and possession of "controlled substances" outside authorized medical or scientific channels. First enacted during the late 19th and early 20th centuries,[a] these laws cover a wide variety of psychoactive substances, many of which have no recognized medical uses. Notwithstanding the prohibitions, many of these drugs, such as heroin, cocaine, and marijuana, are available on an illicit market and are widely used. Drug offenses now account for a substantial proportion of all criminal cases.

Judgments regarding the legitimacy and utility of these prohibitions require attention to all of the considerations explored in the preceding materials. The literature on the subject includes extensive discussion of the ethical dimensions of criminalization as well as the costs and benefits of drug prohibitions.[b] A framework for assessing the social utility of the drug laws, and for identifying the relevant empirical questions, is developed by Professor Bonnie in Discouraging the Use of Alcohol, Tobacco, and Other Drugs: The Effects of Legal Controls and Restrictions, 2 Advances in Substance Abuse: Behavioral and Biological Research 145–84 (1981).

Professor Bonnie begins with the assertion that the utility of drug prohibitions should be assessed from a public-health perspective. He

[a] The history of the drug laws is reviewed by D. Musto, The American Disease: Origins of Narcotic Control (1973). On the history of the marijuana laws, see R. Bonnie & C. Whitebread, The Marihuana Conviction: A History of Marihuana Prohibition in the United States (1974).

[b] For a general discussion of the subject, see N. Zinberg & J. Robertson, Drugs and the Public (1972). On the marijuana laws, see A. Hellman, The Laws Against Marijuana: The Price We Pay (1975); J. Kaplan, Marijuana: The New Prohibition (1970). On the heroin laws, see J. Kaplan, The Hardest Drug: Heroin and Public Policy (1983).

For an elaborate critique of the moral and paternalistic justifications for drug prohibitions, and an argument in favor of a right "to undertake forms of drug experience," see Richards, Drug Use and the Rights of the Person: A Moral Argument for Decriminalization of Certain Forms of Drug Use, 33 Rutgers L.Rev. 607 (1981). Professor Richards' philosophical position on the scope of the criminal law is further developed in Commercial Sex and the Rights of the Person: A Moral Argument for the Decriminalization of Prostitution, 127 U.Pa.L.Rev. 1195 (1979), and Human Rights and the Moral Foundations of the Substantive Criminal Law, 13 Ga.L.Rev. 1395 (1979).

says that the public-health consequences of drug use derive from the resources that are devoted to the treatment and social support of persons whose health and functioning become impaired. He emphasizes that the risks of impaired functioning are associated primarily with chronic or heavy drug use, especially by psychologically vulnerable persons; in contrast "moderate" or occasional use of these drugs by psychologically healthy individuals does not appear to have significant public-health consequences. Accordingly, Professor Bonnie suggests, governmental efforts to discourage and reduce *all* non-medical consumption of psychoactive drugs must be predicated on the conclusion that it is not otherwise possible to prevent undesirable patterns of use.

2. **Prohibition or Regulation.** Professor Bonnie emphasizes that a public-health model of drug control can be implemented either by a regulatory approach, as it is for alcohol and tobacco, or by a prohibitory approach, as it is for controlled substances.[c] A regulatory approach, permitting the substance to be legitimately available for non-medical uses, would obviously maximize human freedom and would be preferred, prima facie, under libertarian principles. In addition, the "costs" of a prohibitory approach toward sumptuary behavior are well-known. Accordingly, Professor Bonnie notes, a decision "to utilize a prohibitory approach—to proscribe production and distribution outside medical channels—would seem to be predicated on the following hypothesis: that the social costs sustained in the effort to enforce the prohibition, together with the aggregate social costs of illicit use, are less than the social costs that would be incurred in connection with less restrictive policies." It follows, Professor Bonnie observes, that a comprehensive assessment of the utility of an existing prohibitory scheme requires (i) estimation of its current effect on aggregate levels and patterns of consumption and (ii) speculation regarding the conditions of consumption that would exist under alternative schemes of availability.

Assessments of this nature will vary in connection with specific drugs. Professor Bonnie illustrates this inquiry in the two contexts in which the existing law has been most strongly challenged:

"Critics of marijuana prohibition have challenged the basic premises of the public-health approach to this drug. They argue, for example, that the risk of individual impairment arising from use of the drug is not great enough to justify restrictions on personal choice and that government may not legitimately aim to

[c] From a purely economic standpoint, the legal distinction between regulation and prohibition is an artificial one. As Professor Bonnie notes, the behavioral effects of a prohibitory scheme—and its costs and benefits—are intimately related to the patterns of enforcement:

"[T]he promulgation and enforcement of controls against non-medical availability of controlled substances has the primary effect of shaping the behavior of those who operate on the legitimate market; however, since a 'black' market inevitably will spring up to meet the demand for proscribed uses, the manner in which the law is enforced against the illicit suppliers will affect the price and accessibility of the illegally marketed substances and can presumably affect thereby the patterns and consequences of their illicit use. A focus on enforcement behavior calls attention to the 'regulatory' effects (influencing price and other conditions of availability) that can be achieved within the framework of a prohibitory regime. . . ."

discourage all use in order to prevent excessive or otherwise unhealthy use. [They] also argue that prohibition is not an effective way to implement the public-health model, contending that the costs of current prohibitory policies exceed the presumed aggregate costs that would be incurred under a regulatory regime, even one which resulted in substantially increased consumption.

"It seems logical to assume that cannabis products, though widely available on the illicit market, are currently less accessible and more costly than they would be under a different legal regime and that the inconvenience, cost, and social risk associated with black-market transactions depresses consumption. But how much? Obviously this question cannot be answered with confidence, as the answer would depend on unverifiable assertions about what would happen to consumption under any of several alternative legal arrangements. But the question deserves more systematic attention than it has thus far received. . . .

"Similarly, the restriction of access to heroin—especially the unavailability of the substance on a more or less controlled basis to heroin-dependent persons—has been challenged on the ground that the costs of the total prohibition exceed the presumed aggregate costs that would be incurred under a regime that permitted heroin to be available to addicts, even if this resulted in an increase in the number of addicts and an increase in the intensity or duration of their addiction. Again, the consequences of an alternative legal regime cannot be established with confidence; however, many commentators have speculated about the likely effects of alternative schemes under which heroin would be legitimately available to the heroin-dependent population. The key variables in this discussion are the relationship between heroin use and criminal behavior and the likely impact of licitly available heroin on the incidence and prevalence of heroin use and dependency. . . ."

Defenders of the existing drug prohibitions do not gainsay the costs of this approach—in expenditure of criminal-justice resources, in official corruption, and in the generation of criminal activity necessitated by the high cost of illicit drugs. However, they argue that the social costs incurred under a regulatory regime would be even higher. In support of this position, public-health officials frequently point out that the estimated social cost of alcohol use under the present regulatory system is $50 billion per year. Should the use of criminal law in this context be predicated on this type of speculation? Is there some point at which the institutional costs of criminalization become intolerable? Does the experience with alcohol prohibition provide a useful comparison?

3. **Consumption-Related Offenses.** Assume that the present prohibitions against producing or distributing drugs for non-medical purposes are to remain intact. Does such a policy necessarily entail a

decision to criminalize consumption itself? Most contemporary commentators have agreed that the use of criminal sanctions for consumption-related behavior raises questions that are ethically and empirically distinct from those raised by laws that restrict legitimate availability. This point was developed in the Final Report of the National Commission on Marihuana and Drug Abuse, Drug Use in America: Problem in Perspective 242–43 (1973), as follows:

"In determining conditions of availability for a psychoactive substance, policy-makers should err in the direction of too much restriction rather than too little. Philosophical and constitutional concerns for individual privacy and freedom of action are touched only indirectly by society's legitimate efforts to resist the adverse consequences of drug availability. Therefore, a presumption exists in favor of restriction, and decisions limiting availability may be defended on speculative grounds. 'What would happen if there were widespread availability?' is a perfectly valid inquiry.

"Too often, however, policy-makers have taken the same perspective and employed a similar line of reasoning in connection with an entirely distinct policy decision: whether and under what circumstances society should intervene in the life of the individual who has chosen to consume a substance outside the legal channels of availability. Here, for philosophical, constitutional, and practical reasons, the presumption in favor of control is reversed: the policy-making perspective must emphasize personal freedom rather than the protection of society. In a free society, the state is obliged to justify restraints on individual liberty, and this justification must rest on facts, not on speculation.

"At the present time, any person who chooses to consume a psychoactive substance outside legally prescribed channels is subject to prosecution and incarceration. In the Commission's view the burden rests on those who would continue this policy."

Obviously, Mill would object to punishment of an individual for choosing to use a drug in a way that does not endanger another person. For the libertarian, criminalization of the consumer would be categorically forbidden, regardless of the aggregate costs and benefits of the prohibition. However, in most contemporary commentary on the drug laws,[d] the inquiry is framed in cost-benefit terms. Professor Bonnie describes the variables relevant to such an inquiry as follows:

"If no categorical bar is posed against consumption sanctions, the legislator must somehow 'weigh' the 'benefits' of sanctions against their 'costs' . . . . On the 'benefit' side, one is presumably measuring 'deterrence' and its derivative social benefits. One is asking how many fewer persons use [the drug] and how

d See generally R. Bonnie, Marijuana Use and Criminal Sanctions: Essays on the Theory and Practice of Decriminalization (1980); M. Rosenthal, Partial Prohibition of Nonmedical Use of Mind-Altering Drugs: Proposals for Change, 16 Hous.L.Rev. 603 (1979).

many more use it less frequently 'because of' the sanctions against use, how many adverse health reactions or behavioral problems are thereby avoided, and how much in the way of public-health and welfare resources are thereby 'saved.'

"On the 'cost' side, one must consider the *individual* costs of perceived injustice, loss of liberty, unfairness and stigma associated with involvement in the legal process. In addition, the policy-maker must consider the *institutional* costs of disrespect for law when an offense is widely ignored and arbitrarily enforced. Finally, there are the *enforcement* costs—the criminal justice resources which are consumed in connection with the enforcement of possession laws and the processing of these cases, resources which might have been 'better' spent [elsewhere]."

Empirical questions regarding the costs of criminalizing the user are relatively easily framed, and data have been compiled on many of them. However, the benefits of these prohibitions are not so easily assessed through empirical investigation. The question is: What do sanctions against consumption-related behavior add to the preventive effect of the proscription on non-medical availability? In the following excerpt, Professor Bonnie summarizes what is known about the deterrent effect of drug possession offenses:

"The first thing to be said is 'not much.' As possession of all [controlled substances] other than marijuana is a crime in every jurisdiction, there is no way of knowing whether use patterns would be significantly different if consumption-related behavior were not punishable as a crime. Variations clearly do exist among jurisdictions in the severity of the penalty threatened, the severity of the penalties actually imposed, and the likelihood that a detected offense will be prosecuted at all. Patterns of police behavior—and therefore the likelihood that offenses will be detected—undoubtedly differ from jurisdiction to jurisdiction. However, the degree to which these differences are perceived by the 'at risk' population and therefore the degree to which they influence decisions to initiate or continue use of particular illicit drugs are virtual mysteries. There is considerable speculation about these matters, but very few investigators have attempted to tackle what is obviously a very complicated question.

"The issues are considerably easier to investigate (i) if the law is in transition, especially if it involves proscription of previously lawful behavior (or a *significant* increase in the severity of threatened sanctions) or, alternatively, the repeal of (or *significant* reduction in) sanctions against previously proscribed behavior; or (ii) if the behavior occurs in public and is therefore more easily detected, and more likely to be influenced by legal sanctions, than behavior that occurs in private. There is a relevant body of research [regarding] possession of marijuana because 'criminal' sanctions have been removed in 11 states since 1973.

. . .

"Although these 11 states share the common feature of having eliminated incarceration as a penalty for some consumption-related behavior, at least for first offenders, the reform statutes vary in significant respects. The conduct that has been 'decriminalized' is not uniformly defined and the reform jurisdictions also differ in their prescriptions of the residual sanctions that can still be imposed on persons who are apprehended for, and convicted of, 'decriminalized' offenses. For present purposes, however, I will assume that the elimination of incarceration, and of the usual record consequences of a criminal conviction, is perceived as a significant reduction in the penalty—and therefore in the 'costs' of being apprehended and 'convicted' for the unlawful activity.

"The question, of course, is whether, as a result of this change, fewer persons are 'deterred' from initiating or continuing marijuana use or whether users use more frequently than would have been the case under the previous legal regime. Or, to put it another way, what is the marginal effect on aggregate consumption patterns of 'criminal' penalties against consumption-related behavior as compared with non-criminal ones or no sanctions at all?

"Several studies have compared the prevalence and patterns of consumption before and after decriminalization in decriminalized jurisdictions and in jurisdictions where the law has remained unchanged. Although the methodologies of these studies vary in strength, these data consistently show that (i) there is no significant immediate change in consumption patterns after decriminalization and (ii) consumption trends are essentially the same in decriminalized and non-decriminalized jurisdictions. Of course, the issue merits more systematic research; but from the standpoint of the 'deterrent' process, the available data strongly suggest that little incremental preventive effect is attributable to the extant 'criminal' misdemeanor sanctions, which are so sporadically applied, when compared with 'civil' penalties. On the other hand, it is possible that changes in the law do influence attitudes and beliefs about the behavior and that these 'symbolic' effects can be assessed only over a longer period of time.

". . . Criminal sanctions against 'simple possession' of controlled substances are frequently regarded as indispensable symbols of social disapproval. Moreover, graded or stratified penalty schemes, which punish possession of 'more harmful' drugs more severely than possession of 'less harmful' drugs, are generally regarded as necessary devices for expressing and communicating the relative seriousness of these transgressions even though there may be no reason to believe that the threat of more severe sanctions exerts a significantly greater deterrent effect than the lesser penalties would.

"The ethical complexity of symbolic uses of the criminal law, especially in the drug area, was a matter of some concern to the National Commission on Marihuana and Drug Abuse:

'If society feels strongly about the impropriety of certain conduct, it may choose to express this norm through the criminal law even though the behavior is largely invisible and will be reduced only through effective operation of other institutions of control. Laws against incest and child beating are good examples. To weigh the costs and benefits of such symbolism requires a special, non-quantitative method of measurement. The benefits consist of the value to society in reaffirming certain norms, together with a reinforcement of self-restraint by those who accept society's judgment. The costs include the effect on the integrity and functioning of the legal system of having a law that is largely unenforcible, plus the resentment of those who reject society's judgment. The scale that balances these two sets of intangibles indicates, among other things, how widely and deeply the values in question are held. . . .

'In light of (society's) ambivalent attitude toward drug use, the relative ineffectiveness of the possession penalty as a deterrent, and the high social costs of its enforcement, the Commission believes that the criminal law is not a very useful symbol for the discouragement policy.'

Nonetheless, the Commission concluded that the criminal law was, for the present at least, a socially indispensable symbol of disapproval for use of drugs other than marijuana:

'Yet, until society develops a replacement symbol and other institutions assume their share of responsibility for control, [the criminal law] may be a necessary codification of public policy. Unfortunately, 60 years of coercive policy have so exaggerated the symbolic importance of the criminal law that it has become interwoven with social attitudes regarding drug use. Removing it suddenly would connote a change in values rather than merely a shift in emphasis. . . .'

"Despite the frequent reliance on symbolism in the formulation of [drug laws] virtually nothing is actually known about the validity of the underlying hypothesis. Do legal declarations of disapproval have any independent effect on the development of attitudes and beliefs about the use of these substances? [The] hypothesis may defy rigorous empirical investigation, but it is surprising how little research has been conducted in the area.

". . . Because the deterrent value of criminal sanctions [for possession of marijuana] is dubious, we are left with the contention that the repeal of [these sanctions] will send the *wrong* message and will connote societal approval of, and thereby encourage, marijuana use—even though the drug is still contraband and even though its cultivation and distribution remain illegal. The available data suggest that any such message is not immediately communicated by a change in the law; attitudes about the wisdom of the law or the morality of use remain unchanged, and consumption patterns also remain substantially unchanged. However, the data in Oregon do suggest that the change in the law may contribute to and reinforce the underlying societal trend toward more tolerant attitudes regarding use of the drug.

"Although the incidence and patterns of use remained virtually unchanged in Oregon for the two years immediately following decriminalization in 1973, the 1976 data did show a large increase relative to the two previous years: the proportion of [persons who had ever used marijuana] among adults rose from 20 percent to 24 percent and the proportion of current users rose from nine percent to 12 percent. Although both figures were slightly above the national average at that time, they were *not* higher than the regional average for the western states. That aside, however, one is led to ask *why* the acceleration in experimentation and recreational use occurred when it did and whether the change in the law had anything to do with it.

"The most plausible hypothesis is that the incidence of experimental and recreational use in Oregon, as well as elsewhere, has been largely restrained by exaggerated perceptions of the harmfulness of using the drug. More realistic assessments of the effects of the drug played a major role in the increase in its use in the late 1960s and early 1970s, an escalation which occurred throughout the country; regional variations in use patterns were entirely unrelated to the prescribed penalties or the patterns of enforcement. The Oregon data suggest that the change in the law, abetted by its national publicity, symbolized and communicated this message: 'It's not as harmful as you thought.' Thus, what is operating here is not deterrence in the classic sense, as the reduced penalty did not quickly lead to increased experimentation among those who had been interested in it but were previously fearful of arrest and punishment. Instead, the educative and declaratory functions of the law may be implicated. That is, the law formerly communicated the message: 'This is awful and dangerous; that's why it's a crime.' Then, when it became apparent to large segments of the population that occasional marijuana use was not 'that dangerous,' use increased despite the law, and the legislature followed along by changing the law, thus reflecting and symbolizing these changing attitudes and perceptions. The pattern does not simply stop once the law is changed. Because the law is intertwined with other sociocultural factors that shape the attitudes of potential users, it is conceivable that one long-term effect of decriminalization is to reinforce the public's increasingly accurate perceptions about the effects of occasional or recreational use."

Do you think criminal penalties for possession of marijuana should be repealed? What about penalties for possession of other drugs? Do you know how to "weigh" the costs and benefits of such laws? Do you accept the legitimacy of symbolic arguments against decriminalization?

*

Appendix A

INTRODUCTORY NOTE ON THE MODEL PENAL CODE

The American Law Institute was founded in 1923. It is a private organization of lawyers, judges, and law teachers. Together with the American Bar Association, the Institute sponsors an extensive program of continuing legal education. It has published Restatements of American law in several areas, including property, torts, and contracts; has prepared model statutes on subjects as diverse as federal income taxation, federal securities, criminal procedure, federal jurisdiction, and land development; and was a major contributor to the drafting of the Uniform Commercial Code. Of more relevance to students of the criminal law, the Institute published the Model Penal Code in 1962.

Examination of the substantive criminal law in the United States was on the Institute's initial agenda in 1923. An early proposal to restate the law was rejected, however, largely on the ground that a more prescriptive document, looking toward major reform, should be attempted. The first proposal for a "model code" of criminal law was considered in 1931. For various reasons, the project was sidetracked until 1950, when an Advisory Committee was established to take another look at the problem. By 1952, funds had been secured from the Rockefeller Foundation, and the drafting of a model penal code began in earnest.

Professor Herbert Wechsler of the Columbia University Law School was appointed the Chief Reporter for the project. Professor Louis B. Schwartz of the University of Pennsylvania Law School became the Reporter for Part II of the Code, dealing with substantive crimes. The elaborate process of producing the Model Code extended over a period of 10 years. Drafts were reviewed by a specially appointed Advisory Committee, by the Council of the Institute, and by the entire Institute membership at annual meetings. During the period from 1953 to 1962, Tentative Drafts of the Model Code, numbered one through 13, were published and reviewed at the annual meetings. A Proposed Final Draft was reviewed by the membership in 1961, and the text of the Proposed Official Draft was approved in 1962.

Extensive explanatory commentary was included in the various Tentative Drafts. This commentary provides a rich source of research and reflection on the content of the criminal law. Shortly after the completion of the text of the Model Code in 1962, an effort was undertaken to prepare a final commentary on each provision. Although that project was also delayed for various reasons, three volumes, consisting of commentary on Part II (specific crimes), were published in the fall of 1980. Three additional volumes on Part I (the general provisions) were published in 1985, together with a fourth volume containing the final text of the Code. This commentary explains the rationale underlying each section of the Model Code and examines the extent to which the Code provisions have been influential in recent reform efforts.

It is impossible to estimate the number of people who have had a hand in the Model Penal Code since the inception of the project in 1950. What can be said, however, is that the list of those who participated at one time or another is a virtual Who's Who of practitioners, judges, and academics interested in the subject of criminal law both in the United States and abroad. Additionally, the Tentative Drafts of the Code sparked a considerable body of commentary from academics, judges, and practitioners, all of which was taken into account as the drafting process progressed. Suffice it to say that the Model Penal Code is the product of an impressive intellectual effort. Moreover, it has been, as Professor Kadish put it, "stunningly successful in accomplishing the comprehensive rethinking of the criminal law that Wechsler and his colleagues sought." [a]

Professor Wechsler stated the objective of the Institute in promulgating a Model Penal Code in his article, Codification of Criminal Law in the United States: The Model Penal Code, 68 Colum.L.Rev. 1425, 1427 (1968), as follows:

"It should be noted, however, that it was not the purpose of the Institute to achieve uniformity in penal law throughout the nation, since it was deemed inevitable that substantial differences of social situation or of point of view among the states should be reflected in substantial variation in their penal laws. The hope was rather than the model would stimulate and facilitate the systematic re-examination of the subject needed to assure that the prevailing law does truly represent the mature sentiment of our respective jurisdictions, sentiment formed after a fresh appraisal of the problems and their possible solutions. Of course, the Institute was not without ambition that in such an enterprise the model might seem worthy of adoption or, at least, of adaptation. . . ." [b]

One need only examine the volume of criminal code reform that has occurred in this country since the Model Code project was undertaken in order to appreciate the extent to which this ambition has been achieved. Prior to 1952, the date the drafting of the Model Code was begun, only one state, Louisiana in 1942, had significantly revised its criminal code in the 20th century. As a result, criminal codes in the United States were a clumsy collection of common-law principles and ad hoc modifications. Dramatic inconsistencies, particularly in penalty structure but also in the definition of offenses, could easily be found in virtually any penal code. Legislatures responded piecemeal to particular problems as they arose, and little effort was devoted to examining the criminal code as a whole or to integrating newly adopted provisions into an overall scheme or plan.

Although four states prepared new codes while the Model Code itself was being drafted, the first new enactment that was animated entirely by the spirit of the Model Code was adopted in New York in 1965 and became effective in 1967. The New York code itself became a kind of model. Subsequent enactments were influenced substantially both by the fact that criminal code reform had been successful in New York and by the particular adaptations of the Model Code enacted in that state.

Code revision proceeded at a moderate pace over the next several years. During the decade of the 1970's, however, substantial reform was achieved in a majority of American jurisdictions. By May of 1982, new legislation in 37 American jurisdictions had been substantially influenced by the Model Penal Code: [c] Alabama (1980), Alaska (1980), American Samoa (1980), Arizona (1978), Arkansas (1976), Colorado (1972), Connecticut (1971), Delaware (1973), Florida

---

[a] Kadish, Codifiers of the Criminal Law: Wechsler's Predecessors, 78 Colum.L.Rev. 1098, 1140 (1978).

[b] In addition to the article by Professor Wechsler from which this excerpt is taken, students will find it helpful to read his

article, The Challenge of a Model Penal Code, 65 Harv.L.Rev. 1097 (1952), prepared at the outset of the Model Code project.

[c] The dates in parenthesis indicate the year in which the legislation was enacted.

(1975), Georgia (1969), Hawaii (1973), Illinois (1962), Indiana (1977), Iowa (1978), Kansas (1970), Kentucky (1975), Maine (1976), Minnesota (1963), Missouri (1979), Montana (1974), Nebraska (1979), New Hampshire (1973), New Jersey (1979), New Mexico (1963), New York (1967), North Dakota (1975), Ohio (1974), Oregon (1972), Pennsylvania (1973), Puerto Rico (1975), South Dakota (1977), Texas (1974), Utah (1973), Virginia (1975), Washington (1976), Wisconsin (1956), and Wyoming (1982). Also as of 1982, all but one state (Nevada) had at least studied the question of reform. In at least 11 jurisidictions (California, District of Columbia, Idaho,[d] Maryland, Massachusetts, Michigan, Oklahoma, Tennessee, Vermont, West Virgina, and the federal government), new criminal codes had been completed as of 1982, but had failed of enactment. The remaining states were at one stage or another in study of the question.[e]

A few of the states in which new legislation has been enacted have adopted only minor revisions, essentially retaining the common-law orientation of their previous codes. But in most of the 37 jurisdictions listed above, a thorough re-examination of fundamental issues was conducted by a locally-appointed drafting body and the codes were substantially revised along lines suggested by the Model Penal Code.

The extent to which the judiciary has been influenced by the Model Code should also be taken into account. Many of the cases reproduced in this book illustrate that influence. More subtly, many of the analytical techniques of the Model Code have become an integral part of judicial reasoning about the criminal law. The vocabulary of the Model Code, particularly in its culpability structure, has also been influential in this manner. The Model Code is thus to a considerable degree working its way into the common law of the country even in jurisdictions that have not explicitly adopted its provisions by legislation.

To a large extent, the Model Penal Code actually illustrates existing law in most American jurisdictions. More importantly, the provisions of the Model Code define the terms of the debate on virtually every issue of penal law of general significance. Thus, it is now clear after more than three decades of effort that the development of the criminal law in the United States will be dominated by the Model Penal Code for many years to come.

---

[d] Idaho enacted the Model Penal Code virtually intact, with an effective date of January 1, 1972. It was then repealed, effective April 1, 1972.

[e] This information was extracted from the Annual Report of the American Law Institute, May 1982.

AMERICAN LAW INSTITUTE
MODEL PENAL CODE [a]
(Official Draft, 1962)

Table of Contents

PART I. GENERAL PROVISIONS

ARTICLE 1. PRELIMINARY

Section   **Page**

1.01 Title and Effective Date _____ 9
1.02 Purposes; Principles of Construction _____ 10
1.03 Territorial Applicability _____ 11
1.04 Classes of Crimes; Violations _____ 12
1.05 All Offenses Defined by Statute; Application of General Provisions of the Code _____ 12
1.06 Time Limitations _____ 12
1.07 Method of Prosecution When Conduct Constitutes More Than One Offense _____ 13
1.08 When Prosecution Barred by Former Prosecution for the Same Offense _____ 14
1.09 When Prosecution Barred by Former Prosecution for Different Offense _____ 15
1.10 Former Prosecution in Another Jurisdiction: When a Bar _____ 15
1.11 Former Prosecution Before Court Lacking Jurisdiction or When Fraudulently Procured by the Defendant _____ 16
1.12 Proof Beyond a Reasonable Doubt; Affirmative Defenses; Burden of Proving Fact When Not an Element of an Offense; Presumptions _____ 16
1.13 General Definitions _____ 17

ARTICLE 2. GENERAL PRINCIPLES OF LIABILITY

2.01 Requirement of Voluntary Act; Omission as Basis of Liability; Possession as an Act _____ 18
2.02 General Requirements of Culpability _____ 18
2.03 Causal Relationship Between Conduct and Result; Divergence Between Result Designed or Contemplated and Actual Result or Between Probable and Actual Result _____ 20
2.04 Ignorance or Mistake _____ 21
2.05 When Culpability Requirements Are Inapplicable to Violations and to Offenses Defined by Other Statutes; Effect of Absolute Liability in Reducing Grade of Offense to Violation _____ 21
2.06 Liability for Conduct of Another; Complicity _____ 22
2.07 Liability of Corporations, Unincorporated Associations and Persons Acting, or Under a Duty to Act, in Their Behalf _____ 23

[a] The Model Penal Code consists of four parts. Parts I and II are reproduced in full on the following pages. Part III (dealing with treatment and correction) and Part IV (dealing with organization of correctional facilities) have been omitted.

MODEL PENAL CODE

Section		Page
2.08	Intoxication	24
2.09	Duress	25
2.10	Military Orders	25
2.11	Consent	25
2.12	De Minimis Infractions	26
2.13	Entrapment	26

ARTICLE 3. GENERAL PRINCIPLES OF JUSTIFICATION

3.01	Justification an Affirmative Defense; Civil Remedies Unaffected	26
3.02	Justification Generally: Choice of Evils	27
3.03	Execution of Public Duty	27
3.04	Use of Force in Self-Protection	27
3.05	Use of Force for the Protection of Other Persons	29
3.06	Use of Force for the Protection of Property	29
3.07	Use of Force in Law Enforcement	31
3.08	Use of Force by Persons with Special Responsibility for Care, Discipline or Safety of Others	33
3.09	Mistake of Law as to Unlawfulness of Force or Legality of Arrest; Reckless or Negligent Use of Otherwise Justifiable Force; Reckless or Negligent Injury or Risk of Injury to Innocent Persons	34
3.10	Justification in Property Crimes	35
3.11	Definitions	35

ARTICLE 4. RESPONSIBILITY

4.01	Mental Disease or Defect Excluding Responsibility	35
4.02	Evidence of Mental Disease or Defect Admissible When Relevant to Element of the Offense; [Mental Disease or Defect Impairing Capacity as Ground for Mitigation of Punishment in Capital Cases]	36
4.03	Mental Disease or Defect Excluding Responsibility Is Affirmative Defense; Requirement of Notice; Form of Verdict and Judgment When Finding of Irresponsibility Is Made	36
4.04	Mental Disease or Defect Excluding Fitness to Proceed	36
4.05	Psychiatric Examination of Defendant with Respect to Mental Disease or Defect	36
4.06	Determination of Fitness to Proceed; Effect of Finding of Unfitness; Proceedings if Fitness Is Regained [; Post-Commitment Hearing]	37
4.07	Determination of Irresponsibility on Basis of Report; Access to Defendant by Psychiatrist of His Own Choice; Form of Expert Testimony When Issue of Responsibility Is Tried	38
4.08	Legal Effect of Acquittal on the Ground of Mental Disease or Defect Excluding Responsibility; Commitment; Release or Discharge	39
4.09	Statements for Purposes of Examination or Treatment Inadmissible Except on Issue of Mental Condition	40
4.10	Immaturity Excluding Criminal Conviction; Transfer of Proceedings to Juvenile Court	40

ARTICLE 5. INCHOATE CRIMES

5.01	Criminal Attempt	41
5.02	Criminal Solicitation	42
5.03	Criminal Conspiracy	42
5.04	Incapacity, Irresponsibility or Immunity of Party to Solicitation or Conspiracy	43
5.05	Grading of Criminal Attempt, Solicitation and Conspiracy; Mitigation in Cases of Lesser Danger; Multiple Convictions Barred	44
5.06	Possessing Instruments of Crime; Weapons	44
5.07	Prohibited Offensive Weapons	45

ARTICLE 6. AUTHORIZED DISPOSITION OF OFFENDERS

Section **Page**

6.01 Degrees of Felonies 45

6.02 Sentence in Accordance with Code; Authorized Dispositions 45

6.03 Fines 46

6.04 Penalties Against Corporations and Unincorporated Associations; Forfeiture of Corporate Charter or Revocation of Certificate Authorizing Foreign Corporation to Do Business in the State 46

6.05 Young Adult Offenders 47

6.06 Sentence of Imprisonment for Felony; Ordinary Terms 47

6.06 (Alternate) Sentence of Imprisonment for Felony; Ordinary Terms 48

6.07 Sentence of Imprisonment for Felony; Extended Terms 48

6.08 Sentence of Imprisonment for Misdemeanors and Petty Misdemeanors; Ordinary Terms 48

6.09 Sentence of Imprisonment for Misdemeanors and Petty Misdemeanors; Extended Terms 49

6.10 First Release of All Offenders on Parole; Sentence of Imprisonment Includes Separate Parole Term; Length of Parole Term; Length of Recommitment and Reparole After Revocation of Parole; Final Unconditional Release 49

6.11 Place of Imprisonment 50

6.12 Reduction of Conviction by Court to Lesser Degree of Felony or to Misdemeanor 50

6.13 Civil Commitment in Lieu of Prosecution or of Sentence 50

ARTICLE 7. AUTHORITY OF COURT IN SENTENCING

7.01 Criteria for Withholding Sentence of Imprisonment and for Placing Defendant on Probation 50

7.02 Criteria for Imposing Fines 51

7.03 Criteria for Sentence of Extended Term of Imprisonment; Felonies 52

7.04 Criteria for Sentence of Extended Term of Imprisonment; Misdemeanors and Petty Misdemeanors 52

7.05 Former Conviction in Another Jurisdiction; Definition and Proof of Conviction; Sentence Taking Into Account Admitted Crimes Bars Subsequent Conviction for Such Crimes 53

7.06 Multiple Sentences; Concurrent and Consecutive Terms 54

7.07 Procedure on Sentence; Pre-sentence Investigation and Report; Remand for Psychiatric Examination; Transmission of Records to Department of Correction 55

7.08 Commitment for Observation; Sentence of Imprisonment for Felony Deemed Tentative for Period of One Year; Re-sentence on Petition of Commissioner of Correction 56

7.09 Credit for Time of Detention Prior to Sentence; Credit for Imprisonment Under Earlier Sentence for the Same Crime 57

PART II. DEFINITION OF SPECIFIC CRIMES

OFFENSES AGAINST EXISTENCE OR STABILITY OF THE STATE

Reporter's Note 58

OFFENSES INVOLVING DANGER TO THE PERSON

ARTICLE 210. CRIMINAL HOMICIDE

210.0 Definitions 58

210.1 Criminal Homicide 58

210.2 Murder 58

210.3 Manslaughter 59

MODEL PENAL CODE

Section		Page
210.4	Negligent Homicide	59
210.5	Causing or Aiding Suicide	59
210.6	Sentence of Death for Murder; Further Proceedings to Determine Sentence	59

ARTICLE 211. ASSAULT; RECKLESS ENDANGERING; THREATS

211.0	Definitions	62
211.1	Assault	62
211.2	Recklessly Endangering Another Person	62
211.3	Terroristic Threats	62

ARTICLE 212. KIDNAPPING AND RELATED OFFENSES; COERCION

212.0	Definitions	63
212.1	Kidnapping	63
212.2	Felonious Restraint	63
212.3	False Imprisonment	63
212.4	Interference with Custody	63
212.5	Criminal Coercion	64

ARTICLE 213. SEXUAL OFFENSES

213.0	Definitions	64
213.1	Rape and Related Offenses	64
213.2	Deviate Sexual Intercourse by Force or Imposition	65
213.3	Corruption of Minors and Seduction	66
213.4	Sexual Assault	66
213.5	Indecent Exposure	66
213.6	Provisions Generally Applicable to Article 213	67

OFFENSES AGAINST PROPERTY

ARTICLE 220. ARSON, CRIMINAL MISCHIEF, AND OTHER PROPERTY DESTRUCTION

220.1	Arson and Related Offenses	67
220.2	Causing or Risking Catastrophe	68
220.3	Criminal Mischief	68

ARTICLE 221. BURGLARY AND OTHER CRIMINAL INTRUSION

221.0	Definitions	69
221.1	Burglary	69
221.2	Criminal Trespass	69

ARTICLE 222. ROBBERY

222.1	Robbery	70

ARTICLE 223. THEFT AND RELATED OFFENSES

223.0	Definitions	70
223.1	Consolidation of Theft Offenses; Grading; Provisions Applicable to Theft Generally	71
223.2	Theft by Unlawful Taking or Disposition	72
223.3	Theft by Deception	72
223.4	Theft by Extortion	72
223.5	Theft of Property Lost, Mislaid, or Delivered by Mistake	73
223.6	Receiving Stolen Property	73
223.7	Theft of Services	73

Section **Page**

223.8   Theft by Failure to Make Required Disposition of Funds Received 74
223.9   Unauthorized Use of Automobiles and Other Vehicles.......................... 74

ARTICLE 224.   FORGERY AND FRAUDULENT PRACTICES

224.0   Definitions.. 74
224.1   Forgery 74
224.2   Simulating Objects of Antiquity, Rarity, Etc. 75
224.3   Fraudulent Destruction, Removal or Concealment of Recordable Instruments... 75
224.4   Tampering with Records 75
224.5   Bad Checks 75
224.6   Credit Cards.. 75
224.7   Deceptive Business Practices 76
224.8   Commercial Bribery and Breach of Duty to Act Disinterestedly.............. 76
224.9   Rigging Publicly Exhibited Contest 77
224.10   Defrauding Secured Creditors 77
224.11   Fraud in Insolvency 77
224.12   Receiving Deposits in a Failing Financial Institution 77
224.13   Misapplication of Entrusted Property and Property of Government or Financial Institution... 78
224.14   Securing Execution of Documents by Deception 78

OFFENSES AGAINST THE FAMILY

ARTICLE 230.   OFFENSES AGAINST THE FAMILY

230.1   Bigamy and Polygamy 78
230.2   Incest.. 79
230.3   Abortion.. 79
230.4   Endangering Welfare of Children 80
230.5   Persistent Non-Support 80

OFFENSES AGAINST PUBLIC ADMINISTRATION

ARTICLE 240.   BRIBERY AND CORRUPT INFLUENCE

240.0   Definitions 80
240.1   Bribery in Official and Political Matters 81
240.2   Threats and Other Improper Influence in Official and Political Matters .. 81
240.3   Compensation for Past Official Behavior................................ 82
240.4   Retaliation for Past Official Action 82
240.5   Gifts to Public Servants by Persons Subject to Their Jurisdiction.......... 82
240.6   Compensating Public Servant for Assisting Private Interests in Relation to Matters Before Him... 83
240.7   Selling Political Endorsement; Special Influence..................... 83

ARTICLE 241.   PERJURY AND OTHER FALSIFICATION IN OFFICIAL MATTERS

241.0   Definitions 84
241.1   Perjury 84
241.2   False Swearing 84
241.3   Unsworn Falsification to Authorities 85
241.4   False Alarms to Agencies of Public Safety 85
241.5   False Reports to Law Enforcement Authorities 85
241.6   Tampering With Witnesses and Informants; Retaliation Against Them ... 86
241.7   Tampering With or Fabricating Physical Evidence.................. 86
241.8   Tampering With Public Records or Information 86
241.9   Impersonating a Public Servant 86

ARTICLE 242.   OBSTRUCTING GOVERNMENTAL OPERATIONS; ESCAPES

Section   **Page**
242.0   Definitions _____ 87
242.1   Obstructing Administration of Law or Other Governmental Function _____ 87
242.2   Resisting Arrest or Other Law Enforcement _____ 87
242.3   Hindering Apprehension or Prosecution _____ 87
242.4   Aiding Consummation of Crime_____ 87
242.5   Compounding_____ 88
242.6   Escape_____ 88
242.7   Implements for Escape; Other Contraband _____ 88
242.8   Bail Jumping; Default in Required Appearance_____ 89

ARTICLE 243.   ABUSE OF OFFICE

243.0   Definitions _____ 89
243.1   Official Oppression _____ 89
243.2   Speculating or Wagering on Official Action or Information _____ 89

OFFENSES AGAINST PUBLIC ORDER AND DECENCY

ARTICLE 250.   RIOT, DISORDERLY CONDUCT, AND RELATED OFFENSES

250.1   Riot; Failure to Disperse _____ 90
250.2   Disorderly Conduct _____ 90
250.3   False Public Alarms _____ 90
250.4   Harassment_____ 91
250.5   Public Drunkenness; Drug Incapacitation _____ 91
250.6   Loitering or Prowling _____ 91
250.7   Obstructing Highways and Other Public Passages_____ 91
250.8   Disrupting Meetings and Processions _____ 92
250.9   Desecration of Venerated Objects _____ 92
250.10 Abuse of Corpse _____ 92
250.11 Cruelty to Animals_____ 92
250.12 Violation of Privacy_____ 92

ARTICLE 251.   PUBLIC INDECENCY

251.1   Open Lewdness_____ 93
251.2   Prostitution and Related Offenses_____ 93
251.3   Loitering to Solicit Deviate Sexual Relations _____ 94
251.4   Obscenity _____ 94

ADDITIONAL ARTICLES

Reporter's Note _____ 95

PART I.   GENERAL PROVISIONS

ARTICLE 1.   PRELIMINARY

Section 1.01.   Title and Effective Date

(1) This Act is called the Penal and Correctional Code and may be cited as P.C.C.   It shall become effective on   .   .   ..

(2) Except as provided in Subsections (3) and (4) of this Section, the Code does not apply to offenses committed prior to its effective date and prosecutions for such offenses shall be governed by the prior law, which is continued in effect for that purpose, as if this Code were not in force. For the purposes of this Section, an offense was committed prior to the effective date of the Code if any of the elements of the offense occurred prior thereto.

(3) In any case pending on or after the effective date of the Code, involving an offense committed prior to such date:

(a) procedural provisions of the Code shall govern, insofar as they are justly applicable and their application does not introduce confusion or delay;

(b) provisions of the Code according a defense or mitigation shall apply, with the consent of the defendant;

(c) the Court, with the consent of the defendant, may impose sentence under the provisions of the Code applicable to the offense and the offender.

(4) Provisions of the Code governing the treatment and the release or discharge of prisoners, probationers and parolees shall apply to persons under sentence for offenses committed prior to the effective date of the Code, except that the minimum or maximum period of their detention or supervision shall in no case be increased.

Section 1.02. Purposes; Principles of Construction

(1) The general purposes of the provisions governing the definition of offenses are:

(a) to forbid and prevent conduct that unjustifiably and inexcusably inflicts or threatens substantial harm to individual or public interests;

(b) to subject to public control persons whose conduct indicates that they are disposed to commit crimes;

(c) to safeguard conduct that is without fault from condemnation as criminal;

(d) to give fair warning of the nature of the conduct declared to constitute an offense;

(e) to differentiate on reasonable grounds between serious and minor offenses.

(2) The general purposes of the provisions governing the sentencing and treatment of offenders are:

(a) to prevent the commission of offenses;

(b) to promote the correction and rehabilitation of offenders;

(c) to safeguard offenders against excessive, disproportionate or arbitrary punishment;

(d) to give fair warning of the nature of the sentences that may be imposed on conviction of an offense;

(e) to differentiate among offenders with a view to a just individualization in their treatment;

(f) to define, coordinate and harmonize the powers, duties and functions of the courts and of administrative officers and agencies responsible for dealing with offenders;

(g) to advance the use of generally accepted scientific methods and knowledge in the sentencing and treatment of offenders;

(h) to integrate responsibility for the administration of the correctional system in a State Department of Correction [or other single department or agency].

(3) The provisions of the Code shall be construed according to the fair import of their terms but when the language is susceptible of differing constructions it shall be interpreted to further the general purposes stated in this Section and the special purposes of the particular provision involved. The discretionary powers conferred by the Code shall be exercised in accordance with the criteria stated in the Code and, insofar as such criteria are not decisive, to further the general purposes stated in this Section.

Section 1.03. Territorial Applicability

(1) Except as otherwise provided in this Section, a person may be convicted under the law of this State of an offense committed by his own conduct or the conduct of another for which he is legally accountable if:

(a) either the conduct which is an element of the offense or the result which is such an element occurs within this State; or

(b) conduct occurring outside the State is sufficient under the law of this State to constitute an attempt to commit an offense within the State; or

(c) conduct occurring outside the State is sufficient under the law of this State to constitute a conspiracy to commit an offense within the State and an overt act in furtherance of such conspiracy occurs within the State; or

(d) conduct occurring within the State establishes complicity in the commission of, or an attempt, solicitation or conspiracy to commit, an offense in another jurisdiction which also is an offense under the law of this State; or

(e) the offense consists of the omission to perform a legal duty imposed by the law of this State with respect to domicile, residence or a relationship to a person, thing or transaction in the State; or

(f) the offense is based on a statute of this State which expressly prohibits conduct outside the State, when the conduct bears a reasonable relation to a legitimate interest of this State and the actor knows or should know that his conduct is likely to affect that interest.

(2) Subsection (1)(a) does not apply when either causing a specified result or a purpose to cause or danger of causing such a result is an element of an offense and the result occurs or is designed or likely to occur only in another jurisdiction where the conduct charged would not constitute an offense, unless a legislative purpose plainly appears to declare the conduct criminal regardless of the place of the result.

(3) Subsection (1)(a) does not apply when causing a particular result is an element of an offense and the result is caused by conduct occurring outside the State which would not constitute an offense if the result had occurred there, unless the actor purposely or knowingly caused the result within the State.

(4) When the offense is homicide, either the death of the victim or the bodily impact causing death constitutes a "result," within the meaning of Subsection (1)(a) and if the body of a homicide victim is found within the State, it is presumed that such result occurred within the State.

(5) This State includes the land and water and the air space above such land and water with respect to which the State has legislative jurisdiction.

Section 1.04. Classes of Crimes; Violations

(1) An offense defined by this Code or by any other statute of this State, for which a sentence of [death or of] imprisonment is authorized, constitutes a crime. Crimes are classified as felonies, misdemeanors or petty misdemeanors.

(2) A crime is a felony if it is so designated in this Code or if persons convicted thereof may be sentenced [to death or] to imprisonment for a term which, apart from an extended term, is in excess of one year.

(3) A crime is a misdemeanor if it is so designated in this Code or in a statute other than this Code enacted subsequent thereto.

(4) A crime is a petty misdemeanor if it is so designated in this Code or in a statute other than this Code enacted subsequent thereto or if it is defined by a statute other than this Code which now provides that persons convicted thereof may be sentenced to imprisonment for a term of which the maximum is less than one year.

(5) An offense defined by this Code or by any other statute of this State constitutes a violation if it is so designated in this Code or in the law defining the offense or if no other sentence than a fine, or fine and forfeiture or other civil penalty is authorized upon conviction or if it is defined by a statute other than this Code which now provides that the offense shall not constitute a crime. A violation does not constitute a crime and conviction of a violation shall not give rise to any disability or legal disadvantage based on conviction of a criminal offense.

(6) Any offense declared by law to constitute a crime, without specification of the grade thereof or of the sentence authorized upon conviction, is a misdemeanor.

(7) An offense defined by any statute of this State other than this Code shall be classified as provided in this Section and the sentence that may be imposed upon conviction thereof shall hereafter be governed by this Code.

Section 1.05. All Offenses Defined by Statute; Application of General Provisions of the Code

(1) No conduct constitutes an offense unless it is a crime or violation under this Code or another statute of this State.

(2) The provisions of Part I of the Code are applicable to offenses defined by other statutes, unless the Code otherwise provides.

(3) This Section does not affect the power of a court to punish for contempt or to employ any sanction authorized by law for the enforcement of an order or a civil judgment or decree.

Section 1.06. Time Limitations

(1) A prosecution for murder may be commenced at any time.

(2) Except as otherwise provided in this Section, prosecutions for other offenses are subject to the following periods of limitation:

(a) a prosecution for a felony of the first degree must be commenced within six years after it is committed;

(b) a prosecution for any other felony must be commenced within three years after it is committed;

(c) a prosecution for a misdemeanor must be commenced within two years after it is committed;

(d) a prosecution for a petty misdemeanor or a violation must be commenced within six months after it is committed.

(3) If the period prescribed in Subsection (2) has expired, a prosecution may nevertheless be commenced for:

(a) any offense a material element of which is either fraud or a breach of fiduciary obligation within one year after discovery of the offense by an aggrieved party or by a person who has legal duty to represent an aggrieved party and who is himself not a party to the offense, but in no case shall this provision extend the period of limitation otherwise applicable by more than three years; and

(b) any offense based upon misconduct in office by a public officer or employee at any time when the defendant is in public office or employment or within two years thereafter, but in no case shall this provision extend the period of limitation otherwise applicable by more than three years.

(4) An offense is committed either when every element occurs, or, if a legislative purpose to prohibit a continuing course of conduct plainly appears, at the time when the course of conduct or the defendant's complicity therein is terminated. Time starts to run on the day after the offense is committed.

(5) A prosecution is commenced either when an indictment is found [or an information filed] or when a warrant or other process is issued, provided that such warrant or process is executed without unreasonable delay.

(6) The period of limitation does not run:

(a) during any time when the accused is continuously absent from the State or has no reasonably ascertainable place of abode or work within the State, but in no case shall this provision extend the period of limitation otherwise applicable by more than three years; or

(b) during any time when a prosecution against the accused for the same conduct is pending in this State.

Section 1.07. Method of Prosecution When Conduct Constitutes More Than One Offense

(1) Prosecution for Multiple Offenses; Limitation on Convictions. When the same conduct of a defendant may establish the commission of more than one offense, the defendant may be prosecuted for each such offense. He may not, however, be convicted of more than one offense if:

(a) one offense is included in the other, as defined in Subsection (4) of this Section; or

(b) one offense consists only of a conspiracy or other form of preparation to commit the other; or

(c) inconsistent findings of fact are required to establish the commission of the offenses; or

(d) the offenses differ only in that one is defined to prohibit a designated kind of conduct generally and the other to prohibit a specific instance of such conduct; or

(e) the offense is defined as a continuing course of conduct and the defendant's course of conduct was uninterrupted, unless the law provides that specific periods of such conduct constitute separate offenses.

(2) Limitation on Separate Trials for Multiple Offenses. Except as provided in Subsection (3) of this Section, a defendant shall not be subject to separate

trials for multiple offenses based on the same conduct or arising from the same criminal episode, if such offenses are known to the appropriate prosecuting officer at the time of the commencement of the first trial and are within the jurisdiction of a single court.

(3) <u>Authority of Court to Order Separate Trials.</u> When a defendant is charged with two or more offenses based on the same conduct or arising from the same criminal episode, the Court, on application of the prosecuting attorney or of the defendant, may order any such charge to be tried separately, if it is satisfied that justice so requires.

(4) <u>Conviction of Included Offense Permitted.</u> A defendant may be convicted of an offense included in an offense charged in the indictment [or the information]. An offense is so included when:

(a) it is established by proof of the same or less than all the facts required to establish the commission of the offense charged; or

(b) it consists of an attempt or solicitation to commit the offense charged or to commit an offense otherwise included therein; or

(c) it differs from the offense charged only in the respect that a less serious injury or risk of injury to the same person, property or public interest or a lesser kind of culpability suffices to establish its commission.

(5) <u>Submission of Included Offense to Jury.</u> The Court shall not be obligated to charge the jury with respect to an included offense unless there is a rational basis for a verdict acquitting the defendant of the offense charged and convicting him of the included offense.

Section 1.08. When Prosecution Barred by Former Prosecution for the Same Offense

When a prosecution is for a violation of the same provision of the statutes and is based upon the same facts as a former prosecution, it is barred by such former prosecution under the following circumstances:

(1) The former prosecution resulted in an acquittal. There is an acquittal if the prosecution resulted in a finding of not guilty by the trier of fact or in a determination that there was insufficient evidence to warrant a conviction. A finding of guilty of a lesser included offense is an acquittal of the greater inclusive offense, although the conviction is subsequently set aside.

(2) The former prosecution was terminated, after the information had been filed or the indictment found, by a final order or judgment for the defendant, which has not been set aside, reversed, or vacated and which necessarily required a determination inconsistent with a fact or a legal proposition that must be established for conviction of the offense.

(3) The former prosecution resulted in a conviction. There is a conviction if the prosecution resulted in a judgment of conviction which has not been reversed or vacated, a verdict of guilty which has not been set aside and which is capable of supporting a judgment, or a plea of guilty accepted by the Court. In the latter two cases failure to enter judgment must be for a reason other than a motion of the defendant.

(4) The former prosecution was improperly terminated. Except as provided in this Subsection, there is an improper termination of a prosecution if the termination is for reasons not amounting to an acquittal, and it takes place

after the first witness is sworn but before verdict. Termination under any of the following circumstances is not improper:

(a) The defendant consents to the termination or waives, by motion to dismiss or otherwise, his right to object to the termination.

(b) The trial court finds that the termination is necessary because:

(1) it is physically impossible to proceed with the trial in conformity with law; or

(2) there is a legal defect in the proceedings which would make any judgment entered upon a verdict reversible as a matter of law; or

(3) prejudicial conduct, in or outside the courtroom, makes it impossible to proceed with the trial without injustice to either the defendant or the State; or

(4) the jury is unable to agree upon a verdict; or

(5) false statements of a juror on voir dire prevent a fair trial.

Section 1.09. When Prosecution Barred by Former Prosecution for Different Offense

Although a prosecution is for a violation of a different provision of the statutes than a former prosecution or is based on different facts, it is barred by such former prosecution under the following circumstances:

(1) The former prosecution resulted in an acquittal or in a conviction as defined in Section 1.08 and the subsequent prosecution is for:

(a) any offense of which the defendant could have been convicted on the first prosecution; or

(b) any offense for which the defendant should have been tried on the first prosecution under Section 1.07, unless the Court ordered a separate trial of the charge of such offense; or

(c) the same conduct, unless (i) the offense of which the defendant was formerly convicted or acquitted and the offense for which he is subsequently prosecuted each requires proof of a fact not required by the other and the law defining each of such offenses is intended to prevent a substantially different harm or evil, or (ii) the second offense was not consummated when the former trial began.

(2) The former prosecution was terminated, after the information was filed or the indictment found, by an acquittal or by a final order or judgment for the defendant which has not been set aside, reversed or vacated and which acquittal, final order or judgment necessarily required a determination inconsistent with a fact which must be established for conviction of the second offense.

(3) The former prosecution was improperly terminated, as improper termination is defined in Section 1.08, and the subsequent prosecution is for an offense of which the defendant could have been convicted had the former prosecution not been improperly terminated.

Section 1.10. Former Prosecution in Another Jurisdiction: When a Bar

When conduct constitutes an offense within the concurrent jurisdiction of this State and of the United States or another State, a prosecution in any such other jurisdiction is a bar to a subsequent prosecution in this State under the following circumstances:

(1) The first prosecution resulted in an acquittal or in a conviction as defined in Section 1.08 and the subsequent prosecution is based on the same conduct, unless (a) the offense of which the defendant was formerly convicted or acquitted and the offense for which he is subsequently prosecuted each requires proof of a fact not required by the other and the law defining each of such offenses is intended to prevent a substantially different harm or evil or (b) the second offense was not consummated when the former trial began; or

(2) The former prosecution was terminated, after the information was filed or the indictment found, by an acquittal or by a final order or judgment for the defendant which has not been set aside, reversed or vacated and which acquittal, final order or judgment necessarily required a determination inconsistent with a fact which must be established for conviction of the offense of which the defendant is subsequently prosecuted.

Section 1.11. Former Prosecution Before Court Lacking Jurisdiction or When Fraudulently Procured by the Defendant

A prosecution is not a bar within the meaning of Sections 1.08, 1.09 and 1.10 under any of the following circumstances:

(1) The former prosecution was before a court which lacked jurisdiction over the defendant or the offense; or

(2) The former prosecution was procured by the defendant without the knowledge of the appropriate prosecuting officer and with the purpose of avoiding the sentence which might otherwise be imposed; or

(3) The former prosecution resulted in a judgment of conviction which was held invalid in a subsequent proceeding on a writ of habeas corpus, coram nobis or similar process.

Section 1.12. Proof Beyond a Reasonable Doubt; Affirmative Defenses; Burden of Proving Fact When Not an Element of an Offense; Presumptions

(1) No person may be convicted of an offense unless each element of such offense is proved beyond a reasonable doubt. In the absence of such proof, the innocence of the defendant is assumed.

(2) Subsection (1) of this Section does not:

(a) require the disproof of an affirmative defense unless and until there is evidence supporting such defense; or

(b) apply to any defense which the Code or another statute plainly requires the defendant to prove by a preponderance of evidence.

(3) A ground of defense is affirmative, within the meaning of Subsection (2)(a) of this Section, when:

(a) it arises under a section of the Code which so provides; or

(b) it relates to an offense defined by a statute other than the Code and such statute so provides; or

(c) it involves a matter of excuse or justification peculiarly within the knowledge of the defendant on which he can fairly be required to adduce supporting evidence.

(4) When the application of the Code depends upon the finding of a fact which is not an element of an offense, unless the Code otherwise provides:

(a) the burden of proving the fact is on the prosecution or defendant, depending on whose interest or contention will be furthered if the finding should be made; and

(b) the fact must be proved to the satisfaction of the Court or jury, as the case may be.

(5) When the Code establishes a presumption with respect to any fact which is an element of an offense, it has the following consequences:

(a) when there is evidence of the facts which give rise to the presumption, the issue of the existence of the presumed fact must be submitted to the jury, unless the Court is satisfied that the evidence as a whole clearly negatives the presumed fact; and

(b) when the issue of the existence of the presumed fact is submitted to the jury, the Court shall charge that while the presumed fact must, on all the evidence, be proved beyond a reasonable doubt, the law declares that the jury may regard the facts giving rise to the presumption as sufficient evidence of the presumed fact.

(6) A presumption not established by the Code or inconsistent with it has the consequences otherwise accorded it by law.

Section 1.13. General Definitions

In this Code, unless a different meaning plainly is required:

(1) "statute" includes the Constitution and a local law or ordinance of a political subdivision of the State;

(2) "act" or "action" means a bodily movement whether voluntary or involuntary;

(3) "voluntary" has the meaning specified in Section 2.01;

(4) "omission" means a failure to act;

(5) "conduct" means an action or omission and its accompanying state of mind, or, where relevant, a series of acts and omissions;

(6) "actor" includes, where relevant, a person guilty of an omission;

(7) "acted" includes, where relevant, "omitted to act";

(8) "person," "he" and "actor" include any natural person and, where relevant, a corporation or an unincorporated association;

(9) "element of an offense" means (i) such conduct or (ii) such attendant circumstances or (iii) such a result of conduct as

(a) is included in the description of the forbidden conduct in the definition of the offense; or

(b) establishes the required kind of culpability; or

(c) negatives an excuse or justification for such conduct; or

(d) negatives a defense under the statute of limitations; or

(e) establishes jurisdiction or venue;

(10) "material element of an offense" means an element that does not relate exclusively to the statute of limitations, jurisdiction, venue or to any other matter similarly unconnected with (i) the harm or evil, incident to conduct, sought to be prevented by the law defining the offense, or (ii) the existence of a justification or excuse for such conduct;

(11) "purposely" has the meaning specified in Section 2.02 and equivalent terms such as "with purpose," "designed" or "with design" have the same meaning;

(12) "intentionally" or "with intent" means purposely;

(13) "knowingly" has the meaning specified in Section 2.02 and equivalent terms such as "knowing" or "with knowledge" have the same meaning;

(14) "recklessly" has the meaning specified in Section 2.02 and equivalent terms such as "recklessness" or "with recklessness" have the same meaning;

(15) "negligently" has the meaning specified in Section 2.02 and equivalent terms such as "negligence" or "with negligence" have the same meaning;

(16) "reasonably believes" or "reasonable belief" designates a belief which the actor is not reckless or negligent in holding.

ARTICLE 2. GENERAL PRINCIPLES OF LIABILITY

Section 2.01. Requirement of Voluntary Act; Omission as Basis of Liability; Possession as an Act

(1) A person is not guilty of an offense unless his liability is based on conduct which includes a voluntary act or the omission to perform an act of which he is physically capable.

(2) The following are not voluntary acts within the meaning of this Section:

(a) a reflex or convulsion;

(b) a bodily movement during unconsciousness or sleep;

(c) conduct during hypnosis or resulting from hypnotic suggestion;

(d) a bodily movement that otherwise is not a product of the effort or determination of the actor, either conscious or habitual.

(3) Liability for the commission of an offense may not be based on an omission unaccompanied by action unless:

(a) the omission is expressly made sufficient by the law defining the offense; or

(b) a duty to perform the omitted act is otherwise imposed by law.

(4) Possession is an act, within the meaning of this Section, if the possessor knowingly procured or received the thing possessed or was aware of his control thereof for a sufficient period to have been able to terminate his possession.

Section 2.02. General Requirements of Culpability

(1) <u>Minimum Requirements of Culpability.</u> Except as provided in Section 2.05, a person is not guilty of an offense unless he acted purposely, knowingly, recklessly or negligently, as the law may require, with respect to each material element of the offense.

(2) Kinds of Culpability Defined.

(a) Purposely.

A person acts purposely with respect to a material element of an offense when:

(i) if the element involves the nature of his conduct or a result thereof, it is his conscious object to engage in conduct of that nature or to cause such a result; and

(ii) if the element involves the attendant circumstances, he is aware of the existence of such circumstances or he believes or hopes that they exist.

(b) Knowingly.

A person acts knowingly with respect to a material element of an offense when:

(i) if the element involves the nature of his conduct or the attendant circumstances, he is aware that his conduct is of that nature or that such circumstances exist; and

(ii) if the element involves a result of his conduct, he is aware that it is practically certain that his conduct will cause such a result.

(c) Recklessly.

A person acts recklessly with respect to a material element of an offense when he consciously disregards a substantial and unjustifiable risk that the material element exists or will result from his conduct. The risk must be of such a nature and degree that, considering the nature and purpose of the actor's conduct and the circumstances known to him, its disregard involves a gross deviation from the standard of conduct that a law-abiding person would observe in the actor's situation.

(d) Negligently.

A person acts negligently with respect to a material element of an offense when he should be aware of a substantial and unjustifiable risk that the material element exists or will result from his conduct. The risk must be of such a nature and degree that the actor's failure to perceive it, considering the nature and purpose of his conduct and the circumstances known to him, involves a gross deviation from the standard of care that a reasonable person would observe in the actor's situation.

(3) Culpability Required Unless Otherwise Provided. When the culpability sufficient to establish a material element of an offense is not prescribed by law, such element is established if a person acts purposely, knowingly or recklessly with respect thereto.

(4) Prescribed Culpability Requirement Applies to All Material Elements. When the law defining an offense prescribes the kind of culpability that is sufficient for the commission of an offense, without distinguishing among the material elements thereof, such provision shall apply to all the material elements of the offense, unless a contrary purpose plainly appears.

(5) Substitutes for Negligence, Recklessness and Knowledge. When the law provides that negligence suffices to establish an element of an offense, such element also is established if a person acts purposely, knowingly or recklessly. When recklessness suffices to establish an element, such element also is established if a person acts purposely or knowingly. When acting knowingly suffices to establish an element, such element also is established if a person acts purposely.

(6) Requirement of Purpose Satisfied if Purpose Is Conditional. When a particular purpose is an element of an offense, the element is established although such purpose is conditional, unless the condition negatives the harm or evil sought to be prevented by the law defining the offense.

(7) Requirement of Knowledge Satisfied by Knowledge of High Probability. When knowledge of the existence of a particular fact is an element of an offense, such knowledge is established if a person is aware of a high probability of its existence, unless he actually believes that it does not exist.

(8) Requirement of Wilfulness Satisfied by Acting Knowingly. A require-ment that an offense be committed wilfully is satisfied if a person acts knowingly with respect to the material elements of the offense, unless a purpose to impose further requirements appears.

(9) Culpability as to Illegality of Conduct. Neither knowledge nor reckless-ness or negligence as to whether conduct constitutes an offense or as to the existence, meaning or application of the law determining the elements of an offense is an element of such offense, unless the definition of the offense or the Code so provides.

(10) Culpability as Determinant of Grade of Offense. When the grade or degree of an offense depends on whether the offense is committed purposely, knowingly, recklessly or negligently, its grade or degree shall be the lowest for which the determinative kind of culpability is established with respect to any material element of the offense.

Section 2.03. Causal Relationship Between Conduct and Result; Divergence Between Result Designed or Contem-plated and Actual Result or Between Probable and Actual Result

(1) Conduct is the cause of a result when:

(a) it is an antecedent but for which the result in question would not have occurred; and

(b) the relationship between the conduct and result satisfies any addi-tional causal requirements imposed by the Code or by the law defining the offense.

(2) When purposely or knowingly causing a particular result is an element of an offense, the element is not established if the actual result is not within the purpose or the contemplation of the actor unless:

(a) the actual result differs from that designed or contemplated, as the case may be, only in the respect that a different person or different property is injured or affected or that the injury or harm designed or contemplated would have been more serious or more extensive than that caused; or

(b) the actual result involves the same kind of injury or harm as that designed or contemplated and is not too remote or accidental in its occur-rence to have a [just] bearing on the actor's liability or on the gravity of his offense.

(3) When recklessly or negligently causing a particular result is an element of an offense, the element is not established if the actual result is not within the risk of which the actor is aware or, in the case of negligence, of which he should be aware unless:

(a) the actual result differs from the probable result only in the respect that a different person or different property is injured or affected or that the probable injury or harm would have been more serious or more extensive than that caused; or

(b) the actual result involves the same kind of injury or harm as the probable result and is not too remote or accidental in its occurrence to have a [just] bearing on the actor's liability or on the gravity of his offense.

(4) When causing a particular result is a material element of an offense for which absolute liability is imposed by law, the element is not established unless the actual result is a probable consequence of the actor's conduct.

Section 2.04. Ignorance or Mistake

(1) Ignorance or mistake as to a matter of fact or law is a defense if:

(a) the ignorance or mistake negatives the purpose, knowledge, belief, recklessness or negligence required to establish a material element of the offense; or

(b) the law provides that the state of mind established by such ignorance or mistake constitutes a defense.

(2) Although ignorance or mistake would otherwise afford a defense to the offense charged, the defense is not available if the defendant would be guilty of another offense had the situation been as he supposed. In such case, however, the ignorance or mistake of the defendant shall reduce the grade and degree of the offense of which he may be convicted to those of the offense of which he would be guilty had the situation been as he supposed.

(3) A belief that conduct does not legally constitute an offense is a defense to a prosecution for that offense based upon such conduct when:

(a) the statute or other enactment defining the offense is not known to the actor and has not been published or otherwise reasonably made available prior to the conduct alleged; or

(b) he acts in reasonable reliance upon an official statement of the law, afterward determined to be invalid or erroneous, contained in (i) a statute or other enactment; (ii) a judicial decision, opinion or judgment; (iii) an administrative order or grant of permission; or (iv) an official interpretation of the public officer or body charged by law with responsibility for the interpretation, administration or enforcement of the law defining the offense.

(4) The defendant must prove a defense arising under Subsection (3) of this Section by a preponderance of evidence.

Section 2.05. When Culpability Requirements Are Inapplicable to Violations and to Offenses Defined by Other Statutes; Effect of Absolute Liability in Reducing Grade of Offense to Violation

(1) The requirements of culpability prescribed by Sections 2.01 and 2.02 do not apply to:

(a) offenses which constitute violations, unless the requirement involved is included in the definition of the offense or the Court determines that its application is consistent with effective enforcement of the law defining the offense; or

(b) offenses defined by statutes other than the Code, insofar as a legislative purpose to impose absolute liability for such offenses or with respect to any material element thereof plainly appears.

A–21

(2) Notwithstanding any other provision of existing law and unless a subsequent statute otherwise provides:

(a) when absolute liability is imposed with respect to any material element of an offense defined by a statute other than the Code and a conviction is based upon such liability, the offense constitutes a violation; and

(b) although absolute liability is imposed by law with respect to one or more of the material elements of an offense defined by a statute other than the Code, the culpable commission of the offense may be charged and proved, in which event negligence with respect to such elements constitutes sufficient culpability and the classification of the offense and the sentence that may be imposed therefor upon conviction are determined by Section 1.04 and Article 6 of the Code.

Section 2.06. Liability for Conduct of Another; Complicity

(1) A person is guilty of an offense if it is committed by his own conduct or by the conduct of another person for which he is legally accountable, or both.

(2) A person is legally accountable for the conduct of another person when:

(a) acting with the kind of culpability that is sufficient for the commission of the offense, he causes an innocent or irresponsible person to engage in such conduct; or

(b) he is made accountable for the conduct of such other person by the Code or by the law defining the offense; or

(c) he is an accomplice of such other person in the commission of the offense.

(3) A person is an accomplice of another person in the commission of an offense if:

(a) with the purpose of promoting or facilitating the commission of the offense, he

(i) solicits such other person to commit it; or

(ii) aids or agrees or attempts to aid such other person in planning or committing it; or

(iii) having a legal duty to prevent the commission of the offense, fails to make proper effort so to do; or

(b) his conduct is expressly declared by law to establish his complicity.

(4) When causing a particular result is an element of an offense, an accomplice in the conduct causing such result is an accomplice in the commission of that offense, if he acts with the kind of culpability, if any, with respect to that result that is sufficient for the commission of the offense.

(5) A person who is legally incapable of committing a particular offense himself may be guilty thereof if it is committed by the conduct of another person for which he is legally accountable, unless such liability is inconsistent with the purpose of the provision establishing his incapacity.

(6) Unless otherwise provided by the Code or by the law defining the offense, a person is not an accomplice in an offense committed by another person if:

(a) he is a victim of that offense; or

(b) the offense is so defined that his conduct is inevitably incident to its commission; or

(c) he terminates his complicity prior to the commission of the offense and

(i) wholly deprives it of effectiveness in the commission of the offense; or

(ii) gives timely warning to the law enforcement authorities or otherwise makes proper effort to prevent the commission of the offense.

(7) An accomplice may be convicted on proof of the commission of the offense and of his complicity therein, though the person claimed to have committed the offense has not been prosecuted or convicted or has been convicted of a different offense or degree of offense or has an immunity to prosecution or conviction or has been acquitted.

Section 2.07. Liability of Corporations, Unincorporated Associations and Persons Acting, or Under a Duty to Act, in Their Behalf

(1) A corporation may be convicted of the commission of an offense if:

(a) the offense is a violation or the offense is defined by a statute other than the Code in which a legislative purpose to impose liability on corporations plainly appears and the conduct is performed by an agent of the corporation acting in behalf of the corporation within the scope of his office or employment, except that if the law defining the offense designates the agents for whose conduct the corporation is accountable or the circumstances under which it is accountable, such provisions shall apply; or

(b) the offense consists of an omission to discharge a specific duty of affirmative performance imposed on corporations by law; or

(c) the commission of the offense was authorized, requested, commanded, performed or recklessly tolerated by the board of directors or by a high managerial agent acting in behalf of the corporation within the scope of his office or employment.

(2) When absolute liability is imposed for the commission of an offense, a legislative purpose to impose liability on a corporation shall be assumed, unless the contrary plainly appears.

(3) An unincorporated association may be convicted of the commission of an offense if:

(a) the offense is defined by a statute other than the Code which expressly provides for the liability of such an association and the conduct is performed by an agent of the association acting in behalf of the association within the scope of his office or employment, except that if the law defining the offense designates the agents for whose conduct the association is accountable or the circumstances under which it is accountable, such provisions shall apply; or

(b) the offense consists of an omission to discharge a specific duty of affirmative performance imposed on associations by law.

(4) As used in this Section:

(a) "corporation" does not include an entity organized as or by a governmental agency for the execution of a governmental program;

(b) "agent" means any director, officer, servant, employee or other person authorized to act in behalf of the corporation or association and, in the case of an unincorporated association, a member of such association;

(c) "high managerial agent" means an officer of a corporation or an unincorporated association, or, in the case of a partnership, a partner, or any other agent of a corporation or association having duties of such responsibility that his conduct may fairly be assumed to represent the policy of the corporation or association.

(5) In any prosecution of a corporation or an unincorporated association for the commission of an offense included within the terms of Subsection (1)(a) or Subsection (3)(a) of this Section, other than an offense for which absolute liability has been imposed, it shall be a defense if the defendant proves by a preponderance of evidence that the high managerial agent having supervisory responsibility over the subject matter of the offense employed due diligence to prevent its commission. This paragraph shall not apply if it is plainly inconsistent with the legislative purpose in defining the particular offense.

(6)(a) A person is legally accountable for any conduct he performs or causes to be performed in the name of the corporation or an unincorporated association or in its behalf to the same extent as if it were performed in his own name or behalf.

(b) Whenever a duty to act is imposed by law upon a corporation or an unincorporated association, any agent of the corporation or association having primary responsibility for the discharge of the duty is legally accountable for a reckless omission to perform the required act to the same extent as if the duty were imposed by law directly upon himself.

(c) When a person is convicted of an offense by reason of his legal accountability for the conduct of a corporation or an unincorporated association, he is subject to the sentence authorized by law when a natural person is convicted of an offense of the grade and the degree involved.

Section 2.08. Intoxication

(1) Except as provided in Subsection (4) of this Section, intoxication of the actor is not a defense unless it negatives an element of the offense.

(2) When recklessness establishes an element of the offense, if the actor, due to self-induced intoxication, is unaware of a risk of which he would have been aware had he been sober, such unawareness is immaterial.

(3) Intoxication does not, in itself, constitute mental disease within the meaning of Section 4.01.

(4) Intoxication which (a) is not self-induced or (b) is pathological is an affirmative defense if by reason of such intoxication the actor at the time of his conduct lacks substantial capacity either to appreciate its criminality [wrongfulness] or to conform his conduct to the requirements of law.

(5) Definitions. In this Section unless a different meaning plainly is required:

(a) "intoxication" means a disturbance of mental or physical capacities resulting from the introduction of substances into the body;

(b) "self-induced intoxication" means intoxication caused by substances which the actor knowingly introduces into his body, the tendency of which to cause intoxication he knows or ought to know, unless he introduces them pursuant to medical advice or under such circumstances as would afford a defense to a charge of crime;

(c) "pathological intoxication" means intoxication grossly excessive in degree, given the amount of the intoxicant, to which the actor does not know he is susceptible.

Section 2.09. Duress

(1) It is an affirmative defense that the actor engaged in the conduct charged to constitute an offense because he was coerced to do so by the use of, or a threat to use, unlawful force against his person or the person of another, which a person of reasonable firmness in his situation would have been unable to resist.

(2) The defense provided by this Section is unavailable if the actor recklessly placed himself in a situation in which it was probable that he would be subjected to duress. The defense is also unavailable if he was negligent in placing himself in such a situation, whenever negligence suffices to establish culpability for the offense charged.

(3) It is not a defense that a woman acted on the command of her husband, unless she acted under such coercion as would establish a defense under this Section. [The presumption that a woman, acting in the presence of her husband, is coerced is abolished.]

(4) When the conduct of the actor would otherwise be justifiable under Section 3.02, this Section does not preclude such defense.

Section 2.10. Military Orders

It is an affirmative defense that the actor, in engaging in the conduct charged to constitute an offense, does no more than execute an order of his superior in the armed services which he does not know to be unlawful.

Section 2.11. Consent

(1) In General. The consent of the victim to conduct charged to constitute an offense or to the result thereof is a defense if such consent negatives an element of the offense or precludes the infliction of the harm or evil sought to be prevented by the law defining the offense.

(2) Consent to Bodily Harm. When conduct is charged to constitute an offense because it causes or threatens bodily harm, consent to such conduct or to the infliction of such harm is a defense if:

(a) the bodily harm consented to or threatened by the conduct consented to is not serious; or

(b) the conduct and the harm are reasonably foreseeable hazards of joint participation in a lawful athletic contest or competitive sport; or

(c) the consent establishes a justification for the conduct under Article 3 of the Code.

(3) Ineffective Consent. Unless otherwise provided by the Code or by the law defining the offense, assent does not constitute consent if:

(a) it is given by a person who is legally incompetent to authorize the conduct charged to constitute the offense; or

(b) it is given by a person who by reason of youth, mental disease or defect or intoxication is manifestly unable or known by the actor to be unable to make a reasonable judgment as to the nature or harmfulness of the conduct charged to constitute the offense; or

(c) it is given by a person whose improvident consent is sought to be prevented by the law defining the offense; or

(d) it is induced by force, duress or deception of a kind sought to be prevented by the law defining the offense.

Section 2.12. De Minimis Infractions

The Court shall dismiss a prosecution if, having regard to the nature of the conduct charged to constitute an offense and the nature of the attendant circumstances, it finds that the defendant's conduct:

(1) was within a customary license or tolerance, neither expressly negatived by the person whose interest was infringed nor inconsistent with the purpose of the law defining the offense; or

(2) did not actually cause or threaten the harm or evil sought to be prevented by the law defining the offense or did so only to an extent too trivial to warrant the condemnation of conviction; or

(3) presents such other extenuations that it cannot reasonably be regarded as envisaged by the legislature in forbidding the offense.

The Court shall not dismiss a prosecution under Subsection (3) of this Section without filing a written statement of its reasons.

Section 2.13. Entrapment

(1) A public law enforcement official or a person acting in cooperation with such an official perpetrates an entrapment if for the purpose of obtaining evidence of the commission of an offense, he induces or encourages another person to engage in conduct constituting such offense by either:

(a) making knowingly false representations designed to induce the belief that such conduct is not prohibited; or

(b) employing methods of persuasion or inducement which create a substantial risk that such an offense will be committed by persons other than those who are ready to commit it.

(2) Except as provided in Subsection (3) of this Section, a person prosecuted for an offense shall be acquitted if he proves by a preponderance of evidence that his conduct occurred in response to an entrapment. The issue of entrapment shall be tried by the Court in the absence of the jury.

(3) The defense afforded by this Section is unavailable when causing or threatening bodily injury is an element of the offense charged and the prosecution is based on conduct causing or threatening such injury to a person other than the person perpetrating the entrapment.

ARTICLE 3. GENERAL PRINCIPLES OF JUSTIFICATION

Section 3.01. Justification an Affirmative Defense; Civil Remedies Unaffected

(1) In any prosecution based on conduct which is justifiable under this Article, justification is an affirmative defense.

(2) The fact that conduct is justifiable under this Article does not abolish or impair any remedy for such conduct which is available in any civil action.

Section 3.02. Justification Generally: Choice of Evils

(1) Conduct which the actor believes to be necessary to avoid a harm or evil to himself or to another is justifiable, provided that:

(a) the harm or evil sought to be avoided by such conduct is greater than that sought to be prevented by the law defining the offense charged; and

(b) neither the Code nor other law defining the offense provides exceptions or defenses dealing with the specific situation involved; and

(c) a legislative purpose to exclude the justification claimed does not otherwise plainly appear.

(2) When the actor was reckless or negligent in bringing about the situation requiring a choice of harms or evils or in appraising the necessity for his conduct, the justification afforded by this Section is unavailable in a prosecution for any offense for which recklessness or negligence, as the case may be, suffices to establish culpability.

Section 3.03. Execution of Public Duty

(1) Except as provided in Subsection (2) of this Section, conduct is justifiable when it is required or authorized by:

(a) the law defining the duties or functions of a public officer or the assistance to be rendered to such officer in the performance of his duties; or

(b) the law governing the execution of legal process; or

(c) the judgment or order of a competent court or tribunal; or

(d) the law governing the armed services or the lawful conduct of war; or

(e) any other provision of law imposing a public duty.

(2) The other sections of this Article apply to:

(a) the use of force upon or toward the person of another for any of the purposes dealt with in such sections; and

(b) the use of deadly force for any purpose, unless the use of such force is otherwise expressly authorized by law or occurs in the lawful conduct of war.

(3) The justification afforded by Subsection (1) of this Section applies:

(a) when the actor believes his conduct to be required or authorized by the judgment or direction of a competent court or tribunal or in the lawful execution of legal process, notwithstanding lack of jurisdiction of the court or defect in the legal process; and

(b) when the actor believes his conduct to be required or authorized to assist a public officer in the performance of his duties, notwithstanding that the officer exceeded his legal authority.

Section 3.04. Use of Force in Self-Protection

(1) <u>Use of Force Justifiable for Protection of the Person.</u> Subject to the provisions of this Section and of Section 3.09, the use of force upon or toward another person is justifiable when the actor believes that such force is immediately necessary for the purpose of protecting himself against the use of unlawful force by such other person on the present occasion.

(2) Limitations on Justifying Necessity for Use of Force.

(a) The use of force is not justifiable under this Section:

(i) to resist an arrest which the actor knows is being made by a peace officer, although the arrest is unlawful; or

(ii) to resist force used by the occupier or possessor of property or by another person on his behalf, where the actor knows that the person using the force is doing so under a claim of right to protect the property, except that this limitation shall not apply if:

(1) the actor is a public officer acting in the performance of his duties or a person lawfully assisting him therein or a person making or assisting in a lawful arrest; or

(2) the actor has been unlawfully dispossessed of the property and is making a re-entry or recaption justified by Section 3.06; or

(3) the actor believes that such force is necessary to protect himself against death or serious bodily harm.

(b) The use of deadly force is not justifiable under this Section unless the actor believes that such force is necessary to protect himself against death, serious bodily harm, kidnapping or sexual intercourse compelled by force or threat; nor is it justifiable if:

(i) the actor, with the purpose of causing death or serious bodily harm, provoked the use of force against himself in the same encounter; or

(ii) the actor knows that he can avoid the necessity of using such force with complete safety by retreating or by surrendering possession of a thing to a person asserting a claim of right thereto or by complying with a demand that he abstain from any action which he has no duty to take, except that:

(1) the actor is not obliged to retreat from his dwelling or place of work, unless he was the initial aggressor or is assailed in his place of work by another person whose place of work the actor knows it to be; and

(2) a public officer justified in using force in the performance of his duties or a person justified in using force in his assistance or a person justified in using force in making an arrest or preventing an escape is not obliged to desist from efforts to perform such duty, effect such arrest or prevent such escape because of resistance or threatened resistance by or on behalf of the person against whom such action is directed.

(c) Except as required by paragraphs (a) and (b) of this Subsection, a person employing protective force may estimate the necessity thereof under the circumstances as he believes them to be when the force is used, without retreating, surrendering possession, doing any other act which he has no legal duty to do or abstaining from any lawful action.

(3) Use of Confinement as Protective Force. The justification afforded by this Section extends to the use of confinement as protective force only if the actor takes all reasonable measures to terminate the confinement as soon as he knows that he safely can, unless the person confined has been arrested on a charge of crime.

Section 3.05. Use of Force for the Protection of Other Persons

(1) Subject to the provisions of this Section and of Section 3.09, the use of force upon or toward the person of another is justifiable to protect a third person when:

(a) the actor would be justified under Section 3.04 in using such force to protect himself against the injury he believes to be threatened to the person whom he seeks to protect; and

(b) under the circumstances as the actor believes them to be, the person whom he seeks to protect would be justified in using such protective force; and

(c) the actor believes that his intervention is necessary for the protection of such other person.

(2) Notwithstanding Subsection (1) of this Section:

(a) when the actor would be obliged under Section 3.04 to retreat, to surrender the possession of a thing or to comply with a demand before using force in self-protection, he is not obliged to do so before using force for the protection of another person, unless he knows that he can thereby secure the complete safety of such other person; and

(b) when the person whom the actor seeks to protect would be obliged under Section 3.04 to retreat, to surrender the possession of a thing or to comply with a demand if he knew that he could obtain complete safety by so doing, the actor is obliged to try to cause him to do so before using force in his protection if the actor knows that he can obtain complete safety in that way; and

(c) neither the actor nor the person whom he seeks to protect is obliged to retreat when in the other's dwelling or place of work to any greater extent than in his own.

Section 3.06. Use of Force for the Protection of Property

(1) Use of Force Justifiable for Protection of Property. Subject to the provisions of this Section and of Section 3.09, the use of force upon or toward the person of another is justifiable when the actor believes that such force is immediately necessary:

(a) to prevent or terminate an unlawful entry or other trespass upon land or a trespass against or the unlawful carrying away of tangible, movable property, provided that such land or movable property is, or is believed by the actor to be, in his possession or in the possession of another person for whose protection he acts; or

(b) to effect an entry or re-entry upon land or to retake tangible movable property, provided that the actor believes that he or the person by whose authority he acts or a person from whom he or such other person derives title was unlawfully dispossessed of such land or movable property and is entitled to possession, and provided, further, that:

(i) the force is used immediately or on fresh pursuit after such dispossession; or

(ii) the actor believes that the person against whom he uses force has no claim of right to the possession of the property and, in the case of land, the circumstances, as the actor believes them to be, are of such urgency that it would be an exceptional hardship to postpone the entry or re-entry until a court order is obtained.

(2) Meaning of Possession. For the purposes of Subsection (1) of this Section:

(a) a person who has parted with the custody of property to another who refuses to restore it to him is no longer in possession, unless the property is movable and was and still is located on land in his possession;

(b) a person who has been dispossessed of land does not regain possession thereof merely by setting foot thereon;

(c) a person who has a license to use or occupy real property is deemed to be in possession thereof except against the licensor acting under claim of right.

(3) Limitations on Justifiable Use of Force.

(a) Request to Desist. The use of force is justifiable under this Section only if the actor first requests the person against whom such force is used to desist from his interference with the property, unless the actor believes that:

(i) such request would be useless; or

(ii) it would be dangerous to himself or another person to make the request; or

(iii) substantial harm will be done to the physical condition of the property which is sought to be protected before the request can effectively be made.

(b) Exclusion of Trespasser. The use of force to prevent or terminate a trespass is not justifiable under this Section if the actor knows that the exclusion of the trespasser will expose him to substantial danger or serious bodily harm.

(c) Resistance of Lawful Re-entry or Recaption. The use of force to prevent an entry or re-entry upon land or the recaption of movable property is not justifiable under this Section, although the actor believes that such re-entry or recaption is unlawful, if:

(i) the re-entry or recaption is made by or on behalf of a person who was actually dispossessed of the property; and

(ii) it is otherwise justifiable under paragraph (1)(b) of this Section.

(d) Use of Deadly Force. The use of deadly force is not justifiable under this Section unless the actor believes that:

(i) the person against whom the force is used is attempting to dispossess him of his dwelling otherwise than under a claim of right to its possession; or

(ii) the person against whom the force is used is attempting to commit or consummate arson, burglary, robbery or other felonious theft or property destruction and either:

(1) has employed or threatened deadly force against or in the presence of the actor; or

(2) the use of force other than deadly force to prevent the commission or the consummation of the crime would expose the actor or another in his presence to substantial danger of serious bodily harm.

(4) Use of Confinement as Protective Force. The justification afforded by this Section extends to the use of confinement as protective force only if the actor takes all reasonable measures to terminate the confinement as soon as he

knows that he can do so with safety to the property, unless the person confined has been arrested on a charge of crime.

(5) Use of Device to Protect Property. The justification afforded by this Section extends to the use of a device for the purpose of protecting property only if:

(a) the device is not designed to cause or known to create a substantial risk of causing death or serious bodily harm; and

(b) the use of the particular device to protect the property from entry or trespass is reasonable under the circumstances, as the actor believes them to be; and

(c) the device is one customarily used for such a purpose or reasonable care is taken to make known to probable intruders the fact that it is used.

(6) Use of Force to Pass Wrongful Obstructor. The use of force to pass a person whom the actor believes to be purposely or knowingly and unjustifiably obstructing the actor from going to a place to which he may lawfully go is justifiable, provided that:

(a) the actor believes that the person against whom he uses force has no claim of right to obstruct the actor; and

(b) the actor is not being obstructed from entry or movement on land which he knows to be in the possession or custody of the person obstructing him, or in the possession or custody of another person by whose authority the obstructor acts, unless the circumstances, as the actor believes them to be, are of such urgency that it would not be reasonable to postpone the entry or movement on such land until a court order is obtained; and

(c) the force used is not greater than would be justifiable if the person obstructing the actor were using force against him to prevent his passage.

Section 3.07. Use of Force in Law Enforcement

(1) Use of Force Justifiable to Effect an Arrest. Subject to the provisions of this Section and of Section 3.09, the use of force upon or toward the person of another is justifiable when the actor is making or assisting in making an arrest and the actor believes that such force is immediately necessary to effect a lawful arrest.

(2) Limitations on the Use of Force.

(a) The use of force is not justifiable under this Section unless:

(i) the actor makes known the purpose of the arrest or believes that it is otherwise known by or cannot reasonably be made known to the person to be arrested; and

(ii) when the arrest is made under a warrant, the warrant is valid or believed by the actor to be valid.

(b) The use of deadly force is not justifiable under this Section unless:

(i) the arrest is for a felony; and

(ii) the person effecting the arrest is authorized to act as a peace officer or is assisting a person whom he believes to be authorized to act as a peace officer; and

(iii) the actor believes that the force employed creates no substantial risk of injury to innocent persons; and

(iv) the actor believes that:

(1) the crime for which the arrest is made involved conduct including the use or threatened use of deadly force; or

(2) there is a substantial risk that the person to be arrested will cause death or serious bodily harm if his apprehension is delayed.

(3) Use of Force to Prevent Escape from Custody. The use of force to prevent the escape of an arrested person from custody is justifiable when the force could justifiably have been employed to effect the arrest under which the person is in custody, except that a guard or other person authorized to act as a peace officer is justified in using any force, including deadly force, which he believes to be immediately necessary to prevent the escape of a person from a jail, prison, or other institution for the detention of persons charged with or convicted of a crime.

(4) Use of Force by Private Person Assisting an Unlawful Arrest.

(a) A private person who is summoned by a peace officer to assist in effecting an unlawful arrest, is justified in using any force which he would be justified in using if the arrest were lawful, provided that he does not believe the arrest is unlawful.

(b) A private person who assists another private person in effecting an unlawful arrest, or who, not being summoned, assists a peace officer in effecting an unlawful arrest, is justified in using any force which he would be justified in using if the arrest were lawful, provided that (i) he believes the arrest is lawful, and (ii) the arrest would be lawful if the facts were as he believes them to be.

(5) Use of Force to Prevent Suicide or the Commission of a Crime.

(a) The use of force upon or toward the person of another is justifiable when the actor believes that such force is immediately necessary to prevent such other person from committing suicide, inflicting serious bodily harm upon himself, committing or consummating the commission of a crime involving or threatening bodily harm, damage to or loss of property or a breach of the peace, except that:

(i) any limitations imposed by the other provisions of this Article on the justifiable use of force in self-protection, for the protection of others, the protection of property, the effectuation of an arrest or the prevention of an escape from custody shall apply notwithstanding the criminality of the conduct against which such force is used; and

(ii) the use of deadly force is not in any event justifiable under this Subsection unless:

(1) the actor believes that there is a substantial risk that the person whom he seeks to prevent from committing a crime will cause death or serious bodily harm to another unless the commission or the consummation of the crime is prevented and that the use of such force presents no substantial risk of injury to innocent persons; or

(2) the actor believes that the use of such force is necessary to suppress a riot or mutiny after the rioters or mutineers have been ordered to disperse and warned, in any particular manner that the law may require, that such force will be used if they do not obey.

(b) The justification afforded by this Subsection extends to the use of confinement as preventive force only if the actor takes all reasonable measures to terminate the confinement as soon as he knows that he safely can, unless the person confined has been arrested on a charge of crime.

Section 3.08. Use of Force by Persons with Special Responsibility for Care, Discipline or Safety of Others

The use of force upon or toward the person of another is justifiable if:

(1) the actor is the parent or guardian or other person similarly responsible for the general care and supervision of a minor or a person acting at the request of such parent, guardian or other responsible person and:

(a) the force is used for the purpose of safeguarding or promoting the welfare of the minor, including the prevention or punishment of his misconduct; and

(b) the force used is not designed to cause or known to create a substantial risk of causing death, serious bodily harm, disfigurement, extreme pain or mental distress or gross degradation; or

(2) the actor is a teacher or a person otherwise entrusted with the care or supervision for a special purpose of a minor and:

(a) the actor believes that the force used is necessary to further such special purpose, including the maintenance of reasonable discipline in a school, class or other group, and that the use of such force is consistent with the welfare of the minor; and

(b) the degree of force, if it had been used by the parent or guardian of the minor, would not be unjustifiable under Subsection (1)(b) of this Section; or

(3) the actor is the guardian or other person similarly responsible for the general care and supervision of an incompetent person; and:

(a) the force is used for the purpose of safeguarding or promoting the welfare of the incompetent person, including the prevention of his misconduct, or, when such incompetent person is in a hospital or other institution for his care and custody, for the maintenance of reasonable discipline in such institution; and

(b) the force used is not designed to cause or known to create a substantial risk of causing death, serious bodily harm, disfigurement, extreme or unnecessary pain, mental distress, or humiliation; or

(4) the actor is a doctor or other therapist or a person assisting him at his direction, and:

(a) the force is used for the purpose of administering a recognized form of treatment which the actor believes to be adapted to promoting the physical or mental health of the patient; and

(b) the treatment is administered with the consent of the patient or, if the patient is a minor or an incompetent person, with the consent of his parent or guardian or other person legally competent to consent in his behalf, or the treatment is administered in an emergency when the actor believes that no one competent to consent can be consulted and that a reasonable person, wishing to safeguard the welfare of the patient, would consent; or

(5) the actor is a warden or other authorized official of a correctional institution, and:

(a) he believes that the force used is necessary for the purpose of enforcing the lawful rules or procedures of the institution, unless his belief in the lawfulness of the rule or procedure sought to be enforced is erroneous and his error is due to ignorance or mistake as to the provisions of the Code, any other provision of the criminal law or the law governing the administration of the institution; and

(b) the nature or degree of force used is not forbidden by Article 303 or 304 of the Code; and

(c) if deadly force is used, its use is otherwise justifiable under this Article; or

(6) the actor is a person responsible for the safety of a vessel or an aircraft or a person acting at his direction, and

(a) he believes that the force used is necessary to prevent interference with the operation of the vessel or aircraft or obstruction of the execution of a lawful order, unless his belief in the lawfulness of the order is erroneous and his error is due to ignorance or mistake as to the law defining his authority; and

(b) if deadly force is used, its use is otherwise justifiable under this Article; or

(7) the actor is a person who is authorized or required by law to maintain order or decorum in a vehicle, train or other carrier or in a place where others are assembled, and:

(a) he believes that the force used is necessary for such purpose; and

(b) the force used is not designed to cause or known to create a substantial risk of causing death, bodily harm, or extreme mental distress.

Section 3.09. Mistake of Law as to Unlawfulness of Force or Legality of Arrest; Reckless or Negligent Use of Otherwise Justifiable Force; Reckless or Negligent Injury or Risk of Injury to Innocent Persons

(1) The justification afforded by Sections 3.04 to 3.07, inclusive, is unavailable when:

(a) the actor's belief in the unlawfulness of the force or conduct against which he employs protective force or his belief in the lawfulness of an arrest which he endeavors to effect by force is erroneous; and

(b) his error is due to ignorance or mistake as to the provisions of the Code, any other provision of the criminal law or the law governing the legality of an arrest or search.

(2) When the actor believes that the use of force upon or toward the person of another is necessary for any of the purposes for which such belief would establish a justification under Sections 3.03 to 3.08 but the actor is reckless or negligent in having such belief or in acquiring or failing to acquire any knowledge or belief which is material to the justifiability of his use of force, the justification afforded by those Sections is unavailable in a prosecution for an offense for which recklessness or negligence, as the case may be, suffices to establish culpability.

(3) When the actor is justified under Sections 3.03 to 3.08 in using force upon or toward the person of another but he recklessly or negligently injures or creates a risk of injury to innocent persons, the justification afforded by those Sections is unavailable in a prosecution for such recklessness or negligence towards innocent persons.

Section 3.10. Justification in Property Crimes

Conduct involving the appropriation, seizure or destruction of, damage to, intrusion on or interference with property is justifiable under circumstances which would establish a defense of privilege in a civil action based thereon, unless:

(1) the Code or the law defining the offense deals with the specific situation involved; or

(2) a legislative purpose to exclude the justification claimed otherwise plainly appears.

Section 3.11. Definitions

In this Article, unless a different meaning plainly is required:

(1) "unlawful force" means force, including confinement, which is employed without the consent of the person against whom it is directed and the employment of which constitutes an offense or actionable tort or would constitute such offense or tort except for a defense (such as the absence of intent, negligence, or mental capacity; duress; youth; or diplomatic status) not amounting to a privilege to use the force. Assent constitutes consent, within the meaning of this Section, whether or not it otherwise is legally effective, except assent to the infliction of death or serious bodily harm.

(2) "deadly force" means force which the actor uses with the purpose of causing or which he knows to create a substantial risk of causing death or serious bodily harm. Purposely firing a firearm in the direction of another person or at a vehicle in which another person is believed to be constitutes deadly force. A threat to cause death or serious bodily harm, by the production of a weapon or otherwise, so long as the actor's purpose is limited to creating an apprehension that he will use deadly force if necessary, does not constitute deadly force;

(3) "dwelling" means any building or structure, though movable or temporary, or a portion thereof, which is for the time being the actor's home or place of lodging.

ARTICLE 4. RESPONSIBILITY

Section 4.01. Mental Disease or Defect Excluding Responsibility

(1) A person is not responsible for criminal conduct if at the time of such conduct as a result of mental disease or defect he lacks substantial capacity either to appreciate the criminality [wrongfulness] of his conduct or to conform his conduct to the requirements of law.

(2) As used in this Article, the terms "mental disease or defect" do not include an abnormality manifested only by repeated criminal or otherwise antisocial conduct.

Section 4.02. Evidence of Mental Disease or Defect Admissible When Relevant to Element of the Offense; [Mental Disease or Defect Impairing Capacity as Ground for Mitigation of Punishment in Capital Cases]

(1) Evidence that the defendant suffered from a mental disease or defect is admissible whenever it is relevant to prove that the defendant did or did not have a state of mind which is an element of the offense.

[(2) Whenever the jury or the Court is authorized to determine or to recommend whether or not the defendant shall be sentenced to death or imprisonment upon conviction, evidence that the capacity of the defendant to appreciate the criminality [wrongfulness] of his conduct or to conform his conduct to the requirements of law was impaired as a result of mental disease or defect is admissible in favor of sentence of imprisonment.]

Section 4.03. Mental Disease or Defect Excluding Responsibility Is Affirmative Defense; Requirement of Notice; Form of Verdict and Judgment When Finding of Irresponsibility Is Made

(1) Mental disease or defect excluding responsibility is an affirmative defense.

(2) Evidence of mental disease or defect excluding responsibility is not admissible unless the defendant, at the time of entering his plea of not guilty or within ten days thereafter or at such later time as the Court may for good cause permit, files a written notice of his purpose to rely on such defense.

(3) When the defendant is acquitted on the ground of mental disease or defect excluding responsibility, the verdict and the judgment shall so state.

Section 4.04. Mental Disease or Defect Excluding Fitness to Proceed

No person who as a result of mental disease or defect lacks capacity to understand the proceedings against him or to assist in his own defense shall be tried, convicted or sentenced for the commission of an offense so long as such incapacity endures.

Section 4.05. Psychiatric Examination of Defendant with Respect to Mental Disease or Defect

(1) Whenever the defendant has filed a notice of intention to rely on the defense of mental disease or defect excluding responsibility, or there is reason to doubt his fitness to proceed, or reason to believe that mental disease or defect of the defendant will otherwise become an issue in the cause, the Court shall appoint at least one qualified psychiatrist or shall request the Superintendent of the _____ Hospital to designate at least one qualified psychiatrist, which designation may be or include himself, to examine and report upon the mental condition of the defendant. The Court may order the defendant to be committed to a hospital or other suitable facility for the purpose of the examination for a period of not exceeding sixty days or such longer period as the Court determines to be necessary for the purpose and may direct that a qualified psychiatrist retained by the defendant be permitted to witness and participate in the examination.

(2) In such examination any method may be employed which is accepted by the medical profession for the examination of those alleged to be suffering from mental disease or defect.

(3) The report of the examination shall include the following: (a) a description of the nature of the examination; (b) a diagnosis of the mental condition of the defendant; (c) if the defendant suffers from a mental disease or defect, an opinion as to his capacity to understand the proceedings against him and to assist in his own defense; (d) when a notice of intention to rely on the defense of irresponsibility has been filed, an opinion as to the extent, if any, to which the capacity of the defendant to appreciate the criminality [wrongfulness] of his conduct or to conform his conduct to the requirements of law was impaired at the time of the criminal conduct charged; and (e) when directed by the Court, an opinion as to the capacity of the defendant to have a particular state of mind which is an element of the offense charged.

If the examination can not be conducted by reason of the unwillingness of the defendant to participate therein, the report shall so state and shall include, if possible, an opinion as to whether such unwillingness of the defendant was the result of mental disease or defect.

The report of the examination shall be filed [in triplicate] with the clerk of the Court, who shall cause copies to be delivered to the district attorney and to counsel for the defendant.

Section 4.06. Determination of Fitness to Proceed; Effect of Finding of Unfitness; Proceedings if Fitness Is Regained [; Post-Commitment Hearing]

(1) When the defendant's fitness to proceed is drawn in question, the issue shall be determined by the Court. If neither the prosecuting attorney nor counsel for the defendant contests the finding of the report filed pursuant to Section 4.05, the Court may make the determination on the basis of such report. If the finding is contested, the Court shall hold a hearing on the issue. If the report is received in evidence upon such hearing, the party who contests the finding thereof shall have the right to summon and to cross-examine the psychiatrists who joined in the report and to offer evidence upon the issue.

(2) If the Court determines that the defendant lacks fitness to proceed, the proceeding against him shall be suspended, except as provided in Subsection (3) [Subsections (3) and (4)] of this Section, and the Court shall commit him to the custody of the Commissioner of Mental Hygiene [Public Health or Correction] to be placed in an appropriate institution of the Department of Mental Hygiene [Public Health or Correction] for so long as such unfitness shall endure. When the Court, on its own motion or upon the application of the Commissioner of Mental Hygiene [Public Health or Correction] or the prosecuting attorney, determines, after a hearing if a hearing is requested, that the defendant has regained fitness to proceed, the proceeding shall be resumed. If, however, the Court is of the view that so much time has elapsed since the commitment of the defendant that it would be unjust to resume the criminal proceeding, the Court may dismiss the charge and may order the defendant to be discharged or, subject to the law governing the civil commitment of persons suffering from mental disease or defect, order the defendant to be committed to an appropriate institution of the Department of Mental Hygiene [Public Health].

(3) The fact that the defendant is unfit to proceed does not preclude any legal objection to the prosecution which is susceptible of fair determination prior to trial and without the personal participation of the defendant.

[Alternative: (3) At any time within ninety days after commitment as provided in Subsection (2) of this Section, or at any later time with permission of the Court granted for good cause, the defendant or his counsel or the Commissioner of Mental Hygiene [Public Health or Correction] may apply for a special post-commitment hearing. If the application is made by or on behalf of a defendant not represented by counsel, he shall be afforded a reasonable opportunity to obtain counsel, and if he lacks funds to do so, counsel shall be assigned by the Court. The application shall be granted only if the counsel for the defendant satisfies the Court by affidavit or otherwise that as an attorney he has reasonable grounds for a good faith belief that his client has, on the facts and the law, a defense to the charge other than mental disease or defect excluding responsibility.

[(4) If the motion for a special post-commitment hearing is granted, the hearing shall be by the Court without a jury. No evidence shall be offered at the hearing by either party on the issue of mental disease or defect as a defense to, or in mitigation of, the crime charged. After hearing, the Court may in an appropriate case quash the indictment or other charge, or find it to be defective or insufficient, or determine that it is not proved beyond a reasonable doubt by the evidence, or otherwise terminate the proceedings on the evidence or the law. In any such case, unless all defects in the proceedings are promptly cured, the Court shall terminate the commitment ordered under Subsection (2) of this Section and order the defendant to be discharged or, subject to the law governing the civil commitment of persons suffering from mental disease or defect, order the defendant to be committed to an appropriate institution of the Department of Mental Hygiene [Public Health].]

Section 4.07. Determination of Irresponsibility on Basis of Report; Access to Defendant by Psychiatrist of His Own Choice; Form of Expert Testimony When Issue of Responsibility Is Tried

(1) If the report filed pursuant to Section 4.05 finds that the defendant at the time of the criminal conduct charged suffered from a mental disease or defect which substantially impaired his capacity to appreciate the criminality [wrongfulness] of his conduct or to conform his conduct to the requirements of law, and the Court, after a hearing if a hearing is requested by the prosecuting attorney or the defendant, is satisfied that such impairment was sufficient to exclude responsibility, the Court on motion of the defendant shall enter judgment of acquittal on the ground of mental disease or defect excluding responsibility.

(2) When, notwithstanding the report filed pursuant to Section 4.05, the defendant wishes to be examined by a qualified psychiatrist or other expert of his own choice, such examiner shall be permitted to have reasonable access to the defendant for the purposes of such examination.

(3) Upon the trial, the psychiatrists who reported pursuant to Section 4.05 may be called as witnesses by the prosecution, the defendant or the Court. If the issue is being tried before a jury, the jury may be informed that the psychiatrists were designated by the Court or by the Superintendent of the _____ Hospital at the request of the Court, as the case may be. If called by the Court, the witness shall be subject to cross-examination by the prosecution and by the defendant. Both the prosecution and the defendant may summon any other qualified psychiatrist or other expert to testify, but no one who has not examined the defendant shall be competent to testify to an expert opinion with

respect to the mental condition or responsibility of the defendant, as distinguished from the validity of the procedure followed by, or the general scientific propositions stated by, another witness.

(4) When a psychiatrist or other expert who has examined the defendant testifies concerning his mental condition, he shall be permitted to make a statement as to the nature of his examination, his diagnosis of the mental condition of the defendant at the time of the commission of the offense charged and his opinion as to the extent, if any, to which the capacity of the defendant to appreciate the criminality [wrongfulness] of his conduct or to conform his conduct to the requirements of law or to have a particular state of mind which is an element of the offense charged was impaired as a result of mental disease or defect at that time. He shall be permitted to make any explanation reasonably serving to clarify his diagnosis and opinion and may be cross-examined as to any matter bearing on his competency or credibility or the validity of his diagnosis or opinion.

Section 4.08. Legal Effect of Acquittal on the Ground of Mental Disease or Defect Excluding Responsibility; Commitment; Release or Discharge

(1) When a defendant is acquitted on the ground of mental disease or defect excluding responsibility, the Court shall order him to be committed to the custody of the Commissioner of Mental Hygiene [Public Health] to be placed in an appropriate institution for custody, care and treatment.

(2) If the Commissioner of Mental Hygiene [Public Health] is of the view that a person committed to his custody, pursuant to paragraph (1) of this Section, may be discharged or released on condition without danger to himself or to others, he shall make application for the discharge or release of such person in a report to the Court by which such person was committed and shall transmit a copy of such application and report to the prosecuting attorney of the county [parish] from which the defendant was committed. The Court shall thereupon appoint at least two qualified psychiatrists to examine such person and to report within sixty days, or such longer period as the Court determines to be necessary for the purpose, their opinion as to his mental condition. To facilitate such examination and the proceedings thereon, the Court may cause such person to be confined in any institution located near the place where the Court sits, which may hereafter be designated by the Commissioner of Mental Hygiene [Public Health] as suitable for the temporary detention of irresponsible persons.

(3) If the Court is satisfied by the report filed pursuant to paragraph (2) of this Section and such testimony of the reporting psychiatrists as the Court deems necessary that the committed person may be discharged or released on condition without danger to himself or others, the Court shall order his discharge or his release on such conditions as the Court determines to be necessary. If the Court is not so satisfied, it shall promptly order a hearing to determine whether such person may safely be discharged or released. Any such hearing shall be deemed a civil proceeding and the burden shall be upon the committed person to prove that he may safely be discharged or released. According to the determination of the Court upon the hearing, the committed person shall thereupon be discharged or released on such conditions as the Court determines to be necessary, or shall be recommitted to the custody of the Commissioner of Mental Hygiene [Public Health], subject to discharge or

release only in accordance with the procedure prescribed above for a first hearing.

(4) If, within [five] years after the conditional release of a committed person, the court shall determine, after hearing evidence, that the conditions of release have not been fulfilled and that for the safety of such person or for the safety of others his conditional release should be revoked, the Court shall forthwith order him to be recommitted to the Commissioner of Mental Hygiene [Public Health], subject to discharge or release only in accordance with the procedure prescribed above for a first hearing.

(5) A committed person may make application for his discharge or release to the Court by which he was committed, and the procedure to be followed upon such application shall be the same as that prescribed above in the case of an application by the Commissioner of Mental Hygiene [Public Health]. However, no such application by a committed person need be considered until he has been confined for a period of not less than [six months] from the date of the order of commitment, and if the determination of the Court be adverse to the application, such person shall not be permitted to file a further application until [one year] has elapsed from the date of any preceding hearing on an application for his release or discharge.

Section 4.09. Statements for Purposes of Examination or Treatment Inadmissible Except on Issue of Mental Condition

A statement made by a person subjected to psychiatric examination or treatment pursuant to Sections 4.05, 4.06 or 4.08 for the purposes of such examination or treatment shall not be admissible in evidence against him in any criminal proceeding on any issue other than that of his mental condition but it shall be admissible upon that issue, whether or not it would otherwise be deemed a privileged communication [, unless such statement constitutes an admission of guilt of the crime charged].

Section 4.10. Immaturity Excluding Criminal Conviction; Transfer of Proceedings to Juvenile Court

(1) A person shall not be tried for or convicted of an offense if:

(a) at the time of the conduct charged to constitute the offense he was less than sixteen years of age [, in which case the Juvenile Court shall have exclusive jurisdiction]; or

(b) at the time of the conduct charged to constitute the offense he was sixteen or seventeen years of age, unless:

(i) the Juvenile Court has no jurisdiction over him, or,

(ii) the Juvenile Court has entered an order waiving jurisdiction and consenting to the institution of criminal proceedings against him.

(2) No court shall have jurisdiction to try or convict a person of an offense if criminal proceedings against him are barred by Subsection (1) of this Section. When it appears that a person charged with the commission of an offense may be of such an age that criminal proceedings may be barred under Subsection (1) of this Section, the Court shall hold a hearing thereon, and the burden shall be on the prosecution to establish to the satisfaction of the Court that the criminal proceeding is not barred upon such grounds. If the Court determines that the proceeding is barred, custody of the person charged shall be surrendered to the

Juvenile Court, and the case, including all papers and processes relating thereto, shall be transferred.

ARTICLE 5. INCHOATE CRIMES

Section 5.01. Criminal Attempt

(1) <u>Definition of Attempt.</u> A person is guilty of an attempt to commit a crime if, acting with the kind of culpability otherwise required for commission of the crime, he:

(a) purposely engages in conduct which would constitute the crime if the attendant circumstances were as he believes them to be; or

(b) when causing a particular result is an element of the crime, does or omits to do anything with the purpose of causing or with the belief that it will cause such result without further conduct on his part; or

(c) purposely does or omits to do anything which, under the circumstances as he believes them to be, is an act or omission constituting a substantial step in a course of conduct planned to culminate in his commission of the crime.

(2) <u>Conduct Which May Be Held Substantial Step Under Subsection (1)(c).</u> Conduct shall not be held to constitute a substantial step under Subsection (1)(c) of this Section unless it is strongly corroborative of the actor's criminal purpose. Without negativing the sufficiency of other conduct, the following, if strongly corroborative of the actor's criminal purpose, shall not be held insufficient as a matter of law:

(a) lying in wait, searching for or following the contemplated victim of the crime;

(b) enticing or seeking to entice the contemplated victim of the crime to go to the place contemplated for its commission;

(c) reconnoitering the place contemplated for the commission of the crime;

(d) unlawful entry of a structure, vehicle or enclosure in which it is contemplated that the crime will be committed;

(e) possession of materials to be employed in the commission of the crime, which are specially designed for such unlawful use or which can serve no lawful purpose of the actor under the circumstances;

(f) possession, collection or fabrication of materials to be employed in the commission of the crime, at or near the place contemplated for its commission, where such possession, collection or fabrication serves no lawful purpose of the actor under the circumstances;

(g) soliciting an innocent agent to engage in conduct constituting an element of the crime.

(3) <u>Conduct Designed to Aid Another in Commission of a Crime.</u> A person who engages in conduct designed to aid another to commit a crime which would establish his complicity under Section 2.06 if the crime were committed by such other person, is guilty of an attempt to commit the crime, although the crime is not committed or attempted by such other person.

(4) <u>Renunciation of Criminal Purpose.</u> When the actor's conduct would otherwise constitute an attempt under Subsection (1)(b) or (1)(c) of this Section, it is an affirmative defense that he abandoned his effort to commit the crime or otherwise prevented its commission, under circumstances manifesting a com-

plete and voluntary renunciation of his criminal purpose. The establishment of such defense does not, however, affect the liability of an accomplice who did not join in such abandonment or prevention.

Within the meaning of this Article, renunciation of criminal purpose is not voluntary if it is motivated, in whole or in part, by circumstances, not present or apparent at the inception of the actor's course of conduct, which increase the probability of detection or apprehension or which make more difficult the accomplishment of the criminal purpose. Renunciation is not complete if it is motivated by a decision to postpone the criminal conduct until a more advantageous time or to transfer the criminal effort to another but similar objective or victim.

Section 5.02. Criminal Solicitation

(1) Definition of Solicitation. A person is guilty of solicitation to commit a crime if with the purpose of promoting or facilitating its commission he commands, encourages or requests another person to engage in specific conduct which would constitute such crime or an attempt to commit such crime or which would establish his complicity in its commission or attempted commission.

(2) Uncommunicated Solicitation. It is immaterial under Subsection (1) of this Section that the actor fails to communicate with the person he solicits to commit a crime if his conduct was designed to effect such communication.

(3) Renunciation of Criminal Purpose. It is an affirmative defense that the actor, after soliciting another person to commit a crime, persuaded him not to do so or otherwise prevented the commission of the crime, under circumstances manifesting a complete and voluntary renunciation of his criminal purpose.

Section 5.03. Criminal Conspiracy

(1) Definition of Conspiracy. A person is guilty of conspiracy with another person or persons to commit a crime if with the purpose of promoting or facilitating its commission he:

(a) agrees with such other person or persons that they or one or more of them will engage in conduct which constitutes such crime or an attempt or solicitation to commit such crime; or

(b) agrees to aid such other person or persons in the planning or commission of such crime or of an attempt or solicitation to commit such crime.

(2) Scope of Conspiratorial Relationship. If a person guilty of conspiracy, as defined by Subsection (1) of this Section, knows that a person with whom he conspires to commit a crime has conspired with another person or persons to commit the same crime, he is guilty of conspiring with such other person or persons, whether or not he knows their identity, to commit such crime.

(3) Conspiracy With Multiple Criminal Objectives. If a person conspires to commit a number of crimes, he is guilty of only one conspiracy so long as such multiple crimes are the object of the same agreement or continuous conspiratorial relationship.

(4) Joinder and Venue in Conspiracy Prosecutions.

(a) Subject to the provisions of paragraph (b) of this Subsection, two or more persons charged with criminal conspiracy may be prosecuted jointly if:

(i) they are charged with conspiring with one another; or

(ii) the conspiracies alleged, whether they have the same or different parties, are so related that they constitute different aspects of a scheme of organized criminal conduct.

(b) In any joint prosecution under paragraph (a) of this Subsection:

(i) no defendant shall be charged with a conspiracy in any county [parish or district] other than one in which he entered into such conspiracy or in which an overt act pursuant to such conspiracy was done by him or by a person with whom he conspired; and

(ii) neither the liability of any defendant nor the admissibility against him of evidence of acts or declarations of another shall be enlarged by such joinder; and

(iii) the Court shall order a severance or take a special verdict as to any defendant who so requests, if it deems it necessary or appropriate to promote the fair determination of his guilt or innocence, and shall take any other proper measures to protect the fairness of the trial.

(5) Overt Act. No person may be convicted of conspiracy to commit a crime, other than a felony of the first or second degree, unless an overt act in pursuance of such conspiracy is alleged and proved to have been done by him or by a person with whom he conspired.

(6) Renunciation of Criminal Purpose. It is an affirmative defense that the actor, after conspiring to commit a crime, thwarted the success of the conspiracy, under circumstances manifesting a complete and voluntary renunciation of his criminal purpose.

(7) Duration of Conspiracy. For purposes of Section 1.06(4):

(a) conspiracy is a continuing course of conduct which terminates when the crime or crimes which are its object are committed or the agreement that they be committed is abandoned by the defendant and by those with whom he conspired; and

(b) such abandonment is presumed if neither the defendant nor anyone with whom he conspired does any overt act in pursuance of the conspiracy during the applicable period of limitation; and

(c) if an individual abandons the agreement, the conspiracy is terminated as to him only if and when he advises those with whom he conspired of his abandonment or he informs the law enforcement authorities of the existence of the conspiracy and of his participation therein.

Section 5.04. Incapacity, Irresponsibility or Immunity of Party to Solicitation or Conspiracy

(1) Except as provided in Subsection (2) of this Section, it is immaterial to the liability of a person who solicits or conspires with another to commit a crime that:

(a) he or the person whom he solicits or with whom he conspires does not occupy a particular position or have a particular characteristic which is an element of such crime, if he believes that one of them does; or

(b) the person whom he solicits or with whom he conspires is irresponsible or has an immunity to prosecution or conviction for the commission of the crime.

(2) It is a defense to a charge of solicitation or conspiracy to commit a crime that if the criminal object were achieved, the actor would not be guilty of a

crime under the law defining the offense or as an accomplice under Section 2.06(5) or 2.06(6)(a) or (b).

Section 5.05.　Grading of Criminal Attempt, Solicitation and Conspiracy; Mitigation in Cases of Lesser Danger; Multiple Convictions Barred

(1) Grading.　Except as otherwise provided in this Section, attempt, solicitation and conspiracy are crimes of the same grade and degree as the most serious offense which is attempted or solicited or is an object of the conspiracy. An attempt, solicitation or conspiracy to commit a [capital crime or a] felony of the first degree is a felony of the second degree.

(2) Mitigation.　If the particular conduct charged to constitute a criminal attempt, solicitation or conspiracy is so inherently unlikely to result or culminate in the commission of a crime that neither such conduct nor the actor presents a public danger warranting the grading of such offense under this Section, the Court shall exercise its power under Section 6.12 to enter judgment and impose sentence for a crime of lower grade or degree or, in extreme cases, may dismiss the prosecution.

(3) Multiple Convictions.　A person may not be convicted of more than one offense defined by this Article for conduct designed to commit or to culminate in the commission of the same crime.

Section 5.06.　Possessing Instruments of Crime; Weapons

(1) Criminal Instruments Generally.　A person commits a misdemeanor if he possesses any instrument of crime with purpose to employ it criminally. "Instrument of crime" means:

> (a) anything specially made or specially adapted for criminal use; or

> (b) anything commonly used for criminal purposes and possessed by the actor under circumstances which do not negative unlawful purpose.

(2) Presumption of Criminal Purpose from Possession of Weapon.　If a person possesses a firearm or other weapon on or about his person, in a vehicle occupied by him, or otherwise readily available for use, it is presumed that he had the purpose to employ it criminally, unless:

> (a) the weapon is possessed in the actor's home or place of business;

> (b) the actor is licensed or otherwise authorized by law to possess such weapon; or

> (c) the weapon is of a type commonly used in lawful sport.

"Weapon" means anything readily capable of lethal use and possessed under circumstances not manifestly appropriate for lawful uses which it may have; the term includes a firearm which is not loaded or lacks a clip or other component to render it immediately operable, and components which can readily be assembled into a weapon.

(3) Presumptions as to Possession of Criminal Instruments in Automobiles. Where a weapon or other instrument of crime is found in an automobile, it shall be presumed to be in the possession of the occupant if there is but one. If there is more than one occupant, it shall be presumed to be in the possession of all, except under the following circumstances:

> (a) where it is found upon the person of one of the occupants;

(b) where the automobile is not a stolen one and the weapon or instrument is found out of view in a glove compartment, car trunk, or other enclosed customary depository, in which case it shall be presumed to be in the possession of the occupant or occupants who own or have authority to operate the automobile;

(c) in the case of a taxicab, a weapon or instrument found in the passengers' portion of the vehicle shall be presumed to be in the possession of all the passengers, if there are any, and, if not, in the possession of the driver.

Section 5.07. Prohibited Offensive Weapons

A person commits a misdemeanor if, except as authorized by law, he makes, repairs, sells, or otherwise deals in, uses, or possesses any offensive weapon. "Offensive weapon" means any bomb, machine gun, sawed-off shotgun, firearm specially made or specially adapted for concealment or silent discharge, any blackjack, sandbag, metal knuckles, dagger, or other implement for the infliction of serious bodily injury which serves no common lawful purpose. It is a defense under this Section for the defendant to prove by a preponderance of evidence that he possessed or dealt with the weapon solely as a curio or in a dramatic performance, or that he possessed it briefly in consequence of having found it or taken it from an aggressor, or under circumstances similarly negativing any purpose or likelihood that the weapon would be used unlawfully. The presumptions provided in Section 5.06(3) are applicable to prosecutions under this Section.

ARTICLE 6. AUTHORIZED DISPOSITION OF OFFENDERS

Section 6.01. Degrees of Felonies

(1) Felonies defined by this Code are classified, for the purpose of sentence, into three degrees, as follows:

(a) felonies of the first degree;

(b) felonies of the second degree;

(c) felonies of the third degree.

A felony is of the first or second degree when it is so designated by the Code. A crime declared to be a felony, without specification of degree, is of the third degree.

(2) Notwithstanding any other provision of law, a felony defined by any statute of this State other than this Code shall constitute for the purpose of sentence a felony of the third degree.

Section 6.02. Sentence in Accordance with Code; Authorized Dispositions

(1) No person convicted of an offense shall be sentenced otherwise than in accordance with this Article.

[(2) The Court shall sentence a person who has been convicted of murder to death or imprisonment, in accordance with Section 210.6.]

(3) Except as provided in Subsection (2) of this Section and subject to the applicable provisions of the Code, the Court may suspend the imposition of sentence on a person who has been convicted of a crime, may order him to be

committed in lieu of sentence, in accordance with Section 6.13, or may sentence him as follows:

    (a) to pay a fine authorized by Section 6.03; or

    (b) to be placed on probation [, and, in the case of a person convicted of a felony or misdemeanor to imprisonment for a term fixed by the Court not exceeding thirty days to be served as a condition of probation]; or

    (c) to imprisonment for a term authorized by Sections 6.05, 6.06, 6.07, 6.08, 6.09, or 7.06; or

    (d) to fine and probation or fine and imprisonment, but not to probation and imprisonment [, except as authorized in paragraph (b) of this Subsection].

(4) The Court may suspend the imposition of sentence on a person who has been convicted of a violation or may sentence him to pay a fine authorized by Section 6.03.

(5) This Article does not deprive the Court of any authority conferred by law to decree a forfeiture of property, suspend or cancel a license, remove a person from office, or impose any other civil penalty. Such a judgment or order may be included in the sentence.

Section 6.03. Fines

A person who has been convicted of an offense may be sentenced to pay a fine not exceeding:

    (1) $10,000, when the conviction is of a felony of the first or second degree;

    (2) $5,000, when the conviction is of a felony of the third degree;

    (3) $1,000, when the conviction is of a misdemeanor;

    (4) $500, when the conviction is of a petty misdemeanor or a violation;

    (5) any higher amount equal to double the pecuniary gain derived from the offense by the offender;

    (6) any higher amount specifically authorized by statute.

Section 6.04. Penalties Against Corporations and Unincorporated Associations; Forfeiture of Corporate Charter or Revocation of Certificate Authorizing Foreign Corporation to Do Business in the State

(1) The Court may suspend the sentence of a corporation or an unincorporated association which has been convicted of an offense or may sentence it to pay a fine authorized by Section 6.03.

(2) (a) The [prosecuting attorney] is authorized to institute civil proceedings in the appropriate court of general jurisdiction to forfeit the charter of a corporation organized under the laws of this State or to revoke the certificate authorizing a foreign corporation to conduct business in this State. The Court may order the charter forfeited or the certificate revoked upon finding (i) that the board of directors or a high managerial agent acting in behalf of the corporation has, in conducting the corporation's affairs, purposely engaged in a persistent course of criminal conduct and (ii) that for the prevention of future criminal conduct of the same character, the public interest requires the charter of the corporation to be forfeited and the corporation to be dissolved or the certificate to be revoked.

(b) When a corporation is convicted of a crime or a high managerial agent of a corporation, as defined in Section 2.07, is convicted of a crime committed in the conduct of the affairs of the corporation, the Court, in sentencing the corporation or the agent, may direct the [prosecuting attorney] to institute proceedings authorized by paragraph (a) of this Subsection.

(c) The proceedings authorized by paragraph (a) of this Subsection shall be conducted in accordance with the procedures authorized by law for the involuntary dissolution of a corporation or the revocation of the certificate authorizing a foreign corporation to conduct business in this State. Such proceedings shall be deemed additional to any other proceedings authorized by law for the purpose of forfeiting the charter of a corporation or revoking the certificate of a foreign corporation.

Section 6.05. Young Adult Offenders

(1) Specialized Correctional Treatment. A young adult offender is a person convicted of a crime who, at the time of sentencing, is sixteen but less than twenty-two years of age. A young adult offender who is sentenced to a term of imprisonment which may exceed thirty days [alternatives: (1) ninety days; (2) one year] shall be committed to the custody of the Division of Young Adult Correction of the Department of Correction, and shall receive, as far as practicable, such special and individualized correctional and rehabilitative treatment as may be appropriate to his needs.

(2) Special Term. A young adult offender convicted of a felony may, in lieu of any other sentence of imprisonment authorized by this Article, be sentenced to a special term of imprisonment without a minimum and with a maximum of four years, regardless of the degree of the felony involved, if the Court is of the opinion that such special term is adequate for his correction and rehabilitation and will not jeopardize the protection of the public.

[(3) Removal of Disabilities; Vacation of Conviction.

(a) In sentencing a young adult offender to the special term provided by this Section or to any sentence other than one of imprisonment, the Court may order that so long as he is not convicted of another felony, the judgment shall not constitute a conviction for the purposes of any disqualification or disability imposed by law upon conviction of a crime.

(b) When any young adult offender is unconditionally discharged from probation or parole before the expiration of the maximum term thereof, the Court may enter an order vacating the judgment of conviction.]

[(4) Commitment for Observation. If, after pre-sentence investigation, the Court desires additional information concerning a young adult offender before imposing sentence, it may order that he be committed, for a period not exceeding ninety days, to the custody of the Division of Young Adult Correction of the Department of Correction for observation and study at an appropriate reception or classification center. Such Division of the Department of Correction and the [Young Adult Division of the] Board of Parole shall advise the Court of their findings and recommendations on or before the expiration of such ninety-day period.]

Section 6.06. Sentence of Imprisonment for Felony; Ordinary Terms

A person who has been convicted of a felony may be sentenced to imprisonment, as follows:

(1) in the case of a felony of the first degree, for a term the minimum of which shall be fixed by the Court at not less than one year nor more than ten years, and the maximum of which shall be life imprisonment;

(2) in the case of a felony of the second degree, for a term the minimum of which shall be fixed by the Court at not less than one year nor more than three years, and the maximum of which shall be ten years;

(3) in the case of a felony of the third degree, for a term the minimum of which shall be fixed by the Court at not less than one year nor more than two years, and the maximum of which shall be five years.

Alternate Section 6.06. Sentence of Imprisonment for Felony; Ordinary Terms

A person who has been convicted of a felony may be sentenced to imprisonment, as follows:

(1) in the case of a felony of the first degree, for a term the minimum of which shall be fixed by the Court at not less than one year nor more than ten years, and the maximum at not more than twenty years or at life imprisonment;

(2) in the case of a felony of the second degree, for a term the minimum of which shall be fixed by the Court at not less than one year nor more than three years, and the maximum at not more than ten years;

(3) in the case of a felony of the third degree, for a term the minimum of which shall be fixed by the Court at not less than one year nor more than two years, and the maximum at not more than five years.

No sentence shall be imposed under this Section of which the minimum is longer than one-half the maximum, or, when the maximum is life imprisonment, longer than ten years.

Section 6.07. Sentence of Imprisonment for Felony; Extended Terms

In the cases designated in Section 7.03, a person who has been convicted of a felony may be sentenced to an extended term of imprisonment, as follows:

(1) in the case of a felony of the first degree, for a term the minimum of which shall be fixed by the Court at not less than five years nor more than ten years, and the maximum of which shall be life imprisonment;

(2) in the case of a felony of the second degree, for a term the minimum of which shall be fixed by the Court at not less than one year nor more than five years, and the maximum of which shall be fixed by the Court at not less than ten nor more than twenty years;

(3) in the case of a felony of the third degree, for a term the minimum of which shall be fixed by the Court at not less than one year nor more than three years, and the maximum of which shall be fixed by the Court at not less than five nor more than ten years.

Section 6.08 Sentence of Imprisonment for Misdemeanors and Petty Misdemeanors; Ordinary Terms

A person who has been convicted of a misdemeanor or a petty misdemeanor may be sentenced to imprisonment for a definite term which shall be fixed by the Court and shall not exceed one year in the case of a misdemeanor or thirty days in the case of a petty misdemeanor.

Section 6.09. Sentence of Imprisonment for Misdemeanors and Petty Misdemeanors; Extended Terms

(1) In the cases designated in Section 7.04, a person who has been convicted of a misdemeanor or a petty misdemeanor may be sentenced to an extended term of imprisonment, as follows:

(a) in the case of a misdemeanor, for a term the minimum of which shall be fixed by the Court at not more than one year and the maximum of which shall be three years;

(b) in the case of a petty misdemeanor, for a term the minimum of which shall be fixed by the Court at not more than six months and the maximum of which shall be two years.

(2) No such sentence for an extended term shall be imposed unless:

(a) the Director of Correction has certified that there is an institution in the Department of Correction, or in a county, city [or other appropriate political subdivision of the State] which is appropriate for the detention and correctional treatment of such misdemeanants or petty misdemeanants, and that such institution is available to receive such commitments; and

(b) the [Board of Parole] [Parole Administrator] has certified that the Board of Parole is able to visit such institution and to assume responsibility for the release of such prisoners on parole and for their parole supervision.

Section 6.10. First Release of All Offenders on Parole; Sentence of Imprisonment Includes Separate Parole Term; Length of Parole Term; Length of Recommitment and Reparole After Revocation of Parole; Final Unconditional Release

(1) First Release of All Offenders on Parole. An offender sentenced to an indefinite term of imprisonment in excess of one year under Section 6.05, 6.06, 6.07, 6.09 or 7.06 shall be released conditionally on parole at or before the expiration of the maximum of such term, in accordance with Article 305.

(2) Sentence of Imprisonment Includes Separate Parole Term; Length of Parole Term. A sentence to an indefinite term of imprisonment in excess of one year under Section 6.05, 6.06, 6.07, 6.09 or 7.06 includes as a separate portion of the sentence a term of parole or of recommitment for violation of the conditions of parole which governs the duration of parole or recommitment after the offender's first conditional release on parole. The minimum of such term is one year and the maximum is five years, unless the sentence was imposed under Section 6.05(2) or Section 6.09, in which case the maximum is two years.

(3) Length of Recommitment and Reparole After Revocation of Parole. If an offender is recommitted upon revocation of his parole, the term of further imprisonment upon such recommitment and of any subsequent reparole or recommitment under the same sentence shall be fixed by the Board of Parole but shall not exceed in aggregate length the unserved balance of the maximum parole term provided by Subsection (2) of this Section.

(4) Final Unconditional Release. When the maximum of his parole term has expired or he has been sooner discharged from parole under Section 305.12, an offender shall be deemed to have served his sentence and shall be released unconditionally.

Section 6.11. Place of Imprisonment

(1) When a person is sentenced to imprisonment for an indefinite term with a maximum in excess of one year, the Court shall commit him to the custody of the Department of Correction [or other single department or agency] for the term of his sentence and until released in accordance with law.

(2) When a person is sentenced to imprisonment for a definite term, the Court shall designate the institution or agency to which he is committed for the term of his sentence and until released in accordance with law.

Section 6.12. Reduction of Conviction by Court to Lesser Degree of Felony or to Misdemeanor

If, when a person has been convicted of a felony, the Court, having regard to the nature and circumstances of the crime and to the history and character of the defendant, is of the view that it would be unduly harsh to sentence the offender in accordance with the Code, the Court may enter judgment of conviction for a lesser degree of felony or for a misdemeanor and impose sentence accordingly.

Section 6.13. Civil Commitment in Lieu of Prosecution or of Sentence

(1) When a person prosecuted for a [felony of the third degree,] misdemeanor or petty misdemeanor is a chronic alcoholic, narcotic addict [or prostitute] or person suffering from mental abnormality and the Court is authorized by law to order the civil commitment of such person to a hospital or other institution for medical, psychiatric or other rehabilitative treatment, the Court may order such commitment and dismiss the prosecution. The order of commitment may be made after conviction, in which event the Court may set aside the verdict or judgment of conviction and dismiss the prosecution.

(2) The Court shall not make an order under Subsection (1) of this Section unless it is of the view that it will substantially further the rehabilitation of the defendant and will not jeopardize the protection of the public.

ARTICLE 7. AUTHORITY OF COURT IN SENTENCING

Section 7.01. Criteria for Withholding Sentence of Imprisonment and for Placing Defendant on Probation

(1) The Court shall deal with a person who has been convicted of a crime without imposing sentence of imprisonment unless, having regard to the nature and circumstances of the crime and the history, character and condition of the defendant, it is of the opinion that his imprisonment is necessary for protection of the public because:

(a) there is undue risk that during the period of a suspended sentence or probation the defendant will commit another crime; or

(b) the defendant is in need of correctional treatment that can be provided most effectively by his commitment to an institution; or

(c) a lesser sentence will depreciate the seriousness of the defendant's crime.

(2) The following grounds, while not controlling the discretion of the Court, shall be accorded weight in favor of withholding sentence of imprisonment:

(a) the defendant's criminal conduct neither caused nor threatened serious harm;

(b) the defendant did not contemplate that his criminal conduct would cause or threaten serious harm;

(c) the defendant acted under a strong provocation;

(d) there were substantial grounds tending to excuse or justify the defendant's criminal conduct, though failing to establish a defense;

(e) the victim of the defendant's criminal conduct induced or facilitated its commission;

(f) the defendant has compensated or will compensate the victim of his criminal conduct for the damage or injury that he sustained;

(g) the defendant has no history of prior delinquency or criminal activity or has led a law-abiding life for a substantial period of time before the commission of the present crime;

(h) the defendant's criminal conduct was the result of circumstances unlikely to recur;

(i) the character and attitudes of the defendant indicate that he is unlikely to commit another crime;

(j) the defendant is particularly likely to respond affirmatively to probationary treatment;

(k) the imprisonment of the defendant would entail excessive hardship to himself or his dependents.

(3) When a person who has been convicted of a crime is not sentenced to imprisonment, the Court shall place him on probation if he is in need of the supervision, guidance, assistance or direction that the probation service can provide.

Section 7.02. Criteria for Imposing Fines

(1) The Court shall not sentence a defendant only to pay a fine, when any other disposition is authorized by law, unless having regard to the nature and circumstances of the crime and to the history and character of the defendant, it is of the opinion that the fine alone suffices for protection of the public.

(2) The Court shall not sentence a defendant to pay a fine in addition to a sentence of imprisonment or probation unless:

(a) the defendant has derived a pecuniary gain from the crime; or

(b) the Court is of opinion that a fine is specially adapted to deterrence of the crime involved or to the correction of the offender.

(3) The Court shall not sentence a defendant to pay a fine unless:

(a) the defendant is or will be able to pay the fine; and

(b) the fine will not prevent the defendant from making restitution or reparation to the victim of the crime.

(4) In determining the amount and method of payment of a fine, the Court shall take into account the financial resources of the defendant and the nature of the burden that its payment will impose.

Section 7.03. Criteria for Sentence of Extended Term of Imprisonment; Felonies

The Court may sentence a person who has been convicted of a felony to an extended term of imprisonment if it finds one or more of the grounds specified in this Section. The finding of the Court shall be incorporated in the record.

(1) The defendant is a persistent offender whose commitment for an extended term is necessary for protection of the public.

The Court shall not make such a finding unless the defendant is over twenty-one years of age and has previously been convicted of two felonies or of one felony and two misdemeanors, committed at different times when he was over [insert Juvenile Court age] years of age.

(2) The defendant is a professional criminal whose commitment for an extended term is necessary for protection of the public.

The Court shall not make such a finding unless the defendant is over twenty-one years of age and:

(a) the circumstances of the crime show that the defendant has knowingly devoted himself to criminal activity as a major source of livelihood; or

(b) the defendant has substantial income or resources not explained to be derived from a source other than criminal activity.

(3) The defendant is a dangerous, mentally abnormal person whose commitment for an extended term is necessary for protection of the public.

The Court shall not make such a finding unless the defendant has been subjected to a psychiatric examination resulting in the conclusions that his mental condition is gravely abnormal; that his criminal conduct has been characterized by a pattern of repetitive or compulsive behavior or by persistent aggressive behavior with heedless indifference to consequences; and that such condition makes him a serious danger to others.

(4) The defendant is a multiple offender whose criminality was so extensive that a sentence of imprisonment for an extended term is warranted.

The Court shall not make such a finding unless:

(a) the defendant is being sentenced for two or more felonies, or is already under sentence of imprisonment for felony, and the sentences of imprisonment involved will run concurrently under Section 7.06; or

(b) the defendant admits in open court the commission of one or more other felonies and asks that they be taken into account when he is sentenced; and

(c) the longest sentences of imprisonment authorized for each of the defendant's crimes, including admitted crimes taken into account, if made to run consecutively would exceed in length the minimum and maximum of the extended term imposed.

Section 7.04. Criteria for Sentence of Extended Term of Imprisonment; Misdemeanors and Petty Misdemeanors

The Court may sentence a person who has been convicted of a misdemeanor or petty misdemeanor to an extended term of imprisonment if it finds one or more of the grounds specified in this Section. The finding of the Court shall be incorporated in the record.

(1) The defendant is a persistent offender whose commitment for an extended term is necessary for protection of the public.

The Court shall not make such a finding unless the defendant has previously been convicted of two crimes, committed at different times when he was over [insert Juvenile Court age] years of age.

(2) The defendant is a professional criminal whose commitment for an extended term is necessary for protection of the public.

The Court shall not make such a finding unless:

(a) the circumstances of the crime show that the defendant has knowingly devoted himself to criminal activity as a major source of livelihood; or

(b) the defendant has substantial income or resources not explained to be derived from a source other than criminal activity.

(3) The defendant is a chronic alcoholic, narcotic addict, prostitute or person of abnormal mental condition who requires rehabilitative treatment for a substantial period of time.

The Court shall not make such a finding unless, with respect to the particular category to which the defendant belongs, the Director of Correction has certified that there is a specialized institution or facility which is satisfactory for the rehabilitative treatment of such persons and which otherwise meets the requirements of Section 6.09, Subsection (2).

(4) The defendant is a multiple offender whose criminality was so extensive that a sentence of imprisonment for an extended term is warranted.

The Court shall not make such a finding unless:

(a) the defendant is being sentenced for a number of misdemeanors or petty misdemeanors or is already under sentence of imprisonment for crime of such grades, or admits in open court the commission of one or more such crimes and asks that they be taken into account when he is sentenced; and

(b) maximum fixed sentences of imprisonment for each of the defendant's crimes, including admitted crimes taken into account, if made to run consecutively, would exceed in length the maximum period of the extended term imposed.

Section 7.05. Former Conviction in Another Jurisdiction; Definition and Proof of Conviction; Sentence Taking into Account Admitted Crimes Bars Subsequent Conviction for Such Crimes

(1) For purposes of paragraph (1) of Section 7.03 or 7.04, a conviction of the commission of a crime in another jurisdiction shall constitute a previous conviction. Such conviction shall be deemed to have been of a felony if sentence of death or of imprisonment in excess of one year was authorized under the law of such other jurisdiction, of a misdemeanor if sentence of imprisonment in excess of thirty days but not in excess of a year was authorized and of a petty misdemeanor if sentence of imprisonment for not more than thirty days was authorized.

(2) An adjudication by a court of competent jurisdiction that the defendant committed a crime constitutes a conviction for purposes of Sections 7.03 to 7.05 inclusive, although sentence or the execution thereof was suspended, provided that the time to appeal has expired and that the defendant was not pardoned on the ground of innocence.

(3) Prior conviction may be proved by any evidence, including fingerprint records made in connection with arrest, conviction or imprisonment, that reasonably satisfies the Court that the defendant was convicted.

(4) When the defendant has asked that other crimes admitted in open court be taken into account when he is sentenced and the Court has not rejected such request, the sentence shall bar the prosecution or conviction of the defendant in this State for any such admitted crime.

Section 7.06. Multiple Sentences; Concurrent and Consecutive Terms

(1) Sentences of Imprisonment for More Than One Crime. When multiple sentences of imprisonment are imposed on a defendant for more than one crime, including a crime for which a previous suspended sentence or sentence of probation has been revoked, such multiple sentences shall run concurrently or consecutively as the Court determines at the time of sentence, except that:

(a) a definite and an indefinite term shall run concurrently and both sentences shall be satisfied by service of the indefinite term; and

(b) the aggregate of consecutive definite terms shall not exceed one year; and

(c) the aggregate of consecutive indefinite terms shall not exceed in minimum or maximum length the longest extended term authorized for the highest grade and degree of crime for which any of the sentences was imposed; and

(d) not more than one sentence for an extended term shall be imposed.

(2) Sentences of Imprisonment Imposed at Different Times. When a defendant who has previously been sentenced to imprisonment is subsequently sentenced to another term for a crime committed prior to the former sentence, other than a crime committed while in custody:

(a) the multiple sentences imposed shall so far as possible conform to Subsection (1) of this Section; and

(b) whether the Court determines that the terms shall run concurrently or consecutively, the defendant shall be credited with time served in imprisonment on the prior sentence in determining the permissible aggregate length of the term or terms remaining to be served; and

(c) when a new sentence is imposed on a prisoner who is on parole, the balance of the parole term on the former sentence shall be deemed to run during the period of the new imprisonment.

(3) Sentence of Imprisonment for Crime Committed While on Parole. When a defendant is sentenced to imprisonment for a crime committed while on parole in this State, such term of imprisonment and any period of reimprisonment that the Board of Parole may require the defendant to serve upon the revocation of his parole shall run concurrently, unless the Court orders them to run consecutively.

(4) Multiple Sentences of Imprisonment in Other Cases. Except as otherwise provided in this Section, multiple terms of imprisonment shall run concurrently or consecutively as the Court determines when the second or subsequent sentence is imposed.

(5) Calculation of Concurrent and Consecutive Terms of Imprisonment.

(a) When indefinite terms run concurrently, the shorter minimum terms merge in and are satisfied by serving the longest minimum term and the shorter maximum terms merge in and are satisfied by discharge of the longest maximum term.

(b) When indefinite terms run consecutively, the minimum terms are added to arrive at an aggregate minimum to be served equal to the sum of all minimum terms and the maximum terms are added to arrive at an aggregate maximum equal to the sum of all maximum terms.

(c) When a definite and an indefinite term run consecutively, the period of the definite term is added to both the minimum and maximum of the indefinite term and both sentences are satisfied by serving the indefinite term.

(6) Suspension of Sentence or Probation and Imprisonment; Multiple Terms of Suspension and Probation. When a defendant is sentenced for more than one offense or a defendant already under sentence is sentenced for another offense committed prior to the former sentence:

(a) the Court shall not sentence to probation a defendant who is under sentence of imprisonment [with more than thirty days to run] or impose a sentence of probation and a sentence of imprisonment [, except as authorized by Section 6.02(3)(b)]; and

(b) multiple periods of suspension or probation shall run concurrently from the date of the first such disposition; and

(c) when a sentence of imprisonment is imposed for an indefinite term, the service of such sentence shall satisfy a suspended sentence on another count or a prior suspended sentence or sentence to probation; and

(d) when a sentence of imprisonment is imposed for a definite term, the period of a suspended sentence on another count or a prior suspended sentence or sentence to probation shall run during the period of such imprisonment.

(7) Offense Committed While Under Suspension of Sentence or Probation. When a defendant is convicted of an offense committed while under suspension of sentence or on probation and such suspension or probation is not revoked:

(a) if the defendant is sentenced to imprisonment for an indefinite term, the service of such sentence shall satisfy the prior suspended sentence or sentence to probation; and

(b) if the defendant is sentenced to imprisonment for a definite term, the period of the suspension or probation shall not run during the period of such imprisonment; and

(c) if sentence is suspended or the defendant is sentenced to probation, the period of such suspension or probation shall run concurrently with or consecutively to the remainder of the prior periods, as the Court determines at the time of sentence.

Section 7.07. Procedure on Sentence; Pre-sentence Investigation and Report; Remand for Psychiatric Examination; Transmission of Records to Department of Correction

(1) The Court shall not impose sentence without first ordering a presentence investigation of the defendant and according due consideration to a written report of such investigation where:

(a) the defendant has been convicted of a felony; or

(b) the defendant is less than twenty-two years of age and has been convicted of a crime; or

(c) the defendant will be [placed on probation or] sentenced to imprisonment for an extended term.

(2) The Court may order a pre-sentence investigation in any other case.

(3) The pre-sentence investigation shall include an analysis of the circumstances attending the commission of the crime, the defendant's history of delinquency or criminality, physical and mental condition, family situation and background, economic status, education, occupation and personal habits and any other matters that the probation officer deems relevant or the Court directs to be included.

(4) Before imposing sentence, the Court may order the defendant to submit to psychiatric observation and examination for a period of not exceeding sixty days or such longer period as the Court determines to be necessary for the purpose. The defendant may be remanded for this purpose to any available clinic or mental hospital or the Court may appoint a qualified psychiatrist to make the examination. The report of the examination shall be submitted to the Court.

(5) Before imposing sentence, the Court shall advise the defendant or his counsel of the factual contents and the conclusions of any pre-sentence investigation or psychiatric examination and afford fair opportunity, if the defendant so requests, to controvert them. The sources of confidential information need not, however, be disclosed.

(6) The Court shall not impose a sentence of imprisonment for an extended term unless the ground therefor has been established at a hearing after the conviction of the defendant and on written notice to him of the ground proposed. Subject to the limitation of Subsection (5) of this Section, the defendant shall have the right to hear and controvert the evidence against him and to offer evidence upon the issue.

(7) If the defendant is sentenced to imprisonment, a copy of the report of any pre-sentence investigation or psychiatric examination shall be transmitted forthwith to the Department of Correction [or other state department or agency] or, when the defendant is committed to the custody of a specific institution, to such institution.

Section 7.08. Commitment for Observation; Sentence of Imprisonment for Felony Deemed Tentative for Period of One Year; Re-sentence on Petition of Commissioner of Correction

(1) If, after pre-sentence investigation, the Court desires additional information concerning an offender convicted of a felony or misdemeanor before imposing sentence, it may order that he be committed, for a period not exceeding ninety days, to the custody of the Department of Correction, or, in the case of a young adult offender, to the custody of the Division of Young Adult Correction, for observation and study at an appropriate reception or classification center. The Department and the Board of Parole, or the Young Adult Divisions thereof, shall advise the Court of their findings and recommendations on or before the expiration of such ninety-day period. If the offender is thereafter sentenced to imprisonment, the period of such commitment for observation shall be deducted from the maximum term and from the minimum, if any, of such sentence.

(2) When a person has been sentenced to imprisonment upon conviction of a felony, whether for an ordinary or extended term, the sentence shall be deemed tentative, to the extent provided in this Section, for the period of one year

following the date when the offender is received in custody by the Department of Correction [or other state department or agency].

(3) If, as a result of the examination and classification by the Department of Correction [or other state department or agency] of a person under sentence of imprisonment upon conviction of a felony, the Commissioner of Correction [or other department head] is satisfied that the sentence of the Court may have been based upon a misapprehension as to the history, character or physical or mental condition of the offender, the Commissioner, during the period when the offender's sentence is deemed tentative under Subsection (2) of this Section shall file in the sentencing Court a petition to re-sentence the offender. The petition shall set forth the information as to the offender that is deemed to warrant his re-sentence and may include a recommendation as to the sentence to be imposed.

(4) The Court may dismiss a petition filed under Subsection (3) of this Section without a hearing if it deems the information set forth insufficient to warrant reconsideration of the sentence. If the Court is of the view that the petition warrants such reconsideration, a copy of the petition shall be served on the offender, who shall have the right to be heard on the issue and to be represented by counsel.

(5) When the Court grants a petition filed under Subsection (3) of this Section, it shall re-sentence the offender and may impose any sentence that might have been imposed originally for the felony of which the defendant was convicted. The period of his imprisonment prior to re-sentence and any reduction for good behavior to which he is entitled shall be applied in satisfaction of the final sentence.

(6) For all purposes other than this Section, a sentence of imprisonment has the same finality when it is imposed that it would have if this Section were not in force.

(7) Nothing in this Section shall alter the remedies provided by law for vacating or correcting an illegal sentence.

Section 7.09. Credit for Time of Detention Prior to Sentence; Credit for Imprisonment Under Earlier Sentence for the Same Crime

(1) When a defendant who is sentenced to imprisonment has previously been detained in any state or local correctional or other institution following his [conviction of] [arrest for] the crime for which such sentence is imposed, such period of detention following his [conviction] [arrest] shall be deducted from the maximum term, and from the minimum, if any, of such sentence. The officer having custody of the defendant shall furnish a certificate to the Court at the time of sentence, showing the length of such detention of the defendant prior to sentence in any state or local correctional or other institution, and the certificate shall be annexed to the official records of the defendant's commitment.

(2) When a judgment of conviction is vacated and a new sentence is thereafter imposed upon the defendant for the same crime, the period of detention and imprisonment theretofore served shall be deducted from the maximum term, and from the minimum, if any, of the new sentence. The officer having custody of the defendant shall furnish a certificate to the Court at the time of sentence, showing the period of imprisonment served under the original sentence, and the certificate shall be annexed to the official records of the defendant's new commitment.

A-57

PART II. DEFINITION OF SPECIFIC CRIMES

OFFENSES AGAINST EXISTENCE OR STABILITY OF THE STATE

[Reporter's note: This category of offenses, including treason, sedition, espionage and like crimes, was excluded from the scope of the Model Penal Code. These offenses are peculiarly the concern of the federal government. The Constitution itself defines treason: "Treason against the United States shall consist only in levying War against them, or in adhering to their Enemies, giving them Aid and Comfort. . . ." Article III, Section 3; cf. Pennsylvania v. Nelson, 350 U.S. 497 (1956) (supersession of state sedition legislation by federal law). Also, the definition of offenses against the stability of the state is inevitably affected by special political considerations. These factors militated against the use of the Institute's limited resources to attempt to draft "model" provisions in this area. However we provide at this point in the Plan of the Model Penal Code for an Article 200, where definitions of offenses against the existence or stability of the state may be incorporated.]

OFFENSES INVOLVING DANGER TO THE PERSON

ARTICLE 210. CRIMINAL HOMICIDE

Section 210.0. Definitions

In Articles 210–213, unless a different meaning plainly is required:

(1) "human being" means a person who has been born and is alive;

(2) "bodily injury" means physical pain, illness or any impairment of physical condition;

(3) "serious bodily injury" means bodily injury which creates a substantial risk of death or which causes serious, permanent disfigurement, or protracted loss or impairment of the function of any bodily member or organ;

(4) "deadly weapon" means any firearm, or other weapon, device, instrument, material or substance, whether animate or inanimate, which in the manner it is used or is intended to be used is known to be capable of producing death or serious bodily injury.

Section 210.1. Criminal Homicide

(1) A person is guilty of criminal homicide if he purposely, knowingly, recklessly or negligently causes the death of another human being.

(2) Criminal homicide is murder, manslaughter or negligent homicide.

Section 210.2. Murder

(1) Except as provided in Section 210.3(1)(b), criminal homicide constitutes murder when:

(a) it is committed purposely or knowingly; or

(b) it is committed recklessly under circumstances manifesting extreme indifference to the value of human life. Such recklessness and indifference are presumed if the actor is engaged or is an accomplice in the commission of, or an attempt to commit, or flight after committing or attempting to commit robbery, rape or deviate sexual intercourse by force or threat of force, arson, burglary, kidnapping or felonious escape.

(2) Murder is a felony of the first degree [but a person convicted of murder may be sentenced to death, as provided in Section 210.6].[b]

Section 210.3. Manslaughter

(1) Criminal homicide constitutes manslaughter when:

(a) it is committed recklessly; or

(b) a homicide which would otherwise be murder is committed under the influence of extreme mental or emotional disturbance for which there is reasonable explanation or excuse. The reasonableness of such explanation or excuse shall be determined from the viewpoint of a person in the actor's situation under the circumstances as he believes them to be.

(2) Manslaughter is a felony of the second degree.

Section 210.4. Negligent Homicide

(1) Criminal homicide constitutes negligent homicide when it is committed negligently.

(2) Negligent homicide is a felony of the third degree.

Section 210.5. Causing or Aiding Suicide

(1) Causing Suicide as Criminal Homicide. A person may be convicted of criminal homicide for causing another to commit suicide only if he purposely causes such suicide by force, duress or deception.

(2) Aiding or Soliciting Suicide as an Independent Offense. A person who purposely aids or solicits another to commit suicide is guilty of a felony of the second degree if his conduct causes such suicide or an attempted suicide, and otherwise of a misdemeanor.

[Section 210.6. Sentence of Death for Murder; Further Proceedings to Determine Sentence

(1) Death Sentence Excluded. When a defendant is found guilty of murder, the Court shall impose sentence for a felony of the first degree if it is satisfied that:

(a) none of the aggravating circumstances enumerated in Subsection (3) of this Section was established by the evidence at the trial or will be established if further proceedings are initiated under Subsection (2) of this Section; or

(b) substantial mitigating circumstances, established by the evidence at the trial, call for leniency; or

[b] The American Law Institute took no position on whether the capital sanction should be provided. The bracketed portion of this provision, as well as Section 210.6, was included to address the procedures for imposition of the death penalty for jurisdictions that wished to retain it. [Footnote by eds.]

(c) the defendant, with the consent of the prosecuting attorney and the approval of the Court, pleaded guilty to murder as a felony of the first degree; or

(d) the defendant was under 18 years of age at the time of the commission of the crime; or

(e) the defendant's physical or mental condition calls for leniency; or

(f) although the evidence suffices to sustain the verdict, it does not foreclose all doubt respecting the defendant's guilt.

(2) Determination by Court or by Court and Jury. Unless the Court imposes sentence under Subsection (1) of this Section, it shall conduct a separate proceeding to determine whether the defendant should be sentenced for a felony of the first degree or sentenced to death. The proceeding shall be conducted before the Court alone if the defendant was convicted by a Court sitting without a jury or upon his plea of guilty or if the prosecuting attorney and the defendant waive a jury with respect to sentence. In other cases it shall be conducted before the Court sitting with the jury which determined the defendant's guilt or, if the Court for good cause shown discharges that jury, with a new jury empanelled for the purpose.

In the proceeding, evidence may be presented as to any matter that the Court deems relevant to sentence, including but not limited to the nature and circumstances of the crime, the defendant's character, background, history, mental and physical condition and any of the aggravating or mitigating circumstances enumerated in Subsections (3) and (4) of this Section. Any such evidence, not legally privileged, which the Court deems to have probative force, may be received, regardless of its admissibility under the exclusionary rules of evidence, provided that the defendant's counsel is accorded a fair opportunity to rebut such evidence. The prosecuting attorney and the defendant or his counsel shall be permitted to present argument for or against sentence of death.

The determination whether sentence of death shall be imposed shall be in the discretion of the Court, except that when the proceeding is conducted before the Court sitting with a jury, the Court shall not impose sentence of death unless it submits to the jury the issue whether the defendant should be sentenced to death or to imprisonment and the jury returns a verdict that the sentence should be death. If the jury is unable to reach a unanimous verdict, the Court shall dismiss the jury and impose sentence for a felony of the first degree.

The Court, in exercising its discretion as to sentence, and the jury, in determining upon its verdict, shall take into account the aggravating and mitigating circumstances enumerated in Subsections (3) and (4) and any other facts that it deems relevant, but it shall not impose or recommend sentence of death unless it finds one of the aggravating circumstances enumerated in Subsection (3) and further finds that there are no mitigating circumstances sufficiently substantial to call for leniency. When the issue is submitted to the jury, the Court shall so instruct and also shall inform the jury of the nature of the sentence of imprisonment that may be imposed, including its implication with respect to possible release upon parole, if the jury verdict is against sentence of death.

Alternative formulation of Subsection (2):

(2) Determination by Court. Unless the Court imposes sentence under Subsection (1) of this Section, it shall conduct a separate proceeding to determine whether the defendant should be sentenced for a felony of the first degree

or sentenced to death. In the proceeding, the Court, in accordance with Section 7.07, shall consider the report of the pre-sentence investigation and, if a psychiatric examination has been ordered, the report of such examination. In addition, evidence may be presented as to any matter that the Court deems relevant to sentence, including but not limited to the nature and circumstances of the crime, the defendant's character, background, history, mental and physical condition and any of the aggravating or mitigating circumstances enumerated in Subsections (3) and (4) of this Section. Any such evidence, not legally privileged, which the Court deems to have probative force, may be received, regardless of its admissibility under the exclusionary rules of evidence, provided that the defendant's counsel is accorded a fair opportunity to rebut such evidence. The prosecuting attorney and the defendant or his counsel shall be permitted to present argument for or against sentence of death.

The determination whether sentence of death shall be imposed shall be in the discretion of the Court. In exercising such discretion, the Court shall take into account the aggravating and mitigating circumstances enumerated in Subsections (3) and (4) and any other facts that it deems relevant but shall not impose sentence of death unless it finds one of the aggravating circumstances enumerated in Subsection (3) and further finds that there are no mitigating circumstances sufficiently substantial to call for leniency.

(3) Aggravating Circumstances.

(a) The murder was committed by a convict under sentence of imprisonment.

(b) The defendant was previously convicted of another murder or of a felony involving the use or threat of violence to the person.

(c) At the time the murder was committed the defendant also committed another murder.

(d) The defendant knowingly created a great risk of death to many persons.

(e) The murder was committed while the defendant was engaged or was an accomplice in the commission of, or an attempt to commit, or flight after committing or attempting to commit robbery, rape or deviate sexual intercourse by force or threat of force, arson, burglary or kidnapping.

(f) The murder was committed for the purpose of avoiding or preventing a lawful arrest or effecting an escape from lawful custody.

(g) The murder was committed for pecuniary gain.

(h) The murder was especially heinous, atrocious or cruel, manifesting exceptional depravity.

(4) Mitigating Circumstances.

(a) The defendant has no significant history of prior criminal activity.

(b) The murder was committed while the defendant was under the influence of extreme mental or emotional disturbance.

(c) The victim was a participant in the defendant's homicidal conduct or consented to the homicidal act.

(d) The murder was committed under circumstances which the defendant believed to provide a moral justification or extenuation for his conduct.

(e) The defendant was an accomplice in a murder committed by another person and his participation in the homicidal act was relatively minor.

(f) The defendant acted under duress or under the domination of another person.

(g) At the time of the murder, the capacity of the defendant to appreciate the criminality [wrongfulness] of his conduct or to conform his conduct to the requirements of law was impaired as a result of mental disease or defect or intoxication.

(h) The youth of the defendant at the time of the crime.]

ARTICLE 211. ASSAULT; RECKLESS ENDANGERING; THREATS

Section 211.0. Definitions

In this Article, the definitions given in Section 210.0 apply unless a different meaning plainly is required.

Section 211.1. Assault

(1) <u>Simple Assault.</u> A person is guilty of assault if he:

(a) attempts to cause or purposely, knowingly or recklessly causes bodily injury to another; or

(b) negligently causes bodily injury to another with a deadly weapon; or

(c) attempts by physical menace to put another in fear of imminent serious bodily injury.

Simple assault is a misdemeanor unless committed in a fight or scuffle entered into by mutual consent, in which case it is a petty misdemeanor.

(2) <u>Aggravated Assault.</u> A person is guilty of aggravated assault if he:

(a) attempts to cause serious bodily injury to another, or causes such injury purposely, knowingly or recklessly under circumstances manifesting extreme indifference to the value of human life; or

(b) attempts to cause or purposely or knowingly causes bodily injury to another with a deadly weapon.

Aggravated assault under paragraph (a) is a felony of the second degree; aggravated assault under paragraph (b) is a felony of the third degree.

Section 211.2. Recklessly Endangering Another Person

A person commits a misdemeanor if he recklessly engages in conduct which places or may place another person in danger of death or serious bodily injury. Recklessness and danger shall be presumed where a person knowingly points a firearm at or in the direction of another, whether or not the actor believed the firearm to be loaded.

Section 211.3. Terroristic Threats

A person is guilty of a felony of the third degree if he threatens to commit any crime of violence with purpose to terrorize another or to cause evacuation of a building, place of assembly, or facility of public transportation, or otherwise to cause serious public inconvenience, or in reckless disregard of the risk of causing such terror or inconvenience.

ARTICLE 212. KIDNAPPING AND RELATED OFFENSES; COERCION

Section 212.0. Definitions

In this Article, the definitions given in Section 210.0 apply unless a different meaning plainly is required.

Section 212.1. Kidnapping

A person is guilty of kidnapping if he unlawfully removes another from his place of residence or business, or a substantial distance from the vicinity where he is found, or if he unlawfully confines another for a substantial period in a place of isolation, with any of the following purposes:

(a) to hold for ransom or reward, or as a shield or hostage; or

(b) to facilitate commission of any felony or flight thereafter; or

(c) to inflict bodily injury on or to terrorize the victim or another; or

(d) to interfere with the performance of any governmental or political function.

Kidnapping is a felony of the first degree unless the actor voluntarily releases the victim alive and in a safe place prior to trial, in which case it is a felony of the second degree. A removal or confinement is unlawful within the meaning of this Section if it is accomplished by force, threat or deception, or, in the case of a person who is under the age of 14 or incompetent, if it is accomplished without the consent of a parent, guardian or other person responsible for general supervision of his welfare.

Section 212.2. Felonious Restraint

A person commits a felony of the third degree if he knowingly:

(a) restrains another unlawfully in circumstances exposing him to risk of serious bodily injury; or

(b) holds another in a condition of involuntary servitude.

Section 212.3. False Imprisonment

A person commits a misdemeanor if he knowingly restrains another unlawfully so as to interfere substantially with his liberty.

Section 212.4. Interference with Custody

(1) Custody of Children. A person commits an offense if he knowingly or recklessly takes or entices any child under the age of 18 from the custody of its parent, guardian or other lawful custodian, when he has no privilege to do so. It is an affirmative defense that:

(a) the actor believed that his action was necessary to preserve the child from danger to its welfare; or

(b) the child, being at the time not less than 14 years old, was taken away at its own instigation without enticement and without purpose to commit a criminal offense with or against the child.

Proof that the child was below the critical age gives rise to a presumption that the actor knew the child's age or acted in reckless disregard thereof. The offense is a misdemeanor unless the actor, not being a parent or person in equivalent relation to the child, acted with knowledge that his conduct would cause serious alarm for the child's safety, or in reckless disregard of a likelihood of causing such alarm, in which case the offense is a felony of the third degree.

(2) Custody of Committed Persons. A person is guilty of a misdemeanor if he knowingly or recklessly takes or entices any committed person away from lawful custody when he is not privileged to do so. "Committed person" means, in addition to anyone committed under judicial warrant, any orphan, neglected or delinquent child, mentally defective or insane person, or other dependent or incompetent person entrusted to another's custody by or through a recognized social agency or otherwise by authority of law.

Section 212.5. Criminal Coercion

(1) Offense Defined. A person is guilty of criminal coercion if, with purpose unlawfully to restrict another's freedom of action to his detriment, he threatens to:

(a) commit any criminal offense; or

(b) accuse anyone of a criminal offense; or

(c) expose any secret tending to subject any person to hatred, contempt or ridicule, or to impair his credit or business repute; or

(d) take or withhold action as an official, or cause an official to take or withhold action.

It is an affirmative defense to prosecution based on paragraphs (b), (c) or (d) that the actor believed the accusation or secret to be true or the proposed official action justified and that his purpose was limited to compelling the other to behave in a way reasonably related to the circumstances which were the subject of the accusation, exposure or proposed official action, as by desisting from further misbehavior, making good a wrong done, refraining from taking any action or responsibility for which the actor believes the other disqualified.

(2) Grading. Criminal coercion is a misdemeanor unless the threat is to commit a felony or the actor's purpose is felonious, in which cases the offense is a felony of the third degree.

ARTICLE 213. SEXUAL OFFENSES

Section 213.0. Definitions

In this Article, unless a different meaning plainly is required:

(1) the definitions given in Section 210.0 apply;

(2) "Sexual intercourse" includes intercourse per os or per anum, with some penetration however slight; emission is not required;

(3) "Deviate sexual intercourse" means sexual intercourse per os or per anum between human beings who are not husband and wife, and any form of sexual intercourse with an animal.

Section 213.1. Rape and Related Offenses

(1) Rape. A male who has sexual intercourse with a female not his wife is guilty of rape if:

(a) he compels her to submit by force or by threat of imminent death, serious bodily injury, extreme pain or kidnapping, to be inflicted on anyone; or

(b) he has substantially impaired her power to appraise or control her conduct by administering or employing without her knowledge drugs, intoxicants or other means for the purpose of preventing resistance; or

(c) the female is unconscious; or

(d) the female is less than 10 years old.

Rape is a felony of the second degree unless (i) in the course thereof the actor inflicts serious bodily injury upon anyone, or (ii) the victim was not a voluntary social companion of the actor upon the occasion of the crime and had not previously permitted him sexual liberties, in which cases the offense is a felony of the first degree.

(2) Gross Sexual Imposition. A male who has sexual intercourse with a female not his wife commits a felony of the third degree if:

(a) he compels her to submit by any threat that would prevent resistance by a woman of ordinary resolution; or

(b) he knows that she suffers from a mental disease or defect which renders her incapable of appraising the nature of her conduct; or

(c) he knows that she is unaware that a sexual act is being committed upon her or that she submits because she mistakenly supposes that he is her husband.

Section 213.2. Deviate Sexual Intercourse by Force or Imposition

(1) By Force or Its Equivalent. A person who engages in deviate sexual intercourse with another person, or who causes another to engage in deviate sexual intercourse, commits a felony of the second degree if:

(a) he compels the other person to participate by force or by threat of imminent death, serious bodily injury, extreme pain or kidnapping, to be inflicted on anyone; or

(b) he has substantially impaired the other person's power to appraise or control his conduct, by administering or employing without the knowledge of the other person drugs, intoxicants or other means for the purpose of preventing resistance; or

(c) the other person is unconscious; or

(d) the other person is less than 10 years old.

(2) By Other Imposition. A person who engages in deviate sexual intercourse with another person, or who causes another to engage in deviate sexual intercourse, commits a felony of the third degree if:

(a) he compels the other person to participate by any threat that would prevent resistance by a person of ordinary resolution; or

(b) he knows that the other person suffers from a mental disease or defect which renders him incapable of appraising the nature of his conduct; or

(c) he knows that the other person submits because he is unaware that a sexual act is being committed upon him.

Section 213.3. Corruption of Minors and Seduction

(1) <u>Offense Defined.</u> A male who has sexual intercourse with a female not his wife, or any person who engages in deviate sexual intercourse or causes another to engage in deviate sexual intercourse, is guilty of an offense if:

(a) the other person is less than [16] years old and the actor is at least [four] years older than the other person; or

(b) the other person is less than 21 years old and the actor is his guardian or otherwise responsible for general supervision of his welfare; or

(c) the other person is in custody of law or detained in a hospital or other institution and the actor has supervisory or disciplinary authority over him; or

(d) the other person is a female who is induced to participate by a promise of marriage which the actor does not mean to perform.

(2) <u>Grading.</u> An offense under paragraph (a) of Subsection (1) is a felony of the third degree. Otherwise an offense under this section is a misdemeanor.

Section 213.4. Sexual Assault

A person who has sexual contact with another not his spouse, or causes such other to have sexual contact with him, is guilty of sexual assault, a misdemeanor, if:

(1) he knows that the contact is offensive to the other person; or

(2) he knows that the other person suffers from a mental disease or defect which renders him or her incapable of appraising the nature of his or her conduct; or

(3) he knows that the other person is unaware that a sexual act is being committed; or

(4) the other person is less than 10 years old; or

(5) he has substantially impaired the other person's power to appraise or control his or her conduct, by administering or employing without the other's knowledge drugs, intoxicants or other means for the purpose of preventing resistance; or

(6) the other person is less than [16] years old and the actor is at least [four] years older than the other person; or

(7) the other person is less than 21 years old and the actor is his guardian or otherwise responsible for general supervision of his welfare; or

(8) the other person is in custody of law or detained in a hospital or other institution and the actor has supervisory or disciplinary authority over him.

Sexual contact is any touching of the sexual or other intimate parts of the person for the purpose of arousing or gratifying sexual desire.

Section 213.5. Indecent Exposure

A person commits a misdemeanor if, for the purpose of arousing or gratifying sexual desire of himself or of any person other than his spouse, he exposes his genitals under circumstances in which he knows his conduct is likely to cause affront or alarm.

Section 213.6. Provisions Generally Applicable to Article 213

(1) <u>Mistake as to Age.</u> Whenever in this Article the criminality of conduct depends on a child's being below the age of 10, it is no defense that the actor did not know the child's age, or reasonably believed the child to be older than 10. When criminality depends on the child's being below a critical age other than 10, it is a defense for the actor to prove by a preponderance of the evidence that he reasonably believed the child to be above the critical age.

(2) <u>Spouse Relationships.</u> Whenever in this Article the definition of an offense excludes conduct with a spouse, the exclusion shall be deemed to extend to persons living as man and wife, regardless of the legal status of their relationship. The exclusion shall be inoperative as respects spouses living apart under a decree of judicial separation. Where the definition of an offense excludes conduct with a spouse or conduct by a woman, this shall not preclude conviction of a spouse or woman as accomplice in a sexual act which he or she causes another person, not within the exclusion, to perform.

(3) <u>Sexually Promiscuous Complainants.</u> It is a defense to prosecution under Section 213.3 and paragraphs (6), (7) and (8) of Section 213.4 for the actor to prove by a preponderance of the evidence that the alleged victim had, prior to the time of the offense charged, engaged promiscuously in sexual relations with others.

(4) <u>Prompt Complaint.</u> No prosecution may be instituted or maintained under this Article unless the alleged offense was brought to the notice of public authority within [3] months of its occurrence or, where the alleged victim was less than [16] years old or otherwise incompetent to make complaint, within [3] months after a parent, guardian or other competent person specially interested in the victim learns of the offense.

(5) <u>Testimony of Complainants.</u> No person shall be convicted of any felony under this Article upon the uncorroborated testimony of the alleged victim. Corroboration may be circumstantial. In any prosecution before a jury for an offense under this Article, the jury shall be instructed to evaluate the testimony of a victim or complaining witness with special care in view of the emotional involvement of the witness and the difficulty of determining the truth with respect to alleged sexual activities carried out in private.

OFFENSES AGAINST PROPERTY

ARTICLE 220. ARSON, CRIMINAL MISCHIEF, AND OTHER PROPERTY DESTRUCTION

Section 220.1. Arson and Related Offenses

(1) <u>Arson.</u> A person is guilty of arson, a felony of the second degree, if he starts a fire or causes an explosion with the purpose of:

(a) destroying a building or occupied structure of another; or

(b) destroying or damaging any property, whether his own or another's, to collect insurance for such loss. It shall be an affirmative defense to prosecution under this paragraph that the actor's conduct did not recklessly endanger any building or occupied structure of another or place any other person in danger of death or bodily injury.

(2) Reckless Burning or Exploding. A person commits a felony of the third degree if he purposely starts a fire or causes an explosion, whether on his own property or another's, and thereby recklessly:

(a) places another person in danger of death or bodily injury; or

(b) places a building or occupied structure of another in danger of damage or destruction.

(3) Failure to Control or Report Dangerous Fire. A person who knows that a fire is endangering life or a substantial amount of property of another and fails to take reasonable measures to put out or control the fire, when he can do so without substantial risk to himself, or to give a prompt fire alarm, commits a misdemeanor if:

(a) he knows that he is under an official, contractual, or other legal duty to prevent or combat the fire; or

(b) the fire was started, albeit lawfully, by him or with his assent, or on property in his custody or control.

(4) Definitions. "Occupied structure" means any structure, vehicle or place adapted for overnight accommodation of persons, or for carrying on business therein, whether or not a person is actually present. Property is that of another, for the purposes of this section, if anyone other than the actor has a possessory or proprietory interest therein. If a building or structure is divided into separately occupied units, any unit not occupied by the actor is an occupied structure of another.

Section 220.2. Causing or Risking Catastrophe

(1) Causing Catastrophe. A person who causes a catastrophe by explosion, fire, flood, avalanche, collapse of building, release of poison gas, radioactive material or other harmful or destructive force or substance, or by any other means of causing potentially widespread injury or damage, commits a felony of the second degree if he does so purposely or knowingly, or a felony of the third degree if he does so recklessly.

(2) Risking Catastrophe. A person is guilty of a misdemeanor if he recklessly creates a risk of catastrophe in the employment of fire, explosives or other dangerous means listed in Subsection (1).

(3) Failure to Prevent Catastrophe. A person who knowingly or recklessly fails to take reasonable measures to prevent or mitigate a catastrophe commits a misdemeanor if:

(a) he knows that he is under an official, contractual or other legal duty to take such measures; or

(b) he did or assented to the act causing or threatening the catastrophe.

Section 220.3. Criminal Mischief

(1) Offense Defined. A person is guilty of criminal mischief if he:

(a) damages tangible property of another purposely, recklessly, or by negligence in the employment of fire, explosives, or other dangerous means listed in Section 220.2(1); or

(b) purposely or recklessly tampers with tangible property of another so as to endanger person or property; or

(c) purposely or recklessly causes another to suffer pecuniary loss by deception or threat.

(2) Grading. Criminal mischief is a felony of the third degree if the actor purposely causes pecuniary loss in excess of $5,000, or a substantial interruption or impairment of public communication, transportation, supply of water, gas or power, or other public service. It is a misdemeanor if the actor purposely causes pecuniary loss in excess of $100, or a petty misdemeanor if he purposely or recklessly causes pecuniary loss in excess of $25. Otherwise criminal mischief is a violation.

ARTICLE 221. BURGLARY AND OTHER CRIMINAL INTRUSION

Section 221.0. Definitions

In this Article, unless a different meaning plainly is required:

(1) "occupied structure" means any structure, vehicle or place adapted for overnight accommodation of persons, or for carrying on business therein, whether or not a person is actually present.

(2) "night" means the period between thirty minutes past sunset and thirty minutes before sunrise.

Section 221.1. Burglary

(1) Burglary Defined. A person is guilty of burglary if he enters a building or occupied structure, or separately secured or occupied portion thereof, with purpose to commit a crime therein, unless the premises are at the time open to the public or the actor is licensed or privileged to enter. It is an affirmative defense to prosecution for burglary that the building or structure was abandoned.

(2) Grading. Burglary is a felony of the second degree if it is perpetrated in the dwelling of another at night, or if, in the course of committing the offense, the actor:

(a) purposely, knowingly or recklessly inflicts or attempts to inflict bodily injury on anyone; or

(b) is armed with explosives or a deadly weapon.

Otherwise, burglary is a felony of the third degree. An act shall be deemed "in the course of committing" an offense if it occurs in an attempt to commit the offense or in flight after the attempt or commission.

(3) Multiple Convictions. A person may not be convicted both for burglary and for the offense which it was his purpose to commit after the burglarious entry or for an attempt to commit that offense, unless the additional offense constitutes a felony of the first or second degree.

Section 221.2. Criminal Trespass

(1) Buildings and Occupied Structures. A person commits an offense if, knowing that he is not licensed or privileged to do so, he enters or surreptitiously remains in any building or occupied structure, or separately secured or occupied portion thereof. An offense under this Subsection is a misdemeanor if it is committed in a dwelling at night. Otherwise it is a petty misdemeanor.

(2) <u>Defiant Trespasser.</u> A person commits an offense if, knowing that he is not licensed or privileged to do so, he enters or remains in any place as to which notice against trespass is given by:

(a) actual communication to the actor; or

(b) posting in a manner prescribed by law or reasonably likely to come to the attention of intruders; or

(c) fencing or other enclosure manifestly designed to exclude intruders.

An offense under this Subsection constitutes a petty misdemeanor if the offender defies an order to leave personally communicated to him by the owner of the premises or other authorized person. Otherwise it is a violation.

(3) <u>Defenses.</u> It is an affirmative defense to prosecution under this Section that:

(a) a building or occupied structure involved in an offense under Subsection (1) was abandoned; or

(b) the premises were at the time open to members of the public and the actor complied with all lawful conditions imposed on access to or remaining in the premises; or

(c) the actor reasonably believed that the owner of the premises, or other person empowered to license access thereto, would have licensed him to enter or remain.

ARTICLE 222. ROBBERY

Section 222.1. Robbery

(1) <u>Robbery Defined.</u> A person is guilty of robbery if, in the course of committing a theft, he:

(a) inflicts serious bodily injury upon another; or

(b) threatens another with or purposely puts him in fear of immediate serious bodily injury; or

(c) commits or threatens immediately to commit any felony of the first or second degree.

An act shall be deemed "in the course of committing a theft" if it occurs in an attempt to commit theft or in flight after the attempt or commission.

(2) <u>Grading.</u> Robbery is a felony of the second degree, except that it is a felony of the first degree if in the course of committing the theft the actor attempts to kill anyone, or purposely inflicts or attempts to inflict serious bodily injury.

ARTICLE 223. THEFT AND RELATED OFFENSES

Section 223.0. Definitions

In this Article, unless a different meaning plainly is required:

(1) "deprive" means: (a) to withhold property of another permanently or for so extended a period as to appropriate a major portion of its economic value, or with intent to restore only upon payment of reward or other compensation; or (b) to dispose of the property so as to make it unlikely that the owner will recover it.

(2) "financial institution" means a bank, insurance company, credit union, building and loan association, investment trust or other organization held out to the public as a place of deposit of funds or medium of savings or collective investment.

(3) "government" means the United States, any State, county, municipality, or other political unit, or any department, agency or subdivision of any of the foregoing, or any corporation or other association carrying out the functions of government.

(4) "movable property" means property the location of which can be changed, including things growing on, affixed to, or found in land, and documents although the rights represented thereby have no physical location. "Immovable property" is all other property.

(5) "obtain" means: (a) in relation to property, to bring about a transfer or purported transfer of a legal interest in the property, whether to the obtainer or another; or (b) in relation to labor or service, to secure performance thereof.

(6) "property" means anything of value, including real estate, tangible and intangible personal property, contract rights, choses-in-action and other interests in or claims to wealth, admission or transportation tickets, captured or domestic animals, food and drink, electric or other power.

(7) "property of another" includes property in which any person other than the actor has an interest which the actor is not privileged to infringe, regardless of the fact that the actor also has an interest in the property and regardless of the fact that the other person might be precluded from civil recovery because the property was used in an unlawful transaction or was subject to forfeiture as contraband. Property in possession of the actor shall not be deemed property of another who has only a security interest therein, even if legal title is in the creditor pursuant to a conditional sales contract or other security agreement.

Section 223.1. Consolidation of Theft Offenses; Grading; Provisions Applicable to Theft Generally

(1) Consolidation of Theft Offenses. Conduct denominated theft in this Article constitutes a single offense. An accusation of theft may be supported by evidence that it was committed in any manner that would be theft under this Article, notwithstanding the specification of a different manner in the indictment or information, subject only to the power of the Court to ensure fair trial by granting a continuance or other appropriate relief where the conduct of the defense would be prejudiced by lack of fair notice or by surprise.

(2) Grading of Theft Offenses.

(a) Theft constitutes a felony of the third degree if the amount involved exceeds $500, or if the property stolen is a firearm, automobile, airplane, motorcycle, motorboat, or other motor-propelled vehicle, or in the case of theft by receiving stolen property, if the receiver is in the business of buying or selling stolen property.

(b) Theft not within the preceding paragraph constitutes a misdemeanor, except that if the property was not taken from the person or by threat, or in breach of a fiduciary obligation, and the actor proves by a preponderance of the evidence that the amount involved was less than $50, the offense constitutes a petty misdemeanor.

(c) The amount involved in a theft shall be deemed to be the highest value, by any reasonable standard, of the property or services which the actor stole or attempted to steal. Amounts involved in thefts committed pursuant to one scheme or course of conduct, whether from the same person or several persons, may be aggregated in determining the grade of the offense.

(3) Claim of Right. It is an affirmative defense to prosecution for theft that the actor:

(a) was unaware that the property or service was that of another; or

(b) acted under an honest claim of right to the property or service involved or that he had a right to acquire or dispose of it as he did; or

(c) took property exposed for sale, intending to purchase and pay for it promptly, or reasonably believing that the owner, if present, would have consented.

(4) Theft from Spouse. It is no defense that theft was from the actor's spouse, except that misappropriation of household and personal effects, or other property normally accessible to both spouses, is theft only if it occurs after the parties have ceased living together.

Section 223.2. Theft by Unlawful Taking or Disposition

(1) Movable Property. A person is guilty of theft if he unlawfully takes, or exercises unlawful control over, movable property of another with purpose to deprive him thereof.

(2) Immovable Property. A person is guilty of theft if he unlawfully transfers immovable property of another or any interest therein with purpose to benefit himself or another not entitled thereto.

Section 223.3. Theft by Deception

A person is guilty of theft if he purposely obtains property of another by deception. A person deceives if he purposely:

(1) creates or reinforces a false impression, including false impressions as to law, value, intention or other state of mind; but deception as to a person's intention to perform a promise shall not be inferred from the fact alone that he did not subsequently perform the promise; or

(2) prevents another from acquiring information which would affect his judgment of a transaction; or

(3) fails to correct a false impression which the deceiver previously created or reinforced, or which the deceiver knows to be influencing another to whom he stands in a fiduciary or confidential relationship; or

(4) fails to disclose a known lien, adverse claim or other legal impediment to the enjoyment of property which he transfers or encumbers in consideration for the property obtained, whether such impediment is or is not valid, or is or is not a matter of official record.

The term "deceive" does not, however, include falsity as to matters having no pecuniary significance, or puffing by statements unlikely to deceive ordinary persons in the group addressed.

Section 223.4. Theft by Extortion

A person is guilty of theft if he purposely obtains property of another by threatening to:

(1) inflict bodily injury on anyone or commit any other criminal offense; or

(2) accuse anyone of a criminal offense; or

(3) expose any secret tending to subject any person to hatred, contempt or ridicule, or to impair his credit or business repute; or

(4) take or withhold action as an official, or cause an official to take or withhold action; or

(5) bring about or continue a strike, boycott or other collective unofficial action, if the property is not demanded or received for the benefit of the group in whose interest the actor purports to act; or

(6) testify or provide information or withhold testimony or information with respect to another's legal claim or defense; or

(7) inflict any other harm which would not benefit the actor.

It is an affirmative defense to prosecution based on paragraphs (2), (3) or (4) that the property obtained by threat of accusation, exposure, lawsuit or other invocation of official action was honestly claimed as restitution or indemnification for harm done in the circumstances to which such accusation, exposure, lawsuit or other official action relates, or as compensation for property or lawful services.

Section 223.5. Theft of Property Lost, Mislaid, or Delivered by Mistake

A person who comes into control of property of another that he knows to have been lost, mislaid, or delivered under a mistake as to the nature or amount of the property or the identity of the recipient is guilty of theft if, with purpose to deprive the owner thereof, he fails to take reasonable measures to restore the property to a person entitled to have it.

Section 223.6. Receiving Stolen Property

(1) <u>Receiving.</u> A person is guilty of theft if he purposely receives, retains, or disposes of movable property of another knowing that it has been stolen, or believing that it has probably been stolen, unless the property is received, retained, or disposed with purpose to restore it to the owner. "Receiving" means acquiring possession, control or title, or lending on the security of the property.

(2) <u>Presumption of Knowledge.</u> The requisite knowledge or belief is presumed in the case of a dealer who:

(a) is found in possession or control of property stolen from two or more persons on separate occasions; or

(b) has received stolen property in another transaction within the year preceding the transaction charged; or

(c) being a dealer in property of the sort received, acquires it for a consideration which he knows is far below its reasonable value.

"Dealer" means a person in the business of buying or selling goods including a pawnbroker.

Section 223.7. Theft of Services

(1) A person is guilty of theft if he purposely obtains services which he knows are available only for compensation, by deception or threat, or by false token or other means to avoid payment for the service. "Services" includes labor, professional service, transportation, telephone or other public service, accommodation in hotels, restaurants or elsewhere, admission to exhibitions, use of vehicles or other movable property. Where compensation for service is

ordinarily paid immediately upon the rendering of such service, as in the case of hotels and restaurants, refusal to pay or absconding without payment or offer to pay gives rise to a presumption that the service was obtained by deception as to intention to pay.

(2) A person commits theft if, having control over the disposition of services of others, to which he is not entitled, he knowingly diverts such services to his own benefit or to the benefit of another not entitled thereto.

Section 223.8.   Theft by Failure to Make Required Disposition of Funds Received

A person who purposely obtains property upon agreement, or subject to a known legal obligation, to make specified payment or other disposition, whether from such property or its proceeds or from his own property to be reserved in equivalent amount, is guilty of theft if he deals with the property obtained as his own and fails to make the required payment or disposition. The foregoing applies notwithstanding that it may be impossible to identify particular property as belonging to the victim at the time of the actor's failure to make the required payment or disposition. An officer or employee of the government or of a financial institution is presumed: (i) to know any legal obligation relevant to his criminal liability under this Section, and (ii) to have dealt with the property as his own if he fails to pay or account upon lawful demand, or if an audit reveals a shortage or falsification of accounts.

Section 223.9.   Unauthorized Use of Automobiles and Other Vehicles

A person commits a misdemeanor if he operates another's automobile, airplane, motorcycle, motorboat, or other motor-propelled vehicle without consent of the owner. It is an affirmative defense to prosecution under this Section that the actor reasonably believed that the owner would have consented to the operation had he known of it.

ARTICLE 224.   FORGERY AND FRAUDULENT PRACTICES

Section 224.0.   Definitions

In this Article, the definitions given in Section 223.0 apply unless a different meaning plainly is required.

Section 224.1.   Forgery

(1) Definition. A person is guilty of forgery if, with purpose to defraud or injure anyone, or with knowledge that he is facilitating a fraud or injury to be perpetrated by anyone, the actor:

(a) alters any writing of another without his authority; or

(b) makes, completes, executes, authenticates, issues or transfers any writing so that it purports to be the act of another who did not authorize that act, or to have been executed at a time or place or in a numbered sequence other than was in fact the case, or to be a copy of an original when no such original existed; or

(c) utters any writing which he knows to be forged in a manner specified in paragraphs (a) or (b).

"Writing" includes printing or any other method of recording information, money, coins, tokens, stamps, seals, credit cards, badges, trade-marks, and other symbols of value, right, privilege, or identification.

(2) *Grading.* Forgery is a felony of the second degree if the writing is or purports to be part of an issue of money, securities, postage or revenue stamps, or other instruments issued by the government, or part of an issue of stock, bonds or other instruments representing interests in or claims against any property or enterprise. Forgery is a felony of the third degree if the writing is or purports to be a will, deed, contract, release, commercial instrument, or other document evidencing, creating, transferring, altering, terminating, or otherwise affecting legal relations. Otherwise forgery is a misdemeanor.

Section 224.2. Simulating Objects of Antiquity, Rarity, Etc.

A person commits a misdemeanor if, with purpose to defraud anyone or with knowledge that he is facilitating a fraud to be perpetrated by anyone, he makes, alters or utters any object so that it appears to have value because of antiquity, rarity, source, or authorship which it does not possess.

Section 224.3. Fraudulent Destruction, Removal or Concealment of Recordable Instruments

A person commits a felony of the third degree if, with purpose to deceive or injure anyone, he destroys, removes or conceals any will, deed, mortgage, security instrument or other writing for which the law provides public recording.

Section 224.4. Tampering with Records

A person commits a misdemeanor if, knowing that he has no privilege to do so, he falsifies, destroys, removes or conceals any writing or record, with purpose to deceive or injure anyone or to conceal any wrongdoing.

Section 224.5. Bad Checks

A person who issues or passes a check or similar sight order for the payment of money, knowing that it will not be honored by the drawee, commits a misdemeanor. For the purposes of this Section as well as in any prosecution for theft committed by means of a bad check, an issuer is presumed to know that the check or order (other than a post-dated check or order) would not be paid, if:

(1) the issuer had no account with the drawee at the time the check or order was issued; or

(2) payment was refused by the drawee for lack of funds, upon presentation within 30 days after issue, and the issuer failed to make good within 10 days after receiving notice of that refusal.

Section 224.6. Credit Cards

A person commits an offense if he uses a credit card for the purpose of obtaining property or services with knowledge that:

(1) the card is stolen or forged; or

(2) the card has been revoked or cancelled; or

(3) for any other reason his use of the card is unauthorized by the issuer.

It is an affirmative defense to prosecution under paragraph (c) if the actor proves by a preponderance of the evidence that he had the purpose and ability to meet all obligations to the issuer arising out of his use of the card. "Credit card" means a writing or other evidence of an undertaking to pay for property or services delivered or rendered to or upon the order of a designated person or bearer. An offense under this Section is a felony of the third degree if the value of the property or services secured or sought to be secured by means of the credit card exceeds $500; otherwise it is a misdemeanor.

Section 224.7. Deceptive Business Practices

A person commits a misdemeanor if in the course of business he:

(1) uses or possesses for use a false weight or measure, or any other device for falsely determining or recording any quality or quantity; or

(2) sells, offers or exposes for sale, or delivers less than the represented quantity of any commodity or service; or

(3) takes or attempts to take more than the represented quantity of any commodity or service when as buyer he furnishes the weight or measure; or

(4) sells, offers or exposes for sale adulterated or mislabeled commodities. "Adulterated" means varying from the standard of composition or quality prescribed by or pursuant to any statute providing criminal penalties for such variance, or set by established commercial usage. "Mislabeled" means varying from the standard of truth or disclosure in labeling prescribed by or pursuant to any statute providing criminal penalties for such variance, or set by established commercial usage; or

(5) makes a false or misleading statement in any advertisement addressed to the public or to a substantial segment thereof for the purpose of promoting the purchase or sale of property or services; or

(6) makes a false or misleading written statement for the purpose of obtaining property or credit; or

(7) makes a false or misleading written statement for the purpose of promoting the sale of securities, or omits information required by law to be disclosed in written documents relating to securities.

It is an affirmative defense to prosecution under this Section if the defendant proves by a preponderance of the evidence that his conduct was not knowingly or recklessly deceptive.

Section 224.8. Commercial Bribery and Breach of Duty to Act Disinterestedly

(1) A person commits a misdemeanor if he solicits, accepts or agrees to accept any benefit as consideration for knowingly violating or agreeing to violate a duty of fidelity to which he is subject as:

(a) partner, agent, or employee of another;

(b) trustee, guardian, or other fiduciary;

(c) lawyer, physician, accountant, appraiser, or other professional adviser or informant;

(d) officer, director, manager or other participant in the direction of the affairs of an incorporated or unincorporated association; or

(e) arbitrator or other purportedly disinterested adjudicator or referee.

(2) A person who holds himself out to the public as being engaged in the business of making disinterested selection, appraisal, or criticism of commodities or services commits a misdemeanor if he solicits, accepts or agrees to accept any benefit to influence his selection, appraisal or criticism.

(3) A person commits a misdemeanor if he confers, or offers or agrees to confer, any benefit the acceptance of which would be criminal under this Section.

Section 224.9. Rigging Publicly Exhibited Contest

(1) A person commits a misdemeanor if, with purpose to prevent a publicly exhibited contest from being conducted in accordance with the rules and usages purporting to govern it, he:

(a) confers or offers or agrees to confer any benefit upon, or threatens any injury to a participant, official or other person associated with the contest or exhibition; or

(b) tampers with any person, animal or thing.

(2) Soliciting or Accepting Benefit for Rigging. A person commits a misdemeanor if he knowingly solicits, accepts or agrees to accept any benefit the giving of which would be criminal under Subsection (1).

(3) Participation in Rigged Contest. A person commits a misdemeanor if he knowingly engages in, sponsors, produces, judges, or otherwise participates in a publicly exhibited contest knowing that the contest is not being conducted in compliance with the rules and usages purporting to govern it, by reason of conduct which would be criminal under this Section.

Section 224.10. Defrauding Secured Creditors

A person commits a misdemeanor if he destroys, removes, conceals, encumbers, transfers or otherwise deals with property subject to a security interest with purpose to hinder enforcement of that interest.

Section 224.11. Fraud in Insolvency

A person commits a misdemeanor if, knowing that proceedings have been or are about to be instituted for the appointment of a receiver or other person entitled to administer property for the benefit of creditors, or that any other composition or liquidation for the benefit of creditors has been or is about to be made, he:

(1) destroys, removes, conceals, encumbers, transfers, or otherwise deals with any property with purpose to defeat or obstruct the claim of any creditor, or otherwise to obstruct the operation of any law relating to administration of property for the benefit of creditors; or

(2) knowingly falsifies any writing or record relating to the property; or

(3) knowingly misrepresents or refuses to disclose to a receiver or other person entitled to administer property for the benefit of creditors, the existence, amount or location of the property, or any other information which the actor could be legally required to furnish in relation to such administration.

Section 224.12. Receiving Deposits in a Failing Financial Institution

An officer, manager or other person directing or participating in the direction of a financial institution commits a misdemeanor if he receives or permits the receipt of a deposit, premium payment or other investment in the institution knowing that:

(1) due to financial difficulties the institution is about to suspend operations or go into receivership or reorganization; and

(2) the person making the deposit or other payment is unaware of the precarious situation of the institution.

Section 224.13. Misapplication of Entrusted Property and Property of Government or Financial Institution

A person commits an offense if he applies or disposes of property that has been entrusted to him as a fiduciary, or property of the government or of a financial institution, in a manner which he knows is unlawful and involves substantial risk of loss or detriment to the owner of the property or to a person for whose benefit the property was entrusted. The offense is a misdemeanor if the amount involved exceeds $50; otherwise it is a petty misdemeanor. "Fiduciary" includes trustee, guardian, executor, administrator, receiver and any person carrying on fiduciary functions on behalf of a corporation or other organization which is a fiduciary.

Section 224.14. Securing Execution of Documents by Deception

A person commits a misdemeanor if by deception he causes another to execute any instrument affecting, purporting to affect, or likely to affect the pecuniary interest of any person.

OFFENSES AGAINST THE FAMILY

ARTICLE 230. OFFENSES AGAINST THE FAMILY

Section 230.1. Bigamy and Polygamy

(1) Bigamy. A married person is guilty of bigamy, a misdemeanor, if he contracts or purports to contract another marriage, unless at the time of the subsequent marriage:

(a) the actor believes that the prior spouse is dead; or

(b) the actor and the prior spouse have been living apart for five consecutive years throughout which the prior spouse was not known by the actor to be alive; or

(c) a Court has entered a judgment purporting to terminate or annul any prior disqualifying marriage, and the actor does not know that judgment to be invalid; or

(d) the actor reasonably believes that he is legally eligible to remarry.

(2) Polygamy. A person is guilty of polygamy, a felony of the third degree, if he marries or cohabits with more than one spouse at a time in purported exercise of the right of plural marriage. The offense is a continuing one until all cohabitation and claim of marriage with more than one spouse terminates. This section does not apply to parties to a polygamous marriage, lawful in the country of which they are residents or nationals, while they are in transit through or temporarily visiting this State.

(3) Other Party to Bigamous or Polygamous Marriage. A person is guilty of bigamy or polygamy, as the case may be, if he contracts or purports to contract marriage with another knowing that the other is thereby committing bigamy or polygamy.

Section 230.2. Incest

A person is guilty of incest, a felony of the third degree, if he knowingly marries or cohabits or has sexual intercourse with an ancestor or descendant, a brother or sister of the whole or half blood [or an uncle, aunt, nephew or niece of the whole blood]. "Cohabit" means to live together under the representation or appearance of being married. The relationships referred to herein include blood relationships without regard to legitimacy, and relationship of parent and child by adoption.

Section 230.3. Abortion

(1) Unjustified Abortion. A person who purposely and unjustifiably terminates the pregnancy of another otherwise than by a live birth commits a felony of the third degree or, where the pregnancy has continued beyond the twenty-sixth week, a felony of the second degree.

(2) Justifiable Abortion. A licensed physician is justified in terminating a pregnancy if he believes there is substantial risk that continuance of the pregnancy would gravely impair the physical or mental health of the mother or that the child would be born with grave physical or mental defect, or that the pregnancy resulted from rape, incest, or other felonious intercourse. All illicit intercourse with a girl below the age of 16 shall be deemed felonious for purposes of this Subsection. Justifiable abortions shall be performed only in a licensed hospital except in case of emergency when hospital facilities are unavailable. [Additional exceptions from the requirement of hospitalization may be incorporated here to take account of situations in sparsely settled areas where hospitals are not generally accessible.]

(3) Physicians' Certificates; Presumption from Non-Compliance. No abortion shall be performed unless two physicians, one of whom may be the person performing the abortion, shall have certified in writing the circumstances which they believe to justify the abortion. Such certificate shall be submitted before the abortion to the hospital where it is to be performed and, in the case of abortion following felonious intercourse, to the prosecuting attorney or the police. Failure to comply with any of the requirements of this Subsection gives rise to a presumption that the abortion was unjustified.

(4) Self-Abortion. A woman whose pregnancy has continued beyond the twenty-sixth week commits a felony of the third degree if she purposely terminates her own pregnancy otherwise than by a live birth, or if she uses instruments, drugs or violence upon herself for that purpose. Except as justified under Subsection (2), a person who induces or knowingly aids a woman to use instruments, drugs or violence upon herself for the purpose of terminating her pregnancy otherwise than by a live birth commits a felony of the third degree whether or not the pregnancy has continued beyond the twenty-sixth week.

(5) Pretended Abortion. A person commits a felony of the third degree if, representing that it is his purpose to perform an abortion, he does an act adapted to cause abortion in a pregnant woman although the woman is in fact not pregnant, or the actor does not believe she is. A person charged with

unjustified abortion under Subsection (1) or an attempt to commit that offense may be convicted thereof upon proof of conduct prohibited by this Subsection.

(6) Distribution of Abortifacients. A person who sells, offers to sell, possesses with intent to sell, advertises, or displays for sale anything specially designed to terminate a pregnancy, or held out by the actor as useful for that purpose, commits a misdemeanor, unless:

(a) the sale, offer or display is to a physician or druggist or to an intermediary in a chain of distribution to physicians or druggists; or

(b) the sale is made upon prescription or order of a physician; or

(c) the possession is with intent to sell as authorized in paragraphs (a) and (b); or

(d) the advertising is addressed to persons named in paragraph (a) and confined to trade or professional channels not likely to reach the general public.

(7) Section Inapplicable to Prevention of Pregnancy. Nothing in this Section shall be deemed applicable to the prescription, administration or distribution of drugs or other substances for avoiding pregnancy, whether by preventing implantation of a fertilized ovum or by any other method that operates before, at or immediately after fertilization.

Section 230.4. Endangering Welfare of Children

A parent, guardian, or other person supervising the welfare of a child under 18 commits a misdemeanor if he knowingly endangers the child's welfare by violating a duty of care, protection or support.

Section 230.5. Persistent Non-Support

A person commits a misdemeanor if he persistently fails to provide support which he can provide and which he knows he is legally obliged to provide to a spouse, child or other dependent.

———

OFFENSES AGAINST PUBLIC ADMINISTRATION

———

ARTICLE 240. BRIBERY AND CORRUPT INFLUENCE

Section 240.0. Definitions

In Articles 240–243, unless a different meaning plainly is required:

(1) "benefit" means gain or advantage, or anything regarded by the beneficiary as gain or advantage, including benefit to any other person or entity in whose welfare he is interested, but not an advantage promised generally to a group or class of voters as a consequence of public measures which a candidate engages to support or oppose;

(2) "government" includes any branch, subdivision or agency of the government of the State or any locality within it;

(3) "harm" means loss, disadvantage or injury, or anything so regarded by the person affected, including loss, disadvantage or injury to any other person or entity in whose welfare he is interested;

(4) "official proceeding" means a proceeding heard or which may be heard before any legislative, judicial, administrative or other governmental agency or official authorized to take evidence under oath, including any referee, hearing examiner, commissioner, notary or other person taking testimony or deposition in connection with any such proceeding;

(5) "party official" means a person who holds an elective or appointive post in a political party in the United States by virtue of which he directs or conducts, or participates in directing or conducting party affairs at any level of responsibility;

(6) "pecuniary benefit" is benefit in the form of money, property, commercial interests or anything else the primary significance of which is economic gain;

(7) "public servant" means any officer or employee of government, including legislators and judges, and any person participating as juror, advisor, consultant or otherwise, in performing a governmental function; but the term does not include witnesses;

(8) "administrative proceeding" means any proceeding, other than a judicial proceeding, the outcome of which is required to be based on a record or documentation prescribed by law, or in which law or regulation is particularized in application to individuals.

Section 240.1. Bribery in Official and Political Matters

A person is guilty of bribery, a felony of the third degree, if he offers, confers or agrees to confer upon another, or solicits, accepts or agrees to accept from another:

(1) any pecuniary benefit as consideration for the recipient's decision, opinion, recommendation, vote or other exercise of discretion as a public servant, party official or voter; or

(2) any benefit as consideration for the recipient's decision, vote, recommendation or other exercise of official discretion in a judicial or administrative proceeding; or

(3) any benefit as consideration for a violation of a known legal duty as public servant or party official.

It is no defense to prosecution under this section that a person whom the actor sought to influence was not qualified to act in the desired way whether because he had not yet assumed office, or lacked jurisdiction, or for any other reason.

Section 240.2. Threats and Other Improper Influence in Official and Political Matters

(1) Offenses Defined. A person commits an offense if he:

(a) threatens unlawful harm to any person with purpose to influence his decision, opinion, recommendation, vote or other exercise of discretion as a public servant, party official or voter; or

(b) threatens harm to any public servant with purpose to influence his decision, opinion, recommendation, vote or other exercise of discretion in a judicial or administrative proceeding; or

(c) threatens harm to any public servant or party official with purpose to influence him to violate his known legal duty; or

(d) privately addresses to any public servant who has or will have an official discretion in a judicial or administrative proceeding any representation, entreaty, argument or other communication with purpose to influence the outcome on the basis of considerations other than those authorized by law.

It is no defense to prosecution under this Section that a person whom the actor sought to influence was not qualified to act in the desired way, whether because he had not yet assumed office, or lacked jurisdiction, or for any other reason.

(2) Grading. An offense under this Section is a misdemeanor unless the actor threatened to commit a crime or made a threat with purpose to influence a judicial or administrative proceeding, in which cases the offense is a felony of the third degree.

Section 240.3. Compensation for Past Official Behavior

A person commits a misdemeanor if he solicits, accepts or agrees to accept any pecuniary benefit as compensation for having, as public servant, given a decision, opinion, recommendation or vote favorable to another, or for having otherwise exercised a discretion in his favor, or for having violated his duty. A person commits a misdemeanor if he offers, confers or agrees to confer compensation acceptance of which is prohibited by this Section.

Section 240.4. Retaliation for Past Official Action

A person commits a misdemeanor if he harms another by any unlawful act in retaliation for anything lawfully done by the latter in the capacity of public servant.

Section 240.5. Gifts to Public Servants by Persons Subject to Their Jurisdiction

(1) Regulatory and Law Enforcement Officials. No public servant in any department or agency exercising regulatory functions, or conducting inspections or investigations, or carrying on civil or criminal litigation on behalf of the government, or having custody of prisoners, shall solicit, accept or agree to accept any pecuniary benefit from a person known to be subject to such regulation, inspection, investigation or custody, or against whom such litigation is known to be pending or contemplated.

(2) Officials Concerned with Government Contracts and Pecuniary Transactions. No public servant having any discretionary function to perform in connection with contracts, purchases, payments, claims or other pecuniary transactions of the government shall solicit, accept or agree to accept any pecuniary benefit from any person known to be interested in or likely to become interested in any such contract, purchase, payment, claim or transaction.

(3) Judicial and Administrative Officials. No public servant having judicial or administrative authority and no public servant employed by or in a court or other tribunal having such authority, or participating in the enforcement of its decisions, shall solicit, accept or agree to accept any pecuniary benefit from a person known to be interested in or likely to become interested in any matter before such public servant or a tribunal with which he is associated.

(4) Legislative Officials. No legislator or public servant employed by the legislature or by any committee or agency thereof shall solicit, accept or agree

to accept any pecuniary benefit from any person known to be interested in a bill, transaction or proceeding, pending or contemplated, before the legislature or any committee or agency thereof.

(5) Exceptions. This Section shall not apply to:

(a) fees prescribed by law to be received by a public servant, or any other benefit for which the recipient gives legitimate consideration or to which he is otherwise legally entitled; or

(b) gifts or other benefits conferred on account of kinship or other personal, professional or business relationship independent of the official status of the receiver; or

(c) trivial benefits incidental to personal, professional or business contacts and involving no substantial risk of undermining official impartiality.

(6) Offering Benefits Prohibited. No person shall knowingly confer, or offer or agree to confer, any benefit prohibited by the foregoing Subsections.

(7) Grade of Offense. An offense under this Section is a misdemeanor.

Section 240.6. Compensating Public Servant for Assisting Private Interests in Relation to Matters Before Him

(1) Receiving Compensation. A public servant commits a misdemeanor if he solicits, accepts or agrees to accept compensation for advice or other assistance in preparing or promoting a bill, contract, claim, or other transaction or proposal as to which he knows that he has or is likely to have an official discretion to exercise.

(2) Paying Compensation. A person commits a misdemeanor if he pays or offers or agrees to pay compensation to a public servant with knowledge that acceptance by the public servant is unlawful.

Section 240.7. Selling Political Endorsement; Special Influence

(1) Selling Political Endorsement. A person commits a misdemeanor if he solicits, receives, agrees to receive, or agrees that any political party or other person shall receive, any pecuniary benefit as consideration for approval or disapproval of an appointment or advancement in public service, or for approval or disapproval of any person or transaction for any benefit conferred by an official or agency of government. "Approval" includes recommendation, failure to disapprove, or any other manifestation of favor or acquiescence. "Disapproval" includes failure to approve, or any other manifestation of disfavor or nonacquiescence.

(2) Other Trading in Special Influence. A person commits a misdemeanor if he solicits, receives or agrees to receive any pecuniary benefit as consideration for exerting special influence upon a public servant or procuring another to do so. "Special influence" means power to influence through kinship, friendship or other relationship, apart from the merits of the transaction.

(3) Paying for Endorsement or Special Influence. A person commits a misdemeanor if he offers, confers or agrees to confer any pecuniary benefit receipt of which is prohibited by this Section.

ARTICLE 241. PERJURY AND OTHER FALSIFICATION IN OFFICIAL MATTERS

Section 241.0. Definitions

In this Article, unless a different meaning plainly is required:

(1) the definitions given in Section 240.0 apply; and

(2) "statement" means any representation, but includes a representation of opinion, belief or other state of mind only if the representation clearly relates to state of mind apart from or in addition to any facts which are the subject of the representation.

Section 241.1. Perjury

(1) Offense Defined. A person is guilty of perjury, a felony of the third degree, if in any official proceeding he makes a false statement under oath or equivalent affirmation, or swears or affirms the truth of a statement previously made, when the statement is material and he does not believe it to be true.

(2) Materiality. Falsification is material, regardless of the admissibility of the statement under rules of evidence, if it could have affected the course or outcome of the proceeding. It is no defense that the declarant mistakenly believed the falsification to be immaterial. Whether a falsification is material in a given factual situation is a question of law.

(3) Irregularities No Defense. It is not a defense to prosecution under this Section that the oath or affirmation was administered or taken in an irregular manner or that the declarant was not competent to make the statement. A document purporting to be made upon oath or affirmation at any time when the actor presents it as being so verified shall be deemed to have been duly sworn or affirmed.

(4) Retraction. No person shall be guilty of an offense under this Section if he retracted the falsification in the course of the proceeding in which it was made before it became manifest that the falsification was or would be exposed and before the falsification substantially affected the proceeding.

(5) Inconsistent Statements. Where the defendant made inconsistent statements under oath or equivalent affirmation, both having been made within the period of the statute of limitations, the prosecution may proceed by setting forth the inconsistent statements in a single count alleging in the alternative that one or the other was false and not believed by the defendant. In such case it shall not be necessary for the prosecution to prove which statement was false but only that one or the other was false and not believed by the defendant to be true.

(6) Corroboration. No person shall be convicted of an offense under this Section where proof of falsity rests solely upon contradiction by testimony of a single person other than the defendant.

Section 241.2. False Swearing

(1) False Swearing in Official Matters. A person who makes a false statement under oath or equivalent affirmation, or swears or affirms the truth of such a statement previously made, when he does not believe the statement to be true, is guilty of a misdemeanor if:

(a) the falsification occurs in an official proceeding; or

(b) the falsification is intended to mislead a public servant in performing his official function.

(2) Other False Swearing. A person who makes a false statement under oath or equivalent affirmation, or swears or affirms the truth of such a statement previously made, when he does not believe the statement to be true, is guilty of a petty misdemeanor, if the statement is one which is required by law to be sworn or affirmed before a notary or other person authorized to administer oaths.

(3) Perjury Provisions Applicable. Subsections (3) to (6) of Section 241.1 apply to the present Section.

Section 241.3. Unsworn Falsification to Authorities

(1) In General. A person commits a misdemeanor if, with purpose to mislead a public servant in performing his official function, he:

(a) makes any written false statement which he does not believe to be true; or

(b) purposely creates a false impression in a written application for any pecuniary or other benefit, by omitting information necessary to prevent statements therein from being misleading; or

(c) submits or invites reliance on any writing which he knows to be forged, altered or otherwise lacking in authenticity; or

(d) submits or invites reliance on any sample, specimen, map, boundary-mark, or other object which he knows to be false.

(2) Statements "Under Penalty." A person commits a petty misdemeanor if he makes a written false statement which he does not believe to be true, on or pursuant to a form bearing notice, authorized by law, to the effect that false statements made therein are punishable.

(3) Perjury Provisions Applicable. Subsections (3) to (6) of Section 241.1 apply to the present section.

Section 241.4. False Alarms to Agencies of Public Safety

A person who knowingly causes a false alarm of fire or other emergency to be transmitted to or within any organization, official or volunteer, for dealing with emergencies involving danger to life or property commits a misdemeanor.

Section 241.5. False Reports to Law Enforcement Authorities

(1) Falsely Incriminating Another. A person who knowingly gives false information to any law enforcement officer with purpose to implicate another commits a misdemeanor.

(2) Fictitious Reports. A person commits a petty misdemeanor if he:

(a) reports to law enforcement authorities an offense or other incident within their concern knowing that it did not occur; or

(b) pretends to furnish such authorities with information relating to an offense or incident when he knows he has no information relating to such offense or incident.

Section 241.6. Tampering With Witnesses and Informants; Retaliation Against Them

(1) <u>Tampering.</u> A person commits an offense if, believing that an official proceeding or investigation is pending or about to be instituted, he attempts to induce or otherwise cause a witness or informant to:

(a) testify or inform falsely; or

(b) withhold any testimony, information, document or thing; or

(c) elude legal process summoning him to testify or supply evidence; or

(d) absent himself from any proceeding or investigation to which he has been legally summoned.

The offense is a felony of the third degree if the actor employs force, deception, threat or offer of pecuniary benefit. Otherwise it is a misdemeanor.

(2) <u>Retaliation Against Witness or Informant.</u> A person commits a misdemeanor if he harms another by any unlawful act in retaliation for anything lawfully done in the capacity of witness or informant.

(3) <u>Witness or Informant Taking Bribe.</u> A person commits a felony of the third degree if he solicits, accepts or agrees to accept any benefit in consideration of his doing any of the things specified in clauses (a) to (d) of Subsection (1).

Section 241.7. Tampering With or Fabricating Physical Evidence

A person commits a misdemeanor if, believing that an official proceeding or investigation is pending or about to be instituted, he:

(1) alters, destroys, conceals or removes any record, document or thing with purpose to impair its verity or availability in such proceeding or investigation; or

(2) makes, presents or uses any record, document or thing knowing it to be false and with purpose to mislead a public servant who is or may be engaged in such proceeding or investigation.

Section 241.8. Tampering With Public Records or Information

(1) <u>Offense Defined.</u> A person commits an offense if he:

(a) knowingly makes a false entry in, or false alteration of, any record, document or thing belonging to, or received or kept by, the government for information or record, or required by law to be kept by others for information of the government; or

(b) makes, presents or uses any record, document or thing knowing it to be false, and with purpose that it be taken as a genuine part of information or records referred to in paragraph (a); or

(c) purposely and unlawfully destroys, conceals, removes or otherwise impairs the verity or availability of any such record, document or thing.

(2) <u>Grading.</u> An offense under this Section is a misdemeanor unless the actor's purpose is to defraud or injure anyone, in which case the offense is a felony of the third degree.

Section 241.9. Impersonating a Public Servant

A person commits a misdemeanor if he falsely pretends to hold a position in the public service with purpose to induce another to submit to such pretended official authority or otherwise to act in reliance upon that pretense to his prejudice.

ARTICLE 242. OBSTRUCTING GOVERNMENTAL OPERATIONS; ESCAPES

Section 242.0. Definitions

In this Article, unless another meaning plainly is required, the definitions given in Section 240.0 apply.

Section 242.1. Obstructing Administration of Law or Other Governmental Function

A person commits a misdemeanor if he purposely obstructs, impairs or perverts the administration of law or other governmental function by force, violence, physical interference or obstacle, breach of official duty, or any other unlawful act, except that this Section does not apply to flight by a person charged with crime, refusal to submit to arrest, failure to perform a legal duty other than an official duty, or any other means of avoiding compliance with law without affirmative interference with governmental functions.

Section 242.2. Resisting Arrest or Other Law Enforcement

A person commits a misdemeanor if, for the purpose of preventing a public servant from effecting a lawful arrest or discharging any other duty, the person creates a substantial risk of bodily injury to the public servant or anyone else, or employs means justifying or requiring substantial force to overcome the resistance.

Section 242.3. Hindering Apprehension or Prosecution

A person commits an offense if, with purpose to hinder the apprehension, prosecution, conviction or punishment of another for crime, he:

(1) harbors or conceals the other; or

(2) provides or aids in providing a weapon, transportation, disguise or other means of avoiding apprehension or effecting escape; or

(3) conceals or destroys evidence of the crime, or tampers with a witness, informant, document or other source of information, regardless of its admissibility in evidence; or

(4) warns the other of impending discovery or apprehension, except that this paragraph does not apply to a warning given in connection with an effort to bring another into compliance with law; or

(5) volunteers false information to a law enforcement officer.

The offense is a felony of the third degree if the conduct which the actor knows has been charged or is liable to be charged against the person aided would constitute a felony of the first or second degree. Otherwise it is a misdemeanor.

Section 242.4. Aiding Consummation of Crime

A person commits an offense if he purposely aids another to accomplish an unlawful object of a crime, as by safeguarding the proceeds thereof or converting the proceeds into negotiable funds. The offense is a felony of the third degree if the principal offense was a felony of the first or second degree. Otherwise it is a misdemeanor.

Section 242.5. Compounding

A person commits a misdemeanor if he accepts or agrees to accept any pecuniary benefit in consideration of refraining from reporting to law enforcement authorities the commission or suspected commission of any offense or information relating to an offense. It is an affirmative defense to prosecution under this Section that the pecuniary benefit did not exceed an amount which the actor believed to be due as restitution or indemnification for harm caused by the offense.

Section 242.6. Escape

(1) Escape. A person commits an offense if he unlawfully removes himself from official detention or fails to return to official detention following temporary leave granted for a specific purpose or limited period. "Official detention" means arrest, detention in any facility for custody of persons under charge or conviction of crime or alleged or found to be delinquent, detention for extradition or deportation, or any other detention for law enforcement purposes; but "official detention" does not include supervision of probation or parole, or constraint incidental to release on bail.

(2) Permitting or Facilitating Escape. A public servant concerned in detention commits an offense if he knowingly or recklessly permits an escape. Any person who knowingly causes or facilitates an escape commits an offense.

(3) Effect of Legal Irregularity in Detention. Irregularity in bringing about or maintaining detention, or lack of jurisdiction of the committing or detaining authority, shall not be a defense to prosecution under this Section if the escape is from a prison or other custodial facility or from detention pursuant to commitment by official proceedings. In the case of other detentions, irregularity or lack of jurisdiction shall be a defense only if:

(a) the escape involved no substantial risk of harm to the person or property of anyone other than the detainee; or

(b) the detaining authority did not act in good faith under color of law.

(4) Grading of Offenses. An offense under this Section is a felony of the third degree where:

(a) the actor was under arrest for or detained on a charge of felony or following conviction of crime; or

(b) the actor employs force, threat, deadly weapon or other dangerous instrumentality to effect the escape; or

(c) a public servant concerned in detention of persons convicted of crime purposely facilitates or permits an escape from a detention facility.

Otherwise an offense under this section is a misdemeanor.

Section 242.7. Implements for Escape; Other Contraband

(1) Escape Implements. A person commits a misdemeanor if he unlawfully introduces within a detention facility, or unlawfully provides an inmate with, any weapon, tool or other thing which may be useful for escape. An inmate commits a misdemeanor if he unlawfully procures, makes, or otherwise provides himself with, or has in his possession, any such implement of escape. "Unlawfully" means surreptitiously or contrary to law, regulation or order of the detaining authority.

(2) Other Contraband. A person commits a petty misdemeanor if he provides an inmate with anything which the actor knows it is unlawful for the inmate to possess.

Section 242.8. Bail Jumping; Default in Required Appearance

A person set at liberty by court order, with or without bail, upon condition that he will subsequently appear at a specified time and place, commits a misdemeanor if, without lawful excuse, he fails to appear at that time and place. The offense constitutes a felony of the third degree where the required appearance was to answer to a charge of felony, or for disposition of any such charge, and the actor took flight or went into hiding to avoid apprehension, trial or punishment. This Section does not apply to obligations to appear incident to release under suspended sentence or on probation or parole.

ARTICLE 243. ABUSE OF OFFICE

Section 243.0. Definitions

In this Article, unless a different meaning plainly is required, the definitions given in Section 240.0 apply.

Section 243.1. Official Oppression

A person acting or purporting to act in an official capacity or taking advantage of such actual or purported capacity commits a misdemeanor if, knowing that his conduct is illegal, he:

(1) subjects another to arrest, detention, search, seizure, mistreatment, dispossession, assessment, lien or other infringement of personal or property rights; or

(2) denies or impedes another in the exercise or enjoyment of any right, privilege, power or immunity.

Section 243.2. Speculating or Wagering on Official Action or Information

A public servant commits a misdemeanor if, in contemplation of official action by himself or by a governmental unit with which he is associated, or in reliance on information to which he has access in his official capacity and which has not been made public, he:

(1) acquires a pecuniary interest in any property, transaction or enterprise which may be affected by such information or official action; or

(2) speculates or wagers on the basis of such information or official action; or

(3) aids another to do any of the foregoing.

OFFENSES AGAINST PUBLIC ORDER AND DECENCY

ARTICLE 250. RIOT, DISORDERLY CONDUCT, AND RELATED OFFENSES

Section 250.1. Riot; Failure to Disperse

(1) Riot. A person is guilty of riot, a felony of the third degree, if he participates with [two] or more others in a course of disorderly conduct:

(a) with purpose to commit or facilitate the commission of a felony or misdemeanor;

(b) with purpose to prevent or coerce official action; or

(c) when the actor or any other participant to the knowledge of the actor uses or plans to use a firearm or other deadly weapon.

(2) Failure of Disorderly Persons to Disperse Upon Official Order. Where [three] or more persons are participating in a course of disorderly conduct likely to cause substantial harm or serious inconvenience, annoyance or alarm, a peace officer or other public servant engaged in executing or enforcing the law may order the participants and others in the immediate vicinity to disperse. A person who refuses or knowingly fails to obey such an order commits a misdemeanor.

Section 250.2. Disorderly Conduct

(1) Offense Defined. A person is guilty of disorderly conduct if, with purpose to cause public inconvenience, annoyance or alarm, or recklessly creating a risk thereof, he:

(a) engages in fighting or threatening, or in violent or tumultuous behavior; or

(b) makes unreasonable noise or offensively coarse utterance, gesture or display, or addresses abusive language to any person present; or

(c) creates a hazardous or physically offensive condition by any act which serves no legitimate purpose of the actor.

"Public" means affecting or likely to affect persons in a place to which the public or a substantial group has access; among the places included are highways, transport facilities, schools, prisons, apartment houses, places of business or amusement, or any neighborhood.

(2) Grading. An offense under this Section is a petty misdemeanor if the actor's purpose is to cause substantial harm or serious inconvenience, or if he persists in disorderly conduct after reasonable warning or request to desist. Otherwise disorderly conduct is a violation.

Section 250.3. False Public Alarms

A person is guilty of a misdemeanor if he initiates or circulates a report or warning of an impending bombing or other crime or catastrophe, knowing that the report or warning is false or baseless and that it is likely to cause evacuation of a building, place of assembly, or facility of public transport, or to cause public inconvenience or alarm.

Section 250.4. Harassment

A person commits a petty misdemeanor if, with purpose to harass another, he:

(1) makes a telephone call without purpose of legitimate communication; or

(2) insults, taunts or challenges another in a manner likely to provoke violent or disorderly response; or

(3) makes repeated communications anonymously or at extremely inconvenient hours, or in offensively coarse language; or

(4) subjects another to an offensive touching; or

(5) engages in any other course of alarming conduct serving no legitimate purpose of the actor.

Section 250.5. Public Drunkenness; Drug Incapacitation

A person is guilty of an offense if he appears in any public place manifestly under the influence of alcohol, narcotics or other drug, not therapeutically administered, to the degree that he may endanger himself or other persons or property, or annoy persons in his vicinity. An offense under this Section constitutes a petty misdemeanor if the actor has been convicted hereunder twice before within a period of one year. Otherwise the offense constitutes a violation.

Section 250.6. Loitering or Prowling

A person commits a violation if he loiters or prowls in a place, at a time, or in a manner not usual for law-abiding individuals under circumstances that warrant alarm for the safety of persons or property in the vicinity. Among the circumstances which may be considered in determining whether such alarm is warranted is the fact that the actor takes flight upon appearance of a peace officer, refuses to identify himself, or manifestly endeavors to conceal himself or any object. Unless flight by the actor or other circumstance makes it impracticable, a peace officer shall prior to any arrest for an offense under this section afford the actor an opportunity to dispel any alarm which would otherwise be warranted, by requesting him to identify himself and explain his presence and conduct. No person shall be convicted of an offense under this Section if the peace officer did not comply with the preceding sentence, or if it appears at trial that the explanation given by the actor was true and, if believed by the peace officer at the time, would have dispelled the alarm.

Section 250.7. Obstructing Highways and Other Public Passages

(1) A person, who, having no legal privilege to do so, purposely or recklessly obstructs any highway or other public passage, whether alone or with others, commits a violation, or, in case he persists after warning by a law officer, a petty misdemeanor. "Obstructs" means renders impassable without unreasonable inconvenience or hazard. No person shall be deemed guilty of recklessly obstructing in violation of this Subsection solely because of a gathering of persons to hear him speak or otherwise communicate, or solely because of being a member of such a gathering.

(2) A person in a gathering commits a violation if he refuses to obey a reasonable official request or order to move:

(a) to prevent obstruction of a highway or other public passage; or

(b) to maintain public safety by dispersing those gathered in dangerous proximity to a fire or other hazard.

An order to move, addressed to a person whose speech or other lawful behavior attracts an obstructing audience, shall not be deemed reasonable if the obstruction can be readily remedied by police control of the size or location of the gathering.

Section 250.8. Disrupting Meetings and Processions

A person commits a misdemeanor if, with purpose to prevent or disrupt a lawful meeting, procession or gathering, he does any act tending to obstruct or interfere with it physically, or makes any utterance, gesture or display designed to outrage the sensibilities of the group.

Section 250.9. Desecration of Venerated Objects

A person commits a misdemeanor if he purposely desecrates any public monument or structure, or place of worship or burial, or if he purposely desecrates the national flag or any other object of veneration by the public or a substantial segment thereof in any public place. "Desecrate" means defacing, damaging, polluting or otherwise physically mistreating in a way that the actor knows will outrage the sensibilities of persons likely to observe or discover his action.

Section 250.10. Abuse of Corpse

Except as authorized by law, a person who treats a corpse in a way that he knows would outrage ordinary family sensibilities commits a misdemeanor.

Section 250.11. Cruelty to Animals

A person commits a misdemeanor if he purposely or recklessly:

(1) subjects any animal to cruel mistreatment; or

(2) subjects any animal in his custody to cruel neglect; or

(3) kills or injures any animal belonging to another without legal privilege or consent of the owner.

Subsections (1) and (2) shall not be deemed applicable to accepted veterinary practices and activities carried on for scientific research.

Section 250.12. Violation of Privacy

(1) Unlawful Eavesdropping or Surveillance. A person commits a misdemeanor if, except as authorized by law, he:

(a) trespasses on property with purpose to subject anyone to eavesdropping or other surveillance in a private place; or

(b) installs in any private place, without the consent of the person or persons entitled to privacy there, any device for observing, photographing, recording, amplifying or broadcasting sounds or events in such place, or uses any such unauthorized installation; or

(c) installs or uses outside a private place any device for hearing, recording, amplifying or broadcasting sounds originating in such place which would not ordinarily be audible or comprehensible outside, without the consent of the person or persons entitled to privacy there.

"Private place" means a place where one may reasonably expect to be safe from casual or hostile intrusion or surveillance, but does not include a place to which the public or a substantial group thereof has access.

(2) Other Breach of Privacy of Messages. A person commits a misdemeanor if, except as authorized by law, he:

(a) intercepts without the consent of the sender or receiver a message by telephone, telegraph, letter or other means of communicating privately; but this paragraph does not extend to (i) overhearing of messages through a regularly installed instrument on a telephone party line or on an extension, or (ii) interception by the telephone company or subscriber incident to enforcement of regulations limiting use of the facilities or incident to other normal operation and use; or

(b) divulges without the consent of the sender or receiver the existence or contents of any such message if the actor knows that the message was illegally intercepted, or if he learned of the message in the course of employment with an agency engaged in transmitting it.

ARTICLE 251.   PUBLIC INDECENCY

Section 251.1.   Open Lewdness

A person commits a petty misdemeanor if he does any lewd act which he knows is likely to be observed by others who would be affronted or alarmed.

Section 251.2.   Prostitution and Related Offenses

(1) Prostitution. A person is guilty of prostitution, a petty misdemeanor, if he or she:

(a) is an inmate of a house of prostitution or otherwise engages in sexual activity as a business; or

(b) loiters in or within view of any public place for the purpose of being hired to engage in sexual activity.

"Sexual activity" includes homosexual and other deviate sexual relations. A "house of prostitution" is any place where prostitution or promotion of prostitution is regularly carried on by one person under the control, management or supervision of another. An "inmate" is a person who engages in prostitution in or through the agency of a house of prostitution. "Public place" means any place to which the public or any substantial group thereof has access.

(2) Promoting Prostitution. A person who knowingly promotes prostitution of another commits a misdemeanor or felony as provided in Subsection (3). The following acts shall, without limitation of the foregoing, constitute promoting prostitution:

(a) owning, controlling, managing, supervising or otherwise keeping, alone or in association with others, a house of prostitution or a prostitution business; or

(b) procuring an inmate for a house of prostitution or a place in a house of prostitution for one who would be an inmate; or

(c) encouraging, inducing, or otherwise purposely causing another to become or remain a prostitute; or

(d) soliciting a person to patronize a prostitute; or

(e) procuring a prostitute for a patron; or

A–93

(f) transporting a person into or within this state with purpose to promote that person's engaging in prostitution, or procuring or paying for transportation with that purpose; or

(g) leasing or otherwise permitting a place controlled by the actor, alone or in association with others, to be regularly used for prostitution or the promotion of prostitution, or failure to make reasonable effort to abate such use by ejecting the tenant, notifying law enforcement authorities, or other legally available means; or

(h) soliciting, receiving, or agreeing to receive any benefit for doing or agreeing to do anything forbidden by this Subsection.

(3) Grading of Offenses Under Subsection (2). An offense under Subsection (2) constitutes a felony of the third degree if:

(a) the offense falls within paragraph (a), (b) or (c) of Subsection (2); or

(b) the actor compels another to engage in or promote prostitution; or

(c) the actor promotes prostitution of a child under 16, whether or not he is aware of the child's age; or

(d) the actor promotes prostitution of his wife, child, ward or any person for whose care, protection or support he is responsible.

Otherwise the offense is a misdemeanor.

(4) Presumption from Living off Prostitutes. A person, other than the prostitute or the prostitute's minor child or other legal dependent incapable of self-support, who is supported in whole or substantial part by the proceeds of prostitution is presumed to be knowingly promoting prostitution in violation of Subsection (2).

(5) Patronizing Prostitutes. A person commits a violation if he hires a prostitute to engage in sexual activity with him, or if he enters or remains in a house of prostitution for the purpose of engaging in sexual activity.

(6) Evidence. On the issue whether a place is a house of prostitution the following shall be admissible evidence: its general repute; the repute of the persons who reside in or frequent the place; the frequency, timing and duration of visits by non-residents. Testimony of a person against his spouse shall be admissible to prove offenses under this Section.

Section 251.3. Loitering to Solicit Deviate Sexual Relations

A person is guilty of a petty misdemeanor if he loiters in or near any public place for the purpose of soliciting or being solicited to engage in deviate sexual relations.

Section 251.4. Obscenity

(1) Obscene Defined. Material is obscene if, considered as a whole, its predominant appeal is to prurient interest, that is, a shameful or morbid interest, in nudity, sex or excretion, and if in addition it goes substantially beyond customary limits of candor in describing or representing such matters. Predominant appeal shall be judged with reference to ordinary adults unless it appears from the character of the material or the circumstances of its dissemination to be designed for children or other specially susceptible audience. Undeveloped photographs, molds, printing plates, and the like, shall be deemed obscene notwithstanding that processing or other acts may be required to make the obscenity patent or to disseminate it.

(2) <u>Offenses.</u> Subject to the affirmative defense provided in Subsection (3), a person commits a misdemeanor if he knowingly or recklessly:

(a) sells, delivers or provides, or offers or agrees to sell, deliver or provide, any obscene writing, picture, record or other representation or embodiment of the obscene; or

(b) presents or directs an obscene play, dance or performance, or participates in that portion thereof which makes it obscene; or

(c) publishes, exhibits or otherwise makes available any obscene material; or

(d) possesses any obscene material for purposes of sale or other commercial dissemination; or

(e) sells, advertises or otherwise commercially disseminates material, whether or not obscene, by representing or suggesting that it is obscene.

A person who disseminates or possesses obscene material in the course of his business is presumed to do so knowingly or recklessly.

(3) <u>Justifiable and Non-Commercial Private Dissemination.</u> It is an affirmative defense to prosecution under this Section that dissemination was restricted to:

(a) institutions or persons having scientific, educational, governmental or other similar justification for possessing obscene material; or

(b) non-commercial dissemination to personal associates of the actor.

(4) <u>Evidence; Adjudication of Obscenity.</u> In any prosecution under this Section evidence shall be admissible to show:

(a) the character of the audience for which the material was designed or to which it was directed;

(b) what the predominant appeal of the material would be for ordinary adults or any special audience to which it was directed, and what effect, if any, it would probably have on conduct of such people;

(c) artistic, literary, scientific, educational or other merits of the material;

(d) the degree of public acceptance of the material in the United States;

(e) appeal to prurient interest, or absence thereof, in advertising or other promotion of the material; and

(f) the good repute of the author, creator, publisher or other person from whom the material originated.

Expert testimony and testimony of the author, creator, publisher or other person from whom the material originated, relating to factors entering into the determination of the issue of obscenity, shall be admissible. The Court shall dismiss a prosecution for obscenity if it is satisfied that the material is not obscene.

ADDITIONAL ARTICLES

[Reporter's note: At this point, a State enacting a new Penal Code may insert additional Articles dealing with special topics such as narcotics, alcoholic beverages, gambling and offenses against tax and trade laws. The Model Penal Code project did not extend to these, partly because a higher priority on limited time and resources was accorded to branches of the penal law which have not received close legislative scrutiny. Also, in legislation dealing with narcotics, liquor, tax evasion, and the like, penal provisions have been so intermingled with regulatory and procedural provisions that the task of segregating one group from the other presents special difficulty for model legislation.]

TABLE OF MODEL PENAL CODE REFERENCES

Sec.	Page	Sec.	Page
1.02	103	2.04(1)(a) (Cont'd)	256
1.04	237		272
1.04(5)	307		273
1.05	43		274
1.07(1)(b)	462	2.04(1)(b)	255
1.12	975	2.04(2)	256
1.12(5)	938	2.04(3)	263
1.13	238		267
1.13(5)	121	2.04(3)(b)(iv)	630
1.13(9)	238	2.05	237
	535		307
1.13(10)	238	2.06	399
1.13(16)	245		620
2.01	15	2.06(1)	411
2.01(4)	121	2.06(2)	411
2.02	235	2.06(3)(a)	391
	237	2.06(4)	398
	244	2.06(6)	413
	245	2.07	421
	256	2.07(1)	422
	331	2.07(2)	425
	332	2.07(3)	430
	922	2.07(6)(a)	432
2.02(1)	238	2.07(6)(b)	433
2.02(2)(a)(ii)	243	2.08	726
	399	2.08(2)	278
2.02(2)(c)	240	2.08(4)	731
2.02(3)	237	2.08(5)(b)	284
	241	2.09	606
	242		608
	243		609
	244		612
	255		620
	256	2.09(2)	608
2.02(3)(c)	239	2.10	601
2.02(4)	237		603
	242	2.11(2)	121
	243	2.11.1(1)(b)	241
	244	2.12	362
2.02(5)	244	2.13	628
2.02(9)	263	2.13(1)(a)	630
	267	3.02	519
	274		523
	535		527
	596		612
2.03	929		620
2.03(1)(a)	930	3.02(2)	526
2.03(2)(a)	931		608
2.03(3)(b)	932	3.03	595
2.04	267		601
	391	3.03(1)(a)	603
	396	3.03(3)(b)	604
	477	3.04(1)	533
2.04(1)	535	3.04(2)(a)(i)	536
	536	3.04(2)(b)	533
2.04(1)(a)	255	3.04(2)(b)(ii)	548

TABLE OF MODEL PENAL CODE REFERENCES

Sec.	Page	Sec.	Page
3.04(2)(b)(ii)(1)	551	6.08	7
3.05	576	7.01(1)(b)	25
3.06(1)(b)	536	7.01(1)(c)	15
3.06(3)(d)	547	7.03(2)	462
3.07	584	7.03(4)	462
3.07(1)	547	210.2	218
3.07(2)	547	210.2(1)(b)	921
3.07(2)(b)	536		931
	589		937
3.07(2)(b)(ii)	589	210.3	399
3.07(4)	601		922
3.07(4)(a)	603	210.3(1)(b)	71
3.07(5)	547		842
3.09(1)	535	210.4	218
	601		241
3.09(2)	533		399
4.01	661		911
	662		922
4.01(1)	843	210.5	31
4.01(2)	711	210.6(4)	842
	712	210.6(4)(b)	842
4.02	662		843
4.02(1)	756	210.6(4)(g)	842
5.01	132		843
	351	211.1(1)(a)	534
	352	211.1(1)(b)	241
	370	211.1(2)(b)	240
	371	211.2	926
	392	212.3	242
	459	212.4	255
5.01(1)	351		256
	352	213.1	256
	361		342
5.01(1)(a)	351		1010
	352	213.1(1)(d)	245
5.01(1)(b)	351		353
	352	213.3(1)(a)	234
5.01(1)(c)	136		245
	351		353
	352	213.6(1)	245
	392	220.1(2)(a)	243
5.01(2)	364	220.1(3)	113
	392	221.1	256
5.01(4)	376		353
5.02	139	221.2(1)	245
5.02(3)	376	222.1	342
5.03	450	223	229
	455	223.0(7)	95
	459	223.1	459
	462	223.1(2)	256
	484	223.1(3)	255
5.03(3)	483	223.2	459
5.03(5)	449	223.2(1)	245
5.03(6)	376		256
5.03(7)	499		376
5.03(7)(a)	499	223.3	369
5.03(7)(b)	499	223.6	362
5.03(7)(c)	499	230.1	273
5.05(1)	341	230.1(1)	255
5.05(2)	362	230.1(3)	411
6.01	7	230.1(3)(iii)	411
6.06	7	230.5	270
	218	241.1	370

TABLE OF MODEL PENAL CODE REFERENCES

Sec.	Page	Sec.	Page
241.1 (Cont'd)	371	242.6	612
241.1(4)	376	242.6(1)	243
241.5	244	242.7(1)	245
242.3	244	250.2	1067
	382	250.4(2)	245
242.3(5)	243	250.6	147
	244	251.1	1067

*

Appendix B

SELECTED PENAL STATUTES

(A) VIRGINIA HOMICIDE STATUTES.

1. 2 Va.Stat. §§ 2, 4, 14 (Shepherd 1796):

II. And whereas, The several offenses which are included under the general denomination of murder, differ so greatly from each other in the degree of their atrociousness, that it is unjust to involve them in the same punishment; Be it . . . enacted, That all murder which shall be perpetrated by means of poison, or by lying in wait, or by any other kind of wilful, deliberate, and premeditated killing, or which shall be committed in the perpetration or attempt to perpetrate any arson, rape, robbery or burglary, shall be deemed murder of the first degree; and all other kinds of murder shall be deemed murder of the second degree . . . .

IV. . . . Every person duly convicted of the crime of murder in the second degree, shall be sentenced to . . . confinement for a period not less than five years, nor more than 18 years . . . .

XIV. Every person convicted of murder of the first degree . . . shall suffer death by hanging by the neck.

2. Va.Code, tit. 52 (1887):

§ 3662. Murder, first and second degree, defined.—Murder by poison, lying in wait, imprisonment, starving, or any wilful, deliberate, and premeditated killing, or in the commission of, or attempt to commit arson, rape, robbery, or burglary, is murder of the first degree. All other murder is murder of the second degree.

§ 3663. First degree, how punished.—Murder of the first degree shall be punished with death.

§ 3664. Second degree, how punished.—Murder of the second degree shall be punished by confinement in the penitentiary not less than five nor more than 18 years.

§ 3665. Voluntary manslaughter, how punished.—Voluntary manslaughter, shall be punished by confinement in the penitentiary not less than one nor more than five years.

§ 3666. Involuntary manslaughter, a misdemeanor.—Involuntary manslaughter, shall be a misdemeanor.

3. Va.Acts, ch. 240, § 1 (1914):

1. Be it enacted by the General Assembly of Virginia, That section 3663, be amended and reenacted so as to read as follows:

Sec. 3663. Murder of the first degree shall be punished with death, or in the discretion of the jury by confinement in the penitentiary for life.

4. Va.Code Ann. (1975 Repl.Vol. and 1985 Cum.Supp.):

§ 18.2–10. Punishment for conviction of felony.—The authorized punishments for conviction of a felony are:

(a) For Class 1 felonies, death, or imprisonment for life.[a]

---

[a] As originally enacted in 1975, the only authorized punishment for a Class 1 felony under § 18.2–10(a) was death. The current version was enacted in 1977 when

(b) For Class 2 felonies, imprisonment for life or for any term not less than 20 years.

(c) For Class 3 felonies, a term of imprisonment of not less than five years nor more than 20 years.

(d) For Class 4 felonies, a term of imprisonment of not less than two years nor more than 10 years.

(e) For Class 5 felonies, a term of imprisonment of not less than one year nor more than 10 years, or in the discretion of the jury or the court trying the case without a jury, confinement in jail for not more than 12 months and a fine of not more than $1,000, either or both.

(f) For Class 6 felonies, a term of imprisonment of not less than one year nor more than five years, or in the discretion of the jury or the court trying the case without a jury, confinement in jail for not more than 12 months and a fine of not more than $1,000, either or both.

§ 18.2–30. Murder and manslaughter declared felonies.—Any person who commits capital murder, murder of the first degree, murder of the second degree, voluntary manslaughter, or involuntary manslaughter, shall be guilty of a felony.

§ 18.2–31. Capital murder defined; punishment.—The following offenses shall constitute capital murder, punishable as a Class 1 felony: [b]

(a) The willful, deliberate and premeditated killing of any person in the commission of abduction, as defined in § 18.2–48, when such abduction was committed with the intent to extort money, or a pecuniary benefit;

(b) The willful, deliberate and premeditated killing of any person by another for hire;

(c) The willful, deliberate and premeditated killing of any person by an inmate in a penal institution as defined in § 53–11.1, or while in the custody of an employee thereof;

(d) The willful, deliberate and premeditated killing of any person in the commission of robbery while armed with a deadly weapon;

(e) The willful, deliberate and premeditated killing of a person during the commission of, or subsequent to, rape;

(f) The willful, deliberate and premeditated killing of a law-enforcement officer . . . when such killing is for the purpose of interfering with the performance of his official duties; and

(g) The willful, deliberate and premeditated killing of more than one person as part of the same act or transaction.

§ 18.2–32. First- and second-degree murder defined; punishment.—Murder, other than capital murder, by poison, lying in wait, imprisonment, starving, or by any willful, deliberate, and premeditated killing, or in the commission of, or attempt to commit, arson, rape, forcible sodomy, inanimate object sexual penetration, robbery, burglary or abduction, except as provided in § 18.2–31, is murder of the first degree, punishable as a Class 2 felony.

All murder other than capital murder and murder in the first degree is murder of the second degree and is punishable as a Class 3 felony.

---

§§ 19.2–264.2 et seq. and § 17.110.1 were also enacted.

[b] As originally enacted in 1975, the capital murder provision (§ 18.2–31) included only paragraphs (a), (b), and (c). Paragraphs (d) and (e) were added in 1976; paragraph (f) was added in 1977; and paragraph (g) was added in 1981.

§ 18.2–33. Felony homicide defined; punishment.—The killing of one accidentally, contrary to the intention of the parties, while in the prosecution of some felonious act other than those specified in §§ 18.2–31 and 18.2–32, is murder of the second degree and is punishable as a Class 3 felony.

§ 18.2–35. How voluntary manslaughter punished.—Voluntary manslaughter is punishable as a Class 5 felony.

§ 18.2–36. How involuntary manslaughter punished.—Involuntary manslaughter is punishable as a Class 6 felony.

§ 19.2–264.2. Conditions for imposition of death sentence.—In assessing the penalty of any person convicted of an offense for which the death penalty may be imposed, a sentence of death shall not be imposed unless the court or jury shall (1) after consideration of the past criminal record of convictions of the defendant, find that there is a probability that the defendant would commit criminal acts of violence that would constitute a continuing serious threat to society or that his conduct in committing the offense for which he stands charged was outrageously or wantonly vile, horrible or inhuman in that it involved torture, depravity of mind or an aggravated battery to the victim; and (2) recommend that the penalty of death be imposed.

§ 19.2–264.3. Procedure for trial by jury.—

A. In any case in which the offense may be punishable by death which is tried before a jury the court shall first submit to the jury the issue of guilt or innocence of the defendant of the offense charged in the indictment, or any other offense supported by the evidence for which a lesser punishment is provided by law and the penalties therefor.

B. If the jury finds the defendant guilty of an offense for which the death penalty may not be imposed, it shall fix the punishment for such offense as provided by law.

C. If the jury finds the defendant guilty of an offense which may be punishable by death, then a separate proceeding before the same jury shall be held as soon as is practicable on the issue of the penalty, which shall be fixed as is provided in § 19.2–264.4.

§ 19.2–264.4. Sentence proceeding.—

A. Upon a finding that the defendant is guilty of an offense which may be punishable by death, a proceeding shall be held which shall be limited to a determination as to whether the defendant shall be sentenced to death or life imprisonment. In case of trial by jury, where a sentence of death is not recommended, the defendant shall be sentenced to imprisonment for life.

B. In cases of trial by jury, evidence may be presented as to any matter which the court deems relevant to sentence, except that reports under the provisions of § 19.2–299, or under any Rule of Court, shall not be admitted into evidence.

Evidence which may be admissible, subject to the rules of evidence governing admissibility, may include the circumstances surrounding the offense, the history and background of the defendant, and any other facts in mitigation of the offense. Facts in mitigation may include, but shall not be limited to, the following: (i) The defendant has no significant history of prior criminal activity, or (ii) the capital felony was committed while the defendant was under the influence of extreme mental or emotional disturbance or (iii) the victim was a participant in the defendant's conduct or consented to the act, or (iv) at the time of the commission of the capital felony, the capacity of the defendant to appreciate the criminality of his conduct or to conform his conduct to the requirements of law was significantly impaired; or (v) the age of the defendant at the time of the commission of the capital offense.

C. The penalty of death shall not be imposed unless the Commonwealth shall prove beyond a reasonable doubt that there is a probability based upon evidence of the prior history of the defendant or of the circumstances surrounding the commission of the offense of which he is accused that he would commit criminal acts of violence that would constitute a continuing serious threat to society, or that his conduct in committing the offense was outrageously or wantonly vile, horrible or inhuman, in that it involved torture, depravity of mind or aggravated battery to the victim.

D. The verdict of the jury shall be in writing, and in one of the following forms:

(1) "We, the jury, on the issue joined, having found the defendant guilty of (here set out statutory language of the offense charged) and that (after consideration of his prior history that there is a probability that he would commit criminal acts of violence that would constitute a continuing serious threat to society) or his conduct in committing the offense is outrageously or wantonly vile, horrible or inhuman in that it involved (torture) (depravity of mind) (aggravated battery to the victim), and having considered the evidence in mitigation of the offense, unanimously fix his punishment at death.

Signed _____ foreman"

or

(2) "We, the jury, on the issue joined, having found the defendant guilty of (here set out statutory language of the offense charged) and having considered all of the evidence in aggravation and mitigation of such offense, fix his punishment at imprisonment for life.

Signed _____ foreman"

E. In the event the jury cannot agree as to the penalty, the court shall dismiss the jury, and impose a sentence of imprisonment for life. If the sentence of death is subsequently set aside or found invalid, and the defendant or the Commonwealth requests a jury for purposes of resentencing, the court shall impanel a different jury on the issue of penalty.

§ 19.2–264.5. Post sentence reports.—When the punishment of any person has been fixed at death, the court shall, before imposing sentence, direct a probation officer of the court to thoroughly investigate upon the history of the defendant and any and all other relevant facts, to the end that the court may be fully advised as to whether the sentence of death is appropriate and just. Reports shall be made, presented and filed as provided in § 19.2–299. After consideration of the report, and upon good cause shown, the court may set aside the sentence of death, and impose a sentence of imprisonment for life.

§ 17–110.1. Review of death sentence.—

A. A sentence of death, upon the judgment thereon becoming final in the circuit court, shall be reviewed on the record by the Supreme Court.

B. The proceeding in the circuit court shall be transcribed as expeditiously as practicable, and the transcript filed forthwith upon transcription with the clerk of the circuit court, who shall within ten days after receipt of the transcript, compile the record as provided in Rule 5:14 and transmit it to the Supreme Court.

C. In addition to consideration of any errors in the trial enumerated by appeal, the court shall consider and determine:

    1. Whether the sentence of death was imposed under the influence of passion, prejudice or any other arbitrary factor; and

    2. Whether the sentence of death is excessive or disproportionate to the penalty imposed in similar cases, considering both the crime and the defendant.

D. In addition to the review and correction of errors in the trial of the case, with respect to review of the sentence of death, the court may:

    1. Affirm the sentence of death; or

    2. Commute the sentence of death to imprisonment for life.

    3. Remand to the trial court for a new sentence proceeding.

E. The Supreme Court may accumulate the records of all capital felony cases tried within such period of time as the court may determine. The court shall consider such records as are available as a guide in determining whether the sentence imposed in the case under review is excessive. Such records as are accumulated shall be made available to the circuit courts.

F. Sentence review shall be in addition to appeals, if taken, and review and appeal may be consolidated. The defendant and the Commonwealth shall have the right to submit briefs within time limits imposed by the court, either by rule or order, and to present oral argument.

§ 17–110.2. Priority given to such review.—The Supreme Court shall, in setting its docket, give priority to the review of cases in which the sentence of death has been imposed over other cases pending in the Court.

(B) PRE-*FURMAN* GEORGIA HOMICIDE STATUTES.

    1. **Ga.Laws, 1968 Sess., pp. 1276–77, 1335, before the Supreme Court in Furman v. Georgia, 408 U.S. 238 (1972):**

§ 26–1101. Murder.—(a) A person commits murder when he unlawfully and with malice aforethought, either express or implied, causes the death of another human being. Express malice is that deliberate intention unlawfully to take away the life of a fellow creature, which is manifested by external circumstances capable of proof. Malice shall be implied where no considerable provocation appears, and where all the circumstances of the killing show an abandoned and malignant heart.

(b) A person also commits the crime of murder when in the commission of a felony he causes the death of another human being, irrespective of malice.

(c) A person convicted of murder shall be punished by death or by imprisonment for life.

§ 26–1102. Voluntary Manslaughter. A person commits voluntary manslaughter when he causes the death of another human being, under circumstances which would otherwise be murder, if he acts solely as the result of a sudden, violent, and irresistible passion resulting from serious provocation sufficient to excite such passion in a reasonable person; however, if there should have been an interval between the provocation and the killing sufficient for the voice of reason and humanity to be heard, of which the jury in all cases shall be the judge, the killing shall be attributed to deliberate revenge and be punished as murder. A person convicted of voluntary manslaughter shall be punished by imprisonment for not less than one nor more than 20 years.

§ 26–1103. Involuntary Manslaughter. (a) A person commits involuntary manslaughter in the commission of an unlawful act when he causes the death of another human being without any intention to do so, by the commission of an unlawful act other than a felony. A person convicted under this subsection shall be punished by imprisonment for not less than one year nor more than five years.

(b) A person commits involuntary manslaughter in the commission of a lawful act in an unlawful manner when he causes the death of another human being, without any intention to do so, by the commission of a lawful act in an unlawful manner likely to cause death or great bodily harm. A person convicted under this subsection shall be punished as for a misdemeanor.

§ 26–3102. Capital Offenses.—Jury Verdict and Sentence. Where, upon a trial by jury, a person is convicted of an offense which may be punishable by death, a sentence of death shall not be imposed unless the jury verdict includes a recommendation that such sentence be imposed. Where a recommendation of death is made, the court shall sentence the defendant to death. Where a sentence of death is not recommended by the jury, the court shall sentence the defendant to imprisonment as provided by law. Unless the jury trying the case recommends the death sentence in its verdict, the court shall not sentence the defendant to death.

(C) NEW YORK HOMICIDE STATUTES.

1. Bender's N.Y. Penal Law (1942):

§ 1044. Murder in first degree defined.

The killing of a human being, unless it is excusable or justifiable, is murder in the first degree, when committed:

1. From a deliberate and premeditated design to effect the death of the person killed, or of another; or,

2. By an act imminently dangerous to others, and evincing a depraved mind, regardless of human life, although without a premeditated design to effect the death of any individual; or without a design to effect death, by a person engaged in the commission of, or in an attempt to commit a felony, either upon or affecting the person killed or otherwise; or

3. When perpetrated in committing the crime of arson in the first degree.

. . .

§ 1045. Punishment for murder in first degree.

Murder in the first degree is punishable by death, unless the jury recommends life imprisonment as provided by section 1045–a.

§ 1045–a. Life imprisonment for felony murder; jury may recommend.

A jury finding a person guilty of murder in the first degree, as defined by Section 1044(2), may, as a part of its verdict, recommend that the defendant be imprisoned for the term of his natural life. Upon such recommendation, the court may sentence the defendant to imprisonment for the term of his natural life.

§ 1046. Murder in second degree defined.

Such killing of a human being is murder in the second degree, when committed with a design to effect the death of the person killed, or of another, but without deliberation and premeditation.

§ 1048. Punishment for murder in the second degree.

Murder in the second degree is punishable by imprisonment under an indeterminate sentence, the minimum of which shall be not less than 20 years and the maximum of which shall be for the offender's natural life . . . .

§ 1049. Manslaughter defined.

In a case other than one of those specified in Sections 1044 [and] 1046 . . . , homicide, not being justifiable or excusable, is manslaughter.

§ 1050. Manslaughter in first degree.

Such homicide is manslaughter in the first degree, when committed without a design to effect death:

1. By a person engaged in committing, or attempting to commit a misdemeanor, affecting the person or property, either of the person killed, or of another; or,

2. In the heat of passion, but in a cruel and unusual manner, or by means of a dangerous weapon. . . .

§ 1051. Punishment for manslaughter in first degree.

Manslaughter in the first degree is punishable by imprisonment for a term not exceeding 20 years.

§ 1052. Manslaughter in second degree defined.

Such homicide is manslaughter in the second degree, when committed without a design to effect death:

1. By a person committing or attempting to commit a trespass, or other invasion of a private right, either of the person killed, or of another, not amounting to a crime; or,

2. In the heat of passion, but not by a dangerous weapon or by the use of means of either cruel or unusual; or,

3. By any act, procurement or culpable negligence of any person, which, according to the provisions of this article, does not constitute the crime of murder in the first or second degree, nor manslaughter in the first degree. . . .

§ 1053. Punishment for manslaughter in second degree.

Manslaughter in the second degree is punishable by imprisonment for a term not exceeding 15 years, or by a fine of not more than $1,000, or by both.

§ 1053–a. Criminal negligence in operation of a vehicle resulting in death.

A person who operates or drives any vehicle of any kind in a reckless or culpably negligent manner, whereby a human being is killed, is guilty of criminal negligence in the operation of a vehicle resulting in death.

§ 1053–b. Punishment for criminal negligence in operation of vehicle resulting in death.

A person convicted of the crime defined by section 1053–a is punishable by imprisonment for a term of not exceeding five years or by a fine of not more than $1000, or by both.

2. **N.Y. Laws, 1965, ch. 1030, effective Sept. 1, 1967, as subsequently amended:**

§ 125.10. Criminally negligent homicide.

A person is guilty of criminally negligent homicide when, with criminal negligence, he causes the death of another person.

B–7

Criminally negligent homicide is a class E felony [four-year maximum].

§ 125.15. Manslaughter in the second degree.

A person is guilty of manslaughter in the second degree when:

1. He recklessly causes the death of another person . . . .

Manslaughter in the second degree is a class C felony [15-year maximum].

§ 125.20. Manslaughter in the first degree.

A person is guilty of manslaughter in the first degree when:

1. With intent to cause serious physical injury to another person, he causes the death of such person or of a third person; or

2. With intent to cause the death of another person, he causes the death of such person or of a third person under circumstances which do not constitute murder because he acts under the influence of extreme emotional disturbance, as defined in paragraph (a) of subdivision one of section 125.25. The fact that homicide was committed under the influence of extreme emotional disturbance constitutes a mitigating circumstance reducing murder to manslaughter in the first degree and need not be proved in any prosecution initiated under this subdivision . . . .

Manslaughter in the first degree is a class B felony [25-year maximum].

§ 125.25. Murder.

A person is guilty of murder in the second degree when:

1. With intent to cause the death of another person, he causes the death of such person or of a third person; except that in any prosecution under this subdivision, it is an affirmative defense that:

(a) The defendant acted under the influence of extreme emotional disturbance for which there was a reasonable explanation or excuse, the reasonableness of which is to be determined from the viewpoint of a person in the defendant's situation under the circumstances as the defendant believed them to be. Nothing contained in this paragraph shall constitute a defense to a prosecution for, or preclude a conviction of, manslaughter in the first degree or any other crime; or . . .

2. Under circumstances evincing a depraved indifference to human life, he recklessly engages in conduct which creates a grave risk of death to another person, and thereby causes the death of another person; or

3. Acting either alone or with one or more other persons, he commits or attempts to commit robbery, burglary, kidnapping, arson, rape in the first degree, sodomy in the first degree, sexual abuse in the first degree, aggravated sexual abuse, escape in the first degree, or escape in the second degree, and, in the course of and in furtherance of such crime or of immediate flight therefrom, he, or another participant, if there be any, causes the death of a person other than one of the participants, except that in any prosecution under this subdivision, in which the defendant was not the only participant in the underlying crime, it is an affirmative defense that the defendant:

(a) Did not commit the homicidal act or in any way solicit, request, command, importune, cause or aid the commission thereof; and

(b) Was not armed with a deadly weapon, or any instrument, article or substance readily capable of causing death or serious physical injury and of a sort not ordinarily carried in public places by law-abiding persons; and

(c) Had no reasonable ground to believe that any other participant was armed with such a weapon, instrument, article or substance; and

(d) Had no reasonable ground to believe that any other participant intended to engage in conduct likely to result in death or serious physical injury.[c]

(D) OREGON HOMICIDE AND ASSAULT OFFENSES AND PROVISIONS ON ATTEMPT.

1. Ore.Rev.Stat. 1972, as amended:

HOMICIDE

§ 163.005. Criminal homicide. (1) A person commits criminal homicide if, without justification or excuse, he intentionally, knowingly, recklessly or with criminal negligence causes the death of another human being.

(2) "Criminal homicide" is murder, manslaughter or criminally negligent homicide.

(3) "Human being" means a person who has been born and was alive at the time of the criminal act.

§ 163.115. Murder; affirmative defense to certain felony murders; sentence required. (1) Except as provided in ORS 163.118 and 163.125, criminal homicide constitutes murder when:

(a) It is committed intentionally, except that it is an affirmative defense that, at the time of the homicide, the defendant was under the influence of an extreme emotional disturbance; or

(b) It is committed by a person, acting either alone or with one or more persons, who commits or attempts to commit any of the following crimes and in the course of and in furtherance of the crime the person is committing or attempting to commit, or during the immediate flight therefrom, the person, or another participant if there be any, causes the death of a person other than one of the participants:

(A) Arson in the first degree as defined in ORS 164.325;

(B) Criminal mischief in the first degree by means of an explosive as defined in ORS 164.365;

(C) Burglary in the first degree as defined in ORS 164.225;

(D) Escape in the first degree as defined in ORS 162.165;

(E) Kidnapping in the second degree as defined in ORS 163.225;

(F) Kidnapping in the first degree as defined in ORS 163.235;

(G) Robbery in the first degree as defined in ORS 164.415;

(H) Any felony sexual offense in the first degree defined in this chapter; or

(I) Compelling prostitution as defined in ORS 167.017.

[c] Murder in the second degree is a class A–1 felony, punishable by a maximum sentence of life imprisonment.

In 1974, the New York legislature enacted § 125.27, defining as first-degree murder the intentional killing of a police officer or a correctional officer and the intentional killing of anyone by a prisoner serving a life sentence. The penalty was a mandatory death sentence. These provisions were declared unconstitutional by the New York Court of Appeals in People v. Davis, 43 N.Y.2d 17, 400 N.Y.S.2d 735, 371 N.E.2d 456 (1977) and People v. Smith, 63 N.Y.2d 41, 479 N.Y.S.2d 706, 468 N.E.2d 879 (1984).

(2) It is an affirmative defense to a charge of violating paragraph (b) of subsection (1) of this section that the defendant:

(a) Was not the only participant in the underlying crime; and

(b) Did not commit the homicidal act or in any way solicit, request, command, importune, cause or aid in the commission thereof; and

(c) Was not armed with a dangerous or deadly weapon; and

(d) Had no reasonable ground to believe that any other participant was armed with a dangerous or deadly weapon; and

(e) Had no reasonable ground to believe that any other participant intended to engage in conduct likely to result in death.

(3) A person convicted of murder shall be punished by imprisonment for life.

§ 163.118. Manslaughter in the first degree. (1) Criminal homicide constitutes manslaughter in the first degree when:

(a) It is committed recklessly under circumstances manifesting extreme indifference to the value of human life; or

(b) It is committed intentionally by a defendant under the influence of extreme emotional disturbance as provided in ORS 163.135. The fact that the homicide was committed under the influence of extreme emotional disturbance constitutes a mitigating circumstance reducing the homicide which would otherwise be murder to manslaughter in the first degree and need not be proved in any prosecution.

(2) Manslaughter in the first degree is a Class A felony.

§ 163.125. [This section punishes reckless homicide as manslaughter in the second degree, a Class B felony.]

§ 163.135. Extreme emotional disturbance as affirmative defense to murder . . .. (1) It is an affirmative defense to murder for purposes of ORS 163.115(1)(a) that the homicide was committed under the influence of extreme emotional disturbance when such disturbance is not the result of the person's own intentional, knowing, reckless or criminally negligent act, and for which disturbance there is a reasonable explanation. The reasonableness of the explanation for the disturbance shall be determined from the standpoint of an ordinary person in the actor's situation under the circumstances as the actor reasonably believes them to be. . . .

§ 163.145. [This section punishes criminally negligent homicide as a Class C felony.]

ASSAULT AND RELATED OFFENSES

§ 163.160. Assault in the fourth degree. (1) A person commits the crime of assault in the fourth degree if he:

(a) Intentionally, knowingly or recklessly causes physical injury to another; or

(b) With criminal negligence causes physical injury to another by means of a deadly weapon.

(2) Assault in the fourth degree is a Class A misdemeanor.

§ 163.165. Assault in the third degree. (1) A person commits the crime of assault in the third degree if he:

(a) Recklessly causes serious physical injury to another by means of a deadly or dangerous weapon;

(b) Recklessly causes serious physical injury to another under circumstances manifesting extreme indifference to the value of human life; or

(c) Recklessly causes physical injury to another by means of a deadly or dangerous weapon under circumstances manifesting extreme indifference to the value of human life.

(2) Assault in the third degree is a Class C felony.

§ 163.175. Assault in the second degree. (1) A person commits the crime of assault in the second degree if he:

(a) Intentionally or knowingly causes serious physical injury to another; or

(b) Intentionally or knowingly causes physical injury to another by means of a deadly or dangerous weapon; or

(c) Recklessly causes serious physical injury to another by means of a deadly or dangerous weapon under circumstances manifesting extreme indifference to the value of human life.

(2) Assault in the second degree is a Class B felony.

§ 163.185. Assault in the first degree. (1) A person commits the crime of assault in the first degree if he intentionally causes serious physical injury to another by means of a deadly or dangerous weapon.

(2) Assault in the first degree is a Class A felony.

§ 163.190. Menacing. (1) A person commits the crime of menacing if by word or conduct he intentionally attempts to place another person in fear of imminent serious physical injury.

(2) Menacing is a Class A misdemeanor.

§ 163.195. Recklessly endangering another person. (1) A person commits the crime of recklessly endangering another person if he recklessly engages in conduct which creates a substantial risk of serious physical injury to another person.

(2) Recklessly endangering another person is a Class A misdemeanor.

INCHOATE CRIMES

§ 161.405. "Attempt" described. (1) A person is guilty of an attempt to commit a crime when he intentionally engages in conduct which constitutes a substantial step toward commission of the crime.

(2) An attempt is a:

(a) Class A felony if the offense attempted is murder or treason.

(b) Class B felony if the offense attempted is a Class A felony.

(c) Class C felony if the offense attempted is a Class B felony.

(d) Class A misdemeanor if the offense attempted is a Class C felony or an unclassified felony.

(e) Class B misdemeanor if the offense attempted is a Class A misdemeanor.

(f) Class C misdemeanor if the offense attempted is a Class B misdemeanor.

(g) Violation if the offense attempted is a Class C misdemeanor or an unclassified misdemeanor.

§ 161.425.   Impossibility not a defense.   In a prosecution for an attempt, it is no defense that it was impossible to commit the crime which was the object of the attempt where the conduct engaged in by the actor would be a crime if the circumstances were as the actor believed them to be.

§ 161.430.   Renunciation as a defense to attempt.   (1) A person is not liable under ORS 161.405 if, under circumstances manifesting a voluntary and complete renunciation of his criminal intent, he avoids the commission of the crime attempted by abandoning his criminal effort and, if mere abandonment is insufficient to accomplish this avoidance, doing everything necessary to prevent the commission of the attempted crime.

(2) The defense of renunciation is an affirmative defense.

DISPOSITION OF OFFENDERS

§ 161.605.   Maximum prison terms for felonies.   The maximum term of an indeterminate sentence of imprisonment for a felony is as follows:

(1) For a Class A felony, 20 years.

(2) For a Class B felony, 10 years.

(3) For a Class C felony, 5 years.

(4) For an unclassified felony as provided in the statute defining the crime.

§ 161.615.   Prison terms for misdemeanors.   Sentences for misdemeanors shall be for a definite term.   The court shall fix the term of imprisonment within the following maximum limitations:

(1) For a Class A misdemeanor, 1 year.

(2) For a Class B misdemeanor, 6 months.

(3) For a Class C misdemeanor, 30 days.

(4) For an unclassified misdemeanor, as provided in the statute defining the crime.

(E) CAPITAL PUNISHMENT STATUTES BEFORE THE SUPREME COURT IN 1976 DECISIONS.

1.   **Ga.Laws, 1973 Sess., pp. 164–67, 170, before the Supreme Court in Gregg v. Georgia, 428 U.S. 153 (1976):**

§ 26–3102.   Capital offenses; jury verdict and sentence.   Where, upon a trial by jury, a person is convicted of an offense which may be punishable by death, a sentence of death shall not be imposed unless the jury verdict includes a finding of at least one statutory aggravating circumstance and a recommendation that such sentence be imposed.   Where a statutory aggravating circumstance is found and a recommendation of death is made, the court shall sentence the defendant to death.   Where a sentence of death is not recommended by the jury, the court shall sentence the defendant to imprisonment as provided by law.   Unless the jury trying the case makes a finding of at least one statutory aggravating circumstance and recommends the death sentence in its verdict, the court shall not sentence the defendant to death, provided that no such finding of statutory aggravating circumstance shall be necessary in offenses of treason or aircraft hijacking.   The provisions of this section shall not affect a sentence when the case is tried without a jury or when the judge accepts a plea of guilty.

§ 27–2534.1. Mitigating and aggravating circumstances; death penalty.—(a) The death penalty may be imposed for the offenses of aircraft hijacking or treason, in any case.

(b) In all cases of other offenses for which the death penalty may be authorized, the judge shall consider, or he shall include in his instructions to the jury for it to consider, any mitigating circumstances or aggravating circumstances otherwise authorized by law and any of the following statutory aggravating circumstances which may be supported by the evidence:

(1) The offense of murder, rape, armed robbery, or kidnapping was committed by a person with a prior record of conviction for a capital felony, or the offense of murder was committed by a person who has a substantial history of serious assaultive criminal convictions.

(2) The offense of murder, rape, armed robbery, or kidnapping was committed while the offender was engaged in the commission of another capital felony, or aggravated battery, or the offense of murder was committed while the offender was engaged in the commission of burglary or arson in the first degree.

(3) The offender by his act of murder, armed robbery, or kidnapping knowingly created a great risk of death to more than one person in a public place by means of a weapon or device which would normally be hazardous to the lives of more than one person.

(4) The offender committed the offense of murder for himself or another, for the purpose of receiving money or any other thing of monetary value.

(5) The murder of a judicial officer, former judicial officer, district attorney or solicitor or former district attorney or solicitor during or because of the exercise of his official duty.

(6) The offender caused or directed another to commit murder or committed murder as an agent or employee of another person.

(7) The offense of murder, rape, armed robbery, or kidnapping was outrageously or wantonly vile, horrible or inhuman in that it involved torture, depravity of mind, or an aggravated battery to the victim.

(8) The offense of murder was committed against any peace officer, corrections employee or fireman while engaged in the performance of his official duties.

(9) The offense of murder was committed by a person in, or who has escaped from, the lawful custody of a peace officer or place of lawful confinement.

(10) The murder was committed for the purpose of avoiding, interfering with, or preventing a lawful arrest or custody in a place of lawful confinement, of himself or another.

(c) The statutory instructions as determined by the trial judge to be warranted by the evidence shall be given in charge and in writing to the jury for its deliberation. The jury, if its verdict be a recommendation of death, shall designate in writing, signed by the foreman of the jury, the aggravating circumstance or circumstances which it found beyond a reasonable doubt. In non-jury cases the judge shall make such designation. Except in cases of treason or aircraft hijacking, unless at least one of the statutory aggravating circumstances enumerated in Code Section 27–2534.1(b) is so found, the death penalty shall not be imposed.

§ 27–2537. Review of death sentences.—(a) Whenever the death penalty is imposed, and upon the judgment becoming final in the trial court, the sentence shall be reviewed on the record by the Supreme Court of Georgia. The clerk of the trial court, within ten days after receiving the transcript, shall transmit the entire record and transcript to the Supreme Court of Georgia together with a notice prepared by the clerk and a report prepared by the trial judge. The notice shall set forth the title and docket number of the case, the name of the defendant and the name and address of his attorney, a narrative statement of the judgment, the offense, and the punishment prescribed. The report shall be in the form of a standard questionnaire prepared and supplied by the Supreme Court of Georgia.

(b) The Supreme Court of Georgia shall consider the punishment as well as any errors enumerated by way of appeal.

(c) With regard to the sentence, the court shall determine:

(1) Whether the sentence of death was imposed under the influence of passion, prejudice, or any other arbitrary factor, and

(2) Whether, in cases other than treason or aircraft hijacking, the evidence supports the jury's or judge's finding of a statutory aggravating circumstance as enumerated in Code Section 27–2534.1(b), and

(3) Whether the sentence of death is excessive or disproportionate to the penalty imposed in similar cases, considering both the crime and the defendant.

(d) Both the defendant and the State shall have the right to submit briefs within the time provided by the court, and to present oral argument to the court.

(e) The court shall include in its decision a reference to those similar cases which it took into consideration. In addition to its authority regarding correction of errors, the court, with regard to review of death sentences, shall be authorized to:

(1) Affirm the sentence of death; or

(2) Set the sentence aside and remand the case for resentencing by the trial judge based on the record and argument of counsel. The records of those similar cases referred to by the Supreme Court of Georgia in its decision, and the extracts prepared as hereinafter provided for, shall be provided to the resentencing judge for his consideration.

(f) There shall be an Assistant to the Supreme Court, who shall be an attorney appointed by the Chief Justice of Georgia and who shall serve at the pleasure of the court. The court shall accumulate the records of all capital felony cases in which sentence was imposed after January 1, 1970, or such earlier date as the court may deem appropriate. The Assistant shall provide the court with whatever extracted information it desires with respect thereto, including but not limited to a synopsis or brief of the facts in the record concerning the crime and the defendant.

(g) The court shall be authorized to employ an appropriate staff and such methods to compile such data as are deemed by the Chief Justice to be appropriate and relevant to the statutory questions concerning the validity of the sentence.

(h) The office of the Assistant shall be attached to the office of the Clerk of the Supreme Court of Georgia for administrative purposes.

(i) The sentence review shall be in addition to direct appeal, if taken, and the review and appeal shall be consolidated for consideration. The court shall render its decision on legal errors enumerated, the factual substantiation of the verdict, and the validity of the sentence.

2. **Fla.Laws, 1975, ch. 75–298, § 6; Fla.Laws, 1972, ch. 72–724, §§ 2, 9, before the Supreme Court in Proffitt v. Florida, 428 U.S. 242 (1976):**

§ 782.04. Murder—

(1)(a) The unlawful killing of a human being, when perpetrated from a premeditated design to effect the death of the person killed or any human being, or when committed by a person engaged in the perpetration of, or in the attempt to perpetrate, any arson, involuntary sexual battery, robbery, burglary, kidnapping, aircraft piracy, or unlawful throwing, placing, or discharging of a destructive device or bomb, or which resulted from the unlawful distribution of heroin by a person 18 years of age or older when such drug is proven to be the proximate cause of the death of the user, shall be murder in the first degree and shall constitute a capital felony, punishable as provided in § 775.082.

(b) In all cases under this section, the procedure set forth in § 921.141 shall be followed in order to determine sentence of death or life imprisonment.

§ 775.082. Penalties for felonies and misdemeanors.—

(1) A person who has been convicted of a capital felony shall be punished by life imprisonment and shall be required to serve no less than 25 calendar years before becoming eligible for parole unless the proceeding held to determine sentence according to the procedure set forth in § 921.141 results in findings by the court that such person shall be punished by death, and in the latter event such person shall be punished by death.

§ 921.141. Sentence of death or life imprisonment for capital felonies; further proceedings to determine sentence.—

(1) Upon conviction or adjudication of guilt of a defendant of a capital felony the court shall conduct a separate sentencing proceeding to determine whether the defendant should be sentenced to death or life imprisonment as authorized by Section 775.082. The proceeding shall be conducted by the trial judge before the trial jury as soon as practicable. If the trial jury has been waived or if the defendant pleaded guilty, the sentencing proceeding shall be conducted before a jury empaneled for that purpose unless waived by the defendant. In the proceeding, evidence may be presented as to any matter that the court deems relevant to sentence, and shall include matters relating to any of the aggravating or mitigating circumstances enumerated in Subsections (6) and (7) of this section. Any such evidence which the court deems to have probative value may be received, regardless of its admissibility under the exclusionary rules of evidence, provided that the defendant is accorded a fair opportunity to rebut any hearsay statements; and further provided that this subsection shall not be construed to authorize the introduction of any evidence secured in violation of the Constitution of the United States or of the State of Florida. The state and the defendant or his counsel shall be permitted to present argument for or against sentence of death.

(2) After hearing all the evidence, the jury shall deliberate and render an advisory sentence to the court based upon the following matters:

(a) Whether sufficient aggravating circumstances exist as enumerated in Subsection (6), and

(b) Whether sufficient mitigating circumstances exist as enumerated in Subsection (7), which outweigh aggravating circumstances found to exist, and

(c) Based on these considerations whether the defendant should be sentenced to life or death.

(3) Notwithstanding the recommendation of a majority of the jury, the court after weighing the aggravating and mitigating circumstances shall enter a sentence of life imprisonment or death, but if the court imposes a sentence of death, it shall set forth in writing its findings upon which the sentence of death is based as to the facts:

(a) That sufficient aggravating circumstances exist as enumerated in Subsection (6), and

(b) That there are insufficient mitigating circumstances, as enumerated in Subsection (7), to outweigh the aggravating circumstances.

In each case in which the court imposes the death sentence, the determination of the court shall be supported by specific written findings of fact based upon the circumstances in Subsections (6) and (7) and based upon the records of the trial and the sentencing proceedings.

(4) If the court does not make the findings requiring the death sentence, the court shall impose sentence of life imprisonment in accordance with Section 775.082.

(5) The judgment of conviction and sentence of death shall be subject to automatic review by the Supreme Court of Florida within 60 days after certification by the sentencing court of the entire record unless time is extended an additional period not to exceed 30 days by the Supreme Court for good cause shown. Such review by the Supreme Court shall have priority over all other cases, and shall be heard in accordance with rules promulgated by the Supreme Court.

(6) Aggravating circumstances.—Aggravating circumstances shall be limited to the following:

(a) The capital felony was committed by a person under sentence of imprisonment;

(b) The defendant was previously convicted of another capital felony or of a felony involving the use or threat of violence to the person;

(c) The defendant knowingly created a great risk of death to many persons;

(d) The capital felony was committed while the defendant was engaged or was an accomplice in the commission of, or an attempt to commit, or flight after committing or attempting to commit any robbery, rape, arson, burglary, kidnaping, aircraft piracy, or the unlawful throwing, placing or discharging of a destructive device or bomb;

(e) The capital felony was committed for the purpose of avoiding or preventing a lawful arrest or effecting an escape from custody;

(f) The capital felony was committed for pecuniary gain;

(g) The capital felony was committed to disrupt or hinder the lawful exercise of any governmental function or the enforcement of laws.

(h) The capital felony was especially heinous, atrocious or cruel.

(7) Mitigating circumstances.—Mitigating circumstances shall be the following:

(a) The defendant has no significant history of prior criminal activity;

(b) The capital felony was committed while the defendant was under the influence of extreme mental or emotional disturbance;

(c) The victim was a participant in the defendant's conduct or consented to the act;

(d) The defendant was an accomplice in the capital felony committed by another person and his participation was relatively minor;

(e) The defendant acted under extreme duress or under the substantial domination of another person;

(f) The capacity of the defendant to appreciate the criminality of his conduct or to conform his conduct to the requirements of law was substantially impaired;

(g) The age of the defendant at the time of the crime.

3. Tex.Gen.Laws, 63rd Leg., ch. 426, art. 1, § 1, p. 1122, art. 3, § 1, pp. 1125–26, before the Supreme Court in Jurek v. Texas, 428 U.S. 262 (1976):

Art. 1257. Punishment for murder

(a) Except as provided in Subsection (b) of this Article, the punishment for murder shall be confinement in the penitentiary for life or for any term of years not less than two.

(b) The punishment for murder with malice aforethought shall be death or imprisonment for life if:

(1) the person murdered a peace officer or fireman who was acting in the lawful discharge of an official duty and who the defendant knew was a peace officer or fireman;

(2) the person intentionally committed the murder in the course of committing or attempting to commit kidnapping, burglary, robbery, forcible rape, or arson;

(3) the person committed the murder for remuneration or the promise of remuneration or employed another to commit the murder for remuneration or the promise of remuneration;

(4) the person committed the murder while escaping or attempting to escape from a penal institution;

(5) the person, while incarcerated in a penal institution, murdered another who was employed in the operation of the penal institution.

(c) If the jury does not find beyond a reasonable doubt that the murder was committed under one of the circumstances or conditions enumerated in Subsection (b) of this Article, the defendant may be convicted of murder, with or without malice, under Subsection (a) of this Article or of any other lesser included offense. . . .

Art. 37.071. Procedure in capital case.

(a) Upon a finding that the defendant is guilty of a capital offense, the court shall conduct a separate sentencing proceeding to determine whether the defendant shall be sentenced to death or life imprisonment. The proceeding shall be conducted in the trial court before the trial jury as soon as practicable. In the proceeding, evidence may be presented as to any matter that the court deems relevant to sentence. This subsection shall not be construed to authorize the introduction of any evidence secured in violation of the Constitution of the United States or of the State of Texas. The state and the defendant or his counsel shall be permitted to present argument for or against sentence of death.

(b) On conclusion of the presentation of the evidence, the court shall submit the following issues to the jury:

(1) whether the conduct of the defendant that caused the death of the deceased was committed deliberately and with the reasonable expectation that the death of the deceased or another would result;

(2) whether there is a probability that the defendant would commit criminal acts of violence that would constitute a continuing threat to society; and

(3) if raised by the evidence, whether the conduct of the defendant in killing the deceased was unreasonable in response to the provocation, if any, by the deceased.

(c) The state must prove each issue submitted beyond a reasonable doubt, and the jury shall return a special verdict of "yes" or "no" on each issue submitted.

(d) The court shall charge the jury that:

(1) it may not answer any issue "yes" unless it agrees unanimously; and

(2) it may not answer any issue "no" unless 10 or more jurors agree.

(e) If the jury returns an affirmative finding on each issue submitted under this article, the court shall sentence the defendant to death. If the jury returns a negative finding on any issue submitted under this article, the court shall sentence the defendant to confinement in the Texas Department of Corrections for life.

(f) The judgment of conviction and sentence of death shall be subject to automatic review by the Court of Criminal Appeals within 60 days after certification by the sentencing court of the entire record unless time is extended an additional period not to exceed 30 days by the Court of Criminal Appeals for good cause shown. Such review by the Court of Criminal Appeals shall have priority over all other cases, and shall be heard in accordance with rules promulgated by the Court of Criminal Appeals.

4. **N.C.Sess.Laws, 1973, ch. 1201, § 1, p. 323, before the Supreme Court in Woodson v. North Carolina, 428 U.S. 280 (1976):**

§ 14–17. Murder in the first and second degree defined; punishment.—A murder which shall be perpetrated by means of poison, lying in wait, imprisonment, starving, torture, or by any other kind of willful, deliberate and premeditated killing, or which shall be committed in the perpetration or attempt to perpetrate any arson, rape, robbery, kidnapping, burglary or other felony, shall be deemed to be murder in the first degree and shall be punished with death. All other kinds of murder shall be deemed murder in the second degree, and shall be punished by imprisonment for a term of not less than two years nor more than life imprisonment in the State's prison.

5. **La.Acts, 1973, No. 109, § 1, p. 218, before the Supreme Court in Roberts v. Louisiana, 428 U.S. 325 (1976):**

§ 30. First-degree murder.

First-degree murder is the killing of a human being:

(1) When the offender has a specific intent to kill or to inflict great bodily harm and is engaged in the perpetration or attempted perpetration of aggravated kidnapping, aggravated rape or armed robbery; or

(2) When the offender has a specific intent to kill, or to inflict great bodily harm upon, a fireman or a peace officer who was engaged in the performance of his lawful duties; or

(3) Where the offender has a specific intent to kill or to inflict great bodily harm and has previously been convicted of an unrelated murder or is serving a life sentence; or

(4) When the offender has a specific intent to kill or to inflict great bodily harm upon more than one person.

(5) When the offender has specific intent to commit murder and has been offered or has received anything of value for committing the murder.

For the purposes of Paragraph (2) herein, the term peace officer shall be defined and include any constable, sheriff, deputy sheriff, local or state policeman, game warden, federal law enforcement officer, jail or prison guard, parole officer, probation officer, judge, district attorney, assistant district attorney or district attorneys' investigator.

Whoever commits the crime of first-degree murder shall be punished by death.

(F) ADDITIONAL CONTEMPORARY CAPITAL SENTENCING STATUTES:

1. Alabama Code, Title 13A:

§ 13A–6–1. Definitions.

The following terms shall have the meanings ascribed to them by this section:

(1) <u>Homicide.</u> A person commits criminal homicide if he intentionally, knowingly, recklessly or with criminal negligence causes the death of another person.

(2) <u>Person.</u> Such term, when referring to the victim of a criminal homicide, means a human being who had been born and was alive at the time of the homicidal act.

(3) <u>Criminal Homicide.</u> Murder, manslaughter, or criminally negligent homicide.

§ 13A–6–2. Murder.

(a) A person commits the crime of murder if:

(1) With intent to cause the death of another person, he causes the death of that person or of another person; or

(2) Under circumstances manifesting extreme indifference to human life, he recklessly engages in conduct which creates a grave risk of death to a person other than himself, and thereby causes the death of another person; or

(3) He commits or attempts to commit arson in the first degree, burglary in the first or second degree, escape in the first degree, kidnapping in the first degree, rape in the first degree, robbery in any degree, sodomy in the first degree or any other felony clearly dangerous to human life and, in the course of and in furtherance of the crime that he is committing or attempt-

ing to commit, or in immediate flight therefrom, he, or another participant if there be any, causes the death of any person.

(b) A person does not commit murder under subdivisions (a)(1) or (a)(2) of this section if he was moved to act by a sudden heat of passion caused by provocation recognized by law, and before there had been a reasonable time for the passion to cool and for reason to reassert itself. The burden of injecting the issue of killing under legal provocation is on the defendant, but this does not shift the burden of proof. This subsection does not apply to a prosecution for, or preclude a conviction of, manslaughter or other crime.

(c) Murder is a Class A felony; provided, that the punishment for murder or any offense committed under aggravated circumstances, as provided by article 2 of chapter 5 of this title, is death or life imprisonment without parole, which punishment shall be determined and fixed as provided by article 2 of chapter 5 of this title or any amendments thereto.

§ 13A–5–40. Capital offenses.

(a) The following are capital offenses:

(1) Murder by the defendant during a kidnapping in the first degree or an attempt thereof committed by the defendant;

(2) Murder by the defendant during a robbery in the first degree or an attempt thereof committed by the defendant;

(3) Murder by the defendant during a rape in the first or second degree or an attempt thereof committed by the defendant; or murder by the defendant during sodomy in the first or second degree or an attempt thereof committed by the defendant;

(4) Murder by the defendant during a burglary in the first or second degree or an attempt thereof committed by the defendant;

(5) Murder of any police officer, sheriff, deputy, state trooper, federal law enforcement officer, or any other state or federal peace officer of any kind, or prison or jail guard, while such officer or guard is on duty or because of some official or job-related act or performance of such officer or guard;

(6) Murder committed while the defendant is under sentence of life imprisonment;

(7) Murder done for a pecuniary or other valuable consideration or pursuant to a contract or for hire;

(8) Murder by the defendant during sexual abuse in the first or second degree or an attempt thereof committed by the defendant;

(9) Murder by the defendant during arson in the first or second degree committed by the defendant; or murder by the defendant by means of explosives or explosion;

(10) Murder wherein two or more persons are murdered by the defendant by one act or pursuant to one scheme or course of conduct;

(11) Murder by the defendant when the victim is a state or federal public official or former public official and the murder stems from or is caused by or is related to his official position, act, or capacity;

(12) Murder by the defendant during the act of unlawfully assuming control of any aircraft by use of threats or force with intent to obtain any valuable consideration for the release of said aircraft or any passenger or crewmen thereon or to direct the route or movement of said aircraft, or otherwise exert control over said aircraft;

(13) Murder by a defendant who has been convicted of any other murder in the 20 years preceding the crime; provided that the murder which constitutes the capital crime shall be murder as defined in subsection (b) of this section; and provided further that the prior murder conviction referred to shall include murder in any degree as defined at the time and place of the prior conviction; and

(14) Murder when the victim is subpoenaed, or has been subpoenaed, to testify, or the victim had testified, in any preliminary hearing, grand jury proceeding, criminal trial or criminal proceeding of whatever nature, or civil trial or civil proceeding of whatever nature, in any municipal, state, or federal court, when the murder stems from, is caused by, or is related to the capacity or role of the victim as a witness.

(b) Except as specifically provided to the contrary in the last part of subdivision (a)(13) of this section, the terms "murder" and "murder by the defendant" as used in this section to define capital offenses mean murder as defined in section 13A–6–2(a)(1), but not as defined in section 13A–6–2(a)(2) and (3). Subject to the provisions of section 13A–5–41, murder as defined in section 13A–6–2(a)(2) and (3), as well as murder as defined in section 13A–6–2(a)(1), may be a lesser included offense of the capital offenses defined in subsection (a) of this section.

(c) A defendant who does not personally commit the act of killing which constitutes the murder is not guilty of a capital offense defined in subsection (a) of this section unless that defendant is legally accountable for the murder because of complicity in the murder itself under the provisions of section 13A–2–23, in addition to being guilty of the other elements of the capital offense as defined in subsection (a) of this section.

(d) To the extent that a crime other than murder is an element of a capital offense defined in subsection (a) of this section, a defendant's guilt of that other crime may also be established under section 13A–2–23. When the defendant's guilt of that other crime is established under section 13A–2–23, that crime shall be deemed to have been "committed by the defendant" within the meaning of that phrase as it is used in subsection (a) of this section.

§ 13A–5–47. Determination of sentence by court; pre-sentence investigation report; presentation of arguments on aggravating and mitigating circumstances; court to enter written findings; court not bound by sentence recommended by jury.

(a) After the sentence hearing has been conducted, and after the jury has returned an advisory verdict, or after such a verdict has been waived as provided in section 13A–5–46(a) or section 13A–5–46(g), the trial court shall proceed to determine the sentence.

(b) Before making the sentence determination, the trial court shall order and receive a written pre-sentence investigation report. The report shall contain the information prescribed by law or court rule for felony cases generally and any additional information specified by the trial court. No part of the report shall be kept confidential, and the parties shall have the right to respond to it and to present evidence to the court about any part of the report which is the subject of factual dispute. The report and any evidence submitted in connection with it shall be made part of the record in the case.

(c) Before imposing sentence the trial court shall permit the parties to present arguments concerning the existence of aggravating and mitigating circumstances and the proper sentence to be imposed in the case. The order of the arguments shall be the same as at the trial of a case.

(d) Based upon the evidence presented at trial, the evidence presented during the sentence hearing, and the pre-sentence investigation report and any evidence submitted in connection with it, the trial court shall enter specific written findings concerning the existence or nonexistence of each aggravating circumstance enumerated in section 13A–5–49, each mitigating circumstance enumerated in section 13A–5–51, and any additional mitigating circumstances offered pursuant to section 13A–5–52. The trial court shall also enter written findings of facts summarizing the crime and the defendant's participation in it.

(e) In deciding upon the sentence, the trial court shall determine whether the aggravating circumstances it finds to exist outweigh the mitigating circumstances it finds to exist, and in doing so the trial court shall consider the recommendation of the jury contained in its advisory verdict, unless such a verdict has been waived pursuant to section 13A–5–46(a) or 13A–5–46(g). While the jury's recommendation concerning sentence shall be given consideration, it is not binding upon the court.

§ 13A–5–48. Process of weighing aggravating and mitigating circumstances defined.

The process described in sections 13A–5–46(e)(2), 13A–5–46(e)(3) and section 13A–5–47(e) of weighing the aggravating and mitigating circumstances to determine the sentence shall not be defined to mean a mere tallying of aggravating and mitigating circumstances for the purpose of numerical comparison. Instead, it shall be defined to mean a process by which circumstances relevant to sentence are marshalled and considered in an organized fashion for the purpose of determining whether the proper sentence in view of all the relevant circumstances in an individual case is life imprisonment without parole or death.

§ 13A–5–49. Aggravating circumstances.

Aggravating circumstances shall be the following:

(1) The capital offense was committed by a person under sentence of imprisonment;

(2) The defendant was previously convicted of another capital offense or a felony involving the use or threat of violence to the person;

(3) The defendant knowingly created a great risk of death to many persons;

(4) The capital offense was committed while the defendant was engaged or was an accomplice in the commission of, or an attempt to commit, or flight after committing, or attempting to commit, rape, robbery, burglary or kidnapping;

(5) The capital offense was committed for the purpose of avoiding or preventing a lawful arrest or effecting an escape from custody;

(6) The capital offense was committed for pecuniary gain;

(7) The capital offense was committed to disrupt or hinder the lawful exercise of any governmental function or the enforcement of laws; or

(8) The capital offense was especially heinous, atrocious or cruel compared to other capital offenses.

§ 13A–5–50. Consideration of aggravating circumstances in sentence determination.

The fact that a particular capital offense as defined in section 13A–5–40(a) necessarily includes one or more aggravating circumstances as specified in section 13A–5–49 shall not be construed to preclude the finding and consideration of that relevant circumstance or circumstances in determining sentence. By way of illustration and not limitation, the aggravating circumstance specified in section 13A–5–49(4) shall be found and considered in determining sentence in every case in which a defendant is convicted of the capital offenses defined in subdivisions (1) through (4) of subsection (a) of section 13A–5–40.

§ 13A–5–51. Mitigating circumstances—Generally.

Mitigating circumstances shall include, but not be limited to, the following:

(1) The defendant has no significant history of prior criminal activity;

(2) The capital offense was committed while the defendant was under the influence of extreme mental or emotional disturbance;

(3) The victim was a participant in the defendant's conduct or consented to it;

(4) The defendant was an accomplice in the capital offense committed by another person and his participation was relatively minor;

(5) The defendant acted under extreme duress or under the substantial domination of another person;

(6) The capacity of the defendant to appreciate the criminality of his conduct or to conform his conduct to the requirements of law was substantially impaired; and

(7) The age of the defendant at the time of the crime.

§ 13A–5–52. Same—Inclusion of defendant's character, record, etc.

In addition to the mitigating circumstances specified in section 13A–5–51, mitigating circumstances shall include any aspect of a defendant's character or record and any of the circumstances of the offense that the defendant offers as a basis for a sentence of life imprisonment without parole instead of death, and any other relevant mitigating circumstance which the defendant offers as a basis for a sentence of life imprisonment without parole instead of death.

§ 13A–5–53. Appellate review of death sentence; scope; remand; specific determinations to be made by court; authority of court following review.

(a) In any case in which the death penalty is imposed, in addition to reviewing the case for any error involving the conviction, the Alabama court of criminal appeals, subject to review by the Alabama supreme court, shall also review the propriety of the death sentence. This review shall include the determination of whether any error adversely affecting the rights of the defendant was made in the sentence proceedings, whether the trial court's findings concerning the aggravating and mitigating circumstances were supported by the evidence, and whether death was the proper sentence in the case. If the court determines that an error adversely affecting the rights of the defendant was made in the sentence proceedings or that one or more of the trial court's findings concerning aggravating and mitigating circumstances were not supported by the evidence, it shall remand the case for new proceedings to the extent necessary to correct the error or errors. If the appellate court finds that no error adversely affecting the rights of the defendant was made in the sentence proceedings and that the trial court's findings concerning aggravating and mitigating circumstances were supported by the evidence, it shall proceed to review the propriety of the decision that death was the proper sentence.

(b) In determining whether death was the proper sentence in the case the Alabama court of criminal appeals, subject to review by the Alabama supreme court, shall determine:

(1) Whether the sentence of death was imposed under the influence of passion, prejudice, or any other arbitrary factor;

(2) Whether an independent weighing of the aggravating and mitigating circumstances at the appellate level indicates that death was the proper sentence; and

(3) Whether the sentence of death is excessive or disproportionate to the penalty imposed in similar cases, considering both the crime and the defendant.

(c) The court of criminal appeals shall explicitly address each of the three questions specified in subsection (b) of this section in every case it reviews in which a sentence of death has been imposed.

(d) After performing the review specified in this section, the Alabama court of criminal appeals, subject to review by the Alabama supreme court, shall be authorized to:

(1) Affirm the sentence of death;

(2) Set the sentence of death aside and remand to the trial court for correction of any errors occurring during the sentence proceedings and for imposition of the appropriate penalty after any new sentence proceedings that are necessary, provided that such errors shall not affect the determination of guilt and shall not preclude the imposition of a sentence of death where it is determined to be proper after any new sentence proceedings that are deemed necessary; or

(3) In cases in which the death penalty is deemed inappropriate under subdivision (b)(2) or (b)(3) of this section, set the sentence of death aside and remand to the trial court with directions that the defendant be sentenced to life imprisonment without parole.

§ 13A–5–55.   Conviction and sentence of death subject to automatic review.

In all cases in which a defendant is sentenced to death, the judgment of conviction shall be subject to automatic review.   The sentence of death shall be subject to review as provided in section 13A–5–53.

   2.   **Gen.Stat. of North Carolina, Vol. 1B (Repl.1981):**

ARTICLE 6.   HOMICIDE

§ 14–17.   Murder in the first and second degree defined; punishment.

A murder which shall be perpetrated by means of poison, lying in wait, imprisonment, starving, torture, or by any other kind of willful, deliberate, and premeditated killing, or which shall be committed in the perpetration or attempted perpetration of any arson, rape or a sex offense, robbery, kidnapping, burglary, or other felony committed or attempted with the use of a deadly weapon shall be deemed to be murder in the first degree, and any person who commits such murder shall be punished with death or imprisonment in the State's prison for life as the court shall determine pursuant to G.S. 15A–2000. All other kinds of murder, including that which shall be proximately caused by the unlawful distribution of opium or any synthetic or natural salt, compound, derivative, or preparation of opium when the ingestion of such substance causes the death of the user, shall be deemed murder in the second degree, and any person who commits such murder shall be punished as a Class C felon.

ARTICLE 100. CAPITAL PUNISHMENT

§ 15A–2000. Sentence of death or life imprisonment for capital felonies; further proceedings to determine sentence.

(a) Separate Proceedings on Issue of Penalty.—

(1) Upon conviction or adjudication of guilt of a defendant of a capital felony, the court shall conduct a separate sentencing proceeding to determine whether the defendant should be sentenced to death or life imprisonment. A capital felony is one which may be punishable by death.

(2) The proceeding shall be conducted by the trial judge before the trial jury as soon as practicable after the guilty verdict is returned. If prior to the time that the trial jury begins its deliberations on the issue of penalty, any juror dies, becomes incapacitated or disqualified, or is discharged for any reason, an alternate juror shall become a part of the jury and serve in all respects as those selected on the regular trial panel. An alternate juror shall become a part of the jury in the order in which he was selected. If the trial jury is unable to reconvene for a hearing on the issue of penalty after having determined the guilt of the accused, the trial judge shall impanel a new jury to determine the issue of the punishment. If the defendant pleads guilty, the sentencing proceeding shall be conducted before a jury impaneled for that purpose. A jury selected for the purpose of determining punishment in a capital case shall be selected in the same manner as juries are selected for the trial of capital cases.

(3) In the proceeding there shall not be any requirement to resubmit evidence presented during the guilt determination phase of the case, unless a new jury is impaneled, but all such evidence is competent for the jury's consideration in passing on punishment. Evidence may be presented as to any matter that the court deems relevant to sentence, and may include matters relating to any of the aggravating or mitigating circumstances enumerated in subsections (e) and (f). Any evidence which the court deems to have probative value may be received.

(4) The State and the defendant or his counsel shall be permitted to present argument for or against sentence of death. The defendant or defendant's counsel shall have the right to the last argument.

(b) Sentence Recommendation by the Jury.—Instructions determined by the trial judge to be warranted by the evidence shall be given by the court in its charge to the jury prior to its deliberation in determining sentence. In all cases in which the death penalty may be authorized, the judge shall include in his instructions to the jury that it must consider any aggravating circumstance or circumstances or mitigating circumstance or circumstances from the lists provided in subsections (e) and (f) which may be supported by the evidence, and shall furnish to the jury a written list of issues relating to such aggravating or mitigating circumstance or circumstances.

After hearing the evidence, argument of counsel, and instructions of the court, the jury shall deliberate and render a sentence recommendation to the court, based upon the following matters:

(1) Whether any sufficient aggravating circumstance or circumstances as enumerated in subsection (e) exist;

(2) Whether any sufficient mitigating circumstance or circumstances as enumerated in subsection (f), which outweigh the aggravating circumstance or circumstances found, exist; and

(3) Based on these considerations, whether the defendant should be sentenced to death or to imprisonment in the State's prison for life.

The sentence recommendation must be agreed upon by a unanimous vote of the 12 jurors. Upon delivery of the sentence recommendation by the foreman of the jury, the jury shall be individually polled to establish whether each juror concurs and agrees to the sentence recommendation returned.

If the jury cannot, within a reasonable time, unanimously agree to its sentence recommendation, the judge shall impose a sentence of life imprisonment; provided, however, that the judge shall in no instance impose the death penalty when the jury cannot agree unanimously to its sentence recommendation.

(c) Findings in Support of Sentence of Death.—When the jury recommends a sentence of death, the foreman of the jury shall sign a writing on behalf of the jury which writing shall show:

(1) The statutory aggravating circumstance or circumstances which the jury finds beyond a reasonable doubt; and

(2) That the statutory aggravating circumstance or circumstances found by the jury are sufficiently substantial to call for the imposition of the death penalty; and

(3) That the mitigating circumstance or circumstances are insufficient to outweigh the aggravating circumstance or circumstances found.

(d) Review of Judgment and Sentence.—

(1) The judgment of conviction and sentence of death shall be subject to automatic review by the Supreme Court of North Carolina pursuant to procedures established by the Rules of Appellate Procedure. In its review, the Supreme Court shall consider the punishment imposed as well as any errors assigned on appeal.

(2) The sentence of death shall be overturned and a sentence of life imprisonment imposed in lieu thereof by the Supreme Court upon a finding that the record does not support the jury's findings of any aggravating circumstance or circumstances upon which the sentencing court based its sentence of death, or upon a finding that the sentence of death was imposed under the influence of passion, prejudice, or any other arbitrary factor, or upon a finding that the sentence of death is excessive or disproportionate to the penalty imposed in similar cases, considering both the crime and the defendant. The Supreme Court may suspend consideration of death penalty cases until such time as the court determines it is prepared to make the comparisons required under the provisions of this section.

(3) If the sentence of death and the judgment of the trial court are reversed on appeal for error in the post-verdict sentencing proceeding, the Supreme Court shall order that a new sentencing hearing be conducted in conformity with the procedures of this Article.

(e) Aggravating Circumstances.—Aggravating circumstances which may be considered shall be limited to the following:

(1) The capital felony was committed by a person lawfully incarcerated.

(2) The defendant had been previously convicted of another capital felony.

(3) The defendant had been previously convicted of a felony involving the use or threat of violence to the person.

(4) The capital felony was committed for the purpose of avoiding or preventing a lawful arrest or effecting an escape from custody.

(5) The capital felony was committed while the defendant was engaged, or was an aider or abettor, in the commission of, or an attempt to commit, or flight after committing or attempting to commit, any homicide, robbery, rape or a sex offense, arson, burglary, kidnapping, or aircraft piracy or the unlawful throwing, placing, or discharging of a destructive device or bomb.

(6) The capital felony was committed for pecuniary gain.

(7) The capital felony was committed to disrupt or hinder the lawful exercise of any governmental function or the enforcement of laws.

(8) The capital felony was committed against a law-enforcement officer, employee of the Department of Correction, jailer, fireman, judge or justice, former judge or justice, prosecutor or former prosecutor, juror or former juror, or witness or former witness against the defendant, while engaged in the performance of his official duties or because of the exercise of his official duty.

(9) The capital felony was especially heinous, atrocious, or cruel.

(10) The defendant knowingly created a great risk of death to more than one person by means of a weapon or device which would normally be hazardous to the lives of more than one person.

(11) The murder for which the defendant stands convicted was part of a course of conduct in which the defendant engaged and which included the commission by the defendant of other crimes of violence against another person or persons.

(f) Mitigating Circumstances.—Mitigating circumstances which may be considered shall include, but not be limited to, the following:

(1) The defendant has no significant history of prior criminal activity.

(2) The capital felony was committed while the defendant was under the influence of mental or emotional disturbance.

(3) The victim was a voluntary participant in the defendant's homicidal conduct or consented to the homicidal act.

(4) The defendant was an accomplice in or accessory to the capital felony committed by another person and his participation was relatively minor.

(5) The defendant acted under duress or under the domination of another person.

(6) The capacity of the defendant to appreciate the criminality of his conduct or to conform his conduct to the requirements of law was impaired.

(7) The age of the defendant at the time of the crime.

(8) The defendant aided in the apprehension of another capital felon or testified truthfully on behalf of the prosecution in another prosecution of a felony.

(9) Any other circumstance arising from the evidence which the jury deems to have mitigating value.

*

INDEX

References are to Pages

ABANDONMENT
Generally, 371–377
Model Penal Code, 376
Scope of the defense, 376–377
Traditional position, 374–375

ACCESSORIES
See Complicity

ACCOMPLICE
See Complicity

ACT, CRIMINAL
See, also, Attempt; Conduct; Vague-
ness Doctrine; Voluntariness
Generally, 29–192
Definition of the offense, 85–122
Acts, 85–107
See, also, Conduct
Omissions, 107–122
See, also, Conduct
Previously defined conduct, requirement of,
29–85
See, also, Conduct
Vagueness doctrine, 45–85
See, also, Vagueness Doctrine

ACTUS REUS
See Conduct, Acts; Impossibility

ADDICTION
See, also, Civil Coercive Intervention;
Drugs, Offenses; Insanity
Generally, 158–187, 189–191
Alcoholism, 168–182
Recent trends, 189–191
Narcotic, 158–168
See, also, Drugs, Offenses
Recent trends, 189–191

ALCOHOLISM
See Addiction; Civil Coercive Intervention;
Insanity

ANTICIPATORY OFFENSES
See Attempt; Conspiracy; Solicitation

ARSON
Mens rea requirement, 196–198
Reckless burning,
Model Penal Code and mens rea, 243

ATTEMPT
Generally, 126–137, 339–377
Abandonment, 371–377
See, also, Abandonment
Equivocal conduct in completed offenses,
366–371
Felony murder, 954
Grading, 341
History,
Origins, 339–340
United States, 340–341
Impossibility and, 353–366
See, also, Impossibility
Mens rea of, 342–353
Circumstance elements, 346–348
Completed conduct but no result, 348–350
Specific-intent requirement, rationale for,
345–346
Model Penal Code, 341–342, 351–353
Grading of attempt, 341
Overt act requirement, 127–131
Preparation vs. attempt,
Dangerous-proximity test, 134
Indispensable-element test, 133–134
Last-proximate-act doctrine, 132
Model Penal Code approach, 136–137
Physical proximity test, 132–133
Res-ipsa-loquitur test, 134–136
Solicitation vs., 137–138

AUTOMATISM
See Insanity; Voluntariness, Impaired consciousness

BATTERED WOMAN SYNDROME
Defenses to homicide,
Duress or domination by another, 835
Self-defense, 559–570

BENTHAM
Deterrence, classical concept of, 8–10

BIGAMY
Mistake or ignorance of law, 271

BLAMEWORTHINESS
Deterrence and, 13–14
Retribution and, 4–6

BRAINWASHING
Excuse, situational, 624–625

[1]

CANON LAW
Mens rea, 194–195

CAPITAL PUNISHMENT
Generally, 786–882
Aggravating circumstances,
Accompanying criminal offenses, 825
Custody, committed while in, 826
Hazardous conduct (creating risk of death
to more than one person), 824, 825
Hindrance of law enforcement, 826
Identity of victim, 825
Pecuniary motive, 825
Prediction of future criminal conduct,
826–827
Prior criminal conduct, 826
Unusual cruelty or depravity, 826
Case-by-case proportionality review on ap-
peal, 850–851
Comparative review on appeal, 815–816,
850–868
Defining the universe of relevant cases,
859–864
Efficacy of, 867–868
Selecting and comparing "similar" cases,
864–866
Efficacy and morality of, 787–791
Felony-murder rule, 1020–1028
See, also, Homicide
Leniency,
Intracase disparity as basis for, 848–850
Limits on discretion, 847–848
Mitigating circumstances, 834–850
Degree of participation, 840
Diminished responsibility, 841–843
Extreme mental or emotional distur-
bance, 842–843
Impaired capacity for appreciation or
control, 843
Duress or domination by another, 833,
836, 840–841
Limits on mitigating evidence, 847
Youth, 833, 837, 838–840
Proportionality, 1004–1028
See, also, Punishment
Rape, 1004–1019
Race, 868–882
Studies on discriminatory sentencing pat-
terns, 869–878
Recent history, 786–787
Statutes, 814–868
Aggravating and mitigating circum-
stances, 824–826, 834–850
See, also, Aggravating circumstances
and Mitigating circumstances, both
this topic
Overview of modern capital sentencing
statutes,
Comparative review on appeal, 815–816
Exclusion, criteria of, 814–815
Inclusion, criteria of, 814
Mitigation and selection, criteria of, 815
Premeditation-deliberation formula, con-
tinued relevance of, 827
Supreme Court and, 792–816

CAPITAL PUNISHMENT—Cont'd
Character and record of convicted defen-
dant must be considered, 798, 799–
800
Cruel and unusual punishment, 793–795
Discretion by jury in sentencing,
lack of, 797–798
Unguided, 792–793, 795, 801–813
Individualized determination, 799–801
Mandatory death penalty statutes, 796,
797–798
Proper role of the court, 813
Rape, 1004–1019

CIVIL COERCIVE INTERVENTION
Generally, 183–191
Alcoholism,
See, also, Addiction; Insanity; Intoxi-
cation
Recent trends, 189–191
Children in need of supervision, 188
Civil commitment, 183–184
Legality, 184–186
Limits, 186
Mentally disordered sex offenders, 187–188
Narcotic addicts, 186–187
See, also, Addiction
Recent trends, 189–191
Purpose, 184
Quarantine, 183
Treatment vs. punishment, 186–189
Venereal disease, treatment for, 188–189

COERCIVE PERSUASION
Excuse, situational, 625

COMMITMENT
See Civil Coervice Intervention; Insanity

COMMON LAW
See, also, Mistake or Ignorance, Fact
Accessorial liability, 379–381
Causation, 928–929
Conspiracy, 440
Culpability, 193–233
Justification,
Necessity, 512–519
Presumptions,
Juveniles, 632–633, 640–642

COMPLICITY
See, also, Conspiracy
Generally, 379–413
Accessories after the fact, 381–383
Accomplice,
Felony-murder rule, 962–963
Common law concept of accessorial liability,
379–380
Abrogation of, 380–381
Conduct required for, 383–392
Conspiracy, relation to, 463–480
See, also, Conspiracy
Culpability required for, 392–404
Circumstances of accomplice's conduct,
attaching importance to, 399
Facilitation, offense of, 397–398

COMPLICITY—Cont'd
Knowledge vs. stake in the venture, 395–397
Compromise solutions, 397
Natural and probable consequences, rule of, 400–404
Results of accomplice's conduct, 398–399
Excusable wrong, 408
Limits of accomplice liability, 412–413
Implied exemption, 413
Withdrawal, 413
Mens rea of principal,
Absence of mens rea, 404–409
Secondary party charged with higher degree of liability than principal, 409–410
Model Penal Code, 382–383, 391–392, 396–397, 411
Modern statutes,
Describing the proscribed conduct, 390–391
Parties to crime, 379–383
Vicarious liability, compared, 417

COMPULSION, SITUATIONAL
New defense to fill gap between duress and necessity, 622–623

CONCUSSION
Form of impaired consciousness, 154

CONDUCT
Acts, 85–107
Abortional homicide, 85–94
Model Penal Code, 233–235
Partner's stealing of partnership property, 94–97
Retroactive application of unforeseeable judicial enlargement of criminal statute, 89–101
Culpability and, 339–377
Definition of the offense, 85–122
Equivocal conduct in completed offense,
Perjury charge based on literally true but unresponsive answer, 366–370
Minimum conduct requirements, 122–191
Anticipatory offenses, 126–139
See, also, Attempt; Solicitation
Completed offenses, 140–152
Voluntariness, 152–191
See, also, Addiction; Civil Coercive Intervention
Omissions, 107–122
Child neglect, 107–109
Duty to act, 109–111
Duty to rescue, 111–113
Life-sustaining treatment, 114–121
Outside the law of homicide, 113–114
Possession, 141–146
Constructive, 145–146
Liability for, 121–122
Possession-or-control statute, 142–143, 146
Previously defined conduct, requirement of, 29–85
Legality, principle of, 29–44

CONDUCT—Cont'd
Vagueness doctrine, 45–85
See, also, Vagueness Doctrine
Status crimes,
See, also, Addiction
"Stop-and-identify" statutes, 151–152
Vagrancy and loitering laws, 146–151
Void for vagueness, 148–150
Vagueness doctrine, 45–85
See, also, Vagueness Doctrine

CONSPIRACY
See, also, Complicity
Generally, 434–509
Agreement,
Bilateral or unilateral, 453–457
Necessity of, 449–450
Sufficiency of, 450–452
Complicity, relation to, 463–480
See, also, Complicity
Corrupt motive or *Powell* doctrine, 444
Cumulative punishment, 461–462
Defined, 139
Defraud the United States, conspiracy to, 442–444
Duration, 493–500
Conspiracies to conceal, 493–498, 499–500
Model Penal Code, 499
Functions of law of conspiracy, 434
Hearsay rule,
Co-conspirator's exception to, 434–435
Impossibility, 460–461
Inchoate offense, as, 445–462
Joint trial, 435–436
Legality, principle of, 440–442
Limits on liability for, 500–509
Mann Act,
Woman being transported not guilty of conspiracy to violate, 500–502
Mens rea, 457–459, 472–473
Attempt, compared, 457–458
Circumstances, 458–459
Conduct, 458
Results, 458
Objectives that make conspiracy criminal, 437–444
Pinkerton rule, 473–480
Rationale for the common-law rule, 440
Renunciation, 461
Scope, 482–493
Model Penal Code, 483–484
Object dimension, 482–484
Party dimension, 484–493
Model Penal Code, 486–487
Wheels and chains, 485–486
Statutes, 444
Venue, 436
Wharton's rule, 502–508
Withdrawal, 461

CORPORATE CRIMINALITY
Generally, 420–434
Individual responsibility for corporate acts, 432–434
Partnerships and other unincorporated associations, 430–431

CORPORATE CRIMINALITY—Cont'd
Racketeer Influenced and Corrupt Organizations Act (RICO), 429–430
Sanctions, 426–429
"True" crimes, different approaches to, 420–426

CRIMINALIZATION
Generally, 1053–1089
Benefits, assessing, 1074–1075
Weighing costs and benefits, 1080–1081
Costs,
Assessing, 1075–1080
Under-enforcement, 1077–1079
Weighing costs and benefits, 1080–1081
"Crime tariff," social consequences of, 1079–1080
Decency, offenses against, 1067–1071
Deterrence of socially valuable behavior, 1075–1076
Drug offenses, 1081–1089
See, also, Drugs, Offenses
Effects of, 1073–1081
Criminogenic, 1077
Individual, on the, 1076
Privacy, on, 1076
Enforcement expenditures, 1076
Health and safety, paternalism in, 1071–1073
Morals, enforcement of, 1053–1073
Mill, John Stuart, 1053–1058
Response of James Fitzjames Stephen, 1059
Wolfenden report, 1059–1060
Response of Lord Devlin, 1060–1065
Rejoinder of Professor Hart, 1065–1067
Under-enforcement, costs of, 1077–1079

CRUEL AND UNUSUAL PUNISHMENT
Capital punishment, 793–795

CULPABILITY
See, also, Mens Rea
Generally, 193–245
Common law, 193–233
Model Penal Code, 233–245
See, also, Model Penal Code
Statutes, 233–245

DEATH PENALTY
See Capital Punishment

DECENCY, OFFENSES AGAINST
See Criminalization, Morals, enforcement of

DECRIMINALIZATION
See Criminalization

DEFENSIVE ACTIONS
See, generally, Justification

DELINQUENCY PROCEEDINGS
See Juveniles

DEPROGRAMMING
Justified, 520–521

DETERRENCE
Generally, 7–21
Blameworthiness and, 13–14
Concept,
Bentham's "The Rationale of Punishment," 8–10
Posner's "Economic Analysis of Law," 10
Criticisms of deterrence theory, responses to, 10–12
General,
Defined, 7–8
Limits of, 12–13
Measurement of, 16–17
Severity and certainty, relation of, 17–21
Socializing effect of criminal law, 15–16
Special, 21–22
Defined, 7

DIMINISHED RESPONSIBILITY
Capital sentencing proceedings, 841–842
Extreme mental or emotional disturbance, 842–843
Impaired capacity for appreciation or control, 843
Homicide, 904
Partial responsibility, 753–754
Rule of logical relevance, 752–753, 756–758

DISCRIMINATION
See Race

DISEASE OR ILLNESS
See Insanity

DOMESTIC VIOLENCE
Self-defense,
Battered child, 570–573
Battered woman, 559–570

DRUGS
See, also, Addiction; Insanity; Intoxication
Felony-murder rule,
Distribution of controlled substances, 952–954
Insanity,
See, also, Insanity
"Functional" psychosis, precipitation of a, 729–730
Psychoactive effects, 728–729
Toxic psychosis, 730–731
Offenses, 1081–1089
Consumption-related, 1083–1089
Prohibition or regulation, 1082–1083
Volitional impairment and drug dependence, 716–720

DURESS
See, also, Excuse, Situational
Involuntariness and, 604–606

ENTRAPMENT
See Excuse, Situational

EPILEPTIC CONDITION
Driving with knowledge of, 156–157

ESCAPE
Model Penal Code and mens rea, 243

EXCUSE, SITUATIONAL
Generally, 511–512, 604–630
Brainwashing, 624–625
Coercive persuasion, 625
Duress, 604–625
Battered woman syndrome, 835
Capital punishment, 833, 836, 840–841
Elements of the defense, 606–607
Escaping prisoner's claim of intolerable conditions, 609–619, 621–622
Insanity defense's control inquiry compared with, 695–696
Involuntariness and, 604–606
Murder, 607–608
Necessity vs., 612, 619–620
See, also, Justification
Voluntary exposure to, 608–609
Entrapment, 625–630
Approaches to the defense, 627–628
Questions on the defense, 628–629
Mens rea and situational excuse, 624
Situational compulsion as new defense to fill gap between duress and necessity, 622–623

FALSE IMPRISONMENT
Model Penal Code and mens rea, 242–243

FELONY–MURDER RULE
See Homicide

FOURTH AMENDMENT
Use of deadly force in the arrest of fleeing felon, 581–589

GAMBLING, COMPULSIVE
Insanity defense, grounds for, 713–716

HABITUAL OFFENDER STATUTES
Sentencing, proportionality in, 1028–1048

HINDERING PROSECUTION
Model Penal Code and mens rea, 243–244

HOLMES, OLIVER WENDELL
Ignorance of law, 261–263
Mens rea, theories on, 211–214, 229–231

HOMICIDE
Generally, 779–966
Capital punishment, 786–882
See, also, Capital Punishment
Causation, 923–932
Common law approach, 928–929
Felony-murder rule,
Application of the rule, 962
Independent prosecution for murder, 962
Model Penal Code
Approach of, 929–930
Problems with, 930–932
Relevance of, 926–928
Diminished responsibility,
England, 903

HOMICIDE—Cont'd
Extreme emotional disturbance, 904
Emotional disturbance, extreme, 896–904
Burden of persuasion, 904
Diminished responsibility, 904
Felony murder rule, 932–965
Accomplice liability, 962–963
Attempted felony murder, 954
Capital punishment and, 1020–1028
Causation, relation to principles of,
Application of felony-murder rule, 962
Independent prosecution for murder, 962
Defenses, availability of, 952
Distribution of controlled substances, 952–954
Duration of the felony, 963–964
Inherent dangerousness, determination of, 951
Judicial rejection, 935–937
Lesser-included-offense instruction, 951–952
Limitations, traditional, 932–933
Merger, 949–950
Mitigation, availability of, 952
Model Penal Code, 937–938
Modern statutes, 964
Non-participant, homicide committed by, 954–961
Rationale, 933–935
Unlawful possession of firearm by convicted felon, 938–949
History of criminal homicide, 779–786
Intentional, 882–904
Justifiable,
Necessity, 523–526
Manslaughter,
Involuntary,
Degree of culpability sufficient for, 912–914, 922
Misdemeanor-manslaughter rule, 965–966
Murder and, distinction between, 780–781
Murder,
Degree of culpability sufficient for, 911–912, 921–922
Duress, 607–608
Manslaughter and, distinction between, 780–781
Negligent homicide,
Degree of culpability sufficient for, 922
Premeditation-deliberation formula, 781–786
Abandonment of, 785–786
Continued relevance of, 827
Provocation, 882–895
Cooling time, 890–892
Development of formula, 884–886
Heat of passion, 886–887
Legally adequate, 887
Mental abnormality, relevance of, 895
Mistake, relevance of, 893–895
Objective standard, 887–890
Characteristics, 892–893
Unintentional, 905–923

HYPOGLYCEMIA
Form of impaired consciousness, 154–155

IGNORANCE
See Mistake or Ignorance

IMMATURITY
See, generally, Juveniles

IMPOSSIBILITY
Actus reus, importance of, 363–365
Attempt and, 353–366
  Previously consummated attempt, 358–359
Conspiracy, 460–461
Factual, 357
Intent, distinguish between primary and secondary, 359–360
Legal, 356–357
  True legal impossibility, 366
Legality, principle of, 365–366
Model Penal Code, 361–363
Previously consummated attempt, 358–359
Reasonable expectations, 360–361

INFANTS
See Juveniles

INSANITY
Generally, 654–778
Abolition of insanity defense, proposals for, 770–778
Automatism and insanity defense, relation between, 749–750
Bifurcated procedure trying issues of guilt or innocence and insanity in successive stages, 769–770
Cognitive impairment, significance of, 682–684
Commitment,
  Automatic, constitutionality of, 746–747
  Eligibility for release, 747–749
  Persons acquitted by reason of insanity, 734–749
    Automatic commitment, constitutionality of, 746–747
    Controversy over, release of such persons, 735–749
    Eligibility for release from automatic commitment, 747–749
  Persons incompetent to stand trial, 733–734
Compulsive gambling as grounds for insanity defense, 713–716
Disease or illness,
  Approaches to use as threshold for all insanity defense tests, 709–712
    Abandonment of the requirement, 712
    Intermediate position, 711–712
    Restrictive definition, 710–711
  Existence of, 673–675
Disposition of mentally disordered offenders, 733–752
  See, also, Commitment, this topic
Drug dependence and volitional impairment, 716–720
Guilty but mentally ill, verdict of, 750–752
History of insanity defense, 656–658
Intoxication, 720–732

INSANITY—Cont'd
Chronic, 725, 726–728
Drugs other than alcohol, 728–731
  Precipitation of a "functional" psychosis, 729–730
  Psychoactive effects, 728–729
  Toxic psychosis, 730–731
Involuntary, 725–728
Pathological, 731–732
Voluntary, 723–725
Mens rea, 752–770
  Bifurcation of insanity and guilt or innocence (mens rea) issues, 769–770
  Boundaries of psychiatric testimony on, 758–769
  Expert psychiatric testimony on mens rea issues, argument for excluding, 758–761
  Mental abnormality and, 290–291
  Relevance rules governing testimony on mental abnormality, 752–753, 756–758
Mental disorder, major, 664
M'Naghten's case, 658–659
Knowledge,
  Act, of the, 677
  Meaning of "knowing", 680–682
  Wrongfulness, of, 677–678
  Objections to, 676, 680–682, 683–684
Post-Hinkley reforms of insanity defense,
  Federal statute eliminating volitional prong and placing burden of proof on defendant, 664
  State statutes restricting or abolishing the defense, 663–664
Sentencing, 734
Tests,
  Analysis of, 675–676, 682–684
  Control, 660–661, 685–720
    Criticism and defense, 696–700
    Illustrative cases, 704–709
    Psychotic defendants, 685–686
    Relation to other doctrines, 695–696
      Duress, 695–696
      Voluntariness, 695
  Federal statute eliminating volitional prong and placing burden of proof on defendant, 664
  M'Naghten, 658–659
    See, also, *M'Naghten's* case, this topic
  Model Penal Code, 661–663
  Post-Hinkley reforms, 663–664
  Product, 660
Unconscious motivation, 700–704

INTENT
See Mens Rea

INTOXICATION
See, also, Drugs; Insanity
"Dangerous intoxication" offense, proposal for creation of, 288–290
General-intent crimes, 283–285
Mens rea, 274–288
Specific-intent crimes, 285–288
Voluntary act doctrine, 283

JUDICIAL CRIME CREATION
English examples, 29–33
Principle of legality vs., 33–44

JUSTIFICATION
Generally, 511–603
Accidental, 534–535
Defense against aggression, 537–580
  Reasonable perception of danger, 551–573
    Battered child, 570–573
    Battered woman, 559–570
    Model Penal Code, 559
    Objective standard, 556–558
    Subjective standard, 558–559
Defense of habitation, 537–541
Defense of others, 573–580
Defensive use of deadly force, approaches to, 542–545
  Accommodating autonomy and proportionality, 544–545
  Law of nature, 542–543
  Social utility, 543
Deprogramming, 520–521
Domestic violence and the law of self-defense,
  Battered child, 570–573
  Battered woman, 559–570
Escaping prisoner's claim of intolerable conditions, 609–619, 621–622
Excessive use of deadly force, 545–546
Fourth Amendment and the arrest of fleeing felon,
  Use of deadly force, 581–589
General principle of, 512–529
Homicide, 523–526
Imperfect justification, 532–533, 895–896
Mistake, 530–536
  See, also, Mistake or Ignorance
  Law, of, 535–536
  Model Penal Code vs. proposed federal code, 533–534
  Reasonable, 530–531
  Unreasonable, 531–532
    Imperfect justification and, 532
Model Penal Code,
  Choice-of-evils defense, 519–520
  Imperfect justification, 532–533
  Mistake of law, 535
Necessity, 512–529
  Common law, 512–519
  Deprogramming, 520–521
  Desirability of such a defense, 526–529
  Duress vs., 612, 619–620
  Economic, 521
  Fault of actor, created by, 526
  Homicide, 523–526
  Medical, 521–523
  Statutes, 519–520
Prevention of dangerous felonies, 541
Prevention of escape, 546–547
Public authority, 581–603
  Citizen reliance on apparent official authority, 597–603
  Deadly force used against fleeing felon, 581–591
    Private citizens, authority of, 589–591

JUSTIFICATION—Cont'd
  Mistakes by public officials regarding their own authority, 591–597
Retreat rule, 547–551
  "Castle" exception, 550–551
  Rule stated, 547–549
  Wisdom of rule discussed, 549–550
Self-defense, 537–540
  Domestic violence,
    Battered child, 570–573
    Battered woman, 559–570
Situational compulsion as new defense to fill gap between duress and necessity, 622–623
Statutes, 545
Strict liability in claims of, 536

JUVENILES
Generally, 632–654
Court, juvenile,
  Antecedents, 633–634
  Juvenile-court movement, 634–636
Delinquency proceedings,
  Infancy presumptions, 642–645
  Mens rea, 642–643
  Minimum age for jurisdiction, 645–646
  Statutory purpose, 643–644
Mens rea,
  Delinquency and, 642–643
Presumptions, common-law, 632–633, 640–642
  Delinquency proceedings, 642–645
Proof beyond a reasonable doubt, 967
  See, also, Proof Beyond A Reasonable Doubt
Reform of juvenile justice, 636–640
Transfer of juveniles to criminal court, 646–654

LEGALITY, PRINCIPLE OF
Generally, 29–44
American experience,
  History, 36–38
  Recent, 38–39
Defined, 33–34
European origins, 34–36
Growing acceptance and evolving meaning, 39–43
Judicial crime creation vs.,
  Common law, continuing significance of, 43–44
  English examples of judicial crime creation, 29–33

MANN ACT
Conspiracy to violate, woman being transported not guilty of, 500–502

MENS REA
  See, also, Attempt; Culpability; Insanity; Intoxication; Juveniles; Mistakes or Ignorance; Model Penal Code, Culpability
Generally, 193 et seq.
Abandonment of mens rea for all crimes, arguments for and against, 334–339
Arson, 196–198

MENS REA—Cont'd
Canon law, 194–195
Criminal responsibility defenses, compared,
    631–632
Early development of concept, 194–196
Excuse, situational, 624
    See, also, Excuse, situational
General malevolence, mens rea as, 199–201
Holmes' theory, 211–214, 229–231
Intent,
    General, 219–220
    Specific, 228–233
Intoxication, 274–290
    See also, generally, Intoxication
Juvenile delinquency and, 642–643
Language of, 198–199, 201–203
Legal fictions and, 220
"Malicious", meaning of, 196–198, 201–208
Mental abnormality and, 290–291
Negligence as basis for criminal liability,
    214–219
Particular state of mind, as a, 201
Presumption one intends the natural and
    probable consequences of one's acts,
    208–211
    Statutory response, 221
Retributive vs. deterrent theories, 211–214
Roman law, 194–195
Strict liability, 220
    Ignorance of the law is no excuse vs.
        mens rea requirement, 323–334

MENTAL ABNORMALITY
See Insanity; Mens Rea

MILL, JOHN STUART
See Criminalization, Morals, enforcement of

MIND, CRIMINAL
See, generally, Mens Rea

MISTAKE OR IGNORANCE
    See, also, Intoxication; Justification,
        Mistake
Generally, 246–274
Fact, 246–257
    Common law,
        General intent, 250–254
            Grading elements, 253–254
            Negligence, as, 250
            Recklessness, as, 252–253
            Specific-intent crimes and, 253
        Methodology, 248
        Specific intent, 248–250
            General-intent elements of, 253
    Law mistakes, compared, 271–274, 330
Law, 257–274
    Bigamy, 271
    Blanket Act, 268–270, 272
    Criminality, mistake or ignorance as to,
        257–268
        Maxim "ignorance of the law is no ex-
            cuse,"
            Application of, 258–259
            Justifications for, 260–263
            Mens rea vs., 323–334
            Problems with, 259–260

MISTAKE OR IGNORANCE—Cont'd
    New Jersey Code, 264
        Official misstatement of criminal law,
            reliance on, 264–268
        Reform, proposals for, 263–264
    Divorce, validity of, 268–270
    Fact mistakes, compared, 271–274, 330
    Specific intent or other special mental
        element, mistake negating, 270
    Model Penal Code, 254–257
        Fact, mistake of,
            Grading elements and, 256–257
            Innovations of, 255–256
            Methodology of, 255
        Law, mistake of, 263
            Official misstatement of criminal law,
                reliance on, 267–268
    Rape, assault with intent to, 246–248

MODEL PENAL CODE
Generally, App. A
Abandonment, 376
    Actus reus, 233–235
Attempt, 341–342, 351–353
    Grading, 341
Complicity, 382–383, 391–392, 396–397,
    411
Conspiracy,
    Duration, 499
    Scope, 483–484, 486–487
Culpability, 235–245
    Ambiguous provision of, 236, 242–244
    Hierarchy of terms, 237, 244–245
    Knowledge, 236, 238–239
    Material element, 236, 238
    Minimum requirements of, 235, 237–238
    Negligence, 240–241
    Offense silent on, 241–242
    Purpose, 236, 238
    Recklessness, 239–240
    Strict liability, 237
    Types, 236, 237–238
Felony-murder rule, 937–938
Impossibility, 361–363
Insanity defense, 661–663
Justification,
    Choice-of-evils defense, 519–520
    Imperfect justification, 532–533
    Mistake of law, 535
Mens rea,
    See Culpability, this topic
Mistake or ignorance,
    Fact, mistake of, 254–257, 272–273
    Law, mistake of, 263, 270, 272–273
        Official misstatement of law, reliance
            on, 267–268

MORAL STATEMENT
Criminal Law as, 3–4

MORALS
Enforcement of, 1059–1073
See, also, Criminalization

NATURAL AND PROBABLE CONSE-QUENCES
Rule, 208–211, 400–404, 993–1000
Statutory response, 221

NECESSITY
See Justification

NEGLIGENCE
Criminal liability, as basis for, 214–219

NEGLIGENT HOMICIDE
Degree of culpability sufficient for, 922

OBSCENITY
Vagueness doctrine, case study of, 76–85

OVERBREATH DOCTRINE
Vagueness doctrine, relation between over-breadth doctrine and,
Doctrines compared, 73–74
Facial review, 73–75

PARTNERSHIPS
See Corporate Criminality

PERJURY
Literally true but unresponsive answer, 366–370
Misrepresentation of erroneous belief, 371

PRESUMPTIONS
See Juveniles; Proof Beyond a Reasonable Doubt

PRINCIPALS
See Complicity

PRIVACY
Dangers of criminalizing private behavior, 1076–1077

PROOF BEYOND A REASONABLE DOUBT
Generally, 967–1004
Mitigations and defenses, 968–993
Presumptions, 993–1004
Conclusive, 1000–1001
Inferences, permissive, 1002
Intends the ordinary consequences of his acts, unconstitutional instruction stating that a person, 993–1000
Legislative candor, argument that presumptions should be declared unconstitutional in order to induce, 1002–1003
Rebuttable, 1001
Shift in burden of production, 1001–1002
Substantive justice, 991–993
Winship opinion,
Procedural interpretation of, 986–989
Criticisms of procedural approach, 989–991
Scope of reasonable-doubt requirement, 967 et seq.

PROOF BEYOND A REASONABLE DOUBT—Cont'd
Absence of heat of passion required to be proved beyond a reasonable doubt, 968–974
Affirmative defense of extreme emotional disturbance not required to be disproved beyond a reasonable doubt, 975–986
Presumption of one intending the ordinary consequences of one's acts held unconstitutional, 993–1000

PROPORTIONALITY
See Punishment

PROVOCATION
See Homicide

PUBLIC AUTHORITY
See Justification

PUBLIC–WELFARE OFFENSES
See Strict Liability

PUNISHMENT
Generally, 1–28
Deterrence, 7–21
See, also, Deterrence
Prevention, 21–28
Incapacitation, 22–24
Rehabilitation, 24–28
Special deterrence, 21–22
Proportionality,
Capital punishment and, 1004–1028
Accomplice, 1020–1028
Rape, 1004–1019
Sixteen-year-old defendant, 1019–1020
Imprisonment and, 1028–1053
Eighth Amendment proscribes a life sentence with possibility of parole for seventh nonviolent felony (uttering "no account" check), 1028–1048
Parole possibility as factor in determining constitutionality of alleged disproportionate sentence, 1037, 1039, 1050
Rehabilitation, 24–28
Retribution, 2–7
See, also, Retribution
Deterrent vs. retributive theories and the concept of mens rea, 211–214
Sentencing,
See Proportionality, this topic

RACE
See, also, Capital Punishment
Capital punishment and, 868–882

RACKETEER INFLUENCED AND CORRUPT ORGANIZATIONS ACT (RICO)
See, also, Corporate Criminality
Corporate misconduct, 429–430

RAPE
Mistake or ignorance,
    Assault with intent to rape, 246–248
Proportionality and capital punishment,
    1004–1019

REGULATORY OFFENSES
See Strict Liability

REHABILITATION
Purpose or goal, 24–28

RENUNCIATION
Conspiracy and, 461

RESPONSIBILITY, CRIMINAL
    See, also, Diminished responsibility; In-
        sanity; Juveniles
Generally, 631–778
Mens rea,
    Compared with criminal responsibility de-
        fenses, 631–632

RETREAT RULE
See Justification

RETRIBUTION
Generally, 2–7
Blameworthiness, 4–6
Mens rea,
    Retributive vs. deterrent theories, 211–
        214
Moral statement, criminal law as, 3–4
Proportionality, 7

ROMAN LAW
Mens rea, 194–195

SELF–DEFENSE
See Justification

SENTENCING
Insanity, 734

SOLICITATION
    Generally,
Attempt vs., 137–138
Independent offense, solicitation as, 139

SOMNAMBULISM
Form of impaired consciousness, 154

STATUTES, SELECTED PENAL, App. B

STRICT CONSTRUCTION, DOCTRINE OF
Generally, 101–107
Federal-state balance and, 106
Legislative response, 102–103
Lenity, ambiguity to be resolved in favor of,
    105–106
Origin, 101–102
Vagueness doctrine, junior version of, 103–
    104

STRICT LIABILITY
Generally, 291–339
Constitutional limits on, 308–313

STRICT LIABILITY—Cont'd
Federal Food, Drug, and Cosmetic Act,
    prosecutions under, 293–304
Mens rea,
    Arguments for and against the abandon-
        ment of mens rea for all crimes, 334–
        339
    Ignorance of the law is no excuse vs.
        mens rea requirement, 323–334
Public welfare offenses,
    See Regulatory offenses, this topic
Regulatory offenses, 291–308
    Alternatives to strict liability, 307–308
    Debate over use of criminal law in such
        situations, 304–305
    Unauthorized acquisition or possession of
        food stamps, 328
Serious crimes, 313–322

VAGUENESS DOCTRINE
Generally, 45–85
Arbitrary and discriminatory enforcement,
    potential of indefinite law for, 67–68
Limits of, 64–66
Military context,
    Misconduct resulting in conviction by
        court-martial, 45–60
    Significance of, 62–63
Obscenity and, 76–85
Overbreadth doctrine, relation between
    vagueness doctrine and,
    Doctrines compared, 73–74
    Facial review, 73–75
Protected freedoms, intolerable vagueness
    and impact of indefinite laws on, 71–72
Rationales of, 64
    Limits of rationales, 64–66
Strict construction doctrine as junior ver-
    sion of, 103–104
Tolerable vagueness,
    Demands of necessity and, 68–69
    Questions of degree and, 69–71
Warning to prospective offenders, potential
    of indefinite law to deny, 66–67

VICARIOUS LIABILITY
Generally, 414–420
Background, 417–418
Liquor regulation, 414–417
Minor offenses, confined to, 418

VOLUNTARINESS
    See, also, Addiction; Civil Coercive In-
        tervention
Generally, 152–191
Codification, 155
Definition by examples of involuntary con-
    duct, 152–153
    Muscular contraction or paralysis pro-
        duced by disease, 153
    Physically coerced movement, 153
    Reflex movements, 153
    Unconsciousness, 153
Duress and involuntariness, 157, 604–606
Function of voluntary-act requirement, 156
Impaired consciousness, forms of, 153–155

VOLUNTARINESS—Cont'd
  Concussion, 154
  Hypnosis, 154
  Hypoglycemia, 154–155
  Somnambulism, 154
Insanity defense,
  Control inquiry of insanity defense compared with issue of voluntariness, 695
Intoxication and voluntary act doctrine, 283
Involuntary act embedded in otherwise voluntary conduct,
  Driving with knowledge of epileptic condition, 156–157
Mental illness vs., 157

WARNING, REQUIREMENT OF FAIR
Due process, essential of, 89
Ex post facto laws, constitutional prohibition against, 89–90
Vagueness doctrine and, 66–67

WHARTON'S RULE
Limit on liability for conspiracy, 502–508

WITHDRAWAL
Conspiracy and, 461

WOLFENDEN REPORT
See Criminalization, Morals, enforcement of

†